JOAN DIDION

WE TELL OURSELVES STORIES IN ORDER TO LIVE

COLLECTED NONFICTION

WITH AN INTRODUCTION
BY JOHN LEONARD

EVERYMAN'S LIBRARY
Alfred A. Knopf   New York   London   Toronto

304

THIS IS A BORZOI BOOK

PUBLISHED BY ALFRED A. KNOPF

First included in Everyman's Library, 2006
Introduction Copyright © 2006 by John Leonard
Bibliography and Chronology Copyright © 2006 by Everyman's Library
Typography by Peter B. Willberg

www.randomhouse.com/everymans

ISBN 0-307-26487-4

Library of Congress Cataloging-in-Publication Data
Didion, Joan
We tell ourselves stories in order to live: the collected nonfiction / Joan Didion.
p. cm.—(Everyman's library)
Includes bibliographical references.
Contents: Slouching towards Bethlehem – The white album – Salvador – Miami –
After Henry – Political fictions – Where I was from.
ISBN 0-307-26487-4 (alk. paper)
I. Title.

PS3554.I33W3   2006   2006041043
814'.54–dc22   CIP

Book design by Barbara de Wilde and Carol Devine Carson

Printed and bound in Germany by GGP Media GmbH, Pössneck

JOAN DIDION

EVERYMAN'S LIBRARY

EVERYMAN,
I WILL GO WITH THEE,
AND BE THY GUIDE,
IN THY MOST NEED
TO GO BY THY SIDE

CONTENTS

INTRODUCTION

"My only advantage as a reporter," Joan Didion explained in *Slouching Towards Bethlehem*, "is that I am so physically small, so temperamentally unobtrusive, and so neurotically inarticulate that people tend to forget that my presence runs counter to their best interests." For awhile there back in the bliss of acid and guitars, she was practically counterrevolutionary, a poster girl for anomie, wearing a bikini but also a migraine to the bonfires of the zeitgeist. Then as the essays and novels and screenplays proliferated, she turned into a desert lioness of the style pages, part sybilline icon and part Stanford seismograph, alert on the faultlines of the culture to every tremor of tectonic fashion plate. She seemed sometimes so sensitive that whole decades hurt her feelings, and the prose on the page suggested Valéry's "shiverings of an effaced leaf," as if her next trick might be evaporation. But always anterior to the shiverings and effacements, the staccatos and crescendos in an echo chamber of blank uneasiness, there was a pessimism she appeared to have been born to, a hard-wired chill. Of the glum T. S. Eliot, Randall Jarrell once said that he'd have written *The Waste Land* about the Garden of Eden. Likewise it was possible to imagine Didion bee-stung by blue meanies even at Walden Pond.

Still, just because Eliot felt bad most of the time doesn't mean he didn't get it exactly right about water, rock and the Unreal City. So was Didion on pure Zen target.

We were neophytes together in Manhattan during the late-Fifties Ike Snooze, both published by William F. Buckley Jr. in *National Review* alongside such equally unlikely beginning writers as Garry Wills, Renata Adler, and Arlene Croce, back when Buckley hired the unknown young just because he liked our zippy lip and figured he would take care of our politics with the charismatic science of his own personality. Later, ruefully, he would call us "the apostates." So I have been reading Didion ever since she started doing it for money, have known her well enough to nod at for almost as long, have reviewed most of her books since her second novel, *Play It As*

It Lays, even published a couple of her essays when I edited the *New York Times Book Review* in the early 1970s, and cannot pretend to objectivity. While I might have taken furious exception to something she said—about Joan Baez, for instance: "So now the girl whose life is a crystal teardrop has her own place, a place where the sun shines and the ambiguities can be set aside a little while longer"; or such condescension as "the kind of jazz people used to have on their record players when everyone who believed in the Family of Man bought Scandinavian stainless-steel flatware and voted for Adai Stevenson"— I remain a partisan. To some degree, this is because she is a fellow Westerner, like Pauline Kael, and we have to stick together against the provincialism of the East. But in larger part it is because I have been trying forever to figure out why her sentences are better than mine or yours … something about cadence. They come at you, if not from ambush, then in gnomic haikus, icepick laser beams, or waves. Even the space on the page around these sentences is more interesting than it ought to be, as if to square a sandbox for a Sphinx.

And looking back, it seems to me that *The Year of Magical Thinking* should not have come as a surprise. All these years, Didion has been writing about loss. All these years, she has been rehearsing death. Her whole career has been a disenchantment from which pages fall like brilliant autumn leaves and arrange themselves as sermons in the stones.

*

The most terrifying verse I know: merrily merrily merrily life is but a dream.
—The Last Thing He Wanted

As early as *The White Album* she had her doubts about California, but did her best to blame time instead of space, as in this much-quoted passage:

Quite often during the past several years I have felt myself a sleepwalker, moving through the world unconscious of the moment's high issues, oblivious to its data, alert only to the stuff of bad dreams, the children burning in the locked car in the supermarket parking lot, the bike boys stripping down stolen cars on the captive cripple's ranch, the freeway sniper who feels "real bad" about picking off the family

of five, the hustlers, the insane, the cunning Okie faces that turn up in military investigations, the sullen lurking in doorways, the lost children, all the ignorant armies jostling in the night.

But if this geomancer of deracination can be said to have any roots at all, they are here at the edge, on the cliff. She is usually, if not more forgiving, then at least bemused. "Love and death in the golden land" has been one of her themes. Los Angeles she has described as "a city not only largely conceived as a series of real estate promotions but largely supported by a series of confidence games, a city currently afloat on motion pictures and junk bonds and the B-2 Stealth bomber." In Hollywood, "as in all cultures in which gambling is the central activity," she would find "a lowered sexual energy, an inability to devote more than token attention to the preoccupations of the society outside." And there is so much everywhere else: lemon groves and Thriftimarts; tumbleweeds and cyclotrons; Big Sur and Death Valley; Scientologists, Maharishis, and baby-sitters who see death in your aura; where "a boom mentality and a sense of Chekhovian loss meet in uneasy suspension; in which the mind is troubled by some buried but ineradicable suspicion that things had better work here, because here, beneath that immense bleached sky, is where we ran out of continent."

Then look what happened when she returned to these roots in *Where I Was From*, a book of lamentations entirely devoted to California dreamtime—to crossing stories and origin myths like the Donner Party and the Dust Bowl; to railroads, oil companies, agribiz and aerospace; to water rights, defense contracts, absentee owners and immigration; to such novelists as Jack London and Frank Norris, such philosophers as Josiah Royce, and such painters as Thomas Kinkade; to freeways, strip malls, meth labs, San Francisco's Bohemian Club, Lakewood's Spur Posse, and a state legislature that spends more money on California's prisons than it does on its colleges.

Didions have lived in California, with a ranchero sense of entitlement, since the middle of the nineteenth century, when Joan's great-great-great grandmother brought a cornbread recipe and a potato masher across the plains from Arkansas to the Sierras. As a nine-year-old girl scout Joan sang songs in the sunroom of the Sacramento insane asylum. As a trapped teen, she spent summers reading Eugene O'Neill and dreaming about Bennington (although she would graduate instead from Berkeley just like her melancholy father). As a first novelist with *Run River* in 1963, she blamed outsiders and newcomers for paving her childhood paradise to make freeways and parking lots. But eleven books and forty years later, she decides that selling their future to the highest bidder had been a habit among the earliest Californians, including her own family. If the whole state has turned into "an entirely dependent colony of the invisible empire" of corporate and political greed, the Didions are complicit.

As usual, of course, this bad news is fun to read, in a prose that moseys from sinew to schadenfreude to incantation, with some liturgical/fatidic tendencies toward the enigmatic and oracular, seasoned sarcastically. When *Where I Was From* was published in 2003, my only gripe as a reviewer was that it omitted so much she'd written about California elsewhere. Ideally, I said, there ought to be a Library of America Golden State Didion, including everything she had ever said about Alcatraz and mall culture, poker parlors and Malibu—*where horses caught fire and were shot on the beach, where birds exploded in the air*—all the bloody butter on her crust of dread.

Everyman answers that plea with this omnibus. And so we see that Didion is now skeptical not only about her home state, but, like her anthropologist in *A Book of Common Prayer*, about everything she thought she knew:

> I studied under Kroeber at California and worked with Levi-Strauss at Sao Paulo, classified several societies, catalogued their rites and attitudes on occasions of birth, copulation, initiation and death; did extensive and well-regarded studies on the rearing of female children in the Mato Grosso and along certain tributaries of the Rio Xingu, and still I did not know why any one of these female children did or did not do anything at all.
> Let me go further.
> I did not know why I did or did not do anything at all.

*

INTRODUCTION

*I realized that my impression of myself had been of someone who could
look for, and find, the upside in any situation. I had believed in the
logic of popular songs. I had looked for the silver lining. I had walked
on through the storm. It occurs to me now that these were not even the
songs of my generation.*

— The Year of Magical Thinking

No one else has ever thought looking for the upside was a big
part of her repertoire. She is a declared agnostic about history,
narrative, and reasons why, a devout disbeliever in social
action, moral imperatives, American exemptions, and the primacy of personal conscience. Inside this agnosticism, in both
the essays and the novels, there is a a fugitive who drinks
bourbon to cure herself of "bad attitudes, unpleasant tempers,
[and] wrongthink," a neurasthenic beating herself up for bad
sexual conduct and nameless derelictions, a female human
being who endures "the usual intimations of erratic cell multiplication, dust and dry wind, sexual dyaesthesia, sloth, flatu-
lence, root canal"—who has discovered "that not all of the
promises would be kept, that some things are in fact irrevocable
and that it had counted after all, every evasion and every
procrastination, every mistake, every word, all of it"; who has
misplaced "whatever slight faith she ever had in the social
contract, in the meliorative principle, in the whole grand
pattern of human endeavor"; who got married instead of seeing a shrink; who puts her head in a paper bag to keep from
crying; who has not been the witness she wanted to be; whose
nights are troubled by peacocks screaming in the olive trees—
an Alcestis back from the tunnel and half in love with death.
You know me, or think you do.

Although this Alcestis may have sometimes fudged the
difference between fatalism and lassitude, what she *does* believe
in, besides "tropism[s] towards disorder" and the dark troika of
dislocation, dread, and dreams, is Original Sin. She tells her
stories in self-defense: "The princess is caged in the consulate.
The man with the candy will lead the children into the sea."
Over and over again in her novels, wounded women make
strange choices in hot places with calamitous consequences.
This is the fictionalizing Didion, a closet romantic, who actually

JOAN DIDION

rooted for Elena McMahon, the journalist, and Treat Morrison, the American diplomat, to make a go of it in *The Last Thing He Wanted*: "I want those two to have been together all their lives."

But it's personal—intuition and anxiety, frazzled nerves and love gone wrong: nothing apparently to do with the rest of us or the world's mean work. As she explained in *The White Album*, "I am not the society in microcosm. I am a thirty-four-year-old woman with long straight hair and an old bikini bathing suit and bad nerves sitting on an island in the middle of the Pacific waiting for a tidal wave that will not come." To which she added, in *A Book of Common Prayer*: "Fear of the dark can be synthesized in the laboratory. Fear of the dark is an arrangement of fifteen amino acids. Fear of the dark is a protein."

Thus she'd seem the unlikeliest of writers to turn into a disillusioned legionnaire "on the far frontiers of the Monroe Doctrine." Somehow, though, she went left and south, to discover in the Latin latitudes more than her own unbearable whiteness of being. In Mexico, for instance, in the Sonoran desert: "The point is to become disoriented, shriven, by the heat and the deceptive perspectives and the oppressive sense of carrion.... Graham Greene might have written it: a shadowy square with a filigree pergola for the Sunday band, a racket of birds, a cathedral in bad repair with a robin's-egg-blue tile dome, a turkey buzzard on the cross." In Yucatán and Bogotá: white skies, idle casinos, shawls, and salt mines; parrots and termites; "obscurely sexual misunderstandings and bewilderment" among mineral geologists and CIA operatives; banana palms, kidnappings. El Salvador is Conrad's heart of darkness: "Exterminate all the brutes!" Ghost resorts on the empty beaches; mongrel dogs, bulletproof Plexiglas, and "a prolonged amnesiac fugue"; Archibishop Romero, El Mozote, students, nuns ... On one hand, in the "vast brutalist space" that was the cathedral, "the unlit altar seemed to offer a single ineluctable message: at this time and in this space the light of the world could be construed as out, off, extinguished." On the other, "Central America's Largest Shopping Mall"—where, just past the weapons check, Muzak is playing "I Left My Heart in San Francisco" and *pâté de foie gras* is on sale to matrons in tight Sergio Valente jeans, along with Bloomingdale beach towels, Halazone tablets, and bottles of Stolichynaya vodka. In El Salvador, between "grimgrams," body dumps, and midnight screenings on video cassettes of *Apocalypse Now* and *Bananas*, Joan Didion decides that Gabriel García Márquez is in fact "a social realist."

In El Salvador one learns that vultures go first for the soft tissue, for the eyes, the exposed genitalia, the open mouth. One learns that an open mouth can be used to make a specific point, can be stuffed with something emblematic; stuffed, say, with a penis, or, if the point has to do with land title, stuffed with some of the dirt in question. One learns that hair deteriorates less rapidly than flesh, and that a skull surrounded by a perfect corona of hair is not an uncommon sight in the body dumps.

So the essayist who in *Slouching Towards Bethlehem* liked Howard Hughes and John Wayne more than Joan Baez and the flower children, who in *The White Album* found more fault with Doris Lessing, Hollywood liberals and feminism than with mall culture and Manson groupies, ends up in *Salvador, Miami*, and *After Henry* savagely disdainful of Reagan and the "dreamwork" of American foreign policy ('a dreamwork devised to obscure any intelligence that might trouble the dreamer'). And the writer of fiction who started out with *Play It As It Lays*, a scary manual on narcissism, leaves town not for Hawaii but for Panama, Costa Rica, "Boca Grande" and other tropics of "morbidity and paranoia"; for Managua and Santiago, Haiti and Rwalpindi, Jakarta and Saigon, Tunis and Penang, Dakar and Jedda, where she talks to absolutely anybody—embassy drivers, airline stewardesses, Fulbright scholars, tropical agronomists, bar girls, desk clerks, wild cards, salesmen of coco dryers and rice converters, dealers in information and weapons-grade uranium, cash transfers and end-user certificates, Uzis and unction—graduating overnight from the middle school of Raymond Chandler and Nathanael West to a doctoral program with Nadine Gordimer, Octavio Paz, and Andre Malraux, after which she will write postcolonial NAFTA novels.

And the daughter of conservative Republicans who tells us that she voted "ardently" for Barry Goldwater in 1964 will describe in *Political Fictions* the abduction of American democracy.

It's not just that the momentum Didion worries so much about has taken her in surprising directions. It's that we shouldn't perhaps have been surprised. As early as *Bethlehem*, for every syllable on rattlesnakes and mesquite, there was an inquiry into Alcatraz and body bags from Vietnam. The *White Album*, an almanac of nameless blue-eyed willies, had nevertheless a lot to say about Huey Newton and the Panthers, Bogotá, Hoover Dam, and the storage of nerve gas in an army arsenal in Oregon. In *After Henry*, one morning she visits a transit camp for Vietnamese refugees near Kowloon, Hong Kong, where "a woman of indeterminate age was crouched on the pavement near the washing pumps bleeding out a live chicken." On another morning she just happens to stop in on the Berkeley nuclear reactor, flashing back to her Fifties grammar-school days of atom bomb drills and her Fifties nightmares of death light while chatting up the engineer and inspecting the core, the radiation around the fuel rods, and the blue shimmer of the shock wave under twenty feet of water—water "the exact blue of the glass at Chartres."

Political Fictions was perhaps inevitable. In 1988, the *New York Review of Books* invited her to feel bad on the campaign trail as George Bush and Michael Dukakis competed for those Reagan Democrats believed by politicians in both parties to be crucial to the election of any U.S. President. Off and on for the next twelve years, Didion would engage the legacy of Ronald Reagan, the conundrum of Jesse Jackson, the woo-woo of Newt Gingrich, the culture wars and wet dreams of Bill Clinton and Ken Starr, the perfidy of the pundit caste, "faith-based" vote-grubbing, and the "process" itself—a slick mechanism not usefully to be distinguished from the perpetual-motion clock bug in Kobo Abe's *The Ark Sakura*, eating as it eliminates, thriving on a diet of its own feces, circling always to face the sun.

Political Fictions may be many variations on a single theme, but, as in Bach, they are Goldberg Variations. By whom has democracy been abducted? By a "permanent political class," an oligarchy consisting not only of the best candidates big money can buy, plus their ancillary focus groups, advance teams, donor bases and consultants, but also, crucially, the journalists who cover the prefab story, sell the "sedative fantasy of a fixable imperial America," and are themselves eager cogwheels in the clock bug, along with the Op-Ed smogball sermonizers, the spayed creatures of the talkshow ether who handicap the horse race, and the apparatchiks who leak "scoops" upon them for the greater glory of career advancement, agenda enhancement, a book contract or a coup d'état:

> When we talk about process, then, we are talking, increasingly, not about the "democratic process," or the general mechanism affording the citizens of a state a voice in its affairs, but the reverse: a mechanism seen as so specialized that access to it is correctly limited to its own professionals, to those who manage policy and those who report on it, to those who run the polls and those who quote them, to those who ask and those who answer the questions on the Sunday shows, to the media consultants, to the columnists, to the issues advisers, to those who give the off-the-record breakfasts and those who attend them; to that handful of insiders who invent, year in and year out, the narrative of public life.

It is this narrative—part fable, part Zeigeist, part code, all ideology—that Didion synthesizes from convention oratory, cable chat, stump speeches, bull sessions, tell-all memoirs, the dailies, weeklies and transcripts; the white noise, the "rapture of the feed," and the shadow on the scan. As in her novels, she condenses slanguages to a sort of antipoetry. But instead of Black Flights, Tiger Ops, assets, and extractions, or "drop fuel, jettison cargo, eject crew, lose track," what we hear is all about game plans and trade-offs, talking points and wimp factors, how it will play and "staying on message," Willie Horton and Sister Souljah. Translated, this means that in the scrum for votes among the affluent, educated, suburban and wired, those who are "poor, Hispanic, urban, homeless, hungry and other people out of favor in Middle America" will no longer get the "freebies" they got from "mushy" liberals in the Sixties and Seventies. The gatekeepers, border guards, hierophants, jackalheads, and flacks who tend the eternal flame of a safe center "in which both parties are committed to calibrating the precise level of incremental tinkering required to be elected" aren't interested any more in civil liberties, organized labor, affirmative action, due process, or child care. They oppose all entitlements but their own, like tax exemptions for mortgage interest.

Now even the Didion who went to El Salvador is no left-wing herbivorous feminazi. She has elsewhere explained that hers was a generation "distrustful of political highs ... convinced that the heart of darkness lay not in some error of social organization but in man's own blood." About this heart of darkness she has sounded over the years more like a nineteenth-century New Englander than a twentieth-century Californian—the way Herman Melville read Nathaniel Hawthorne: "For in certain moods, no man can weigh this world without throwing in something, somehow like Original Sin, to strike the uneven balance."

But to *Political Fictions*, besides her black conceit, her sonar ear, her radar eye, and her nightscope-sniper prose, she brings Tiger Ops assets of temperament. She is more than a match for any political class of I'm-All-Right Jacks. She is not likely to be snowed by the best boys and gaffers of this music-video, with their nostalgia for an imaginary America and their contempt for everybody who has failed to prosper. When she isn't taking topics like the politics of the death penalty, social control through drug enforcement, the Super Tuesday sellout of grassroots protest, the "cargo cult" of Ronald Reagan, and the Florida fiasco out for a ride in her tumbrel, she is as hard on centrist politicians as we'd expect of someone who seemed almost thrilled by the Jesse Jackson insurrection in 1988, and who let Jerry Brown camp out in her apartment during the 1992 Democratic convention. About Joe Lieberman, for instance, every Republican's favorite Democratic senator: "His speech patterns, grounded as they were in the burden he bore for the rest of us and the personal rewards he had received from God for bearing it, tended to self-congratulation." And that conscience he always followed "came to seem a kind of golden retriever bounding ever to the right."

And she's harder still on the shill game of a complicit media. *The New York Times* takes its lumps for failing to back reporter Ray Bonner on his absolutely accurate account of the El Mozote massacre. Michael Isikoff of *Newsweek* gets a woodshed thrashing. In alphabetical order, Jonathan Alter, Wolf Blitzer, David Broder, Sam Donaldson, Maureen Dowd, Thomas J. Friedman, Jeff Greenfield, Al Hunt, Joe Klein, William Kristol, Andrea Mitchell, Cokie Roberts and George Will may want to check for minor lacerations. Bob Woodward of the *Washington Post* might consider a career change. In all his books, Didion says, "measurable cerebral activity is virtually absent," but "this disinclination ... to exert cognitive energy reaches critical mass in *The Choice*."

We need no longer wonder how come the largest political party in America is "the party of those who see no reason to vote." And if Didion is short on remedies for our sickness, doctoring is not her job. As Chinua Achebe explained in *Anthills of the Savannah*: "Writers don't give prescriptions. They give headaches!"

*

We might expect if death is sudden to feel shock. We do not expect this shock to be obliterative, dislocating to both body and mind. We might expect that we will be prostrate, inconsolable, crazy with loss. We do not expect to be literally crazy, cool customers who believe that their husband is about to return and need his shoes.
The Year of Magical Thinking

Nor can we know ahead of the fact (and here lies the heart of the difference between grief as we imagine it and grief as it is) the unending absence that follows, the void, the very opposite of meaning, the relentless succession of moments during which we will confront the experience of meaninglessness itself.
The Year of Magical Thinking

Three times the mother had to repeat herself, telling the daughter her father was dead. The daughter, Quintana, kept forgetting because she was in and out of comas, septic shock, extubation, or neurosurgery, in one or another intensive care unit on the West Coast or the East. Halfway through *The Year of Magical Thinking*—Didion's *Life Studies* and her *Kaddish*, her Robert Lowell and Allen Ginsberg—the daughter is medevacked from the UCLA Medical Center in Los Angeles to the Rusk Institute in New York, but the transfer is complicated. Through a guerrilla action by wildcat truckers who have jack-knifed a semitrailer on the interstate the ambulance must feel its way to an airport that could be in Burbank, Santa Monica, or Van Nuys, nobody seems to know for sure, where a Cessna waits with just enough room for two pilots, two paramedics, the stretcher to which Quintana is strapped and the bench on which her mother sits on top of oxygen canisters. And they have to make a heartland stop.

Later we landed in a cornfield in Kansas to refuel. The pilots struck a deal with the two teenagers who managed the airstrip: during the refueling they would take their pickup to a McDonald's and bring back hamburgers. While we waited the paramedics suggested that we take turns getting some exercise. When my turn came I stood frozen on the tarmac for a moment, ashamed to be free and outside when Quintana could not be, then walked to where the runway ended and the corn started. There was a little rain and unstable air and I imagined a tornado coming. Quintana and I were Dorothy. We were both free. In fact we were out of here.

If Didion is reminded of Oz, I am reminded of Didion. We've met this runway woman more than once before. In *Democracy* her name was Inez Victor, and after the death of her lover, Jack Lovett, in the shallow end of a hotel swimming pool in Jakarta, she moved to Kuala Lumpur: "A woman who had once thought of living in the White House was flicking termites from her teacup and telling me about landing on a series of atolls in a seven-passenger plane with a man in a body bag." In *The Last Thing He Wanted* her name was Elena McMahon, a journalist who washed up on the wet grass runway on one of those Caribbean islands we only pay attention to when they pop up on the Bad Weather Channel, after which she disappeared into the lost clusters and corrupted data of Iran/Contra. The novelist wonders "what made her think a black shift bought off a rack sale at Bergdrof Goodman during the New York primary was the appropriate thing to wear on an unscheduled flight at one-thirty in the morning out of Fort Lauderdale-Hollywood International Airport, destination San Jose Costa Rica but not quite."

Women are always rehearsing a kind of death on Didion's tarmac. It's her preferred tropic as skepticism is her preferred meridian. Maria in *Play It As It Lays* not only expects to die soon but believes that planes crash if she boards them in "bad spirit," that loveless marriages cause cancer, and fatal accidents happen to the children of adulterers. Charlotte in *A Book of Common Prayer* dreams of "sexual surrender and infant death" and has come to Boca Grande because it's "at the very cervix of the world, the place through which a child lost to history must eventually pass." The body count in *Democracy* is remarkable not even counting the AID analyst and the Reuters correspondent who are poisoned in Saigon in 1970 by oleander leaves, "a chiffonade of hemotoxins." In *The Last Thing He Wanted*, everybody we care about dies, leaving only Arthur Schlesinger Jr. to eat by candlelight and Ted Sorensen to swim with the dolphins.

Later in *Magical Thinking*, Didion will dream two dreams. In one, after her dead husband has boarded without her, she is "left alone on the tarmac at Santa Monica Airport watching the planes take off one by one." In the other, she imagines a rough flight with Quintana between Honolulu and Los Angeles: "The plane would go down. Miraculously, she and I would survive the crash, adrift in the Pacific, clinging to the debris. The dilemma was this: I would need, because I was menstruating and the blood would attract sharks, to abandon her, swim away, leave her alone."

She has always juxtaposed the hardware and the soft: hummingbirds and the F.B.I.; the disposable needle in the Snoopy wastebasket, the light at dawn for a Pacific bomb test, and the cost of a visa to leave Phnom Penh; four-year-olds in burning cars, rattlesnakes in playpens and lizards in a crèche; earthquakes, tidal waves, and Patty Hearst. Against the "hydraulic imagery" of the clandestine world, its conduits, pipelines, and diversions, she opposes a gravitational imagery of black holes and weightlessness. Against dummy corporations, phantom payrolls and fragmentation mines, she opposes wild orchids washed by rain into a milky ditch of waste. Half of her last novel was depositions, cable traffic, brokered accounts, and classified secrets. The other half was jasmine, jacaranda petals, twilight, vertigo.

In *Magical Thinking*, these conjunctions and abutments—scraps of poetry, cramps of memory, medical terms, body parts, bad dreams, readouts, breakdowns—amount to a kind of liturgical sing-song, a whistling in the dark against a "vortex" that would otherwise swallow her whole with a hum. This then is how she passes the evil hours of an evil year, with spells and amulets. Her seventy-year-old husband, John Gregory Dunne, has dropped dead of a massive heart attack in their living room in New York City, shortly before their fortieth wedding anniversary. Except for the first five months of that marriage, when John still worked at *Time*, they had both stayed home, writing together and reading to each other, "twenty-four hours a day"—an amazing intimacy. You would think they needed each other to breathe. She can't erase his voice from the answering machine, and refuses to get rid of his shoes. She puts his cellphone in its charger. She puts his money clip in the box where they keep passports and proof of jury service. She calls a friend at the *Los Angeles Times* so they won't feel scooped by the *New York Times*. She will not authorize an organ harvest: "How could he come back if they took away his organs, how could he come back if he had no shoes?" Besides: "His blue eyes. His blue imperfect eyes." She can't eat, can't sleep, can't think without remembering, can't remember without hurting, and for six long months can't even dream. She rereads John's books, finding them darker. She understands, for the first time, "the power in the image of the rivers, the Styx, the Lethe, the cloaked ferry-man with his pole," the burning raft of grief.

Meanwhile, her thirty-eight-year-old daughter, Quintana Roo Dunne Michael, has only been married five months before she is out of one hospital into another, a flu that somehow "morphs" into pneumonia and is followed by a stroke. One morning in the ICU Didion is startled to see that the monitor above her daughter's head is dark, "that her brain waves were gone." Without telling Quintana's mother, the doctors have turned off her EEG. But "I had grown used to watching her brain waves. It was a way of hearing her talk."

So we watch her listen—to the obscene susurrus of electrodes, syringes, catheter lines, breathing tubes, ultrasound, white cell counts, anticoagulants, ventricular fibbing, tracheostomy, Thallium scan, fixed pupils and brain death, not to neglect such euphemisms as "leave the table" (which means to survive surgery) and "subacute rehab facility" (which means a nursing

INTRODUCTION

home). But she also consults texts by Shakespeare, Philippe Aries, William Styron, Sigmund Freud, W. H. Auden, Melanie Klein, C. S. Lewis, Matthew Arnold, D. H. Lawrence, Dylan Thomas, Emily Post and Euripedes. And, simultaneously, she is watching and listening to herself. How does she measure up to the stalwart grieving behaviors of dolphins and geese?

"It's okay. She's a pretty cool customer," said a social worker to a doctor at New York Presbyterian Hospital, where John Gregory Dunne was pronounced dead, about the brand-new widow. Little did they know. What she was really thinking was, "I needed to be alone so that he could come back." Later on it would occur to her that "I had to believe he was dead all along. If I did not believe he was dead all along I would have thought I should have been able to save him." But then again: "I had allowed other people to think he was dead. I had allowed him to be buried alive." If Joan Didion, of all cool customers, went crazy, what are the chances for the rest of us? Not so good, except that we have her black album, this habitation of a brave heart and radiant intellect, an ice palace and a greenhouse, her example to instruct us and the sentences we can almost sing.

John Leonard

JOHN LEONARD is a former editor of *The New York Times Book Review*. He reviews books for *Harper's Magazine* and *The Nation*, television for *New York* magazine, and movies for "CBS News Sunday Morning."

SELECT BIBLIOGRAPHY

———

BIOGRAPHY/BIBLIOGRAPHY

HENDERSON, KATHERINE U., *Joan Didion*, NY: Ungar, 1981.

OLENDORF, DONNA, "Joan Didion: A Checklist, 1955–1980", Bulletin of Bibliography 38.1, (Jan.–Mar. 1981): 32–44.

JACOBS, FRED RUE, *Joan Didion: Bibliography*, Keene, CA: The Loop Press, 1977.

CRITICISM

BOYNTON, ROBERT, *The New New Journalism: Conversations with America's Best Nonfiction Writers on Their Craft*, New York, NY: Vintage, 2005.

FELTON, SHARON, ed., *The Critical Response to Joan Didion*, Westport, CN: Greenwood Press, 1994.

FRIEDMAN, ELLEN G., ed., *Joan Didion: Essays and Conversations*, Princeton, NJ: Ontario Rev., 1984.

WINCHELL, MARK R., *Joan Didion*, Boston, MA: Twayne, 1989.

CHRONOLOGY

DATE	AUTHOR'S LIFE	LITERARY CONTEXT
1925		1925 *The New Yorker* is founded by American journalist Harold Ross.
1929		1929 Woolf: *A Room of One's Own*.
1932		1932 Hammett: *The Thin Man*.
1933		1933 Orwell: *Down and Out in Paris and London*. N. West: *Miss Lonelyhearts*.
1934	Joan Didion is born at Mercy Hospital, Sacramento, California to Eduene Jerrett Didion and Frank Reese Didion (5 December).	1934 Fitzgerald: *Tender is the Night*. Miller: *Tropic of Cancer*. Waugh: *A Handful of Dust*; *Ninety-two Days*.
1935–41	Lives in Sacramento, California.	1935 Lewis: *It Can't Happen Here*. 1936 Orwell: 'Shooting an Elephant'.
		1937 Orwell: *The Road to Wigan Pier*. 1938 Orwell: *Homage to Catalonia*. 1939 Steinbeck: *The Grapes of Wrath*. 1940 Hemingway: *For Whom the Bell Tolls*. 1941 Fitzgerald: *The Last Tycoon*.
1942–43	Lives in Tacoma, Washington; Durham, North Carolina; and Colorado Springs, Colorado, where her father is stationed with Army Air Corps.	1942 Eliot: *Four Quartets*. Camus: *The Stranger*. 1943 Chandler: *The Lady in the Lake*.
1944	Returns to Sacramento with her mother and brother (father returns in 1945).	1944 Borges: *Ficciones*.
1945		1945 Orwell: *Animal Farm*.
1946		1946 Orwell: 'A Nice Cup of Tea'; 'Decline of the English Murder'. Hersey: *Hiroshima* (report).

1932 La Matanza, massacre in El Salvador by government troops following a peasant rebellion in western part of the country.
1933 Roosevelt announces 'New Deal'. Hitler becomes German Chancellor.

1936 Outbreak of Spanish Civil War. Hitler and Mussolini form Rome–Berlin Axis. Edward VIII abdicates; George VI crowned in UK. Stalin's 'Great Purge' of the Communist Party (to 1938).
1937 Japanese invasion of China.

1938 Germany annexes Austria; Munich crisis.
1939 Nazi–Soviet Pact. Hitler invades Poland; World War II begins.

1940 Churchill becomes Prime Minister in UK. Dunkirk evacuation. Fall of France. Battle of Britain. The Blitz.
1941 Japan attacks Pearl Harbor; US enters war. Germans invade USSR.
1942 Fall of Singapore. Russian troops halt German advance at Stalingrad. North Africa campaign; Battle of El Alamein.

1944 Attempted military coup in Colombia. Normandy landings and liberation of Paris. Red Army reaches Belgrade and Budapest.

1945 Unconditional surrender of Germany; Hitler commits suicide. US drops atomic bombs on Hiroshima and Nagasaki. End of World War II. United Nations founded. Death of Roosevelt; Truman becomes US President.
1946 Nuremberg trials. 'Iron Curtain' speech by Churchill.

DATE	AUTHOR'S LIFE	LITERARY CONTEXT
1947		1947 Robert Penn Warren: *All the King's Men.*
		1948 Mailer: *The Naked and the Dead.*
1949		1949 Orwell: *Nineteen Eighty-Four.* Beauvoir: *The Second Sex.*
1950		1950 Lessing: *The Grass is Singing.*
1951		1951 Salinger: *The Catcher in the Rye.*
1952	Graduates from C. K. McClatchy High School, Sacramento.	1952 Beckett: *Waiting for Godot.* McCarthy: *The Groves of Academe.*
1953		1953 Bellow: *The Adventures of Augie March.*
1954		1954 K. Amis: *Lucky Jim.*
1955		1955 Nabokov: *Lolita.* Greene: *The Quiet American.* Baldwin: *Notes of a Native Son* (essays). Miller: *A View from the Bridge.*
1956–63	Graduates from the University of California at Berkeley (1956). Lives in New York while working for *Vogue.*	1956 Mahfouz: *The Cairo Trilogy* (to 1957). 1957 Kerouac: *On the Road.* Pasternak: *Doctor Zhivago.* 1958 Lampedusa: *The Leopard* Achebe: *Things Fall Apart.* 1959 Burroughs: *Naked Lunch* Bellow: *Henderson the Rain King.* Gellhorn: *The Face of War.* Grass: *The Tin Drum* 1960 Updike: *Rabbit, Run.* 1961 Naipaul: *A House for Mr Biswas.* Heller: *Catch-22.* 1962 Lessing: *The Golden Notebook.* Solzhenitsyn: *One Day in the Life of Ivan Denisovich.*
1963	First novel, *Run River.*	1963 *The New York Review of Books* is founded by Robert Silvers, Barbara Epstein and publisher A. Whitney Ellsworth. Arendt: *Eichmann in Jerusalem.* McCarthy: *The Group.* Plath: *The Bell Jar.*

CHRONOLOGY

1948 Jewish state of Israel comes into existence. Russian blockade of West Berlin. Assassination of Gandhi in India. Apartheid introduced in South Africa.
1949 Communists win Chinese civil war. North Atlantic Treaty signed.

1950 Korean War (to 1953).

1952 Eisenhower elected US President. Accession of Elizabeth II in UK.

1953 Death of Stalin.

1954 Vietnam War (to 1975).
1955 UN refuses to discontinue discussions on 1952 Cruz Report on apartheid; South Africa withdraws from UN.

1956 Khrushchev delivers 'Secret Speech' at 20th Party Congress. Suez crisis in Egypt. California repeals all Alien Land Laws.
1957 Civil Rights Commission established in US to safeguard voting rights.

1959 Castro seizes power in Cuba and forms a Socialist government.

1960 John F. Kennedy wins the US presidency.
1961 Anti-Castro force of Cuban exiles backed by CIA attempts invasion of Cuba at the Bay of Pigs. Yuri Gagarin becomes first man in space. Construction of the Berlin Wall.
1962 Cuban missile crisis.

1963 Assassination of Kennedy; Johnson becomes President.

JOAN DIDION

DATE	AUTHOR'S LIFE	LITERARY CONTEXT
1964	Marries writer John Gregory Dunne at Mission San Juan Bautista, San Benito County, California (30 January). Moves from New York to Portuguese Bend, Los Angeles County, California (June).	1964 Naipaul: *An Area of Darkness*. Bellow: *Herzog*.
1965		1965 Wolfe: *The Kandy-Kolored Tangerine-Flake Streamline Baby* (essays). Mailer: *An American Dream*. Scott: *The Raj Quartet* (to 1975).
1966	Only child, Quintana Roo Dunne is born at St John's Hospital, Santa Monica (3 March). Moves with family from Portuguese Bend to Franklin Avenue in Hollywood.	1966 Sontag: *Against Interpretation* (essays). Gellhorn: *Vietnam: A New Kind of War*. Rhys: *Wide Sargasso Sea*.
1967		1967 McCarthy: reports on Vietnam from Saigon and Hanoi (to 1968). William Styron: *The Confessions of Nat Turner*. Dunne: *Delano*. Márquez: *One Hundred Years of Solitude*.
1968	*Slouching Towards Bethlehem*.	1968 Solzhenitsyn: *Cancer Ward*.
1969		1969 Hersh: *Vietnam War: My Lai Massacre* (report). Nader: *The Great American Gyp* (report). Dunne: *The Studio*. Sontag: *Styles of Radical Will*. Oates: *Them*.
1970	*Play It As It Lays*.	1970 Bellow: *Mr Sammler's Planet*. Gordimer: *A Guest of Honour*.
1971	Moves with family to the Pacific Coast Highway in Malibu. *The Panic in Needle Park* is released, starring Al Pacino and Kitty Winn. It is the first motion picture credited to Didion and Dunne, and also first to Pacino.	1971 Updike: *Rabbit Redux*. Lessing: *Briefing for a Descent into Hell*. McCarthy: *Birds of America*. Flannery O'Connor: *The Complete Stories*.

CHRONOLOGY

1964 Civil Rights Act prohibits discrimination in the US. Nobel Peace Prize is awarded to Martin Luther King.

1965 Human rights activist Malcolm X is assassinated. President Johnson orders US intervention in the Dominican Republic when civil war breaks out.

1966 Mao launches Cultural Revolution in China. Revolutionary Black nationalist organization the Black Panther Party is founded in Oakland, California.

1967 Six-Day War between Israel and Arab states. Outbreaks of racial violence mount in many US cities; President Johnson appoints a commission to look into causes. 75,000 young people gather at Haight-Ashbury, California for 'Summer of Love'. Argentinian-born Cuban guerrilla hero Che Guevara is shot dead in Bolivia.

1968 Martin Luther King assassinated in Memphis, Tennessee, triggering violent reaction throughout the USA. Czechoslovakia is invaded by Soviet troops seeking to reinstate Communism. Richard Nixon is elected US President.
1969 US troops begin to withdraw from Vietnam. US astronaut Neil Armstrong becomes first man on the moon. Woodstock rock festival, New York State attracts 400,000 fans.

1970 Salvador Allende becomes first Socialist President of Chile in a democratic election. Death of de Gaulle in France.

JOAN DIDION

DATE	AUTHOR'S LIFE	LITERARY CONTEXT
1972		
1973		1973 Pynchon: *Gravity's Rainbow.* Solzhenitsyn: *The Gulag Archipelago* (to 1975).
1974		1974 Dunne: *Vegas.* Gordimer: *The Conservationist.*
1975		1975 Bellow: *Humboldt's Gift.* Levi: *The Periodic Table.*
1976		1976 Gordimer: *Letter from South Africa* (report). Hong Kingston: *The Woman Warrior.*
1977	*A Book of Common Prayer.*	1977 Dunne: *True Confessions.* Morrison: *Song of Solomon.*
1978	Moves with family from Malibu to Brentwood Park. Receives the Morton Dauwen Zabel Award for Fiction from the American Academy of Arts and Letters	1978 French: *The Woman's Room.* Munro: *The Beggar Maid.*
1979	*The White Album.*	1979 Calvino: *If on a winter's night a traveler.* Mailer: *The Executioner's Story.*
1980		1980 Hong Kingston: *China Men.* McCarthy: *Cannibals and Missionaries.*
1981		1981 Vargas Llosa: *The War of the End of the World.* Márquez: *Chronicle of a Death Foretold.* Rushdie: *Midnight's Children.* Updike: *Rabbit Is Rich.*
1982		1982 Dunne: *Dutch Shea, Jr.* Allende: *The House of the Spirits.* Levi: *If not Now, When?* Walker: *The Color Purple.*
1983	*Salvador.*	1983 Updike: *Hugging the Shore* (essays). Walker: *In Search of our Mothers' Gardens* (essays).
1984	*Democracy.*	1984 Brookner: *Hotel du Lac.* Barnes: *Flaubert's Parrot.* Naipaul: *Among the Republicans* (report).

CHRONOLOGY

1972 Strategic Arms Limitation Treaty (SALT I) signed by US and USSR.
Eleven Israeli athletes are killed at the Olympic Village near Munich.
1973 US Supreme Court suspends capital punishment (until 1976). Chilean
President Allende and at least 2,700 others are killed in a coup led by
General Pinochet.
1974 Nixon resigns in wake of Watergate scandal; Ford becomes US
President.
1975 Vietnam War ends.

1976 Death of Chairman Mao in China. Jimmy Carter elected US President.

1978 Camp David Agreement between Carter, Egyptian President Sadat and
Israeli Prime Minister Begin.

1979 Margaret Thatcher elected first female Prime Minister in UK. Carter
and Brezhnev sign SALT II Arms Limitation Treaty. Soviets occupy
Afghanistan.
1980 Mariel Boatlift, mass exodus of Cuban refugees to US. Shipyard worker
Lech Walsea leads strikes in Gdansk, Poland. Iran–Iraq war begins (to 1988).
The Farabundo Martí National Liberation Front established in El Salvador;
launches armed struggle against the government. Ronald Reagan elected US
President.
1981 Attempted assassination of Reagan in Washington. President Sadat
killed by Islamic fundamentalists in Egypt. El Mozote Massacre: hundreds of
civilians die at hands of Salvadoran armed forces.

1982 Argentina occupies Falkland Islands, resulting in war with Britain.

1983 US troops invade Grenada after the government is overthrown.

1984 Famine in Ethiopia. Indira Gandhi assassinated in India.

DATE	AUTHOR'S LIFE	LITERARY CONTEXT
1985		1985 Márquez: *Love in the Time of Cholera.*
1986		1986 DeLillo: *End Zone.* Levi: *The Drowned and the Saved.* Munro: *The Progress of Love.* Atwood: *The Handmaid's Tale*
1987	*Miami.*	1987 Dunne: *The Red White and Blue.* Wolfe: *The Bonfire of the Vanities.* Morrison: *Beloved.*
1988	Moves from California to New York.	1988 Rushdie: *The Satanic Verses.* Carey: *Oscar and Lucinda.* Gellhorn: *A View From the Ground.* Carver: *Where I'm Calling From.*
1989		1989 Márquez: *The General in His Labyrinth.* Atwood: *Cat's Eye.* Ozick: *The Shawl.* Dunne: *Harp.*
1990		1990 Pynchon: *Vineland.* Updike: *Rabbit at Rest.*
1991		1991 Updike: *Odd Jobs* (essays). Jung Chang: *Wild Swans.*
1992	*After Henry.*	1992 Ondaatje: *The English Patient.* Oates: *Black Water.*
1993		1993 Roth: *Operation Shylock.*
1994		1994 Allende: *Paula.* Heller: *Closing Time.* Dunne: *Playland.* Murakami: *The Wind-Up Bird Chronicle.*
1995		1995 Guterson: *Snow Falling on Cedars.* M. Amis: *The Information.*
1996	*The Last Thing He Wanted.* Receives Edward MacDowell Medal from The MacDowell Colony.	1996 Updike: *In the Beauty of the Lilies.*

CHRONOLOGY

1985 Gorbachev becomes General Secretary in USSR; period of reform begins. South African government declares State of Emergency.
1986 Nuclear explosion at Chernobyl. US bombs Libya. New State of Emergency declared in South Africa. Gorbachev–Reagan summit.

1988 George Bush elected US President. Gorbachev announces significant troop reductions and withdrawal from Afghanistan.

1989 Collapse of Communism in Eastern Europe. Fall of the Berlin Wall. First democratic elections in USSR. Tiananmen Square massacre in China.

1990 Pinochet stands down as President of Chile. End of Communist monopoly in USSR. Yeltsin elected first leader of Russian Federation. Nelson Mandela released from jail after 27 years' imprisonment. John Major becomes Prime Minister in UK.
1991 Gulf War. Bush and Gorbachev sign START arms reduction treaty. Central government in USSR suspended. War begins in former Yugoslavia. End of apartheid in South Africa.
1992 Peace accords signed in El Salvador, signalling end to 12-year civil war. Riots in Los Angeles. Bill Clinton elected US President.

1993 Palestinian leader Arafat and Israeli Prime Minister Rabin sign peace agreement in US. Maastricht Treaty ratified.
1994 Massacres in Rwanda. Mandela leads the ANC to victory in South African elections. Russian military actions against Chechen Republic. IRA ceasefire announced. The Channel Tunnel is opened.

1995 Israeli Prime Minister Rabin assassinated.

1996 President Clinton re-elected.

DATE	AUTHOR'S LIFE	LITERARY CONTEXT
1997		1997 Dunne: *Monster: Living Off the Big Screen.* Roth: *American Pastoral.* McEwan: *Enduring Love.* Bellow: *The Actual.*
1998		1998 Morrison: *Paradise.* DeLillo: *Underworld.* Roth: *I Married a Communist.* Heller: *Now and Then.*
1999		1999 Sontag: *In America.*
2000		2000 Bellow: *Ravelstein.* Roth: *The Human Stain.* Atwood: *The Blind Assassin.*
2001	*Political Fictions*; wins George Polk Book Award.	2001 Franzen: *The Corrections.* Munro: *Hateship, Friendship, Courtship, Loveship, Marriage.*
2002		2002 Safran Foer: *Everything is Illuminated.*
2003	Quintana Roo Dunne marries Gerald Michael at the Cathedral Church of St John the Divine, New York (26 July). *Where I Was From* (October). John Gregory Dunne dies of cardiac arrest, New York (30 December).	2003 Hersh: *Lunch with the Chairman; Selective Intelligence* (reports). Atwood: *Oryx and Crake.*
2004		2004 Dunne: *Nothing Lost.* Hersh: *Torture at Abu Ghraib* (report).
2005	Quintana Roo Dunne Michael dies of septic shock, New York (26 August). *The Year of Magical Thinking* (November); wins 2005 National Book Award for Nonfiction.	2005 Mayer: *Outsourcing Terror: The secret history of America's 'extraordinary rendition' program* (report). Safran Foer: *Extremely Loud and Incredibly Close.*

CHRONOLOGY

1997 Tony Blair elected Prime Minister in the UK. UK hands sovereignty of Hong Kong to People's Republic of China.

1998 Iraq disarmament crisis. Referendum in Northern Ireland accepts Good Friday Agreement; an assembly is elected. General Pinochet is arrested and detained in UK on an extradition request from Spain. Lewinsky scandal; President Clinton is impeached (acquitted February 1999).
1999 Serbs attack ethnic Albanians in Kosovo; US leads NATO in bombing of Belgrade.
2000 Putin succeeds Yeltsin as Russian President. Further violence in Chechen Republic. Pinochet returns to Chile; Supreme Court rules that he is unfit to stand trial. Milosevic's regime in former Yugoslavia collapses; Vojislav Kostunica elected President. George W. Bush elected US President.
2001 Al-Qaeda terrorist attacks of 9/11. US and allied military attacks against the Taliban in Afghanistan.

2003 Iraq weapons crisis; American and British troops invade Iraq. Saddam Hussein captured in Iraq by US troops.

2004 Terrorist bombings in Madrid. Beslan school hostage crisis. George W. Bush re-elected as US President. Indian Ocean tsunami.

2005 Blair re-elected as Prime Minister in UK. Terrorist bombings in London. Provisional IRA formally orders an end to its armed campaign (since 1969). First forced evacuation of settlers under Israel Unilateral Disengagement Plan.

SLOUCHING TOWARDS
BETHLEHEM

For Quintana

Turning and turning in the widening gyre
The falcon cannot hear the falconer;
Things fall apart; the center cannot hold;
Mere anarchy is loosed upon the world,
The blood-dimmed tide is loosed, and everywhere
The ceremony of innocence is drowned;
The best lack all conviction, while the worst
Are full of passionate intensity.

Surely some revelation is at hand;
Surely the Second Coming is at hand.
The Second Coming! Hardly are those words out
When a vast image out of Spiritus Mundi
Troubles my sight: somewhere in the sands of the desert
A shape with lion body and the head of a man,
A gaze blank and pitiless as the sun,
Is moving its slow thighs, while all about it
Reel shadows of the indignant desert birds.
The darkness drops again; but now I know
That twenty centuries of stony sleep
Were vexed to nightmare by a rocking cradle,
And what rough beast, its hour come round at last,
Slouches towards Bethlehem to be born?

W. B. YEATS

I learned courage from Buddha, Jesus, Lincoln, Einstein,
and Cary Grant.

MISS PEGGY LEE

A PREFACE

THIS BOOK IS called *Slouching Towards Bethlehem* because for several years now certain lines from the Yeats poem which appears two pages back have reverberated in my inner ear as if they were surgically implanted there. The widening gyre, the falcon which does not hear the falconer, the gaze blank and pitiless as the sun; those have been my points of reference, the only images against which much of what I was seeing and hearing and thinking seemed to make any pattern. "Slouching Towards Bethlehem" is also the title of one piece in the book, and that piece, which derived from some time spent in the Haight-Ashbury district of San Francisco, was for me both the most imperative of all these pieces to write and the only one that made me despondent after it was printed. It was the first time I had dealt directly and flatly with the evidence of atomization, the proof that things fall apart: I went to San Francisco because I had not been able to work in some months, had been paralyzed by the conviction that writing was an irrelevant act, that the world as I had understood it no longer existed. If I was to work again at all, it would be necessary for me to come to terms with disorder. That was why the piece was important to me. And after it was printed I saw that, however directly and flatly I thought I had said it, I had failed to get through to many of the people who read and even liked the piece, failed to suggest that I was talking about something more general than a handful of children wearing mandalas on their foreheads. Disc jockeys telephoned my house and wanted to discuss (on the air) the incidence of "filth" in the Haight-Ashbury, and acquaintances congratulated me on having finished the piece "just in time," because "the whole fad's dead now, *fini, kaput.*" I suppose almost everyone who writes is afflicted some of the time by the suspicion that nobody out there is listening, but it seemed to me then (perhaps because the piece was important to me) that I had never gotten a feedback so universally beside the point.

Almost all of the pieces here were written for magazines during 1965, 1966, and 1967, and most of them, to get that question out of the way at the outset, were "my idea." I was asked to go up to the Carmel Valley and report on Joan Baez's school there; I was asked to go to Hawaii; I think I was asked to write about John Wayne; and I was asked for the short essays on "morality," by *The American Scholar*, and on "self-respect," by *Vogue*. Thirteen of the twenty pieces were published in *The Saturday Evening Post*. Quite often people write me from places like Toronto and want to know (demand to know) how I can reconcile my conscience with writing for *The Saturday Evening Post*; the answer is quite simple. The *Post* is extremely receptive to what the writer wants to do, pays enough for him to be able to do it right, and is meticulous about not changing copy. I lose a nicety of inflection now and then to the *Post*, but do not count myself compromised. Of course not all of the pieces in this book have to do, in a "subject" sense, with the general breakup, with things falling apart; that is a large and rather presumptuous notion, and many of these pieces are small and personal. But since I am neither a camera eye nor much given to writing pieces which do not interest me, whatever I do write reflects, sometimes gratuitously, how I feel.

I am not sure what more I could tell you about these pieces. I could tell you that I liked doing some of them more than others, but that all of them were hard for me to do, and took more time than perhaps they were worth; that there is always a point in the writing of a piece when I sit in a room literally papered with false starts and cannot put one word after another and imagine that I have suffered a small stroke, leaving me apparently undamaged but actually aphasic. I was in fact as sick as I have ever been when I was writing "Slouching Towards Bethlehem"; the pain kept me awake at night and so for twenty and twenty-one hours a day I drank gin-and-hot-water to blunt the pain and took Dexedrine to blunt the gin and wrote the piece. (I would like you to believe that I kept working out of some real professionalism, to meet the deadline, but that would not be entirely true; I did have a deadline, but it was also a troubled time, and working did to the trouble what gin did to the pain.) What else is there to tell? I am bad at interviewing people. I avoid situations in which I have to talk to anyone's press agent. (This precludes doing pieces on most actors, a bonus in itself.) I do not like to make telephone calls, and would not like to count the mornings I have sat on some Best Western motel bed somewhere and tried to force myself to put through the call to the assistant district attorney. My only advantage as a reporter is that I am so physically small, so temperamentally unobtrusive, and so neurotically inarticulate that people tend to forget that my presence runs counter to their best interests. And it always does. That is one last thing to remember: *writers are always selling somebody out.*

CONTENTS

I
LIFE STYLES IN THE
GOLDEN LAND

THIS IS A story about love and death in the golden land, and begins with the country. The San Bernardino Valley lies only an hour east of Los Angeles by the San Bernardino Freeway but is in certain ways an alien place: not the coastal California of the subtropical twilights and the soft westerlies off the Pacific but a harsher California, haunted by the Mojave just beyond the mountains, devastated by the hot dry Santa Ana wind that comes down through the passes at 100 miles an hour and whines through the eucalyptus windbreaks and works on the nerves. October is the bad month for the wind, the month when breathing is difficult and the hills blaze up spontaneously. There has been no rain since April. Every voice seems a scream. It is the season of suicide and divorce and prickly dread, wherever the wind blows.

The Mormons settled this ominous country, and then they abandoned it, but by the time they left the first orange tree had been planted and for the next hundred years the San Bernardino Valley would draw a kind of people who imagined they might live among the talismanic fruit and prosper in the dry air, people who brought with them Midwestern ways of building and cooking and praying and who tried to graft those ways upon the land. The graft took in curious ways. This is the California where it is possible to live and die without ever eating an artichoke, without ever meeting a Catholic or a Jew. This is the California where it is easy to Dial-A-Devotion, but hard to buy a book. This is the country in which a belief in the literal interpretation of Genesis has slipped imperceptibly into a belief in the literal interpretation of *Double Indemnity*, the country of the teased hair and the Capris and the girls for whom all life's promise comes down to a waltz-length white wedding dress and the birth of a Kimberly or a Sherry or a Debbi and a Tijuana divorce and a return to hairdressers' school. "We were just crazy kids," they say without regret, and look to the future. The future always looks good in the golden land, because no one remembers the past.

Here is where the hot wind blows and the old ways do not seem relevant, where the divorce rate is double the national average and where one person in every thirty-eight lives in a trailer. Here is the last stop for all those who come from somewhere else, for all those who drifted away from the cold and the past and the old ways. Here is where they are trying to find a new life style, trying to find it in the only places they know to look: the movies and the newspapers. The case of Lucille Marie Maxwell Miller is a tabloid monument to that new life style.

Imagine Banyan Street first, because Banyan is where it happened. The way to Banyan is to drive west from San Bernardino out Foothill Boulevard, Route 66: past the Santa Fe switching yards, the Forty Winks Motel. Past the motel that is nineteen stucco tepees: "SLEEP IN A WIGWAM—GET MORE FOR YOUR WAMPUM." Past Fontana Drag City and the Fontana Church of the Nazarene and the Pit Stop A Go-Go; past Kaiser Steel, through Cucamonga, out to the Kapu Kai Restaurant-Bar and Coffee Shop, at the corner of Route 66 and Carnelian Avenue. Up Carnelian Avenue from the Kapu Kai, which means "Forbidden Seas," the subdivision flags whip in the harsh wind. "HALF-ACRE RANCHES! SNACK BARS! TRAVERTINE ENTRIES! $95 DOWN." It is the trail of an intention gone haywire, the flotsam of the New California. But after a while the signs thin out on Carnelian Avenue, and the houses are no longer the bright pastels of the Springtime Home owners but the faded bungalows of the people who grow a few grapes and keep a few chickens out here, and then the hill gets steeper and the road climbs and even the bungalows are few, and here—desolate, roughly surfaced, lined with eucalyptus and lemon groves—is Banyan Street.

Like so much of this country, Banyan suggests something curious and unnatural. The lemon groves are sunken, down a three- or four-foot retaining wall, so that one looks directly into their dense foliage, too lush, unsettlingly glossy, the greenery of nightmare; the fallen eucalyptus bark is too dusty, a place for snakes to breed. The stones look not like natural stones but like the rubble of some unmentioned upheaval. There are smudge pots, and a closed cistern. To one side of Banyan there is the flat valley, and to the other the San Bernardino Mountains, a dark mass looming too high, too fast, nine, ten, eleven thousand feet, right there above the lemon groves. At midnight on Banyan

Street there is no light at all, and no sound except the wind in the eucalyptus and a muffled barking of dogs. There may be a kennel somewhere, or the dogs may be coyotes.

Banyan Street was the route Lucille Miller took home from the twenty-four-hour Mayfair Market on the night of October 7, 1964, a night when the moon was dark and the wind was blowing and she was out of milk, and Banyan Street was where, at about 12:30 a.m., her 1964 Volkswagen came to a sudden stop, caught fire, and began to burn. For an hour and fifteen minutes Lucille Miller ran up and down Banyan calling for help, but no cars passed and no help came. At three o'clock that morning, when the fire had been put out and the California Highway Patrol officers were completing their report, Lucille Miller was still sobbing and incoherent, for her husband had been asleep in the Volkswagen. "What will I tell the children, when there's nothing left, nothing left in the casket," she cried to the friend called to comfort her. "How can I tell them there's nothing left?"

In fact there was something left, and a week later it lay in the Draper Mortuary Chapel in a closed bronze coffin blanketed with pink carnations. Some 200 mourners heard Elder Robert E. Denton of the Seventh-Day Adventist Church of Ontario speak of "the temper of fury that has broken out among us." For Gordon Miller, he said, there would be "no more death, no more heartaches, no more misunderstandings." Elder Ansel Bristol mentioned the "peculiar" grief of the hour. Elder Fred Jensen asked "what shall it profit a man, if he shall gain the whole world, and lose his own soul?" A light rain fell, a blessing in a dry season, and a female vocalist sang "Safe in the Arms of Jesus." A tape recording of the service was made for the widow, who was being held without bail in the San Bernardino County Jail on a charge of first-degree murder.

Of course she came from somewhere else, came off the prairie in search of something she had seen in a movie or heard on the radio, for this is a Southern California story. She was born on January 17, 1930, in Winnipeg, Manitoba, the only child of Gordon and Lily Maxwell, both schoolteachers and both dedicated to the Seventh-Day Adventist Church, whose members observe the Sabbath on Saturday, believe in an apocalyptic Second Coming, have a strong missionary tendency, and, if they are strict, do not smoke, drink, eat meat, use makeup, or wear jewelry, including wedding rings. By the time Lucille Maxwell enrolled at Walla Walla College in College Place, Washington, the Adventist school where her parents then taught, she was an eighteen-year-old possessed of unremarkable good looks and remarkable high spirits. "Lucille wanted to see the world," her father would say in retrospect, "and I guess she found out."

The high spirits did not seem to lend themselves to an extended course of study at Walla Walla College, and in the spring of 1949 Lucille Maxwell met and married Gordon ("Cork") Miller, a twenty-four-old graduate of Walla Walla and of the University of Oregon dental school, then stationed at Fort Lewis as a medical officer. "Maybe you could say it was love at first sight," Mr. Maxwell recalls. "Before they were ever formally introduced, he sent Lucille a dozen and a half roses with a card that said even if she didn't come out on a date with him, he hoped she'd find the roses pretty anyway." The Maxwells remember their daughter as a "radiant" bride.

Unhappy marriages so resemble one another that we do not need to know too much about the course of this one. There may or may not have been trouble on Guam, where Cork and Lucille Miller lived while he finished his Army duty. There may or may not have been problems in the small Oregon town where he first set up private practice. There appears to have been some disappointment about their move to California: Cork Miller had told friends that he wanted to become a doctor, that he was unhappy as a dentist and planned to enter the Seventh-Day Adventist College of Medical Evangelists at Loma Linda, a few miles south of San Bernardino. Instead he bought a dental practice in the west end of San Bernardino County, and the family settled there, in a modest house on the kind of street where there are always tricycles and revolving credit and dreams about bigger houses, better streets. That was 1957. By the summer of 1964 they had achieved the bigger house on the better street and the familiar accouterments of a family on its way up: the $30,000 a year, the three children for the Christmas card, the picture window, the family room, the newspaper photographs that showed "Mrs. Gordon Miller, Ontario Heart Fund Chairman...." They were paying the familiar price for it. And they had reached the familiar season of divorce.

It might have been anyone's bad summer, anyone's siege of heat and nerves and migraine and money worries, but this one began particularly early and particularly badly. On April 24 an old friend, Elaine Hayton, died suddenly; Lucille Miller had seen her only the night before. During the month of May, Cork Miller was hospitalized briefly with a bleeding ulcer, and his usual reserve deepened into depression. He told his accountant that he was "sick of looking at open mouths," and threatened suicide. By July 8, the conventional tensions of love and money had reached the conventional impasse in the new house on the acre lot at 8488 Bella Vista, and Lucille Miller filed for divorce. Within a month, however, the Millers seemed reconciled. They saw a marriage counselor. They talked about a fourth child. It seemed that the marriage had reached the traditional truce, the point at which so many resign themselves to cutting both their losses and their hopes.

But the Millers' season of trouble was not to end that easily. October 7 began as a commonplace enough day, one of those days that sets the teeth on edge with its tedium, its small frustrations. The temperature reached 102° in San Bernardino that afternoon, and the Miller children were home from school because of Teachers' Institute. There was ironing to be dropped off. There was a trip to pick up a prescription for Nembutal, a trip to a self-service dry cleaner. In the early evening, an unpleasant accident with the Volkswagen: Cork Miller hit and killed a German shepherd, and afterward said that his head felt "like it had a Mack truck on it." It was something he often said. As of that evening Cork Miller was $63,479 in debt, including the $29,637 mortgage on the new house, a debt load which seemed oppressive to him. He was a man who wore his responsibilities uneasily, and complained of migraine headaches almost constantly.

He ate alone that night, from a TV tray in the living room. Later the Millers watched John Forsythe and Senta Berger in *See How They Run*, and when the movie ended, about eleven, Cork Miller suggested that they go out for milk. He wanted some hot chocolate. He took a blanket and pillow from the couch and climbed into the passenger seat of the Volkswagen. Lucille Miller remembers reaching over to lock his door as she backed down the driveway. By the time she left the Mayfair Market, and long before they reached Banyan Street, Cork Miller appeared to be asleep.

There is some confusion in Lucille Miller's mind about what happened between 12:30 a.m., when the fire broke out, and 1:50 a.m., when it was reported. She says that she was driving east on Banyan Street at about 35 m.p.h. when she felt the Volkswagen pull sharply to the right. The next thing she knew the car was on the embankment, quite near the edge of the retaining wall, and flames were shooting up behind her. She does not remember jumping out. She does remember prying up a stone with which she broke the window next to her husband, and then scrambling down the retaining wall to try to find a stick. "I don't know how I was going to push him out," she says. "I just thought if I had a stick, I'd push him out." She could not, and after a while she ran to the intersection of Banyan and Carnelian Avenue. There are no houses at that corner, and almost no traffic. After one car had passed without stopping, Lucille Miller ran back down Banyan toward the burning Volkswagen. She did not stop, but she slowed down, and in the flames she could see her husband. He was, she said, "just black."

At the first house up Sapphire Avenue, half a mile from the Volkswagen, Lucille Miller finally found help. There Mrs. Robert Swenson called the sheriff, and then, at Lucille Miller's request, she called Harold Lance, the Millers' lawyer and their close friend. When Harold Lance arrived he took Lucille Miller home to his wife, Joan. Twice Harold Lance and Lucille Miller returned to Banyan Street and talked to the Highway Patrol officers. A third time Harold Lance returned alone, and when he came back he said to Lucille Miller, "O.K. ... you don't talk any more."

When Lucille Miller was arrested the next afternoon, Sandy Slagle was with her. Sandy Slagle was the intense, relentlessly loyal medical student who used to baby-sit for the Millers, and had been living as a member of the family since she graduated from high school in 1959. The Millers took her away from a difficult home situation, and she thinks of Lucille Miller not only as "more or less a mother or a sister" but as "the most wonderful character" she has ever known. On the night of the accident, Sandy Slagle was in her dormitory at Loma Linda University, but Lucille Miller called her early in the morning and asked her to come home. The doctor was there when Sandy Slagle arrived, giving Lucille Miller an injection of Nembutal. "She was crying as she was going under," Sandy Slagle recalls. "Over and over she'd say,

'Sandy, all the hours I spent trying to save him and now what are they trying to *do* to me?'"

At 1:30 that afternoon, Sergeant William Paterson and Detectives Charles Callahan and Joseph Karr of the Central Homicide Division arrived at 8488 Bella Vista. "One of them appeared at the bedroom door," Sandy Slagle remembers, "and said to Lucille, 'You've got ten minutes to get dressed or we'll take you as you are.' She was in her nightgown, you know, so I tried to get her dressed."

Sandy Slagle tells the story now as if by rote, and her eyes do not waver. "So I had her panties and bra on her and they opened the door again, so I got some Capris on her, you know, and a scarf." Her voice drops. "And then they just took her."

The arrest took place just twelve hours after the first report that there had been an accident on Banyan Street, a rapidity which would later prompt Lucille Miller's attorney to say that the entire case was an instance of trying to justify a reckless arrest. Actually what first caused the detectives who arrived on Banyan Street toward dawn that morning to give the accident more than routine attention were certain apparent physical inconsistencies. While Lucille Miller had said that she was driving about 35 m.p.h. when the car swerved to a stop, an examination of the cooling Volkswagen showed that it was in low gear, and that the parking rather than the driving lights were on. The front wheels, moreover, did not seem to be in exactly the position that Lucille Miller's description of the accident would suggest, and the right rear wheel was dug in deep, as if it had been spun in place. It seemed curious to the detectives, too, that a sudden stop from 35 m.p.h.—the same jolt which was presumed to have knocked over a gasoline can in the back seat and somehow started the fire—should have left two milk cartons upright on the back floorboard, and the remains of a Polaroid camera box lying apparently undisturbed on the back seat.

No one, however, could be expected to give a precise account of what did and did not happen in a moment of terror, and none of these inconsistencies seemed in themselves incontrovertible evidence of criminal intent. But they did interest the Sheriff's Office, as did Gordon Miller's apparent unconsciousness at the time of the accident, and the length of time it had taken Lucille Miller to get help. Something, moreover, struck the investigators as wrong about Harold Lance's attitude when he came back to

Banyan Street the third time and found the investigation by no means over. "The way Lance was acting," the prosecuting attorney said later, "they thought maybe they'd hit a nerve."

And so it was that on the morning of October 8, even before the doctor had come to give Lucille Miller an injection to calm her, the San Bernardino County Sheriff's Office was trying to construct another version of what might have happened between 12:30 and 1:50 a.m. The hypothesis they would eventually present was based on the somewhat tortuous premise that Lucille Miller had undertaken a plan which failed: a plan to stop the car on the lonely road, spread gasoline over her presumably drugged husband, and, with a stick on the accelerator, gently "walk" the Volkswagen over the embankment, where it would tumble four feet down the retaining wall into the lemon grove and almost certainly explode. If this happened, Lucille Miller might then have somehow negotiated the two miles up Carnelian to Bella Vista in time to be home when the accident was discovered. This plan went awry, according to the Sheriff's Office hypothesis, when the car would not go over the rise of the embankment. Lucille Miller might have panicked then—after she had killed the engine the third or fourth time, say, out there on the dark road with the gasoline already spread and the dogs baying and the wind blowing and the unspeakable apprehension that a pair of headlights would suddenly light up Banyan Street and expose her there—and set the fire herself.

Although this version accounted for some of the physical evidence—the car in low because it had been started from a dead stop, the parking lights on because she could not do what needed doing without some light, a rear wheel spun in repeated attempts to get the car over the embankment, the milk cartons upright because there had been no sudden stop—it did not seem on its own any more or less credible than Lucille Miller's own story. Moreover, some of the physical evidence did seem to support her story: a nail in a front tire, a nine-pound rock found in the car, presumably the one with which she had broken the window in an attempt to save her husband. Within a few days an autopsy had established that Gordon Miller was alive when he burned, which did not particularly help the State's case, and that he had enough Nembutal and Sandoptal in his blood to put the average person to sleep, which did: on the other hand

Gordon Miller habitually took both Nembutal and Fiorinal (a common headache prescription which contains Sandoptal), and had been ill besides.

It was a spotty case, and to make it work at all the State was going to have to find a motive. There was talk of unhappiness, talk of another man. That kind of motive, during the next few weeks, was what they set out to establish. They set out to find it in accountants' ledgers and double-indemnity clauses and motel registers, set out to determine what might move a woman who believed in all the promises of the middle class—a woman who had been chairman of the Heart Fund and who always knew a reasonable little dressmaker and who had come out of the bleak wild of prairie fundamentalism to find what she imagined to be the good life—what should drive such a woman to sit on a street called Bella Vista and look out her new picture window into the empty California sun and calculate how to burn her husband alive in a Volkswagen. They found the wedge they wanted closer at hand than they might have at first expected, for, as testimony would reveal later at the trial, it seemed that in December of 1963 Lucille Miller had begun an affair with the husband of one of her friends, a man whose daughter called her "Auntie Lucille," a man who might have seemed to have the gift for people and money and the good life that Cork Miller so noticeably lacked. The man was Arthwell Hayton, a well-known San Bernardino attorney and at one time a member of the district attorney's staff.

In some ways it was the conventional clandestine affair in a place like San Bernardino, a place where little is bright or graceful, where it is routine to misplace the future and easy to start look-ing for it in bed. Over the seven weeks that it would take to try Lucille Miller for murder, Assistant District Attorney Don A. Turner and defense attorney Edward P. Foley would between them unfold a curiously predictable story. There were the falsi-fied motel registrations. There were the lunch dates, the afternoon drives in Arthwell Hayton's red Cadillac convertible. There were the interminable discussions of the wronged partners. There were the confidantes ("I knew everything," Sandy Slagle would insist fiercely later. "I knew every time, places, everything") and there were the words remembered from bad magazine stories

("Don't kiss me, it will trigger things," Lucille Miller remembered telling Arthwell Hayton in the parking lot of Harold's Club in Fontana after lunch one day) and there were the notes, the sweet exchanges: "Hi Sweetie Pie! You are my cup of tea!! Happy Birthday—you don't look a day over 29!! Your baby, Arthwell."

And, toward the end, there was the acrimony. It was April 24, 1964, when Arthwell Hayton's wife, Elaine, died suddenly, and nothing good happened after that. Arthwell Hayton had taken his cruiser, *Captain's Lady*, over to Catalina that weekend; he called home at nine o'clock Friday night, but did not talk to his wife because Lucille Miller answered the telephone and said that Elaine was showering. The next morning the Haytons' daughter found her mother in bed, dead. The newspapers reported the death as accidental, perhaps the result of an allergy to hair spray. When Arthwell Hayton flew home from Catalina that weekend, Lucille Miller met him at the airport, but the finish had already been written.

It was in the breakup that the affair ceased to be in the conventional mode and began to resemble instead the novels of James M. Cain, the movies of the late 1930's, all the dreams in which violence and threats and blackmail are made to seem commonplaces of middle-class life. What was most startling about the case that the State of California was preparing against Lucille Miller was something that had nothing to do with law at all, something that never appeared in the eight-column afternoon headlines but was always there between them: the revelation that the dream was teaching the dreamers how to live. Here is Lucille Miller talking to her lover sometime in the early summer of 1964, after he had indicated that, on the advice of his minister, he did not intend to see her any more: "First, I'm going to go to that dear pastor of yours and tell him a few things.... When I do tell him that, you won't be in the Redlands Church any more.... Look, Sonny Boy, if you think your reputation is going to be ruined, your life won't be worth two cents." Here is Arthwell Hayton, to Lucille Miller: "I'll go to Sheriff Frank Bland and tell him some things that I know about you until you'll wish you'd never heard of Arthwell Hayton." For an affair between a Seventh-Day Adventist dentist's wife and a Seventh-Day Adventist personal-injury lawyer, it seems a curious kind of dialogue.

"Boy, I could get that little boy coming and going," Lucille Miller later confided to Erwin Sprengle, a Riverside contractor

22

who was a business partner of Arthwell Hayton's and a friend to both the lovers. (Friend or no, on this occasion he happened to have an induction coil attached to his telephone in order to tape Lucille Miller's call.) "And he hasn't got one thing on me that he can prove. I mean, I've got concrete—he has nothing concrete." In the same taped conversation with Erwin Sprengle, Lucille Miller mentioned a tape that she herself had surreptitiously made, months before, in Arthwell Hayton's car.

"I said to him, I said 'Arthwell, I just feel like I'm being used.'... He started sucking his thumb and he said 'I love you.... This isn't something that happened yesterday. I'd marry you tomorrow if I could. I don't love Elaine.' He'd love to hear that played back, wouldn't he?"

"Yeah," drawled Sprengle's voice on the tape. "That would be just a little incriminating, wouldn't it?"

"Just a *little* incriminating," Lucille Miller agreed. "It really *is*."

Later on the tape, Sprengle asked where Cork Miller was.

"He took the children down to the church."

"You didn't go?"

"No."

"You're naughty."

It was all, moreover, in the name of "love"; everyone involved placed a magical faith in the efficacy of the very word. There was the significance that Lucille Miller saw in Arthwell's saying that he "loved" her, that he did not "love" Elaine. There was Arthwell insisting, later, at the trial, that he had never said it, that he may have "whispered sweet nothings in her ear" (as her defense hinted that he had whispered in many ears), but he did not remember bestowing upon her the special seal, saying the word, declaring "love." There was the summer evening when Lucille Miller and Sandy Slagle followed Arthwell Hayton down to his new boat in its mooring at Newport Beach and untied the lines with Arthwell aboard, Arthwell and a girl with whom he later testified he was drinking hot chocolate and watching television. "I did that on purpose," Lucille Miller told Erwin Sprengle later, "to save myself from letting my heart do something crazy."

January 11, 1965, was a bright warm day in Southern California, the kind of day when Catalina floats on the Pacific horizon and the air smells of orange blossoms and it is a long way from the bleak and difficult East, a long way from the cold, a long way from the past. A woman in Hollywood staged an all-night sit-in on the hood of her car to prevent repossession by a finance company. A seventy-year-old pensioner drove his station wagon at five miles an hour past three Gardena poker parlors and emptied three pistols and a twelve-gauge shotgun through their windows, wounding twenty-nine people. "Many young women become prostitutes just to have enough money to play cards," he explained in a note. Mrs. Nick Adams said that she was "not surprised" to hear her husband announce his divorce plans on the Les Crane Show, and, farther north, a sixteen-year-old jumped off the Golden Gate Bridge and lived.

And, in the San Bernardino County Courthouse, the Miller trial opened. The crowds were so bad that the glass courtroom doors were shattered in the crush, and from then on identification disks were issued to the first forty-three spectators in line. The line began forming at 6 a.m., and college girls camped at the courthouse all night, with stores of graham crackers and No-Cal.

All they were doing was picking a jury, those first few days, but the sensational nature of the case had already suggested itself. Early in December there had been an abortive first trial, a trial at which no evidence was ever presented because on the day the jury was seated the San Bernardino *Sun-Telegram* ran an "inside" story quoting Assistant District Attorney Don Turner, the prosecutor, as saying, "We are looking into the circumstances of Mrs. Hayton's death. In view of the current trial concerning the death of Dr. Miller, I do not feel I should comment on Mrs. Hayton's death." It seemed that there had been barbiturates in Elaine Hayton's blood, and there had seemed some irregularity about the way she was dressed on that morning when she was found under the covers, dead. Any doubts about the death at the time, however, had never gotten as far as the Sheriff's Office. "I guess somebody didn't want to rock the boat," Turner said later. "These were prominent people."

Although all of that had not been in the *Sun-Telegram*'s story, an immediate mistrial had been declared. Almost as immediately, there had been another development: Arthwell Hayton had asked newspapermen to an 11 a.m. Sunday morning press conference in his office. There had been television cameras, and flash bulbs popping. "As you gentlemen may know," Hayton had said, striking a note of stiff bonhomie, "there are very often women who become amorous toward their doctor or lawyer. This does not mean on the physician's or lawyer's part that there is any romance toward the patient or client."

"Would you deny that you were having an affair with Mrs. Miller?" a reporter had asked.

"I would deny that there was any romance on my part whatsoever."

It was a distinction he would maintain through all the wearing weeks to come.

So they had come to see Arthwell, these crowds who now milled beneath the dusty palms outside the courthouse, and they had also come to see Lucille, who appeared as a slight, intermittently pretty woman, already pale from lack of sun, a woman who would turn thirty-five before the trial was over and whose tendency toward haggardness was beginning to show, a meticulous woman who insisted, against her lawyer's advice, on coming to court with her hair piled high and lacquered. "I would've been happy if she'd come in with it hanging loose, but Lucille wouldn't do that," her lawyer said. He was Edward P. Foley, a small, emotional Irish Catholic who several times wept in the courtroom. "She has a great honesty, this woman," he added, "but this honesty about her appearance always worked against her."

By the time the trial opened, Lucille Miller's appearance included maternity clothes, for an official examination on December 18 had revealed that she was then three and a half months pregnant, a fact which made picking a jury even more difficult than usual, for Turner was asking the death penalty. "It's unfortunate but there it is," he would say of the pregnancy to each juror in turn, and finally twelve were seated, seven of them women, the youngest forty-one, an assembly of the very peers— housewives, a machinist, a truck driver, a grocery-store manager, a filing clerk—above whom Lucille Miller had wanted so badly to rise.

That was the sin, more than the adultery, which tended to reinforce the one for which she was being tried. It was implicit in both the defense and the prosecution that Lucille Miller was an erring woman, a woman who perhaps wanted too much. But to the prosecution she was not merely a woman who would want a new house and want to go to parties and run up high telephone bills ($1,152 in ten months), but a woman who would go so far as to murder her husband for his $80,000 in insurance, making it appear an accident in order to collect another $40,000 in double indemnity and straight accident policies. To Turner she was a woman who did not want simply her freedom and a reasonable alimony (she could have had that, the defense contended, by going through with her divorce suit), but wanted everything, a woman motivated by "love and greed." She was a "manipulator." She was a "user of people."

To Edward Foley, on the other hand, she was an impulsive woman who "couldn't control her foolish little heart." Where Turner skirted the pregnancy, Foley dwelt upon it, even calling the dead man's mother down from Washington to testify that her son had told her they were going to have another baby because Lucille felt that it would "do much to weld our home again in the pleasant relations that we used to have." Where the prosecution saw a "calculator," the defense saw a "blabber-mouth," and in fact Lucille Miller did emerge as an ingenuous conversationalist. Just as, before her husband's death, she had confided in her friends about her love affair, so she chatted about it after his death, with the arresting sergeant. "Of course Cork lived with it for years, you know," her voice was heard to tell Sergeant Paterson on a tape made the morning after her arrest. "After Elaine died, he pushed the panic button one night and just asked me right out, and that, I think, was when he really—the first time he really faced it." When the sergeant asked why she had agreed to talk to him, against the specific instructions of her lawyers, Lucille Miller said airily, "Oh, I've always been basically quite an honest person.... I mean I can put a hat in the cupboard and say it cost ten dollars less, but basically I've always kind of just lived my life the way I wanted to, and if you don't like it you can take off."

The prosecution hinted at men other than Arthwell, and even, over Foley's objections, managed to name one. The defense called Miller suicidal. The prosecution produced experts who said that the Volkswagen fire could not have been accidental. Foley produced witnesses who said that it could have been. Lucille's father, now a junior-high-school teacher in Oregon, quoted Isaiah to reporters: "*Every tongue that shall rise against thee in judgment thou shalt condemn.*" "Lucille did wrong, her affair," her mother said judiciously. "With her it was love. But with some I guess it's just passion." There was Debbie, the Millers' fourteen-year-old, testifying in a steady voice about how she and her mother had gone to a supermarket to buy the gasoline can the week before the accident. There was Sandy Slagle, in the courtroom every day, declaring that on at least one occasion Lucille Miller had prevented her husband not only from committing suicide but from committing suicide in such a way that it would appear an accident and ensure the double-indemnity payment. There was Wenche Berg, the pretty twenty-seven-year-old Norwegian governess to Arthwell Hayton's children, testifying that Arthwell had instructed her not to allow Lucille Miller to see or talk to the children.

Two months dragged by, and the headlines never stopped. Southern California's crime reporters were headquartered in San Bernardino for the duration: Howard Hertel from the *Times*, Jim Bennett and Eddy Jo Bernal from the *Herald-Examiner*. Two months in which the Miller trial was pushed off the *Examiner*'s front page only by the Academy Award nominations and Stan Laurel's death. And finally, on March 2, after Turner had reiterated that it was a case of "love and greed," and Foley had protested that his client was being tried for adultery, the case went to the jury.

They brought in the verdict, guilty of murder in the first degree, at 4:50 p.m. on March 5. "She didn't do it," Debbie Miller cried, jumping up from the spectators' section. "She didn't *do* it." Sandy Slagle collapsed in her seat and began to scream. "Sandy, for God's sake please *don't*," Lucille Miller said in a voice that carried across the courtroom, and Sandy Slagle was momentarily subdued. But as the jurors left the courtroom she screamed again: "You're murderers. …Every last one of you is a *murderer*." Sheriff's deputies moved in then, each wearing a string tie that read "1965 SHERIFF'S RODEO," and Lucille Miller's father, that sad-faced junior-high-school teacher who believed in the word of Christ and the dangers of wanting to see the world, blew her a kiss off his fingertips.

The California Institution for Women at Frontera, where Lucille Miller is now, lies down where Euclid Avenue turns into country road, not too many miles from where she once lived and shopped and organized the Heart Fund Ball. Cattle graze across the road, and Rainbirds sprinkle the alfalfa. Frontera has a softball field and tennis courts, and looks as if it might be a California junior college, except that the trees are not yet high enough to conceal the concertina wire around the top of the Cyclone fence. On visitors' day there are big cars in the parking area, big Buicks and Pontiacs that belong to grandparents and sisters and fathers (not many of them belong to husbands), and some of them have bumper stickers that say "SUPPORT YOUR LOCAL POLICE."

A lot of California murderesses live here, a lot of girls who somehow misunderstood the promise. Don Turner put Sandra Garner here (and her husband in the gas chamber at San Quentin) after the 1959 desert killings known to crime reporters as "the soda-pop murders." Carole Tregoff is here, and has been ever since she was convicted of conspiring to murder Dr. Finch's wife in West Covina, which is not too far from San Bernardino. Carole Tregoff is in fact a nurse's aide in the prison hospital, and might have attended Lucille Miller had her baby been born at Frontera; Lucille Miller chose instead to have it outside, and paid for the guard who stood outside the delivery room in St. Bernardine's Hospital. Debbie Miller came to take the baby home from the hospital, in a white dress with pink ribbons, and Debbie was allowed to choose a name. She named the baby Kimi Kai. The children live with Harold and Joan Lance now, because Lucille Miller will probably spend ten years at Frontera. Don Turner waived his original request for the death penalty (it was generally agreed that he had demanded it only, in Edward Foley's words, "to get anybody with the slightest trace of human kindness in their veins off the jury"), and settled for life imprisonment with the possibility of parole. Lucille Miller does not like it at Frontera, and has had trouble adjusting. "She's going to have to learn humility," Turner says. "She's going to have to use her ability to charm, to manipulate."

The new house is empty now, the house on the street with the sign that says

PRIVATE ROAD
BELLA VISTA
DEAD END

The Millers never did get it landscaped, and weeds grow up around the fieldstone siding. The television aerial has toppled on the roof, and a trash can is stuffed with the debris of family life: a cheap suitcase, a child's game called "Lie Detector." There is a sign on what would have been the lawn, and the sign reads "ESTATE SALE." Edward Foley is trying to get Lucille Miller's case appealed, but there have been delays. "A trial always comes down to a matter of sympathy," Foley says wearily now. "I couldn't create sympathy for her." Everyone is a little weary now, weary and resigned, everyone except Sandy Slagle, whose bitterness is still raw. She lives in an apartment near the medical school in Loma Linda, and studies reports of the case in *True Police Cases* and *Official Detective Stories*. "I'd much rather we not talk about the Hayton business too much," she tells visitors, and she keeps a tape recorder running. "I'd rather talk about Lucille and what a wonderful person she is and how her rights were violated." Harold Lance does not talk to visitors at all. "We don't want to give away what we can sell," he explains pleasantly; an attempt was made to sell Lucille Miller's personal story to *Life*, but *Life* did not want to buy it. In the district attorney's offices they are prosecuting other murders now, and do not see why the Miller trial attracted so much attention. "It wasn't a very interesting murder as murders go," Don Turner says laconically. Elaine Hayton's death is no longer under investigation. "We know everything we want to know," Turner says.

Arthwell Hayton's office is directly below Edward Foley's. Some people around San Bernardino say that Arthwell Hayton suffered; others say that he did not suffer at all. Perhaps he did not, for time past is not believed to have any bearing upon time present or future, out in the golden land where every day the world is born anew. In any case, on October 17, 1965, Arthwell Hayton married again, married his children's pretty governess, Wenche Berg, at a service in the Chapel of the Roses at a retirement village near Riverside. Later the newlyweds were feted at a reception for seventy-five in the dining room of Rose Garden Village. The bridegroom was in black tie, with a white carnation in his buttonhole. The bride wore a long white *peau de soie* dress and carried a shower bouquet of sweetheart roses with stephanotis streamers. A coronet of seed pearls held her illusion veil.

1966

JOHN WAYNE: A LOVE SONG

IN THE SUMMER of 1943 I was eight, and my father and mother and small brother and I were at Peterson Field in Colorado Springs. A hot wind blew through that summer, blew until it seemed that before August broke, all the dust in Kansas would be in Colorado, would have drifted over the tar-paper barracks and the temporary strip and stopped only when it hit Pikes Peak. There was not much to do, a summer like that: there was the day they brought in the first B-29, an event to remember but scarcely a vacation program. There was an Officers' Club, but no swimming pool; all the Officers' Club had of interest was artificial blue rain behind the bar. The rain interested me a good deal, but I could not spend the summer watching it, and so we went, my brother and I, to the movies.

We went three and four afternoons a week, sat on folding chairs in the darkened Quonset hut which served as a theater, and it was there, that summer of 1943 while the hot wind blew outside, that I first saw John Wayne. Saw the walk, heard the voice. Heard him tell the girl in a picture called *War of the Wildcats* that he would build her a house, "at the bend in the river where the cottonwoods grow." As it happened I did not grow up to be the kind of woman who is the heroine in a Western, and although the men I have known have had many virtues and have taken me to live in many places I have come to love, they have never been John Wayne, and they have never taken me to that bend in the river where the cottonwoods grow. Deep in that part of my heart where the artificial rain forever falls, that is still the line I wait to hear.

I tell you this neither in a spirit of self-revelation nor as an exercise in total recall, but simply to demonstrate that when John Wayne rode through my childhood, and perhaps through yours, he determined forever the shape of certain of our dreams. It did not seem possible that such a man could fall ill, could carry within him that most inexplicable and ungovernable of diseases. The rumor struck some obscure anxiety, threw our very childhoods into question. In John Wayne's world, John Wayne was supposed to give the orders. "Let's ride," he said, and "Saddle up." "Forward *ho*," and "A man's gotta do what he's got to do." "Hello, there," he said when he first saw the girl, in a construction camp or on a train or just standing around on the front porch waiting for somebody to ride up through the tall grass. When John Wayne spoke, there was no mistaking his intentions; he had a sexual authority so strong that even a child could perceive it. And in a world we understood early to be characterized by venality and doubt and paralyzing ambiguities, he suggested another world, one which may or may not have existed ever but in any case existed no more: a place where a man could move free, could make his own code and live by it; a world in which, if a man did what he had to do, he could one day take the girl and go riding through the draw and find himself home free, not in a hospital with something going wrong inside, not in a high bed with the flowers and the drugs and the forced smiles, but there at the bend in the bright river, the cottonwoods shimmering in the early morning sun.

"Hello, there." Where did he come from, before the tall grass? Even his history seemed right, for it was no history at all, nothing to intrude upon the dream. Born Marion Morrison in Winterset, Iowa, the son of a druggist. Moved as a child to Lancaster, California, part of the migration to that promised land sometimes called "the west coast of Iowa." Not that Lancaster was the promise fulfilled; Lancaster was a town on the Mojave where the dust blew through. But Lancaster was still California, and it was only a year from there to Glendale, where desolation had a different flavor: antimacassars among the orange groves, a middle-class prelude to Forest Lawn. Imagine Marion Morrison in Glendale. A Boy Scout, then a student at Glendale High. A tackle for U.S.C., a Sigma Chi. Summer vacations, a job moving props on the old Fox lot. There, a meeting with John Ford, one of the several directors who were to sense that into this perfect mold might be poured the inarticulate longings of a nation wondering at just what pass the trail had been lost. "Dammit," said Raoul Walsh later, "the son of a bitch looked like a man." And so after a while the boy from Glendale became a star. He did not become an actor, as he has always been careful to point out to interviewers

("How many times do I gotta tell you, I don't act at all, I *re*-act"), but a star, and the star called John Wayne would spend most of the rest of his life with one or another of those directors, out on some forsaken location, in search of the dream.

> *Out where the skies are a trifle bluer*
> *Out where friendship's a little truer*
> *That's where the West begins.*

Nothing very bad could happen in the dream, nothing a man could not face down. But something did. There it was, the rumor, and after a while the headlines. "I licked the Big C," John Wayne announced, as John Wayne would, reducing those outlaw cells to the level of any other outlaws, but even so we all sensed that this would be the one unpredictable confrontation, the one shoot-out Wayne could lose. I have as much trouble as the next person with illusion and reality, and I did not much want to see John Wayne when he must be (or so I thought) having some trouble with it himself, but I did, and it was down in Mexico when he was making the picture his illness had so long delayed, down in the very country of the dream.

It was John Wayne's 165th picture. It was Henry Hathaway's 84th. It was number 34 for Dean Martin, who was working off an old contract to Hal Wallis, for whom it was independent production number 65. It was called *The Sons of Katie Elder*, and it was a Western, and after the three-month delay they had finally shot the exteriors up in Durango, and now they were in the waning days of interior shooting at Estudio Churubusco outside Mexico City, and the sun was hot and the air was clear and it was lunch-time. Out under the pepper trees the boys from the Mexican crew sat around sucking caramels, and down the road some of the technical men sat around a place which served a stuffed lobster and a glass of tequila for one dollar American, but it was inside the cavernous empty commissary where the talent sat around, the reasons for the exercise, all sitting around the big table picking at *huevos con queso* and Carta Blanca beer. Dean Martin, unshaven. Mack Gray, who goes where Martin goes. Bob Goodfried, who was in charge of Paramount publicity and who had flown down to arrange for a trailer and who had a delicate stomach. "Tea and toast," he warned repeatedly. "That's the ticket. You can't trust the lettuce." And Henry Hathaway, the director, who did not seem to be listening to Goodfried. And John Wayne, who did not seem to be listening to anyone.

"This week's gone slow," Dean Martin said, for the third time.

"How can you say that?" Mack Gray demanded.

"*This … week's … gone … slow*, that's how I can say it."

"You don't mean you want it to end."

"I'll say it right out, Mack, I want it to *end*. Tomorrow night I shave this beard, I head for the airport, I say *adiós amigos*! Bye-bye *muchachos*!"

Henry Hathaway lit a cigar and patted Martin's arm fondly. "Not tomorrow, Dino."

"Henry, what are you planning to add? A World War?"

Hathaway patted Martin's arm again and gazed into the middle distance. At the end of the table someone mentioned a man who, some years before, had tried unsuccessfully to blow up an airplane.

"He's still in jail," Hathaway said suddenly.

"In jail?" Martin was momentarily distracted from the question whether to send his golf clubs back with Bob Goodfried or consign them to Mack Gray. "What's he in jail for if nobody got killed?"

"Attempted murder, Dino," Hathaway said gently. "A felony."

"You mean some guy just *tried* to kill me he'd end up in jail?"

Hathaway removed the cigar from his mouth and looked across the table. "Some guy just tried to kill *me* he wouldn't end up in jail. How about you, Duke?"

Very slowly, the object of Hathaway's query wiped his mouth, pushed back his chair, and stood up. It was the real thing, the authentic article, the move which had climaxed a thousand scenes on 165 flickering frontiers and phantasmagoric battlefields before, and it was about to climax this one, in the commissary at Estudio Churubusco outside Mexico City. "Right," John Wayne drawled. "I'd kill him."

Almost all the cast of *Katie Elder* had gone home, that last week; only the principals were left, Wayne, and Martin, and Earl Holliman, and Michael Anderson, Jr., and Martha Hyer. Martha Hyer was not around much, but every now and then someone referred to her, usually as "the girl." They had all been together nine weeks, six of them in Durango. Mexico City was not quite Durango; wives like to come along to places like Mexico City, like to shop for handbags, go to parties at Merle Oberon Pagliai's, like to look at her paintings. But Durango. The very name hallucinates. Man's country. Out where the West begins. There had been ahuehuete trees in Durango; a waterfall, rattlesnakes. There had been weather, nights so cold that they had postponed one or two exteriors until they could shoot inside at Churubusco. "It was the girl," they explained. "You couldn't keep the girl out in cold like that." Henry Hathaway had cooked in Durango, *gazpacho* and ribs and the steaks that Dean Martin had ordered flown down from the Sands; he had wanted to cook in Mexico City, but the management of the Hotel Bamer refused to let him set up a brick barbecue in his room. "You really missed something, *Durango*," they would say, sometimes joking and sometimes not, until it became a refrain, Eden lost.

But if Mexico City was not Durango, neither was it Beverly Hills. No one else was using Churubusco that week, and there inside the big sound stage that said LOS HIJOS DE KATIE ELDER on the door, there with the pepper trees and the bright sun outside, they could still, for just so long as the picture lasted, maintain a world peculiar to men who like to make Westerns, a world of loyalties and fond raillery, of sentiment and shared cigars, of interminable desultory recollections; campfire talk, its only point to keep a human voice raised against the night, the wind, the rustlings in the brush.

"Stuntman got hit accidentally on a picture of mine once," Hathaway would say between takes of an elaborately choreographed fight scene. "What was his name, married Estelle Taylor, met her down in Arizona."

The circle would close around him, the cigars would be fingered. The delicate art of the staged fight was to be contemplated.

"I only hit one guy in my life," Wayne would say. "Accidentally, I mean. That was Mike Mazurki."

"Some guy. Hey, Duke says he only hit one guy in his life, Mike Mazurki."

"Some choice." Murmurings, assent.

"It wasn't a choice, it was an accident."

"I can believe it."

"You bet."

"Oh boy. Mike Mazurki."

And so it would go. There was Web Overlander, Wayne's makeup man for twenty years, hunched in a blue Windbreaker, passing out sticks of Juicy Fruit. "*Insect* spray," he would say. "Don't tell us about insect spray. We saw insect spray in Africa, all right. Remember Africa?" Or, "*Steamer* clams. Don't tell us about steamer clams. We got our fill of steamer clams all right, on the *Hatari!* appearance tour. Remember Bookbinder's?" There was Ralph Volkie, Wayne's trainer for eleven years, wearing a red baseball cap and carrying around a clipping from Hedda Hopper, a tribute to Wayne. "This Hopper's some lady," he would say again and again. "Not like some of these guys, all they write is sick, sick, sick, how can you call that guy *sick*, when he's got pains, coughs, works all day, *never complains*. That guy's got the best hook since Dempsey, not *sick*."

And there was Wayne himself, fighting through number 165. There was Wayne, in his thirty-three-year-old spurs, his dusty neckerchief, his blue shirt. "You don't have too many worries about what to wear in these things," he said. "You can wear a blue shirt, or, if you're down in Monument Valley, you can wear a yellow shirt." There was Wayne, in a relatively new hat, a hat which made him look curiously like William S. Hart. "I had this old cavalry hat I loved, but I lent it to Sammy Davis. I got it back, it was unwearable. I think they all pushed it down on his head and said *O.K., John Wayne*—you know, a joke."

There was Wayne, working too soon, finishing the picture with a bad cold and a racking cough, so tired by late afternoon that he kept an oxygen inhalator on the set. And still nothing mattered but the Code. "That guy," he muttered of a reporter who had incurred his displeasure. "I admit I'm balding. I admit I got a tire around my middle. What man fifty-seven doesn't? Big news. Anyway, that guy."

He paused, about to expose the heart of the matter, the root of the distaste, the fracture of the rules that bothered him more than the alleged misquotations, more than the intimation that he was no longer the Ringo Kid. "He comes down, uninvited, but I ask him over anyway. So we're sitting around drinking mescal out of a water jug."

He paused again and looked meaningfully at Hathaway, readying him for the unthinkable denouement. "He had to be *assisted* to his room."

They argued about the virtues of various prizefighters, they argued about the price of J & B in pesos. They argued about dialogue.

"As rough a guy as he is, Henry, I still don't think he'd raffle off his mother's *Bible*."

"I like a shocker, Duke."

They exchanged endless training-table jokes. "You know why they call this memory sauce?" Martin asked, holding up a bowl of chili.

"Why?"

"Because you *remember it in the morning*."

"Hear that, Duke? Hear why they call this memory sauce?"

They delighted one another by blocking out minute variations in the free-for-all fight which is a set piece in Wayne pictures; motivated or totally gratuitous, the fight sequence has to be in the picture, because they so enjoy making it. "Listen—this'll really be funny. Duke picks up the kid, see, and then it takes both Dino and Earl to throw him out the door—*how's that*?"

They communicated by sharing old jokes; they sealed their camaraderie by making gentle, old-fashioned fun of wives, those civilizers, those tamers. "So Señora Wayne takes it into her head to stay up and have one brandy. So for the rest of the night it's 'Yes, Pilar, you're right, dear. I'm a bully, Pilar, you're right, I'm impossible.'"

"You hear that? Duke says Pilar threw a table at him."

"Hey, Duke, here's something funny. That finger you hurt today, get the Doc to bandage it up, go home tonight, show it to Pilar, tell her she did it when she threw the table. You know, make her think she was really cutting up."

They treated the oldest among them respectfully; they treated the youngest fondly. "You see that kid?" they said of Michael Anderson, Jr. "What a kid."

"He don't act, it's right from the heart," said Hathaway, patting his heart.

"Hey kid," Martin said. "You're gonna be in my next picture. We'll have the whole thing, no beards. The striped shirts, the girls, the hi-fi, the eye lights."

They ordered Michael Anderson his own chair, with "BIG MIKE" tooled on the back. When it arrived on the set, Hathaway hugged him. "You see that?" Anderson asked Wayne, suddenly too shy to look him in the eye. Wayne gave him the smile, the nod, the final accolade. "I saw it, kid."

On the morning of the day they were to finish *Katie Elder*, Web Overlander showed up not in his Windbreaker but in a blue blazer. "Home, Mama," he said, passing out the last of his Juicy Fruit. "I got on my getaway clothes." But he was subdued. At noon, Henry Hathaway's wife dropped by the commissary to tell him that she might fly over to Acapulco. "Go ahead," he told her. "I get through here, all I'm gonna do is take Seconal to a point just this side of suicide." They were all subdued. After Mrs. Hathaway left, there were desultory attempts at reminiscing, but man's country was receding fast; they were already halfway home, and all they could call up was the 1961 Bel Air fire, during which Henry Hathaway had ordered the Los Angeles Fire Department off his property and saved the place himself by, among other measures, throwing everything flammable into the swimming pool. "Those fire guys might've just given it up," Wayne said. "Just let it burn." In fact this was a good story, and one incorporating several of their favorite themes, but a Bel Air story was still not a Durango story.

In the early afternoon they began the last scene, and although they spent as much time as possible setting it up, the moment finally came when there was nothing to do but shoot it. "Second team out, first team in, *doors closed*," the assistant director shouted one last time. The stand-ins walked off the set, John Wayne and Martha Hyer walked on. "All right, boys, *silencio*, this is a picture." They took it twice. Twice the girl offered John Wayne the tattered Bible. Twice John Wayne told her that "there's a lot of places I go where that wouldn't fit in." Everyone was very still. And at 2:30 that Friday afternoon Henry Hathaway turned away from the camera, and in the hush that followed he ground out his cigar in a sand bucket. "O.K.," he said. "That's it."

* * *

37

Since that summer of 1943 I had thought of John Wayne in a number of ways. I had thought of him driving cattle up from Texas, and bringing airplanes in on a single engine, thought of him telling the girl at the Alamo that "Republic is a beautiful word." I had never thought of him having dinner with his family and with me and my husband in an expensive restaurant in Chapultepec Park, but time brings odd mutations, and there we were, one night that last week in Mexico. For a while it was only a nice evening, an evening anywhere. We had a lot of drinks and I lost the sense that the face across the table was in certain ways more familiar than my husband's.

And then something happened. Suddenly the room seemed suffused with the dream, and I could not think why. Three men appeared out of nowhere, playing guitars. Pilar Wayne leaned slightly forward, and John Wayne lifted his glass almost imperceptibly toward her. "We'll need some Pouilly-Fuissé for the rest of the table," he said, "and some red Bordeaux for the Duke." We all smiled, and drank the Pouilly-Fuissé for the rest of the table and the red Bordeaux for the Duke, and all the while the men with the guitars kept playing, until finally I realized what they were playing, what they had been playing all along: "The Red River Valley" and the theme from *The High and the Mighty*. They did not quite get the beat right, but even now I can hear them, in another country and a long time later, even as I tell you this.

1965

OUTSIDE THE MONTEREY county courthouse in Salinas, California, the Downtown Merchants' Christmas decorations glittered in the thin sunlight that makes the winter lettuce grow. Inside, the crowd blinked uneasily in the blinding television lights. The occasion was a meeting of the Monterey County Board of Supervisors, and the issue, on this warm afternoon before Christmas 1965, was whether or not a small school in the Carmel Valley, the Institute for the Study of Nonviolence, owned by Miss Joan Baez, was in violation of Section 32-C of the Monterey County Zoning Code, which prohibits land use "detrimental to the peace, morals, or general welfare of Monterey County." Mrs. Gerald Petkuss, who lived across the road from the school, had put the problem another way. "We wonder what kind of people would go to a school like this," she asked quite early in the controversy. "Why they aren't out working and making money."

Mrs. Petkuss was a plump young matron with an air of bewildered determination, and she came to the rostrum in a strawberry-pink knit dress to say that she had been plagued "by people associated with Miss Baez's school coming up to ask where it was although they knew perfectly *well* where it was— one gentleman I remember had a beard."

"Well I don't *care*," Mrs. Petkuss cried when someone in the front row giggled. "I have three small children, that's a big responsibility, and I don't like to have to worry about…" Mrs. Petkuss paused delicately. "About who's around."

The hearing lasted from two until 7:15 p.m., five hours and fifteen minutes of participatory democracy during which it was suggested, on the one hand, that the Monterey County Board of Supervisors was turning our country into Nazi Germany, and, on the other, that the presence of Miss Baez and her fifteen students in the Carmel Valley would lead to "Berkeley-type" demonstrations, demoralize trainees at Fort Ord, paralyze Army convoys using the Carmel Valley road, and send property values plummeting throughout the county. "Frankly, I can't conceive of anyone buying property near such an operation," declared Mrs. Petkuss's husband, who is a veterinarian. Both Dr. and Mrs. Petkuss, the latter near tears, said that they were particularly offended by Miss Baez's presence on her property during weekends. It seemed that she did not always stay inside. She sat out under trees, and walked around the property.

"We don't start until one," someone from the school objected. "Even if we did make noise, which we don't, the Petkusses could sleep until one, I don't see what the problem is."

The Petkusses' lawyer jumped up. "The *prob*lem is that the Petkusses happen to have a very beautiful swimming pool, they'd like to have guests out on weekends, like to use the pool."

"They'd have to stand up on a table to see the school."

"They will, too," shouted a young woman who had already indicated her approval of Miss Baez by reading aloud to the supervisors a passage from John Stuart Mill's *On Liberty*. "They'll be out with spyglasses."

"That is *not* true," Mrs. Petkuss keened. "We see the school out of three bedroom windows, out of one living-room window, it's the only direction we can *look*."

Miss Baez sat very still in the front row. She was wearing a long-sleeved navy-blue dress with an Irish lace collar and cuffs, and she kept her hands folded in her lap. She is extraordinary looking, far more so than her photographs suggest, since the camera seems to emphasize an Indian cast to her features and fails to record either the startling fineness and clarity of her bones and eyes or, her most striking characteristic, her absolute directness, her absence of guile. She has a great natural style, and she is what used to be called a lady. "Scum," hissed an old man with a snap-on bow tie who had identified himself as "a veteran of two wars" and who is a regular at such meetings. "*Spaniel*." He seemed to be referring to the length of Miss Baez's hair, and was trying to get her attention by tapping with his walking stick, but her eyes did not flicker from the rostrum. After a while she got up, and stood until the room was completely quiet. Her opponents sat tensed, ready to spring up and counter whatever defense she was planning to make of her politics, of her school, of beards, of "Berkeley-type" demonstrations and disorder in general.

"Everybody's talking about their forty- and fifty-thousand-dollar houses and their property values going down," she drawled finally, keeping her clear voice low and gazing levelly at the supervisors. "I'd just like to say one thing. I have more than one *hundred* thousand dollars invested in the Carmel Valley, and I'm interested in protecting my property too." The property owner smiled disingenuously at Dr. and Mrs. Petkuss then, and took her seat amid complete silence.

She is an interesting girl, a girl who might have interested Henry James, at about the time he did Verena Tarrant, in *The Bostonians*. Joan Baez grew up in the more evangelistic thickets of the middle class, the daughter of a Quaker physics teacher, the granddaughter of two Protestant ministers, an English-Scottish Episcopalian on her mother's side, a Mexican Methodist on her father's. She was born on Staten Island, but raised on the edges of the academic community all over the country; until she found Carmel, she did not really come from anywhere. When it was time to go to high school, her father was teaching at Stanford, and so she went to Palo Alto High School, where she taught herself "House of the Rising Sun" on a Sears, Roebuck guitar, tried to achieve a vibrato by tapping her throat with her finger, and made headlines by refusing to leave the school during a bomb drill. When it was time to go to college, her father was at M.I.T. and Harvard, and so she went a month to Boston University, dropped out, and for a long while sang in coffee bars around Harvard Square. She did not much like the Harvard Square life ("They just lie in their pads, smoke pot, and do stupid things like that," said the ministers' granddaughter of her acquaintances there), but she did not yet know another.

In the summer of 1959, a friend took her to the first Newport Folk Festival. She arrived in Newport in a Cadillac hearse with "JOAN BAEZ" painted on the side, sang a few songs to 13,000 people, and there it was, the new life. Her first album sold more copies than the work of any other female folksinger in record history. By the end of 1961 Vanguard had released her second album, and her total sales were behind those of only Harry Belafonte, the Kingston Trio, and the Weavers. She had finished her first long tour, had given a concert at Carnegie Hall which was sold out two months in advance, and had turned down $100,000 worth of concert dates because she would work only a few months a year.

She was the right girl at the right time. She had only a small repertory of Child ballads ("What's Joanie still doing with this Mary Hamilton?" Bob Dylan would fret later), never trained her pure soprano and annoyed some purists because she was indifferent to the origins of her material and sang everything "sad." But she rode in with the folk wave just as it was cresting. She could reach an audience in a way that neither the purists nor the more commercial folksingers seemed to be able to do. If her interest was never in the money, neither was it really in the music: she was interested instead in something that went on between her and the audience. "The easiest kind of relationship for me is with ten thousand people," she said. "The hardest is with one."

She did not want, then or ever, to entertain; she wanted to move people, to establish with them some communion of emotion. By the end of 1963 she had found, in the protest movement, something upon which she could focus the emotion. She went into the South. She sang at Negro colleges, and she was always there where the barricade was, Selma, Montgomery, Birmingham. She sang at the Lincoln Memorial after the March on Washington. She told the Internal Revenue Service that she did not intend to pay the sixty percent of her income tax that she calculated went to the defense establishment. She became the voice that meant protest, although she would always maintain a curious distance from the movement's more ambiguous moments. ("I got pretty sick of those Southern marches after a while," she could say later. "All these big entertainers renting little planes and flying down, always about 35,000 people in town.") She had recorded only a handful of albums, but she had seen her face on the cover of *Time*. She was just twenty-two.

Joan Baez was a personality before she was entirely a person, and, like anyone to whom that happens, she is in a sense the hapless victim of what others have seen in her, written about her, wanted her to be and not to be. The roles assigned to her are various, but variations on a single theme. She is the Madonna of the disaffected. She is the pawn of the protest movement. She is the unhappy analysand. She is the singer who would not train her voice, the rebel who drives the Jaguar too fast, the Rima who hides with the birds and the deer. Above all, she is the girl who "feels" things, who has hung on to the freshness and pain of adolescence, the girl ever wounded, ever young. Now, at an age when the wounds begin to heal whether one wants them to or not, Joan Baez rarely leaves the Carmel Valley.

Although all Baez activities tend to take on certain ominous overtones in the collective consciousness of Monterey County, what actually goes on at Miss Baez's Institute for the Study of Nonviolence, which was allowed to continue operating in the Carmel Valley by a three-two vote of the supervisors, is so apparently ingenuous as to disarm even veterans of two wars who wear snap-on bow ties. Four days a week, Miss Baez and her fifteen students meet at the school for lunch: potato salad, Kool-Aid, and hot dogs broiled on a portable barbecue. After lunch they do ballet exercises to Beatles records, and after that they sit around on the bare floor beneath a photomural of Cypress Point and discuss their reading: *Gandhi on Nonviolence*, Louis Fischer's *Life of Mahatma Gandhi*, Jerome Frank's *Breaking the Thought Barrier*, Thoreau's *On Civil Disobedience*, Krishnamurti's *The First and Last Freedom* and *Think on These Things*, C. Wright Mills's *The Power Elite*, Huxley's *Ends and Means*, and Marshall McLuhan's *Understanding Media*. On the fifth day, they meet as usual but spend the afternoon in total silence, which involves not only not talking but also not reading, not writing, and not smoking. Even on discussion days, this silence is invoked for regular twenty-minute or hour intervals, a regimen described by one student as "invaluable for clearing your mind of personal hangups" and by Miss Baez as "just about the most important thing about the school."

There are no admission requirements, other than that applicants must be at least eighteen years old; admission to each session is granted to the first fifteen who write and ask to come. They come from all over, and they are on the average very young, very earnest, and not very much in touch with the larger scene, less refugees from it than children who do not quite apprehend it. They worry a great deal about "responding to one another with beauty and tenderness," and their response to one another is in

JOAN DIDION

fact so tender that an afternoon at the school tends to drift perilously into the never-never. They debate whether or not it was a wise tactic for the Vietnam Day Committee at Berkeley to try to reason with Hell's Angels "on the hip level."

"O.K.," someone argues. "So the Angels just shrug and say 'our thing's violence.' How can the V.D.C. guy answer that?"

They discuss a proposal from Berkeley for an International Nonviolent Army:"The idea is, we go to Vietnam and we go into these villages, and then if they burn them, we burn too."

"It has a beautiful simplicity," someone says.

Most of them are too young to have been around for the memorable events of protest, and the few who have been active tell stories to those who have not, stories which begin "One night at the Scranton Y ..." or "Recently when we were sitting in at the A.E.C...." and "We had this eleven-year-old on the Canada-to-Cuba march who was at the time corresponding with a Gandhian, and he...." They talk about Allen Ginsberg, "the only one, the only beautiful voice, the only one talking." Ginsberg had suggested that the V.D.C. send women carrying babies and flowers to the Oakland Army Terminal.

"Babies and flowers," a pretty little girl breathes."But that's so *beautiful*, that's the whole *point*."

"Ginsberg was down here one weekend," recalls a dreamy boy with curly golden hair. "He brought a copy of the *Fuck Songbag*, but we burned it." He giggles. He is holding a clear violet marble up to the window, turning it in the sunlight."Joan gave it to me," he says. "One night at her house, when we all had a party and gave each other presents. It was like Christmas but it wasn't."

The school itself is an old whitewashed adobe house quite far out among the yellow hills and dusty scrub oaks of the Upper Carmel Valley. Oleanders support a torn wire fence around the school, and there is no sign, no identification at all. The adobe was a one-room county school until 1950; after that it was occupied in turn by the So Help Me Hannah Poison Oak Remedy Laboratory and by a small shotgun-shell manufacturing business, two enterprises which apparently did not present the threat to property values that Miss Baez does. She bought the place in the fall of 1965, after the County Planning Commission told her

44

that zoning prohibited her from running the school in her house, which is on a ten-acre piece a few miles away. Miss Baez is the vice president of the Institute, and its sponsor; the $120 fee paid by each student for each six-week session includes lodging, at an apartment house in Pacific Grove, and does not meet the school's expenses. Miss Baez not only has a $40,000 investment in the school property but is responsible as well for the salary of Ira Sandperl, who is the president of the Institute, the leader of the discussions, and in fact the *eminence grise* of the entire project. "You might think we're starting in a very small way," Ira Sandperl says. "Sometimes the smallest things can change the course of history. Look at the Benedictine order."

In a way it is impossible to talk about Joan Baez without talking about Ira Sandperl. "One of the men on the Planning Commission said I was being led down the primrose path by the lunatic fringe," Miss Baez giggles. "Ira said maybe he's the lunatic and his beard's the fringe." Ira Sandperl is a forty-two-year-old native of St. Louis who has, besides the beard, a shaved head, a large nuclear-disarmament emblem on his corduroy jacket, glittering and slightly messianic eyes, a high cracked laugh and the general look of a man who has, all his life, followed some imperceptibly but fatally askew rainbow. He has spent a good deal of time in pacifist movements around San Francisco, Berkeley, and Palo Alto, and was, at the time he and Miss Baez hit upon the idea of the Institute, working in a Palo Alto bookstore.

Ira Sandperl first met Joan Baez when she was sixteen and was brought by her father to a Quaker meeting in Palo Alto. "There was something magic, something different about her even then," he recalls. "I remember once she was singing at a meeting where I was speaking. The audience was so responsive that night that I said 'Honey, when you grow up we'll have to be an evangelical team.'" He smiles, and spreads his hands.

The two became close, according to Ira Sandperl, after Miss Baez's father went to live in Paris as a UNESCO advisor. "I was the oldest friend around, so naturally she turned to me." He was with her at the time of the Berkeley demonstrations in the fall of 1964. "We were actually the outside agitators you heard so much about," he says. "Basically we wanted to turn an *un*violent movement into a *non*violent one. Joan was *enor*mously instrumental in pulling the movement out of its slump, although the boys may not admit it now."

A month or so after her appearance at Berkeley, Joan Baez talked to Ira Sandperl about the possibility of tutoring her for a year. "She found herself among politically knowledgeable people," he says, "and while she had strong *feel*ings, she didn't know any of the socio-economic-political-historical terms of nonviolence."

"It was all vague," she interrupts, nervously brushing her hair back. "I want it to be less vague."

They decided to make it not a year's private tutorial but a school to go on indefinitely, and enrolled the first students late in the summer of 1965. The Institute aligns itself with no movements ("Some of the kids are just leading us into another long, big, violent mess," Miss Baez says), and there is in fact a marked distrust of most activist organizations. Ira Sandperl, for example, had little use for the V.D.C., because the V.D.C. believed in nonviolence only as a limited tactic, accepted conventional power blocs, and even ran one of its leaders for Congress, which is anathema to Sandperl. "Darling, let me put it this way. In civil rights, now, the President signs a bill, who does he call to witness it? Adam Powell? No. He calls Rustin, Farmer, King, *none* of them in the conventional power structure." He pauses, as if envisioning a day when he and Miss Baez will be called upon to witness the signing of a bill outlawing violence. "I'm not optimistic, darling, but I'm hopeful. There's a difference. I'm hopeful."

The gas heater sputters on and off and Miss Baez watches it, her duffel coat drawn up around her shoulders. "Everybody says I'm politically naïve, and I am," she says after a while. It is something she says frequently to people she does not know. "So are the people running politics, or we wouldn't be in wars, would we."

The door opens and a short middle-aged man wearing hand-made sandals walks in. He is Manuel Greenhill, Miss Baez's manager, and although he has been her manager for five years, he has never before visited the Institute, and he has never before met Ira Sandperl.

"At last!" Ira Sandperl cries, jumping up. "The disembodied voice on the telephone is here at last! There *is* a Manny Greenhill! There *is* an Ira Sandperl! Here I am! Here's the villain!"

* * *

It is difficult to arrange to see Joan Baez, at least for anyone not tuned to the underground circuits of the protest movement. The New York company for which she records, Vanguard, will give only Manny Greenhill's number, in Boston. "Try Area Code 415, prefix DA 4, number 4321," Manny Greenhill will rasp. Area Code 415, DA 4-4321 will connect the caller with Keppler's Bookstore in Palo Alto, which is where Ira Sandperl used to work. Someone at the bookstore will take a number, and, after checking with Carmel to see if anyone there cares to hear from the caller, will call back, disclosing a Carmel number. The Carmel number is not, as one might think by now, for Miss Baez, but for an answering service. The service will take a number, and, after some days or weeks, a call may or may not be received from Judy Flynn, Miss Baez's secretary. Miss Flynn says that she will "try to contact" Miss Baez. "I don't see people," says the heart of this curiously improvised web of wrong numbers, disconnected telephones, and unreturned calls. "I lock the gate and hope nobody comes, but they come anyway. Somebody's been telling them where I live."

She lives quietly. She reads, and she talks to the people who have been told where she lives, and occasionally she and Ira Sandperl go to San Francisco, to see friends, to talk about the peace movement. She sees her two sisters and she sees Ira Sandperl. She believes that her days at the Institute talking and listening to Ira Sandperl are bringing her closer to contentment than anything she has done so far. "Certainly than the singing. I used to stand up there and think I'm getting so many thousand dollars, and for what?" She is defensive about her income ("Oh, I have some money from somewhere"), vague about her plans. "There are some things I want to do. I want to try some rock 'n' roll and some classical music. But I'm not going to start worrying about the charts and the sales because then where are you?"

Exactly where it is she wants to be seems an open question, bewildering to her and even more so to her manager. If he is asked what his most celebrated client is doing now and plans to do in the future, Many Greenhill talks about "lots of plans," "other areas," and "her own choice." Finally he hits upon something: "Listen, she just did a documentary for Canadian television, *Variety* gave it a great review, let me read you."

Manny Greenhill reads. "Let's see. Here *Variety* says '*planned only a twenty-minute interview but when CBC officials in Toronto saw the film they decided to go with a special*—'" He interrupts himself. "That's pretty newsworthy right there. Let's see now. Here they quote her ideas on peace ... you know those ... here she says '*every time I go to Hollywood I want to throw up*' ... let's not get into that ... here now, '*her impersonations of Ringo Starr and George Harrison were dead-on,*' get that, that's good."

Manny Greenhill is hoping to get Miss Baez to write a book, to be in a movie, and to get around to recording the rock 'n' roll songs. He will not discuss her income, although he will say, at once jaunty and bleak, "but it won't be much *this* year." Miss Baez let him schedule only one concert for 1966 (down from an average of thirty a year), has accepted only one regular club booking in her entire career, and is virtually never on television. "What's she going to do on Andy Williams?" Manny Greenhill shrugs. "One time she sang one of Pat Boone's songs with him," he adds, "which proves she can get along, but still. We don't want her up there with some dance routine behind her." Greenhill keeps an eye on her political appearances, and tries to prevent the use of her name. "We say, if they use her name it's a concert. The point is, if they haven't used her name, then if she doesn't like the looks of it she can get out." He is resigned to the school's cutting into her schedule. "Listen," he says. "I've always encouraged her to be political. I may not be active, but let's say I'm concerned." He squints into the sun. "Let's say maybe I'm just too old."

To encourage Joan Baez to be "political" is really only to encourage Joan Baez to continue "feeling" things, for her politics are still, as she herself said, "all vague." Her approach is instinctive, pragmatic, not too far from that of any League of Women Voters member. "Frankly, I'm down on Communism," is her latest word on that subject. On recent events in the pacifist movement, she has this to say: "Burning draft cards doesn't make sense, and burning themselves makes even less." When she was at Palo Alto High School and refused to leave the building during a bomb drill, she was not motivated by theory; she did it because "it was the practical thing to do, I mean it seemed to me this drill was impractical, all these people thinking they could get into some kind of little shelter and be saved with canned water." She has

48

made appearances for Democratic administrations, and is frequently quoted as saying: "There's never been a good Republican folksinger"; it is scarcely the diction of the new radicalism. Her concert program includes some of her thoughts about "waiting on the eve of destruction," and her thoughts are these:

> *My life is a crystal teardrop. There are snowflakes falling in the teardrop and little figures trudging around in slow motion. If I were to look into the teardrop for the next million years, I might never find out who the people are, and what they are doing.*

> *Sometimes I get lonesome for a storm. A full-blown storm where everything changes. The sky goes through four days in an hour, the trees wail, little animals skitter in the mud and everything gets dark and goes completely wild. But it's really God—playing music in his favorite cathedral in heaven—shattering stained glass—playing a gigantic organ—thundering on the keys—perfect harmony—perfect joy.*

Although Miss Baez does not actually talk this way when she is kept from the typewriter, she does try, perhaps unconsciously, to hang on to the innocence and turbulence and capacity for wonder, however ersatz or shallow, of her own or of anyone's adolescence. This openness, this vulnerability, is of course precisely the reason why she is so able to "come through" to all the young and lonely and inarticulate, to all those who suspect that no one else in the world understands about beauty and hurt and love and brotherhood. Perhaps because she is older now, Miss Baez is sometimes troubled that she means, to a great many of her admirers, everything that is beautiful and true.

"I'm not very happy with my thinking about it," she says. "Sometimes I tell myself, 'Come on, Baez, you're just like everybody else,' but then I'm not happy with that either."

"Not everybody else has the voice," Ira Sandperl interrupts dotingly.

"Oh, it's all right to have the *voice*, the *voice* is all right …"

She breaks off and concentrates for a long while on the buckle of her shoe.

* * *

So now the girl whose life is a crystal teardrop has her own place, a place where the sun shines and the ambiguities can be set aside a little while longer, a place where everyone can be warm and loving and share confidences. "One day we went around the room and told a little about ourselves," she confides, "and I discovered that *boy*, I'd had it pretty easy." The late afternoon sun streaks the clean wooden floor and the birds sing in the scrub oaks and the beautiful children sit in their coats on the floor and listen to Ira Sandperl.

"Are you a vegetarian, Ira?" someone asks idly.

"Yes. Yes, I am."

"Tell them, Ira," Joan Baez says. "It's nice."

He leans back and looks toward the ceiling. "I was in the Sierra once." He pauses, and Joan Baez smiles approvingly. "I saw this magnificent tree *growing* out of bare rock, *thrust*ing itself ... and I thought *all right, tree*, if you want to live that much, *all right*! All *right*! O.K.! I won't chop you! I won't eat you! The one thing we all have in common is that we all want to *live*!"

"But what about vegetables," a girl murmurs.

"Well, I realized, of course, that as long as I was in *this flesh* and *this blood* I couldn't be *per*fectly nonviolent."

It is getting late. Fifty cents apiece is collected for the next day's lunch, and someone reads a request from the Monterey County Board of Supervisors that citizens fly American flags to show that "Kooks, Commies, and Cowards do not represent our County," and someone else brings up the Vietnam Day Committee, and a dissident member who had visited Carmel.

"Marv's an honest-to-God nonviolenter," Ira Sandperl declares. "A man of honesty and love."

"He said he's an anarchist," someone interjects doubtfully.

"Right," Ira Sandperl agrees. "Absolutely."

"Would the V.D.C. call Gandhi bourgeois?"

"Oh, they must know better, but they lead such bourgeois lives themselves ..."

"That's so true," says the dreamy blond boy with the violet marble. "You walk into their office, they're so unfriendly, so unfriendly and cold ..."

Everyone smiles lovingly at him. By now the sky outside is the color of his marble, but they are all reluctant about gathering up their books and magazines and records, about finding their car keys and ending the day, and by the time they are ready to leave Joan Baez is eating potato salad with her fingers from a bowl in the refrigerator, and everyone stays to share it, just a little while longer where it is warm.

1966

COMRADE LASKI, C.P.U.S.A. (M.-L.)

MICHAEL LASKI, ALSO known as M. I. Laski, is a relatively obscure young man with deep fervent eyes, a short beard, and a pallor which seems particularly remarkable in Southern California. With his striking appearance and his relentlessly ideological diction, he looks and talks precisely like the popular image of a professional revolutionary, which in fact he is. He was born twenty-six years ago in Brooklyn, moved as a child to Los Angeles, dropped out of U.C.L.A. his sophomore year to organize for the Retail Clerks, and now, as General Secretary of the Central Committee of the Communist Party U.S.A. (Marxist-Leninist), a splinter group of Stalinist-Maoists who divide their energies between Watts and Harlem, he is rigidly committed to an immutable complex of doctrine, including the notions that the traditional American Communist Party is a "revisionist bourgeois clique," that the Progressive Labor Party, the Trotskyites, and "the revisionist clique headed by Gus Hall" prove themselves opportunistic bourgeois lackeys by making their peace appeal not to the "workers" but to the liberal imperialists; and that H. Rap Brown is the tool, if not the conscious agent, of the ruling imperialist class.

Not long ago I spent some time with Michael Laski, down at the Workers' International Bookstore in Watts, the West Coast headquarters of the C.P.U.S.A. (M.-L.). We sat at a kitchen table beneath the hammer-and-sickle flag and the portraits of Marx, Engels, Mao Tse-tung, Lenin, and Stalin (Mao in the favored center position), and we discussed the revolution necessary to bring about the dictatorship of the proletariat. Actually I was interested not in the revolution but in the revolutionary. He had with him a small red book of Mao's poems, and as he talked he squared it on the table, aligned it with the table edge first vertically and then horizontally. To understand who Michael Laski is you must have a feeling for that kind of compulsion. One does not think of him eating, or in bed. He has nothing in common with the passionate personalities who tend to turn up on the New Left. Michael

Laski scorns deviationist reformers. He believes with Mao that political power grows out of the barrel of a gun, a point he insists upon with blazing and self-defeating candor. His place in the geography of the American Left is, in short, an almost impossibly lonely and quixotic one, unpopular, unpragmatic. He believes that there are "workers" in the United States, and that, when the time comes, they will "arise," not in anarchy but in conscious concert, and he also believes that "the ruling class" is self-conscious, and possessed of demonic powers. He is in all ways an idealist.

As it happens I am comfortable with the Michael Laskis of this world, with those who live outside rather than in, those in whom the sense of dread is so acute that they turn to extreme and doomed commitments; I know something about dread myself, and appreciate the elaborate systems with which some people manage to fill the void, appreciate all the opiates of the people, whether they are as accessible as alcohol and heroin and promiscuity or as hard to come by as faith in God or History.

But of course I did not mention dread to Michael Laski, whose particular opiate is History. I did suggest "depression," did venture that it might have been "depressing" for him to see only a dozen or so faces at his last May Day demonstration, but he told me that depression was an impediment to the revolutionary process, a disease afflicting only those who do not have ideology to sustain them. Michael Laski, you see, did not feel as close to me as I did to him. "I talk to you at all," he said, "only as a calculated risk. Of course your function is to gather information for the intelligence services. Basically you want to conduct the same probe the F.B.I. would carry out if they could put us in a chair." He paused and tapped the small red book with his fingernails. "And yet," he said finally, "there's a definite advantage to me in talking to you. Because of one fact: these interviews provide a public record of my existence."

Still, he was not going to discuss with me what he called "the underground apparatus" of the C.P.U.S.A. (M.-L.), any more than he would tell me how many members constituted the cadre. "Obviously I'm not going to give you that kind of information," he said. "We know as a matter of course that we'll be outlawed." The Workers' International Bookstore, however, was "an open facility," and I was free to look around. I leafed through some of the literature out of Peking (*Vice-Premier Chen Yi Answers*

Questions Put by Correspondents), Hanoi (*President Ho Chi Minh Answers President L. B. Johnson*), and Tirana, Albania (*The Hue and Cry About a Change in Tito's Policy and the Undeniable Truth*), and I tried to hum, from a North Vietnamese song book, "When the Party Needs Us Our Hearts Are Filled with Hatred." The literature was in the front of the store, along with a cash register and the kitchen table; in back, behind a plywood partition, were a few cots and the press and mimeograph machine on which the Central Committee prints its "political organ," *People's Voice*, and its "theoretical organ," *Red Flag*. "There's a cadre assigned to this facility in order to guarantee the security," Michael Laski said when I mentioned the cots. "They have a small arsenal in back, a couple of shotguns and a number of other items."

So much security may seem curious when one considers what the members of the cadre actually do, which is, aside from selling the *People's Voice* and trying to set up People's Armed Defense Groups, largely a matter of perfecting their own ideology, searching out "errors" and "mistakes" in one another's attitudes. "What we do may seem a waste of time to some people," Michael Laski said suddenly. "Not having any ideology yourself, you might wonder what the Party offers. It offers nothing. It offers thirty or forty years of putting the Party above everything. It offers beatings. Jail. On the high levels, assassination."

But of course that was offering a great deal. The world Michael Laski had constructed for himself was one of labyrinthine intricacy and immaculate clarity, a world made meaningful not only by high purpose but by external and internal threats, intrigues and apparatus, an immutably ordered world in which things mattered. Let me tell you about another day at the Workers' International Bookstore. The Marxist-Leninists had been out selling the *People's Voice*, and now Michael Laski and three other members of the cadre were going over the proceeds, a ceremony as formal as a gathering of the Morgan partners.

"Mr.—*Comrade*—Simmons—what was the total income?" Michael Laski asked.

"Nine dollars and ninety-one cents."

"Over what period of time?"

"Four hours."

"What was the total number of papers sold?"

"Seventy-five."

"And the average per hour?"

"Nineteen."

"The average contribution?"

"Thirteen and a half cents."

"The largest contribution?"

"Sixty cents."

"The smallest?"

"Four cents."

"It was not a very good day, Comrade Simmons. Can you explain?"

"It's always bad the day before welfare and unemployment checks arrive."

"Very good, Comrade Simmons."

You see what the world of Michael Laski is: a minor but perilous triumph of being over nothingness.

1967

SEVEN THOUSAND ROMAINE Street is in that part of Los Angeles familiar to admirers of Raymond Chandler and Dashiell Hammett: the underside of Hollywood, south of Sunset Boulevard, a middle-class slum of "model studios" and warehouses and two-family bungalows. Because Paramount and Columbia and Desilu and the Samuel Goldwyn studios are nearby, many of the people who live around here have some tenuous connection with the motion-picture industry. They once processed fan photographs, say, or knew Jean Harlow's manicurist. 7000 Romaine looks itself like a faded movie exterior, a pastel building with chipped *art moderne* detailing, the windows now either boarded or paned with chicken-wire glass and, at the entrance, among the dusty oleander, a rubber mat that reads WELCOME.

Actually no one is welcome, for 7000 Romaine belongs to Howard Hughes, and the door is locked. That the Hughes "communications center" should lie here in the dull sunlight of Hammett-Chandler country is one of those circumstances that satisfy one's suspicion that life is indeed a scenario, for the Hughes empire has been in our time the only industrial complex in the world—involving, over the years, machinery manufacture, foreign oil-tool subsidiaries, a brewery, two airlines, immense real-estate holdings, a major motion-picture studio, and an electronics and missile operation—run by a man whose *modus operandi* most closely resembles that of a character in *The Big Sleep*.

As it happens, I live not far from 7000 Romaine, and I make a point of driving past it every now and then, I suppose in the same spirit that Arthurian scholars visit the Cornish coast. I am interested in the folklore of Howard Hughes, in the way people react to him, in the terms they use when they talk about him. Let me give you an example. A few weeks ago I lunched with an old friend at the Beverly Hills Hotel. One of the other guests was a well-married woman in her thirties who had once been a Hughes contract starlet, and another was a costume designer who had worked on a lot of Hughes pictures and who still receives a weekly salary from 7000 Romaine, on the understanding that he work for no one else. He has done nothing but cash that weekly check for some years now. They sat there in the sun, the one-time starlet and the sometime costume designer for a man whose public appearances are now somewhat less frequent than those of The Shadow, and they talked about him. They wondered how he was and why he was devoting 1967 to buying up Las Vegas.

"You can't tell me it's like they say, that he bought the Desert Inn just because the high rollers were coming in and they wouldn't let him keep the penthouse," the ex-starlet mused, fingering a diamond as big as the Ritz. "It must be part of some larger mission."

The phrase was exactly right. Anyone who skims the financial press knows that Hughes never has business "transactions," or "negotiations"; he has "missions." His central mission, as *Fortune* once put it in a series of love letters, has always been "to preserve his power as the proprietor of the largest pool of industrial wealth still under the absolute control of a single individual." Nor does Hughes have business "associates"; he has only "adversaries." When the adversaries "appear to be" threatening his absolute control, Hughes "might or might not" take action. It is such phrases as "appear to be" and "might or might not," peculiar to business reportage involving Hughes, that suggested the special mood of a Hughes mission. And here is what the action might or might not be: Hughes might warn, at the critical moment, "You're holding a gun to my head." If there is one thing Hughes dislikes, it is a gun to his head (generally this means a request for an appearance, or a discussion of policy), and at least one president of T.W.A., a company which, as Hughes ran it, bore an operational similarity only to the government of Honduras, departed on this note.

The stories are endless, infinitely familiar, traded by the faithful like baseball cards, fondled until they fray around the edges and blur into the apocryphal. There is the one about the barber, Eddie Alexander, who was paid handsomely to remain on "day and night standby" in case Hughes wanted a haircut. "Just checking, Eddie," Hughes once said when he called Alexander at two in the morning. "Just wanted to see if you were standing by." There was the time Convair wanted to sell Hughes 340 transports and

Hughes insisted that, to insure "secrecy," the mission be discussed only between midnight and dawn, by flashlight, in the Palm Springs Municipal Dump. There was the evening when both Hughes and Greg Bautzer, then his lawyer, went incommunicado while, in the conference room of the Chemical Bank in New York, the money men waited to lend T.W.A. $165 million. There they were, $165 million in hand, the men from two of the country's biggest insurance companies and nine of its most powerful banks, all waiting, and it was 7 p.m. of the last day the deal could be made and the bankers found themselves talking by phone not to Hughes, not even to Bautzer, but to Bautzer's wife, the movie star Dana Wynter. "I hope he takes it in pennies," a Wall Street broker said when Hughes, six years later, sold T.W.A. for $546 million, "and drops it on his toes."

Then there are the more recent stories. Howard Hughes is en route to Boston aboard the Super Chief with the Bel Air Patrol riding shotgun. Howard Hughes is in Peter Bent Brigham Hospital. Howard Hughes commandeers the fifth floor of the Boston Ritz. Howard Hughes is or is not buying 37½ percent of Columbia Pictures through the Swiss Banque de Paris. Howard Hughes is ill. Howard Hughes is dead. No, Howard Hughes is in Las Vegas. Howard Hughes pays $13 million for the Desert Inn. $15 million for the Sands. Gives the State of Nevada $6 million for a medical school. Negotiates for ranches, Alamo Airways, the North Las Vegas Air Terminal, more ranches, the rest of the Strip. By July of 1967 Howard Hughes is the largest single landholder in Clark Country, Nevada. "Howard likes Las Vegas," an acquaintance of Hughes's once explained, "because he likes to be able to find a restaurant open in case he wants a sandwich."

Why do we like those stories so? Why do we tell them over and over? Why have we made a folk hero of a man who is the antithesis of all our official heroes, a haunted millionaire out of the West, trailing a legend of desperation and power and white sneakers? But then we have always done that. Our favorite people and our favorite stories become so not by any inherent virtue, but because they illustrate something deep in the grain, something unadmitted. Shoeless Joe Jackson, Warren Gamaliel Harding, the *Titanic: how the mighty are fallen.* Charles Lindbergh, Scott and Zelda Fitzgerald, Marilyn Monroe: *the beautiful and damned.* And Howard Hughes. That we have made a hero of Howard Hughes tells us something interesting about ourselves, something only dimly remembered, tells us that the secret point of money and power in America is neither the things that money can buy nor power for power's sake (Americans are uneasy with their possessions, guilty about power, all of which is difficult for Europeans to perceive because they are themselves so truly materialistic, so versed in the uses of power), but absolute personal freedom, mobility, privacy. It is the instinct which drove America to the Pacific, all through the nineteenth century, the desire to be able to find a restaurant open in case you want a sandwich, to be a free agent, live by one's own rules.

Of course we do not admit that. The instinct is socially suicidal, and because we recognize that this is so we have developed workable ways of saying one thing and believing quite another. A long time ago, Lionel Trilling pointed out what he called "the fatal separation" between "the ideas of our educated liberal class and the deep places of the imagination." "I mean only," he wrote, "that our educated class has a ready if mild suspiciousness of the profit motive, a belief in progress, science, social legislation, planning and international cooperation.... Those beliefs do great credit to those who hold them. Yet it is a comment, if not on our beliefs then on our way of holding them, that not a single first-rate writer has emerged to deal with these ideas, and the emotions that are consonant with them, in a great literary way." Officially we admire men who exemplify those ideas. We admire the Adlai Stevenson character, the rational man, the enlightened man, the man not dependent upon the potentially psychopathic mode of action. Among rich men, we officially admire Paul Mellon, a socially responsible inheritor in the European mold. There has always been that divergence between our official and our unofficial heroes. It is impossible to think of Howard Hughes without seeing the apparently bottomless gulf between what we say we want and what we do want, between what we officially admire and secretly desire, between, in the largest sense, the people we marry and the people we love. In a nation which increasingly appears to prize social virtues, Howard Hughes remains not merely antisocial but grandly, brilliantly, surpassingly, asocial. He is the last private man, the dream we no longer admit.

1967

CALIFORNIA DREAMING

EVERY WEEKDAY MORNING at eleven o'clock, just about the time the sun burns the last haze off the Santa Barbara hills, fifteen or twenty men gather in what was once the dining room of a shirt manufacturer's mansion overlooking the Pacific Ocean and begin another session of what they like to call "clarifying the basic issues." The place is the Center for the Study of Democratic Institutions, the current mutation of the Fund for the Republic, and since 1959, when the Fund paid $250,000 for the marble villa and forty-one acres of eucalyptus, a favored retreat for people whom the Center's president, Robert M. Hutchins, deems controversial, stimulating, and, perhaps above all, cooperative, or *our kind*. "If they just want to work on their own stuff," Hutchins has said, "then they ought not to come here. Unless they're willing to come in and work with the group as a group, then this place is not for them."

Those invited to spend time at the Center get an office (there are no living quarters at the Center) and a salary, the size of which is reportedly based on the University of California pay scale. The selection process is usually described as "mysterious," but it always involves "people we know." Paul Hoffman, who was at one time president of the Ford Foundation and then director of the Fund for the Republic, is now the Center's honorary chairman, and his son is there quite a bit, and Robert Hutchins's son-in-law. Rexford Tugwell, one of the New Deal "brain trust," is there ("Why not?" he asked me. "If I weren't here I'd be in a rest home"), and Harvey Wheeler, the co-author of *Fail-Safe*. Occasionally someone might be asked to the Center because he has built-in celebrity value, *e.g.*, Bishop James Pike. "What we are is a group of highly skilled public-relations experts," Harry Ashmore says. Harry Ashmore is a fixture at the Center, and he regards Hutchins—or, as the president of the Center is inflexibly referred to in the presence of outsiders, Dr. Hutchins—as "a natural intellectual resource." What these highly skilled public-relations

60

experts do, besides clarifying the basic issues and giving a lift to Bennett Cerf ("My talk with Paul Hoffman on the Coast gave me a lift I won't forget," Bennett Cerf observed some time ago), is to gather every weekday for a few hours of discussion, usually about one of several broad areas that the Center is concentrating upon at any given time—The City, say, or The Emerging Constitution. Papers are prepared, read, revised, reread, and sometimes finally published. This process is variously described by those who participate in it as "pointing the direction for all of us toward a greater understanding" and "applying human reason to the complex problems of our brand-new world."

I have long been interested in the Center's rhetoric, which has about it the kind of ectoplasmic generality that always makes me sense I am on the track of the real soufflé, the genuine American *kitsch*, and so not long ago I arranged to attend a few sessions in Santa Barbara. It was in no sense time wasted. The Center is the most perfectly indigenous cultural phenomenon since the Encyclopaedia Britannica's *Syntopicon*, which sets forth "The 102 Great Ideas of Western Man" and which we also owe to Robert, or Dr., Hutchins. "Don't make the mistake of taking a chair at the big table," I was warned *sotto voce* on my first visit to the Center. "The talk there is pretty high-powered."

"Is there any evidence that living in a violent age encourages violence?" someone was asking at the big table.

"That's hard to measure."

"I think it's the Westerns on television."

"I tend [*pause*] to agree."

Every word uttered at the Center is preserved on tape, and not only colleges and libraries but thousands of individuals receive Center tapes and pamphlets. Among the best-selling pamphlets have been A. A. Berle, Jr.'s *Economic Power and the Free Society*, Clark Kerr's *Unions and Union Leaders of Their Own Choosing*, Donald Michael's *Cybernation: The Silent Conquest*, and Harrison Brown's *Community of Fear*. Seventy-five thousand people a year then write fan letters to the Center, confirming the staff in its conviction that everything said around the place mystically improves the national, and in fact the international, weal. From a Colorado country-day-school teacher: "I use the Center's various papers in my U.S. history-current events course. It seems to me that there is no institution in the U.S. today engaged in more valuable and first-rate work than the Center." From a California mother: "Now my fifteen-year-old daughter has discovered your publications. This delights me as she is one of those regular teenagers. But when she curls up to read, it is with your booklets."

The notion that providing useful papers for eighth-grade current-events classes and reading for regular teenagers might not be at all times compatible with establishing "a true intellectual community" (another Hutchins aim) would be considered, at the Center, a downbeat and undemocratic cavil. "People are entitled to learn what we're thinking," someone there told me. The place is in fact avidly anti-intellectual, the deprecatory use of words like "egghead" and "ivory tower" reaching heights matched only in a country-club locker room. Hutchins takes pains to explain that by "an intellectual community" he does not mean a community "whose members regard themselves as 'intellectuals.'" Harry Ashmore frets particularly that "men of affairs" may fail to perceive the Center's "practical utility." Hutchins likes to quote Adlai Stevenson on this point: "The Center can be thought of as a kind of national insurance plan, a way of making certain that we will deserve better and better."

Although one suspects that this pragmatic Couéism as a mode of thought comes pretty naturally to most of the staff at the Center, it is also vital to the place's survival. In 1959 the Fund for the Republic bequeathed to the Center the $4 million left of its original $15 million Ford Foundation grant, but that is long gone, and because there was never any question of more Ford money, the Center must pay its own way. Its own way costs about a million dollars a year. Some twelve thousand contributors provide the million a year, and it helps if they can think of a gift to the Center not as a gift to support some visionaries who never met a payroll but "as an investment [tax-exempt] in the preservation of our free way of life." It helps, too, to present the donor with a fairly broad-stroke picture of how the Center is besieged by the forces of darkness, and in this effort the Center has had an invaluable, if unintentional, ally in the Santa Barbara John Birch Society. "You can't let the fascists drive them out of town," I was advised by an admirer of the Center.

Actually, even without the Birch Society as a foil, Hutchins has evolved the $E = mc^2$ of all fund-raising formulae. The Center is supported on the same principle as a vanity press. People who are in a position to contribute large sums of money are encouraged to participate in clarifying the basic issues. Dinah Shore, a founding member, is invited up to discuss civil rights with Bayard Rustin. Steve Allen talks over "Ideology and Intervention" with Senator Fulbright and Arnold Toynbee, and Kirk Douglas, a founding member, speaks his piece on "The Arts in a Democratic Society." Paul Newman, in the role of "concerned citizen," is on hand to discuss "The University in America" with Dr. Hutchins, Supreme Court Justice William O. Douglas, Arnold Grant, Rosemary Park, and another concerned citizen, Jack Lemmon. "Apropos of absolutely nothing," Mr. Lemmon says, pulling on a pipe, "just for my own amazement—I don't *know*, but I *want* to know—" At this juncture he wants to know about student unrest, and, at another, he worries that government contracts will corrupt "pure research."

"You mean maybe they get a grant to develop some new kind of *plastic*," Mr. Newman muses, and Mr. Lemmon picks up the cue: "What happens then to the humanities?"

Everyone goes home flattered, and the Center prevails. Well, why not? One morning I was talking with the wife of a big contributor as we waited on the terrace for one of the Center's ready-mixed martinis and a few moments' chat with Dr. Hutchins. "These sessions are way over my head," she confided, "but I go out floating on air."

1967

MARRYING ABSURD

TO BE MARRIED in Las Vegas, Clark County, Nevada, a bride must swear that she is eighteen or has parental permission and a bridegroom that he is twenty-one or has parental permission. Someone must put up five dollars for the license. (On Sundays and holidays, fifteen dollars. The Clark County Courthouse issues marriage licenses at any time of the day or night except between noon and one in the afternoon, between eight and nine in the evening, and between four and five in the morning.) Nothing else is required. The State of Nevada, alone among these United States, demands neither a premarital blood test nor a waiting period before or after the issuance of a marriage license. Driving in across the Mojave from Los Angeles, one sees the signs way out on the desert, looming up from that moonscape of rattlesnakes and mesquite, even before the Las Vegas lights appear like a mirage on the horizon: "GETTING MARRIED? Free License Information First Strip Exit." Perhaps the Las Vegas wedding industry achieved its peak operational efficiency between 9:00 p.m. and midnight of August 26, 1965, an otherwise unremarkable Thursday which happened to be, by Presidential order, the last day on which anyone could improve his draft status merely by getting married. One hundred and seventy-one couples were pronounced man and wife in the name of Clark County and the State of Nevada that night, sixty-seven of them by a single justice of the peace, Mr. James A. Brennan. Mr. Brennan did one wedding at the Dunes and the other sixty-six in his office, and charged each couple eight dollars. One bride lent her veil to six others. "I got it down from five to three minutes," Mr. Brennan said later of his feat. "I could've married them *en masse*, but they're people, not cattle. People expect more when they get married."

What people who get married in Las Vegas actually do expect— what, in the largest sense, their "expectations" are—strikes one as a curious and self-contradictory business. Las Vegas is the most extreme and allegorical of American settlements, bizarre and beautiful in its venality and in its devotion to immediate gratification,

64

a place the tone of which is set by mobsters and call girls and ladies' room attendants with amyl nitrite poppers in their uniform pockets. Almost everyone notes that there is no "time" in Las Vegas, no night and no day and no past and no future (no Las Vegas casino, however, has taken the obliteration of the ordinary time sense quite so far as Harold's Club in Reno, which for a while issued, at odd intervals in the day and night, mimeographed "bulletins" carrying news from the world outside); neither is there any logical sense of where one is. One is standing on a highway in the middle of a vast hostile desert looking at an eighty-foot sign which blinks "STAR-DUST" or "CAESAR'S PALACE." Yes, but what does that explain? This geographical implausibility reinforces the sense that what happens there has no connection with "real" life; Nevada cities like Reno and Carson are ranch towns, Western towns, places behind which there is some historical imperative. But Las Vegas seems to exist only in the eye of the beholder. All of which makes it an extraor-dinarily stimulating and interesting place, but an odd one in which to want to wear a candlelight satin Priscilla of Boston wedding dress with Chantilly lace insets, tapered sleeves and a detachable modified train.

And yet the Las Vegas wedding business seems to appeal to precisely that impulse. "Sincere and Dignified Since 1954," one wedding chapel advertises. There are nineteen such wedding chapels in Las Vegas, intensely competitive, each offering better, faster, and, by implication, more sincere services than the next: Our Photos Best Anywhere, Your Wedding on A Phonograph Record, Candlelight with Your Ceremony, Honeymoon Accommodations, Free Transportation from Your Motel to Courthouse to Chapel and Return to Motel, Religious or Civil Ceremonies, Dressing Rooms, Flowers, Rings, Announcements, Witnesses Available, and Ample Parking. All of these services, like most others in Las Vegas (sauna baths, payroll-check cashing, chinchilla coats for sale or rent) are offered twenty-four hours a day, seven days a week, presumably on the premise that marriage, like craps, is a game to be played when the table seems hot.

But what strikes one most about the Strip chapels, with their wishing wells and stained-glass paper windows and their artificial bouvardia, is that so much of their business is by no means a matter of simple convenience, of late-night liaisons between show girls and baby Crosbys. Of course there is some of that. (One night

JOAN DIDION

about eleven o'clock in Las Vegas I watched a bride in an orange minidress and masses of flame-colored hair stumble from a Strip chapel on the arm of her bridegroom, who looked the part of the expendable nephew in movies like *Miami Syndicate*. "I gotta get the kids," the bride whimpered. "I gotta pick up the sitter, I gotta get to the midnight show." "What you gotta get," the bridegroom said, opening the door of a Cadillac Coupe de Ville and watching her crumple on the seat, "is sober.") But Las Vegas seems to offer something other than "convenience"; it is merchandising "nice-ness," the facsimile of proper ritual, to children who do not know how else to find it, how to make the arrangements, how to do it "right." All day and evening long on the Strip, one sees actual wedding parties, waiting under the harsh lights at a crosswalk, standing uneasily in the parking lot of the Frontier while the photographer hired by The Little Church of the West ("Wedding Place of the Stars") certifies the occasion, takes the picture: the bride in a veil and white satin pumps, the bridegroom usually in a white dinner jacket, and even an attendant or two, a sister or a best friend in hot-pink *peau de soie*, a flirtation veil, a carnation nosegay. "When I Fall in Love It Will Be Forever," the organist plays, and then a few bars of Lohengrin. The mother cries; the stepfather, awkward in his role, invites the chapel hostess to join them for a drink at the Sands. The hostess declines with a profes-sional smile; she has already transferred her interest to the group waiting outside. One bride out, another in, and again the sign goes up on the chapel door: "One moment please—Wedding."

I sat next to one such wedding party in a Strip restaurant the last time I was in Las Vegas. The marriage had just taken place; the bride still wore her dress, the mother her corsage. A bored waiter poured out a few swallows of pink champagne ("on the house") for everyone but the bride, who was too young to be served. "You'll need something with more kick than that," the bride's father said with heavy jocularity to his new son-in-law; the ritual jokes about the wedding night had a certain Panglossian charac-ter, since the bride was clearly several months pregnant. Another round of pink champagne, this time not on the house, and the bride began to cry. "It was just as nice," she sobbed, "as I hoped and dreamed it would be."

1967

THE CENTER WAS not holding. It was a country of bankruptcy notices and public-auction announcements and commonplace reports of casual killings and misplaced children and abandoned homes and vandals who misplaced even the four-letter words they scrawled. It was a country in which families routinely disappeared, trailing bad checks and repossession papers. Adolescents drifted from city to torn city, sloughing off both the past and the future as snakes shed their skins, children who were never taught and would never now learn the games that had held the society together. People were missing. Children were missing. Parents were missing. Those left behind filed desultory missing-persons reports, then moved on themselves.

It was not a country in open revolution. It was not a country under enemy siege. It was the United States of America in the cold late spring of 1967, and the market was steady and the G.N.P. high and a great many articulate people seemed to have a sense of high social purpose and it might have been a spring of brave hopes and national promise, but it was not, and more and more people had the uneasy apprehension that it was not. All that seemed clear was that at some point we had aborted ourselves and butchered the job, and because nothing else seemed so relevant I decided to go to San Francisco. San Francisco was where the social hemorrhaging was showing up. San Francisco was where the missing children were gathering and calling themselves "hippies." When I first went to San Francisco in that cold late spring of 1967 I did not even know what I wanted to find out, and so I just stayed around awhile, and made a few friends.

A sign on Haight Street, San Francisco:

> *Last Easter Day*
> *My Christopher Robin wandered away.*
> *He called April 10th*

But he hasn't called since
He said he was coming home
But he hasn't shown.

If you see him on Haight
Please tell him not to wait
I need him now
I don't care how
If he needs the bread
I'll send it ahead.

If there's hope
Please write me a note
If he's still there
Tell him how much I care
Where he's at I need to know
For I really love him so!

> Deeply,
> Marla

Marla Pence
12702 NE. Multnomah
Portland, Ore. 97230
503/252-2720.

I am looking for somebody called Deadeye and I hear he is on the Street this afternoon doing a little business, so I keep an eye out for him and pretend to read the signs in the Psychedelic Shop on Haight Street when a kid, sixteen, seventeen, comes in and sits on the floor beside me.

"What are you looking for," he says.

I say nothing much.

"I been out of my mind for three days," he says. He tells me he's been shooting crystal, which I already pretty much know because he does not bother to keep his sleeves rolled down over the needle tracks. He came up from Los Angeles some number of weeks ago, he doesn't remember what number, and now he'll take off for New York, if he can find a ride. I show him a sign offering a ride to Chicago. He wonders where Chicago is. I ask where he comes from. "Here," he says. I mean before here. "San Jose, Chula Vista, I dunno. My mother's in Chula Vista."

A few days later I run into him in Golden Gate Park when the Grateful Dead are playing. I ask if he found a ride to New York. "I hear New York's a bummer," he says.

Deadeye never showed up that day on the Street, and somebody says maybe I can find him at his place. It is three o'clock and Deadeye is in bed. Somebody else is asleep on the living-room couch, and a girl is sleeping on the floor beneath a poster of Allen Ginsberg, and there are a couple of girls in pajamas making instant coffee. One of the girls introduces me to the friend on the couch, who extends one arm but does not get up because he is naked. Deadeye and I have a mutual acquaintance, but he does not mention his name in front of the others. "The man you talked to," he says, or "that man I was referring to earlier." The man is a cop.

The room is overheated and the girl on the floor is sick. Deadeye says she has been sleeping for twenty-four hours now. "Lemme ask you something," he says. "You want some grass?" I say I have to be moving on. "You want it," Deadeye says, "it's yours." Deadeye used to be an Angel around Los Angeles but that was a few years ago. "Right now," he says, "I'm trying to set up this groovy religious group—'Teenage Evangelism.'"

Don and Max want to go out to dinner but Don is only eating macrobiotic so we end up in Japantown again. Max is telling me how he lives free of all the old middle-class Freudian hang-ups. "I've had this old lady for a couple of months now, maybe she makes something special for my dinner and I come in three days late and tell her I've been balling some other chick, well, maybe she shouts a little but then I say 'That's me, baby,' and she laughs and says 'That's you, Max.'" Max says it works both ways. "I mean if she comes in and tells me she wants to ball Don, maybe, I say 'O.K., baby, it's your trip.'"

Max sees his life as a triumph over "don'ts." Among the don'ts he had done before he was twenty-one were peyote, alcohol, mescaline, and Methedrine. He was on a Meth trip for three years in New York and Tangier before he found acid. He first tried peyote when he was in an Arkansas boys' school and got down to the Gulf and met "an Indian kid who was doing a don't. Then every weekend I could get loose I'd hitchhike seven hundred miles to Brownsville, Texas, so I could cop peyote. Peyote went for thirty cents a button down in Brownsville on the street." Max dropped in and out of most of the schools and fashionable clinics in the eastern half of America, his standard technique for dealing with boredom being to leave. Example: Max was in a hospital in New York and "the night nurse was a groovy spade, and in the afternoon for therapy there was a chick from Israel who was interesting, but there was nothing much to do in the morning, so I left."

We drink some more green tea and talk about going up to Malakoff Diggings in Nevada County because some people are starting a commune there and Max thinks it would be a groove to take acid in the diggings. He says maybe we could go next week, or the week after, or anyway sometime before his case comes up. Almost everybody I meet in San Francisco has to go to court at some point in the middle future. I never ask why.

I am still interested in how Max got rid of his middle-class Freudian hang-ups and I ask if he is now completely free.

"Nah," he says. "I got acid."

Max drops a 250- or 350-microgram tab every six or seven days.

Max and Don share a joint in the car and we go over to North Beach to find out if Otto, who has a temporary job there, wants to go to Malakoff Diggings. Otto is pitching some electronics engineers. The engineers view our arrival with some interest, maybe, I think, because Max is wearing bells and an Indian headband. Max has a low tolerance for straight engineers and their Freudian hang-ups. "Look at 'em," he says. "They're always yelling 'queer' and then they come sneaking down to the Haight-Ashbury trying to get the hippie chick because she fucks."

We do not get around to asking Otto about Malakoff Diggings because he wants to tell me about a fourteen-year-old he knows who got busted in the Park the other day. She was just walking through the Park, he says, minding her own, carrying her schoolbooks, when the cops took her in and booked her and gave her a pelvic. "*Fourteen years old*," Otto says. "A *pelvic*."

"Coming down from acid," he adds, "that could be a real bad trip."

I call Otto the next afternoon to see if he can reach the fourteen-year-old. It turns out she is tied up with rehearsals for her junior-high-school play, *The Wizard of Oz*. "Yellow-brick-road time," Otto says. Otto was sick all day. He thinks it was some cocaine-and-wheat somebody gave him.

There are always little girls around rock groups—the same little girls who used to hang around saxophone players, girls who live on the celebrity and power and sex a band projects when it plays—and there are three of them out here this afternoon in Sausalito where the Grateful Dead rehearse. They are all pretty and two of them still have baby fat and one of them dances by herself with her eyes closed.

I ask a couple of the girls what they do.

"I just kind of come out here a lot," one of them says.

"I just sort of know the Dead," the other says.

The one who just sort of knows the Dead starts cutting up a loaf of French bread on the piano bench. The boys take a break and one of them talks about playing the Los Angeles Cheetah, which is in the old Aragon Ballroom. "We were up there drinking beer where Lawrence Welk used to sit," Jerry Garcia says.

The little girl who was dancing by herself giggles. "Too much," she says softly. Her eyes are still closed.

Somebody said that if I was going to meet some runaways I better pick up a few hamburgers and Cokes on the way, so I did, and we are eating them in the Park together, me, Debbie who is fifteen, and Jeff who is sixteen. Debbie and Jeff ran away twelve days ago, walked out of school one morning with $100 between them. Because a missing-juvenile is out on Debbie—she was already on probation because her mother had once taken her down to the police station and declared her incorrigible—this is only the second time they have been out of a friend's apartment since they got to San Francisco. The first time they went over to the Fairmont Hotel and rode the outside elevator, three times up and three times down. "Wow," Jeff says, and that is all he can think to say, about that.

I ask why they ran away.

"My parents said I had to go to church," Debbie says. "And they wouldn't let me dress the way I wanted. In the seventh grade my skirts were longer than anybody's—it got better in the eighth grade, but still."

"Your mother was kind of a bummer," Jeff agrees.

"They didn't like Jeff. They didn't like my girlfriends. My father thought I was cheap and he told me so. I had a C average and he told me I couldn't date until I raised it, and that bugged me too."

"My mother was just a genuine all-American bitch," Jeff says. "She was really troublesome about hair. Also she didn't like boots. It was really weird."

"Tell about the chores," Debbie says.

"For example I had chores. If I didn't finish ironing my shirts for the week I couldn't go out for the weekend. It was weird. Wow."

Debbie giggles and shakes her head. "This year's gonna be wild."

"We're just gonna let it all happen," Jeff says. "Everything's in the future, you can't pre-plan it. First we get jobs, then a place to live. Then, I dunno."

Jeff finishes off the French fries and gives some thought to what kind of job he could get. "I always kinda dug metal shop, welding, stuff like that." Maybe he could work on cars, I say. "I'm not too mechanically minded," he says. "Anyway you can't pre-plan."

"I could get a job baby-sitting," Debbie says. "Or in a dime store."

"You're always talking about getting a job in a dime store," Jeff says.

"That's because I worked in a dime store already."

Debbie is buffing her fingernails with the belt to her suède jacket. She is annoyed because she chipped a nail and because I do not have any polish remover in the car. I promise to get her to a friend's apartment so that she can redo her manicure, but something has been bothering me and as I fiddle with the ignition I finally ask it. I ask them to think back to when they were children, to tell me what they had wanted to be when they were grown up, how they had seen the future then.

Jeff throws a Coca-Cola bottle out the car window. "I can't remember I ever thought about it," he says.

"I remember I wanted to be a veterinarian once," Debbie says. "But now I'm more or less working in the vein of being an artist or a model or a cosmetologist. Or something."

I hear quite a bit about one cop, Officer Arthur Gerrans, whose name has become a synonym for zealotry on the Street. "He's our Officer Krupke," Max once told me. Max is not personally wild about Officer Gerrans because Officer Gerrans took Max in after the Human Be-In last winter, that's the big Human Be-In in Golden Gate Park where 20,000 people got turned on free, or 10,000 did, or some number did, but then Officer Gerrans has busted almost everyone in the District at one time or another. Presumably to forestall a cult of personality, Officer Gerrans was transferred out of the District not long ago, and when I see him it is not at the Park Station but at the Central Station on Greenwich Avenue.

We are in an interrogation room, and I am interrogating Officer Gerrans. He is young and blond and wary and I go in slow. I wonder what he thinks "the major problems" in the Haight are.

Officer Gerrans thinks it over. "I would say the major problems there," he says finally, "the major problems are narcotics and juveniles. Juveniles and narcotics, those are your major problems."

I write that down.

"Just one moment," Officer Gerrans says, and leaves the room. When he comes back he tells me that I cannot talk to him without permission from Chief Thomas Cahill.

"In the meantime," Officer Gerrans adds, pointing at the notebook in which I have written *major problems: juveniles, narcotics*, "I'll take those notes."

The next day I apply for permission to talk to Officer Gerrans and also to Chief Cahill. A few days later a sergeant returns my call.

"We have finally received clearance from the Chief per your request," the sergeant says, "and that is taboo."

I wonder why it is taboo to talk to Officer Gerrans.

Officer Gerrans is involved in court cases coming to trial.

I wonder why it is taboo to talk to Chief Cahill.

The Chief has pressing police business.

I wonder if I can talk to anyone at all in the Police Department.

"No," the sergeant says, "not at the particular moment."

Which was my last official contact with the San Francisco Police Department.

Norris and I are standing around the Panhandle and Norris is telling me how it is all set up for a friend to take me to Big Sur. I say what I really want to do is spend a few days with Norris and his wife and the rest of the people in their house. Norris says it would be a lot easier if I'd take some acid. I say I'm unstable. Norris says all right, anyway, *grass*, and he squeezes my hand.

One day Norris asks how old I am. I tell him I am thirty-two. It takes a few minutes, but Norris rises to it. "Don't worry," he says at last. "There's old hippies too."

It is a pretty nice evening and nothing much happening and Max brings his old lady, Sharon, over to the Warehouse. The Warehouse, which is where Don and a floating number of other people live, is not actually a warehouse but the garage of a condemned hotel. The Warehouse was conceived as total theater, a continual happening, and I always feel good there. What happened ten minutes ago or what is going to happen a half hour from now tends to fade from mind in the Warehouse. Somebody is usually doing something interesting, like working on a light show, and there are a lot of interesting things around, like an old Chevrolet touring car which is used as a bed and a vast American flag fluttering up in the shadows and an overstuffed chair suspended like a swing from the rafters, the point of that being that it gives you a sensory-deprivation high.

One reason I particularly like the Warehouse is that a child named Michael is staying there now. Michael's mother, Sue Ann, is a sweet wan girl who is always in the kitchen cooking seaweed or baking macrobiotic bread while Michael amuses himself with joss sticks or an old tambourine or a rocking horse with the paint worn off. The first time I ever saw Michael was on that rocking horse, a very blond and pale and dirty child on a rocking horse with no paint. A blue theatrical spotlight was the only light in the Warehouse that afternoon, and there was Michael in it, crooning softly to the wooden horse. Michael is three years old. He is a bright child but does not yet talk.

This particular night Michael is trying to light his joss sticks and there are the usual number of people floating through and they all drift into Don's room and sit on the bed and pass joints. Sharon is very excited when she arrives. "*Don*," she cries, breathless. "We got some STP today." At this time STP is a pretty big deal, remember; nobody yet knew what it was and it was relatively, although just relatively, hard to come by. Sharon is blond and scrubbed and probably seventeen, but Max is a little vague about that since his court case comes up in a month or so and he doesn't need statutory rape on top of it. Sharon's parents were living apart when last she saw them. She does not miss school or anything much about her past, except her younger brother. "I want to turn him on," she confided one day. "He's fourteen now, that's the perfect age. I know where he goes to high school and someday I'll just go get him."

Time passes and I lose the thread and when I pick it up again Max seems to be talking about what a beautiful thing it is the way Sharon washes dishes.

"Well it *is* beautiful," Sharon says. "*Everything* is. I mean you watch that blue detergent blob run on the plate, watch the grease cut—well, it can be a real trip."

Pretty soon now, maybe next month, maybe later, Max and Sharon plan to leave for Africa and India, where they can live off the land. "I got this little trust fund, see," Max says, "which is useful in that it tells cops and border patrols I'm O.K., but living off the land is the thing. You can get your high and get your dope in the city, O.K., but we gotta get out somewhere and live organically."

"Roots and things," Sharon says, lighting another joss stick for Michael. Michael's mother is still in the kitchen cooking seaweed. "You can eat them."

Maybe eleven o'clock, we move from the Warehouse to the place where Max and Sharon live with a couple named Tom and Barbara. Sharon is pleased to get home ("I hope you got some hash joints fixed in the kitchen," she says to Barbara by way of greeting) and everybody is pleased to show off the apartment, which has a lot of flowers and candles and paisleys. Max and

Sharon and Tom and Barbara get pretty high on hash, and everyone dances a little and we do some liquid projections and set up a
strobe and take turns getting a high on that. Quite late, somebody
called Steve comes in with a pretty, dark girl. They have been to a
meeting of people who practice a Western yoga, but they do not
seem to want to talk about that. They lie on the floor awhile, and
then Steve stands up.

"Max," he says, "I want to say one thing."

"It's your trip." Max is edgy.

"I found love on acid. But I lost it. And now I'm finding it
again. With nothing but grass."

Max mutters that heaven and hell are both in one's karma.

"That's what bugs me about psychedelic art," Steve says.

"What about psychedelic art," Max says. "I haven't seen much
psychedelic art."

Max is lying on a bed with Sharon, and Steve leans down to
him. "Groove, baby," he says. "You're a groove."

Steve sits down then and tells me about one summer when he
was at a school of design in Rhode Island and took thirty trips,
the last ones all bad. I ask why they were bad. "I could tell you it
was my neuroses," he says, "but fuck that."

A few days later I drop by to see Steve in his apartment.
He paces nervously around the room he uses as a studio and
shows me some paintings. We do not seem to be getting to the
point.

"Maybe you noticed something going on at Max's," he says
abruptly.

It seems that the girl he brought, the dark pretty one, had once
been Max's girl. She had followed him to Tangier and now to San
Francisco. But Max has Sharon. "So she's kind of staying around
here," Steve says.

Steve is troubled by a lot of things. He is twenty-three, was
raised in Virginia, and has the idea that California is the beginning of the end. "I feel it's insane," he says, and his voice drops.
"This chick tells me there's no meaning to life but it doesn't
matter, we'll just flow right out. There've been times I felt like
packing up and taking off for the East Coast again, at least there
I had a *target*. At least there you expect that it's going to *happen*."
He lights a cigarette for me and his hands shake. "Here you know
it's not going to."

I ask what it is that is supposed to happen.

"I don't know," he says. "Something. Anything."

Arthur Lisch is on the telephone in his kitchen, trying to sell VISTA a program for the District. "We already *got* an emergency," he says into the telephone, meanwhile trying to disentangle his daughter, age one and a half, from the cord. "We don't get help here, nobody can guarantee what's going to happen. We've got people sleeping in the streets here. We've got people starving to death." He pauses. "All right," he says then, and his voice rises. "So they're doing it by choice. So what."

By the time he hangs up he has limned what strikes me as a pretty Dickensian picture of life on the edge of Golden Gate Park, but then this is my first exposure to Arthur Lisch's "riot-on-the-Street-unless" pitch. Arthur Lisch is a kind of leader of the Diggers, who, in the official District mythology, are supposed to be a group of anonymous good guys with no thought in their collective head but to lend a helping hand. The official District mythology also has it that the Diggers have no "leaders," but nonetheless Arthur Lisch is one. Arthur Lisch is also a paid worker for the American Friends' Service Committee and he lives with his wife, Jane, and their two small children in a railroad flat, which on this particular day lacks organization. For one thing the telephone keeps ringing. Arthur promises to attend a hearing at city hall. Arthur promises to "send Edward, he's O.K." Arthur promises to get a good group, maybe the Loading Zone, to play free for a Jewish benefit. For a second thing the baby is crying, and she does not stop until Jane Lisch appears with a jar of Gerber's Junior Chicken Noodle Dinner. Another confusing element is somebody named Bob, who just sits in the living room and looks at his toes. First he looks at the toes on one foot, then at the toes on the other. I make several attempts to include Bob in the conversation before I realize he is on a bad trip. Moreover, there are two people hacking up what looks like a side of beef on the kitchen floor, the idea being that when it gets hacked up, Jane Lisch can cook it for the daily Digger feed in the Park.

Arthur Lisch does not seem to notice any of this. He just keeps talking about cybernated societies and the guaranteed annual wage and riot on the Street, unless.

I call the Lisches a day or so later and ask for Arthur. Jane Lisch says he's next door taking a shower because somebody is coming down from a bad trip in their bathroom. Besides the freak-out in the bathroom they are expecting a psychiatrist in to look at Bob. Also a doctor for Edward, who is not O.K. at all but has the flu. Jane says maybe I should talk to Chester Anderson. She will not give me his number.

Chester Anderson is a legacy of the Beat Generation, a man in his middle thirties whose peculiar hold on the District derives from his possession of a mimeograph machine, on which he prints communiqués signed "the communication company." It is another tenet of the official District mythology that the communication company will print anything anybody has to say, but in fact Chester Anderson prints only what he writes himself, agrees with, or considers harmless or dead matter. His statements, which are left in piles and pasted on windows around Haight Street, are regarded with some apprehension in the District and with considerable interest by outsiders, who study them, like China watchers, for subtle shifts in obscure ideologies. An Anderson communiqué might be doing something as specific as fingering someone who is said to have set up a marijuana bust, or it might be working in a more general vein:

> Pretty little 16-year-old middle-class chick comes to the Haight to see what it's all about & gets picked up by a 17-year-old street dealer who spends all day shooting her full of speed again & again, then feeds her 3,000 mikes & raffles off her temporarily unemployed body for the biggest Haight Street gangbang since the night before last. The politics and ethics of ecstasy. Rape is as common as bullshit on Haight Street. Kids are starving on the Street. Minds and bodies are being maimed as we watch, a scale model of Vietnam.

Somebody other than Jane Lisch gave me an address for Chester Anderson, 443 Arguello, but 443 Arguello does not exist. I telephone the wife of the man who gave me 443 Arguello and she says it's 742 Arguello.

"But don't go up there," she says.

I say I'll telephone.

"There's no number," she says. "I can't give it to you."

"742 Arguello," I say.

"No," she says. "I don't know. And don't go there. And don't use either my name or my husband's name if you do."

She is the wife of a full professor of English at San Francisco State College. I decide to lie low on the question of Chester Anderson for awhile.

> Paranoia strikes deep—
> Into your life it will creep—
>> is a song the Buffalo
>> Springfield sings.

The appeal of Malakoff Diggings has kind of faded out but Max says why don't I come to his place, just be there, the next time he takes acid. Tom will take it too, probably Sharon, maybe Barbara. We can't do it for six or seven days because Max and Tom are in STP space now. They are not crazy about STP but it has advantages. "You've still got your forebrain," Tom says. "I could write behind STP, but not behind acid." This is the first time I have heard of anything you can't do behind acid, also the first time I have heard that Tom writes.

Otto is feeling better because he discovered it wasn't the cocaine-and-wheat that made him sick. It was the chicken pox, which he caught baby-sitting for Big Brother and the Holding Company one night when they were playing. I go over to see him and meet Vicki, who sings now and then with a group called the Jook Savages and lives at Otto's place. Vicki dropped out of Laguna High "because I had mono," followed the Grateful Dead up to San Francisco one time and has been here "for a while." Her mother and father are divorced, and she does not see her father, who works for a network in New York. A few months ago he came out to do a documentary on the District and tried to find her, but couldn't. Later he wrote her a letter in care of her mother urging her to go back to school. Vicki guesses maybe she will sometime but she doesn't see much point in it right now.

* * *

We are eating a little tempura in Japantown, Chet Helms and I, and he is sharing some of his insights with me. Until a couple of years ago Chet Helms never did much besides hitchhiking, but now he runs the Avalon Ballroom and flies over the Pole to check out the London scene and says things like "Just for the sake of clarity I'd like to categorize the aspects of primitive religion as I see it." Right now he is talking about Marshall McLuhan and how the printed word is finished, out, over. "The *East Village Other* is one of the few papers in America whose books are in the black," he says. "I know that from reading *Barron's*."

A new group is supposed to play in the Panhandle today but they are having trouble with the amplifier and I sit in the sun listening to a couple of little girls, maybe seventeen years old. One of them has a lot of makeup and the other wears Levi's and cowboy boots. The boots do not look like an affectation, they look like she came up off a ranch about two weeks ago. I wonder what she is doing here in the Panhandle trying to make friends with a city girl who is snubbing her but I do not wonder long, because she is homely and awkward and I think of her going all the way through the consolidated union high school out there where she comes from and nobody ever asking her to go into Reno on Saturday night for a drive-in movie and a beer on the riverbank, so she runs. "I know a thing about dollar bills," she is saying now. "You get one that says 'IIII' in one corner and 'IIII' in another, you take it down to Dallas, Texas, they'll give you $15 for it."

"Who will?" the city girl asks.

"I don't know."

"There are only three significant pieces of data in the world today," is another thing Chet Helms told me one night. We were at the Avalon and the big strobe was going and the colored lights and the Day-Glo painting and the place was full of high-school kids trying to look turned on. The Avalon sound system projects 126 decibels at 100 feet but to Chet Helms the sound is just there, like the air, and he talks through it. "The first is," he said, "God died last year and was obited by the press. The second is, fifty percent of the population is or will be under twenty-five." A boy shook a tambourine toward us and Chet smiled benevolently at him. "The third," he said, "is that they got twenty billion irresponsible dollars to spend."

Thursday comes, some Thursday, and Max and Tom and Sharon and maybe Barbara are going to take some acid. They want to drop it about three o'clock. Barbara has baked fresh bread, Max has gone to the Park for fresh flowers, and Sharon is making a sign for the door which reads "DO NOT DISTURB, RING, KNOCK, OR IN ANY OTHER WAY DISTURB. LOVE." This is not how I would put it to either the health inspector, who is due this week, or any of the several score narcotics agents in the neighborhood, but I figure the sign is Sharon's trip.

Once the sign is finished Sharon gets restless. "Can I at least play the new record?" she asks Max.

"Tom and Barbara want to save it for when we're high."

"I'm getting bored, just sitting around here."

Max watches her jump up and walk out. "That's what you call pre-acid uptight jitters," he says.

Barbara is not in evidence. Tom keeps walking in and out. "All these innumerable last-minute things you have to do," he mutters.

"It's a tricky thing, acid," Max says after a while. He is turning the stereo on and off. "When a chick takes acid, it's all right if she's alone, but when she's living with somebody this edginess comes out. And if the hour-and-a-half process before you take the acid doesn't go smooth …" He picks up a roach and studies it, then adds, "They're having a little thing back there with Barbara."

Sharon and Tom walk in.

"You pissed off too?" Max asks Sharon.

Sharon does not answer.

Max turns to Tom. "Is she all right?"

"Yeh."

"Can we take acid?" Max is on edge.

"I don't know what she's going to do."

"What do you want to do?"

"What I want to do depends on what she wants to do." Tom is rolling some joints, first rubbing the papers with a marijuana resin he makes himself. He takes the joints back to the bedroom, and Sharon goes with him.

"Something like this happens every time people take acid," Max says. After a while he brightens and develops a theory around it. "Some people don't like to go out of themselves, that's the trouble. You probably wouldn't. You'd probably like only a quarter of a tab. There's still an ego on a quarter tab, and it wants things. Now if that thing is balling—and your old lady or your old man is off somewhere flashing and doesn't want to be touched—well, you get put down on acid, you can be on a bummer for months."

Sharon drifts in, smiling. "Barbara might take some acid, we're all feeling better, we smoked a joint."

At three-thirty that afternoon Max, Tom, and Sharon placed tabs under their tongues and sat down together in the living room to wait for the flash. Barbara stayed in the bedroom, smoking hash. During the next four hours a window banged once in Barbara's room, and about five-thirty some children had a fight on the street. A curtain billowed in the afternoon wind. A cat scratched a beagle in Sharon's lap. Except for the sitar music on the stereo there was no other sound or movement until seven-thirty, when Max said "Wow."

I spot Deadeye on Haight Street, and he gets in the car. Until we get off the Street he sits very low and inconspicuous. Deadeye wants me to meet his old lady, but first he wants to talk to me about how he got hip to helping people.

"Here I was, just a tough kid on a motorcycle," he says, "and suddenly I see that young people don't have to walk alone." Deadeye has a clear evangelistic gaze and the reasonable rhetoric of a car salesman. He is society's model product. I try to meet his gaze directly because he once told me he could read character in people's eyes, particularly if he has just dropped acid, which he did, about nine o'clock this morning. "They just have to remember one thing," he says. "The Lord's Prayer. And that can help them in more ways than one."

He takes a much-folded letter from his wallet. The letter is from a little girl he helped. "My loving brother," it begins. "I thought I'd write you a letter since I'm a part of you. Remember that: When you feel happiness, I do, when you feel …"

"What I want to do now," Deadeye says, "is set up a house where a person of any age can come, spend a few days, talk over his problems. *Any age*. People your age, they've got problems too."

I say a house will take money.

"I've found a way to make money," Deadeye says. He hesitates only a few seconds. "I could've made eighty-five dollars on the Street just then. See, in my pocket I had a hundred tabs of acid. I had to come up with twenty dollars by tonight or we're out of the house we're in, so I knew somebody who had acid, and I knew somebody who wanted it, so I made the connection."

Since the Mafia moved into the LSD racket, the quantity is up and the quality is down ... Historian Arnold Toynbee celebrated his 78th birthday Friday night by snapping his fingers and tapping his toes to the Quicksilver Messenger Service ... are a couple of items from Herb Caen's column one morning as the West declined in the spring of 1967.

When I was in San Francisco a tab, or a cap, of LSD-25 sold for three to five dollars, depending upon the seller and the district. LSD was slightly cheaper in the Haight-Ashbury than in the Fillmore, where it was used rarely, mainly as a sexual ploy, and sold by pushers of hard drugs, *e.g.*, heroin, or "smack." A great deal of acid was being cut with Methedrine, which is the trade name for an amphetamine, because Methedrine can simulate the flash that low-quality acid lacks. Nobody knows how much LSD is actually in a tab, but the standard trip is supposed to be 250 micrograms. Grass was running ten dollars a lid, five dollars a matchbox. Hash was considered "a luxury item." All the amphetamines, or "speed"—Benzedrine, Dexedrine, and particularly Methedrine—were in far more common use in the late spring than they had been in the early spring. Some attributed this to the presence of the Syndicate; others to a general deterioration of the scene, to the incursions of gangs and younger part-time, or "plastic," hippies, who like the amphetamines and the illusions of action and power they give. Where Methedrine is in wide use, heroin tends to be available, because, I was told, "You can get awful damn high shooting crystal, and smack can be used to bring you down."

* * *

Deadeye's old lady, Gerry, meets us at the door of their place. She is a big, hearty girl who has always counseled at Girl Scout camps during summer vacations and was "in social welfare" at the University of Washington when she decided that she "just hadn't done enough living" and came to San Francisco. "Actually the heat was bad in Seattle," she adds.

"The first night I got down here," she says, "I stayed with a gal I met over at the Blue Unicorn. I looked like I'd just arrived, had a knapsack and stuff." After that, Gerry stayed at a house the Diggers were running, where she met Deadeye. "Then it took time to get my bearings, so I haven't done much work yet."

I ask Gerry what work she does. "Basically I'm a poet," she says, "but I had my guitar stolen right after I arrived, and that kind of hung up my thing."

"Get your books," Deadeye orders. "Show her your books."

Gerry demurs, then goes into the bedroom and comes back with several theme books full of verse. I leaf through them but Deadeye is still talking about helping people. "Any kid that's on speed," he says, "I'll try to get him off it. The only advantage to it from the kids' point of view is that you don't have to worry about sleeping or eating."

"Or sex," Gerry adds.

"That's right. When you're strung out on crystal you don't need *nothing.*"

"It can lead to the hard stuff," Gerry says. "Take your average Meth freak, once he's started putting the needle in his arm, it's not too hard to say, well, let's shoot a little smack."

All the while I am looking at Gerry's poems. They are a very young girl's poems, each written out in a neat hand and finished off with a curlicue. Dawns are roseate, skies silver-tinted. When Gerry writes "crystal" in her books, she does not mean Meth.

"You gotta get back to your writing," Deadeye says fondly, but Gerry ignores this. She is telling about somebody who propositioned her yesterday. "He just walked up to me on the Street, offered me six hundred dollars to go to Reno and do the thing."

"You're not the only one he approached," Deadeye says.

"If some chick wants to go with him, fine," Gerry says. "Just don't bum my trip." She empties the tuna-fish can we are using for an ashtray and goes over to look at a girl who is asleep on the floor. It is the same girl who was sleeping on the floor the first day I came to Deadeye's place. She has been sick a week now, ten days. "Usually when somebody comes up to me on the Street like that," Gerry adds, "I hit him for some change."

When I saw Gerry in the Park the next day I asked her about the sick girl, and Gerry said cheerfully that she was in the hospital, with pneumonia.

Max tells me about how he and Sharon got together. "When I saw her the first time on Haight Street, I flashed. I mean flashed. So I started some conversation with her about her beads, see, but I didn't care about her beads." Sharon lived in a house where a friend of Max's lived, and the next time he saw her was when he took the friend some bananas. "It was during the great banana bubble. You had to kind of force your personality and the banana peels down their throats. Sharon and I were like kids—we just smoked bananas and looked at each other and smoked more bananas and looked at each other."

But Max hesitated. For one thing he thought Sharon was his friend's girl. "For another I didn't know if I wanted to get hung up with an old lady." But the next time he visited the house, Sharon was on acid.

"So everybody yelled 'Here comes the banana man,'" Sharon interrupts, "and I got all excited."

"She was living in this crazy house," Max continues. "There was this one kid, all he did was scream. His whole trip was to practice screams. It was too much." Max still hung back from Sharon. "But then she offered me a tab, and I knew."

Max walked to the kitchen and back with the tab, wondering whether to take it. "And then I decided to flow with it, and that was that. Because once you drop acid with somebody you flash on, you see the whole world melt in her eyes."

"It's stronger than anything in the world," Sharon says.

"Nothing can break it up," Max says. "As long as it lasts."

No milk today—
My love has gone away ...

The end of my hopes—
The end of all my dreams—
is a song I heard every morning in the
cold late spring of 1967 on KFRC, the
Flower Power Station, San Francisco.

Deadeye and Gerry tell me they plan to be married. An Episcopal priest in the District has promised to perform the wedding in Golden Gate Park, and they will have a few rock groups there, "a real community thing." Gerry's brother is also getting married, in Seattle. "Kind of interesting," Gerry muses, "because, you know, his is the traditional straight wedding, and then you have the contrast with ours."

"I'll have to wear a tie to his," Deadeye says.

"Right," Gerry says.

"Her parents came down to meet me, but they weren't ready for me," Deadeye notes philosophically.

"They finally gave it their blessing," Gerry says. "In a way."

"They came to me and her father said, 'Take care of her,'" Deadeye reminisces. "And her mother said, 'Don't let her go to jail.'"

Barbara baked a macrobiotic apple pie and she and Tom and Max and Sharon and I are eating it. Barbara tells me how she learned to find happiness in "the woman's thing." She and Tom had gone somewhere to live with the Indians, and although she first found it hard to be shunted off with the women and never to enter into any of the men's talk, she soon got the point. "That was where the *trip* was," she says.

Barbara is on what is called the woman's trip to the exclusion of almost everything else. When she and Tom and Max and Sharon need money, Barbara will take a part-time job, modeling or teaching kindergarten, but she dislikes earning more than ten or twenty dollars a week. Most of the time she keeps house and bakes. "Doing something that shows your love that way," she says, "is just about the most beautiful thing I know." Whenever I hear about the woman's trip, which is often, I think a lot about nothin'-says-lovin'-like-something-from-the-oven and the Feminine Mystique and how it is possible for people to be the unconscious instruments of values they would strenuously reject on a conscious level, but I do not mention this to Barbara.

It is a pretty nice day and I am just driving down the Street and I see Barbara at a light.

What am I doing, she wants to know.

I am just driving around.

"Groovy," she says.

It's a beautiful day, I say.

"Groovy," she agrees.

She wants to know if I will come over. Sometime soon, I say.

"Groovy," she says.

I ask if she wants to drive in the Park but she is too busy. She is out to buy wool for her loom.

Arthur Lisch gets pretty nervous whenever he sees me now because the Digger line this week is that they aren't talking to "media poisoners," which is me. So I still don't have a tap on Chester Anderson, but one day in the Panhandle I run into a kid who says he is Chester's "associate." He has on a black cape, black slouch hat, mauve Job's Daughters sweatshirt and dark glasses, and he says his name is Claude Hayward, but never mind that because I think of him just as The Connection. The Connection offers to "check me out."

I take off my dark glasses so he can see my eyes. He leaves his on.

"How much you get paid for doing this kind of media poisoning?" he says for openers.

I put my dark glasses back on.

"There's only one way to find out where it's at," The Connection says, and jerks his thumb at the photographer I'm with. "Dump him and get out on the Street. Don't take money. You won't need money." He reaches into his cape and pulls out a Mimeographed sheet announcing a series of classes at the Digger Free Store on How to Avoid Getting Busted, Gangbangs, VD, Rape, Pregnancy, Beatings, and Starvation. "You oughta come," The Connection says. "You'll need it."

I say maybe, but meanwhile I would like to talk to Chester Anderson.

"If we decide to get in touch with you at all," The Connection says, "we'll get in touch with you real quick." He kept an eye on me in the Park after that but never called the number I gave him.

It is twilight and cold and too early to find Deadeye at the Blue Unicorn so I ring Max's bell. Barbara comes to the door.

"Max and Tom are seeing somebody on a kind of business thing," she says. "Can you come back a little later?"

I am hard put to think what Max and Tom might be seeing somebody about in the way of business, but a few days later in the Park I find out.

"Hey," Max calls. "Sorry you couldn't come up the other day, but *business* was being done." This time I get the point. "We got some great stuff," he says, and begins to elaborate. Every third person in the Park this afternoon looks like a narcotics agent and I try to change the subject. Later I suggest to Max that he be more wary in public. "Listen, I'm very cautious," he says. "You can't be too careful."

By now I have an unofficial taboo contact with the San Francisco Police Department. What happens is that this cop and I meet in various late-movie ways, like I happen to be sitting in the bleachers at a baseball game and he happens to sit down next to me, and we exchange guarded generalities. No information actually passes between us, but after a while we get to kind of like each other.

"The kids aren't too bright," he is telling me on this particular day. "They'll tell you they can always spot an undercover, they'll tell you about 'the kind of car he drives.' They aren't talking about undercovers, they're talking about plainclothesmen who just happen to drive unmarked cars, like I do. They can't tell an undercover. An undercover doesn't drive some black Ford with a two-way radio."

He tells me about an undercover who was taken out of the District because he was believed to be overexposed, too familiar. He was transferred to the narcotics squad, and by error was sent immediately back into the District as a narcotics undercover.

The cop plays with his keys. "You want to know how smart these kids are?" he says finally. "The first week, this guy makes forty-three cases."

The Jook Savages are supposed to be having a May Day party in Larkspur and I go by the Warehouse and Don and Sue Ann think it would be nice to drive over there because Sue Ann's three-year-old, Michael, hasn't been out lately. The air is soft and there is a sunset haze around the Golden Gate and Don asks Sue Ann how many flavors she can detect in a single grain of rice and Sue Ann tells Don maybe she better learn to cook *yang*, maybe they are all too *yin* at the Warehouse, and I try to teach Michael "Frère Jacques." We each have our own trip and it is a nice drive. Which is just as well because there is nobody at all at the Jook Savages' place, not even the Jook Savages. When we get back Sue Ann decides to cook up a lot of apples they have around the Warehouse and Don starts working with his light show and I go down to see Max for a minute. "Out of sight," Max says about the Larkspur caper. "Somebody thinks it would be groovy to turn on five hundred people the first day in May, and it would be, but then they turn on the last day in April instead, so it doesn't happen. If it happens, it happens. If it doesn't, it doesn't. Who cares. Nobody cares."

Some kid with braces on his teeth is playing his guitar and boasting that he got the last of the STP from Mr. O. himself and somebody else is talking about how five grams of acid will be liberated within the next month and you can see that nothing much is happening this afternoon around the *San Francisco Oracle* office. A boy sits at a drawing board drawing the infinitesimal figures that people do on speed, and the kid with the braces watches him. "*I'm gonna shoot my wo–man*," he sings softly. "*She been with a–noth–er man.*" Someone works out the numerology of my name and the name of the photographer I'm with. The photographer's is all white and the sea ("If I were to make you some beads, see, I'd do it mainly in white," he is told), but mine has a double death symbol. The afternoon does not seem to be getting anywhere, so it is suggested that we go over to Japantown and find somebody named Sandy who will take us to the Zen temple.

Four boys and one middle-aged man are sitting on a grass mat at Sandy's place, sipping anise tea and watching Sandy read Laura Huxley's *You Are Not the Target*.

We sit down and have some anise tea. "Meditation turns us on," Sandy says. He has a shaved head and the kind of cherubic face usually seen in newspaper photographs of mass murderers. The middle-aged man, whose name is George, is making me uneasy because he is in a trance next to me and stares at me without seeing me.

I feel that my mind is going—George is *dead*, or we *all* are—when the telephone rings.

"It's for George," Sandy says.

"George, *tele*phone."

"*George.*"

Somebody waves his hand in front of George and George finally gets up, bows, and moves toward the door on the balls of his feet.

"I think I'll take George's tea," somebody says. "George—are you coming back?"

George stops at the door and stares at each of us in turn. "In a *mo*ment," he snaps.

> *Do you know who is the first eternal spaceman of this universe?*
> *The first to send his wild wild vibrations*
> *To all those cosmic superstations?*
> *For the song he always shouts*
> *Sends the planets flipping out …*
> *But I'll tell you before you think me loony*
> *That I'm talking about Narada Muni …*
> *Singing*
> HARE KRISHNA HARE KRISHNA
> KRISHNA KRISHNA HARE HARE
> HARE RAMA HARE RAMA
> RAMA RAMA HARE HARE
> is a Krishna song. Words by
> Howard Wheeler and music by
> Michael Grant.

Maybe the trip is not in Zen but in Krishna, so I pay a visit to Michael Grant, the Swami A.C. Bhaktivedanta's leading disciple in San Francisco. Michael Grant is at home with his brother-in-law and his wife, a pretty girl wearing a cashmere pullover, a jumper, and a red caste mark on her forehead.

"I've been associated with the Swami since about last July," Michael says. "See, the Swami came here from India and he was at this ashram in upstate New York and he just kept to himself and chanted a lot. For a couple of months. Pretty soon I helped him get his storefront in New York. Now it's an international movement, which we spread by teaching this chant." Michael is fingering his red wooden beads and I notice that I am the only person in the room with shoes on. "It's catching on like wildfire."

"If everybody chanted," the brother-in-law says, "there wouldn't be any problem with the police or anybody."

"Ginsberg calls the chant ecstasy, but the Swami says that's not exactly it." Michael walks across the room and straightens a picture of Krishna as a baby. "Too bad you can't meet the Swami," he adds. "The Swami's in New York now."

"Ecstasy's not the right word at all," says the brother-in-law, who has been thinking about it. "It makes you think of some ... mun*dane* ecstasy."

The next day I drop by Max and Sharon's, and find them in bed smoking a little morning hash. Sharon once advised me that half a joint even of grass would make getting up in the morning a beautiful thing. I ask Max how Krishna strikes him.

"You can get a high on a mantra," he says. "But I'm holy on acid."

Max passes the joint to Sharon and leans back. "Too bad you couldn't meet the Swami," he says. "The Swami was the turn-on."

Anybody who thinks this is all about drugs has his head in a bag. It's a social movement, quintessentially romantic, the kind that recurs in times of real social crisis. The themes are always the same. A return to innocence. The invocation of an earlier authority and control. The mysteries of the blood. An itch for the transcendental, for purification. Right there you've got the ways that romanticism historically ends up in trouble, lends itself to authoritarianism. When the direction appears. How long do you think it'll take for that to happen? is a question a San Francisco psychiatrist asked me.

At the time I was in San Francisco the political potential of what was then called the movement was just becoming clear. It had always been clear to the revolutionary core of the Diggers, whose every guerrilla talent was now bent toward open confrontations and the creation of a summer emergency, and it was clear to many of the straight doctors and priests and sociologists who had occasion to work in the District, and it could rapidly become clear to any outsider who bothered to decode Chester Anderson's call-to-action communiqués or to watch who was there first at the street skirmishes which now set the tone for life in the District. One did not have to be a political analyst to see it; the boys in the rock groups saw it, because they were often where it was happening. "In the Park there are always twenty or thirty people below the stand," one of the Dead complained to me. "Ready to take the crowd on some militant trip."

But the peculiar beauty of this political potential, as far as the activists were concerned, was that it remained not clear at all to most of the inhabitants of the District, perhaps because the few seventeen-year-olds who are political realists tend not to adopt romantic idealism as a life style. Nor was it clear to the press, which at varying levels of competence continued to report "the hippie phenomenon" as an extended panty raid; an artistic avant-garde led by such comfortable YMHA regulars as Allen Ginsberg; or a thoughtful protest, not unlike joining the Peace Corps, against the culture which had produced Saran-Wrap and the Vietnam War. This last, or they're-trying-to-tell-us-something approach, reached its apogee in a *Time* cover story which revealed that hippies "scorn money—they call it 'bread'" and remains the most remarkable, if unwitting, extant evidence that the signals between the generations are irrevocably jammed.

Because the signals the press was getting were immaculate of political possibilities, the tensions of the District went unremarked upon, even during the period when there were so many observers on Haight Street from *Life* and *Look* and CBS that they were largely observing one another. The observers believed roughly what the children told them: that they were a generation dropped out of political action, beyond power games, that the New Left was just another ego trip. *Ergo*, there really were no activists in the Haight-Ashbury, and those things which happened every Sunday were spontaneous demonstrations because, just as the Diggers say, the police are brutal and juveniles have no rights and runaways are deprived of their right to self-determination and people are starving to death on Haight Street, a scale model of Vietnam.

Of course the activists—not those whose thinking had become rigid, but those whose approach to revolution was imaginatively anarchic—had long ago grasped the reality which still eluded the press: we were seeing something important. We were seeing the desperate attempt of a handful of pathetically unequipped children to create a community in a social vacuum. Once we had seen these children, we could no longer overlook the vacuum, no longer pretend that the society's atomization could be reversed. This was not a traditional generational rebellion. At some point between 1945 and 1967 we had somehow neglected to tell these children the rules of the game we happened to be playing. Maybe we had stopped believing in the rules ourselves, maybe we were having a failure of nerve about the game. Maybe there were just too few people around to do the telling. These were children who grew up cut loose from the web of cousins and great-aunts and family doctors and lifelong neighbors who had traditionally suggested and enforced the society's values. They are children who have moved around a lot, *San Jose, Chula Vista, here*. They are less in rebellion against the society than ignorant of it, able only to feed back certain of its most publicized self-doubts, *Vietnam, Saran-Wrap, diet pills, the Bomb*.

They feed back exactly what is given them. Because they do not believe in words—words are for "typeheads," Chester Anderson tells them, and a thought which needs words is just one more of those ego trips—their only proficient vocabulary is in the society's platitudes. As it happens I am still committed to the idea that the ability to think for one's self depends upon one's mastery of the language, and I am not optimistic about children who will settle for saying, to indicate that their mother and father do not live together, that they come from "a broken home." They are sixteen, fifteen, fourteen years old, younger all the time, an army of children waiting to be given the words.

Peter Berg knows a lot of words.

"Is Peter Berg around?" I ask.

"Maybe."

"Are you Peter Berg?"

"Yeh."

The reason Peter Berg does not bother sharing too many words with me is because two of the words he knows are "media poisoning." Peter Berg wears a gold earring and is perhaps the only person in the District on whom a gold earring looks obscurely ominous. He belongs to the San Francisco Mime Troupe, some of whose members started the Artist's Liberation Front for "those who seek to combine their creative urge with socio-political involvement." It was out of the Mime Troupe that the Diggers grew, during the 1966 Hunter's Point riots, when it seemed a good idea to give away food and do puppet shows in the streets making fun of the National Guard. Along with Arthur Lisch, Peter Berg is part of the shadow leadership of the Diggers, and it was he who more or less invented and first introduced to the press the notion that there would be an influx into San Francisco during the summer of 1967 of 200,000 indigent adolescents. The only conversation I ever have with Peter Berg is about how he holds me personally responsible for the way *Life* captioned Henri Cartier-Bresson's pictures out of Cuba, but I like to watch him at work in the Park.

Janis Joplin is singing with Big Brother in the Panhandle and almost everybody is high and it is a pretty nice Sunday afternoon between three and six o'clock, which the activists say are the three hours of the week when something is most likely to happen in the Haight-Ashbury, and who turns up but Peter Berg. He is with his wife and six or seven other people, along with Chester Anderson's associate The Connection, and the first peculiar thing is, they're in blackface.

I mention to Max and Sharon that some members of the Mime Troupe seem to be in blackface.

"It's street theater," Sharon assures me. "It's supposed to be really groovy."

The Mime Troupers get a little closer, and there are some other peculiar things about them. For one thing they are tapping people on the head with dime-store plastic night-sticks, and for another they are wearing signs on their backs. "HOW MANY TIMES YOU BEEN RAPED, YOU LOVE FREAKS?" and "WHO STOLE CHUCK BERRY'S MUSIC?", things like that. Then they are distributing communication company fliers which say:

> & this summer thousands of un-white un-suburban bop-pers are going to want to know why you've given up what they can't get & how you get away with it & how come you not a faggot with hair so long & they want haight street one way or the other. IF YOU DON'T KNOW, BY AUGUST HAIGHT STREET WILL BE A CEMETERY.

Max reads the flier and stands up. "I'm getting bad vibes," he says, and he and Sharon leave.

I have to stay around because I'm looking for Otto so I walk over to where the Mime Troupers have formed a circle around a Negro. Peter Berg is saying if anybody asks that this is street theater, and I figure the curtain is up because what they are doing right now is jabbing the Negro with the nightsticks. They jab, and they bare their teeth, and they rock on the balls of their feet and they wait.

"I'm beginning to get annoyed here," the Negro says. "I'm gonna get mad."

By now there are several Negroes around, reading the signs and watching.

"Just beginning to get annoyed, are you?" one of the Mime Troupers says. "Don't you think it's about time?"

"Nobody *stole* Chuck Berry's music, man," says another Negro who has been studying the signs. "Chuck Berry's music belongs to *every*body."

"Yeh?" a girl in blackface says. "Everybody *who*?"

"Why," he says, confused. "Everybody. In America."

"In *America*," the blackface girl shrieks. "Listen to him talk about *America*."

"Listen," he says helplessly. "Listen here."

"What'd *America* ever do for you?" the girl in blackface jeers. "White kids here, they can sit in the Park all summer long, listen-ing to the music they stole, because their bigshot parents keep sending them money. Who ever sends you money?"

"Listen," the Negro says, his voice rising. "You're gonna start something here, this isn't right—"

"You tell us what's right, black boy," the girl says.

The youngest member of the blackface group, an earnest tall kid about nineteen, twenty, is hanging back at the edge of the scene. I offer him an apple and ask what is going on. "Well," he says, "I'm new at this, I'm just beginning to study it, but you see the capitalists are taking over the District, and that's what Peter—well, ask Peter."

I did not ask Peter. It went on for a while. But on that particular Sunday between three and six o'clock everyone was too high and the weather was too good and the Hunter's Point gangs who usually come in between three and six on Sunday afternoon had come in on Saturday instead, and nothing started. While I waited for Otto I asked a little girl I knew slightly what she had thought of it. "It's something groovy they call street theater," she said. I said I had wondered if it might not have political overtones. She was seventeen years old and she worked it around in her mind awhile and finally she remembered a couple of words from somewhere. "Maybe it's some John Birch thing," she said.

When I finally find Otto he says "I got something at my place that'll blow your mind," and when we get there I see a child on the living-room floor, wearing a reefer coat, reading a comic book. She keeps licking her lips in concentration and the only off thing about her is that she's wearing white lipstick.

"Five years old," Otto says. "On acid."

The five-year-old's name is Susan, and she tells me she is in High Kindergarten. She lives with her mother and some other people, just got over the measles, wants a bicycle for Christmas, and particularly likes Coca-Cola, ice cream, Marty in the Jefferson Airplane, Bob in the Grateful Dead, and the beach. She remembers going to the beach once a long time ago, and wishes she had taken a bucket. For a year now her mother has given her both acid and peyote. Susan describes it as getting stoned.

I start to ask if any of the other children in High Kindergarten get stoned, but I falter at the key words.

"She means do the other kids in your class turn on, *get stoned*," says the friend of her mother's who brought her to Otto's.

"Only Sally and Anne," Susan says.

"What about Lia?" her mother's friend prompts.

"Lia," Susan says, "is not in High Kindergarten."

Sue Ann's three-year-old Michael started a fire this morning before anyone was up, but Don got it out before much damage was done. Michael burned his arm though, which is probably why Sue Ann was so jumpy when she happened to see him chewing on an electric cord. "You'll fry like rice," she screamed. The only people around were Don and one of Sue Ann's macrobiotic friends and somebody who was on his way to a commune in the Santa Lucias, and they didn't notice Sue Ann screaming at Michael because they were in the kitchen trying to retrieve some very good Moroccan hash which had dropped down through a floorboard damaged in the fire.

1967

II
PERSONALS

ON KEEPING A NOTEBOOK

" 'THAT WOMAN ESTELLE,'" the note reads, " 'is partly the reason why George Sharp and I are separated today.' *Dirty crepe-de-Chine wrapper, hotel bar, Wilmington RR, 9:45 a.m. August Monday morning.*"

Since the note is in my notebook, it presumably has some meaning to me. I study it for a long while. At first I have only the most general notion of what I was doing on an August Monday morning in the bar of the hotel across from the Pennsylvania Railroad station in Wilmington, Delaware (waiting for a train? missing one? 1960? 1961? why Wilmington?), but I do remember being there. The woman in the dirty crepe-de-Chine wrapper had come down from her room for a beer, and the bartender had heard before the reason why George Sharp and she were separated today. "Sure," he said, and went on mopping the floor. "You told me." At the other end of the bar is a girl. She is talking, pointedly, not to the man beside her but to a cat lying in the triangle of sunlight cast through the open door. She is wearing a plaid silk dress from Peck & Peck, and the hem is coming down.

Here is what it is: the girl has been on the Eastern Shore, and now she is going back to the city, leaving the man beside her, and all she can see ahead are the viscous summer sidewalks and the 3 a.m. long-distance calls that will make her lie awake and then sleep drugged through all the steaming mornings left in August (1960? 1961?). Because she must go directly from the train to lunch in New York, she wishes that she had a safety pin for the hem of the plaid silk dress, and she also wishes that she could forget about the hem and the lunch and stay in the cool bar that smells of disinfectant and malt and make friends with the woman in the crepe-de-Chine wrapper. She is afflicted by a little self-pity, and she wants to compare Estelles. That is what that was all about.

Why did I write it down? In order to remember, of course, but exactly what was it I wanted to remember? How much of it actually happened? Did any of it? Why do I keep a notebook at all? It is easy to deceive oneself on all those scores. The impulse to write things down is a peculiarly compulsive one, inexplicable to those who do not share it, useful only accidentally, only secondarily, in the way that any compulsion tries to justify itself. I suppose that it begins or does not begin in the cradle. Although I have felt compelled to write things down since I was five years old, I doubt that my daughter ever will, for she is a singularly blessed and accepting child, delighted with life exactly as life presents itself to her, unafraid to go to sleep and unafraid to wake up. Keepers of private notebooks are a different breed altogether, lonely and resistant rearrangers of things, anxious malcontents, children afflicted apparently at birth with some presentiment of loss.

My first notebook was a Big Five tablet, given to me by my mother with the sensible suggestion that I stop whining and learn to amuse myself by writing down my thoughts. She returned the tablet to me a few years ago; the first entry is an account of a woman who believed herself to be freezing to death in the Arctic night, only to find, when day broke, that she had stumbled onto the Sahara Desert, where she would die of the heat before lunch. I have no idea what turn of a five-year-old's mind could have prompted so insistently "ironic" and exotic a story, but it does reveal a certain predilection for the extreme which has dogged me into adult life; perhaps if I were analytically inclined I would find it a truer story than any I might have told about Donald Johnson's birthday party or the day my cousin Brenda put Kitty Litter in the aquarium.

So the point of my keeping a notebook has never been, nor is it now, to have an accurate factual record of what I have been doing or thinking. That would be a different impulse entirely, an instinct for reality which I sometimes envy but do not possess. At no point have I ever been able successfully to keep a diary; my approach to daily life ranges from the grossly negligent to the merely absent, and on those few occasions when I have tried dutifully to record a day's events, boredom has so overcome me that the results are mysterious at best. What is this business about "shopping, typing piece, dinner with E, depressed"? Shopping for what? Typing what piece? Who is E? Was this "E" depressed, or was I depressed? Who cares?

In fact I have abandoned altogether that kind of pointless entry; instead I tell what some would call lies. "That's simply not true," the members of my family frequently tell me when they come up against my memory of a shared event. "The party was *not* for you, the spider was *not* a black widow, *it wasn't that way at all*." Very likely they are right, for not only have I always had trouble distinguishing between what happened and what merely might have happened, but I remain unconvinced that the distinction, for my purposes, matters. The cracked crab that I recall having for lunch the day my father came home from Detroit in 1945 must certainly be embroidery, worked into the day's pattern to lend verisimilitude; I was ten years old and would not now remember the cracked crab. The day's events did not turn on cracked crab. And yet it is precisely that fictitious crab that makes me see the afternoon all over again, a home movie run all too often, the father bearing gifts, the child weeping, an exercise in family love and guilt. Or that is what it was to me. Similarly, perhaps it never did snow that August in Vermont; perhaps there never were flurries in the night wind, and maybe no one else felt the ground hardening and summer already dead even as we pretended to bask in it, but that was how it felt to me, and it might as well have snowed, could have snowed, did snow.

How it felt to me: that is getting closer to the truth about a notebook. I sometimes delude myself about why I keep a notebook, imagine that some thrifty virtue derives from preserving everything observed. See enough and write it down, I tell myself, and then some morning when the world seems drained of wonder, some day when I am only going through the motions of doing what I am supposed to do, which is write—on that bankrupt morning I will simply open my notebook and there it will all be, a forgotten account with accumulated interest, paid passage back to the world out there: dialogue overheard in hotels and elevators and at the hatcheck counter in Pavillon (one middle-aged man shows his hat check to another and says, "That's my old football number"); impressions of Bettina Aptheker and Benjamin Sonnenberg and Teddy ("Mr. Acapulco") Stauffer; careful *aperçus* about tennis bums and failed fashion models and Greek shipping heiresses, one of whom taught me a significant lesson (a lesson I could have learned from F. Scott Fitzgerald, but perhaps we all must meet the very rich for ourselves) by asking, when I arrived to interview her in her orchid-filled sitting room on the second day of a paralyzing New York blizzard, whether it was snowing outside.

I imagine, in other words, that the notebook is about other people. But of course it is not. I have no real business with what one stranger said to another at the hat-check counter in Pavillon; in fact I suspect that the line "That's my old football number" touched not my own imagination at all, but merely some memory of something once read, probably "The Eighty-Yard Run." Nor is my concern with a woman in a dirty crepe-de-Chine wrapper in a Wilmington bar. My stake is always, of course, in the unmentioned girl in the plaid silk dress. *Remember what it was to be me:* that is always the point.

It is a difficult point to admit. We are brought up in the ethic that others, any others, all others, are by definition more interesting than ourselves; taught to be diffident, just this side of self-effacing. ("You're the least important person in the room and don't forget it," Jessica Mitford's governess would hiss in her ear on the advent of any social occasion; I copied that into my notebook because it is only recently that I have been able to enter a room without hearing some such phrase in my inner ear.) Only the very young and the very old may recount their dreams at breakfast, dwell upon self, interrupt with memories of beach picnics and favorite Liberty lawn dresses and the rainbow trout in a creek near Colorado Springs. The rest of us are expected, rightly, to affect absorption in other people's favorite dresses, other people's trout.

And so we do. But our notebooks give us away, for however dutifully we record what we see around us, the common denominator of all we see is always, transparently, shamelessly, the implacable "I." We are not talking here about the kind of notebook that is patently for public consumption, a structural conceit for binding together a series of graceful *pensées*; we are talking about something private, about bits of the mind's string too short to use, an indiscriminate and erratic assemblage with meaning only for its maker.

And sometimes even the maker has difficulty with the meaning. There does not seem to be, for example, any point in my knowing for the rest of my life that, during 1964, 720 tons of soot fell on every square mile of New York City, yet there it is in my notebook, labeled "FACT." Nor do I really need to remember that Ambrose Bierce liked to spell Leland Stanford's name "£eland $tanford," or that "smart women almost always wear black in Cuba," a fashion hint without much potential for practical application. And does not the relevance of these notes seem marginal at best?:

> In the basement museum of the Inyo County Courthouse in Independence, California, sign pinned to a mandarin coat: "This MANDARIN COAT was often worn by Mrs. Minnie S. Brooks when giving lectures on her TEAPOT COLLECTION."

> Redhead getting out of car in front of Beverly Wilshire Hotel, chinchilla stole, Vuitton bags with tags reading:

> MRS LOU FOX
> HOTEL SAHARA
> VEGAS

Well, perhaps not entirely marginal. As a matter of fact, Mrs. Minnie S. Brooks and her MANDARIN COAT pull me back into my own childhood, for although I never knew Mrs. Brooks and did not visit Inyo County until I was thirty, I grew up in just such a world, in houses cluttered with Indian relics and bits of gold ore and ambergris and the souvenirs my Aunt Mercy Farnsworth brought back from the Orient. It is a long way from that world to Mrs. Lou Fox's world, where we all live now, and is it not just as well to remember that? Might not Mrs. Minnie S. Brooks help me to remember what I am? Might not Mrs. Lou Fox help me to remember what I am not?

But sometimes the point is harder to discern. What exactly did I have in mind when I noted down that it cost the father of someone I know $650 a month to light the place on the Hudson in which he lived before the Crash? What use was I planning to make of this line by Jimmy Hoffa: "I may have my faults, but

being wrong ain't one of them"? And although I think it interesting to know where the girls who travel with the Syndicate have
their hair done when they find themselves on the West Coast,
will I ever make suitable use of it? Might I not be better off just
passing it on to John O'Hara? What is a recipe for sauerkraut
doing in my notebook? What kind of magpie keeps this notebook? "*He was born the night the Titanic went down.*" That seems a
nice enough line, and I even recall who said it, but is it not really
a better line in life than it could ever be in fiction?

But of course that is exactly it: not that I should ever use the
line, but that I should remember the woman who said it and the
afternoon I heard it. We were on her terrace by the sea, and we
were finishing the wine left from lunch, trying to get what sun
there was, a California winter sun. The woman whose husband
was born the night the *Titanic* went down wanted to rent her
house, wanted to go back to her children in Paris. I remember
wishing that I could afford the house, which cost $1,000 a month.
"Someday you will," she said lazily. "Someday it all comes." There
in the sun on her terrace it seemed easy to believe in someday,
but later I had a low-grade afternoon hangover and ran over a
black snake on the way to the supermarket and was flooded with
inexplicable fear when I heard the checkout clerk explaining to
the man ahead of me why she was finally divorcing her husband.
"He left me no choice," she said over and over as she punched
the register. "He has a little seven-month-old baby by her, he left
me no choice." I would like to believe that my dread then was
for the human condition, but of course it was for me, because I
wanted a baby and did not then have one and because I wanted
to own the house that cost $1,000 a month to rent and because
I had a hangover.

It all comes back. Perhaps it is difficult to see the value in
having one's self back in that kind of mood, but I do see it; I
think we are well advised to keep on nodding terms with the
people we used to be, whether we find them attractive company
or not. Otherwise they turn up unannounced and surprise us,
come hammering on the mind's door at 4 a.m. of a bad night
and demand to know who deserted them, who betrayed them,
who is going to make amends. We forget all too soon the things
we thought we could never forget. We forget the loves and the
betrayals alike, forget what we whispered and what we screamed,

forget who we were. I have already lost touch with a couple of people I used to be; one of them, a seventeen-year-old, presents little threat, although it would be of some interest to me to know again what it feels like to sit on a river levee drinking vodka-and-orange-juice and listening to Les Paul and Mary Ford and their echoes sing "How High the Moon" on the car radio. (You see I still have the scenes, but I no longer perceive myself among those present, no longer could even improvise the dialogue.) The other one, a twenty-three-year-old, bothers me more. She was always a good deal of trouble, and I suspect she will reappear when I least want to see her, skirts too long, shy to the point of aggravation, always the injured party, full of recriminations and little hurts and stories I do not want to hear again, at once saddening me and angering me with her vulnerability and ignorance, an apparition all the more insistent for being so long banished.

It is a good idea, then, to keep in touch, and I suppose that keeping in touch is what notebooks are all about. And we are all on our own when it comes to keeping those lines open to ourselves: your notebook will never help me, nor mine you. "*So what's new in the whiskey business?*" What could that possibly mean to you? To me it means a blonde in a Pucci bathing suit sitting with a couple of fat men by the pool at the Beverly Hills Hotel. Another man approaches, and they all regard one another in silence for a while. "So what's new in the whiskey business?" one of the fat men finally says by way of welcome, and the blonde stands up, arches one foot and dips it in the pool, looking all the while at the cabaña where Baby Pignatari is talking on the telephone. That is all there is to that, except that several years later I saw the blonde coming out of Saks Fifth Avenue in New York with her California complexion and a voluminous mink coat. In the harsh wind that day she looked old and irrevocably tired to me, and even the skins in the mink coat were not worked the way they were doing them that year, not the way she would have wanted them done, and there is the point of the story. For a while after that I did not like to look in the mirror, and my eyes would skim the newspapers and pick out only the deaths, the cancer victims, the premature coronaries, the suicides, and I stopped riding the Lexington Avenue IRT because I noticed for the first time that all the strangers I had seen for years—the man with the seeing-eye dog, the spinster who read the classified pages every day, the fat girl who always got off with me at Grand Central—looked older than they once had.

It all comes back. Even that recipe for sauerkraut: even that brings it back. I was on Fire Island when I first made that sauerkraut, and it was raining, and we drank a lot of bourbon and ate the sauerkraut and went to bed at ten, and I listened to the rain and the Atlantic and felt safe. I made the sauerkraut again last night and it did not make me feel any safer, but that is, as they say, another story.

1966

ON SELF-RESPECT

ONCE, IN A DRY season, I wrote in large letters across two pages of a notebook that innocence ends when one is stripped of the delusion that one likes oneself. Although now, some years later, I marvel that a mind on the outs with itself should have nonetheless made painstaking record of its every tremor, I recall with embarrassing clarity the flavor of those particular ashes. It was a matter of misplaced self-respect.

I had not been elected to Phi Beta Kappa. This failure could scarcely have been more predictable or less ambiguous (I simply did not have the grades), but I was unnerved by it; I had somehow thought myself a kind of academic Raskolnikov, curiously exempt from the cause-effect relationships which hampered others. Although even the humorless nineteen-year-old that I was must have recognized that the situation lacked real tragic stature, the day that I did not make Phi Beta Kappa nonetheless marked the end of something, and innocence may well be the word for it. I lost the conviction that lights would always turn green for me, the pleasant certainty that those rather passive virtues which had won me approval as a child automatically guaranteed me not only Phi Beta Kappa keys but happiness, honor, and the love of a good man; lost a certain touching faith in the totem power of good manners, clean hair, and proven competence on the Stanford-Binet scale. To such doubtful amulets had my self-respect been pinned, and I faced myself that day with the non-plused apprehension of someone who has come across a vampire and has no crucifix at hand.

Although to be driven back upon oneself is an uneasy affair at best, rather like trying to cross a border with borrowed credentials, it seems to me now the one condition necessary to the beginnings of real self-respect. Most of our platitudes notwithstanding, self-deception remains the most difficult deception. The tricks that work on others count for nothing in that very well-lit back alley where one keeps assignations with oneself: no winning smiles will do here, no prettily drawn lists of good intentions. One shuffles flashily but in vain through one's marked cards—the kindness done for the wrong reason, the apparent triumph which involved no real effort, the seemingly heroic act into which one had been shamed. The dismal fact is that self-respect has nothing to do with the approval of others—who are, after all, deceived easily enough; has nothing to do with reputation, which, as Rhett Butler told Scarlett O'Hara, is something people with courage can do without.

To do without self-respect, on the other hand, is to be an unwilling audience of one to an interminable documentary that details one's failings, both real and imagined, with fresh footage spliced in for every screening. *There's the glass you broke in anger, there's the hurt on X's face; watch now, this next scene, the night Y came back from Houston, see how you muff this one.* To live without self-respect is to lie awake some night, beyond the reach of warm milk, phenobarbital, and the sleeping hand on the coverlet, counting up the sins of commission and omission, the trusts betrayed, the promises subtly broken, the gifts irrevocably wasted through sloth or cowardice or carelessness. However long we postpone it, we eventually lie down alone in that notoriously uncomfortable bed, the one we make ourselves. Whether or not we sleep in it depends, of course, on whether or not we respect ourselves.

To protest that some fairly improbable people, some people who *could not possibly respect themselves,* seem to sleep easily enough is to miss the point entirely, as surely as those people miss it who think that self-respect has necessarily to do with not having safety pins in one's underwear. There is a common superstition that "self-respect" is a kind of charm against snakes, something that keeps those who have it locked in some unblighted Eden, out of strange beds, ambivalent conversations, and trouble in general. It does not at all. It has nothing to do with the face of things, but concerns instead a separate peace, a private reconciliation. Although the careless, suicidal Julian English in *Appointment in Samarra* and the careless, incurably dishonest Jordan Baker in *The Great Gatsby* seem equally improbable candidates for self-respect, Jordan Baker had it, Julian English did not. With that genius for accommodation more often seen in women than in men, Jordan took her own measure, made her own peace, avoided threats to that peace: "I hate careless people," she told Nick Carraway. "It takes two to make an accident."

Like Jordan Baker, people with self-respect have the courage of their mistakes. They know the price of things. If they choose to commit adultery, they do not then go running, in an access of bad conscience, to receive absolution from the wronged parties; nor do they complain unduly of the unfairness, the undeserved embarrassment, of being named co-respondent. In brief, people with self-respect exhibit a certain toughness, a kind of moral nerve; they display what was once called *character*, a quality which, although approved in the abstract, sometimes loses ground to other, more instantly negotiable virtues. The measure of its slipping prestige is that one tends to think of it only in connection with homely children and United States senators who have been defeated, preferably in the primary, for reelection. Nonetheless, character—the willingness to accept responsibility for one's own life—is the source from which self-respect springs.

Self-respect is something that our grandparents, whether or not they had it, knew all about. They had instilled in them, young, a certain discipline, the sense that one lives by doing things one does not particularly want to do, by putting fears and doubts to one side, by weighing immediate comforts against the possibility of larger, even intangible, comforts. It seemed to the nineteenth century admirable, but not remarkable, that Chinese Gordon put on a clean white suit and held Khartoum against the Mahdi; it did not seem unjust that the way to free land in California involved death and difficulty and dirt. In a diary kept during the winter of 1846, an emigrating twelve-year-old named Narcissa Cornwall noted coolly: "Father was busy reading and did not notice that the house was being filled with strange Indians until Mother spoke about it." Even lacking any clue as to what Mother said, one can scarcely fail to be impressed by the entire incident: the father reading, the Indians filing in, the mother choosing the words that would not alarm, the child duly recording the event and noting further that those particular Indians were not, "fortunately for us," hostile. Indians were simply part of the *donnée*.

In one guise or another, Indians always are. Again, it is a question of recognizing that anything worth having has its price. People who respect themselves are willing to accept the risk that the Indians will be hostile, that the venture will go bankrupt, that the liaison may not turn out to be one in which *every day is a holiday because you're married to me*. They are willing to invest something of themselves; they may not play at all, but when they do play, they know the odds.

That kind of self-respect is a discipline, a habit of mind that can never be faked but can be developed, trained, coaxed forth. It was once suggested to me that, as an antidote to crying, I put my head in a paper bag. As it happens, there is a sound physiological reason, something to do with oxygen, for doing exactly that, but the psychological effect alone is incalculable: it is difficult in the extreme to continue fancying oneself Cathy in *Wuthering Heights* with one's head in a Food Fair bag. There is a similar case for all the small disciplines, unimportant in themselves; imagine maintaining any kind of swoon, commiserative or carnal, in a cold shower.

But those small disciplines are valuable only insofar as they represent larger ones. To say that Waterloo was won on the playing fields of Eton is not to say that Napoleon might have been saved by a crash program in cricket; to give formal dinners in the rain forest would be pointless did not the candlelight flickering on the liana call forth deeper, stronger disciplines, values instilled long before. It is a kind of ritual, helping us to remember who and what we are. In order to remember it, one must have known it.

To have that sense of one's intrinsic worth which constitutes self-respect is potentially to have everything: the ability to discriminate, to love and to remain indifferent. To lack it is to be locked within oneself, paradoxically incapable of either love or indifference. If we do not respect ourselves, we are on the one hand forced to despise those who have so few resources as to consort with us, so little perception as to remain blind to our fatal weaknesses. On the other, we are peculiarly in thrall to everyone we see, curiously determined to live out—since our self-image is untenable—their false notions of us. We flatter ourselves by thinking this compulsion to please others an attractive trait: a gist for imaginative empathy, evidence of our willingness to give. *Of course* I will play Francesca to your Paolo, Helen Keller to anyone's Annie Sullivan: no expectation is too misplaced, no role too ludicrous. At the mercy of those we cannot but hold in contempt, we play roles doomed to failure before they are begun, each defeat generating fresh despair at the urgency of divining and meeting the next demand made upon us.

It is the phenomenon sometimes called "alienation from self." In its advanced stages, we no longer answer the telephone, because someone might want something; that we could say *no* without drowning in self-reproach is an idea alien to this game. Every encounter demands too much, tears the nerves, drains the will, and the specter of something as small as an unanswered letter arouses such disproportionate guilt that answering it becomes out of the question. To assign unanswered letters their proper weight, to free us from the expectations of others, to give us back to ourselves—there lies the great, the singular power of self-respect. Without it, one eventually discovers the final turn of the screw: one runs away to find oneself, and finds no one at home.

1961

QUITE EARLY IN the action of an otherwise unmemorable monster movie (I do not even remember its name), having to do with a mechanical man who walks underwater down the East River as far as Forty-ninth Street and then surfaces to destroy the United Nations, the heroine is surveying the grounds of her country place when the mechanical monster bobs up from a lake and attempts to carry off her child. (Actually we are aware that the monster wants only to make friends with the little girl, but the young mother, who has presumably seen fewer monster movies than we have, is not. This provides pathos, and dramatic tension.) Later that evening, as the heroine sits on the veranda reflecting upon the day's events, her brother strolls out, tamps his pipe, and asks: "Why the brown study, Deborah?" Deborah smiles, ruefully. "It's nothing, Jim, really," she says. "I just can't get that monster out of my mind."

I just can't get that monster out of my mind. It is a useful line, and one that frequently occurs to me when I catch the tone in which a great many people write or talk about Hollywood. In the popular imagination, the American motion-picture industry still represents a kind of mechanical monster, programmed to stifle and destroy all that is interesting and worthwhile and "creative" in the human spirit. As an adjective, the very word "Hollywood" has long been pejorative and suggestive of something referred to as "the System," a phrase delivered with the same sinister emphasis that James Cagney once lent to "the Syndicate." The System not only strangles talent but poisons the soul, a fact supported by rich webs of lore. Mention Hollywood, and we are keyed to remember Scott Fitzgerald, dying at Malibu, attended only by Sheilah Graham while he ground out college-weekend movies (he was also writing *The Last Tycoon*, but that is not part of the story); we are conditioned to recall the brightest minds of a generation, deteriorating around the swimming pool at the Garden of Allah while they waited for calls from the Thalberg Building.

(Actually it takes a fairly romantic sensibility to discern why the Garden of Allah should have been a more insidious ambiance than the Algonquin, or why the Thalberg Building, and Metro-Goldwyn-Mayer, should have been more morally debilitating than the Graybar Building, and *Vanity Fair*. Edmund Wilson, who has this kind of sensibility, once suggested that it has something to do with the weather. Perhaps it does.)

Hollywood the Destroyer. It was essentially a romantic vision, and before long Hollywood was helping actively to perpetuate it: think of Jack Palance, as a movie star finally murdered by the System in *The Big Knife;* think of Judy Garland and James Mason (and of Janet Gaynor and Fredric March before them), their lives blighted by the System, or by the Studio—the two phrases were, when the old major studios still ran Hollywood, more or less interchangeable—in *A Star Is Born*. By now, the corruption and venality and restrictiveness of Hollywood have become such firm tenets of American social faith—and of Hollywood's own image of itself—that I was only mildly surprised, not long ago, to hear a young screenwriter announce that Hollywood was "ruining" him. "As a writer," he added. "As a writer," he had previously written, over a span of ten years in New York, one comedy (as opposed to "comic") novel, several newspaper reviews of other people's comedy novels, and a few years' worth of captions for a picture magazine.

Now. It is not surprising that the specter of Hollywood the Destroyer still haunts the rote middle intelligentsia (the monster lurks, I understand, in the wilds between the Thalia and the Museum of Modern Art), or at least those members of it who have not yet perceived the *chic* conferred upon Hollywood by the *Cahiers du Cinéma* set. (Those who have perceived it adopt an equally extreme position, speculating endlessly about what Vincente Minelli was up to in *Meet Me in St. Louis*, attending seminars on Nicholas Ray, that kind of thing.) What is surprising is that the monster still haunts Hollywood itself—and Hollywood knows better, knows that the monster was laid to rest, dead of natural causes, some years ago. The Fox back lot is now a complex of office buildings called Century City; Paramount makes not forty movies a year but "Bonanza." What was once The Studio is now a releasing operation, and even the Garden of Allah is no more. Virtually every movie made is an independent production—and is that not what we once wanted? Is that not what we once said could revolutionize American movies? The millennium is here, the era of "fewer and better" motion pictures, and what have we? We have fewer pictures, but not necessarily better pictures. Ask Hollywood why, and Hollywood resorts to murmuring about the monster. It has been, they say, impossible to work "honestly" in Hollywood. Certain things have prevented it. The studios, or what is left of the studios, thwart their every dream. The money-men conspire against them. New York spirits away their prints before they have finished cutting. They are bound by clichés. There is something wrong with "the intellectual climate." If only they were allowed some freedom, if only they could exercise an individual voice....

If only. These protests have about them an engaging period optimism, depending as they do upon the Rousseauean premise that most people, left to their own devices, think not in clichés but with originality and brilliance; that most individual voices, once heard, turn out to be voices of beauty and wisdom. I think we would all agree that a novel is nothing if it is not the expression of an individual voice, of a single view of experience—and how many good or even interesting novels, of the thousands published, appear each year? I doubt that more can be expected of the motion-picture industry. Men who do have interesting individual voices have for some time now been making movies in which those voices are heard; I think of Elia Kazan's *America America*, and, with a good deal less enthusiasm for the voice, of Stanley Kubrick's *Dr. Strangelove*.

But it is not only the "interesting" voices who now have the opportunity to be heard. John Frankenheimer was quoted in *Life* as admitting: "You can't call Hollywood 'The Industry' any more. Today we have a chance to put our personal fantasies on film." Frankenheimer's own personal fantasies have included *All Fall Down*, in which we learned that Warren Beatty and Eva Marie Saint were in love when Frankenheimer dissolved to some swans shimmering on a lake, and *Seven Days in May*, which, in its misapprehension of the way the American power elite thinks and talks and operates (the movie's United States Senator from California, as I recall, drove a Rolls-Royce), appeared to be fantasy in the most clinical sense of that word. Carl Foreman, who, before he was given a chance to put his personal fantasies on film, worked on some very good (of their type) movies—*High Noon* and *The Guns of Navarone*, for two—later released what he called his "personal statement": *The Victors*, a phenomenon which suggests only that two heads are perhaps better than one, if that one is Foreman's.

One problem is that American directors, with a handful of exceptions, are not much interested in style; they are at heart didactic. Ask what they plan to do with their absolute freedom, with their chance to make a personal statement, and they will pick an "issue," a "problem." The "issues" they pick are generally no longer real issues, if indeed they ever were—but I think it a mistake to attribute this to any calculated venality, to any conscious playing it safe. (I am reminded of a screenwriter who just recently discovered dwarfs—although he, like the rest of us, must have lived through that period when dwarfs turned up on the fiction pages of the glossier magazines with the approximate frequency that Suzy Parker turned up on the advertising pages. This screenwriter sees dwarfs as symbols of modern man's crippling anomie. There is a certain cultural lag.) Call it instead—this apparent calculation about what "issues" are now safe—an absence of imagination, a sloppiness of mind in some ways encouraged by a comfortable feedback from the audience, from the bulk of the reviewers, and from some people who ought to know better. Stanley Kramer's *Judgment at Nuremberg*, made in 1961, was an intrepid indictment not of authoritarianism in the abstract, not of the trials themselves, not of the various moral and legal issues involved, but of Nazi war atrocities, about which there would have seemed already to be some consensus. (You may remember that *Judgment at Nuremberg* received an Academy Award, which the screenwriter Abby Mann accepted on the behalf of "all intellectuals.") Later, Kramer and Abby Mann collaborated on *Ship of Fools*, into which they injected "a little more compassion and humor" and in which they advanced the action from 1931 to 1933—the better to register another defiant protest against the National Socialist Party. Foreman's *The Victors* set forth, interminably, the proposition that war defeats the victors equally with the vanquished, a notion not exactly radical. (Foreman is a director who at first gives the impression of having a little style, but the impression is entirely spurious, and prompted mostly by his total recall for old Eisenstein effects.) Stanley Kubrick's *Dr. Strangelove*, which did have a little style, was scarcely a picture of relentless originality; rarely have we seen so much made over so little. John Simon, in the *New Leader*, declared that the "altogether admirable thing" about *Dr. Strangelove* was that it managed to be "thoroughly irreverent about everything the Establishment takes seriously: atomic war, government, the army, international relations, heroism, sex, and what not." I don't know who John Simon thinks makes up the Establishment, but skimming back at random from "what not," sex is our most durable communal joke; Billy Wilder's *One, Two, Three* was a boffo (*cf. Variety*) spoof of international relations; the army as a laugh line has filtered right down to Phil Silvers and "Sergeant Bilko"; and, if "government" is something about which the American Establishment is inflexibly reverent, I seem to have been catching some pretty underground material on prime time television. And what not. *Dr. Strangelove* was essentially a one-line gag, having to do with the difference between all other wars and nuclear war. By the time George Scott had said "I think I'll mosey on over to the War Room" and Sterling Hayden had said "Looks like we got ourselves a shootin' war" and the SAC bomber had begun heading for its Soviet targets to the tune of "When Johnny Comes Marching Home Again," Kubrick had already developed a full fugue upon the theme, and should have started counting the minutes until it would begin to pall.

What we have, then, are a few interesting minds at work; and a great many less interesting ones. The European situation is not all that different. Antonioni, among the Italians, makes beautiful, intelligent, intricately and subtly built pictures, the power of which lies entirely in their structure; Visconti, on the other hand, has less sense of form than anyone now directing. One might as well have viewed a series of stills, in no perceptible order, as his *The Leopard*. Federico Fellini and Ingmar Bergman share a stunning visual intelligence and a numbingly banal view of human experience; Alain Resnais, in *Last Year at Marienbad* and *Muriel*, demonstrated a style so intrusive that one suspected it to be a smoke screen, suspected that it was intruding upon a vacuum. As for the notion that European movies tend to be more original than American movies, no one who saw *Boccaccio '70* could ever again automatically modify the word "formula" with "Hollywood."

* * *

So. With perhaps a little prodding from abroad, we are all grown up now in Hollywood, and left to set out in the world on our own. We are no longer in the grip of a monster; Harry Cohn no longer runs Columbia like, as the saying went, a concentration camp. Whether or not a picture receives a Code seal no longer matters much at the box office. No more curfew, no more Daddy, *anything goes*. Some of us do not quite like this permissiveness; some of us would like to find "reasons" why our pictures are not as good as we know in our hearts they might be. Not long ago I met a producer who complained to me of the difficulties he had working within what I recognized as the System, although he did not call it that. He longed, he said, to do an adaptation of a certain Charles Jackson short story. "Some really terrific stuff," he said. "Can't touch it, I'm afraid. About masturbation."

1964

ON MORALITY

AS IT HAPPENS I am in Death Valley, in a room at the Enterprise Motel and Trailer Park, and it is July, and it is hot. In fact it is 119°. I cannot seem to make the air conditioner work, but there is a small refrigerator, and I can wrap ice cubes in a towel and hold them against the small of my back. With the help of the ice cubes I have been trying to think, because *The American Scholar* asked me to, in some abstract way about "morality," a word I distrust more every day, but my mind veers inflexibly toward the particular.

Here are some particulars. At midnight last night, on the road in from Las Vegas to Death Valley Junction, a car hit a shoulder and turned over. The driver, very young and apparently drunk, was killed instantly. His girl was found alive but bleeding internally, deep in shock. I talked this afternoon to the nurse who had driven the girl to the nearest doctor, 185 miles across the floor of the Valley and three ranges of lethal mountain road. The nurse explained that her husband, a talc miner, had stayed on the highway with the boy's body until the coroner could get over the mountains from Bishop, at dawn today. "You can't just leave a body on the highway," she said. "It's immoral."

It was one instance in which I did not distrust the word, because she meant something quite specific. She meant that if a body is left alone for even a few minutes on the desert, the coyotes close in and eat the flesh. Whether or not a corpse is torn apart by coyotes may seem only a sentimental consideration, but of course it is more: one of the promises we make to one another is that we will try to retrieve our casualties, try not to abandon our dead to the coyotes. If we have been taught to keep our promises—if, in the simplest terms, our upbringing is good enough—we stay with the body, or have bad dreams.

I am talking, of course, about the kind of social code that is sometimes called, usually pejoratively, "wagon-train morality." In fact that is precisely what it is. For better or worse, we are what we learned as children: my own childhood was illuminated by graphic litanies of the grief awaiting those who failed in their loyalties to each other. The Donner-Reed Party, starving in the Sierra snows, all the ephemera of civilization gone save that one vestigial taboo, the provision that no one should eat his own blood kin. The Jayhawkers, who quarreled and separated not far from where I am tonight. Some of them died in the Funerals and some of them died down near Badwater and most of the rest of them died in the Panamints. A woman who got through gave the Valley its name. Some might say that the Jayhawkers were killed by the desert summer, and the Donner Party by the mountain winter, by circumstances beyond control; we were taught instead that they had somewhere abdicated their responsibilities, somehow breached their primary loyalties, or they would not have found themselves helpless in the mountain winter or the desert summer, would not have given way to acrimony, would not have deserted one another, would not have *failed*. In brief, we heard such stories as cautionary tales, and they still suggest the only kind of "morality" that seems to me to have any but the most potentially mendacious meaning.

You are quite possibly impatient with me by now; I am talking, you want to say, about a "morality" so primitive that it scarcely deserves the name, a code that has as its point only survival, not the attainment of the ideal good. Exactly. Particularly out here tonight, in this country so ominous and terrible that to live in it is to live with antimatter, it is difficult to believe that "the good" is a knowable quantity. Let me tell you what it is like out here tonight. Stories travel at night on the desert. Someone gets in his pickup and drives a couple of hundred miles for a beer, and he carries news of what is happening, back wherever he came from. Then he drives another hundred miles for another beer, and passes along stories from the last place as well as from the one before; it is a network kept alive by people whose instincts tell them that if they do not keep moving at night on the desert they will lose all reason. Here is a story that is going around the desert tonight: over across the Nevada line, sheriff's deputies are diving in some underground pools, trying to retrieve a couple of bodies known to be in the hole. The widow of one of the drowned boys is over there; she is eighteen, and pregnant, and is said not to leave the hole. The divers go down and come up, and she just stands there and stares into the water. They have been diving for ten days but have found no bottom to the caves, no bodies and no trace of them, only the black 90° water going down and down and down, and a single translucent fish, not classified. The story tonight is that one of the divers has been hauled up incoherent, out of his head, shouting—until they got him out of there so that the widow could not hear—about water that got hotter instead of cooler as he went down, about light flickering through the water, about magma, about underground nuclear testing.

That is the tone stories take out here, and there are quite a few of them tonight. And it is more than the stories alone. Across the road at the Faith Community Church a couple of dozen old people, come here to live in trailers and die in the sun, are holding a prayer sing. I cannot hear them and do not want to. What I can hear are occasional coyotes and a constant chorus of "Baby the Rain Must Fall" from the jukebox in the Snake Room next door, and if I were also to hear those dying voices, those Midwestern voices drawn to this lunar country for some unimaginable atavistic rites, *rock of ages cleft for me,* I think I would lose my own reason. Every now and then I imagine I hear a rattlesnake, but my husband says that it is a faucet, a paper rustling, the wind. Then he stands by a window, and plays a flashlight over the dry wash outside.

What does it mean? It means nothing manageable. There is some sinister hysteria in the air out here tonight, some hint of the monstrous perversion to which any human idea can come. "I followed my own conscience." "I did what I thought was right." How many madmen have said it and meant it? How many murderers? Klaus Fuchs said it, and the men who committed the Mountain Meadows Massacre said it, and Alfred Rosenberg said it. And, as we are rotely and rather presumptuously reminded by those who would say it now, Jesus said it. Maybe we have all said it, and maybe we have been wrong. Except on that most primitive level—our loyalties to those we love—what could be more arrogant than to claim the primacy of personal conscience? ("Tell me," a rabbi asked Daniel Bell when he said, as a child, that he did not believe in God. "Do you think God cares?") At least some of the time, the world appears to me as a painting by Hieronymous

Bosch; were I to follow my conscience then, it would lead me out onto the desert with Marion Faye, out to where he stood in *The Deer Park* looking east to Los Alamos and praying, as if for rain, that it would happen: *"... let it come and clear the rot and the stench and the stink, let it come for all of everywhere, just so it comes and the world stands clear in the white dead dawn."*

Of course you will say that I do not have the right, even if I had the power, to inflict that unreasonable conscience upon you; nor do I want you to inflict your conscience, however reasonable, however enlightened, upon me. ("We must be aware of the dangers which lie in our most generous wishes," Lionel Trilling once wrote. "Some paradox of our nature leads us, when once we have made our fellow men the objects of our enlightened interest, to go on to make them the objects of our pity, then of our wisdom, ultimately of our coercion.") That the ethic of conscience is intrinsically insidious seems scarcely a revelatory point, but it is one raised with increasing infrequency; even those who do raise it tend to *segue* with troubling readiness into the quite contradictory position that the ethic of conscience is dangerous when it is "wrong," and admirable when it is "right."

You see I want to be quite obstinate about insisting that we have no way of knowing—beyond that fundamental loyalty to the social code—what is "right" and what is "wrong," what is "good" and what "evil." I dwell so upon this because the most disturbing aspect of "morality" seems to me to be the frequency with which the word now appears; in the press, on television, in the most perfunctory kinds of conversation. Questions of straightforward power (or survival) politics, questions of quite indifferent public policy, questions of almost anything: they are all assigned these factitious moral burdens. There is something facile going on, some self-indulgence at work. Of course we would all like to "believe" in something, like to assuage our private guilts in public causes, like to lose our tiresome selves; like, perhaps, to transform the white flag of defeat at home into the brave white banner of battle away from home. And of course it is all right to do that; that is how, immemorially, things have gotten done. But I think it is all right only so long as we do not delude ourselves about what we are doing, and why. It is all right only so long as we remember that all the *ad hoc* committees, all the picket lines, all the brave signatures in *The New York Times*, all the tools of agitprop straight across the spectrum, do not confer upon anyone any *ipso facto* virtue. It is all right only so long as we recognize that the end may or may not be expedient, may or may not be a good idea, but in any case has nothing to do with "morality." Because when we start deceiving ourselves into thinking not that we want something or need something, not that it is a pragmatic necessity for us to have it, but that it is a *moral imperative* that we have it, then is when we join the fashionable madmen, and then is when the thin whine of hysteria is heard in the land, and then is when we are in bad trouble. And I suspect we are already there.

1965

ON GOING HOME

I AM HOME for my daughter's first birthday. By "home" I do not mean the house in Los Angeles where my husband and I and the baby live, but the place where my family is, in the Central Valley of California. It is a vital although troublesome distinction. My husband likes my family but is uneasy in their house, because once there I fall into their ways, which are difficult, oblique, deliberately inarticulate, not my husband's ways. We live in dusty houses ("D-U-S-T," he once wrote with his finger on surfaces all over the house, but no one noticed it) filled with mementos quite without value to him (what could the Canton dessert plates mean to him? how could he have known about the assay scales, why should he care if he did know?), and we appear to talk exclusively about people we know who have been committed to mental hospitals, about people we know who have been booked on drunk-driving charges, and about property, particularly about property, land, price per acre and C-2 zoning and assessments and freeway access. My brother does not understand my husband's inability to perceive the advantage in the rather common real-estate transaction known as "sale-leaseback," and my husband in turn does not understand why so many of the people he hears about in my father's house have recently been committed to mental hospitals or booked on drunk-driving charges. Nor does he understand that when we talk about sale-leasebacks and right-of-way condemnations we are talking in code about the things we like best, the yellow fields and the cottonwoods and the rivers rising and falling and the mountain roads closing when the heavy snow comes in. We miss each other's points, have another drink and regard the fire. My brother refers to my husband, in his presence, as "Joan's husband." Marriage is the classic betrayal.

Or perhaps it is not any more. Sometimes I think that those of us who are now in our thirties were born into the last generation to carry the burden of "home," to find in family life the source of all tension and drama. I had by all objective accounts a "normal"

125

and a "happy" family situation, and yet I was almost thirty years old before I could talk to my family on the telephone without crying after I had hung up. We did not fight. Nothing was wrong. And yet some nameless anxiety colored the emotional charges between me and the place that I came from. The question of whether or not you could go home again was a very real part of the sentimental and largely literary baggage with which we left home in the fifties; I suspect that it is irrelevant to the children born of the fragmentation after World War II. A few weeks ago in a San Francisco bar I saw a pretty young girl on crystal take off her clothes and dance for the cash prize in an "amateur-topless" contest. There was no particular sense of moment about this, none of the effect of romantic degradation, of "dark journey," for which my generation strived so assiduously. What sense could that girl possibly make of, say, *Long Day's Journey into Night*? Who is beside the point?

That I am trapped in this particular irrelevancy is never more apparent to me than when I am home. Paralyzed by the neurotic lassitude engendered by meeting one's past at every turn, around every corner, inside every cupboard, I go aimlessly from room to room. I decide to meet it head-on and clean out a drawer, and I spread the contents on the bed. A bathing suit I wore the summer I was seventeen. A letter of rejection from *The Nation*, an aerial photograph of the site for a shopping center my father did not build in 1954. Three teacups hand-painted with cabbage roses and signed "E.M.," my grandmother's initials. There is no final solution for letters of rejection from *The Nation* and teacups hand-painted in 1900. Nor is there any answer to snapshots of one's grandfather as a young man on skis, surveying around Donner Pass in the year 1910. I smooth out the snapshot and look into his face, and do and do not see my own. I close the drawer, and have another cup of coffee with my mother. We get along very well, veterans of a guerrilla war we never understood.

Days pass. I see no one. I come to dread my husband's evening call, not only because he is full of news of what by now seems to me our remote life in Los Angeles, people he has seen, letters which require attention, but because he asks what I have been doing, suggests uneasily that I get out, drive to San Francisco or Berkeley. Instead I drive across the river to a family graveyard. It has been vandalized since my last visit and the monuments are broken, overturned in the dry grass. Because I once saw a rattlesnake in the grass I stay in the car and listen to a country-and-Western station. Later I drive with my father to a ranch he has in the foothills. The man who runs his cattle on it asks us to the roundup, a week from Sunday, and although I know that I will be in Los Angeles I say, in the oblique way my family talks, that I will come. Once home I mention the broken monuments in the graveyard. My mother shrugs.

I go to visit my great-aunts. A few of them think now that I am my cousin, or their daughter who died young. We recall an anecdote about a relative last seen in 1948, and they ask if I still like living in New York City. I have lived in Los Angeles for three years, but I say that I do. The baby is offered a horehound drop, and I am slipped a dollar bill "to buy a treat." Questions trail off, answers are abandoned, the baby plays with the dust motes in a shaft of afternoon sun.

It is time for the baby's birthday party: a white cake, strawberry-marshmallow ice cream, a bottle of champagne saved from another party. In the evening, after she has gone to sleep, I kneel beside the crib and touch her face, where it is pressed against the slats, with mine. She is an open and trusting child, unprepared for and unaccustomed to the ambushes of family life, and perhaps it is just as well that I can offer her little of that life. I would like to give her more. I would like to promise her that she will grow up with a sense of her cousins and of rivers and of her great-grandmother's teacups, would like to pledge her a picnic on a river with fried chicken and her hair uncombed, would like to give her *home* for her birthday, but we live differently now and I can promise her nothing like that. I give her a xylophone and a sundress from Madeira, and promise to tell her a funny story.

1967

III
SEVEN PLACES OF THE MIND

NOTES FROM A NATIVE DAUGHTER

IT IS VERY easy to sit at the bar in, say, La Scala in Beverly Hills, or Ernie's in San Francisco, and to share in the pervasive delusion that California is only five hours from New York by air. The truth is that La Scala and Ernie's are only five hours from New York by air. California is somewhere else.

Many people in the East (or "back East," as they say in California, although not in La Scala or Ernie's) do not believe this. They have been to Los Angeles or to San Francisco, have driven through a giant redwood and have seen the Pacific glazed by the afternoon sun off Big Sur, and they naturally tend to believe that they have in fact been to California. They have not been, and they probably never will be, for it is a longer and in many ways a more difficult trip than they might want to undertake, one of those trips on which the destination flickers chimerically on the horizon, ever receding, ever diminishing. I happen to know about that trip because I come from California, come from a family, or a congeries of families, that has always been in the Sacramento Valley.

You might protest that no family has been in the Sacramento Valley for anything approaching "always." But it is characteristic of Californians to speak grandly of the past as if it had simultaneously begun, *tabula rasa*, and reached a happy ending on the day the wagons started west. *Eureka*—"I Have Found It"—as the state motto has it. Such a view of history casts a certain melancholia over those who participate in it; my own childhood was suffused with the conviction that we had long outlived our finest hour. In fact that is what I want to tell you about: what it is like to come from a place like Sacramento. If I could make you understand that, I could make you understand California and perhaps something else besides, for Sacramento *is* California, and California is a place in which a boom mentality and a sense of Chekhovian loss meet in uneasy suspension; in which the mind is troubled by some buried but ineradicable suspicion that things had better work here, because here, beneath that immense bleached sky, is where we run out of continent.

In 1847 Sacramento was no more than an adobe enclosure, Sutter's Fort, standing alone on the prairie; cut off from San Francisco and the sea by the Coast Range and from the rest of the continent by the Sierra Nevada, the Sacramento Valley was then a true sea of grass, grass so high a man riding into it could tie it across his saddle. A year later gold was discovered in the Sierra foothills, and abruptly Sacramento was a town, a town any moviegoer could map tonight in his dreams—a dusty collage of assay offices and wagonmakers and saloons. Call that Phase Two. Then the settlers came—the farmers, the people who for two hundred years had been moving west on the frontier, the peculiar flawed strain who had cleared Virginia, Kentucky, Missouri; they made Sacramento a farm town. Because the land was rich, Sacramento became eventually a rich farm town, which meant houses in town, Cadillac dealers, a country club. In that gentle sleep Sacramento dreamed until perhaps 1950, when something happened. What happened was that Sacramento woke to the fact that the outside world was moving in, fast and hard. At the moment of its waking Sacramento lost, for better or for worse, its character, and that is part of what I want to tell you about.

But the change is not what I remember first. First I remember running a boxer dog of my brother's over the same flat fields that our great-great-grandfather had found virgin and had planted; I remember swimming (albeit nervously, for I was a nervous child, afraid of sinkholes and afraid of snakes, and perhaps that was the beginning of my error) the same rivers we had swum for a century: the Sacramento, so rich with silt that we could barely see our hands a few inches beneath the surface; the American, running clean and fast with melted Sierra snow until July, when it would slow down, and rattlesnakes would sun themselves on its newly exposed rocks. The Sacramento, the American, sometimes the Cosumnes, occasionally the Feather. Incautious children died every day in those rivers; we read about it in the paper, how they had miscalculated a current or stepped into a hole down where the American runs into the Sacramento, how the Berry Brothers had been called in from Yolo County to drag the river but how the bodies remained unrecovered. "They were from away," my grandmother would extrapolate from the newspaper stories. "Their parents had no

business letting them in the river. They were visitors from Omaha."
It was not a bad lesson, although a less than reliable one; children
we knew died in the rivers too.

When summer ended—when the State Fair closed and the
heat broke, when the last green hop vines had been torn down
along the H Street road and the tule fog began rising off the low
ground at night—we would go back to memorizing the Products
of Our Latin American Neighbors and to visiting the great-aunts
on Sunday, dozens of great-aunts, year after year of Sundays.
When I think now of those winters I think of yellow elm leaves
wadded in the gutters outside the Trinity Episcopal Pro-Cathedral
on M Street. There are actually people in Sacramento now who
call M Street Capitol Avenue, and Trinity has one of those fea-
tureless new buildings, but perhaps children still learn the same
things there on Sunday mornings:

> *Q. In what way does the Holy Land resemble the Sacramento
> Valley?*
> *A. In the type and diversity of its agricultural products.*

And I think of the rivers rising, of listening to the radio to hear
at what height they would crest and wondering if and when and
where the levees would go. We did not have as many dams in
those years. The bypasses would be full, and men would sandbag
all night. Sometimes a levee would go in the night, somewhere
upriver; in the morning the rumor would spread that the Army
Engineers had dynamited it to relieve the pressure on the city.

After the rains came spring, for ten days or so; the drenched
fields would dissolve into a brilliant ephemeral green (it would be
yellow and dry as fire in two or three weeks) and the real-estate
business would pick up. It was the time of year when people's
grandmothers went to Carmel; it was the time of year when girls
who could not even get into Stephens or Arizona or Oregon, let
alone Stanford or Berkeley, would be sent to Honolulu, on the
Lurline. I have no recollection of anyone going to New York, with
the exception of a cousin who visited there (I cannot imagine
why) and reported that the shoe salesmen at Lord & Taylor were
"intolerably rude." What happened in New York and Washington
and abroad seemed to impinge not at all upon the Sacramento
mind. I remember being taken to call upon a very old woman, a

rancher's widow, who was reminiscing (the favored conversational mode in Sacramento) about the son of some contemporaries of hers. "That Johnston boy never did amount to much," she said. Desultorily, my mother protested: Alva Johnston, she said, had won the Pulitzer Prize, when he was working for *The New York Times*. Our hostess looked at us impassively. "He never amounted to anything in Sacramento," she said.

Hers was the true Sacramento voice, and, although I did not realize it then, one not long to be heard, for the war was over and the boom was on and the voice of the aerospace engineer would be heard in the land. VETS NO DOWN! EXECUTIVE LIVING ON LOW FHA!

Later, when I was living in New York, I would make the trip back to Sacramento four and five times a year (the more comfortable the flight, the more obscurely miserable I would be, for it weighs heavily upon my kind that we could perhaps not make it by wagon), trying to prove that I had not meant to leave at all, because in at least one respect California—the California we are talking about—resembles Eden: it is assumed that those who absent themselves from its blessings have been banished, exiled by some perversity of heart. Did not the Donner-Reed Party, after all, eat its own dead to reach Sacramento?

I have said that the trip back is difficult, and it is—difficult in a way that magnifies the ordinary ambiguities of sentimental journeys. Going back to California is not like going back to Vermont, or Chicago; Vermont and Chicago are relative constants, against which one measures one's own change. All that is constant about the California of my childhood is the rate at which it disappears. An instance: on Saint Patrick's Day of 1948 I was taken to see the legislature "in action," a dismal experience; a handful of florid assemblymen, wearing green hats, were reading Pat-and-Mike jokes into the record. I still think of the legislators that way—wearing green hats, or sitting around on the veranda of the Senator Hotel fanning themselves and being entertained by Artie Samish's emissaries. (Samish was the lobbyist who said, "Earl Warren may be the governor of the state, but I'm the governor of the legislature.") In fact there is no longer a veranda at the Senator Hotel—it was turned into an airline ticket office, if you

want to embroider the point—and in any case the legislature has
largely deserted the Senator for the flashy motels north of town,
where the tiki torches flame and the steam rises off the heated
swimming pools in the cold Valley night.

It is hard to *find* California now, unsettling to wonder how
much of it was merely imagined or improvised; melancholy to
realize how much of anyone's memory is no true memory at all
but only the traces of someone else's memory, stories handed
down on the family network. I have an indelibly vivid "memory,"
for example, of how Prohibition affected the hop growers around
Sacramento: the sister of a grower my family knew brought home
a mink coat from San Francisco, and was told to take it back,
and sat on the floor of the parlor cradling that coat and crying.
Although I was not born until a year after Repeal, that scene is
more "real" to me than many I have played myself.

I remember one trip home, when I sat alone on a night
jet from New York and read over and over some lines from a
W. S. Merwin poem I had come across in a magazine, a poem
about a man who had been a long time in another country and
knew that he must go home:

> ... But it should be
> Soon. Already I defend hotly
> Certain of our indefensible faults,
> Resent being reminded; already in my mind
> Our language becomes freighted with a richness
> No common tongue could offer, while the mountains
> Are like nowhere on earth, and the wide rivers.

You see the point. I want to tell you the truth, and already I have
told you about the wide rivers.

It should be clear by now that the truth about the place is elusive,
and must be tracked with caution. You might go to Sacramento
tomorrow and someone (although no one I know) might take
you out to Aerojet-General, which has, in the Sacramento
phrase, "something to do with rockets." Fifteen thousand people work for Aerojet, almost all of them imported; a Sacramento
lawyer's wife told me, as evidence of how Sacramento was

opening up, that she believed she had met one of them, at an open house two Decembers ago. ("Couldn't have been nicer, actually," she added enthusiastically. "I think he and his wife bought the house next *door* to Mary and Al, something like that, which of course was how *they* met him.") So you might go to Aerojet and stand in the big vendors' lobby where a couple of thousand components salesmen try every week to sell their wares and you might look up at the electrical wallboard that lists Aerojet personnel, their projects and their location at any given time, and you might wonder if I have been in Sacramento lately. MINUTEMAN, POLARIS, TITAN, the lights flash, and all the coffee tables are littered with airline schedules, very now, very much in touch.

But I could take you a few miles from there into towns where the banks still bear names like The Bank of Alex Brown, into towns where the one hotel still has an octagonal-tile floor in the dining room and dusty potted palms and big ceiling fans; into towns where everything—the seed business, the Harvester franchise, the hotel, the department store and the main street—carries a single name, the name of the man who built the town. A few Sundays ago I was in a town like that, a town smaller than that, really, no hotel, no Harvester franchise, the bank burned out, a river town. It was the golden anniversary of some of my relatives and it was 110° and the guests of honor sat on straight-backed chairs in front of a sheaf of gladioluses in the Rebekah Hall. I mentioned visiting Aerojet-General to a cousin I saw there, who listened to me with interested disbelief. Which is the true California? That is what we all wonder.

Let us try out a few irrefutable statements, on subjects not open to interpretation. Although Sacramento is in many ways the least typical of the Valley towns, it *is* a Valley town, and must be viewed in that context. When you say "the Valley" in Los Angeles, most people assume that you mean the San Fernando Valley (some people in fact assume that you mean Warner Brothers), but make no mistake: we are talking not about the valley of the sound stages and the ranchettes but about the real Valley, the Central Valley, the fifty thousand square miles drained by the Sacramento and the San Joaquin Rivers and further irrigated by a complex network of sloughs, cutoffs, ditches, and the Delta-Mendota and Friant-Kern Canals.

A hundred miles north of Los Angeles, at the moment when you drop from the Tehachapi Mountains into the outskirts of Bakersfield, you leave Southern California and enter the Valley. "You look up the highway and it is straight for miles, coming at you, with the black line down the center coming at you and at you ... and the heat dazzles up from the white slab so that only the black line is clear, coming at you with the whine of the tires, and if you don't quit staring at that line and don't take a few deep breaths and slap yourself hard on the back of the neck you'll hypnotize yourself."

Robert Penn Warren wrote that about another road, but he might have been writing about the Valley road, U.S. 99, three hundred miles from Bakersfield to Sacramento, a highway so straight that when one flies on the most direct pattern from Los Angeles to Sacramento one never loses sight of U.S. 99. The landscape it runs through never, to the untrained eye, varies. The Valley eye can discern the point where miles of cotton seedlings fade into miles of tomato seedlings, or where the great corporation ranches—Kern County Land, what is left of DiGiorgio—give way to private operations (somewhere on the horizon, if the place is private, one sees a house and a stand of scrub oaks), but such distinctions are in the long view irrelevant. All day long, all that moves is the sun, and the big Rainbird sprinklers.

Every so often along 99 between Bakersfield and Sacramento there is a town: Delano, Tulare, Fresno, Madera, Merced, Modesto, Stockton. Some of these towns are pretty big now, but they are all the same at heart, one- and two- and three-story buildings artlessly arranged, so that what appears to be the good dress shop stands beside a W. T. Grant store, so that the big Bank of America faces a Mexican movie house. *Dos Peliculas, Bingo Bingo Bingo*. Beyond the downtown (pronounced *down*town, with the Okie accent that now pervades Valley speech patterns) lie blocks of old frame houses—paint peeling, sidewalks cracking, their occasional leaded amber windows overlooking a Foster's Freeze or a five-minute car wash or a State Farm Insurance office; beyond those spread the shopping centers and the miles of tract houses, pastel with redwood siding, the unmistakable signs of cheap building already blossoming on those houses which have survived the first rain. To a stranger driving 99 in an air-conditioned car (he would be on business, I suppose, any stranger driving 99, for 99 would never get a tourist to Big Sur or San Simeon, never get him to the California he came to see), these towns must seem so flat, so impoverished, as to drain the imagination. They hint at evenings spent hanging around gas stations, and suicide pacts sealed in drive-ins.

But remember:

Q. In what way does the Holy Land resemble the Sacramento Valley?
A. In the type and diversity of its agricultural products.

U.S. 99 in fact passes through the richest and most intensely cultivated agricultural region in the world, a giant outdoor hot-house with a billion-dollar crop. It is when you remember the Valley's wealth that the monochromatic flatness of its towns takes on a curious meaning, suggests a habit of mind some would consider perverse. There is something in the Valley mind that reflects a real indifference to the stranger in his air-conditioned car, a failure to perceive even his presence, let alone his thoughts or wants. An implacable insularity is the seal of these towns. I once met a woman in Dallas, a most charming and attractive woman accustomed to the hospitality and social hypersensitivity of Texas, who told me that during the four war years her husband had been stationed in Modesto, she had never once been invited inside anyone's house. No one in Sacramento would find this story remarkable ("She probably had no *rel*atives there," said someone to whom I told it), for the Valley towns understand one another, share a peculiar spirit. They think alike and they look alike. *I* can tell Modesto from Merced, but I have visited there, gone to dances there; besides, there is over the main street of Modesto an arched sign which reads:

WATER — WEALTH
CONTENTMENT — HEALTH

There is no such sign in Merced.

* * *

I said that Sacramento was the least typical of the Valley towns, and it is—but only because it is bigger and more diverse, only because it has had the rivers and the legislature; its true character remains the Valley character, its virtues the Valley virtues, its sadness the Valley sadness. It is just as hot in the summertime, so hot that the air shimmers and the grass bleaches white and the blinds stay drawn all day, so hot that August comes on not like a month but like an affliction; it is just as flat, so flat that a ranch of my family's with a slight rise on it, perhaps a foot, was known for the hundred-some years which preceded this year as "the hill ranch." (It is known this year as a subdivision in the making, but that is another part of the story.) Above all, in spite of its infusions from outside, Sacramento retains the Valley insularity.

To sense that insularity a visitor need do no more than pick up a copy of either of the two newspapers, the morning *Union* or the afternoon *Bee*. The *Union* happens to be Republican and impoverished and the *Bee* Democratic and powerful ("THE VALLEY OF THE BEES!" as the McClatchys, who own the Fresno, Modesto, and Sacramento *Bees*, used to headline their advertisements in the trade press. "ISOLATED FROM ALL OTHER MEDIA INFLUENCE!"), but they read a good deal alike, and the tone of their chief editorial concerns is strange and wonderful and instructive. The *Union*, in a county heavily and reliably Democratic, frets mainly about the possibility of a local takeover by the John Birch Society; the *Bee*, faithful to the letter of its founder's will, carries on overwrought crusades against phantoms it still calls "the power trusts." Shades of Hiram Johnson, whom the *Bee* helped elect governor in 1910. Shades of Robert La Follette, to whom the *Bee* delivered the Valley in 1924. There is something about the Sacramento papers that does not quite connect with the way Sacramento lives now, something pronouncedly beside the point. The aerospace engineers, one learns, read the San Francisco *Chronicle*.

The Sacramento papers, however, simply mirror the Sacramento peculiarity, the Valley fate, which is to be paralyzed by a past no longer relevant. Sacramento is a town which grew up on farming and discovered to its shock that land has more profitable uses. (The chamber of commerce will give you crop figures, but pay them no mind—what matters is the feeling, the knowledge that where the green hops once grew is now Larchmont Riviera, that what used to be the Whitney ranch is now Sunset City, thirty-three thousand houses and a country-club complex.) It is a town in which defense industry and its absentee owners are suddenly the most important facts; a town which has never had more people or more money, but has lost its *raison d'être*. It is a town many of whose most solid citizens sense about themselves a kind of functional obsolescence. The old families still see only one another, but they do not see even one another as much as they once did; they are closing ranks, preparing for the long night, selling their rights-of-way and living on the proceeds. Their children still marry one another, still play bridge and go into the real-estate business together. (There is no other business in Sacramento, no reality other than land—even I, when I was living and working in New York, felt impelled to take a University of California correspondence course in Urban Land Economics.) But late at night when the ice has melted there is always somebody now, some Julian English, whose heart is not quite in it. For out there on the outskirts of town are marshaled the legions of aerospace engineers, who talk their peculiar condescending language and tend their dichondra and plan to stay in the promised land; who are raising a new generation of native Sacramentans and who do not care, really do not care, that they are not asked to join the Sutter Club. It makes one wonder, late at night when the ice is gone; introduces some air into the womb, suggests that the Sutter Club is perhaps not, after all, the Pacific Union or the Bohemian; that Sacramento is not *the city*. In just such self-doubts do small towns lose their character.

I want to tell you a Sacramento story. A few miles out of town is a place, six or seven thousand acres, which belonged in the beginning to a rancher with one daughter. That daughter went abroad and married a title, and when she brought the title home to live on the ranch, her father built them a vast house—music rooms, conservatories, a ballroom. They needed a ballroom because they entertained: people from abroad, people from San Francisco, house parties that lasted weeks and involved special trains. They are long dead, of course, but their only son, aging and unmarried, still lives on the place. He does not live in the house, for the house is no longer there. Over the years it burned, room by room, wing by wing. Only the chimneys of the great house are still standing, and its heir lives in their shadow, lives by himself on the charred site, in a house trailer.

That is a story my generation knows; I doubt that the next will know it, the children of the aerospace engineers. Who would tell it to them? Their grandmothers live in Scarsdale, and they have never met a great-aunt. "Old" Sacramento to them will be something colorful, something they read about in *Sunset*. They will probably think that the Redevelopment has always been there, that the Embarcadero, down along the river, with its amusing places to shop and its picturesque fire houses turned into bars, has about it the true flavor of the way it was. There will be no reason for them to know that in homelier days it was called Front Street (the town was not, after all, settled by the Spanish) and was a place of derelicts and missions and itinerant pickers in town for a Saturday-night drunk: VICTORIOUS LIFE MISSION, JESUS SAVES, BEDS 25¢ A NIGHT, CROP INFORMATION HERE. They will have lost the real past and gained a manufactured one, and there will be no way for them to know, no way at all, why a house trailer should stand alone on seven thousand acres outside town.

But perhaps it is presumptuous of me to assume that they will be missing something. Perhaps in retrospect this has been a story not about Sacramento at all, but about the things we lose and the promises we break as we grow older; perhaps I have been playing out unawares the Margaret in the poem:

> *Margaret, are you grieving*
> *Over Goldengrove unleaving?…*
> *It is the blight man was born for,*
> *It is Margaret you mourn for.*

1965

LETTER FROM PARADISE, 21° 19′N., 157° 52′ W.

BECAUSE I HAD been tired too long and quarrelsome too much and too often frightened of migraine and failure and the days getting shorter, I was sent, a recalcitrant thirty-one-year-old child, to Hawaii, where winter does not come and no one fails and the median age is twenty-three. There I could become a new woman, there with the life-insurance salesmen on million-dollar-a-year incentive trips, there with the Shriners and the San Francisco divorcées and the splurging secretaries and the girls in the string bikinis and the boys in search of the perfect wave, children who understood the insouciant economy of buying a Honda or a surfboard for one dollar down and $2.50 a week and then abandoning it, children who have never been told, as I was told, that golden lads and girls all must as chimney sweepers come to dust. I was to lie beneath the same sun that had kept Doris Duke and Henry Kaiser forever hopeful. I was to play at sipping frozen daiquiris and wear flowers in my hair as if ten years had never happened. I was to see for myself that just beyond the end of the line lay not Despond but Diamond Head.

I went, a wary visitor. I do not believe that the stories told by lovely hula hands merit extensive study. I have never heard a Hawaiian word, including and perhaps most particularly *aloha*, which accurately expressed anything I had to say. I have neither enough capacity for surprise nor enough heart for twice-told tales to make you listen again to tedious vignettes about Midwesterners in souvenir shirts and touring widows in muumuus and simulated pearls, about the Kodak Hula Show or the Sunday Night Luau or the Schoolteacher and the Beach Boy. And so, now that it is on the line between us that I lack all temperament for paradise, real or facsimile, I am going to find it difficult to tell you precisely how and why Hawaii moves me, touches me, saddens and troubles and engages my imagination, what it is in the air that will linger long after I have forgotten the smell of pikake and pineapple and the way the palms sound in the trade winds.

Perhaps because I grew up in California, Hawaii figured large in my fantasies. I sat as a child on California beaches and imagined that I saw Hawaii, a certain shimmer in the sunset, a barely perceptible irregularity glimpsed intermittently through squinted eyes. The curious void in this fantasy was that I had not the slightest idea what Hawaii would look like if I did see it, for in my child's mind there were three distant Hawaiis, and I could perceive no connections among the three.

There was, to begin with, the Hawaii first shown to me in an atlas on December 7, 1941, the pastel pinpoints that meant war and my father going away and makeshift Christmases in rented rooms near Air Corps bases and nothing the same ever again. Later, when the war was over, there was another Hawaii, a big rock candy mountain in the Pacific which presented itself to me in newspaper photographs of well-fed Lincoln-Mercury dealers relaxing beside an outrigger at the Royal Hawaiian Hotel or disembarking *en famille* from the *Lurline*, a Hawaii where older cousins might spend winter vacations learning to surfboard (for that is what it was called in those simpler days, surfboarding, and it was peculiar to Hawaii) and where godmothers might repair to rest and to learn all the lyrics to "My Little Grass Shack in Kealakekua Hawaii." I do not remember how many nights I lay awake in bed and listened to someone downstairs singing "My Little Grass Shack in Kealakekua Hawaii," but I do remember that I made no connection between that Hawaii and the Hawaii of December 7, 1941.

And then, always, there was a third Hawaii, a place which seemed to have to do neither with war nor with vacationing godmothers but only with the past, and with loss. The last member of my direct family ever to live in Hawaii was a great-great-grandfather who taught there as a young missionary in 1842, and I was given to understand that life in the Islands, as we called Hawaii on the West Coast, had been declining steadily since. My aunt married into a family which had lived for generations in the Islands, but they did not even visit there any more; "Not since Mr. *Kaiser*," they would say, as if the construction of the Hawaiian Village Hotel on a few acres of reclaimed tidal flat near Fort De Russy had in one swing of the builder's crane wiped out their childhoods and their parents' childhoods, blighted forever some subtropical cherry orchard where every night in the soft blur of memory the table was set for forty-eight in case someone dropped by; as if Henry Kaiser had personally condemned them to live out their lives in California exile among only their token mementos, the calabashes and the carved palace chairs and the flat silver for forty-eight and the diamond that had been Queen Liliuokalani's and the heavy linens embroidered on all the long golden afternoons that were no more.

Of course as I grew older I recognized that the name "Henry Kaiser" carried more symbolic than literal freight, but even then I missed the point, imagined that it was merely the proliferation of hotels and hundred-dollar thrift flights that had disturbed the old order, managed to dismiss the Hawaii of my first memory, the Hawaii which meant war, as an accident of history, a freak relevant neither to the gentle idyll that must have been the past nor to the frenetic paean to middle-income leisure that must be the present. In so doing I misapprehended Hawaii completely, for if there is a single aura which pervades Honolulu, one mood which lends the lights a feverish luster and the pink catamarans a heartbreaking absurdity and which engages the imagination as mere paradise never could, that mood is, inescapably, one of war.

It begins, of course, in what we remember.

Hawaii is our Gibraltar, and almost our Channel Coast. Planes, their eyes sharpened by the year-round clearness of blue Pacific days, can keep easy watch over an immense sea-circle, of which Hawaii is the centre. With Hawaii on guard, a surprise attack on us from Asia, the experts believe, would be quite impossible. So long as the great Pearl Harbor Naval Base, just down the road from Honolulu, is ours, American warships and submarines can run their un-Pacific errands with a maximum of ease. Pearl Harbor is one of the greatest, if not the very greatest, maritime fortresses in the world. Pearl Harbor has immense reserves of fuel and food, and huge and clanging hospitals for the healing of any wounds which steel can suffer. It is the one sure sanctuary in the whole of the vast Pacific both for ships and men.

John W. Vandercook, in
Vogue, January 1, 1941

Every afternoon now, twenty-five years after the fact, the bright pink tour boats leave Kewalo Basin for Pearl Harbor. It has a kind of sleazy festivity at first, the prospect of an outing on a fine day, the passengers comparing complaints about their tour directors and their accommodations and the food at Canlis' Charcoal Broiler, the boys diving for coins around the boats; "Hey Mister Big," they scream. "How's about a coin." Sometimes a woman will throw a bill, and then be outraged when the insolent brown bodies pluck it from the air and jeer at her expectations. As the boat leaves the basin the boys swim back, their cheeks stuffed with money, and the children pout that they would rather be at the beach, and the women in their new Liberty House shifts and leftover leis sip papaya juice and study a booklet billed as *An Ideal Gift—Picture Story of December* 7.

It is, after all, a familiar story that we have come to hear—familiar even to the children, for of course they have seen John Wayne and John Garfield at Pearl Harbor, have spent countless rainy afternoons watching Kirk Douglas and Spencer Tracy and Van Johnson wonder out loud why Hickam does not answer this morning—and no one listens very closely to the guide. Sugar cane now blows where the *Nevada* went aground. An idle figure practices putting on Ford Island. The concessionaire breaks out more papaya juice. It is hard to remember what we came to remember.

And then something happens. I took that bright pink boat to Pearl Harbor on two afternoons, but I still do not know what I went to find out, which is how other people respond a quarter of a century later. I do not know because there is a point at which I began to cry, and to notice no one else. I began to cry at the place where the *Utah* lies in fifty feet of water, water neither turquoise nor bright blue here but the gray of harbor waters everywhere, and I did not stop until after the pink boat had left the *Arizona*, or what is visible of the *Arizona*: the rusted after-gun turret breaking the gray water, the flag at full mast because the Navy considers the *Arizona* still in commission, a full crew aboard, 1,102 men from forty-nine states. All I know about how other people respond is what I am told: that everyone is quiet at the *Arizona*.

A few days ago someone just four years younger than I am told me that he did not see why a sunken ship should affect me so, that John Kennedy's assassination, not Pearl Harbor, was the single most indelible event of what he kept calling "our generation." I could tell him only that we belonged to different generations, and I did not tell him what I want to tell you, about a place in Honolulu that is quieter still than the *Arizona*: the National Memorial Cemetery of the Pacific. They all seem to be twenty years old, the boys buried up there in the crater of an extinct volcano named Punchbowl, twenty and nineteen and eighteen and sometimes not that old. "SAMUEL FOSTER HARMON," one stone reads. "PENNSYLVANIA. PVT 27 REPL DRAFT 5 MARINE DIV. WORLD WAR II. APRIL 10 1928—MARCH 25 1945." Samuel Foster Harmon died, at Iwo Jima, fifteen days short of his seventeenth birthday. Some of them died on December 7 and some of them died after the *Enola Gay* had already bombed Hiroshima and some of them died on the dates of the landings at Okinawa and Iwo Jima and Guadalcanal and one whole long row of them, I am told, died on the beach of an island we no longer remember. There are 19,000 graves in the vast sunken crater above Honolulu.

I would go up there quite a bit. If I walked to the rim of the crater I could see the city, look down over Waikiki and the harbor and the jammed arterials, but up there it was quiet, and high enough into the rain forest so that a soft mist falls most of the day. One afternoon a couple came and left three plumeria leis on the grave of a California boy who had been killed, at nineteen, in 1945. The leis were already wilting by the time the woman finally placed them on the grave, because for a long time she only stood there and twisted them in her hands. On the whole I am able to take a very long view of death, but I think a great deal about what there is to remember, twenty-one years later, of a boy who died at nineteen. I saw no one else there but the men who cut the grass and the men who dig new graves, for they are bringing in bodies now from Vietnam. The graves filled last week and the week before that and even last month do not yet have stones, only plastic identification cards, streaked by the mist and splattered with mud. The earth is raw and trampled in that part of the crater, but the grass grows fast, up there in the rain cloud.

It is not very far from the crater down to Hotel Street, which is to Honolulu what Market Street is to San Francisco, the bright night street in a port city. The carrier *Coral Sea* was in Honolulu that week, and 165 men in from Vietnam on rest-and-recuperation leave, and 3,500 Marines on their way to Okinawa and then to Vietnam (they were part of the reactivated 5th Marine Division, and it was the 5th, if you will remember, to which the sixteen-year-old Samuel Foster Harmon belonged), and besides that there was the regular complement of personnel for Pearl and Hickam and Camp H. M. Smith and Fort Shafter and Fort De Russy and Bellows A.F.B. and the Kaneohe Marine Air Station and Schofield Barracks, and sooner or later they all got downtown to Hotel Street. They always have. The Navy cleaned out the red-light houses at the end of World War II, but the Hotel Streets of this world do not change perceptibly from war to war. The girls with hibiscus in their hair stroll idly in front of the penny arcades and the Japanese pool halls and the massage studios. "GIRLS WANTED FOR MASSAGE WORK," the signs say. "WHAT A REFRESHING NEW TINGLE." The fortune-tellers sit and file their nails behind flowered paper curtains. The boys from the cast of the Boys Will Be Girls Revue stand out on the sidewalk in lamé evening dresses, smoking cigarettes and looking the sailors over.

And the sailors get drunk. They all seem to be twenty years old on Hotel Street, too, twenty and nineteen and eighteen and drunk because they are no longer in Des Moines and not yet in Danang. They look in at the taxi-dance places and they look in at the strip places with the pictures of Lili St. Cyr and Tempest Storm outside (Lili St. Cyr was in California and Tempest Storm in Baltimore, but never mind, they all look alike on Saturday night in Honolulu) and they fish in their pockets for quarters to see the Art Movie in the back of the place that sells *Sunshine* and *Nude* and all the paperbacks with chained girls on the cover. They have snapshots laminated. They record their own voices (*Hi, Sweetheart, I'm in Honolulu tonight*) and they talk to the girls with hibiscus in their hair.

But mostly they just get a little drunker, and jostle around on the sidewalk avoiding the Hawaii Armed Forces Patrol and daring one another to get tattooed. In a show of bravado they rip off their shirts a half block before they reach Lou Normand's Tattoo Parlor and then they sit with glazed impassivity while the needle brands them with a heart or an anchor or, if they are particularly flush or particularly drunk, a replica of Christ on the cross with the stigmata in red. Their friends cluster outside the glass cubicle watching the skin redden and all the while, from a country-and-Western bar on the corner, "King of the Road" reverberates down Hotel Street. The songs change and the boys come and go but Lou Normand has been Thirty Years in the Same Location.

Perhaps it seems not surprising that there should be a mood of war at the scenes of famous defeats and at the graves of seventeen-year-olds and downtown in a port city. But the mood is not only there. War is in the very fabric of Hawaii's life, ineradicably fixed in both its emotions and its economy, dominating not only its memory but its vision of the future. There is a point at which every Honolulu conversation refers back to war. People sit in their gardens up on Makiki Heights among their copa de oro and their star jasmine and they look down toward Pearl Harbor and get another drink and tell you about the morning it happened. Webley Edwards was on the radio, they remember that, and what he said that morning again and again was "This is an air raid, take cover, *this is the real McCoy.*" That is not a remarkable thing to say, but it is a remarkable thing to have in one's memory. And they remember how people drove up into the hills and parked to watch the fires, just as they do now when a tsunami wave is due. They remember emergency wards in school auditoriums and how the older children were dispatched to guard reservoirs with unloaded guns. They laugh about trying to drive over the Pali in the fog after the 9 p.m. blackout, and about how their wives took thick books and large handkerchiefs down to the Y.W.C.A. and used them to show girls from the outer islands how to make a hospital bed, and they remember how it was when there were only three hotels on all two miles of Waikiki, the Royal for the Navy, the Halekulani for the press, and the Moana. In fact they contrive to leave an indistinct impression that it was in 1945, or perhaps '46, that they last got down to Waikiki. "I suppose the Royal hasn't changed," one Honolulan who lives within eight minutes of the Royal remarked to me. "The Halekulani," another said, as if it had just flickered into memory and she was uncertain it still existed. "*That* used to be kind of fun for drinks." Everyone was younger then, and in the telling a certain glow suffuses those years.

And then, if they have a stake in selling Hawaii, and there are very few people left in Hawaii who refuse to perceive that they do have a stake in selling it, they explain why Hawaii's future is so bright. In spite of what might be considered a classic false economy, based first upon the military, next upon the tourist, and third upon subsidized sugar, Hawaii's future is bright because Hawaii is the hub of the Pacific, a phrase employed in Honolulu only slightly less frequently than "our wonderful *aloha* spirit." They point out that Hawaii is the hub of the Pacific as far as the travel industry goes, and that Hawaii is also the hub of the Pacific as far as—they pause, and perhaps pick up a glass and study it before continuing. "And, well, frankly, if it goes the other way, what I mean by that is if the *situation* goes the other way, we're in the right spot for that, too." Perhaps nowhere else in the United States is the prospect of war regarded with so much equanimity.

Of course it is easy to suggest reasons, to say that after all Hawaii has already lived through one war, or to point out that Honolulu is even now in a war zone, steeped in the vocabulary of the military, deeply committed to the business of war. But it runs deeper than that. War is viewed with a curious ambivalence in Hawaii because the largest part of its population interprets war, however unconsciously, as a force for good, an instrument of social progress. And of course it was precisely World War II which cracked the spine of sugar feudalism, opened up a contracting economy and an immobile society, shattered forever the pleasant but formidable colonial world in which a handful of families controlled everything Hawaii did, where it shopped, how it shipped its goods, who could come in and how far they could go and at what point they would be closed out.

We have, most of us, some image of prewar Hawaii. We have heard the phrase "Big Five," and we have a general notion that certain families acquired a great deal of money and power in Hawaii and kept that money and that power for a very long while. The reality of Hawaiian power was at once more obvious and more subtle than one might imagine it to have been. The Big Five companies—C. Brewer, Theo. H. Davies, American Factors, Castle & Cooke, and Alexander & Baldwin—began as "factors" for the sugar planters; in effect they were plantation management. Over the years, the Big Five families and a few others—the Dillinghams, say, who were descended from a stranded sailor who built Hawaii's first railroad—intermarried, sat on one another's boards, got into shipping and insurance and money, and came to comprise a benevolent oligarchy unlike any on the mainland.

For almost half a century this interlocking directorate extended into every area of Hawaiian life, and its power could be exercised immediately and personally. American Factors, for example, owned (and still owns) the major Hawaiian department store, Liberty House. In 1941, Sears, Roebuck, working secretly through intermediaries, bought land for a store in suburban Honolulu. Sears finally opened its store, but not until the Sears president, Robert E. Wood, had threatened to buy his own ship; there had been some question as to whether Matson Navigation, controlled by Castle & Cooke and Alexander & Baldwin, would ship merchandise for anyone so baldly attempting to compete with a Big Five enterprise.

That was Hawaii. And then World War II came. Island boys went to war, and came home with new ideas. Mainland money came in, against all Island opposition. After World War II, the late Walter Dillingham could come down to a public hearing from his house on Diamond Head and cast at Henry Kaiser the most meaningful epithet of ante-bellum Hawaii—"*visitor*"—and have its significance lost on perhaps half his audience. In spirit if never quite in fact, World War II made everyone a Dillingham, and anyone in Hawaii too slow to perceive this for himself was constantly told it, by politicians and by labor leaders and by mainland observers.

The extent of the change, of course, has often been overstated, for reasons sometimes sentimental and sometimes strategic, but it is true that Hawaii is no more what it once was. There is still only one "Lowell" in Honolulu, and that is Lowell Dillingham, still only one "Ben," and that is his brother—but Ben Dillingham was overwhelmingly defeated in his 1962 campaign for the United States Senate by Daniel Inouye, a Nisei. (In the 1920's, when a congressional committee asked Ben Dillingham's father and Henry Baldwin why so few Japanese voted in Hawaii, they could suggest only that perhaps the Japanese were under instructions from Tokyo not to register.) There is still a strong feeling in old-line Honolulu that the Big Five "caved in" to labor—but Jack Hall, the tough I.L.W.U. leader who was once convicted under the Smith Act for conspiring to teach the overthrow of the United States Government by force and violence, now sits on the

board of the Hawaii Visitors' Bureau and commends the ladies of
the Outdoor Circle for their efforts in "preserving the loveliness
that is Hawaii." And Chinn Ho, who as a schoolboy used to chalk
up quotations for a downtown broker, now owns not only a few
score million dollars' worth of real estate but also that broker's
own house, out on Diamond Head, hard by Ben Dillingham's.
"The thing is," the broker's niece told me, "I suppose he wanted
it when he was fourteen."

But perhaps there is no clearer way to understand the
change than to visit Punahou School, the school the missionaries founded "for their children and their children's children,"
a statement of purpose interpreted rather literally until quite
recently. To leaf through Punahou's old class books is a briefing
in Hawaiian oligarchy, for the same names turn up year after
year, and the names are the same as those which appear in cut
stone or discreet brass letters down around what Honolulu calls
The Street, Merchant Street, down on those corners where the
Big Five have their offices and most Island business is done. In
1881 an Alexander delivered the commencement address and
a Dillingham the commencement poem; at the 1882 graduation a Baldwin spoke on "Chinese Immigration," an Alexander
on "Labor Ipse Voluptas," and a Bishop on "Sunshine." And
although high-caste Hawaiians have always coexisted with and
in fact intermarried with the white oligarchy, their Punahou
classmates usually visualized them, when it came time for class
prophecies, "playing in a band."

It is not that Punahou is not still the school of the Island
power elite; it is. "There will always be room at Punahou for
those children who belong here," Dr. John Fox, headmaster since
1944, assured alumni in a recent bulletin. But where in 1944 there
were 1,100 students and they had a median IQ of 108, now there
are 3,400 with a median IQ of 125. Where once the enrollment
was ten percent Oriental, now it is a fraction under thirty percent. And so it is that outside Punahou's new Cooke Library,
where the archives are kept by a great-great-granddaughter of the
Reverend Hiram Bingham, there sit, among the plumeria blossoms drifted on the steps, small Chinese boys with their books in
Pan American flight bags.

"John Fox is rather controversial, I guess you know," old-
family alumni will sometimes say now, but they do not say

exactly wherein the controversy lies. Perhaps because Hawaii sells itself so assiduously as the very model of a modern melting pot, the entire area of race relations is conversationally delicate. "I wouldn't exactly say we had discrimination here," one Honolulu woman explained tactfully. "I'd say we had a wonderful, wonderful competitive feeling." Another simply shrugs. "It's just something that's never pressed. The Orientals are—well, discreet's not really the word, but they aren't like the Negroes and the Jews, they don't push in where they're not wanted."

Even among those who are considered Island liberals, the question of race has about it, to anyone who has lived through these hypersensitive past years on the mainland, a curious and rather engaging ingenuousness. "There are very definitely people here who know the Chinese socially," one woman told me. "They have them to their houses. The uncle of a friend of mine, for example, has Chinn Ho to his house all the time." Although this seemed a statement along the lines of "Some of my best friends are Rothschilds," I accepted it in the spirit in which it was offered—just as I did the primitive progressivism of an Island teacher who was explaining, as we walked down a corridor of her school, about the miracles of educational integration the war had wrought. "Look," she said suddenly, grabbing a pretty Chinese girl by the arm and wheeling her around to face me. "You wouldn't have seen this here before the war. Look at those eyes."

And so, in the peculiar and still insular mythology of Hawaii, the dislocations of war became the promises of progress. Whether or not the promises have been fulfilled depends of course upon who is talking, as does whether or not progress is a virtue, but in any case it is war that is pivotal to the Hawaiian imagination, war that fills the mind, war that seems to hover over Honolulu like the rain clouds on Tantalus. Not very many people talk about that. They talk about freeways on Oahu and condominiums on Maui and beer cans at the Sacred Falls and how much wiser it is to bypass Honolulu altogether in favor of going directly to Laurance Rockefeller's Mauna Kea, on Hawaii. (In fact the notion that the only place to go in the Hawaiian Islands is somewhere on Maui or Kauai or Hawaii has by now filtered down to such wide acceptance that one can only suspect Honolulu to be due for a revival.)

Or, if they are of a more visionary turn, they talk, in a kind of James Michener rhetoric, about how Hawaii is a multiracial paradise and a labor-management paradise and a progressive paradise in which the past is now reconciled with the future, where the I.L.W.U.'s Jack Hall lunches at the Pacific Club and where that repository of everything old-line in Hawaii, the Bishop Estate, works hand in hand with Henry Kaiser to transform Koko Head into a $350 million development named Hawaii Kai. If they are in the travel business they talk about The Million Visitor Year (1970) and The Two Million Visitor Year (1980) and twenty thousand Rotarians convening in Honolulu in 1969, and they talk about The Product. "The reports show what we need," one travel man told me. "We need more attention to shaping and molding the product." The product is the place they live.

If they are from Honolulu but a little *arriviste*—say if they have been here only thirty years—they drop the name "Lowell" and talk about their charity work. If they are from Honolulu but not at all *arriviste* they talk about opening boutiques and going into the real-estate business and whether or not it was rude for Jacqueline Kennedy to appear for dinner at Henry Kaiser's in a muumuu and bare feet. ("I mean I *know* people come here to relax and not get dressed up, but still....") They get to the mainland quite often but not often enough to be well-informed about what is going on there. They like to entertain and to be entertained and to have people coming through. ("What would it be like without them?" one woman asked me rhetorically. "It'd be Saturday night at the club in Racine, Wisconsin.") They are very gracious and very enthusiastic, and give such an appearance of health and happiness and hope that I sometimes find it difficult to talk to them. I think that they would not understand why I came to Hawaii, and I think that they will perhaps not understand what I am going to remember.

1966

ROCK OF AGES

ALCATRAZ ISLAND IS covered with flowers now: orange and yellow nasturtiums, geraniums, sweet grass, blue iris, black-eyed Susans. Candytuft springs up through the cracked concrete in the exercise yard. Ice plant carpets the rusting catwalks. "WARNING! KEEP OFF! U.S. PROPERTY," the sign still reads, big and yellow and visible for perhaps a quarter of a mile, but since March 21, 1963, the day they took the last thirty or so men off the island and sent them to prisons less expensive to maintain, the warning has been only *pro forma*, the gun turrets empty, the cell blocks abandoned. It is not an unpleasant place to be, out there on Alcatraz with only the flowers and the wind and a bell buoy moaning and the tide surging through the Golden Gate, but to like a place like that you have to want a moat.

I sometimes do, which is what I am talking about here. Three people live on Alcatraz Island now. John and Marie Hart live in the same apartment they had for the sixteen years that he was a prison guard; they raised five children on the island, back when their neighbors were the Birdman and Mickey Cohen, but the Birdman and Mickey Cohen are gone now and so are the Harts' children, moved away, the last married in a ceremony on the island in June 1966. One other person lives on Alcatraz, a retired merchant seaman named Bill Doherty, and, between them, John Hart and Bill Doherty are responsible to the General Services Administration for maintaining a twenty-four-hour watch over the twenty-two-acre island. John Hart has a dog named Duffy, and Bill Doherty has a dog named Duke, and although the dogs are primarily good company they are also the first line of defense on Alcatraz Island. Marie Hart has a corner window which looks out to the San Francisco skyline, across a mile and a half of bay, and she sits there and paints "views" or plays her organ, songs like "Old Black Joe" and "Please Go 'Way and Let Me Sleep." Once a week the Harts take their boat to San Francisco to pick up their mail and shop at the big Safeway in the Marina, and occasionally

Marie Hart gets off the island to visit her children. She likes to keep in touch with them by telephone, but for ten months recently, after a Japanese freighter cut the cable, there was no telephone service to or from Alcatraz. Every morning the KGO traffic reporter drops the San Francisco *Chronicle* from his helicopter, and when he has time he stops for coffee. No one else comes out there except a man from the General Services Administration named Thomas Scott, who brings out an occasional congressman or somebody who wants to buy the island or, once in a while, his wife and small son, for a picnic. Quite a few people would like to buy the island, and Mr. Scott reckons that it would bring about five million dollars in a sealed-bid auction, but the General Services Administration is powerless to sell it until Congress acts on a standing proposal to turn the island into a "peace park." Mr. Scott says that he will be glad to get Alcatraz off his hands, but the charge of a fortress island could not be something a man gives up without ambivalent thoughts.

I went out there with him a while ago. Any child could imagine a prison more like a prison than Alcatraz looks, for what bars and wires there are seem perfunctory, beside the point; the island itself was the prison, and the cold tide its wall. It is precisely what they called it: the Rock. Bill Doherty and Duke lowered the dock for us, and in the station wagon on the way up the cliff Bill Doherty told Mr. Scott about small repairs he had made or planned to make. Whatever repairs get made on Alcatraz are made to pass the time, a kind of caretaker's scrimshaw, because the government pays for no upkeep at all on the prison; in 1963 it would have cost five million dollars to repair, which is why it was abandoned, and the $24,000 a year that it costs to maintain Alcatraz now is mostly for surveillance, partly to barge in the 400,000 gallons of water that Bill Doherty and the Harts use every year (there is no water at all on Alcatraz, one impediment to development), and the rest to heat two apartments and keep some lights burning. The buildings seem quite literally abandoned. The key locks have been ripped from the cell doors and the big electrical locking mechanisms disconnected. The tear-gas vents in the cafeteria are empty and the paint is buckling everywhere, corroded by the sea air, peeling off in great scales of pale green and ocher. I stood for a while in Al Capone's cell, five by nine feet, number 200 on the second tier of B Block, not one of the view cells, which were awarded on seniority, and I walked through the solitary block, totally black when the doors were closed. "Snail Mitchel," read a pencil scrawl on the wall of Solitary 14. "The only man that ever got shot for walking too slow." Beside it was a calendar, the months penciled on the wall with the days scratched off, May, June, July, August of some unnumbered year.

Mr. Scott, whose interest in penology dates from the day his office acquired Alcatraz as a potential property, talked about escapes and security routines and pointed out the beach where Ma Barker's son Doc was killed trying to escape. (They told him to come back up, and he said he would rather be shot, and he was.) I saw the shower room with the soap still in the dishes. I picked up a yellowed program from an Easter service (*Why seek ye the living among the dead? He is not here, but is risen*) and I struck a few notes on an upright piano with the ivory all rotted from the keys and I tried to imagine the prison as it had been, with the big lights playing over the windows all night long and the guards patrolling the gun galleries and the silverware clattering into a bag as it was checked in after meals, tried dutifully to summon up some distaste, some night terror of the doors locking and the boat pulling away. But the fact of it was that I liked it out there, a ruin devoid of human vanities, clean of human illusions, an empty place reclaimed by the weather where a woman plays an organ to stop the wind's whining and an old man plays ball with a dog named Duke. I could tell you that I came back because I had promises to keep, but maybe it was because nobody asked me to stay.

1967

THE SEACOAST OF DESPAIR

I WENT TO Newport not long ago, to see the great stone *fin-de-siècle* "cottages" in which certain rich Americans once summered. The places loom still along Bellevue Avenue and Cliff Walk, one after another, silk curtains frayed but gargoyles intact, monuments to something beyond themselves; houses built, clearly, to some transcendental point. No one had made clear to me exactly what that point was. I had been promised that the great summer houses were museums and warned that they were monstrosities, had been assured that the way of life they suggested was graceful beyond belief and that it was gross beyond description, that the very rich were different from you and me and yes, they had lower taxes, and if "The Breakers" was perhaps not entirely tasteful, still, *où sont les croquet wickets d'antan.* I had read Edith Wharton and I had read Henry James, who thought that the houses should stand there always, reminders "of the peculiarly awkward vengeances of affronted proportion and discretion."

But all that turns out to be beside the point, all talk of taxes and taste and affronted proportion. If, for example, one pursues the course, as Mrs. Richard Gambrill did in 1900, of engaging the architect who did the New York Public Library, approving plans for an eighteenth-century French château on a Rhode Island beach, ordering the garden copied after one Henry VIII gave to Anne Boleyn, and naming the result "Vernon Court," one moves somehow beyond the charge of breached "discretion." Something else is at work here. No aesthetic judgment could conceivably apply to the Newport of Bellevue Avenue, to those vast follies behind their hand-wrought gates; they are products of the metastasis of capital, the Industrial Revolution carried to its logical extreme, and what they suggest is how recent are the notions that life should be "comfortable," that those who live it should be "happy."

"Happiness" is, after all, a consumption ethic, and Newport is the monument of a society in which production was seen as the moral point, the reward if not exactly the end, of the economic process. The place is devoid of the pleasure principle. To have had the money to build "The Breakers" or "Marble House" or "Ochre Court" and to choose to build at Newport is in itself a denial of possibilities; the island is physically ugly, mean without the saving grace of extreme severity, a landscape less to be enjoyed than dominated. The prevalence of topiary gardening in Newport suggests the spirit of the place. And it was not as if there were no other options for these people: William Randolph Hearst built not at Newport but out on the edge of the Pacific. San Simeon, whatever its peculiarities, is in fact *la cuesta encantada*, swimming in golden light, sybaritic air, a deeply romantic place. But in Newport the air proclaims only the sources of money. Even as the sun dapples the great lawns and the fountains plash all around, there is something in the air that has nothing to do with pleasure and nothing to do with graceful tradition, a sense not of how prettily money can be spent but of how harshly money is made, an immediate presence of the pits and the rails and the foundries, of turbines and pork-belly futures. So insistent is the presence of money in Newport that the mind springs ineluctably to the raw beginnings of it. A contemplation of "Rosecliff" dissolves into the image of Big Jim Fair, digging the silver out of a mountain in Nevada so that his daughter might live in Newport. "Old Man Berwind, he'd turn in his grave to see that oil truck parked in the driveway," a guard at "The Elms" said to me as we surveyed the sunken garden there. "He made it in coal, soft coal." It had been on my mind as well as on the guard's, even as we stood in the sunlight outside the marble summer house, coal, soft coal, words like *bituminous* and *anthracite*, not the words of summer fancy.

In that way Newport is curiously Western, closer in spirit to Virginia City than to New York, to Denver than to Boston. It has the stridency usually credited to the frontier. And, like the frontier, it was not much of a game for women. Men paid for Newport, and granted to women the privilege of living in it. Just as gilt vitrines could be purchased for the correct display of biscuit Sèvres, so marble stairways could be bought for the advantageous display of women. In the filigreed gazebos they could be exhibited in a different light; in the French sitting rooms, in still another setting. They could be cajoled, flattered, indulged, given pretty rooms and Worth dresses, allowed to imagine that they ran their own houses and their own lives, but when it came time to negotiate, their freedom proved *trompe l'oeil*. It was the world of Bailey's Beach which made a neurasthenic of Edith Wharton, and, against her will, the Duchess of Marlborough of Consuelo Vanderbilt. The very houses are men's houses, factories, undermined by tunnels and service railways, shot through with plumbing to collect salt water, tanks to store it, devices to collect rain water, vaults for table silver, equipment inventories of china and crystal and "Tray cloths—fine" and "Tray cloths—ordinary." Somewhere in the bowels of "The Elms" is a coal bin twice the size of Julia Berwind's bedroom. The mechanics of such hous-es take precedence over all desires or inclinations; neither for great passions nor for morning whims can the factory be shut down, can production—of luncheons, of masked balls, of *marrons glacés*—be slowed. To stand in the dining room of "The Breakers" is to imagine fleeing from it, pleading migraine.

What Newport turns out to be, then, is homiletic, a fantas-tically elaborate stage setting for an American morality play in which money and happiness are presented as antithetical. It is a curious theatrical for these particular men to have conceived, but then we all judge ourselves sometime; it is hard for me to believe that Cornelius Vanderbilt did not sense, at some point in time, in some dim billiard room of his unconscious, that when he built "The Breakers" he damned himself. The world must have seemed greener to all of them, out there when they were young and began laying the rails or digging for high-grade ore in the Comstock or daring to think that they might corner copper. More than anyone else in the society, these men had apparently dreamed the dream and made it work. And what they did then was to build a place which seems to illustrate, as in a child's primer, that the production ethic led step by step to unhappiness, to restrictiveness, to entrap-ment in the mechanics of living. In that way the lesson of Bellevue Avenue is more seriously radical than the idea of Brook Farm. Who could fail to read the sermon in the stones of Newport? Who could think that the building of a railroad could guarantee salva-tion, when there on the lawns of the men who built the railroad nothing is left but the shadows of migrainous women, and the pony carts waiting for the long-dead children?

1967

GUAYMAS, SONORA

IT HAD RAINED in Los Angeles until the cliff was crumbling into the surf and I did not feel like getting dressed in the morning, so we decided to go to Mexico, to Guaymas, where it was hot. We did not go for marlin. We did not go to skin-dive. We went to get away from ourselves, and the way to do that is to drive, down through Nogales some day when the pretty green places pall and all that will move the imagination is some place difficult, some desert. The desert, any desert, is indeed the valley of the shadow of death; come back from the desert and you feel like Alcestis, reborn. After Nogales on Route 15 there is nothing but the Sonoran desert, nothing but mesquite and rattlesnakes and the Sierra Madre floating to the east, no trace of human endeavor but an occasional Pemex truck hurtling north and once in a while in the distance the dusty Pullman cars of the Ferrocarril del Pacífico. Magdalena is on Route 15, and then Hermosillo, where the American ore and cattle buyers gather in the bar at the Hotel San Alberto. There is an airport in Hermosillo, and Hermosillo is only eighty-five miles above Guaymas, but to fly is to miss the point. The point is to become disoriented, shriven, by the heat and the deceptive perspectives and the oppressive sense of carrion. The road shimmers. The eyes want to close.

And then, just past that moment when the desert has become the only reality, Route 15 hits the coast and there is Guaymas, a lunar thrust of volcanic hills and islands with the warm Gulf of California lapping idly all around, lapping even at the cactus, the water glassy as a mirage, the ships in the harbor whistling unsettlingly, moaning, ghost schooners, landlocked, lost. That is Guaymas. As far as the town goes, Graham Greene might have written it: a shadowy square with a filigree pergola for the Sunday band, a racket of birds, a cathedral in bad repair with a robin's-egg-blue tile dome, a turkey buzzard on the cross. The wharves are piled with bales of Sonoran cotton and mounds of dark copper concentrates; out on the freighters with the Panamanian and Liberian flags the Greek and German boys stand in the hot twilight and stare sullenly at the grotesque and claustrophobic hills, at the still town, a curious limbo at which to call.

Had we really been intent upon losing ourselves we might have stayed in town, at a hotel where faded and broken turquoise-blue shutters open onto the courtyard, where old men sit in the doorways and nothing moves, but instead we stayed outside town, at the Playa de Cortés, the big old hotel built by the Southern Pacific before the railways were nationalized. That place was a mirage, too, lovely and cool with thick whitewashed walls and dark shutters and bright tiles, tables made from ebony railroad ties, pale appliqued muslin curtains, shocks of corn wrapped around the heavy beams. Pepper trees grew around the swimming pool, and lemons and bananas in the courtyard. The food was unremarkable, but after dinner one could lie in a hammock on the terrace and listen to the fountains and the sea. For a week we lay in hammocks and fished desultorily and went to bed early and got very brown and lazy. My husband caught eight sharks, and I read an oceanography textbook, and we did not talk much. At the end of the week we wanted to do something, but all there was to do was visit the tracking station for an old space program or go see John Wayne and Claudia Cardinale in *Circus World*, and we knew it was time to go home.

1965

THERE IS SOMETHING uneasy in the Los Angeles air this afternoon, some unnatural stillness, some tension. What it means is that tonight a Santa Ana will begin to blow, a hot wind from the northeast whining down through the Cajon and San Gorgonio Passes, blowing up sandstorms out along Route 66, drying the hills and the nerves to the flash point. For a few days now we will see smoke back in the canyons, and hear sirens in the night. I have neither heard nor read that a Santa Ana is due, but I know it, and almost everyone I have seen today knows it too. We know it because we feel it. The baby frets. The maid sulks. I rekindle a waning argument with the telephone company, then cut my losses and lie down, given over to whatever it is in the air. To live with the Santa Ana is to accept, consciously or unconsciously, a deeply mechanistic view of human behavior.

I recall being told, when I first moved to Los Angeles and was living on an isolated beach, that the Indians would throw themselves into the sea when the bad wind blew. I could see why. The Pacific turned ominously glossy during a Santa Ana period, and one woke in the night troubled not only by the peacocks screaming in the olive trees but by the eerie absence of surf. The heat was surreal. The sky had a yellow cast, the kind of light sometimes called "earthquake weather." My only neighbor would not come out of her house for days, and there were no lights at night, and her husband roamed the place with a machete. One day he would tell me that he had heard a trespasser, the next a rattlesnake.

"On nights like that," Raymond Chandler once wrote about the Santa Ana, "every booze party ends in a fight. Meek little wives feel the edge of the carving knife and study their husbands' necks. Anything can happen." That was the kind of wind it was. I did not know then that there was any basis for the effect it had on all of us, but it turns out to be another of those cases in which science bears out folk wisdom. The Santa Ana, which is named for one of the canyons it rushes through, is a *foehn* wind, like the *foehn* of Austria and Switzerland and the *hamsin* of Israel. There are a number of persistent malevolent winds, perhaps the best known of which are the mistral of France and the Mediterranean sirocco, but a *foehn* wind has distinct characteristics: it occurs on the leeward slope of a mountain range and, although the air begins as a cold mass, it is warmed as it comes down the mountain and appears finally as a hot dry wind. Whenever and wherever a *foehn* blows, doctors hear about headaches and nausea and allergies, about "nervousness," about "depression." In Los Angeles some teachers do not attempt to conduct formal classes during a Santa Ana, because the children become unmanageable. In Switzerland the suicide rate goes up during the *foehn*, and in the courts of some Swiss cantons the wind is considered a mitigating circumstance for crime. Surgeons are said to watch the wind, because blood does not clot normally during a *foehn*. A few years ago an Israeli physicist discovered that not only during such winds, but for the ten or twelve hours which precede them, the air carries an unusually high ratio of positive to negative ions. No one seems to know exactly why that should be; some talk about friction and others suggest solar disturbances. In any case the positive ions are there, and what an excess of positive ions does, in the simplest terms, is make people unhappy. One cannot get much more mechanistic than that.

Easterners commonly complain that there is no "weather" at all in Southern California, that the days and the seasons slip by relentlessly, numbingly bland. That is quite misleading. In fact the climate is characterized by infrequent but violent extremes: two periods of torrential subtropical rains which continue for weeks and wash out the hills and send subdivisions sliding toward the sea; about twenty scattered days a year of the Santa Ana, which, with its incendiary dryness, invariably means fire. At the first prediction of a Santa Ana, the Forest Service flies men and equipment from northern California into the southern forests, and the Los Angeles Fire Department cancels its ordinary non-firefighting routines. The Santa Ana caused Malibu to burn the way it did in 1956, and Bel Air in 1961, and Santa Barbara in 1964. In the winter of 1966–67 eleven men were killed fighting a Santa Ana fire that spread through the San Gabriel Mountains.

Just to watch the front-page news out of Los Angeles during a Santa Ana is to get very close to what it is about the place.

The longest single Santa Ana period in recent years was in 1957, and it lasted not the usual three or four days but fourteen days, from November 21 until December 4. On the first day 25,000 acres of the San Gabriel Mountains were burning, with gusts reaching 100 miles an hour. In town, the wind reached Force 12, or hurricane force, on the Beaufort Scale; oil derricks were toppled and people ordered off the downtown streets to avoid injury from flying objects. On November 22 the fire in the San Gabriels was out of control. On November 24 six people were killed in automobile accidents, and by the end of the week the Los Angeles *Times* was keeping a box score of traffic deaths. On November 26 a prominent Pasadena attorney, depressed about money, shot and killed his wife, their two sons, and himself. On November 27 a South Gate divorcée, twenty-two, was murdered and thrown from a moving car. On November 30 the San Gabriel fire was still out of control, and the wind in town was blowing eighty miles an hour. On the first day of December four people died violently, and on the third the wind began to break.

It is hard for people who have not lived in Los Angeles to realize how radically the Santa Ana figures in the local imagination. The city burning is Los Angeles's deepest image of itself: Nathanael West perceived that, in *The Day of the Locust*; and at the time of the 1965 Watts riots what struck the imagination most indelibly were the fires. For days one could drive the Harbor Freeway and see the city on fire, just as we had always known it would be in the end. Los Angeles weather is the weather of catastrophe, of apocalypse, and, just as the reliably long and bitter winters of New England determine the way life is lived there, so the violence and the unpredictability of the Santa Ana affect the entire quality of life in Los Angeles, accentuate its impermanence, its unreliability. The wind shows us how close to the edge we are.

2

"Here's why I'm on the beeper, Ron," said the telephone voice on the all-night radio show. "I just want to say that this *Sex for the Secretary* creature—whatever her name is—certainly isn't contributing anything to the morals in this country. It's pathetic. Statistics *show*."

"It's *Sex and the Office*, honey," the disc jockey said. "That's the title. By Helen Gurley Brown. Statistics show what?"

"I haven't got them right here at my fingertips, naturally. But they *show*."

"I'd be interested in hearing them. Be constructive, you Night Owls."

"All right, let's take *one* statistic," the voice said, truculent now. "Maybe I haven't read the book, but what's this business she recommends about *going out with married men for lunch*?"

So it went, from midnight until 5 a.m., interrupted by records and by occasional calls debating whether or not a rattlesnake can swim. Misinformation about rattlesnakes is a leitmotiv of the insomniac imagination in Los Angeles. Toward 2 a.m. a man from "out Tarzana way" called to protest. "The Night Owls who called earlier must have been thinking about, uh, *The Man in the Gray Flannel Suit* or some other book," he said, "because Helen's one of the few authors trying to tell us what's really going *on*. Hefner's another, and he's also controversial, working in, uh, another area."

An old man, after testifying that he "personally" had seen a swimming rattlesnake, in the Delta-Mendota Canal, urged "moderation" on the Helen Gurley Brown question. "We shouldn't get on the beeper to call things pornographic before we've read them," he complained, pronouncing it pornee-oh-graphic. "I say, get the book. Give it a chance." The original *provocateur* called back to agree that she would get the book. "And then I'll burn it," she added.

"Book burner, eh?" laughed the disc jockey good-naturedly.

"I wish they still burned witches," she hissed.

3

It is three o'clock on a Sunday afternoon and 105° and the air so thick with smog that the dusty palm trees loom up with a sudden and rather attractive mystery. I have been playing in the sprinklers with the baby and I get in the car and go to Ralph's Market on the corner of Sunset and Fuller wearing an old bikini bathing suit. That is not a very good thing to wear to the market but neither is it, at Ralph's on the corner of Sunset and Fuller, an unusual costume. Nonetheless a large woman in a cotton muumuu jams her cart into mine at the butcher counter. "*What a thing to wear to the market,*" she says in a loud but strangled voice. Everyone looks the other way and I study a plastic package of rib lamb chops and she repeats it. She follows me all over the store, to the Junior Foods, to the Dairy Products, to the Mexican Delicacies, jamming my cart whenever she can. Her husband plucks at her sleeve. As I leave the check-out counter she raises her voice one last time: "*What a thing to wear to Ralph's,*" she says.

4

A party at someone's house in Beverly Hills: a pink tent, two orchestras, a couple of French Communist directors in Cardin evening jackets, chili and hamburgers from Chasen's. The wife of an English actor sits at a table alone; she visits California rarely although her husband works here a good deal. An American who knows her slightly comes over to the table.

"Marvelous to see you here," he says.

"Is it," she says.

"How long have you been here?"

"Too long."

She takes a fresh drink from a passing waiter and smiles at her husband, who is dancing.

The American tries again. He mentions her husband.

"I hear he's marvelous in this picture."

She looks at the American for the first time. When she finally speaks she enunciates every word very clearly. "He … is … also … a … fag," she says pleasantly.

5

The oral history of Los Angeles is written in piano bars. "Moon River," the piano player always plays, and "Mountain Greenery." "There's a Small Hotel" and "This Is Not the First Time." People talk to each other, tell each other about their first wives and last husbands. "Stay funny," they tell each other, and "This is to die over." A construction man talks to an unemployed screenwriter who is celebrating, alone, his tenth wedding anniversary. The construction man is on a job in

Montecito: "Up in Montecito," he says, "they got one square mile with 135 millionaires."

"Putrescence," the writer says.

"That's all you got to say about it?"

"Don't read me wrong, I think Santa Barbara's one of the most—Christ, *the* most—beautiful places in the world, but it's a beautiful place that contains a ... *putrescence*. They just live on their putrescent millions."

"So give me putrescent."

"No, no," the writer says. "I just happen to think millionaires have some sort of lacking in their ... in their elasticity."

A drunk requests "The Sweetheart of Sigma Chi." The piano player says he doesn't know it. "Where'd you learn to play the piano?" the drunk asks. "I got two degrees," the piano player says. "One in musical education." I go to a coin telephone and call a friend in New York. "Where are you?" he says. "In a piano bar in Encino," I say. "Why?" he says. "Why not," I say.

1965–67

GOODBYE TO ALL THAT

How many miles to Babylon?
Three score miles and ten—
Can I get there by candlelight?
Yes, and back again—
If your feet are nimble and light
You can get there by candlelight.

IT IS EASY to see the beginnings of things, and harder to see the ends. I can remember now, with a clarity that makes the nerves in the back of my neck constrict, when New York began for me, but I cannot lay my finger upon the moment it ended, can never cut through the ambiguities and second starts and broken resolves to the exact place on the page where the heroine is no longer as optimistic as she once was. When I first saw New York I was twenty, and it was summertime, and I got off a DC-7 at the old Idlewild temporary terminal in a new dress which had seemed very smart in Sacramento but seemed less smart already, even in the old Idlewild temporary terminal, and the warm air smelled of mildew and some instinct, programmed by all the movies I had ever seen and all the songs I had ever heard sung and all the stories I had ever read about New York, informed me that it would never be quite the same again. In fact it never was. Some time later there was a song on all the jukeboxes on the upper East Side that went "but where is the schoolgirl who used to be me," and if it was late enough at night I used to wonder that. I know now that almost everyone wonders something like that, sooner or later and no matter what he or she is doing, but one of the mixed blessings of being twenty and twenty-one and even twenty-three is the conviction that nothing like this, all evidence to the contrary notwithstanding, has ever happened to anyone before.

Of course it might have been some other city, had circumstances been different and the time been different and had

I been different, might have been Paris or Chicago or even San Francisco, but because I am talking about myself I am talking here about New York. That first night I opened my window on the bus into town and watched for the skyline, but all I could see were the wastes of Queens and the big signs that said MIDTOWN TUNNEL THIS LANE and then a flood of summer rain (even that seemed remarkable and exotic, for I had come out of the West where there was no summer rain), and for the next three days I sat wrapped in blankets in a hotel room air-conditioned to 35° and tried to get over a bad cold and a high fever. It did not occur to me to call a doctor, because I knew none, and although it did occur to me to call the desk and ask that the air conditioner be turned off, I never called, because I did not know how much to tip whoever might come—was anyone ever so young? I am here to tell you that someone was. All I could do during those three days was talk long-distance to the boy I already knew I would never marry in the spring. I would stay in New York, I told him, just six months, and I could see the Brooklyn Bridge from my window. As it turned out the bridge was the Triborough, and I stayed eight years.

In retrospect it seems to me that those days before I knew the names of all the bridges were happier than the ones that came later, but perhaps you will see that as we go along. Part of what I want to tell you is what it is like to be young in New York, how six months can become eight years with the deceptive ease of a film dissolve, for that is how those years appear to me now, in a long sequence of sentimental dissolves and old-fashioned trick shots—the Seagram Building fountains dissolve into snowflakes, I enter a revolving door at twenty and come out a good deal older, and on a different street. But most particularly I want to explain to you, and in the process perhaps to myself, why I no longer live in New York. It is often said that New York is a city for only the very rich and the very poor. It is less often said that New York is also, at least for those of us who came there from somewhere else, a city for only the very young.

I remember once, one cold bright December evening in New York, suggesting to a friend who complained of having been around too long that he come with me to a party where there would be, I assured him with the bright resourcefulness of twenty-three, "new faces." He laughed literally until he choked, and I had to roll down the taxi window and hit him on the back. "New faces," he said finally, "don't tell me about *new faces*." It seemed that the last time he had gone to a party where he had been promised "new faces," there had been fifteen people in the room, and he had already slept with five of the women and owed money to all but two of the men. I laughed with him, but the first snow had just begun to fall and the big Christmas trees glittered yellow and white as far as I could see up Park Avenue and I had a new dress and it would be a long while before I would come to understand the particular moral of the story.

It would be a long while because, quite simply, I was in love with New York. I do not mean "love" in any colloquial way, I mean that I was in love with the city, the way you love the first person who ever touches you and never love anyone quite that way again. I remember walking across Sixty-second Street one twilight that first spring, or the second spring, they were all alike for a while. I was late to meet someone but I stopped at Lexington Avenue and bought a peach and stood on the corner eating it and knew that I had come out of the West and reached the mirage. I could taste the peach and feel the soft air blowing from a subway grating on my legs and I could smell lilac and garbage and expensive perfume and I knew that it would cost something sooner or later—because I did not belong there, did not come from there—but when you are twenty-two or twenty-three, you figure that later you will have a high emotional balance, and be able to pay whatever it costs. I still believed in possibilities then, still had the sense, so peculiar to New York, that something extraordinary would happen any minute, any day, any month. I was making only $65 or $70 a week then ("Put yourself in Hattie Carnegie's hands," I was advised without the slightest trace of irony by an editor of the magazine for which I worked), so little money that some weeks I had to charge food at Bloomingdale's gourmet shop in order to eat, a fact which went unmentioned in the letters I wrote to California. I never told my father that I needed money because then he would have sent it, and I would never know if I could do it by myself. At that time making a living seemed a game to me, with arbitrary but quite inflexible rules. And except on a certain kind of winter evening—six-thirty in the Seventies, say, already dark and bitter with a wind off the river, when I would be walking very fast toward a bus and would look in the bright windows of brownstones and see cooks working in clean kitchens and imagine women lighting candles on the floor above and beautiful children being bathed on the floor above that—except on nights like those, I never felt poor; I had the feeling that if I needed money I could always get it. I could write a syndicated column for teenagers under the name "Debbi Lynn" or I could smuggle gold into India or I could become a $100 call girl, and none of it would matter.

Nothing was irrevocable; everything was within reach. Just around every corner lay something curious and interesting, something I had never before seen or done or known about. I could go to a party and meet someone who called himself Mr. Emotional Appeal and ran The Emotional Appeal Institute or Tina Onassis Blandford or a Florida cracker who was then a regular on what he called "the Big C," the Southampton-El Morocco circuit ("I'm well-connected on the Big C, honey," he would tell me over collard greens on his vast borrowed terrace), or the widow of the celery king of the Harlem market or a piano salesman from Bonne Terre, Missouri, or someone who had already made and lost two fortunes in Midland, Texas. I could make promises to myself and to other people and there would be all the time in the world to keep them. I could stay up all night and make mistakes, and none of it would count.

You see I was in a curious position in New York: it never occurred to me that I was living a real life there. In my imagination I was always there for just another few months, just until Christmas or Easter or the first warm day in May. For that reason I was most comfortable in the company of Southerners. They seemed to be in New York as I was, on some indefinitely extended leave from wherever they belonged, disinclined to consider the future, temporary exiles who always knew when the flights left for New Orleans or Memphis or Richmond or, in my case, California. Someone who lives always with a plane schedule in the drawer lives on a slightly different calendar. Christmas, for example, was a difficult season. Other people could take it in stride, going to Stowe or going abroad or going for the day to their mothers' places in Connecticut; those of us who believed that we lived somewhere else would spend it making and canceling airline reservations, waiting for weatherbound flights as if for the last plane out of Lisbon in 1940, and finally comforting one another, those of us who were left, with the oranges and mementos and smoked-oyster stuffings of childhood, gathering close, colonials in a far country.

Which is precisely what we were. I am not sure that it is possible for anyone brought up in the East to appreciate entirely what New York, the idea of New York, means to those of us who came out of the West and the South. To an Eastern child, particularly a child who has always had an uncle on Wall Street and who has spent several hundred Saturdays first at F. A. O. Schwarz and being fitted for shoes at Best's and then waiting under the Biltmore clock and dancing to Lester Lanin, New York is just a city, albeit *the* city, a plausible place for people to live. But to those of us who came from places where no one had heard of Lester Lanin and Grand Central Station was a Saturday radio program, where Wall Street and Fifth Avenue and Madison Avenue were not places at all but abstractions ("Money," and "High Fashion," and "The Hucksters"), New York was no mere city. It was instead an infinitely romantic notion, the mysterious nexus of all love and money and power, the shining and perishable dream itself. To think of "living" there was to reduce the miraculous to the mundane; one does not "live" at Xanadu.

In fact it was difficult in the extreme for me to understand those young women for whom New York was not simply an ephemeral Estoril but a real place, girls who bought toasters and installed new cabinets in their apartments and committed themselves to some reasonable future. I never bought any furniture in New York. For a year or so I lived in other people's apartments; after that I lived in the Nineties in an apartment furnished entirely with things taken from storage by a friend whose wife had moved away. And when I left the apartment in the Nineties (that was when I was leaving everything, when it was all breaking up) I left everything in it, even my winter clothes and the map of Sacramento County I had hung on the bedroom wall to remind me who I was, and I moved into a monastic four-room floor-through on Seventy-fifth Street. "Monastic" is perhaps misleading here, implying some chic severity; until after I was married and my husband moved some furniture in, there was nothing at all in those four rooms except a cheap double mattress and box springs, ordered by telephone the day I decided to move, and two French garden chairs lent me by a friend who imported them. (It strikes me now that the people I knew in New York all had curious and self-defeating sidelines. They imported garden chairs which did not sell very well at Hammacher Schlemmer or they tried to market hair straighteners in Harlem or they ghosted exposés of Murder Incorporated for Sunday supplements. I think that perhaps none of us was very serious, *engagé* only about our most private lives.)

All I ever did to that apartment was hang fifty yards of yellow theatrical silk across the bedroom windows, because I had some idea that the gold light would make me feel better, but I did not bother to weight the curtains correctly and all that summer the long panels of transparent golden silk would blow out the windows and get tangled and drenched in the afternoon thunderstorms. That was the year, my twenty-eighth, when I was discovering that not all of the promises would be kept, that some things are in fact irrevocable and that it had counted after all, every evasion and every procrastination, every mistake, every word, all of it.

That is what it was all about, wasn't it? Promises? Now when New York comes back to me it comes in hallucinatory flashes, so clinically detailed that I sometimes wish that memory would effect the distortion with which it is commonly credited. For a lot of the time I was in New York I used a perfume called *Fleurs de Rocaille*, and then *L'Air du Temps*, and now the slightest trace of either can short-circuit my connections for the rest of the day. Nor can I smell Henri Bendel jasmine soap without falling back into the past, or the particular mixture of spices used for boiling crabs. There were barrels of crab boil in a Czech place in the Eighties where I once shopped. Smells, of course, are notorious memory stimuli, but there are other things which affect me the same way. Blue-and-white striped sheets. Vermouth cassis. Some faded nightgowns which were new in 1959 or 1960, and some chiffon scarves I bought about the same time.

I suppose that a lot of us who have been young in New York have the same scenes on our home screens. I remember sitting in a lot of apartments with a slight headache about five o'clock in the morning. I had a friend who could not sleep, and he knew a few other people who had the same trouble, and we would watch the sky lighten and have a last drink with no ice and then go home in the early morning light, when the streets were clean and wet (had it rained in the night? we never knew) and the few cruising taxis still had their headlights on and the only color was the red and green of traffic signals. The White Rose bars opened very early in the morning; I recall waiting in one of them to watch an astronaut go into space, waiting so long that at the moment it actually happened I had my eyes not on the television screen but on a cockroach on the tile floor. I liked the bleak branches above Washington Square at dawn, and the monochromatic flatness of Second Avenue, the fire escapes and the grilled storefronts peculiar and empty in their perspective.

It is relatively hard to fight at six-thirty or seven in the morning without any sleep, which was perhaps one reason we stayed up all night, and it seemed to me a pleasant time of day. The windows were shuttered in that apartment in the Nineties and I could sleep a few hours and then go to work. I could work then on two or three hours' sleep and a container of coffee from Chock Full O' Nuts. I liked going to work, liked the soothing and satisfactory rhythm of getting out a magazine, liked the orderly progression of four-color closings and two-color closings and black-and-white closings and then The Product, no abstraction but something which looked effortlessly glossy and could be picked up on a newsstand and weighed in the hand. I liked all the minutiae of proofs and layouts, liked working late on the nights the magazine went to press, sitting and reading *Variety* and waiting for the copy desk to call. From my office I could look across town to the weather signal on the Mutual of New York Building and the lights that alternately spelled out TIME and LIFE above Rockefeller Plaza; that pleased me obscurely, and so did walking uptown in the mauve eight o'clocks of early summer evenings and looking at things, Lowestoft tureens in Fifty-seventh Street windows, people in evening clothes trying to get taxis, the trees just coming into full leaf, the lambent air, all the sweet promises of money and summer.

Some years passed, but I still did not lose that sense of wonder about New York. I began to cherish the loneliness of it, the sense that at any given time no one need know where I was or what I was doing. I liked walking, from the East River over to the Hudson and back on brisk days, down around the Village on warm days. A friend would leave me the key to her apartment in the West Village when she was out of town, and sometimes I would just move down there, because by that time the telephone was beginning to bother me (the canker, you see, was already in the rose) and not many people had that number. I remember one day when someone who did have the West Village number came to pick me up for lunch there, and we both had hangovers, and I cut my finger opening him a beer and burst into tears, and we walked to a Spanish restaurant and drank Bloody Marys and *gazpacho* until we felt better. I was not then guilt-ridden about spending afternoons that way, because I still had all the afternoons in the world.

And even that late in the game I still liked going to parties, all parties, bad parties, Saturday-afternoon parties given by recently married couples who lived in Stuyvesant Town, West Side parties given by unpublished or failed writers who served cheap red wine and talked about going to Guadalajara, Village parties where all the guests worked for advertising agencies and voted for Reform Democrats, press parties at Sardi's, the worst kinds of parties. You will have perceived by now that I was not one to profit by the experience of others, that it was a very long time indeed before I stopped believing in new faces and began to understand the lesson in that story, which was that it is distinctly possible to stay too long at the Fair.

I could not tell you when I began to understand that. All I know is that it was very bad when I was twenty-eight. Everything that was said to me I seemed to have heard before, and I could no longer listen. I could no longer sit in little bars near Grand Central and listen to someone complaining of his wife's inability to cope with the help while he missed another train to Connecticut. I no longer had any interest in hearing about the advances other people had received from their publishers, about plays which were having second-act trouble in Philadelphia, or about people I would like very much if only I would come out and meet them. I had already met them, always. There were certain parts of the city which I had to avoid. I could not bear upper Madison Avenue on weekday mornings (this was a particularly inconvenient aversion, since I then lived just fifty or sixty feet east of Madison), because I would see women walking Yorkshire terriers and shopping at Gristede's, and some Veblenesque gorge would rise in my throat. I could not go to Times Square in the afternoon, or to the New York Public Library for any reason whatsoever. One day I could not go into a Schrafft's; the next day it would be Bonwit Teller.

I hurt the people I cared about, and insulted those I did not. I cut myself off from the one person who was closer to me than any other. I cried until I was not even aware when I was crying and when I was not, cried in elevators and in taxis and in Chinese laundries, and when I went to the doctor he said only that I seemed to be depressed, and should see a "specialist." He wrote down a psychiatrist's name and address for me, but I did not go.

Instead I got married, which as it turned out was a very good thing to do but badly timed, since I still could not walk on upper Madison Avenue in the mornings and still could not talk to people and still cried in Chinese laundries. I had never before understood what "despair" meant, and I am not sure that I understand now, but I understood that year. Of course I could not work. I could not even get dinner with any degree of certainty, and I would sit in the apartment on Seventy-fifth Street paralyzed until my husband would call from his office and say gently that I did not have to get dinner, that I could meet him at Michael's Pub or at Toots Shor's or at Sardi's East. And then one morning in April (we had been married in January) he called and told me that he wanted to get out of New York for a while, that he would take a six-month leave of absence, that we would go somewhere.

It was three years ago that he told me that, and we have lived in Los Angeles since. Many of the people we knew in New York think this a curious aberration, and in fact tell us so. There is no possible, no adequate answer to that, and so we give certain stock answers, the answers everyone gives. I talk about how difficult it would be for us to "afford" to live in New York right now, about how much "space" we need. All I mean is that I was very young in New York, and that at some point the golden rhythm was broken, and I am not that young any more. The last time I was in New York was in a cold January, and everyone was ill and tired. Many of the people I used to know there had moved to Dallas or had gone on Antabuse or had bought a farm in New Hampshire.

We stayed ten days, and then we took an afternoon flight back to Los Angeles, and on the way home from the airport that night I could see the moon on the Pacific and smell jasmine all around and we both knew that there was no longer any point in keeping the apartment we still kept in New York. There were years when I called Los Angeles "the Coast," but they seem a long time ago.

1967

THE WHITE ALBUM

For Earl McGrath, and for Lois Wallace

CONTENTS

I

THE WHITE ALBUM

I

WE TELL OURSELVES stories in order to live. The princess is caged
in the consulate. The man with the candy will lead the children
into the sea. The naked woman on the ledge outside the window
on the sixteenth floor is a victim of accidie, or the naked woman
is an exhibitionist, and it would be "interesting" to know which.
We tell ourselves that it makes some difference whether the naked
woman is about to commit a mortal sin or is about to register a
political protest or is about to be, the Aristophanic view, snatched
back to the human condition by the fireman in priest's clothing
just visible in the window behind her, the one smiling at the tele-
photo lens. We look for the sermon in the suicide, for the social or
moral lesson in the murder of five. We interpret what we see, select
the most workable of the multiple choices. We live entirely, especially if we are writers, by the imposition of a narrative line upon
disparate images, by the "ideas" with which we have learned to
freeze the shifting phantasmagoria which is our actual experience.

Or at least we do for a while. I am talking here about a time
when I began to doubt the premises of all the stories I had ever
told myself, a common condition but one I found troubling. I
suppose this period began around 1966 and continued until 1971.
During those five years I appeared, on the face of it, a competent
enough member of some community or another, a signer of
contracts and Air Travel cards, a citizen: I wrote a couple of times
a month for one magazine or another, published two books,
worked on several motion pictures; participated in the paranoia
of the time, in the raising of a small child, and in the entertainment of large numbers of people passing through my house;
made gingham curtains for spare bedrooms, remembered to ask
agents if any reduction of points would be *pari passu* with the
financing studio, put lentils to soak on Saturday night for lentil
soup on Sunday, made quarterly F.I.C.A. payments and renewed
my driver's license on time, missing on the written examination
only the question about the financial responsibility of California

drivers. It was a time of my life when I was frequently "named." I was named godmother to children. I was named lecturer and panelist, colloquist and conferee. I was even named, in 1968, a *Los Angeles Times* "Woman of the Year," along with Mrs. Ronald Reagan, the Olympic swimmer Debbie Meyer, and ten other California women who seemed to keep in touch and do good works. I did no good works but I tried to keep in touch. I was responsible. I recognized my name when I saw it. Once in a while I even answered letters addressed to me, not exactly upon receipt but eventually, particularly if the letters had come from strangers. "During my absence from the country these past eighteen months," such replies would begin.

This was an adequate enough performance, as improvisations go. The only problem was that my entire education, everything I had ever been told or had told myself, insisted that the production was never meant to be improvised: I was supposed to have a script, and had mislaid it. I was supposed to hear cues, and no longer did. I was meant to know the plot, but all I knew was what I saw: flash pictures in variable sequence, images with no "meaning" beyond their temporary arrangement, not a movie but a cutting-room experience. In what would probably be the middle of my life I wanted still to believe in the narrative and in the narrative's intelligibility, but to know that one could change the sense with every cut was to begin to perceive the experience as rather more electrical than ethical.

During this period I spent what were for me the usual proportions of time in Los Angeles and New York and Sacramento. I spent what seemed to many people I knew an eccentric amount of time in Honolulu, the particular aspect of which lent me the illusion that I could any minute order from room service a revisionist theory of my own history, garnished with a vanda orchid. I watched Robert Kennedy's funeral on a verandah at the Royal Hawaiian Hotel in Honolulu, and also the first reports from My Lai. I reread all of George Orwell on the Royal Hawaiian Beach, and I also read, in the papers that came one day late from the mainland, the story of Betty Lansdown Fouquet, a 26-year-old woman with faded blond hair who put her five-year-old daughter out to die on the center divider of Interstate 5 some miles south of the last Bakersfield exit. The child, whose fingers had to be pried loose from the Cyclone fence when she was rescued twelve hours later by the California Highway Patrol, reported that she had run after the car carrying her mother and stepfather and brother and sister for "a long time." Certain of these images did not fit into any narrative I knew.

Another flash cut:

"In June of this year patient experienced an attack of vertigo, nausea, and a feeling that she was going to pass out. A thorough medical evaluation elicited no positive findings and she was placed on Elavil, Mg 20, tid.... The Rorschach record is interpreted as describing a personality in process of deterioration with abundant signs of failing defenses and increasing inability of the ego to mediate the world of reality and to cope with normal stress.... Emotionally, patient has alienated herself almost entirely from the world of other human beings. Her fantasy life appears to have been virtually completely preempted by primitive, regressive libidinal preoccupations many of which are distorted and bizarre.... In a technical sense basic affective controls appear to be intact but it is equally clear that they are insecurely and tenuously maintained for the present by a variety of defense mechanisms including intellectualization, obsessive-compulsive devices, projection, reaction-formation, and somatization, all of which now seem inadequate to their task of controlling or containing an underlying psychotic process and are therefore in process of failure. The content of patient's responses is highly unconventional and frequently bizarre, filled with sexual and anatomical preoccupations, and basic reality contact is obviously and seriously impaired at times. In quality and level of sophistication patient's responses are characteristic of those of individuals of high average or superior intelligence but she is now functioning intellectually in impaired fashion at barely average level. Patient's thematic productions on the Thematic Apperception Test emphasize her fundamentally pessimistic, fatalistic, and depressive view of the world around her. It is as though she feels deeply that all human effort is foredoomed to failure, a conviction which seems to push her further into a dependent, passive withdrawal. In her view she lives in a world of people moved by strange, conflicted, poorly comprehended, and, above all, devious motivations which commit them inevitably to conflict and failure ..."

The patient to whom this psychiatric report refers is me. The tests mentioned—the Rorschach, the Thematic Apperception Test, the Sentence Completion Test and the Minnesota Multiphasic Personality Index—were administered privately, in the outpatient psychiatric clinic at St. John's Hospital in Santa Monica, in the summer of 1968, shortly after I suffered the "attack of vertigo and nausea" mentioned in the first sentence and shortly before I was named a *Los Angeles Times* "Woman of the Year." By way of comment I offer only that an attack of vertigo and nausea does not now seem to me an inappropriate response to the summer of 1968.

2

In the years I am talking about I was living in a large house in a part of Hollywood that had once been expensive and was now described by one of my acquaintances as a "senseless-killing neighborhood." This house on Franklin Avenue was rented, and paint peeled inside and out, and pipes broke and window sashes crumbled and the tennis court had not been rolled since 1933, but the rooms were many and high-ceilinged and, during the five years that I lived there, even the rather sinistral inertia of the neighborhood tended to suggest that I should live in the house indefinitely.

In fact I could not, because the owners were waiting only for a zoning change to tear the house down and build a high-rise apartment building, and for that matter it was precisely this anticipation of imminent but not exactly immediate destruction that lent the neighborhood its particular character. The house across the street had been built for one of the Talmadge sisters, had been the Japanese consulate in 1941, and was now, although boarded up, occupied by a number of unrelated adults who seemed to constitute some kind of therapy group. The house next door was owned by Synanon. I recall looking at a house around the corner with a rental sign on it: this house had once been the Canadian consulate, had 28 large rooms and two refrigerated fur closets, and could be rented, in the spirit of the neighborhood, only on a month-to-month basis, unfurnished. Since the inclination to rent an unfurnished 28-room house for a month or two is a distinctly special one, the neighborhood was peopled mainly by rock-and-roll bands, therapy groups, very old women wheeled down the street by practical nurses in soiled uniforms, and by my husband, my daughter and me.

Q. *And what else happened, if anything....*
A. *He said that he thought that I could be a star, like, you know, a young Burt Lancaster, you know, that kind of stuff.*
Q. *Did he mention any particular name?*
A. *Yes, sir.*
Q. *What name did he mention?*
A. *He mentioned a lot of names. He said Burt Lancaster. He said Clint Eastwood. He said Fess Parker. He mentioned a lot of names....*
Q. *Did you talk after you ate?*
A. *While we were eating, after we ate. Mr. Novarro told our fortunes with some cards and he read our palms.*
Q. *Did he tell you you were going to have a lot of good luck or bad luck or what happened?*
A. *He wasn't a good palm reader.*

These are excerpts from the testimony of Paul Robert Ferguson and Thomas Scott Ferguson, brothers, ages 22 and 17 respectively, during their trial for the murder of Ramon Novarro, age 69, at his house in Laurel Canyon, not too far from my house in Hollywood, on the night of October 30, 1968. I followed this trial quite closely, clipping reports from the newspapers and later borrowing a transcript from one of the defense attorneys. The younger of the brothers, "Tommy Scott" Ferguson, whose girl friend testified that she had stopped being in love with him "about two weeks after Grand Jury," said that he had been unaware of Mr. Novarro's career as a silent film actor until he was shown, at some point during the night of the murder, a photograph of his host as Ben-Hur. The older brother, Paul Ferguson, who began working carnivals when he was 12 and described himself at 22 as having had "a fast life and a good one," gave the jury, upon request, his definition of a hustler: "A hustler is someone who can talk—not just to men, to women, too. Who can cook. Can keep company. Wash a car. Lots of things make up a hustler. There are a lot of lonely people in this town, man." During the course of the trial each of the brothers accused the other of the murder. Both were convicted. I read the transcript several times, trying to bring the picture into some focus which did not suggest that I lived, as my psychiatric report had put it, "in a world of people moved by strange, conflicted, poorly comprehended and, above all, devious motivations"; I never met the Ferguson brothers.

I did meet one of the principals in another Los Angeles County murder trial during those years: Linda Kasabian, star witness for the prosecution in what was commonly known as the Manson Trial. I once asked Linda what she thought about the apparently chance sequence of events which had brought her first to the Spahn Movie Ranch and then to the Sybil Brand Institute for Women on charges, later dropped, of murdering Sharon Tate Polanski, Abigail Folger, Jay Sebring, Voytek Frykowski, Steven Parent, and Rosemary and Leno LaBianca. "Everything was to teach me something," Linda said. Linda did not believe that chance was without pattern. Linda operated on what I later recognized as dice theory, and so, during the years I am talking about, did I.

It will perhaps suggest the mood of those years if I tell you that during them I could not visit my mother-in-law without averting my eyes from a framed verse, a "house blessing," which hung in a hallway of her house in West Hartford, Connecticut.

> God bless the corners of this house,
> And be the lintel blest—
> And bless the hearth and bless the board
> And bless each place of rest—
> And bless the crystal windowpane that lets the starlight in
> And bless each door that opens wide, to stranger as to kin.

This verse had on me the effect of a physical chill, so insistently did it seem the kind of "ironic" detail the reporters would seize upon, the morning the bodies were found. In my neighborhood in California we did not bless the door that opened wide to stranger as to kin. Paul and Tommy Scott Ferguson were the strangers at Ramon Novarro's door, up on Laurel Canyon. Charles Manson was the stranger at Rosemary and Leno LaBianca's door, over in

Los Feliz. Some strangers at the door knocked, and invented a reason to come inside: a call, say, to the Triple A, about a car not in evidence. Others just opened the door and walked in, and I would come across them in the entrance hall. I recall asking one such stranger what he wanted. We looked at each other for what seemed a long time, and then he saw my husband on the stair landing. "Chicken Delight," he said finally, but we had ordered no Chicken Delight, nor was he carrying any. I took the license number of his panel truck. It seems to me now that during those years I was always writing down the license numbers of panel trucks, panel trucks circling the block, panel trucks parked across the street, panel trucks idling at the intersection. I put these license numbers in a dressing-table drawer where they could be found by the police when the time came.

That the time would come I never doubted, at least not in the inaccessible places of the mind where I seemed more and more to be living. So many encounters in those years were devoid of any logic save that of the dreamwork. In the big house on Franklin Avenue many people seemed to come and go without relation to what I did. I knew where the sheets and towels were kept but I did not always know who was sleeping in every bed. I had the keys but not the key. I remember taking a 25-mg. Compazine one Easter Sunday and making a large and elaborate lunch for a number of people, many of whom were still around on Monday. I remember walking barefoot all day on the worn hardwood floors of that house and I remember "Do You Wanna Dance" on the record player, "Do You Wanna Dance" and "Visions of Johanna" and a song called "Midnight Confessions." I remember a babysitter telling me that she saw death in my aura. I remember chatting with her about reasons why this might be so, paying her, opening all the French windows and going to sleep in the living room.

It was hard to surprise me in those years. It was hard to even get my attention. I was absorbed in my intellectualization, my obsessive-compulsive devices, my projection, my reaction-formation, my somatization, and in the transcript of the Ferguson trial. A musician I had met a few years before called from a Ramada Inn in Tuscaloosa to tell me how to save myself through Scientology. I had met him once in my life, had talked to him for maybe half an hour about brown rice and the charts, and now he was telling me from Alabama about E-meters, and how I might become a Clear. I received a telephone call from a stranger in Montreal who seemed to want to enlist me in a narcotics operation. "Is it cool to talk on this telephone?" he asked several times. "Big Brother isn't listening?"

I said that I doubted it, although increasingly I did not.

"Because what we're talking about, basically, is applying the Zen philosophy to money and business, dig? And if I say we are going to finance the underground, and if I mention major money, you know what I'm talking about because you know what's going down, right?"

Maybe he was not talking about narcotics. Maybe he was talking about turning a profit on M-1 rifles: I had stopped looking for the logic in such calls. Someone with whom I had gone to school in Sacramento and had last seen in 1952 turned up at my house in Hollywood in 1968 in the guise of a private detective from West Covina, one of very few licensed women private detectives in the State of California. "They call us Dickless Tracys," she said, idly but definitely fanning out the day's mail on the hall table. "I have a lot of very close friends in law enforcement," she said then. "You might want to meet them." We exchanged promises to keep in touch but never met again: a not atypical encounter of the period. The Sixties were over before it occurred to me that this visit might have been less than entirely social.

3

It was six, seven o'clock of an early spring evening in 1968 and I was sitting on the cold vinyl floor of a sound studio on Sunset Boulevard, watching a band called The Doors record a rhythm track. On the whole my attention was only minimally engaged by the preoccupations of rock-and-roll bands (I had already heard about acid as a transitional stage and also about the Maharishi and even about Universal Love, and after a while it all sounded like marmalade skies to me), but The Doors were different, The Doors interested me. The Doors seemed unconvinced that love was brotherhood and the Kama Sutra. The Doors' music insisted that love was sex and sex was death and therein lay salvation. The Doors were the Norman Mailers of the Top Forty, missionaries of apocalyptic sex. *Break on through*, their lyrics urged, and *Light my fire*, and:

> *Come on baby, gonna take a little ride*
> *Goin' down by the ocean side*
> *Gonna get real close*
> *Get real tight*
> *Baby gonna drown tonight—*
> *Goin' down, down, down.*

On this evening in 1968 they were gathered together in uneasy symbiosis to make their third album, and the studio was too cold and the lights were too bright and there were masses of wires and banks of the ominous blinking electronic circuitry with which musicians live so easily. There were three of the four Doors. There was a bass player borrowed from a band called Clear Light. There were the producer and the engineer and the road manager and a couple of girls and a Siberian husky named Nikki with one gray eye and one gold. There were paper bags half filled with hard-boiled eggs and chicken livers and cheeseburgers and empty bottles of apple juice and California rosé. There was everything and everybody The Doors needed to cut the rest of this third album except one thing, the fourth Door, the lead singer, Jim Morrison, a 24-year-old graduate of U.C.L.A. who wore black vinyl pants and no underwear and tended to suggest some range of the possible just beyond a suicide pact. It was Morrison who had described The Doors as "erotic politicians." It was Morrison who had defined the group's interests as "anything about revolt, disorder, chaos, about activity that appears to have no meaning." It was Morrison who got arrested in Miami in December of 1967 for giving an "indecent" performance. It was Morrison who wrote most of The Doors' lyrics, the peculiar character of which was to reflect either an ambiguous paranoia or a quite unambiguous insistence upon the love-death as the ultimate high. And it was Morrison who was missing. It was Ray Manzarek and Robby Krieger and John Densmore who made The Doors sound the way they sounded, and maybe it was Manzarek and Krieger and Densmore who made seventeen out of twenty interviewees on *American Bandstand* prefer The Doors over all other bands, but it was Morrison who got up there in his black vinyl pants with no underwear and projected the idea, and it was Morrison they were waiting for now.

"Hey listen," the engineer said. "I was listening to an FM station on the way over here, they played three Doors songs, first they played 'Back Door Man' and then 'Love Me Two Times' and 'Light My Fire.'"

"I heard it," Densmore muttered. "I heard it."

"So what's wrong with somebody playing three of your songs?"

"This cat dedicates it to his family."

"Yeah? To his family?"

"To his family. Really crass."

Ray Manzarek was hunched over a Gibson keyboard. "You think *Morrison's* going to come back?" he asked to no one in particular.

No one answered.

"So we can do some *vocals?*" Manzarek said.

The producer was working with the tape of the rhythm track they had just recorded. "I hope so," he said without looking up.

"Yeah," Manzarek said. "So do I."

My leg had gone to sleep, but I did not stand up; unspecific tensions seemed to be rendering everyone in the room catatonic. The producer played back the rhythm track. The engineer said that he wanted to do his deep-breathing exercises. Manzarek ate a hard-boiled egg. "Tennyson made a mantra out of his own name," he said to the engineer. "I don't know if he said 'Tennyson Tennyson Tennyson' or 'Alfred Alfred Alfred' or 'Alfred Lord Tennyson,' but anyway, he did it. Maybe he just said 'Lord Lord Lord.'"

"Groovy," the Clear Light bass player said. He was an amiable enthusiast, not at all a Door in spirit.

"I wonder what Blake said," Manzarek mused. "Too bad *Morrison's* not here. *Morrison* would know."

It was a long while later. Morrison arrived. He had on his black vinyl pants and he sat down on a leather couch in front of the four big blank speakers and he closed his eyes. The curious aspect of Morrison's arrival was this: no one acknowledged it. Robby

Krieger continued working out a guitar passage. John Densmore tuned his drums. Manzarek sat at the control console and twirled a corkscrew and let a girl rub his shoulders. The girl did not look at Morrison, although he was in her direct line of sight. An hour or so passed, and still no one had spoken to Morrison. Then Morrison spoke to Manzarek. He spoke almost in a whisper, as if he were wresting the words from behind some disabling aphasia.

"It's an hour to West Covina," he said. "I was thinking maybe we should spend the night out there after we play."

Manzarek put down the corkscrew. "Why?" he said.

"Instead of coming back."

Manzarek shrugged. "We were planning to come back."

"Well, I was thinking, we could rehearse out there."

Manzarek said nothing.

"We could get in a rehearsal, there's a Holiday Inn next door."

"We could do that," Manzarek said. "Or we could rehearse Sunday, in town."

"I guess so." Morrison paused. "Will the place be ready to rehearse Sunday?"

Manzarek looked at him for a while. "No," he said then.

I counted the control knobs on the electronic console. There were seventy-six. I was unsure in whose favor the dialogue had been resolved, or if it had been resolved at all. Robby Krieger picked at his guitar, and said that he needed a fuzz box. The producer suggested that he borrow one from the Buffalo Springfield, who were recording in the next studio. Krieger shrugged. Morrison sat down again on the leather couch and leaned back. He lit a match. He studied the flame awhile and then very slowly, very deliberately, lowered it to the fly of his black vinyl pants. Manzarek watched him. The girl who was rubbing Manzarek's shoulders did not look at anyone. There was a sense that no one was going to leave the room, ever. It would be some weeks before The Doors finished recording this album. I did not see it through.

4

Someone once brought Janis Joplin to a party at the house on Franklin Avenue: she had just done a concert and she wanted brandy-and-Benedictine in a water tumbler. Music people never wanted ordinary drinks. They wanted sake, or champagne cocktails, or tequila neat. Spending time with music people was confusing, and required a more fluid and ultimately a more passive approach than I ever acquired. In the first place time was never of the essence: we would have dinner at nine unless we had it at eleven-thirty, or we could order in later. We would go down to U.S.C. to see the Living Theater if the limo came at the very moment when no one had just made a drink or a cigarette or an arrangement to meet Ultra Violet at the Montecito. In any case David Hockney was coming by. In any case Ultra Violet was not at the Montecito. In any case we would go down to U.S.C. and see the Living Theater tonight or we would see the Living Theater another night, in New York, or Prague. First we wanted sushi for twenty, steamed clams, vegetable vindaloo and many rum drinks with gardenias for our hair. First we wanted a table for twelve, fourteen at the most, although there might be six more, or eight more, or eleven more: there would never be one or two more, because music people did not travel in groups of "one" or "two." John and Michelle Phillips, on their way to the hospital for the birth of their daughter Chynna, had the limo detour into Hollywood in order to pick up a friend, Anne Marshall. This incident, which I often embroider in my mind to include an imaginary second detour, to the Luau for gardenias, exactly describes the music business to me.

5

Around five o'clock on the morning of October 28, 1967, in the desolate district between San Francisco Bay and the Oakland estuary that the Oakland police call Beat 101A, a 25-year-old black militant named Huey P. Newton was stopped and questioned by a white police officer named John Frey, Jr. An hour later Huey Newton was under arrest at Kaiser Hospital in Oakland, where he had gone for emergency treatment of a gunshot wound in his stomach, and a few weeks later he was indicted by the Alameda County Grand Jury on charges of murdering John Frey, wounding another officer, and kidnapping a bystander.

In the spring of 1968, when Huey Newton was awaiting trial, I went to see him in the Alameda County Jail. I suppose I went because I was interested in the alchemy of issues, for an issue is what Huey Newton had by then become. To understand how that had happened you must first consider Huey Newton, who he was. He came from an Oakland family, and for a while he went to Merritt College. In October of 1966 he and a friend named Bobby Seale organized what they called the Black Panther Party. They borrowed the name from the emblem used by the Freedom Party in Lowndes County, Alabama, and, from the beginning, they defined themselves as a revolutionary political group. The Oakland police knew the Panthers, and had a list of the twenty or so Panther cars. I am telling you neither that Huey Newton killed John Frey nor that Huey Newton did not kill John Frey, for in the context of revolutionary politics Huey Newton's guilt or innocence was irrelevant. I am telling you only how Huey Newton happened to be in the Alameda County Jail, and why rallies were held in his name, demonstrations organized whenever he appeared in court. LET'S SPRING HUEY, the buttons read (fifty cents each), and here and there on the courthouse steps, among the Panthers with their berets and sunglasses, the chants would go up:

Get your M-
31.
'Cause baby we gonna
Have some fun.
BOOM BOOM. BOOM BOOM.

"Fight on, brother," a woman would add in the spirit of a good-natured amen. "Bang-bang."

Bullshit bullshit
Can't stand the game
White man's playing.
One way out, one way out.
BOOM BOOM. BOOM BOOM.

In the corridor downstairs in the Alameda County Courthouse there was a crush of lawyers and CBC correspondents and cameramen and people who wanted to "visit Huey."

JOAN DIDION

"Eldridge doesn't mind if I go up," one of the latter said to one of the lawyers.

"If Eldridge doesn't mind, it's all right with me," the lawyer said. "If you've got press credentials."

"I've got kind of dubious credentials."

"I can't take you up then. *Eldridge* has got dubious credentials. One's bad enough. I've got a good working relationship up there, I don't want to blow it." The lawyer turned to a cameraman. "You guys rolling yet?"

On that particular day I was allowed to go up, and a *Los Angeles Times* man, and a radio newscaster. We all signed the police register and sat around a scarred pine table and waited for Huey Newton. "The only thing that's going to free Huey Newton," Rap Brown had said recently at a Panther rally in Oakland Auditorium, "is gunpowder." "Huey Newton laid down his life for us," Stokely Carmichael had said the same night. But of course Huey Newton had not yet laid down his life at all, was just here in the Alameda County Jail waiting to be tried, and I wondered if the direction these rallies were taking ever made him uneasy, ever made him suspect that in many ways he was more useful to the revolution behind bars than on the street. He seemed, when he finally came in, an extremely likable young man, engaging, direct, and I did not get the sense that he had intended to become a political martyr. He smiled at us all and waited for his lawyer, Charles Garry, to set up a tape recorder, and he chatted softly with Eldridge Cleaver, who was then the Black Panthers' Minister of Information. (Huey Newton was still the Minister of Defense.) Eldridge Cleaver wore a black sweater and one gold earring and spoke in an almost inaudible drawl and was allowed to see Huey Newton because he had those "dubious credentials," a press card from *Ramparts*. Actually his interest was in getting "statements" from Huey Newton, "messages" to take outside; in receiving a kind of prophecy to be interpreted as needed.

"We need a statement, Huey, about the ten-point program," Eldridge Cleaver said, "so I'll ask you a question, see, and you answer it ..."

"How's Bobby," Huey Newton asked.

"He's got a hearing on his misdemeanors, see ..."

"I thought he had a felony."

"Well, that's another thing, the felony, he's also got a couple of misdemeanors …"

Once Charles Garry had set up the tape recorder Huey Newton stopped chatting and started lecturing, almost without pause. He talked, running the words together because he had said them so many times before, about "the American capitalistic-materialistic system" and "so-called free enterprise" and "the fight for the liberation of black people throughout the world." Every now and then Eldridge Cleaver would signal Huey Newton and say something like, "There are a lot of people interested in the Executive Mandate Number Three you've issued to the Black Panther Party, Huey. Care to comment?"

And Huey Newton would comment. "Yes. Mandate Number Three is this demand from the Black Panther Party speaking for the black community. Within the Mandate we admonish the racist police force …" I kept wishing that he would talk about himself, hoping to break through the wall of rhetoric, but he seemed to be one of those autodidacts for whom all things specific and personal present themselves as mine fields to be avoided even at the cost of coherence, for whom safety lies in generalization. The newspaperman, the radio man, they tried:

Q. *Tell us something about yourself, Huey, I mean your life before the Panthers.*

A. *Before the Black Panther Party my life was very similar to that of most black people in this country.*

Q. *Well, your family, some incidents you remember, the influences that shaped you—*

A. *Living in America shaped me.*

Q. *Well, yes, but more specifically—*

A. *It reminds me of a quote from James Baldwin: "To be black and conscious in America is to be in a constant state of rage."*

"To be black and conscious in America is to be in a constant state of rage," Eldridge Cleaver wrote in large letters on a pad of paper, and then he added: *"Huey P. Newton quoting James Baldwin."* I could see it emblazoned above the speakers' platform at a rally, imprinted on the letterhead of an ad hoc committee still unborn. As a matter of fact almost everything Huey Newton said had the ring of being a "quotation," a "pronouncement" to be employed when the need arose. I had heard Huey P. Newton

On Racism ("The Black Panther Party is against racism"), Huey P. Newton On Cultural Nationalism ("The Black Panther Party believes that the only culture worth holding on to is revolutionary culture"), Huey P. Newton On White Radicalism, On Police Occupation of the Ghetto, On the European Versus the African. "The European started to be sick when he denied his sexual nature," Huey Newton said, and Charles Garry interrupted then, bringing it back to first principles. "Isn't it true, though, Huey," he said, "that racism got its start for *economic* reasons?"

This weird interlocution seemed to take on a life of its own. The small room was hot and the fluorescent light hurt my eyes and I still did not know to what extent Huey Newton understood the nature of the role in which he was cast. As it happened I had always appreciated the logic of the Panther position, based as it was on the proposition that political power began at the end of the barrel of a gun (exactly what gun had even been specified, in an early memorandum from Huey P. Newton: "*Army .45; carbine; 12-gauge Magnum shotgun with 18″ barrel, preferably the brand of High Standard; M-16; .357 Magnum pistols; P-38*"), and I could appreciate as well the particular beauty in Huey Newton as "issue." In the politics of revolution everyone was expendable, but I doubted that Huey Newton's political sophistication extended to seeing himself that way: the value of a Scottsboro case is easier to see if you are not yourself the Scottsboro boy. "Is there anything else you want to ask Huey?" Charles Garry asked. There did not seem to be. The lawyer adjusted his tape recorder. "I've had a request, Huey," he said, "from a high-school student, a reporter on his school paper, and he wanted a statement from you, and he's going to call me tonight. Care to give me a message for him?"

Huey Newton regarded the microphone. There was a moment in which he seemed not to remember the name of the play, and then he brightened. "I would like to point out," he said, his voice gaining volume as the memory disks clicked, *high school, student, youth, message to youth*, "that America is becoming a very young nation …"

I heard a moaning and a groaning, and I went over and it was— this Negro fellow was there. He had been shot in the stomach and

*at the time he didn't appear in any acute distress and so I said I'd
see, and I asked him if he was a Kaiser, if he belonged to Kaiser,
and he said, "Yes, yes. Get a doctor. Can't you see I'm bleeding?
I've been shot. Now get someone out here." And I asked him
if he had his Kaiser card and he got upset at this and he said,
"Come on, get a doctor out here, I've been shot." I said, "I see
this, but you're not in any acute distress." ... So I told him we'd
have to check to make sure he was a member.... And this kind
of upset him more and he called me a few nasty names and said,
"Now get a doctor out here right now, I've been shot and I'm
bleeding." And he took his coat off and his shirt and he threw
it on the desk there and he said, "Can't you see all this blood?"
And I said, "I see it." And it wasn't that much, and so I said,
"Well, you'll have to sign our admission sheet before you can be
seen by a doctor." And he said, "I'm not signing anything." And
I said, "You cannot be seen by a doctor unless you sign the admission sheet," and he said, "I don't have to sign anything" and a
few more choice words ...*

This is an excerpt from the testimony before the Alameda
County Grand Jury of Corrine Leonard, the nurse in charge of
the Kaiser Foundation Hospital emergency room in Oakland at
5:30 A.M. on October 28, 1967. The "Negro fellow" was of course
Huey Newton, wounded that morning during the gunfire which
killed John Frey. For a long time I kept a copy of this testimony
pinned to my office wall, on the theory that it illustrated a collision
of cultures, a classic instance of an historical outsider confronting
the established order at its most petty and impenetrable level. This
theory was shattered when I learned that Huey Newton was in
fact an enrolled member of the Kaiser Foundation Health Plan,
i.e., in Nurse Leonard's words, "a Kaiser."

6

One morning in 1968 I went to see Eldridge Cleaver in the
San Francisco apartment he then shared with his wife, Kathleen.
To be admitted to this apartment it was necessary to ring first and
then stand in the middle of Oak Street, at a place which could be
observed clearly from the Cleavers' apartment. After this scrutiny
the visitor was, or was not, buzzed in. I was, and I climbed the

stairs to find Kathleen Cleaver in the kitchen frying sausage and Eldridge Cleaver in the living room listening to a John Coltrane record and a number of other people all over the apartment, people everywhere, people standing in doorways and people moving around in one another's peripheral vision and people making and taking telephone calls. "When can you move on that?" I would hear in the background, and "You can't bribe me with a dinner, man, those *Guardian* dinners are all Old Left, like a wake." Most of these other people were members of the Black Panther Party, but one of them, in the living room, was Eldridge Cleaver's parole officer. It seems to me that I stayed about an hour. It seems to me that the three of us—Eldridge Cleaver, his parole officer and I—mainly discussed the commercial prospects of *Soul on Ice*, which, it happened, was being published that day. We discussed the advance ($5,000). We discussed the size of the first printing (10,000 copies). We discussed the advertising budget and we discussed the bookstores in which copies were or were not available. It was a not unusual discussion between writers, with the difference that one of the writers had his parole officer there and the other had stood out on Oak Street and been visually frisked before coming inside.

7

To Pack and Wear:

2 *skirts*
2 *jerseys or leotards*
1 *pullover sweater*
2 *pair shoes*
stockings
bra
nightgown, robe, slippers
cigarettes
bourbon
bag with:
    shampoo
    toothbrush and paste
    Basis soap

> *razor, deodorant*
> *aspirin, prescriptions, Tampax*
> *face cream, powder, baby oil*

To Carry:

> *mohair throw*
> *typewriter*
> *2 legal pads and pens*
> *files*
> *house key*

This is a list which was taped inside my closet door in Hollywood during those years when I was reporting more or less steadily. The list enabled me to pack, without thinking, for any piece I was likely to do. Notice the deliberate anonymity of costume: in a skirt, a leotard, *and stockings*, I could pass on either side of the culture. Notice the mohair throw for trunk-line flights (i.e., no blankets) and for the motel room in which the air conditioning could not be turned off. Notice the bourbon for the same motel room. Notice the typewriter for the airport, coming home: the idea was to turn in the Hertz car, check in, find an empty bench, and start typing the day's notes.

It should be clear that this was a list made by someone who prized control, yearned after momentum, someone determined to play her role as if she had the script, heard her cues, knew the narrative. There is on this list one significant omission, one article I needed and never had: a watch. I needed a watch not during the day, when I could turn on the car radio or ask someone, but at night, in the motel. Quite often I would ask the desk for the time every half hour or so, until finally, embarrassed to ask again, I would call Los Angeles and ask my husband. In other words I had skirts, jerseys, leotards, pullover sweater, shoes, stockings, bra, nightgown, robe, slippers, cigarettes, bourbon, shampoo, toothbrush and paste, Basis soap, razor, deodorant, aspirin, prescriptions, Tampax, face cream, powder, baby oil, mohair throw, typewriter, legal pads, pens, files and a house key, but I didn't know what time it was. This may be a parable, either of my life as a reporter during this period or of the period itself.

8

Driving a budget Rent-A-Car between Sacramento and San Francisco one rainy morning in November of 1968 I kept the radio on very loud. On this occasion I kept the radio on very loud not to find out what time it was but in an effort to erase six words from my mind, six words which had no significance for me but which seemed that year to signal the onset of anxiety or fright. The words, a line from Ezra Pound's "In a Station of the Metro," were these: *Petals on a wet black bough.* The radio played "Wichita Lineman" and "I Heard It Through the Grapevine." *Petals on a wet black bough.* Somewhere between the Yolo Causeway and Vallejo it occurred to me that during the course of any given week I met too many people who spoke favorably about bombing power stations. Somewhere between the Yolo Causeway and Vallejo it also occurred to me that the fright on this particular morning was going to present itself as an inability to drive this Budget Rent-A-Car across the Carquinas Bridge. *The Wichita Lineman was still on the line.* I closed my eyes and drove across the Carquinas Bridge, because I had appointments, because I was working, because I had promised to watch the revolution being made at San Francisco State College and because there was no place in Vallejo to turn in a Budget Rent-A-Car and because nothing on my mind was in the script as I remembered it.

9

At San Francisco State College on that particular morning the wind was blowing the cold rain in squalls across the muddied lawns and against the lighted windows of empty classrooms. In the days before there had been fires set and classes invaded and finally a confrontation with the San Francisco Police Tactical Unit, and in the weeks to come the campus would become what many people on it were pleased to call "a battlefield." The police and the Mace and the noon arrests would become the routine of life on the campus, and every night the combatants would review their day on television: the waves of students advancing, the commotion at the edge of the frame, the riot sticks flashing, the instant of jerky camera that served to suggest at what risk the film was obtained; then a cut to the weather map. In the beginning there had been the necessary "issue," the suspension of a 22-year-old instructor who happened as well to be Minister of Education for the Black Panther Party, but that issue, like most, had soon ceased to be the point in the minds of even the most dense participants. Disorder was its own point.

I had never before been on a campus in disorder, had missed even Berkeley and Columbia, and I suppose I went to San Francisco State expecting something other than what I found there. In some not at all trivial sense, the set was wrong. The very architecture of California state colleges tends to deny radical notions, to reflect instead a modest and hopeful vision of progressive welfare bureaucracy, and as I walked across the campus that day and on later days the entire San Francisco State dilemma— the gradual politicization, the "issues" here and there, the obligatory "Fifteen Demands," the continual arousal of the police and the outraged citizenry—seemed increasingly off-key, an instance of the *enfants terribles* and the Board of Trustees unconsciously collaborating on a wishful fantasy (Revolution on Campus) and playing it out in time for the six o'clock news. "Adjet-prop committee meeting in the Redwood Room," read a scrawled note on the cafeteria door one morning; only someone who needed very badly to be alarmed could respond with force to a guerrilla band that not only announced its meetings on the enemy's bulletin board but seemed innocent of the spelling, and so the meaning, of the words it used. "Hitler Hayakawa," some of the faculty had begun calling S. I. Hayakawa, the semanticist who had become the college's third president in a year and had incurred considerable displeasure by trying to keep the campus open. "*Eichmann*," Kay Boyle had screamed at him at a rally. In just such broad strokes was the picture being painted in the fall of 1968 on the pastel campus at San Francisco State.

The place simply never seemed serious. The headlines were dark that first day, the college had been closed "indefinitely," both Ronald Reagan and Jesse Unruh were threatening reprisals; still, the climate inside the Administration Building was that of a musical comedy about college life. "No *chance* we'll be open tomorrow," secretaries informed callers. "Go skiing, have a good time." Striking black militants dropped in to chat with the deans; striking white radicals exchanged gossip in the corridors. "No interviews, no press," announced a student strike leader who happened into a dean's office where I was sitting; in the next moment he was piqued because no one had told him that a Huntley-Brinkley camera crew was on campus. "We can still plug into that," the dean said soothingly. Everyone seemed joined in a rather festive camaraderie, a shared jargon, a shared sense of moment: the future was no longer arduous and indefinite but immediate and programmatic, aglow with the prospect of problems to be "addressed," plans to be "implemented." It was agreed all around that the confrontations could be "a very healthy development," that maybe it took a shutdown "to get something done." The mood, like the architecture, was 1948 functional, a model of pragmatic optimism.

Perhaps Evelyn Waugh could have gotten it down exactly right: Waugh was good at scenes of industrious self-delusion, scenes of people absorbed in odd games. Here at San Francisco State only the black militants could be construed as serious: they were at any rate picking the games, dictating the rules, and taking what they could from what seemed for everyone else just an amiable evasion of routine, of institutional anxiety, of the tedium of the academic calendar. Meanwhile the administrators could talk about programs. Meanwhile the white radicals could see themselves, on an investment of virtually nothing, as urban guerrillas. It was working out well for everyone, this game at San Francisco State, and its peculiar virtues had never been so clear to me as they became one afternoon when I sat in on a meeting of fifty or sixty SDS members. They had called a press conference for later that day, and now they were discussing "just what the format of the press conference should be."

"This has to be on our terms," someone warned. "Because they'll ask very leading questions, they'll ask *questions*."

"Make them submit any questions in writing," someone else suggested. "The Black Student Union does that very successfully, then they just don't answer anything they don't want to answer."

"That's it, don't fall into their trap."

"Something we should stress at this press conference is *who owns the media*."

"You don't think it's common knowledge that the papers represent corporate interests?" a realist among them interjected doubtfully.

"I don't think it's *understood*."

Two hours and several dozen hand votes later, the group had selected four members to tell the press who owned the media, had decided to appear *en masse* at an opposition press conference, and had debated various slogans for the next day's demonstration. "Let's see, first we have 'Hearst Tells It Like It Ain't,' then 'Stop Press Distortion'—that's the one there was some political controversy about...."

And, before they broke up, they had listened to a student who had driven up for the day from the College of San Mateo, a junior college down the peninsula from San Francisco. "I came up here today with some Third World students to tell you that we're with you, and we hope you'll be with *us* when we try to pull off a strike next week, because we're really into it, we carry our motorcycle helmets all the time, can't think, can't go to class."

He had paused. He was a nice-looking boy, and fired with his task. I considered the tender melancholy of life in San Mateo, which is one of the richest counties per capita in the United States of America, and I considered whether or not the Wichita Lineman and the petals on the wet black bough represented the aimlessness of the bourgeoisie, and I considered the illusion of aim to be gained by holding a press conference, the only problem with press conferences being that the press asked questions. "I'm here to tell you that at College of San Mateo we're living like *revolutionaries*," the boy said then.

10

We put "Lay Lady Lay" on the record player, and "Suzanne." We went down to Melrose Avenue to see the Flying Burritos. There was a jasmine vine grown over the verandah of the big house on Franklin Avenue, and in the evenings the smell of jasmine came in through all the open doors and windows. I made bouillabaisse for people who did not eat meat. I imagined that my own life was simple and sweet, and sometimes it was, but there were odd things going around town. There were rumors. There were stories. Everything was unmentionable but nothing was unimaginable. This mystical flirtation with the idea of "sin"—this sense that it was possible to go "too far," and that many people were doing it—was very much with us in Los Angeles in 1968 and 1969.

A demented and seductive vortical tension was building in the community. The jitters were setting in. I recall a time when the dogs barked every night and the moon was always full. On August 9, 1969, I was sitting in the shallow end of my sister-in-law's swimming pool in Beverly Hills when she received a telephone call from a friend who had just heard about the murders at Sharon Tate Polanski's house on Cielo Drive. The phone rang many times during the next hour. These early reports were garbled and contradictory. One caller would say hoods, the next would say chains. There were twenty dead, no, twelve, ten, eighteen. Black masses were imagined, and bad trips blamed. I remember all of the day's misinformation very clearly, and I also remember this, and wish I did not: *I remember that no one was surprised.*

II

When I first met Linda Kasabian in the summer of 1970 she was wearing her hair parted neatly in the middle, no makeup, Elizabeth Arden "Blue Grass" perfume, and the unpressed blue uniform issued to inmates at the Sybil Brand Institute for Women in Los Angeles. She was at Sybil Brand in protective custody, waiting out the time until she could testify about the murders of Sharon Tate Polanski, Abigail Folger, Jay Sebring, Voytek Frykowski, Steven Parent, and Rosemary and Leno LaBianca, and, with her lawyer, Gary Fleischman, I spent a number of evenings talking to her there. Of these evenings I remember mainly my dread at entering the prison, at leaving for even an hour the infinite possibilities I suddenly perceived in the summer twilight. I remember driving downtown on the Hollywood Freeway in Gary Fleischman's Cadillac convertible with the top down. I remember watching a rabbit graze on the grass by the gate as Gary Fleischman signed the prison register. Each of the half-dozen doors that locked behind us as we entered Sybil Brand was a little death, and I would emerge after the interview like Persephone from the underworld, euphoric, elated. Once home I would have two drinks and make myself a hamburger and eat it ravenously.

"Dig it," Gary Fleischman was always saying. One night when we were driving back to Hollywood from Sybil Brand in the Cadillac convertible with the top down he demanded that I tell him the population of India. I said that I did not know the population of India. "Take a guess," he prompted. I made a guess, absurdly low, and he was disgusted. He had asked the same question of his niece ("a college girl"), of Linda, and now of me, and none of us had known. It seemed to confirm some idea he had of women, their essential ineducability, their similarity under the skin. Gary Fleischman was someone of a type I met only rarely, a comic realist in a porkpie hat, a business traveler on the far frontiers of the period, a man who knew his way around the courthouse and Sybil Brand and remained cheerful, even jaunty, in the face of the awesome and impenetrable mystery at the center of what he called "the case." In fact we never talked about "the case," and referred to its central events only as "Cielo Drive" and "LaBianca." We talked instead about Linda's childhood pastimes and disappointments, her high-school romances and her concern for her children. This particular juxtaposition of the spoken and the unspeakable was eerie and unsettling, and made my notebook a litany of little ironies so obvious as to be of interest only to dedicated absurdists. An example: Linda dreamed of opening a combination restaurant-boutique and pet shop.

12

Certain organic disorders of the central nervous system are characterized by periodic remissions, the apparent complete recovery of the afflicted nerves. What happens appears to be this: as the lining of a nerve becomes inflamed and hardens into scar tissue, thereby blocking the passage of neural impulses, the nervous system gradually changes its circuitry, finds other, unaffected nerves to carry the same messages. During the years when I found it necessary to revise the circuitry of my mind I discovered that I was no longer interested in whether the woman on the ledge outside the window on the sixteenth floor jumped or did not jump, or in why. I was interested only in the picture of her in my mind: her hair incandescent in the floodlights, her bare toes curled inward on the stone ledge.

In this light all narrative was sentimental. In this light all connections were equally meaningful, and equally senseless. Try these: on the morning of John Kennedy's death in 1963 I was buying, at Ransohoff's in San Francisco, a short silk dress in which to be married. A few years later this dress of mine was ruined when, at a dinner party in Bel-Air, Roman Polanski accidentally spilled a glass of red wine on it. Sharon Tate was also a guest at this party, although she and Roman Polanski were not yet married. On July 27, 1970, I went to the Magnin-Hi Shop on the third floor of I. Magnin in Beverly Hills and picked out, at Linda Kasabian's request, the dress in which she began her testimony about the murders at Sharon Tate Polanski's house on Cielo Drive. "Size 9 Petite," her instructions read. "Mini but not extremely mini. In velvet if possible. Emerald green or gold. Or: A Mexican peasant-style dress, smocked or embroidered." She needed a dress that morning because the district attorney, Vincent Bugliosi, had expressed doubts about the dress she had planned to wear, a long white homespun shift. "Long is for evening," he had advised Linda. Long was for evening and white was for brides. At her own wedding in 1965 Linda Kasabian had worn a white brocade suit. Time passed, times changed. Everything was to teach us something. At 11:20 on that July morning in 1970 I delivered the dress in which she would testify to Gary Fleischman, who was waiting in front of his office on Rodeo Drive in Beverly Hills. He was wearing his porkpie hat and he was standing with Linda's second husband, Bob Kasabian, and their friend Charlie Melton, both of whom were wearing long white robes. Long was for Bob and Charlie, the dress in the I. Magnin box was for Linda. The three of them took the I. Magnin box and got into Gary Fleischman's Cadillac convertible with the top down and drove off in the sunlight toward the freeway downtown, waving back at me. I believe this to be an authentically senseless chain of correspondences, but in the jingle-jangle morning of that summer it made as much sense as anything else did.

13

I recall a conversation I had in 1970 with the manager of a motel in which I was staying near Pendleton, Oregon. I had been doing a piece for *Life* about the storage of VX and GB nerve gas at an Army arsenal in Umatilla County, and now I was done, and trying to check out of the motel. During the course of checking out I was asked this question by the manager, who was a Mormon: *If you can't believe you're going to heaven in your own body and on a first-name basis with all the members of your family, then what's the point of dying?* At that time I believed that my basic affective controls were no longer intact, but now I present this to you as a more cogent question than it might at first appear, a kind of koan of the period.

14

Once I had a rib broken, and during the few months that it was painful to turn in bed or raise my arms in a swimming pool I had, for the first time, a sharp apprehension of what it would be like to be old. Later I forgot. At some point during the years I am talking about here, after a series of periodic visual disturbances, three electroencephalograms, two complete sets of skull and neck X-rays, one five-hour glucose tolerance test, two electromyelograms, a battery of chemical tests and consultations with two ophthalmologists, one internist and three neurologists, I was told that the disorder was not really in my eyes, but in my central nervous system. I might or might not experience symptoms of neural damage all my life. These symptoms, which might or might not appear, might or might not involve my eyes. They might or might not involve my arms or legs, they might or might not be disabling. Their effects might be lessened by cortisone injections, or they might not. It could not be predicted. The condition had a name, the kind of name usually associated with telethons, but the name meant nothing and the neurologist did not like to use it. The name was multiple sclerosis, but the name had no meaning. This was, the neurologist said, an exclusionary diagnosis, and meant nothing.

I had, at this time, a sharp apprehension not of what it was like to be old but of what it was like to open the door to the stranger and find that the stranger did indeed have the knife. In a few lines of dialogue in a neurologist's office in Beverly Hills, the improbable had become the probable, the norm: things which happened only to other people could in fact happen to me. I could be struck by lightning, could dare to eat a peach and be poisoned by the cyanide in the stone. The startling fact was this: my body was offering a precise physiological equivalent to what had been going on in my mind. "Lead a simple life," the neurologist advised. "Not that it makes any difference we know about." In other words it was another story without a narrative.

Many people I know in Los Angeles believe that the Sixties ended abruptly on August 9, 1969, ended at the exact moment when word of the murders on Cielo Drive traveled like brushfire through the community, and in a sense this is true. The tension broke that day. The paranoia was fulfilled. In another sense the Sixties did not truly end for me until January of 1971, when I left the house on Franklin Avenue and moved to a house on the sea. This particular house on the sea had itself been very much a part of the Sixties, and for some months after we took possession I would come across souvenirs of that period in its history—a piece of Scientology literature beneath a drawer lining, a copy of *Stranger in a Strange Land* stuck deep on a closet shelf—but after a while we did some construction, and between the power saws and the sea wind the place got exorcised.

I have known, since then, very little about the movements of the people who seemed to me emblematic of those years. I know of course that Eldridge Cleaver went to Algeria and came home an entrepreneur. I know that Jim Morrison died in Paris. I know that Linda Kasabian fled in search of the pastoral to New Hampshire, where I once visited her; she also visited me in New York, and we took our children on the Staten Island Ferry to see the Statue of Liberty. I also know that in 1975 Paul Ferguson, while serving a life sentence for the murder of Ramon Novarro, won first prize in a PEN fiction contest and announced plans to "continue my writing." Writing had helped him, he said, to "reflect on experience and see what it means." Quite often I reflect on the big house in Hollywood, on "Midnight Confessions" and on Ramon Novarro and on the fact that Roman Polanski and I are godparents to the same child, but writing has not yet helped me to see what it means.

1968–78

II
CALIFORNIA REPUBLIC

IT IS A curious and arrogantly secular monument, Grace Episcopal Cathedral in San Francisco, and it imposes its tone on everything around it. It stands directly upon the symbolic nexus of all old California money and power, Nob Hill. Its big rose window glows at night and dominates certain views from the Mark Hopkins and the Fairmont, as well as from Randolph and Catherine Hearst's apartment on California Street. In a city dedicated to the illusion that all human endeavor tends mystically west, toward the Pacific, Grace Cathedral faces resolutely east, toward the Pacific Union Club. As a child I was advised by my grandmother that Grace was "unfinished," and always would be, which was its point. In the years after World War I my mother had put pennies for Grace in her mite box but Grace would never be finished. In the years after World War II I would put pennies for Grace in my mite box but Grace would never be finished. In 1964 James Albert Pike, who had come home from St. John the Divine in New York and *The Dean Pike Show* on ABC to be Bishop of California, raised three million dollars, installed images of Albert Einstein, Thurgood Marshall and John Glenn in the clerestory windows, and, in the name of God (James Albert Pike had by then streamlined the Trinity, eliminating the Son and the Holy Ghost), pronounced Grace "finished." This came to my attention as an odd and unsettling development, an extreme missing of the point—at least as I had understood the point in my childhood—and it engraved James Albert Pike on my consciousness more indelibly than any of his previous moves.

What was one to make of him. Five years after he finished Grace, James Albert Pike left the Episcopal Church altogether, detailing his pique in the pages of *Look*, and drove into the Jordanian desert in a white Ford Cortina rented from Avis. He went with his former student and bride of nine months, Diane. Later she would say that they wanted to experience the wilderness as Jesus had. They equipped themselves for this mission with an Avis map and two bottles of Coca-Cola. The young Mrs. Pike got out alive. Five days after James Albert Pike's body was retrieved from a canyon near the Dead Sea a Solemn Requiem Mass was offered for him at the cathedral his own hubris had finished in San Francisco. Outside on the Grace steps the cameras watched the Black Panthers demonstrating to free Bobby Seale. Inside the Grace nave Diane Kennedy Pike and her two predecessors, Jane Alvies Pike and Esther Yanovsky Pike, watched the cameras and one another.

That was 1969. For some years afterward I could make nothing at all of this peculiar and strikingly "now" story, so vast and atavistic was my irritation with the kind of man my grandmother would have called "just a damn old fool," the kind of man who would go into the desert with the sappy Diane and two bottles of Coca-Cola, but I see now that Diane and the Coca-Cola are precisely the details which lift the narrative into apologue. James Albert Pike has been on my mind quite a bit these past few weeks, ever since I read a biography of him by William Stringfellow and Anthony Towne, *The Death and Life of Bishop Pike*, an adoring but instructive volume from which there emerges the shadow of a great literary character, a literary character in the sense that Howard Hughes and Whittaker Chambers were literary characters, a character so ambiguous and driven and revealing of his time and place that his gravestone in the Protestant Cemetery in Jaffa might well have read only JAMES PIKE, AMERICAN.

Consider his beginnings. He was the only child of an ambitious mother and an ailing father who moved from Kentucky a few years before his birth in 1913 to homestead forty acres of mesquite in Oklahoma. There had been for a while a retreat to a one-room shack in Alamogordo, New Mexico, there had been always the will of the mother to improve the family's prospects. She taught school. She played piano with a dance band, she played piano in a silent-movie theater. She raised her baby James a Catholic and she entered him in the Better Babies Contest at the Oklahoma State Fair and he took first prize, two years running. "I thought you would like that," she told his biographers almost sixty years later. "He started out a winner."

He also started out dressing paper dolls in priests' vestments. The mother appears to have been a woman of extreme determination. Her husband died when James was two. Six years later the widow moved to Los Angeles, where she devoted herself to maintaining a world in which nothing "would change James' life or thwart him in any way," a mode of upbringing which would show in the son's face and manner all his life. "Needless to say this has all been a bit tedious for me to relive," he complained when the question of his first divorce and remarriage seemed to stand between him and election as Bishop of California; his biography is a panoply of surprised petulance in the face of other people's attempts to "thwart" him by bringing up an old marriage or divorce or some other "long-dead aspect of the past."

In Los Angeles there was Hollywood High, there was Mass every morning at Blessed Sacrament on Sunset Boulevard. After Hollywood High there was college with the Jesuits, at Santa Clara, at least until James repudiated the Catholic Church and convinced his mother that she should do the same. He was eighteen at the time, but it was characteristic of both mother and son to have taken this adolescent "repudiation" quite gravely: they give the sense of having had no anchor but each other, and to have reinvented their moorings every day. After Santa Clara, for the freshly invented agnostic, there was U.C.L.A., then U.S.C., and finally the leap east. Back East. Yale Law. A job in Washington with the Securities and Exchange Commission. "You have to understand that he was very lonely in Washington," his mother said after his death. "He really wanted to come home. I wish he had." And yet it must have seemed to such a western child that he had at last met the "real" world, the "great" world, the world to beat. The world in which, as the young man who started out a winner soon discovered and wrote to his mother, "practically every churchgoer you meet in our level of society is Episcopalian, and an R.C. or straight Protestant is as rare as hen's teeth."

One thinks of Gatsby, coming up against the East. One also thinks of Tom Buchanan, and his vast carelessness. (Some 25 years later, in Santa Barbara, when the Bishop of California's mistress swallowed 55 sleeping pills, he appears to have moved her from his apartment into her own before calling an ambulance, and to have obscured certain evidence before she died.) One even thinks of Dick Diver, who also started out a winner, and who tried to embrace the essence of the American continent in Nicole as James Albert Pike would now try to embrace it in the Episcopal Church. "*Practically every churchgoer you meet in our level of society is Episcopalian.*"

JOAN DIDION

It is an American Adventure of Barry Lyndon, this Westerner going East to seize his future, equipped with a mother's love and with what passed in the makeshift moorage from which he came as a passion for knowledge. As evidence of this passion his third wife, Diane, would repeat this curious story: he "had read both the dictionary and the phone book from cover to cover by the time he was five, and a whole set of the Encyclopaedia Britannica before he was ten." Diane also reports his enthusiasm for the Museum of Man in Paris, which seemed to him to offer, in the hour he spent there, "a complete education," the "entire history of the human race … in summary form."

In summary form. One gets a sense of the kind of mindless fervor that a wife less rapt than Diane might find unhinging. In the late thirties, as Communion was about to be served at the first Christmas Mass of James Albert Pike's new career as an Episcopalian, his first wife, Jane, another transplanted Californian, is reported to have jumped up and run screaming from the church. There would have been nothing in the phone book to cover that, or in the Britannica either. Later he invented an ecclesiastical annulment to cover his divorce from Jane, although no such annulment was actually granted. "In his mind," his biographers explain, "the marriage was not merely a mistake, but a nullity in the inception." In his mind. He needed to believe in the annulment because he wanted to be Bishop of California. "At heart he was a Californian," a friend said. "He had grown up with the idea that San Francisco was it…he was obsessed with the idea of being Bishop of California. Nothing in heaven or hell could have stopped him." In his mind. "Tom and Gatsby, Daisy and Jordan and I, were all Westerners," as Nick Carraway said, "and perhaps we possessed some deficiency in common which made us subtly unadaptable to Eastern life."

In his mind. I recall standing in St. Thomas Church in New York one Monday morning in 1964 debating whether or not to steal a book by James Albert Pike, a pastoral tract called *If You Marry Outside Your Faith*. I had only a twenty-dollar bill and could not afford to leave it in the box but I wanted to read the book more closely, because a few weeks before I had in fact married a

Catholic, which was what Bishop Pike seemed to have in mind. I had not been brought up to think it made much difference what I married, as long as I steered clear of odd sects where they didn't drink at the wedding (my grandmother was an Episcopalian only by frontier chance; her siblings were Catholics but there was no Catholic priest around the year she needed christening), and I was struck dumb by Bishop Pike's position, which appeared to be that I had not only erred but had every moral right and obligation to erase this error by regarding my marriage as null, and any promises I had made as invalid. In other words the way to go was to forget it and start over.

In the end I did not steal *If You Marry Outside Your Faith*, and over the years I came to believe that I had doubtless misread it. After considering its source I am no longer so sure. "Jim never cleaned up after himself," a friend notes, recalling his habit of opening a shirt and letting the cardboards lie where they fell, and this *élan* seems to have applied to more than his laundry. Here was a man who moved through life believing that he was entitled to forget it and start over, to shed women when they became difficult and allegiances when they became tedious and simply *move on*, dismissing those who quibbled as petty and "judgmental" and generally threatened by his superior and more dynamic view of human possibility. That there was an ambivalence and a speciousness about this moral frontiersmanship has not gone unnoticed, but in the rush to call the life "only human" I suspect we are overlooking its real interest, which is as social history. The man was a Michelin to his time and place. At the peak of his career James Albert Pike carried his peace cross (he had put away his pectoral cross for the duration of the Vietnam War, which outlived him) through every charlatanic thicket in American life, from the Center for the Study of Democratic Institutions to the Aspen Institute of Humanistic Studies to Spiritual Frontiers, which was at the time the Ford Foundation of the spirit racket. James Albert Pike was everywhere at the right time. He was in Geneva for *Pacem in Terris*. He was in Baltimore for the trial of the Catonsville Nine, although he had to be briefed on the issue in the car from the airport. He was in the right room at the right time to reach his son, Jim Jr., an apparent suicide on Romilar, via séance. The man kept moving. If death was troubling then start over, and reinvent it as "The Other Side." If faith was troubling then leave the Church, and reinvent it as "The Foundation for Religious Transition."

This sense that the world can be reinvented smells of the Sixties in this country, those years when no one at all seemed to have any memory or mooring, and in a way the Sixties were the years for which James Albert Pike was born. When the man who started out a winner was lying dead in the desert his brother-in-law joined the search party, and prayed for the assistance of God, Jim Jr., and Edgar Cayce. I think I have never heard a more poignant trinity.

1976

HOLY WATER

SOME OF US who live in arid parts of the world think about water with a reverence others might find excessive. The water I will draw tomorrow from my tap in Malibu is today crossing the Mojave Desert from the Colorado River, and I like to think about exactly where that water is. The water I will drink tonight in a restaurant in Hollywood is by now well down the Los Angeles Aqueduct from the Owens River, and I also think about exactly where that water is: I particularly like to imagine it as it cascades down the 45-degree stone steps that aerate Owens water after its airless passage through the mountain pipes and siphons. As it happens my own reverence for water has always taken the form of this constant meditation upon where the water is, of an obsessive interest not in the politics of water but in the waterworks themselves, in the movement of water through aqueducts and siphons and pumps and forebays and afterbays and weirs and drains, in plumbing on the grand scale. I know the data on water projects I will never see. I know the difficulty Kaiser had closing the last two sluiceway gates on the Guri Dam in Venezuela. I keep watch on evaporation behind the Aswan in Egypt. I can put myself to sleep imagining the water dropping a thousand feet into the turbines at Churchill Falls in Labrador. If the Churchill Falls Project fails to materialize, I fall back on waterworks closer at hand—the tailrace at Hoover on the Colorado, the surge tank in the Tehachapi Mountains that receives California Aqueduct water pumped higher than water has ever been pumped before—and finally I replay a morning when I was seventeen years old and caught, in a military-surplus life raft, in the construction of the Nimbus Afterbay Dam on the American River near Sacramento. I remember that at the moment it happened I was trying to open a tin of anchovies with capers. I recall the raft spinning into the narrow chute through which the river had been temporarily diverted. I recall being deliriously happy.

I suppose it was partly the memory of that delirium that led me to visit, one summer morning in Sacramento, the Operations

Control Center for the California State Water Project. Actually so much water is moved around California by so many different agencies that maybe only the movers themselves know on any given day whose water is where, but to get a general picture it is necessary only to remember that Los Angeles moves some of it, San Francisco moves some of it, the Bureau of Reclamation's Central Valley Project moves some of it and the California State Water Project moves most of the rest of it, moves a vast amount of it, moves more water farther than has ever been moved anywhere. They collect this water up in the granite keeps of the Sierra Nevada and they store roughly a trillion gallons of it behind the Oroville Dam and every morning, down at the Project's head-quarters in Sacramento, they decide how much of their water they want to move the next day. They make this morning deci-sion according to supply and demand, which is simple in theory but rather more complicated in practice. In theory each of the Project's five field divisions—the Oroville, the Delta, the San Luis, the San Joaquin and the Southern divisions—places a call to headquarters before nine A.M. and tells the dispatchers how much water is needed by its local water contractors, who have in turn based their morning estimates on orders from growers and other big users. A schedule is made. The gates open and close according to schedule. The water flows south and the deliveries are made.

In practice this requires prodigious coordination, precision, and the best efforts of several human minds and that of a Univac 418. In practice it might be necessary to hold large flows of water for power production, or to flush out encroaching salinity in the Sacramento-San Joaquin Delta, the most ecologically sensitive point on the system. In practice a sudden rain might obviate the need for a delivery when that delivery is already on its way. In practice what is being delivered here is an enormous volume of water, not quarts of milk or spools of thread, and it takes two days to move such a delivery down through Oroville into the Delta, which is the great pooling place for California water and has been for some years alive with electronic sensors and tele-metering equipment and men blocking channels and diverting flows and shoveling fish away from the pumps. It takes perhaps another six days to move this same water down the California Aqueduct from the Delta to the Tehachapi and put it over the hill to Southern California. "Putting some over the hill" is what they say around the Project Operations Control Center when they want to indicate that they are pumping Aqueduct water from the floor of the San Joaquin Valley up and over the Tehachapi Mountains. "Pulling it down" is what they say when they want to indicate that they are lowering a water level somewhere in the system. They can put some over the hill by remote control from this room in Sacramento with its Univac and its big board and its flashing lights. They can pull down a pool in the San Joaquin by remote control from this room in Sacramento with its locked doors and its ringing alarms and its constant print-outs of data from sensors out there in the water itself. From this room in Sacramento the whole system takes on the aspect of a perfect three-billion-dollar hydraulic toy, and in certain ways it is. "LET'S START DRAINING QUAIL AT 12:00" was the 10:51 A.M. entry on the electronically recorded communications log the day I visited the Operations Control Center. "Quail" is a reservoir in Los Angeles County with a gross capacity of 1,636,018,000 gallons. "OK" was the response recorded in the log. I knew at that moment that I had missed the only vocation for which I had any instinctive affinity: I wanted to drain Quail myself.

Not many people I know carry their end of the conversation when I want to talk about water deliveries, even when I stress that these deliveries affect their lives, indirectly, every day. "Indirectly" is not quite enough for most people I know. This morning, however, several people I know were affected not "indirectly" but "directly" by the way the water moves. They had been in New Mexico shooting a picture, one sequence of which required a river deep enough to sink a truck, the kind with a cab and a trailer and fifty or sixty wheels. It so happened that no river near the New Mexico location was running that deep this year. The production was therefore moved today to Needles, California, where the Colorado River normally runs, depending upon releases from Davis Dam, eighteen to twenty-five feet deep. Now. Follow this closely: yesterday we had a freak tropical storm in Southern California, two inches of rain in a normally dry month, and because this rain flooded the fields and provided more irrigation than any grower could possibly want for several days, no water was ordered from Davis Dam.

No orders, no releases.

Supply and demand.

As a result the Colorado was running only seven feet deep past Needles today, Sam Peckinpah's desire for eighteen feet of water in which to sink a truck not being the kind of demand anyone at Davis Dam is geared to meet. The production closed down for the weekend. Shooting will resume Tuesday, providing some grower orders water and the agencies controlling the Colorado release it. Meanwhile many gaffers, best boys, cameramen, assistant directors, script supervisors, stunt drivers and maybe even Sam Peckinpah are waiting out the weekend in Needles, where it is often 110 degrees at five P.M. and hard to get dinner after eight. This is a California parable, but a true one.

I have always wanted a swimming pool, and never had one. When it became generally known a year or so ago that California was suffering severe drought, many people in water-rich parts of the country seemed obscurely gratified, and made frequent reference to Californians having to brick up their swimming pools. In fact a swimming pool requires, once it has been filled and the filter has begun its process of cleaning and recirculating the water, virtually no water, but the symbolic content of swimming pools has always been interesting: a pool is misapprehended as a trapping of affluence, real or pretended, and of a kind of hedonistic attention to the body. Actually a pool is, for many of us in the West, a symbol not of affluence but of order, of control over the uncontrollable. A pool is water, made available and useful, and is, as such, infinitely soothing to the western eye.

It is easy to forget that the only natural force over which we have any control out here is water, and that only recently. In my memory California summers were characterized by the coughing in the pipes that meant the well was dry, and California winters by all-night watches on rivers about to crest, by sandbagging, by dynamite on the levees and flooding on the first floor. Even now the place is not all that hospitable to extensive settlement. As I write a fire has been burning out of control for two weeks in the ranges behind the Big Sur coast. Flash floods last night wiped out all major roads into Imperial County. I noticed this morning a

hairline crack in a living-room tile from last week's earthquake, a
4.4 I never felt. In the part of California where I now live aridity
is the single most prominent feature of the climate, and I am not
pleased to see, this year, cactus spreading wild to the sea. There will
be days this winter when the humidity will drop to ten, seven, four.
Tumbleweed will blow against my house and the sound of the
rattlesnake will be duplicated a hundred times a day by dried bougainvillea drifting in my driveway. The apparent ease of California
life is an illusion, and those who believe the illusion real live here
in only the most temporary way. I know as well as the next person
that there is considerable transcendent value in a river running
wild and undammed, a river running free over granite, but I have
also lived beneath such a river when it was running in flood, and
gone without showers when it was running dry.

"The West begins," Bernard DeVoto wrote, "where the average
annual rainfall drops below twenty inches." This is maybe the
best definition of the West I have ever read, and it goes a long way
toward explaining my own passion for seeing the water under
control, but many people I know persist in looking for psycho-
analytical implications in this passion. As a matter of fact I have
explored, in an amateur way, the more obvious of these implications, and come up with nothing interesting. A certain external
reality remains, and resists interpretation. The West begins where
the average annual rainfall drops below twenty inches. Water is
important to people who do not have it, and the same is true of
control. Some fifteen years ago I tore a poem by Karl Shapiro
from a magazine and pinned it on my kitchen wall. This fragment
of paper is now on the wall of a sixth kitchen, and crumbles a
little whenever I touch it, but I keep it there for the last stanza,
which has for me the power of a prayer:

It is raining in California, a straight rain
Cleaning the heavy oranges on the bough,
Filling the gardens till the gardens flow,
Shining the olives, tiling the gleaming tile,
Waxing the dark camellia leaves more green,
Flooding the daylong valleys like the Nile.

I thought of those lines almost constantly on the morning in Sacramento when I went to visit the California State Water Project Operations Control Center. If I had wanted to drain Quail at 10:51 that morning, I wanted, by early afternoon, to do a great deal more. I wanted to open and close the Clifton Court Forebay intake gate. I wanted to produce some power down at the San Luis Dam. I wanted to pick a pool at random on the Aqueduct and pull it down and then refill it, watching for the hydraulic jump. I wanted to put some water over the hill and I wanted to shut down all flow from the Aqueduct into the Bureau of Reclamation's Cross Valley Canal, just to see how long it would take somebody over at Reclamation to call up and complain. I stayed as long as I could and watched the system work on the big board with the lighted checkpoints. The Delta salinity report was coming in on one of the teletypes behind me. The Delta tidal report was coming in on another. The earthquake board, which has been desensitized to sound its alarm (a beeping tone for Southern California, a high-pitched tone for the north) only for those earthquakes which register at least 3.0 on the Richter Scale, was silent. I had no further business in this room and yet I wanted to stay the day. I wanted to be the one, that day, who was shining the olives, filling the gardens, and flooding the daylong valleys like the Nile. I want it still.

1977

THE NEW OFFICIAL residence for governors of California, unlandscaped, unfurnished, and unoccupied since the day construction stopped in 1975, stands on eleven acres of oaks and olives on a bluff overlooking the American River outside Sacramento. This is the twelve-thousand-square-foot house that Ronald and Nancy Reagan built. This is the sixteen-room house in which Jerry Brown declined to live. This is the vacant house which cost the State of California one-million-four, not including the property, which was purchased in 1969 and donated to the state by such friends of the Reagans as Leonard K. Firestone of Firestone Tire and Rubber and Taft Schreiber of the Music Corporation of America and Holmes Tuttle, the Los Angeles Ford dealer. All day at this empty house three maintenance men try to keep the bulletproof windows clean and the cobwebs swept and the wild grass green and the rattlesnakes down by the river and away from the thirty-five exterior wood and glass doors. All night at this empty house the lights stay on behind the eight-foot chainlink fence and the guard dogs lie at bay and the telephone, when it rings, startles by the fact that it works. "Governor's Residence," the guards answer, their voices laconic, matter-of-fact, quite as if there were some phantom governor to connect. Wild grass grows where the tennis court was to have been. Wild grass grows where the pool and sauna were to have been. The American is the river in which gold was discovered in 1848, and it once ran fast and full past here, but lately there have been upstream dams and dry years. Much of the bed is exposed. The far bank has been dredged and graded. That the river is running low is of no real account, however, since one of the many peculiarities of the new Governor's Residence is that it is so situated as to have no clear view of the river.

It is an altogether curious structure, this one-story one-million-four dream house of Ronald and Nancy Reagan's. Were the house on the market (which it will probably not be, since, at the time it was costing a million-four, local real estate agents

JOAN DIDION

seemed to agree on $300,000 as the top price ever paid for a house in Sacramento County), the words used to describe it would be "open" and "contemporary," although technically it is neither. "Flow" is a word that crops up quite a bit when one is walking through the place, and so is "resemble." The walls "resemble" local adobe, but they are not: they are the same concrete blocks, plastered and painted a rather stale yellowed cream, used in so many supermarkets and housing projects and Coca-Cola bottling plants. The door frames and the exposed beams "resemble" native redwood, but they are not: they are construction-grade lumber of indeterminate quality, stained brown. If anyone ever moves in, the concrete floors will be carpeted, wall to wall. If anyone ever moves in, the thirty-five exterior wood and glass doors, possibly the single distinctive feature in the house, will be, according to plan, "draped." The bathrooms are small and standard. The family bedrooms open directly onto the nonexistent swimming pool, with all its potential for noise and distraction. To one side of the fireplace in the formal living room there is what is known in the trade as a "wet bar," a cabinet for bottles and glasses with a sink and a long vinyl-topped counter. (This vinyl "resembles" slate.) In the entire house there are only enough bookshelves for a set of the World Book and some Books of the Month, plus maybe three Royal Doulton figurines and a back file of *Connoisseur*, but there is $90,000 worth of other teak cabinetry, including the "refreshment center" in the "recreation room." There is that most ubiquitous of all "luxury features," a bidet in the master bathroom. There is one of those kitchens which seem designed exclusively for defrosting by microwave and compacting trash. It is a house built for a family of snackers.

And yet, appliances notwithstanding, it is hard to see where the million-four went. The place has been called, by Jerry Brown, a "Taj Mahal." It has been called a "white elephant," a "resort," a "monument to the colossal ego of our former governor." It is not exactly any of these things. It is simply and rather astonishingly an enlarged version of a very common kind of California tract house, a monument not to colossal ego but to a weird absence of ego, a case study in the architecture of limited possibilities, insistently and malevolently "democratic," flattened out, mediocre and "open" and as devoid of privacy or personal eccentricity as the lobby area in a Ramada Inn. It is the architecture of "background

228

music," decorators, "good taste." I recall once interviewing Nancy Reagan, at a time when her husband was governor and the construction on this house had not yet begun. We drove down to the State Capitol Building that day, and Mrs. Reagan showed me how she had lightened and brightened offices there by replacing the old burnished leather on the walls with the kind of beige burlap then favored in new office buildings. I mention this because it was on my mind as I walked through the empty house on the American River outside Sacramento.

From 1903 until Ronald Reagan, who lived in a rented house in Sacramento while he was governor ($1,200 a month, payable by the state to a group of Reagan's friends), the governors of California lived in a large white Victorian Gothic house at 16th and H Streets in Sacramento. This extremely individual house, three stories and a cupola and the face of Columbia the Gem of the Ocean worked into the molding over every door, was built in 1877 by a Sacramento hardware merchant named Albert Gallatin. The state paid $32,500 for it in 1903 and my father was born in a house a block away in 1908. This part of town has since run to seed and small business, the kind of place where both Squeaky Fromme and Patricia Hearst could and probably did go about their business unnoticed, but the Governor's Mansion, unoccupied and open to the public as State Historical Landmark Number 823, remains Sacramento's premier example of eccentric domestic architecture.

As it happens I used to go there once in a while, when Earl Warren was governor and his daughter Nina was a year ahead of me at C. K. McClatchy Senior High School. Nina was always called "Honey Bear" in the papers and in *Life* magazine but she was called "Nina" at C. K. McClatchy Senior High School and she was called "Nina" (or sometimes "Warren") at weekly meetings of the Mañana Club, a local institution to which we both belonged. I recall being initiated into the Mañana Club one night at the old Governor's Mansion, in a ceremony which involved being blindfolded and standing around Nina's bedroom in a state of high apprehension about secret rites which never materialized. It was the custom for the members to hurl mild insults at

JOAN DIDION

the initiates, and I remember being dumbfounded to hear Nina, by my fourteen-year-old lights the most glamorous and unapproachable fifteen-year-old in America, characterize me as "stuck on herself." There in the Governor's Mansion that night I learned for the first time that my face to the world was not necessarily the face in my mirror. "No smoking on the third floor," everyone kept saying. "Mrs. Warren *said*. No smoking on the third floor *or else*."

Firetrap or not, the old Governor's Mansion was at that time my favorite house in the world, and probably still is. The morning after I was shown the new "Residence" I visited the old "Mansion," took the public tour with a group of perhaps twenty people, none of whom seemed to find it as ideal as I did. "All those stairs," they murmured, as if stairs could no longer be tolerated by human physiology. "All those stairs," and "all that waste space." The old Governor's Mansion does have stairs and waste space, which is precisely why it remains the kind of house in which sixty adolescent girls might gather and never interrupt the real life of the household. The bedrooms are big and private and high-ceilinged and they do not open on the swimming pool and one can imagine reading in one of them, or writing a book, or closing the door and crying until dinner. The bathrooms are big and airy and they do not have bidets but they do have room for hampers, and dressing tables, and chairs on which to sit and read a story to a child in the bathtub. There are hallways wide and narrow, stairs front and back, sewing rooms, ironing rooms, secret rooms. On the gilt mirror in the library there is worked a bust of Shakespeare, a pretty fancy for a hardware merchant in a California farm town in 1877. In the kitchen there is no trash compactor and there is no "island" with the appliances built in but there are two pantries, and a nice old table with a marble top for rolling out pastry and making divinity fudge and chocolate leaves. The morning I took the tour our guide asked if anyone could think why the old table had a marble top. There were a dozen or so other women in the group, each of an age to have cooked unnumbered meals, but not one of them could think of a single use for a slab of marble in the kitchen. It occurred to me that we had finally evolved a society in which knowledge of a pastry marble, like a taste for stairs and closed doors, could be construed as "elitist," and as I left the Governor's Mansion I felt very like the heroine of Mary McCarthy's *Birds of America*, the one who located America's moral decline in the disappearance of the first course.

A guard sleeps at night in the old mansion, which has been condemned as a dwelling by the state fire marshal. It costs about $85,000 a year to keep guards at the new official residence. Meanwhile the current governor of California, Edmund G. Brown, Jr., sleeps on a mattress on the floor in the famous apartment for which he pays $275 a month out of his own $49,100 annual salary. This has considerable and potent symbolic value, as do the two empty houses themselves, most particularly the house the Reagans built on the river. It is a great point around the Capitol these days to have "never seen" the house on the river. The governor himself has "never seen" it. The governor's press secretary, Elisabeth Coleman, has "never seen" it. The governor's chief of staff, Gray Davis, admits to having seen it, but only once, when "Mary McGrory wanted to see it." This unseen house on the river is, Jerry Brown has said, "not my style."

As a matter of fact this is precisely the point about the house on the river—the house is not Jerry Brown's style, not Mary McGrory's style, *not our style*—and it is a point which presents a certain problem, since the house so clearly *is* the style not only of Jerry Brown's predecessor but of millions of Jerry Brown's constituents. Words are chosen carefully. Reasonable objections are framed. One hears about how the house is too far from the Capitol, too far from the Legislature. One hears about the folly of running such a lavish establishment for an unmarried governor and one hears about the governor's temperamental austerity. One hears every possible reason for not living in the house except the one that counts: it is the kind of house that has a wet bar in the living room. It is the kind of house that has a refreshment center. It is the kind of house in which one does not live, but there is no way to say this without getting into touchy and evanescent and finally inadmissible questions of taste, and ultimately of class. I have seldom seen a house so evocative of the unspeakable.

1977

THE GETTY

THE PLACE MIGHT have been commissioned by The Magic Christian. Mysteriously and rather giddily splendid, hidden in a grove of sycamores just above the Pacific Coast Highway in Malibu, a commemoration of high culture so immediately productive of crowds and jammed traffic that it can now be approached by appointment only, the seventeen-million-dollar villa built by the late J. Paul Getty to house his antiquities and paintings and furniture manages to strike a peculiar nerve in almost everyone who sees it. From the beginning, the Getty was said to be vulgar. The Getty was said to be "Disney." The Getty was even said to be Jewish, if I did not misread the subtext in "like a Beverly Hills nouveau-riche dining room" (*Los Angeles Times*, January 6, 1974) and "gussied up like a Bel-Air dining room" (*New York Times*, May 28, 1974).

The Getty seems to stir up social discomforts at levels not easily plumbed. To mention this museum in the more enlightened of those very dining rooms it is said to resemble is to invite a kind of nervous derision, as if the place were a local hoax, a perverse and deliberate affront to the understated good taste and general class of everyone at the table. The Getty's intricately patterned marble floors and walls are "garish." The Getty's illusionistic portico murals are "back lot." The entire building, an informed improvisation on a villa buried by mud from Vesuvius in 79 A.D. and seen again only dimly during some eighteenth-century tunneling around Herculaneum, is ritually dismissed as "inauthentic," although what "authentic" could mean in this context is hard to say.

Something about the place embarrasses people. The collection itself is usually referred to as "that kind of thing," as in "not even the best of that kind of thing," or "absolutely top-drawer if you like that kind of thing," both of which translate "not our kind of thing." The Getty's damask-lined galleries of Renaissance and Baroque paintings are distinctly that kind of thing, there being little in the modern temperament that responds immediately to popes and libertine babies, and so are the Getty's rather unrelenting arrangements of French furniture. A Louis XV writing table tends to please the modern eye only if it has been demystified by a glass of field flowers and some silver-framed snapshots, as in a Horst photograph for *Vogue*. Even the Getty's famous antiquities are pretty much that kind of thing, evoking as they do not their own period but the eighteenth- and nineteenth-century rage for antiquities. The sight of a Greek head depresses many people, strikes an unliberated chord, reminds them of books in their grandmother's parlor and of all they were supposed to learn and never did. This note of "learning" pervades the entire Getty collection. Even the handful of Impressionists acquired by Getty were recently removed from the public galleries, put away as irrelevant. The Getty collection is in certain ways unremittingly reproachful, and quite inaccessible to generations trained in the conviction that a museum is meant to be fun, with Calder mobiles and Barcelona chairs.

In short the Getty is a monument to "fine art," in the old-fashioned didactic sense, which is part of the problem people have with it. The place resists contemporary notions about what art is or should be or ever was. A museum is now supposed to kindle the untrained imagination, but this museum does not. A museum is now supposed to set the natural child in each of us free, but this museum does not. This was art acquired to teach a lesson, and there is also a lesson in the building which houses it: the Getty tells us that the past was perhaps different from the way we like to perceive it. Ancient marbles were not always attractively faded and worn. Ancient marbles once appeared just as they appear here: as strident, opulent evidence of imperial power and acquisition. Ancient murals were not always bleached and mellowed and "tasteful." Ancient murals once looked as they do here: as if dreamed by a Mafia don. Ancient fountains once worked, and drowned out that very silence we have come to expect and want from the past. Ancient bronze once gleamed ostentatiously. The old world was once discomfitingly new, or even nouveau, as people like to say about the Getty. (I have never been sure what the word "nouveau" can possibly mean in America, implying as it does that the speaker is gazing down six hundred years of rolled lawns.) At a time when all our public conventions remain rooted in a kind of knocked-down roman-ticism, when the celebration of natural man's capacity for mov-ing onward and upward has become a kind of official tic, the Getty presents us with an illustrated lesson in classical doubt. The Getty advises us that not much changes. The Getty tells us that we were never any better than we are and will never be any better than we were, and in so doing makes a profoundly unpopular political statement.

The Getty's founder may or may not have had some such statement in mind. In a way he seems to have wanted only to do something no one else could or would do. In his posthumous book, *As I See It*, he advises us that he never wanted "one of those concrete-bunker-type structures that are the fad among museum architects." He refused to pay for any "tinted-glass-and-stainless-steel monstrosity." He assures us that he was "neither shaken nor surprised" when his villa was finished and "certain critics sniffed." He had "calculated the risks." He knew that he was flouting the "doctrinaire and elitist" views he believed endemic in "many Art World (or should I say Artsy-Craftsy?) quarters."

Doctrinaire and elitist. Artsy-craftsy. On the surface the Getty would appear to have been a case of he-knew-what-he-liked-and-he-built-it, a tax dodge from the rather louche world of the international rich, and yet the use of that word "elitist" strikes an interesting note. The man who built himself the Getty never saw it, although it opened a year and a half before his death. He seems to have liked the planning of it. He personally approved every paint sample. He is said to have taken immense pleasure in every letter received from anyone who visited the museum and liked it (such letters were immediately forwarded to him by the museum staff), but the idea of the place seems to have been enough, and the idea was this: here was a museum built not for those elitist critics but for "the public." Here was a museum that would be forever supported by its founder alone, a museum that need never depend on any city or state or federal funding, a place forever "open to the public and free of all charges."

As a matter of fact large numbers of people who do not ordinarily visit museums like the Getty a great deal, just as its founder knew they would. There is one of those peculiar social secrets at work here. On the whole "the critics" distrust great wealth, but "the public" does not. On the whole "the critics" subscribe to the romantic view of man's possibilities, but "the public" does not. In the end the Getty stands above the Pacific Coast Highway as one of those odd monuments, a palpable contract between the very rich and the people who distrust them least.

1977

BUREAUCRATS

THE CLOSED DOOR upstairs at 120 South Spring Street in downtown Los Angeles is marked OPERATIONS CENTER. In the windowless room beyond the closed door a reverential hush prevails.
From six A.M. until seven P.M. in this windowless room men sit at
consoles watching a huge board flash colored lights. "There's the
heart attack," someone will murmur, or "we're getting the gawk
effect." 120 South Spring is the Los Angeles office of Caltrans, or
the California Department of Transportation, and the Operations
Center is where Caltrans engineers monitor what they call "the
42-Mile Loop." The 42-Mile Loop is simply the rough triangle
formed by the intersections of the Santa Monica, the San Diego
and the Harbor freeways, and 42 miles represents less than ten per
cent of freeway mileage in Los Angeles County alone, but these
particular 42 miles are regarded around 120 South Spring with a
special veneration. The Loop is a "demonstration system," a phrase
much favored by everyone at Caltrans, and is part of a "pilot project," another two words carrying totemic weight on South Spring.
  The Loop has electronic sensors embedded every half-mile out
there in the pavement itself, each sensor counting the crossing cars
every twenty seconds. The Loop has its own mind, a Xerox Sigma
V computer which prints out, all day and night, twenty-second
readings on what is and is not moving in each of the Loop's eight
lanes. It is the Xerox Sigma V that makes the big board flash red
when traffic out there drops below fifteen miles an hour. It is the
Xerox Sigma V that tells the Operations crew when they have an
"incident" out there. An "incident" is the heart attack on the San
Diego, the jackknifed truck on the Harbor, the Camaro just now
tearing out the Cyclone fence on the Santa Monica. "Out there"
is where incidents happen. The windowless room at 120 South
Spring is where incidents get "verified." "Incident verification"
is turning on the closed-circuit TV on the console and watching
the traffic slow down to see (this is "the gawk effect") where the
Camaro tore out the fence.

As a matter of fact there is a certain closed-circuit aspect to the entire mood of the Operations Center. "Verifying" the incident does not after all "prevent" the incident, which lends the enterprise a kind of tranced distance, and on the day recently when I visited 120 South Spring it took considerable effort to remember what I had come to talk about, which was that particular part of the Loop called the Santa Monica Freeway. The Santa Monica Freeway is 16.2 miles long, runs from the Pacific Ocean to downtown Los Angeles through what is referred to at Caltrans as "the East-West Corridor," carries more traffic every day than any other freeway in California, has what connoisseurs of freeways concede to be the most beautiful access ramps in the world, and appeared to have been transformed by Caltrans, during the several weeks before I went downtown to talk about it, into a 16.2-mile parking lot.

The problem seemed to be another Caltrans "demonstration," or "pilot," a foray into bureaucratic terrorism they were calling "The Diamond Lane" in their promotional literature and "The Project" among themselves. That the promotional literature consisted largely of schedules for buses (or "Diamond Lane Expresses") and invitations to join a car pool via computer ("Commuter Computer") made clear not only the putative point of The Project, which was to encourage travel by car pool and bus, but also the actual point, which was to eradicate a central Southern California illusion, that of individual mobility, without anyone really noticing. This had not exactly worked out. "FREEWAY FIASCO," the *Los Angeles Times* was headlining page-one stories. "THE DIAMOND LANE: ANOTHER BUST BY CALTRANS." "CALTRANS PILOT EFFORT ANOTHER IN LONG LIST OF FAILURES." "OFFICIAL DIAMOND LANE STANCE: LET THEM HOWL."

All "The Diamond Lane" theoretically involved was reserving the fast inside lanes on the Santa Monica for vehicles carrying three or more people, but in practice this meant that 25 per cent of the freeway was reserved for 3 per cent of the cars, and there were other odd wrinkles here and there suggesting that Caltrans had dedicated itself to making all movement around Los Angeles as arduous as possible. There was for example the matter of surface streets. A "surface street" is anything around Los Angeles that is not a freeway ("going surface" from one part of town to another is generally regarded as idiosyncratic), and surface streets do not fall directly within the Caltrans domain, but now the engineer in charge of surface streets was accusing Caltrans of threatening and intimidating him. It appeared that Caltrans wanted him to create a "confused and congested situation" on his surface streets, so as to force drivers back to the freeway, where they would meet a still more confused and congested situation and decide to stay home, or take a bus. "We are beginning a process of deliberately making it harder for drivers to use freeways," a Caltrans director had in fact said at a transit conference some months before. "We are prepared to endure considerable public outcry in order to pry John Q. Public out of his car.... I would emphasize that this is a political decision, and one that can be reversed if the public gets sufficiently enraged to throw us rascals out."

Of course this political decision was in the name of the greater good, was in the interests of "environmental improvement" and "conservation of resources," but even there the figures had about them a certain Caltrans opacity. The Santa Monica normally carried 240,000 cars and trucks every day. These 240,000 cars and trucks normally carried 260,000 people. What Caltrans described as its ultimate goal on the Santa Monica was to carry the same 260,000 people, "but in 7,800 fewer, or 232,200 vehicles." The figure "232,200" had a visionary precision to it that did not automatically create confidence, especially since the only effect so far had been to disrupt traffic throughout the Los Angeles basin, triple the number of daily accidents on the Santa Monica, prompt the initiation of two lawsuits against Caltrans, and cause large numbers of Los Angeles County residents to behave, most uncharacteristically, as an ignited and conscious proletariat. Citizen guerrillas splashed paint and scattered nails in the Diamond Lanes. Diamond Lane maintenance crews expressed fear of hurled objects. Down at 120 South Spring the architects of the Diamond Lane had taken to regarding "the media" as the architects of their embarrassment, and Caltrans statements in the press had been cryptic and contradictory, reminiscent only of old communiqués out of Vietnam.

To understand what was going on it is perhaps necessary to have participated in the freeway experience, which is the only secular communion Los Angeles has. Mere driving on the freeway is in no way the same as participating in it. Anyone can "drive" on the freeway, and many people with no vocation for it do, hesitating here and resisting there, losing the rhythm of the lane change, thinking about where they came from and where they are going. Actual participants think only about where they are. Actual participation requires a total surrender, a concentration so intense as to seem a kind of narcosis, a rapture-of-the-freeway. The mind goes clean. The rhythm takes over. A distortion of time occurs, the same distortion that characterizes the instant before an accident. It takes only a few seconds to get off the Santa Monica Freeway at National-Overland, which is a difficult exit requiring the driver to cross two new lanes of traffic streamed in from the San Diego Freeway, but those few seconds always seem to me the longest part of the trip. The moment is dangerous. The exhilaration is in doing it. "As you acquire the special skills involved," Reyner Banham observed in an extraordinary chapter about the freeways in his 1971 *Los Angeles: The Architecture of Four Ecologies*, "the freeways become a special way of being alive ... the extreme concentration required in Los Angeles seems to bring on a state of heightened awareness that some locals find mystical."

Indeed some locals do, and some nonlocals too. Reducing the number of lone souls careering around the East-West Corridor in a state of mechanized rapture may or may not have seemed socially desirable, but what it was definitely not going to seem was easy. "We're only seeing an initial period of unfamiliarity," I was assured the day I visited Caltrans. I was talking to a woman named Eleanor Wood and she was thoroughly and professionally grounded in the diction of "planning" and it did not seem likely that I could interest her in considering the freeway as regional mystery. "Any time you try to rearrange people's daily habits, they're apt to react impetuously. All this project requires is a certain rearrangement of people's daily planning. That's really all we want."

It occurred to me that a certain rearrangement of people's daily planning might seem, in less rarefied air than is breathed at 120 South Spring, rather a great deal to want, but so impenetrable was the sense of higher social purpose there in the Operations Center that I did not express this reservation. Instead I changed the subject, mentioned an earlier "pilot project" on the Santa Monica: the big electronic message boards that Caltrans had installed a year or two before. The idea was that traffic information transmitted from the Santa Monica to the Xerox Sigma V could be translated, here in the Operations Center, into suggestions to the driver, and flashed right back out to the Santa Monica. This operation, in that it involved telling drivers electronically what they already knew empirically, had the rather spectral circularity that seemed to mark a great many Caltrans schemes, and I was interested in how Caltrans thought it worked.

"Actually the message boards were part of a larger pilot project," Mrs. Wood said. "An ongoing project in incident management. With the message boards we hoped to learn if motorists would modify their behavior according to what we told them on the boards."

I asked if the motorists had.

"Actually no," Mrs. Wood said finally. "They didn't react to the signs exactly as we'd hypothesized they would, no. *But.* If we'd *known* what the motorist would do … then we wouldn't have needed a pilot project in the first place, would we."

The circle seemed intact. Mrs. Wood and I smiled, and shook hands. I watched the big board until all lights turned green on the Santa Monica and then I left and drove home on it, all 16.2 miles of it. All the way I remembered that I was watched by the Xerox Sigma V. All the way the message boards gave me the number to call for CAR POOL INFO. As I left the freeway it occurred to me that they might have their own rapture down at 120 South Spring, and it could be called Perpetuating the Department. Today the California Highway Patrol reported that, during the first six weeks of the Diamond Lane, accidents on the Santa Monica, which normally range between 49 and 72 during a six-week period, totaled 204. Yesterday plans were announced to extend the Diamond Lane to other freeways at a cost of $42,500,000.

1976

GOOD CITIZENS

I

I WAS ONCE invited to a civil rights meeting at Sammy Davis, Jr.'s house, in the hills above the Sunset Strip. "Let me tell you how to get to Sammy's," said the woman to whom I was talking. "You turn left at the old Mocambo." I liked the ring of this line, summing up as it did a couple of generations of that peculiar vacant fervor which is Hollywood political action, but acquaintances to whom I repeated it seemed uneasy. Politics are not widely considered a legitimate source of amusement in Hollywood, where the borrowed rhetoric by which political ideas are reduced to choices between the good (equality is good) and the bad (genocide is bad) tends to make even the most casual political small talk resemble a rally. "Those who cannot remember the past are condemned to repeat it," someone said to me at dinner not long ago, and before we had finished our *fraises des bois* he had advised me as well that "no man is an island." As a matter of fact I hear that no man is an island once or twice a week, quite often from people who think they are quoting Ernest Hemingway. "What a sacrifice on the altar of nationalism," I heard an actor say about the death in a plane crash of the president of the Philippines. It is a way of talking that tends to preclude further discussion, which may well be its intention: the public life of liberal Hollywood comprises a kind of dictatorship of good intentions, a social contract in which actual and irreconcilable disagreement is as taboo as failure or bad teeth, a climate devoid of irony. "Those men are our unsung heroes," a quite charming and intelligent woman once said to me at a party in Beverly Hills. She was talking about the California State Legislature.

I remember spending an evening in 1968, a week or so before the California primary and Robert Kennedy's death, at Eugene's in Beverly Hills, one of the "clubs" opened by supporters of Eugene McCarthy. The Beverly Hills Eugene's, not unlike Senator McCarthy's campaign itself, had a certain *déjà vu* aspect to it, a glow of 1952 humanism: there were Ben Shahn posters

241

JOAN DIDION

on the walls, and the gesture toward a strobe light was nothing
that might interfere with "good talk," and the music was not 1968
rock but the kind of jazz people used to have on their record
players when everyone who believed in the Family of Man
bought Scandinavian stainless-steel flatware and voted for Adlai
Stevenson. There at Eugene's I heard the name "Erich Fromm"
for the first time in a long time, and many other names cast out for
the sympathetic magic they might work ("I saw the Senator in
San Francisco, where I was with Mrs. Leonard Bernstein…"), and
then the evening's main event: a debate between William Styron
and the actor Ossie Davis. It was Mr. Davis' contention that in
writing *The Confessions of Nat Turner* Mr. Styron had encouraged
racism ("Nat Turner's love for a white maiden, I feel my country can become psychotic about this"), and it was Mr. Styron's
contention that he had not. (David Wolper, who had bought the
motion picture rights to *Nat Turner*, had already made his position clear: "How can anyone protest a book," he had asked in
the trade press, "that has withstood the critical test of time since
last October?") As the evening wore on, Mr. Styron said less and
less, and Mr. Davis more and more ("So you might ask, why
didn't *I* spend five years and write *Nat Turner?* I won't go into
my reasons why, but…"), and James Baldwin sat between them,
his eyes closed and his head thrown back in understandable but
rather theatrical agony. Mr. Baldwin summed up: "If Bill's book
does no more than what it's done tonight, it's a very important event." "Hear, hear," cried someone sitting on the floor, and
there was general agreement that it had been a stimulating and
significant evening.

Of course there was nothing crucial about that night at
Eugene's in 1968, and of course you could tell me that there was
certainly no harm and perhaps some good in it. But its curious
vanity and irrelevance stay with me, if only because those qualities characterize so many of Hollywood's best intentions. Social
problems present themselves to many of these people in terms of
a scenario, in which, once certain key scenes are licked (the confrontation on the courthouse steps, the revelation that the opposition leader has an anti-Semitic past, the presentation of the bill
of particulars to the President, a Henry Fonda cameo), the plot
will proceed inexorably to an upbeat fade. Marlon Brando does
not, in a well-plotted motion picture, picket San Quentin in vain:

what we are talking about here is faith in a dramatic convention. Things "happen" in motion pictures. There is always a resolution, always a strong cause-effect dramatic line, and to perceive the world in those terms is to assume an ending for every social scenario. If Budd Schulberg goes into Watts and forms a Writers' Workshop, then "Twenty Young Writers" must emerge from it, because the scenario in question is the familiar one about how the ghetto teems with raw talent and vitality. If the poor people march on Washington and camp out, there to receive bundles of clothes gathered on the Fox lot by Barbra Streisand, then some good must come of it (the script here has a great many dramatic staples, not the least of them a sentimental notion of Washington as an open forum, *cf. Mr. Deeds Goes to Washington*), and doubts have no place in the story.

There are no bit players in Hollywood politics: everyone makes things "happen." As it happens I live in a house in Hollywood in which, during the late thirties and early fifties, a screenwriters' cell of the Communist Party often met. Some of the things that are in the house now were in it then: a vast Stalinist couch, the largest rag rug I have ever seen, cartons of *New Masses*. Some of the people who came to meetings in the house were blacklisted, some of them never worked again and some of them are now getting several hundred thousand dollars a picture; some of them are dead and some of them are bitter and most of them lead very private lives. Things did change, but in the end it was not they who made things change, and their enthusiasms and debates sometimes seem very close to me in this house. In a way the house suggests the particular vanity of perceiving social life as a problem to be solved by the good will of individuals, but I do not mention that to many of the people who visit me here.

2

Pretty Nancy Reagan, the wife then of the governor of California, was standing in the dining room of her rented house on 45th Street in Sacramento, listening to a television newsman explain what he wanted to do. She was listening attentively. Nancy Reagan is a very attentive listener. The television crew wanted to watch her, the newsman said, while she was doing precisely what she would ordinarily be doing on a Tuesday morning at home. Since I was also there to watch her doing precisely what she would ordinarily be doing on a Tuesday morning at home, we seemed to be on the verge of exploring certain media frontiers: the television newsman and the two cameramen could watch Nancy Reagan being watched by me, or I could watch Nancy Reagan being watched by the three of them, or one of the cameramen could step back and do a *cinéma vérité* study of the rest of us watching and being watched by one another. I had the distinct sense that we were on the track of something revelatory, the truth about Nancy Reagan at 24 frames a second, but the television newsman opted to overlook the moment's peculiar essence. He suggested that we watch Nancy Reagan pick flowers in the garden. "That's something you might ordinarily do, isn't it?" he asked. "Indeed it is," Nancy Reagan said with spirit. Nancy Reagan says almost everything with spirit, perhaps because she was once an actress and has the beginning actress's habit of investing even the most casual lines with a good deal more dramatic emphasis than is ordinarily called for on a Tuesday morning on 45th Street in Sacramento. "Actually," she added then, as if about to disclose a delightful surprise, "actually, I really *do* need flowers."

She smiled at each of us, and each of us smiled back. We had all been smiling quite a bit that morning. "And then," the television newsman said thoughtfully, surveying the dining-room table, "even though you've got a beautiful arrangement right now, we could set up the pretense of your arranging, you know, the flowers."

We all smiled at one another again, and then Nancy Reagan walked resolutely into the garden, equipped with a decorative straw basket about six inches in diameter. "Uh, Mrs. Reagan," the newsman called after her. "May I ask what you're going to select for flowers?"

"Why, I don't know," she said, pausing with her basket on a garden step. The scene was evolving its own choreography.

"Do you think you could use rhododendrons?"

Nancy Reagan looked critically at a rhododendron bush. Then she turned to the newsman and smiled. "Did you know there's a Nancy Reagan rose now?"

"Uh, no," he said. "I didn't."

"It's awfully pretty, it's a kind of, of, a kind of coral color."

"Would the … the Nancy Reagan rose be something you might be likely to pick now?"

A silvery peal of laughter. "I could certainly *pick* it. But I won't be *using* it." A pause. "I *can* use the rhododendron."

"Fine," the newsman said. "Just fine. Now I'll ask a question, and if you could just be nipping a bud as you answer it…"

"Nipping a bud," Nancy Reagan repeated, taking her place in front of the rhododendron bush.

"Let's have a dry run," the cameraman said.

The newsman looked at him. "In other words, by a dry run, you mean you want her to fake nipping the bud."

"Fake the nip, yeah," the cameraman said. "Fake the nip."

3

Outside the Miramar Hotel in Santa Monica a hard subtropical rain had been falling for days. It scaled still more paint from the faded hotels and rooming houses that front the Pacific along Ocean Avenue. It streamed down the blank windows of unleased offices, loosened the soft coastal cliffs and heightened the most characteristic Santa Monica effect, that air of dispirited abandon which suggests that the place survives only as illustration of a boom gone bankrupt, evidence of some irreversible flaw in the laissez-faire small-business ethic. In any imaginative sense Santa Monica seemed an eccentric place for the United States Junior Chamber of Commerce to be holding a national congress, but there they were, a thousand delegates and wives, gathered in the Miramar Hotel for a relentless succession of keynote banquets and award luncheons and prayer breakfasts and outstanding-young-men forums. Now it was the President's Luncheon and everyone was listening to an animated singing group called The New Generation and I was watching the pretty young wife of one delegate pick sullenly at her lunch. "Let someone else eat this slop," she said suddenly, her voice cutting through not only the high generalities of the occasion but The New Generation's George M. Cohan medley as well. Her husband looked away, and she repeated it. To my left another delegate was urging me to ask every man in the room how the Jaycees had changed his life. I watched the girl down the table and asked the delegate how the

Jaycees had changed his life. "It saved my marriage and it built my business," he whispered. "You could find a thousand inspirational stories right here at this President's Luncheon." Down the table the young wife was sobbing into a pink napkin. The New Generation marched into "Supercalifragilisticexpialidocious." In many ways the Jaycees' 32nd Annual Congress of America's Ten Outstanding Young Men was a curious and troubling way to spend a few days in the opening weeks of 1970.

I suppose I went to Santa Monica in search of the abstraction lately called "Middle America," went to find out how the Jaycees, with their Couéistic emphasis on improving one's world and one's self simultaneously, had weathered these past several years of cultural shock. In a very real way the Jaycees have exemplified, usually so ingenuously that it was popular to deride them, certain ideas shared by almost all of the people in America's small cities and towns and by at least some of the people in America's large cities, ideas shared in an unexamined way even by those who laughed at the Jaycees' boosterism and pancake breakfasts and safe-driving Road-e-os. There was the belief in business success as a transcendent ideal. There was the faith that if one transforms oneself from an "introvert" into an "extrovert," if one learns to "speak effectively" and "do a job," success and its concomitant, spiritual grace, follow naturally. There was the approach to international problems which construed the underdeveloped world as a temporarily depressed area in need mainly of People-to-People programs. ("Word of Operation Brotherhood swept through the teeming masses of Asia like a fresh wind from the sea," reads a Jaycee report on one such program in the late Fifties.) If only because these ideas, these last rattles of Social Darwinism, had in fact been held in common by a great many people who never bothered to articulate them, I wondered what the Jaycees were thinking now, wondered what their mood might be at a time when, as their national president put it one day at the Miramar, "so much of America seems to be looking at the negative."

At first I thought I had walked out of the rain into a time warp: the Sixties seemed not to have happened. All these Jaycees were, by definition, between 21 and 35 years old, but there was a disquieting tendency among them to have settled foursquare into middle age. There was the heavy jocularity, the baroque rhetoric of another generation entirely, a kind of poignant attempt to circumnavigate social conventions that had in fact broken down in the Twenties. Wives were lovely and forbearing. Getting together for drinks was having a cocktail reception. Rain was liquid sunshine and the choice of a table for dinner was making an executive decision. They knew that this was a brave new world and they said so. It was time to "put brotherhood into action," to "open our neighborhoods to those of all colors." It was time to "turn attention to the cities," to think about youth centers and clinics and the example set by a black policeman-preacher in Philadelphia who was organizing a decency rally patterned after Miami's. It was time to "decry apathy."

The word "apathy" cropped up again and again, an odd word to use in relation to the past few years, and it was a while before I realized what it meant. It was not simply a word remembered from the Fifties, when most of these men had frozen their vocabularies: it was a word meant to indicate that not enough of "our kind" were speaking out. It was a cry in the wilderness, and this resolute determination to meet 1950 head-on was a kind of refuge. Here were some people who had been led to believe that the future was always a rational extension of the past, that there would ever be world enough and time for "turning attention," for "problems" and "solutions." Of course they would not admit their inchoate fears that the world was not that way any more. Of course they would not join the "fashionable doubters." Of course they would ignore the "pessimistic pundits." Late one afternoon I sat in the Miramar lobby, watching the rain fall and the steam rise off the heated pool outside and listening to a couple of Jaycees discussing student unrest and whether the "solution" might not lie in on-campus Jaycee groups. I thought about this astonishing notion for a long time. It occurred to me finally that I was listening to a true underground, to the voice of all those who have felt themselves not merely shocked but personally betrayed by recent history. It was supposed to have been their time. It was not.

1968–70

NOTES TOWARD A DREAMPOLITIK

I

ELDER ROBERT J. THEOBOLD, pastor of what was until October 12, 1968, the Friendly Bible Apostolic Church in Port Hueneme, California, is twenty-eight years old, born and bred in San Jose, a native Californian whose memory stream could encompass only the boom years; in other words a young man who until October 12, 1968, had lived his entire life in the nerve center of the most elaborately technological and media-oriented society in the United States, and so the world. His looks and to some extent his background are indistinguishable from those of a legion of computer operators and avionics technicians. Yet this is a young man who has remained immaculate of the constant messages with which a technological society bombards itself, for at the age of sixteen he was saved, received the Holy Spirit in a Pentecostal church. Brother Theobold, as the eighty-some members of his congregation call him, now gets messages only from the Lord, "forcible impressions" instructing him, for example, to leave San Jose and start a church in Port Hueneme, or, more recently, to lead his congregation on the 12th of October, 1968, from Port Hueneme to Murfreesboro, Tennessee, in order to avoid destruction by earthquake.

"We're leaving the 12th but I don't have any message that it's going to happen before the end of 1968," Brother Theobold told me one morning a few weeks before he and his congregation piled their belongings into campers and cars and left California for Tennessee. He was minding the children that morning, and his two-year-old walked around sucking on a plastic bottle while Brother Theobold talked to me and fingered the pages of a tooled-leather Bible. "This one minister I heard, he definitely said it would happen before the end of 1970, but as far as I'm concerned, the Lord has shown me that it's definitely coming but he hasn't shown me *when*."

I mentioned to Brother Theobold that most seismologists were predicting an imminent major earthquake on the San Andreas Fault, but he did not seem unduly interested: Brother Theobold's perception of the apocalypse neither began with nor depended upon the empirical. In a way the Pentecostal mind reveals itself most clearly in something like Brother Theobold's earthquake prophecy. Neither he nor the members of his congregation to whom I talked had ever been particularly concerned by reports in the newspapers that an earthquake was overdue. "Of course we'd *heard* of earthquakes," a soft-voiced woman named Sister Mosley told me. "Because the Bible mentions there'll be more and more toward the end of time." Nor was there any need to think twice about pulling up stakes and joining a caravan to a small town few of them had ever seen. I kept asking Brother Theobold how he had chosen Murfreesboro, and over and over he tried to tell me: he had "received a telephone call from a man there," or "God had directed this particular man to call on this particular day." The man did not seem to have made a direct entreaty to Brother Theobold to bring his flock to Tennessee, but there had been no question in Brother Theobold's mind that God's intention was exactly that. "From the natural point of view I didn't care to go to Murfreesboro at all," he said. "We just bought this place, it's the nicest place we ever had. But I put it up to the Lord, and the Lord said *put it up for sale*. Care for a Dr. Pepper?"

We might have been talking in different languages, Brother Theobold and I; it was as if I knew all the words but lacked the grammar, and so kept questioning him on points that seemed to him ineluctably clear. He seemed to be one of those people, so many of whom gravitate to Pentecostal sects, who move around the West and the South and the Border States forever felling trees in some interior wilderness, secret frontiersmen who walk around right in the ganglia of the fantastic electronic pulsing that is life in the United States and continue to receive information only through the most tenuous chains of rumor, hearsay, haphazard trickledown. In the social conventions by which we now live there is no category for people like Brother Theobold and his congregation, most of whom are young and white and nominally literate; they are neither the possessors nor the dispossessed. They participate in the national anxieties only through a glass darkly. They teach their daughters to eschew makeup and to cover their knees, and they believe in divine healing, and in speaking in tongues. Other people leave towns like Murfreesboro, and they move into them. To an astonishing extent they keep

JOAN DIDION

themselves unviolated by common knowledge, by the ability to make routine assumptions; when Brother Theobold first visited Murfreesboro he was dumbfounded to learn that the courthouse there had been standing since the Civil War. "The *same building*," he repeated twice, and then he got out a snapshot as corroboration. In the interior wilderness no one is bloodied by history, and it is no coincidence that the Pentecostal churches have their strongest hold in places where Western civilization has its most superficial hold. There are more than twice as many Pentecostal as Episcopal churches in Los Angeles.

2

The scene is quite near the end of Roger Corman's 1966 *The Wild Angels*, which was the first and in many ways the classic exploitation bike movie. Here it is: the Angels, led by Peter Fonda, are about to bury one of their number. They have already torn up the chapel, beaten and gagged the preacher, and held a wake, during which the dead man's girl was raped on the altar and the corpse itself, propped up on a bench in full biker colors, dark goggles over the eyes and a marijuana cigarette between the lips, was made an object of necrophilia. Now they stand at the grave, and, uncertain how to mark the moment, Peter Fonda shrugs. "Nothing to say," he says.

What we have here is an obligatory bike-movie moment, the outlaw-hero embracing man's fate: I tell you about it only to suggest the particular mood of these pictures. Many of them are extraordinarily beautiful in their instinct for the real look of the American West, for the faded banners fluttering over abandoned gas stations and for the bleached streets of desert towns. These are the movies known to the trade as "programmers," and very few adults have ever seen one. Most of them are made for less than $200,000. They are shown in New York only occasionally. Yet for several years bike movies have constituted a kind of underground folk literature for adolescents, have located an audience and fabricated a myth to exactly express that audience's every inchoate resentment, every yearning for the extreme exhilaration of death. To die violently is "righteous," a flash. To keep on living, as Peter Fonda points out in *The Wild Angels*, is just to keep on paying rent. A successful bike movie is a perfect Rorschach of its audience.

I saw nine of them recently, saw the first one almost by accident and the rest of them with a notebook. I saw *Hell's Angels on Wheels* and *Hell's Angels '9*. I saw *Run Angel Run* and *The Glory Stompers* and *The Losers*. I saw *The Wild Angels*, I saw *Violent Angels*, I saw *The Savage Seven* and I saw *The Cycle Savages*. I was not even sure why I kept going. To have seen one bike movie is to have seen them all, so meticulously observed are the rituals of getting the bikers out of town and onto the highway, of "making a run," of terrorizing the innocent "citizens" and fencing with the Highway Patrol and, finally, meeting death in a blaze, usually quite a literal blaze, of romantic fatalism. There is always that instant in which the outlaw leader stands revealed as existential hero. There is always that "perverse" sequence in which the bikers batter at some psychic sound barrier, degrade the widow, violate the virgin, defile the rose and the cross alike, break on through to the other side and find, once there, "nothing to say." The brutal images glaze the eye. The senseless insouciance of all the characters in a world of routine stompings and casual death takes on a logic better left unplumbed.

I suppose I kept going to these movies because there on the screen was some news I was not getting from *The New York Times*. I began to think I was seeing ideograms of the future. To watch a bike movie is finally to apprehend the extent to which the toleration of small irritations is no longer a trait much admired in America, the extent to which a nonexistent frustration threshold is seen not as psychopathic but as a "right." A biker is goaded on the job about the swastika on his jacket, so he picks up a wrench, threatens the foreman, and later describes the situation as one in which the foreman "got uptight." A biker runs an old man off the road: the old man was "in the way," and his subsequent death is construed as further "hassling." A nurse happens into a hospital room where a biker beats her unconscious and rapes her: that she later talks to the police is made to seem a betrayal, evidence only of some female hysteria, vindictiveness, sexual deprivation. Any girl who "acts dumb" deserves what she gets, and what she gets is beaten and turned out from the group. Anything less than instant service in a restaurant constitutes intolerable provocation, or "hassling": tear the place apart, leave the owner for dead, gangbang the waitress. Rev up the Harleys and ride.

To imagine the audience for whom these sentiments are tailored, maybe you need to have sat in a lot of drive-ins yourself, to have gone to school with boys who majored in shop and worked in gas stations and later held them up. Bike movies are made for all these children of vague "hill" stock who grow up absurd in the West and Southwest, children whose whole lives are an obscure grudge against a world they think they never made. These children are, increasingly, everywhere, and their style is that of an entire generation.

3

Palms, California, is a part of Los Angeles through which many people drive on their way from 20th Century-Fox to Metro-Goldwyn-Mayer, and vice versa. It is an area largely unnoticed by those who drive though it, an invisible prairie of stucco bungalows and two-story "units," and I mention it at all only because it is in Palms that a young woman named Dallas Beardsley lives. Dallas Beardsley has spent all of her twenty-two years on this invisible underside of the Los Angeles fabric, living with her mother in places like Palms and Inglewood and Westchester: she went to Airport Junior High School, out near Los Angeles International Airport, and to Westchester High School, where she did not go out with boys but did try out for cheerleader. She remembers not being chosen cheerleader as her "biggest discouragement." After that she decided to become an actress, and one morning in October of 1968 she bought the fifth page of *Daily Variety* for an advertisement which read in part: "There is no one like me in the world. I'm going to be a movie star."

It seemed an anachronistic ambition, wanting to be a movie star; girls were not supposed to want that in 1968. They were supposed to want only to perfect their *karma*, to give and get what were called good vibrations and to renounce personal ambition as an ego game. They were supposed to know that wanting things leads in general to grief, and that wanting to be a movie star leads in particular to U.C.L.A. Neuropsychiatric. Such are our conventions. But here was Dallas Beardsley, telling the world what she wanted for $50 down and $35 a month on an eight-month contract with *Variety*. *I'm going to be a movie star.*

I called Dallas, and one hot afternoon we drove around the Hollywood hills and talked. Dallas had long blond hair and a sundress and she was concerned about a run in her stocking and she did not hesitate when I asked what it meant to be a movie star. "It means being known all over the world," she said. "And bringing my family a bunch of presents on Christmas Day, you know, like carloads, and putting them by the tree. And it means happiness, and living by the ocean in a huge house." She paused. "But being *known*. It's important to me to be *known*." That morning she had seen an agent, and she was pleased because he had said that his decision not to handle her was "nothing personal." "The big agents are nice," she said. "They answer letters, they return your calls. It's the little ones who're nasty. But I understand, I really do." Dallas believes that all people, even agents, are "basically good inside," and that "when they hurt you, it's because they've been hurt themselves, and anyway maybe God means for you to be hurt, so some beautiful thing can happen later." Dallas attends the Unity Church in Culver City, the general thrust of which is that everything works out for the best, and she described herself as "pretty religious" and "politically less on the liberal side than most actors."

Her dedication to the future is undiluted. The jobs she takes to support herself—she has been a Kelly Girl, and worked in restaurants—do not intrude upon her ambitions. She does not go out to parties or on dates. "I work till six-thirty, then I have a dance lesson, then I rehearse at the workshop—when would I have time? Anyway I'm not interested in that." As I drove home that day through the somnolent back streets of Hollywood I had the distinct sense that everyone I knew had some fever which had not yet infected the invisible city. In the invisible city girls were still disappointed at not being chosen cheerleader. In the invisible city girls still got discovered at Schwab's and later met their true loves at the Mocambo or the Troc, still dreamed of big houses by the ocean and carloads of presents by the Christmas tree, still prayed to be known.

4

Another part of the invisible city.

"Speaking for myself," the young woman said, "in this seven months since I been on the program it's been real good. I was strictly a Gardena player, low-ball. I'd play in the nighttime after

JOAN DIDION

I got my children to bed, and of course I never got home before five A.M., and my problem was, I couldn't sleep then, I'd replay every hand, so the next day I'd be, you know, tired. Irritable. With the children."

Her tone was that of someone who had adapted her mode of public address from analgesic commercials, but she was not exactly selling a product. She was making a "confession" at a meeting of Gamblers Anonymous: nine o'clock on a winter evening in a neighborhood clubhouse in Gardena, California. Gardena is the draw-poker capital of Los Angeles County (no stud, no alcoholic beverages, clubs closed between five A.M. and nine A.M. and all day on Christmas Day), and the proximity of the poker clubs hung over this meeting like a paraphysical substance, almost as palpable as the American flag, the portraits of Washington and Lincoln, and the table laid by the Refreshments Committee. There it was, just around the corner, the action, and here in this overheated room were forty people, shifting uneasily on folding chairs and blinking against the cigarette smoke, who craved it. "I never made this Gardena meeting before," one of them said, "for one simple reason only, which is I break out in a cold sweat every time I pass Gardena on the freeway even, but I'm here tonight because every night I make a meeting is a night I don't place a bet, which with the help of God and you people is 1,223 nights now." Another: "I started out for a Canoga Park meeting and turned around on the freeway, that was last Wednesday, I ended up in Gardena and now I'm on the verge of divorce again." And a third: "I didn't lose no fortune, but I lost all the money I could get my hands on, it began in the Marine Corps, I met a lot of pigeons in Vietnam, I was making easy money and it was, you might say, this period in my life that, uh, led to my downfall." This last speaker was a young man who said that he had done OK in mechanical drawing at Van Nuys High School. He wore his hair in a sharp 1951 ducktail. He was, like Dallas Beardsley, twenty-two years old. Tell me the name of the elected representative from the invisible city.

1968–70

III
WOMEN

TO MAKE AN omelette you need not only those broken eggs but someone "oppressed" to break them: every revolutionist is presumed to understand that, and also every woman, which either does or does not make fifty-one percent of the population of the United States a potentially revolutionary class. The creation of this revolutionary "class" was from the virtual beginning the "idea" of the women's movement, and the tendency for popular discussion of the movement to center for so long around day-care centers is yet another instance of that studied resistance to political ideas which characterizes our national life.

"The new feminism is not just the revival of a serious political movement for social equality," the feminist theorist Shulamith Firestone announced flatly in 1970. "It is the second wave of the most important revolution in history." This was scarcely a statement of purpose anyone could find cryptic, and it was scarcely the only statement of its kind in the literature of the movement. Nonetheless, in 1972, in a "special issue" on women, *Time* was still musing genially that the movement might well succeed in bringing about "fewer diapers and more Dante."

That was a very pretty image, the idle ladies sitting in the gazebo and murmuring *lasciate ogni speranza*, but it depended entirely upon the popular view of the movement as some kind of collective inchoate yearning for "fulfillment," or "self-expression," a yearning absolutely devoid of ideas and capable of engendering only the most *pro forma* benevolent interest. In fact there was an idea, and the idea was Marxist, and it was precisely to the extent that there was this Marxist idea that the curious historical anomaly known as the women's movement would have seemed to have any interest at all. Marxism in this country had ever been an eccentric and quixotic passion. One oppressed class after another had seemed finally to miss the point. The have-nots, it turned out, aspired mainly to having. The minorities seemed to promise more, but finally disappointed: it developed that they actually cared about the issues, that they tended to see the integration of the luncheonette and the seat in the front of the bus as real goals, and only rarely as ploys, counters in a larger game. They resisted that essential inductive leap from the immediate reform to the social ideal, and, just as disappointingly, they failed to perceive their common cause with other minorities, continued to exhibit a self-interest disconcerting in the extreme to organizers steeped in the rhetoric of "brotherhood."

And then, at that exact dispirited moment when there seemed no one at all willing to play the proletariat, along came the women's movement, and the invention of women as a "class." One could not help admiring the radical simplicity of this instant transfiguration. The notion that, in the absence of a cooperative proletariat, a revolutionary class might simply be invented, made up, "named" and so brought into existence, seemed at once so pragmatic and so visionary, so precisely Emersonian, that it took the breath away, exactly confirmed one's idea of where nine-teenth-century transcendental instincts, crossed with a late read-ing of Engels and Marx, might lead. To read the theorists of the women's movement was to think not of Mary Wollstonecraft but of Margaret Fuller at her most high-minded, of rushing position papers off to mimeo and drinking tea from paper cups in lieu of eating lunch; of thin raincoats on bitter nights. If the family was the last fortress of capitalism, then let us abolish the family. If the necessity for conventional reproduction of the species seemed unfair to women, then let us transcend, via technology, "the very organization of nature," the oppression, as Shulamith Firestone saw it, "that goes back through recorded history to the animal kingdom itself." *I accept the universe*, Margaret Fuller had finally allowed: Shulamith Firestone did not.

It seemed very New England, this febrile and cerebral passion. The solemn *a priori* idealism in the guise of radical material-ism somehow bespoke old-fashioned self-reliance and prudent sacrifice. The clumsy torrent of words became a principle, a renunciation of style as unserious. The rhetorical willingness to break eggs became, in practice, only a thrifty capacity for find-ing the sermon in every stone. Burn the literature, Ti-Grace Atkinson said in effect when it was suggested that, even come the revolution, there would still remain the whole body of "sexist" Western literature. But of course no books would be burned:

the women of this movement were perfectly capable of crafting didactic revisions of whatever apparently intractable material
came to hand. "As a parent you should become an interpreter
of myths," advised Letty Cottin Pogrebin in the preview issue
of *Ms*. "Portions of any fairy tale or children's story can be salvaged during a critique session with your child." Other literary
analysts devised ways to salvage other books: Isabel Archer in *The
Portrait of a Lady* need no longer be the victim of her own idealism. She could be, instead, the victim of a sexist society, a woman
who had "internalized the conventional definition of wife." The
narrator of Mary McCarthy's *The Company She Keeps* could be
seen as "enslaved because she persists in looking for her identity
in a man." Similarly, Miss McCarthy's *The Group* could serve to
illustrate "what happens to women who have been educated at
first-rate women's colleges—taught philosophy and history—and
then are consigned to breast-feeding and gourmet cooking."

The idea that fiction has certain irreducible ambiguities
seemed never to occur to these women, nor should it have, for
fiction is in most ways hostile to ideology. They had invented
a class; now they had only to make that class conscious. They
seized as a political technique a kind of shared testimony at
first called a "rap session," then called "consciousness-raising,"
and in any case a therapeutically oriented American reinter-
pretation, according to the British feminist Juliet Mitchell, of a
Chinese revolutionary practice known as "speaking bitterness."
They purged and regrouped and purged again, worried out one
another's errors and deviations, the "elitism" here, the "careerism"
there. It would have been merely sententious to call some of their
thinking Stalinist: of course it was. It would have been pointless
even to speak of whether one considered these women "right"
or "wrong," meaningless to dwell upon the obvious, upon the
coarsening of moral imagination to which such social idealism so
often leads. To believe in "the greater good" is to operate, necessarily, in a certain ethical suspension. Ask anyone committed to
Marxist analysis how many angels stand on the head of a pin, and
you will be asked in return to never mind the angels, tell me who
controls the production of pins.

To those of us who remain committed mainly to the
exploration of moral distinctions and ambiguities, the feminist
analysis may have seemed a particularly narrow and cracked

determinism. Nonetheless it was serious, and for these high-strung idealists to find themselves out of the mimeo room and onto the Cavett show must have been in certain ways more unsettling to them than it ever was to the viewers. They were being heard, and yet not really. Attention was finally being paid, and yet that attention was mired in the trivial. Even the brightest movement women found themselves engaged in sullen public colloquies about the inequities of dishwashing and the intolerable humiliations of being observed by construction workers on Sixth Avenue. (This grievance was not atypical in that discussion of it seemed always to take on unexplored Ms. Scarlett overtones, suggestions of fragile cultivated flowers being "spoken to," and therefore violated, by uppity proles.) They totted up the pans scoured, the towels picked off the bathroom floor, the loads of laundry done in a lifetime. Cooking a meal could only be "dogwork," and to claim any pleasure from it was evidence of craven acquiescence in one's own forced labor. Small children could only be odious mechanisms for the spilling and digesting of food, for robbing women of their "freedom." It was a long way from Simone de Beauvoir's grave and awesome recognition of woman's role as "the Other" to the notion that the first step in changing that role was Alix Kates Shulman's marriage contract ("wife strips beds, husband remakes them"), a document reproduced in *Ms.*, but it was toward just such trivialization that the women's movement seemed to be heading.

Of course this litany of trivia was crucial to the movement in the beginning, a key technique in the politicizing of women who had perhaps been conditioned to obscure their resentments even from themselves. Mrs. Shulman's discovery that she had less time than her husband seemed to have was precisely the kind of chord the movement had hoped to strike in all women (the "click! of recognition," as Jane O'Reilly described it), but such discoveries could be of no use at all if one refused to perceive the larger point, failed to make that inductive leap from the personal to the political. Splitting up the week into hours during which the children were directed to address their "personal questions" to either one parent or another might or might not have improved the quality of Mr. and Mrs. Shulman's marriage, but the improvement of marriages would not a revolution make. It could be very useful to call housework, as Lenin did, "the most unproductive, the most barbarous and the most arduous work a woman can do," but it could be useful only as the first step in a political process, only in the "awakening" of a class to its position, useful only as a metaphor: to believe, during the late Sixties and early Seventies in the United States of America, that the words had literal meaning was not only to stall the movement in the personal but to seriously delude oneself.

More and more, as the literature of the movement began to reflect the thinking of women who did not really understand the movement's ideological base, one had the sense of this stall, this delusion, the sense that the drilling of the theorists had struck only some psychic hardpan dense with superstitions and little sophistries, wish fulfillment, self-loathing and bitter fancies. To read even desultorily in this literature was to recognize instantly a certain dolorous phantasm, an imagined Everywoman with whom the authors seemed to identify all too entirely. This ubiquitous construct was everyone's victim but her own. She was persecuted even by her gynecologist, who made her beg in vain for contraceptives. She particularly needed contraceptives because she was raped on every date, raped by her husband, and raped finally on the abortionist's table. During the fashion for shoes with pointed toes, she, like "many women," had her toes amputated. She was so intimidated by cosmetics advertising that she would sleep "huge portions" of her day in order to forestall wrinkling, and when awake she was enslaved by detergent commercials on television. She sent her child to a nursery school where the little girls huddled in a "doll corner," and were forcibly restrained from playing with building blocks. Should she work she was paid "three to ten times less" than an (always) unqualified man holding the same job, was prevented from attending business lunches because she would be "embarrassed" to appear in public with a man not her husband, and, when she traveled alone, faced a choice between humiliation in a restaurant and "eating a doughnut" in her hotel room.

The half-truths, repeated, authenticated themselves. The bitter fancies assumed their own logic. To ask the obvious—why she did not get herself another gynecologist, another job, why she did not get out of bed and turn off the television set, or why, the most eccentric detail, she stayed in hotels where only doughnuts could be obtained from room service—was to join this argument at its own spooky level, a level which had only the most tenuous and unfortunate relationship to the actual condition of being a woman. That many women are victims of condescension and exploitation and sex-role stereotyping was scarcely news, but neither was it news that other women are not: nobody forces women to buy the package.

But of course something other than an objection to being "discriminated against" was at work here, something other than an aversion to being "stereotyped" in one's sex role. Increasingly it seemed that the aversion was to adult sexual life itself: how much cleaner to stay forever children. One is constantly struck, in the accounts of lesbian relationships which appear from time to time in movement literature, by the emphasis on the superior "tenderness" of the relationship, the "gentleness" of the sexual connection, as if the participants were wounded birds. The derogation of assertiveness as "machismo" has achieved such currency that one imagines several million women too delicate to deal at any level with an overtly heterosexual man. Just as one had gotten the unintended but inescapable suggestion, when told about the "terror and revulsion" experienced by women in the vicinity of construction sites, of creatures too "tender" for the abrasiveness of daily life, too fragile for the streets, so now one was getting, in the later literature of the movement, the impression of women too "sensitive" for the difficulties of adult life, women unequipped for reality and grasping at the movement as a rationale for denying that reality. The transient stab of dread and loss which accompanies menstruation simply never happens: we only thought it happened, because a male-chauvinist psychiatrist told us so. No woman need have bad dreams after an abortion: she has only been told she should. The power of sex is just an oppressive myth, no longer to be feared, because what the sexual connection really amounts to, we learn in one woman's account of a postmarital affair presented as liberated and liberating, is "wisecracking and laughing" and "lying together and then leaping up to play and sing the entire *Sesame Street Songbook*." All one's actual apprehension of what it is like to be a woman, the irreconcilable difference of it—that sense of living one's deepest life underwater, that dark involvement with blood and birth and death—could now be declared invalid, unnecessary, *one never felt it at all*.

One was only told it, and now one is to be reprogrammed, fixed up, rendered again as inviolate and unstained as the "modern" little girls in the Tampax advertisements. More and more we have been hearing the wishful voices of just such perpetual adolescents, the voices of women scarred not by their class position as women but by the failure of their childhood expectations and misapprehensions. "Nobody ever so much as mentioned" to Susan Edmiston "that when you say 'I do,' what you are doing is not, as you thought, vowing your eternal love, but rather subscribing to a whole system of rights, obligations and responsibilities that may well be anathema to your most cherished beliefs." To Ellen Peck "the birth of children too often means the dissolution of romance, the loss of freedom, the abandonment of ideals to economics." A young woman described on the cover of *New York* as "The Suburban Housewife Who Bought the Promises of Women's Lib and Came to the City to Live Them" tells us what promises she bought: "The chance to respond to the bright lights and civilization of the Big Apple, yes. The chance to compete, yes. But most of all, the chance to have some fun. Fun is what's been missing."

Eternal love, romance, fun. The Big Apple. These are relatively rare expectations in the arrangements of consenting adults, although not in those of children, and it wrenches the heart to read about these women in their brave new lives. An ex-wife and mother of three speaks of her plan to "play out my college girl's dream. I am going to New York to become this famous writer. Or this working writer. Failing that, I will get a job in publishing." She mentions a friend, another young woman who "had never had any other life than as a daughter or wife or mother" but who is "just discovering herself to be a gifted potter." The childlike resourcefulness—to get a job in publishing, to become a gifted potter!—bewilders the imagination. The astral discontent with actual lives, actual men, the denial of the real generative possibilities of adult sexual life, somehow touches beyond words. "It is the right of the oppressed to organize around their oppression *as they see and define it*," the movement theorists insist doggedly in an effort to solve the question of these women, to convince themselves that what is going on is still a political process, but the handwriting is already on the wall. These are converts who want not a revolution but "romance," who believe not in the oppression of women but in their own chances for a new life in exactly the mold of their old life. In certain ways they tell us sadder things about what the culture has done to them than the theorists ever did, and they also tell us, I suspect, that the movement is no longer a cause but a symptom.

1972

DORIS LESSING

TO READ A great deal of Doris Lessing over a short span of time is to feel that the original hound of heaven has commandeered the attic. She holds the mind's other guests in ardent contempt. She appears for meals only to dismiss as decadent the household's own preoccupations with writing well. For more than twenty years now she has been registering, in a torrent of fiction that increasingly seems conceived in a stubborn rage against the very idea of fiction, every tremor along her emotional fault system, every slippage in her self-education. *Look here*, she is forever demanding, a missionary devoid of any but the most didactic irony: *The Communist Party is not the answer. There is a life beyond vaginal orgasm. St. John of the Cross was not as dotty as certain Anglicans would have had you believe.* She comes hard to ideas, and, once she has collared one, worries it with Victorian doggedness.

That she is a writer of considerable native power, a "natural" writer in the Dreiserian mold, someone who can close her eyes and "give" a situation by the sheer force of her emotional energy, seems almost a stain on her conscience. She views her real gift for fiction much as she views her own biology, as another trick to entrap her. She does not want to "write well." Her leaden disregard for even the simplest rhythms of language, her arrogantly bad ear for dialogue—all of that is beside her own point. More and more, Mrs. Lessing writes exclusively in the service of immediate cosmic reform: she wants to write, as the writer Anna in *The Golden Notebook* wanted to write, only to "create a new way of looking at life."

Consider *Briefing for a Descent into Hell*. Here Mrs. Lessing gave us a novel exclusively of "ideas," not a novel about the play of ideas in the lives of certain characters but a novel in which the characters exist only as markers in the presentation of an idea. The situation in the novel was this: a well-dressed but disheveled man is found wandering, an amnesiac, on the embankment near the Waterloo Bridge in London. He is taken by the police to a psychiatric hospital where, in the face of total indifference on his part, attempts are made to identify him. He is Charles Watkins, a professor of classics at Cambridge. An authority in his field, an occasional lecturer on more general topics. Lately a stammerer. Lately prone to bad evenings during which he condemns not only his own but all academic disciplines as "pigswill." A fifty-year-old man who finally cracked, and in cracking personified Mrs. Lessing's conviction that "the millions who have cracked" were "making cracks where the light could shine through at last." For of course the "nonsense" that Charles Watkins talks in the hospital makes, to the reader although not to the doctors, unmistakable "sense."

So pronounced was Charles Watkins' acumen about the inner reality of those around him that much of the time *Briefing for a Descent into Hell* read like a selective case study from an R. D. Laing book. The reality Charles Watkins describes is familiar to anyone who has ever had a high fever, or been exhausted to the point of breaking, or is just on the whole only marginally engaged in the dailiness of life. He experiences the loss of ego, the apprehension of the cellular nature of all matter, the "oneness" of things that seems always to lie just past the edge of controlled conscious thought. He hallucinates, or "remembers," the nature of the universe. He "remembers"—or is on the verge of remembering, before electroshock obliterates the memory and returns him to "sanity"—something very like a "briefing" for life on earth.

The details of this briefing were filled in by Mrs. Lessing, only too relieved to abandon the strain of creating character and slip into her own rather more exhortative voice. Imagine an interplanetary conference, convened on Venus to discuss once again the problem of the self-destructive planet Earth. (The fancy that extraterrestrial life is by definition of a higher order than our own is one that soothes all children, and many writers.) The procedure is this: certain superior beings descend to Earth brainprinted with the task of arousing the planet to its folly. These emissaries have, once on Earth, no memory of their more enlightened life. They wake slowly to their mission. They recognize one another only vaguely, and do not remember why. We are to understand, of course, that Charles Watkins is among those who have made the Descent, whether literal or metaphorical, and is now, for just so long as he can resist therapy, awake. This is the initial revelation in the book, and it is also the only one.

Even given Mrs. Lessing's tendency to confront all ideas *tabula rasa*, we are dealing here with less than astonishing stuff. The idea that there is sanity in insanity, that truth lies on the far side of madness, informs not only a considerable spread of Western literature but also, so commonly is it now held, an entire generation's experiment with hallucinogens. Most of Mrs. Lessing's thoughts about the cultural definition of insanity reflect or run parallel to those of Laing, and yet the idea was already so prevalent that Laing cannot even be said to have popularized it: his innovation was only to have taken it out of the realm of instinctive knowledge and into the limited context of psychiatric therapy. Although Mrs. Lessing apparently thought the content of *Briefing for a Descent into Hell* so startling that she was impelled to add an explanatory afterword, a two-page parable about the ignorance of certain psychiatrists at large London teaching hospitals, she had herself dealt before with this very material. In *The Golden Notebook* Anna makes this note for a story: "A man whose 'sense of reality' has gone; and because of it, has a deeper sense of reality than 'normal' people." By the time Mrs. Lessing finished *The Four-Gated City* she had refined the proposition: Lynda Coldridge's deeper sense of reality is not the result but the definition of her madness. So laboriously is this notion developed in the closing three hundred pages of *The Four-Gated City* that one would have thought that Mrs. Lessing had more or less exhausted its literary possibilities.

But she was less and less interested in literary possibilities, which is where we strike the faultline. "If I saw it in terms of an artistic problem, then it'd be easy, wouldn't it," Anna tells her friend Molly, in *The Golden Notebook*, as explanation of her disinclination to write another book. "We could have ever such intelligent chats about the modern novel." This may seem a little on the easy side, even to the reader who is willing to overlook Anna's later assertion that she cannot write because "a Chinese peasant" is looking over her shoulder. ("Or one of Castro's guerrilla fighters. Or an Algerian fighting in the F.L.N.") *Madame Bovary* told us more about bourgeois life than several generations of Marxists have, but there does not seem much doubt that Flaubert saw it as an artistic problem.

That Mrs. Lessing does not suggests her particular dilemma. What we are witnessing here is a writer undergoing a profound and continuing cultural trauma, a woman of determinedly utopian and distinctly teleological bent assaulted at every turn by fresh evidence that the world is not exactly improving as promised. And, because such is the particular quality of her mind, she is compelled in the face of this evidence to look even more frenetically for the final cause, the unambiguous answer.

In the beginning her search was less frenzied. She came out of Southern Rhodesia imprinted ineradicably by precisely the kind of rigid agrarian world that most easily makes storytellers of its exiled children. What British Africa gave her, besides those images of a sky so empty and a society so inflexible as to make the slightest tremor in either worth remarking upon, was a way of perceiving the rest of her life: for a long time to come she could interpret all she saw in terms of "injustice," not merely the injustice of white man to black, of colonizer to colonized, but the more general injustices of class and particularly of sex. She grew up knowing not only what hard frontiers do to women but what women then do to the men who keep them there. She could hear in all her memories that "voice of the suffering female" passed on from mothers to daughters in a chain broken only at great cost.

Of these memories she wrote a first novel, *The Grass Is Singing*, entirely traditional in its conventions. Reality was *there*, waiting to be observed by an omniscient third person. *The Grass Is Singing* was neat in its construction, relatively scrupulous in its maintenance of tone, predicated upon a world of constants. Its characters moved through that world unconscious of knowledge shared by author and reader. The novel was, in brief, everything Mrs. Lessing was to reject as "false" and "evasive" by the time she wrote *The Golden Notebook*. "Why not write down, simply, what happened between Molly and her son today?" Anna demands of herself. "Why do I never write down, simply, what happens? Why don't I keep a diary? Obviously, my changing everything into fiction is simply a means of concealing something from myself. ... I shall keep a diary."

It would be hard to imagine a character more unrelievedly self-conscious, or more insistently the author's surrogate, than Anna Gould in *The Golden Notebook*. The entire intention of the novel is to shatter the conventional distance of fiction, to deny all distinction between toad and garden, to "write down, simply, what happens." Call the writer Anna Gould or call her Doris Lessing, *The Golden Notebook* is the diary of a writer in shock. There she is in London, 1950. A young woman determined to forge a life as a "free woman," as an "intellectual," she has come out of a simple society into what Robert Penn Warren once called the convulsion of the world, and she is finding some equivocation in the answers so clear to her in Africa. Her expectations give off a bright and dated valiance. Her disenchantments are all too familiar. The sheer will, the granitic ambitiousness of *The Golden Notebook* overrides everything else about it. Great raw hunks of undigested experience, unedited transcripts of what happened between Molly and her son today, overwhelming memories and rejections of those memories as sentimental, the fracturing of a sensibility beginning for the first time to doubt its perceptions: all of it runs out of the teller's mind and into the reader's with deliberate disregard for the nature of the words in between. The teller creates "characters" and "scenes" only to deny their validity. She berates herself for clinging to the "certainty" of her memories in the face of the general uncertainty. Mrs. Lessing looms through *The Golden Notebook* as a woman driven by doubts not only about what to tell but about the validity of telling it at all.

Yet she continued to write, and to write fiction. Not until the end of the five-volume *Children of Violence* series did one sense a weakening of that compulsion to remember, and a metastasis of that cognitive frenzy for answers. She had seen, by then, a great deal go, had seized a great many answers and lost them. Organized politics went early. Freudian determinism seemed incompatible. The Africa of her memory was another country. The voice she felt most deeply, that of women trying to define their relationships to one another and to men, first went shrill and then, appropriated by and reduced to a "movement," slipped below the range of her attention. She had been betrayed by all those answers and more, and yet, increasingly possessed, her only response has been to look for another. That she is scarcely alone in this possession is what lends her quest its great interest: the impulse to final solutions has been not only Mrs. Lessing's dilemma but the guiding delusion of her time. It is not an impulse I hold high, but there is something finally very moving about her tenacity.

1971

GEORGIA O'KEEFFE

"WHERE I WAS born and where and how I have lived is unimportant," Georgia O'Keeffe told us in the book of paintings and words published in her ninetieth year on earth. She seemed to be advising us to forget the beautiful face in the Stieglitz photographs. She appeared to be dismissing the rather condescending romance that had attached to her by then, the romance of extreme good looks and advanced age and deliberate isolation. "It is what I have done with where I have been that should be of interest." I recall an August afternoon in Chicago in 1973 when I took my daughter, then seven, to see what Georgia O'Keeffe had done with where she had been. One of the vast O'Keeffe "Sky Above Clouds" canvases floated over the back stairs in the Chicago Art Institute that day, dominating what seemed to be several stories of empty light, and my daughter looked at it once, ran to the landing, and kept on looking. "Who drew it," she whispered after a while. I told her. "I need to talk to her," she said finally.

My daughter was making, that day in Chicago, an entirely unconscious but quite basic assumption about people and the work they do. She was assuming that the glory she saw in the work reflected a glory in its maker, that the painting was the painter as the poem is the poet, that every choice one made alone—every word chosen or rejected, every brush stroke laid or not laid down—betrayed one's character. *Style is character.* It seemed to me that afternoon that I had rarely seen so instinctive an application of this familiar principle, and I recall being pleased not only that my daughter responded to style as character but that it was Georgia O'Keeffe's particular style to which she responded: this was a hard woman who had imposed her 192 square feet of clouds on Chicago.

"Hardness" has not been in our century a quality much admired in women, nor in the past twenty years has it even been in official

271

favor for men. When hardness surfaces in the very old we tend
to transform it into "crustiness" or eccentricity, some tonic pep-
periness to be indulged at a distance. On the evidence of her
work and what she has said about it, Georgia O'Keeffe is neither
"crusty" nor eccentric. She is simply hard, a straight shooter, a
woman clean of received wisdom and open to what she sees. This
is a woman who could early on dismiss most of her contemporaries as "dreamy," and would later single out one she liked as "a
very poor painter." (And then add, apparently by way of softening
the judgment: "I guess he wasn't a painter at all. He had no courage and I believe that to create one's own world in any of the arts
takes courage.") This is a woman who in 1939 could advise her
admirers that they were missing her point, that their appreciation
of her famous flowers was merely sentimental. "When I paint a
red hill," she observed coolly in the catalogue for an exhibition
that year, "you say it is too bad that I don't always paint flowers.
A flower touches almost everyone's heart. A red hill doesn't touch
everyone's heart." This is a woman who could describe the genesis of one of her most well-known paintings—the "Cow's Skull:
Red, White and Blue" owned by the Metropolitan—as an act of
quite deliberate and derisive orneriness. "I thought of the city
men I had been seeing in the East," she wrote. "They talked so
often of writing the Great American Novel—the Great American
Play—the Great American Poetry. ... So as I was painting my
cow's head on blue I thought to myself, 'I'll make it an American
painting. They will not think it great with the red stripes down
the sides—Red, White and Blue—but they will notice it.'"

The city men. The men. They. The words crop up again and
again as this astonishingly aggressive woman tells us what was
on her mind when she was making her astonishingly aggressive paintings. It was those city men who stood accused of sen-
timentalizing her flowers: "I made you take time to look at what
I saw and when you took time to really notice my flower you
hung all your associations with flowers on my flower and you
write about my flower as if I think and see what you think and
see—and I don't." *And I don't.* Imagine those words spoken, and
the sound you hear is *don't tread on me.* "The men" believed it
impossible to paint New York, so Georgia O'Keeffe painted New
York. "The men" didn't think much of her bright color, so she
made it brighter. The men yearned toward Europe so she went

to Texas, and then New Mexico. The men talked about Cézanne, "long involved remarks about the 'plastic quality' of his form and color," and took one another's long involved remarks, in the view of this angelic rattlesnake in their midst, altogether too seriously. "I can paint one of those dismal-colored paintings like the men," the woman who regarded herself always as an outsider remembers thinking one day in 1922, and she did: a painting of a shed "all low-toned and dreary with the tree beside the door." She called this act of rancor "The Shanty" and hung it in her next show. "The men seemed to approve of it," she reported fifty-four years later, her contempt undimmed. "They seemed to think that maybe I was beginning to paint. That was my only low-toned dismal-colored painting."

Some women fight and others do not. Like so many successful guerrillas in the war between the sexes, Georgia O'Keeffe seems to have been equipped early with an immutable sense of who she was and a fairly clear understanding that she would be required to prove it. On the surface her upbringing was conventional. She was a child on the Wisconsin prairie who played with china dolls and painted watercolors with cloudy skies because sunlight was too hard to paint and, with her brother and sisters, listened every night to her mother read stories of the Wild West, of Texas, of Kit Carson and Billy the Kid. She told adults that she wanted to be an artist and was embarrassed when they asked what kind of artist she wanted to be: she had no idea "what kind." She had no idea what artists did. She had never seen a picture that interested her, other than a pen-and-ink Maid of Athens in one of her mother's books, some Mother Goose illustrations printed on cloth, a tablet cover that showed a little girl with pink roses, and the painting of Arabs on horseback that hung in her grandmother's parlor. At thirteen, in a Dominican convent, she was mortified when the sister corrected her drawing. At Chatham Episcopal Institute in Virginia she painted lilacs and sneaked time alone to walk out to where she could see the line of the Blue Ridge Mountains on the horizon. At the Art Institute in Chicago she was shocked by the presence of live models and wanted to abandon anatomy lessons. At the Art Students League in New York one of her fellow students advised her that, since he would be a great painter and she would end up teaching painting in a girls' school, any work of hers was less important than modeling for him. Another painted over her work to show her how the Impressionists did trees. She had not before heard how the Impressionists did trees and she did not much care.

At twenty-four she left all those opinions behind and went for the first time to live in Texas, where there were no trees to paint and no one to tell her how not to paint them. In Texas there was only the horizon she craved. In Texas she had her sister Claudia with her for a while, and in the late afternoons they would walk away from town and toward the horizon and watch the evening star come out. "That evening star fascinated me," she wrote. "It was in some way very exciting to me. My sister had a gun, and as we walked she would throw bottles into the air and shoot as many as she could before they hit the ground. I had nothing but to walk into nowhere and the wide sunset space with the star. Ten watercolors were made from that star." In a way one's interest is compelled as much by the sister Claudia with the gun as by the painter Georgia with the star, but only the painter left us this shining record. Ten watercolors were made from that star.

1976

IV

SOJOURNS

1969: I HAD better tell you where I am, and why. I am sitting in a high-ceilinged room in the Royal Hawaiian Hotel in Honolulu watching the long translucent curtains billow in the trade wind and trying to put my life back together. My husband is here, and our daughter, age three. She is blond and barefoot, a child of paradise in a frangipani lei, and she does not understand why she cannot go to the beach. She cannot go to the beach because there has been an earthquake in the Aleutians, 7.5 on the Richter scale, and a tidal wave is expected. In two or three minutes the wave, if there is one, will hit Midway Island, and we are awaiting word from Midway. My husband watches the television screen. I watch the curtains, and imagine the swell of the water.

The bulletin, when it comes, is a distinct anticlimax: Midway reports no unusual wave action. My husband switches off the television set and stares out the window. I avoid his eyes, and brush the baby's hair. In the absence of a natural disaster we are left again to our own uneasy devices. We are here on this island in the middle of the Pacific in lieu of filing for divorce.

I tell you this not as aimless revelation but because I want you to know, as you read me, precisely who I am and where I am and what is on my mind. I want you to understand exactly what you are getting: you are getting a woman who for some time now has felt radically separated from most of the ideas that seem to interest other people. You are getting a woman who somewhere along the line misplaced whatever slight faith she ever had in the social contract, in the meliorative principle, in the whole grand pattern of human endeavor. Quite often during the past several years I have felt myself a sleepwalker, moving through the world unconscious of the moment's high issues, oblivious to its data, alert only to the stuff of bad dreams, the children burning in the locked car in the supermarket parking lot, the bike boys stripping down stolen cars on the captive cripple's ranch, the freeway sniper who feels "real bad" about picking off the family of five, the hustlers, the insane, the cunning Okie faces that turn up in military investigations, the sullen lurkers in doorways, the lost children, all the ignorant armies jostling in the night. Acquaintances read *The New York Times*, and try to tell me the news of the world. I listen to call-in shows.

You will perceive that such a view of the world presents difficulties. I have trouble making certain connections. I have trouble maintaining the basic notion that keeping promises matters in a world where everything I was taught seems beside the point. The point itself seems increasingly obscure. I came into adult life equipped with an essentially romantic ethic, holding always before me the examples of Axel Heyst in *Victory* and Milly Theale in *The Wings of the Dove* and Charlotte Rittenmayer in *The Wild Palms* and a few dozen others like them, believing as they did that salvation lay in extreme and doomed commitments, promises made and somehow kept outside the range of normal social experience. I still believe that, but I have trouble reconciling salvation with those ignorant armies camped in my mind. I could indulge here in a little idle generalization, could lay off my own state of profound emotional shock on the larger cultural breakdown, could talk fast about convulsions in the society and alienation and anomie and maybe even assassination, but that would be just one more stylish shell game. I am not the society in microcosm. I am a thirty-four-year-old woman with long straight hair and an old bikini bathing suit and bad nerves sitting on an island in the middle of the Pacific waiting for a tidal wave that will not come.

We spend, my husband and I and the baby, a restorative week in paradise. We are each the other's model of consideration, tact, restraint at the very edge of the precipice. He refrains from noticing when I am staring at nothing, and in turn I refrain from dwelling at length upon a newspaper story about a couple who apparently threw their infant and then themselves into the boiling crater of a live volcano on Maui. We also refrain from mentioning any kicked-down doors, hospitalized psychotics, any chronic anxieties or packed suitcases. We lie in the sun, drive out through the cane to Waimea Bay. We breakfast on the terrace, and gray-haired women smile benevolently at us. I smile back. Happy families are all alike on the terrace of the Royal Hawaiian Hotel in Honolulu. My husband comes in from Kalakaua Avenue one morning and tells me that he has seen a six-foot-two drag queen we know in Los Angeles. Our acquaintance was shopping, my husband reports, for a fishnet bikini and did not speak. We both laugh. I am reminded that we laugh at the same things, and read him this complaint from a very old copy of *Honolulu* magazine I picked up in someone's office: "When President Johnson recently came to Honolulu, the morning paper's banner read something like 'PICKETS TO GREET PRESIDENT.' Would it not have been just as newsworthy to say 'WARM ALOHA TO GREET PRESIDENT'?" At the end of the week I tell my husband that I am going to try harder to make things matter. My husband says that he has heard that before, but the air is warm and the baby has another frangipani lei and there is no rancor in his voice. Maybe it can be all right, I say. Maybe, he says.

1970: Quite early every morning in Honolulu, on that stretch of Waikiki Beach which fronts the Royal Hawaiian Hotel, an employee of the hotel spends fifteen or twenty minutes raking the sand within a roped enclosure reserved for registered guests. Since this "private" beach differs from the "public" beach only by its raked sand, its rope, and its further remove from the water, it is at first difficult to see why anyone would sit there, but people do. They sit there all day long and in great numbers, facing the sea in even rows.

I had been an occasional visitor to Honolulu for several years before I entirely perceived that the roped beach was central to the essence of the Royal Hawaiian, that the point of sitting there was not at all exclusivity, as is commonly supposed on Waikiki, but inclusivity. Anyone behind the rope is presumed to be, by tacit definition, "our kind." Anyone behind the rope will watch over our children as we will watch over theirs, will not palm room keys or smoke dope or listen to Creedence Clearwater on a transistor when we are awaiting word from the Mainland on the prime rate. Anyone behind the rope, should we venture conversation, will "know people we know": the Royal's roped beach is an enclave of apparent strangers ever on the verge of discovering that their nieces roomed in Lagunita at Stanford the same year, or that their best friends lunched together during the last Crosby. The fact that anyone behind the rope would understand the word "Crosby" to signify a golf tournament at Pebble Beach

JOAN DIDION

suggests the extent to which the Royal Hawaiian is not merely
a hotel but a social idea, one of the few extant clues to a certain
kind of American life.

Of course great hotels have always been social ideas, flawless
mirrors to the particular societies they service. Had there never
been an Empire there would not have been a Raffles. To understand what the Royal is now you must first understand what it
was, from 1927 through the Thirties, the distant and mildly exotic
"pink palace" of the Pacific, the resort built by the Matson Line to
rival and surpass such hotels as the Coronado, the Broadmoor, Del
Monte. Standing then almost alone on Waikiki, the Royal made
Honolulu a place to go, made all things "Hawaiian"—leis, ukule-
les, luaus, coconut-leaf hats and the singing of "I Wanna Learn to
Speak Hawaiian"—a decade's craze at country-club dances across
the United States. During the fourteen years between the Royal's
opening and Pearl Harbor people came in on the Matson Line's
Malolo and *Lurline* and they brought with them not only steamer
trunks but children and grandchildren and valets and nurses and
silver Rolls-Royces and ultramarine-blue Packard roadsters. They
"wintered" at the Royal, or "summered" there, or "spent several
months." They came to the Royal to rest "after hunting in South
Africa." They went home "by way of Banff and Lake Louise."
In Honolulu there was polo, golf, bowling on the green. Every
afternoon the Royal served tea on rattan tables. The maids wove
leis for every guest. The chefs constructed, as table decoration, the
United States Capitol Building in Hawaiian sugar.

The Royal's scrapbooks for those years survive as an index to
America's industrial fortunes, large and small. Mellons and Du
Ponts and Gettys and the man who had just patented the world's
largest incubator (47,000-egg capacity) seem to differ not at all
from one another, photographed at the Royal in 1928. Dorothy
Spreckels strums a ukulele on the verandah. Walter P. Chrysler,
Jr., arrives with his mother and father for a season at the Royal.
A figure on the beach is described as "a Colorado Springs soci-
ety woman," a young couple as "prominently identified with the
young-married set in Akron." At the Royal they met not only
one another but a larger world as well: Australian station owners,
Ceylonese tea planters, Cuban sugar operators.

In the faded photographs one sees mostly mothers and
daughters. The men, when they are present, display in the main

an affecting awkwardness, an awareness that they have harsher roles, say as mayor of Seattle or president of the Overland Motor Company, a resistance to the world of summering and wintering. In 1931 the son of President Hoover spent time at the Royal, was widely entertained, caught thirty-eight fish off the Kona coast of Hawaii, and had his picture taken on the Royal beach shaking hands with Duke Kahanamoku. This photograph appeared in *Town and Country*, which also reported in 1931 that "the diving boys in Honolulu harbor say that fishing has been good and there are no indications of hard times in the denominations of coins flipped to them as bait from incoming steamers."

Nor did the turnings of the Sixties effect much change at the Royal. What the place reflected in the Thirties it reflects still, in less flamboyant mutations: a kind of life lived always on the streets where the oldest trees grow. It is a life so secure in its traditional concerns that the cataclysms of the larger society disturb it only as surface storms disturb the sea's bottom, a long time later and in oblique ways. It is a life lived by millions of people in this country and largely forgotten by most of us. Sometimes I think I remember it only at the Royal Hawaiian. There in the warm early evenings, the women in turquoise-blue and buttercup-yellow chiffons seem, as they wait for cars under the pink porte-cochere, the natural inheritors of a style later seized upon by Patricia Nixon and her daughters. In the mornings, when the beach is just raked and the air damp and sweet from the dawn rain, I see the same women, now in printed silks and lined cashmere cardigans, eating papaya on the terrace just as they have done every few seasons since they were young girls, in the late Twenties, and came to the Royal with their mothers and sisters. Their husbands scan the San Francisco and Los Angeles papers with the practiced disinterest of men who believe their lives safe in municipal bonds. These papers arrive at the Royal one and sometimes two days late, which lends the events of the day a peculiar and unsettling distance. I recall overhearing a conversation at the Royal's newsstand on the morning after the California primary in June 1968, the morning Robert Kennedy lay dying in Good Samaritan Hospital in Los Angeles. "How'd the primary go?" a man buying cigarettes asked his wife. She studied the day-old headlines. "'Early Turnout Heavy,'" she said. Later in the morning I overheard this woman discussing the assassination: her

JOAN DIDION

husband had heard the news when he dropped by a brokerage office to get the day's New York closings.

To sit by the Royal pool and read *The New York Review of Books* is to feel oneself an asp, disguised in a voile beach robe, in the very bosom of the place. I put *The New York Review of Books* aside and talk to a pretty young woman who has honeymooned at the Royal, because honeymoons at the Royal are a custom in her family, with each of her three husbands. My daughter makes friends at the pool with another four-year-old, Jill, from Fairbanks, Alaska, and it is taken for granted by Jill's mother and aunt that the two children will meet again, year after year, in the immutable pleasant rhythms of a life that used to be, and at the Royal Hawaiian seems still to be. I sit in my voile beach robe and watch the children and wish, against all the evidence I know, that it might be so.

1970: To look down upon Honolulu from the high rain forest that divides windward Oahu from the leeward city is to see, in the center of an extinct volcano named Puowaina, a place so still and private that once seen it is forever in the mind. There are banyan trees in the crater, and rain trees, and 19,500 graves. Yellow primavera blazes on the hills above. Whole slopes seem clouded in mauve jacaranda. This is the place commonly called Punchbowl, the National Memorial Cemetery of the Pacific, and 13,000 of the dead in its crater were killed during World War II. Some of the rest died in Korea. For almost a decade now, in the outer sections just inside the rim of the crater, they have been digging graves for Americans killed in Vietnam, not many, a fraction of the total, one, two, three a week, most of them Island boys but some of them carried here by families who live thousands of miles across the Pacific, a gesture that touches by its very difficulty. Because the Vietnam dead are shipped first to Travis A.F.B. in California and then to the next of kin, those Mainland families burying their sons or husbands in Honolulu must bring the bodies back over the Pacific one last time. The superintendent of Punchbowl, Martin T. Corley, refers to such burials as his "ship-in Vietnams."

"A father or an uncle calls me from the Mainland and he says they're bringing their boy here, I don't ask why," Mr. Corley said when I talked to him not long ago. We were sitting in his office in the crater and on the wall hung the Bronze Star and Silver Star citations he had received in Europe in 1944, Martin T. Corley, a man in an aloha shirt who had gone from South Ozone Park in Queens to the Battle of the Bulge to a course in cemetery management at Fort Sam Houston and finally, twenty-some years later, to an office in an extinct volcano in the Pacific from which he could watch the quick and the dead in still another war.

I watched him leafing through a stack of what he called "transmittals," death forms from Vietnam. There in Martin T. Corley's office Vietnam seemed considerably less chimerical than it had seemed on the Mainland for some months, less last year's war, less successfully consigned to that limbo of benign neglect in which any mention of continuing casualties was made to seem a little counterproductive, a little démodé. There in the crater it seemed less easy to believe that weekly killed-in-action figures under 100 might by some sleight-of-hand add up to zero, a nonexistent war. There in sight of the automatic gravediggers what the figures added up to, for the first twelve weeks of 1970, was 1,078 dead. Martin T. Corley gets a transmittal on each of them. He holds these transmittal forms for fifteen or twenty days before throwing them away, just in case a family wants to bring its dead to Punchbowl. "See, we had a family bring a boy in from Oregon a few days ago," he said. "We've got a California coming in now. We figure they've got their reasons. We pick the plot, open the grave. These ship-in families, we don't see them until the hearse comes through the gate."

On a warm windy afternoon a few days later I stood with Mr. Corley on the soft grass up in Section K of the crater and waited for one such family to come through the gate. They had flown out from the Mainland with the body the night before, six of them, the mother and father and a sister and her husband and a couple of other relatives, and they would bury their boy in the afternoon sun and fly back a few hours later. We waited, and we watched, and then, on the road below, the six Air Force pallbearers snapped to attention. The bugler jumped up from beneath a banyan tree and took his place behind the honor guard. We could see the hearse then, winding up and around the circular road to Section K, the hearse and two cars, their headlights dim in the tropical sun. "Two of us from the office come to all the Vietnams," Mr. Corley said suddenly. "I mean in case the family breaks down or something."

All I can tell you about the next ten minutes is that they seemed a very long time. We watched the coffin being carried to the grave and we watched the pallbearers lift the flag, trying to hold it taut in the warm trade wind. The wind was blowing hard, toppling the vases of gladioli set by the grave, obliterating some of the chaplain's words. "If God is for us then who can be against us," the chaplain said, a red-headed young major in suntans, and then I did not hear any more for a while. I was standing behind the six canvas chairs where the family sat, standing there with Mr. Corley and an Air Force survival assistance officer, and I was looking beyond the chaplain to a scattering of graves so fresh they had no headstones, just plastic markers stuck in the ground. "We tenderly commit this body to the ground," the chaplain said then. The men in the honor guard raised their rifles. Three shots cracked out. The bugler played taps. The pallbearers folded the flag until only the blue field and a few stars showed, and one of them stepped forward to present the flag to the father. For the first time the father looked away from the coffin, looked away from the pallbearers and out across the expanse of graves. A slight man with his face trembling and his eyes wet, he stood facing Mr. Corley and me, and for a moment we looked directly at each other, but he was seeing not me, not Mr. Corley, not anyone.

It was not quite three o'clock. The father, transferring the flag from hand to hand as if it burned, said a few halting words to the pallbearers. I walked away from the grave then, down to my car, and waited for Mr. Corley to talk to the father. He wanted to tell the father that if he and his wife wanted to come back before their plane left, the grave would be covered by four o'clock. "Sometimes it makes them feel better to see it," Mr. Corley said when he caught up with me. "Sometimes they get on the plane and they worry, you know, it didn't get covered." His voice trailed off. "We cover within thirty minutes," he said finally. "Fill, cover, get the marker on. That's one thing I remember from my training." We stood there a moment in the warm wind, then said goodbye. The pallbearers filed onto the Air Force bus. The bugler walked past, whistling "Raindrops Keep Fallin' on My Head." Just after four o'clock the father and mother came back and looked for a long while at the covered grave, then took a night flight back to the Mainland. Their son was one of 101 Americans killed that week in Vietnam.

1975: The 8:45 A.M. Pan American to Honolulu this morning was delayed half an hour before takeoff from Los Angeles. During this delay the stewardesses served orange juice and coffee and two children played tag in the aisles and, somewhere behind me, a man began screaming at a woman who seemed to be his wife. I say that the woman seemed to be his wife only because the tone of his invective sounded practiced, although the only words I heard clearly were these: "You are driving me to murder." After a moment I was aware of the door to the plane being opened a few rows behind me, and of the man rushing off. There were many Pan American employees rushing on and off then, and considerable confusion. I do not know whether the man reboarded the plane before takeoff or whether the woman came on to Honolulu alone, but I thought about it all the way across the Pacific. I thought about it while I was drinking a sherry-on-the-rocks and I thought about it during lunch and I was still thinking about it when the first of the Hawaiian Islands appeared off the left wing tip. It was not until we had passed Diamond Head and were coming in low over the reef for landing at Honolulu, however, that I realized what I most disliked about this incident: I disliked it because it had the aspect of a short story, one of those "little epiphany" stories in which the main character glimpses a crisis in a stranger's life—a woman weeping in a tearoom, often, or an accident seen from the window of a train, "tearooms" and "trains" still being fixtures of short stories although not of real life—and is moved to see his or her own life in a new light. I was not going to Honolulu because I wanted to see life reduced to a short story. I was going to Honolulu because I wanted to see life expanded to a novel, and I still do. I wanted room for flowers, and reef fish, and people who may or may not be driving one another to murder but in any case are not impelled, by the demands of narrative convention, to say so out loud on the 8:45 A.M. Pan American to Honolulu.

* * *

1977: I have never seen a postcard of Hawaii that featured Schofield Barracks. Schofield is off the track, off the tour, hard by the shadowy pools of the Wahiawa Reservoir, and to leave Honolulu and drive inland to Schofield is to sense a clouding of the atmosphere, a darkening of the color range. The translucent pastels of the famous coast give way to the opaque greens of interior Oahu. Crushed white coral gives way to red dirt, sugar dirt, deep red laterite soil that crumbles soft in the hand and films over grass and boots and hubcaps. Clouds mass over the Waianae Range. Cane fires smoke on the horizon and rain falls fitfully. BUY SOME COLLARD GREENS, reads a sign on a weathered frame grocery in Wahiawa, just across the two-lane bridge from the Schofield gate. MASSAGE PARLOR, CHECKS CASHED, 50TH STATE POOLROOM, HAPPY HOUR, CASH FOR CARS. Schofield Loan. Schofield Pawn. Schofield Sands Motor Lodge. Then, finally, Schofield itself, the Schofield we all know from James Jones's *From Here to Eternity*, the Schofield that is Home of the 25th "Tropic Lightning" Infantry Division, formerly the Hawaii Division, James Jones's own division, Robert E. Lee Prewitt's division, Maggio's and Warden's and Stark's and Dynamite Holmes's division, *Fit to Fight, Trained to Win, Ready to Go. All Wars Are Won in the End by the Infantryman. Through These Portals Pass the Finest Soldiers in the World*—25TH INFANTRY DIVISION SOLDIERS. TROPIC LIGHTNING REENLISTMENT. I have never driven into Schofield and seen those words without hearing the blues that end *From Here to Eternity*:

> *Got paid out on Monday*
> *Not a dog soldier no more*
> *They gimme all that money*
> *So much my pockets is sore*
> *More dough than I can use. Reenlistment Blues.*
> *Ain't no time to lose. Reenlistment Blues.*

Certain places seem to exist mainly because someone has written about them. Kilimanjaro belongs to Ernest Hemingway. Oxford, Mississippi, belongs to William Faulkner, and one hot

July week in Oxford I was moved to spend an afternoon walking the graveyard looking for his stone, a kind of courtesy call on the owner of the property. A place belongs forever to whoever claims it hardest, remembers it most obsessively, wrenches it from itself, shapes it, renders it, loves it so radically that he remakes it in his image, and not only Schofield Barracks but a great deal of Honolulu itself has always belonged for me to James Jones. The first time I ever saw Hotel Street in Honolulu was on a Saturday night in 1966 when all the bars and tattoo parlors were full of military police and girls looking for a dollar and nineteen-year-olds, on their way to or from Saigon, looking for a girl. I recall looking that night for the particular places that had figured in *From Here to Eternity*: the Black Cat, the Blue Anchor, the whorehouse Jones called the New Congress Hotel. I remember driving up Wilhemina Rise to look for Alma's house and I remember walking out of the Royal Hawaiian Hotel and expecting to see Prewitt and Maggio sitting on the curb and I remember walking the Waialae Country Club golf course, trying to figure exactly where Prewitt died. I think it was in the trap near the fifth green.

It is hard to see one of these places claimed by fiction without a sudden blurring, a slippage, a certain vertiginous occlusion of the imagined and the real, and this slippage was particularly acute the last time I arrived in Honolulu, on a June day when the author of *From Here to Eternity* had been dead just a few weeks. In New York the death of James Jones had been the occasion for many considerations and reconsiderations. Many mean guilts had been recalled and exorcised. Many lessons had been divined, in both the death and the life. In Honolulu the death of James Jones had been marked by the publication, in the *Honolulu Star-Bulletin*, of an excerpt from the author's *Viet Journal*, the epilogue, the part in which he talked about returning to Honolulu in 1973 and looking for the places he had remembered in *From Here to Eternity* but had last seen in 1942, when he was twenty-one years old and shipped out for Guadalcanal with the 25th Division. In 1973 the five pillboxes on Makapuu Head had seemed to James Jones exactly as he had left them in 1942. In 1973 the Royal Hawaiian Hotel had seemed to James Jones less formidably rich than he had left it in 1942, and it had occurred to him with considerable poignance that he was a man in his fifties who could walk into the Royal Hawaiian and buy whatever he wanted.

He had bought a beer and gone back to Paris. In June of 1977 he was dead and it was not possible to buy a copy of his great novel, his living novel, the novel in which he so loved Honolulu that he remade it in his image, in any of Honolulu's largest book-stores. "Is it a best-seller?" I was asked in one, and the golden child in charge of another suggested that I try the psychic-science shelf. In that instant I thought I grieved for James Jones, a man I never met, but I think I grieved for all of us: for Jones, for myself, for the sufferers of mean guilts and for their exorcists, for Robert E. Lee Prewitt, for the Royal Hawaiian Hotel and for this golden nitwit who believed eternity to be a psychic science.

I have never been sure whether the extreme gravity of *From Here to Eternity* is an exact reflection of the light at Schofield Barracks or whether I see the light as grave because I have read James Jones. "It had rained all morning and then suddenly cleared at noon, and the air, freshly washed today, was like dark crystal in the sharp clarity and sombre focus it gave to every image." It was in this sombre focus that James Jones rendered Schofield, and it was in this sombre focus that I last saw Schofield, one Monday during that June. It had rained in the morning and the smell of eucalyptus was sharp in the air and I had again that familiar sense of having left the bright coast and entered a darker country. The black outline of the Waianae Range seemed obscurely oppressive. A foursome on the post golf course seemed to have been playing since 1940, and to be doomed to continue. A soldier in fatigues appeared to be trimming a bougainvillea hedge, swinging at it with a scythe, but his movements were hypnotically slowed, and the scythe never quite touched the hedge. Around the tropical frame bungalows where the families of Schofield officers have always lived there was an occasional tricycle but no child, no wife, no sign of life but one: a Yorkshire terrier yapping on the lawn of a colonel's bungalow. As it happens I have spent time around Army posts in the role of an officer's child, have even played with lap dogs on the lawns of colonels' quarters, but I saw this Yorkshire with Prewitt's eyes, and I hated it.

I had driven out to Schofield in other seasons, but this trip was different. I was making this trip for the same reason I had walked the Oxford graveyard, a courtesy call on the owner. This trip I made appointments, spoke to people, asked questions and wrote down answers, had lunch with my hosts at the Aloha Lightning NCO Club and was shown the regimental trophies and studied the portraits of commanding officers in every corridor I walked down. Unlike the golden children in the Honolulu bookstores these men I met at Schofield, these men in green fatigues, all knew exactly who James Jones was and what he had written and even where he had slept and eaten and probably gotten drunk during the three years he spent at Schofield. They recalled the incidents and locations of *From Here to Eternity* in minute detail. They anticipated those places that I would of course want to see: D Quad, the old stockade, the stone quarry, Kolekole Pass. Some weeks before, there had been at the post theater a special screening of the movie *From Here to Eternity*, an event arranged by the Friends of the Tropic Lightning Historical Society, and everyone to whom I spoke at Schofield had turned out for this screening. Many of these men were careful to qualify their obvious attachment to James Jones's view of their life by pointing out that the Army had changed. Others did not mention the change. One, a young man who had re-upped once and now wanted out, mentioned that it had not changed at all. We were standing on the lawn in D Quad, Jones's quad, Robert E. Lee Prewitt's quad, and I was watching the idle movement around the square, a couple of soldiers dropping a basketball through a hoop, another cleaning an M-16, a desultory argument at the Dutch door of the supply room—when he volunteered a certain inchoate dissatisfaction with his six years in the 25th Division. "I read this book *From Here to Eternity*," he said, "and they still got the same little games around here."

I suppose everything had changed and nothing had. A mess hall was now called a "dining facility," but they still served chipped beef on toast and they still called it "S.O.S." A stockade was now called a "confinement facility," and the confinement facility for all military installations on Oahu was now at Pearl Harbor, but the old stockade at Schofield was now the headquarters for the military police, and during the time I was there the M.P.s brought in a handcuffed soldier, bare to the waist and shoeless.

Investigators in aloha shirts chatted in the exercise yard. Office supplies were stored in some of the "close confinement" cells, but there were still the plain wooden bunks, "plate beds," beds for those occasions, it was explained to me by a major who had once been in charge of the Schofield stockade, "when a guy is completely berserk and starts ripping up his mattress." On the wall there were still the diagrams detailing the order in which belongings were to be arranged: WHITE TOWEL, SOAP WITH DISH, DEODORANT, TOOTHPASTE, TOOTHBRUSH, COMB, SHAVING CREAM, RAZOR.

In many ways I found it difficult to leave Schofield that day. I had fallen into the narcoleptic movements of the Army day. I had picked up the liquid speech patterns of the Army voice. I took a copy of the *Tropic Lightning News* back into Honolulu with me, and read it that night in my hotel room. During the month of May the Schofield military police had reported 32 arrests for driving under the influence of alcohol, 115 arrests for possession of marijuana, and the theft of a number of items, including one Sansui amplifier, one Sansui pre-amp and tuner, one Kenwood receiver and turntable, two Bose speakers and the tachometer from a 1969 Ford Mustang. One private, two spec fours and one sergeant were asked in the "Troop Talk" column to name their ideal, or favorite, post. One chose Fort Hood. Another chose Fort Sam Houston. None chose Schofield Barracks. In the letters column one correspondent advised a WAC who had objected to the shows at the NCO Club to stay home ("We once had it set up where you girls didn't have to see the entertainment, but the loverly libbers put an end to that"), and another advised "barracks rats" to stop limiting their lives to "erasing Army hatred by indulging in smoke or drink or listening to Peter Frampton at eighty decibels." I thought about barracks rats and I thought about Prewitt and Maggio and I thought about Army hatred and it seemed to me that night in Honolulu that only the details had changed, that James Jones had known a great simple truth: the Army was nothing more or less than life itself. I wish I could tell you that on the day in May when James Jones died someone had played a taps for him at Schofield Barracks, but I think this is not the way life goes.

1969–77

"YOU CAN TAKE Hollywood for granted like I did," Cecilia Brady tells the reader in *The Last Tycoon*, "or you can dismiss it with the contempt we reserve for what we don't understand. It can be understood, too, but only dimly and in flashes. Not half a dozen men have ever been able to keep the whole equation of pictures in their heads." To the extent that *The Last Tycoon* is "about" Hollywood it is about not Monroe Stahr but Cecilia Brady, as anyone who understands the equation of pictures even dimly or in flashes would apprehend immediately: the Monroe Stahrs come and go, but the Cecilia Bradys are the second generation, the survivors, the inheritors of a community as intricate, rigid, and deceptive in its mores as any devised on this continent. At midwinter in the survivors' big houses off Benedict Canyon the fireplaces blaze all day with scrub oak and eucalyptus, the French windows are opened wide to the subtropical sun, the rooms filled with white phalaenopsis and cymbidium orchids and needlepoint rugs and the requisite scent of Rigaud candles. Dinner guests pick with vermeil forks at broiled fish and limestone lettuce *vinaigrette*, decline dessert, adjourn to the screening room, and settle down to *The Heartbreak Kid* with a little seltzer in a Baccarat glass.

After the picture the women, a significant number of whom seem to have ascended through chronic shock into an elusive dottiness, discuss for a ritual half-hour the transpolar move-ments of acquaintances and the peace of spirit to be derived from exercise class, ballet class, the use of paper napkins at the beach. Quentin Bell's *Virginia Woolf* was an approved event this winter, as were the Chinese acrobats, the recent visits to Los Angeles of Bianca Jagger, and the opening in Beverly Hills of a branch Bonwit Teller. The men talk pictures, grosses, the deal, the morning line on the talent. "Face it," I heard someone say the other night of a director whose current picture had opened a few days before to tepid business. "Last week he was bankable."

Such evenings end before midnight. Such couples leave together. Should there be marital unhappiness it will go unmentioned until one of the principals is seen lunching with a lawyer. Should there be illness it will go unadmitted until the onset of the terminal coma. Discretion is "good taste," and discretion is also good business, since there are enough imponderables in the business of Hollywood without handing the dice to players too distracted to concentrate on the action. This is a community whose notable excesses include virtually none of the flesh or spirit: heterosexual adultery is less easily tolerated than respectably settled homosexual marriages or well-managed liaisons between middle-aged women. "A nice lesbian relationship, the most common thing in the world," I recall Otto Preminger insisting when my husband and I expressed doubt that the heroine of the Preminger picture we were writing should have one. "Very easy to arrange, does not threaten the marriage."

Flirtations between men and women, like drinks after dinner, remain largely the luxury of character actors out from New York, one-shot writers, reviewers being courted by Industry people, and others who do not understand the *mise* of the local *scène*. In the houses of the inheritors the preservation of the community is paramount, and it is also Universal, Columbia, Fox, Metro, and Warner's. It is in this tropism toward survival that Hollywood sometimes presents the appearance of the last extant stable society.

One afternoon not long ago, at a studio where my husband was doing some work, the director of a picture in production collapsed of cardiac arrest. At six o'clock the director's condition was under discussion in the executives' steam room.

"I called the hospital," the head of production for the studio said. "I talked to his wife."

"Hear what Dick did," one of the other men in the steam room commanded. "Wasn't that a nice thing for Dick to do."

This story illustrates many elements of social reality in Hollywood, but few of the several non-Industry people to whom I have told it have understood it. For one thing it involves a "studio," and many people outside the Industry are gripped by the delusion that "studios" have nothing to do with the making of motion pictures in modern times. They have heard the phrase "independent production," and have fancied that the phrase means what the words mean. They have been told about "runaways," about "empty sound stages," about "death knell" after "death knell" sounding for the Industry.

In fact the byzantine but very efficient economics of the business render such rhetoric even more meaningless than it sounds: the studios still put up almost all the money. The studios still control all effective distribution. In return for financing and distributing the average "independent" picture, the studio gets not only the largest share (at least half) of any profit made by the picture, but, more significantly, 100 per cent of what the picture brings in up to a point called the "break," or break-even, an arbitrary figure usually set at 2.7 or 2.8 times the actual, or "negative," cost of the picture.

Most significant of all, the "break-even" never represents the point at which the studio actually breaks even on any given production: that point occurs, except on paper, long before, since the studio has already received 10 to 25 percent of the picture's budget as an "overhead" charge, has received additional rental and other fees for any services actually rendered the production company, and continues to receive, throughout the picture's release, a fee amounting to about a third of the picture's income as a "distribution" charge. In other words there is considerable income hidden in the risk itself, and the ideal picture from the studio's point of view is often said to be the picture that makes one dollar less than break-even. More perfect survival bookkeeping has been devised, but mainly in Chicago and Las Vegas.

Still, it is standard for anyone writing about Hollywood to slip out of the economic reality and into a catchier metaphor, usually paleontological, *vide* John Simon: "I shall not rehearse here the well-known facts of how the industry started dying from being too bulky, toothless, and dated—just like all those other saurians of a few aeons ago...." So pervasive is this vocabulary of extinction (Simon forgot the mandatory illusion to the La Brea Tar Pits) that I am frequently assured by visitors that the studios are "morgues," that they are "shuttered up," that in "the new Hollywood" the "studio has no power." The studio has.

* * *

January in the last extant stable society. I know that it is January for an empirical fact only because wild mustard glazes the hills an acid yellow, and because there are poinsettias in front of all the bungalows down around Goldwyn and Technicolor, and because many people from Beverly Hills are at La Costa and Palm Springs and many people from New York are at the Beverly Hills Hotel.

"This whole town's dead," one such New York visitor tells me. "I dropped into the Polo Lounge last night, the place was a wasteland." He tells me this every January, and every January I tell him that people who live and work here do not frequent hotel bars either before or after dinner, but he seems to prefer his version. On reflection I can think of only three non-Industry people in New York whose version of Hollywood corresponds at any point with the reality of the place, and they are Johanna Mankiewicz Davis, Jill Schary Robinson and Jean Stein van-den Heuvel, the daughters respectively of the late screenwriter Herman Mankiewicz; the producer and former production chief at Metro, Dore Schary; and the founder of the Music Corporation of America and Universal Pictures, Jules Stein. "We don't go for strangers in Hollywood," Cecilia Brady said.

Days pass. Visitors arrive, scout the Polo Lounge, and leave, confirmed in their conviction that they have penetrated an art-fully camouflaged disaster area. The morning mail contains a statement from 20th Century-Fox on a picture in which my husband and I are supposed to have "points," or a percentage. The picture cost $1,367,224.57. It has so far grossed $947,494.86. The statement might suggest to the casual subtracter that the picture is about $400,000 short of breaking even, but this is not the case: the statement reports that the picture is $1,389,112.72 short of breaking even. "$1,389,112.72 unrecovered" is, literally, the bottom line.

In lieu of contemplating why a venture that cost a million-three and has recovered almost a million remains a million-three in the red, I decide to get my hair cut, pick up the trades, learn that *The Poseidon Adventure* is grossing four million dollars a week, that Adolph "Papa" Zukor will celebrate his 100th birthday at a dinner sponsored by Paramount, and that James Aubrey, Ted Ashley and Freddie Fields rented a house together in Acapulco over Christmas. At this moment in the action, James Aubrey is Metro-Goldwyn-Mayer. Ted Ashley is Warner Brothers. Freddie

Fields is Creative Management Associates, First Artists and the Directors Company. The players will change but the game will stay the same. The bottom line seems clear on the survival of Adolph "Papa" Zukor, but not yet on that of James Aubrey, Ted Ashley and Freddie Fields.

"Listen, I got this truly beautiful story," the man who cuts my hair says to me. "Think about some new Dominique-Sanda-type unknown. *Comprenez* so far?"

So far *comprends*. The man who cuts my hair, like everyone else in the community, is looking for the action, the game, a few chips to lay down. Here in the grand casino no one needs capital. One needs only this truly beautiful story. Or maybe if no truly beautiful story comes to mind one needs $500 to go halves on a $1,000 option payment for someone else's truly beautiful but (face it) three-year-old property. (A book or a story is a "property" only until the deal; after that it is "the basic material," as in "I haven't read the basic material on *Gatsby*.") True, the casino is not now so wide open as it was in '69, summer and fall of '69 when every studio in town was narcotized by *Easy Rider*'s grosses and all that was needed to get a picture off the ground was the suggestion of a $750,000 budget, a low-cost NABET or even a nonunion crew, and this terrific 22-year-old kid director. As it turned out most of these pictures were shot as usual by IATSE rather than NABET crews and they cost as usual not seven-fifty but a million-two and many of them ended up unreleased, shelved. And so there was one very bad summer there, the hangover summer of 1970, when nobody could get past the gate without a commitment from Barbra Streisand.

That was the summer when all the terrific 22-year-old directors went back to shooting television commercials and all the creative 24-year-old producers used up the leases on their office space at Warner Brothers by sitting out there in the dull Burbank sunlight smoking dope before lunch and running one another's unreleased pictures after lunch. But that period is over and the game is back on, development money available, the deal dependent only upon the truly beautiful story and the right elements. The elements matter. "We like the *elements*," they say at studios when they are maybe going to make the deal. That is why the man who cuts my hair is telling me his story. A writer might be an element. I listen because in certain ways I am a captive but willing audience, not only to the hairdresser but at the grand casino.

The place makes everyone a gambler. Its spirit is speedy, obsessive, immaterial. The action itself is the art form, and is described in aesthetic terms: "A very imaginative deal," they say, or, "He writes the most creative deals in the business." There is in Hollywood, as in all cultures in which gambling is the central activity, a lowered sexual energy, an inability to devote more than token attention to the preoccupations of the society outside. The action is everything, more consuming than sex, more immediate than politics; more important always than the acquisition of money, which is never, for the gambler, the true point of the exercise.

I talk on the telephone to an agent, who tells me that he has on his desk a check made out to a client for $1,275,000, the client's share of first profits on a picture now in release. Last week, in someone's office, I was shown another such check, this one made out for $4,850,000. Every year there are a few such checks around town. An agent will speak of such a check as being "on my desk," or "on Guy McElwaine's desk," as if the exact physical location lent the piece of paper its credibility. One year they might be the *Midnight Cowboy* and *Butch Cassidy* checks, another year the *Love Story* and *Godfather* checks.

In a curious way these checks are not "real," not real money in the sense that a check for a thousand dollars can be real money; no one "needs" $4,850,000, nor is it really disposable income. It is instead the unexpected payoff on dice rolled a year or two before, and its reality is altered not only by the time lapse but by the fact that no one ever counted on the payoff. A four-million-dollar windfall has the aspect only of Monopoly money, but the actual pieces of paper which bear such figures have, in the community, a totemic significance. They are totems of the action. When I hear of these totems I think reflexively of Sergius O'Shaugnessy, who sometimes believed what he said and tried to take the cure in the very real sun of Desert D'Or with its cactus, its mountain, and the bright green foliage of its love and its money.

* * *

Since any survivor is believed capable in the community of conferring on others a ritual and lucky kinship, the birthday dinner for Adolph "Papa" Zukor turns out also to have a totemic significance. It is described by Robert Evans, head of production at Paramount, as "one of the memorable evenings in our Industry.... There's never been anyone who's reached one hundred before." Hit songs from old Paramount pictures are played throughout dinner. Jack Valenti speaks of the guest of honor as "the motion picture world's living proof that there is a connection between us and our past."

Zukor himself, who is described in *Who's Who* as a "motion picture mfr." and in *Daily Variety* as a "firm believer in the philosophy that today is the first day of the rest of your life," appears after dinner to express his belief in the future of motion pictures and his pleasure at Paramount's recent grosses. Many of those present have had occasion over the years to regard Adolph "Papa" Zukor with some rancor, but on this night there is among them a resigned warmth, a recognition that they will attend one another's funerals. This ceremonial healing of old and recent scars is a way of life among the survivors, as is the scarring itself. "Having some fun" is what the scarring is called. "Let's go see Nick, I think we'll have some fun," David O. Selznick remembered his father saying to him when the elder Selznick was on his way to tell Nick Schenk that he was going to take 50 percent of the gross of *Ben-Hur* away from him.

The winter progresses. My husband and I fly to Tucson with our daughter for a few days of meetings on a script with a producer on location. We go out to dinner in Tucson: the sitter tells me that she has obtained, for her crippled son, an autographed picture of Paul Newman. I ask how old her son is. "Thirty-four," she says.

We came for two days, we stay for four. We rarely leave the Hilton Inn. For everyone on the picture this life on location will continue for twelve weeks. The producer and the director collect Navajo belts and speak every day to Los Angeles, New York, London. They are setting up other deals, other action. By the time this picture is released and reviewed they will be on location in

other cities. A picture in release is gone. A picture in release tends
to fade from the minds of the people who made it. As the four-
million-dollar check is only the totem of the action, the picture
itself is in many ways only the action's by-product. "We can have
some fun with this one," the producer says as we leave Tucson.
"Having some fun" is also what the action itself is called.

I pass along these notes by way of suggesting that much of what is
written about pictures and about picture people approaches reality only occasionally and accidentally. At one time the assurance
with which many writers about film palmed off their miscon-
ceptions puzzled me a good deal. I used to wonder how Pauline
Kael, say, could slip in and out of such airy subordinate clauses as
"now that the studios are collapsing," or how she could so misread the labyrinthine propriety of Industry evenings as to characterize "Hollywood wives" as women "whose jaws get a hard set
from the nights when they sit soberly at parties waiting to take
their sloshed geniuses home." (This fancy, oddly enough, cropped
up in a review of *Alex in Wonderland*, a Paul Mazursky picture
which, whatever its faults, portrayed with meticulous accuracy
that level of "young" Hollywood on which the average daily nar-
cotic intake is one glass of a three-dollar Mondavi white and two
marijuana cigarettes shared by six people.) These "sloshed" husbands and "collapsing" studios derive less from Hollywood life
than from some weird West Side *Playhouse* 90 about Hollywood
life, presumably the same one Stanley Kauffmann runs on his
mind's screen when he speaks of a director like John Huston as
"corrupted by success."

What is there to be said about this particular cast of mind?
Some people who write about film seem so temperamentally at
odds with what both Fellini and Truffaut have called the "circus"
aspect of making film that there is flatly no question of their ever
apprehending the social or emotional reality of the process. In
this connection I think particularly of Kauffmann, whose idea
of a nasty disclosure about the circus is to reveal that the aerialist
is up there to get our attention. I recall him advising his readers
that Otto Preminger (the same Otto Preminger who cast Joseph
Welch in *Anatomy of a Murder* and engaged Louis Nizer to write a

script about the Rosenbergs) was a "commercial showman," and also letting them know that he was wise to the "phoniness" in the chase sequence in *Bullitt*: "Such a chase through the normal streets of San Francisco would have ended in deaths much sooner than it does."

A curious thing about Kauffmann is that in both his dogged rightmindedness and his flatulent diction he is indistinguishable from many members of the Industry itself. He is a man who finds R. D. Laing "blazingly humane." Lewis Mumford is "civilized and civilizing" and someone to whom we owe a "long debt," Arthur Miller a "tragic agonist" hampered in his artistry only by "the shackles of our time." It is the vocabulary of the Jean Hersholt Humanitarian Award. Kauffmann divined in *Bullitt* not only its "phoniness" but a "possible propagandistic motive": "to show (particularly to the young) that law and order are not necessarily Dullsville." The "motive" in *Bullitt* was to show that several million people would pay three dollars apiece to watch Steve McQueen drive fast, but Kauffmann, like my acquaintance who reports from the Polo Lounge, seems to prefer his version. "People in the East pretend to be interested in how pictures are made," Scott Fitzgerald observed in his notes on Hollywood. "But if you actually tell them anything, you find … they never see the ventriloquist for the doll. Even the intellectuals, who ought to know better, like to hear about the pretensions, extravagances and vulgarities—tell them pictures have a private grammar, like politics or automobile production or society, and watch the blank look come into their faces."

Of course there is good reason for this blank look, for this almost queasy uneasiness with pictures. To recognize that the picture is but the by-product of the action is to make rather more arduous the task of maintaining one's self-image as (Kauffmann's own job definition) "a critic of new works." Making judgments on films is in many ways so peculiarly vaporous an occupation that the only question is why, beyond the obvious opportunities for a few lecture fees and a little careerism at a dispiritingly self-limiting level, anyone does it in the first place. A finished picture defies all attempts to analyze what makes it work or not work: the responsibility for its every frame is clouded not only in the accidents and compromises of production but in the clauses of its financing. *The Getaway* was Sam Peckinpah's picture, but Steve

McQueen had the "cut," or final right to edit. *Up the Sandbox* was Irvin Kershner's picture, but Barbra Streisand had the cut. In a series of interviews with directors, Charles Thomas Samuels asked Carol Reed why he had used the same cutter on so many pictures. "I had no control," Reed said. Samuels asked Vittorio De Sica if he did not find a certain effect in one of his Sophia Loren films a bit artificial. "It was shot by the second unit," De Sica said. "I didn't direct it." In other words, Carlo Ponti wanted it.

Nor does calling film a "collaborative medium" exactly describe the situation. To read David O. Selznick's instructions to his directors, writers, actors and department heads in *Memo from David O. Selznick* is to come very close to the spirit of actually making a picture, a spirit not of collaboration but of armed conflict in which one antagonist has a contract assuring him nuclear capability. Some reviewers make a point of trying to understand whose picture it is by "looking at the script": to understand whose picture it is one needs to look not particularly at the script but at the deal memo.

About the best a writer on film can hope to do, then, is to bring an engaging or interesting intelligence to bear upon the subject, a kind of *petit-point*-on-Kleenex effect which rarely stands much scrutiny. "Motives" are inferred where none existed; allegations spun out of thin speculation. Perhaps the difficulty of knowing who made which choices in a picture makes this airiness so expedient that it eventually infects any writer who makes a career of reviewing; perhaps the initial error is in making a career of it. Reviewing motion pictures, like reviewing new cars, may or may not be a useful consumer service (since people respond to a lighted screen in a dark room in the same secret and powerfully irrational way they respond to most sensory stimuli, I tend to think much of it beside the point, but never mind that); the review of pictures has been, as well, a traditional diversion for writers whose actual work is somewhere else. Some 400 mornings spent at press screenings in the late Thirties were, for Graham Greene, an "escape," a way of life "adopted quite voluntarily from a sense of fun." Perhaps it is only when one inflates this sense of fun into (Kauffmann again) "a continuing relation with an art" that one passes so headily beyond the reality principle.

* * *

February in the last extant stable society. A few days ago I went to lunch in Beverly Hills. At the next table were an agent and a director who should have been, at that moment, on his way to a location to begin a new picture. I knew what he was supposed to be doing because this picture had been talked about around town: six million dollars above the line. There was two million for one actor. There was a million and a quarter for another actor. The director was in for $800,000. The property had cost more than half a million; the first-draft screenplay $200,000, the second draft a little less. A third writer had been brought in, at $6,000 a week. Among the three writers were two Academy Awards and one New York Film Critics Award. The director had an Academy Award for his last picture but one.

And now the director was sitting at lunch in Beverly Hills and he wanted out. The script was not right. Only 38 pages worked, the director said. The financing was shaky. "They're in breach, we all recognize your right to pull out," the agent said carefully. The agent represented many of the principals, and did not want the director to pull out. On the other hand he also represented the director, and the director seemed unhappy. It was difficult to ascertain what anyone involved did want, except for the action to continue. "You pull out," the agent said, "it dies right here, not that I want to influence your decision." The director picked up the bottle of Margaux they were drinking and examined the label.

"Nice little red," the agent said.

"Very nice."

I left as the Sanka was being served. No decision had been reached. Many people have been talking these past few days about this aborted picture, always with a note of regret. It had been a very creative deal and they had run with it as far as they could run and they had had some fun and now the fun was over, as it also would have been had they made the picture.

1973

IN BED

THREE, FOUR, SOMETIMES five times a month, I spend the day in bed with a migraine headache, insensible to the world around me. Almost every day of every month, between these attacks, I feel the sudden irrational irritation and the flush of blood into the cerebral arteries which tell me that migraine is on its way, and I take certain drugs to avert its arrival. If I did not take the drugs, I would be able to function perhaps one day in four. The physiological error called migraine is, in brief, central to the given of my life. When I was 15, 16, even 25, I used to think that I could rid myself of this error by simply denying it, character over chemistry. "Do you have headaches *sometimes? frequently? never?*" the application forms would demand. "Check one." Wary of the trap, wanting whatever it was that the successful circumnavigation of that particular form could bring (a job, a scholarship, the respect of mankind and the grace of God), I would check one. "*Sometimes,*" I would lie. That in fact I spent one or two days a week almost unconscious with pain seemed a shameful secret, evidence not merely of some chemical inferiority but of all my bad attitudes, unpleasant tempers, wrongthink.

For I had no brain tumor, no eyestrain, no high blood pressure, nothing wrong with me at all: I simply had migraine headaches, and migraine headaches were, as everyone who did not have them knew, imaginary. I fought migraine then, ignored the warnings it sent, went to school and later to work in spite of it, sat through lectures in Middle English and presentations to advertisers with involuntary tears running down the right side of my face, threw up in washrooms, stumbled home by instinct, emptied ice trays onto my bed and tried to freeze the pain in my right temple, wished only for a neurosurgeon who would do a lobotomy on house call, and cursed my imagination.

It was a long time before I began thinking mechanistically enough to accept migraine for what it was: something with which I would be living, the way some people live with diabetes.

Migraine is something more than the fancy of a neurotic imagination. It is an essentially hereditary complex of symptoms, the most frequently noted but by no means the most unpleasant of which is a vascular headache of blinding severity, suffered by a surprising number of women, a fair number of men (Thomas Jefferson had migraine, and so did Ulysses S. Grant, the day he accepted Lee's surrender), and by some unfortunate children as young as two years old. (I had my first when I was eight. It came on during a fire drill at the Columbia School in Colorado Springs, Colorado. I was taken first home and then to the infirmary at Peterson Field, where my father was stationed. The Air Corps doctor prescribed an enema.) Almost anything can trigger a specific attack of migraine: stress, allergy, fatigue, an abrupt change in barometric pressure, a contretemps over a parking ticket. A flashing light. A fire drill. One inherits, of course, only the predisposition. In other words I spent yesterday in bed with a headache not merely because of my bad attitudes, unpleasant tempers and wrongthink, but because both my grandmothers had migraine, my father has migraine and my mother has migraine.

No one knows precisely what it is that is inherited. The chemistry of migraine, however, seems to have some connection with the nerve hormone named serotonin, which is naturally present in the brain. The amount of serotonin in the blood falls sharply at the onset of migraine, and one migraine drug, methysergide, or Sansert, seems to have some effect on serotonin. Methysergide is a derivative of lysergic acid (in fact Sandoz Pharmaceuticals first synthesized LSD-25 while looking for a migraine cure), and its use is hemmed about with so many contraindications and side effects that most doctors prescribe it only in the most incapacitating cases. Methysergide, when it is prescribed, is taken daily, as a preventive; another preventive which works for some people is old-fashioned ergotamine tartrate, which helps to constrict the swelling blood vessels during the "aura," the period which in most cases precedes the actual headache.

Once an attack is under way, however, no drug touches it. Migraine gives some people mild hallucinations, temporarily blinds others, shows up not only as a headache but as a gastrointestinal disturbance, a painful sensitivity to all sensory stimuli, an abrupt overpowering fatigue, a strokelike aphasia, and a crippling inability to make even the most routine connections. When I am in a migraine aura (for some people the aura lasts fifteen minutes, for others several hours), I will drive through red lights, lose the house keys, spill whatever I am holding, lose the ability to focus my eyes or frame coherent sentences, and generally give the appearance of being on drugs, or drunk. The actual headache, when it comes, brings with it chills, sweating, nausea, a debility that seems to stretch the very limits of endurance. That no one dies of migraine seems, to someone deep into an attack, an ambiguous blessing.

My husband also has migraine, which is unfortunate for him but fortunate for me: perhaps nothing so tends to prolong an attack as the accusing eye of someone who has never had a headache. "Why not take a couple of aspirin," the unafflicted will say from the doorway, or "I'd have a headache, too, spending a beautiful day like this inside with all the shades drawn." All of us who have migraine suffer not only from the attacks themselves but from this common conviction that we are perversely refusing to cure ourselves by taking a couple of aspirin, that we are making ourselves sick, that we "bring it on ourselves." And in the most immediate sense, the sense of why we have a headache this Tuesday and not last Thursday, of course we often do. There certainly is what doctors call a "migraine personality," and that personality tends to be ambitious, inward, intolerant of error, rather rigidly organized, perfectionist. "You don't look like a migraine personality," a doctor once said to me. "Your hair's messy. But I suppose you're a compulsive housekeeper." Actually my house is kept even more negligently than my hair, but the doctor was right nonetheless: perfectionism can also take the form of spending most of a week writing and rewriting and not writing a single paragraph.

But not all perfectionists have migraine, and not all migrainous people have migraine personalities. We do not escape heredity. I have tried in most of the available ways to escape my own migrainous heredity (at one point I learned to give myself two daily injections of histamine with a hypodermic needle, even though the needle so frightened me that I had to close my eyes when I did it), but I still have migraine. And I have learned now to live with it, learned when to expect it, how to outwit it, even how to regard it, when it does come, as more friend than lodger. We have reached a certain understanding, my migraine and I. It never comes when I am in real trouble. Tell me that my house is burned down, my husband has left me, that there is gunfighting in the streets and panic in the banks, and I will not respond by getting a headache. It comes instead when I am fighting not an open but a guerrilla war with my own life, during weeks of small household confusions, lost laundry, unhappy help, canceled appointments, on days when the telephone rings too much and I get no work done and the wind is coming up. On days like that my friend comes uninvited.

And once it comes, now that I am wise in its ways, I no longer fight it. I lie down and let it happen. At first every small apprehension is magnified, every anxiety a pounding terror. Then the pain comes, and I concentrate only on that. Right there is the usefulness of migraine, there in that imposed yoga, the concentration on the pain. For when the pain recedes, ten or twelve hours later, everything goes with it, all the hidden resentments, all the vain anxieties. The migraine has acted as a circuit breaker, and the fuses have emerged intact. There is a pleasant convalescent euphoria. I open the windows and feel the air, eat gratefully, sleep well. I notice the particular nature of a flower in a glass on the stair landing. I count my blessings.

1968

WHERE ARE WE *heading*, they asked in all the television and radio studios. They asked it in New York and Los Angeles and they asked it in Boston and Washington and they asked it in Dallas and Houston and Chicago and San Francisco. Sometimes they made eye contact as they asked it. Sometimes they closed their eyes as they asked it. Quite often they wondered not just where we were heading but where we were heading "as Americans," or "as concerned Americans," or "as American women," or, on one occasion, "as the American guy and the American woman." I never learned the answer, nor did the answer matter, for one of the eerie and liberating aspects of broadcast discourse is that nothing one says will alter in the slightest either the form or the length of the conversation. Our voices in the studios were those of manic actors assigned to do three-minute, four-minute, seven-minute improvs. Our faces on the monitors were those of concerned Americans. On my way to one of those studios in Boston I had seen the magnolias bursting white down Marlborough Street. On my way to another in Dallas I had watched the highway lights blazing and dimming pink against the big dawn sky. Outside one studio in Houston the afternoon heat was sinking into the deep primeval green of the place and outside the next, that night in Chicago, snow fell and glittered in the lights along the lake. Outside all these studios America lay in all its exhilaratingly volatile weather and eccentricity and specificity, but inside the studios we shed the specific and rocketed on to the general, for they were The Interviewers and I was The Author and the single question we seemed able to address together was *where are we heading*.

> "8:30 *A.M. to* 9:30 *A.M.: LIVE on WFSB TV/THIS MORNING.*
> "10 *A.M. to* 10:30 *A.M.: LIVE on WINF AM/THE WORLD TODAY.*
> "10:45 *A.M. to* 11:45 *A.M.: PRESS INTERVIEW with HARTFORD COURANT.*

"12 *noon to* 1:30 *P.M.: AUTOGRAPHING at BARNES AND NOBLE.*

"2 *P.M. to* 2:30 *P.M.: TAPE at WDRC AM/FM.*

"3 *P.M. to* 3:30 *P.M.: PRESS INTERVIEW with THE HILL INK.*

"7:30 *P.M. to* 9 *P.M.: TAPE at WHNB TV/WHAT ABOUT WOMEN.*"

From 12 noon to 1:30 P.M., that first day in Hartford, I talked to a man who had cut a picture of me from a magazine in 1970 and had come round to Barnes and Noble to see what I looked like in 1977. From 2 P.M. to 2:30 P.M., that first day in Hartford, I listened to the receptionists at WDRC AM/FM talk about the new records and I watched snow drop from the pine boughs in the cemetery across the street. The name of the cemetery was Mt. St. Benedict and my husband's father had been buried there. "Any Steely Dan come in?" the receptionists kept asking. From 8:30 A.M. until 9 P.M., that first day in Hartford, I neglected to mention the name of the book I was supposed to be promoting. It was my fourth book but I had never before done what is called in the trade a book tour. I was not sure what I was doing or why I was doing it. I had left California equipped with two "good" suits, a box of unanswered mail, Elizabeth Hardwick's *Seduction and Betrayal*, Edmund Wilson's *To the Finland Station*, six Judy Blume books and my eleven-year-old daughter. The Judy Blume books were along to divert my daughter. My daughter was along to divert me. Three days into the tour I sent home the box of unanswered mail to make room for a packet of Simon and Schuster press releases describing me in favorable terms. Four days into the tour I sent home *Seduction and Betrayal* and *To the Finland Station* to make room for a thousand-watt hair blower. By the time I reached Boston, ten days into the tour, I knew that I had never before heard and would possibly never again hear America singing at precisely this pitch: ethereal, speedy, an angel choir on Dexamyl.

Where were we heading. The set for this discussion was always the same: a cozy oasis of wicker and ferns in the wilderness of cables and cameras and Styrofoam coffee cups that was the actual studio. On wicker settees across the nation I expressed my conviction that we were heading "into an era" of whatever the clock seemed to demand. In green rooms across the nation I listened to other people talk about where we were heading, and also about their vocations, avocations, and secret interests. I discussed L-dopa and biorhythm with a woman whose father invented prayer breakfasts. I exchanged makeup tips with a former Mouseketeer. I stopped reading newspapers and started relying on bulletins from limo drivers, from Mouseketeers, from the callers-in on call-in shows and from the closed-circuit screens in airports that flashed random stories off the wire ("CARTER URGES BARBITURATE BAN" is one that got my attention at La Guardia) between advertisements for *Shenandoah*. I gravitated to the random. I swung with the nonsequential.

I began to see America as my own, a child's map over which my child and I could skim and light at will. We spoke not of cities but of airports. If rain fell at Logan we could find sun at Dulles. Bags lost at O'Hare could be found at Dallas/Fort Worth. In the first-class cabins of the planes on which we traveled we were often, my child and I, the only female passengers, and I apprehended for the first time those particular illusions of mobility which power American business. Time was money. Motion was progress. Decisions were snap and the ministrations of other people were constant. Room service, for example, assumed paramount importance. We needed, my eleven-year-old and I, instant but erratically timed infusions of consommé, oatmeal, crab salad and asparagus vinaigrette. We needed Perrier water and tea to drink when we were working. We needed bourbon on the rocks and Shirley Temples to drink when we were not. A kind of irritable panic came over us when room service went off, and also when no one answered in the housekeeping department. In short we had fallen into the peculiar hormonal momentum of business travel, and I had begun to understand the habituation many men and a few women have to planes and telephones and schedules. I had begun to regard my own schedule—a sheaf of thick cream-colored pages printed with the words "SIMON & SCHUSTER/A DIVISION OF GULF & WESTERN CORPORATION"—with a reverence approaching the mystical. We wanted 24-hour room service.

We wanted direct-dial telephones. We wanted to stay on the road forever.

We saw air as our element. In Houston the air was warm and rich and suggestive of fossil fuel and we pretended we owned a house in River Oaks. In Chicago the air was brilliant and thin and we pretended we owned the 27th floor of the Ritz. In New York the air was charged and crackling and shorting out with opinions, and we pretended we had some. Everyone in New York had opinions. Opinions were demanded in return. The absence of opinion was construed as opinion. Even my daughter was developing opinions. "Had an interesting talk with Carl Bernstein," she noted in the log she had been assigned to keep for her fifth-grade teacher in Malibu, California. Many of these New York opinions seemed intended as tonic revisions, bold corrections to opinions in vogue during the previous week, but since I had just dropped from the sky it was difficult for me to distinguish those opinions which "bold" and "revisionist" from those which were merely "weary" and "rote." At the time I left New York many people were expressing a bold belief in "joy"—joy in children, joy in wedlock, joy in the dailiness of life—but joy was trickling down fast to show-business personalities. Mike Nichols, for example, was expressing his joy in the pages of *Newsweek*, and also his weariness with "lapidary bleakness." Lapidary bleakness was definitely rote.

We were rethinking the Sixties that week, or Morris Dickstein was.

We were taking another look at the Fifties that week, or Hilton Kramer was.

I agreed passionately. I disagreed passionately. I called room service on one phone and listened attentively on the other to people who seemed convinced that the "texture" of their lives had been agreeably or adversely affected by conversion to the politics of joy, by regression to lapidary bleakness, by the Sixties, by the Fifties, by the recent change in administrations and by the sale of *The Thorn Birds* to paper for one-million-nine.

I lost track of information.

I was blitzed by opinion.

I began to see opinions arcing in the air, intersecting flight patterns. The Eastern shuttle was cleared for landing and so was lapidary bleakness. John Leonard and joy were on converging vectors. I began to see the country itself as a projection on air, a kind of hologram, an invisible grid of image and opinion and electronic impulse. There were opinions in the air and there were planes in the air and there were even people in the air: one afternoon in New York my husband saw a man jump from a window and fall to the sidewalk outside the Yale Club. I mentioned this to a *Daily News* photographer who was taking my picture. "You have to catch a jumper in the act to make the paper," he advised me. He had caught two in the act but only the first had made the paper. The second was a better picture but coincided with the crash of a DC-10 at Orly. "They're all over town," the photographer said. "Jumpers. A lot of them aren't even jumpers. They're window washers. Who fall."

What does that say about us as a nation, I was asked the next day when I mentioned the jumpers and window washers on the air. *Where are we headed*. On the 27th floor of the Ritz in Chicago my daughter and I sat frozen at the breakfast table until the window washers glided safely out of sight. At a call-in station in Los Angeles I was told by the guard that there would be a delay because they had a jumper on the line. "I say let him jump," the guard said to me. I imagined a sky dense with jumpers and fallers and DC-10s. I held my daughter's hand at takeoff and landing and watched for antennae on the drive into town. The big antennae with the pulsing red lights had been for a month our landmarks. The big antennae with the pulsing red lights had in fact been for a month our destinations. "Out I-10 to the antenna" was the kind of direction we had come to understand, for we were on the road, on the grid, on the air and also in it. *Where were we heading*. I don't know where you're heading, I said in the studio attached to the last of these antennae, my eyes fixed on still another of the neon FLEETWOOD MAC signs that flickered that spring in radio stations from coast to coast, but I'm heading home.

1977

ON THE MALL

THEY FLOAT ON the landscape like pyramids to the boom years, all those Plazas and Malls and Esplanades. All those Squares and Fairs. All those Towns and Dales, all those Villages, all those Forests and Parks and Lands. Stonestown. Hillsdale. Valley Fair, Mayfair, Northgate, Southgate, Eastgate, Westgate. Gulfgate. They are toy garden cities in which no one lives but everyone consumes, profound equalizers, the perfect fusion of the profit motive and the egalitarian ideal, and to hear their names is to recall words and phrases no longer quite current. Baby Boom. Consumer Explosion. Leisure Revolution. Do-It-Yourself Revolution. Backyard Revolution. Suburbia. "The Shopping Center," the Urban Land Institute could pronounce in 1957, "is today's extraordinary retail business evolvement. ... The automobile accounts for suburbia, and suburbia accounts for the shopping center."

It was a peculiar and visionary time, those years after World War II to which all the Malls and Towns and Dales stand as climate-controlled monuments. Even the word "automobile," as in "the automobile accounts for suburbia and suburbia accounts for the shopping center," no longer carries the particular freight it once did: as a child in the late Forties in California I recall reading and believing that the "freedom of movement" afforded by the automobile was "America's fifth freedom." The trend was up. The solution was in sight. The frontier had been reinvented, and its shape was the subdivision, that new free land on which all settlers could recast their lives *tabula rasa*. For one perishable moment there the American idea seemed about to achieve itself, via F.H.A. housing and the acquisition of major appliances, and a certain enigmatic glamour attached to the architects of this newfound land. They made something of nothing. They gambled and sometimes lost. They staked the past to seize the future. I have difficulty now imagining a childhood in which a man named Jere Strizek, the developer of Town and Country Village outside Sacramento (143,000 square feet gross floor area, 68 stores, 1000 parking spaces, the Urban Land Institute's "prototype for centers using heavy timber and tile construction for informality"), could materialize as a role model, but I had such a childhood, just after World War II, in Sacramento. I never met or even saw Jere Strizek, but at the age of 12 I imagined him a kind of frontiersman, a romantic and revolutionary spirit, and in the indigenous grain he was.

I suppose James B. Douglas and David D. Bohannon were too.

I first heard of James B. Douglas and David D. Bohannon not when I was 12 but a dozen years later, when I was living in New York, working for *Vogue*, and taking, by correspondence, a University of California Extension course in shopping-center theory. This did not seem to me eccentric at the time. I remember sitting on the cool floor in Irving Penn's studio and reading, in *The Community Builders Handbook*, advice from James B. Douglas on shopping-center financing. I recall staying late in my pale-blue office on the twentieth floor of the Graybar Building to memorize David D. Bohannon's parking ratios. My "real" life was to sit in this office and describe life as it was lived in Djakarta and Caneel Bay and in the great châteaux of the Loire Valley, but my dream life was to put together a Class-A regional shopping center with three full-line department stores as major tenants.

That I was perhaps the only person I knew in New York, let alone on the Condé Nast floors of the Graybar Building, to have memorized the distinctions among "A," "B," and "C" shopping centers did not occur to me (the defining distinction, as long as I have your attention, is that an "A," or "regional," center has as its major tenant a full-line department store which carries major appliances; a "B," or "community," center has as its major tenant a junior department store which does not carry major appliances; and a "C," or "neighborhood," center has as its major tenant only a supermarket): my interest in shopping centers was in no way casual. I did want to build them. I wanted to build them because I had fallen into the habit of writing fiction, and I had it in my head that a couple of good centers might support this habit less taxingly than a pale-blue office at *Vogue*. I had even devised an original scheme by which I planned to gain enough capital and credibility to enter the shopping-center game: I would lease warehouses in, say, Queens, and offer Manhattan delicatessens the opportunity to sell competitively by buying cooperatively, from my trucks. I see a few wrinkles in this scheme now (the words "concrete overcoat" come to mind), but I did not then. In fact I planned to run it out of the pale-blue office.

James B. Douglas and David D. Bohannon. In 1950 James B. Douglas had opened Northgate, in Seattle, the first regional center to combine a pedestrian mall with an underground truck tunnel. In 1954 David D. Bohannon had opened Hillsdale, a forty-acre regional center on the peninsula south of San Francisco. That is the only solid bio I have on James B. Douglas and David D. Bohannon to this day, but many of their opinions are engraved on my memory. David D. Bohannon believed in preserving the integrity of the shopping center by not cutting up the site with any dedicated roads. David D. Bohannon believed that architectural setbacks in a center looked "pretty on paper" but caused "customer resistance." James B. Douglas advised that a small-loan office could prosper in a center only if it was placed away from foot traffic, since people who want small loans do not want to be observed getting them. I do not now recall whether it was James B. Douglas or David D. Bohannon or someone else altogether who passed along this hint on how to paint the lines around the parking spaces (actually this is called "striping the lot," and the spaces are "stalls"): make each space a foot wider than it need be—ten feet, say, instead of nine—when the center first opens and business is slow. By this single stroke the developer achieves a couple of important objectives, the appearance of a popular center and the illusion of easy parking, and no one will really notice when business picks up and the spaces shrink.

Nor do I recall who first solved what was once a crucial center dilemma: the placement of the major tenant vis-à-vis the parking lot. The dilemma was that the major tenant—the draw, the *raison d'être* for the financing, the Sears, the Macy's, the May Company—wanted its customer to walk directly from car to store. The smaller tenants, on the other hand, wanted that same customer to *pass their stores* on the way from the car to, say, Macy's. The solution to this conflict of interests was actually very simple: *two major tenants*, one at each end of a mall. This is called "anchoring the mall," and represents seminal work in shopping-center theory. One thing you will note about shopping-center theory is that you could have thought of it yourself, and a course in it will go a long way toward dispelling the notion that business proceeds from mysteries too recondite for you and me.

A few aspects of shopping-center theory do in fact remain impenetrable to me. I have no idea why the Community Builders' Council ranks "Restaurant" as deserving a Number One (or "Hot Spot") location but exiles "Chinese Restaurant" to a Number Three, out there with "Power and Light Office" and "Christian Science Reading Room." Nor do I know why the Council approves of enlivening a mall with "small animals" but specifically, vehemently, and with no further explanation, excludes "monkeys." If I had a center I would have monkeys, and Chinese restaurants, and Mylar kites and bands of small girls playing tambourine.

A few years ago at a party I met a woman from Detroit who told me that the Joyce Carol Oates novel with which she identified most closely was *Wonderland*.

I asked her why.

"Because," she said, "my husband has a branch there."

I did not understand.

"In Wonderland the center," the woman said patiently. "My husband has a branch in Wonderland."

I have never visited Wonderland but imagine it to have bands of small girls playing tambourine.

A few facts about shopping centers.

The "biggest" center in the United States is generally agreed to be Woodfield, outside Chicago, a "super" regional or "leviathan" two-million-square-foot center with four major tenants.

The "first" shopping center in the United States is generally agreed to be Country Club Plaza in Kansas City, built in the twenties. There were some other early centers, notably Edward H. Bouton's 1907 Roland Park in Baltimore, Hugh Prather's 1931 Highland Park Shopping Village in Dallas, and Hugh Potter's

1937 River Oaks in Houston, but the developer of Country Club Plaza, the late J. C. Nichols, is referred to with ritual frequency in the literature of shopping centers, usually as "pioneering J. C. Nichols," "trailblazing J. C. Nichols," or "J. C. Nichols, father of the center as we know it."

Those are some facts I know about shopping centers because I still want to be Jere Strizek or James B. Douglas or David D. Bohannon. Here are some facts I know about shopping centers because I never will be Jere Strizek or James B. Douglas or David D. Bohannon: a good center in which to spend the day if you wake feeling low in Honolulu, Hawaii, is Ala Moana, major tenants Liberty House and Sears. A good center in which to spend the day if you wake feeling low in Oxnard, California, is The Esplanade, major tenants the May Company and Sears. A good center in which to spend the day if you wake feeling low in Biloxi, Mississippi, is Edgewater Plaza, major tenant Godchaux's. Ala Moana in Honolulu is larger than The Esplanade in Oxnard, and The Esplanade in Oxnard is larger than Edgewater Plaza in Biloxi. Ala Moana has carp pools. The Esplanade and Edgewater Plaza do not.

These marginal distinctions to one side, Ala Moana, The Esplanade, and Edgewater Plaza are the same place, which is precisely their role not only as equalizers but in the sedation of anxiety. In each of them one moves for a while in an aqueous suspension not only of light but of judgment, not only of judgment but of "personality." One meets no acquaintances at The Esplanade. One gets no telephone calls at Edgewater Plaza. "It's a hard place to run in to for a pair of stockings," a friend complained to me recently of Ala Moana, and I knew that she was not yet ready to surrender her ego to the idea of the center. The last time I went to Ala Moana it was to buy *The New York Times*. Because *The New York Times* was not in, I sat on the mall for a while and ate caramel corn. In the end I bought not *The New York Times* at all but two straw hats at Liberty House, four bottles of nail enamel at Woolworth's, and a toaster, on sale at Sears. In the literature of shopping centers these would be described as impulse purchases, but the impulse here was obscure. I do not wear hats, nor do I like caramel corn. I do not use nail enamel. Yet flying back across the Pacific I regretted only the toaster.

1975

IN BOGOTÁ

ON THE COLOMBIAN coast it was hot, fevered, eleven degrees off the equator with evening trades that did not relieve but blew hot and dusty. The sky was white, the casino idle. I had never meant to leave the coast but after a week of it I began to think exclusively of Bogotá, floating on the Andes an hour away by air. In Bogotá it would be cool. In Bogotá one could get *The New York Times* only two days late and the *Miami Herald* only one day late and also emeralds, and bottled water. In Bogotá there would be fresh roses in the bathrooms at the Hotel Tequendama and hot water twenty-four hours a day and numbers to be dialed for chicken sandwiches from room service and Xerox *rápido* and long-distance operators who could get Los Angeles in ten minutes. In my room in Cartagena I would wake to the bleached coastal morning and find myself repeating certain words and phrases under my breath, an incantation: *Bogotá, Bacatá*. El Dorado. Emeralds. Hot water. Madeira consommé in cool dining rooms. *Santa Fé de Bogotá del Nuevo Reino de Granada de las Indias del Mar Océano*. The Avianca flight to Bogotá left Cartagena every morning at ten-forty, but such was the slowed motion of the coast that it took me another four days to get on it.

Maybe that is the one true way to see Bogotá, to have it float in the mind until the need for it is visceral, for the whole history of the place has been to seem a mirage, a delusion on the high savannah, its gold and its emeralds unattainable, inaccessible, its isolation so splendid and unthinkable that the very existence of a city astonishes. There on the very spine of the Andes gardeners espalier roses on embassy walls. Swarms of little girls in proper navy-blue school blazers line up to enter the faded tent of a tatty traveling circus: the elephant, the strong man, the tattooed man from Maracaibo. I arrived in Bogotá on a day in 1973 when the streets seemed bathed in mist and thin brilliant light and in the amplified pop voice of Nelson Ned, a Brazilian dwarf whose records played in every *disco* storefront. Outside the sixteenth-century Church of

San Francisco, where the Spanish viceroys took office when the country was Nueva Granada and where Simón Bolívar assumed the presidency of the doomed republic called Gran Colombia, small children and old women hawked Cuban cigars and cartons of American cigarettes and newspapers with the headline "JACKIE Y ARI." I lit a candle for my daughter and bought a paper to read about Jackie and Ari, how the princess *de los norteamericanos* ruled the king of the Greek sea by demanding of him pink champagne every night and *medialunas* every morning, a story a child might invent. Later, in the Gold Museum of the Banco de la República, I looked at the gold the Spaniards opened the Americas to get, the vision of El Dorado which was to animate a century and is believed to have begun here, outside Bogotá, at Lake Guatavita. "Many golden offerings were cast into the lake," wrote the anthropologist Olivia Vlahos of the nights when the Chibcha Indians lit bonfires on the Andes and confirmed their rulers at Guatavita.

> *Many more were heaped on a raft. … Then into the firelight stepped the ruler-to-be, his nakedness coated with a sticky resin. Onto the resin his priests applied gold dust and more gold dust until he gleamed like a golden statue. He stepped onto the raft, which was cut loose to drift into the middle of the lake. Suddenly he dived into the black water. When he emerged, the gold was gone, washed clean from his body. And he was king.*

Until the Spaniards heard the story, and came to find El Dorado for themselves. "One thing you must understand," a young Colombian said to me at dinner that night. We were at Eduardo's out in the Chico district and the piano player was playing "Love Is Blue" and we were drinking an indifferent bottle of Château Léoville-Poyferré which cost $20 American. "Spain sent all its highest aristocracy to South America." In fact I had heard variations on this hallucination before, on the coast: when Colombians spoke about the past I often had the sense of being in a place where history tended to sink, even as it happened, into the traceless solitude of autosuggestion. The princess was drinking pink champagne. High in the mountains the men were made of gold. Spain sent its highest aristocracy to South America. They were all stories a child might invent.

*Many years later, as he faced the firing squad, Colonel Aureliano
Buendía was to remember that distant afternoon when his father took
him to discover ice.*

—The opening line of *One Hundred Years of Solitude,* by the
Colombian novelist Gabriel García Márquez.

At the big movie theaters in Bogotá in the spring of 1973
The Professionals was playing, and *It's a Mad Mad Mad Mad World,*
two American pictures released in, respectively, 1967 and 1964.
The English-language racks of paperback stands were packed
with Edmund Wilson's *The Cold War and the Income Tax,* the 1964
Signet edition. This slight but definite dislocation of time fixed on
the mind the awesome isolation of the place, as did dislocations of
other kinds. On the fourth floor of the glossy new Bogotá Hilton
one could lunch in an orchid-filled gallery that overlooked the
indoor swimming pool, and also overlooked a shantytown of
packing-crate and tin-can shacks where a small boy, his body
hideously scarred and his face obscured by a knitted mask, played
listlessly with a yo-yo. In the lobby of the Hotel Tequendama two
Braniff stewardesses in turquoise-blue Pucci pantsuits flirted desultorily with a German waiting for the airport limousine; a third
ignored the German and stood before a relief map on which buttons could be pressed to light up the major cities of Colombia.
Santa Marta, on the coast; Barranquilla, Cartagena. Medellín, on
the Central Cordillera. Cali, on the Cauca River, San Agustín on
the Magdalena. Leticia, on the Amazon.

I watched her press the buttons one by one, transfixed by
the vast darkness each tiny bulb illumined. The light for Bogotá
blinked twice and went out. The girl in the Pucci pantsuit traced
the Andes with her index finger. *Alto arrecife de la aurora humana,*
the Chilean poet Pablo Neruda called the Andes. *High reef of the
human dawn.* It cost the *conquistador* Gonzalo Jiménez de Quesada
two years and the health of most of his men to reach Bogotá from
the coast. It cost me $26.

"I knew they were your bags," the man at the airport said,
producing them triumphantly from a moraine of baggage and
cartons and rubble from the construction that seemed all over
Bogotá a chronic condition. "They smelled American." *Parece
una turista norteamericana,* I read about myself in *El Espectador*
a few mornings later. She resembles an American tourist. In

fact I was aware of being an American in Colombia in a way I had not been in other places. I kept running into Americans, compatriots for whom the emotional center of Bogotá was the massive concrete embassy on Carrera 10, members of a phantom colony called "the American presence" which politesse prevented them from naming out loud. Several times I met a young American who ran an "information" office, which he urged me to visit; he had extremely formal manners, appeared for the most desultory evening in black tie, and was, according to the Colombian I asked, CIA. I recall talking at a party to a USIS man who spoke in a low mellifluous voice of fevers he had known, fevers in Sierra Leone, fevers in Monrovia, fevers on the Colombian coast. Our host interrupted this litany, demanded to know why the ambassador had not come to the party. "Little situation in Cali," the USIS man said, and smiled professionally. He seemed very concerned that no breach of American manners be inferred, and so, absurdly, did I. We had nothing in common except the eagles on our passports, but those eagles made us, in some way I did not entirely understand, co-conspirators, two strangers heavy with responsibility for seeing that the eagle should not offend. We would prefer the sweet local Roman-Cola to the Coca-Cola the Colombians liked. We would think of Standard Oil as Esso Colombiano. We would not speak of fever except to one another. Later I met an American actor who had spent two weeks taking cold showers in Bogotá before he discovered that the hot and cold taps in the room assigned him were simply reversed: he had never asked, he said, because he did not want to be considered an arrogant *gringo*.

In *El Tiempo* that morning I had read that General Gustavo Rojas Pinilla, who took over Colombia in a military coup in 1953 and closed down the press before he was overthrown in 1957, was launching a new bid for power on a Peronist platform, and I had thought that perhaps people at the party would be talking about that, but they were not. Why had the American film industry not made films about the Vietnam War, was what the Colombian stringer for the Caribbean newspaper wanted to talk about. The young Colombian filmmakers looked at him incredulously.

"What would be the point," one finally shrugged. "They run that war on television."

The filmmakers had lived in New York, spoke of Rip Torn, Norman Mailer, Ricky Leacock, Super 8. One had come to the party in a stovepipe preacher's hat; another in a violet macramé shawl to the knees. The girl with them, a famous beauty from the coast, wore a flamingo-pink sequinned midriff, and her pale red hair was fluffed around her head in an electric halo. She watched the *cumbia* dancers and fondled a baby ocelot and remained impassive both to the possibility of General Gustavo Rojas Pinilla's comeback and to the question of why the American film industry had not made films about the Vietnam War. Later, outside the gate, the filmmakers lit thick marijuana cigarettes in view of the uniformed *policia* and asked if I knew Paul Morrissey's and Andy Warhol's address in Rome. The girl from the coast cradled her ocelot against the wind.

Of the time I spent in Bogotá I remember mainly images, indelible but difficult to connect. I remember the walls on the second floor of the Museo Nacional, white and cool and lined with portraits of the presidents of Colombia, a great many presidents. I remember the emeralds in shop windows, lying casually in trays, all of them oddly pale at the center, somehow watered, cold at the very heart where one expects the fire. I asked the price of one: "Twenty-thousand American," the woman said. She was reading a booklet called *Horóscopo: Sagitario* and did not look up. I remember walking across Plaza Bolívar, the great square from which all Colombian power emanates, at mid-afternoon when men in dark European suits stood talking on the steps of the Capitol and the mountains floated all around, their perspective made fluid by sun and shadow; I remember the way the mountains dwarfed a deserted Ferris wheel in the Parque Nacional in late afternoon.

In fact the mountains loom behind every image I remember, and perhaps are themselves the connection. Some afternoons I would drive out along their talus slopes through the Chico district, out Carrera 7 where the grounds of the great houses were immaculately clipped and the gates bore brass plaques with the names of European embassies and American foundations and Argentinian neurologists. I recall stopping in El Chico to make a telephone call one day, from a small shopping center off Carrera 7; the shopping center adjoined a church where a funeral mass had just taken place. The mourners were leaving the church, talking on the street, the women, most of them, in black pantsuits and violet-tinted glasses and pleated silk dresses and Givenchy coats that had not been bought in Bogotá. In El Chico it did not seem so far to Paris or New York, but there remained the mountains, and beyond the mountains that dense world described by Gabriel García Márquez as so recent that many things lacked names.

And even just a little farther, out where Carrera 7 became the Carretera Central del Norte, the rutted road that plunged through the mountains to Tunja and eventually to Caracas, it was in many ways a perpetual frontier, vertiginous in its extremes. Rickety buses hurtled dizzyingly down the center of the road, swerving now and then to pick up a laborer, to avoid a pothole or a pack of children. Back from the road stretched large *haciendas*, their immense main houses barely visible in the folds of the slopes, their stone walls splashed occasionally with red paint, crude representations of the hammer and sickle and admonitions to vote *comunista*. One day when I was out there a cloud burst, and because my rented car with 110,000 miles on it had no windshield wipers, I stopped by the side of the road. Rain streamed over the MESA ARIZONA WESTWOOD WARRIORS and GO TIDE decals on the car windows. Gullies formed on the road. Up in the high gravel quarries men worked on, picking with shovels at the Andes for twelve and a half pesos a load.

> *Through another of our cities without a center, as hideous*
> *as Los Angeles, and with as many cars*
> *per head, and past the 20-foot neon sign*
> *for* Coppertone *on a church, past the population*
> *earning $700 per capita*
> *in jerry skyscraper living-slabs, and on to the White House*
> *of El Presidente Leoni, his small men with 18-*
> *inch repeating pistols, firing 45 bullets a minute,*
> *the two armed guards petrified beside us, while we had*
>   *champagne,*

and someone bugging the President: "Where are the girls?"
And the enclosed leader, quite a fellow, saying,
"I don't know where yours are, but I know where to find
   mine." ...
This house, this pioneer democracy, built
on foundations, not of rock, but blood as hard as rock.

          —Robert Lowell, "Caracas"

There is one more image I remember, and it comes in
two parts. First there was the mine. Tunneled into a mountain in Zipaquirá, fifty kilometers north of Bogotá, is a salt
mine. This single mine produces, each year, enough salt for
all of South America, and has done so since before Europeans
knew the continent existed: salt, not gold, was the economic
basis of the Chibcha Empire, and Zipaquirá one of its capitals.
The mine is vast, its air oppressive. I happened to be inside the
mine because inside the mine there is, carved into the mountain
450 feet below the surface, a cathedral in which 10,000 people
can hear mass at the same time. Fourteen massive stone pilas-
ters support the vault. Recessed fluorescent tubes illuminate the
Stations of the Cross, the dense air absorbing and dimming the
light unsteadily. One could think of Chibcha sacrifices here, of
the *conquistador* priests struggling to superimpose the European
mass on the screams of the slaughtered children.

But one would be wrong. The building of this enigmatic excavation in the salt mountain was undertaken not by the Chibcha
but by the Banco de la República, in 1954. In 1954 General
Gustavo Rojas Pinilla and his colonels were running Colombia,
and the country was wrenched by *La Violencia*, the fifteen years of
anarchy that followed the assassination of Jorge Gaitán in Bogotá
in 1948. In 1954 people were fleeing the terrorized countryside
to squat in shacks in the comparative safety of Bogotá. In 1954
Colombia still had few public works projects, no transportation
to speak of: Bogotá would not be connected by rail with the
Caribbean until 1961. As I stood in the dim mountain reading
the Banco de la República's dedicatory plaque, 1954 seemed to
me an extraordinary year to have hit on the notion of building
a cathedral of salt, but the Colombians to whom I mentioned it
only shrugged.

* * *

The second part of the image. I had come up from the mine and was having lunch on the side of the salt mountain, in the chilly dining room of the Hostería del Libertador. There were heavy draperies that gave off a faint muskiness when touched. There were white brocade tablecloths, carefully darned. For every stalk of blanched asparagus served, there appeared another battery of silverplated flatware and platters and *vinaigrette* sauceboats, and also another battery of "waiters": little boys, twelve or thirteen years old, dressed in tailcoats and white gloves and taught to serve as if this small inn on an Andean precipice were Vienna under the Hapsburgs.

I sat there for a long time. All around us the wind was sweeping the clouds off the Andes and across the savannah. Four hundred and fifty feet beneath us was the cathedral built of salt in the year 1954. *This house, this pioneer democracy, built on foundations, not of rock, but blood as hard as rock.* One of the little boys in white gloves picked up an empty wine bottle from a table, fitted it precisely into a wine holder, and marched toward the kitchen holding it stiffly before him, glancing covertly at the *maître d'hôtel* for approval. It seemed to me later that I had never before seen and would perhaps never again see the residuum of European custom so movingly and pointlessly observed.

1974

AT THE DAM

SINCE THE AFTERNOON in 1967 when I first saw Hoover Dam, its image has never been entirely absent from my inner eye. I will be talking to someone in Los Angeles, say, or New York, and suddenly the dam will materialize, its pristine concave face gleaming white against the harsh rusts and taupes and mauves of that rock canyon hundreds or thousands of miles from where I am. I will be driving down Sunset Boulevard, or about to enter a freeway, and abruptly those power transmission towers will appear before me, canted vertiginously over the tailrace. Sometimes I am confronted by the intakes and sometimes by the shadow of the heavy cable that spans the canyon and sometimes by the ominous outlets to unused spillways, black in the lunar clarity of the desert light. Quite often I hear the turbines. Frequently I wonder what is happening at the dam this instant, at this precise intersection of time and space, how much water is being released to fill downstream orders and what lights are flashing and which generators are in full use and which just spinning free.

I used to wonder what it was about the dam that made me think of it at times and in places where I once thought of the Mindanao Trench, or of the stars wheeling in their courses, or of the words *As it was in the beginning, is now and ever shall be, world without end, amen*. Dams, after all, are commonplace: we have all seen one. This particular dam had existed as an idea in the world's mind for almost forty years before I saw it. Hoover Dam, showpiece of the Boulder Canyon project, the several million tons of concrete that made the Southwest plausible, the *fait accompli* that was to convey, in the innocent time of its construction, the notion that mankind's brightest promise lay in American engineering.

Of course the dam derives some of its emotional effect from precisely that aspect, that sense of being a monument to a faith since misplaced. "They died to make the desert bloom," reads a plaque dedicated to the 96 men who died building this first of the great high dams, and in context the worn phrase touches, suggests

324

all of that trust in harnessing resources, in the meliorative power of the dynamo, so central to the early Thirties. Boulder City, built in 1931 as the construction town for the dam, retains the ambience of a model city, a new town, a toy triangular grid of green lawns and trim bungalows, all fanning out from the Reclamation building. The bronze sculptures at the dam itself evoke muscular citizens of a tomorrow that never came, sheaves of wheat clutched heavenward, thunderbolts defied. Winged Victories guard the flagpole. The flag whips in the canyon wind. An empty Pepsi-Cola can clatters across the terrazzo. The place is perfectly frozen in time.

But history does not explain it all, does not entirely suggest what makes that dam so affecting. Nor, even, does energy, the massive involvement with power and pressure and the transparent sexual overtones to that involvement. Once when I revisited the dam I walked through it with a man from the Bureau of Reclamation. For a while we trailed behind a guided tour, and then we went on, went into parts of the dam where visitors do not generally go. Once in a while he would explain something, usually in that recondite language having to do with "peaking power," with "outages" and "dewatering," but on the whole we spent the afternoon in a world so alien, so complete and so beautiful unto itself that it was scarcely necessary to speak at all. We saw almost no one. Cranes moved above us as if under their own volition. Generators roared. Transformers hummed. The gratings on which we stood vibrated. We watched a hundred-ton steel shaft plunging down to that place where the water was. And finally we got down to that place where the water was, where the water sucked out of Lake Mead roared through thirty-foot penstocks and then into thirteen-foot penstocks and finally into the turbines themselves. "Touch it," the Reclamation said, and I did, and for a long time I just stood there with my hands on the turbine. It was a peculiar moment, but so explicit as to suggest nothing beyond itself.

There was something beyond all that, something beyond energy, beyond history, something I could not fix in my mind. When I came up from the dam that day the wind was blowing harder, through the canyon and all across the Mojave. Later, toward Henderson and Las Vegas, there would be dust blowing, blowing past the Country-Western Casino FRI & SAT NITES and blowing past the Shrine of Our Lady of Safe Journey STOP

& PRAY, but out at the dam there was no dust, only the rock and the dam and a little greasewood and a few garbage cans, their tops chained, banging against a fence. I walked across the marble star map that traces a sidereal revolution of the equinox and fixes forever, the Reclamation man had told me, for all time and for all people who can read the stars, the date the dam was dedicated. The star map was, he had said, for when we were all gone and the dam was left. I had not thought much of it when he said it, but I thought of it then, with the wind whining and the sun dropping behind a mesa with the finality of a sunset in space. Of course that was the image I had seen always, seen it without quite realizing what I saw, a dynamo finally free of man, splendid at last in its absolute isolation, transmitting power and releasing water to a world where no one is.

1970

V

ON THE MORNING AFTER THE SIXTIES

ON THE MORNING AFTER THE SIXTIES

I AM TALKING here about being a child of my time. When I think about the Sixties now I think about an afternoon not of the Sixties at all, an afternoon early in my sophomore year at Berkeley, a bright autumn Saturday in 1953. I was lying on a leather couch in a fraternity house (there had been a lunch for the alumni, my date had gone on to the game, I do not now recall why I had stayed behind), lying there alone reading a book by Lionel Trilling and listening to a middle-aged man pick out on a piano in need of tuning the melodic line to "Blue Room." All that afternoon he sat at the piano and all that afternoon he played "Blue Room" and he never got it right. I can hear and see it still, the wrong note in "We will thrive on / Keep alive on," the sunlight falling through the big windows, the man picking up his drink and beginning again and telling me, without ever saying a word, something I had not known before about bad marriages and wasted time and looking backward. That such an afternoon would now seem implausible in every detail— the idea of having had a "date" for a football lunch now seems to me so exotic as to be almost czarist—suggests the extent to which the narrative on which many of us grew up no longer applies.

The distance we have come from the world in which I went to college was on my mind quite a bit during those seasons when not only Berkeley but dozens of other campuses were periodically shut down, incipient battlegrounds, their borders sealed. To think of Berkeley as it was in the Fifties was not to think of barricades and reconstituted classes. "Reconstitution" would have sounded to us then like Newspeak, and barricades are never personal. We were all very personal then, sometimes relentlessly so, and, at that point where we either act or do not act, most of us are still. I suppose I am talking about just that: the ambiguity of belonging to a generation distrustful of political highs, the historical irrelevancy of growing up convinced that the heart of darkness lay not in some error of social organization but in man's own blood. If man was bound to err, then any social organization was bound to be in error. It was a premise which still seems to me accurate enough, but one which robbed us early of a certain capacity for surprise.

At Berkeley in the Fifties no one was surprised by anything at all, a *donnée* which tended to render discourse less than spirited, and debate nonexistent. The world was by definition imperfect, and so of course was the university. There was some talk even then about IBM cards, but on balance the notion that free education for tens of thousands of people might involve automation did not seem unreasonable. We took it for granted that the Board of Regents would sometimes act wrongly. We simply avoided those students rumored to be FBI informers. We were that generation called "silent," but we were silent neither, as some thought, because we shared the period's official optimism nor, as others thought, because we feared its official repression. We were silent because the exhilaration of social action seemed to many of us just one more way of escaping the personal, of masking for a while that dread of the meaningless which was man's fate.

To have assumed that particular fate so early was the peculiarity of my generation. I think now that we were the last generation to identify with adults. That most of us have found adulthood just as morally ambiguous as we expected it to be falls perhaps into the category of prophecies self-fulfilled: I am simply not sure. I am telling you only how it was. The mood of Berkeley in those years was one of mild but chronic "depression," against which I remember certain small things that seemed to me somehow explications, dazzling in their clarity, of the world I was about to enter: I remember a woman picking daffodils in the rain one day when I was walking in the hills. I remember a teacher who drank too much one night and revealed his fright and bitterness. I remember my real joy at discovering for the first time how language worked, at discovering, for example, that the central line of *Heart of Darkness* was a postscript. All such images were personal, and the personal was all that most of us expected to find. We would make a separate peace. We would do graduate work in Middle English, we would go abroad. We would make some money and live on a ranch. We would survive outside history, in a kind of *idée fixe* referred to always, during the years I spent at Berkeley, as "some little town with a decent beach."

As it worked out I did not find or even look for the little town with the decent beach. I sat in the large bare apartment in which I lived my junior and senior years (I had lived awhile in a sorority, the Tri Delt house, and had left it, typically, not over any "issue" but because I, the implacable "I," did not like living with sixty people) and I read Camus and Henry James and I watched a flowering plum come in and out of blossom and at night, most nights, I walked outside and looked up to where the cyclotron and the bevatron glowed on the dark hillside, unspeakable mysteries which engaged me, in the style of my time, only personally. Later I got out of Berkeley and went to New York and later I got out of New York and came to Los Angeles. What I have made for myself is personal, but is not exactly peace. Only one person I knew at Berkeley later discovered an ideology, dealt himself into history, cut himself loose from both his own dread and his own time. A few of the people I knew at Berkeley killed themselves not long after. Another attempted suicide in Mexico and then, in a recovery which seemed in many ways a more advanced derangement, came home and joined the Bank of America's three-year executive-training program. Most of us live less theatrically, but remain the survivors of a peculiar and inward time. If I could believe that going to a barricade would affect man's fate in the slightest I would go to that barricade, and quite often I wish that I could, but it would be less than honest to say that I expect to happen upon such a happy ending.

1970

QUIET DAYS IN MALIBU

1

IN A WAY it seems the most idiosyncratic of beach communities, twenty-seven miles of coastline with no hotel, no passable restaurant, nothing to attract the traveler's dollar. It is not a resort. No one "vacations" or "holidays," as those words are conventionally understood, at Malibu. Its principal residential street, the Pacific Coast Highway, is quite literally a highway, California 1, which runs from the Mexican border to the Oregon line and brings Greyhound buses and refrigerated produce trucks and sixteen-wheel gasoline tankers hurtling past the front windows of houses frequently bought and sold for over a million dollars. The water off Malibu is neither as clear nor as tropically colored as the water off La Jolla. The beaches at Malibu are neither as white nor as wide as the beach at Carmel. The hills are scrubby and barren, infested with bikers and rattlesnakes, scarred with cuts and old burns and new R.V. parks. For these and other reasons Malibu tends to astonish and disappoint those who have never before seen it, and yet its very name remains, in the imagination of people all over the world, a kind of shorthand for the easy life. I had not before 1971 and will probably not again live in a place with a Chevrolet named after it.

2

Dick Haddock, a family man, a man twenty-six years in the same line of work, a man who has on the telephone and in his office the crisp and easy manner of technological middle management, is in many respects the prototypical Southern California solid citizen. He lives in a San Fernando Valley subdivision near a freshwater marina and a good shopping plaza. His son is a high-school swimmer. His daughter is "into tennis." He drives thirty miles to and from work, puts in a forty-hour week, regularly takes courses to maintain his professional skills, keeps in shape and looks it. When he discusses his career he talks, in a kind of politely impersonal second person, about how "you would want like any other individual to advance yourself," about "improving your rating" and "being more of an asset to your department," about "really knowing your business." Dick Haddock's business for all these twenty-six years has been that of a professional life-guard for the Los Angeles County Department of Beaches, and his office is a $190,000 lookout on Zuma Beach in northern Malibu.

It was Thanksgiving morning, 1975. A Santa Ana wind was just dying after blowing in off the Mojave for three weeks and setting 69,000 acres of Los Angeles County on fire. Squadrons of planes had been dropping chemicals on the fires to no effect. Querulous interviews with burned-out householders had become a fixed element of the six o'clock news. Smoke from the fires had that week stretched a hundred miles out over the Pacific and darkened the days and lit the nights and by Thanksgiving morning there was the sense all over Southern California of living in some grave solar dislocation. It was one of those weeks when Los Angeles seemed most perilously and breathtakingly itself, a cartoon of natural disaster, and it was a peculiar week in which to spend the day with Dick Haddock and the rest of the Zuma headquarters crew.

Actually I had wanted to meet the lifeguards ever since I moved to Malibu. I would drive past Zuma some cold win-ter mornings and see a few of them making their mandatory daily half-mile swims in open ocean. I would drive past Zuma some late foggy nights and see others moving around behind the lookout's lighted windows, the only other souls awake in all of northern Malibu. It seemed to me a curious, almost beati-fied career choice, electing to save those in peril upon the sea forty hours a week, and as the soot drifted down around the Zuma lookout on that Thanksgiving morning the laconic rou-tines and paramilitary rankings of these civil servants in red trunks took on a devotionary and dreamlike inevitability. There was the "captain," John McFarlane, a man who had already taken his daily half-mile run and his daily half-mile swim and was putting on his glasses to catch up on paperwork. Had the

JOAN DIDION

water been below 56 degrees he would have been allowed to swim in a wet suit, but the water was not below 56 degrees and so he had swum as usual in his red trunks. The water was 58 degrees. John McFarlane is 48. There was the "lieutenant," Dick Haddock, telling me about how each of the Department's 125 permanent lifeguards (there are also 600 part-time or "recurrent" lifeguards) learns crowd control at the Los Angeles County Sheriff's Academy, learns emergency driving techniques at the California Highway Patrol Academy, learns medical procedures at the U.S.C. Medical Center, and, besides running the daily half-mile and swimming the daily half-mile, does a monthly 500-meter paddle and a monthly pier jump. A "pier jump" is just what it sounds like, and its purpose is to gain practice around pilings in heavy surf.

There was as well the man out on patrol.

There were as well the "call-car personnel," two trained divers and cliff-climbers "ready to roll at any time" in what was always referred to as "a Code 3 vehicle with red light and siren," two men not rolling this Thanksgiving morning but sitting around the lookout, listening to the Los Angeles Rams beat the Detroit Lions on the radio, watching the gray horizon and waiting for a call.

No call came. The radios and the telephones crackled occasionally with reports from the other "operations" supervised by the Zuma crew: the "rescue-boat operation" at Paradise Cove, the "beach operations" at Leo Carrillo, Nicholas, Point Dume, Corral, Malibu Surfrider, Malibu Lagoon, Las Tunas, Topanga North and Topanga South. Those happen to be the names of some Malibu public beaches but in the Zuma lookout that day the names took on the sound of battle stations during a doubtful cease-fire. All quiet at Leo. Situation normal at Surfrider.

The lifeguards seemed most comfortable when they were talking about "operations" and "situations," as in "a phone-watch situation" or "a riptide situation." They also talked easily about "functions," as in "the function of maintaining a secure position on the beach." Like other men at war they had charts, forms, logs, counts kept current to within twelve hours: 1405 *surf rescues off Zuma between* 12:01 *A.M. January* 1, 1975 *and* 11:59 *P.M. Thanksgiving Eve* 1975. As well as: 36,120 *prevention rescues,* 872 *first aids,* 176 *beach emergency calls,* 12 *resuscitations,*

334

8 *boat distress calls*, 107 *boat warnings*, 438 *lost-and-found children*, and 0 *deaths*. Zero. No body count. When he had occasion to use the word "body" Dick Haddock would hesitate and glance away.

On the whole the lifeguards favored a diction as flat and finally poetic as that of Houston Control. Everything that morning was "real fine." The headquarters crew was "feeling good." The day was "looking good." Malibu surf was "two feet and shape is poor." Earlier that morning there had been a hundred or so surfers in the water, a hundred or so of those bleached children of indeterminate age and sex who bob off Zuma and appear to exist exclusively on packaged beef jerky, but by ten they had all pocketed their Thanksgiving jerky and moved on to some better break. "It heats up, we could use some more personnel," Dick Haddock said about noon, assessing the empty guard towers. "That happened, we might move on a decision to open Towers One and Eleven, I'd call and say we need two recurrents at Zuma, plus I might put an extra man at Leo."

It did not heat up. Instead it began to rain, and on the radio the morning N.F.L. game gave way to the afternoon N.F.L. game, and after a while I drove with one of the call-car men to Paradise Cove, where the rescue-boat crew needed a diver. They did not need a diver to bring up a body, or a murder weapon, or a crate of stolen ammo, or any of the things Department divers sometimes get their names in the paper for bringing up. They needed a diver, with scuba gear and a wet suit, because they had been removing the propeller from the rescue boat and had dropped a metal part the size of a dime in twenty feet of water. I had the distinct impression that they particularly needed a diver in a wet suit because nobody on the boat crew wanted to go back in the water in his trunks to replace the propeller, but there seemed to be some tacit agreement that the lost part was to be considered the point of the dive.

"I guess you know it's fifty-eight down there," the diver said.

"Don't need to tell me how cold it is," the boat lieutenant said. His name was Leonard McKinley and he had "gone permanent" in 1942 and he was of an age to refer to Zuma as a "bathing" beach. "After you find that little thing you could put the propeller back on for us, you wanted. As long as you're in the water anyway? In your suit?"

"I had a feeling you'd say that."

Leonard McKinley and I stood on the boat and watched the diver disappear. In the morning soot from the fires had coated the surface but now the wind was up and the soot was clouding the water. Kelp fronds undulated on the surface. The boat rocked. The radio sputtered with reports of a yacht named *Ursula* in distress.

"One of the other boats is going for it," Leonard McKinley said. "We're not. Some days we just sit here like firemen. Other days, a day with rips, I been out ten hours straight. You get your big rips in the summer, swells coming up from Mexico. A Santa Ana, you get your capsized boats, we got one the other day, it was overdue out of Santa Monica, they were about drowned when we picked them up."

I tried to keep my eyes on the green-glass water but could not. I had been sick on boats in the Catalina Channel and in the Gulf of California and even in San Francisco Bay, and now I seemed to be getting sick on a boat still moored at the end of the Paradise Cove pier. The radio reported the *Ursula* under tow to Marina del Rey. I concentrated on the pilings.

"He gets the propeller on," Leonard McKinley said, "you want to go out?"

I said I thought not.

"You come back another day," Leonard McKinley said, and I said that I would, and although I have not gone back there is no day when I do not think of Leonard McKinley and Dick Haddock and what they are doing, what situations they face, what operations, what green-glass water. The water today is 56 degrees.

3

Amado Vazquez is a Mexican national who has lived in Los Angeles County as a resident alien since 1947. Like many Mexicans who have lived for a long time around Los Angeles he speaks of Mexico as "over there," remains more comfortable in Spanish than in English, and transmits, in his every movement, a kind of "different" propriety, a correctness, a cultural reserve. He is in no sense a Chicano. He is rather what California-born Mexicans sometimes call "Mexican-from-Mexico," pronounced as one word and used to suggest precisely that difference, that rectitude, that personal conservatism. He was born in Ahualulco, Jalisco. He was trained as a barber at the age of ten. Since the age of twenty-seven, when he came north to visit his brother and find new work for himself, he has married, fathered two children, and become, to the limited number of people who know and understand the rather special work he found for himself in California, a kind of legend. Amado Vazquez was, at the time I first met him, head grower at Arthur Freed Orchids, a commercial nursery in Malibu founded by the late motion-picture producer Arthur Freed, and he is one of a handful of truly great orchid breeders in the world.

In the beginning I met Amado Vazquez not because I knew about orchids but because I liked greenhouses. All I knew about orchids was that back in a canyon near my house someone was growing them *in greenhouses*. All I knew about Amado Vazquez was that he was the man who would let me spend time alone in these greenhouses. To understand how extraordinary this seemed to me you would need to have craved the particular light and silence of greenhouses as I did: all my life I had been trying to spend time in one greenhouse or another, and all my life the person in charge of one greenhouse or another had been trying to hustle me out. When I was nine I would deliberately miss the school bus in order to walk home, because by walking I could pass a greenhouse. I recall being told at that particular greenhouse that the purchase of a nickel pansy did not entitle me to "spend the day," and at another that my breathing was "using up the air."

And yet back in this canyon near my house twenty-five years later were what seemed to me the most beautiful greenhouses in the world—the most aqueous filtered light, the softest tropical air, the most silent clouds of flowers—and the person in charge, Amado Vazquez, seemed willing to take only the most benign notice of my presence. He seemed to assume that I had my own reasons for being there. He would speak only to offer a nut he had just cracked, or a flower cut from a plant he was pruning. Occasionally Arthur Freed's brother Hugo, who was then running the business, would come into the greenhouse with real customers, serious men in dark suits who appeared to have just flown in from Taipei or Durban and who spoke in hushed voices,

JOAN DIDION

as if they had come to inspect medieval enamels, or uncut diamonds.

But then the buyers from Taipei or Durban would go into the office to make their deal and the silence in the greenhouse would again be total. The temperature was always 72 degrees. The humidity was always 60 per cent. Great arcs of white phalaenopsis trembled overhead. I learned the names of the crosses by studying labels there in the greenhouse, the exotic names whose value I did not then understand. *Amabilis* × *Rimestadiana* = *Elisabethae*. *Aphrodite* × *Rimestadiana* = *Gilles Gratiot*. *Amabilis* × *Gilles Gratiot* = *Katherine Siegwart* and *Katherine Siegwart* × *Elisabethae* = *Doris*. *Doris* after Doris Duke. *Doris* which first flowered at Duke Farms in 1940. At least once each visit I would remember the nickel pansy and find Amado Vazquez and show him a plant I wanted to buy, but he would only smile and shake his head. "For breeding," he would say, or "not for sale today." And then he would lift the spray of flowers and show me some point I would not have noticed, some marginal difference in the substance of the petal or the shape of the blossom. "Very beautiful," he would say. "Very nice you like it." What he would not say was that these plants he was letting me handle, these plants "for breeding" or "not for sale today," were stud plants, and that the value of such a plant at Arthur Freed could range from ten thousand to more than three-quarters of a million dollars.

I suppose the day I realized this was the day I stopped using the Arthur Freed greenhouses as a place to eat my lunch, but I made a point of going up one day in 1976 to see Amado Vazquez and to talk to Marvin Saltzman, who took over the business in 1973 and is married to Arthur Freed's daughter Barbara. (As in *Phal. Barbara Freed Saltzman* "Jean McPherson," *Phal. Barbara Freed Saltzman* "Zuma Canyon," and *Phal. Barbara Freed Saltzman* "Malibu Queen," three plants "not for sale today" at Arthur Freed.) It was peculiar talking to Marvin Saltzman because I had never before been in the office at Arthur Freed, never seen the walls lined with dulled silver awards, never seen the genealogical charts on the famous Freed hybrids, never known anything at all about the actual business of orchids.

"Frankly it's an expensive business to get into," Marvin Saltzman said. He was turning the pages of *Sander's List*, the standard orchid studbook, published every several years and showing the parentage

338

of every hybrid registered with the Royal Horticultural Society, and he seemed oblivious to the primeval silence of the greenhouse beyond the office window. He had shown me how Amado Vazquez places the pollen from one plant into the ovary of a flower on another. He had explained that the best times to do this are at full moon and high tide, because phalaenopsis plants are more fertile then. He had explained that a phalaenopsis is more fertile at full moon because in nature it must be pollinated by a night-flying moth, and over sixty-five million years of evolution its period of highest fertility began to coincide with its period of highest visibility. He had explained that a phalaenopsis is more fertile at high tide because the moisture content of every plant responds to tidal movement. It was all an old story to Marvin Saltzman. I could not take my eyes from the window.

"You bring back five thousand seedlings from the jungle and you wait three years for them to flower," Marvin Saltzman said. "You find two you like and you throw out the other four thousand nine hundred ninety-eight and you try to breed the two. Maybe the pollenization takes, eighty-five percent of the time it doesn't. Say you're lucky, it takes, you'll still wait another four years before you see a flower. Meanwhile you've got a big capital investment. An Arthur Freed could take $400,000 a year from M-G-M and put $100,000 of it into getting this place started, but not many people could. You see a lot of what we call backyard nurseries—people who have fifty or a hundred plants, maybe they have two they think are exceptional, they decide to breed them—but you talk about major nurseries, there are maybe only ten in the United States, another ten in Europe. That's about it. Twenty."

Twenty is also about how many head growers there are, which is part of what lends Amado Vazquez his legendary aspect, and after a while I left the office and went out to see him in the greenhouse. There in the greenhouse everything was operating as usual to approximate that particular level of a Malaysian rain forest—not on the ground but perhaps a hundred feet up—where epiphytic orchids grow wild. In the rain forest these orchids get broken by wind and rain. They get pollinated randomly and rarely by insects. Their seedlings are crushed by screaming monkeys and tree boas and the orchids live unseen and die young. There in the greenhouse nothing would break the orchids and they would be pollinated at full moon and high tide by Amado Vazquez, and their seedlings would be tended in a sterile box with sterile gloves and sterile tools by Amado Vazquez's wife, Maria, and the orchids would not seem to die at all. "We don't know how long they'll live," Marvin Saltzman told me. "They haven't been bred under protected conditions that long. The botanists estimate a hundred and fifty, two hundred years, but we don't know. All we know is that a plant a hundred years old will show no signs of senility."

It was very peaceful there in the greenhouse with Amado Vazquez and the plants that would outlive us both. "We grew in osmunda then," he said suddenly. Osmunda is a potting medium. Amado Vazquez talks exclusively in terms of how the orchids grow. He had been talking about the years when he first came to this country and got a job with his brother tending a private orchid collection in San Marino, and he had fallen silent. "I didn't know orchids then, now they're like my children. You wait for the first bloom like you wait for a baby to come. Sometimes you wait four years and it opens and it isn't what you expected, maybe your heart wants to break, but you love it. You never say, 'that one was prettier.' You just love them. My whole life is orchids."

And in fact it was. Amado Vazquez's wife, Maria (as in *Phal. Maria Vasquez* "Malibu," the spelling of Vazquez being mysteriously altered by everyone at Arthur Freed except the Vazquezes themselves), worked in the laboratory at Arthur Freed. His son, George (as in *Phal. George Vasquez* "Malibu"), was the sales manager at Arthur Freed. His daughter, Linda (as in *Phal. Linda Mia* "Innocence"), worked at Arthur Freed before her marriage. Amado Vazquez will often get up in the night to check a heater, adjust a light, hold a seed pod in his hand and try to sense if morning will be time enough to sow the seeds in the sterile flask. When Amado and Maria Vazquez go to Central or South America, they go to look for orchids. When Amado and Maria Vazquez went for the first time to Europe a few years ago, they looked for orchids. "I asked all over Madrid for orchids," Amado Vazquez recalled. "Finally they tell me about this one place. I go there, I knock. The woman finally lets me in. She agrees to let me see the orchids. She takes me into a house and ..."

Amado Vazquez broke off, laughing.

"She has three orchids," he finally managed to say. "Three. One of them dead. All three from Oregon."

We were standing in a sea of orchids, an extravagance of orchids, and he had given me an armful of blossoms from his own cattleyas to take to my child, more blossoms maybe than in all of Madrid. It seemed to me that day that I had never talked to anyone so direct and unembarrassed about the things he loved. He had told me earlier that he had never become a United States citizen because he had an image in his mind which he knew to be false but could not shake: the image was that of standing before a judge and stamping on the flag of Mexico. "And I love my country," he had said. Amado Vazquez loved his country. Amado Vazquez loved his family. Amado Vazquez loved orchids. "You want to know how I feel about the plants," he said as I was leaving. "I'll tell you. I will die in orchids."

4

In the part of Malibu where I lived from January of 1971 until quite recently we all knew one another's cars, and watched for them on the highway and at the Trancas Market and at the Point Dume Gulf station. We exchanged information at the Trancas Market. We left packages and messages for one another at the Gulf station. We called one another in times of wind and fire and rain, we knew when one another's septic tanks needed pumping, we watched for ambulances on the highway and helicopters on the beach and worried about one another's dogs and horses and children and corral gates and Coastal Commission permits. An accident on the highway was likely to involve someone we knew. A rattlesnake in my driveway meant its mate in yours. A stranger's campfire on your beach meant fire on both our slopes.

In fact this was a way of life I had not expected to find in Malibu. When I first moved in 1971 from Hollywood to a house on the Pacific Coast Highway I had accepted the conventional notion that Malibu meant the easy life, had worried that we would be cut off from "the real world," by which I believe I meant daily exposure to the Sunset Strip. By the time we left Malibu, seven years later, I had come to see the spirit of the place as one of shared isolation and adversity, and I think now that I never loved the house on the Pacific Coast Highway more than on those many days when it was impossible to leave it, when fire or flood had in fact closed the highway. We moved to this house on the highway in the year of our daughter's fifth birthday. In the year of her twelfth it rained until the highway collapsed, and one of her friends drowned at Zuma Beach, a casualty of Quaaludes.

One morning during the fire season of 1978, some months after we had sold the house on the Pacific Coast Highway, a brush fire caught in Agoura, in the San Fernando Valley. Within two hours a Santa Ana wind had pushed this fire across 25,000 acres and thirteen miles to the coast, where it jumped the Pacific Coast Highway as a half-mile fire storm generating winds of 100 miles per hour and temperatures up to 2500 degrees Fahrenheit. Refugees huddled on Zuma Beach. Horses caught fire and were shot on the beach, birds exploded in the air. Houses did not explode but imploded, as in a nuclear strike. By the time this fire storm had passed 197 houses had vanished into ash, many of them houses which belonged or had belonged to people we knew. A few days after the highway reopened I drove out to Malibu to see Amado Vazquez, who had, some months before, bought from the Freed estate all the stock at Arthur Freed Orchids, and had been in the process of moving it a half-mile down the canyon to his own new nursery, Zuma Canyon Orchids. I found him in the main greenhouse at what had been Arthur Freed Orchids. The place was now a range not of orchids but of shattered glass and melted metal and the imploded shards of the thousands of chemical beakers that had held the Freed seedlings, the new crosses. "I lost three years," Amado Vazquez said, and for an instant I thought we would both cry. "You want today to see flowers," he said then, "we go down to the other place." I did not want that day to see flowers. After I said goodbye to Amado Vazquez my husband and daughter and I went to look at the house on the Pacific Coast Highway in which we had lived for seven years. The fire had come to within 125 feet of the property, then stopped or turned or been beaten back, it was hard to tell which. In any case it was no longer our house.

1976–78

SALVADOR

"All Europe contributed to the making of Kurtz; and by-and-by I learned that, most appropriately, the International Society for the Suppression of Savage Customs had intrusted him with the making of a report, for its future guidance. And he had written it, too. I've seen it. I've read it. It was eloquent, vibrating with eloquence.... 'By the simple exercise of our will we can exert a power for good practically unbounded,' etc. etc. From that point he soared and took me with him. The peroration was magnificent, although difficult to remember, you know. It gave me the notion of an exotic Immensity ruled by an august Benevolence. It made me tingle with enthusiasm. This was the unbounded power of eloquence—of words—of burning noble words. There were no practical hints to interrupt the magic current of phrases, unless a kind of note at the foot of the last page, scrawled evidently much later, in an unsteady hand, may be regarded as the exposition of a method. It was very simple, and at the end of that moving appeal to every altruistic sentiment it blazed at you, luminous and terrifying, like a flash of lightning in a serene sky: 'Exterminate all the brutes!'"

—Joseph Conrad,
Heart of Darkness

THE THREE-YEAR-OLD El Salvador International Airport is glassy and white and splendidly isolated, conceived during the waning of the Molina "National Transformation" as convenient less to the capital (San Salvador is forty miles away, until recently a drive of several hours) than to a central hallucination of the Molina and Romero regimes, the projected beach resorts, the Hyatt, the Pacific Paradise, tennis, golf, water-skiing, condos, *Costa del Sol*; the visionary invention of a tourist industry in yet another republic where the leading natural cause of death is gastrointestinal infection. In the general absence of tourists these hotels have since been abandoned, ghost resorts on the empty Pacific beaches, and to land at this airport built to service them is to plunge directly into a state in which no ground is solid, no depth of field reliable, no perception so definite that it might not dissolve into its reverse.

The only logic is that of acquiescence. Immigration is negotiated in a thicket of automatic weapons, but by whose authority the weapons are brandished (Army or National Guard or National Police or Customs Police or Treasury Police or one of a continuing proliferation of other shadowy and overlapping forces) is a blurred point. Eye contact is avoided. Documents are scrutinized upside down. Once clear of the airport, on the new highway that slices through green hills rendered phosphorescent by the cloud cover of the tropical rainy season, one sees mainly underfed cattle and mongrel dogs and armored vehicles, vans and trucks and Cherokee Chiefs fitted with reinforced steel and bulletproof Plexiglas an inch thick. Such vehicles are a fixed feature of local life, and are popularly associated with disappearance and death. There was the Cherokee Chief seen following the Dutch television crew killed in Chalatenango province in March of 1982. There was the red Toyota three-quarter-ton pickup sighted near the van driven by the four American Catholic workers on the night they were killed in 1980. There were, in the late spring and

347

summer of 1982, the three Toyota panel trucks, one yellow, one blue, and one green, none bearing plates, reported present at each of the mass detentions (a "detention" is another fixed feature of local life, and often precedes a "disappearance") in the Amatepec district of San Salvador. These are the details—the models and colors of armored vehicles, the makes and calibers of weapons, the particular methods of dismemberment and decapitation used in particular instances—on which the visitor to Salvador learns immediately to concentrate, to the exclusion of past or future concerns, as in a prolonged amnesiac fugue.

Terror is the given of the place. Black-and-white police cars cruise in pairs, each with the barrel of a rifle extruding from an open window. Roadblocks materialize at random, soldiers fanning out from trucks and taking positions, fingers always on triggers, safeties clicking on and off. Aim is taken as if to pass the time. Every morning *El Diario de Hoy* and *La Prensa Gráfica* carry cautionary stories. "*Una madre y sus dos hijos fueron asesinados con arma cortante (corvo) por ocho sujetos desconocidos el lunes en la noche*": A mother and her two sons hacked to death in their beds by eight *desconocidos*, unknown men. The same morning's paper: the unidentified body of a young man, strangled, found on the shoulder of a road. Same morning, different story: the unidentified bodies of three young men, found on another road, their faces partially destroyed by bayonets, one faced carved to represent a cross.

It is largely from these reports in the newspapers that the United States embassy compiles its body counts, which are transmitted to Washington in a weekly dispatch referred to by embassy people as "the grimgram." These counts are presented in a kind of tortured code that fails to obscure what is taken for granted in El Salvador, that government forces do most of the killing. In a January 15 1982 memo to Washington, for example, the embassy issued a "guarded" breakdown on its count of 6,909 "reported" political murders between September 16 1980 and September 15 1981. Of these 6,909, according to the memo, 922 were "believed committed by security forces," 952 "believed committed by leftist terrorists," 136 "believed committed by rightist terrorists," and 4,889 "committed by unknown assailants," the famous *desconocidos* favored by those San Salvador newspapers still publishing. (The figures actually add up not to 6,909 but to 6,899, leaving ten in a kind of official limbo.) The memo continued:

> The uncertainty involved here can be seen in the fact that responsibility cannot be fixed in the majority of cases. We note, however, that it is generally believed in El Salvador that a large number of the unexplained killings are carried out by the security forces, officially or unofficially. The Embassy is aware of dramatic claims that have been made by one interest group or another in which the security forces figure as the primary agents of murder here. El Salvador's tangled web of attack and vengeance, traditional criminal violence and political mayhem make this an impossible charge to sustain. In saying this, however, we make no attempt to lighten the responsibility for the deaths of many hundreds, and perhaps thousands, which can be attributed to the security forces....

The body count kept by what is generally referred to in San Salvador as "the Human Rights Commission" is higher than the embassy's, and documented periodically by a photographer who goes out looking for bodies. These bodies he photographs are often broken into unnatural positions, and the faces to which the bodies are attached (when they are attached) are equally unnatural, sometimes unrecognizable as human faces, obliterated by acid or beaten to a mash of misplaced ears and teeth or slashed ear to ear and invaded by insects. "*Encontrado en Antiguo Cuscatlán el día 25 de Marzo 1982: camison de dormir celeste,*" the typed caption reads on one photograph: found in Antiguo Cuscatlán March 25 1982 wearing a sky-blue nightshirt. The captions are laconic. Found in Soyapango May 21 1982. Found in Mejicanos June 11 1982. Found at El Playón May 30 1982, white shirt, purple pants, black shoes.

The photograph accompanying that last caption shows a body with no eyes, because the vultures got to it before the photographer did. There is a special kind of practical information that the visitor to El Salvador acquires immediately, the way visitors to other places acquire information about the currency rates, the hours for the museums. In El Salvador one learns that vultures go first for the soft tissue, for the eyes, the exposed genitalia, the open mouth.

One learns that an open mouth can be used to make a specific point, can be stuffed with something emblematic; stuffed, say, with a penis, or, if the point has to do with land title, stuffed with some of the dirt in question. One learns that hair deteriorates less rapidly than flesh, and that a skull surrounded by a perfect corona of hair is a not uncommon sight in the body dumps.

All forensic photographs induce in the viewer a certain protective numbness, but dissociation is more difficult here. In the first place these are not, technically, "forensic" photographs, since the evidence they document will never be presented in a court of law. In the second place the disfigurement is too routine. The locations are too near, the dates too recent. There is the presence of the relatives of the disappeared: the women who sit every day in this cramped office on the grounds of the archdiocese, waiting to look at the spiral-bound photo albums in which the photographs are kept. These albums have plastic covers bearing soft-focus color photographs of young Americans in dating situations (strolling through autumn foliage on one album, recumbent in a field of daisies on another), and the women, looking for the bodies of their husbands and brothers and sisters and children, pass them from hand to hand without comment or expression.

> One of the more shadowy elements of the violent scene here [is] the death squad. Existence of these groups has long been disputed, but not by many Salvadorans.... Who constitutes the death squads is yet another difficult question. We do not believe that these squads exist as permanent formations but rather as ad hoc vigilante groups that coalesce according to perceived need. Membership is also uncertain, but in addition to civilians we believe that both on- and off-duty members of the security forces are participants. This was unofficially confirmed by right-wing spokesman Maj. Roberto D'Aubuisson who stated in an interview in early 1981 that security force members utilize the guise of the death squad when a potentially embarrassing or odious task needs to be performed.

> —From the confidential but later declassified January 15, 1982 memo previously cited, drafted for the State Department by the political section at the embassy in San Salvador.

The dead and pieces of the dead turn up in El Salvador everywhere, every day, as taken for granted as in a nightmare, or a horror movie. Vultures of course suggest the presence of a body. A knot of children on the street suggests the presence of a body. Bodies turn up in the brush of vacant lots, in the garbage thrown down ravines in the richest districts, in public rest rooms, in bus stations. Some are dropped in Lake Ilopango, a few miles east of the city, and wash up near the lakeside cottages and clubs frequented by what remains in San Salvador of the sporting bourgeoisie. Some still turn up at El Playón, the lunar lava field of rotting human flesh visible at one time or another on every television screen in America but characterized in June of 1982 in the *El Salvador News Gazette*, an English-language weekly edited by an American named Mario Rosenthal, as an "uncorroborated story … dredged up from the files of leftist propaganda." Others turn up at Puerta del Diablo, above Parque Balboa, a national *Turicentro* described as recently as the April–July 1982 issue of *Aboard TACA*, the magazine provided passengers on the national airline of El Salvador, as "offering excellent subjects for color photography."

I drove up to Puerta del Diablo one morning in June of 1982, past the Casa Presidencial and the camouflaged watch towers and heavy concentrations of troops and arms south of town, on up a narrow road narrowed further by landslides and deep crevices in the roadbed, a drive so insistently premonitory that after a while I began to hope that I would pass Puerta del Diablo without knowing it, just miss it, write it off, turn around and go back. There was however no way of missing it. Puerta del Diablo is a "view site" in an older and distinctly literary tradition, nature as lesson, an immense cleft rock through which half of El Salvador seems framed, a site so romantic and "mystical," so theatrically sacrificial in aspect, that it might be a cosmic parody of nineteenth-century landscape painting. The place presents itself as pathetic fallacy: the sky "broods," the stones "weep," a constant seepage of water weighting the ferns and moss. The foliage is thick and slick with moisture. The only sound is a steady buzz, I believe of cicadas.

Body dumps are seen in El Salvador as a kind of visitors' must-do, difficult but worth the detour. "Of course you have seen El Playón," an aide to President Alvaro Magaña said to me one day, and proceeded to discuss the site geologically, as evidence of the country's geothermal resources. He made no mention of the bodies. I was unsure if he was sounding me out or simply found the geothermal aspect of overriding interest. One difference between El Playón and Puerta del Diablo is that most bodies at El Playón appear to have been killed somewhere else, and then dumped; at Puerta del Diablo the executions are believed to occur in place, at the top, and the bodies thrown over. Sometimes reporters will speak of wanting to spend the night at Puerta del Diablo, in order to document the actual execution, but at the time I was in Salvador no one had.

The aftermath, the daylight aspect, is well documented. "Nothing fresh today, I hear," an embassy officer said when I mentioned that I had visited Puerta del Diablo. "Were there any on top?" someone else asked. "There were supposed to have been three on top yesterday." The point about whether or not there had been any on top was that usually it was necessary to go down to see bodies. The way down is hard. Slabs of stone, slippery with moss, are set into the vertiginous cliff, and it is down this cliff that one begins the descent to the bodies, or what is left of the bodies, pecked and maggoty masses of flesh, bone, hair. On some days there have been helicopters circling, tracking those making the descent. Other days there have been militia at the top, in the clearing where the road seems to run out, but on the morning I was there the only people on top were a man and a woman and three small children, who played in the wet grass while the woman started and stopped a Toyota pickup. She appeared to be learning how to drive. She drove forward and then back toward the edge, apparently following the man's signals, over and over again.

We did not speak, and it was only later, down the mountain and back in the land of the provisionally living, that it occurred to me that there was a definite question about why a man and a woman might choose a well-known body dump for a driving lesson. This was one of a number of occasions, during the two weeks my husband and I spent in El Salvador, on which I came to understand, in a way I had not understood before, the exact mechanism of terror.

Whenever I had nothing better to do in San Salvador I would walk up in the leafy stillness of the San Benito and Escalón districts, where the hush at midday is broken only by the occasional crackle of a walkie-talkie, the click of metal moving on a weapon. I recall a day in San Benito when I opened my bag to check an address, and heard the clicking of metal on metal all up and down the street. On the whole no one walks up here, and pools of blossoms lie undisturbed on the sidewalks. Most of the houses in San Benito are more recent than those in Escalón, less idiosyncratic and probably smarter, but the most striking architectural features in both districts are not the houses but their walls, walls built upon walls, walls stripped of the usual copa de oro and bougainvillea, walls that reflect successive generations of violence: the original stone, the additional five or six or ten feet of brick, and finally the barbed wire, sometimes concertina, sometimes electrified; walls with watch towers, gun ports, closed-circuit television cameras, walls now reaching twenty and thirty feet.

San Benito and Escalón appear on the embassy security maps as districts of relatively few "incidents," but they remain districts in which a certain oppressive uneasiness prevails. In the first place there are always "incidents"—detentions and deaths and disappearances—in the *barrancas*, the ravines lined with shanties that fall down behind the houses with the walls and the guards and the walkie-talkies; one day in Escalón I was introduced to a woman who kept the lean-to that served as a grocery in a *barranca* just above the Hotel Sheraton. She was sticking prices on bars of Camay and Johnson's baby soap, stopping occasionally to sell a plastic bag or two filled with crushed ice and Coca-Cola, and all the while she talked in a low voice about her fear, about her eighteen-year-old son, about the boys who had been taken out and shot on successive nights recently in a neighboring *barranca*.

In the second place there is, in Escalón, the presence of the Sheraton itself, a hotel that has figured rather too prominently in certain local stories involving the disappearance and death of Americans. The Sheraton always seems brighter and more mildly festive than either the Camino Real or the Presidente, with children in the pool and flowers and pretty women in pastel dresses, but there are usually several bulletproofed Cherokee Chiefs in the parking area, and the men drinking in the lobby often carry the little zippered purses that in San Salvador suggest not passports or credit cards but Browning 9-mm. pistols.

It was at the Sheraton that one of the few American *desa-parecidos*, a young free-lance writer named John Sullivan, was last seen, in December of 1980. It was also at the Sheraton, after eleven on the evening of January 3 1981, that the two American advisers on agrarian reform, Michael Hammer and Mark Pearlman, were killed, along with the Salvadoran director of the Institute for Agrarian Transformation, José Rodolfo Viera. The three were drinking coffee in a dining room off the lobby, and whoever killed them used an Ingram MAC-10, without sound suppressor, and then walked out through the lobby, unapprehended. The Sheraton has even turned up in the investigation into the December 1980 deaths of the four American churchwomen, Sisters Ita Ford and Maura Clarke, the two Maryknoll nuns; Sister Dorothy Kazel, the Ursuline nun; and Jean Donovan, the lay volunteer. In *Justice in El Salvador: A Case Study*, prepared and released in July of 1982 in New York by the Lawyers' Committee for International Human Rights, there appears this note:

On December 19, 1980, the [Duarte government's] Special Investigative Commission reported that "a red Toyota ¾-ton pickup was seen leaving (the crime scene) at about 11:00 P.M. on December 2" and that "a red splotch on the burned van" of the churchwomen was being checked to determine whether the paint splotch "could be the result of a collision between that van and the red Toyota pickup." By February 1981, the Maryknoll Sisters' Office of Social Concerns, which has been actively monitoring the investigation, received word from a source which it considered reliable that the FBI had matched the red splotch on the burned van with a red Toyota pickup belonging to the Sheraton hotel in San Salvador.... Subsequent to the FBI's alleged matching of the paint splotch and a Sheraton truck, the State Department has claimed, in a communication with the families of the churchwomen, that "the FBI could not determine the source of the paint scraping."

There is also mention in this study of a young Salvadoran businessman named Hans Christ (his father was a German who arrived in El Salvador at the end of World War II), a part owner of the Sheraton. Hans Christ lives now in Miami, and that his name should have even come up in the Maryknoll investigation made many people uncomfortable, because it was Hans Christ, along with his brother-in-law, Ricardo Sol Meza, who, in April of 1981, was first charged with the murders of Michael Hammer and Mark Pearlman and José Rodolfo Viera at the Sheraton. These charges were later dropped, and were followed by a series of other charges, arrests, releases, expressions of "dismay" and "incredulity" from the American embassy, and even, in the fall of 1982, confessions to the killings from two former National Guard corporals, who testified that Hans Christ had led them through the lobby and pointed out the victims. Hans Christ and Ricardo Sol Meza have said that the dropped case against them was a government frame-up, and that they were only having drinks at the Sheraton the night of the killings, with a National Guard intelligence officer. It was logical for Hans Christ and Ricardo Sol Meza to have drinks at the Sheraton because they both had interests in the hotel, and Ricardo Sol Meza had just opened a roller disco, since closed, off the lobby into which the killers walked that night. The killers were described by witnesses as well dressed, their faces covered. The room from which they walked was at the time I was in San Salvador no longer a restaurant, but the marks left by the bullets were still visible, on the wall facing the door.

Whenever I had occasion to visit the Sheraton I was apprehensive, and this apprehension came to color the entire Escalón district for me, even its lower reaches, where there were people and movies and restaurants. I recall being struck by it on the canopied porch of a restaurant near the Mexican embassy, on an evening when rain or sabotage or habit had blacked out the city and I became abruptly aware, in the light cast by a passing car, of two human shadows, silhouettes illuminated by the headlights and then invisible again. One shadow sat behind the smoked glass windows of a Cherokee Chief parked at the curb in front of the restaurant; the other crouched between the pumps at the Esso station next door, carrying a rifle. It seemed to me unencouraging that my husband and I were the only people seated on the porch. In the absence of the headlights the candle on our table provided the only light, and I fought the impulse to blow it out.

We continued talking, carefully. Nothing came of this, but I did not forget the sensation of having been in a single instant demoralized, undone, humiliated by fear, which is what I meant when I said that I came to understand in El Salvador the mechanism of terror.

3/3/81: ROBERTO D'AUBUISSON, a former Salvadoran army intelligence officer, holds a press conference and says that before the U.S. presidential election he had been in touch with a number of Reagan advisers and those contacts have continued. The armed forces should ask the junta to resign, D'Aubuisson says. He refuses to name a date for the action, but says "March is, I think, a very interesting month." He also calls for the abandonment of the economic reforms. D'Aubuisson had been accused of plotting to overthrow the government on two previous occasions. Observers speculate that since D'Aubuisson is able to hold the news conference and pass freely between Salvador and Guatemala, he must enjoy considerable support among some sections of the army.... 3/4/81: In San Salvador, the U.S. embassy is fired upon; no one is injured. Chargé d'Affaires Frederic Chapin says, "This incident has all the hallmarks of a D'Aubuisson operation. Let me state to you that we oppose coups and we have no intention of being intimidated."

—From the "Chronology of Events Related to Salvadoran Situation" prepared periodically by the United States embassy in San Salvador.

Since the Exodus from Egypt, historians have written of those who sacrificed and struggled for freedom: the stand at Thermopylae, the revolt of Spartacus, the storming of the Bastille, the Warsaw uprising in World War II. More recently we have seen evidence of this same human impulse in one of the developing nations in Central America. For months and months the world news media covered the fighting in El Salvador. Day after day, we were treated to stories and film slanted toward the brave freedom fighters battling oppressive government forces in behalf of the

357

silent, suffering people of that tortured country. Then one day those silent suffering people were offered a chance to vote to choose the kind of government they wanted. Suddenly the freedom fighters in the hills were exposed for what they really are: Cuban-backed guerrillas.... On election day the people of El Salvador, an unprecedented [1.5 million] of them, braved ambush and gunfire, trudging miles to vote for freedom.

> —*President Reagan, in his June 8 1982 speech before both houses of the British Parliament, referring to the March 28 1982 election which resulted in the ascension of Roberto D'Aubuisson to the presidency of the Constituent Assembly.*

From whence he shall come to judge the quick and the dead. I happened to read President Reagan's speech one evening in San Salvador when President Reagan was in fact on television, with Doris Day, in *The Winning Team*, a 1952 Warner Brothers picture about the baseball pitcher Grover Cleveland Alexander. I reached the stand at Thermopylae at about the time that *el salvador del Salvador* began stringing cranberries and singing "Old St. Nicholas" with Miss Day. "*Muy bonita*," he said when she tried out a rocking chair in her wedding dress. "*Feliz Navidad*," they cried, and, in accented English, "*Play ball!*"

As it happened "play ball" was a phrase I had come to associate in El Salvador with Roberto D'Aubuisson and his followers in the Nationalist Republican Alliance, or ARENA. "It's a process of letting certain people know they're going to have to play ball," embassy people would say, and: "You take a guy who's young, and everything 'young' implies, you send him signals, he plays ball, then we play ball." American diction in this situation tends toward the studied casual, the can-do, as if sheer cool and Bailey bridges could shape the place up. Elliott Abrams told *The New York Times* in July of 1982 that punishment within the Salvadoran military could be "a very important sign that you can't do this stuff any more," meaning kill the citizens. "If you clean up your act, all things are possible," is the way Jeremiah O'Leary, a special assistant to U.S. national security adviser William Clark, described the American diplomatic effort in an interview given *The Los Angeles Times* just after the March 28 1982 election. He was speculating on how Ambassador Deane Hinton might be dealing with D'Aubuisson. "I kind of picture him saying, 'Goddamnit, Bobbie, you've got a problem and … if you're what everyone said you are, you're going to make it hard for everybody.'"

Roberto D'Aubuisson is a chain smoker, as were many of the people I met in El Salvador, perhaps because it is a country in which the possibility of achieving a death related to smoking remains remote. I never met Major D'Aubuisson, but I was always interested in the adjectives used to describe him. "Pathological" was the adjective, modifying "killer," used by former ambassador Robert E. White (it was White who refused D'Aubuisson a visa, after which, according to the embassy's "Chronology of Events" for June 30 1980, "D'Aubuisson manages to enter the U.S. illegally and spends two days in Washington holding press conferences and attending luncheons before turning himself in to immigration authorities"), but "pathological" is not a word one heard in-country, where meaning tends to be transmitted in code.

In-country one heard "young" (the "and everything 'young' implies" part was usually left tacit), even "immature";"impetuous," "impulsive," "impatient," "nervous," "volatile," "high-strung," "kind of coiled-up," and, most frequently,"intense," or just "tense." Offhand it struck me that Roberto D'Aubuisson had some reason to be tense, in that General José Guillermo García, who had remained a main player through several changes of government, might logically perceive him as the wild card who could queer everybody's ability to refer to his election as a vote for freedom. As I write this I realize that I have fallen into the Salvadoran mindset, which turns on plot, and, since half the players at any given point in the game are in exile, on the phrase "in touch with."

"I've known D'Aubuisson a long time," I was told by Alvaro Magaña, the banker the Army made, over D'Aubuisson's rather frenzied objections ("We stopped that one on the one-yard line," Deane Hinton told me about D'Aubuisson's play to block Magaña), provisional president of El Salvador. We were sitting in his office upstairs at the Casa Presidencial, an airy and spacious building in the tropical colonial style, and he was drinking cup after Limoges cup of black coffee, smoking one cigarette with each, carefully, an unwilling actor who intended to survive the accident of being cast in this production. "Since Molina was president. I used to come here to see Molina, D'Aubuisson would be here, he was a young man in military intelligence, I'd see him here." He gazed toward the corridor that opened onto the interior courtyard, with cannas, oleander, a fountain not in operation. "When we're alone now I try to talk to him. I do talk to him, he's coming for lunch today. He never calls me Alvaro, it's always *usted, Señor, Doctor*. I call him Roberto. I say, Roberto, don't do this, don't do that, you know."

Magaña studied in the United States, at Chicago, and his four oldest children are now in the United States, one son at Vanderbilt, a son and a daughter at Santa Clara, and another daughter near Santa Clara, at Notre Dame in Belmont. He is connected by money, education, and temperament to oligarchal families. All the players here are densely connected: Magaña's sister, who lives in California, is the best friend of Nora Ungo, the wife of Guillermo Ungo, and Ungo spoke to Magaña's sister in August of 1982 when he was in California raising money for the FMLN–FDR, which is what the opposition to the Salvadoran government was called this year. The membership and even the initials of this opposition tend to the fluid, but the broad strokes are these: the FMLN–FDR is the coalition between the Revolutionary Democratic Front (FDR) and the five guerrilla groups joined together in the Farabundo Martí National Liberation Front (FMLN). These five groups are the Salvadoran Communist Party (PCS), the Popular Forces of Liberation (FPL), the Revolutionary Party of Central American Workers (PRTC), the People's Revolutionary Army (ERP), and the Armed Forces of National Resistance (FARN). Within each of these groups, there are further factions, and sometimes even further initials, as in the PRS and LP-28 of the ERP.

During the time that D'Aubuisson was trying to stop Magaña's appointment as provisional president, members of ARENA, which is supported heavily by other oligarchal elements, passed out leaflets referring to Magaña, predictably, as a communist, and, more interestingly, as "the little Jew." The manipulation of anti-Semitism is an undercurrent in Salvadoran life that is not much discussed and probably worth some study, since it refers to

a tension within the oligarchy itself, the tension between those
families who solidified their holdings in the mid-nineteenth century and those later families, some of them Jewish, who arrived
in El Salvador and entrenched themselves around 1900. I recall
asking a well-off Salvadoran about the numbers of his acquaintances within the oligarchy who have removed themselves and
their money to Miami. "Mostly the Jews," he said.

In San Salvador
in the year 1965
the best sellers
of the three most important
book stores
were:
The Protocols of the Elders of Zion;
a few books by
diarrhetic Somerset Maugham;
a book of disagreeably
obvious poems
by a lady with a European name
who nonetheless writes in Spanish about our
country
and a collection of
Reader's Digest condensed novels.

> —"San Salvador" by Roque Dalton, translated by
> Edward Baker.

The late Roque Dalton García was born into the Salvadoran
bourgeoisie in 1935, spent some years in Havana, came home in
1973 to join the ERP, or the People's Revolutionary Army, and,
in 1975, was executed, on charges that he was a CIA agent, by
his own comrades. The actual executioner was said to be Joaquín
Villalobos, who is now about thirty years old, commander of the
ERP, and a key figure in the FMLN, which, as the Mexican writer
Gabriel Zaid pointed out in the winter 1982 issue of *Dissent*, has
as one of its support groups the Roque Dalton Cultural Brigade.
The Dalton execution is frequently cited by people who want to
stress that "the other side kills people too, you know," an argument
common mainly among those, like the State Department, with a
stake in whatever government is current in El Salvador, since, if it

is taken for granted in Salvador that the government kills, it is also taken for granted that the other side kills; that everyone has killed, everyone kills now, and, if the history of the place suggests any pattern, everyone will continue to kill.

"Don't say I said this, but there are no issues here," I was told by a high-placed Salvadoran. "There are only ambitions." He meant of course not that there were no ideas in conflict but that the conflicting ideas were held exclusively by people he knew, that, whatever the outcome of any fighting or negotiation or coup or countercoup, the Casa Presidencial would ultimately be occupied not by *campesinos* and Maryknolls but by the already entitled, by a Guillermo Ungo or a Joaquín Villalobos or even by Roque Dalton's son, Juan José Dalton, or by Juan José Dalton's comrade in the FPL, José Antonio Morales Carbonell, the guerrilla son of José Antonio Morales Ehrlich, a former member of the Duarte junta who had himself been in exile during the Romero regime. In an open letter written shortly before his arrest in San Salvador in June 1980, José Antonio Morales Carbonell had charged his father with an insufficient appreciation of "Yankee imperialism." José Antonio Morales Carbonell and Juan José Dalton tried together to enter the United States in the summer of 1982, for a speaking engagement in San Francisco, but were refused visas by the American embassy in Mexico City.

Whatever the issues were that had divided Morales Carbonell and his father and Roque Dalton and Joaquín Villalobos, the prominent Salvadoran to whom I was talking seemed to be saying, they were issues that fell somewhere outside the lines normally drawn to indicate "left" and "right." That this man saw *la situación* as only one more realignment of power among the entitled, a conflict of "ambitions" rather than "issues," was, I recognized, what many people would call a conventional bourgeois view of civil conflict, and offered no solutions, but the people with solutions to offer were mainly somewhere else, in Mexico or Panama or Washington.

The place brings everything into question. One afternoon when I had run out of the Halazone tablets I dropped every night in a pitcher of tap water (a demented *gringa* gesture, I knew even then, in a country where everyone not born there was at least mildly ill, including the nurse at the American embassy), I walked across the street from the Camino Real to the Metrocenter, which is referred to locally as "Central America's Largest Shopping Mall." I found no Halazone at the Metrocenter but became absorbed in making notes about the mall itself, about the Muzak playing "I Left My Heart in San Francisco" and "American Pie" ("... *singing this will be the day that I die....*") although the record store featured a cassette called *Classics of Paraguay*, about the *pâté de foie gras* for sale in the supermarket, about the guard who did the weapons check on everyone who entered the supermarket, about the young matrons in tight Sergio Valente jeans, trailing maids and babies behind them and buying towels, big beach towels printed with maps of Manhattan that featured Bloomingdale's; about the number of things for sale that seemed to suggest a fashion for "smart drinking," to evoke modish cocktail hours. There were bottles of Stolichnaya vodka packaged with glasses and mixer, there were ice buckets, there were bar carts of every conceivable design, displayed with sample bottles.

This was a shopping center that embodied the future for which El Salvador was presumably being saved, and I wrote it down dutifully, this being the kind of "color" I knew how to interpret, the kind of inductive irony, the detail that was supposed to illuminate the story. As I wrote it down I realized that I was no longer much interested in this kind of irony, that this was a story that would not be illuminated by such details, that this was a story that would perhaps not be illuminated at all, that this was perhaps even less a "story" than a true *noche obscura*. As I waited to cross back over the Boulevard de los Heroes to the Camino Real I noticed soldiers herding a young civilian into a van, their guns at the boy's back, and I walked straight ahead, not wanting to see anything at all.

12/11/81:EL SALVADOR'S ATLACATL Battalion begins a 6-day offensive sweep against guerrilla strongholds in Morazán.
— *From the U.S. Embassy "Chronology of Events."*

The department of Morazán, one of the country's most embattled areas, was the scene of another armed forces operation in December, the fourth in Morazán during 1981.... The hamlet of Mozote was completely wiped out. For this reason, the several massacres which occurred in the same area at the same time are collectively known as the "Mozote massacre." The apparent sole survivor from Mozote, Rufina Amaya, thirty-eight years old, escaped by hiding behind trees near the house where she and the other women had been imprisoned. She has testified that on Friday, December 11, troops arrived and began taking people from their homes at about 5 in the morning.... At noon, the men were blindfolded and killed in the town's center. Among them was Amaya's husband, who was nearly blind. In the early afternoon the young women were taken to the hills nearby, where they were raped, then killed and burned. The old women were taken next and shot.... From her hiding place, Amaya heard soldiers discuss choking the children to death; subsequently she heard the children calling for help, but no shots. Among the children murdered were three of Amaya's, all under ten years of age.... It should be stressed that the villagers in the area had been warned of the impending military operation by the FMLN and some did leave. Those who chose to stay, such as the evangelical Protestants and others, considered themselves neutral in the conflict and friendly with the army. According to Rufina Amaya, "Because we knew the Army people, we felt safe." Her husband, she said, had

364

been on good terms with the local military and even had what she called "a military safe-conduct." Amaya and other survivors [of the nine hamlets in which the killing took place] accused the Atlacatl Battalion of a major role in the killing of civilians in the Mozote area.

—From the July 20 1982 Supplement to the "Report on Human Rights in El Salvador" prepared by Americas Watch Committee and the American Civil Liberties Union.

At the time I was in El Salvador, six months after the events referred to as the Mozote massacre and a month or so before President Reagan's July 1982 certification that sufficient progress was being made in specified areas ("human rights," and "land reform," and "the initiation of a democratic political process," phrases so remote *in situ* as to render them hallucinatory) to qualify El Salvador for continuing aid, a major offensive was taking place in Morazán, up in the mean hill country between the garrison town of San Francisco Gotera and the Honduran border. This June 1982 fighting was referred to by both sides as the heaviest of the war to date, but actual information, on this as on all subjects in San Salvador, was hard to come by.

Reports drifted back. The Atlacatl, which was trained by American advisers in 1981, was definitely up there again, as were two other battalions, the Atonal, trained, like the Atlacatl, by Americans in El Salvador, and the Ramón Belloso, just back from training at Fort Bragg. Every morning COPREFA, the press office at the Ministry of Defense, reported many FMLN casualties but few government. Every afternoon Radio Venceremos, the clandestine guerrilla radio station, reported many government casualties but few FMLN. The only way to get any sense of what was happening was to go up there, but Morazán was hard to reach: a key bridge between San Salvador and the eastern half of the country, the Puente de Oro on the Río Lempa, had been dynamited by the FMLN in October 1981, and to reach San Francisco Gotera it was now necessary either to cross the Lempa on a railroad bridge or to fly, which meant going out to the military airport, Ilopango, and trying to get one of the seven-passenger prop planes that the Gutierrez Flying Service operated between Ilopango and a grassy field outside San Miguel. At San

Miguel one could sometimes get a taxi willing to go on up to San Francisco Gotera, or a bus, the problem with a bus being that even a roadblock that ended well (no one killed or detained) could take hours, while every passenger was questioned. Between San Miguel and Gotera, moreover, there was a further problem, another blown bridge, this one on the Río Seco, which was *seco* enough in the dry months but often impassable in the wet.

June was wet. The Río Seco seemed doubtful. Everything about the day ahead, on the morning I started for Gotera, seemed doubtful, and that I set out on such a venture with a real lightening of the spirit suggests to me now how powerfully I wanted to get out of San Salvador, to spend a day free of its ambiguous tension, its overcast, its mood of wary somnambulism. It was only a trip of perhaps eighty miles, but getting there took most of the morning. There was, first of all, the wait on the runway at Ilopango while the pilot tried to get the engines to catch. "*Cinco minutos*," he kept saying, and, as a wrench was produced, "*Momentito*." Thunderclouds were massing on the mountains to the east. Rain spattered the fuselage. The plane was full, seven paying passengers at ninety-five *colones* the round trip, and we watched the tinkering without comment until one and finally both of the engines turned over.

Once in the air I was struck, as always in Salvador, by the miniature aspect of the country, an entire republic smaller than some California counties (smaller than San Diego County, smaller than Kern or Inyo, smaller by two-and-a-half times than San Bernardino), the very circumstance that has encouraged the illusion that the place can be managed, salvaged, a kind of pilot project, like TVA. There below us in a twenty-five-minute flight lay half the country, a landscape already densely green from the rains that had begun in May, intensely cultivated, deceptively rich, the coffee spreading down every ravine, the volcanic ranges looming abruptly and then receding. I watched the slopes of the mountains for signs of fighting but saw none. I watched for the hydroelectric works on the Lempa but saw only the blown bridge.

There were four of us on the flight that morning who wanted to go on to Gotera, my husband and I and Christopher Dickey from *The Washington Post* and Joseph Harmes from *Newsweek*, and when the plane set down on the grass strip outside San Miguel a deal was struck with a taxi driver willing to take us at least to the Río Seco. We shared the taxi as far as San Miguel with a local woman who, although she and I sat on a single bucket seat, did not speak, only stared straight ahead, clutching her bag with one hand and trying with the other to keep her skirt pulled down over her black lace slip. When she got out at San Miguel there remained in the taxi a trace of her perfume, Arpège.

In San Miguel the streets showed the marks of January's fighting, and many structures were boarded up, abandoned. There had been a passable motel in San Miguel, but the owners had managed to leave the country. There had been a passable place to eat in San Miguel, but no more. Occasional troop trucks hurtled past, presumably returning empty from the front, and we all made note of them, dutifully. The heat rose. Sweat from my hand kept blurring my tally of empty troop trucks, and I copied it on a clean page, painstakingly, as if it mattered.

The heat up here was drier than that in the capital, harsher, dustier, and by now we were resigned to it, resigned to the jolting of the taxi, resigned to the frequent occasions on which we were required to stop, get out, present our identification (carefully, reaching slowly into an outer pocket, every move calculated not to startle the soldiers, many of whom seemed barely pubescent, with the M-16s), and wait while the taxi was searched. Some of the younger soldiers wore crucifixes wrapped with bright yarn, the pink and green of the yarn stained now with dust and sweat. The taxi driver was perhaps twenty years older than most of these soldiers, a stocky, well-settled citizen wearing expensive sunglasses, but at each roadblock, in a motion so abbreviated as to be almost imperceptible, he would touch each of the two rosaries that hung from the rearview mirror and cross himself.

By the time we reached the Río Seco the question of whether or not we could cross it seemed insignificant, another minor distraction in a day that had begun at six and was now, before nine, already less a day than a way of being alive. We would try, the driver announced, to ford the river, which appeared that day to be running shallow and relatively fast over an unpredictable bed of sand and mud. We stood for a while on the bank and watched a man with an earthmover and winch try again and again to hook up his equipment to a truck that had foundered midstream. Small boys dove repeatedly with hooks, and repeatedly surfaced, unsuccessful. It did not seem entirely promising, but there it was, and there, in due time, we were: in the river, first following the sand-bar in a wide crescent, then off the bar, stuck, the engine dead. The taxi rocked gently in the current. The water bubbled inch by inch through the floorboards. There were women bathing naked in the shallows, and they paid no attention to the earthmover, the small boys, the half-submerged taxi, the *gringos* inside it. As we waited for our turn with the earthmover it occurred to me that fording the river in the morning meant only that we were going to have to ford it again in the afternoon, when the earthmover might or might not be around, but this was thinking ahead, and out of synch with the day at hand.

When I think now of that day in Gotera I think mainly of waiting, hanging around, waiting outside the *cuartel* ("COMANDO," the signs read on the gates, and "BOINAS VERDES," with a green beret) and waiting outside the church and waiting outside the Cine Morazán, where the posters promised *Fright* and *The Abominable Snowman* and the open lobby was lined with .50-caliber machine guns and 120-mm. mobile mortars. There were soldiers billeted in the Cine Morazán, and a few of them kicked a soccer ball, idly, among the mortars. Others joked among themselves at the corner, outside the saloon, and flirted with the women selling Coca-Cola in the stalls between the Cine Morazán and the parish house. The parish house and the church and the stalls and the saloon and the Cine Morazán and the *cuartel* all faced one another, across what was less a square than a dusty widening in the road, an arrangement that lent Gotera a certain proscenium aspect. Any event at all—the arrival of an armored personnel carrier, say, or a funeral procession outside the church—tended to metamorphose instantly into an opera, with all players onstage: the Soldiers of the Garrison, the Young Ladies of the Town, the Vendors, the Priests, the Mourners, and, since we were onstage as well, a dissonant and provocative element, the *norteamericanos*, in *norteamericano* costume, old Abercrombie khakis here, Adidas sneakers there, a Lone Star Beer cap.

We stood in the sun and tried to avoid adverse attention. We drank Coca-Cola and made surreptitious notes. We looked for the priests in the parish office but found only the receptionist, a dwarf. We presented our credentials again and again at the *cuartel*, trying to see the colonel who could give us permission to go up the few kilometers to where the fighting was, but the colonel was out, the colonel would be back, the colonel was delayed. The young officer in charge during the colonel's absence could not give us permission, but he had graduated from the Escuela Militar in one of the classes trained in the spring of 1982 at Fort Benning ("Mar-vel-*ous!*" was his impression of Fort Benning) and seemed at least amenable to us as Americans. Possibly there would be a patrol going up. Possibly we could join it.

In the end no patrol went up and the colonel never came back (the reason the colonel never came back is that he was killed that afternoon, in a helicopter crash near the Honduran border, but we did not learn this in Gotera) and nothing came of the day but overheard rumors, indefinite observations, fragments of information that might or might not fit into a pattern we did not perceive. One of the six A-37B Dragonfly attack jets that the United States had delivered just that week to Ilopango screamed low overhead, then disappeared. A company of soldiers burst through the *cuartel* gates and double-timed to the river, but when we caught up they were only bathing, shedding their uniforms and splashing in the shallow water. On the bluff above the river work was being completed on a helipad that was said to cover two mass graves of dead soldiers, but the graves were no longer apparent. The taxi driver heard, from the soldiers with whom he talked while he waited (talked and played cards and ate tortillas and sardines and listened to rock-and-roll on the taxi radio), that two whole companies were missing in action, lost or dead somewhere in the hills, but this was received information, and equivocal.

In some ways the least equivocal fact of the day was the single body we had seen that morning on the road between the Río Seco and Gotera, near San Carlos, the naked corpse of a man about thirty with a clean bullet-hole drilled neatly between his eyes. He could have been stripped by whoever killed him or, since this was a country in which clothes were too valuable to leave on the dead, by someone who happened past: there was no way of telling. In any case his genitals had been covered with a leafy branch, presumably by the *campesinos* who were even then digging a grave. A *subversivo*, the driver thought, because there was no family in evidence (to be related to someone killed in El Salvador is a prima facie death warrant, and families tend to vanish), but all anyone in Gotera seemed to know was that there had been another body at precisely that place the morning before, and five others before that. One of the priests in Gotera had happened to see the body the morning before, but when he drove past San Carlos later in the day the body had been buried. It was agreed that someone was trying to make a point. The point was unclear.

We spent an hour or so that day with the priests, or with two of them, both Irish, and two of the nuns, one Irish and one American, all of whom lived together in the parish house facing the *cuartel* in a situation that remains in my mind as the one actual instance I have witnessed of grace not simply under pressure but under siege. Except for the American, Sister Phyllis, who had arrived only a few months before, they had all been in Gotera a long time, twelve years, nine years, long enough to have established among themselves a grave companionableness, a courtesy and good humor that made the courtyard porch where we sat with them seem civilization's last stand in Morazán, which in certain ways it was.

The light on the porch was cool and aqueous, filtered through ferns and hibiscus, and there were old wicker rockers and a map of PARROQUIA SAN FRANCISCO GOTERA and a wooden table with a typewriter, a can of Planter's Mixed Nuts, copies of *Lives of the Saints: Illustrated* and *The Rules of the Secular Franciscan Order*. In the shadows beyond the table was a battered refrigerator from which, after a while, one of the priests got bottles of Pilsener beer, and we sat in the sedative half-light and drank the cold beer and talked in a desultory way about nothing in particular, about the situation, but no solutions.

These were not people much given to solutions, to abstracts: their lives were grounded in the specific. There had been the funeral that morning of a parishioner who had died in the night of cerebral hemorrhage. There had been the two children who died that week, of diarrhea, dehydration, in the squatter camps outside town where some 12,000 refugees were then gathered, many of them ill. There was no medicine in the camps. There was no water anywhere, and had been none since around the time of the election, when the tank that supplied Gotera with water had been dynamited. Five or six weeks after the tank was blown the rains had begun, which was bad in one way, because the rain washed out the latrines at the camps, but good in another, because at the parish house they were no longer dependent entirely on water from the river, soupy with bacteria and amoebae and worms. "We have the roof water now," Sister Jean, the Irish nun, said. "Much cleaner. It's greenish yellow, the river water, we only use it for the toilets."

There had been, they agreed, fewer dead around since the election, fewer bodies, they thought, than in the capital, but as they began reminding one another of this body or that there still seemed to have been quite a few. They spoke of these bodies in the matter-of-fact way that they might have spoken, in another kind of parish, of confirmation candidates, or cases of croup. There had been the few up the road, the two at Yoloaiquin. Of course there had been the forty-eight near Barrios, but Barrios was in April. "A *guardia* was killed last Wednesday," one of them recalled.

"Thursday."

"Was it Thursday then, Jerry?"

"A sniper."

"That's what I thought. A sniper."

We left the parish house that day only because rain seemed about to fall, and it was clear that the Río Seco had to be crossed now or perhaps not for days. The priests kept a guest book, and I thought as I signed it that I would definitely come back to this porch, come back with antibiotics and Scotch and time to spend, but I did not get back, and some weeks after I left El Salvador I heard in a third-hand way that the parish house had been at least temporarily abandoned, that the priests, who had been under threats and pressure from the garrison, had somehow been forced to leave Gotera. I recalled that on the day before I left El Salvador Deane Hinton had asked me, when I mentioned Gotera, if I had seen the priests, and had expressed concern for their situation. He was particularly concerned about the American, Sister Phyllis (an American nun in a parish under siege in a part of the country even then under attack from American A-37Bs was nothing the American embassy needed in those last delicate weeks before certification), and had at some point expressed this concern to the *comandante* at the garrison. The *comandante*, he said, had been surprised to learn the nationalities of the nuns and priests; he had thought them French, because the word used to describe them was always "Franciscan." This was one of those occasional windows that open onto the heart of El Salvador and then close, a glimpse of the impenetrable interior.

At the time I was in El Salvador the hostilities at hand were referred to by those reporters still in the country as "the number-four war," after Beirut, Iran-Iraq, and the aftermath of the Falklands. So many reporters had in fact abandoned the Hotel Camino Real in San Salvador (gone home for a while, or gone to the Intercontinental in Managua, or gone to whatever hotels they frequented in Guatemala and Panama and Tegucigalpa) that the dining room had discontinued its breakfast buffet, a fact often remarked upon: no breakfast buffet meant no action, little bang-bang, a period of editorial indifference in which stories were filed and held, and film rarely made the network news. "Get an NBC crew up from the Falklands, we might get the buffet back," they would say, and, "It hots up a little, we could have the midnight movies." It seemed that when the networks arrived in force they brought movies down, and showed them at midnight on their video recorders, *Apocalypse Now*, and Woody Allen's *Bananas*.

Meanwhile only the regulars were there. "Are you going out today?" they would say to one another at breakfast, and, "This might not be a bad day to look around." The Avis counter in the bar supplied signs reading "PRENSA INTERNACIONAL" with every car and van, and modified its insurance agreements with a typed clause excluding damage incurred by terrorists. The American embassy delivered translated transcripts of Radio Venceremos, prepared by the CIA in Panama. The COPREFA office at the Ministry of Defense sent over "urgent" notices, taped to the front desk, announcing events specifically devised, in those weeks before certification, for the American press: the ceremonial transfer of land titles, and the ritual display of "defectors," terrified-looking men who were reported in *La Prensa Gráfica* to have "abandoned the ranks of subversion, weary of so many lies and false promises."

A handful of reporters continued to cover these events, particularly if they were staged in provincial garrisons and offered the possibility of action en route, but action was less than certain, and the situation less accessible than it had seemed in the days of the breakfast buffet. The American advisers would talk to no one, although occasionally a reporter could find a few drinking at the Sheraton on Saturday night and initiate a little general conversation. (That the American advisers were still billeted at the Sheraton struck me as somewhat perverse, particularly because I knew that the embassy had moved its visiting AID people to a guarded house in San Benito. "Frankly, I'd rather stay at the Sheraton," an AID man had told me. "But since the two union guys got killed at the Sheraton, they want us here.") The era in which the guerrillas could be found just by going out on the highway had largely ended; the only certain way to spend time with them now was to cross into their territory from Honduras, through contact with the leadership in Mexico. This was a process that tended to discourage day-tripping, and in any case it was no longer a war in which the dateline "SOMEWHERE BEHIND GUERRILLA LINES, EL SALVADOR" was presumed automatically to illuminate much at all.

Everyone had already spent time, too, with the available government players, most of whom had grown so practiced in the process that their interviews were now performances, less apt to be reported than reviewed, and analyzed for subtle changes in delivery. Roberto D'Aubuisson had even taken part, wittingly or unwittingly, in an actual performance: a scene shot by a Danish film crew on location in Haiti and El Salvador for a movie about a foreign correspondent, in which the actor playing the correspondent "interviewed" D'Aubuisson, on camera, in his office. This Danish crew treated the Camino Real not only as a normal location hotel (the star, for example, was the only person I ever saw swim in the Camino Real pool) but also as a story element, on one occasion shooting a scene in the bar, which lent daily life during their stay a peculiar extra color. They left San Salvador without making it entirely clear whether or not they had ever told D'Aubuisson it was just a movie.

AT TWENTY-TWO MINUTES past midnight on Saturday June 19, 1982, there was a major earthquake in El Salvador, one that collapsed shacks and set off landslides and injured several hundred people but killed only about a dozen (I say "about" a dozen because figures on this, as on everything else in Salvador, varied), surprisingly few for an earthquake of this one's apparent intensity (Cal Tech registered it at 7.0 on the Richter scale, Berkeley at 7.4) and length, thirty-seven seconds. For the several hours that preceded the earthquake I had been seized by the kind of amorphous bad mood that my grandmother believed an adjunct of what is called in California "earthquake weather," a sultriness, a stillness, an unnatural light; the jitters. In fact there was no particular prescience about my bad mood, since it is always earthquake weather in San Salvador, and the jitters are endemic.

I recall having come back to the Camino Real about ten-thirty that Friday night, after dinner in a Mexican restaurant on the Paseo Escalón with a Salvadoran painter named Victor Barriere, who had said, when we met at a party a few days before, that he was interested in talking to Americans because they so often came and went with no understanding of the country and its history. Victor Barriere could offer, he explained, a special perspective on the country and its history, because he was a grandson of the late General Maximiliano Hernández Martínez, the dictator of El Salvador between 1931 and 1944 and the author of what Salvadorans still call *la matanza*, the massacre, or "killing," those weeks in 1932 when the government killed uncountable thousands of citizens, a lesson. ("Uncountable" because estimates of those killed vary from six or seven thousand to thirty thousand. Even higher figures are heard in Salvador, but, as Thomas P. Anderson pointed out in *Matanza: El Salvador's Communist Revolt of 1932*, "Salvadorans, like medieval people, tend to use numbers like fifty thousand simply to indicate a great number—statistics are not their strong point.")

As it happened I had been interested for some years in General Martínez, the spirit of whose regime would seem to have informed Gabriel García Márquez's *The Autumn of the Patriarch*. This original patriarch, who was murdered in exile in Honduras in 1966, was a rather sinister visionary who entrenched the military in Salvadoran life, was said to have held séances in the Casa Presidencial, and conducted both the country's and his own affairs along lines dictated by eccentric insights, which he sometimes shared by radio with the remaining citizens:

> It is good that children go barefoot. That way they can better receive the beneficial effluvia of the planet, the vibrations of the earth. Plants and animals don't use shoes.

> Biologists have discovered only five senses. But in reality there are ten. Hunger, thirst, procreation, urination, and bowel movements are the senses not included in the lists of biologists.

I had first come across this side of General Martínez in the United States Government Printing Office's *Area Handbook for El Salvador*, a generally straightforward volume ("designed to be useful to military and other personnel who need a convenient compilation of basic facts") in which, somewhere between the basic facts about General Martínez's program for building schools and the basic facts about General Martínez's program for increasing exports, there appears this sentence: "He kept bottles of colored water that he dispensed as cures for almost any disease, including cancer and heart trouble, and relied on complex magical formulas for the solution of national problems." This sentence springs from the *Area Handbook for El Salvador* as if printed in neon, and is followed by one even more arresting: "During an epidemic of smallpox in the capital, he attempted to halt its spread by stringing the city with a web of colored lights."

Not a night passed in San Salvador when I did not imagine it strung with those colored lights, and I asked Victor Barriere what it had been like to grow up as the grandson of General Martínez. Victor Barriere had studied for a while in the United States, at the San Diego campus of the University of California, and he spoke perfect unaccented English, with the slightly formal constructions of the foreign speaker, in a fluted, melodic voice that seemed always to suggest a higher reasonableness. The general had been, he said, sometimes misunderstood. Very strong men often were. Certain excesses had been inevitable. Someone had to take charge. "It was sometimes strange going to school with boys whose fathers my grandfather had ordered shot," he allowed, but he remembered his grandfather mainly as a "forceful" man, a man "capable of inspiring great loyalty," a theosophist from whom it had been possible to learn an appreciation of "the classics," "a sense of history," "the Germans." The Germans especially had influenced Victor Barriere's sense of history. "When you've read Schopenhauer, Nietzsche, what's happened here, what's happening here, well ..."

Victor Barriere had shrugged, and the subject changed, although only fractionally, since El Salvador is one of those places in the world where there is just one subject, the situation, the *problema*, its various facets presented over and over again, as on a stereopticon. One turn, and the facet was former ambassador Robert White: "A real jerk." Another, the murder in March of 1980 of Archbishop Oscar Arnulfo Romero: "A real bigot." At first I thought he meant whoever stood outside an open door of the chapel in which the Archbishop was saying mass and drilled him through the heart with a .22-caliber dumdum bullet, but he did not: "Listening to that man on the radio every Sunday," he said, "was like listening to Adolf Hitler or Benito Mussolini." In any case: "We don't really know who killed him, do we? It could have been the right..." He drew the words out, *cantabile*. "Or ... it could have been the left. We have to ask ourselves, who gained? Think about it, Joan."

I said nothing. I wanted only for dinner to end. Victor Barriere had brought a friend along, a young man from Chalatenango whom he was teaching to paint, and the friend brightened visibly when we stood up. He was eighteen years old and spoke no English and had sat through the dinner in polite misery. "He can't even speak Spanish properly," Victor Barriere said, in front of him. "However. If he were cutting cane in Chalatenango, he'd be taken by the Army and killed. If he were out on the street here he'd be killed. So. He comes every day to my studio, he learns to be a primitive painter, and I keep him from getting killed. It's better for him, don't you agree?"

I said that I agreed. The two of them were going back to the house Victor Barriere shared with his mother, a diminutive woman he addressed as "Mommy," the daughter of General Martínez, and after I dropped them there it occurred to me that this was the first time in my life that I had been in the presence of obvious "material" and felt no professional exhilaration at all, only personal dread. One of the most active death squads now operating in El Salvador calls itself the Maximiliano Hernández Martínez Brigade, but I had not asked the grandson about that.

In spite of or perhaps because of the fact that San Salvador had been for more than two years under an almost constant state of siege, a city in which arbitrary detention had been legalized (Revolutionary Governing Junta Decree 507), curfew violations had been known to end in death, and many people did not leave their houses after dark, a certain limited frivolity still obtained. When I got back to the Camino Real after dinner with Victor Barriere that Friday night there was for example a private party at the pool, with live music, dancing, an actual conga line.

There were also a number of people in the bar, many of them watching, on television monitors, "Señorita El Salvador 1982," the selection of El Salvador's entry in "Señorita Universo 1982," scheduled for July 1982 in Lima. Something about "Señorita Universo" struck a familiar note, and then I recalled that the Miss Universe contest itself had been held in San Salvador in 1975, and had ended in what might have been considered a predictable way, with student protests about the money the government was spending on the contest, and the government's predictable response, which was to shoot some of the students on the street and disappear others. (*Desaparecer*, or "disappear," is in Spanish both an intransitive and a transitive verb, and this flexibility has been adopted by those speaking English in El Salvador, as in *John Sullivan was disappeared from the Sheraton; the government disappeared the students*, there being no equivalent situation, and so no equivalent word, in English-speaking cultures.)

No mention of "Señorita Universo 1975" dampened "Señorita El Salvador 1982," which, by the time I got upstairs, had reached the point when each of the finalists was asked to pick a question from a basket and answer it. The questions had to do with the hopes and dreams of the contestants, and the answers ran to "*Dios*," "*Paz*," "El Salvador." A local entertainer wearing a white dinner jacket and a claret-colored bow tie sang "The Impossible Dream," in Spanish. The judges began their deliberations, and the moment of decision arrived: Señorita El Salvador 1982 would be Señorita San Vicente, Miss Jeannette Marroquín, who was several inches taller than the other finalists, and more *gringa*-looking. The four runners-up reacted, on the whole, with rather less grace than is the custom on these occasions, and it occurred to me that this was a contest in which winning meant more than a scholarship or a screen test or a new wardrobe; winning here could mean the difference between life and casual death, a provisional safe-conduct not only for the winner but for her entire family.

> God damn it, he cut inaugural ribbons, he showed himself large as life in public taking on the risks of power as he had never done in more peaceful times, what the hell, he played endless games of dominoes with my lifetime friend General Rodrigo de Aguilar and my old friend the minister of health who were the only ones who ... dared ask him to receive in a special audience the beauty queen of the poor, an incredible creature from that miserable wallow we call the dogfight district. ... I'll not only receive her in a special audience but I'll dance the first waltz with her, by God, have them write it up in the newspapers, he ordered, this kind of crap makes a big hit with the poor. Yet, the night after the audience, he commented with a certain bitterness to General Rodrigo de Aguilar that the queen of the poor wasn't even worth dancing with, that she was as common as so many other slum Manuela Sánchezes with her nymph's dress of muslin petticoats and the gilt crown with artificial jewels and a rose in her hand under the watchful eye of a mother who looked after her as if she were made of gold, so he gave her everything she wanted which was only electricity and running water for the dogfight district. ...

That is Gabriel García Márquez, *The Autumn of the Patriarch.* On this evening that began with the grandson of General

Maximiliano Hernández Martínez and progressed to "Señorita El Salvador 1982" and ended, at 12:22 A.M., with the earthquake, I began to see Gabriel García Márquez in a new light, as a social realist.

There were a number of metaphors to be found in this earthquake, not the least of them being that the one major building to suffer extensive damage happened also to be the major building most specifically and elaborately designed to withstand earthquakes, the American embassy. When this embassy was built, in 1965, the idea was that it would remain fluid under stress, its deep pilings shifting and sliding on Teflon pads, but over the past few years, as shelling the embassy came to be a favorite way of expressing dissatisfaction on all sides, the structure became so fortified—the steel exterior walls, the wet sandbags around the gun emplacements on the roof, the bomb shelter dug out underneath—as to render it rigid. The ceiling fell in Deane Hinton's office that night. Pipes burst on the third floor, flooding everything below. The elevator was disabled, the commissary a sea of shattered glass.

The Hotel Camino Real, on the other hand, which would appear to have been thrown together in the insouciant tradition of most tropical construction, did a considerable amount of rolling (I recall crouching under a door frame in my room on the seventh floor and watching, through the window, the San Salvador volcano appear to rock from left to right), but when the wrenching stopped and candles were found and everyone got downstairs nothing was broken, not even the glasses behind the bar. There was no electricity, but there was often no electricity. There were sporadic bursts of machine-gun fire on the street (this had made getting downstairs more problematic than it might have been, since the emergency stairway was exposed to the street), but sporadic bursts of machine-gun fire on the street were not entirely unusual in San Salvador. ("Sometimes it happens when it rains," someone from the embassy had told me about this phenomenon. "They get excited.") On the whole it was business as usual at the Camino Real, particularly in the discothèque off the lobby, where, by the time I got downstairs, an emergency generator seemed already to have been activated,

waiters in black cowboy hats darted about the dance floor
carrying drinks, and dancing continued, to Jerry Lee Lewis's
"Great Balls of Fire."

Actual information was hard to come by in El Salvador,
perhaps because this is not a culture in which a high value is
placed on the definite. The only hard facts on the earthquake,
for example, arrived at the Camino Real that night from New
York, on the AP wire, which reported the Cal Tech reading
of 7.0 Richter on an earthquake centered in the Pacific some
sixty miles south of San Salvador. Over the next few days, as
damage reports appeared in the local papers, the figure varied.
One day the earthquake had been a 7.0 Richter, another day
a 6.8. By Tuesday it was again a 7 in *La Prensa Gráfica*, but on
a different scale altogether, not the Richter but the Modified
Mercalli.

All numbers in El Salvador tended to materialize and vanish and rematerialize in a different form, as if numbers denoted
only the "use" of numbers, an intention, a wish, a recognition
that someone, somewhere, for whatever reason, needed to hear
the ineffable expressed as a number. At any given time in El
Salvador a great deal of what goes on is considered ineffable,
and the use of numbers in this context tends to frustrate people
who try to understand them literally, rather than as propositions to be floated, "heard," "mentioned." There was the case
of the March 28 1982 election, about which there continued
into that summer the rather scholastic argument first posed by
Central American Studies, the publication of the Jesuit university
in San Salvador: Had it taken an average of 2.5 minutes to cast
a vote, or less? Could each ballot box hold 500 ballots, or more?
The numbers were eerily Salvadoran. There were said to be 1.3
million people eligible to vote on March 28, but 1.5 million
people were said to have voted. These 1.5 million people were
said, in turn, to represent not 115 percent of the 1.3 million
eligible voters but 80 percent (or, on another float, "62–68 percent") of the eligible voters, who accordingly no longer numbered 1.3 million, but a larger number. In any case no one
really knew how many eligible voters there were in El Salvador,
or even how many people. In any case it had seemed necessary

to provide a number. In any case the election was over, a success, *la solución pacífica*.

Similarly, there was the question of how much money had left the country for Miami since 1979: Deane Hinton, in March of 1982, estimated $740 million. The Salvadoran minister of planning estimated, the same month, twice that. I recall asking President Magaña, when he happened to say that he had gone to lunch every Tuesday for the past ten years with the officers of the Central Reserve Bank of El Salvador, which reviews the very export and import transactions through which money traditionally leaves troubled countries, how much he thought was gone. "You hear figures mentioned," he said. I asked what figures he heard mentioned at these Tuesday lunches. "The figure they mentioned is six hundred million," he said. He watched as I wrote that down, *600,000,000, central bank El Salvador*. "The figure the Federal Reserve in New York mentioned," he added, "is one thousand million." He watched as I wrote that down too, *1,000,000,000, Fed NY*. "Those people don't want to stay for life in Miami," he said then, but this did not entirely address the question, nor was it meant to.

Not only numbers but names are understood locally to have only a situational meaning, and the change of a name is meant to be accepted as a change in the nature of the thing named. ORDEN, for example, the paramilitary organization formally founded in 1968 to function, along classic patronage lines, as the government's eyes and ears in the countryside, no longer exists as ORDEN, or the Organización Democrática Nacionalista, but as the Frente Democrática Nacionalista, a transubstantiation noted only cryptically in the State Department's official "justification" for the January 28 1982 certification: "The Salvadoran government, since the overthrow of General Romero, has taken explicit actions to end human rights abuses. The paramilitary organization 'ORDEN' has been outlawed, *although some of its former members may still be active*." (Italics added.)

This tactic of solving a problem by changing its name is by no means limited to the government. The small office on the arch-diocese grounds where the scrapbooks of the dead are kept is still called, by virtually everyone in San Salvador, "the Human Rights Commission" (Comisión de los Derechos Humanos), but in fact both the Human Rights Commission and Socorro Jurídico, the archdiocesan legal aid office, were ordered in the spring of 1982 to vacate the church property, and, in the local way, did so: everything pretty much stayed in place, but the scrapbooks of the dead were thereafter kept, officially, in the "Oficina de Tutela Legal" of the "Comisión Arquidiocesana de Justicia y Paz." (This "Human Rights Commission," in any case, is not to be confused with the Salvadoran government's "Commission on Human Rights," the formation of which was announced the day before a scheduled meeting between President Magaña and Ronald Reagan. This official *comisión* is a seven-member panel notable for its inclusion of Colonel Carlos Reynaldo López Nuila, the director of the National Police.) This renaming was referred to as a "reorganization," which is one of many words in El Salvador that tend to signal the presence of the ineffable.

Other such words are "improvement," "perfection" (reforms are never abandoned or ignored, only "perfected" or "improved"), and that favorite from other fronts, "pacification." Language has always been used a little differently in this part of the world (an apparent statement of fact often expresses something only wished for, or something that might be true, a story, as in García Márquez's *many years later, as he faced the firing squad, Colonel Aureliano Buendía was to remember that distant afternoon when his father took him to discover ice*), but "improvement" and "perfection" and "pacification" derive from another tradition. Language as it is now used in El Salvador is the language of advertising, of persuasion, the product being one or another of the *soluciones* crafted in Washington or Panama or Mexico, which is part of the place's pervasive obscenity.

This language is shared by Salvadorans and Americans, as if a linguistic deal had been cut. "Perhaps the most striking measure of progress [in El Salvador]," Assistant Secretary of State Thomas Enders was able to say in August of 1982 in a speech at the Commonwealth Club in San Francisco, "is the transform-ation of the military from an institution dedicated to the status quo to one that spearheads land reform and supports consti-tutional democracy." Thomas Enders was able to say this pre-cisely because the Salvadoran minister of defense, General José Guillermo García, had so superior a dedication to his own status quo that he played the American card as Roberto D'Aubuisson did not, played the game, played ball, understood the importance to Americans of symbolic action: the importance of letting the

Americans have their land reform program, the importance of letting the Americans pretend that while "democracy in El Salvador" may remain "a slender reed" (that was Elliott Abrams in *The New York Times*), the situation is one in which "progress" is measurable ("the minister of defense has ordered that all violations of citizens' rights be stopped immediately," the State Department noted on the occasion of the July 1982 certification, a happy ending); the importance of giving the Americans an acceptable president, Alvaro Magaña, and of pretending that this acceptable president was in fact commander-in-chief of the armed forces, *el generalísimo* as *la solución*.

La solución changed with the market. Pacification, although those places pacified turned out to be in need of repeated pacification, was *la solución*. The use of the word "negotiations," however abstract that use may have been, was *la solución*. The election, although it ended with the ascension of a man, Roberto D'Aubuisson, essentially hostile to American policy, was *la solución* for Americans. The land reform program, grounded as it was in political rather than economic reality, was *la solución* as symbol. "It has not been a total economic success," Peter Askin, the AID director working with the government on the program, told *The New York Times* in August 1981, "but up to this point it has been a political success. I'm firm on that. There does seem to be a direct correlation between the agrarian reforms and the peasants not having become more radicalized." The land reform program, in other words, was based on the principle of buying off, buying time, giving a little to gain a lot, *minifundismo* in support of *latifundismo*, which, in a country where the left had no interest in keeping the peasants less "radicalized" and the right remained unconvinced that these peasants could not simply be eliminated, rendered it a program about which only Americans could be truly enthusiastic, less a "reform" than an exercise in public relations.

Even *la verdad*, the truth, was a degenerated phrase in El Salvador: on my first evening in the country I was asked by a Salvadoran woman at an embassy party what I hoped to find out in El Salvador. I said that ideally I hoped to find out *la verdad*, and she beamed approvingly. Other journalists, she said, did not want *la verdad*. She called over two friends, who also approved: no one told *la verdad*. If I wrote *la verdad* it would be good for El Salvador.

I realized that I had stumbled into a code, that these women used *la verdad* as it was used on the bumper stickers favored that spring and summer by ARENA people. "JOURNALISTS, TELL THE TRUTH!" the bumper stickers warned in Spanish, and they meant the truth according to Roberto D'Aubuisson.

In the absence of information (and the presence, often, of disinformation) even the most apparently straightforward event takes on, in El Salvador, elusive shadows, like a fragment of retrieved legend. On the afternoon that I was in San Francisco Gotera trying to see the commander of the garrison there, this *comandante*, Colonel Salvador Beltrán Luna, was killed, or was generally believed to have been killed, in the crash of a Hughes 500-D helicopter. The crash of a helicopter in a war zone would seem to lend itself to only a limited number of interpretations (the helicopter was shot down, or the helicopter suffered mechanical failure, are the two that come to mind), but the crash of this particular helicopter became, like everything else in Salvador, an occasion of rumor, doubt, suspicion, conflicting reports, and finally a kind of listless uneasiness.

The crash occurred either near the Honduran border in Morazán or, the speculation went, actually in Honduras. There were or were not four people aboard the helicopter: the pilot, a bodyguard, Colonel Beltrán Luna, and the assistant secretary of defense, Colonel Francisco Adolfo Castillo. At first all four were dead. A day later only three were dead: Radio Venceremos broadcast news of Colonel Castillo (followed a few days later by a voice resembling that of Colonel Castillo), not dead but a prisoner, or said to be a prisoner, or perhaps only claiming to be a prisoner. A day or so later another of the dead materialized, or appeared to: the pilot was, it seemed, neither dead nor a prisoner but hospitalized, incommunicado.

Questions about what actually happened to (or on, or after the crash of, or after the clandestine landing of) this helicopter provided table talk for days (one morning the newspapers emphasized that the Hughes 500-D had been *comprado en Guatemala*, bought in Guatemala, a detail so solid in this otherwise vaporous story that it suggested rumors yet unheard, intrigues yet unimagined), and remained unresolved at the time I left. At one point I asked

President Magaña, who had talked to the pilot, what had happened. "They don't say," he said. Was Colonel Castillo a prisoner? "I read that in the paper, yes." Was Colonel Beltrán Luna dead? "I have that impression." Was the bodyguard dead? "Well, the pilot said he saw someone lying on the ground, either dead or unconscious, he doesn't know, but he believes it may have been Castillo's security man, yes." Where exactly had the helicopter crashed? "I didn't ask him." I looked at President Magaña, and he shrugged. "This is very delicate," he said. "I have a problem there. I'm supposed to be the commander-in-chief, so if I ask him, he should tell me. But he might say he's not going to tell me, then I would have to arrest him. So I don't ask." This is in many ways the standard development of a story in El Salvador, and is also illustrative of the position of the provisional president of El Salvador.

News of the outside world drifted in only fitfully, and in peculiar details. *La Prensa Gráfica* carried a regular column of news from San Francisco, California, and I recall reading in this column one morning that a man identified as a former president of the Bohemian Club had died, at age seventy-two, at his home in Tiburon. Most days *The Miami Herald* came in at some point, and sporadically *The New York Times* or *The Washington Post*, but there would be days when nothing came in at all, and I would find myself rifling back sports sections of *The Miami Herald* for installments of *Chrissie: My Own Story*, by Chris Evert Lloyd with Neil Amdur, or haunting the paperback stand at the hotel, where the collection ran mainly to romances and specialty items, like *The World's Best Dirty Jokes*, a volume in which all the jokes seemed to begin: "A midget went into a whorehouse …"

In fact the only news I wanted from outside increasingly turned out to be that which had originated in El Salvador: all other information seemed beside the point, the point being here, now, the situation, the *problema*, what did they mean the Hughes 500-D was *comprado en Guatemala*, was the Río Seco passable, were there or were there not American advisers on patrol in Usulután, who was going out, where were the roadblocks, were they burning cars today. In this context the rest of the world tended to recede, and word from the United States seemed profoundly remote, even inexplicable. I recall one morning picking up this message, from my secretary in Los Angeles: "JDD: Alessandra Stanley from *Time*, 213/273–1530. They heard you were in El Salvador and wanted some input from you for the cover story they're preparing on the women's movement. Ms. Stanley wanted their correspondent in Central America to contact you—I said that you could not be reached but would be calling me. She wanted you to call: Jay Cocks 212/841–2633." I studied this message for a long time, and tried to imagine the scenario in which a *Time* stringer in El Salvador received, by Telex from Jay Cocks in New York, a request to do an interview on the women's movement with someone who happened to be at the Camino Real Hotel. This was not a scenario that played, and I realized then that El Salvador was as inconceivable to Jay Cocks in the high keep of the Time-Life Building in New York as this message was to me in El Salvador.

I WAS TOLD in the summer of 1982 by both Alvaro Magaña and Guillermo Ungo that although each of course knew the other they were of "different generations." Magaña was fifty-six. Ungo was fifty-one. Five years is a generation in El Salvador, it being a place in which not only the rest of the world but time itself tends to contract to the here and now. History is *la matanza*, and then current events, which recede even as they happen: General José Guillermo García was in the summer of 1982 widely perceived as a fixture of long standing, an immovable object through several governments and shifts in the national temperament, a survivor. In context he was a survivor, but the context was just three years, since the Majano coup. All events earlier than the Majano coup had by then vanished into uncertain memory, and the coup itself, which took place on October 15 1979, was seen as so distant that there was common talk of the next *juventud militar*, of the cyclical readiness for rebellion of what was always referred to as "the new generation" of young officers. "We think in five-year horizons," the economic officer at the American embassy told me one day. "Anything beyond that is evolution." He was talking about not having what he called "the luxury of the long view," but there is a real sense in which the five-year horizons of the American embassy constitute the longest view taken in El Salvador, either forward or back.

One reason no one looks back is that the view could only dispirit: this is a national history peculiarly resistant to heroic interpretation. There is no *libertador* to particularly remember. Public statues in San Salvador tend toward representations of abstracts, the Winged Liberty downtown, the *Salvador del Mundo* at the junction of Avenida Roosevelt and Paseo Escalón and the Santa Tecla highway; the expressionist spirit straining upward, outsized hands thrust toward the sky, at the Monument of the Revolution up by the Hotel Presidente. If the country's history as a republic seems devoid of shared purpose or unifying event, a record of insensate ambitions and their accidental consequences, its three centuries as a colony seem blanker still: Spanish colonial life was centered in Colombia and Panama to the south and Guatemala to the north, and Salvador lay between, a neglected frontier of the Captaincy General of Guatemala from 1525 until 1821, the year Guatemala declared its independence from Spain. So attenuated was El Salvador's sense of itself in its moment of independence that it petitioned the United States for admission to the union as a state. The United States declined.

In fact El Salvador had always been a frontier, even before the Spaniards arrived. The great Mesoamerican cultures penetrated this far south only shallowly. The great South American cultures thrust this far north only sporadically. There is a sense in which the place remains marked by the meanness and discontinuity of all frontier history, by a certain frontier proximity to the cultural zero. Some aspects of the local culture were imposed. Others were borrowed. An instructive moment: at an exhibition of native crafts in Nahuizalco, near Sonsonate, it was explained to me that a traditional native craft was the making of wicker furniture, but that little of this furniture was now seen because it was hard to obtain wicker in the traditional way. I asked what the traditional way of obtaining wicker had been. The traditional way of obtaining wicker, it turned out, had been to import it from Guatemala.

In fact there were a number of instructive elements about this day I spent in Nahuizalco, a hot Sunday in June. The event for which I had driven down from San Salvador was not merely a craft exhibit but the opening of a festival that would last several days, the sixth annual Feria Artesanal de Nahuizalco, sponsored by the Casa de la Cultura program of the Ministry of Education as part of its effort to encourage indigenous culture. Since public policy in El Salvador has veered unerringly toward the elimination of the indigenous population, this official celebration of its culture seemed an undertaking of some ambiguity, particularly in Nahuizalco: the uprising that led to the 1932 *matanza* began and ended among the Indian workers on the coffee *fincas* in this part of the country, and Nahuizalco and the other Indian villages around Sonsonate lost an entire generation to the *matanza*. By the early sixties estimates of the remaining Indian population in all of El Salvador ranged only between four and sixteen percent;

the rest of the population was classified as *ladino*, a cultural rather than an ethnic designation, denoting only Hispanization, including both acculturated Indians and *mestizos*, and rejected by those upper-class members of the population who preferred to emphasize their Spanish ancestry.

Nineteen thirty-two was a year around Nahuizalco when Indians were tied by their thumbs and shot against church walls, shot on the road and left for the dogs, shot and bayoneted into the mass graves they themselves had dug. Indian dress was abandoned by the survivors. Nahuatl, the Indian language, was no longer spoken in public. In many ways race remains the ineffable element at the heart of this particular darkness: even as he conducted the *matanza*, General Maximiliano Hernández Martínez was dismissed, by many of the very oligarchs whose interests he was protecting by killing Indians, as "the little Indian." On this hot Sunday fifty years later the celebrants of Nahuizalco's indigenous culture would arrange themselves, by noon, into two distinct camps, the *ladinos* sitting in the shade of the schoolyard, the Indians squatting in the brutal sun outside. In the schoolyard there were trees, and tables, where the Queen of the Fair, who had a wicker crown and European features, sat with the local *guardia*, each of whom had an automatic weapon, a sidearm, and a bayonet. The *guardia* drank beer and played with their weapons. The Queen of the Fair studied her ox-blood-red fingernails. It took twenty centavos to enter the schoolyard, and a certain cultural confidence.

There had been Indian dances that morning. There had been music. There had been the "blessing of the market": the statue of San Juan Bautista carried, on a platform trimmed with wilted gladioli, from the church to the market, the school, the homes of the bedridden. To the extent that Catholic mythology has been over four centuries successfully incorporated into local Indian life, this blessing of the market was at least part of the "actual" indigenous culture, but the dances and the music derived from other traditions. There was a Suprema Beer sound truck parked in front of the Casa de la Cultura office on the plaza, and the music that blared all day from its loudspeakers was "Roll Out the Barrel," "La Cucaracha," "Everybody Salsa."

The provenance of the dances was more complicated. They were Indian, but they were less remembered than recreated, and as such derived not from local culture but from a learned idea of local culture, an official imposition made particularly ugly by the cultural impotence of the participants. The women, awkward and uncomfortable in an approximation of native costume, moved with difficulty into the dusty street and performed a listless and unpracticed dance with baskets. Whatever men could be found (mainly little boys and old men, since those young men still alive in places like Nahuizalco try not to be noticed) had been dressed in "warrior" costume: headdresses of crinkled foil, swords of cardboard and wood. Their hair was lank, their walk furtive. Some of them wore sunglasses. The others averted their eyes. Their role in the fair involved stamping and lunging and brandishing their cardboard weapons, a display of warrior *machismo*, and the extent to which each of them had been unmanned—unmanned not only by history but by a factor less abstract, unmanned by the real weapons in the schoolyard, by the G-3 assault rifles with which the *guardia* played while they drank beer with the Queen of the Fair—rendered this display deeply obscene.

I had begun before long to despise the day, the dirt, the blazing sun, the pervasive smell of rotting meat, the absence of even the most rudimentary skill in the handicrafts on exhibit (there were sewn items, for example, but they were sewn by machine of sleazy fabric, and the simplest seams were crooked), the brutalizing music from the sound truck, the tedium; had begun most of all to despise the fair itself, which seemed contrived, pernicious, a kind of official opiate, an attempt to recreate or perpetuate a way of life neither economically nor socially viable. There was no pleasure in this day. There was a great deal of joyless milling. There was some shade in the plaza, from trees plastered with ARENA posters, but nowhere to sit. There was a fountain painted bright blue inside, but the dirty water was surrounded by barbed wire, and the sign read: "SE PROHIBE SENTARSE AQUI," no sitting allowed.

I stood for a while and watched the fountain. I bought a John Deere cap for seven *colones* and stood in the sun and watched the little ferris wheel, and the merry-go-round, but there seemed to be no children with the money or will to ride them, and after a while I crossed the plaza and went into the church, avoiding the bits of masonry which still fell from the bell tower damaged that week in the earthquake and its aftershocks. In the church a mass baptism was taking place: thirty or forty infants and older babies, and probably a few hundred mothers and grandmothers and aunts and godmothers. The altar was decorated with asters in condensed milk cans. The babies fretted, and several of the mothers produced bags of Fritos to quiet them. A piece of falling masonry bounced off a scaffold in the back of the church, but no one looked back. In this church full of women and babies there were only four men present. The reason for this may have been cultural, or may have had to do with the time and the place, and the G-3s in the schoolyard.

During the week before I flew down to El Salvador a Salvadoran woman who works for my husband and me in Los Angeles gave me repeated instructions about what we must and must not do. We must not go out at night. We must stay off the street whenever possible. We must never ride in buses or taxis, never leave the capital, never imagine that our passports would protect us. We must not even consider the hotel a safe place: people were killed in hotels. She spoke with considerable vehemence, because two of her brothers had been killed in Salvador in August of 1981, in their beds. The throats of both brothers had been slashed. Her father had been cut but stayed alive. Her mother had been beaten. Twelve of her other relatives, aunts and uncles and cousins, had been taken from their houses one night the same August, and their bodies had been found some time later, in a ditch. I assured her that we would remember, we would be careful, we would in fact be so careful that we would probably (trying for a light touch) spend all our time in church.

She became still more agitated, and I realized that I had spoken as a *norteamericana*: churches had not been to this woman the neutral ground they had been to me. I must remember: Archbishop Romero killed saying mass in the chapel of the Divine Providence Hospital in San Salvador. I must remember: more than thirty people killed at Archbishop Romero's funeral in the Metropolitan Cathedral in San Salvador. I must remember: more than twenty people killed before that on the steps of the Metropolitan Cathedral. CBS had filmed it. It had been on television, the bodies jerking, those still alive crawling over the dead as they tried to get out of range. I must understand: the Church was dangerous.

I told her that I understood, that I knew all that, and I did, abstractly, but the specific meaning of the Church she knew eluded me until I was actually there, at the Metropolitan Cathedral in San Salvador, one afternoon when rain sluiced down its corrugated plastic windows and puddled around the supports of the Sony and Phillips billboards near the steps. The effect of the Metropolitan Cathedral is immediate, and entirely literary. This is the cathedral that the late Archbishop Oscar Arnulfo Romero refused to finish, on the premise that the work of the Church took precedence over its display, and the high walls of raw concrete bristle with structural rods, rusting now, staining the concrete, sticking out at wrenched and violent angles. The wiring is exposed. Fluorescent tubes hang askew. The great high altar is backed by warped ply-board. The cross on the altar is of bare incandescent bulbs, but the bulbs, that afternoon, were unlit: there was in fact no light at all on the main altar, no light on the cross, no light on the globe of the world that showed the northern American continent in gray and the southern in white; no light on the dove above the globe, *Salvador del Mundo*. In this vast brutalist space that was the cathedral, the unlit altar seemed to offer a single ineluctable message: at this time and in this place the light of the world could be construed as out, off, extinguished.

In many ways the Metropolitan Cathedral is an authentic piece of political art, a statement for El Salvador as *Guernica* was for Spain. It is quite devoid of sentimental relief. There are no decorative or architectural references to familiar parables, in fact no stories at all, not even the Stations of the Cross. On the afternoon I was there the flowers laid on the altar were dead. There were no traces of normal parish activity. The doors were open to the barricaded main steps, and down the steps there was a spill of red paint, lest anyone forget the blood shed there. Here and there on the cheap linoleum inside the cathedral there was what seemed to be actual blood, dried in spots, the kind of spots dropped by a slow hemorrhage, or by a woman who does not know or does not care that she is menstruating.

There were several women in the cathedral during the hour or so I spent there, a young woman with a baby, an older woman in house slippers, a few others, all in black. One of the women walked the aisles as if by compulsion, up and down, across and back, crooning loudly as she walked. Another knelt without moving at the tomb of Archbishop Romero in the right transept. "LOOR A MONSENOR ROMERO," the crude needlepoint tapestry by the tomb read, "Praise to Monsignor Romero from the Mothers of the Imprisoned, the Disappeared, and the Murdered," the *Comité de Madres y Familiares de Presos, Desaparecidos, y Asesinados Politicos de El Salvador.*

The tomb itself was covered with offerings and petitions, notes decorated with motifs cut from greeting cards and cartoons. I recall one with figures cut from a Bugs Bunny strip, and another with a pencil drawing of a baby in a crib. The baby in this drawing seemed to be receiving medication or fluid or blood intravenously, through the IV line shown on its wrist. I studied the notes for a while and then went back and looked again at the unlit altar, and at the red paint on the main steps, from which it was possible to see the guardsmen on the balcony of the National Palace hunching back to avoid the rain. Many Salvadorans are offended by the Metropolitan Cathedral, which is as it should be, because the place remains perhaps the only unambiguous political statement in El Salvador, a metaphorical bomb in the ultimate power station.

> ... I had nothing more to do in San Salvador. I had given a lecture on the topic that had occurred to me on the train to Tapachula: Little-known Books by Famous American Authors—*Pudd'nhead Wilson, The Devil's Dictionary, The Wild Palms.* I had looked at the university; and no one could explain why there was a mural of Marx, Engels, and Lenin in the university of this right-wing dictatorship.
>
> —Paul Theroux, *The Old Patagonian Express.*

The university Paul Theroux visited in San Salvador was the National University of El Salvador. This visit (and, given the context, this extraordinary lecture) took place in the late seventies, a period when the National University was actually open. In 1972 the Molina government had closed it, forcibly, with tanks and artillery and planes, and had kept it closed until 1974. In 1980 the Duarte government again moved troops onto the campus, which then had an enrollment of about 30,000, leaving fifty dead and offices and laboratories systematically smashed. By the time I visited El Salvador a few classes were being held in storefronts around San Salvador, but no one other than an occasional reporter had been allowed to enter the campus since the day the troops came in. Those reporters allowed to look had described walls still splashed with the spray-painted slogans left by the students, floors littered with tangled computer tape and with copies of what the National Guardsmen in charge characterized as *subversivo* pamphlets, for example a reprint of an article on inherited enzyme deficiency from *The New England Journal of Medicine.*

In some ways the closing of the National University seemed another of those Salvadoran situations in which no one came out well, and everyone was made to bleed a little, not excluding the National Guardsmen left behind to have their ignorance exposed by *gringo* reporters. The Jesuit university, UCA, or La Universidad Centroamericana José Simeón Cañas, had emerged as the most important intellectual force in the country, but the Jesuits had been so widely identified with the left that some local scholars would not attend lectures or seminars held on the UCA campus. (Those Jesuits still in El Salvador had in fact been under a categorical threat of death from the White Warriors Union since 1977. The Carter administration forced President Romero to protect the Jesuits, and on the day the killing was to have begun, July 22, 1977, the National Police are said to have sat outside the Jesuit residence in San Salvador on their motorcycles, with UZIs.) In any case UCA could manage an enrollment of only about 5,000. The scientific disciplines, which never had a particularly tenacious hold locally, had largely vanished from local life.

Meanwhile many people spoke of the National University in the present tense, as if it still existed, or as if its closing were a routine event on some long-term academic calendar. I recall talking one day to a former member of the faculty at the National University, a woman who had not seen her office since the morning she noticed the troops massing outside and left it. She lost her books and her research and the uncompleted manuscript of the book she was then writing, but she described this serenely, and seemed to find no immediate contradiction in losing her work to the Ministry of Defense and the work she did later with the Ministry of Education. The campus of the National University is said to be growing over, which is one way contradictions get erased in the tropics.

I was invited one morning to a gathering of Salvadoran writers, a kind of informal coffee hour arranged by the American embassy. For some days there had been a question about where to hold this *café literario*, since there seemed to be no single location that was not considered off-limits by at least one of the guests, and at one point the ambassador's residence was put forth as the most neutral setting. On the day before the event it was finally decided that UCA was the more appropriate place ("and just never mind," as one of the embassy people put it, that some people would not go to UCA), and at ten the next morning we gathered there in a large conference room and drank coffee and talked, at first in platitudes, and then more urgently.

These are some of the sentences spoken to me that morning: *It's not possible to speak of intellectual life in El Salvador. Every day we lose more. We are regressing constantly. Intellectual life is drying up. You are looking at the intellectual life of El Salvador. Here. In this room. We are the only survivors. Some of the others are out of the country, others are not writing because they are engaged in political activity. Some have been disappeared, many of the teachers have been disappeared. Teaching is very dangerous, if a student misinterprets what a teacher says, then the teacher may be arrested. Some are in exile, the rest are dead. Los muertos, you know? We are the only ones left. There is no one after us, no young ones. It is all over, you know?* At noon there was an exchange of books and *curricula vitae*. The cultural attaché from the embassy said that she, for one, would like to see this *café literario* close on a hopeful note, and someone provided one: it was a hopeful note that *norteamericanos* and *centroamericanos* could have such a meeting. This is what passed for a hopeful note in San Salvador in the summer of 1982.

THE AMBASSADOR OF the United States of America in El Salvador, Deane Hinton, received on his desk every morning in the summer of 1982 a list of the American military personnel in-country that day. The number on this list, I was told, was never to exceed 55. Some days there were as few as 35. If the number got up to 55, and it was thought essential to bring in someone else, then a trade was made: the incoming American was juggled against an outgoing American, one normally stationed in Salvador but shunted down to Panama for as long as necessary to maintain the magic number.

Everything to do with the United States Military Group, or MILGP, was treated by the embassy as a kind of magic, a totemic presence circumscribed by potent taboos. The American A-37Bs presented to El Salvador in June of that year were actually flown up from Panama not by Americans but by Salvadorans trained at the United States Southern Air Command in Panama for this express purpose. American advisers could participate in patrols for training purposes but could not participate in patrols in combat situations. When both CBS and *The New York Times*, one day that June, reported having seen two or three American advisers in what the reporters construed as a combat situation in Usulután province, Colonel John D. Waghelstein, the MILGP commander, was called back from playing tennis in Panama (his wife had met him in Panama, there being no dependents allowed in El Salvador) in order, as he put it, "to deal with the press."

I happened to arrive for lunch at the ambassador's residence just as Colonel Waghelstein reported in from Panama that day, and the two of them, along with the embassy public affairs officer, walked to the far end of the swimming pool to discuss the day's problem out of my hearing. Colonel Waghelstein is massively built, crew-cut, tight-lipped, and very tanned, almost a cartoon of the American military presence, and the notion that he had come up from Panama to deal with the press was novel and interesting, in that he had made, during his tour in El Salvador, a pretty terse point of not dealing with the press. Some months later in Los Angeles I saw an NBC documentary in which I noticed the special effort Colonel Waghelstein had made in this case. American advisers had actually been made available to NBC, which in turn adopted a chiding tone toward CBS for the June "advisers in action" story. The total effect was mixed, however, since even as the advisers complained on camera about how "very few people" asked them what they did and about how some reporters "spend all their time with the other side," the camera angles seemed such that no adviser's face was distinctly seen. There were other points in this NBC documentary when I thought I recognized a certain official hand, for example the mention of the "sometimes cruel customs" of the Pipil Indians in El Salvador. The custom in question was that of flaying one another alive, a piece of pre-Columbian lore often tendered by embassy people as evidence that from a human-rights point of view, the trend locally is up, or at any rate holding.

Colonel Waghelstein stayed at the ambassador's that day only long enough for a drink (a Bloody Mary, which he nursed morosely), and, after he left, the ambassador and the public affairs officer and my husband and I sat down to lunch on the covered terrace. We watched a lime-throated bird in the garden. We watched the ambassador's English sheep dog bound across the lawn at the sound of shots, rifle practice at the Escuela Militar beyond the wall and down the hill. "Only time we had any quiet up here," the ambassador said in his high Montana twang, "was when we sent the whole school up to Benning." The shots rang out again. The sheep dog barked. "*Quieto*," the houseman crooned.

I have thought since about this lunch a great deal. The wine was chilled and poured into crystal glasses. The fish was served on porcelain plates that bore the American eagle. The sheep dog and the crystal and the American eagle together had on me a certain anesthetic effect, temporarily deadening that receptivity to the sinister that afflicts everyone in Salvador, and I experienced for a moment the official American delusion, the illusion of plausibility, the sense that the American undertaking in El Salvador might turn out to be, from the right angle, in the right light, just another difficult but possible mission in another troubled but possible country.

Deane Hinton is an interesting man. Before he replaced Robert White in San Salvador he had served in Europe, South America, and Africa. He had been married twice, once to an American, who bore him five children before their divorce, and once to a Chilean, who had died not long before, leaving him the stepfather of her five children by an earlier marriage. At the time I met him he had just announced his engagement to a Salvadoran named Patricia de Lopez. Someone who is about to marry a third time, who thinks of himself as the father of ten, and who has spent much of his career in chancey posts—Mombasa, Kinshasa, Santiago, San Salvador—is apt to be someone who believes in the possible.

His predecessor, Robert White, was relieved of the San Salvador embassy in February 1981, in what White later characterized as a purge, by the new Reagan people, of the State Department's entire Latin American section. This circumstance made Deane Hinton seem, to many in the United States, the bearer of the administration's big stick in El Salvador, but what Deane Hinton actually said about El Salvador differed from what Robert White said about El Salvador more in style than in substance. Deane Hinton believed, as Robert White believed, that the situation in El Salvador was bad, terrible, squalid beyond anyone's power to understand it without experiencing it. Deane Hinton also believed, as Robert White believed to a point, that the situation would be, in the absence of one or another American effort, still worse.

Deane Hinton believes in doing what he can. He had gotten arrests on the deaths of the four American churchwomen. He had even ("by yelling some more," he said) gotten the government to announce these arrests, no small accomplishment, since El Salvador was a country in which the "announcement" of an arrest did not necessarily follow the arrest itself. In the case of the murders of Michael Hammer and Mark Pearlman and José Rodolfo Viera at the Sheraton, for example, it was not the government but the American embassy which announced at least two of the various successive arrests, those of the former guardsmen Abel Campos and Rodolfo Orellana Osorio. This embassy "announcement" was reported by the American press on September 15 1982, and was followed immediately by another announcement: on September 16 1982, "a police spokesman" in San Salvador announced not the arrest but the "release" of the same suspects, after what was described as a month in custody.

To persist in so distinctly fluid a situation required a personality of considerable resistance. Deane Hinton was even then working on getting new arrests in the Sheraton murders. He was even then working on getting trials in the murders of the four American women, a trial being another step that did not, in El Salvador, necessarily follow an arrest. There had been progress. There had been the election, a potent symbol for many Americans and perhaps even for some Salvadorans, although the symbolic content of the event showed up rather better in translation than on the scene. "There was some shooting in the morning," I recall being told by a parish priest about election day in his district, "but it quieted down around nine A.M. The army had a truck going around to go out and vote—*Tu Voto Es La Solución*, you know—so they went out and voted. They wanted that stamp on their identity cards to show they voted. The stamp was the proof of their good will. Whether or not they actually wanted to vote is hard to say. I guess you'd have to say they were more scared of the army than of the guerrillas, so they voted."

Four months after the fact, in *The New York Times Magazine*, former ambassador Robert White wrote about the election: "Nothing is more symbolic of our current predicament in El Salvador than the Administration's bizarre attempt to recast D'Aubuisson in a more favorable light." Even the fact that the election had resulted in what White called "political disaster" could be presented, with a turn of the mirror, positively: one man's political disaster could be another's democratic turbulence, the birth pangs of what Assistant Secretary of State Thomas Enders persisted in calling "nascent democratic institutions." "The new Salvadoran democracy," Enders was saying five months after the election, not long after Justice of the Peace Gonzalo Alonso García, the twentieth prominent Christian Democrat to be kidnapped or killed since the election, had been dragged from his house in San Cayetano Itepeque by fifteen armed men, "is doing what it is supposed to do—bringing a broad spectrum of forces and factions into a functioning democratic system."

In other words even the determination to eradicate the opposition could be interpreted as evidence that the model worked. There was still, moreover, a certain obeisance to the land reform program, the lustrous intricacies of which were understood by so few that almost any interpretation could be construed as possible. "About

207, 207 always applied only to 1979, that is what no one under-stands," I had been told by President Magaña when I tried at one point to get straight the actual status of Decree 207, the legislation meant to implement the "Land-to-the-Tiller" program by provid-ing that title to all land farmed by tenants be transferred immediately to those tenants. "There is no one more conservative than a small farmer," Peter Shiras, a former consultant to the Inter-American Development Bank, had quoted an AID official as saying about 207. "We're going to be breeding capitalists like rabbits."

Decree 207 had been the source of considerable confusion and infighting during the weeks preceding my arrival in El Salvador, suspended but not suspended, on and off and on again, but I had not before heard anyone describe it, as President Magaña seemed to be describing it, as a proposition wound up to self-destruct. Did he mean, I asked carefully, that Decree 207, implementing Land-to-the-Tiller, applied only to 1979 because no landowner, in practice, would work against his own interests by allowing ten-ants on his land after 207 took effect? "Right!" President Magaña had said, as if to a slow student. "Exactly! This is what no one understands. There were no new rental contracts in 1980 or 1981. No one would rent out land under 207, they would have to be crazy to do that."

What he said was obvious, but out of line with the rhetoric, and this conversation with President Magaña about Land-to-the-Tiller, which I had heard described through the spring as a center-piece of United States policy in El Salvador, had been one of many occasions when the American effort in El Salvador seemed based on auto-suggestion, a dreamwork devised to obscure any intelligence that might trouble the dreamer. This impression per-sisted, and I was struck, a few months later, by the suggestion in the report on El Salvador released by the Permanent Select Committee on Intelligence of the House of Representatives (*U.S. Intelligence Performance in Central America: Achievements and Selected Instances of Concern*) that the intelligence was itself a dreamwork, tending to support policy, the report read, "rather than inform it," providing "reinforcement more than illumination," "'ammuni-tion' rather than analysis."

A certain tendency to this kind of dreamwork, to improving upon rather than illuminating the situation, may have been inevitable, since the unimproved situation in El Salvador was such that to consider it was to consider moral extinction. "This time they won't get away with it," Robert White was reported to have said as he watched the bodies of the four American women dragged from their common grave, but they did, and White was brought home. This is a country that cracks Americans, and Deane Hinton gave the sense of a man determined not to crack. There on the terrace of the official residence on Avenida La Capilla in the San Benito district it was all logical. One step followed another, progress was slow. We were Americans, we would not be demoralized. It was not until late in the lunch, at a point between the salad and the profiteroles, that it occurred to me that we were talking exclusively about the appearances of things, about how the situation might be made to look better, about trying to get the Salvadoran government to "appear" to do what the American government needed done in order to make it "appear" that the American aid was justified.

It was sometimes necessary to stop Roberto D'Aubuisson "on the one-yard line" (Deane Hinton's phrase about the ARENA attempt to commandeer the presidency) because Roberto D'Aubuisson made a negative appearance in the United States, made things, as Jeremiah O'Leary, the assistant to national security adviser William Clark, had imagined Hinton advising D'Aubuisson after the election, "hard for everybody." What made a positive appearance in the United States, and things easier for everybody, were elections, and the announcement of arrests in cases involving murdered Americans, and ceremonies in which tractable *campesinos* were awarded land titles by army officers, and the Treasury Police sat on the platform, and the president came, by helicopter. "Our land reform program," Leonel Gómez, who had worked with the murdered José Rodolfo Viera in the Salvadoran Institute of Agrarian Transformation, noted in *Food Monitor*, "gave them an opportunity to build up points for the next U.S. AID grant." By "them" Leonel Gómez meant not his compatriots but Americans, meant the American Institute for Free Labor Development, meant Roy Prosterman, the architect of the Land-to-the-Tiller programs in both El Salvador and Vietnam.

In this light the American effort had a distinctly circular aspect (the aid was the card with which we got the Salvadorans to do it our way, and appearing to do it our way was the card with which the Salvadorans got the aid), and the question of

why the effort was being made went unanswered. It was possible to talk about Cuba and Nicaragua, and by extension the
Soviet Union, and national security, but this seemed only to
justify a momentum already underway: no one could doubt that
Cuba and Nicaragua had at various points supported the armed
opposition to the Salvadoran government, but neither could
anyone be surprised by this, or, given what could be known
about the players, be unequivocally convinced that American
interests lay on one side or another of what even Deane Hinton
referred to as a civil war.

It was certainly possible to describe some members of the
opposition, as Deane Hinton had, as "out-and-out Marxists,"
but it was equally possible to describe other members of the
opposition, as the embassy had at the inception of the FDR in
April of 1980, as "a broad-based coalition of moderate and center-left groups." The right in El Salvador never made this distinction: to the right, anyone in the opposition was a communist,
along with most of the American press, the Catholic Church,
and, as time went by, all Salvadoran citizens not of the right. In
other words there remained a certain ambiguity about political
terms as they were understood in the United States and in El
Salvador, where "left" may mean, in the beginning, only a resistance to seeing one's family killed or disappeared. That it comes
eventually to mean something else may be, to the extent that
the United States has supported the increasing polarization in El
Salvador, the Procrustean bed we made ourselves.

It was a situation in which American interests would seem
to have been best served by attempting to isolate the "out-
and-out Marxists" while supporting the "broad-based coalition of moderate and center-left groups," discouraging the
one by encouraging the other, co-opting the opposition; but
American policy, by accepting the invention of "communism,"
as defined by the right in El Salvador, as a daemonic element to
be opposed at even the most draconic cost, had in fact achieved
the reverse. "We believe in gringos," Hugh Barrera, an ARENA
contender for the presidency, told Laurie Becklund of *The Los
Angeles Times* when she asked in April of 1982 if ARENA did
not fear losing American aid by trying to shut the Christian
Democrats out of the government. "Congress would not risk
losing a whole country over one party. That would be turning

against a U.S. ally and encouraging Soviet intervention here. It would not be intelligent." In other words "anti-communism" was seen, correctly, as the bait the United States would always take.

That we had been drawn, both by a misapprehension of the local rhetoric and by the manipulation of our own rhetorical weaknesses, into a game we did not understand, a play of power in a political tropic alien to us, seemed apparent, and yet there we remained. In this light all arguments tended to trail off. Pros and cons seemed equally off the point. At the heart of the American effort there was something of the familiar ineffable, as if it were taking place not in El Salvador but in a mirage of El Salvador, the mirage of a society not unlike our own but "sick," a temporarily fevered republic in which the antibodies of democracy needed only to be encouraged, in which words had stable meanings north and south ("election," say, and "Marxist") and in which there existed, waiting to be tapped by our support, some latent good will. A few days before I arrived in El Salvador there appeared in *Diario de Hoy* a full-page advertisement placed by leaders of the Women's Crusade for Peace and Work. This advertisement accused the United States, in the person of its ambassador, Deane Hinton, of "blackmailing us with your miserable aid, which only keeps us subjugated in underdevelopment so that powerful countries like yours can continue exploiting our few riches and having us under your boot." The Women's Crusade for Peace and Work is an organization of the right, with links to ARENA, which may suggest how latent that good will remains.

This "blackmail" motif, and its arresting assumption that trying to keep Salvadorans from killing one another constituted a new and particularly crushing imperialism, began turning up more and more frequently. By October of 1982 advertisements were appearing in the San Salvador papers alleging that the blackmail was resulting in a "betrayal" of El Salvador by the military, who were seen as "lackeys" of the United States. At a San Salvador Chamber of Commerce meeting in late October, Deane Hinton said that "in the first two weeks of this month at least sixty-eight human beings were murdered in El Salvador under circumstances which are familiar to everyone here," stressed that American aid was dependent upon "progress" in this area, and fielded some fifty written questions, largely hostile, one of which read, "Are you trying to blackmail us?"

I was read this speech over the telephone by an embassy officer, who described it as "the ambassador's strongest statement yet." I was puzzled by this, since the ambassador had made most of the same points, at a somewhat lower pitch, in a speech on February 11, 1982; it was hard to discern a substantive advance between, in February, "If there is one issue which could force our Congress to withdraw or seriously reduce its support for El Salvador, it is the issue of human rights," and, in October: "If not, the United States—in spite of our other interests, in spite of our commitment to the struggle against communism, could be forced to deny assistance to El Salvador." In fact the speeches seemed almost cyclical, seasonal events keyed to the particular rhythm of the six-month certification process; midway in the certification cycle things appear "bad," and are then made, at least rhetorically, to appear "better," "improvement" being the key to certification.

I mentioned the February speech on the telephone, but the embassy officer to whom I was speaking did not see the similarity; this was, he said, a "stronger" statement, and would be "front-page" in both *The Washington Post* and *The Los Angeles Times*. In fact the story did appear on the front pages of both *The Washington Post* and *The Los Angeles Times*, suggesting that every six months the news is born anew in El Salvador.

Whenever I hear someone speak now of one or another *solución* for El Salvador I think of particular Americans who have spent time there, each in his or her own way inexorably altered by the fact of having been in a certain place at a certain time. Some of these Americans have since moved on and others remain in Salvador, but, like survivors of a common natural disaster, they are equally marked by the place.

There are a lot of options that aren't playable. We could come in militarily and shape the place up. That's an option, but it's not playable, because of public opinion. If it weren't for public opinion, however, El Salvador would be the ideal laboratory for a full-scale military operation. It's small. It's self-contained. There are hemispheric cultural similarities.

—*A United States embassy officer in San Salvador.*

June 15th was not only a great day for El Salvador, receiving $5 million in additional U.S. aid for the private sector and a fleet of fighter planes and their corresponding observation units, but also a great day for me. Ray Bonner [of *The New York Times*] actually spoke to me at Ilopango airport and took my hand and shook it when I offered it to him.... Also, another correspondent pulled me aside and said that if I was such a punctilious journalist why the hell had I written something about him that wasn't true. Here I made no attempt to defend myself but only quoted my source. Later we talked and ironed out some wrinkles. It is a great day when journalists with opposing points of view can get together and learn something from each other, after all, we are all on the same side. I even wrote a note to Robert E. White (which he ignored) not long ago after he protested that I had not published his Letter to the Editor (which I had) suggesting that we be friendly enemies. The only enemy is totalitarianism, in any guise: communistic, socialistic, capitalistic or militaristic. Man is unique because he has free will and the capacity to choose. When this is suppressed he is no longer a man but an animal. That is why I say that despite differing points of view, we are none of us enemies.

—*Mario Rosenthal, editor of the* El Salvador News Gazette, *in his June 14–20 1982 column, "A Great Day."*

You would have had the last interview with an obscure Salvadoran.

—*An American reporter to whom I had mentioned that I had been trying to see Colonel Salvador Beltrán Luna on the day he died in a helicopter crash.*

JOAN DIDION

It's not as bad as it could be. I was talking to the political risk people at one of the New York banks and in 1980 they gave El Salvador only a ten percent chance of as much stability in 1982 as we have now. So you see.

—The same embassy officer.

Normally I wouldn't have a guard at my level, but there were death threats against my predecessor, he was on a list. I'm living in his old house. In fact something kind of peculiar happened today. Someone telephoned and wanted to know, very urgent, how to reach the Salvadoran woman with whom my predecessor lived. This person on the phone claimed that the woman's family needed to reach her, a death, or illness, and she had left no address. This might have been true and it might not have been true. Naturally I gave no information.

—Another embassy officer.

AMBASSADOR WHITE: My embassy also sent in several months earlier these captured documents. There is no doubt about the provenance of these documents as they were handed to me directly by Colonel Adolfo Majano, then a member of the junta. They were taken when they captured ex-Major D'Aubuisson and a number of other officers who were conspiring against the Government of El Salvador.
SENATOR ZORINSKY: ... Please continue, Mr. Ambassador.
AMBASSADOR WHITE: I would be glad to give you copies of these documents for your record. In these documents there are over a hundred names of people who are participating, both within the Salvadoran military as active conspirers against the Government, and also the names of people living in the United States and in Guatemala City who are actively funding the death squads. I gave this document, in Spanish, to three of the most skilled political analysts I know in El Salvador without orienting them in any way. I just asked them to read this and tell me what conclusions they came up with. All three of them came up with the conclusion that there is, within this document, evidence

that is compelling, if not 100 percent conclusive, that
D'Aubuisson and his group are responsible for the murder
of Archbishop Romero.
SENATOR CRANSTON: What did you say? Responsible for
whose murder?
AMBASSADOR WHITE: Archbishop Romero ...

—*From the record of hearings before the Committee on Foreign
Relations, U.S. Senate, April 9, 1981, two months after
Robert White left San Salvador.*

Of all these Americans I suppose I think especially of Robert
White, for his is the authentic American voice afflicted by El
Salvador: *You will find one of the pages with Monday underlined and
with quotation marks*, he said that April day in 1981 about his documents, which were duly admitted into the record and, as the
report of the House Permanent Select Committee on Intelligence
later concluded, ignored by the CIA; he talked about Operation
Pineapple, and blood sugar, and 257 Roberts guns, about addresses
in Miami, about Starlight scopes; about *documents handed to him
directly by Colonel Majano,* about *compelling if not conclusive evidence*
of activities that continued to fall upon the ears of his auditors as
signals from space, unthinkable, inconceivable, dim impulses from
a black hole. In the serene light of Washington that spring day in
1981, two months out of San Salvador, Robert White's distance
from the place was already lengthening: in San Salvador he might
have wondered, the final turn of the mirror, *what Colonel Majano
had to gain by handing him the documents.*

That the texture of life in such a situation is essentially
untranslatable became clear to me only recently, when I tried
to describe to a friend in Los Angeles an incident that occurred
some days before I left El Salvador. I had gone with my husband
and another American to the San Salvador morgue, which, unlike
most morgues in the United States, is easily accessible, through
an open door on the ground floor around the back of the court
building. We had been too late that morning to see the day's
bodies (there is not much emphasis on embalming in El Salvador,
or for that matter on identification, and bodies are dispatched fast
for disposal), but the man in charge had opened his log to show
us the morning's entries, seven bodies, all male, none identified,

none believed older than twenty-five. Six had been certified dead by *arma de fuego*, firearms, and the seventh, who had also been shot, of shock. The slab on which the bodies had been received had already been washed down, and water stood on the floor. There were many flies, and an electric fan.

The other American with whom my husband and I had gone to the morgue that morning was a newspaper reporter, and since only seven unidentified bodies bearing evidence of *arma de fuego* did not in San Salvador in the summer of 1982 constitute a newspaper story worth pursuing, we left. Outside in the parking lot there were a number of wrecked or impounded cars, many of them shot up, upholstery chewed by bullets, windshield shattered, thick pastes of congealed blood on pearlized hoods, but this was also unremarkable, and it was not until we walked back around the building to the reporter's rented car that each of us began to sense the potentially remarkable.

Surrounding the car were three men in uniform, two on the sidewalk and the third, who was very young, sitting on his motorcycle in such a way as to block our leaving. A second motorcycle had been pulled up directly behind the car, and the space in front was occupied. The three had been joking among themselves, but the laughter stopped as we got into the car. The reporter turned the ignition on, and waited. No one moved. The two men on the sidewalk did not meet our eyes. The boy on the motorcycle stared directly, and caressed the G-3 propped between his thighs. The reporter asked in Spanish if one of the motorcycles could be moved so that we could get out. The men on the sidewalk said nothing, but smiled enigmatically. The boy only continued staring, and began twirling the flash suppressor on the barrel of his G-3.

This was a kind of impasse. It seemed clear that if we tried to leave and scraped either motorcycle the situation would deteriorate. It also seemed clear that if we did not try to leave the situation would deteriorate. I studied my hands. The reporter gunned the motor, forced the car up onto the curb far enough to provide a minimum space in which to maneuver, and managed to back out clean. Nothing more happened, and what did happen had been a common enough kind of incident in El Salvador, a pointless confrontation with aimless authority, but I have heard of no *solución* that precisely addresses this local vocation for terror.

Any situation can turn to terror. The most ordinary errand can go bad. Among Americans in El Salvador there is an endemic apprehension of danger in the apparently benign. I recall being told by a network anchor man that one night in his hotel room (it was at the time of the election, and because the Camino Real was full he had been put up at the Sheraton) he took the mattress off the bed and shoved it against the window. He happened to have with him several bulletproof vests that he had brought from New York for the camera crew, and before going to the Sheraton lobby he put one on. Managers of American companies in El Salvador (Texas Instruments is still there, and Cargill, and some others) are replaced every several months, and their presence is kept secret. Some companies bury their managers in a number-two or number-three post. American embassy officers are driven in armored and unmarked vans (no eagle, no seal, no CD plates) by Salvadoran drivers and Salvadoran guards, because, I was told, "if someone gets blown away, obviously the State Department would prefer it done by a local security man, then you don't get headlines saying 'American Shoots Salvadoran Citizen.'" These local security men carry automatic weapons on their laps.

In such a climate the fact of being in El Salvador comes to seem a sentence of indeterminate length, and the prospect of leaving doubtful. On the night before I was due to leave I did not sleep, lay awake and listened to the music drifting up from a party at the Camino Real pool, heard the band play "Malaguena" at three and at four and again at five A.M., when the party seemed to end and light broke and I could get up. I was picked up to go to the airport that morning by one of the embassy vans, and a few blocks from the hotel I was seized by the conviction that this was not the most direct way to the airport, that this was not an embassy guard sitting in front with the Remington on his lap; that this was someone else. That the van turned out in fact to be the embassy van, detouring into San Benito to pick up an AID official, failed to relax me: once at the airport I sat without moving and averted my eyes from the soldiers patrolling the empty departure lounges.

When the nine A.M. TACA flight to Miami was announced I boarded without looking back, and sat rigid until the plane left the ground. I did not fasten my seat belt. I did not lean back. The plane stopped that morning at Belize, setting down on the runway lined with abandoned pillboxes and rusting camouflaged tanks to pick up what seemed to be every floater on two continents, wildcatters, collectors of information, the fantasts of the hemisphere. Even a team of student missionaries got on at Belize, sallow children from the piney woods of Georgia and Alabama who had been teaching the people of Belize, as the team member who settled down next to me explained, to know Jesus as their personal savior.

He was perhaps twenty, with three hundred years of American hill stock in his features, and as soon as the plane left Belize he began filling out a questionnaire on his experience there, laboriously printing out the phrases, *in obedience to God, opportunity to renew commitment, most rewarding part of my experience, most disheartening part.* Somewhere over the Keys I asked him what the most disheartening part of his experience had been. The most disheartening part of his experience, he said, had been seeing people leave the Crusade as empty as they came. The most rewarding part of his experience had been renewing his commitment to bring the Good News of Jesus as personal savior to all these different places. The different places to which he was committed to bring the Good News were New Zealand, Iceland, Finland, Colorado, and El Salvador. This was *la solución* not from Washington or Panama or Mexico but from Belize, and the piney woods of Georgia. This flight from San Salvador to Belize to Miami took place at the end of June 1982. In the week that I am completing this report, at the end of October 1982, the offices in the Hotel Camino Real in San Salvador of the Associated Press, United Press International, United Press International Television News, NBC News, CBS News, and ABC News were raided and searched by members of the El Salvador National Police carrying submachine guns; fifteen leaders of legally recognized political and labor groups opposing the government of El Salvador were disappeared in San Salvador; Deane Hinton said that he was "reasonably certain" that these disappearances had not been conducted under Salvadoran government orders; the Salvadoran Ministry of Defense announced that eight of the fifteen disappeared citizens were in fact in government custody; and the State Department announced that the Reagan administration believed that it had "turned the corner" in its campaign for political stability in Central America.

MIAMI

This book is for Eduene Jerrett Didion and Frank Reese Didion

Part I

I

HAVANA VANITIES COME to dust in Miami. On the August night in 1933 when General Gerardo Machado, then president of Cuba, flew out of Havana into exile, he took with him five revolvers, seven bags of gold, and five friends, still in their pajamas. Gerardo Machado is buried now in a marble crypt at Woodlawn Park Cemetery in Miami, Section Fourteen, the mausoleum. On the March night in 1952 when Carlos Prío Socarrás, who had helped depose Gerardo Machado in 1933 and had fifteen years later become president himself, flew out of Havana into exile, he took with him his foreign minister, his minister of the interior, his wife and his two small daughters. A photograph of the occasion shows Señora de Prío, quite beautiful, boarding the plane in what appears to be a raw silk suit, and a hat with black fishnet veiling. She wears gloves, and earrings. Her makeup is fresh. The husband and father, recently the president, wears dark glasses, and carries the younger child, María Elena, in his arms.

Carlos Prío is now buried himself at Woodlawn Park Cemetery in Miami, Section Three, not far from Gerardo Machado, in a grave marked by a six-foot marble stone on which the flag of Cuba waves in red, white and blue ceramic tile. CARLOS PRÍO SOCARRÁS 1903–1977, the stone reads, and directly below that, as if Carlos Prío Socarrás's main hedge against oblivion had been that period at the University of Havana when he was running actions against Gerardo Machado: MIEMBRO DEL DIRECTORIO ESTUDIANTIL UNIVERSITARIO 1930. Only then does the legend PRESIDENTE DE LA REPÚBLICA DE CUBA 1948–1952 appear, an anticlimax. Presidencies are short and the glamours of action long, there among the fallen frangipani and crepe myrtle blossoms at Woodlawn Park Cemetery in Miami. "They say that I was a terrible president of Cuba," Carlos Prío once said to Arthur M. Schlesinger, Jr., during a visit to the Kennedy White House some ten years into the quarter-century Miami epilogue to his

415

four-year Havana presidency. "That may be true. But I was the best president Cuba ever had."

Many Havana epilogues have been played in Florida, and some prologues. Florida is that part of the Cuban stage where declamatory exits are made, and side deals. Florida is where the chorus waits to comment on the action, and sometimes to join it. The exiled José Martí raised money among the Cuban tobacco workers in Key West and Tampa, and in 1894 attempted to mount an invasionary expedition from north of Jacksonville. The exiled Fidel Castro Ruz came to Miami in 1955 for money to take the 26 Julio into the Sierra Maestra, and got it, from Carlos Prío. Fulgencio Batista had himself come back from Florida to take Havana away from Carlos Prío in 1952, but by 1958 Fidel Castro, with Carlos Prío's money, was taking it away from Fulgencio Batista, at which turn Carlos Prío's former prime minister tried to land a third force in Camagüey Province, the idea being to seize the moment from Fidel Castro, a notably failed undertaking encouraged by the Central Intelligence Agency and financed by Carlos Prío, at home in Miami Beach.

This is all instructive. In the continuing opera still called, even by Cubans who have now lived the largest part of their lives in this country, *el exilio*, the exile, meetings at private houses in Miami Beach are seen to have consequences. The actions of individuals are seen to affect events directly. Revolutions and counterrevolutions are framed in the private sector, and the state security apparatus exists exclusively to be enlisted by one or another private player. That this particular political style, indigenous to the Caribbean and to Central America, has now been naturalized in the United States is one reason why, on the flat coastal swamps of South Florida, where the palmettos once blew over the detritus of a dozen failed booms and the hotels were boarded up six months a year, there has evolved since the early New Year's morning in 1959 when Fulgencio Batista flew for the last time out of Havana (for this flight, to the Dominican Republic on an Aerovías Q DC-4, the women still wore the evening dresses in which they had gone to dinner) a settlement of considerable interest, not exactly an American city as American cities have until recently been understood but a tropical capital: long on rumor, short on memory, overbuilt on the chimera of runaway money and referring not to New York or Boston or Los Angeles or Atlanta but to Caracas and Mexico, to Havana and to Bogotá and to Paris and Madrid. Of American cities Miami has since 1959 connected only to Washington, which is the peculiarity of both places, and increasingly the warp.

In the passion of *el exilio* there are certain stations at which the converged, or colliding, fantasies of Miami and Washington appear in fixed relief. Resentments are recited, rosaries of broken promises. Occasions of error are recounted, imperfect understandings, instances in which the superimposition of Washington abstractions on Miami possibilities may or may not have been, in a word Washington came to prefer during the 1980s, flawed. On April 17, 1985, the twenty-fourth anniversary of the aborted invasion referred to by most Americans and even some Cubans as the Bay of Pigs, what seems in retrospect a particularly poignant progression of events was held in Miami to commemorate those losses suffered in 1961 at Playa Girón, on the southern coast of Matanzas Province, by the 2506 Brigade, the exile invasion force trained and supported—up to a point, the famous point, the midnight hour when John F. Kennedy sent down the decision to preserve deniability by withholding air cover—by the United States government.

The actual events of this 1985 anniversary were ritual, and as such differed only marginally from those of other years, say 1986, when Jeane Kirkpatrick would be present, to wave small souvenir flags, American and Cuban, and to speak of "how different the world would have been" had the brigade prevailed. By one minute past midnight on the morning of the 1985 anniversary, as in years before and after, some thirty members of the 2506, most of them men in their forties and fifties wearing camouflage fatigues and carrying AR-15 rifles, veterans of the invasion plus a few later recruits, had assembled at the Martyrs of Girón monument on Southwest Eighth Street in Miami and posted a color guard, to stand watch through the soft Florida night. A tape recording of "The Star Spangled Banner" had been played, and one of "La Bayamesa," the Cuban national anthem. *No temáis una muerte gloriosa*, the lyric of "La Bayamesa" runs, striking the exact note of transcendent nationalism on which the occasion turned. *Do not fear a glorious death: To die for patria is to live.*

By late morning the police had cordoned off the weathered bungalow on Southwest Ninth Street which was meant to be the Casa, Museo y Biblioteca de la Brigada 2506 del Exilio Cubano, the projected repository for such splinters of the true cross as the 2506 flag presented to John F. Kennedy at the Orange Bowl, twenty months after the Bay of Pigs, when he promised to return the flag to the brigade "in a free Havana" and took it back to Washington, later expanding its symbolic content geometrically by consigning it to storage in what explicators of this parable usually refer to as a dusty basement. On the morning of the anniversary ground was being broken for the renovation of the bungalow, an occasion for Claude Pepper, fresh from the continuing debate in the House of Representatives over aid to the Nicaraguan contras, to character-ize the landing at Girón as "one of the most heroic events in the history of the world" and for many of those present to voice what had become by that spring the most urgent concern of the exile community, the very concern which now lends the occasion its retrospective charge, that "the freedom fighters of the eighties" not be treated by the Reagan administration as the men of the 2506 had been treated, or believed that they had been treated, by the Kennedy administration.

Sometimes the word used to describe that treatment was "abandonment," and sometimes the word was "betrayal," but the meaning was the same, and the ardor behind the words cut across all class lines, not only that morning at the bungalow but later at the roll call at the monument and still later, at the Mass said that evening for the 2506 at the chapel on Biscayne Bay which is so situated as to face Cuba. There were men that morning in combat fatigues, but there were also men in navy-blue blazers, with the bright patch of the 2506 pinned discreetly to the pocket. There were National Rifle Association windbreakers and there were T-shirts featuring the American flag and the legend THESE COLORS DON'T RUN and there were crucifixes on bare skin and there were knife sheaths on belts slung so low that Jockey shorts showed, but there were also Brooks Brothers shirts, and rep ties, and briefcases of supple leather. There were men who would go later that day to offices in the new glass towers along Brickell Avenue, offices with Barcelona chairs and floor-to-ceiling views of the bay and the harbor and Miami Beach and Key Biscayne, and there were men whose only offices were the gun stores and the shooting ranges and the flying clubs out off Krome Avenue, where the West Dade subdivisions give way to the Everglades and only the sudden glitter of water reveals its encroaching presence and drugs get dropped and bodies dumped.

They have been construed since as political flotsam, these men of the 2506, uniformly hard cases, drifters among the more doubtful venues serviced by Southern Air Transport, but this is misleading. Some members of the 2506 had lived in Miami since before Fidel Castro entered Havana and some had arrived as recently as 1980, the year of the Mariel exodus. Some were American citizens and some never would be, but they were all Cuban first, and they proceeded equally from a kind of collective spell, an occult enchantment, from that febrile complex of resentments and revenges and idealizations and taboos which renders exile so potent an organizing principle. They shared not just Cuba as a birthplace but Cuba as a construct, the idea of birthright lost. They shared a definition of *patria* as indivisible from personal honor, and therefore of personal honor as that which had been betrayed and must be revenged. They shared, not only with one another but with virtually every other Cuban in Miami, a political matrix in which the very shape of history, its dialectic, its tendency, had traditionally presented itself as *la lucha*, the struggle.

For most of them as children there had of course been the formative story of *la lucha* against Spain, the central scenario of nineteenth-century Cuba. For some of their fathers there had been *la lucha* against Gerardo Machado and for some of them there had been *la lucha* against Fulgencio Batista and for all of them—for those who had fought originally with the 26 Julio and for those who had fought against it, for *barbudos* and *Batistianos* alike—there was now *la lucha* on the grand canvas of a quarter century, *la lucha* purified, *la lucha* in a preservative vacuum, *la lucha* not only against Fidel Castro but against his allies, and his agents, and all those who could conceivably be believed to have aided or encouraged him.

What constituted such aid or encouragement remained the great Jesuitical subject of *el exilio*, defined and redefined, distilled finally to that point at which a notably different angle obtained on certain events in the recent American past. The 1972 burglary at the Watergate headquarters of the Democratic National

Committee, say, appeared from this angle as a patriotic mission, and the Cubans who were jailed for it as *mártires de la lucha*. Mariel appeared as a betrayal on the part of yet another administration, a deal with Fidel Castro, a decision by the Carter people to preserve the status quo in Cuba by siphoning off the momentum of what could have been, in the dreamtime of *el exilio*, where the betrayal which began with the Kennedy administration continued to the day at hand, a popular uprising. DOWN WITH THE KENNEDY-KHRUSHCHEV PACT was the legend, in Spanish, on one of the placards bobbing for attention in front of the minicams that day. ENOUGH TREASONS. On the back of another placard there was lettered a chant: CONTADORA / TRAIDORA / VENDA / PATRIA. That traitor who would back a political settlement in Central America, in other words, sold out his country, and so his honor.

In many ways the Bay of Pigs continued to offer Miami an ideal narrative, one in which the men of the 2506 were forever the valiant and betrayed and the United States was forever the seducer and betrayer and the blood of *los mártires* remained forever fresh. When the names of the 114 brigade members who died in Cuba were read off that day at the Playa Girón monument, the survivors had called out the responses in unison, the rhythm building, clenched fists thrust toward the sky: *Presente*, 114 times. The women, in silk dresses and high-heeled sandals, dabbed at their eyes behind dark glasses. "*Es triste*," one woman murmured, again and again, to no one in particular.

La tristeza de Miami. "We must attempt to strengthen the non-Batista democratic anti-Castro forces in exile," a Kennedy campaign statement had declared in 1960, and Miami had for a time believed John F. Kennedy a communicant in its faith. "We cannot have the United States walk away from one of the greatest moral challenges in postwar history," Ronald Reagan had declared two nights before this 1985 anniversary of the Bay of Pigs, at a Nicaraguan Refugee Fund benefit dinner in Washington, and Miami once again believed an American president a communicant in its faith. Even the paper thimbles of sweet Cuban coffee distributed after the 2506 Mass that April evening in Miami, on the steps of the chapel which faces Cuba and has over its altar a sequined Virgin, a Virgin dressed for her *quince*, had the aspect of a secular communion, the body and blood of *patria, machismo, la lucha*, sentimental trinity. That *la lucha* had become, during the

years since the Bay of Pigs, a matter of assassinations and bombings on the streets of American cities, of plots and counterplots
and covert dealings involving American citizens and American
institutions, of attitudes and actions which had shadowed the
abrupt termination of two American presidencies and would
eventually shadow the immobilization of a third, was a peculiarity left, that one evening, officially unexplored.

Part II

"THE GENERAL WILDNESS, the eternal labyrinths of waters and marshes, interlocked and apparently never ending; the whole surrounded by interminable swamps…. Here I am then in the Floridas, thought I," John James Audubon wrote to the editor of *The Monthly American Journal of Geology and Natural Science* during the course of an 1831 foray in the territory then still called the Floridas. The place came first, and to touch down there is to begin to understand why at least six administrations now have found South Florida so fecund a colony. I never passed through security for a flight to Miami without experiencing a certain weightlessness, the heightened wariness of having left the developed world for a more fluid atmosphere, one in which the native distrust of extreme possibilities that tended to ground the temperate United States in an obeisance to democratic institutions seemed rooted, if at all, only shallowly. At the gate for such flights the preferred language was already Spanish. Delays were explained by weather in Panama. The very names of the scheduled destinations suggested a world in which many evangelical inclinations had historically been accommodated, many yearnings toward empire indulged. The Eastern 5:59 P.M. from New York/Kennedy to Miami and Panama and Santiago and Buenos Aires carried in its magazine racks, along with the usual pristine copies of *Golf* and *Ebony* and *U.S. News & World Report*, a monthly called *South: The Third World Magazine*, edited in London and tending to brisk backgrounders on coup rumors and capital flight.

In Miami itself this kind of news was considerably less peripheral than it might have seemed farther north, since to set foot in South Florida was already to be in a place where coup rumors and capital flight were precisely what put money on the street, and also what took it off. The charts on the wall in a Coral Gables investment office gave the time in Panama, San Salvador, Asunción. A chain of local gun shops advertised, as a "Father's Day Sale," the semiautomatic Intratec TEC-9, with extra ammo

JOAN DIDION

clip, case, and flash suppressor, reduced from $347.80 to $249.95 and available on layaway. I recall picking up the *Miami Herald* one morning in July of 1985 to read that the Howard Johnson's hotel near the Miami airport had been offering "guerrilla discounts," rooms at seventeen dollars a day under what an employee, when pressed by the *Herald* reporter, described as "a freedom fighters program" that was "supposed to be under wraps."

As in other parts of the world where the citizens shop for guerrilla discounts and bargains in semiautomatic weapons, there was in Miami an advanced interest in personal security. The security installations in certain residential neighborhoods could have been transplanted intact from Bogotá or San Salvador, and even modest householders had detailed information about perimeter defenses, areas of containment, motion monitors and closed-circuit television surveillance. Decorative grilles on doors and windows turned out to have a defensive intent. Break-ins were referred to by the Metro-Dade Police Department as "home invasions," a locution which tended to suggest a city under systematic siege. A firm specializing in security for the home and automobile offered to install bullet-proof windows tested to withstand a 7.62mm NATO round of ammunition, for example one fired by an M60. A ten-page pamphlet found, along with $119,500 in small bills, in the Turnberry Isle apartment of an accused cocaine importer gave these tips for maintaining a secure profile: "Try to imitate an American in all his habits. Mow the lawn, wash the car, etc.... Have an occasional barbecue, inviting trusted relatives." The wary citizen could on other occasions, the pamphlet advised, "appear as the butler of the house. To any question, he can answer: the owners are traveling."

This assumption of extralegal needs dominated the advertisements for more expensive residential properties. The Previews brochure for a house on Star Island, built originally as the Miami Beach Yacht Club and converted to residential use in the 1920s by Hetty Green's son, emphasized, in the headline, not the house's twenty-one rooms, not its multiple pools, not even its 255 feet of bay frontage, but its "Unusual Security and Ready Access to the Ocean." Grove Isle, a luxury condominium complex with pieces by Isamu Noguchi and Alexander Calder and Louise Nevelson in its sculpture garden, presented itself as "a bridge away from

426

Coconut Grove," which meant, in the local code, that access was controlled, in this case by one of the "double security" systems favored in new Miami buildings, requiring that the permit acquired at the gate, or "perimeter," be surrendered at the second line of defense, the entrance to the building itself. A bridge, I was told by several people in Miami, was a good thing to have between oneself and the city, because it could be drawn up, or blocked, during times of unrest.

For a city even then being presented, in news reports and in magazine pieces and even in advertising and fashion promotions which had adopted their style from the television show "Miami Vice," as a rich and wicked pastel boomtown, Miami seemed, at the time I began spending time there, rather spectacularly depressed, again on the southern model. There were new condominiums largely unsold. There were new office towers largely unleased. There were certain signs of cutting and running among those investors who had misread the constant cash moving in and out of Miami as the kind of reliable American money they understood, and been left holding the notes. Helmsley-Spear, it was reported, had let an undeveloped piece on Biscayne Bay go into foreclosure, saving itself $3 million a year in taxes. Tishman Speyer had jettisoned plans for an $800-million medical complex in Broward County. WELL-HEELED INVESTORS RETURNING NORTH was a *Herald* headline in June of 1985. COSTLY CONDOS THREATENED WITH MASSIVE FORECLOSURES was a *Herald* headline in August of 1985. FORECLOSURES SOARING IN S. FLORIDA was a *Herald* headline in March of 1986.

The feel was that of a Latin capital, a year or two away from a new government. Space in shopping malls was unrented, or rented to the wrong tenants. There were too many shoe stores for an American city, and video arcades. There were also too many public works projects: a new mass transit system which did not effectively transport anyone, a projected "people mover" around the downtown area which would, it was said, salvage the new mass transit system. On my first visits to Miami the gleaming new Metrorail cars glided empty down to the Dadeland Mall and back, ghost trains above the jammed traffic on the South Dixie Highway. When I returned a few months later service had

427

already been cut back, and the billion-dollar Metrorail ran only until early evening.

A tropical entropy seemed to prevail, defeating grand schemes even as they were realized. Minor drug deals took place beneath the then unfinished people-mover tracks off Biscayne Boulevard, and plans were under way for yet another salvage operation, "Biscayne Centrum," a twenty-eight-acre sports arena and convention hall that could theoretically be reached by either Metrorail or people mover and offered the further advantage, since its projected site lay within the area sealed off during the 1982 Overtown riot, a district of generally apathetic but occasionally volatile poverty, of defoliating at least twenty-eight acres of potential trouble. ARENA FINANCING PLAN RELIES ON HOTEL GUESTS was a *Herald* headline one morning. S. FLORIDA HOTEL ROOMS GET EMPTIER was a *Herald* headline four months later. A business reporter for the *Herald* asked a local real-estate analyst when he thought South Florida would turn around. "Tell me when South America is going to turn around," the analyst said.

Meanwhile the construction cranes still hovered on the famous new skyline, which, floating as it did between a mangrove swamp and a barrier reef, had a kind of perilous attraction, like a mirage. I recall walking one October evening through the marble lobby of what was then the Pavillon Hotel, part of the massive new Miami Center which Pietro Belluschi had designed for a Virginia developer named Theodore Gould. There was in this vast travertine public space that evening one other person, a young Cuban woman in a short black dinner dress who seemed to be in charge of table arrangements for a gala not in evidence. I could hear my heels clicking on the marble. I could hear the young woman in the black taffeta dinner dress drumming her lacquered fingernails on the table at which she sat. It occurred to me that she and I might be the only people in the great empty skyline itself. Later that week control of the Pavillon, and of Miami Center, passed, the latest chapter in a short dolorous history of hearings and defaults and Chapter 11 filings, from Theodore Gould to the Bank of New York, and it was announced that the Inter-Continental chain would henceforth operate the hotel. The occupancy rate at the Pavillon was, at the time Inter-Continental assumed its management, 7 percent. Theodore Gould was said by the chairman of the Greater Miami Chamber of Commerce to have made "a very unique contribution to downtown Miami."

DURING THE SPRING when I began visiting Miami all of Florida was reported to be in drought, with dropping water tables and unfilled aquifers and SAVE WATER signs, but drought, in a part of the world which would be in its natural state a shelf of porous oolitic limestone covered most of the year by a shallow sheet flow of fresh water, proved relative. During this drought the city of Coral Gables continued, as it had every night since 1924, to empty and refill its Venetian Pool with fresh unchlorinated water, 820,000 gallons a day out of the water supply and into the storm sewer. There was less water than there might have been in the Biscayne Aquifer but there was water everywhere above it. There were rains so hard that windshield wipers stopped working and cars got swamped and stalled on I-95. There was water roiling and bubbling over the underwater lights in decorative pools. There was water sluicing off the six-story canted window at the Omni, a hotel from which it was possible to see, in the Third World way, both the slums of Overtown and those island houses with the Unusual Security and Ready Access to the Ocean, equally wet. Water plashed off banana palms, water puddled on flat roofs, water streamed down the CARNE U.S. GOOD & U.S. STANDARD signs on Flagler Street. Water rocked the impounded drug boats which lined the Miami River and water lapped against the causeways on the bay. I got used to the smell of incipient mildew in my clothes. I stuffed Kleenex in wet shoes and stopped expecting them to dry.

A certain liquidity suffused everything about the place. Causeways and bridges and even Brickell Avenue did not stay put but rose and fell, allowing the masts of ships to glide among the marble and glass facades of the unleased office buildings. The buildings themselves seemed to swim free against the sky: there had grown up in Miami during the recent money years an architecture which appeared to have slipped its moorings, a not inappropriate style for a terrain with only a provisional claim on being land at all. Surfaces were reflective, opalescent. Angles were oblique, intersecting to disorienting effect. The Arquitectonica office, which produced the celebrated glass condominium on Brickell Avenue with the fifty-foot cube cut from its center, the frequently photographed "sky patio" in which there floated a palm tree, a Jacuzzi, and a lipstick-red spiral staircase, accompanied its elevations with crayon sketches, all moons and starry skies and airborne maidens, as in a Chagall. Skidmore, Owings and Merrill managed, in its Southeast Financial Center, the considerable feat of rendering fifty-five stories of polished gray granite incorporeal, a sky-blue illusion.

Nothing about Miami was exactly fixed, or hard. Hard consonants were missing from the local speech patterns, in English as well as in Spanish. Local money tended to move on hydraulic verbs: when it was not being washed it was being diverted, or channeled through Mexico, or turned off in Washington. Local stories tended to turn on underwater plot points, submerged snappers: on unsoundable extradition proceedings in the Bahamas, say, or fluid connections with the Banco Nacional de Colombia. I recall trying to touch the bottom of one such story in the *Herald*, about six hand grenades which had just been dug up in the bayfront backyard of a Biscayne Boulevard pawnbroker who had been killed in his own bed a few years before, shot at close range with a .25-caliber automatic pistol.

There were some other details on the surface of this story, for example the wife who fired the .25-caliber automatic pistol and the nineteen-year-old daughter who was up on federal weapons charges and the flight attendant who rented the garage apartment and said that the pawnbroker had collected "just basic things like rockets, just defused things," but the underwater narrative included, at last sounding, the Central Intelligence Agency (with which the pawnbroker was said to have been associated), the British intelligence agency M16 (with which the pawnbroker was also said to have been associated), the late Anastasio Somoza Debayle (whose family the pawnbroker was said to have spirited into Miami shortly before the regime fell in Managua), the late shah of Iran (whose presence in Panama was said to have queered an arms deal about which the pawnbroker had been told), Dr. Josef Mengele (for whom the pawnbroker was said to be searching), and a Pompano Beach resident last seen cruising

Miami in a cinnamon-colored Cadillac Sedan de Ville and looking to buy, he said for the Salvadoran insurgents, a million rounds
of ammunition, thirteen thousand assault rifles, and "at least a
couple" of jeep-mounted machine guns.

In this mood Miami seemed not a city at all but a tale, a romance
of the tropics, a kind of waking dream in which any possibility
could and would be accommodated. The most ordinary morning, say at the courthouse, could open onto the distinctly lurid.
"I don't think he came out with me, that's all," I recall hearing
someone say one day in an elevator at the Miami federal courthouse. His voice had kept rising. "What happened to all that stuff
about how next time, he gets twenty keys, he could run wher-
ever-it-is-Idaho, now he says he wouldn't know what to do with
five keys, what is this shit?" His companion had shrugged. We had
continued in silence to the main floor. Outside one courtroom
that day a group of Colombians, the women in silk shirts and
Chanel necklaces and Charles Jourdan suede pumps, the children
in appliquéd dresses from Baby Dior, had been waiting for the
decision in a pretrial detention hearing, one in which the government was contending that the two defendants, who between
them lived in houses in which eighty-three kilos of cocaine and
a million-three in cash had been found, failed to qualify as good
bail risks.

"That doesn't make him a longtime drug dealer," one of the
two defense lawyers, both of whom were Anglo and one of
whom drove a Mercedes 380 SEL with the license plate DEFENSE,
had argued about the million-three in cash. "That could be one
transaction." Across the hall that day closing arguments were
being heard in a boat case, a "boat case" being one in which a
merchant or fishing vessel has been boarded and drugs seized
and eight or ten Colombian crew members arrested, the kind
of case in which pleas were typically entered so that one of the
Colombians would get eighteen months and the others deported.
There were never any women in Chanel necklaces around a
boat case, and the lawyers (who were usually hired and paid for
not by the defendants but by the unnamed owner of the "load,"
or shipment) tended to be Cuban. "You had the great argument,
you got to give me some good ideas," one of the eight Cuban

defense lawyers on this case joked with the prosecutor during a recess. "But you haven't heard my argument yet," another of the defense lawyers said. "The stuff about communism. Fabulous closing argument."

Just as any morning could turn lurid, any moment could turn final, again as in a dream. "I heard a loud, short noise and then there was just a plain moment of dullness," the witness to a shooting in a Miami Beach supermarket parking lot told the *Herald*. "There was no one around except me and two bagboys." I happened to be in the coroner's office one morning when autopsies were being performed on the bodies of two Mariels, shot and apparently pushed from a car on I-95 about nine the evening before, another plain moment of dullness. The story had been on television an hour or two after it happened: I had seen the crime site on the eleven o'clock news, and had not expected to see the victims in the morning. "When he came here in Mariel he stayed at our house but he didn't get along with my mom," a young girl was saying in the anteroom to one of the detectives working the case. "These two guys were killed together," the detective had pressed. "They probably knew each other."

"For sure," the young girl had said, agreeably. Inside the autopsy room the hands of the two young men were encased in the brown paper bags which indicated that the police had not yet taken what they needed for laboratory studies. Their flesh had the marbleized yellow look of the recently dead. There were other bodies in the room, in various stages of autopsy, and a young woman in a white coat taking eyes, for the eye bank. "Who are we going to start on next?" one of the assistant medical examiners was saying. "The fat guy? Let's do the fat guy."

It was even possible to enter the waking dream without leaving the house, just by reading the *Herald*. A Mariel named Jose "Coca-Cola" Yero gets arrested, with nine acquaintances, in a case involving 1,664 pounds of cocaine, a thirty-seven-foot Cigarette boat named *The Connection*, two Lamborghinis, a million-six in cash, a Mercedes 500 SEL with another $350,000 in cash in the trunk, one dozen Rolex watches color-coordinated to match Jose "Coca-Cola" Yero's wardrobe, and various houses in Dade and Palm Beach counties, a search of one of which turns up not just a photograph of Jose "Coca-Cola" Yero face down in a pile of white powder but also a framed poster of Al

Pacino as Tony Montana, the Mariel who appears at a dramatic moment in *Scarface* face down in a pile of white powder. "They got swept up in the fast lane," a Metro-Dade narcotics detective advises the *Herald*. "The fast lane is what put this whole group in jail." A young woman in South Palm Beach goes out to the parking lot of her parents' condominium and gets into her 1979 Pontiac Firebird, opens the T-top, starts the ignition and loses four toes when the bomb goes off. "She definitely knows some-one is trying to kill her," the sheriff's investigator tells the *Herald*. "She knew they were coming, but she didn't know when."

Surfaces tended to dissolve here. Clear days ended less so. I recall an October Sunday when my husband and I were taken, by Gene Miller, a *Herald* editor who had won two Pulitzer Prizes for investigative reporting and who had access to season tickets exactly on the fifty-yard line at the Orange Bowl, to see the Miami Dolphins beat the Pittsburgh Steelers, 21–17. In the row below us the former Dolphin quarterback Earl Morrall signed autographs for the children who wriggled over seats to slip him their programs and steal surreptitious glances at his Super Bowl ring. A few rows back an Anglo teenager in sandals and shorts and a black T-shirt smoked a marijuana cigarette in full view of the Hispanic police officer behind him. Hot dogs were passed, and Coca-Cola spilled. Sony Watchmans were compared, for the defi-nition on the instant replay. The NBC cameras dollied along the sidelines and the Dolphin cheerleaders kneeled on their white pom-poms and there was a good deal of talk about red dogging and weak secondaries and who would be seen and what would be eaten in New Orleans, come Super Bowl weekend.

The Miami on display in the Orange Bowl that Sunday after-noon would have seemed another Miami altogether, one with less weather and harder, more American surfaces, but by dinner we were slipping back into the tropical: in a virtually empty res-taurant on top of a virtually empty condominum off Biscayne Boulevard, with six people at the table, one of whom was Gene Miller and one of whom was Martin Dardis, who as the chief investigator for the state attorney's office in Miami had led Carl Bernstein through the local angles on Watergate and who remained a walking data bank on CDs at the Biscayne Bank and on who called who on what payoff and on how to follow a money chain, we sat and we talked and we watched a storm break over Biscayne Bay. Sheets of warm rain washed down the big windows. Lightning began to fork somewhere around Bal Harbour. Gene Miller mentioned the Alberto Duque trial, then entering its fourth week at the federal courthouse, the biggest bank fraud case ever tried in the United States. Martin Dardis mentioned the ESM Government Securities collapse, just then breaking into a fraud case maybe bigger than the Duque.

The lightning was no longer forking now but illuminating the entire sky, flashing a dead strobe white, turning the bay fluorescent and the islands black, as if in negative. I sat and I listened to Gene Miller and Martin Dardis discuss these old and new turns in the underwater narrative and I watched the lightning backlight the islands. During the time I had spent in Miami many people had mentioned, always as something extraordinary, something I should have seen if I wanted to understand Miami, the *Surrounded Islands* project executed in Biscayne Bay in 1983 by the Bulgarian artist Christo. *Surrounded Islands*, which had involved surrounding eleven islands with two-hundred-foot petals, or skirts, of pink polypropylene fabric, had been mentioned both by people who were knowledgeable about conceptual art and by people who had not before heard and could not then recall the name of the man who had surrounded the islands. All had agreed. It seemed that the pink had shimmered in the water. It seemed that the pink had kept changing color, fading and reemerging with the movement of the water and the clouds and the sun and the night lights. It seemed that this period when the pink was in the water had for many people exactly defined, as the backlit islands and the fluorescent water and the voices at the table were that night defining for me, Miami.

ON MY FIRST visits to Miami I was always being told that there were places I should not go. There were things I should and should not do. I should not walk the block and a half from the Omni to the *Herald* alone after dark. I should lock my car doors when I drove at night. If I hit a red light as I was about to enter I-95 I should not stop but look both ways, and accelerate. I should not drive through Liberty City, or walk around Overtown. If I had occasion to drive through what was called "the black Grove," those several dozen blocks of project housing which separated the expensive greenery of Coral Gables from the expensive greenery of Coconut Grove, I should rethink my route, avoid at all costs the territory of the disentitled, which in fact was hard to do, since Miami was a city, like so many to the south of it, in which it was possible to pass from walled enclaves to utter desolation while changing stations on the car radio.

In the end I went without incident to all of the places I had been told not to go, and did not or did do most of the things I had been told to do or not to do, but the subtext of what I had been told, that this was a city in which black people and white people viewed each other with some discontent, stayed with me, if only because the most dramatic recent season of that discontent, the spring of 1980, the season when certain disruptive events in Havana happened to coincide with a drama then being played out in a Florida courtroom, still figured so large in the local memory. Many people in Miami mentioned the spring of 1980 to me, speaking always of its "mood," which appeared to have been one of collective fever. In the spring of 1980 everyone had been, it was said, "nervous," or "tense." This tension had built, it was said, "to a point of just no return," or "to the breaking point." "It could drive you mad, just waiting for something to happen," one woman said. "The Cuban kids were all out leaning on their horns and the blacks were all out sitting on their porches," someone else said. "You knew it was going to happen but you didn't know when. And anyway it was going to happen. There was no doubt about that. It was like, well, a bad dream. When you try to wake up and you can't."

The Miami part of what happened that spring, the part people in Miami refer to as "McDuffie," had its proximate beginning early on the morning of December 17, 1979, when a thirty-three-year-old black insurance agent named Arthur McDuffie was said by police to have made a rolling stop at a red light, to have executed the maneuver called "popping a wheelie" on his borrowed Kawasaki motorcycle, and to have given the finger to a Dade County Public Safety Department officer parked nearby. The officer gave chase. By the time Arthur McDuffie was apprehended, eight minutes later, more than a dozen Dade County and city of Miami police units had converged on the scene.

Accounts of the next several minutes conflict. What is known is that at some point a rescue unit was called, for the victim of an "accident," and that four days later Arthur McDuffie died, without regaining consciousness, in Jackson Memorial Hospital. On March 31, 1980, four Dade County Public Safety Department officers, all four of them white, each charged with having played some role in the beating of Arthur McDuffie or in the subsequent attempt to make his injuries seem the result of a motorcycle accident, went on trial before an all-white jury in Tampa, where the case had been moved after a Miami judge granted a change of venue with these words: "This case is a time bomb. I don't want to see it go off in my courtroom or in this community."

The Havana part of what happened in the spring of 1980 was also a time bomb. There had been all that spring a dispute between Fidel Castro and the government of Peru over the disposition of a handful of disaffected Cubans who had claimed asylum at the Peruvian embassy in Havana. Castro wanted the Cubans turned out. Peru insisted that they be brought to Lima. It was April 4, four days after jury selection began in the McDuffie case in Tampa, when the Cuban government, as an apparently quixotic move in this dispute, bulldozed down the gates at the Peruvian embassy in Havana and set into motion, whether deliberately or inadvertently, that chain of events referred to as "Mariel," by which people in Miami mean not just the place and not just the boatlift and not just what many see as the "trick," the way in which Fidel Castro managed to take his own problem and make it Miami's, but the entire range of dislocations attendant upon the unloading of 125,000 refugees, 26,000 of them with prison records, onto an already volatile community.

The first Mariel refugees arrived in South Florida on April 21, 1980. By May 17, the day the McDuffie case went to the jury in Tampa, there were already some 57,000 Mariels camped under the bleachers at the Orange Bowl and in makeshift tent cities in the Orange Bowl parking area and on the public land under I-95, downtown, in the most visible and frequently traveled part of the city, in case it had escaped anybody's notice that the needs of the black community might not in the immediate future have Miami's full attention. May 17 was a Saturday. The temperature was in the mid-seventies. There was, in Miami, no rain in view.

There appears to have been an astonishing innocence about what happened that day. In another part of the country the judge in a trial as sensitive as the McDuffie trial might not have allowed the case to go to the jury on a clear Saturday morning, but the judge in Tampa did. In another part of the country the jury in such a case might not have brought in its verdicts, complete acquittal for all four defendants, in just two hours and forty-five minutes, which came down to something less than forty-two minutes per defendant, but the jury in Tampa did, in many ways predictably, for among the citizens of South Florida the urge to conciliate one another remained remarkably undeveloped. The president of the Orange Bowl Committee, which pretty much represents the established order in Miami, thought as recently as 1985, and said so, for attribution, that it was "not offensive" for the committee to entertain the participating college teams at the Indian Creek Country Club, which admitted no blacks or Jews as members but did allow them to visit the club as guests at private parties. "At the hospital where I work, the black doctors are intellectually fine and wonderful people, but they aren't able to handle the cosmopolitan aspects of circulating in society," a Miami surgeon said a few weeks later, also for attribution, to the *Herald* reporter who had asked him about restrictive policies at another local institution, the Bath Club, on Collins Avenue in Miami Beach.

Symbolic moves seemed to be missing here. A University of Miami study released the month of the 1968 Miami Riot had found it necessary to suggest that local black males resented being addressed by police as "boy," or "nigger." When a delegation of black citizens had asked the same year that a certain police officer be transferred, after conduct which had troubled the community, off his Liberty City beat, they were advised by the Miami chief of police that their complaint was "silly." Several weeks later it was reported that the officer in question and his partner had picked up a black seventeen-year-old, charged him with carrying a concealed knife, forced him to strip naked, and dangled him by his heels a hundred feet over the Miami River, from an unfinished span of the Dolphin Expressway.

During the twelve years between the 1968 Miami Riot and the Saturday in 1980 when the McDuffie case went to the jury, there had been, in Dade County, thirteen occasions on which the rage of some part of the black community went, for periods of time ranging from a few hours to a few days, out of control. This regular evidence of discontent notwithstanding, those gestures with which other troubled cities gradually learn to accommodate their citizens seemed not, in South Florida, to take hold. Blacks continued to be excluded for cause from juries in trials involving police officers accused of killing blacks. The juries in such cases continued to stay out two hours, and to bring in acquittals, on clear days, in the summer.

The McDuffie acquittals were on the Associated Press wire, that clear Saturday in 1980, by 2:42 P.M. The first police call reporting rioting in Liberty City came in at 6:02 P.M., from Miami Police Department Unit 621. By 9:44 P.M., when a call was placed to Tallahassee asking that the National Guard be sent in, there was rioting not only in Liberty City but in Overtown and in the black Grove and around the entire Metro Justice complex, where doctors and nurses answering emergency calls to Jackson Memorial Hospital were being stoned and beaten and the Metro Justice building itself was being torched. Four days later, when the 1980 Liberty City Riot, called that because Liberty City was where it had begun, had run its course, there were eighteen dead or fatally injured, eight of them whites who had driven down the wrong streets and been stoned or doused with gasoline and set afire or, in the case of one, a twenty-two-year-old Burdines warehouse loader on his way home from a day at the beach with his girlfriend and younger brother, dragged from the car to be beaten, kicked, struck not only with bottles and bricks and a twenty-three-pound chunk of concrete but also with a *Miami Herald* street dispenser, shot, stabbed with a screwdriver, run over by a green Cadillac and left, one ear cut off and lying on his chest and his tongue cut out, with a red rose in his mouth.

An instinct for self-preservation would have seemed at this point to encourage negotiations, or at least the appearance of negotiations, but few lessons get learned in tropical cities under attack from their own citizens. Lines only harden. Positions become more fixed, and privileges more fiercely defended. In December of 1982 another police killing of another black man occasioned another riot, the 1982 Overtown Riot, on the second night of which there happened to be held, in the ballroom of the Surf Club on Collins Avenue, which numbered among its 680 members no blacks and no Jews, one of the most expensive parties given that year in Miami, a debutante party at which actors performed the story of Little Red Riding Hood under two hundred freshly cut fir trees arranged to represent the Black Forest of Bavaria. In this case too the police officer in question, a Cuban, was eventually tried before an all-white jury, which again stayed out two hours and again brought in an acquittal. This verdict came in early one Thursday evening in March of 1984, and order was restored in Miami just after midnight on Saturday morning, which was applauded locally as progress, not even a riot.

There are between the street and the lobby levels of the Omni International Hotel on Biscayne Boulevard, one block east of the hundred-block area sealed off by police during the 1982 Overtown Riot, two levels of shops and movie theaters and carnival attractions: a mall, so designed that the teenagers, most of them black and most of them male, who hang out around the carousel in the evenings, waiting for a movie to break or for a turn at the Space Walk or at the Sea of Balls or just for something to happen, can look up to the Omni ballroom and lobby levels, but only with some ingenuity reach them, since a steel grille blocks

JOAN DIDION

the floating stairway after dark and armed security men patrol the
elevator areas. The visible presence of this more or less forbidden
upstairs lends the mall in the evening an unspecific atmosphere
of incipient trouble, an uneasiness which has its equivalent in the
hotel itself, where the insistent and rather sinister music from
the carousel downstairs comes to suggest, particularly on those
weekend nights when the mall is at its loosest and the hotel often
given over to one or another of the lavish *quinces* or charity galas
which fill the local Cuban calendar, a violent night world just
underfoot, and perhaps not underfoot for long.

Not often does a social dynamic seem to present itself in a
single tableau, but at the Omni in Miami one did, and during
the time I spent there I came to see the hotel and its mall as the
most theatrical possible illustration of how a native proletariat
can be left behind in a city open to the convulsions of the Third
World, something which had happened in the United States
first and most dramatically in Miami but had been happening
since in other parts of the country. Black Miami had of course
been particularly unprepared to have the world move in. Its
common experience was of the cracker South. Black assertiveness had been virtually nonexistent, black political organization
absent. Into the 1960s, according to *The Miami Riot of* 1980, a
study of the Liberty City Riot by Bruce Porter of Brooklyn
College and Marvin Dunn of Florida International University,
the latter a black candidate for mayor of Miami who lost in
1985 to a Cuban, Xavier Suarez, Miami blacks did not swim
at Dade County beaches. When Miami blacks paid taxes at the
Dade County Courthouse they did so at a separate window,
and when Miami blacks shopped at Burdines, where they were
allowed to buy although not to try on clothes, they did so without using the elevators.

This had been a familiar enough pattern throughout the South,
but something else had happened here. Desegregation had not just
come hard and late to South Florida but it had also coincided, as
it had not in other parts of the South, with another disruption of
the local status quo, the major Cuban influx, which meant that
jobs and services which might have helped awaken an inchoate
black community went instead to Cubans, who tended to be
overtrained but willing. Havana bankers took jobs as inventory
clerks at forty-five dollars a week. Havana newspaper publishers

drove taxis. That these were the men in black tie who now danced with the women in the Chanel and Valentino evening dresses on the ballroom level of the Omni was an irony lost in its precise detail, although not in its broad outline, on the sons of the men who did not get jobs as inventory clerks or taxi drivers, the children downstairs, in the high-topped sneakers, fanning in packs through the dim avenues of the locked-up mall.

ON THE ONE hundred and fiftieth anniversary of the founding of Dade County, in February of 1986, the *Miami Herald* asked four prominent amateurs of local history to name "the ten people and the ten events that had the most impact on the county's history." Each of the four submitted his or her own list of "The Most Influential People in Dade's History," and among the names mentioned were Julia Tuttle ("pioneer businesswoman"), Henry Flagler ("brought the Florida East Coast Railway to Miami"), Alexander Orr, Jr. ("started the research that saved Miami's drinking water from salt"), Everest George Sewell ("publicized the city and fostered its deepwater seaport"), Carl Fisher ("creator of Miami Beach"), Hugh M. Anderson ("to whom we owe Biscayne Boulevard, Miami Shores, and more"), Charles H. Crandon ("father of Dade County's park system"), Glenn Curtiss ("developer and promoter of the area's aviation potential"), and James L. Knight ("whose creative management enabled the *Miami Herald* to become a force for good"), this last nominee the choice of a retired *Herald* editorial writer.

There were more names. There were John Pennekamp ("conceived Dade's metropolitan form of government and fathered the Everglades National Park") and Father Theodore Gibson ("inspirational spokesman for racial justice and social change"). There were Maurice Ferre ("mayor for twelve years") and Marjorie Stoneman Douglas ("indefatigable environmentalist") and Dr. Bowman F. Ashe ("first and longtime president of the University of Miami"). There was David Fairchild, who "popularized tropical plants and horticulture that have made the county a more attractive place to live." There was William A. Graham, "whose Miami Lakes is a model for real estate development," Miami Lakes being the area developed by William A. Graham and his brother, Senator Bob Graham, at the time of Dade's one hundred and fiftieth anniversary the governor of Florida, on three thousand acres their father had just west of the Opa-Locka Airport.

There was another Graham, Ernest R., the father of Bob and William A., nominated for his "experiments with sugarcane culture and dairying." There was another developer, John Collins, as in Collins Avenue, Miami Beach. There were, as a dual entry, Richard Fitzpatrick, who "owned four square miles between what is now Northeast 14th Street and Coconut Grove," and William F. English, who "platted the village of Miami." There was Dr. James M. Jackson, an early Miami physician. There was Napoleon Bonaparte Broward, the governor of Florida who initiated the draining of the Everglades. There appeared on three of the four lists the name of the developer of Coral Gables, George Merrick. There appeared on one of the four lists the name of the coach of the Miami Dolphins, Don Shula.

On none of these lists of "The Most Influential People in Dade's History" did the name Fidel Castro appear, nor for that matter did the name of any Cuban, although the presence of Cubans in Dade County did not go entirely unnoted by the *Herald* panel. When it came to naming the Ten Most Important "Events," as opposed to "People," all four panelists mentioned the arrival of the Cubans, but at slightly off angles ("Mariel Boatlift of 1980" was the way one panelist saw it), and as if this arrival had been just another of those isolated disasters or innovations which deflect the course of any growing community, on an approximate par with the other events mentioned, for example the Freeze of 1895, the Hurricane of 1926, the opening of the Dixie Highway, the establishment of Miami International Airport, and the adoption, in 1957, of the metropolitan form of government, "enabling the Dade County Commission to provide urban services to the increasingly populous unincorporated area."

This set of mind, in which the local Cuban community was seen as a civic challenge determinedly met, was not uncommon among Anglos to whom I talked in Miami, many of whom persisted in the related illusions that the city was small, manageable, prosperous in a predictable broad-based way, southern in a progressive sunbelt way, American, and belonged to them. In fact 43 percent of the population of Dade County was by that time "Hispanic," which meant mostly Cuban. Fifty-six percent of the population of Miami itself was Hispanic. The most visible new buildings on the Miami skyline, the Arquitectonica buildings along Brickell Avenue, were by a firm with a Cuban founder. There were Cubans in the board rooms of the major banks, Cubans in the clubs that did not admit Jews or blacks, and four Cubans in the most recent mayoralty campaign, two of whom, Raul Masvidal and Xavier Suarez, had beaten out the incumbent and all other candidates to meet in a runoff, and one of whom, Xavier Suarez, a thirty-six-year-old lawyer who had been brought from Cuba to the United States as a child, was by then mayor of Miami.

The entire tone of the city, the way people looked and talked and met one another, was Cuban. The very image the city had begun presenting of itself, what was then its newfound glamour, its "hotness" (hot colors, hot vice, shady dealings under the palm trees), was that of prerevolutionary Havana, as perceived by Americans. There was even in the way women dressed in Miami a definable Havana look, a more distinct emphasis on the hips and décolletage, more black, more veiling, a generalized flirtatiousness of style not then current in American cities. In the shoe departments at Burdines and Jordan Marsh there were more platform soles than there might have been in another American city, and fewer displays of the running-shoe ethic. I recall being struck, during an afternoon spent at La Liga Contra el Cancer, a prominent exile charity which raises money to help cancer patients, by the appearance of the volunteers who had met that day to stuff envelopes for a benefit. Their hair was sleek, of a slightly other period, immaculate page boys and French twists. They wore Bruno Magli pumps, and silk and linen dresses of considerable expense. There seemed to be a preference for strictest gray or black, but the effect remained lush, tropical, like a room full of perfectly groomed mangoes.

This was not, in other words, an invisible 56 percent of the population. Even the social notes in *Diario Las Americas* and in *El Herald*, the daily Spanish edition of the *Herald* written and edited for *el exilio*, suggested a dominant culture, one with money to spend and a notable willingness to spend it in public. La Liga Contra el Cancer alone sponsored, in a single year, two benefit dinner dances, one benefit ball, a benefit children's fashion show, a benefit telethon, a benefit exhibition of jewelry, a benefit presentation of Miss Universe contestants, and a benefit showing, with Saks Fifth Avenue and chicken *vol-au-vent*, of the Adolfo (as it happened, a Cuban) fall collection. One morning *El Herald* would bring news of the gala at the Pavillon of the Amigos Latinamericanos del Museo de Ciencia y Planetarium; another morning, of an upcoming event at the Big Five Club, a Miami club founded by former members of five fashionable clubs in prerevolutionary Havana: a *coctel*, or cocktail party, at which tables would be assigned for yet another gala, the annual "Baile Imperial de las Rosas" of the American Cancer Society, Hispanic Ladies Auxiliary. Some members of the community were honoring Miss America Latina with dinner dancing at the Doral. Some were being honored themselves, at the Spirit of Excellence Awards Dinner at the Omni. Some were said to be enjoying the skiing at Vail; others to prefer Bariloche, in Argentina. Some were reported unable to attend (but sending checks for) the gala at the Pavillon of the Amigos Latinamericanos del Museo de Ciencia y Planetarium because of a scheduling conflict, with *el coctel de* Paula Hawkins.

Fete followed fete, all high visibility. Almost any day it was possible to drive past the limestone arches and fountains which marked the boundaries of Coral Gables and see little girls being photographed in the tiaras and ruffled hoop skirts and maribou-trimmed illusion capes they would wear at their *quinces*, the elaborate fifteenth-birthday parties at which the community's female children came of official age. The favored facial expression for a *quince* photograph was a classic smolder. The favored backdrop was one suggesting Castilian grandeur, which was how the Coral Gables arches happened to figure. Since the idealization of the virgin implicit in the *quince* could exist only in the presence of its natural foil, *machismo*, there was often a brother around, or a boyfriend. There was also a mother, in dark glasses, not only to protect the symbolic virgin but to point out the better angle, the more aristocratic location. The *quinceañera* would pick up her hoop skirts and move as directed, often revealing the scuffed Jellies she had worn that day to school. A few weeks later there she would be, transformed in *Diario Las Americas*, one of the morning battalion of smoldering fifteen-year-olds, each with her arch, her fountain, her borrowed scenery, the gift if not exactly the intention of the late George Merrick, who built the arches when he developed Coral Gables.

Neither the photographs of the Cuban *quinceañeras* nor the notes about the *coctel* at the Big Five were apt to appear in the newspapers read by Miami Anglos, nor, for that matter, was much information at all about the daily life of the Cuban majority. When, in the fall of 1986, Florida International University offered an evening course called "Cuban Miami: A Guide for Non-Cubans," the *Herald* sent a staff writer, who covered the classes as if from a distant beat. "Already I have begun to make some sense out of a culture that, while it totally surrounds us, has remained inaccessible and alien to me," the *Herald* writer was reporting by the end of the first meeting, and, by the end of the fourth: "What I see day to day in Miami, moving through mostly Anglo corridors of the community, are just small bits and pieces of that other world, the tip of something much larger than I'd imagined. ... We may frequent the restaurants here, or wander into the occasional festival. But mostly we try to ignore Cuban Miami, even as we rub up against this teeming, incomprehensible presence."

Only thirteen people, including the *Herald* writer, turned up for the first meeting of "Cuban Miami: A Guide for Non-Cubans" (two more appeared at the second meeting, along with a security guard, because of telephone threats prompted by what the *Herald* writer called "somebody's twisted sense of national pride"), an enrollment which tended to suggest a certain willingness among non-Cubans to let Cuban Miami remain just that, Cuban, the "incomprehensible presence." In fact there had come to exist in South Florida two parallel cultures, separate but not exactly equal, a key distinction being that only one of the two, the Cuban, exhibited even a remote interest in the activities of the other. "The American community is not really aware of what is happening in the Cuban community," an exile banker named Luis Botifoll said in a 1983 *Herald* Sunday magazine piece about ten prominent local Cubans. "We are clannish, but at least we know who is who in the American establishment. They do not." About another of the ten Cubans featured in this piece, Jorge Mas Canosa, the *Herald* had this to say: "He is an advisor to U.S. Senators, a confidant of federal bureaucrats, a lobbyist for anti-Castro U.S. policies, a near unknown in Miami. When his political group sponsored a luncheon speech in Miami by Secretary of Defense Caspar Weinberger, almost none of the American business leaders attending had ever heard of their Cuban host."

The general direction of this piece, which appeared under the cover line "THE CUBANS: *They're ten of the most powerful men in*

Miami. Half the population doesn't know it," was, as the *Herald* put it, "to challenge the widespread presumption that Miami's Cubans are not really Americans, that they are a foreign presence here, an exile community that is trying to turn South Florida into North Cuba. ... The top ten are not separatists; they have achieved success in the most traditional ways. They are the solid, bedrock citizens, hard-working humanitarians who are role models for a community that seems determined to assimilate itself into American society."

This was interesting. It was written by one of the few Cubans then on the *Herald* staff, and yet it described, however unwittingly, the precise angle at which Miami Anglos and Miami Cubans were failing to connect: Miami Anglos were in fact interested in Cubans only to the extent that they could cast them as aspiring immigrants, "determined to assimilate," a "hard-working" minority not different in kind from other groups of resident aliens. (But had I met any Haitians, a number of Anglos asked when I said that I had been talking to Cubans.) Anglos (who were, significantly, referred to within the Cuban community as "Americans") spoke of cross-culturalization, and of what they believed to be a meaningful second-generation preference for hamburgers, and rock and roll. They spoke of "diversity," and of Miami's "Hispanic flavor," an approach in which 56 percent of the population was seen as decorative, like the Coral Gables arches.

Fixed as they were on this image of the melting pot, of immigrants fleeing a disruptive revolution to find a place in the American sun, Anglos did not on the whole understand that assimilation would be considered by most Cubans a doubtful goal at best. Nor did many Anglos understand that living in Florida was still at the deepest level construed by Cubans as a temporary condition, an accepted political option shaped by the continuing dream, if no longer the immediate expectation, of a vindicatory return. *El exilio* was for Cubans a ritual, a respected tradition. *La revolución* was also a ritual, a trope fixed in Cuban political rhetoric at least since José Martí, a concept broadly interpreted to mean reform, or progress, or even just change. Ramón Grau San Martín, the president of Cuba during the autumn of 1933 and again from 1944 until 1948, had presented himself as a revolutionary, as had his 1948 successor, Carlos Prío. Even Fulgencio Batista had entered Havana life calling for *la revolución*, and had later been accused of betraying it, even as Fidel Castro was now.

This was a process Cuban Miami understood, but Anglo Miami did not, remaining as it did arrestingly innocent of even the most general information about Cuba and Cubans. Miami Anglos, for example, still had trouble with Cuban names, and Cuban food. When the Cuban novelist Guillermo Cabrera Infante came from London to lecture at Miami-Dade Community College, he was referred to by several Anglo faculty members to whom I spoke as "Infante." Cuban food was widely seen not as a minute variation on that eaten throughout both the Caribbean and the Mediterranean but as "exotic," and full of garlic. A typical Thursday food section of the *Herald* included recipes for Broiled Lemon-Curry Cornish Game Hens, Chicken Tetrazzini, King Cake, Pimiento Cheese, Raisin Sauce for Ham, Sautéed Spiced Peaches, Shrimp Scampi, Easy Beefy Stir-Fry, and four ways to use dried beans ("Those cheap, humble beans that have long sustained the world's poor have become the trendy set's new pet"), none of them Cuban.

This was all consistent, and proceeded from the original construction, that of the exile as an immigration. There was no reason to be curious about Cuban food, because Cuban teenagers preferred hamburgers. There was no reason to get Cuban names right, because they were complicated, and would be simplified by the second generation, or even by the first. "Jorge L. Mas" was the way Jorge Más Canosa's business card read. "Raul Masvidal" was the way Raúl Masvidal y Jury ran for mayor of Miami. There was no reason to know about Cuban history, because history was what immigrants were fleeing. Even the revolution, the reason for the immigration, could be covered in a few broad strokes: "Batista," "Castro," "26 Julio," this last being the particular broad stroke that inspired the Miami Springs Holiday Inn, on July 26, 1985, the thirty-second anniversary of the day Fidel Castro attacked the Moncada Barracks and so launched his six-year struggle for power in Cuba, to run a bar special on Cuba Libres, thinking to attract local Cubans by commemorating their holiday. "It was a mistake," the manager said, besieged by outraged exiles. "The gentleman who did it is from Minnesota."

There was in fact no reason, in Miami as well as in Minnesota, to know anything at all about Cubans, since Miami Cubans were now, if not Americans, at least aspiring Americans, and worthy of Anglo attention to the exact extent that they were proving themselves, in the *Herald*'s words, "role models for a community that seems determined to assimilate itself into American society"; or, as Vice President George Bush put it in a 1986 Miami address to the Cuban American National Foundation, "the most eloquent testimony I know to the basic strength and success of America, as well as to the basic weakness and failure of Communism and Fidel Castro."

The use of this special lens, through which the exiles were seen as a tribute to the American system, a point scored in the battle of the ideologies, tended to be encouraged by those outside observers who dropped down from the northeast corridor for a look and a column or two. George Will, in *Newsweek*, saw Miami as "a new installment in the saga of America's absorptive capacity," and Southwest Eighth Street as the place where "these exemplary Americans," the seven Cubans who had been gotten together to brief him, "initiated a columnist to fried bananas and black-bean soup and other Cuban contributions to the tanginess of American life." George Gilder, in *The Wilson Quarterly*, drew pretty much the same lesson from Southwest Eighth Street, finding it "more effervescently thriving than its crushed prototype," by which he seemed to mean Havana. In fact Eighth Street was for George Gilder a street that seemed to "percolate with the forbidden commerce of the dying island to the south ... the Refrescos Cawy, the Competidora and El Cuño cigarettes, the *guayaberas*, the Latin music pulsing from the storefronts, the pyramids of mangoes and tubers, gourds and plantains, the iced coconuts served with a straw, the new theaters showing the latest anti-Castro comedies."

There was nothing on this list, with the possible exception of the "anti-Castro comedies," that could not most days be found on Southwest Eighth Street, but the list was also a fantasy, and a particularly gringo fantasy, one in which Miami Cubans, who came from a culture which had represented western civilization in this hemisphere since before there was a United States of America, appeared exclusively as vendors of plantains, their native music "pulsing" behind them. There was in any such view of Miami Cubans an extraordinary element of condescension, and it was the very condescension shared by Miami Anglos, who were inclined to reduce the particular liveliness and sophistication of local Cuban life to a matter of shrines on the lawn and love potions in the *botánicas*, the primitive exotica of the tourist's Caribbean.

Cubans were perceived as most satisfactory when they appeared to most fully share the aspirations and manners of middle-class Americans, at the same time adding "color" to the city on appropriate occasions, for example at their *quinces* (the *quinces* were one aspect of Cuban life almost invariably mentioned by Anglos, who tended to present them as evidence of Cuban extravagance, *i.e.*, Cuban irresponsibility, or childishness), or on the day of the annual Calle Ocho Festival, when they could, according to the *Herald*, "samba" in the streets and stir up a paella for two thousand (10 cooks, 2,000 mussels, 220 pounds of lobster and 440 pounds of rice), using rowboat oars as spoons. Cubans were perceived as least satisfactory when they "acted clannish," "kept to themselves," "had their own ways," and, two frequent flash points, "spoke Spanish when they didn't need to" and "got political"; complaints, each of them, which suggested an Anglo view of what Cubans should be at significant odds with what Cubans were.

THIS QUESTION OF language was curious. The sound of spoken Spanish was common in Miami, but it was also common in Los Angeles, and Houston, and even in the cities of the northeast. What was unusual about Spanish in Miami was not that it was so often spoken, but that it was so often heard: in, say, Los Angeles, Spanish remained a language only barely registered by the Anglo population, part of the ambient noise, the language spoken by the people who worked in the car wash and came to trim the trees and cleared the tables in restaurants. In Miami Spanish was spoken by the people who ate in the restaurants, the people who owned the cars and the trees, which made, on the socioauditory scale, a considerable difference. Exiles who felt isolated or declassed by language in New York or Los Angeles thrived in Miami. An entrepreneur who spoke no English could still, in Miami, buy, sell, negotiate, leverage assets, float bonds, and, if he were so inclined, attend galas twice a week, in black tie. "I have been after the *Herald* ten times to do a story about millionaires in Miami who do not speak more than two words in English," one prominent exile told me. "'Yes' and 'no.' Those are the two words. They come here with five dollars in their pockets and without speaking another word of English they are millionaires."

The truculence a millionaire who spoke only two words of English might provoke among the less resourceful native citizens of a nominally American city was predictable, and manifested itself rather directly. In 1980, the year of Mariel, Dade County voters had approved a referendum requiring that county business be conducted exclusively in English. Notwithstanding the fact that this legislation was necessarily amended to exclude emergency medical and certain other services, and notwithstanding even the fact that many local meetings continued to be conducted in that unbroken alternation of Spanish and English which had become the local patois ("I will be in Boston on Sunday and desafortunadamente yo tengo un compromiso en Boston que no puedo

romper y yo no podré estar con Vds.,'' read the minutes of a 1984
Miami City Commission meeting I had occasion to look up.
"En espíritu, estaré, pero the other members of the commission
I am sure are invited ..."), the very existence of this referendum
was seen by many as ground regained, a point made. By 1985
a St. Petersburg optometrist named Robert Melby was launching his third attempt in four years to have English declared the
official language of the state of Florida, as it would be in 1986 of
California. "I don't know why your legislators here are so, how
should I put it?—spineless," Robert Melby complained about
those South Florida politicians who knew how to count. "No
one down here seems to want to run with the issue."

Even among those Anglos who distanced themselves from such
efforts, Anglos who did not perceive themselves as economically or
socially threatened by Cubans, there remained considerable uneasiness on the matter of language, perhaps because the inability or the
disinclination to speak English tended to undermine their conviction that assimilation was an ideal universally shared by those who
were to be assimilated. This uneasiness had for example shown
up repeatedly during the 1985 mayoralty campaign, surfacing at
odd but apparently irrepressible angles. The winner of that contest,
Xavier Suarez, who was born in Cuba but educated in the United
States, was reported in a wire service story to speak, an apparently
unexpected accomplishment, "flawless English."

A less prominent Cuban candidate for mayor that year had
unsettled reporters at a televised "meet the candidates" forum by
answering in Spanish the questions they asked in English. "For all
I or my dumbstruck colleagues knew," the *Herald* political editor
complained in print after this event, "he was reciting his high
school's alma mater or the ten Commandments over and over
again. The only thing I understood was the occasional *Cubano
vota Cubano* he tossed in." It was noted by another *Herald* columnist that of the leading candidates, only one, Raul Masvidal, had
a listed telephone number, but: "... if you call Masvidal's 661-
0259 number on Kiaora Street in Coconut Grove—during the
day, anyway—you'd better speak Spanish. I spoke to two women
there, and neither spoke enough English to answer the question
of whether it was the candidate's number."

On the morning this last item came to my attention in the
Herald I studied it for some time. Raul Masvidal was at that time

the chairman of the board of the Miami Savings Bank and the Miami Savings Corporation. He was a former chairman of the Biscayne Bank, and a minority stockholder in the M Bank, of which he had been a founder. He was a member of the Board of Regents for the state university system of Florida. He had paid $600,000 for the house on Kiaora Street in Coconut Grove, buying it specifically because he needed to be a Miami resident (Coconut Grove is part of the city of Miami) in order to run for mayor, and he had sold his previous house, in the incorporated city of Coral Gables, for $1,100,000. The Spanish words required to find out whether the number listed for the house on Kiaora Street was in fact the candidate's number would have been roughly these: "*Es la casa de Raúl Masvidal?*" The answer might have been "*Sí,*" or the answer might have been "*No.*" It seemed to me that there must be very few people working on daily newspapers along the southern borders of the United States who would consider this exchange entirely out of reach, and fewer still who would not accept it as a commonplace of American domestic life that daytime telephone calls to middle-class urban households will frequently be answered by women who speak Spanish.

Something else was at work in this item, a real resistance, a balkiness, a coded version of the same message Dade County voters had sent when they decreed that their business be done only in English. WILL THE LAST AMERICAN TO LEAVE MIAMI PLEASE BRING THE FLAG, the famous bumper stickers had read the year of Mariel. "It was the last American stronghold in Dade County," the owner of Gator Kicks Longneck Saloon, out where Southwest Eight Street runs into the Everglades, had said after he closed the place for good the night of Super Bowl Sunday, 1986. "Fortunately or unfortunately, I'm not alone in my inability," a *Herald* columnist named Charles Whited had written a week or so later, in a column about not speaking Spanish. "A good many Americans have left Miami because they want to live someplace where everybody speaks one language: theirs." In this context the call to the house on Kiaora Street in Coconut Grove which did or did not belong to Raul Masvidal appeared not as a statement of literal fact but as shorthand, a glove thrown down, a stand, a cry from the heart of a beleaguered raj.

7

ON THE WHOLE the members of the beleaguered raj and the 56 percent of the population whose affairs they continued to believe they directed did not see politics on the same canvas, which tended to complicate the Anglo complaint about the way in which Cubans "got political."

> Every election in the city of Miami produces its share of rumors involving the *Herald*, and last Tuesday's mayoral runoff between Raul Masvidal and Xavier Suarez produced one that I think I'll have bronzed and hang on my office wall. It was *that* bizarre.
>
> Political Editor Tom Fiedler reported it in his column on Thursday. The previous day, Mr. Suarez was sworn in as mayor after readily defeating Mr. Masvidal, whom this newspaper had recommended, in the runoff. Tom wrote that "the rumor going around Little Havana is that the *Herald* really preferred Suarez the best and only used Masvidal as a feint. Follow this reasoning closely, now: because the newspaper knows that its endorsement actually hurts candidates in Little Havana, it endorsed Masvidal with the knowledge that Suarez would be the beneficiary of a backlash. Thus, according to this rationale, the *Herald* actually got what it wanted. Clever, huh?"
>
> I wish I knew where behind the looking glass the authors of these contortions reside. I'd like to meet them, really I would. Maybe if we chatted I could begin to understand the thought processes that make them see up as down, black as white, alpha as omega. Or maybe I simply would be left where I am now: scratching my head and chortling in baffled amusement.
>
> —Jim Hampton, Editor,
> the *Miami Herald,* November 17, 1985

Miami Anglos continued, as the editor of the *Herald* did, to regard the density and febrility of exile political life with "baffled amusement." They continued, as the editor of the *Herald* did, to find that life "bizarre." They thought of politics exactly the way most of their elected representatives thought of politics, not as the very structure of everything they did but as a specific and usually programmatic kind of activity: an election, a piece of legislation, the deals made and the trade-offs extracted during the course of the campaign or the legislative markup. Any more general notions tended to be amorphous, the detritus of a desultory education in the confident latitudes: politics were part of "civics," one of the "social studies," something taught with audiovisual aids and having as its goal the promotion of good citizenship.

Politics, in other words, remained a "subject," an assortment of maxims once learned and still available to be learned by those not blessed with American birth, which may have been why, on those infrequent occasions when the city's parallel communities contrived an opportunity to express their actual feelings about each other, Miami Anglos tended unveeringly toward the didactic. On March 7, 1986, a group called the South Florida Peace Coalition applied for and received a Miami police permit authorizing a demonstration, scheduled for a Saturday noon some two weeks later at the Torch of Friendship monument on Biscayne Boulevard, against American aid to the Nicaraguan contras. Since the cause of the Nicaraguan contras was one with which many Miami Cubans had come to identify their most febrile hopes and fears, the prospect of such a demonstration was not likely to go unremarked upon, nor did it: in due course, after what was apparently a general sounding of the alarm on local Cuban radio, a second police permit was applied for and issued, this one to Andres Nazario Sargen, the executive director of Alpha 66, one of the most venerable of the exile action groups and one which had regularly claimed, ever since what had appeared to be its original encouragement in 1962 by the CIA, to be running current actions against the government of Cuba.

This second permit authorized a counterdemonstration, intended not so much to show support for the contras, which in context went without saying, as to show opposition to those Anglos presumed to be working for hemispheric communism. "We took it as a challenge," Andres Nazario Sargen said of the original permit and its holders. "They know very well they are defending a communist regime, and that hurts the Cuban exile's sensibility." That the permits would allow the South Florida Peace Coalition demonstration and the Alpha 66 counterdemonstration to take place at exactly the same time and within a few yards of each other was a point defended by Miami police, the day before the scheduled events, as a "manpower" decision, a question of not wanting to "split resources." "With the number of police officers who will be there," a police spokesman was quoted as saying, "someone would have to be foolish to try anything."

This was not an assessment which suggested a particularly close reading, over the past twenty-five years, of either Alpha 66 or Andres Nazario Sargen, and I was not unduly surprised, on the Sunday morning after the fact, to find the front page of the *Herald* given over to double headlines (DEMONSTRATIONS TURN UGLY and VIOLENCE MARS PRO-CONTRA PROTEST) and a four-color photograph showing a number of exiles brandishing Cuban and American flags as they burned the placards abandoned by the routed South Florida Peace Coalition. It appeared that many eggs had been hurled, and some rocks. It appeared that at least one onion had been hurled, hitting the president of the Dade County Young Democrats, who later expressed his thoughts on the matter by describing himself as "an eleventh-generation American."

It appeared, moreover, that these missiles had been hurled in just one direction, that of the South Florida Peace Coalition demonstrators, a group of about two hundred which included, besides the president of the Dade County Young Democrats, some state and local legislators, some members of the American Friends Service Committee, a few people passing out leaflets bearing the name of the Revolutionary Communist Party, one schoolteacher who advised the *Herald* that she was there because "Americans need to reclaim Miami from these foreigners," and, the most inflammatory cut of all for the Alpha 66 demonstrators on the other side of the metal police barricades, at least one Cuban, a leader of the Antonio Maceo Brigade, a heretical exile group founded in the mid-seventies to sponsor student visits to Cuba.

From noon of that Saturday until about three, when a riot squad was called and the South Florida Peace Coalition physically extracted from the fray, the police had apparently managed to keep the Alpha 66 demonstrators on the Alpha 66 side of the barricades. The two hundred Peace Coalition demonstrators had apparently spent those three hours listening to speeches and singing folk songs. The two thousand Alpha 66 demonstrators had apparently spent the three hours trying to rush the barricades, tangling with police, and shouting down the folksingers with chants of "*Comunismo no, Democracia sí*," and "*Rusia no, Reagan sí*." The mayor of Miami, Xavier Suarez, had apparently stayed on the Alpha 66 side of the barricades, at one point speaking from the back of a Mazda pickup, a technique he later described in a letter to the *Herald* as "mingling with the people and expressing my own philosophical agreement with their ideas—as well as my disagreement with the means by which some would implement those ideas," and also as "an effective way to control the crowd."

"Unfortunately, they have the right to be on the other side of the street" was what he apparently said at the time, from the back of the Mazda pickup. "I'm sure you've all looked clearly to see who is on that side, senators and representatives included, and surely some members of Marxist groups." This method of crowd control notwithstanding, nothing much seemed actually to have happened that Saturday afternoon at the Torch of Friendship (only one demonstrator had been arrested, only one required hospital treatment), but the fevers of the moment continued for some weeks to induce a certain exhortatory delirium in the pages of the *Herald*. Statements were framed, and letters to the editor written, mostly along the preceptive lines favored by the Anglo community.

"I was raised to believe that the right to peaceful dissent was vital to our freedoms," one such letter read, from a woman who noted that she had been present at the Peace Coalition demonstration but had "fortunately" been "spared the vocal vituperation—as it was totally in the Spanish language." "Apparently," she continued, "some in the Cuban community do not recognize my right. ... Evidently, their definition of human rights is not the same as that of most native-born Americans. It is as simple as that. No, my Cuban brothers and sisters, this is not the American way. Shame!"

Voltaire was quoted, somewhat loosely ("'I disagree with what you say, but I will defend to the death your right to say it'"), and even Wendell Willkie, the inscription on whose grave marker

JOAN DIDION

("'Because we are generous with our freedom, we share our rights with those who disagree with us'") was said to be "our American creed, as spelled out in the Constitution." One correspondent mentioned how "frightening" it was to realize "that although we live in a democracy that guarantees the right of free speech, when we exercise this right we can be physically attacked by a group of people whom we have given refuge here in our country."

The subtext here, that there were some people who belonged in Miami and other people who did not, became, as the letters mounted, increasingly explicit, taking on finally certain aspects of a crusade. "Perhaps," another correspondent suggested, taking the point a step further, "it is time for a change of venue to countries in which they may vent their spleen at risk only to the governments they oppose and themselves." A *Herald* columnist, Carl Hiaasen, put the matter even more flatly: "They have come to the wrong country," he wrote about those pro-contra demonstrators who had that Saturday afternoon attacked a young man named David Camp, "a carpenter and stagehand who was born here, and has always considered himself patriotic ... They need to go someplace where they won't have to struggle so painfully with the concept of free speech, or the right to dissent. Someplace where the names of Paine and Jefferson have no meaning, where folks wouldn't know the Bill of Rights if it was stapled to their noses."

If this native reduction of politics to a Frank Capra movie was not an approach which provided much of a libretto for the tropical Ring of exile and conspiracy that had been Cuban political experience, neither had the Cubans arrived in Miami equipped with much instinctive feeling for the native way. Miami Cubans were not the heirs to a tradition in which undue effort had been spent defining the rights and responsibilities of "good citizens," nor to one in which loosely organized democracies on the American model were widely admired. They were the heirs instead to the Spanish Inquisition, and after that to a tradition of anti-Americanism so sturdy that it had often been for Cubans a motive force. "It is my duty," José Martí had written to a friend in May of 1895, a few days before he was killed on his white horse fighting for the independence of Cuba at Dos Ríos, "to prevent,

458

through the independence of Cuba, the U.S.A. from spreading over the West Indies and falling with added weight upon other lands of Our America. All I have done up to now and shall do hereafter is to that end. ... I know the Monster, because I have lived in its lair—and my weapon is only the slingshot of David."

From within this matrix, which was essentially autocratic, Miami Cubans looked at the merely accidental in American life and found a design, often sinister. They looked at what amounted to Anglo indifference (on the question, say, of which of two Cubans, neither of whom could be expected to recall the Hurricane of 1926 or the opening of the Dixie Highway, was to be mayor of Miami) and divined a conspiratorial intention. They looked at American civil rights and saw civil disorder. They had their own ideas about how order should be maintained, even in the lair of the Monster that was the United States. "All underaged children will not be allowed to leave their homes by themselves," one Cuban candidate in the 1985 Miami mayoralty campaign promised to ensure if elected. "They should always be accompanied by an adult, with parents or guardians being responsible for compliance with the law." Another Cuban candidate in the same election, General Manuel Benítez, who had been at one time chief of the Batista security forces, promised this: "... you can rest assured that within six months there will be no holdups, life in general will be protected and stores will be able to open their doors without fear of robberies or murders. ... A powerful force of security guards, the county school personnel, teachers, professionals, retirees, Boy Scouts and church people will all take part in a program of citizen education and in the constant fight against evil and immorality."

"Unfortunately," as the winning candidate in that campaign, Mayor Xavier Suarez, had said of the Peace Coalition demonstrators at the Torch of Friendship, "they have the right to be on the other side of the street." That this was a right devised to benefit those who would subvert civil order was, for many Cubans, a given, because this was a community in which nothing could be inadvertent, nothing without its place in a larger, usually hostile, scheme. The logic was close, even claustrophobic. That the *Herald* should have run, on the 1985 anniversary of the Bay of Pigs, a story about Canadian and Italian tourists vacationing on what had been the invasion beaches (RESORT SELLS

SUN, FUN—IN CUBA: TOPLESS BATHERS FROLIC AS HAVANA TRIES HAND AT TOURISM) was, in this view, not just a minor historical irony, not just an arguably insensitive attempt to find a news peg for a twenty-four-year-old annual story, but a calculated affront to the Cuban community, "a slap," I was repeatedly told, "in the face." That the *Herald* should have run, a few weeks before, a story suggesting a greater availability of consumer goods in Cuba (FREE MARKETS ALLOW HAVANA TO SPIFF UP) not only sealed the affront but indicated that it was systematic, directed by Washington and signaling a rapprochement between the Americans and Havana, the imminence of which was a fixed idea among Miami Cubans.

Fixed ideas about Americans seemed, among Miami Cubans, general. Americans, I was frequently told, never touched one another, nor did they argue. Americans did not share the attachment to family which characterized Cuban life. Americans did not share the attachment to *patria* which characterized Cuban life. Americans placed undue importance on being on time. Americans were undereducated. Americans, at one and the same time, acted exclusively in their own interests and failed to see their own interests, not only because they were undereducated but because they were by temperament "naive," a people who could live and die without ever understanding those nuances of conspiracy and allegiance on which, in the Cuban view, the world turned.

Americans, above all, lacked "passion," which was the central failing from which most of these other national peculiarities flowed. If I wanted evidence that Americans lacked passion, I was advised repeatedly, I had only to consider their failure to appreciate *la lucha*. If I wanted further evidence that Americans lacked passion, I had only to turn on a television set and watch Ted Koppel's "Nightline," a program on which, I was told a number of times, it was possible to observe Americans "with very opposing points of view" talking "completely without passion," "without any gestures at all," and "seemingly without any idea in the world of conspiring against each other, despite being totally opposed."

This repeated reference to "Nightline" was arresting. At the end of a day or an evening in Miami I would look through my notes and find the references underlined and boxed in my notebook, with arrows, and the notation, "Ch.: NIGHTLINE???" The mode of discourse favored by Ted Koppel (it was always, for reasons I never discerned, Ted Koppel, no one else) and his guests seemed in fact so consistent a source of novelty and derision among the Cubans to whom I spoke in Miami that I began to see these mentions of "Nightline" as more shorthand, the Cuban version of the Anglo telephone call to the house on Kiaora Street in Coconut Grove which did or did not belong to Raul Masvidal, another glove thrown down, another stand; the code which indicated that the speaker, like José Martí, knew the Monster, and did not mean to live easily in its lair.

"Let those who desire a secure homeland conquer it," José Martí also wrote. "Let those who do not conquer it live under the whip and in exile, watched over like wild animals, cast from one country to another, concealing the death of their souls with a beggar's smile from the scorn of free men." The humiliation of the continuing exile was what the Monster, lacking passion, did not understand. It was taken for granted in this continuing exile that the Monster, lacking passion or understanding, could be utilized. It was also taken for granted in this continuing exile that the Monster, lacking passion or understanding, could not be trusted. "We must attempt to strengthen the non-Batista democratic anti-Castro forces in exile," a John F. Kennedy campaign statement had declared in the course of working up an issue against Richard Nixon in 1960. "We cannot have the United States walk away from one of the greatest moral challenges in postwar history," Ronald Reagan had declared in the course of working up support for the Nicaraguan freedom fighters in 1985.

"We have seen that movie before," one prominent exile had said to me about the matter of the United States not, as Ronald Reagan had put it, walking away from the Nicaraguan freedom fighters. Here between the mangrove swamp and the barrier reef was an American city largely populated by people who believed that the United States had walked away before, had betrayed them at the Bay of Pigs and later, with consequences we have since seen. Here between the swamp and the reef was an American city populated by people who also believed that the United States would betray them again, in Honduras and in El Salvador and in Nicaragua, betray them at all the barricades of a phantom war they had once again taken not as the projection of another Washington abstraction but as their own struggle, *la lucha, la causa*, with consequences we have not yet seen.

Part III

"DON'T FORGET THAT we have a disposal problem" is what Arthur M. Schlesinger, Jr., tells us that Allen Dulles said on March 11, 1961, by way of warning John F. Kennedy about the possible consequences of aborting the projected Cuban invasion and cutting loose what the CIA knew to be a volatile and potentially vengeful asset, the 2506 Brigade. What John F. Kennedy was said to have said, four weeks later, to Arthur M. Schlesinger, Jr., is this: "If we have to get rid of these 800 men, it is much better to dump them in Cuba than in the United States, especially if that is where they want to go." This is dialogue recalled by someone without much ear for it, and the number of men involved in the invasion force was closer to fifteen hundred than to eight hundred, but the core of it, the "dump them in Cuba" construction, has an authentic ring, as does "disposal problem" itself. Over the years since the publication of *A Thousand Days* I had read the chapter in which these two lines appear several times, but only after I had spent time in Miami did I begin to see them as curtain lines, or as the cannon which the protagonist brings onstage in the first act so that it may be fired against him in the third.

"I would say that John F. Kennedy is still the number two most hated man in Miami," Raul Masvidal said to me one afternoon, not long after he had announced his candidacy for mayor, in a cool and immaculate office on the top floor of one of the Miami banks in which he has an interest. Raul Masvidal, who was born in Havana in 1942, would seem in many ways a model for what both Anglo Miami and the rest of the United States like to see as Cuban assimilation. He was named by both Cubans and non-Cubans in a 1983 *Miami Herald* poll as the most powerful Cuban in Miami. He received the endorsement of the *Herald* in his campaign to become mayor of Miami, the election he ultimately lost to Xavier Suarez. He was, at the time we spoke, one of two Cuban members (the other being Armando Codina, a Miami entrepreneur and member of the advisory board of the

Southeast First National Bank) of The Non-Group, an unofficial and extremely private organization which had been called
the shadow government of South Florida and included among
its thirty-eight members, who met once a month for dinner at
one another's houses or clubs, the ownership or top management
of Knight-Ridder, Eastern Airlines, Arvida Disney, Burdines, the
Miami Dolphins, and the major banks and utilities.

"Castro is of course the number one most hated," Raul
Masvidal added. "Then Kennedy. The entire Kennedy family." He
opened and closed a leather folder, the only object on his marble
desk, then aligned it with the polished edge of the marble. On
the wall behind him hung a framed poster with the legend, in
English, YOU HAVE NOT CONVERTED A MAN BECAUSE YOU HAVE
SILENCED HIM, a sentiment so outside the thrust of local Cuban
thinking that it lent the office an aspect of having been dressed
exclusively for visits from what Cubans sometimes call, with a
slight ironic edge, the mainstream population.

"Something I did which involved Ted Kennedy became
very controversial here," Raul Masvidal said then. "Jorge asked
me to contact Senator Kennedy." He was talking about Jorge
Mas Canosa, the Miami engineering contractor (the "advisor to
U.S. Senators," "confidant of federal bureaucrats," "lobbyist for
anti-Castro U.S. policies" and "near unknown in Miami," as the
Herald had described him a few years before) who had been,
through the Washington office of the Cuban American National
Foundation and its companion PAC, the National Coalition for a
Free Cuba, instrumental in the lobbying for Radio Martí. "To see
if we could get him to reverse his position on Radio Martí. We
needed Kennedy to change his vote, to give that bill the famous
luster. I did that. And the Cubans here took it as if it had been an
attempt to make peace with the Kennedys."

The man who had been accused of attempting to make peace
with the Kennedys arrived in this country in 1960, when he was
eighteen. He enrolled at the University of Miami, then took two
semesters off to train with the 2506 for the Bay of Pigs. After
the 1962 Cuban missile crisis, which was then and is still perceived in Miami as another personal betrayal on the part of John
F. Kennedy, Raul Masvidal again dropped out of the University of
Miami, this time to join a unit of Cubans recruited by the United
States Army for training at Fort Knox, Kentucky, part of what

Theodore C. Sorensen, in *Kennedy*, recalled in rather soft focus as a "special arrangement" under which Bay of Pigs veterans "were quietly entering the American armed forces."

This seems to have been, even through the filter offered by diarists of the Kennedy administration, a gray area. Like other such ad hoc attempts to neutralize the 2506, the recruitment program involved, if not outright deception, a certain encouragement of self-deception, an apparent willingness to allow those Cubans who "were quietly entering the American armed forces" to do so under the misapprehension that the United States was in fact preparing to invade Cuba. Sentences appear to have been left unfinished, and hints dropped. Possibilities appear to have been floated, and not exclusively, as it has become the convention in this kind of situation to suggest, by some uncontrollable element in the field, some rogue agent. "President Kennedy came to the Orange Bowl and made us a promise," Jorge Mas Canosa, who is also a veteran of the 2506, repeated insistently to me one morning, his voice rising in the retelling of what has become for Miami a primal story. "December. Nineteen sixty-two. What he said turned out to be another—I won't say deception, let us call it a misconception—another misconception on the part of President Kennedy."

Jorge Mas Canosa had drawn the words "President" and "Kennedy" out, inflecting all syllables with equal emphasis. This was the same Jorge Mas Canosa who had enlisted Raul Masvidal in the effort to secure the luster of the Kennedy name for Radio Martí, the Jorge Mas Canosa who had founded the Cuban American National Foundation and was one of those funding its slick offices overlooking the Potomac in Georgetown; the Jorge Mas Canosa who had become so much a figure in Washington that it was sometimes hard to catch up with him in Miami. I had driven finally down the South Dixie Highway that morning to meet him at his main construction yard, the cramped office of which was decorated with a LONG LIVE FREE GRENADA poster and framed photographs of Jorge Mas Canosa with Ronald Reagan and Jorge Mas Canosa with Jeane Kirkpatrick and Jorge Mas Canosa with Paula Hawkins. "And at the Orange Bowl he was given the flag," Jorge Mas Canosa continued. "The flag the invasion forces had taken to Playa Girón. And he took this flag in his hands and he promised that he would return it to us in a free Havana. And he called on us to join the United States armed forces. To get training. And try again."

This particular effort to get the cannon offstage foundered, as many such efforts foundered, on the familiar shoal of Washington hubris. In this instance the hubris took the form of simultaneously underestimating the exiles' distrust of the United States and overestimating their capacity for self-deception, which, although considerable, was tempered always by a rather more extensive experience in the politics of conspiracy than the Kennedy administration's own. The exiles had not, once they put it together that the point of the exercise was to keep them occupied, served easily. Jorge Mas Canosa, who had been sent to Fort Benning, had stayed only long enough to finish OCS, then resigned his commission and returned to Miami. At Fort Knox, according to Raul Masvidal, there had been, "once it became evident that the United States and Russia had reached an agreement and the United States had no intention of invading Cuba," open rebellion.

"A lot of things happened," Raul Masvidal said. "For example we had a strike, which was unheard of for soldiers. One day we just decided we were going to remain in our barracks for a few days. They threatened us with all kinds of things. But at that point we didn't care much for the threats." A representative of the Kennedy White House had finally been dispatched to Fort Knox to try to resolve the situation, and a deal had been struck, a renegotiated "special arrangement," under which the exiles agreed to end their strike in return for an immediate transfer to Fort Jackson, South Carolina (they had found Kentucky, they said, too cold), and an almost immediate discharge. At this point Raul Masvidal went back to the University of Miami, to parking cars at the Everglades Hotel, and to the more fluid strategies of CIA/Miami, which was then running, through a front operation on the south campus of the University of Miami called Zenith Technological Services and codenamed JM/WAVE, a kind of action about which everybody in Miami and nobody in Washington seemed to know.

"I guess during that period I was kind of a full-time student and part-time warrior," Raul Masvidal had recalled the afternoon we spoke. "In those days the CIA had these infiltration teams in the Florida Keys, and they ran sporadic missions to Cuba."

These training camps in the Keys, which appear to have been simultaneously run by the CIA and, in what was after the Cuban missile crisis a further convolution of the disposal problem, periodically raided by the FBI, do not much figure in the literature of the Kennedy administration. Theodore C. Sorensen, in *Kennedy*, mentioned "a crackdown by Federal authorities on the publicity-seeking Cuban refugee groups who conducted hit-and-run raids on Cuban ports and shipping," further distancing the "publicity-seeking Cuban refugee groups" from the possessive plural of the White House by adding that they damaged "little other than our efforts to persuade the Soviets to leave." Arthur M. Schlesinger, Jr., elided this Miami action altogether in *A Thousand Days*, an essentially antihistorical work in which the entire matter of the Cuban exiles is seen to have resolved itself on an inspirational note in December of 1962, when Jacqueline Kennedy stood at the Orange Bowl before the Bay of Pigs veterans, 1,113 of whom had just returned from imprisonment in Cuba, and said, in Spanish, that she wanted her son to be "a man at least half as brave as the members of Brigade 2506." In his more complex reconsideration of the period, *Robert Kennedy and His Times*, Schlesinger did deal with the Miami action, but with so profound a queasiness as to suggest that the question of whether the United States government had or had not been involved with it ("But had CIA been up to its old tricks?") remained obscure, as if unknowable.

Such accounts seem, in Miami, where an impressive amount of the daily business of the city is carried on by men who speak casually of having run missions for the CIA, remote to the point of the delusional. According to reports published in 1975 and 1976 and prompted by hearings before the Church committee, the Senate Select Committee to Study Governmental Operations with Respect to Intelligence Operations, the CIA's JM/WAVE station on the University of Miami campus was by 1962 the largest CIA installation, outside Langley, in the world, and one of the largest employers in the state of Florida. There were said to have been at JM/WAVE headquarters between 300 and 400 case officers from the CIA's clandestine services branch. Each case officer was said to have run between four and ten Cuban "principal agents," who were referred to in code as "amots." Each principal agent was said to have run in turn between ten and thirty "regular agents," again mainly exiles.

JOAN DIDION

The arithmetic here is impressive. Even the minimum figures, 300 case officers each running 4 principal agents who in turn ran 10 regular agents, yield 12,000 regular agents. The maximum figures yield 120,000 regular agents, each of whom might be presumed to have contacts of his own. There were, all operating under the JM/WAVE umbrella, flotillas of small boats. There were mother ships, disguised as merchant vessels, what an unidentified CIA source described to the *Herald* as "the third largest navy in the western hemisphere." There was the CIA's Miami airline, Southern Air Transport, acquired in 1960 and subsequently financed through its holding company, Actus Technology Inc., and through another CIA holding company, the Pacific Corporation, with more than $16.7 million in loans from the CIA's Air America and an additional $6.6 million from the Manufacturers Hanover Trust Company. There were hundreds of pieces of Miami real estate, residential bungalows maintained as safe houses, waterfront properties maintained as safe harbors. There were, besides the phantom "Zenith Technological Services" that was JM/WAVE headquarters itself, fifty-four other front businesses, providing employment and cover and various services required by JM/WAVE operations. There were CIA boat shops. There were CIA gun shops. There were CIA travel agencies and there were CIA real-estate agencies and there were CIA detective agencies.

Anyone who spent any time at all on the street in Miami during the early 1960s, then, was likely to have had dealings with the CIA, to have known what actions were being run, to have known who was running them, and for whom. Among Cubans of his generation in Miami, Raul Masvidal was perhaps most unusual in that he did not actually run the missions himself. "I was more an assistant to the person who was running the program," he had said the day we talked. "Helping with the logistics. Making sure the people got fed and had the necessary weapons. It was a frustrating time, because you could see the pattern right away. The pattern was for a decline in activity toward Castro. We were just being kept busy. For two reasons. One reason was that it provided a certain amount of intelligence in which the CIA was interested."

Raul Masvidal is wary, almost impassive. He speaks carefully, in the even cadences of American management, the cadences

470

of someone who received a degree in international business at
Thunderbird, the American Graduate School of International
Management in Arizona, and had been by the time he was thirty
a vice president of Citibank in New York and Madrid, and this
was one of the few occasions during our conversation when he
allowed emotion to enter his voice. "The other reason," he said,
"was that it was supposed to keep people in Miami thinking that
something was being done. The fact that there were a few Cubans
running around Miami saying that they were being trained, that
they were running missions—well, it kept up a few hopes." Raul
Masvidal paused. "So I guess that was important to the CIA,"
he said then. "To try to keep people here from facing the very
hard and very frustrating fact that they were not going home
because their strongest and best ally had made a deal. Behind
their backs."

Bottom soundings are hard to come by here. We are talking about 1963, the year which ended in the death of John F.
Kennedy. It was a year described by Arthur M. Schlesinger, Jr., as
one in which "the notion of invading Cuba had been dead for
years" (since the notion of invading Cuba had demonstrably not
been dead as recently as April of 1961, the "for years" is interesting on its face, and suggestive of the way in which Washington's
perception of time expands and contracts with its agenda); a year
in which, in the wake of the missile crisis and John F. Kennedy's
1962 agreement not to invade Cuba, the administration's anti-
Castro policy had been "drastically modified" and in which the
White House was in fact, as Schlesinger put it, "drifting toward
accommodation." It was a year in which the official and well-
publicized Washington policy toward Miami exile operations was
one of unequivocal discouragement and even prosecution, a year
of repeated exile arrests and weapons seizures; a year that was
later described by the chief of station for JM/WAVE, in testimony before the Church committee, as one in which "the whole
apparatus of government, Coast Guard, Customs, Immigration
and Naturalization, FBI, CIA, were working together to try to
keep these operations from going to Cuba." (The chief of station
for JM/WAVE in 1963 happened to be Theodore Shackley, who
left Miami in 1965, spent from 1966 until 1972 as political officer and chief of station in Vientiane and Saigon, and turned up
in 1987 in the Tower Commission report, meeting on page B-3

in Hamburg with Manucher Ghorbanifar and with the former head of SAVAK counterespionage; discussing on page B-11 the hostage problem over lunch with Michael Ledeen.)

On the one hand "the whole apparatus of government" did seem to be "working together to try to keep these operations from going to Cuba," and on the other hand the whole apparatus of government seemed not to be doing this. There was still, it turned out, authorized CIA funding for such "autonomous operations" (a concept devised by Walt Whitman Rostow at the State Department) as the exile action group JURE, or Junta Revolucionaria Cubana, an "autonomous operation" being an operation, according to guidelines summarized in a CIA memorandum, with which the United States, "if ever charged with complicity," would deny having anything to do. "Autonomous operations" were, it turned out, part of the "track two" approach, which, whatever it meant in theory, meant for example in practice that JURE could, on "track two," request and receive explosives and grenades from the CIA even as, on track one, JURE was being investigated for possession of illegal firearms by the FBI and the INS.

"Track two" and "autonomous operations" were of course Washington phrases, phrases from the special vocabulary of Special Groups and Standing Groups and "guidelines" and "approaches," words from a language in which deniability was built into the grammar, and as such may or may not have had a different meaning, or any meaning, in 1963 in Miami, where deniability had become in many ways the very opposite of the point. In a CIA review of various attempts between 1960 and 1963 to assassinate Fidel Castro (which were "merely one aspect of the overall active effort to overthrow the regime," in other words not exactly a third track), an internal report prepared in 1967 by the Inspector General of the CIA and declassified in 1978 for release to the House Select Committee on Assassinations, there appears, on the matter of Washington language, this instructive reflection:

> ... There is a third point, which was not directly made by any of those we interviewed, but which emerges clearly from the interviews and from reviews of files. The point is that of frequent resort to synecdoche—the mention of a part when the whole is to be understood, or vice versa. Thus, we encounter repeated references to phrases such as "disposing

of Castro," which may be read in the narrow, literal sense
of assassinating him, when it is intended that it be read in
the broader, figurative sense of dislodging the Castro regime.
Reversing the coin, we find people speaking vaguely of
"doing something about Castro" when it is clear that what
they have specifically in mind is killing him. In a situation
wherein those speaking may not have actually meant what
they seemed to say or may not have said what they actually
meant, they should not be surprised if their oral shorthand is
interpreted differently than was intended.

In the superimposition of the Washington dreamwork on that
of Miami there has always been room, in other words, for everyone
to believe what they need to believe. Arthur M. Schlesinger, Jr., in
Robert Kennedy and His Times, finally went so far as to conclude
that the CIA had during 1963 in Miami continued to wage what
he still preferred to call "its private war against Castro," or had "evidently" done so, "despite," as he put it, in a clause that suggests the
particular angle of deflection in the superimposition, "the lack of
Special Group authorization." Asked at a press conference in May
of 1963 whether either the CIA or the White House was supporting exile paramilitary operations, John F. Kennedy said this: "We
may well be ... well, none that I am familiar with ... I don't think
as of today that we are." What James Angleton, who was then chief
of counterintelligence for the CIA, was later quoted as having said
about the year 1963 in Miami, and about what the CIA was or was
not doing, with or without Special Group authorization, was this:
"The concept of Miami was correct. In a Latino area, it made sense
to have a base in Miami for Latin American problems, as an extension of the desk. If it had been self-contained, then it would have
had the quality of being a foreign base of sorts. It was a novel idea.
But it got out of hand, it became a power unto itself. And when
the target diminishes, it's very difficult for a bureaucracy to adjust.
What do you do with your personnel? We owed a deep obligation
to the men in Miami."

In Washington in 1962, according to a footnote in *Robert Kennedy
and His Times*, "the regular Special Group—[Maxwell] Taylor,
McGeorge Bundy, Alexis Johnson, [Roswell] Gilpatric, [Lyman]

Lemnitzer and [John] McCone—would meet at two o'clock every Thursday afternoon. When its business was finished, Robert Kennedy would arrive, and it would expand into the Special Group (CI). At the end of the day, Cuba would become the subject, and the group, with most of the same people, would metamorphose into Special Group (Augmented)." 12.756 ptThat was the context in which those people with the most immediate interest in the policy of the United States toward Cuba appear, during the years of the Kennedy administration, to have been talking in Washington. This was the context in which those people with the same interest during the same years appear, according to testimony later given before the Church committee by the 1963 chief of station for JM/WAVE, to have been talking in Miami: "'Assassination' was part of the ambience of that time ... nobody could be involved in Cuban operations without having had some sort of discussion at some time with some Cuban who said ... the way to create a revolution is to shoot Fidel and Raúl ... so the fact that somebody would talk about assassination just wasn't anything really out of the ordinary at that time."

What John F. Kennedy actually said when he held the 2506 flag in his hands at the Orange Bowl on December 29, 1962, was this: "I can assure you that this flag will be returned to this brigade in a free Havana." How Theodore C. Sorensen described this was as "a supposed Kennedy promise for a second invasion." How Arthur M. Schlesinger, Jr., described it was as "a promise," but one "not in the script," a promise made "in the emotion of the day." What Jorge Mas Canosa said about it, that morning in the office with the LONG LIVE FREE GRENADA poster and the framed photographs of figures from yet another administration, the office in the construction yard forty minutes down the South Dixie Highway, a forty-minute drive down a flat swamp of motor home rentals and discount water-bed sales and boat repairs and bird and reptile sales and Midas Mufflers and Radio Shacks, was this: "I remember that later some people here made a joke about President Kennedy and that promise." Jorge Mas Canosa had again drawn out the syllables, *Pre-see-dent Ken-ned-ee*, and I listened closely, because, during a considerable amount of time spent listening to exiles in Miami talk about the promise John F. Kennedy made at the Orange Bowl, I had not before heard anything approaching a joke. "The joke," Jorge Mas Canosa said, "was that the 'Free Havana' he meant was a bar by that name here in Miami."

9

TO SPEND TIME in Miami is to acquire a certain fluency in cognitive dissonance. What Allen Dulles called the disposal problem is what Miami calls *la lucha*. One man's loose cannon is another's freedom fighter, or, in the local phrase, man of action, or man of valor. "This is a thing for men of valor, not for weaklings like you," an exile named Miriam Arocena had told the *Miami Herald* reporter who tried to interview her after the arrest of her husband, Eduardo Arocena, who was finally convicted, in a series of trials which ended a few days before the Bay of Pigs twenty-fourth anniversary observances at the 2506 bungalow and at the Martyrs of Girón monument and at the chapel which faces Cuba, of seventy-one federal counts connected with bombings in New York and Miami and with the 1980 assassination in New York of Félix García Rodríguez, an attaché at the Cuban mission to the United Nations, as well as with the attempted assassination the same year of Raúl Roa Kouri, at that time the Cuban ambassador to the United Nations.

The Florida bombings in question had taken place, between 1979 and 1983, at the Mexican consulate in Miami, at the Venezuelan consulate in Miami, and at various Miami businesses rumored in the exile community to have had dealings with, or sympathy for, or perhaps merely indifference toward, the current government of Cuba. None of these bombings had caused deaths or mutilations, although bombings which did had become commonplace enough in Miami during the 1970s to create a market for devices designed to flick the ignition in a parked car by remote signal, enabling the intended victim to watch what might have been his own incineration from across the street, an interested bystander.

Many of the bombings mentioned in the government's case against Eduardo Arocena involved what the FBI called his signature, a pocket-watch timer with a floral backpiece. All had been claimed, in communiqués to local Spanish radio stations

476

and newspapers, by Omega 7, which was by the time of these Arocena trials perhaps the most extensively prosecuted and so the most widely known of all the exile action groups operating out of Miami and New Jersey, where there had been since the beginning of the exile a small but significant exile concentration. Omega 7, the leader of which used the code name "Omar," was said by the FBI to have been involved in not only the machine-gunning in Queens of Felíx García Rodríguez and the attempted car-bombing in Manhattan of Raúl Roa Kouri (whose driver had discovered the bag of plastique under the car, which was parked at 12 East Eighty-first Street) but also in the 1979 murder in Union City, New Jersey, of Eulalio José Negrin, an exile who supported the normalization of relations between the United States and Cuba and so was killed by a fusillade of semiautomatic fire as he got into a car with his thirteen-year-old son.

Omega 7 had claimed, in New York, the 1979 TWA terminal bombing at Kennedy airport. Omega 7 had claimed the 1978 Avery Fisher Hall bombing at Lincoln Center. Omega 7 had claimed, in Manhattan alone, the 1975 and 1977 bombings of the Venezuelan Mission to the United Nations on East Fifty-first Street, the 1976 and 1978 bombings at the Cuban Mission to the United Nations on East Sixty-seventh Street, the two 1979 bombings of the relocated Cuban Mission to the United Nations on Lexington Avenue, the 1979 bombing of the Soviet Mission to the United Nations on East Sixty-seventh Street, the 1978 bombing of the office of *El Diario–La Prensa* on Hudson Street, the 1980 bombing of the Soviet Union's Aeroflot ticket office on Fifth Avenue, and, by way of protesting the inclusion of Cuban boxers on the card at Madison Square Garden, the 1978 bomb-ing of the adjacent Gerry Cosby Sporting Goods store at 2 Penn Plaza.

The issue in dispute, then, during the three trials that made up *United States of America* v. *Eduardo Arocena*, the first in New York and the second and third in Miami, was not whether Omega 7 had committed the acts mentioned in the indictments, but whether Eduardo Arocena was in fact its leader, "Omar." The government continued to maintain, with considerable success, that he was. Eduardo Arocena continued to maintain that he was not, notwithstanding the fact that he had in 1982 talked at some length to the FBI, in a room at the Ramada Inn near the Miami airport, about Omega 7 actions; had declared during his New York trial that he "unconditionally supported" those actions; and had advised the second of his Miami juries that they had in him "the most confirmed terrorist of all," one who would never repent. "*Padre*, forgive them," Eduardo Arocena had said when this jury handed down its verdicts of guilty on all counts. "For they know not what they do." Miriam Arocena, a small intense woman who strained forward in her seat during testimony and moved to crouch protectively behind her husband whenever the lawyers were conferring with the judge, had called the trial a "comedy," "a farce the government of the United States is carrying out in order to benefit Fidel Castro."

Early in the course of this third Arocena trial I had spent some time at the federal courthouse in downtown Miami, watching the federal prosecutors enter their physical evidence, the wigs and the hairpieces and the glue and the Samsonite attaché cases ("Contents—one pair black gloves, one cheesecloth Handi Wipe rag," or "Contents—one .38-caliber revolver") seized at the bungalow on Southwest Seventh Street in which Eduardo Arocena had been apprehended: an entire modus operandi for the hypothetical Omar, conjured up from the brassbound trunks which the prosecution hauled into court every morning. There was the Browning 9mm pistol. There was the sales receipt for the Browning, as well as for the .25-caliber Beretta Jetfire, the AR-15, and the UZI. There were the timers and there were the firecracker fuses. There were the Eveready Energizer alkaline batteries. There was the target list, with the names and the locations of offending businesses, some of them underscored: *Réplica* magazine, Padron Cigars, Almacén El Español, Ebenezer Trading Agency, a half dozen others. All that was missing finally was the explosive material itself, the stuff, the dynamite or the plastique, but the defendant, according to the government, had already advised the FBI that the military plastique called C-4 could be readily obtained on the street in Miami.

This was all engrossing, not least because it was curiously artless, devoid of much instinct for the clandestine, the wigs and the hairpieces notwithstanding. The sales receipts for the Browning and for the Beretta and for the AR-15 and for the UZI were in the defendant's own name. The target list bore on its upper-left-hand corner the notation TARGETS, suggesting an indifference to discovery which tended to undermine the government's exhaustive cataloging of that which had been discovered. A man who buys a Browning and a Beretta and an AR-15 and an UZI under his own name does not have as his first interest the successful evasion of American justice. A man who compiles a target list under the heading TARGETS may in fact have a first interest best served by disclosure, the inclination toward public statement natural to someone who sees himself as engaged not in a crime but a crusade. HEROES DE OMEGA 7, as the Omega 7 stencils were lettered. The stencils were Exhibit 3036, recovered by the FBI from a self-storage locker on Southwest Seventy-second Street. LA VERDAD ES NUESTROS.

There was flickering all through this presentation of the government's evidence a certain stubborn irritability, a sense of crossed purposes, crossed wires, of cultures not exactly colliding but glancing off one another, at unpromising angles. Eduardo Arocena's attorney, a rather rumpled Cuban who had adopted as his general strategy the argument that this trial was taking place at all only because the United States had caved in to what he called "the international community," looked on with genial contempt. The government attorneys, young and well-pressed, rummaged doggedly through their trunks, property masters for what had become in Miami, after some years of trials in which the defense talked about the international community and the prosecution about cheesecloth Handi Wipe rags, a kind of local puppet theater, to which the audience continued to respond in ways novel to those unfamiliar with the form.

This was a theater in which the defendant was always cast as the hero and martyr, not at all because the audience believed him wrongly accused, innocent of whatever charges had been trumped up against him, but precisely because the audience believed him to be guilty. The applause, in other words, was for the action, not for the actor. "Anybody who fights communism has my sympathy," the head of the 2506 Brigade told the *Miami Herald* at the time of Eduardo Arocena's arrest. "The best communist is a dead communist. If that is his way to fight, I won't condemn him." Andres Nazario Sargen of Alpha 66 had said this: "He is a person who chose that path for the liberation of Cuba. We have to respect his position but we think our methods are more effective."

479

Nor was this response confined exclusively to those members of the audience who, like the men of the 2506 or Alpha 66, might be expected to exhibit a certain institutional tolerance toward bombing as a political tactic. "It's like asking the Palestinian people about Arafat," the news director of WQBA, the Miami radio station that calls itself *La Cubanísima*, had said to the *Herald* about Eduardo Arocena. "He may be a terrorist, but to the Palestinian people he's not thought of that way." All *el exilio* stood by its men of action. When, for example, after Eduardo Arocena's arrest in July of 1983, a fund for his defense was organized within the exile community, one of the contributors was Xavier Suarez, who was that year running a losing campaign for the post to which he was later elected, mayor of Miami. Xavier Suarez was brought to this country as a child, in 1960. He is a graduate of Villanova. He is a graduate of Harvard Law. He has a master's degree in public policy from the John F. Kennedy School of Government at Harvard. He said about Eduardo Arocena that he preferred to think of him not as a terrorist, but a freedom fighter.

Sometimes (when, say, Xavier Suarez says that he prefers to think of Eduardo Arocena not as a terrorist but a freedom fighter, or when, say, Xavier Suarez stands on the back of a Mazda pickup and speaks of the right to be on the other side of the street as unfortunate) words are believed in Miami to be without consequence. Other times they are not. Among the bombs which Omega 7 was credited with having left around Miami in January of 1983, a period of considerable industry for Omega 7, was one at the office of *Réplica*, a Spanish-language weekly largely devoted to soft news and entertainment gossip (CATHY LEE CROSBY: EL SEXO ES MUY IMPORTANTE PARA ELLA is a not atypical photo caption) and edited by an exile named Max Lesnik. Max Lesnik was, in the period after Fidel Castro's 1953 attack on the Moncada Barracks, a youth leader in the Cuban People's Party, the party founded by Eduardo Chibás and known as the "Ortodoxo" party. Opposed to Batista, Max Lesnik was also opposed to Castro, on the grounds that he and his 26 Julio were destructive to the anti-Batista movement. During the time Castro was in the Sierra Maestra, Max Lesnik was working underground in Havana against Batista, not with the 26 Julio but with the Segundo Frente del Escambray, and it was he, in the waning days of 1958, who interested the CIA in the last-ditch attempt to bring Carlos Prío back from Miami as Batista's successor. He made his final break with Castro, and with Cuba, in 1961.

This demonstrable lack of enthusiasm for Fidel Castro notwithstanding, Max Lesnik was considered, by some people in Miami, insufficiently anti-Castro, principally because he, or *Réplica*, had a history of using what were seen to be the wrong words. "Negotiation," for example, was a wrong word, and so, in this context, was "political," as in "a political approach." A political approach implied give-and-take, even compromise, an unthinkable construct in a community organized exclusively around the principle of implacable resistance, and it was the occasional discussion of such an approach in the pages of *Réplica* that had caused *Réplica* to be underscored on Eduardo Arocena's target list, and five bombs to have been left at the *Réplica* office between 1981 and 1984.

Some of *Réplica*'s trouble on this point dated from 1974, when a contributor named Luciano Nieves suggested that the way to bring Fidel Castro down might be "politically," by working with Cubans within Cuba in an effort to force elections and the acceptance of a legal opposition. Someone who did not agree with Luciano Nieves broke a chair over his head in the Versailles, a Cuban restaurant on Southwest Eighth Street where many of the more visible figures in *el exilio* turn up late in the evening. Several other people who did not agree with Luciano Nieves conspired to try, in November of 1974, to assassinate him, a count on which three members of an action group called the Pragmatistas were later tried and convicted, but Luciano Nieves, and *Réplica*, persisted.

In February of 1975, two days after *Réplica* published his declaration that he would return to Cuba to participate in any election Fidel Castro should call, Luciano Nieves was shot and killed, in the parking lot of Variety Children's Hospital in Miami, an event construed locally as his own fault. "I'm glad I never finally came out publicly in favor of peaceful coexistence with Castro," an unidentified professor at what was then Miami-Dade Junior College was quoted as having said a few days later in the *Miami News*, in a story headlined INTELLECTUALS FEARFUL AFTER

CUBAN KILLING. "Now, I'll be more than careful not to. Cubans are apparently very sensitive to that." The incident in the parking lot of Variety Children's Hospital was mentioned to me by a number of people during the time I spent in Miami, always to this corrective point.

THE BOMB EDUARDO Arocena was believed to have left at the *Réplica* office in January of 1983 did not, as it happened, go off, but another bomb credited that month to Omega 7 did, this one at a factory on Flagler Street owned by an exiled cigar manufacturer named Orlando Padron. Orlando Padron's treason, as it was viewed by many, had been to visit Havana in 1978 (he was said to have been photographed handing Fidel Castro a Padron cigar) as a member of the "Committee of 75," a participant in what was called the *diálogo*, or dialogue, a word with the same reverberations as "political."

The *diálogo* began as an essay into private diplomacy on the part of a prominent exile banker, Bernardo Benes, whose somewhat visionary notion it was that the exiles themselves, with the tacit cooperation of the Carter administration, could, in what was to become a series of visits to Havana, open a continuing discussion with the Cuban government. Secretary of State Cyrus Vance was approached. The National Security Council and the CIA and the FBI were consulted. The visits to Havana took place, and resulted in two concessions, one an agreement by the Cuban government to release certain political prisoners, some thirty-six hundred in all, the other an agreement allowing exiles who wished to visit relatives in Cuba to do so on seven-day package tours.

Such agreements might have seemed, outside Miami, unexceptionable. Such agreements might even have seemed, outside Miami, to serve the interests of the exile community, but to think this would be to miss the drift of the exile style. Americans, it is often said in Miami, will act always in their own interests, an indictment. Miami Cubans, by implicit contrast, take their stand on a higher ground, *la lucha* as a sacred abstraction, and any talk about "interests," or for that matter "agreements," remains alien to the local temperament, which is absolutist, and sacrificial, on the Spanish model.

Which is to say on the Cuban model. "... I feel my belief in sacrifice and struggle getting stronger," Fidel Castro wrote from his prison cell on the Isle of Pines on December 19, 1953. "I despise the kind of existence that clings to the miserly trifles of comfort and self-interest. I think that a man should not live beyond the age when he begins to deteriorate, when the flame that lighted the brightest moment of his life has weakened ..." In exile as well as in situ, this is the preferred Cuban self-perception, the same idealization of gesture and intention which led, in the months and years after the *diálogo*, to bombings and assassinations and to public occasions of excoriation and recantation, to accusations and humiliations which broke some and estranged many; an unloosing of fratricidal furies from which *el exilio* did not entirely recover.

Bernardo Benes, the architect of the *diálogo* and its principal surviving victim, arrived at the Miami airport, alone, on November 11, 1960, a day he recalls as the bleakest of his life. He recalls believing that the exile would last at most nine months. He recalls himself as unprepared in every way to accept the exile as an immigration, and yet, like many of the early exiles, a significant number of whom had been educated to move in the necessarily international commercial life of prerevolutionary Havana, Bernardo Benes apparently managed to maintain the notion of Florida as a kind of colonial opportunity, an India to be tapped, and in this spirit he prospered, first as an officer of a Miami savings and loan, Washington Federal, and then as a local entrepreneur. He was, for example, the first exile to own a major automobile dealership in Miami. He was among the first exiles to start a bank in Miami, the Continental. He was also, and this continued to be, in the culturally resistant world of *el exilio*, a more ambiguous distinction, the first exile to travel what has been in provincial American cities a traditional road to assimilation, the visible doing of approved works, the act of making oneself available for this steering committee, for that kickoff dinner.

"I am frank," Bernardo Benes said when I talked to him one morning at his house on Biscayne Bay. "I do not beat around the bush. Until 1977, 1978, I was The Cuban in Miami. This goes back to when I was still at Washington Federal, I was chief of all the branches, I was the contact for Latin America. So sometimes I was working twenty hours a day to make the time, but believe me, I did. There was nothing important happening in Miami that I wasn't involved with. I was the guerrilla in the establishment, the first person to bring other Cubans into the picture." Bernardo Benes paused. "I and I and I and I," he said finally. "And then came the big change in my life. I was no longer the first token Cuban in Miami. I was the Capitán Dreyfus of Miami."

We were sitting at the kitchen counter, drinking the caffeine and sugar infusion that is Cuban coffee, and as Bernardo Benes began to talk about the *diálogo* and its aftermath he glanced repeatedly at his wife, a strikingly attractive woman who was clearing the breakfast dishes with the brisk, definite movements of someone who has only a limited enthusiasm for the discussion at hand. The *diálogo*, Bernardo Benes said, had come about by "pure chance." There had been, he said, a family vacation in Panama. There had been in Panama, he said, a telephone call from a friend, an entreaty to have lunch with two officers of the Cuban government. This lunch in Panama, he said, had been "the beginning of the end."

There was about this account a certain foretold quality, a collapsing of sequence, as in a dream, or an accident report taken from the sole survivor. Somewhere after the beginning there had been the meetings in Washington with Cyrus Vance and the involvement of the FBI and the CIA and the National Security Council. Somewhere before the end there had been the meetings in Havana with Fidel Castro, 14 meetings, 120 hours during which the first exile to own a major automobile dealership in Miami talked one on one with the number one most hated man in Miami.

The end itself, what Bernardo Benes called the castigation, the casting out, had of course been in Miami, and it had begun, as many such scourgings have begun in Miami, with the long invective exhortations of those Spanish-language radio stations on which *el exilio* depends not only for news but for the daily dissemination of rumor and denunciation. Bernardo Benes was said on the radio to be a communist. Bernardo Benes was said to be a Castro agent. Bernardo Benes was said to be at best a *tonto útil*, or *idiota útil*, a useful fool, which is what exiles call one another when they wish to step back from the precipice of the legally actionable.

"This is Miami," Bernardo Benes said about the radio attacks. "Pure Miami. A million Cubans are blackmailed, totally controlled, by three radio stations. I feel sorry for the Cuban community in Miami. Because they have imposed on themselves, by way of the Right, the same condition that Castro has imposed on Cuba. Total intolerance. And ours is worse. Because it is entirely voluntary."

Bernardo Benes again glanced at his wife, who stood now against the kitchen sink, her arms folded. "My bank was picketed for three weeks." He shrugged. "Every morning when I walked in, twenty or thirty people would be screaming whatever they could think to call me. Carrying signs. Telling people to close their accounts. If I went to a restaurant with my wife, people would come to the table and call me names. But maybe the worst was something I learned only a few months ago. My children never told me at the time, my wife never told me, they knew what I was going through. Here is what I just learned: my children's friends were never allowed to come to our house. Because their parents were afraid. All the parents were afraid their children might be at our house when the bomb went off."

This would not have been a frivolous fear. The *diálogo* took place in the fall of 1978. In April of 1979 a twenty-six-year-old participant in the *diálogo* named Carlos Muñiz Varela was murdered in San Juan, Puerto Rico, by a group calling itself "Comando Cero." In November of 1979 there was the murder in Union City of another participant in the *diálogo*, Eulalio José Negrín, the one who was stepping into his car with his son when two men in ski masks appeared and the fusillade started. The October 1978 bombing at *El Diario-La Prensa* in New York was connected to the *diálogo*: the newspaper had run an editorial in favor of the arrangement allowing exiles to visit Cuba. The March 1979 bombing at Kennedy airport (the bomb was in a suitcase about to be loaded into the hold of an L-1011, TWA #17, due to leave for Los Angeles twelve minutes later with more than 150 people already aboard) was connected to the *diálogo*: TWA had provided equipment for some charters to Cuba.

The scars *el exilio* inflicts upon its own do not entirely heal, nor are they meant to. Seven years after the *diálogo*, when Bernardo Benes's daughter was shopping at Burdines and presented her father's credit card, the saleswoman, a Cuban, looked at the name, handed back the card, and walked away. Bernardo Benes himself sold his business interests, and is no longer so visible a presence around Miami. "You move on," he said. "For example something has happened in my life at age fifty. I have become hedonistic. I lost twenty-five pounds, I joined a sauna, and in my garage you will find a new convertible. Which I drive around Miami. With the top down."

Bernardo Benes and I spoke, that morning in the pleasant house on Biscayne Bay, for an hour or so. From the windows of that house it was possible to look across the bay at the Miami skyline, at buildings through which Bernardo Benes had moved as someone entitled. Mrs. Benes spoke only once, to interrupt her husband with a protective burst of vehement Spanish. "No Cubans will read what she writes," Bernardo Benes said in English. "You will be surprised," his wife said in English. "Anything I say can be printed, that's the price of being married to me, I'm a tough cookie," Bernardo Benes said in English. "All right," his wife said, in English, and she walked away. "You just make your life insurance more."

SOME EXILES IN Miami will now allow that Bernardo Benes was perhaps a sacrificial victim, the available if accidental symbol of a polarization within the exile which had actually begun some years before, and had brought into question the very molecular code of the community, its opposition to Fidel Castro. There were at the time of the *diálogo*, and are still, certain exiles, most of them brought to the United States as children, fewer of them living now in Miami than in New York and Washington, who were not in fact opposed to Fidel Castro. Neither were many of them exactly pro-Castro, except to the extent that they believed that there was still in progress in Cuba a revolutionary process, and that this process, under the direction of Fidel Castro or not under the direction of Fidel Castro, should continue. *Somos Cubanos*, the editors of *Areíto*, published as a quarterly by the Círculo de Cultura Cubana in New York, had declared in their first issue, in April 1974. "While recognizing that the revolutionary process has implied sacrifices, sufferings and errors," the *Areíto* manifesto had continued, "we maintain that Cuba in 1958 needed measures capable of radically transforming its political, social and economic structures. We understand that that process has established the basis for a more just and egalitarian society, and that it has irreversibly taken root in Cuban society."

The editors of *Areíto* had put the name of the Havana poet Roberto Fernández Retamar on their masthead, and also that of Gabriel García Márquez. In 1984, for the tenth anniversary issue, they had reprinted the 1974 manifesto, and added: "Solidarity with the Cuban revolution was and is a position based on principle for our Editorial Board.... The ten years that have passed took us on a return trip to Cuba, to confront for ourselves in its entirety the complexity of that society, and by that token, to rid ourselves of the romantic notions which were typical of our group at that time.... Because of that, today we assume our position with more firmness and awareness of its consequences."

Areíto contributors thought of themselves less as exiles than as "Cubans outside Cuba," and of exile Miami, in the words of this tenth anniversary issue, as "the deformed foetus of Meyer Lansky, the Cuban lumpen bourgeoisie and the North American security state."

The *Grupo Areíto*, as *Areíto*'s editors and contributors came to call themselves, had perhaps never represented more than a very small number of exiles, but these few were young, articulate, and determined to be heard. There had been members of the *Areíto* group involved in the Washington lobby originally called the Cuban-American Committee for the Normalization of Relations with Cuba, not to be confused with its polar opposite, the Cuban American National Foundation. There had been members of the *Areíto* group involved with Bernardo Benes in those visits to Cuba which constituted the *diálogo*. (Carlos Muñiz Varela, the member of the Committee of 75 who had been assassinated in 1979 in San Juan, Puerto Rico, was a founder of *Areíto*.) There had been members of the *Areíto* group involved in the inception of the Antonio Maceo Brigade, which was organized along the lines of the largely Anglo Venceremos Brigade and offered working sojourns in Cuba to, in the words of its 1978 statement of purpose, "any young Cuban who (1) left Cuba by family decision, (2) has not participated in counterrevolutionary activities and would not support violence against the revolution, and (3) defines him or herself as opposed to the blockade and in favor of the normalization of relations between the United States and Cuba."

These children of *el exilio* who had taken to talking about the deformed foetus of the North American security state and to writing articles with such titles as "Introduction to the Sandinista Documentary Cinema" were not, in other words, pursuing a course which was likely to slip the attention of exile Miami, nor did it. There were bombings. There were death threats. Members of the Antonio Maceo Brigade were referred to as *traidores*, traitors, and the brigade itself as a demonic strategy by which Fidel Castro hoped to divide the exile along generational lines. *Areíto* was said in Miami to be directly funded by the Cuban government, a charge its editors dismissed as a slander, in fact a *cantinela*, the kind of repeated refrain that set the teeth on edge. "It's very difficult for people like us, who maintain a position like we

do, to live in Miami," an *Areíto* board member named Marifeli
Pérez-Stable told the *Miami Herald* in 1983, by way of explaining why she lived in New York. "Everybody knows everything,
and it makes it difficult for those who are fingered as having a
pro-Castro position to do something as simple as going to the
market."

Marifeli Pérez-Stable was in 1983, when she spoke to the
Herald, thirty-four. Lourdes Casal, a founder of *Areíto* and for
many people its personification, was in 1981, when she died in
Havana, forty-two. *Areíto* was published not at all during 1985 or
1986. Time passes and heat goes, although less reliably in Miami,
where, at the "First Annual Festival of Hispanic Theatre" in May
of 1986, all scheduled performances of a one-act play by a New
York playwright and former *Areíto* contributor named Dolores
Prida were, after several days of radio alarms and a bomb threat,
canceled.

The play itself, *Coser y Cantar*, described by the *Herald* theater
reviewer as "pleasant if flawed," a "modest piece" about an
Hispanic woman living in New York and her Anglo alter ego (the
latter wants to make lists and march at the United Nations, the
former to read *Vanidades* and shop for sausage at Casa Moneo),
seemed not to be the question here. The question seemed to be
Dolores Prida's past, which included connections with *Areíto* and
with the *diálogo* and with the Cuban-American Committee, three
strikes against her in a city where even one proved allegiance
to what was referred to locally as "the so-called Cuban 'revolution.'" Dolores Prida was said by the news director of WQBA-*La
Cubanísima* to be "an enemy of the exiles." That Dolores Prida
should even think of visiting Miami was said by Metro-Dade
commissioner George Valdes to be "a Castroite and communist
plan ... a tactic of the Cuban government to divide us and make
us look bad."

Nonetheless, at the height of her local celebrity, Dolores
Prida did visit Miami, where, as part of a conference at Miami-
Dade Community College on "The Future of Hispanic Theatre
in Miami: Goals and Constraints," she supervised a previously
unscheduled reading of *Coser y Cantar*, the audience for which
had been frisked by Miami police with handheld metal detectors. Dolores Prida told the *Herald* that the word "communist"
was used so loosely in Miami that she did not know what it

meant. "If you're progressive," Dolores Prida said, "you're a communist." Dolores Prida told the *Herald* that the only card she carried was American Express. Dolores Prida, who was at the time of this dispute forty-three years old, also told the *Herald* that the only city other than Miami in which she had ever been afraid to express herself, the only other place "where people look over their shoulder to see if they can say what they were going to say," was Havana.

In many ways these midlife survivors of what had been a student movement seem familiar to us. We have met, if not them, their American-born counterparts, people who at one time thought and in many cases still think along lines they might or might not call, as the *Areíto* group often called itself, "progressive." These were exiles who, to at least some extent, thought of America's interests as their own, and of America's issues as their own; who seemed to fall, in a way that Miami exiles often did not, within the American experience. They experienced for example the Vietnam War, and the movement against it, as their own, in a way that many Miami exiles, some of whom told me that they had avoided the draft not because they opposed the war but because they had been at the time engaged in a war which meant more to them, did not. They experienced the social changes of the sixties and seventies in a way that many Miami exiles did not, and they had been in some cases confused and torn by those changes, which seemed to be, in a light way, part of what Dolores Prida's play was about.

In other words they were Americans, yet they were not. *Somos Cubanos.* They remained Cubans, and they remained outside Cuba, and as Cubans outside Cuba but estranged from *el exilio* they came to occupy a particularly hermetic vacuum, one in which, as in *el exilio* itself, positions were defined and redefined and schisms were divined and dissected and a great deal of what went on floated somewhere in a diaspora of its own. I recall a 1984 issue of *Areíto* in which several pages were given over to the analysis of a schism between the *Areíto* group and the generally like-minded Institute of Cuban Studies, and of what ideological error had caused the Institute of Cuban Studies not only to suggest that the late Lourdes Casal had "deviated from the canons of socialist realism" but to misrepresent her position on the relationship between the intellectual and the Cuban revolutionary process, a position made clear for example in her later refinement of her original 1972 statement on the case of the poet Heberto Padilla. These were questions which seemed at a significant tonal remove from those then being asked in New York or New Haven or Boston or Berkeley, although not, curiously enough, from those then being asked in Miami.

On January 9, 1961, at a time when the Cuban revolution was two years under way and the 2506 Brigade was training in Guatemala for the April invasion, the United States Department of State granted to a Miami priest, Monsignor Bryan O. Walsh, the authority to grant a visa waiver to any Cuban child between the ages of six and sixteen who wished to enter the United States under the guardianship of the Catholic diocese of Miami. According to *Catholicism in South Florida: 1868–1968*, by Michael J. McNally, a Miami priest and professor of church history at St. Vincent de Paul Seminary in Boynton Beach, such waivers were issued, between January of 1961 and September of 1963, to 14,156 children, each of whom was sent alone, by parents or guardians still living in Cuba, to live in special camps established and operated by the Unaccompanied Children's Program of the Diocese of Miami.

There were, in all, six such camps, the last of which did not close until the middle of 1981. The reason that these camps were established and the Unaccompanied Children's Program was initiated, Father McNally tells us, was that, by the end of 1960, "rumors were rife" that Fidel Castro planned to send Cuban children to work on Soviet farms, and that, during 1961, "rumors spread" that Fidel Castro had still another plan, "to have children ages three to ten live in state-run dormitories, seeing their parents for only two days a month." It was "to avoid these two possibilities" that parents dispatched their children to Miami and the Unaccompanied Children's Program, which was also known, according to Father McNally, as "Operation Pedro Pan."

No spread rumor goes unrewarded. In *Contra Viento y Marea*, edited by Lourdes Casal and published in 1978 by Casa de las

Américas in Havana, there appear a number of descriptions, under the joint byline *Grupo Areíto*, of camp life as it was experienced by those who lived it. These members of the *Areíto* group who arrived in the United States as wards of Operation Pedro Pan characterized this experience, in *Contra Viento y Marea*, as "perhaps the most enduring" of their lives. They described the camps as the "prehistory" of their radicalization, the places in which they first formulated, however inchoately, the only analysis which seemed to them to explain the "lunacy," the "political troglodytism," the "traumatic experience," of having been banished by their parents to live in a barracks in a foreign country. The speakers in this part of *Contra Viento y Marea* are both those who spent time in the camps as children and those who worked in them as adults:

It was said that Monsignor Walsh ... had practically unlimited authority to issue visa waivers to children in order to "save them from communism." This episode in our recent history can be seen in retrospect as a period of near-delirium, based as it was on the insistent propaganda that the revolutionary government would strip parents of their authority and send their children to Russia. ...

The first time I began to see through and reevaluate a few things was when I was working at Opa-Locka, one of the camps where they brought the children who came alone from Cuba. Opa-Locka was managed by the Jesuits. Again and again I asked myself what had motivated these parents to send their children alone to the United States. ...

Sometimes we would give little talks to the American Legion Auxiliary ladies, who were fascinated to see these white Cubans who knew how to eat with knives and forks ... but most of all they wanted to hear the horrible story of how and why we were there: the incredible and sad tale of how communism, in order to destroy parental authority, had been going to put us on boats bound for Russia.... We would sing Cuban songs and the old ladies would go home crying.

It must be said that the Americans were using the Cubans: the mass emigration, the children who came alone ... The departure of the children was used largely as a propaganda ploy. What came out of the camps would be a wounded generation. ...

These accounts, however colored, are suggestive. The parents in Cuba had been, as the children put it together, the victims of *una estafa*, a trick, a deceit, since the distinction between being banished to camps in the USSR and banished to camps in the United States lacked, for the children, significance. The nuns in the camps, who had advised their charges that one day they would appreciate this distinction, were, as the children saw it, equally the victims of *una estafa*. The children themselves, some of whom had later become these Cubans outside Cuba but estranged from *el exilio*, these middle-aged scholars and writers whose visits to Miami necessitated metal detectors, had been, as they saw it then and saw it still, "used" by the government of the United States, "utilized" by the government of the United States, "manipulated" by the government of the United States, made by the government of the United States the victims of a "propaganda ploy"; a way of talking about the government of the United States, as it happened, indistinguishable from what was said every day in exile Miami.

"THE MIAMI EXILES are not anti-communist," an exile named Carlos M. Luis said one night at dinner. It was about eleven o'clock, the preferred hour for dinner in those exile houses where Spanish manners still prevailed, and there were at the table nine people, eight Cubans and me. There had been before Carlos Luis spoke a good deal of spirited argument. There had been a mounting rhythm of declamation and interruption. Now there was a silence. "The Miami exiles are not anti-communist," Carlos Luis repeated. "I believe this. Anti-communism is not their motivation."

Carlos Luis was the director of the Museo Cubano de Arte y Cultura in Miami, an interesting and complicated man who had entered exile with his wife in 1962, deciding to move to New York after the cultural restructuring which began in Cuba with the confiscation of Orlando Jiménez Leal's documentary film *P.M.*, or *Pasado Meridiano*, and led eventually to Fidel Castro's declaration that there was no art, or would be no art, outside the revolution. "The *P.M.* affair," as it was called in Miami, had plunged Havana into a spiral of confrontation and flagellation not unlike that which later characterized *el exilio*, and was for many a kind of turning point.

It was the *P.M.* affair, involving as it did the banning of a film showing "decadent" nightlife in Havana, which more or less codified such repressive moves as the official persecution of homosexuals later examined by Orlando Jiménez Leal and the Academy Award-winning cinematographer Nestor Almendros, by then both in exile, in *Mauvaise Conduite*. It was the *P.M.* affair which had in fact gotten Nestor Almendros, at the time a young filmmaker who had written admiringly about *P.M.*, fired from his job at *Bohemia*, the Havana weekly which had by then closed itself down and been restaffed by people closer to the direction in which the regime seemed to be moving. And it was the *P.M.* affair which had caused a number of Cuban artists and intellectuals

JOAN DIDION

to doubt that there would be room within this revolution for whatever it was that they might have valued above the revolution; to conclude that, as Carlos Luis put it, "it was time to leave, there was no more for me in staying."

"The first group left because they were Batistianos," Carlos Luis said now, reaching for a bottle of wine. "The second group left because they were losing their property." Carlos Luis paused, and poured an inch of wine into his glass. "Then," he said, "the people started coming who were unhappy because they couldn't get toothpaste."

"You mean these exiles were anti-Castro but not necessarily anti-communist," our host, an exile, said, as if to clarify the point not for himself but for me.

"Anti-Castro, yes," Carlos Luis had shrugged. "Anti-Castro it goes without saying."

That the wish to see Fidel Castro removed from power in Cuba did not in itself constitute a political philosophy was a point rather more appreciated in *el exilio*, which had as its legacy a tradition of considerable political sophistication, than in Washington, which tended to accept the issue as an idea, and so to see Cuban exiles as refugees not just from Castro but from politics. In fact exile life in Miami was dense with political distinctions, none of them exactly in the American grain. Miami was for example the only American city I had ever visited in which it was not unusual to hear one citizen describe the position of another as "Falangist," or as "essentially Nasserite." There were in Miami exiles who defined themselves as communists, anti-Castro. There were in Miami a significant number of exile socialists, also anti-Castro, but agreed on only this single issue. There were in Miami two prominent groups of exile anarchists, many still in their twenties, all anti-Castro, and divided from one another, I was told, by "personality differences," "personality differences" being the explanation Cubans tend to offer for anything from a dinner-table argument to a coup.

This urge toward the staking out of increasingly recondite positions, traditional to exile life in Europe and in Latin America, remained, in South Florida, exotic, a nervous urban brilliance not entirely apprehended by local Anglos, who continued to think of exiles as occupying a fixed place on the political spectrum, one usually described as "right-wing," or "ultraconservative." It was true enough that there were a number of exiles in Miami who believed the most effective extant political leaders in the hemisphere (aside from Fidel Castro, to whom diabolic powers were attributed) to be General Augusto Pinochet of Chile and General Alfredo Stroessner of Paraguay. In fact those two names were heard with some frequency even in the conversation of exiles who did not share this belief, usually turning up in the "as" construction, in which the speaker thinks to disarm the listener by declaring himself "every bit as hostile to the Pinochet government," or "just as unalterably opposed to General Stroessner," as to Fidel Castro. It was also true enough that there were a number of Cubans in Miami, most notably those tobacco growers who between the fall of Fulgencio Batista and the fall of Anastasio Somoza had managed to maintain their operations in Nicaragua, who supported the military leadership of the Nicaraguan contras not in spite of but precisely because of whatever association that leadership had with the Somoza militia.

Still, "right-wing," on the American spectrum, where political positions were understood as marginally different approaches to what was seen as a shared goal, seemed not to apply. This was something different, a view of politics as so central to the human condition that there may be no applicable words in the political vocabulary of most Americans. Virtually every sentient member of the Miami exile community was on any given day engaged in what was called an "ideological confrontation" with some other member of the Miami exile community, over points which were passionately debated at meals and on the radio and in the *periodiquitos*, the throwaway newspapers which appeared every week on Southwest Eighth Street. Everything was read. I was asked one day by several different people if I had seen a certain piece that morning, by a writer whose name I did not recognize. The piece, it turned out, had appeared not in the *Miami Herald* or the *Miami News*, not in *El Herald* or *Diario Las Americas*, not in any of the *periodiquitos* and not even in *The New York Times*, but in *El Tiempo*, one day late from Bogotá. Analysis was close, and overcharged. Obscure points were "clarified," and immediately "answered." The whole of exile Miami could engage itself in the morning deconstruction of, say, something said by Roberto

Fernández Retamar in Havana as reported by *El País* in Madrid and "answered" on the radio in Miami.

I talked one evening to Agustin Tamargo, an exile whose radio broadcasts with such prominent exiles as the novelist Guillermo Cabrera Infante and the poet Heberto Padilla and the legendary 26 Julio *comandante* Huber Matos, what Agustin Tamargo called "all the revolutionary people," had tended over the years to attract whatever excess animus happened to be loose in the community. "I come from a different place on the political spectrum than most of the other radio commentators here," Agustin Tamargo said. "There are many Batista people in Miami. They call me a communist because I wrote in *Bohemia*, which was to them a leftist-Marxist paper. Actually it was maybe center."

Agustin Tamargo entered exile in 1960, the year *Bohemia*, which had been perhaps the most influential voice of the anti-Batista movement, suspended its own publication with the declaration "this is a revolution betrayed." After he left Havana he was managing editor of *Bohemia*-in-exile, which was published first in New York, with what Agustin Tamargo believes to have been CIA money, and then in Caracas, with what he calls "different business partners, completely separated from American interests," the entire question of "American interests" remaining in Miami an enduring preoccupation. I recall one visit when everyone to whom I spoke seemed engaged in either an attack on or a defense of the exiled writer and former political prisoner Carlos Alberto Montaner, who had written a column from Madrid which some found, because it seemed to them to suggest that Fidel Castro could be tolerated to the extent that he could be separated from Soviet interests, insufficiently separated from American interests. I was advised by one exile that "Montaner thinks about Fidel exactly the way Reagan thinks about Fidel," not, since even those exiles who voted in large numbers for Ronald Reagan in 1980 and 1984 did so despite their conviction that he was bent on making a secret deal with Fidel Castro, an endorsement.

There seemed in fact very few weeks in Miami when, on the informal network the community used to talk to itself, one or another exile spokesman was not being excoriated on or defended against this charge of being insufficiently separated from American interests. One week it was said that the poet Jorge Valls, because he had left Cuba after twenty years in prison and

suggested on the radio in Miami that there should be "an inter-
change of ideas" between the United States and Havana, was
insufficiently separated from American interests. Another week
it was said that Armando Valladares, whose *Contra Toda Esperanza*,
an account of the twenty-two years he had spent imprisoned by
Fidel Castro, appeared in this country as *Against All Hope*, was,
because he had received support from the National Endowment
for Democracy, insufficiently separated from American interests. "There's nothing wrong with American money," Agustin
Tamargo had said the evening we talked, by way of amending an
impassioned indictment of another exile who was, he believed,
getting it. "Or Chinese money or any other kind. I will take it
if they give it to me. But only to do what I want to do. Not what
they want me to do. There is the difference."

In Miami, where he was at the time we met doing a nightly
broadcast for WOCN-Union Radio about which there was
controversy even within the station itself, Agustin Tamargo was
regarded as an eccentric and even a quixotic figure, which seemed
to be how he construed his role. "Fifty thousand people listen to
me every night," he said. "And every night I say Franco was a
killer. Every night I say Pinochet is an assassin. Most of the other
Cuban commentators here never say anything about Pinochet.
This is a program on which people say every kind of thing about
the Cuban past. We say that maybe things before the revolution
were not so golden as people here like to think. And still they
listen. Which suggests to me that maybe the exile is not so one-
sided as the communists say it is."

We were sitting that evening in an office at WOCN-Union
Radio on Flagler Street, and outside in the reception room there
was an armed security guard who would later walk Agustin
Tamargo to his car, Miami being a city in which people who
express their opinions on the radio every night tend, particularly
since 1976, when a commentator named Emilio Milian got his
legs blown off in the WQBA-*La Cubanísima* parking lot, to put
a little thought into the walk to the car. "Listen to me," Agustin
Tamargo said. "You do see a change here. A few years ago no
one in exile would admit that any kind of solution to the Cuban
situation could come from inside. They wouldn't hear of it. Now
they admit it. They admit that a rebellion inside Cuba could lead
to a military solution, a coup." Agustin Tamargo had shrugged.

"That's a real advance. A few years ago here, you said that, you got killed. Immediately."

Emilio Milian lost his legs because he suggested in a series of editorials on WQBA-*La Cubanísima* that it was counterproductive for exiles to continue bombing and assassinating one another on the streets of Miami. That this was an exceptionable opinion in an American city in 1976 was hard for some Americans to entirely appreciate, just as it was hard for some Americans, accustomed as they were to the official abhorrence of political violence, to appreciate the extent to which many people in Miami regarded such violence as an inevitable and even a necessary thread in the social fabric. The Miami City Commission in 1982 voted a ten-thousand-dollar grant to Alpha 66, which was, however venerable, however fixed an element on the Miami landscape, a serious action group, one of the twenty exile groups believed by the House Select Committee on Assassinations in 1978 to have had "the motivation, capability and resources" to have assassinated President John F. Kennedy, and one of the two, according to the committee's report, about which there were as well "indications of a possible connection with figures named in the Kennedy assassination, specifically with Lee Harvey Oswald." At a 1983 meeting, the same Miami City Commission proclaimed March twenty-fifth "Dr. Orlando Bosch Day," in recognition of the Miami pediatrician who was then imprisoned at Cuartel San Carlos in Caracas on charges of planning the bombing in 1976 of a Cubana DC-8 off Barbados, killing all seventy-three passengers, including twenty-four members of the Cuban national fencing team.

The case of Orlando Bosch was interesting. He had been, before he moved to Miami in July of 1960, the chief of the 26 Julio for Las Villas Province. During his first month in Miami he had helped to launch the insurgent group called the MIRR, the Movimiento Insurreccional de Recuperación Revolucionaria, which became known that August, when four Castro army officers and a hundred of their men deserted their posts and took up arms in the Las Villas mountains. Over the next several years in Miami, Orlando Bosch was arrested repeatedly on charges connected with MIRR activity, but was, until 1968, repeatedly acquitted. In 1968 he was finally convicted on a federal charge, that of shelling a Polish freighter in the Port of Miami, was sentenced to ten years and paroled after four. In 1974, back in Miami and subpoenaed for questioning in the assassination of an exile leader, Orlando Bosch had broken parole by fleeing the country.

There were, in all, four Cuban exiles charged by Venezuela in the 1976 Cubana bombing. Two were accused of actually placing the bomb on the plane and the other two, one of whom was Dr. Bosch and the other of whom was a 2506 member named Luis Posada Carriles, of planning or arranging this placement. Not least because Luis Posada Carriles happened to be a former operations chief of the Venezuelan secret police, DISIP, the Cubana case was a sensitive one for Venezuela, and, after a decade of what appeared to many to be stalling actions, Orlando Bosch was in 1986 acquitted by a Venezuelan judge, who noted that at the time the plane actually fell from the sky "citizen Orlando Bosch was not in the company" of the two men accused of placing the bomb, both of whom were convicted. In the case of the fourth defendant, Luis Posada Carriles, there was no final disposition, since he had the year before escaped from the penitentiary in San Juan de Los Morros (aided, it was reported, by $28,600 in payoffs), some sixty miles southwest of Caracas, and appeared to have next surfaced in the Escalón district of San Salvador, living in a rented house and working on the covert contra supply operation at Ilopango air base under the name "Ramon Medina."

The name "Ramon Medina" began coming up in late 1986, at the time the first details of the contra supply network organized by Lieutenant Colonel Oliver North and Major General Richard V. Secord were becoming known, and there was some speculation that his job at Ilopango had been arranged by Felix Rodriguez, also known as Max Gomez, who in turn had been recommended as an adviser to the Salvadoran armed forces by the office of Vice President George Bush. "We have been asked if Mr. Bush knew or knows Ramon Medina," a spokesman for Vice President George Bush said. "The answer is no. The same answer holds for Ramon Posada or any other names or aliases." Some weeks later, in Miami, an exhibition of Orlando Bosch's paintings was held, some sixty oils, priced at $25 to $500 and listed under such titles as *The Southern Coast of Cuba* and *Nightfall in the Tropics*. Tea sandwiches were served, and wine. The president of the Committee to Free Orlando Bosch pointed out that the paintings had certain common motifs, that doors kept turning up, and roads, and bodies of water; that the painter was "always looking for the way to freedom." (Luis Posada Carriles' oils, of Venezuelan landscapes, had been exhibited in Miami a year before.) Orlando Bosch himself was still in jail in Caracas, waiting for yet another obstacle to be negotiated, the confirmation of his acquittal. He was also still, from the point of view of the United States, a fugitive terrorist, someone who, if he tried to reenter the United States, faced immediate arrest on his parole violation.

That the governing body of an American city should have declared a "day" in honor of someone with so clouded a history might have in most parts of the United States profoundly disturbed the citizens of that city, but Miami was a community in which, as the *Herald* had pointed out in 1985, a significant percentage of the population continued to see Orlando Bosch as a hero. "You are mistaken when you say that 'many exiles believe that Bosch is a hero,'" a letter to *El Herald* complained on this point. "Not just 'many,' as you say, but ALL Cuban exiles believe Dr. Bosch to be so decent a man, so Rambo-like a hero, that, even supposing there were any truth to the allegations about that communist plane crash many years ago, Dr. Bosch would only have been trying to pay back in kind those enemies of this country who, every day, all over the world, are bombing and killing and maiming innocent citizens, including elderly tourists in their wheelchairs." This note of *machismo* was often struck when people mentioned Orlando Bosch. "Most people talk more than they act," an exile named Cosme Barros told the *Herald* after the acquittal in Caracas. "Bosch has acted more than he has talked." "He is how every man should be," an exile named Norma Garcia told the same reporter. "If we had more men like him, today Cuba would be free."

The case of Orlando Bosch and Luis Posada Carriles and the bombing of the Cubana DC-8 had always been complicated, as most stories in this part of the world turned out to be, by more than just one sensitive connection. There had been, besides the line from Luis Posada Carriles to the

Venezuelan secret police, visible lines from both Luis Posada
Carriles and Orlando Bosch to the government of the United
States. According to a 1977 CIA document obtained by the
Miami Herald, Luis Posada Carriles, who was later called
Ramon Medina, had received CIA demolition and weapons
training before the Bay of Pigs, had formally joined the CIA
in 1965, had worked briefly in Guatemala and then moved
on to Venezuela and DISIP, finally resigning as DISIP operations chief in 1974. Throughout this period, according to the
1977 document quoted by the *Herald*, Luis Posada Carriles had
remained on the CIA payroll.

Orlando Bosch himself, according to staff interviews conducted by and to CIA and FBI memos released to the 1978 House
Select Committee on Assassinations, had been under contract to
the CIA during the early 1960s, running, with Evelio Duque of
the Ejército Cubano Anticomunista, a camp in Homestead, the
last Florida town before the Keys. Orlando Bosch told the House
committee staff members who interviewed him in Cuartel San
Carlos that he had soon begun to see this Homestead camp as,
in the committee's words, "an exercise in futility." He had begun
to suspect that such CIA-sponsored camps were, again in the
committee's words, "merely a means of keeping the exiles busy."
His CIA contact had, he said, "privately and unofficially" confirmed this suspicion.

This was a peculiar climate in South Florida, and had been so
since 1960. Signals seemed to get mixed. Transmissions seemed
to jam. Some atmospheric anomaly seemed to create trick mirrors, in which those people (or personnel, or assets) who were
to be kept busy (or disposed of) and those people who could
be strategically deployed (or used) appeared to be one and the
same, their image changing with the light, and the distant agenda,
in Washington. Sometimes even those people who were to be
kept busy (or strategically deployed) and those people who were
running the distant agenda appeared to be one and the same,
or so it might have seemed to anyone looking in the mirror
when the images spoke. "You have to fight violence with violence," Orlando Bosch was quoted as saying in the *Miami News* in
1978. "At times you cannot avoid hurting innocent people." The
same year, 1978, Richard Helms, who had been directing CIA
operations from Washington during the time Orlando Bosch

was running the camp in Homestead, said this to the House Select Committee on Assassinations: "I would like to point out something since we are so deeply into this. When one government is trying to upset another government and the operation is successful, people get killed."

IN 1985 AND 1986 it was said in exile Miami that the coup, the coup in Cuba, the "solution from inside," the "military solution" Agustin Tamargo had mentioned the night we spoke in his office at WOCN-Union Radio, would take place in three, maybe four years. In 1985 and 1986 it was also said in exile Miami that the coup would not take place. In 1985 and 1986 it was also said in exile Miami that the coup, were the coup allowed to take place, which it would not be, would occur along anti-Soviet lines, and could begin among certain officers from the one Cuban military school to which there had been assigned no Soviet trainers. Still, this coup would never take place. The reason this coup would never take place, it was said by various people to whom I spoke in exile Miami in 1985 and 1986, was because "the United States wants a Cuba it can control," because "a coup would mean a new situation," and because "in the changed situation after the coup they would hate the United States even more than the communists do."

The coup which the United States would never allow to take place had in fact by the 1980s largely supplanted, as an exile plot point, the invasion which the United States had never allowed to take place, and was for the time being, until something more concrete came along (the narrative bones for this something, the projected abandonment of the Nicaraguan contras, were of course already in place), the main story line for what *el exilio* continued to see as its betrayal, its utilization, its manipulation, by the government of the United States. A rather unsettling number of exiles to whom I spoke cited, as evidence of Washington's continuing betrayal, the Omega 7 prosecutions. Others cited the Reagan administration's attempts to deport the so-called "Mariel excludables," those refugees whose criminal records would normally be grounds, under American immigration policy, for deportation or exclusion. Many, including Agustin Tamargo, cited Radio Martí, about which there had been, it seemed, considerable controversy within the exile community. "Radio Martí is a department of the Voice of America," Agustin Tamargo had said the evening we met in his office at WOCN-Union Radio. "Which is a guarantee to me that when the American government makes its deal with Fidel Castro, Radio Martí will say amen."

I had then been in Miami only a short time, and had not before been exposed to this local view of Radio Martí as yet another way in which the government of the United States was deceiving the exile community. I said to Agustin Tamargo that I did not quite understand. I said that I, and I believed many other Americans, including several to whom I had talked in Washington who had been involved with the issue as it passed through Congress, had tended to think of Radio Martí as something the Miami exile community specifically wanted. I said that I had in fact met Miami exiles, for example Jorge Mas Canosa, who had gone to some lengths to see the Radio Martí legislation enacted.

"Rich people," Agustin Tamargo said.

I allowed that this was possibly true.

"The same rich people who are Republicans. Listen. I hate communists, but I hate some of these exiles more." Agustin Tamargo was on this subject a dog with a bone. "They are why we are here all these years. If a man like Che Guevara were on our side, we would have been back in Cuba long ago. However. Instead of Che Guevara, we have Mas Canosa. I'm sorry. I mention him only because he is one of the richest."

This was one of those leaps to the ad hominem toward which exile conversation seemed ever to tend. I had known that there was within the community a certain resistance to the leadership claims of Jorge Mas Canosa and the other supporters of the Cuban American National Foundation. I had also known that resistance derived in part from the well-publicized conviction of the Cuban American National Foundation, a group somewhat more attuned than the average Miami exile to the pitch at which an American congressman is apt to lose eye contact, that exile aims could best be achieved by working within the American political system; that, in other words, the time had passed for running raids on Cuba and shelling Soviet-bloc ships in the Port of Miami. Still, even ad hominem, even given the fact that Jorge Mas Canosa and the Cuban American National Foundation had been largely responsible for Radio Martí, the point about Radio Martí as proof of American perfidy remained obscure to me, and I had looked for help to another exile who had joined us that evening, a young man named Daniel Morcate.

"I disagree with Agustin strongly on Radio Martí," Daniel Morcate had said, and then, deferentially: "But then the whole exile community is divided. On that question." Daniel Morcate, whose wife Gina was a writer and an assistant to Carlos Luis at the Museo Cubano de Arte y Cultura, had left Cuba at fourteen, in 1971. He had spent four years in Madrid and lived since (except for one year, 1979, when he returned to Madrid to work for Carlos Alberto Montaner) in Miami, where he was, at the time we met, working for WOCN-Union Radio and teaching philosophy at St. Thomas University, an institution founded in Miami by Augustinian brothers formerly affiliated with Villanueva University in Havana. He was among those younger exiles who defined themselves as philosophical anarchists. He had stressed that evening that he was "not a man of action," but that, at certain times and under certain conditions, he supported the idea of action. He was, he had said, "a man of words," and he chose them carefully.

As this might suggest, Daniel Morcate's position on Radio Martí and the Cuban American National Foundation (which was to say, I was beginning to see, his position on working within the American system) was subtle, even tortured. His own concerns about Radio Martí had been sufficient to keep him from accepting one of the Radio Martí jobs which had been passed around Miami as a particularly exotic form of patronage, and he differed from those of his contemporaries who did work in Washington, both for Radio Martí and for the Cuban American National Foundation, on several key points. Despite the fact that he was not, as he had said, a man of action, Daniel Morcate did believe, as the Cuban American National Foundation pointedly did not believe, that now was as good a time as any for running physical actions against the government of Cuba. He also believed that groups running such actions should seek support not only from the United States but from other nations.

Still, given these exceptions and under certain limited conditions, he agreed in principle with such Washington exiles of his generation as Ramon Mestre at Radio Martí and Frank Calzón, who was at that time director of the Cuban American National Foundation, that it was possible for exiles to coexist with and even to influence the government of the United States. "I think that many goals of the United States government are very legitimate," Daniel Morcate said. "Many Cubans do. And so they believe that they can use the United States government without compromising their own ideals. This is what many people in the Cuban American National Foundation believe."

"They believe in publicity," Agustin Tamargo had said, interrupting.

"I happen to think that someone like Frank Calzón is a deep-rooted nationalist," Daniel Morcate had insisted. "I believe that he thinks he is utilizing the United States government." He had paused, and shrugged. "Of course the United States government thinks the same about him."

Agustin Tamargo had been patient. "Look. Radio Martí is an instrument of American foreign policy." He had ticked off the points on his fingers. "The American government decides that it is going to coexist with Castro and the next day we will have a long story on Radio Martí about our cooperation with the United States government. We have no say in this. In the Reagan administration more than ever. The Reagan administration has one goal in Cuba. Which is to separate Castro from Moscow. Not to overthrow Castro. They put in jail anybody here who says he wants to overthrow Castro. They put in jail the Omega 7. We have been taught to throw bombs, taught to work with every kind of *desgraciado*, and then they throw us in jail. We have no choice in the matter. There is absolutely nothing going on now. There is no bombing, there is no fighting in the customs line, there is no tax, there is no terrorism, there is *nothing*."

I supposed that what Agustin Tamargo meant by "no tax" was that there was no community effort, as there had been on occasion in the past, to finance actions against Cuba by collecting from each exile a part of his or her earnings. I did not know what he meant by "no fighting in the customs line," nor, because he seemed at that moment almost mute with disgust, did I ask.

"Nothing," Agustin Tamargo had repeated finally. "Under Reagan."

* * *

That there was in Miami under the Reagan administration "nothing" going on was something said to me by many exiles, virtually all of whom spoke as if this "nothing," by which they seemed to mean the absence of more or less daily threats of domestic terror, might be only a temporary suspension, an intermission of uncertain duration in an otherwise familiar production. There was in Miami a general sense that the Reagan administration, largely by the way in which it had managed to convince some exiles that its commitment to "freedom fighters" extended to them, had to some extent co-opted exile action. There was also in Miami a general sense that this was on the Reagan administration's part just another trick of another mirror, another camp in Homestead, say, another interim occupation for Luis Posada Carriles or his manifold doubles, and as such could end predictably. Some exiles spoke with considerable foreboding about what they saw as the community's misplaced wish to believe in the historically doubtful notion that its interests would in the long run coincide with those of Washington. Some exiles suggested that this wish to believe, or rather this willing suspension of disbelief, had not in the past been and was by no means now an open ticket, that there would once again come a point when exile and Washington interests would be seen to diverge, and diverge dramatically.

These exiles saw, when and if this happened, a rekindling of certain familiar frustrations, the unloosing of furies still only provisionally contained; saw, in other words, built into the mirror trick, yet another narrative on which to hang the betrayal, the utilization, the manipulation of *el exilio* by the government of the United States. "I wouldn't be surprised to see some Cubans attempting to re-create political violence in the United States," Daniel Morcate had said the evening we met in Agustin Tamargo's office at WOCN-Union Radio. He had been talking about what he saw as the Reagan administration's reluctance to directly confront Fidel Castro. "There is a very clear danger here that nobody is pointing out. I wouldn't be surprised if other Omega *Siete* groups were emerging."

I had asked Raul Masvidal, the day I saw him in the cool office with the poster that read YOU HAVE NOT CONVERTED A MAN BECAUSE YOU HAVE SILENCED HIM, if he believed that a perceived divergence of exile and Washington interests, a perception in Miami that promises were once again being broken, could bring about a resurgence of the kind of action which had characterized the exile until recently. Raul Masvidal had looked at me, and shrugged. "That kind of action is here today," he had said. I had asked the same question of Luis Lauredo, who was then the president of Raul Masvidal's Miami Savings Bank and was, as the president of Cuban-American Democrats, perhaps the most visible and active member of that 35 percent of the Dade County Cuban electorate who were registered Democrats.

Luis Lauredo had nodded, and then shook his head, as if the question did not bear contemplation. "I was talking about this last night," he said finally. "With some of the Republicans." We had been sitting across from each other at lunch that day, and I had watched Luis Lauredo fillet a fish before he continued. "We had a kind of gathering," he said then. "And I said to them, 'listen, when it happens, I'll cover your backs.' Because they are going to lose all credibility. It's like a Greek tragedy. That's the way it's going to be. When it happens."

"Those radio guys who attacked me are just looking for ratings," Carlos Luis said one day when I had met him at the Museo Cubano and we had gone around to get something to eat and a coffee, just out of the rain, in the courtyard of the Malaga restaurant on Eighth Street. "Which is why I never answered them. I did a program with Agustin Tamargo, which was good, but I never answered the attacks."

The rain that day had been blowing the bits of colored glass and mirror strung from the tree in the Malaga courtyard and splashing from the eaves overhanging our table and we had been talking in a general way about action of the Left and action of the Right and Carlos Luis had said that he had come to wonder if silence was not the only moral political response. He had a few weeks before, on the twenty-fifth anniversary of the death of Albert Camus, published in *El Herald* a reflection on Camus which had this as its subtext, and it was to this subtext that the "radio guys" had been responding, there apparently being in Miami no subject so remote or abstruse as to rule out its becoming the focus for several hours of invective on AM radio.

"In any event that's the way things are here," Carlos Luis said. "It's very confusing. The guy who attacked me to begin with was totally incapable of discussing Camus's position. Which was a very tragic one. Because the choices Camus had in front of him were not choices at all. Making a choice between terrorism of the Right and terrorism of the Left was incomprehensible to him. Maybe he was right. As time goes by I think that men who were unable to make choices were more right than those who made them. Because there are no clean choices."

Carlos Luis drummed his fingers absently on the wet metal table. It was possible to walk from the Malaga to the bungalow on Seventh Street where Eduardo Arocena had been arrested with the Beretta and the Browning and the AR-15 and the UZI and the target list. It was also possible to walk from the Malaga to the parking lot where Emilio Milian had lost his legs for suggesting on WQBA-*La Cubanísima* that exiles might be working against their own interests by continuing to bomb and assassinate one another on the streets of Miami. On my way to the Museo Cubano de Arte y Cultura that morning I had noticed in a storefront window this poster: ¡NICARAGUA HOY, CUBA MAÑANA! SUPPORT THE FREEDOM FIGHTERS FUND. COMANDO SATURNINO BELTRAN. FREEDOM FIGHTERS FUND, P.O. BOX 661571, MIAMI SPRINGS FL 33266. JEFATURA MILITAR BRIGADA 2506, P.O. BOX 4086, HIALEAH FL 33014.

This was a year and a half before the Southern Air Transport C-123K carrying Eugene Hasenfus crashed inside Nicaragua. There was between the day of Ronald Reagan's first inauguration and the day the C-123K crashed inside Nicaragua "nothing" going on, but of course there was also "something" going on, something peculiar to the early 1980s in Miami but suggestive of the early 1960s in Miami, something in which certain familiar words and phrases once again figured. It was again possible to hear in Miami about "training," and about air charters and altered manifests and pilots hired for onetime flights from Miami to "somewhere" in Central America. It was again possible to hear in Washington about two-track strategies, about back channels and alternative avenues, about what Robert C. McFarlane, at that time the Reagan administration's National Security Affairs adviser, described variously in the *Washington Post* in 1985 as "a continuity of policy," "a national interest in keeping in touch with what was going on"; a matter of "not breaking faith with the freedom fighters," which in turn came down to "making it clear that the United States believes in what they are doing."

What exactly was involved in making it clear that the United States believed in what the freedom fighters were doing was still, at that time in Miami, the spring of 1985, hard to know in detail, but it was already clear that some of the details were known to some Cubans. There were Cubans around Miami who would later say, about how they happened to end up fighting with the Nicaraguan contras, that they had been during the spring of 1985 "trained" at a camp in the Everglades operated by the Jefatura Militar Brigada 2506. There were Cubans around Miami who would later say, about how they happened to join the Nicaraguan contras, that they had been during the spring of 1985 "recruited" at the little park on Eighth Street a few blocks west of the Malaga. Nothing was happening but certain familiar expectations were being raised, and to speak of choices between terrorism of the Left and terrorism of the Right did not seem, in the courtyard of the Malaga on Eighth Street in Miami during the spring of 1985, an entirely speculative exercise. "There are no choices at all," Carlos Luis said then.

WHEN I THINK now about mirror tricks and what might or might not be built into them, about the ways in which frustrations can be kindled and furies unloosed, I think of Guillermo Novo, called Bill Novo. Guillermo Novo was known to FBI agents and federal prosecutors and the various personnel who made up "terrorist task forces" on the eastern seaboard of the United States as one of the Novo brothers, Ignacio and Guillermo, two exiles who first came to national attention in 1964, when they fired a dud bazooka shell at the United Nations during a speech by Che Guevara. There were certain farcical elements here (the embattled brothers bobbing in a small boat, the shell plopping harmlessly into the East River), and, in a period when Hispanics were seen by many Americans as intrinsically funny, an accent joke, this incident was generally treated tolerantly, a comic footnote to the news. As time went by, however, the names of the Novo brothers began turning up in less comic footnotes, for example this one, on page 93 of volume X of the report made by the House Select Committee on Assassinations on its 1978 investigation of the assassination of John F. Kennedy:

(67) Immunized executive session testimony of Marita Lorenz, May 31, 1978. Hearings before the House Select Committee on Assassinations. Lorenz, who had publicly claimed she was once Castro's mistress (*Miami News*, June 15, 1976), told the committee she was present at a September 1963 meeting in Orlando Bosch's Miami home during which Lee Harvey Oswald, Frank Sturgis, Pedro Diaz Lanz, and Bosch made plans to go to Dallas.... She further testified that around November 15, 1963, she, Jerry Patrick Hemming, the Novo brothers, Pedro Diaz Lanz, Sturgis, Bosch, and Oswald traveled in a two-car caravan to Dallas and stayed in a motel where they were contacted by Jack Ruby. There were several rifles and scopes in the

motel room … Lorenz said she returned to Miami around
November 19 or 20…. The committee found no evidence
to support Lorenz's allegation.

Guillermo Novo himself was among those convicted, in a
1979 trial which rested on the demonstration of connections
between the Cuban defendants and DINA, the Chilean secret
police, of the assassination in Washington of the former Chilean
diplomat Orlando Letelier and of the Institute for Policy Studies
researcher who happened to be with him when his car blew up,
Ronni Moffitt. This conviction was overturned on appeal (the
appellate court ruled that the testimony of two jailhouse infor-
mants had been improperly admitted), and in a 1981 retrial, after
the federal prosecutors turned down a deal in which the defense
offered a plea of guilty on the lesser charge of conspiracy, plus
what Guillermo Novo's attorney called "a sweetener," a "guarantee" by Guillermo Novo "to stop all violence by Cuban exiles in
the United States," Guillermo Novo was acquitted.

I happened to meet Guillermo Novo in 1985, one Monday
morning when I was waiting for someone in the reception room
at WRHC-Cadena Azul, Miami, a station the call letters of which
stood for Radio Havana Cuba. There was about this meeting
nothing of either moment or consequence. A man who introduced himself as "Bill Novo" just appeared beside me, and we
exchanged minor biography for a few minutes. He said that he
had noticed me reading a letter framed on the wall of the reception room. He said that he was the sales manager for WRHC,
and had lived in Miami only three years. He said that he had
however lived in the United States since 1954, mostly in New
York and New Jersey. He was a small sharp-featured man in a
white tropical suit, who in fact spoke English with an accent
which suggested New Jersey, and he had a way of materializing
and dematerializing sideways, of appearing from and then sidling
back into an inner office, which was where he retreated after
he gave me his business card, the exchange of cards remaining
a more or less fixed ritual in Cuban Miami. GUILLERMO NOVO
SAMPOL, the card read. *Gerente de Ventas, WRHC-Cadena Azul.*

That it was possible on a Monday morning in Miami to
have so desultory an encounter with one of the Novo brothers
seemed to me, perhaps because I was not yet accustomed to a

rhythm in which dealings with DINA and unsupported allegations about Dallas motel rooms could be incorporated into the
American business day, remarkable, and later that week I asked an
exile acquaintance who was familiar with WRHC if the Guillermo Novo who was the sales manager there was in fact the
Guillermo Novo who had been tried in the Letelier assassination.
There had been, my acquaintance demurred, "a final acquittal
on the Letelier count." But it was, I persisted, the same man. My
acquaintance had shrugged impatiently, not as if he thought it
best not mentioned, but as if he did not quite see the interest.
"Bill Novo has been a man of action," he said. "Yes. Of course."

To be a man of action in Miami was to receive encouragement from many quarters. On the wall of the reception room
at WRHC-Cadena Azul, Miami, where the sales manager was
Guillermo Novo and an occasional commentator was Fidel and
Raúl Castro's estranged sister Juanita and the host of the most
popular talk show was Felipe Rivero, whose family had from
1832 until 1960 published the powerful *Diario de la Marina* in
Havana and who would in 1986, after a controversy fueled by his
insistence that the Holocaust had not occurred but had been fabricated "to defame and divide the German people," move from
WRHC to WOCN, there hung in 1985 a framed letter, the letter
Guillermo Novo had mentioned when he first materialized that
Monday morning. This letter, which was dated October 1983 and
signed by the President of the United States, read:

> I learned from Becky Dunlop [presumably Becky Norton
> Dunlop, a White House aide who later followed Edwin
> Meese to the Justice Department] about the outstanding
> work being done at WRHC. Many of your listeners have
> also been in touch, praising your news coverage and your
> editorials. Your talented staff deserves special commenda-
> tion for keeping your listeners well-informed.
>
> I've been particularly pleased, of course, that you have been
> translating and airing a Spanish version of my weekly talks.
> This is important because your signal reaches the people
> of Cuba, whose rigidly controlled government media

suppress any news Castro and his communist henchmen do not want them to know. WRHC is performing a great service for all its listeners. Keep up the good work, and God bless you.

[signed] RONALD REAGAN

At the time I first noticed it on the WRHC wall, and attracted Guillermo Novo's attention by reading it, this letter interested me because I had the week before been looking back through the administration's arguments for Radio Martí, none of which, built as they were on the figure of beaming light into utter darkness, had alluded to these weekly talks which the people of Cuba appeared to be getting on WRHC-Cadena Azul, Miami. Later the letter interested me because I had begun reading back through the weekly radio talks themselves, and had come across one from 1978 in which Ronald Reagan, not yet president, had expressed his doubt that either the Pinochet government or the indicted "Cuban anti-Castro exiles," one of whom had been Guillermo Novo, had anything to do with the Letelier assassination.

Ronald Reagan had wondered instead ("I don't know the answer, but it is a question worth asking …") if Orlando Letelier's "connections with Marxists and far-left causes" might not have set him up for assassination, caused him to be, as the script for this talk put it, "murdered by his own masters." Here was the scenario: "Alive," Ronald Reagan had reasoned in 1978, Orlando Letelier "could be compromised; dead he could become a martyr. And the left didn't lose a minute in making him one." Actually this version of the Letelier assassination had first been advanced by Senator Jesse Helms (R-N.C.), who had advised his colleagues on the Senate floor that it was not "plausible" to suspect the Pinochet government in the Letelier case, because terrorism was "most often an organized tool of the left," but the Reagan reworking was interesting on its own, a way of speaking, later to become familiar, in which events could be revised as they happened into illustrations of ideology.

"There was no blacklist of Hollywood," Ronald Reagan told Robert Scheer of the *Los Angeles Times* during the 1980 campaign. "The blacklist in Hollywood, if there was one, was provided by the communists." "I'm going to voice a suspicion now that I've never said aloud before," Ronald Reagan told thirty-six high-school students in Washington in 1983 about death squads in El Salvador. "I wonder if all of this is right wing, or if those guerrilla forces have not realized that by infiltrating into the city of San Salvador and places like that, they can get away with these violent acts, helping to try and bring down the government, and the right wing will be blamed for it." "New intelligence shows," Ronald Reagan told his Saturday radio listeners in March of 1986, by way of explaining why he was asking Congress to provide "the Nicaraguan freedom fighters" with what he called "the means to fight back," that "Tomás Borge, the communist interior minister, is engaging in a brutal campaign to bring the freedom fighters into discredit. You see, Borge's communist operatives dress in freedom fighter uniforms, go into the countryside and murder and mutilate ordinary Nicaraguans."

Such stories were what David Gergen, when he was the White House communications director, had once called "a folk art," the President's way of "trying to tell us how society works." Other members of the White House staff had characterized these stories as the President's "notions," casting them in the genial framework of random avuncular musings, but they were something more than that. In the first place they were never random, but systematic, and rather energetically so. The stories were told to a single point. The language in which the stories were told was not that of political argument but of advertising ("New intelligence shows ..." and "Now it has been learned ..." and, a construction that got my attention in a 1984 address to the National Religious Broadcasters, "Medical science doctors confirm ..."), of the sales pitch.

This was not just a vulgarity of diction. When someone speaks of Orlando Letelier as "murdered by his own masters," or of the WRHC signal reaching a people denied information by "Castro and his communist henchmen," or of the "freedom fighter uniforms" in which the "communist operatives" of the "communist interior minister" disguise themselves, that person is not arguing a case, but counting instead on the willingness of the listener to enter what Hannah Arendt called, in a discussion of propaganda, "the gruesome quiet of an entirely imaginary world." On the morning I met Guillermo Novo in the reception room at WRHC-Cadena Azul I copied the framed commendation from the White House into my notebook, and later typed it out and pinned it to my own office wall, an aide-mémoire to the distance between what is said in the high ether of Washington, which is about the making of those gestures and the sending of those messages and the drafting of those positions which will serve to maintain that imaginary world, about two-track strategies and alternative avenues and Special Groups (Augmented), about "not breaking faith" and "making it clear," and what is heard on the ground in Miami, which is about consequences.

In many ways Miami remains our most graphic lesson in consequences. "I can assure you that this flag will be returned to this brigade in a free Havana," John F. Kennedy said at the Orange Bowl in 1962 (the "supposed promise," the promise "not in the script," the promise "made in the emotion of the day"), meaning it as an abstraction, the rhetorical expression of a collective wish; a kind of poetry, which of course makes nothing happen. "We will not permit the Soviets and their henchmen in Havana to deprive others of their freedom," Ronald Reagan said at the Dade County Auditorium in 1983 (2,500 people inside, 60,000 outside, 12 standing ovations and a *pollo asado* lunch at La Esquina de Tejas with Jorge Mas Canosa and 203 other provisional loyalists), and then Ronald Reagan, the first American president since John F. Kennedy to visit Miami in search of Cuban support, added this: "Someday, Cuba itself will be free."

This was of course just more poetry, another rhetorical expression of the same collective wish, but Ronald Reagan, like John F. Kennedy before him, was speaking here to people whose historical experience has not been that poetry makes nothing happen. On one of the first evenings I spent in Miami I sat at midnight over *carne con papas* in an art-filled condominium in one of the Arquitectonica buildings on Brickell Avenue and listened to several exiles talk about the relationship of what was said in Washington to what was done in Miami. These exiles were all well-educated. They were well-read, well-traveled, comfortable citizens of a larger world than that of either Miami or Washington, with well-cut blazers and French dresses and interests in New York and Madrid and Mexico. Yet what was said that evening in the expensive condominium overlooking Biscayne Bay proceeded from an almost primitive helplessness, a regressive fury at having been, as these exiles saw it, repeatedly used and repeatedly betrayed by the government of the United States. "Let me tell you something," one of them said. "They talk about 'Cuban terrorists.' The guys they call 'Cuban terrorists' are the guys they trained."

This was not, then, the general exile complaint about a government which might have taken up their struggle but had not. This was something more specific, a complaint that the government in question had in fact taken up *la lucha*, but for its own purposes, and, in what these exiles saw as a pattern of deceit stretching back through six administrations, to its own ends. The pattern, as they saw it, was one in which the government of the United States had repeatedly encouraged or supported exile action and then, when policy shifted and such action became an embarrassment, a discordant note in whatever message Washington was sending that month or that year, had discarded the exiles involved, had sometimes not only discarded them but, since the nature of *la lucha* was essentially illegal, turned them in, set them up for prosecution; positioned them, as it were, for the fall.

They mentioned, as many exiles did, the Omega 7 prosecutions. They mentioned, as many exiles did, the Cuban burglars at the Watergate, who were told, because so many exiles had come by that time to distrust the CIA, that the assignment at hand was not just CIA, but straight from the White House. They mentioned the case of Jose Elias de la Torriente, a respected exile leader who had been, in the late 1960s, recruited by the CIA to lend his name and his prestige to what was set forth as a new plan to overthrow Fidel Castro, the "Work Plan for Liberation," or the Torriente Plan.

Money had once again been raised, and expectations. The entire attention of *el exilio* had for a time been focused on the Torriente Plan, a diversion of energy which, as years passed and nothing happened, suggested to many that what the plan may have been from its inception was just another ad hoc solution to the disposal problem, another mirror trick. Jose Elias de la Torriente had been called, by a frustrated community once again left with nowhere to go, a traitor. Jose Elias de la Torriente had been called a CIA stooge. Jose Elias de la Torriente had finally been, at age seventy, as he sat in his house in Coral Gables watching *The Robe* on television about nine o'clock on the evening of Good Friday, 1974, assassinated, shot through the venetian blind

JOAN DIDION

on a window by someone, presumably an exile, who claimed the kill in the name "Zero."

This had, in the telling at the dinner table, the sense of a situation played out to its Aristotelian end, of that inexorable Caribbean progress from cause to effect which I later came to see as central to the way Miami thought about itself. Miami stories tended to have endings. The cannon onstage tended to be fired. One of those who spoke most ardently that evening was a quite beautiful young woman in a white jersey dress, a lawyer, active in Democratic politics in Miami. This dinner in the condominium overlooking Biscayne Bay took place in March of 1985, and the woman in the white jersey dress was María Elena Prío Durán, the child who flew into exile in March of 1952 with her father's foreign minister, her father's minister of the interior, her father, her sister, and her mother, the equally beautiful woman in the hat with the fishnet veiling.

I recall watching María Elena Prío Durán that night as she pushed back her hair and reached across the table for a cigarette. This, like the lunch in the Malaga courtyard when Carlos Luis had talked about Albert Camus and the choice between terror of the Right and terror of the Left, was a long time before the C-123K carrying Eugene Hasenfus fell from the sky inside Nicaragua. This was a long time before Eugene Hasenfus mentioned the names of the 2506 members already in place at Ilopango. NICARAGUA HOY, CUBA MAÑANA. Let me tell you about Cuban terrorists, another of the exiles at dinner that night, a prominent Miami architect named Raúl Rodríguez, was saying at the end of the table. Cuba never grew plastique. Cuba grew tobacco. Cuba grew sugarcane. Cuba never grew C-4. María Elena Prío Durán lit the cigarette and immediately crushed it out. C-4, Raúl Rodríguez said, and he slammed his palm down on the white tablecloth as he said it, grew here.

Part IV

Part IV

EARLY ON THE morning of April 19, 1961, when it was clear in Washington that the invasion then underway at Playa Girón had failed, President John F. Kennedy dispatched Adolf A. Berle of the State Department and Arthur M. Schlesinger, Jr., of the White House staff to Miami, to meet with what had been until a few hours before the projected provisional government for a post-Castro Cuba, the Cuban Revolutionary Council, the members of which were being kept temporarily incommunicado in a CIA barracks at the Opa-Locka Airport. "A couple of hours into our meeting with the Kennedy people, I got the feeling that we were being taken for a ride," one member of the council later told the exile sociologist José Llanes, who quoted but did not name him in *Cuban Americans: Masters of Survival.* "The *comierda* [Llanes translates this as "shit face"] they sent me was only worried about the political popularity of their man." In *A Thousand Days,* Arthur M. Schlesinger, Jr., described his and Adolf Berle's thoughts during the same meeting: "Our hearts sank as we walked out for a moment into the dazzling sun. How could we notify the Cubans that there was no hope, that their sons were abandoned for captivity or death—and at the same time dissuade them from public denunciation of the CIA and the United States government?"

What is interesting here is how closely these two views of the meeting at the Opa-Locka Airport, the Miami and the Washington, appear to coincide. The problem that April morning for Schlesinger and Berle, Schlesinger seems himself to suggest, was one of presentation, of damage control, which is another way of saying that they were worried about the political popularity of their man. The solution, as they devised it, was to take the exiles for a literal ride: to fly them immediately to Washington and give them an afternoon audience in the Oval Office, a meeting at which the members of the Cuban Revolutionary Council (several of whom had sons or brothers on the beachhead that day) would sit by the fireplace and hear the President speak of the responsibilities of leadership, of the struggle against communism on its many fronts and of his own commitment to the "eventual" freedom of Cuba; a meeting which in fact took place, and at which, according to Schlesinger, the President spoke "slowly and thoughtfully" ("I had never seen the President more impressive"), and the members of the Cuban Revolutionary Council had been, "in spite of themselves," "deeply moved." Here, the Washington and the Miami views no longer coincide: the recitative of seduction and betrayal from which Miami took its particular tone was in a key Washington failed then to hear, and does still.

On April 10, 1984, midway through yet another administration during which it was periodically suggested that the struggle against communism on its many fronts included a commitment to the eventual freedom of Cuba, an unexceptional Tuesday morning during a week in which *The New York Times* reported that the mining of Nicaraguan harbors had "rekindled doubts in Congress and among some officials in the Reagan administration about the extensive use of covert activities to advance United States interests in Central America," Ronald Reagan, the fortieth President of the United States, was presented to be photographed in the following Washington settings: greeting President Salvador Jorge Blanco of the Dominican Republic on the South Grounds of the White House (10:00 A.M.), conferring with President Salvador Jorge Blanco of the Dominican Republic in the Oval Office of the White House (10:30 A.M.), and placing a telephone call from the Oval Office to the *Challenger* space shuttle, an event covered only by a pool camera crew but piped live into the press briefing room in the West Wing of the White House:

THE PRESIDENT: Hello, Bob—these calls—

ASTRONAUT CRIPPEN: Good afternoon, Mr. President. Thank you very much for speaking with us.

THE PRESIDENT: Well, these calls between the two of us are becoming a habit. I promise you, though, I won't reverse the charges. Over.

ASTRONAUT CRIPPEN: I don't think I can afford them, Mr. President. (*Laughter.*)

THE PRESIDENT: Well, once again, I'm calling to congratulate you and the rest of the crew aboard the *Challenger* there on an historic mission. The retrieval of the Solar

Max satellite this morning was just great. And you and the crew demonstrated once again just how versatile the space shuttle is and what we can accomplish by having a team in space and on the ground. I know you'll agree that those folks at the Goddard Space Flight Center did a fantastic job maneuvering the satellite for you. And, Terry, I guess you made one long reach for man this morning when you snapped that satellite with the fifty-foot robot arms. And George and Jim, you've done fine work as well. The pictures sent back of you working in space are spectacular. They're also a little scary for those of us who are sitting comfortably anchored to the earth. But, Bob, I understand that satellite you have on board would cost us about two hundred million dollars to build at today's prices, so if you can't fix it up there, would you mind bringing it back? Over.

ASTRONAUT CRIPPEN: Well, we—we're going to do our best to repair it tomorrow, sir, and if, for some reason, that is unsuccessful, which we don't think it will be, we will be able to return it. We certainly concur with all of your remarks. The *Challenger* and its sister ships are magnificent flying machines and I think that they can make a significant road into space in regard to repair and servicing of satellites. And we believe this is the initial step. I would also like to concur with your remarks regarding the people up at Goddard who managed to put this satellite back in a configuration that we could retrieve it after the little problem we ran into the other day. Those people and the people in Houston and everybody that worked on it truly made this recovery possible. It is a team effort all the way. It so happens we get to do the fun part.

THE PRESIDENT: Well, let me tell you, you're all a team that has made all Americans very proud of what you're doing up there, and what the future bodes for all of us with regard to this opening up of that great frontier of space. And, seriously, I just want to again say how proud we all are of all of you, and congratulations to you all. Have a safe mission, a safe trip home, and God bless all of you. I'll sign out and let you get on with your chores.

There was at first a silence in the West Wing briefing room. "Sign off," someone said then. "Not 'sign out,' 'sign *off*.'"

"'And, seriously'?" someone else said. "What does that mean, 'And, seriously'?"

This telephone call between the Oval Office and space lasted four minutes, between 12:01 P.M. and 12:05 P.M., and was followed immediately in the briefing room by a report on the meeting between President Reagan and President Salvador Jorge Blanco of the Dominican Republic, or rather on that part of the meeting which had taken place after the pool camera crew left the Oval Office. This report was delivered by Assistant Secretary of State for Inter-American Affairs Langhorne Motley ("This briefing is on background and is attributable to 'a senior Administration official,'" a voice on the loudspeaker had advised before Langhorne Motley appeared), who said that the meeting between the two presidents, dealing with how best to oppose those who were "destabilizing" and "working against the forces of democracy" in Central America, had in fact ended when the pool camera crew was escorted back into the Oval Office to light the phone call to the astronauts.

On this unexceptional Tuesday midway through his administration the President of the United States was lit and photographed as well in the Old Executive Office Building at a ceremony marking Fair Housing Month (1:30 P.M.); in the Rose Garden signing H.R. 4072, the Agricultural Programs Adjustments Act of 1984 (3:45 P.M.); in the Oval Office signing H.R. 4206, an amendment to the Internal Revenue Code (4:30 P.M.); in the Oval Office greeting the board of directors of the Electronics Industries Association (4:45 P.M.), and, later, in three State Dinner situations: descending the Grand Staircase at 7:45 P.M., toasting President Jorge Blanco in the State Dining Room at 9:15 P.M., and, at 10:35 P.M., addressing his guests, including Wayne Newton and his date, Brooke Shields and her mother, Oscar de la Renta, Pilar Crespi and Tommy Lasorda, in the East Room. Of the day's events, some had been open to the White House press corps at large; others limited to the camera crews and a few pool print reporters, who duly submitted their reports for distribution by the White House press office:

POOL REPORT, Reagan and Fair Housing: The ceremony was attended by representatives of civil rights and fair housing groups, builders and realtors who cooperated with HUD to make sure fair housing law works. The room was half full. Secretary Pierce presented several awards. One celebrity present, Phyllis Hyman, Celebrities for Fair Housing. She is a Broadway musical star. The President stood under a sign:

> Fair Housing
> I support it
> President Reagan supports it
> All America Needs It.

He spoke for about five minutes.

> —*Vic Ostrowidzki*
> *Hearst Newspapers.*

POOL REPORT, Meeting with President Jorge Blanco in the Oval Office: The two presidents sat side by side, exchanging pleasantries. When we were brought in, President Jorge Blanco was in the process of telling President Reagan about his prior visit to the U.S. and that this trip was "an extension of that visit." At one point, President Reagan said "when you were speaking this morning the planes were coming over. They are a big problem at the time they take off. They come every three minutes apart. There is a great deal of public sentiment about that." We never found out what that "sentiment" is because the President suddenly looked up, saw us staring at him expectantly and stopped in mid-sentence. To a question "Are you going to discuss the mining of ports?" Reagan responded "no questions at photo opportunity" and L. Speakes shouted, "lights out."

> —*Vic Ostrowidzki*
> *Hearst Newspapers.*

"Almost everything we do is determined by whether we think it will get on the network news shows in the evening," Larry Speakes, at that time the chief White House spokesman, was quoted as saying in an Associated Press story later that week. "We obviously would like to highlight the positive story of the

day for the President," Michael Deaver, then White House deputy chief of staff, said in the same story, which was about his
efforts to get the President photographed in more "spontaneous"
settings, for example making a surprise visit to Monticello and
eating a hot dog in the Baltimore Orioles' dugout. "I think you
have to give credit to Mike Deaver and to Bill Henkel, our chief
advance man, for setting the scene at the demilitarized zone in
South Korea last December," David Gergen had said not long
before, to *The New York Times*, when asked for highlights of his
three-year tenure as White House director of communications.
"The pictures said as much as anything the President could say."
He was talking about those still photographs and pieces of film
which had shown the President, in the course of a visit to South
Korea, at the 38th parallel, with field glasses and battle helmet.
"Audiences," David Gergen had added, "will listen to you more
if they see the President in an interesting setting. Their memory
of the event will be more vivid. We spend a fair amount of time
thinking about that."

In Washington, then, midway through the Reagan administration, it was taken for granted that the White House schedule should be keyed to the daily network feeds. It was taken
for granted that the efforts of the White House staff should be
directed toward the setting of interesting scenes. It was taken for
granted that the overriding preoccupation of the White House
staff (the subject of a senior staff meeting every morning, an additional meeting every Wednesday, a meeting on foreign coverage
every Thursday, and a "brainstorming" lunch at Blair House every
Friday) should be the invention of what had come to be called
"talking points," the production of "guidance"; the creation and
strategic management of what David Gergen had characterized
as "the story line we are trying to develop that week or that
month."

The story's protagonist, the President himself, was said, even
then, to be "detached," or "disengaged from the decision-making
process," a condition presented, in the accepted cipher, as an
asset in itself: here was a protagonist who "delegated authority,"
who "refused to get mired in details," attractive managerial skills
that suggested a superior purchase on the larger picture. Patrick
Buchanan reported that the President had "mastered the art of
compartmentalization." Morton Kondracke wondered when

"Mr. Reagan's opponents would stop underestimating him and would begin to realize that he has to be pretty smart—even if his intellect does not work like an academic's—and that he has to have a grasp of the large issues confronting the country, even if he has a disconcerting way of not bothering with the details."

"You don't need to know who's playing on the White House tennis court to be a good president," James Baker had liked to say when he was chief of staff. "A president has many roles," White House aides frequently advised reporters, a construct sufficiently supple, even silky, to cover any missed cue, dropped stitch, irreconcilable contradiction or frank looniness that came to light. "I don't have any problem with a reporter or a news person who says the President is uninformed on this issue or that issue," David Gergen had said in the course of a 1984 discussion sponsored by the American Enterprise Institute. "I don't think any of us would challenge that. I do have a problem with the singular focus on this, as if that's the only standard by which we ought to judge a president. What we learned in the last administration was how little having an encyclopedic grasp of all the facts has to do with governing."

Such professed faith in the mystery of "governing," in the ineffable contract that was said to exist between the President and the people (often so called), was only part of what was taken for granted, midway through the Reagan administration. It was also taken for granted that the presidency had been redefined as an essentially passive role, that of "communicator," or "leader," which had been redefined in turn to mean that person whose simple presence before a camera was believed to command support for the policy proposed. It was taken for granted that the key to understanding the policy could be found in the shifts of position and ambition among the President's men. It was taken for granted that the President himself was, if not exactly absent when Larry Speakes ordered lights out, something less than entirely present, the condition expressed even then by the code word "incurious." It was taken for granted, above all, that the reporters and camera operators and still photographers and sound technicians and lighting technicians and producers and electricians and on-camera correspondents showed up at the White House because the President did, and it was also taken for granted, the more innovative construction, that the President showed up at the White House because the reporters and camera operators and still photographers and sound technicians and lighting technicians and producers and electricians and on-camera correspondents did.

In Washington midway through the Reagan administration many things were taken for granted, I learned during time spent there during two consecutive springs, that were not necessarily taken for granted in less abstract venues. I recall talking about the administration's Central American policy, one afternoon in 1984, to David Gergen, and being struck not exactly by what he said but by the way in which he said it, by the terms in which he described what he called the "several stages" of "the same basic policy." The terms David Gergen used that afternoon were exclusively those of presentation. He spoke first of "the very hard line taken in the spring of 1981," a time for "a lot of focus, a lot of attention." He spoke of a period, later the same spring, when "it wasn't looking good, so we kind of moved it back." He spoke of a later period, in 1982, "when some people in the administration thought it could become serious," a time when "we thought we should start laying the groundwork, building some public support for what we might have to do"; a time, then, for moving it not "back" but forward. "I would say this continued to the end of 1983," David Gergen had said finally that afternoon in 1984, his voice trailing off and perhaps his attention: this was to him a familiar chronology, and like many people whose business was the art of the possible he appeared to have only a limited interest in even the most recent past. "Then some people began to see it as a negative issue, and to ask why do we want to make Central America front and center again, so there was an effort to pull it back."

David Gergen had worked in the White House during three administrations, and acquired during the course of them an entire vocabulary of unattributable nods and acquiescent silences, a diction that tended to evaporate like smoke, but the subtext of what he was saying on this spring afternoon in 1984 seemed clear, and to suggest a view of the government of the United States, from someone who had labored at its exact heart for nine of the preceding thirteen years, not substantively different from the view of the government of the United States held by those Cubans to whom I later talked in Miami: the government of the United States was in this view one for which other parts of the world, in this instance Central America, existed only as "issues." In some seasons, during some administrations and in the course of some campaigns, Central America had seemed a useful issue, one to which "focus" and "attention" could profitably be drawn. In other seasons it had seemed a "negative" issue, one which failed to meet, for whatever reason, the test of "looking good."

In all seasons, however, it remained a potentially valuable asset in this business of the art of the possible, and not just an ordinary special-interest, domestic asset, but a national security card, a jeopardy chip, a marker that carried with it the glamour of possible military action, the ultimate interesting setting. As such, it would ideally remain on the board, sometimes available to be moved "back," sometimes available to be moved (whenever the moment seemed to call for a show of determination and resolution, a demonstration, say, of standing tall) "front and center." That each move left a certain residue on the board was what some people in Washington had called their disposal problem, and some people in Miami their betrayal.

16

THERE WERE IN Washington during the Reagan administration a small but significant number of people for whom the commitment to American involvement in Central America did not exist exclusively as an issue, a marker to be moved sometimes front, sometimes back. These were people for whom the commitment to American involvement in Central America was always front, in fact "the" front, the battleground on which, as Ronald Reagan had put it in his second inaugural address and on many occasions before and after, "human freedom" was "on the march." These were people who had believed early on and even formulated what was eventually known as the Reagan Doctrine, people committed to the idea that "rollback," or the reversal of Soviet power which had been part of the rhetoric of the American Right since at least the Eisenhower administration, could now be achieved by supporting guerrilla resistance movements around the world; people who believed that, in the words of *A New Inter-American Policy for the Eighties*, a fifty-three-page policy proposal issued in the summer of 1980 by the Council for Inter-American Security, "containment of the Soviet Union is not enough. Detente is dead. Survival demands a new U.S. foreign policy. America must seize the initiative or perish. For World War III is almost over."

A New Inter-American Policy for the Eighties, usually referred to, because the discussions from which it derived took place in New Mexico, as the Santa Fe statement or the Santa Fe document, was a curious piece of work, less often talked about in this country than in Managua and Havana, where it was generally regarded, according to Edward Cody in the *Washington Post* and Christopher Dickey in *With the Contras*, as a blueprint to Reagan administration intentions in the hemisphere. In fact what seemed most striking about the Santa Fe document was not that it was read in, but that it might have been written in, Managua or Havana. As a document prepared by Americans it seemed not quite authentic, perhaps a piece of "black propaganda," something put forth clandestinely by a foreign government but purporting to be, in the interests of encouraging anti-American sentiment, American. The grasp on the language was not exactly that of native English speakers. The tone of the preoccupations was not exactly that of the American foreign policy establishment:

During the last several years, United States policy toward the other nations within the Western Hemisphere has been one of hoping for the best. Too often it has been a policy described by The Committee of Santa Fe as "anxious accommodation," as if we would prevent the political coloration of Latin America to red crimson by an American-prescribed tint of pale pink. Whatever the pedigree of American policy toward our immediate neighbors, it is not working....

The policies of the past decade regarding arms sales and security assistance are totally bankrupt and discredited at home and abroad.... Combining our arsenal of weaponry with the manpower of the Americas, we can create a free hemisphere of the Americas, that can withstand Soviet-Cuban aggression....

U.S. policy formation must insulate itself from propaganda appearing in the general and specialized media which is inspired by forces specifically hostile to the United States....

U.S. foreign policy must begin to counter (not react against) liberation theology as it is utilized in Latin America by the "liberation theology" clergy....

A campaign to capture the Ibero-American intellectual elite through the media of radio, television, books, articles and pamphlets, plus grants, fellowships and prizes must be initiated. For consideration and recognition are what most intellectuals crave, and such a program would attract them. The U.S. effort must reflect the true sentiments of the American people, not the narrow spectrum of New York and Hollywood....

Human rights, which is a culturally and politically relative concept ... must be abandoned and replaced by a non-interventionist policy of political and ethical realism. The culturally and ethically relative nature of notions of human rights is clear from the fact that Argentines, Brazilians and Chileans find it repugnant that the United States, which legally sanctions the liquidation of more than 1,000,000 unborn children each year, exhibits moral outrage at the killing of a terrorist who bombs and machine-guns innocent citizens. What, they ask, about the human rights of the victims of left-wing terrorism? U.S. policy-makers must discard the illusion that anyone who picks up a Molotov cocktail in the name of human rights is human-righteous....

Havana must be held to account for its policies of aggression against its sister states in the Americas. Among those steps will be the establishment of a Radio Free Cuba, under open U.S. government sponsorship, which will beam objective information to the Cuban people that, among other things, details the costs of Havana's unholy alliance with Moscow. If propaganda fails, a war of national liberation against Castro must be launched.

The five authors of *A New Inter-American Policy for the Eighties*, who called themselves "The Committee of Santa Fe," were all well-known on the Right, regulars on the boards and letter-heads of the various conservative lobbies and foundations around Washington. There was Lynn Francis Bouchey of the Council for Inter-American Security. There was David C. Jordan, a professor of government at the University of Virginia and the coauthor of *Nationalism in Contemporary Latin America*. There was Lieutenant General Gordon Sumner, Jr., at one time chairman of the Inter-American Defense Board and later, during the Reagan administration, special adviser to the assistant secretary of state for inter-American affairs. There was Roger Fontaine, formerly the director for Latin America at the Georgetown University Center for Strategic and International Studies and later, during the Reagan administration, a Latin American specialist at the National Security Council. There was, finally, Lewis Tambs, who had worked in Caracas and Maracaibo as a pipeline engineer for

Creole Petroleum and was later, during the Reagan administration, appointed as ambassador first to Colombia, then to Costa Rica, where, as he eventually told both the Tower Commission and the select committees investigating arms shipments to the contras, he understood himself to have been charged with the task of opening a southern front for the Nicaraguan resistance.

According to these men and to that small but significant group of people who thought as they did, the people with whom they shared the boards and letterheads of the various conservative lobbies and foundations around Washington, the "crisis" facing the United States in Central America was "metaphysical." The war was "for the minds of mankind." What the Santa Fe document had called "ideo-politics" would "prevail." These were not people, as time passed and men like James Baker and Michael Deaver and David Gergen moved into the White House, men who understood that the distinction between a crisis and no crisis was one of "perception," or "setting the scene," particularly close to the center of power. They were all, in varying degrees, ideologues, people who had seized or been seized by an idea, and, as such, they were to the White House only sometimes useful.

Where they were useful, of course, was in voicing the concerns not only of the American Right but in some inchoate way of the President himself: with the Santa Fe document they had even managed, in the rather astonishing context of a foreign policy proposal, to drill through their own discussion of the Roldós Doctrine and the Rio Treaty and into that molten core where "New York" was the problem, and "Hollywood," and women who liquidated their unborn children, the very magma of resentment on which Ronald Reagan's appeal had seemed always to float. Where these conservative spokesmen were less useful, where they were in fact profoundly not useful, was in recognizing when the moment had come to move the war for the minds of mankind "back," or anywhere but "front"; in accepting a place in the wings when the stage was set for a different scene. They tended to lack an appreciation of the full script. They tended not to wait backstage without constant diversion, and it was precisely the contriving of such diversion which seemed to most fully engage, as time went by, the attention and energy of the Reagan White House.

* * *

Sometimes a diversion was referred to as "sending a signal." The White House Outreach Working Group on Central America, or, as it was sometimes called, "Operation Outreach," was a "signal," one of several efforts conceived during 1982 and 1983 when the White House decided that the time was right for, as David Gergen put it, "laying the groundwork," for "building some public support for what we might have to do"; for, in the words of an April 1982 National Security Planning Group document, addressing the "public affairs dimension of the Central American problem" through a "concerted public information effort." There was at first talk about something called "Project Truth." "Project Truth" melted almost immediately into the "Office of Public Diplomacy," which was set up in 1982, put under the direction of a former Miami city official named Otto Juan Reich (who was born in Havana, in 1945, but whose parents had emigrated to Cuba from Austria), and charged with a task which appeared in practice to consist largely of disseminating classified and sometimes "unevaluated" information ("unevaluated" information was that which had not been and in some cases could not be corroborated) tending to support administration contentions about Nicaragua and El Salvador.

The Office of Public Diplomacy, although at the time of its inception controlled by the White House and the National Security Council, was technically under the aegis of the State Department. At the White House itself there was the "Office of Public Liaison" (the word "public," in this administration even more than in others, tended to suggest a sell in progress), and it was out of this "Office of Public Liaison," then under the direction of Faith Ryan Whittlesey, that the White House Outreach Working Group on Central America emerged. The idea was, on its face, straightforward enough: a series of regular briefings, open to the public, at which the administration could "tell its story" about Central America, "make the case" for its interests there. "We hadn't in a systematic way communicated the facts to people who were perfectly willing to do more themselves to support the President but just didn't have access to the information," Faith Ryan Whittlesey told the *Los Angeles Times* not long after the Outreach Working Group began meeting, every Wednesday afternoon at two-thirty, in Room 450 of the Old Executive Office Building. "All the people need is information. They know what to do with it."

The briefings themselves were somewhat less straightforward. For one thing they were not, or the first forty-five of them were not, open to the public at all: they were not open, most specifically, to reporters, the very people who might have been expected to carry the information to a larger number of Americans than were apt to arrange their Wednesday afternoons to include a two-hour session in Room 450 of the Old Executive Office Building. Even after the Outreach briefings had finally been opened to the press, in April of 1984, the White House Office of Public Liaison seemed notably uninterested in talking to reporters: I recall one week in Washington during which, from Monday through Friday, I placed repeated calls to Faith Ryan Whittlesey's office, each time giving my affiliation (I had been asked by a magazine to write a piece about the Reagan administration, and given a kind of introduction to the White House by the magazine's Washington editor), detailing my interest in discussing the Outreach program, and expressing my hope that either Mrs. Whittlesey or someone else in the White House Office of Public Liaison could find a moment to return my call.

Neither Mrs. Whittlesey nor anyone else in the White House Office of Public Liaison did find such a moment, not any day that week or ever, which did not at the time unduly surprise me: it had been my experience that people who worked for the government in Washington were apt to regard anyone who did not work for the government in Washington as a supplicant, a citizen to whom the rightful order must constantly be made clear, and that one of the several ways of asserting this rightful order was by not returning telephone calls. In other words I thought of these unreturned calls to Faith Ryan Whittlesey as unspecific, evidence only of an attitude that came with the particular autointoxication of the territory. Not until later, after I had managed to attend a few Outreach meetings, febrile afternoons in 1984 and 1985 during which the United States was seen to be waging the war for the minds of mankind not only against the Sandinistas in Nicaragua and the FMLN in El Salvador and the Castro government in Cuba and the Machel government in Mozambique but also against its own Congress, against its own State Department, against some members (James Baker, Michael Deaver) of its own executive branch, and, most pointedly, against its own press, did it occur to me that this particular series of unreturned telephone

calls may well have been specific; that there was in the White
House Outreach Working Group on Central America an inherent peculiarity perhaps best left, from the White House point of
view, undiscussed.

This peculiarity was at first hard to assimilate. It did not exactly
derive from the actual briefings, most of which seemed, however
casually inflammatory, however apt to veer vertiginously out of
Central America and into Mozambique and Angola and denun-
ciations of Chester Crocker on the African desk at the State
Department, standard enough. There was Francis X. Gannon, then
adviser to Alejandro Orfila at the Organization of American States,
on "Central America: A Democratic Perspective." ("Somebody
at OAS said about the Kissinger Commission, 'What should we
send them?' And I said, 'Send them a map.'") There was General
Alexander M. Haig, Jr., on "The Imperatives of Central America
in Perspective" ("My opinion of what is happening in Central
America is this: the jury is still out"), a raconteur's version of
American foreign policy during which General Haig referred
to one of its principals with doubtful bonhomie ("So Henry had
one of those Germanic tantrums of his ..."), to another by a
doubtful diminutive ("I again will not make any apologies for
recounting the fact that I was opposed to covert action in 1981, as
Jeannie Kirkpatrick will tell you ..."), and to himself in the third
person, as "Al Haig," or just "Haig."

Some briefings got a little closer to the peculiarity. I recall
one particularly heady Outreach meeting, in 1985, at which one
of the speakers was a fantast named Jack Wheeler, who liked to
say that *Izvestia* had described him as an "ideological gangster"
("When the Soviet Union calls me that, it means I'm starting
to get under their skin") but was identified on the afternoon's
program simply as "Philosopher, Traveler, and Founder of the
Freedom Research Foundation." As it happened I had heard Jack
Wheeler before, at a Conservative Political Action Conference
session on "Rolling Back the Soviet Empire," where he had
received a standing ovation after suggesting that copies of the
Koran be smuggled into the Soviet Union to "stimulate an
Islamic revival" and the subsequent "death of a thousand cuts,"
and I was already familiar not only with many of his exploits
but with his weird and rather punitive enthusiasm. Jack Wheeler
had recently been with the *mujaheddin* in Afghanistan. He had

recently been with Jonas Savimbi in Angola. He had recently been with the insurgents in Cambodia, and Mozambique. He knew of a clandestine radio operating in South Yemen. He saw the first stirrings of democratic liberation in Suriname. He had of course recently been with the contras in Nicaragua, and had, that afternoon in Room 450 of the Old Executive Office Building, brought a few slides to share.

"This is Charley." Jack Wheeler had chuckled as the first slide appeared on the screen. "Charley is a contra. He only looks like he's going to kill you. Actually he's a very nice guy. I told him he looked like Chuck Berry." The slide had changed, and there on the screen was Jack Wheeler himself, his arm around Enrique Bermúdez, the FDN comandante who had been until 1979 a colonel in the Somoza National Guard: "Enrique Bermúdez is convinced—he told me—that only the physical defeat of the Sandinistas will remove the cancer of Soviet-Cuban imperialism and Marxism from Central America." Another slide, this one of a full-breasted young woman carrying a rifle, another chuckle: "One thing that has got to be dispelled is this myth of hopelessness. The myth that they can't win, so why support them ... I wouldn't mind having her fighting alongside of me."

On such afternoons the enemy was manifold, and often within. The "Red Empire" was of course the enemy. "Christian communists" were also the enemy. "Guilt-ridden masochistic liberals" were the enemy, and "the radical chic crowd that always roots for the other side," the "Beverly Hills liberals with their virulent hatred of America." I recall a briefing on the 1984 Salvadoran election in which "people like Tom Brokaw" were the enemy, people like Richard Meislin of *The New York Times* and Sam Dillon of the *Miami Herald*, people whose "sneer was showing," people who "did not need to be in El Salvador to write what they did"; people who were "treated well" ("... although the bar at the Camino Real was closed for the day, they got back to it that night ...") but persisted in following what the briefer of the day, a frequent speaker named Daniel James, who had been in the 1950s managing editor of *The New Leader* and whose distinctly polemical interest in Latin America had led him to the director-ship of the Americas Coalition, one of several amorphous groups formed to support the administration's Central American policy, referred to as "the media party line."

"I'm saying 'party line' in quotes," Daniel James had added quickly. "Because I don't mean to imply that there's any kind of political party involved." This kind of parenthetical disclaimer was not uncommon in Room 450, where irony, or "saying in quotes," was often signaled by raising two fingers on each hand and wiggling them. "Party line" was in quotes, yet there were for Daniel James "just too many similarities" in stories filed from El Salvador. The American press, it seemed, had been "making up deeds of right-wing terror" in El Salvador. The American press, it seemed, had been refusing to "put tough questions to the guerrillas" in El Salvador. "What does that tell you?" Daniel James had asked that afternoon in 1984. "Is this responsible reporting? Or is it done with some kind of political motivation?"

The answer to such questions was, in Room 450, understood, since the meetings of the White House Outreach Working Group on Central America were attended almost exclusively by what might have seemed the already converted, by the convinced, by administration officials and by exiles from the countries in question and by native ideologues from both the heart and the distant fringes of the American Right; true believers who in many cases not only attended the briefings but on occasion gave them. I recall seeing Sam Dickens of the American Security Council, which had co-sponsored the lunch and press conference at which Roberto D'Aubuisson spoke during his illegal 1980 visit to Washington and which was already deeply committed to aiding the Nicaraguan contras. I recall seeing Lynn Francis Bouchey, one of the authors of the Santa Fe document and the chairman of the Council for Inter-American Security, which was equally committed. "Hear, hear," Lynn Francis Bouchey said when Jack Wheeler asked him if the situation in Mozambique did not remind him of the situation in Nicaragua.

This was not a group which would have appeared to need much instruction in administration policy in Central America. This was not a group apt to raise those questions about Central America commonly raised in less special venues. In fact there was for many people in Room 450 just one question about Central America, which was why the United States was compelled to deal through surrogates there when it could be fighting its own war for the minds of mankind, and it was this question that the briefers addressed by tapping into the familiar refrain: the United

States was forced to deal through surrogates because of the defeatists, because of the appeasers, because of the cowards and the useful fools and the traitors, because of what Jack Wheeler had called "that virulent hatred for America as a culture and as a nation and as a society" which was understood, by virtually everyone in the room, to infect the Congress, to infect the State Department, and above all to infect the media, which were, as Otto Juan Reich had said not long after he was appointed coordinator of public diplomacy, "being played like a violin by the Sandinistas."

There were some tricky points in this, although none that the briefers did not negotiate to the apparent satisfaction of most people in the room. The United States was forced to wage the war for the minds of mankind (or, as J. William Middendorf, U.S. ambassador to the OAS, was calling it, "the battle for the freedom of the western world") through surrogates, but in any case these surrogates could, if allowed to do so, win: "The only thing keeping the contras from victory is Congress," as Alexander M. Haig, Jr., had advised the group in Room 450. The war for the minds of mankind was being fought through surrogates only because the United States was thwarted in its wish to enter the war directly, but in any case the entry of the United States could not affect the outcome: "What is needed to shatter the myth of the inevitability of Marxist-Leninism is a genuine peasant rebellion from within a Soviet colony," as Jack Wheeler had advised the group in Room 450. "These heroic freedom fighters ask only for our help, they do not want us to fight for them."

An arresting amount of administration effort went into what might have seemed this marginal project. The weekly planning meetings for the Outreach program were attended not only by Faith Ryan Whittlesey and her aides at the Office of Public Liaison but also by representatives from the United States Information Agency, from the Central Intelligence Agency, from the State Department and from the National Security Council. The National Security Council was often represented by the protean Colonel Oliver North (Colonel North was responsible as well for overseeing Otto Juan Reich's Office of Public Diplomacy at the State Department), who was, according to a *Washington Post* story in August of 1985, a "mainstay" of the Outreach project, not only in the planning meetings but also as a "briefer of choice" in Room 450 itself.

Some of the peculiarity inherent in the Outreach project seemed clear enough at the time. It was of course clear that the program had been designed principally, if not entirely, as a weekly audience between the administration and its most passionate, most potentially schismatic communicants; a bone thrown to those famously restless troops on the far frontiers of the faith. It was also clear that many people in Room 450 on these Wednesday afternoons had links to, or could be useful to, the private funding network then being quite publicly organized, in support of the Reagan Doctrine and the war for the minds of mankind, under the official direction of Major General John K. Singlaub and what was known even then to be the unofficial direction of some of the very administration officials who gave the briefings in Room 450.

Other things were less clear than they might have been. One thing that was less clear, in those high years of the Reagan administration when we had not yet begun to see just how the markers were being moved, was how many questions there might later be about what had been the ends and what the means, what the problem and what the solution; about what, among people who measured the consequences of what they said and did exclusively in terms of approval ratings affected and network news calibrated and pieces of legislation passed or not passed, had come first, the war for the minds of mankind or the private funding network or the need to make a move for those troops on the far frontiers. What was also less clear then, particularly in Washington, most abstract of cities, entirely absorbed by the messages it was sending itself, narcotized by its own action, rapt in the contemplation of its own markers and its own moves, was just how much residue was already on the board.

Steven Carr for example was residue. Jesus Garcia for example was residue. Steven Carr was, at twenty-six, a South Florida lowlife, a sometime Naples construction worker with the motto DEATH BEFORE DISHONOR and a flaming skull tattooed on his left biceps; a discharge from the Navy for alcohol abuse; and a grand-theft conviction for stealing two gold-and-diamond rings, valued at $578, given to his mother by his stepfather. "She only wore them on holidays, I thought she'd never notice they were gone," Steven

Carr later said about the matter of his mother's rings. He did not speak Spanish. He had no interest in any side of the conflict in Nicaragua. Nonetheless, in March of 1985, according to the story he began telling after he had been arrested in Costa Rica on weapons charges and was awaiting trial at La Reforma prison in San José, Steven Carr had collected arms for the contras at various locations around Dade County, loaded them onto a chartered Convair 440 at Fort Lauderdale–Hollywood International Airport, accompanied this shipment to Ilopango airport in San Salvador, and witnessed the eventual delivery of the arms to a unit of 2506 veterans fighting with the contras from a base about three miles south of the Nicaraguan border.

This story later became familiar, but its significance at the time Steven Carr first told it, in the summer of 1985 to Juan Tamayo of the *Miami Herald*, was that he was the first person to publicly claim firsthand knowledge of all stages of a single shipment. By the summer of 1986, after Steven Carr had bonded out of La Reforma and was back in South Florida (the details of how he got there were disputed, but either did or did not involve American embassy officials in Panama and San José who either did or did not give him a plane ticket and instructions to "get the hell out of Dodge"), doing six months in the Collier County jail for violation of probation on the outstanding matter of his mother's rings, he was of course telling it as well to investigators from various congressional committees and from the U.S. attorney's office in Miami. This was the point, in August 1986, at which his lawyers asked that he be released early and placed, on the grounds that the story he was telling endangered his life, in a witness protection program. "I'm not too popular with a lot of people because I'm telling the truth," Steven Carr told the *Miami Herald* a few days before this petition was heard and denied. "I wouldn't feel very safe just walking the streets after all this is over."

Steven Carr was released from the Collier County jail, having served his full sentence, on November 20, 1986. Twenty-three days later, at two-thirty on the morning of December 13, 1986, Steven Carr collapsed outside the room he was renting in Panorama City, California (a room which, according to the woman from whom he had rented it, Jackie Scott, he rarely left, and in which he slept with the doors locked and the lights on), convulsed, and died, of an apparent cocaine overdose. "I'm sorry,"

Steven Carr had said when Jackie Scott, whose daughter had heard "a commotion" and woken her, found him lying in the driveway. Jackie Scott told the *Los Angeles Times* that she had not seen Steven Carr drinking or taking drugs that evening, nor could she shed any light on what he had said next: "I paranoided out—I ate it all."

Jesus Garcia was a former Dade County corrections officer who was, at the time he began telling his story early in 1986, doing time in Miami for illegal possession of a MAC-10 with silencer. Jesus Garcia, who had been born in the United States of Cuban parents and thought of himself as a patriot, talked about having collected arms for the contras during the spring of 1985, and also about the plan, which he said had been discussed in the cocktail lounge of the Howard Johnson's near the Miami airport in February of 1985, to assassinate the new American ambassador to Costa Rica, blow up the embassy there, and blame it on the Sandinistas. The idea, Jesus Garcia said, had been to give the United States the opportunity it needed to invade Nicaragua, and also to collect on a million-dollar contract the Colombian cocaine cartel was said to have out on the new American ambassador to Costa Rica, who had recently been the American ambassador to Colombia and had frequently spoken of what he called "narco-guerrillas."

There were in the story told by Jesus Garcia and in the story told by Steven Carr certain details that appeared to coincide. Both Jesus Garcia and Steven Carr mentioned the Howard Johnson's near the Miami airport, which happened also to be the Howard Johnson's with the seventeen-dollar-a-night "guerrilla discount." Both Jesus Garcia and Steven Carr mentioned meetings in Miami with an American named Bruce Jones, who was said to own a farm on the border between Costa Rica and Nicaragua. Both Jesus Garcia and Steven Carr mentioned Thomas Posey, the Alabama produce wholesaler who had founded the para-military group CMA, or Civilian Materiel Assistance, formerly Civilian Military Assistance. Both Jesus Garcia and Steven Carr mentioned Robert Owen, the young Stanford graduate who had gone to Washington to work on the staff of Senator Dan Quayle (R-Ind.), had then moved into public relations, at Gray and Company, had in January of 1985 founded the nonprofit Institute for Democracy, Education, and Assistance, or IDEA (which was by the fall of 1985 on a consultancy contract to the State Department's Nicaraguan Humanitarian Assistance Office), and had been, it was later revealed, carrying cash to and from Central America for Oliver North.

This was, as described, a small world, and one in which encounters seemed at once random and fated, as in the waking dream that was Miami itself. People in this world spoke of having "tripped into an organization." People saw freedom fighters on "Nightline," and then in Miami. People saw boxes in motel rooms, and concluded that the boxes contained C-4. People received telephone calls from strangers, and picked them up at the airport at three in the morning, and began looking for a private plane to fly to Central America. Some people just turned up out of the nowhere: Jesus Garcia happened to meet Thomas Posey because he was working the afternoon shift at the Dade County jail on the day Thomas Posey was booked for trying to take a .380 automatic pistol through the X-ray machine on Concourse G at the Miami airport. Some people turned up not exactly out of nowhere but all over the map: Jesus Garcia said that he had seen Robert Owen in Miami, more specifically, as an assistant U.S. attorney in Miami put it, "at that Howard Johnson's when they were planning that stuff," by which the assistant U.S. attorney meant weapons flights. Steven Carr said that he had seen Robert Owen in Costa Rica, witnessing a weapons delivery at the base near the Nicaraguan border. Robert Owen, when he eventually appeared before the select committees, acknowledged that he had been present when such a delivery was made, but said that he never saw the actual unloading, and that his presence on the scene was, as the *Miami Herald* put it, "merely coincidental": another random but fated encounter.

There were no particularly novel elements in either the story told by Jesus Garcia or the story told by Steven Carr. They were Miami stories, fragments of the underwater narrative, and as such they were of a genre familiar in this country since at least the Bay of Pigs. Such stories had often been, like these, intrinsically impossible to corroborate. Such stories had often been of doubtful provenance, had been either leaked by prosecutors unable to make a case or elicited, like these, in jailhouse interviews, a circumstance which has traditionally tended, like a DEATH BEFORE DISHONOR tattoo, to work against the credibility of the teller. Any single Miami story, moreover, was hard to follow, and typically required a more extensive recall of other Miami stories than most people outside Miami could offer. Characters would frequently reappear. A convicted bomber named Hector Cornillot, a onetime member of Orlando Bosch's Cuban Power movement, turned out, for example, to have been during the spring of 1985 the night bookkeeper at the Howard Johnson's near the Miami airport. Motivation, often opaque in a first or a second appearance, might come clear only in a third, or a tenth.

Miami stories were low, and lurid, and so radically reliant on the inductive leap that they tended to attract advocates of an ideological or a paranoid bent, which was another reason they remained, for many people, easy to dismiss. Stories like these had been told to the Warren Commission in 1964, but many people had preferred to discuss what was then called the climate of violence, and the healing process. Stories like these had been told during the Watergate investigations in 1974, but the President had resigned, enabling the healing process, it was again said, to begin. Stories like these had been told to the Church committee in 1975 and 1976, and to the House Select Committee on Assassinations in 1977 and 1978, but many people had preferred to focus instead on the constitutional questions raised, not on the hypodermic syringe containing Black Leaf 40 with which the CIA was trying in November of 1963 to get Fidel Castro assassinated, not on Johnny Roselli in the oil drum in Biscayne Bay, not on that motel room in Dallas where Marita Lorenz claimed she had seen the rifles and the scopes and Frank Sturgis and Orlando Bosch and Jack Ruby and the Novo brothers, but on the separation of powers, and the proper role of congressional oversight. "The search for conspiracy," Anthony Lewis had written in *The New York Times* in September of 1975, "only increases the elements of morbidity and paranoia and fantasy in this country. It romanticizes crimes that are terrible because of their lack of purpose. It obscures our necessary understanding, all of us, that in this life there is often tragedy without reason."

This was not at the time an uncommon note, nor was it later. Particularly in Washington, where the logical consequences of any administration's imperial yearnings were thought to be voided when the voting levels were next pulled, the study of the underwater narrative, these stories about what people in Miami may or may not have done on the basis of what people in Washington had or had not said, was believed to serve no useful purpose. That the assassination of John F. Kennedy might or might not have been the specific consequence of his administration's own incursions into the tropic of morbidity and paranoia and fantasy (as early as 1964, two staff attorneys for the Warren Commission, W. David Slawson and William Coleman, had prepared a memorandum urging the commission to investigate the possibility that Lee Harvey Oswald had been acting for, or had been set up by, anti-Castro Cuban exiles) did not recommend, in this view, a closer study of the tropic. That there might or might not be, in the wreckage of the Reagan administration, certain consequences to that administration's similar incursions recommended only, in this view, that it was again time to focus on the mechanical model, time to talk about runaway agencies, arrogance in the executive branch, about constitutional crises and the nature of the presidency, about faults in the structure, flaws in the process; time to talk, above all, about 1988, when the levers would again be pulled and the consequences voided and any lingering morbidity dispelled by the enthusiasms, the energies, of the new team. "Dick Goodwin was handling Latin America and a dozen other problems," Arthur M. Schlesinger, Jr., once told us about the early months of the Kennedy administration, as suggestive a sentence as has perhaps been written about this tabula rasa effect in Washington life.

In the late summer of 1985, some months after the Outreach meeting in Room 450 of the Old Executive Office Building in Washington at which I had heard Jack Wheeler talk about the necessity for supporting freedom fighters around the world, I happened to receive a letter ("Dear Fellow American") from Major General John K. Singlaub, an invitation to the International Freedom Fighters Dinner to be held that September in the Crystal Ballroom of the Registry Hotel in Dallas. This letter was dated August 7, 1985, a date on which Steven Carr was already sitting in La Reforma prison in San José and on which Jesus Garcia was one day short of receiving a call from a twenty-nine-year-old stranger who identified himself as Allen Saum, who said that he was a major in the U.S. Marines and had been sent by the White House, who enlisted Jesus Garcia in a mission he described as "George Bush's baby," and who then telephoned the Miami office of the FBI and told them where they could pick up Jesus Garcia and his MAC-10. "He looked typical Ivy League, I thought he must be CIA," Jesus Garcia later said about "Allen Saum," who did not show up for Jesus Garcia's trial but did appear at a pretrial hearing, where he said that he took orders from a man he knew only as "Sam."

The letter from General Singlaub urged that any recipient unable to attend the Dallas dinner ($500 a plate) plan in any case to have his or her name listed on the International Freedom Fighters Commemorative Program ($50 a copy), which General Singlaub would, in turn, "personally present to President Reagan." Even the smallest donation, General Singlaub stressed, would go far toward keeping "freedom's light burning." The *mujaheddin* in Afghanistan, for example, who would be among the freedom fighters to benefit from the Dallas dinner (along with those in Angola, Laos, South Vietnam, Cambodia, Mozambique, Ethiopia, and of course Nicaragua), had not long before destroyed "approximately twenty-five percent of the Afghan government's Soviet supplied air force" (or, according to General Singlaub, twenty MIGs, worth $100 million) with just "a few hundred dollars spent on plastic explosives."

I recall experiencing, as I read this sentence about the *mujaheddin* and the few hundred dollars spent on plastic explosives, the exact sense of expanding, or contracting, possibility that I had recently experienced during flights to Miami. Many apparently disparate elements seemed to be converging in the letter from General Singlaub, and the convergence was not one which discouraged that "search for conspiracy" deplored by Anthony Lewis a decade before. The narrative in which a few hundred dollars spent on plastic explosives could reverse history, which appeared to be the scenario on which General Singlaub and many of the people I had seen in Room 450 were operating, was the same narrative in which meetings at private houses in Miami Beach had been seen to overturn governments. This was that narrative in which the actions of individuals had been seen to affect events directly, in which revolutions and counterrevolutions had been framed in the private sector; that narrative in which the state security apparatus existed to be enlisted by one or another private player.

This was also the narrative in which words had tended to have consequences, and stories endings. NICARAGUA HOY, CUBA MAÑANA. When Jesus Garcia talked about meeting in the cocktail lounge of the Howard Johnson's near the Miami airport to discuss a plan to assassinate the American ambassador to Costa Rica, bomb the American embassy there, and blame it on the Sandinistas, the American ambassador he was talking about was Lewis Tambs, one of the authors of the Santa Fe document, the fifty-three pages which had articulated for many people in Washington the reasons for the exact American involvement in the politics of the Caribbean which this plan discussed in the cocktail lounge of the Howard Johnson's near the Miami airport was meant to ensure. Let me tell you about Cuban terrorists, Raúl Rodríguez had said at the midnight dinner in the Arquitectonica condominium overlooking Biscayne Bay. Cuba never grew plastique. Cuba grew tobacco, Cuba grew sugarcane. Cuba never grew C-4.

The air that evening in Miami had been warm and soft even at midnight, and the glass doors had been open onto the terrace overlooking the bay. The daughter of the fifteenth president of the Republic of Cuba, María Elena Prío Durán, whose father's grave at Woodlawn Park Cemetery in Miami lay within sight of the private crypt to which the body of another exiled president, Anastasio Somoza Debayle of Nicaragua, was flown forty-eight hours after his assassination in Asunción (no name on this crypt, no dates, no epitaph, only the monogram "AS" worked among the lilies on a stained-glass window, as if the occupant had negotiated himself out of history), had lit her cigarette and immediately put it out. When Raúl Rodríguez said that evening that C-4 grew here, he was talking about what it had cost to forget that decisions made in Washington had effects outside Washington; about the reverberative effect of certain ideas, and about their consequences. This dinner in Miami took place on March 26, 1985. The meetings in Miami described by Jesus Garcia had already taken place. The flights out of Miami described by Jesus Garcia and Steven Carr had already taken place. These meetings and these flights were the least of what had already taken place; of what was to take place; and also of what, in this world where stories have tended to have endings, has yet to take place. "As a matter of fact I was very definitely involved in the decisions about support to the freedom fighters," the fortieth President of the United States said more than two years later, on May 15, 1987. "My idea to begin with."

AFTER HENRY

This book is dedicated to Henry Robbins and to Bret Easton Ellis, each of whom did time with its publisher.

CONTENTS

I
AFTER HENRY

AFTER HENRY

IN THE SUMMER of 1966 I was living in a borrowed house in Brentwood, and had a new baby. I had published one book, three years before. My husband was writing his first. Our daybook for those months shows no income at all for April, $305.06 for May, none for June, and, for July, $5.29, a dividend on our single capital asset, fifty shares of Transamerica stock left to me by my grandmother. This 1966 daybook shows laundry lists and appointments with pediatricians. It shows sixty christening presents received and sixty thank-you notes written, shows the summer sale at Saks and the attempt to retrieve a fifteen-dollar deposit from Southern Counties Gas, but it does not show the date in June on which we first met Henry Robbins.

This seems to me now a peculiar and poignant omission, and one that suggests the particular fractures that new babies and borrowed houses can cause in the moods of people who live largely by their wits. Henry Robbins was until that June night in 1966 an abstract to us, another New York editor, a stranger at Farrar, Straus & Giroux who had called or written and said that he was coming to California to see some writers. I thought so little of myself as a writer that summer that I was obscurely ashamed to go to dinner with still another editor, ashamed to sit down again and discuss this "work" I was not doing, but in the end I did go: in the end I put on a black silk dress and went with my husband to the Bistro in Beverly Hills and met Henry Robbins and began, right away, to laugh. The three of us laughed until two in the morning, when we were no longer at the Bistro but at the Daisy, listening over and over to "In the Midnight Hour" and "Softly As I Leave You" and to one another's funny, brilliant, enchanting voices, voices that transcended lost laundry and babysitters and prospects of $5.29, voices full of promise, *writers'* voices.

In short we got drunk together, and before the summer was out Henry Robbins had signed contracts with each of us, and, from that summer in 1966 until the summer of 1979, very few weeks passed during which one or the other of us did not talk to Henry

Robbins about something which was amusing us or interesting us or worrying us, about our hopes and about our doubts, about work and love and money and gossip; about our news, good or bad. On the July morning in 1979 when we got word from New York that Henry Robbins had died on his way to work a few hours before, had fallen dead, age fifty-one, to the floor of the 14th Street subway station, there was only one person I wanted to talk to about it, and that one person was Henry.

"Childhood is the kingdom where nobody dies" is a line, from the poem by Edna St.Vincent Millay, that has stuck in my mind ever since I first read it, when I was in fact a child and nobody died. Of course people did die, but they were either very old or died unusual deaths, died while rafting on the Stanislaus or loading a shotgun or doing 95 drunk: death was construed as either a "blessing" or an exceptional case, the dramatic instance on which someone else's (never our own) story turned. Illness, in that kingdom where I and most people I knew lingered long past childhood, proved self-limiting. Fever of unknown etiology signaled only the indulgence of a week in bed. Chest pains, investigated, revealed hypochondria.

As time passed it occurred to many of us that our benign experience was less than general, that we had been to date blessed or charmed or plain lucky, players on a good roll, but by that time we were busy: caught up in days that seemed too full, too various, too crowded with friends and obligations and children, dinner parties and deadlines, commitments and overcommitments. "You can't imagine how it is when everyone you know is gone," someone I knew who was old would say to me, and I would nod, uncomprehending, yes I can, I can imagine; would even think, God forgive me, that there must be a certain peace in outliving all debts and claims, in being known to no one, floating free. I believed that days would be too full forever, too crowded with friends there was no time to see. I believed, by way of contemplating the future, that we would all be around for one another's funerals. I was wrong. I had failed to imagine, I had not understood. Here was the way it was going to be: I would be around for Henry's funeral, but he was not going to be around for mine.

* * *

The funeral was not actually a funeral but a memorial service, in the prevailing way, an occasion for all of us to meet on a tropical August New York morning in the auditorium of the Society for Ethical Culture at 64th and Central Park West. A truism about working with language is that other people's arrangements of words are always crowding in on one's actual experience, and this morning in New York was no exception. "Abide with me: do not go away" was a line I kept hearing, unspoken, all through the service; my husband was speaking, and half a dozen other writers and publishers who had been close to Henry Robbins— Wilfrid Sheed, Donald Barthelme, John Irving, Doris Grumbach; Robert Giroux from Farrar, Straus & Giroux; John Macrae from Dutton—but the undersongs I heard were fragments of a poem by Delmore Schwartz, dead thirteen years, the casualty of another New York summer. *Abide with me: do not go away*, and then:

> *Controlling our pace before we get old,*
> *Walking together on the receding road,*
> *Like Chaplin and his orphan sister.*

Five years before, Henry had left Farrar, Straus for Simon and Schuster, and I had gone with him. Two years after that he had left Simon and Schuster and gone to Dutton. This time I had not gone with him, had stayed where my contract was, and yet I remained Henry's orphan sister, Henry's writer. I remember that he worried from time to time about whether we had enough money, and that he would sometimes, with difficulty, ask us if we needed some. I remember that he did not like the title *Play It As It Lays* and I remember railing at him on the telephone from a hotel room in Chicago because my husband's novel *True Confessions* was not yet in the window at Kroch's & Brentano's and I remember a Halloween night in New York in 1970 when our children went trick-or-treating together in the building on West 86th Street in which Henry and his wife and their two children then lived. I remember that this apartment on West 86th Street had white curtains, and that on one hot summer evening we all sat there and ate chicken in tarragon aspic and watched the curtains lift and move in the air off the river and our world seemed one of considerable promise.

I remember arguing with Henry over the use of the second person in the second sentence of *A Book of Common Prayer*. I remember his actual hurt and outrage when any of us, any of his orphan sisters or brothers, got a bad review or a slighting word or even a letter that he imagined capable of marring our most inconsequential moment. I remember him flying to California because I wanted him to read the first 110 pages of *A Book of Common Prayer* and did not want to send them to New York. I remember him turning up in Berkeley one night when I needed him in 1975; I was to lecture that night, an occasion freighted by the fact that I was to lecture many members of the English department who had once lectured me, and I was, until Henry arrived, scared witless, the sacrificial star of my own exposure dream. I remember that he came first to the Faculty Club, where I was staying, and walked me down the campus to 2000 LSB, where I was to speak. I remember him telling me that it would go just fine. I remember believing him.

I always believed what Henry told me, except about two things, the title *Play It As It Lays* and the use of the second person in the second sentence of *A Book of Common Prayer*, believed him even when time and personalities and the difficulty of making a living by either editing books or writing them had complicated our relationship. What editors do for writers is mysterious, and does not, contrary to general belief, have much to do with titles and sentences and "changes." Nor, my railing notwithstanding, does it have much to do with the window at Kroch's & Brentano's in Chicago. The relationship between an editor and a writer is much subtler and deeper than that, at once so elusive and so radical that it seems almost parental: the editor, if the editor was Henry Robbins, was the person who gave the writer the idea of himself, the idea of herself, the image of self that enabled the writer to sit down alone and do it.

This is a tricky undertaking, and requires the editor not only to maintain a faith the writer shares only in intermittent flashes but also to like the writer, which is hard to do. Writers are only rarely likeable. They bring nothing to the party, leave their game at the typewriter. They fear their contribution to the general welfare to be evanescent, even doubtful, and, since the business of publishing is an only marginally profitable enterprise that increasingly attracts people who sense this marginality all too keenly, people who feel defensive or demeaned because they are not at the tables where the high rollers play (not managing mergers, not running motion picture studios, not even principal players in whatever larger concern holds the paper on the publishing house), it has become natural enough for a publisher or an editor to seize on the writer's fear, reinforce it, turn the writer into a necessary but finally unimportant accessory to the "real" world of publishing. Publishers and editors do not, in the real world, get on the night TWA to California to soothe a jumpy midlist writer. Publishers and editors in the real world have access to corporate G-3s, and prefer cruising the Galápagos with the raiders they have so far failed to become. A publisher or editor who has contempt for his own class position can find solace in transferring that contempt to the writer, who typically has no G-3 and can be seen as dependent on the publisher's largesse.

This was not a solace, nor for that matter a contempt, that Henry understood. The last time I saw him was two months before he fell to the floor of the 14th Street subway station, one night in Los Angeles when the annual meeting of the American Booksellers Association was winding to a close. He had come by the house on his way to a party and we talked him into skipping the party, staying for dinner. What he told me that night was indirect, and involved implicit allusions to other people and other commitments and everything that had happened among us since that summer night in 1966, but it came down to this: he wanted me to know that I could do it without him. That was a third thing Henry told me that I did not believe.

II
WASHINGTON

IN THE REALM OF THE FISHER KING

PRESIDENT RONALD REAGAN, we were later told by his speech-writer Peggy Noonan, spent his off-camera time in the White House answering fifty letters a week, selected by the people who ran his mail operation, from citizens. He put the family pictures these citizens sent him in his pockets and desk drawers. When he did not have the zip code, he apologized to his secretary for not looking it up himself. He sharpened his own pencils, we were told by Helene von Damm, his secretary first in Sacramento and then in Washington, and he also got his own coffee.

In the post-Reagan rush to establish that we knew all along about this peculiarity in that particular White House, we forgot the actual peculiarity of the place, which had to do less with the absence at the center than with the amount of centrifugal energy this absence left spinning free at the edges. The Reagan White House was one in which great expectations were allowed into play. Ardor, of a kind that only rarely survives a fully occupied Oval Office, flourished unchecked. "You'd be in someone's home and on the way to the bathroom you'd pass the bedroom and see a big thick copy of Paul Johnson's *Modern Times* lying half open on the table by the bed," Peggy Noonan, who gave Ronald Reagan the boys of Pointe du Hoc and the *Challenger* crew slipping the surly bonds of earth and who gave George Bush the thousand points of light and the kinder, gentler nation, told us in *What I Saw at the Revolution: A Political Life in the Reagan Era.*

"Three months later you'd go back and it was still there," she wrote. "There were words. You had a notion instead of a thought and a dustup instead of a fight, you had a can-do attitude and you were in touch with the zeitgeist. No one had intentions they had an agenda and no one was wrong they were fundamentally wrong and you didn't work on something you broke your pick on it and it wasn't an agreement it was a done deal. All politics is local but more to the point all economics is micro. There were phrases: personnel is policy and ideas have consequences and

ideas drive politics and it's a war of ideas … and to do nothing is
to endorse the status quo and roll back the Brezhnev Doctrine
and there's no such thing as a free lunch, especially if you're dining with the press."

Peggy Noonan arrived in Washington in 1984, thirty-three years
old, out of Brooklyn and Massapequa and Fairleigh Dickinson
and CBS Radio, where she had written Dan Rather's five-minute
commentaries. A few years later, when Rather told her that in lieu
of a Christmas present he wanted to make a donation to her favorite
charity, the charity she specified was The William J. Casey Fund for
the Nicaraguan Resistance. She did not immediately, or for some
months after, meet the man for whose every public utterance she
and the other staff writers were responsible; at the time she checked
into the White House, no speechwriter had spoken to Mr. Reagan
in more than a year. "We wave to him," one said.

   In the absence of an actual president, this resourceful child of a
large Irish Catholic family sat in her office in the Old Executive
Office Building and invented an ideal one: she read Vachel
Lindsay (particularly "I brag and chant of Bryan Bryan Bryan /
Candidate for President who sketched a silver Zion") and she
read Franklin Delano Roosevelt (whom she pictured, again ideally, up in Dutchess County "sitting at a great table with all the
chicks, eating a big spring lunch of beefy red tomatoes and potato
salad and mayonnaise and deviled eggs on the old china with the
flowers almost rubbed off") and she thought "this is how Reagan
should sound." What Miss Noonan had expected Washington to
be, she told us, was "Aaron Copland and 'Appalachian Spring.'"
What she found instead was a populist revolution trying to make
itself, a crisis of raised expectations and lowered possibilities, the
children of an expanded middle class determined to tear down the
established order and what they saw as its repressive liberal ortho-
doxies: "There were libertarians whose girlfriends had just given
birth to their sons, hoisting a Coors with social conservatives
who walked into the party with a wife who bothered to be warm
and a son who carried a Mason jar of something daddy grew in
the backyard. There were Protestant fundamentalists hoping they
wouldn't be dismissed by neocon intellectuals from Queens and
neocons talking to fundamentalists thinking: I wonder if when

they look at me they see what Annie Hall's grandmother saw when she looked down the table at Woody Allen."

She stayed at the White House until the spring of 1986, when she was more or less forced out by the refusal of Donald Regan, at that time chief of staff, to approve her promotion to head speechwriter. Regan thought her, according to Larry Speakes, who did not have a famous feel for the romance of the revolution, too "hard-line," too "dogmatic," too "right-wing," too much "Buchanan's proté-gée." On the occasion of her resignation she received a form letter from the president, signed with the auto-pen. Donald Regan said that there was no need for her to have what was referred to as "a good-bye moment," a farewell shake-hands with the president. On the day Donald Regan himself left the White House, Miss Noonan received this message, left on her answering machine by a friend at the White House:"Hey, Peggy, Don Regan didn't get his good-bye moment." By that time she was hearing the "true tone of Washington" less as "Appalachian Spring" than as something a little more raucous, "nearer," she said, "to Jefferson Starship and 'They Built This City on Rock and Roll.'"

The White House she rendered was one of considerable febrility. Everyone, she told us, could quote Richard John Neuhaus on what was called the collapse of the dogmas of the secular enlightenment. Everyone could quote Michael Novak on what was called the collapse of the assumption that education is or should be "value-free." Everyone could quote George Gilder on what was called the humane nature of the free market. Everyone could quote Jean-François Revel on how democracies perish, and everyone could quote Jeane Kirkpatrick on authoritarian versus totalitarian governments, and everyone spoke of "the movement," as in "he's movement from way back," or "she's good, she's hard-core."

They talked about subverting the pragmatists, who believed that an issue could not be won without the *Washington Post* and the networks, by "going over the heads of the media to the people." They charged one another's zeal by firing off endless letters, mem-os, clippings. "Many thanks for Macedo's new monograph; his brand of judicial activism is more principled than Tribe's," such letters read. "If this gets into the hands of the Russians, it's curtains for the free world!" was the tone to take on the yellow Post-It attached to a clipping. "Soldier on!" was the way to sign off. Those PROF memos we later saw from Robert McFarlane to Lieutenant Colonel Oliver North ("Roger Ollie. Well done—if the world only knew how many times you have kept a semblance of integrity and gumption to US policy, they would make you Secretary of State. But they can't know and would complain if they did—such is the state of democracy in the late 20th century.... Bravo Zulu") do not seem, in this context, quite so unusual.

"Bureaucrats with soft hands adopted the clipped laconic style of John Ford characters," Miss Noonan noted. "A small man from NSC was asked at a meeting if he knew of someone who could work up a statement. Yes, he knew someone at State, a paid pen who's pushed some good paper." To be a moderate was to be a "squish," or a "weenie," or a "wuss." "He got rolled," they would say of someone who had lost the day, or, "He took a lickin' and kept on tickin'." They walked around the White House wearing ties ("slightly stained," according to Miss Noonan, "from the mayonnaise that fell from the sandwich that was wolfed down at the working lunch on judicial reform") embroidered with the code of the movement: eagles, flags, busts of Jefferson. Little gold Laffer curves identified the wearers as "free-market purists." Liberty bells stood for "judicial restraint."

The favored style here, like the favored foreign policy, seems to have been less military than paramilitary, a matter of talking tough. "That's not off my disk," Lieutenant Colonel Oliver North would snap by way of indicating that an idea was not his. "The fellas," as Miss Noonan called them, the sharp, the smooth, the inner circle and those who aspired to it, made a point of not using seat belts on Air Force One. The less smooth flaunted souvenirs of action on the far borders of the Reagan doctrine. "Jack Wheeler came back from Afghanistan with a Russian officer's belt slung over his shoulder," Miss Noonan recalls. "Grover Norquist came back from Africa rubbing his eyes from taking notes in a tent with Savimbi." Miss Noonan herself had lunch in the White House mess with a "Mujahadeen warrior" and his public relations man. "What is the condition of your troops in the field?" she asked. "We need help," he said. The Filipino steward approached, pad and pencil in hand. The mujahadeen leader looked up. "I will have meat," he said.

* * *

This is not a milieu in which one readily places Nancy Reagan, whose preferred style derived from the more structured, if equally rigorous, world from which she had come. The nature of this world was not very well understood. I recall being puzzled, on visits to Washington during the first year or two of the Reagan administration, by the tenacity of certain misapprehensions about the Reagans and the men generally regarded as their intimates, that small group of industrialists and entrepreneurs who had encouraged and financed, as a venture in risk capital, Ronald Reagan's appearances in both Sacramento and Washington. The president was above all, I was told repeatedly, a Californian, a Westerner, as were the acquaintances who made up his kitchen cabinet; it was the "Westernness" of these men that explained not only their rather intransigent views about America's mission in the world but also their apparent lack of interest in or identification with Americans for whom the trend was less reliably up. It was "Westernness," too, that could explain those affronts to the local style so discussed in Washington during the early years, the overwrought clothes and the borrowed jewelry and the Le Cirque hair and the wall-to-wall carpeting and the table settings. In style and substance alike, the Reagans and their friends were said to display what was first called "the California mentality," and then, as the administration got more settled and the social demonology of the exotic landscape more specific, "the California Club mentality."

I recall hearing about this "California Club mentality" at a dinner table in Georgetown, and responding with a certain atavistic outrage (I was from California, my own brother then lived during the week at the California Club); what seems curious in retrospect is that many of the men in question, including the president, had only a convenient connection with California in particular and the West in general. William Wilson was actually born in Los Angeles, and Earle Jorgenson in San Francisco, but the late Justin Dart was born in Illinois, graduated from Northwestern, married a Walgreen heiress in Chicago, and did not move United Rexall, later Dart Industries, from Boston to Los Angeles until he was already its president. The late Alfred Bloomingdale was born in New York, graduated from Brown, and seeded the Diners Club with money from his family's New York store. What these men represented was not "the West" but what was for this century a relatively new kind of monied class in America, a group devoid of social responsibilities precisely because their ties to any one place had been so attenuated.

Ronald and Nancy Reagan had in fact lived most of their adult lives in California, but as part of the entertainment community, the members of which do not belong to the California Club. In 1964, when I first went to live in Los Angeles, and for some years later, life in the upper reaches of this community was, for women, quite rigidly organized. Women left the table after dessert, and had coffee upstairs, isolated in the bedroom or dressing room with demitasse cups and rock sugar ordered from London and cinnamon sticks in lieu of demitasse spoons. On the hostess's dressing table there were always very large bottles of Fracas and Gardenia and Tuberose. The dessert that preceded this retreat (a soufflé or mousse with raspberry sauce) was inflexibly served on Flora Danica plates, and was itself preceded by the ritual of the finger bowls and the doilies. I recall being repeatedly told a cautionary tale about what Joan Crawford had said to a young woman who removed her finger bowl but left the doily. The details of exactly what Joan Crawford had said and to whom and at whose table she had said it differed with the teller, but it was always Joan Crawford, and it always involved the doily; one of the reasons Mrs. Reagan ordered the famous new china was because, she told us in her own account of life in the Reagan White House, *My Turn*, the Johnson china had no finger bowls.

These subtropical evenings were not designed to invigorate. Large arrangements of flowers, ordered from David Jones, discouraged attempts at general conversation, ensuring that the table was turned on schedule. Expensive "resort" dresses and pajamas were worn, Pucci silks to the floor. When the women rejoined the men downstairs, trays of white crème de menthe were passed. Large parties were held in tents, with pink lights and chili from Chasen's. Lunch took place at the Bistro, and later at the Bistro Garden and at Jimmy's, which was owned by Jimmy Murphy, who everyone knew because he had worked for Kurt Niklas at the Bistro.

These forms were those of the local *ancien régime,* and as such had largely faded out by the late sixties, but can be examined in detail in the photographs Jean Howard took over the years and

collected in *Jean Howard's Hollywood: A Photo Memoir*. Although
neither Reagan appears in Miss Howard's book (the people she
saw tended to be stars or powers or famously amusing, and the
Reagans, who fell into hard times and television, were not locally
thought to fill any of these slots), the photographs give a sense
of the rigors of the place. What one notices in a photograph of
the Joseph Cottens' 1955 Fourth of July lunch, the day Jennifer
Jones led the conga line into the pool, is not the pool. There are
people in the pool, yes, and even chairs, but most of the guests sit
decorously on the lawn, wearing rep ties, silk dresses, high-heeled
shoes. Mrs. Henry Hathaway, for a day in the sun at Anatole
Litvak's beach house, wears a strapless dress of embroidered and
scalloped organdy, and pearl earrings. Natalie Wood, lunching on
Minna Wallis's lawn with Warren Beatty and George Cukor and
the Hathaways and the Minnellis and the Axelrods, wears a black
straw hat with a silk ribbon, a white dress, black and white beads,
perfect full makeup, and her hair pinned back.

This was the world from which Nancy Reagan went in 1966
to Sacramento and in 1980 to Washington, and it is in many ways
the world, although it was vanishing *in situ* even before Ronald
Reagan was elected governor of California, she never left. *My
Turn* did not document a life radically altered by later experience. Eight years in Sacramento left so little imprint on Mrs.
Reagan that she described the house in which she lived there—a
house located on 45th Street off M Street in a city laid out on a
numerical and alphabetical grid running from 1st Street to 66th
Street and from A Street to Y Street—as "an English-style country house in the suburbs."

She did not find it unusual that this house should have
been bought for and rented to her and her husband (they paid
$1,250 a month) by the same group of men who gave the State
of California eleven acres on which to build Mrs. Reagan the
"governor's mansion" she actually wanted and who later funded
the million-dollar redecoration of the Reagan White House and
who eventually bought the house on St. Cloud Road in Bel Air
to which the Reagans moved when they left Washington (the
street number of the St. Cloud house was 666, but the Reagans
had it changed to 668, to avoid an association with the Beast
in Revelations); she seemed to construe houses as part of her
deal, like the housing provided to actors on location. Before the

kitchen cabinet picked up Ronald Reagan's contract, the Reagans had lived in a house in Pacific Palisades remodeled by his then sponsor, General Electric.

This expectation on the part of the Reagans that other people would care for their needs struck many people, right away, as remarkable, and was usually characterized as a habit of the rich. But of course it is not a habit of the rich, and in any case the Reagans were not rich: they, and this expectation, were the products of studio Hollywood, a system in which performers performed, and in return were cared for. "I preferred the studio system to the anxiety of looking for work in New York," Mrs. Reagan told us in *My Turn*. During the eight years she lived in Washington, Mrs. Reagan said, she "never once set foot in a supermarket or in almost any other kind of store, with the exception of a card shop at 17th and K, where I used to buy my birthday cards," and carried money only when she went out for a manicure.

She was surprised to learn ("Nobody had told us") that she and her husband were expected to pay for their own food, dry cleaning, and toothpaste while in the White House. She seemed never to understand why it was imprudent of her to have accepted clothes from their makers when so many of them encouraged her to do so. Only Geoffrey Beene, whose clothes for Patricia Nixon and whose wedding dress for Lynda Bird Johnson were purchased through stores at retail prices, seemed to have resisted this impulse. "I don't quite understand how clothes can be 'on loan' to a woman," he told the *Los Angeles Times* in January of 1982, when the question of Mrs. Reagan's clothes was first raised. "I also think they'll run into a great deal of trouble deciding which of all these clothes are of museum quality.... They also claim she's helping to 'rescue' the American fashion industry. I didn't know it was in such dire straits."

The clothes were, as Mrs. Reagan seemed to construe it, "wardrobe"—a production expense, like the housing and the catering and the first-class travel and the furniture and paintings and cars that get taken home after the set is struck—and should rightly have gone on the studio budget. That the producers of this particular production—the men Mrs. Reagan called their "wealthier friends," their "very generous" friends—sometimes misunderstood their own role was understandable: Helene von Damm told us that only after William Wilson was warned that anyone with White House credentials was subject to a full-scale FBI investigation (Fred Fielding, the White House counsel, told him this) did he relinquish Suite 180 of the Executive Office Building, which he had commandeered the day after the inauguration in order to vet the appointment of the nominal, as opposed to the kitchen, cabinet.

"So began my stewardship," Edith Bolling Wilson wrote later about the stroke that paralyzed Woodrow Wilson in October of 1919, eighteen months before he left the White House. The stewardship Nancy Reagan shared first with James Baker and Ed Meese and Michael Deaver and then less easily with Donald Regan was, perhaps because each of its principals was working a different scenario and only one, James Baker, had anything approaching a full script, considerably more Byzantine than most. Baker, whose ultimate role in this White House was to preserve it for the established order, seems to have relied heavily on the tendency of opposing forces, let loose, to neutralize each other. "Usually in a big place there's only one person or group to be afraid of," Peggy Noonan observed. "But in the Reagan White House there were two, the chief of staff and his people and the First Lady and hers—a pincer formation that made everyone feel vulnerable." Miss Noonan showed us Mrs. Reagan moving through the corridors with her East Wing entourage, the members of which were said in the West Wing to be "not serious," readers of *W* and *Vogue*. Mrs. Reagan herself was variously referred to as "Evita," "Mommy," "The Missus," "The Hairdo with Anxiety." Miss Noonan dismissed her as not "a liberal or a leftist or a moderate or a détentist" but "a Galanoist, a wealthy well-dressed woman who followed the common wisdom of her class."

In fact Nancy Reagan was more interesting than that: it was precisely "her class" in which she had trouble believing. She was not an experienced woman. Her social skills, like those of many women trained in the insular life of the motion picture community, were strikingly undeveloped. She and Raisa Gorbachev had "little in common," and "completely different outlooks on the world." She and Betty Ford "were different people who came from different worlds." She seems to have been comfortable in the company of Michael Deaver, of Ted Graber (her decorator), and of only a few other people. She seems not to have had much sense about who goes with who. At a state dinner for José Napoleón Duarte of El Salvador, she seated herself between President Duarte and Ralph Lauren. She had limited social experience and apparently unlimited social anxiety. Helene von Damm complained that Mrs. Reagan would not consent, during the first presidential campaign, to letting the fund-raisers call on "her New York friends"; trying to put together a list for the New York dinner in November of 1979 at which Ronald Reagan was to announce his candidacy, Miss von Damm finally dispatched an emissary to extract a few names from Jerry Zipkin, who parted with them reluctantly, and then said, "Remember, don't use my name."

Perhaps Mrs. Reagan's most endearing quality was this little girl's fear of being left out, of not having the best friends and not going to the parties in the biggest houses. She collected slights. She took refuge in a kind of piss-elegance, a fanciness (the "English-style country house in the suburbs"), in using words like "inappropriate." It was "inappropriate, to say the least" for Geraldine Ferraro and her husband to leave the dais and go "down on the floor, working the crowd" at a 1984 Italian-American Federation dinner at which the candidates on both tickets were speaking. It was "uncalled for—and mean" when, at the time John Koehler had been named to replace Patrick Buchanan as director of communications and it was learned that Koehler had been a member of Hitler Youth, Donald Regan said "blame it on the East Wing."

Mrs. Gorbachev, as Mrs. Reagan saw it, "condescended" to her, and "expected to be deferred to." Mrs. Gorbachev accepted an invitation from Pamela Harriman before she answered one from Mrs. Reagan. The reason Ben Bradlee called Iran-contra "the most fun he'd had since Watergate" was just possibly because, she explained in My Turn, he resented her relationship with Katharine Graham. Betty Ford was given a box on the floor of the 1976 Republican National Convention, and Mrs. Reagan only a skybox. Mrs. Reagan was evenhanded: Maureen Reagan "may have been right" when she called this slight deliberate. When, on the second night of that convention, the band struck up "Tie a Yellow Ribbon Round the Ole Oak Tree" during an ovation for Mrs. Reagan, Mrs. Ford started dancing with Tony Orlando.

Mrs. Reagan was magnanimous: "Some of our people saw this as a deliberate attempt to upstage me, but I never thought that was her intention."

Michael Deaver, in his version of more or less the same events, *Behind the Scenes*, gave us an arresting account of taking the Reagans, during the 1980 campaign, to an Episcopal church near the farm on which they were staying outside Middleburg, Virginia. After advancing the church and negotiating the subject of the sermon with the minister (Ezekiel and the bones rather than what Deaver called "reborn Christians," presumably Christian rebirth), he finally agreed that the Reagans would attend an eleven o'clock Sunday service. "We were not told," Deaver wrote, "and I did not anticipate, that the eleven o'clock service would also be holy communion," a ritual he characterized as "very foreign to the Reagans." He described "nervous glances," and "mildly frantic" whispers about what to do, since the Reagans' experience had been of Bel Air Presbyterian, "a proper Protestant church where trays are passed containing small glasses of grape juice and little squares of bread." The moment arrived: "… halfway down the aisle I felt Nancy clutch my arm…. '*Mike!*' she hissed. '*Are those people drinking out of the same cup?*'"

Here the incident takes on elements of "I Love Lucy." Deaver assures Mrs. Reagan that it will be acceptable to just dip the wafer in the chalice. Mrs. Reagan chances this, but manages somehow to drop the wafer in the wine. Ronald Reagan, cast here as Ricky Ricardo, is too deaf to hear Deaver's whispered instructions, and has been instructed by his wife to "do exactly as I do." He, too, drops the wafer in the wine, where it is left to float next to Mrs. Reagan's. "Nancy was relieved to leave the church," Deaver reports. "The president was chipper as he stepped into the sunlight, satisfied that the service had gone quite well."

I had read this account several times before I realized what so attracted me to it: here we had a perfect model of the Reagan White House. There was the aide who located the correct setting ("I did some quick scouting and found a beautiful Episcopal church"), who anticipated every conceivable problem and handled it adroitly (he had "a discreet chat with the minister," he "gently raised the question"), and yet who somehow missed, as in the visit to Bitburg, a key point. There was the wife, charged with protecting her husband's face to the world, a task requiring, she hinted in *My Turn*, considerable vigilance. This was a husband who could be "naive about people." He had for example "too much trust" in David Stockman. He had "given his word" to Helmut Kohl, and so felt "duty-bound to honor his commitment" to visit Bitburg. He was, Mrs. Reagan disclosed during a "Good Morning America" interview at the time *My Turn* was published, "the softest touch going" when it came to what she referred to as (another instance of somehow missing a key point) "the poor." Mrs. Reagan understood all this. She handled all this. And yet there she was outside Middleburg, Virginia, once again the victim of bad advance, confronted by the "foreign" communion table and rendered stiff with apprehension that a finger bowl might get removed without its doily.

And there, at the center of it all, was Ronald Reagan, insufficiently briefed (or, as they say in the White House, "badly served") on the wafer issue but moving ahead, stepping "into the sunlight" satisfied with his own and everyone else's performance, apparently oblivious of (or inured to, or indifferent to) the crises being managed in his presence and for his benefit. What he had, and the aide and the wife did not have, was the story, the high concept, what Ed Meese used to call "the big picture," as in "he's a big-picture man." The big picture here was of the candidate going to church on Sunday morning; the details obsessing the wife and the aide—what church, what to do with the wafer— remained outside the frame.

From the beginning in California, the principal in this administration was operating on what might have seemed distinctly special information. He had "feelings" about things, for example about the Vietnam War. "I have a feeling that we are doing better in the war than the people have been told," he was quoted as having said in the *Los Angeles Times* on October 16, 1967. With the transforming power of the presidency, this special information that no one else understood—these big pictures, these high concepts—took on a magical quality, and some people in the White House came to believe that they had in their possession, sharpening his own pencils in the Oval Office, the Fisher King himself, the keeper of the grail, the source of that ineffable contact with the electorate that was in turn the source of the power.

There were times, we know now, when this White House had fairly well absented itself from the art of the possible. McFarlane flying to Teheran with the cake and the Bible and ten falsified Irish passports did not derive from our traditional executive tradition. The place was running instead on its own superstition, on the reading of bones, on the belief that a flicker of attention from the president during the presentation of a plan (the ideal presentation, Peggy Noonan explained, was one in which "the president was forced to look at a picture, read a short letter, or respond to a question") ensured the transfer of the magic to whatever was that week exciting the ardor of the children who wanted to make the revolution—to SDI, to the mujahadeen, to Jonas Savimbi, to the contras.

Miss Noonan recalled what she referred to as "the contra meetings," which turned on the magical notion that putting the president on display in the right setting (i.e., "going over the heads of the media to the people") was all that was needed to "inspire a commitment on the part of the American people." They sat in those meetings and discussed having the president speak at the Orange Bowl in Miami on the anniversary of John F. Kennedy's Orange Bowl speech after the Bay of Pigs, never mind that the Kennedy Orange Bowl speech had become over the years in Miami the symbol of American betrayal. They sat in those meetings and discussed having the president go over the heads of his congressional opponents by speaking in Jim Wright's district near the Alamo: "... something like '*Blank* miles to the north of here is the Alamo,'" Miss Noonan wrote in her notebook, sketching out the ritual in which the magic would be transferred. "'... Where brave heroes *blank*, and where the commander of the garrison wrote during those terrible last days *blank* ...'"

But the Fisher King was sketching another big picture, one he had had in mind since California. We have heard again and again that Mrs. Reagan turned the president away from the Evil Empire and toward the meetings with Gorbachev. (Later, on NBC "Nightly News," the San Francisco astrologer Joan Quigley claimed a role in influencing both Reagans on this point, explaining that she had "changed their Evil Empire attitude by briefing them on Gorbachev's horoscope.") Mrs. Reagan herself allowed that she "felt it was ridiculous for these two heav-ily armed superpowers to be sitting there and not talking to each other" and "did push Ronnie a little."

But how much pushing was actually needed remains in question. The Soviet Union appeared to Ronald Reagan as an abstraction, a place where people were helpless to resist "commu-nism," the inanimate evil which, as he had put it in a 1951 speech to a Kiwanis convention and would continue to put it for the next three and a half decades, had "tried to invade our industry" and been "fought" and eventually "licked." This was a construct in which the actual citizens of the Soviet Union could be seen to have been, like the motion picture industry, "invaded"—in need only of liberation. The liberating force might be the appear-ance of a Shane-like character, someone to "lick" the evil, or it might be just the sweet light of reason. "A people free to choose will always choose peace," as President Reagan told students at Moscow State University in May of 1988.

In this sense he was dealing from an entirely abstract deck, and the opening to the East had been his card all along, his big picture, his story. And this is how it went: what he would like to do, he had told any number of people over the years (I recall first hearing it from George Will, who cautioned me not to tell it because conversations with presidents were privileged), was take the leader of the Soviet Union (who this leader would be was another of those details outside the frame) on a flight to Los Angeles. When the plane came in low over the middle-class subdivisions that stretch from the San Bernardino mountains to LAX, he would direct the leader of the Soviet Union to the window, and point out all the swimming pools below. "Those are the pools of the capitalists," the leader of the Soviet Union would say. "No," the leader of the free world would say. "Those are the pools of the workers." *Blank* years further on, when brave heroes *blanked*, and where the leader of the free world *blank*, accidental history took its course, but we have yet to pay for the ardor.

1989

III
CALIFORNIA

THE DOMESTIC DETAILS spring to memory. Early on the evening of February 4, 1974, in her duplex apartment at 2603 Benvenue in Berkeley, Patricia Campbell Hearst, age nineteen, a student of art history at the University of California at Berkeley and a granddaughter of the late William Randolph Hearst, put on a blue terry-cloth bathrobe, heated a can of chicken-noodle soup and made tuna fish sandwiches for herself and her fiancé, Steven Weed; watched "Mission Impossible" and "The Magician" on television; cleaned up the dishes; sat down to study just as the doorbell rang; was abducted at gunpoint and held blindfolded, by three men and five women who called themselves the Symbionese Liberation Army, for the next fifty-seven days.

From the fifty-eighth day, on which she agreed to join her captors and was photographed in front of the SLA's cobra flag carrying a sawed-off M-1 carbine, until September 18, 1975, when she was arrested in San Francisco, Patricia Campbell Hearst participated actively in the robberies of the Hibernia Bank in San Francisco and the Crocker National Bank outside Sacramento; sprayed Crenshaw Boulevard in Los Angeles with a submachine gun to cover a comrade apprehended for shoplifting; and was party or witness to a number of less publicized thefts and several bombings, to which she would later refer as "actions," or "operations."

On trial in San Francisco for the Hibernia Bank operation she appeared in court wearing frosted-white nail polish, and demonstrated for the jury the bolt action necessary to chamber an M-1. On a psychiatric test administered while she was in custody she completed the sentence "Most men ..." with the words "... are assholes." Seven years later she was living with the bodyguard she had married, their infant daughter, and two German shepherds "behind locked doors in a Spanish-style house equipped with the best electronic security system available," describing herself as "older and wiser," and dedicating her account of these events, *Every Secret Thing*, to "Mom and Dad."

* * *

It was a special kind of sentimental education, a public coming-of-age with an insistently literary cast to it, and it seemed at the time to offer a parable for the period. Certain of its images entered the national memory. We had Patricia Campbell Hearst in her first-communion dress, smiling, and we had Patricia Campbell Hearst in the Hibernia Bank surveillance stills, not smiling. We again had her smiling in the engagement picture, an unremarkably pretty girl in a simple dress on a sunny lawn, and we again had her not smiling in the "Tania" snapshot, the famous Polaroid with the M-1. We had her with her father and her sister Anne in a photograph taken at the Burlingame Country Club some months before the kidnapping: all three Hearsts smiling there, not only smiling but wearing leis, the father in maile and orchid leis, the daughters in pikake, that rarest and most expensive kind of lei, strand after strand of tiny Arabian jasmine buds strung like ivory beads.

We had the bank of microphones in front of the Hillsborough house whenever Randolph and Catherine Hearst ("Dad" and "Mom" in the first spectral messages from the absent daughter, "pig Hearsts" as the spring progressed) met the press, the potted flowers on the steps changing with the seasons, domestic upkeep intact in the face of crisis: azaleas, fuchsias, then cymbidium orchids massed for Easter. We had, early on, the ugly images of looting and smashed cameras and frozen turkey legs hurled through windows in West Oakland, the violent result of the Hearsts' first attempt to meet the SLA ransom demand, and we had, on television the same night, the news that William Knowland, the former United States senator from California and the most prominent member of the family that had run Oakland for half a century, had taken the pistol he was said to carry as protection against terrorists, positioned himself on a bank of the Russian River, and blown off the top of his head.

All of these pictures told a story, taught a dramatic lesson, carrying as they did the *frisson* of one another, the invitation to compare and contrast. The image of Patricia Campbell Hearst on the FBI "wanted" fliers was for example cropped from the image of the unremarkably pretty girl in the simple dress on the sunny lawn, schematic evidence that even a golden girl could be pinned in the beam of history. There was no actual connection between turkey legs thrown through windows in West Oakland

and William Knowland lying facedown in the Russian River, but the paradigm was manifest, one California busy being born and another busy dying. Those cymbidiums on the Hearsts' doorstep in Hillsborough dissolved before our eyes into the image of a flaming palm tree in south-central Los Angeles (the model again was two Californias), the palm tree above the stucco bungalow in which Patricia Campbell Hearst was believed for a time to be burning to death on live television. (Actually Patricia Campbell Hearst was in yet a third California, a motel room at Disneyland, watching the palm tree burn as we all were, on television, and it was Donald DeFreeze, Nancy Ling Perry, Angela Atwood, Patricia Soltysik, Camilla Hall, and William Wolfe, one black escaped convict and five children of the white middle class, who were dying in the stucco bungalow.)

Not only the images but the voice told a story, the voice on the tapes, the depressed voice with the California inflection, the voice that trailed off, now almost inaudible, then a hint of whine, a schoolgirl's sarcasm, a voice every parent recognized: *Mom, Dad. I'm OK. I had a few scrapes and stuff, but they washed them up.... I just hope you'll do what they say, Dad.... If you can get the food thing organized before the nineteenth then that's OK.... Whatever you come up with is basically OK, it was never intended that you feed the whole state.... I am here because I am a member of a ruling-class family and I think you can begin to see the analogy.... People should stop acting like I'm dead, Mom should get out of her black dress, that doesn't help at all.... Mom, Dad ... I don't believe you're doing all you can ... Mom, Dad ... I'm starting to think that no one is concerned about me anymore.... And then: Greetings to the people. This is Tania.*

Patricia Campbell Hearst's great-grandfather had arrived in California by foot in 1850, unschooled, unmarried, thirty years old with few graces and no prospects, a Missouri farmer's son who would spend his thirties scratching around El Dorado and Nevada and Sacramento counties looking for a stake. In 1859 he found one, and at his death in 1891 George Hearst could leave the schoolteacher he had married in 1862 a fortune taken from the ground, the continuing proceeds from the most productive mines of the period, the Ophir in Nevada, the Homestake in South Dakota, the Ontario in Utah, the Anaconda in Montana, the San Luis in Mexico. The widow, Phoebe Apperson Hearst, a tiny, strong-minded woman then only forty-eight years old, took this apparently artesian income and financed her only child in the publishing empire he wanted, underwrote a surprising amount of the campus where her great-granddaughter would be enrolled at the time she was kidnapped, and built for herself, on sixty-seven thousand acres on the McCloud River in Siskiyou County, the original Wyntoon, a quarried-lava castle of which its architect, Bernard Maybeck, said simply: "Here you can reach all that is within you."

The extent to which certain places dominate the California imagination is apprehended, even by Californians, only dimly. Deriving not only from the landscape but from the claiming of it, from the romance of emigration, the radical abandonment of established attachments, this imagination remains obdurately symbolic, tending to locate lessons in what the rest of the country perceives only as scenery. Yosemite, for example, remains what Kevin Starr has called "one of the primary California symbols, a fixed factor of identity for all those who sought a primarily Californian aesthetic." Both the community of and the coastline at Carmel have a symbolic meaning lost to the contemporary visitor, a lingering allusion to art as freedom, freedom as craft, the "bohemian" pantheism of the early twentieth century. The Golden Gate Bridge, referring as it does to both the infinite and technology, suggests, to the Californian, a quite complex representation of land's end, and also of its beginning.

Patricia Campbell Hearst told us in *Every Secret Thing* that the place the Hearsts called Wyntoon was "a mystical land," "fantastic, otherworldly," "even more than San Simeon," which was in turn "so emotionally moving that it is still beyond my powers of description." That first Maybeck castle on the McCloud River was seen by most Californians only in photographs, and yet, before it burned in 1933, to be replaced by a compound of rather more playful Julia Morgan chalets ("Cinderella House," "Angel House," "Brown Bear House"), Phoebe Hearst's gothic Wyntoon and her son's baroque San Simeon seemed between them to embody certain opposing impulses in the local consciousness: northern and southern, wilderness sanctified and wilderness banished, the aggrandizement of nature and the aggrandizement of self. Wyntoon had mists, and allusions to the infinite, great trunks of trees left to rot where they fell, a wild river, barbaric fireplaces. San Simeon, swimming in sunlight and the here and now, had two swimming pools, and a zoo.

It was a family in which the romantic impulse would seem to have dimmed. Patricia Campbell Hearst told us that she "grew up in an atmosphere of clear blue skies, bright sunshine, rambling open spaces, long green lawns, large comfortable houses, country clubs with swimming pools and tennis courts and riding horses." At the Convent of the Sacred Heart in Menlo Park she told a nun to "go to hell," and thought herself "quite courageous, although very stupid." At Santa Catalina in Monterey she and Patricia Tobin, whose family founded one of the banks the SLA would later rob, skipped Benediction, and received "a load of demerits." Her father taught her to shoot, duck hunting. Her mother did not allow her to wear jeans into San Francisco. These were inheritors who tended to keep their names out of the paper, to exhibit not much interest in the world at large ("Who the hell is this guy again?" Randolph Hearst asked Steven Weed when the latter suggested trying to approach the SLA through Regis Debray, and then, when told, said, "We need a goddamn South American revolutionary mixed up in this thing like a hole in the head"), and to regard most forms of distinction with the reflexive distrust of the country club.

Yet if the Hearsts were no longer a particularly arresting California family, they remained embedded in the symbolic content of the place, and for a Hearst to be kidnapped from Berkeley, the very citadel of Phoebe Hearst's aspiration, was California as opera. "My thoughts at this time were focused on the single issue of survival," the heiress to Wyntoon and San Simeon told us about the fifty-seven days she spent in the closet. "Concerns over love and marriage, family life, friends, human relationships, my whole previous life, had really become, in SLA terms, bourgeois luxuries."

This abrupt sloughing of the past has, to the California ear, a distant echo, and the echo is of emigrant diaries. "Don't let this letter dishearten anybody, never take no cutoffs and hurry along as fast as you can," one of the surviving children of the Donner Party concluded her account of that crossing. "Don't worry about it," the author of *Every Secret Thing* reported having told herself in the closet after her first sexual encounter with a member of the SLA. "Don't examine your feelings. Never examine your feelings—they're no help at all." At the time Patricia Campbell Hearst was on trial in San Francisco, a number of psychiatrists were brought in to try to plumb what seemed to some an unsoundable depth in the narrative, that moment at which the victim binds over her fate to her captors. "She experienced what I call the death anxiety and the breaking point," Robert Jay Lifton, who was one of these psychiatrists, said. "Her external points of reference for maintenance of her personality had disappeared," Louis Jolyon West, another of the psychiatrists, said. Those were two ways of looking at it, and another was that Patricia Campbell Hearst had cut her losses and headed west, as her great-grandfather had before her.

The story she told in 1982 in *Every Secret Thing* was received, in the main, querulously, just as it had been when she told it during *The United States of America* v. *Patricia Campbell Hearst*, the 1976 proceeding during which she was tried for and convicted of the armed robbery of the Hibernia Bank (one count) and (the second count), the use of a weapon during the commission of a felony. Laconic, slightly ironic, resistant not only to the prosecution but to her own defense, Patricia Hearst was not, on trial in San Francisco, a conventionally ingratiating personality. "I don't know," I recall her saying over and over again during the few days I attended the trial. "I don't remember." "I suppose so." Had there not been, the prosecutor asked one day, telephones in the motels in which she had stayed when she drove across the country with Jack Scott? I recall Patricia Hearst looking at him as if she thought him deranged. I recall Randolph Hearst looking at the floor. I recall Catherine Hearst arranging a Galanos jacket over the back of her seat.

"Yes, I'm sure," their daughter said.

Where, the prosecutor asked, were these motels?

"One was … I think …" Patricia Hearst paused, and then: "Cheyenne? Wyoming?" She pronounced the names as if they were foreign, exotic, information registered and jettisoned. One of these motels had been in Nevada, the place from which the

Hearst money originally came: the heiress pronounced the name *Nevahda*, like a foreigner.

In *Every Secret Thing*, as at her trial, she seemed to project an emotional distance, a peculiar combination of passivity and pragmatic recklessness ("I had crossed over. And I would have to make the best of it ... to live from day to day, to do whatever they said, to play my part, and to pray that I would survive") that many people found inexplicable and irritating. In 1982 as in 1976, she spoke only abstractly about *why*, but quite specifically about *how*. "I could not believe that I had actually fired that submachine gun," she said of the incident in which she shot up Crenshaw Boulevard, but here was how she did it: "I kept my finger pressed on the trigger until the entire clip of thirty shots had been fired.... I then reached for my own weapon, the semi-automatic carbine. I got off three more shots ..."

And, after her book as after her trial, the questions raised were not exactly about her veracity but about her authenticity, her general intention, about whether she was, as the assistant prosecutor put it during the trial, "for real." This was necessarily a vain line of inquiry (whether or not she "loved" William Wolfe was the actual point on which the trial came to turn), and one that encouraged a curious rhetorical regression among the inquisitors. "Why did she choose to write this book?" Mark Starr asked about *Every Secret Thing* in *Newsweek*, and then answered himself: "Possibly she has inherited her family's journalistic sense of what will sell." "The rich get richer," Jane Alpert concluded in *New York* magazine. "Patty," Ted Morgan observed in the *New York Times Book Review*, "is now, thanks to the proceeds of her book, reverting to a more traditional family pursuit, capital formation."

These were dreamy notions of what a Hearst might do to turn a dollar, but they reflected a larger dissatisfaction, a conviction that the Hearst in question was telling less than the whole story, "leaving something out," although what the something might have been, given the doggedly detailed account offered in *Every Secret Thing*, would be hard to define. If "questions still linger," as they did for *Newsweek*, those questions were not about how to lace a bullet with cyanide: the way the SLA did it was to drill into the lead tip to a point just short of the gunpowder, dip the tiny hole in a mound of cyanide crystals, and seal it with paraffin. If

Every Secret Thing "creates more puzzles than it solves," as it did for Jane Alpert, those questions were not about how to make a pipe bomb: the trick here was to pack enough gunpowder into the pipe for a big bang and still leave sufficient oxygen for ignition, a problem, as Patricia Hearst saw it, of "devising the proper proportions of gunpowder, length of pipe and toaster wire, minus Teko's precious toilet paper." "Teko," or Bill Harris, insisted on packing his bombs with toilet paper, and, when one of them failed to explode under a police car in the Mission District, reacted with "one of his worst temper tantrums." Many reporters later found Bill and Emily Harris the appealing defendants that Patricia Hearst never was, but *Every Secret Thing* presented a convincing case for their being, as the author put it, not only "unattractive" but, her most pejorative adjective, "incompetent."

As notes from the underground go, Patricia Hearst's were eccentric in detail. She told us that Bill Harris's favorite television program was "S.W.A.T." (one could, he said, "learn a lot about the pigs' tactics by watching these programs"); that Donald DeFreeze, or "Cinque," drank plum wine from half-gallon jugs and listened to the radio for allusions to the revolution in song lyrics; and that Nancy Ling Perry, who was usually cast by the press in the rather glamorous role of "former cheerleader and Goldwater Girl," was four feet eleven inches tall, and affected a black accent. Emily Harris trained herself to "live with deprivation" by chewing only half sticks of gum. Bill Harris bought a yarmulke, under the impression that this was the way, during the sojourn in the Catskills after the Los Angeles shoot-out, to visit Grossinger's unnoticed.

Life with these people had the distorted logic of dreams, and Patricia Hearst seems to have accepted it with the wary acquiescence of the dreamer. Any face could turn against her. Any move could prove lethal. "My sisters and I had been brought up to believe that we were responsible for what we did and could not blame our transgressions on something being wrong inside our heads. I had joined the SLA because if I didn't they would have killed me. And I remained with them because I truly believed that the FBI would kill me if they could, and if not, the SLA would." She had, as she put it, crossed over. She would, as she put it, make the best of it, and not "reach back to family or friends."

This was the point on which most people foundered, doubted her, found her least explicable, and it was also the point at which she was most specifically the child of a certain culture. Here is the single personal note in an emigrant diary kept by a relative of mine, William Kilgore, the journal of an overland crossing to Sacramento in 1850: "This is one of the trying mornings for me, as I now have to leave my family, or back out. Suffice it to say, we started." Suffice it to say. Don't examine your feelings, they're no help at all. Never take no cutoffs and hurry along as fast as you can. We need a goddamn South American revolutionary mixed up in this thing like a hole in the head. This was a California girl, and she was raised on a history that placed not much emphasis on *why*.

She was never an idealist, and this pleased no one. She was tainted by survival. She came back from the other side with a story no one wanted to hear, a dispiriting account of a situation in which delusion and incompetence were pitted against delusion and incompetence of another kind, and in the febrile rhythms of San Francisco in the mid-seventies it seemed a story devoid of high notes. The week her trial ended in 1976, the *San Francisco Bay Guardian* published an interview in which members of a collective called New Dawn expressed regret at her defection. "It's a question of your self-respect or your ass," one of them said. "If you choose your ass, you live with nothing." This idea that the SLA represented an idea worth defending (if only on the grounds that any idea must be better than none) was common enough at the time, although most people granted that the idea had gone awry. By March of 1977 another writer in the *Bay Guardian* was making a distinction between the "unbridled adventurism" of the SLA and the "discipline and skill" of the New World Liberation Front, whose "fifty-odd bombings without a casualty" made them a "definitely preferable alternative" to the SLA.

As it happened I had kept this issue of the *Bay Guardian*, dated March 31, 1977 (the *Bay Guardian* was not at the time a notably radical paper, by the way, but one that provided a fair guide to local tofu cookery and the mood of the community), and when

I got it out to look at the piece on the SLA I noticed for the first time another piece: a long and favorable report on a San Francisco minister whose practice it was to "confront people and challenge their basic assumptions ... as if he can't let the evil of the world pass him by, a characteristic he shares with other moral leaders." The minister, who was compared at one point to Cesar Chavez, was responsible, according to the writer, for a "mind-boggling" range of social service programs—food distribution, legal aid, drug rehabilitation, nursing homes, free Pap smears—as well as for a "twenty-seven-thousand-acre agricultural station." The agricultural station was in Guyana, and the minister of course was the Reverend Jim Jones, who eventually chose self-respect over his own and nine hundred other asses. This was another local opera, and one never spoiled by a protagonist who insisted on telling it her way.

1982

I

A GOOD PART of any day in Los Angeles is spent driving, alone, through streets devoid of meaning to the driver, which is one reason the place exhilarates some people, and floods others with an amorphous unease. There is about these hours spent in transit a seductive unconnectedness. Conventional information is missing. Context clues are missing. In Culver City as in Echo Park as in East Los Angeles, there are the same pastel bungalows. There are the same leggy poinsettia and the same trees of pink and yellow hibiscus. There are the same laundromats, body shops, strip shopping malls, the same travel agencies offering bargain fares on LACSA and TACA. *San Salvador*, the signs promise, on Beverly Boulevard as on Pico as on Alvarado and Soto. *¡No más barata!* There is the same sound, that of the car radio, tuned in my case to KRLA, an AM station that identifies itself as "the heart and soul of rock and roll" and is given to dislocating programming concepts, for example doing the top hits ("Baby, It's You," "Break It to Me Gently," "The Lion Sleeps Tonight") of 1962. Another day, another KRLA concept: "The Day the Music Died," an exact radio recreation of the day in 1959, including news breaks (Detroit may market compacts), when the plane carrying Buddy Holly, Ritchie Valens, and the Big Bopper crashed near Clear Lake, Iowa. A few days later, KRLA reports a solid response on "The Day the Music Died," including "a call from Ritchie Valens's aunt."

Such tranced hours are, for many people who live in Los Angeles, the dead center of being there, but there is nothing in them to encourage the normal impulse toward "recognition," or narrative connection. Those glosses on the human comedy (the widow's heartbreak, the bad cop, the mother-and-child reunion) that lend dramatic structure to more traditional forms of urban life are hard to come by here. There are, in the pages of the Los Angeles newspapers, no Crack Queens, no Coma Moms or Terror Tots. Events may be lurid, but are rarely personalized. "Mother Apologizes to Her Child, Drives Both Off Cliff," a headline read in the *Los Angeles Times* one morning in December 1988. (Stories like this are relegated in the *Times* either to the Metro Section or to page three, which used to be referred to as "the freak-death page," not its least freaky aspect being that quite arresting accounts of death by Clorox or by rattlesnake or by Dumpster tended to appear and then vanish, with no follow-up.) Here was the story, which had to do with a young woman who had lived with her daughter, Brooke, in a Redondo Beach condominium and was said by a neighbor to have "looked like she was a little down":

> A Redondo Beach woman apologized to her 7-year-old daughter, then apparently tried to take both their lives by driving over a cliff in the Malibu area Tuesday morning, authorities said. The mother, identified by the county cor-oner's office as Susan Sinclair, 29, was killed, but the child survived without serious injury. "I'm sorry I have to do this," the woman was quoted as telling the child just before she suddenly swerved off Malibu Canyon Road about 2½ miles north of Pacific Coast Highway.

"I'm sorry I have to do this." This was the last we heard of Susan and Brooke Sinclair. When I first moved to Los Angeles from New York, in 1964, I found this absence of narrative a deprivation. At the end of two years I realized (quite suddenly, alone one morning in the car) that I had come to find narrative sentimental. This remains a radical difference between the two cities, and also between the ways in which the residents of those cities view each other.

2

Our children remind us of how random our lives have been. I had occasion in 1979 to speak at my daughter's school in Los Angeles, and I stood there, apparently a grown woman, certainly a woman who had stood up any number of times and spoken to students around the country, and tried to confront a question that suddenly seemed to me almost impenetrable: How had I become a writer, how and why had I made the particular choices I had made in my life? I could see my daughter's friends in the back of the room, Claudia, Julie, Anna. I could see my daughter herself, flushed with embarrassment, afraid, she told me later, that her presence would make me forget what I meant to say.

I could tell them only that I had no more idea of how I had become a writer than I had had, at their age, of how I would become a writer. I could tell them only about the fall of 1954, when I was nineteen and a junior at Berkeley and one of perhaps a dozen students admitted to the late Mark Schorer's English 106A, a kind of "fiction workshop" that met for discussion three hours a week and required that each student produce, over the course of the semester, at least five short stories. No auditors were allowed. Voices were kept low. English 106A was widely regarded in the fall of 1954 as a kind of sacramental experience, an initiation into the grave world of real writers, and I remember each meeting of this class as an occasion of acute excitement and dread. I remember each other member of this class as older and wiser than I had hope of ever being (it had not yet struck me in any visceral way that being nineteen was not a long-term proposition, just as it had not yet struck Claudia and Julie and Anna and my daughter that they would recover from being thirteen), not only older and wiser but more experienced, more independent, more interesting, more possessed of an exotic past: marriages and the breaking up of marriages, money and the lack of it, sex and politics and the Adriatic seen at dawn: not only the stuff of grown-up life itself but, more poignantly to me at the time, the very stuff that might be transubstantiated into five short stories. I recall a Trotskyist, then in his forties. I recall a young woman who lived, with a barefoot man and a large white dog, in an attic lit only by candles. I recall classroom discussions that ranged over meetings with Paul and Jane Bowles, incidents involving Djuna Barnes, years spent in Paris, in Beverly Hills, in the Yucatán, on the Lower East Side of New York and on Repulse Bay and even on morphine. I had spent seventeen of my nineteen years more or less in Sacramento, and the other two in the Tri Delt house on Warring Street in Berkeley. I had never read Paul or Jane Bowles, let alone met them, and when, some fifteen years later at a friend's house in Santa Monica Canyon, I did meet Paul Bowles, I was immediately rendered as dumb and awestruck as I had been at nineteen in English 106A.

I suppose that what I really wanted to say that day at my daughter's school is that we never reach a point at which our lives lie before us as a clearly marked open road, never have and never should expect a map to the years ahead, never do close those circles that seem, at thirteen and fourteen and nineteen, so urgently in need of closing. I wanted to tell my daughter and her friends, but did not, about going back to the English department at Berkeley in the spring of 1975 as a Regents' Lecturer, a reversal of positions that should have been satisfying but proved unsettling, moved me profoundly, answered no questions but raised the same old ones. In Los Angeles in 1975 I had given every appearance of being well settled, grown-up, a woman in definite charge of her own work and of a certain kind of bourgeois household that made working possible. In Berkeley in 1975 I had unpacked my clothes and papers in a single room at the Faculty Club, walked once across campus, and regressed, immediately and helplessly, into the ghetto life of the student I had been twenty years before. I hoarded nuts and bits of chocolate in my desk drawer. I ate tacos for dinner (combination plates, *con arroz y frijoles*), wrapped myself in my bedspread and read until two A.M., smoked too many cigarettes and regretted, like a student, only their cost. I found myself making daily notes, as carefully as I had when I was an undergraduate, of expenses, and my room at the Faculty Club was littered with little scraps of envelopes:

> $1.15, *papers, etc.*
> $2.85, *taco plate*
> $ .50, *tips*
> $ .15, *coffee*

I fell not only into the habits but into the moods of the student day. Every morning I was hopeful, determined, energized by the campanile bells and by the smell of eucalyptus and by the day's projected accomplishments. On the way to breakfast I would walk briskly, breathe deeply, review my "plans" for the day: I would write five pages, return all calls, lunch on raisins and answer ten letters. I would at last read E. H. Gombrich. I would once and for all get the meaning of the word "structuralist." And yet every afternoon by four o'clock, the hour when I met my single class, I was once again dulled, glazed, sunk in an excess of carbohydrates and in my own mediocrity, in my failure—still, after twenty years!—to "live up to" the day's possibilities.

In certain ways nothing at all had changed in those twenty years. The clean light and fogs were exactly as I had remembered. The creek still ran clear among the shadows, the rhododendron still bloomed in the spring. On the bulletin boards in the English department there were still notices inviting the reader to apply to Mrs. Diggory Venn for information on the Radcliffe Publishing Procedures course. The less securely tenured members of the department still yearned for dramatic moves to Johns Hopkins. Anything specific was rendered immediately into a general principle. Anything concrete was rendered abstract. That the spring of 1975 was, outside Berkeley, a season of remarkably specific and operatically concrete events seemed, on the campus, another abstract, another illustration of a general tendency, an instance tending only to confirm or not confirm one or another idea of the world. The wire photos from Phnom Penh and Saigon seemed as deliberately composed as symbolist paintings. The question of whether one spoke of Saigon "falling" or of Saigon's "liberation" reduced the fact to a political attitude, a semantic question, another idea.

Days passed. I adopted a shapeless blazer and no makeup. I remember spending considerable time, that spring of 1975, trying to break the code that Telegraph Avenue seemed to present. There, just a block or two off the campus, the campus with its five thousand courses, its four million books, its five million manuscripts, the campus with its cool glades and clear creeks and lucid views, lay this mean wasteland of small venture capital, this unweeded garden in which everything cost more than it was worth. Coffee on Telegraph Avenue was served neither hot nor cold. Food was slopped lukewarm onto chipped plates. Pita bread was stale, curries were rank. Tatty "Indian" stores offered faded posters and shoddy silks. Bookstores featured sections on the occult. Drug buys were in progress up and down the street. The place was an illustration of some tropism toward disorder, and I seemed to understand it no better in 1975 than I had as an undergraduate.

I remember trying to discuss Telegraph Avenue with some people from the English department, but they were discussing a paper we had heard on the plotting of *Vanity Fair*, *Middlemarch*,

and *Bleak House*. I remember trying to discuss Telegraph Avenue
with an old friend who had asked me to dinner, at a place far
enough off campus to get a drink, but he was discussing Jane
Alpert, Eldridge Cleaver, Daniel Ellsberg, Shana Alexander, a
Modesto rancher of his acquaintance, Jules Feiffer, Herbert Gold,
Herb Caen, Ed Janss, and the movement for independence in
Micronesia. I remember thinking that I was still, after twenty
years, out of step at Berkeley, the victim of a different drummer.
I remember sitting in my office in Wheeler Hall one afternoon
when someone, not a student, walked in off the street. He said
that he was a writer, and I asked what he had written. "Nothing
you'll ever dare to read," he said. He admired only Céline and
Djuna Barnes. With the exception of Djuna Barnes, women
could not write. It was possible that I could write but he did
not know, he had not read me. "In any case," he added, sitting
on the edge of my desk, "your time's gone, your fever's over."
It had probably been a couple of decades, English 106A, since
I last heard about Céline and Djuna Barnes and how women
could not write, since I last encountered this particular brand of
extraliterary machismo, and after my caller had left the office I
locked the door and sat there a long time in the afternoon light.
At nineteen I had wanted to write. At forty I still wanted to write,
and nothing that had happened in the years between made me
any more certain that I could.

3

Etcheverry Hall, half a block uphill from the north gate of the
University of California at Berkeley, is one of those postwar classroom and office buildings that resemble parking structures and
seem designed to suggest that nothing extraordinary has been
or will be going on inside. On Etcheverry's east terrace, which
is paved with pebbled concrete and bricks, a few students usually sit studying or sunbathing. There are benches, there is grass.
There are shrubs and a small tree. There is a net for volleyball,
and, on the day in late 1979 when I visited Etcheverry, someone had taken a piece of chalk and printed the word RADIATION
on the concrete beneath the net, breaking the letters in a way
that looked stenciled and official and scary. In fact it was here,
directly below the volleyball court on Etcheverry's east terrace,

that the Department of Nuclear Engineering's TRIGA Mark III nuclear reactor, light-water cooled and reflected, went critical, or achieved a sustained nuclear reaction, on August 10, 1966, and had been in continuous operation since. People who wanted to see the reactor dismantled said that it was dangerous, that it could emit deadly radiation and that it was perilously situated just forty yards west of the Hayward Fault. People who ran the reactor said that it was not dangerous, that any emission of measurable radioactivity was extremely unlikely and that "forty yards west of" the Hayward Fault was a descriptive phrase without intrinsic seismological significance. (This was an assessment with which seismologists agreed.) These differences of opinion represented a difference not only in the meaning of words but in cultures, a difference in images and probably in expectations.

Above the steel door to the reactor room in the basement of Etcheverry Hall was a sign that glowed either green or Roman violet, depending on whether what it said was SAFE ENTRY, which meant that the air lock between the reactor room and the corridor was closed and the radiation levels were normal and the level of pool water was normal, or UNSAFE ENTRY, which meant that at least one of these conditions, usually the first, had not been met. The sign on the steel door itself read only ROOM 1140 / EXCLUSION AREA / ENTRY LIST A, B, or C / CHECK WITH RECEPTIONIST. On the day I visited Etcheverry I was issued a dosimeter to keep in my pocket, then shown the reactor by Tek Lim, at that time the reactor manager, and Lawrence Grossman, a professor of nuclear engineering. They explained that the Etcheverry TRIGA was a modification of the original TRIGA, which is an acronym for Training/Research/Isotopes/General Atomic, and was designed in 1956 by a team, including Edward Teller and Theodore Taylor and Freeman Dyson, that had set for itself the task of making a reactor so safe, in Freeman Dyson's words, "that it could be given to a bunch of high school children to play with, without any fear that they would get hurt."

They explained that the TRIGA operated at a much lower heat level than a power reactor, and was used primarily for "making things radioactive." Nutritionists, for example, used it to measure trace elements in diet. Archaeologists used it for dating. NASA used it for high-altitude pollution studies, and for a study on how weightlessness affects human calcium metabolism.

Stanford was using it to study lithium in the brain. Physicists from the Lawrence Berkeley Laboratory, up the hill, had been coming down to use it for experiments in the development of a fusion, or "clean," reactor. A researcher from Ghana used it for a year, testing samples from African waterholes for the arsenic that could kill the animals.

The reactor was operating at one megawatt as we talked. All levels were normal. We were standing, with Harry Braun, the chief reactor operator, on the metal platform around the reactor pool, and I had trouble keeping my eyes from the core, the Cerenkov radiation around the fuel rods, the blue shimmer under twenty feet of clear water. There was a skimmer on the side of the pool, and a bath mat thrown over the railing. There was a fishing pole, and a rubber duck. Harry Braun uses the fishing rod to extract samples from the specimen rack around the core, and the rubber duck to monitor the water movement. "Or when the little children come on school tours," he added. "Sometimes they don't pay any attention until we put the duck in the pool."

I was ten years old when "the atomic age," as we called it then, came forcibly to the world's attention. At the time the verbs favored for use with "the atomic age" were "dawned" or "ushered in," both of which implied an upward trend to events. I recall being told that the device which ended World War II was "the size of a lemon" (this was not true) and that the University of California had helped build it (this was true). I recall listening all one Sunday afternoon to a special radio report called "The Quick and the Dead," three or four hours during which the people who had built and witnessed the bomb talked about the bomb's and (by extension) their own eerie and apparently unprecedented power, their abrupt elevation to that place from whence they had come to judge the quick and the dead, and I also recall, when summer was over and school started again, being taught to cover my eyes and my brain stem and crouch beneath my desk during atomic-bomb drills.

So unequivocal were these impressions that it never occurred to me that I would not sooner or later—most probably sooner, certainly before I ever grew up or got married or went to college—endure the moment of its happening: first the blinding white light, which appeared in my imagination as a negative photographic image, then the waves of heat, the sound, and, finally, death, instant or prolonged, depending inflexibly on where one was caught in the scale of concentric circles we all imagined pulsing out from ground zero. Some years later, when I was an undergraduate at Berkeley and had an apartment in an old shingled house a few doors from where Etcheverry now stands, I could look up the hill at night and see the lights at the Lawrence Berkeley Laboratory, at what was then called "the rad lab," at the cyclotron and the Bevatron, and I still expected to wake up one night and see those lights in negative, still expected the blinding white light, the heat wave, the logical conclusion.

After I graduated I moved to New York, and after some months or a year I realized that I was no longer anticipating the blinding flash, and that the expectation had probably been one of those ways in which children deal with mortality, learn to juggle the idea that life will end as surely as it began, to perform in the face of definite annihilation. And yet I know that for me, and I suspect for many of us, this single image—this blinding white light that meant death, this seductive reversal of the usual associations around "light" and "white" and "radiance"—became a metaphor that to some extent determined what I later thought and did. In my Modern Library copy of *The Education of Henry Adams*, a book I first read and scored at Berkeley in 1954, I see this passage, about the 1900 Paris Great Exposition, underlined:

> ... to Adams the dynamo became a symbol of infinity. As he grew accustomed to the great gallery of machines, he began to feel the forty-foot dynamos as a moral force, much as the early Christians felt the Cross.

It had been, at the time I saw the TRIGA Mark III reactor in the basement of Etcheverry Hall, seventy-nine years since Henry Adams went to Paris to study Science as he had studied Mont-Saint-Michel and Chartres. It had been thirty-four years since Robert Oppenheimer saw the white light at Alamogordo. The "nuclear issue," as we called it, suggesting that the course of the world since the Industrial Revolution was provisional, open to revision, up for a vote, had been under discussion all those years, and yet something about the fact of the reactor still resisted interpretation: the intense blue in the pool water, the Cerenkov radiation around the fuel rods, the blue past all blue, the blue like light itself, the blue that is actually a shock wave in the water and is the exact blue of the glass at Chartres.

4

At the University of California's Lawrence Livermore Laboratory, a compound of heavily guarded structures in the rolling cattle and orchard country southeast of Oakland, badges had to be displayed not only at the gate but again and again, at various points within the compound, to television cameras mounted between two locked doors. These cameras registered not only the presence but the color of the badge. A red badge meant "No Clearance U.S. Citizen" and might or might not be issued with the white covering badge that meant "Visitor Must Be Escorted." A yellow badge meant "No Higher Than Confidential Access." A green badge banded in yellow indicated that access was to be considered top level but not exactly unlimited: "Does Need to Know Exist?" was, according to a sign in the Badge Office, LLL Building 310, the question to ask as the bearer moved from station to station among the mysteries of the compound.

The symbolic as well as the literal message of a badge at Livermore—or at Los Alamos, or at Sandia, or at any of the other major labs around the country—was that the government had an interest here, that big money was being spent, Big Physics done. Badges were the totems of the tribe, the family. This was the family that used to keep all the plutonium in the world in a cigar box outside Glenn Seaborg's office in Berkeley, the family that used to try different ways of turning on the early twenty-seven-and-one-half-inch Berkeley cyclotron so as not to blow out large sections of the East Bay power grid. "Very gently" was said to work best. I have a copy of a photograph that suggests the day-to-day life of this family with considerable poignance, a snapshot taken during the fifties, when Livermore was testing its atmospheric nuclear weapons in the Pacific. The snapshot shows a very young Livermore scientist, with a flattop haircut and an engaging smile, standing on the beach of an unidentified atoll on an unspecified day just preceding or just following (no clue in the caption) a test shot. He is holding a fishing rod, and, in the other hand, a queen triggerfish, according to the caption "just a few ounces short of a world record." He is wearing only swimming trunks, and his badge.

On the day in February 1980 when I drove down to Livermore from Berkeley the coast ranges were green from the winter rains. The acacia was out along the highway, a haze of chrome yellow in the window. Inside the compound itself, narcissus and daffodil shoots pressed through the asphalt walkways. I had driven down because I wanted to see Shiva, Livermore's twenty-beam laser, the $35 million tool that was then Livermore's main marker in the biggest Big Physics game then going, the attempt to create a controlled fusion reaction. An uncontrolled fusion reaction was easy, and was called a hydrogen bomb. A controlled fusion reaction was harder, so much harder that it was usually characterized as "the most difficult technological feat ever undertaken," but the eventual payoff could be virtually limitless nuclear power produced at a fraction the hazard of the fission plants then operating. The difficulty in a controlled fusion reaction was that it involved achieving a thermonuclear burn of 100 million degrees centigrade, or more than six times the heat of the interior of the sun, without exploding the container. That no one had ever done this was, for the family, the point.

Ideas about how to do it were intensely competitive. Some laboratories had concentrated on what was called the "magnetic bottle" approach, involving the magnetic confinement of plasma; others, on lasers, and the theoretical ability of laser beams to trigger controlled fusion by simultaneously heating and compressing tiny pellets of fuel. Livermore had at that time a magnetic-bottle project but was gambling most heavily on its lasers, on Shiva and on Shiva's then unfinished successor, Nova. This was a high-stakes game: the prizes would end up at those laboratories where the money was, and the money would go to those laboratories where the prizes seemed most likely. It was no accident that Livermore was visited by so many members of Congress, by officials of the Department of Defense and of the Department of Energy, and by not too many other people: friends in high places were essential to the family. The biography of Ernest O. Lawrence, the first of the Berkeley Nobel laureates and the man after whom the Lawrence Berkeley and the Lawrence Livermore laboratories were named, is instructive on this point: there were meetings at the

JOAN DIDION

Pacific Union Club, sojourns at Bohemian Grove and San Simeon, even "a short trip to Acapulco with Randy and Catherine Hearst." The Eniwetok tests during the fifties were typically preceded for Lawrence by stops in Honolulu, where, for example,

> … he was a guest of Admiral John E. Gingrich, a fine host. He reciprocated with a dinner for the admiral and several others at the Royal Hawaiian Hotel the night before departure for Eniwetok, a ten-hour flight from Honolulu. Eniwetok had much the atmosphere of a South Seas resort. A fine officers' club on the beach provided relaxation for congressmen and visitors. The tropical sea invited swimmers and scuba divers. There were no phones to interrupt conversations with interesting and important men … chairs had been placed on the beach when observers assembled at the club near dawn [to witness the shot]. Coffee and sandwiches were served, and dark glasses distributed …

On the day I visited Livermore the staff was still cleaning up after a January earthquake, a Richter 5.5 on the Mount Diablo–Greenville Fault. Acoustical tiles had fallen from the ceilings of the office buildings. Overhead light fixtures had plummeted onto desks, and wiring and insulation and air-conditioning ducts still hung wrenched from the ceilings. "You get damage in the office buildings because the office buildings are only built to local code," I was told by John Emmett, the physicist then in charge of the Livermore laser program. When the ceilings started falling that particular January, John Emmett had been talking to a visitor in his office. He had shown the visitor out, run back inside to see if anyone was trapped under the toppled bookshelves and cabinets, and then run over to the building that houses Shiva. The laser had been affected so slightly that all twenty beams were found, by the sixty-three microcomputers that constantly aligned and realigned the Shiva beams, to be within one-sixteenth of an inch of their original alignment. "We didn't anticipate any real damage and we didn't get any," John Emmett said. "That's the way the gadget is designed."

What John Emmett called "the gadget" was framed in an immaculate white steel scaffolding several stories high and roughly

AFTER HENRY

the size of a football field. This frame was astonishingly beautiful, a piece of pure theater, a kind of abstract set on which the actors wore white coats, green goggles, and hard hats. "You wear the goggles because even when we're not firing we've got some little beams bouncing around," John Emmett said. "The hard hat is because somebody's always dropping something." Within the frame, a single infrared laser beam was split into twenty beams, each of which was amplified and reamplified until, at the instant two or three times a day when all twenty beams hit target, they were carrying sixty times as much power as was produced in the entire (exclusive of this room) United States. The target under bombardment was a glass bead a fraction the size of a grain of salt. The entire shoot took one-half billionth of a second. John Emmett and the Livermore laser team had then achieved with Shiva controlled temperatures of 85 million degrees centigrade, or roughly five times the heat at the center of the sun, but not 100 million. They were gambling on Nova for 100 million, the prize.

I recall, that afternoon at Livermore, asking John Emmett what would happen if I looked at the invisible infrared beam without goggles. "It'll blow a hole in your retina," he said matter-of-factly. It seemed that he had burned out the retina of one of his own eyes with a laser when he was a graduate student at Stanford. I asked if the sight had come back. "All but one little spot," he said. *Give me a mind that is not bored, that does not whimper, whine or sigh / Don't let me worry overmuch about the fussy thing called I*: these are two lines from a popular "prayer," a late-twenties precursor to the "Desiderata" that Ernest O. Lawrence kept framed on his desk until his death. The one little spot was not of interest to John Emmett. Making the laser work was.

5

Wintertime and springtime, Honolulu: in the winter there was the garbage strike, forty-two days during which the city lapsed into a profound and seductive tropicality. Trash drifted in the vines off the Lunalilo Freeway. The airport looked Central American, between governments. Green plastic bags of garbage mounded up on the streets, and orange peels and Tab cans thrown in the canals washed down to the sea and up to the tide line in front of

603

our rented house on Kahala Avenue. A day goes this way: in the morning I rearrange our own green plastic mounds, pick up the orange peels and Tab cans from the tide line, and sit down to work at the wet bar in the living room, a U-shaped counter temporarily equipped with an IBM Selectric typewriter. I turn on the radio for news of a break in the garbage strike: I get a sig-alert for the Lunalilo, roadwork between the Wilder Avenue off-ramp and the Punahou overpass. I get the weather: mostly clear. Actually water is dropping in great glassy sheets on the windward side of the island, fifteen minutes across the Pali, but on leeward Oahu the sky is quicksilver, chiaroscuro, light and dark and sudden falls of rain and rainbow, mostly clear. Some time ago I stopped trying to explain to acquaintances on the mainland the ways in which the simplest routines of a day in Honolulu can please and interest me, but on these winter mornings I am reminded that they do. I keep an appointment with a dermatologist at Kapiolani-Children's Medical Center, and am pleased by the drive down Beretania Street in the rain. I stop for groceries at the Star Market in the Kahala Mall, and am pleased by the sprays of vanda orchids and the foot-long watercress and the little Manoa lettuces in the produce department. Some mornings I am even pleased by the garbage strike.

The undertone of every day in Honolulu, the one fact that colors every other, is the place's absolute remove from the rest of the world. Many American cities began remote, but only Honolulu is fated to remain so, and only in Honolulu do the attitudes and institutions born of extreme isolation continue to set the tone of daily life. The edge of the available world is sharply defined: one turns a corner or glances out an office window and there it is, blue sea. There is no cheap freedom to be gained by getting in a car and driving as far as one can go, since as far as one can go on the island of Oahu takes about an hour and fifteen minutes. "Getting away" involves actual travel, scheduled carriers, involves reservations and reconfirmations and the ambiguous experience of being strapped passive in a darkened cabin and exposed to unwanted images on a flickering screen; involves submission to other people's schedules and involves, most sig-nificantly, money.

I have rarely spent an evening at anyone's house in Honolulu when someone in the room was not just off or about to catch an airplane, and the extent to which ten-hour flights figure in the local imagination tends to reinforce the distinction between those who can afford them and those who cannot. More people probably travel in Honolulu than can actually afford to: one study showed recent trips to the mainland in almost 25 percent of Oahu households and recent trips to countries outside the United States in almost 10 percent. Very few of those trips are to Europe, very few to the east coast of the United States. Not only does it take longer to fly from Honolulu to New York than from Honolulu to Hong Kong (the actual air time is about the same, ten or eleven hours either way, but no carrier now flies non-stop from Honolulu to New York), but Hong Kong seems closer in spirit, as do Manila, Tokyo, Sydney. A druggist suggests that I stock up on a prescription over the counter the next time I am in Hong Kong. The daughter of a friend gets a reward for good grades, a sweet-sixteen weekend on the Great Barrier Reef. The far Pacific is home, or near home in mood and appearance (there are parts of Oahu that bear more resemblance to Southeast Asia than to anywhere in the mainland United States), and the truly foreign lies in the other direction: airline posters feature the New England foliage, the Statue of Liberty, exotic attractions from a distant culture, a culture in which most people in Honolulu have no roots at all and only a fitful interest. This leaning toward Asia makes Honolulu's relation to the rest of America oblique, and divergent at unexpected points, which is part of the place's great but often hidden eccentricity.

To buy a house anywhere on the island of Oahu in the spring of 1980 cost approximately what a similar property would have cost in Los Angeles. Three bedrooms and a bath-and-a-half in the tracts near Pearl Harbor were running over $100,000 ("$138,000" was a figure I kept noticing in advertisements, once under the headline "This Is Your Lucky Day"), although the occasional bungalow with one bath was offered in the nineties. At the top end of the scale (where "life is somehow bigger and disappoint-ment blunted," as one advertisement put it), not quite two-thirds of an acre with a main house, guesthouse, gatehouse, and saltwater pool on the beach at Diamond Head was offered—"fee simple," which was how a piece of property available for actual sale was described in Honolulu—at $3,750,000.

"Fee simple" was a magical phrase in Honolulu, since one of the peculiarities of the local arrangement had been that not much property actually changed hands. The island of Oahu was, at its longest and widest points, forty-five miles long and thirty miles wide, a total land mass—much of it vertical, unbuildable, the sheer volcanic precipices of the Koolau and Waianae ranges—of 380,000 acres. Almost 15 percent of this land was owned by the federal government and an equal amount by the State of Hawaii. Of the remaining privately owned land, more than 70 percent was owned by major landholders, by holders of more than five thousand acres, most notably, on Oahu, by the Campbell Estate, the Damon Estate, Castle and Cooke, and, in the most densely populated areas of Honolulu, the Bishop Estate. The Bishop Estate owned a good part of Waikiki, and the Kahala and Waialae districts, and, farther out, Hawaii Kai, which was a Kaiser development but a Bishop holding. The purchaser of a house on Bishop land bought not title to the property itself but a "lease-hold," a land lease, transferred from buyer to buyer, that might be within a few years of expiration or might be (the preferred situation) recently renegotiated, fixed for a long term. An advertisement in the spring of 1980 for a three-bedroom, two-bath, $230,000 house in Hawaii Kai emphasized its "long, low lease," as did an advertisement for a similar house in the Kahala district offered at $489,000. One Sunday that spring, the Dolman office, a big residential realtor in Honolulu, ran an advertisement in the *Star-Bulletin & Advertiser* featuring forty-seven listings, of which thirty-nine were leasehold. The Earl Thacker office, the same day, featured eighteen listings, ten of which were leasehold, including an oceanfront lease for a house on Kahala Avenue at $1,250,000.

This situation, in which a few owners held most of the land, was relatively unique in the developed world (under 30 percent of the private land in California was held by owners of more than five thousand acres, compared to the more than 70 percent of Oahu) and lent a rather feudal and capricious uncertainty, a note of cosmic transience, to what was in other places a straightforward transaction, a direct assertion of territory, the purchase of a place to live. In some areas the Bishop Estate had offered "conversions," or the opportunity to convert leasehold to fee-simple property at prices then averaging $5.62 a square foot. This was regarded as a kind of land reform, but it worked adversely on the householder who had already invested all he or she could afford in the leasehold. Someone I know whose Bishop lease came up recently was forced to sell the house in which she had lived for some years because she could afford neither the price of the conversion nor the raised payments of what would have been her new lease. I went with another friend in 1980 to look at a house on the "other," or non-oceanfront, side of Kahala Avenue, listed at $695,000. The Bishop lease was fixed for thirty years and graduated: $490 a month until 1989, $735 until 1999, and $979 until 2009. The woman showing the house suggested that a conversion might be obtained. No one could promise it, of course, nor could anyone say what price might be set, if indeed a price were set at all. It was true that nothing on Kahala Avenue itself had at that time been converted. It was also true that the Bishop Estate was talking about Kahala Avenue as a logical place for hotel development. Still, the woman and my friend seemed to agree, it was a pretty house, and a problematic stretch to 2009.

When I first began visiting Honolulu, in 1966, I read in a tourist guidebook that the conventional points of the compass—north, south, east, west—were never employed locally, that one gave directions by saying that a place was either *makai*, toward the sea, or *mauka*, toward the mountains, and, in the city, usually either "diamond head" or "ewa," depending on whether the place in question lay, from where one stood, toward Diamond Head or Ewa Plantation. The Royal Hawaiian Hotel, for example, was diamond head of Ewa, but ewa of Diamond Head. The Kahala Hilton Hotel, since it was situated between Diamond Head and Koko Head, was said to be koko head of Diamond Head, and diamond head of Koko Head. There was about this a resolute colorfulness that did not seem entirely plausible to me at the time, particularly since the federally funded signs on the Lunalilo Freeway read EAST and WEST, but as time passed I came to see not only the chimerical compass but the attitude it seemed to reflect as intrinsic to the local accommodation, a way of maintaining fluidity in the rigid structure and isolation of an island society.

This system of bearings is entirely relative (nothing is absolutely ewa, for instance; the Waianae coast is makaha of Ewa, or toward Makaha, and beyond Makaha the known world metamorphoses again), is used at all levels of Honolulu life, and is common even in courtrooms. I recall spending several days at a murder trial during which the HPD evidence specialist, a quite beautiful young woman who looked as if she had walked off "Hawaii Five-O," spoke of "picking up latents ewa of the sink." The police sergeant with whom she had fingerprinted the site said that he had "dusted the koko head bedroom and the koko head bathroom, also the ewa bedroom and the kitchen floor." The defendant was said to have placed his briefcase, during a visit to the victim's apartment, "toward the ewa-makai corner of the couch." This was a trial, incidentally, during which one of the witnesses, a young woman who had worked a number of call dates with the victim (the victim was a call girl who had been strangled with her own telephone cord in her apartment near Ala Moana), gave her occupation as "fulltime student at the University of Hawaii, carrying sixteen units." Another witness, also a call girl, said, when asked her occupation, that she was engaged in "part-time construction."

The way to get to Ewa was to go beyond Pearl Harbor and down Fort Weaver Road, past the weathered frame building that was once the hospital for Ewa Plantation and past the Japanese graveyard, and turn right. (Going straight instead of turning right would take the driver directly to Ewa Beach, a different proposition. I remember being advised when I first visited Honolulu that if I left the keys in a car in Waikiki I could look for it stripped down in Ewa Beach.) There was no particular reason to go to Ewa, no shops, no businesses, no famous views, no place to eat or even walk far (walk, and you walked right into the cane and the KAPU, or KEEP OUT, signs of the Oahu Sugar Company); there was only the fact that the place was there, intact, operational, a plantation town from another period. There was a school, a post office, a grocery. There were cane tools for sale in the grocery, and the pint bottles of liquor were kept in the office, a kind of wire-mesh cage with a counter. There was the Immaculate Conception Roman Catholic Church, there was the Ewa Hongwanji Mission. On the telephone poles there were torn and rain-stained posters for some revolution past or future, some May Day, a rally, a caucus, a "Mao Tse-tung Memorial Meeting."

Ewa was a company town, and its identical frame houses were arranged down a single street, the street that led to the sugar mill. Just one house on this street stood out: a house built of the same frame as the others but not exactly a bungalow, a house transliterated from the New England style, a *haole* house, a manager's house, a house larger than any other house for miles around. A Honolulu psychiatrist once told me, when I asked if he saw any characteristic island syndrome, that, yes, among the children of the planter families, children raised among the memories of the island's colonial past, he did. These patients shared the conviction that they were being watched, being observed, and not living up to what was expected of them. In Ewa one understood how that conviction might take hold. In Ewa one watched the larger house.

On my desk I used to keep a clock on Honolulu time, and around five o'clock by that clock I would sometimes think of Ewa. I would imagine driving through Ewa at that time of day, when the mill and the frame bungalows swim in the softened light like amber, and I would imagine driving on down through Ewa Beach and onto the tract of military housing at Iroquois Point, a place as rigidly structured and culturally isolated in one way as Ewa was in another. From the shoreline at Iroquois Point one looks across the curve of the coast at Waikiki, a circumstance so poignant, suggesting as it does each of the tensions in Honolulu life, that it stops discussion.

6

On the December morning in 1979 when I visited Kai Tak East, the Caritas transit camp for Vietnamese refugees near Kai Tak airport, Kowloon, Hong Kong, a woman of indeterminate age was crouched on the pavement near the washing pumps bleeding out a live chicken. She worked at the chicken's neck with a small paring knife, opening and reopening the cut and massaging the blood into a tin cup, and periodically she would let the bird run free. The chicken did not exactly run but stumbled, staggered, and finally lurched toward one of the trickles of milky waste water that drained the compound. A flock of small children with bright scarlet rashes on their cheeks giggled and staggered, mimicking the chicken. The woman retrieved the dying chicken and, with what began to seem an almost narcoleptic languor, resumed working the blood from the cut, stroking rhythmically along the matted and stained feathers of the chicken's neck. The chicken had been limp a long time before she finally laid it on the dusty pavement. The children, bored, drifted away. The woman still crouched beside her chicken in the thin December sunlight.

When I think of Hong Kong I remember a particular smell in close places, a smell I construed as jasmine and excrement and sesame oil in varying proportions, and at Kai Tak East, where there were too many people and too few places for them to sleep and cook and eat and wash, this smell pervaded even the wide and dusty exercise yard that was the center of the camp. The smell was in fact what I noticed first, the smell and the dustiness and a certain immediate sense of physical dislocation, a sense of people who had come empty-handed and been assigned odd articles of castoff clothing, which they wore uneasily: a grave little girl in a faded but still garish metallic bolero, an old man in a Wellesley sweatshirt, a wizened woman in a preteen sweater embroidered with dancing cats. In December in Hong Kong the sun lacked real warmth, and the children in the yard seemed bundled in the unfamiliar fragments of other people's habits. Men talking rubbed their hands as if to generate heat. Women cooking warmed their hands over the electric woks. In the corrugated-metal barracks, each with tiers of 144 metal and plywood bunks on which whole families spread their clothes and eating utensils and straw sleeping mats, mothers and children sat huddled in thin blankets. Outside one barrack a little boy about four years old pressed me to take a taste from his rice bowl. Another urinated against the side of the building.

After a few hours at Kai Tak East the intrinsic inertia and tedium of the camp day became vivid. Conversations in one part of the yard gave way only to conversations in another part of the yard. Preparations for one meal melted into preparations for the next. At the time I was in Hong Kong there were some three hundred thousand Vietnamese refugees, the largest number of whom were "ethnic Chinese," or Vietnamese of Chinese ancestry, waiting to be processed in improvised camps in the various countries around the South China Sea, in Hong Kong and Thailand and Malaysia and Macao and Indonesia and the Philippines. More than nine thousand of these were at Kai Tak East, and another fifteen thousand at Kai Tak North, the adjoining Red Cross camp. The details of any given passage from Vietnam to Hong Kong differed, but, in the case of the ethnic Chinese, the journey seemed typically to have begun with the payment of gold and the covert collusion of Vietnamese officials and Chinese syndicates outside Vietnam. The question was shadowy. Refugees were a business in this part of the world. Once in Hong Kong, any refugee who claimed to be Vietnamese underwent, before assignment to Kai Tak East or Kai Tak North or one of the other transit camps in the colony, an initial processing and screening by the Hong Kong police, mostly to establish that he or she was not an illegal immigrant from China looking to be relocated instead of repatriated, or, as they said in Hong Kong, "sent north." Only after this initial screening did refugees receive the yellow photographic identification cards that let them pass freely through the transit camp gates. The Vietnamese at Kai Tak East came and went all day, going out to work and out to market and out just to get out, but the perimeter of the camp was marked by high chain-link fencing, and in some places by concertina wire. The gates were manned by private security officers. The yellow cards were scrutinized closely. "This way we know," a camp administrator told me, "that what we have here is a genuine case of refugee."

They were all waiting, these genuine cases of refugee, for the consular interview that might eventually mean a visa out, and the inert tension of life at Kai Tak East derived mainly from this aspect of waiting, of limbo, of suspended hopes and plans and relationships. Of the 11,573 Vietnamese who had passed through Kai Tak East since the camp opened, in June 1979, only some 2,000 had been, by December, relocated, the largest number of them to the United States and Canada. The rest waited, filled out forms, pretended fluency in languages they had barely heard spoken, and looked in vain for their names on the day's list of interviews. Every week or so a few more would be chosen to go, cut loose from the group and put on the truck and taken to the airport for a flight to a country they had never seen.

Six Vietnamese happened to be leaving Kai Tak East the day I was there, two sisters and their younger brother for Australia, and a father and his two sons for France. The three going to Australia were the oldest children of a family that had lost its home and business in the Cholon district of Saigon and been ordered to a "new economic zone," one of the supervised wastelands in the Vietnamese countryside where large numbers of ethnic Chinese were sent to live off the land and correct their thinking. The parents had paid gold, the equivalent of six ounces, to get these three children out of Saigon via Haiphong, and now the children hoped to earn enough money in Australia to get out their parents and younger siblings. The sisters, who were twenty-three and twenty-four, had no idea how long this would take or if it would be possible. They knew only that they were leaving Hong Kong with their brother on the evening Qantas. They were uncertain in what Australian city the evening Qantas landed, nor did it seem to matter.

I talked to the two girls for a while, and then to the man who was taking his sons to France. This man had paid the equivalent of twelve or thirteen ounces of gold to buy his family out of Hanoi. Because his wife and daughters had left Hanoi on a different day, and been assigned to a different Hong Kong camp, the family was to be, on this day, reunited for the first time in months. The wife and daughters would already be on the truck when it reached Kai Tak East. The truck would take them all to the airport and they would fly together to Nice, "*toute la famille.*" Toward noon, when the truck pulled up to the gate, the man rushed past the guards and leapt up to embrace a pretty woman. "*Ma femme!*" he cried out again and again to those of us watching from the yard. He pointed wildly, and maneuvered the woman and little girls into better view. "*Ma femme, mes filles!*"

I stood in the sun and waved until the truck left, then turned back to the yard. In many ways refugees had become an entrenched fact of Hong Kong life. "They've got to go, there's no room for them here," a young Frenchwoman, Saigon born, had said to me at dinner the night before. Beside me in the yard a man sat motionless while a young woman patiently picked the nits from his hair. Across the yard a group of men and women watched without expression as the administrator posted the names of those selected for the next day's consular interviews. A few days later the *South China Morning Post* carried reports from intelligence sources that hundreds of boats were being assembled in Vietnamese ports to carry out more ethnic Chinese. The headline read, "HK Alert to New Invasion." It was believed that weather would not be favorable for passage to Hong Kong until the advent of the summer monsoon. Almost a dozen years later, the British government, which had agreed to relinquish Hong Kong to the Chinese in 1997, reached an accord with the government of Vietnam providing for the forcible repatriation of Hong Kong's remaining Vietnamese refugees. The flights back to Vietnam began in the fall of 1991. Some Vietnamese were photographed crying and resisting as they were taken to the Hong Kong airport. Hong Kong authorities stressed that the guards escorting the refugees were unarmed.

1979–91

LOS ANGELES DAYS

I

DURING ONE OF the summer weeks I spent in Los Angeles in 1988 there was a cluster of small earthquakes, the most noticeable of which, on the Garlock Fault, a major lateral-slip fracture that intersects the San Andreas in the Tehachapi range north of Los Angeles, occurred at six minutes after four on a Friday afternoon when I happened to be driving in Wilshire Boulevard from the beach. People brought up to believe that the phrase "terra firma" has real meaning often find it hard to understand the apparent equanimity with which earthquakes are accommodated in California, and tend to write it off as regional spaciness. In fact it is less equanimity than protective detachment, the useful adjustment commonly made in circumstances so unthinkable that psychic survival precludes preparation. I know very few people in California who actually set aside, as instructed, a week's supply of water and food. I know fewer still who could actually lay hands on the wrench required to turn off, as instructed, the main gas valve; the scenario in which this wrench will be needed is a catastrophe, and something in the human spirit rejects planning on a daily basis for catastrophe. I once interviewed, in the late sixties, someone who did prepare: a Pentecostal minister who had received a kind of heavenly earthquake advisory, and on its quite specific instructions was moving his congregation from Port Hueneme, north of Los Angeles, to Murfreesboro, Tennessee. A few months later, when a small earthquake was felt not in Port Hueneme but in Murfreesboro, an event so novel that it was reported nationally, I was, I recall, mildly gratified.

A certain fatalism comes into play. When the ground starts moving all bets are off. Quantification, which in this case takes the form of guessing where the movement at hand will rank on the Richter scale, remains a favored way of regaining the illusion of personal control, and people still crouched in the nearest doorjamb will reach for a telephone and try to call Caltech, in Pasadena, for a Richter reading. "Rock and roll," the D.J. said on my car radio

that Friday afternoon at six minutes past four. "This console is definitely shaking ... no word from Pasadena yet, is there?"

"I would say this is a three," the D.J.'s colleague said.

"Definitely a three, maybe I would say a little higher than a
three."

"Say an eight ... just joking."

"It felt like a six where I was."

What it turned out to be was a five-two, followed by a dozen
smaller aftershocks, and it had knocked out four of the six circuit
breakers at the A. D. Edmonston pumping plant on the California
Aqueduct, temporarily shutting down the flow of Northern
California water over the Tehachapi range and cutting off half of
Southern California's water supply for the weekend. This was all
within the range not only of the predictable but of the normal.
No one had been killed or seriously injured. There was plenty of
water for the weekend in the system's four southern reservoirs,
Pyramid, Castaic, Silverwood, and Perris lakes. A five-two earthquake is not, in California, where the movements people remember tend to have Richter numbers well over six, a major event,
and the probability of earthquakes like this one had in fact been
built into the Aqueduct: the decision to pump the water nineteen
hundred feet over the Tehachapi was made precisely because the
Aqueduct's engineers rejected the idea of tunneling through an
area so geologically complex, periodically wrenched by opposing
displacements along the San Andreas and the Garlock, that it has
been called California's structural knot.

Still, this particular five-two, coming as it did when what
Californians call "the Big One" was pretty much overdue (the
Big One is the eight, the Big One is the seven in the wrong
place or at the wrong time, the Big One could even be the six-
five centered near downtown Los Angeles at nine on a weekday
morning), made people a little uneasy. There was some concern
through the weekend that this was not merely an ordinary five-
two but a "foreshock," an earthquake prefiguring a larger event
(the chances of this, according to Caltech seismologists, run about
one in twenty), and by Sunday there was what seemed to many
people a sinister amount of activity on other faults: a three-four
just east of Ontario at twenty-two minutes past two in the
afternoon, a three-six twenty-two minutes later at Lake Berryessa,
and, four hours and one minute later, northeast of San Jose,

a five-five on the Calaveras Fault. On Monday, there was a two-three in Playa del Rey and a three in Santa Barbara.

Had it not been for the five-two on Friday, very few people would have registered these little quakes (the Caltech seismological monitors in Southern California normally record from twenty to thirty earthquakes a day with magnitudes below three), and in the end nothing came of them, but this time people did register them, and they lent a certain moral gravity to the way the city happened to look that weekend, a temporal dimension to the hard white edges and empty golden light. At odd moments during the next few days people would suddenly clutch at tables, or walls. "Is it going," they would say, or "I think it's moving." They almost always said "it," and what they meant by "it" was not just the ground but the world as they knew it. I have lived all my life with the promise of the Big One, but when it starts going now even I get the jitters.

2

What is striking about Los Angeles after a period away is how well it works. The famous freeways work, the supermarkets work (a visit, say, to the Pacific Palisades Gelson's, where the aisles are wide and the shelves full and checkout is fast and free of attitude, remains the zazen of grocery shopping), the beaches work. The 1984 Olympics were not supposed to work, but they did (daily warnings of gridlock and urban misery gave way, during the first week, to a county-wide block party, with pink and aquamarine flags fluttering over empty streets and parking spaces for once available even in Westwood); not only worked but turned a profit, of almost $223 million, about which there was no scandal. Even the way houses are bought and sold seems to work more efficiently than it does in New York (for all practical purposes there are no exclusive listings in Los Angeles, and the various contingencies on which closing the deal depends are arbitrated not by lawyers but by an escrow company), something that came to my attention when my husband and I arranged to have our Los Angeles house shown for the first time to brokers at eleven o'clock one Saturday morning, went out to do a few errands, and came back at one to find that we had three offers, one of them for appreciably more than the asking price.

Selling a house in two hours was not, in 1988 in Los Angeles, an entirely unusual experience. Around February of 1988, midway through what most people call the winter but Californians call the spring ("winter" in California is widely construed as beginning and ending with the Christmas season, reflecting a local preference for the upside), at a time when residential real estate prices in New York were already plunging in response to the October 1987 stock market crash, there had in fact developed on the west side of Los Angeles a heightened enthusiasm for committing large sums of money to marginal improvements in one's domestic situation: to moving, say, from what was called in the listings a "convertible 3" in Santa Monica (three bedrooms, one of which might be converted into a study) to a self-explanatory "4 + lib" in Brentwood Park, or to acquiring what was described in the listings as an "H/F pool," meaning heated and filtered, or a "N/S tennis court," meaning the preferred placement on the lot, the north–south orientation believed to keep sun from the players' eyes.

By June of 1988 a kind of panic had set in, of a kind that occurs periodically in Southern California but had last occurred in 1979. Multiple offers were commonplace, and deals stalled because bank appraisers could not assess sales fast enough to keep up with the rising market. Residential real estate offices were routinely reporting "record months." People were buying one- and two-million-dollar houses as investments, to give their adolescent children what brokers referred to as "a base in the market," which was one reason why small houses on modest lots priced at a million-four were getting, the day they were listed, thirty and forty offers.

All this seemed to assume an infinitely upward trend, and to be one of those instances in which the preoccupations and apprehensions of people in Los Angeles, a city in many ways predicated on the ability to deal with the future at a rather existential remove, did not exactly coincide with those of the country at large. October 19, 1987, which had so immediately affected the New York market that asking prices on some apartments had in the next three or four months dropped as much as a million dollars, seemed, in Los Angeles, not to have happened. Those California brokers to whom I talked, if they mentioned the crash at all, tended to see it as a catalyst for good times, an event that had emphasized the "real" in real estate.

The *Los Angeles Times* had taken to running, every Sunday, a chat column devoted mainly to the buying and selling of houses: Ruth Ryon's "Hot Property," from which one could learn that the highest price paid for a house in Los Angeles to that date was $20.25 million (by Marvin Davis, to Kenny Rogers, for The Knoll in Beverly Hills); that the $2.5 million paid in 1986 for 668 St. Cloud Road in Bel Air (by Earle Jorgenson and Holmes Tuttle and some eighteen other friends of President and Mrs. Reagan, for whom the house was bought and who rent it with an option to buy) was strikingly under value, since even an unbuilt acre in the right part of Bel Air (the house bought by the Reagans' friends is definitely in the right part of Bel Air) will sell for $3 million; and that two houses in the Reagans' new neighborhood sold recently for $13.5 million and $14.75 million respectively. A typical "Hot Property" item ran this way:

> Newlyweds Tracey E. Bregman Recht, star of the daytime soap "The Young and the Restless," and her husband Ron Recht, a commercial real estate developer, just bought their first home, on 2.5 acres in a nifty neighborhood. They're just up the street from Merv Griffin's house (which I've heard is about to be listed at some astronomical price) and they're just down the street from Pickfair, now owned by Pia Zadora and her husband. The Rechts bought a house that was built in 1957 on San Ysidro Drive in Beverly Hills for an undisclosed price, believed to be several million dollars, and now they're fixing it up …

I spent some time, before this 1988 bull market broke, with two West Side brokers, Betty Budlong and Romelle Dunas of the Jon Douglas office, both of whom spoke about the going price of "anything at all" as a million dollars, and of "something decent" as two million dollars. "Right now I've got two clients in the price range of five to six hundred thousand dollars," Romelle Dunas said. "I sat all morning trying to think what I could show them today."

"I'd cancel the appointment," Betty Budlong said.

"I just sold their condo for four. I'm sick. The houses for five-fifty are smaller than their condo."

"I think you could still find something in Ocean Park," Betty Budlong said. "Ocean Park, Sunset Park, somewhere like that. Brentwood Glen, you know, over here, the Rattery tract … of course that's inching towards six."

"Inching toward six and you're living in the right lane of the San Diego Freeway," Romelle Dunas said.

"In seventeen hundred square feet," Betty Budlong said.

"If you're lucky. I saw one that was fifteen hundred square feet. I have a feeling when these people go out today they're not going to close on their condo."

Betty Budlong thought about this. "I think you should make a good friend of Sonny Fox," she said at last.

Sonny Fox was a Jon Douglas agent in Sherman Oaks, in the San Fernando Valley, only a twenty-minute drive from Beverly Hills on the San Diego Freeway but a twenty-minute drive toward which someone living on the West Side—even someone who would drive forty minutes to Malibu—was apt to display considerable sales resistance.

"In the Valley," Romelle Dunas said after a pause.

Betty Budlong shrugged. "In the Valley."

"People are afraid to get out of this market," Romelle Dunas said.

"They can't afford to get out," Betty Budlong said. "I know two people who in any other market would have sold their houses. One of them has accepted a job in Chicago, the other is in Washington for at least two years. They're both leasing their houses. Because until they're sure they're not coming back, they don't want to get out."

The notion that land will be worth more tomorrow than it is worth today has been a real part of the California experience, and remains deeply embedded in the California mentality, but this seemed extreme, and it occurred to me that the buying and selling of houses was perhaps one more area in which the local capacity for protective detachment had come into play, that people capable of compartmentalizing the Big One might be less inclined than others to worry about getting their money out of a 4 + lib, H/F pool. I asked if foreign buyers could be pushing up the market.

Betty Budlong thought not. "These are people who are moving, say, from a seven-fifty house to a million-dollar house."

I asked if the market could be affected by a defense cutback.

Betty Budlong thought not. "Most of the people who buy on the West Side are professionals, or in the entertainment industry. People who work at Hughes and Douglas, say, don't live in Brentwood or Santa Monica or Beverly Hills."

I asked Betty Budlong if she saw anything at all that could affect the market.

"Tight money could affect this market," Betty Budlong said. "For a while."

"Then it always goes higher," Romelle Dunas said.

"Which is why people can't afford to get out," Betty Budlong said.

"They couldn't get back in," Romelle Dunas said.

3

This entire question of houses and what they were worth (and what they should be worth, and what it meant when the roof over someone's head was also his or her major asset) was, during the spring and summer of 1988, understandably more on the local mind than it perhaps should have been, which was one reason why a certain house then under construction just west of the Los Angeles Country Club became the focus of considerable attention, and of emotions usually left dormant on the west side of Los Angeles. The house was that being built by the television producer ("Dynasty," "Loveboat," "Fantasy Island") Aaron Spelling and his wife Candy at the corner of Mapleton and Club View in Holmby Hills, on six acres the Spellings had bought in 1983, for $10,250,000, from Patrick Frawley, the chairman of Schick.

At the time of the purchase there was already a fairly impressive house on the property, a house once lived in by Bing Crosby, but the Spellings, who had become known for expansive domestic gestures (crossing the country in private railroad cars, for example, and importing snow to Beverly Hills for their children's Christmas parties), had decided that the Crosby/Frawley house was what is known locally as a teardown. The progress of the replacement, which was rising from the only residential site I have ever seen with a two-story contractor's office and a sign reading CONSTRUCTION AREA: HARD HATS REQUIRED, became over the next several months not just a form of popular entertainment but, among inhabitants of a city without much common experience, a unifying, even a political, idea.

At first the project was identified, on the kind of site sign usually reserved for office towers in progress, as "THE MANOR"; later "THE MANOR" was modified to what seemed, given the resemblance of the structure to a resort Hyatt, the slightly nutty discretion of "594 SOUTH MAPLETON DRIVE." It was said that the structure ("house" seemed not entirely to cover it) would have 56,500 square feet. It was said that the interior plan would include a bowling alley, and 560 square feet of extra closet space, balconied between the second and the attic floors. It was said, by the owner, that such was the mass of the steel frame construction that to break up the foundation alone would take a demolition crew six months, and cost from four to five million dollars.

Within a few months the site itself had become an established attraction, and evening drive-bys were enlivened by a skittish defensiveness on the part of the guards, who would switch on the perimeter floods and light up the steel girders and mounded earth like a prison yard. The *Los Angeles Times* and *Herald Examiner* published periodic reports on and rumors about the job ("Callers came out of the woodwork yesterday in the wake of our little tale about Candy Spelling having the foundation of her $45-million mansion-in-progress lowered because she didn't want to see the Robinson's department store sign from where her bed-to-be was to sit"), followed by curiously provocative corrections, or "denials," from Aaron Spelling. "The only time Candy sees the Robinson's sign is when she's shopping" was one correction that got everyone's attention, but in many ways the most compelling was this: "They say we have an Olympic-sized swimming pool. Not true. There's no gazebo, no guesthouse.... When people go out to dinner, unless they talk about their movies, they have nothing else to talk about, so they single out Candy."

In that single clause, "unless they talk about their movies," there was hidden a great local truth, and the inchoate heart of the matter: this house was, in the end, that of a television producer, and people who make movies did not, on the average evening, have dinner with people who make television. People who make television had most of the money, but people who make movies still had most of the status, and believed themselves the keepers of the community's unspoken code, of the rules, say, about what constituted excess on the housing front. This was a distinction usually left tacit, but the fact of the Spelling house was making people say things out loud. "There are people in this town worth hundreds of millions of dollars," Richard Zanuck, one of the most successful motion picture producers in the business, once said to my husband, "and they can't get a table at Chasen's." This was a man whose father had run a studio and who had himself run a studio, and his bewilderment was that of someone who had uncovered an anomaly in the wheeling of the stars.

4

When people in Los Angeles talk about "this town," they do not mean Los Angeles, nor do they exactly mean what many of them call "the community." "The community" is more narrowly defined, and generally confined to those inhabitants of this town who can be relied upon to sit at one another's tables on approved evenings (benefiting the American Film Institute, say) and to get one another's daughters into approved schools, say Westlake, in Holmby Hills, not far from the Spellings' house but on eleven acres rather than six. People in the community meet one another for lunch at Hillcrest, but do not, in the main, attend Friars' Club Roasts. People in the community sojourn with their children in Paris, and Aspen, and at the Kahala Hilton in Honolulu, but visit Las Vegas only on business. "The community" is made up of people who can, in other words, get a table at Chasen's.

"This town" is broader, and means just "the industry," which is the way people who make television and motion pictures refer, tellingly, to the environment in which they work. The extent to which the industry in question resembles conventional industries is often obscured by its unconventional product, which requires that its "workers" perform in unconventional ways, for which they are paid unconventional sums of money: some people do make big money writing and directing and producing and acting in television, and some people also make big money, although considerably less big, writing and directing and producing and acting in motion pictures.

Still, as in other entrepreneurial enterprises, it is not those who work on the line in this industry but those who manage it who make the biggest money of all, and who tend to have things their way, which is what the five-month 1988 Writers Guild of America strike, which had become by the time of its settlement in early August 1988 perhaps the most acrimonious union strike in recent industry history, was initially and finally about. It was not about what were inflexibly referred to by both union and management as "the so-called creative issues," nor was it exclusively about the complicated formulas and residuals that were the tokens on the board. It was about respect, and about whether the people who made the biggest money were or were not going to give a little to the people who made the less big money.

In other words, it was a class issue, which was hard for people outside the industry—who in the first place did not understand the essentially adversarial nature of the business (a good contract, it is understood in Hollywood, is one that ensures the other party's breach) and in the second place believed everybody involved to be overpaid—to entirely understand. "Whose side does one take in such a war—that of the writers with their scads of money, or that of the producers with their tons of money?" the *Washington Post*'s television reporter, Tom Shales, demanded (as it turned out, rhetorically) in a June 29, 1988, piece arguing that the writers were "more interested in strutting and swaggering than in reaching a settlement," that "a handful of hotheads" who failed to realize that "the salad days are over" were bringing down an industry beset by "dwindling" profits, and that the only effect of the strike was to crush "those in the lowest-paying jobs," for example a waitress, laid off when Universal shut down its commissary, who Tom Shales perceived to be "not too thrilled with the writers and their grievances" when he saw her interviewed on a television newscast. (This was an example of what became known locally during the strike as "the little people argument," and referred to the traditional practice among struck companies of firing their nonunion hostages. When hard times come to Hollywood, the typing pool goes first, and is understood to symbolize the need of the studio to "cut back," or "slash costs.") "Just because the producers are richer doesn't mean the writers are right. Or righteous," Tom Shales concluded. "These guys haven't just seen too many Rambo movies, they've written too many Rambo movies."

This piece, which reflected with rather impressive fidelity the arguments then being made by the Alliance of Motion Picture and Television Producers, the negotiating body for management, was typical of most coverage of the strike, and also of what had become, by early summer of 1988, the prevailing mood around town. Writers have never been much admired in Hollywood. In an industry predicated on social fluidity, on the daily calibration and reassessment of status and power, screenwriters, who perform a function that remains only dimly understood even by the people who hire them, occupy a notably static place: even the most successful of them have no real power, and therefore no real status. "I can always get a writer," Ray Stark once told my husband, who had expressed a disinclination to join the team on a Stark picture for which he had been, Ray Stark had told him a few weeks before, "the only possible writer."

Writers (even the only possible writers), it is universally believed, can always be replaced, which is why they are so frequently referred to in the plural. Writers, it is believed by many, are even best replaced, hired serially, since they bring, in this view, only a limited amount of talent and energy to bear on what directors often call their "vision." A number of directors prefer to hire fresh writers—usually writers with whom they have previously worked—just before shooting: Sydney Pollack, no matter who wrote the picture he is directing, has the habit of hiring for the period just before and during production David Rayfiel or Elaine May or Kurt Luedtke. "I want it in the contract when David Rayfiel comes in," a writer I know once said when he and Pollack were talking about doing a picture together; this was a practical but unappreciated approach.

The previous writer on a picture is typically described as "exhausted," or "worn-out on this." What is meant by "this" is the task at hand, which is seen as narrow and technical, one color in the larger vision, a matter of taking notes from a producer or an actor or a director, and adding dialogue—something, it is understood, that the producer or actor or director could do without a writer, if only he or she had the time, if only he or she were not required to keep that larger vision in focus. "I've got the ideas," one frequently hears in the industry. "All I need is a writer."

Such "ideas," when explored, typically tend toward the general ("relationships between men and women," say, or "rebel without a cause in the west Valley"), and the necessity for paying a writer to render such ideas specific remains a source of considerable resentment. Writers are generally seen as balky, obstacles to the forward flow of the project. They take time. They want money. They are typically the first element on a picture, the people whose job it is to invent a world sufficiently compelling to interest actors and directors, and, as the first element, they are often unwilling to recognize the necessity for keeping the front money down, for cutting their fees in order to get a project going. "Everyone," they are told, is taking a cut ("everyone" in this instance generally means every one of the writers), yet they insist on "irresponsible" fees. A director who gets several million dollars a picture will often complain, quite bitterly, about being "held up" by the demands of his writers. "You're haggling over pennies," a director once complained to me.

This resentment surfaces most openly in contract negotiations ("We don't give points to writers," studio business-affairs lawyers will say in a negotiation, or, despite the fact that a writer has often delivered one or two drafts on the basis of a deal memo alone, "Our policy is no payment without a fully executed contract"), but in fact suffuses every aspect of life in the community. Writers do not get gross from dollar one, nor do they get the Thalberg Award, nor do they even determine when and where a meeting will take place: these are facts of local life known even to children. Writers who work regularly live comfortably, but not in the houses with the better N/S courts. Writers sometimes get to Paris on business, but rarely on the Concorde. Writers occasionally have lunch at Hillcrest, but only when their agents take them. Writers have at best a provisional relationship with the community in which they live, which is precisely what has made them, over the years, such convenient pariahs. "Fuck 'em, they're weaklings," as one director I know said about the Guild.

As the strike wore on, then, a certain natural irritation, even a bellicosity, was bound to surface when the subject of the writers (or, as some put it, "the writers and their so-called demands") came up, as was an impatience with the whole idea of collective bargaining. "If you're good enough, you can negotiate your own contract," I recall being told by one director. It was frequently suggested that the strike was supported only by those members of the Guild who were not full-time working writers. "A lot of them aren't writers," an Alliance spokesman told the *Los Angeles Times*. "They pay their one-hundred-dollar-a-year dues and get invitations to screenings." A television producer suggested to me that perhaps the answer was "another guild," one that would function, although he did not say this, as a sweetheart union. "A guild for working writers," he said. "That's a guild we could negotiate with."

I heard repeatedly during the strike that I, as a member of the Guild "but an intelligent person," had surely failed to understand what "the leadership" of the Guild was doing to me; when I said that I did understand it, that I had lost three pictures during the course of the strike and would continue to vote against a settlement until certain money issues had been resolved, I was advised that such intransigence would lead nowhere, because "the producers won't budge," because "they're united on this," because "they're going to just write off the Guild," and because, an antic note, "they're going to start hiring college kids—they're even going to start hiring journalists."

In this mounting enthusiasm to punish the industry's own writers by replacing them "even" with journalists ("Why not air traffic controllers?" said a writer to whom I mentioned this threat), certain facts about the strike receded early into the mists of claim and counterclaim. Many people preferred to believe that, as Tom Shales summarized it, the producers had "offered increases," and that the writers had "said they were not enough." In fact the producers had offered, on the key points in the negotiation, rollbacks on a residual payment structure established in 1985, when the WGA contract had been last negotiated. Many people preferred to believe, as Tom Shales seemed to believe, that it was the writers, not the producers, who were refusing to negotiate. In fact the strike had been, from the Alliance's "last and final offer" on March 6, 1988, until a federal mediator called both sides to meet on May 23, 1988, less a strike than a lockout, with the producers agreeing to attend only a single meeting, on April 8, which lasted twenty minutes before the Alliance negotiators walked out. "It looks like the writers are shooting the whole industry in the foot—and they're doing it willfully and stupidly," Grant Tinker, the television producer and former chairman of NBC, told the *Los Angeles Times* after the Guild rejected, by a vote of 2,789 to 933, the June version of the Alliance's series of "last and final" offers. "It's just pigheaded and stupid for the writers to have so badly misread what's going on here."

What was going on here was interesting. This had not been an industry unaccustomed to labor disputes, nor had it been one, plans to hire "journalists" notwithstanding, historically hospitable to outsiders. ("We don't go for strangers in Hollywood," Cecilia Brady said in *The Last Tycoon*; this remains the most succinct description I know of the picture business.) For reasons deep in the structure of the industry, writers' strikes have been a fixed feature of local life, and gains earned by the writers have traditionally been passed on to the other unions—who themselves strike only rarely—in a fairly inflexible ratio: for every dollar in residuals the Writers Guild gets, another dollar goes to the Directors Guild, three dollars go to the Screen Actors Guild, and eight or nine dollars go to IATSE, the principal craft union, which needs the higher take because its pension and health benefits, unlike those of the other unions, are funded entirely from residuals. "So when the WGA negotiates for a dollar increase in residuals, say, the studios don't think just a dollar, they think twelve or thirteen," a former Guild president told me. "The industry is a kind of family, and its members are interdependent."

Something new was at work, and it had to do with a changed attitude among the top executives. I recall being told, quite early in this strike, by someone who had been a studio head of production and had bargained for management in previous strikes, that this strike would be different, and in many ways unpredictable. The problem, he said, was the absence at the bargaining table of "a Lew Wasserman, an Arthur Krim." Lew Wasserman, the chairman of MCA-Universal, it is said in the industry, was always looking for the solution; as he grew less active, Arthur Krim, at United Artists, and to a lesser extent Ted Ashley, at Warner Brothers, fulfilled this function, which was essentially that of the *consigliere*. "The guys who are running the studios now, they don't deal," he said. "Sid Sheinberg bargaining for Universal, Barry Diller for Fox, that's ridiculous. They won't even talk. As far as the Disney guys go, Eisner, Katzenberg, they play hardball, that's the way they run their operation."

Roger Fisher, the Williston Professor of Law at Harvard Law School and director of the Harvard Negotiation Project, suggested, in an analysis of the strike published in the *Los Angeles Times*, that what had been needed between management and labor in this case was "understanding, two-way communication, reliability, and acceptance," the very qualities that natural selection in the

JOAN DIDION

motion picture industry had tended to eliminate. It was in fact June of 1988, three months into the strike, before the people running the studios actually entered the negotiating sessions, which they referred to, significantly, as "downtime." "I talked to Diller, Mancuso, Daly," I was told by one of the two or three most powerful agents in the industry. He meant Barry Diller at Twentieth Century-Fox and Frank Mancuso at Paramount and Robert Daly at Warner Brothers. "I said look, you guys, you want this thing settled, you better indicate you're taking it seriously enough to put in the downtime yourselves. Sheinberg [Sidney Sheinberg of MCA-Universal] and Mancuso have kind of emerged as the point players for management, but you've got to remember, these guys are all prima donnas, they hate each other, so it was a big problem presenting a sufficiently united front to put somebody out there speaking for all of them."

In the context of an industry traditionally organized, like a mob family, around principles of discretion and unity, this notion of the executive as prima donna was a new phenomenon, and not one tending toward an appreciation of the "interdependence" of unions and management. It did not work toward the settlement of this strike that the main players on one side of the negotiations were themselves regarded as stars, the subjects of fan profiles, pieces often written by people who admired and wanted to work in the industry. Michael Eisner of Disney had been on the cover of *Time*. Sidney Sheinberg of Universal had been on the cover of *Manhattan, inc.* Executive foibles had been detailed (Jeffrey Katzenberg of Disney "guzzled" Diet Coke, and "sold his Porsche after he almost killed himself trying to shift gears and dial at the same time"), as had, and this presented a problem, company profits and executive compensation. Nineteen eighty-seven net profit for Warner Communications was up 76.6 percent over 1986. Nineteen eighty-seven net profit for Paramount was up 130 percent over 1986. CBS was up 21 percent, ABC 53 percent. The chairman and CEO of Columbia, Victor Kaufman, received in 1987 $826,154 in salary and an additional $1,506,142 in stock options and bonuses. Michael Eisner was said to have received, including options and bonuses, a figure that ranged from $23 million (this was Disney's own figure) to more than $80 million (this was what the number of shares involved in the stock options seemed to suggest), but was most often given as $63 million.

During a season when management was issuing white papers explaining the "new, colder realities facing the entertainment industry," this last figure in particular had an energizing effect on the local consciousness, and was frequently mentioned in relation to another figure, that for the combined total received in residual payments by all nine thousand members of the Writers Guild. This figure was $58 million, which, against Michael Eisner's $63, made it hard for many people to accept the notion that residual rollbacks were entirely imperative. Trust seemed lacking, as did a certain mutuality of interest. "We used to sit across the table from people we had personally worked with on movies," I was told by a writer who had sat in on negotiating sessions during this and past strikes. "These people aren't movie people. They think like their own business-affairs lawyers. You take somebody like Jeff Katzenberg, he has a very ideological position. He said the other night, 'I'm speaking as a dedicated capitalist. I own this screenplay. So why should I hand anybody else the right to have any say about it?'"

In June of 1988, three months into the strike, it was said around Los Angeles that the strike was essentially over, because the producers said it was over, and that the only problem remaining was to find a way for the Guild negotiators to save face—"a bone," as Jeffrey Katzenberg was said to be calling it, to throw the writers. "This has largely come down to a question of how Brian will look," I was told that month by someone close to management. He was talking about Brian Walton, the Guild's executive director and chief negotiator. "It's a presentation problem, a question of giving him something he can present to the membership, after fifteen weeks, as something approaching win-win." It was generally conceded that the producers, despite disavowals, were determined to break the union; even the disavowals, focusing as they did on the useful clerical work done by the Guild ("If the Guild didn't exist we'd have to invent it," Sidney Sheinberg said at one point), suggested that what the producers had in mind was less a union than a trade association. It was taken for granted that it was not the producers but the writers who, once the situation was correctly "presented," would give in. "Let's get this town back to work," people were saying, and "This strike has to end."

Still, this strike did not end. By late July, it was said around Los Angeles that the negotiations once again in progress were not really negotiations at all; that "they" were meeting only because a federal mediator had ordered them to meet, and that the time spent at the table was just that, time spent at a table, downtime. Twenty-one writers had announced their intention of working in spite of the strike, describing this decision as evidence of "the highest form of loyalty" to the Guild. "What's it for?" people were saying, and "This is lose-lose."

"Writers are children," Monroe Stahr had said almost half a century before, in *The Last Tycoon*, by way of explaining why his own negotiations with the Writers Guild had reached, after a year, a dead end. "They are not equipped for authority. There is no substitute for will. Sometimes you have to fake will when you don't feel it at all.... So I've had to take an attitude in this Guild matter." In the end, the attitude once again was taken and once again prevailed. "This strike has run out of gas," people began to say, and "This is ridiculous, this is enough," as if the writers were not only children but bad children, who had been humored too long. "We've gotten to the end of the road and hit a brick wall," the negotiator for the Alliance of Motion Picture and Television Producers, J. Nicholas Counter III, said on the Sunday afternoon of July 31,1988, at a press conference called by the Alliance to announce that negotiations with the Writers Guild were at an end, "hopelessly" deadlocked. "I suggest it's time for Mr. Walton to look to himself for the answer as to why his guild is still on strike," Jeffrey Katzenberg said that afternoon to Aljean Harmetz of the *New York Times*. That evening, Jeffrey Katzenberg and the other executives of the major studios met with Kenneth Ziffren, a prominent local lawyer who represented several Guild members who, because they had television production companies, had a particular interest in ending the strike; the marginally different formulas suggested by Kenneth Ziffren seemed to many the bone they had been looking for: a way of solving "the presentation problem," of making the strike look, now that the writers understood that it had run out of gas, "like something approaching win-win." On the following Sunday, August 7, 1988, the Guild membership voted to end the strike, on essentially the same terms it had turned down in June.

* * *

During the five months of the dispute many people outside the industry had asked me what the strike was about, and I had heard myself talk about ancillary markets and about the history of pattern bargaining, about the "issues," but the dynamic of the strike, the particular momentum that kept several thousand people with not much in common voting for at least a while against what appeared to be their own best interests, had remained hard to explain. The amounts of money to be gained or lost had seemed, against the money lost during the course of the strike, insignificant. The "creative" issues, the provisions that touched on the right of the writer to have some say in the production, would have been, if won, unenforceable.

Yet I had been for the strike, and felt toward that handful of writers who had declared their intention to desert it, and by so doing encouraged the terms on which it would end, a coolness bordering on distaste, as if we had gone back forty years, and they had named names. "You need to have worked in the industry," I would say by way of explanation, or "You have to live there." Not until July of 1988, at the Democratic National Convention in Atlanta, did the emotional core of the strike come clear to me. I had gone to Atlanta in an extra-industry role, that of "reporter" (or, as we say in Hollywood, "journalist"), with credentials that gave me a seat in the Omni but access to only a rotating pass to go on the floor. I was waiting for this rotating pass one evening when I ran into a director I knew, Paul Mazursky. We talked for a moment, and I noticed that he, like all the other industry people I saw in Atlanta, had a top pass, one of the several all-access passes. In this case it was a floor pass, and, since I was working and he seemed not about to go on the floor, I asked if I might borrow it for half an hour.

He considered this.

He would, he said, "really like" to do this for me, but thought not. He seemed surprised that I had asked, and uncomfortable that I had breached the natural order of the community as we both knew it: directors and actors and producers, I should have understood, have floor passes. Writers do not, which is why they strike.

1988

DOWN AT CITY HALL

JUST INSIDE THE main lobby of City Hall in Los Angeles there was for some time a curious shrine to Tom Bradley, the seventy-one-year-old black former police officer who was in April of 1989 elected to his fifth four-year term as mayor of Los Angeles. There was an Olympic flag, suspended behind glass and lit reverentially, its five interlocking rings worked in bright satin. There were, displayed in a kind of architectural niche, various other mementos of the 1984 Los Angeles Olympics, the event that remained the symbolic centerpiece not only of Tom Bradley's sixteen-year administration (arriving passengers at LAX, for example, were for some years after 1984 confronted on the down escalators by large pictures of Mayor Bradley and the somewhat unsettling legend "Welcome to Los Angeles XXIII Olympiad," as if the plane had touched down in a time warp), but of what Bradley's people liked to present as the city's ascension, under his guidance, to American capital of the Pacific rim.

And there was, behind a crimson silk rope, a sheet of glass on which a three-dimensional holographic image of Tom Bradley, telephone to ear, appeared and disappeared. If the viewer moved to the right, the mayor could be seen to smile; if the viewer moved to the left, the mayor turned grave, and lowered his head to study a paper. From certain angles the mayor vanished altogether, leaving only an eerie blue. It was this disappearing effect, mirroring as it did what many saw as a certain elusiveness about the mayor himself, that most often arrested the passing citizen. "That's the shot on the Jackson endorsement," I recall a television cameraman saying as we passed this dematerializing Tom Bradley one afternoon in June of 1988, a few days before the California presidential primary, on our way from a press conference during which the actual Tom Bradley had successfully, and quite characteristically, managed to appear with Jesse Jackson without in the least recommending him.

In fact it seemed the shot on the entire Bradley administration, the enduring electability of which was something many people in Los Angeles found hard to define, or even to talk about. "I don't think Tom Bradley is beatable," I was told not long before the 1989 mayoralty election by Zev Yaroslavsky, a Los Angeles City Council member who ran an abortive campaign against Bradley in 1985 and aborted a second campaign against him in January of 1989. "At least not by me. His personal popularity transcends the fact that he has been presiding over a city that in some aspects has been experiencing serious difficulties during his term in office. Most people agree that we've got this traffic, that air quality stinks, that they see a hundred and one things wrong with the quality of life. But nobody blames him for it."

In part because of this perceived ability to float free of his own administration and in part because of his presumed attractiveness to black voters, Tom Bradley was over the years repeatedly mentioned, usually in the same clause with Andrew Young, as a potential national figure, even a vice-presidential possibility. This persistent white fantasy to one side, Tom Bradley was never a charismatic, or even a particularly comfortable, candidate. His margin in the April 1989 election, for which a large majority of Los Angeles voters did not bother even to turn out, was surprisingly low. His votes never traveled outside Los Angeles. He twice tried, in 1982 and in 1986, to become governor of California, and was twice defeated by George Deukmejian, not himself noted for much sparkle as a candidate.

Bradley's strength in Los Angeles did not derive exclusively or even principally from the black community, which, in a city where the fastest-growing ethnic groups were Asian and Hispanic, constituted a decreasing percentage of the population and in any case had come to vote for Bradley, who was the first black ever elected to the Los Angeles City Council, grudgingly at best. One city official to whom I spoke during the 1989 campaign pointed out that when Bradley last ran for governor, there was a falling off in even those low-income black precincts in south-central Los Angeles that had previously been, however unenthusiastically, his territory. "He assumed south-central would be there for him," she said. "And so he didn't work it. And having been taken for granted, it wasn't there."

"He is probably less liked in south-central than other elected officials who represent south-central," another city official conceded. "I mean they view him as somebody who is maybe more interested in wining and dining Prince Andrew and Princess Sarah or whatever her name is than in dealing with the crumbling floor in the Nickerson Gardens gymnasium."

Nickerson Gardens was a housing project in Watts, where people may vote but tended not to bid on city contracts, tended not to exhibit interest in the precise location of proposed freeway exits, tended not to have projects that could be made "important" to the mayor because they were "important" to them; tended not, in other words, to require the kind of access that generates contributions to a campaign. Tom Bradley was an access politician in the traditional mold. "We would be rather disappointed if, having supported him, he were inaccessible to us," Eli Broad, a longtime Bradley supporter and the chairman of Kaufman & Broad, told the *Los Angeles Times* during the summer of 1988. "It's not really a quid pro quo. [But] there's no question that … if someone … wants money for the campaign, and if you want to talk to them six months later and don't hear from them, you just don't give any more."

Kaufman & Broad was at that time the largest builder of single-family houses in California, the developer and builder of such subdivisions as California Dawn ("From $108,990, 2, 3, and 4 Bedroom Homes"), California Esprit ("From the low $130,000s, 3 and 4 Bedroom Homes"), and California Gallery ("From $150,000, 3 and 4 Bedroom Homes"). California Dawn, California Esprit, and California Gallery were all in Palmdale, on the Mojave desert, an hour and a half northeast of Los Angeles. According to the final report of the Los Angeles 2000 Committee, a group appointed by Mayor Bradley to recommend a development strategy for the city, the Los Angeles Department of Airports was reviving a languishing plan to build an international airport on 17,750 acres the city happened to own six miles from the center of Palmdale.

The notion of building a Palmdale airport, first proposed in 1968 and more or less dormant since the mid-seventies, had met, over the years, considerable resistance, not the least of which derived from an almost total disinclination on the part of both carriers and passengers to go to Palmdale. But the possibilities were clear at the outset. There would be first of all the acquisition of the 17,750 acres (which would ultimately cost the city about $100 million to buy and to maintain), and the speculative boom that would accompany any such large-scale public acquisition. There would be the need for a highway project, estimated early on at another $100 million, to link Palmdale with the population. There could even be the eventual possibility of a $1.5 billion mountain tunnel, cutting the distance roughly in half. The construction of a monorail could be investigated. The creation of a foreign-trade zone could be studied. There would be the demand not only for housing (as in California Dawn, California Esprit, and California Gallery) but for schools, shopping centers, aircraft-related industry.

This hypothetical Palmdale International Airport, then, had survived as that ideal civic project, the one that just hangs in there, sometimes a threat, sometimes a promise, in either case a money machine. Here was the way the machine worked: with the encouragement of interested investors and an interested city government, the city would eventually reach Palmdale, and the Palmdale International Airport would reach critical mass, at which point many possibilities would be realized and many opportunities generated, both for development and for the access required to facilitate that development. This has been the history of Los Angeles.

Tom Bradley turned up in June of 1988 at a dinner dance honoring Eli Broad. He turned up in September of 1988 as a speaker at a party celebrating Kaufman & Broad's thirtieth anniversary. Bradley's most useful tool as a campaigner may well have been this practice of turning up wherever a supporter or potential supporter asked him to turn up, an impassive and slightly baffling stranger at bar mitzvahs and anniversary cocktail parties and backyard barbecues. "It is just something that I do because I enjoy it," Bradley told the *Los Angeles Times* in the summer of 1988 about another such event, a neighborhood barbecue at the South El Monte home of one of his planning commissioners. "I showed up and I tell you, you've never seen a happier couple in your life than that man and his wife. And the whole family was there.... As we were out in the front yard chatting or taking pictures, everybody who drove by was honking and waving. It was important to him. He enjoyed that. And I enjoyed his enjoyment. I get a pleasure out of that."

This fairly impenetrable style was often referred to locally as "low-keyed," or "conciliatory," which seemed in context to be code words for staying out of the way, not making waves, raising the money and granting the access the money is meant to secure. Tom Bradley was generally regarded as a pro-business, pro-development mayor, a supporter of the kinds of redevelopment and public works projects that tend, however problematical their ultimate public benefit, to suggest considerable opportunity to the kinds of people who are apt to support one or another political campaign. He was often credited with having built the downtown skyline, which translated roughly into having encouraged developers to think of downtown Los Angeles, which was until his tenure a rather somnolent financial district enlivened by the fact that it was also *el centro*, the commercial core of the Mexican and Central American communities, as bulldozable, a raw canvas to be rendered indistinguishable from Atlanta or Houston.

Bradley was redeveloping Watts. He was redeveloping Hollywood. He was redeveloping, in all, more than seven thousand acres around town. He was building—in a city so decentralized as to render conventional mass transit virtually useless and at a time when big transit projects had been largely discredited (one transportation economist had demonstrated that San Francisco's BART system must operate for 535 years before the energy presumably saved by its use catches up with the energy expended on its construction)—one of the world's most expensive mass-transit projects: $3.5 billion for the projected twenty miles of track, from downtown through Hollywood and over Cahuenga Pass to the San Fernando Valley, that would constitute the system's "first phase" and "second phase." This route was one that, according to the project's opponents, could serve at maximum use only 1.5 percent of the work force; most of that 1.5 percent, however, either lived or worked in the heart of the Hollywood Redevelopment. "You go out to where the houses stop and buy land," Bob Hope is supposed to have said when he was asked how he made so much money. This is, in Los Angeles, one way to make money, and the second is to buy land on which the houses have already been built, and get the city to redevelop it.

Metrorail and the Hollywood Redevelopment were of course big projects, major ways of creating opportunity. The true Bradley style was perhaps most apparent when the opportunities were small, for example in the proposal during the spring of 1989 to sell a thirty-five-year-old public housing project, Jordan Downs, to a private developer. Jordan Downs was in Watts, south-central. The price asked for Jordan Downs was reported to be around $10 million. The deal was to include a pledge by the prospective buyer to spend an additional $14 million renovating the project.

Now. When we talk about Jordan Downs we are talking about seven hundred rental units in a virtual war zone, an area where the median family income was $11,427 and even children carried AK-47s. Presented with a developer who wants to spend $24 million to take on the very kind of property that owners all over the country are trying, if not to torch, at least to abandon, the average urban citizen looks for subtext. The subtext in this instance was not hard to find: Jordan Downs was a forty-acre piece of property, only 15 percent of which was developed. This largely undeveloped property bordered both the Century Freeway, which was soon to be completed, and the Watts Redevelopment. In other words the property would very soon, if all went as planned, vastly increase in value, and 85 percent of it would be in hand, available either for resale or for development.

Nor was the developed 15 percent of the property, Jordan Downs itself, the problem it might have seemed at first glance. The project, it turned out, would have to be maintained as low-income rental housing for an estimated period of at most fifteen years, during which time the developer stood in any case to receive, from the federal Department of Housing and Urban Development and the city housing authority, a guaranteed subsidy of $420,000 a month plus federal tax credits estimated at $1.6 million a year. This was the kind of small perfect deal—nobody is actually hurt by it, unless the nobody happens to be a tenant at Jordan Downs, and unable to pay the rent required to make the property break even—that has traditionally been the mother's milk of urban politics. But many people believed Los Angeles to be different, and in one significant aspect it was: the difference in Los Angeles was that very few of its citizens seemed to notice the small perfect deals, or, if they did notice, to much care.

* * *

It was believed for a while during 1988 in Los Angeles that Zev Yaroslavsky, who represented the largely west-side and affluent Fifth District in the Los Angeles City Council (the Fifth includes, in the basin, Beverly-Fairfax, Century City, Bel Air, Westwood, and part of West Los Angeles, and, in the San Fernando Valley, parts of Sherman Oaks, Van Nuys, and North Hollywood), could beat Bradley. It was, people said, "Zev's year." It was said to be "time for Zev." It was to be, Zev Yaroslavsky himself frequently said, "an election about who runs Los Angeles," meaning do a handful of developers run it or do the rest of the citizens run it. He had raised almost $2 million. He had gained the support of a number of local players who had previously backed Bradley, including Marc Nathanson, the chairman of Falcon Cable TV, and Barry Diller, the chairman of Twentieth Century-Fox. He had flat-out won what many saw as an exhibition game for the mayoralty race: a showdown, in November of 1988, between Armand Hammer's Occidental Petroleum Corporation, which had wanted since 1966 to begin drilling for oil on two acres it was holding across the Pacific Coast Highway from Will Rogers State Beach, and the many people who did not want—and had so far, through a series of legal maneuvers, managed to prevent—this drilling.

The showdown took the form of placing opposing propositions, one co-sponsored by Zev Yaroslavsky and the other by an Occidental front calling itself the Los Angeles Public and Coastal Protection Committee, before the voters on the November 8, 1988, ballot. The Los Angeles Public and Coastal Protection Committee had some notable talent prepared to labor on its behalf. It had the support of Mayor Bradley. It would have, by the eve of the election, the endorsement of the *Los Angeles Times*. It had not only Armand Hammer's own attorney, Arthur Groman, but also, and perhaps most importantly, Mickey Kantor, of Manatt, Phelps, Rothenberg, and Phillips, a law firm so deeply connected to Democratic power in California that most people believed Bradley to be backing the Occidental proposition not for Armand Hammer but for Manatt. It had Robert Shrum, of Doak & Shrum, who used to write speeches for Ted Kennedy but was now running campaigns in California. It had, above all, $7.3 million, $7.1 million of it provided directly by Occidental.

There was considerable opacity about this entire endeavor. In the first place, the wording of the Los Angeles Public and Coastal Protection Committee (or Occidental) proposition tended to equate a vote for drilling with a vote for more efficient crime fighting, for more intensive drug-busting, for better schools, and for the cleanup of toxic wastes, all of which were floated as part of Occidental's dedication to public and coastal protection. In the second place, the players themselves had kept changing sides. On the side of the antidrilling proposition there was of course its co-author, Zev Yaroslavsky, but Zev Yaroslavsky had backed Occidental when the drilling question came before the City Council in 1978. On the side of the Occidental proposition there was of course Tom Bradley, but Tom Bradley had first been elected mayor, in 1973, on an anti-Occidental platform, and in 1978 he had vetoed drilling on the Pacific Coast Highway site after the City Council approved it.

During the summer and fall of 1988, when the drilling and the antidrilling propositions were placed fairly insistently before the voters, there were seventeen operating oil fields around town, with tens of thousands of wells. There were more wells along the highways leading north and south. Oil was being pumped from the Beverly Hills High School campus. Oil was being pumped from the golf course at the Hillcrest Country Club. Oil was being pumped from the Twentieth Century-Fox lot. Off Carpinteria, south of Santa Barbara, oil was being pumped offshore, and even people who had expensive beach houses at Rincon del Mar had come to think of the rigs as not entirely unattractive features of the view—something a little mysterious out there in the mist, something a little Japanese on the horizon. In other words the drilling for and pumping of crude oil in Southern California had not historically carried much true political resonance, which made this battle of the propositions a largely symbolic, or "political," confrontation, not entirely about oil drilling. That Zev Yaroslavsky won it—and won it spending only $2.8 million, some $4 million less than Occidental spent—seemed to many to suggest a certain discontent with the way things were going, a certain desire for change: the very desire for change on which Zev Yaroslavsky was planning, in the course of his campaign for the mayor's office, to run.

* * *

There was, early on, considerable interest in this promised may-oralty race between Tom Bradley and Zev Yaroslavsky. Some saw the contest, and this was the way the Bradley people liked to present it, as a long-awaited confrontation between the rest of the city (Bradley) and the West Side (Yaroslavsky), which was well-off, heavily Jewish, and the only part of the city that visitors to Los Angeles normally saw. This scenario had in fact been laid out in the drilling battle, during which Occidental, by way of Mickey Kantor and Robert Shrum, introduced the notion that a vote for Occidental was a vote against "a few selfish people who don't want their beach view obstructed," against "elitists," against, in other words, the West Side. "The euphemism they kept using here was that it was another ploy by the 'rich Westsiders' against the poor minorities and the blacks," I was told by a deputy to Councilman Marvin Braude, who had co-authored the anti-drilling proposition with Zev Yaroslavsky and in whose district Occidental's Pacific Coast Highway property lay. "You always heard about 'rich West-siders' in connection with anything we were doing. It was the euphemism for the Jews."

Others saw the race, and this was increasingly the way the Yaroslavsky people liked to frame it, as a confrontation between the forces of unrestricted growth (developers, the oil business, Bradley) and the proponents of controlled, or "slow," growth (environmentalists, the No Oil lobby, the West Side, Yaroslavsky). Neither version was long on nuance, and both tended to over-look facts that did not support the favored angles (Bradley had for years been the West Side's own candidate, for example, and Yaroslavsky had himself broken bread with a developer or two), but the two scenarios, Yaroslavsky's *Greed* v. *Slow Growth* and Bradley's *The People* v. *the West Side*, continued to provide, for that handful of people in Los Angeles who actually followed city politics, a kind of narrative line. The election would fall, as these people saw it, to whoever told his story best, to whoever had the best tellers, the best fixers.

Only a few people in Los Angeles were believed to be able to fix things, whether the things to be fixed, or arranged, or managed, were labor problems or city permits or elections. There was the master of them all, Paul Ziffren, whose practice as a lawyer had often been indistinguishable from the practice of politics, but he was by the time of this race less active than he had once been. There was his son Kenneth Ziffren, who settled the Writers Guild of America strike in the summer of 1988. There was, operating in a slightly different arena, Sidney Korshak, who settled the Delano grape strike against Schenley in 1966. There was almost anybody at the Manatt office. There was Joseph Cerrell, a political consultant about whom it had been said, "You want to get elected to the judicial, you call him, a campaign can run you fifty thousand dollars." There was Robert Shrum, who worked Alan Cranston's last campaign for the Senate and Representative Richard Gephardt's campaign in the 1988 presidential primaries. There were Michael Berman and Carl D'Agostino, of BAD Campaigns, Inc., who were considered direct mail (most of it negative) geniuses and were central to what was locally called "the Waxman-Berman machine," the Democratic and quite specifically Jewish political organization built by Michael Berman; his brother, Representative Howard Berman; Representative Henry Waxman; and Representative Mel Levine, who was positioning himself to run for Alan Cranston's Senate seat in 1992. It was Michael Berman who figured out how to send Howard Berman and Henry Waxman and Mel Levine to Congress in the first place. It was Michael Berman and Carl D'Agostino who continued to figure out how to elect Waxman-Berman candidates on the state and local levels.

These figures were not without a certain local glamour, and a considerable amount of the interest in this mayoralty race derived from the fact that Doak & Shrum—which, remember, had been part of Mickey Kantor's team on the Occidental proposition—was working for Bradley, while Berman and D'Agostino, who had been hired by Yaroslavsky and Braude to run their antidrilling proposition, were backing Yaroslavsky. A mayoralty contest between Shrum and the Berman-D'Agostino firm, Bill Boyarsky wrote in the *Los Angeles Times*, could be "one of the great matchups of low-down campaigning"; in other words a chance, as I recall being told in June of 1988 by someone else, "for Berman and D'Agostino to knock off Doak & Shrum."

Then something happened, nobody was saying quite how. One Friday in August of 1988, a reporter at the *Los Angeles Times*, Kenneth Reich, got a phone call from a woman who refused to identify herself but said that she was sending him certain material prepared by BAD Campaigns, Inc. The material—delivered the following Monday with a typewritten and unsigned note reading, "You should be interested to see this. Government is bad enough without BAD"— consisted of three strategy memos addressed to Zev Yaroslavsky. One was dated March 29, 1988, another was dated May 4, 1988, and the third, headed "Things to Do," was undated.

Berman and D'Agostino acknowledged that the two dated documents were early drafts of memos prepared by their office, but denied having written the undated memo, which, accordingly, was never printed by the *Times*. The memos that were printed, which Yaroslavsky charged had been stolen from a three-ring binder belonging to one of his aides, had, however, an immediately electrifying effect, not because they said anything that most interested people in Los Angeles did not know or believe but because they violated the local social contract by saying it out loud, and in the vernacular. The memos printed in the *Times* read, in part:

> The reason why BAD thinks you [Yaroslavsky] can beat Bradley is: you've got fifty IQ-points on him (and that's no compliment).... Just because you are more slow-growth than Bradley does not mean you can take anti-growth voters for granted ... many are racially tolerant people who are strongly pulled to Bradley because of his height, skin color, and calm demeanor. They like voting for him— they feel less guilty about how little they used to pay their household help....
>
> Yaroslavsky's vision [should be that] there is no reason on this earth why some flitty restaurateur should be allowed to build a hotel at the corner of Beverly and La Cienega.... The Yaroslavsky vision says "there is no reason on earth why anyone should be building more places to shop in West L.A."... There is no reason for guilt-ridden liberals to vote out of office that fine, dignified "person of color" except that your Vision is total, unwavering and convincing. You want to hug every tree, stop every new building, end the traffic jams and clean up the Bay....

To beat Bradley, you must be intensely, thoroughly and totally committed to your vision of L.A.... It is the way you overcome the racial tug many Jews and non-Jewish liberals feel toward Bradley. It is also the way you overcome the possible Republican preference for the conservative black over the Jewish kid friendly with the Waxman-Berman machine....

Bradley can and will excite black voters to outvote the white electorate especially if there is a runoff where his mayoral office is seen as jeopardized by a perfidious Jew....

What we do know is that Jewish wealth in Los Angeles is endless. That almost every Jewish person who meets you will like you and that asking for $2,000 is not an unreasonable request to people who are both wealthy and like you....

The Yaroslavsky campaign becomes the United Jewish appeal....

This was not, on the face of it, remarkable stuff. The language in the memos was widely described as "cynical," but of course it was not: it was just the working shorthand of people who might even be said, on the evidence of what they wrote down, to have an idealized view of the system, people who noticed the small perfect deals and did not approve of them, or at any rate assumed that there was an electorate out there that did not approve of them. This may have been an erroneous assumption, a strategic miscalculation, but the idea that some of Yaroslavsky's people might have miscalculated the electorate was not, for some people who had supported him and were now beginning to back away, the problem.

"Make a complete list of mainstream Jewish charities," the March 29 memo had advised. "Find a person in each charity to slip us a list with name, address and phone numbers of $1,000-and-above contributors.... Zev begins dialing for dollars.... Make a list of 50 contributors to Zev who have not participated to their ability and who belong to every Jewish country club in the L.A. area.... Make a list of every studio, Hollywood PR firm and 100 top show business personalities in Jewish Los Angeles.... You cannot let Bradley become the chichi, in, campaign against the pushy Jew...."

It was this acknowledgment, even this insistence, that there were in Los Angeles not only Jewish voters but specifically Jewish interests, and Jewish money, that troubled many people, most particularly those very members of the West Side Jewish community on whose support the Yaroslavsky people were counting. What happened next was largely a matter of "perceptions," of a very few people talking among themselves, as they were used to talking whenever there was something to be decided, some candidate or cause to be backed or not backed. The word "divisive" started coming up again and again. It would be, people were saying, a "divisive" campaign, even a "disastrous" campaign, a campaign that would "pit the blacks against the Jews." There was, it was said, "already enough trouble," trouble that had been simmering, as these people saw it, since at least 1985, when Tom Bradley's Jewish supporters on the West Side had insisted that he denounce the Reverend Louis Farrakhan, and some black leaders had protested that Bradley should not be taking orders from the West Side. This issue of race, most people hastened to say, would never be raised by the candidates themselves. The problem would be, as Neil Sandberg of the American Jewish Committee put it to Bill Boyarsky of the *Los Angeles Times*, "undisciplined elements in both communities." The problem would be, in other words, the candidates' "people."

Discussions were held. Many telephone calls were made. In December of 1988, a letter was drafted and signed by some of the most politically active people on the West Side. This letter called on Zev Yaroslavsky to back off, not to run, not to proceed on a course that the signers construed as an invitation, if not to open ethnic conflict, at least to a breaking apart of the coalition between the black and Jewish communities that had given the West Side its recent power over the old-line Los Angeles establishment—the downtown and San Marino money base, which was what people in Los Angeles meant when they referred to the California Club. On the sixth of January, citing a private poll that showed Bradley to be running far ahead, Zev Yaroslavsky announced that he would not run. The BAD memos, he said, had "played absolutely no role" in his decision to withdraw. The "fear of a divisive campaign," he said, had "played no role on my part."

* * *

This "fear of a divisive campaign," and the attendant specter of the membership of the California Club invading City Hall, seemed on the face of it incorporeal, one of those received fears that sometimes overtake a community and redirect the course of its affairs. Still, the convergence of the BAD memos and the polarization implicit in the Occidental campaign had generated a considerable amount of what could only be described as class conflict. "Most of us have known for a long time that the environmentalists are ... white, middle-class groups who have not really shown a lot of concern about the black community or black issues," Maxine Waters, who represented part of south-central in the California State Assembly and was probably the most effective and visible black politician in Southern California, told Bill Boyarsky when he talked to her, after the publication of the BAD memos, about the drilling issue. "Yet we have continued to give support.... I want to tell you I may very well support the oil drilling. I feel such a need to assert independence from this kind of crap, and I feel such a need for the black community not to be led on by someone else's agenda and not even knowing what the agenda was."

One afternoon in February of 1989 when I happened to be in City Hall seeing Zev Yaroslavsky and Marvin Braude, I asked what they made of the "divisive campaign" question. The apprehension, Yaroslavsky said, had been confined to "a very small group of people," whose concern, as he saw it, had been "fueled by my neighbors here in the mayor's office, who were trying to say we could have another Chicago, another Ed Koch."

"Some of it started before your candidacy," Marvin Braude said to him. "With the Farrakhan incident. That set the tone of it."

"Let me tell you," Zev Yaroslavsky said. "If there's any reason why I would have run, it would have been to disprove that notion. Because nothing so offends me—politically and personally—as the notion that I, simply because I'm white or Jewish, don't have the right to run against a fourth-term incumbent just because he happens to be black."

Zev Yaroslavsky, at that point, was mounting a campaign to save his own council seat. He had put the mayoral campaign behind him. Still, it rankled. "Nothing I was talking about had remotely to do with race," he said. "It never would have been an issue, unless Bradley brought it up. But I must say they made every effort to put everything we did into a racial context. They tried to make the Oxy oil initiative racial. They tried to make Proposition U—which was our first slow-growth initiative—racial. They pitted rich against poor, white against black, West Side against South Side—"

"It wasn't only Bradley," Marvin Braude said, interrupting. "It was the people who were using this for their own selfish purposes. It was the developers. It was Occidental."

"I think if the election had gone on…" Zev Yaroslavsky paused. "It doesn't matter. At this point it's speculative. But I think the mayor and his people, especially his people, were running a very risky strategy of trying to make race an issue. For their candidate's benefit."

During the week in February 1989 when I saw Zev Yaroslavsky and Marvin Braude, the *Los Angeles Times* Poll did a telephone sampling to determine local attitudes toward the city and its mayor. About 60 percent of those polled, the *Times* reported a few days later, under the headline "People Turn Pessimistic About Life in Los Angeles," believed that the "quality of life" in Los Angeles had deteriorated during the last fifteen years. About 50 percent said that within the past year they had considered leaving Los Angeles, mainly for San Diego. Sixty-seven percent of those polled, however, believed that Tom Bradley, who had been mayor during this period when the quality of life had so deteriorated that many of them were thinking of moving to San Diego, had done a good job.

This was not actually news. On the whole, life in Los Angeles, perhaps because it is a city so largely populated by people who are ready to drop everything and move to San Diego (just as they or their parents or their grandparents had dropped everything and moved to Los Angeles), seems not to encourage a conventional interest in its elected officials. "Nobody but the press corps and a few elites care anything about the day-to-day workings in city government" is the way this was put in one of the "cynical" BAD memos.

In fact there were maybe a hundred people in Los Angeles, aside from the handful of reporters assigned to the city desk, who followed City Hall. A significant number of the hundred were lawyers at Manatt. All of the hundred were people who understand access. Some of these people said that of course Zev Yaroslavsky would run again, in 1993, when he would be only forty-four and Tom Bradley would be seventy-five and presumably ready to step aside. Nineteen ninety-three, in this revised view, would be "Zev's year." Nineteen ninety-three would be "time for Zev." Others said that 1993 would be too late, that the entire question of whether or not Zev Yaroslavsky could hold together Tom Bradley's famous black-Jewish coalition would be, in a Los Angeles increasingly populated by Hispanics and Asians, irrelevant, history, moot. Nineteen ninety-three, these people said, would be the year for other people altogether, for more recent figures on the local political landscape, for people like Gloria Molina or Richard Alatorre, people like Mike Woo, people whose names would tell a different story, although not necessarily to a different hundred people.

1989

AROUND DIVISION 47, Los Angeles Municipal Court, the downtown courtroom where, for eleven weeks during the spring and
summer of 1989, a preliminary hearing was held to determine if
the charges brought in the 1983 murder of a thirty-three-year-
old road-show promoter named Roy Alexander Radin should be
dismissed or if the defendants should be bound over to superior
court for arraignment and trial, it was said that there were, "in
the works," five movies, four books, and "countless" pieces about
the case. Sometimes it was said that there were four movies and
five books "in the works," or one movie and two books, or two
movies and six books. There were, in any event, "big balls" in the
air. "Everybody's working this one," a reporter covering the trial
said one morning as we waited to get patted down at the entrance
to the courtroom, a security measure prompted by a telephoned
bomb threat and encouraged by the general wish of everyone
involved to make this a noticeable case. "Major money."

    This was curious. Murder cases are generally of interest to
the extent that they suggest some anomaly or lesson in the
world revealed, but there seemed neither anomalies nor lessons
in the murder of Roy Radin, who was last seen alive getting
into a limousine to go to dinner at a Beverly Hills restaurant, La
Scala, and was next seen decomposed, in a canyon off Interstate
5. Among the defendants actually present for the preliminary
hearing was Karen Delayne ("Lanie") Jacobs Greenberger, a fairly
attractive hard case late of South Florida, where her husband was
said to have been the number-two man in the cocaine operation
run by Carlos Lehder, the only major Colombian drug figure
to have been tried and convicted in the United States. (Lanie
Greenberger herself was said to have done considerable business
in this line, and to have had nearly a million dollars in cocaine and
cash stolen from her Sherman Oaks house not long before Roy
Radin disappeared.) The other defendants present were William
Mentzer and Alex Marti, somewhat less attractive hard cases, late

of Larry Flynt's security staff. (Larry Flynt is the publisher of *Hustler*, and one of the collateral artifacts that turned up in the Radin case was a million-dollar check Flynt had written in 1983 to the late Mitchell Livingston WerBell III, a former arms dealer who operated a counterterrorism school outside Atlanta and described himself as a retired lieutenant general in the Royal Free Afghan Army. The Los Angeles County Sheriff's Department said that Flynt had written the check to WerBell as payment on a contract to kill Frank Sinatra, Hugh Hefner, Bob Guccione, and Walter Annenberg. Larry Flynt's lawyer said that there had been no contract, and described the check, on which payment was stopped, as a dinner-party joke.) There was also an absent defendant, a third Flynt security man, fighting extradition from Maryland.

In other words this was a genre case, and the genre, L.A. *noir*, was familiar. There is a *noir* case every year or two in Los Angeles. There was for example the Wonderland case, which involved the 1981 bludgeoning to death of four people. The Wonderland case, so called because the bludgeoning took place in a house on Wonderland Avenue in Laurel Canyon, turned, like the Radin case, on a million-dollar cocaine theft, but featured even more deeply *noir* players, including a nightclub entrepreneur and con-victed cocaine dealer named Adel Nasrallah, aka "Eddie Nash"; a pornographic-movie star, now dead of AIDS, named John C. Holmes, aka "Johnny Wadd"; and a young man named Scott Thorson, who was, at the time he first testified in the case, an inmate in the Los Angeles County Jail (Scott Thorson was, in the natural ecology of the criminal justice system, the star witness for the state in the Wonderland case), and who in 1982 sued Liberace on the grounds that he had been promised $100,000 a year for life in return for his services as Liberace's lover, driver, travel sec-retary, and animal trainer.

In this context there would have seemed nothing particularly novel about the Radin case. It was true that there were, floating around the edges of the story, several other unnatural deaths, for example that of Lanie Greenberger's husband, Larry Greenberger, aka "Vinnie De Angelo," who either shot himself or was shot in the head in September of 1988 on the front porch of his house in Okeechobee, Florida, but these deaths were essentially unsurprising. It was also true that the Radin case offered not bad sidebar details. I was interested for example in how much security Larry Flynt apparently had patrolling Doheny Estates, where his house was, and Century City, where the *Hustler* offices were. I was interested in Dean Kahn, who ran the limousine service that provided the stretch Cadillac with smoked windows in which Roy Radin took, in the language of this particular revealed world, his last ride. I was interested in how Roy Radin, before he came to Los Angeles and decided to go to dinner at La Scala, had endeavored to make his way in the world by touring high school auditoriums with Tiny Tim, Frank Fontaine, and a corps of tap-dancing dwarfs.

Still, promoters of tap-dancing dwarfs who get done in by hard cases have not been, historically, the stuff of which five movies, four books, and countless pieces are made. The almost febrile interest in this case derived not from the principals but from what was essentially a cameo role, played by Robert Evans. Robert Evans had been head of production at Paramount during the golden period of *The Godfather* and *Love Story* and *Rosemary's Baby*, had moved on to produce independently such successful motion pictures as *Chinatown* and *Marathon Man*, and was, during what was generally agreed to be a dry spell in his career (he had recently made a forty-five-minute videotape on the life of John Paul II, and had announced that he was writing an autobiography, to be called *The Kid Stays in the Picture*), a district attorney's dream: a quite possibly desperate, quite famously risk-oriented, high-visibility figure with low-life connections.

It was the contention of the Los Angeles County District Attorney's office that Lanie Greenberger had hired her co-defendants to kill Roy Radin after he refused to cut her in on his share of the profits from Robert Evans's 1984 picture *The Cotton Club*. It was claimed that Lanie Greenberger had introduced Roy Radin, who wanted to get into the movie business, to Robert Evans. It was claimed that Roy Radin had offered to find, in return for 45 percent of the profits from either one Evans picture (*The Cotton Club*) or three Evans pictures (*The Cotton Club*, *The Sicilian*, and *The Two Jakes*), "Puerto Rican investors" willing to put up either thirty-five or fifty million dollars.

Certain objections leap to the nonprosecutorial mind here (the "Puerto Rican investors" turned out to be one Puerto Rican banker with "connections," the money never actually materialized,

Roy Radin therefore had no share of the profits, there were no profits in any case), but seem not to have figured in the state's case. The District Attorney's office was also hinting, if not quite contending, that Robert Evans himself had been in on the pay-off of Radin's killers, and the DA's office had a protected witness (still another Flynt security man, this one receiving $3,000 a month from the Los Angeles County Sheriff's Department) who had agreed to say in court that one of the defendants, William Mentzer, told him that Lanie Greenberger and Robert Evans had, in the witness's words, "paid for the contract." Given the state's own logic, it was hard to know what Robert Evans might have thought to gain by putting out a contract on the goose with the $50 million egg, but the deputy district attorney on the case seemed unwilling to let go of this possibility, and had in fact told reporters that Robert Evans was "one of the people who we have not eliminated as a suspect."

Neither, on the other hand, was Robert Evans one of the people they had arrested, a circumstance suggesting certain lacunae in the case from the major-money point of view, and also from the district attorney's. Among people outside the criminal justice system, it was widely if vaguely assumed that Robert Evans was somehow "on trial" during the summer of 1989. "Evans Linked for First Time in Court to Radin's Murder," the headlines were telling them, and, in the past-tense obituary mode, "Evans' Success Came Early: Career Epitomized Hollywood Dream."

"Bob always had a premonition that his career would peak before he was fifty and fade downhill," Peter Bart, who had worked under Evans at Paramount, told the Los Angeles Times, again in the obituary mode. "He lived by it. He was haunted by it…. To those of us who knew him and knew what a good-spirited person he was, it's a terrible sadness." Here was a case described by the Times as "focused on the dark side of Hollywood deal making," a case offering "an unsparing look at the film capital's unsavory side," a case everyone was calling just Cotton Club, or even just Cotton, as in "'Cotton': Big Movie Deal's Sequel Is Murder."

Inside the system, the fact that no charge had been brought against the single person on the horizon who had a demonstrable connection with The Cotton Club was rendering Cotton Club, qua Cotton Club, increasingly problematic. Not only was Robert Evans not "on trial" in Division 47, but what was going on there was not even a "trial," only a preliminary hearing, intended to determine whether the state had sufficient evidence and cause to prosecute those charged, none of whom was Evans. Since 1978, when a California Supreme Court ruling provided criminal defendants the right to a preliminary hearing even after indictment by a grand jury, preliminary hearings have virtually replaced grand juries as a way of indicting felony suspects in California, and are one of the reasons that criminal cases in Los Angeles now tend to go on for years. The preliminary hearing alone in the McMartin child-abuse case lasted eighteen months.

On the days I dropped by Division 47, the judge, a young black woman with a shock of gray in her hair, seemed fretful, inattentive. The lawyers seemed weary. The bailiffs discussed their domestic arrangements on the telephone. When Lanie Greenberger entered the courtroom, not exactly walking but undulating forward on the balls of her feet, in a little half-time prance, no one bothered to look up. The courtroom had been full on the day Robert Evans appeared as the first witness for the prosecution and took the Fifth, but in the absence of Evans there were only a few reporters and the usual two or three retirees in the courtroom, perhaps a dozen people in all, reduced to interviewing each other and discussing alternative names for the Night Stalker case, which involved a man named Richard Ramirez who had been accused of thirteen murders and thirty other felonies committed in Los Angeles County during 1984 and 1985. One reporter was calling the Ramirez case, which was then in its sixth month of trial after nine weeks of preliminary hearings and six months of jury selection, Valley Intruder. Another had settled on Serial Killer. "I still slug it Night Stalker," a third said, and she turned to me. "Let me ask you," she said. "This is how hard up I am. Is there a story in your being here?"

The preliminary hearing in the Radin case had originally been scheduled for three weeks, and lasted eleven. On July 12, 1989, in Division 47, Judge Patti Jo McKay ruled not only that there was sufficient evidence to bind over Lanie Greenberger, Alex Marti, and William Mentzer for trial but also that the Radin murder may have been committed for financial gain, which meant that the defendants could receive, if convicted, penalties of death. "Mr. Radin was an obstacle to further negotiation involving *The Cotton Club*," the prosecuting attorney had argued in closing. "The deal could not go through until specific issues such as percentages were worked out. It was at that time that Mrs. Greenberger had the motive to murder Mr. Radin."

I was struck by this as a final argument, because it seemed to suggest an entire case based on the notion that an interest in an entirely hypothetical share of the entirely hypothetical profits from an entirely hypothetical motion picture (at the time Roy Radin was killed, *The Cotton Club* had an advertising poster but no shooting script and no money and no cast and no start date) was money in the bank. All that had stood between Lanie Greenberger and Fat City, as the prosecutor saw it, was boiler-plate, a matter of seeing that "percentages were worked out."

The prosecution's certainty on this point puzzled me, and I asked an acquaintance in the picture business if he thought there had ever been money to be made from *The Cotton Club*. He seemed not to believe what I was asking. There had been "gross positions," he reminded me, participants with a piece of the gross rather than the net. There had been previous investors. There had been commitments already made on *The Cotton Club*, paper out all over town. There had been, above all, a $26 million budget going in (it eventually cost $47 million), and a production team not noted for thrift. "It had to make a hundred to a hundred forty million, depending on how much got stolen, before anybody saw gross," he said. "Net on this baby was dreamland. Which could have been figured out, with no loss of life, by a junior agent just out of the William Morris mailroom."

There was always in the Cotton Club case a certain dream-land aspect, a looniness that derived in part from the ardent if misplaced faith of everyone involved, from the belief in windfalls, in sudden changes of fortune (five movies and four books would change someone's fortune, a piece of *The Cotton Club* someone else's, a high-visibility case the district attorney's); in killings, both literal and figurative. In fact this kind of faith is not unusual in Los Angeles. In a city not only largely conceived as a series of real estate promotions but largely supported by a series of confidence games, a city even then afloat on motion pictures and junk bonds and the B-2 Stealth bomber, the conviction that something can be made of nothing may be one of the few narratives in which every-one participates. A belief in extreme possibilities colors daily life. Anyone might have woken up one morning and been discovered at Schwab's, or killed at Bob's Big Boy. "Luck is all around you," a silky voice says on the California State Lottery's Lotto commercials, against a background track of "Dream a Little Dream of Me." "Imagine winning millions ... what would you do?"

During the summer of 1989 this shimmer of the possible still lay on Cotton Club, although there seemed, among those dreamers to whom I spoke in both the picture business and the criminal justice business, a certain impatience with the way the case was actually playing out. There was nobody in either business, including the detectives on the case, who could hear the words "Cotton Club" and not see a possible score, but the material was resistant. It still lacked a bankable element. There was a definite wish to move on, as they say in the picture business, to screenplay. The detectives were keeping in touch with motion picture producers, car phone to car phone, sketching in connecting lines not apparent in the courtroom. "This friend of mine in the sheriff's office laid it out for me three years ago," one producer told me. "The deal was, 'This is all about drugs, Bob Evans is involved, we're going to get him.' And so forth. He wanted me to have the story when and if the movie was done. He called me a week ago, from his car, wanted to know if I was going to move on it."

I heard a number of alternative scenarios. "The story is in this one cop who wouldn't let it go," I was told by a producer. "The story is in the peripheral characters," I was told by a detective I had reached by dialing his car phone. Another producer reported having run into Robert Evans's lawyer, Robert Shapiro, the evening before at Hillcrest Country Club, where the Thomas Hearns–Sugar Ray Leonard fight was being shown closed circuit from Caesars Palace in Las Vegas. "I asked how our boy was doing," he said, meaning Evans. "Shapiro says he's doing fine. Scot-free, he says. Here's the story. A soft guy from our world, just sitting up there in his sixteen-room house, keeps getting visits from these detectives. Big guys. Real hard guys. Apes. Waiting for him to crack."

Here we had the rough line for several quite different stories, but it would have been hard not to notice that each of them depended for its dramatic thrust on the presence of Robert Evans. I mentioned this one day to Marcia Morrissey, who—as co-counsel with the Miami trial lawyer Edward Shohat, who had defended Carlos Lehder—was representing Lanie Greenberger. "Naturally they all *want* him in," Marcia Morrissey said.

I asked if she thought the District Attorney's Office would manage to get him in.

Marcia Morrissey rolled her eyes. "That's what it's called, isn't it? I mean face it. It's called Cotton Club."

1989

FIRE SEASON

"I'VE SEEN FIRE and I've seen rain," I recall James Taylor singing over and over on the news radio station between updates on
the 1978 Mandeville and Kanan fires, both of which started on
October 23 of that year and could be seen burning toward each
other, systematically wiping out large parts of Malibu and Pacific
Palisades, from an upstairs window of my house in Brentwood. It
was said that the Kanan fire was burning on a twenty-mile front
and had already jumped the Pacific Coast Highway at Trancas
Canyon. The stand in the Mandeville fire, it was said, would be
made at Sunset Boulevard. I stood at the window and watched a
house on a hill above Sunset implode, its oxygen sucked out by
the force of the fire.

Some thirty-four thousand acres of Los Angeles County
burned that week in 1978. More than eighty thousand acres
had burned in 1968. Close to a hundred and thirty thousand
acres had burned in 1970. Seventy-four-some thousand had
burned in 1975, sixty-some thousand would burn in 1979. Forty-
six thousand would burn in 1980, forty-five thousand in 1982. In
the hills behind Malibu, where the moist air off the Pacific makes
the brush grow fast, it takes about twelve years before a burn is
ready to burn again. Inland, where the manzanita and sumac and
chamise that make up the native brush in Southern California
grow more slowly (the wild mustard that turns the hills a translucent yellow after rain is not native but exotic, introduced in the
1920s in an effort to reseed burns), regrowth takes from fifteen to
twenty years. Since 1919, when the county began keeping records
of its fires, some areas have burned eight times.

In other words there is nothing unusual about fires in Los
Angeles, which is after all a desert city with only two distinct
seasons, one beginning in January and lasting three or four
months during which storms come in from the northern Pacific
and it rains (often an inch every two or three hours, sometimes
and in some places an inch a minute) and one lasting eight or

nine months during which it burns, or gets ready to burn. Most years it is September or October before the Santa Ana winds start blowing down through the passes and the relative humidity drops to figures like 7 or 6 or 3 percent and the bougainvillea starts rattling in the driveway and people start watching the horizon for smoke and tuning in to another of those extreme local possibilities, in this case that of imminent devastation. What was unusual in 1989, after two years of drought and a third year of less than average rainfall, was that it was ready to burn while the June fogs still lay on the coastline. On the first of May that year, months earlier than ever before, the California Department of Forestry had declared the start of fire season and begun hiring extras crews. By the last week in June there had already been more than two thousand brush and forest fires in California. Three hundred and twenty of them were burning that week alone.

One morning early that summer I drove out the San Bernardino Freeway to the headquarters of the Los Angeles County Fire Department, which was responsible not only for coordinating fire fighting and reseeding operations throughout the county but for sending, under the California Master Mutual Aid agreement, both equipment and strike teams to fires around the state. Los Angeles County sent strike teams to fight the 116,000-acre Wheeler fire in Ventura County in 1985. (The logistics of these big fires are essentially military. Within twelve hours of the first reports on the Wheeler fire, which eventually burned for two weeks and involved three thousand fire fighters flown in from around the country, a camp had materialized, equipped with kitchen, sanitation, transportation and medical facilities, a communications network, a "situation trailer," a "what if" trailer for long-range contingency planning, and a "pool coordinator," to get off-duty crews to and from the houses of residents who had offered the use of their swimming pools. "We simply superimposed a city on top of the incident," a camp spokesman said at the time.) Los Angeles County sent strike teams to fight the 100,000-acre Las Pilitas fire in San Luis Obispo County the same year. It sent specially trained people to act as "overhead" on, or to run, the crews of military personnel brought in from all over the United States to fight the Yellowstone fires in 1988.

On the June morning in 1989 when I visited the headquarters building in East Los Angeles, it was already generally agreed that, as one of the men to whom I spoke put it, "we pretty much know we're going to see some fires this year," with no probable break until January or February. (There is usually some November rain in Los Angeles, often enough to allow crews to gain control of a fire already burning, but only rarely does November rain put enough moisture into the brush to offset the Santa Ana winds that blow until the end of December.) There had been unusually early Santa Ana conditions, a week of temperatures over one hundred. The measurable moisture in the brush, a measurement the Fire Department calls the "fuel stick," was in some areas already down to single digits. The daily "burn index," which rates the probability of fire on a scale running from 0 to 200, was that morning showing figures of 45 for the Los Angeles basin, 41 for what is called the "high country," 125 for the Antelope Valley, and, for the Santa Clarita Valley, 192.

Anyone who has spent fire season in Los Angeles knows some of its special language—knows, for example, the difference between a fire that has been "controlled" and a fire that has so far been merely "contained" (a "contained" fire has been surrounded, usually by a trench half as wide as the brush is high, but is still burning out of control within this line and may well jump it), knows the difference between "full" and "partial" control ("partial" control means, if the wind changes, no control at all), knows about "backfiring" and about "making the stand" and about the difference between a Red Flag Alert (there will probably be a fire today) and a Red Flag Warning (there will probably be a Red Flag Alert within three days).

Still, "burn index" was new to me, and one of the headquarters foresters, Paul Rippens, tried that morning to explain it. "Let's take the Antelope Valley, up around Palmdale, Lancaster," he said. "For today, temperature's going to be ninety-six, humidity's going to be seventeen percent, wind speed's going to be fifteen miles per hour, and the fuel stick is six, which is getting pretty low."

"Six burns very well," another forester, John Haggenmiller, said. "If the fuel stick's up around twelve, it's pretty hard to get it to burn. That's the range that you have. Anything under six and it's ready to burn very well."

"So you correlate all that, you get an Antelope Valley burn index today of one twenty-five, the adjective for which is 'high,'" Paul Rippens continued. "The adjectives we use are 'low,' 'moderate,' 'high,' 'very high,' and 'extreme.' One twenty-five is 'high'. High probability of fire. We had a hundred-plus-acre fire out there yesterday, about a four-hour fire. Divide the burn index by ten and you get the average flame length. So a burn index of one twenty-five is going to give you a twelve-and-a-half-foot flame length out there. If you've got a good fire burning, flame length has a lot to do with it."

"There's a possibility of a grass fire going through and not doing much damage at all," John Haggenmiller said. "Other cases, where the fuel has been allowed to build up—say you had a bug kill or a die-back, a lot of decadent fuel—you're going to get a flame length of thirty, forty feet. And it gets up into the crown of a tree and the whole thing goes down. That does a lot of damage."

Among the men to whom I spoke that morning there was a certain grudging admiration for what they called "the big hitters," the major fires, the ones people remember. "I'd say about ninety-five percent of our fires, we're able to hold down to under five acres," I was told by Captain Garry Oversby, who did community relations and education for the Fire Department. "It's the ones when we have extreme Santa Ana conditions, extreme weather—they get started, all we can do is try to hold the thing in check until the weather lays down a little bit for us. Times like that, we revert to what we call a defensive attack. Just basically go right along the edges of that fire until we can get a break. Reach a natural barrier. Or sometimes we make a stand several miles in advance of the fire—construct a line there, and then maybe set a backfire. Which will burn back toward the main fire and take out the vegetation, rob the main fire of its fuel."

They spoke of the way a true big hitter "moved," of the way it "pushed," of the way it could "spot," or throw embers and firebrands, a mile ahead of itself, rendering any kind of conventional firebreak useless; of the way a big hitter, once it got moving, would "outrun anybody." "You get the right weather conditions in Malibu, it's almost impossible to stop it," Paul Rippens said. He was talking about the fires that typically start somewhere in the brush off the Ventura Freeway and then burn twenty miles to the sea, the fires that roar over a ridge in a matter of seconds and make national news because they tend to take out, just before they hit the beach along Malibu, houses that belong to well-known people. Taking out houses is what the men at head-quarters mean when they talk about "the urban interface."

"We can dump all our resources out there," Paul Rippens said, and he shrugged.

"You can pick up the flanks and channel it," John Haggenmiller said, "but until the wind stops or you run out of fuel, you can't do much else."

"You get into Malibu," Paul Rippens said, "you're looking at what we call two-story brush."

"You know the wind," John Haggenmiller said. "You're not going to change that phenomenon."

"You can dump everything you've got on that fire," Paul Rippens said. "It's still going to go to what we call the big blue break."

It occurred to me then that it had been eleven years since the October night in 1978 when I listened to James Taylor sing-ing "Fire and Rain" between reports on how the Kanan fire had jumped the Pacific Coast Highway to go to the big blue break. On the twelve-year-average fire cycle that regulates life in Malibu, the Kanan burn, which happened to include a beach on which my husband and daughter and I had lived from 1971 until June of 1978, was coming due again. "Beautiful country burn again," I wrote in my notebook, a line from a Robinson Jeffers poem I remember at some point during every fire season, and I got up to leave.

A week or so later 3,700 acres burned in the hills west of the Antelope Valley. The flames reached sixty feet. The wind was gusting at forty miles an hour. There were 250 fire fighters on the ground, and they evacuated 1,500 residents, one of whom returned to find her house gone but managed to recover, according to the *Los Angeles Times*, "an undamaged American flag and a porcelain Nativity set handmade by her mother." A week after this Antelope Valley fire, 1,500 acres burned in the Puente Hills, above Whittier. The temperatures that day were in the high nineties, and the flames were as high as fifty feet. There were more than 970 fire fighters on the line. Two hundred and fifty families were evacuated. They took with them what people always take out of fires, mainly snapshots, mementos small enough to put in the car. "We won't have a stitch of clothing, but at least we'll have these," a woman about to leave the Puente Hills told the *Times* as she packed the snapshots into the trunk of her car.

People who live with fires think a great deal about what will happen "when," as the phrase goes in the instruction leaflets, "the fire comes." These leaflets, which are stuck up on refrigerator doors all over Los Angeles County, never say "if." When the fire comes there will be no water pressure. The roof one watered all the night before will go dry in seconds. Plastic trash cans must be filled with water and wet gunny-sacks kept at hand, for smothering the sparks that blow ahead of the fire. The garden hoses must be connected and left where they can be seen. The cars must be placed in the garage, headed out. Whatever one wants most to save must be placed in the cars. The lights must be left on, so that the house can be seen in the smoke. I remember my daughter's Malibu kindergarten sending home on the first day of the fall semester a detailed contingency plan, with alternative sites where, depending on the direction of the wind when the fire came, the children would be taken to wait for their parents. The last-ditch site was the naval air station at Point Mugu, twenty miles up the coast.

"Dry winds and dust, hair full of knots," our Malibu child wrote when asked, in the fourth grade, for an "autumn" poem. "Gardens are dead, animals not fed.... People mumble as leaves crumble, fire ashes tumble." The rhythm here is not one that many people outside Los Angeles seem to hear. In the *New York Times* this morning I read a piece in which the way people in Los Angeles "persist" in living with fire was described as "denial." "Denial" is a word from a different lyric altogether. This will have been only the second fire season over twenty-five years during which I did not have a house somewhere in Los Angeles County, and the second during which I did not keep the snapshots in a box near the door, ready to go when the fire comes.

1989

TIMES MIRROR SQUARE

HARRISON GRAY OTIS, the first successful editor and publisher of the *Los Angeles Times* and in many ways the prototypical Los Angeles citizen, would seem to have been one of those entrepreneurial drifters at once set loose and energized by the Civil War and the westward expansion. He was born in a log house in Ohio in 1837. He went to work as an apprentice printer at fourteen. He was a delegate at twenty-three to the Republican National Convention at which Abraham Lincoln was nominated for the presidency. He spent forty-nine months in the Ohio Infantry, was wounded at Antietam in 1862 and again in Virginia in 1864, and then parlayed his Army connections into government jobs, first as a journeyman printer at the Government Printing Office in Washington and then at the Patent Office. He made his first foray to Southern California in 1874, to investigate a goat-raising scheme that never materialized, and pronounced the place "the fattest land I was ever in." He drifted first to Santa Barbara, where he published a small daily without notable success (he and his wife and three children, he noted later, were reduced to living in the fattest land on "not enough to keep a rabbit alive"), and struck out then for Alaska, where he had lucked into a $10-a-day government sinecure as the special agent in charge of poaching and liquor control in the Seal Islands.

In 1882, already a forty-five-year-old man with a rather accidental past and unremarkable prospects, Harrison Gray Otis managed finally to seize the moment: he quit the government job, returned to Southern California, and put down $6,000, $5,000 of it borrowed, for a quarter interest in the four-page *Los Angeles Daily Times*, a failed paper started a few months before by a former editor of the *Sacramento Union* (the *Union*, for which Mark Twain was a correspondent, is the oldest California daily still publishing) and abandoned almost immediately to its creditors. "Small beginnings, but great oaks, etc.," Harrison Gray Otis later noted of his purchase. He seems to have known immediately what kind of Los Angeles he wanted, and what role a newspaper could play in getting it: "Los Angeles wants no dudes, loafers and paupers; people who have no means and trust to luck," the new citizen announced in an early editorial, already shedding his previous skin, his middle-aged skin, the skin of a person who had recently had no means and trusted to luck. Los Angeles, as he saw it, was all capital formation, no service. It needed, he said, no "cheap politicians, failures, bummers, scrubs, impecunious clerks, bookkeepers, lawyers, doctors. The market is overstaffed already. We need workers! Hustlers! Men of brains, brawn and guts! Men who have a little capital and a good deal of energy—first-class men!"

The extent to which Los Angeles was literally invented by the *Los Angeles Times* and by its owners, Harrison Gray Otis and his descendants in the Chandler family, remains hard for people in less recent parts of the country to fully apprehend. At the time Harrison Gray Otis bought his paper there were only some five thousand people living in Los Angeles. There was no navigable river. The Los Angeles River was capable of providing ditch water for a population of two or three hundred thousand, but there was little other ground water to speak of. Los Angeles has water today because Harrison Gray Otis and his son-in-law Harry Chandler wanted it, and fought a series of outright water wars to get it. "With this water problem out of the way, the growth of Los Angeles will leap forward as never before," the *Times* advised its readers in 1905, a few weeks before the initial vote to fund the aqueduct meant to bring water from the Owens River, 233 miles to the north. "Adjacent towns will soon be knocking on our doors for admission to secure the benefits to be derived from our never-failing supply of life-giving water, and Greater Los Angeles will become a magnificent reality." Any citizen voting against the aqueduct bonds, the *Times* warned on the day before the election, would be "placing himself in the attitude of an *enemy of the city*."

To oppose the Chandlers, in other words, was to oppose the perfection of Los Angeles, the expansion that was the city's imperial destiny. The false droughts and artful title transactions that brought Northern California water south are familiar stories in Los Angeles, and were made so in other parts of the country by the motion picture *Chinatown*. Without Owens River water the San Fernando Valley could not have been developed. The San Fernando Valley was where Harrison Gray Otis and Harry Chandler, through two interlocking syndicates, the San Fernando Mission Land Company and the Los Angeles Suburban Homes Company, happened to have bought or optioned, before the completion of the aqueduct and in some cases before the aqueduct vote, almost sixty-five thousand acres, virtually the entire valley from what is now Burbank to what is now Tarzana, at strictly dry-land prices, between $31 and $53 an acre. "Have A Contract for A Lot in Your Pocket When the Big Bonds are Voted," the advertisements read in the *Times* during the days before the initial vote on the aqueduct bonds. "Pacoima Will Feel the First Benefits of the Owens River Water and Every Purchaser Investing Now Will Reap the Fruits of his Wisdom in Gratifying Profits."

A great deal of Los Angeles as it appears today derived from this impulse to improve Chandler property. The Los Angeles Civic Center and Union Station and the curiosity known as Olvera Street (Olvera Street is part of El Pueblo de Los Angeles State Historic Park, but it was actually conceived in 1926 as the first local theme mall, the theme being "Mexican marketplace") are where they are because Harry Chandler wanted to develop the north end of downtown, where the *Times* building and many of his other downtown holdings lay. California has an aerospace industry today because Harry Chandler believed that the development of Los Angeles required that new industry be encouraged, and, in 1920, called on his friends to lend Donald Douglas $15,000 to build an experimental torpedo plane.

The same year, Harry Chandler called on his friends to build Caltech, and the year after that to build a facility (the Coliseum, near the University of Southern California) large enough to attract the 1932 Olympics. The Hollywood Bowl exists because Harry Chandler wanted it. The Los Angeles highway system exists because Harry Chandler knew that people would not buy land in his outlying subdivisions unless they could drive to them, and also because Harry Chandler sat on the board of Goodyear Tire & Rubber, which by then had Los Angeles plants. Goodyear Tire & Rubber had Los Angeles plants in the first place because Harry Chandler and his friends made an investment of $7.5 million to build them.

It was this total identification of the Chandler family's destiny with that of Los Angeles that made the *Times* so peculiar an institution, and also such a rich one. Under their corporate umbrella, the Times Mirror Company, the Chandlers now own, for all practical purposes, not only the *Times*, which for a number of years carried more full-run advertising linage than any other newspaper in the United States, but *Newsday, New York Newsday*, the *Baltimore Sun*, the *Hartford Courant*, the *National Journal*, nine specialized book- and educational-publishing houses, seventeen specialized magazines, the CBS affiliates in Dallas and Austin, the ABC affiliate in St. Louis, the NBC affiliate in Birmingham, a cable-television business, and a company that exists exclusively to dispose of what had been Times Mirror's timber and ranchland (this company, since it is meant to self-destruct, is described by Times Mirror as "entropic"): an empire with operating revenues for 1989 of $3,517,493,000.

The climate in which the *Times* prospered was a special one. Los Angeles had been, through its entire brief history, a boom town. People who lived there had tended to believe, and were encouraged to do so by the increasingly fat newspaper dropped at their doors every morning, that the trend would be unfailingly up. It seemed logical that the people who made business work in California should begin to desert San Francisco, which had been since the gold rush the financial center of the West, and look instead to Los Angeles, where the money increasingly was. It seemed logical that shipping should decline in San Francisco, one of the world's great natural ports, even as it flourished in Los Angeles, where a port had to be dredged, and was, at the insistence of the *Times* and Harry Chandler. It seemed logical that the wish to dredge this port should involve, since Los Angeles was originally landlocked, the annexation first of a twenty-mile corridor to the sea and then the "consolidation" with Los Angeles ("annexation" of one incorporated city by another was prohibited by state law) of two entire other cities, San Pedro and Wilmington, both of which lay on the Pacific.

The logic here was based on the declared imperative of unlimited opportunity, which in turn dictated unlimited growth. What was construed by people in the rest of the country as accidental—the sprawl of the city, the apparent absence of a cohesive center—was in fact purposeful, the scheme itself: this would be a new kind of city, one that would seem to have no finite limits, a literal cloud on the land that would eventually touch the Tehachapi range to the north and the Mexican border to the south, the San Bernardino Mountains to the east and the Pacific to the west; not just a city finally but its own nation, The Southland. That the Chandlers had been sufficiently prescient to buy up hundreds of thousands of acres on the far reaches of the expanding cloud—300,000 acres spanning the Tehachapi, 860,000 acres in Baja California, which Harrison Gray Otis and Harry Chandler were at one point trying to get the Taft administration to annex from Mexico, thereby redefining even what might have seemed Southern California's one fixed border (the Pacific was seen locally as not a border but an opportunity, a bridge to Hawaii and on to Asia)—was only what might be expected of any provident citizen: "The best interests of Los Angeles are paramount to the *Times*," Harry Chandler wrote in 1934, and it had been, historically, the *Times* that defined what those best interests were.

The *Times* under Harrison Gray Otis was a paper in which the owners' opponents were routinely described as "thieves," "scoundrels," "blackmailers," "venal," "cowardly," "mean," "un-American," "assassinlike," "petty," "despotic," and "anarchic scum." It was said of General Otis (he had been commissioned a brigadier general when he led an expeditionary force to the Philippines during the Spanish-American War, and he was General Otis forever after, just as his houses were The Bivouac and The Outpost, the *Times* building was The Fortress, and the *Times* staff The Phalanx) that he had a remarkably even temper, that of a hungry tiger. A libel suit or judgment against the paper was seen as neither a problem nor an embarrassment but a journalistic windfall, an opportunity to reprint the offending story, intact and often. In November of 1884, after the election of Grover Cleveland to the presidency, the *Times* continued to maintain for eleven days that the president-elect was James G. Blaine, Harrison Gray Otis's candidate.

Even under Harry Chandler's son Norman, who was publisher from 1944 until 1960, the *Times* continued to exhibit a fitful will-fulness. The Los Angeles for which the *Times* was at that time published was still remote from the sources of national and international power, isolated not only geographically but developmentally, a deliberately adolescent city, intent on its own growth and not much interested in the world outside. In 1960, when Norman Chandler's son Otis was named publisher of the *Times*, the paper had only one foreign correspondent, based in Paris. The city itself was run by a handful of men who worked for the banks and the old-line law firms downtown and drove home at five o'clock to Hancock Park or Pasadena or San Marino. They had lunch at the California Club or the Los Angeles Athletic Club. They held their weddings and funerals in Protestant or Catholic churches and did not, on the whole, know people who lived on the West Side, in Beverly Hills and Bel Air and Brentwood and Pacific Palisades, many of the most prominent of whom were in the entertainment business and were Jewish. As William Severns, the original general manager of the Los Angeles Music Center's operating company, put it in a recent interview with Patt Morrison of the *Times*, there was at that time a "big schism in society" between these downtown people and what he called "the movie group." The movie group, he said, "didn't even know where downtown was, except when they came downtown for a divorce." (This was in itself a cultural crossed connection, since people on the West Side generally got divorced not downtown but in Santa Monica.)

It was Norman Chandler's wife, Dorothy Buffum Chandler, called Buff, who perceived that it was in the interests of the city, and therefore of the *Times*, to draw the West Side into the power structure, and she saw the Music Center, for which she was then raising money, as a natural way to initiate this process. I once watched Mrs. Chandler, at a dinner sometime in 1964, try to talk the late Jules Stein, the founder and at that time the chairman of MCA, into contributing $25,000 toward the construction of the Music Center. Jules Stein said that he would be glad to donate any amount to Mrs. Chandler's Music Center, and would then expect Mrs. Chandler to make a matching contribution, for this was the way things got done on the West Side, to the eye clinic he was then building at the UCLA Medical Center. "I can't do that," Mrs. Chandler said, and then she leaned across the table, and demonstrated what the Chandlers had always seen as the true usefulness of owning a newspaper: "But I can give you twenty-five thousand dollars' worth of free publicity in the paper."

By the time Mrs. Chandler was through, the Music Center and one of its support groups, The Amazing Blue Ribbon, had become the common ground on which the West Side met downtown. This was not to say that all the top editors and managers at the *Times* were entirely comfortable on the West Side; many of them tended still to regard it as alien, a place where people exchanged too many social kisses and held novel, if not dangerous, ideas. "I always enjoy visiting the West Side," I recall being told by Tom Johnson, who had in 1980 become the publisher of the *Times*, when we happened to be seated next to each other at a party in Brentwood. He then took a notepad and a pen from his pocket. "I like to hear what people out here think." Nor was it to say that an occasional citizen of a more self-absorbed Los Angeles did not still surface, and even write querulous letters to the *Times*:

> Regarding "The Party Pace Picks Up During September" (by Jeannine Stein, Aug. 31): the social season in Los Angeles starts the first Friday in October when the Autumn Cotillion is held. This event, started over fifty years ago, brings together the socially prominent folks of Los Angeles who wouldn't be seen in Michael's and haven't yet decided if the opera is here to stay. By the time Cotillion comes around families are back from vacation, dove hunting season is just over and deer hunting season hasn't begun so the gentlemen of the city find no excuse not to attend. Following that comes the annual Assembly Ball and the Chevaliers du Tastevin dinner followed by the Las Madrinas Debutante Ball. If you are invited to these events you are in socially. No *nouveau riche* or publicity seekers nor social climbers need apply.

The *Times* in which this letter appeared, on September 10, 1989, was one that maintained six bureaus in Europe, five in Latin America, five in Asia, three in the Middle East, and two in Africa. It was reaching an area inhabited by between 13 and 14 million people, more than half of whom, a recent Rand Corporation study suggests, had arrived in Los Angeles as adults, eighteen years old or over, citizens whose memories did not include the Las Madrinas Debutante Ball. In fact there is in Los Angeles no memory everyone shares, no monument everyone knows, no historical reference as meaningful as the long sweep of the ramps where the San Diego and Santa Monica freeways intersect, as the way the hard Santa Ana light strikes the palm trees against the white western wall of the Carnation Milk building on Wilshire Boulevard. Mention of "historic" sites tends usually to signal a hustle under way, for example transforming a commercial development into historic Olvera Street, or wrapping a twenty-story office tower and a four-hundred-room hotel around the historic Mann's Chinese Theater (the historic Mann's Chinese Theater was originally Grauman's Chinese, but a significant percentage of the population has no reason to remember this), a featured part of the Hollywood Redevelopment.

Californians until recently spoke of the United States beyond Colorado as "back east." If they went to New York, they went "back" to New York, a way of speaking that carried with it the suggestion of living on a distant frontier. Californians of my daughter's generation speak of going "out" to New York, a meaningful shift in the perception of one's place in the world. The Los Angeles that Norman and Buff Chandler's son Otis inherited in 1960—and, with his mother, proceeded over the next twenty years to reinvent—was, in other words, a new proposition, potentially one of the world's great cities but still unformed, outgrowing its old controlling idea, its tropistic confidence in growth, and not yet seized by a new one. It was Otis Chandler who decided that what Los Angeles needed if it was to be a world-class city was a world-class newspaper, and he set out to get one.

Partly in response to the question of what a daily newspaper could do that television could not do better, and partly in response to geography—papers on the West Coast have a three-hour advantage going to press, and a three-hour disadvantage when they come off the press—Otis Chandler, then thirty-two, decided that the *Times* should be what was sometimes called a daily magazine, a newspaper that would cover breaking news competitively, but remain willing to commit enormous resources to providing a kind of analysis and background no one else was providing. He made it clear at the outset that the paper was no longer his father's but his, antagonizing members of his own family in 1961 by running a five-part report on the John Birch Society, of which his aunt and uncle Alberta and Philip Chandler were influential members. Otis Chandler followed up the John Birch series, in case anyone had missed the point, by signing the Chandler name to a front-page editorial opposing Birch activities. "His legs bestrid the ocean, his reared arm crested the world," as the brass letters read (for no clear reason, since it is what Cleopatra says about Antony as the asps are about to arrive in the fifth act of *Antony and Cleopatra*) at the base of the turning globe in the lobby of the *Times* building. "His voice was propertied to all the tuned spheres." One reason Otis Chandler could property the voice of the *Times* to all the tuned spheres was that his *Times* continued to make more money than his father's. "The paper was published every day and they could see it," he later said about his family. "They disagreed endlessly with my editorial policies. But they never disagreed with the financial results."

In fact an unusual kind of reporting developed at the *Times*, the editorial philosophy of which was frequently said to be "run it long and run it once." The *Times* became a paper on which reporters were allowed, even encouraged, to give the reader the kind of detail that was known to everyone on the scene but rarely got filed. On the night Son of Sam was arrested in New York, according to Charles T. Powers, then in the *Times'* New York bureau, Roone Arledge was walking around Police Headquarters, "dressed as if for a touch football game, a glass of scotch in one hand, a portable two-way radio in the other, directing his network's feed to the Coast," details that told the reader pretty much all there was to know about celebrity police work. In San Salvador in the early spring of 1982, when representatives from the centrist Christian Democrats, the militarist National Conciliation Party, and the rightist ARENA were all meeting under a pito tree on Francisco ("Chachi") Guerrero's patio, Laurie Becklund of the *Times* asked Guerrero, who has since been assassinated, how people so opposed to one another could possibly work together. "We all know each other—we've known each other for years," he said. "You underestimate our *política tropical*." A few days later, when Laurie Becklund asked an ARENA leader why ARENA, then trying to close out the Christian Democrats, did not fear losing American aid, the answer she got, and filed, summed up the entire relationship between the United States and the Salvadoran right: "We believe in gringos."

This kind of detail was sometimes dismissed by reporters at other papers as "L.A. color," but really it was something different: the details gave the tone of the situation, the subtext without which the text could not be understood, and sharing this subtext with the reader was the natural tendency of reporters who, because of the nature of both the paper on which they worked and the city in which it was published, tended not to think of themselves as insiders. "Jesse don't wanna run nothing but his mouth," Mayor Marion Barry of Washington, D.C., was quoted as having said, about Jesse Jackson, early in 1990 in a piece by Bella Stumbo in the *Los Angeles Times*; there was in this piece, I was told in New York, after both the *New York Times* and the *Washington Post* had been forced to report the ensuing controversy, nothing that many *Post* and *New York Times* reporters in Washington did not already know. This was presumably true, but only the *Los Angeles Times* had printed it.

Unconventional choices were made at the *Times*. Otis Chandler had insisted that the best people in the country be courted and hired, regardless of their politics. The political cartoonist Paul Conrad was lured from the *Denver Post*, brought out for an interview, and met at the airport, per his demand, by the editor of the paper. Robert Scheer, who had a considerable reputation as a political journalist at *Ramparts* and *New Times* but no newspaper experience, was not only hired but given whatever he wanted, including the use of the executive dining room, the Picasso Room. "For the money we're paying Scheer, I should hope he'd be abrasive," William Thomas, the editor of the *Times* from 1971 until 1989, said to a network executive who called to complain that Scheer had been abrasive in an interview. The *Times* had by then abandoned traditional ideas of what newspaper reporters and editors should be paid, and was in some cases paying double the going rate. "I don't think newspapers should take a back seat to magazines, TV, or public relations," Otis Chandler had said early on. He had bought the *Times* a high-visibility Washington bureau. He had bought the *Times* a foreign staff.

By 1980, when Otis Chandler named Tom Johnson the publisher of the *Times* and created for himself the new title of editor in chief, the *Times* was carrying, in the average week, more columns

of news than either the *New York Times* or the *Washington Post*. It
was running long analytical background pieces from parts of the
country and of the world that other papers left to the wires. Its
Washington bureau, even Bob Woodward of the *Washington Post*
conceded recently, was frequently beating the *Post*. Its foreign
coverage, particularly from Central America and the Middle East,
was, day for day, stronger than that of the national competition.
"Otis was a little more specific than just indicating he wanted
the *Times* to be among the top U.S. newspapers," Nick Williams,
the editor of the *Times* from 1958 until 1971, said later of Otis
Chandler's ascension to publisher of the *Times*. "He said, 'I want
it to be the number one newspaper in the country.'" What began
worrying people in Los Angeles during the fall of 1989, starting
on the morning in October when the *Times* unveiled the first
edition of what it referred to on billboards and television advertisements and radio spots and bus shelters and bus tails and rack
cards and in-paper advertisements and even in its own house
newsletter as "the new, faster-format *Los Angeles Times*," was
whether having the number one newspaper in the country was a
luxury the Chandlers, and the city, could still afford.

It was hard, that fall at the *Times*, to sort out exactly what was
going on. A series of shoes had already been dropped. There
had been in January 1989 the installation of a new editor,
someone from outside, someone whose particular depths and
shallows many people had trouble sounding, someone from
the East (actually he was from Tennessee, but his basic training
had been under Benjamin Bradlee at the *Washington Post*, and
around the *Times* he continued to be referred to, tellingly, as an
Easterner), Shelby Coffey III. There had been some months later
the announcement of a new approach to what had become the
Times' Orange County problem, the problem being that a few
miles to the south, in Orange County, the *Times'* zoned edition
had so far been unable to unseat the *Orange County Register*, the
leading paper in a market so rich that the *Register* had a few years
earlier become the one paper in the United States with more
full-run advertising linage than the *Times*.

The new approach to this Orange County problem seemed
straightforward enough (the editor of the Orange County edition,

at that time Narda Zacchino, would get twenty-nine additional reporters, an expanded plant, virtual autonomy over what appeared in the *Times* in Orange County, and would report only to Shelby Coffey), although it did involve a new "president," or business person, for Orange County, Lawrence M. Higby, whose particular skills—he was a marketing expert out of Taco Bell, Pepsi, and H. R. Haldeman's office in the Nixon White House, where he had been known as Haldeman's Haldeman—made some people uneasy. Narda Zacchino was liked and respected around the *Times* (she had more or less grown up on the paper, and was married to Robert Scheer), but Higby was an unknown quantity, and there were intimations that not everyone was entirely comfortable with these heightened stakes in Orange County. According to the *Wall Street Journal*, Tom Johnson, the publisher, said in an August 1989 talk to the Washington bureau that the decision to give Narda Zacchino and Lawrence Higby autonomy in Orange County had led to "blood all over the floor" in Los Angeles. He described the situation in Orange County as "a failure of mine," an area in which "I should have done more sooner."

Still, it was September 1989 before people outside the *Times* started noticing the blood, or even the dropped shoes, already on the floor. September was when it was announced, quite unexpectedly, that Tom Johnson, who had been Otis Chandler's own choice as publisher and had in turn picked Shelby Coffey as editor, was moving upstairs to what were described as "broader responsibilities," for example newsprint supply. The publisher's office, it was explained, would now be occupied by David Laventhol, who had spent time at the *New York Herald Tribune* and the *Washington Post*, had moved next to *Newsday* (he was editor, then publisher), had been since 1987 the president of the parent Times Mirror Company, and had achieved, mainly because he was seen to have beat the *New York Times* in Queens with *New York Newsday*, a certain reputation for knowing how to run the kind of regional war the *Los Angeles Times* wanted to run in Orange County. David Laventhol, like Shelby Coffey, was referred to around the office as an Easterner.

Then, on October 11, 1989, there was the format change, to which many of the paper's most vocal readers, a significant number of whom had been comparing the paper favorably every morning with the national edition of the *New York Times*, reacted negatively. It appeared that some readers of the *Los Angeles Times* did not want color photographs on its front page. Nor, it appeared, did these readers want News Highlights or news briefs or boxes summarizing the background of a story in three or four sentences without dependent clauses. A Laguna Niguel subscriber described himself in a letter to the editor as "heartsick." A Temple City reader characterized the changes as "beyond my belief." By the first of December even the student newspaper at Caltech, the *California Tech*, was having a little fun at the *Times'* expense, calling itself the *New, Faster Format Tech* and declaring itself dedicated to "increasing the amount of information on the front page by replacing all stories with pictures." In the lost-and-found classified section of the *Times* itself there appeared, sandwiched among pleas for lost Akitas ("Has Tattoo") and lost Saudi Arabian Airlines ID cards and lost four-carat emerald-cut diamond rings set in platinum ("sentimental value"), this notice, apparently placed by a group of the *Times'* own reporters: "*LA TIMES*: Last seen in a confused state disguised as *USA Today*. If found, please return to Times Mirror Square."

The words "*USA Today*" were heard quite a bit during the first few months of the new, faster format, as were "New Coke" and "Michael Dukakis." It was said that Shelby Coffey and David Laventhol had turned the paper over to its marketing people. It was said that the marketing people were bent on reducing the paper to its zoned editions, especially to its Orange County edition, and reducing the zoned editions to a collection of suburban shoppers. It was said that the paper was conducting a deliberate dumb-down, turning itself over to the interests and whims (less to read, more local service announcements) of the several thousand people who had taken part in the videotaped focus groups the marketing people and key editors had been running down in Orange County. A new format for a newspaper or magazine tends inevitably to suggest a perceived problem with the product, and the insistence with which this particular new format was promoted—the advertising stressed the superior disposability of the new *Times*, how easy it was, how cut down, how little time the reader need spend with it—convinced many people that the paper was determined to be less than it had been. "READ THIS," *Times* rack cards now demanded. "QUICK."

The architects of the new, faster format became, predictably, defensive, even impatient. People with doubts were increasingly seen as balky, resistant to all change, sulky dogs in the manger of progress. "Just look at this," Narda Zacchino, who as editor of the Orange County edition had been one of the central figures in the redesign, ordered me, brandishing first a copy of that morning's *USA Today* and then one of that morning's *Times*. "Do they look alike? No. They look nothing alike. I know there's been a negative response from within the paper. 'This is *USA Today*,' you hear. Well, look at it. It's not *USA Today*. But we're a newspaper. We want people to read the newspaper. I've been struggling down there for seven years, trying to get people to read the paper. And, despite the in-house criticism, we're not getting criticism from outside. Our response has been very, very good."

Shelby Coffey mentioned the redesign that Walter Bernard had done in 1977 for Henry Anatole Grunwald at *Time*. "They got scorched," he said. "They had thousands of letters, cancellations by the hundreds. I remember seeing it the first time and being jarred. In fact I thought they had lost their senses. They had gone to color. They had done the departments and the type in quite a different way. But it stood up over the years as one of the most successful, maybe *the* most successful, of the redesigns. I think you have to accept as a given that it's going to take six months or a year before people get used to this."

Around the paper, where it was understood that the format change had originally been developed in response to the needs of the Orange County edition, a certain paranoia had taken hold. People were exchanging rumors by computer mail. People were debating whether the Orange County edition should be encouraged to run announcements of local events in column one of page one ("Tonight: Tito Puente brings his Latin Jazz All-Stars to San Juan Capistrano.... Puente, a giant among salsa musicians, is a particular favorite at New York's celebrated Blue Note nightclub. Time: 8 P.M. at the Coach House, 33157 Camino Capistrano. Tickets: $19.50. Information: (714) 496–8930") and still call itself the *Los Angeles Times*. People were noticing that the Orange County edition was, as far as that went, not always calling itself the *Los Angeles Times*—that some of its subscription callers were urging telephone contacts to subscribe to "the Orange County *Times*." People were tormenting one another with various forms of the verb "to drive," as in "market-driven" and "customer-driven" and "a lot of people are calling this paper market-driven but it's not, what drives this paper is editorial" and "this paper has different forces driving it than something like *The Nation*." (The necessity for distinguishing the *Los Angeles Times* from *The Nation* was perhaps the most arresting but far from the only straw point made to me in the course of a few days at the *Times*.)

The mood was rendered no less febrile by what began to seem an unusual number of personnel changes. During the first few days of November 1989, the *Los Angeles Herald Examiner* folded, and a visible number of its columnists and its sports and arts and entertainment writers began appearing immediately in the *Times*. A week or so later, Dennis Britton, who had been, with Shelby Coffey and two other editors, a final contender for the editorship of the *Times* (the four candidates had been asked by Tom Johnson to submit written analyses of the content of the *Times* and of the areas in which it needed strengthening), bailed out as one of the *Times'* deputy managing editors, accepting the editorship of the *Chicago Sun-Times*.

A week after that, it was announced that Anthony Day, the editor of the *Times* editorial pages since 1971, would be replaced by Thomas Plate, who had directed the partially autonomous editorial and op-ed pages for *New York Newsday* and was expected to play a role in doing something similar for Orange County. In the fever of the moment it was easy for some people to believe that the changes were all of a piece, that, for example, Anthony Day's leaving the editorial page had something to do with the new fast read, or with the fact that some people on the Times Mirror board had occasionally expressed dissatisfaction with the paper's editorial direction on certain issues, particularly its strong anti-Administration stand on Central American policy. Anthony Day was told only, he reported, that it was "time for a change," that he would be made a reporter and assigned a beat ("ideas and ideology in the modern world"), and that he would report directly to Shelby Coffey. "There was this strange, and strangely moving, party for Tony last Saturday at which Tom Johnson spoke," a friend at the *Times* wrote me not long after Day was fired. "And they sang songs to Tony—among them a version of 'Yesterday' in which the words were changed to 'Tony-day'. ('Why he had to go, we don't know, they wouldn't say')."

Part of the problem, as some people at the *Times* saw it, was that neither Shelby Coffey nor David Laventhol shared much history with anybody at the *Times*. Shelby Coffey was viewed by many people at the *Times* as virtually unfathomable. He seemed to place mysterious demands upon himself. His manner, which was essentially border Southern, was unfamiliar in Los Angeles. His wife, Mary Lee, was for many people at the *Times* equally hard to place, a delicate Southerner who looked like a lifetime Maid of Cotton but was in fact a doctor, not even a gynecologist or a pediatrician but a trauma specialist, working the emergency room at Huntington Hospital in Pasadena. "You know the golden rule of the emergency room," Mary Lee Coffey drawled the first time I met her, not long after her arrival in Los Angeles. She was wearing a white angora sweater. "Keep 'em alive till eight-oh-five."

Together, Shelby Coffey and David Laventhol, a demonstrated corporate player, suggested a new mood at the *Times,* a little leaner and maybe a little meaner, a little more market-oriented. "Since 1881, the *Los Angeles Times* has led the way with award-winning journalism," a *Times* help-wanted advertisement read around that time. "As we progress into our second century, we're positioned as one of America's largest newspapers. To help us maintain our leadership position, we're currently seeking a Promotion Writer." Some people in the newsroom began referring to the two as the First Street Gangster Crips (the Gangster Crips were a prominent Los Angeles gang, and the *Times* building was on First Street), and to their changes as drive-bys. They were repeatedly referred to as "guys whose ties are all in Washington or New York," as "people with Eastern ideas of what Los Angeles wants or deserves." Shelby Coffey's new editors were called "the Stepford Wives," and Shelby Coffey himself was called, to his face, "the Dan Quayle of journalism." (That this was said by a reporter who continued to be employed by the *Times* suggested not only the essentially tolerant nature of the paper but the extent to which Coffey appeared dedicated to the accommodation of dissent.) During the 1989 Christmas season, a blowup of his photograph, with a red hat pinned above it, appeared in one of the departments at the *Times*. "He Knows When You Are Sleeping," the legend read. "And With Whom."

This question of Coffey and Laventhol being "Easterners" was never far below the surface. "Easterner," as the word is

JOAN DIDION

used in Los Angeles, remains somewhat harder to translate than
First Street Gangster Crip. It carries both an arrogance and a
defensiveness, and has to do not exactly with geography (people
who themselves came from the East will quite often dismiss
other people as "Easterners") but with a virtually uncrackable
complex of attitudes. An Easterner, in the local view, believes that
Los Angeles begins and ends on the West Side and is about the
movie business. Easterners, moreover, do not understand even the
movie business: they come out in January and get taken to dinner
at Spago and complain that the view is obscured by billboards,
by advertisements for motion pictures, missing the point that
advertisements for motion pictures are the most comforting
possible view for those people who regularly get window tables
at Spago. Easterners refer to Los Angeles as El Lay, as La La Land,
as the Left Coast. "I suppose you're glad to be here," Easterners
say to Californians when they run into them in New York. "I
suppose you can always read the *Times* here," Easterners say on
their January visits to Los Angeles, meaning the *New York Times*.

Easterners see the *Los Angeles Times* only rarely, and complain,
when they do see it, about the length of its pieces. "They can
only improve it," an editor of the *New York Times* said to me when
I mentioned that the *Los Angeles Times* had undertaken some
changes. He said that the paper had been in the past "unreadable."
It was, he said, "all gray." I asked what he meant. "It's these stories
that cover whole pages," he said. "And then the story breaks to
the next page and keeps going." This was said on a day when, of
eight stories on the front page of the *New York Times*, seven broke
to other sections. "Who back east cares?" I was asked by someone
at the *Los Angeles Times* when I said that I was writing about the
changes at the paper. "If this were happening to the *New York
Times*, you'd have the *Washington Post* all over it."

When people in Los Angeles talked about what was happening
at the *Times*, they were talking about something harder to define,
in the end, than any real or perceived or feared changes in the
paper itself, which in fact was looking good. Day for day, not
much about the *Times* had actually changed. There sometimes
seemed fewer of the analytic national pieces that used to appear
in column one. There seemed to be some increase in syndicated

soft features, picked up with the columnists and arts reviewers when the *Herald Examiner* folded. But the "new, faster-format *Los Angeles Times*" (or, as early advertisements called it, the "new, fast-read *Los Angeles Times*") still carried more words every day than appear in the New Testament. It still carried in the average week more columns of news than the *New York Times* or the *Washington Post*. It still ran pieces at a length few other papers would countenance—David Shaw's January 1990 series on the coverage of the McMartin child-abuse case, for example, ran 17,000 words. The paper's editorials were just as strong under Thomas Plate as they had been under Anthony Day. Its reporters were still filing stories full of details that did not appear in other papers, for example the fact (this was from Kenneth Freed in Panama, January 1, 1990) that nearly 125 journalists, after spending less than twelve hours in Panama without leaving Howard Air Force Base, where they were advised that there was shooting on the streets of Panama City ("It is war out there," the briefing officer told them), had accepted the Southern Command's offer of a charter flight back to Miami.

The *Times* had begun, moreover, to do aggressive local coverage, not historically the paper's strong point, and also to do frequent "special reports," eight-to-fourteen-page sections, with no advertising, offering wrap-up newsmagazine coverage of, say, China, or Eastern Europe, or the October 1989 Northern California earthquake, or the state of the environment in Southern California. A week or so before Christmas 1989, Shelby Coffey initiated a daily "Moscow Edition," a six-to-eight-page selection of stories from that day's *Los Angeles Times*. This Moscow Edition, which was prepared in Los Angeles, faxed to the *Times* bureau in Moscow, and delivered by hand to some 125 Soviet officials, turned out to be sufficiently popular that the Moscow bureau received a call from the Soviet Foreign Ministry requesting that the *Times* extend its publication to weekends and even to Christmas Day.

"Shelby may be fighting more of a fight against the dumbing-down of the newspaper than we know or he can say," one *Times* editor, who had himself been wary of the changes under way but had come to believe that there had been among some members of the staff an unjustified rush to judgment, said to me. "That the *Times* is still essentially the same paper seems to me so plainly the case as to refute the word 'new' in 'the new, faster-format *Los Angeles Times.*' What small novelty there is would have received very little promotion had it begun as a routine editorial modification. But it didn't originate in editorial discussion. It originated in market research, which was why it got promoted so heavily. The *Times* needed a way to declare Orange County a new ball game, and this was it. But you can't change the paper anywhere without changing it everywhere. And once the *Times* throws the switch, a colossal amount of current seems to flow through the whole system."

In a way the uneasiness had to do with the entire difficult question of "Easterners." It was not that Shelby Coffey was an Easterner or that David Laventhol was an Easterner but that Easterners had been brought in, that there was no Chandler in the publisher's office, no one to whom the *Los Angeles Times* was intrinsically more important than, say, *Newsday*, no one who could reliably be expected to have a visceral appreciation not just of how far the *Times* had come but of how far Los Angeles itself had come, of how fragile the idea of the place was and how easily it could be lost. Los Angeles had been the most idealized of American cities, and the least accidental. Its development had proceeded not from the circumstances of geography but from sheer will, from an idea. It had been General Otis and Harry Chandler who conceived the future of Los Angeles as one of ever-expanding possibility, and had instructed the readers of the *Times* in what was needed to achieve that future. It had been Otis Chandler who articulated this vision by defining the *Times*' sphere of influence as regional, from Santa Barbara to the border and from the mountains to the sea, and who told the readers of the *Times* that this was what they wanted.

What the *Times* seemed to be telling its readers now was significantly different, and was based not on the logic of infinite opportunity proceeding from infinite growth but on the logic of minimizing risk, on corporate logic, and it was not impossible to follow that logic to a point at which what might be best for the *Times* and what might be best for Los Angeles would no longer necessarily coincide. "You talk to people in Orange County, they don't want news of Los Angeles," David Laventhol said one afternoon in late November of 1989. "We did a survey. Ask them what news they want, news from Los Angeles rates very, very low."

We were talking about his sense that Southern California was fragmenting more than it was coalescing, about what one *Times* editor had called "the aggressive disidentification with Los Angeles" of the more recent and more uniformly affluent communities in Ventura and San Diego and Orange counties. This aggressive disidentification with Los Angeles was the reason the Orange County Edition had been made autonomous.

"I spent many years in the New York market, and in many ways this is a more complex market," David Laventhol said. "The *New York Times* and some other papers were traditionally able to connect the entire New York community. It's much tougher here. If anything could bind this whole place together—anything that's important, anything beyond baseball teams—it would probably be the *Times*. But people are looking inward right now. They aren't thinking in terms of the whole region. It's partly a function of transportation, jobs, the difficulty of commuting or whatever, but it's also a function of lifestyle. People in Orange County don't like the West Side of Los Angeles. They don't like the South Side of Los Angeles. They don't like whatever. They're lined up at the county line with their backs to Los Angeles."

Some years ago, Otis Chandler was asked how many readers would actually miss the *Times* were it to stop publishing tomorrow. "Probably less than half," Otis Chandler had said, and been so quoted in his own paper. For reasons that might not have been clear to his market-research people, he had nonetheless continued trying to make that paper the best in the country. During the 1989 Christmas season there was at the *Times*, as there had traditionally been, a party, and a Christmas toast was given, as it had traditionally been, by the publisher. In the past the publishers of the *Times* had stressed the growth of the enterprise, both achieved and anticipated. It had been a good year, David Laventhol said at the 1989 Christmas party, and he was glad it was over.

1990

IV
NEW YORK

SENTIMENTAL JOURNEYS

I

WE KNOW HER story, and some of us, although not all of us, which was to become one of the story's several equivocal aspects, know her name. She was a twenty-nine-year-old unmarried white woman who worked as an investment banker in the corporate finance department at Salomon Brothers in downtown Manhattan, the energy and natural resources group. She was said by one of the principals in a Texas oil-stock offering on which she had collaborated as a member of the Salomon team to have done "topnotch" work. She lived alone in an apartment on East 83rd Street, between York and East End, a sublet cooperative she was thinking about buying. She often worked late and when she got home she would change into jogging clothes and at eight-thirty or nine-thirty in the evening would go running, six or seven miles through Central Park, north on the East Drive, west on the less traveled road connecting the East and West Drives at approximately 102nd Street, and south on the West Drive. The wisdom of this was later questioned by some, by those who were accustomed to thinking of the Park as a place to avoid after dark, and defended by others, the more adroit of whom spoke of the citizen's absolute right to public access ("That park belongs to us and this time nobody is going to take it from us," Ronnie Eldridge, at the time a Democratic candidate for the City Council of New York, declared on the op-ed page of the *New York Times*), others of whom spoke of "running" as a preemptive right. "Runners have Type A controlled personalities and they don't like their schedules interrupted," one runner, a securities trader, told the *Times* to this point. "When people run is a function of their lifestyle," another runner said. "I am personally very angry," a third said. "Because women should have the right to run anytime."

For this woman in this instance these notional rights did not prevail. She was found, with her clothes torn off, not far from the 102nd Street connecting road at one-thirty on the morning of April 20, 1989. She was taken near death to Metropolitan Hospital on East 97th Street. She had lost 75 percent of her blood. Her skull had been crushed, her left eyeball pushed back through its socket, the characteristic surface wrinkles of her brain flattened. Dirt and twigs were found in her vagina, suggesting rape. By May 2, when she first woke from coma, six black and Hispanic teenagers, four of whom had made videotaped statements concerning their roles in the attack and another of whom had described his role in an unsigned verbal statement, had been charged with her assault and rape and she had become, unwilling and unwitting, a sacrificial player in the sentimental narrative that is New York public life.

Nightmare in Central Park, the headlines and display type read. *Teen Wolfpack Beats and Rapes Wall Street Exec on Jogging Path. Central Park Horror. Wolf Pack's Prey. Female Jogger Near Death After Savage Attack by Roving Gang. Rape Rampage. Park Marauders Call It "Wilding," Street Slang for Going Berserk. Rape Suspect: "It Was Fun." Rape Suspect's Jailhouse Boast: "She Wasn't Nothing." The teenagers were back in the holding cell, the confessions gory and complete. One shouted "hit the beat" and they all started rapping to "Wild Thing." The Jogger and the Wolf Pack. An Outrage and a Prayer.* And, on the Monday morning after the attack, on the front page of the *New York Post*, with a photograph of Governor Mario Cuomo and the headline "*None of Us Is Safe*," this italic text: "A visibly shaken Governor Cuomo spoke out yesterday on the vicious Central Park rape: 'The people are angry and frightened—my mother is, my family is. To me, as a person who's lived in this city all of his life, this is the ultimate shriek of alarm.'"

Later it would be recalled that 3,254 other rapes were reported that year, including one the following week involving the near decapitation of a black woman in Fort Tryon Park and one two weeks later involving a black woman in Brooklyn who was robbed, raped, sodomized, and thrown down an air shaft of a four-story building, but the point was rhetorical, since crimes are universally understood to be news to the extent that they offer, however erroneously, a story, a lesson, a high concept. In the 1986 Central Park death of Jennifer Levin, then eighteen, at the hands of Robert Chambers, then nineteen, the "story," extrapolated more or less from thin air but left largely uncorrected, had to do not with people living wretchedly and marginally on the underside of where they wanted to be, not with the Dreiserian pursuit of "respectability" that marked the revealed details (Robert Chambers's mother was a private-duty nurse who worked twelve-hour night shifts to enroll her son in private schools and the Knickerbocker Greys), but with "preppies," and the familiar "too much too soon."

Susan Brownmiller, during a year spent monitoring newspaper coverage of rape as part of her research for *Against Our Will: Men, Women and Rape*, found, not surprisingly, that "although New York City police statistics showed that black women were more frequent victims of rape than white women, the favored victim in the tabloid headline ... was young, white, middle class and 'attractive.'" In its quite extensive coverage of rape-murders during the year 1971, according to Ms. Brownmiller, the *Daily News* published in its four-star final edition only two stories in which the victim was not described in the lead paragraph as "attractive": one of these stories involved an eight-year-old child, the other was a second-day follow-up on a first-day story that had in fact described the victim as "attractive." The *Times*, she found, covered rapes only infrequently that year, but what coverage they did "concerned victims who had some kind of middle-class status, such as 'nurse,' 'dancer' or 'teacher,' and with a favored setting of Central Park."

As a news story, "Jogger" was understood to turn on the demonstrable "difference" between the victim and her accused assailants, four of whom lived in Schomburg Plaza, a federally subsidized apartment complex at the northeast corner of Fifth Avenue and 110th Street in East Harlem, and the rest of whom lived in the projects and rehabilitated tenements just to the north and west of Schomburg Plaza. Some twenty-five teenagers were brought in for questioning; eight were held. The six who were finally indicted ranged in age from fourteen to sixteen. That none of the six had previous police records passed, in this context, for achievement; beyond that, one was recalled by his classmates to have taken pride in his expensive basketball shoes, another to have been "a follower." *I'm a smooth type of fellow, cool, calm, and mellow,* one of the six, Yusef Salaam, would say in the rap he presented as part of his statement before sentencing.

> *I'm kind of laid back, but now I'm speaking so that you know /*
> *I got used and abused and even was put on the news....*
>   *I'm not dissing them all, but the some that I called.*
>   *They tried to dis me like I was an inch small, like a midget,*
> *a mouse, something less than a man.*

The victim, by contrast, was a leader, part of what the *Times* would describe as "the wave of young professionals who took over New York in the 1980's," one of those who were "handsome and pretty and educated and white," who, according to the *Times*, not only "believed they owned the world" but "had reason to." She was from a Pittsburgh suburb, Upper St. Clair, the daughter of a retired Westinghouse senior manager. She had been Phi Beta Kappa at Wellesley, a graduate of the Yale School of Management, a congressional intern, nominated for a Rhodes Scholarship, remembered by the chairman of her department at Wellesley as "probably one of the top four or five students of the decade." She was reported to be a vegetarian, and "fun-loving," although only "when time permitted," and also to have had (these were the *Times'* details) "concerns about the ethics of the American business world."

In other words she was wrenched, even as she hung between death and life and later between insentience and sentience, into New York's ideal sister, daughter, Bacharach bride: a young woman of conventional middle-class privilege and promise whose situation was such that many people tended to overlook the fact that the state's case against the accused was not invulnerable. The state could implicate most of the defendants in the assault and rape in their own videotaped words, but had none of the incontrovertible forensic evidence—no matching semen, no matching fingernail scrapings, no matching blood—commonly produced in this kind of case. Despite the fact that jurors in the second trial would eventually mention physical evidence as having been crucial in their bringing guilty verdicts against one defendant, Kevin Richardson, there was not actually much physical evidence at hand. Fragments of hair "similar [to] and consistent" with that of the victim were found on Kevin Richardson's clothing and underwear, but the state's own criminologist had testified that hair samples were necessarily inconclusive since, unlike fingerprints, they could not be traced to a single person. Dirt samples found on the defendants' clothing were, again, similar to dirt found in that part of the park where the attack took place, but the state's criminologist allowed that the samples were also similar to dirt found in other uncultivated areas of the park. To suggest, however, that this minimal physical evidence could open the case to an aggressive defense—to, say, the kind of defense that such celebrated New York criminal lawyers as Jack Litman and Barry Slotnick typically present—would come to be construed, during the weeks and months to come, as a further attack on the victim.

She would be Lady Courage to the *New York Post,* she would be A Profile in Courage to the *Daily News* and *New York Newsday*. She would become for Anna Quindlen in the *New York Times* the figure of "New York rising above the dirt, the New Yorker who has known the best, and the worst, and has stayed on, living somewhere in the middle." She would become for David Dinkins, the first black mayor of New York, the emblem of his apparently fragile hopes for the city itself: "I hope the city will be able to learn a lesson from this event and be inspired by the young woman who was assaulted in the case," he said. "Despite tremendous odds, she is rebuilding her life. What a human life can do, a human society can do as well." She was even then for John Gutfreund, at that time the chairman and chief executive officer of Salomon Brothers, the personification of "what makes this city so vibrant and so great," now "struck down by a side of our city that is as awful and terrifying as the creative side is wonderful." It was precisely in this conflation of victim and city, this confusion of personal woe with public distress, that the crime's "story" would be found, its lesson, its encouraging promise of narrative resolution.

One reason the victim in this case could be so readily abstracted, and her situation so readily made to stand for that of the city itself, was that she remained, as a victim of rape, unnamed in most press reports. Although the American and English press convention of not naming victims of rape (adult rape victims are named in French papers) derives from the understandable wish to protect the victim, the rationalization of this special protection rests on a number of doubtful, even magical, assumptions. The convention assumes, by providing a protection for victims of rape not afforded victims of other assaults, that rape involves a violation absent from other kinds of assault. The convention assumes that this violation is of a nature best kept secret, that the rape victim feels, and would feel still more strongly were she identified, a shame and self-loathing unique to this form of assault; in other words that she has been in an unspecified way party to her own assault, that a special contract exists between this one kind of victim and her assailant. The convention assumes, finally, that the victim would be, were this special contract revealed, the natural object of prurient interest; that the act of male penetration involves such potent mysteries that the woman so penetrated (as opposed, say, to having her face crushed with a brick or her brain penetrated with a length of pipe) is permanently marked, "different," even—especially if there is a perceived racial or social "difference" between victim and assailant, as in nineteenth-century stories featuring white women taken by Indians—"ruined."

These quite specifically masculine assumptions (women do not want to be raped, nor do they want to have their brains smashed, but very few mystify the difference between the two) tend in general to be self-fulfilling, guiding the victim to define her assault as her protectors do. "Ultimately we're doing women a disservice by separating rape from other violent crimes," Deni Elliott, the director of Dartmouth's Ethics Institute, suggested in a discussion of this custom in *Time*. "We are participating in the stigma of rape by treating victims of this crime differently," Geneva Overholser, the editor of the *Des Moines Register*, said about her decision to publish in February of 1990 a five-part piece about a rape victim who agreed to be named. "When we as a society refuse to talk openly about rape, I think we weaken our ability to deal with it." Susan Estrich, a professor of criminal law at Harvard Law School and the manager of Michael Dukakis's 1988 presidential campaign, discussed, in *Real Rape*, the conflicting emotions that followed her own 1974 rape:

> At first, being raped is something you simply don't talk about. Then it occurs to you that people whose houses are broken into or who are mugged in Central Park talk about it *all* the time.... If it isn't my fault, why am I supposed to

be ashamed? If I'm not ashamed, if it wasn't "personal," why look askance when I mention it?

There were, in the 1989 Central Park attack, specific circumstances that reinforced the conviction that the victim should not be named. She had clearly been, according to the doctors who examined her at Metropolitan Hospital and to the statements made by the suspects (she herself remembered neither the attack nor anything that happened during the next six weeks), raped by one or more assailants. She had also been beaten so brutally that, fifteen months later, she could not focus her eyes or walk unaided. She had lost all sense of smell. She could not read without experiencing double vision. She was believed at the time to have permanently lost function in some areas of her brain.

Given these circumstances, the fact that neither the victim's family nor, later, the victim herself wanted her name known struck an immediate chord of sympathy, seemed a belated way to protect her as she had not been protected in Central Park. Yet there was in this case a special emotional undertow that derived in part from the deep and allusive associations and taboos attaching, in American black history, to the idea of the rape of white women. Rape remained, in the collective memory of many blacks, the very core of their victimization. Black men were accused of raping white women, even as black women were, Malcolm X wrote in *The Autobiography of Malcolm X*, "raped by the slavemaster white man until there had begun to emerge a homemade, handmade, brainwashed race that was no longer even of its true color, that no longer even knew its true family names." The very frequency of sexual contact between white men and black women increased the potency of the taboo on any such contact between black men and white women. The abolition of slavery, W. J. Cash wrote in *The Mind of the South*,

... in destroying the rigid fixity of the black at the bottom of the scale, in throwing open to him at least the legal opportunity to advance, had inevitably opened up to the mind of every Southerner a vista at the end of which stood the overthrow of this taboo. If it was given to the black to advance at all, who could say (once more the logic of the doctrine of his inherent inferiority would not hold) that he would not one day advance the whole way and lay claim to complete equality, including, specifically, the ever crucial right of marriage?

What Southerners felt, therefore, was that any assertion of any kind on the part of the Negro constituted in a perfectly real manner an attack on the Southern woman. What they saw, more or less consciously, in the conditions of Reconstruction was a passage toward a condition for her as degrading, in their view, as rape itself. And a condition, moreover, which, logic or no logic, they infallibly thought of as being as absolutely forced upon her as rape, and hence a condition for which the term "rape" stood as truly as for the *de facto* deed.

Nor was the idea of rape the only potentially treacherous undercurrent in this case. There has historically been, for American blacks, an entire complex of loaded references around the question of "naming": slave names, masters' names, African names, call me by my rightful name, nobody knows my name; stories, in which the specific gravity of naming locked directly into that of rape, of black men whipped for addressing white women by their given names. That, in this case, just such an interlocking of references could work to fuel resentments and inchoate hatreds seemed clear, and it seemed equally clear that some of what ultimately occurred—the repeated references to lynchings, the identification of the defendants with the Scottsboro boys, the insistently provocative repetition of the victim's name, the weird and self-defeating insistence that no rape had taken place and little harm been done the victim—derived momentum from this historical freight. "Years ago, if a white woman said a Black man looked at her lustfully, he could be hung higher than a magnolia tree in bloom, while a white mob watched joyfully sipping tea and eating cookies," Yusef Salaam's mother reminded readers of the *Amsterdam News*. "The first thing you do in the United States of America when a white woman is raped is round up a bunch of black youths, and I think that's what happened here," the Reverend Calvin O. Butts III of the Abyssinian Baptist Church in Harlem told the *New York Times*. "You going to arrest me now because I said the jogger's name?" Gary Byrd asked rhetorically on his WLIB show, and was quoted by Edwin Diamond in *New York* magazine:

> I mean, she's obviously a public figure, and a very mysterious one, I might add. Well, it's a funny place we live in called America, and should we be surprised that they're up to their usual tricks? It was a trick that got us here in the first place.

This reflected one of the problems with not naming this victim: she was in fact named all the time. Everyone in the courthouse, everyone who worked for a paper or a television station or who followed the case for whatever professional reason, knew her name. She was referred to by name in all court records and in all court proceedings. She was named, in the days immediately following the attack, on some local television stations. She was also routinely named—and this was part of the difficulty, part of what led to a damaging self-righteousness among those who did not name her and to an equally damaging embattlement among those who did—in Manhattan's black-owned newspapers, the *Amsterdam News* and the *City Sun,* and she was named as well on WLIB, the Manhattan radio station owned by a black partnership that included Percy Sutton and, until 1985, when he transferred his stock to his son, Mayor Dinkins.

That the victim in this case was identified on Centre Street and north of 96th Street but not in between made for a certain cognitive dissonance, especially since the names of even the juvenile suspects had been released by the police and the press before any suspect had been arraigned, let alone indicted. "The police normally withhold the names of minors who are accused of crimes," the *Times* explained (actually the police normally withhold the names of accused "juveniles," or minors under age sixteen, but not of minors sixteen or seventeen), "but officials said they made public the names of the youths charged in the attack on the woman because of the seriousness of the incident." There seemed a debatable point here, the question of whether "the seriousness of the incident" might not have in fact seemed a compelling reason to avoid any appearance of a rush to judgment by preserving the anonymity of a juvenile suspect; one of the names released by the police and published in the *Times* was of a fourteen-year-old who was ultimately not indicted.

There were, early on, certain aspects of this case that seemed not well handled by the police and prosecutors, and others that seemed not well handled by the press. It would seem to have been tactically unwise, since New York State law requires that a parent or guardian be present when children under sixteen are questioned, for police to continue the interrogation of Yusef Salaam, then fifteen, on the grounds that his Transit Authority bus pass said he was sixteen, while his mother was kept waiting outside. It would seem to have been unwise for Linda Fairstein, the assistant district attorney in charge of Manhattan sex crimes, to ignore, at the precinct house, the mother's assertion that the son was fifteen, and later to suggest, in court, that the boy's age had been unclear to her because the mother had used the word "minor."

It would also seem to have been unwise for Linda Fairstein to tell David Nocenti, the assistant U.S. Attorney who was paired with Yusef Salaam in a "Big Brother" program and who had come to the precinct house at the mother's request, that he had "no legal standing" there and that she would file a complaint with his supervisors. It would seem in this volatile a case imprudent of the police to follow their normal procedure by presenting Raymond Santana's initial statement in their own words, cop phrases that would predictably seem to some in the courtroom, as the expression of a fourteen-year-old held overnight and into the next afternoon for interrogation, unconvincing:

On April 19, 1989, at approximately 20:30 hours, I was at the Taft Projects in the vicinity of 113th St. and Madison Avenue. I was there with numerous friends.... At approximately 21:00 hours, we all (myself and approximately 15 others) walked south on Madison Avenue to E. 110th Street, then walked westbound to Fifth Avenue. At Fifth Avenue and 110th Street, we met up with an additional group of approximately 15 other males, who also entered Central Park with us at that location with the intent to rob cyclists and joggers...

In a case in which most of the defendants had made video-taped statements admitting at least some role in the assault and rape, this less than meticulous attitude toward the gathering and dissemination of information seemed peculiar and self-defeat-ing, the kind of pressured or unthinking standard procedure that could not only exacerbate the fears and angers and suspicions of conspiracy shared by many blacks but open what seemed, on the basis of the confessions, a conclusive case to the kind of doubt that would eventually keep juries out, in the trial of the first three defendants, ten days, and, in the trial of the next two defendants, twelve days. One of the reasons the jury in the first trial could not agree, *Manhattan Lawyer* reported in its October 1990 issue, was that one juror, Ronald Gold, remained "deeply troubled by the discrepancies between the story [Antron] McCray tells on his videotaped statement and the prosecution's scenario":

Why did McCray place the rape at the reservoir, Gold demanded, when all evidence indicated it happened at the 102 Street cross-drive? Why did McCray say the jogger was raped where she fell, when the prosecution said she'd been dragged 300 feet into the woods first? Why did McCray talk about having to hold her arms down, if she was found bound and gagged?

The debate raged for the last two days, with jurors drop-ping in and out of Gold's acquittal [for McCray] camp....

After the jurors watched McCray's video for the fifth time, Miranda [Rafael Miranda, another juror] knew it well enough to cite the time-code numbers imprinted at the bottom of the videotape as he rebuffed Gold's argu-ments with specific statements from McCray's own lips. [McCray, on the videotape, after admitting that he had held the victim by her left arm as her clothes were pulled off, volunteered that he had "got on top" of her, and said that he had rubbed against her without an erection "so every-body would ... just know I did it."] The pressure on Gold was mounting. Three jurors agree that it was evident Gold, worn down perhaps by his own displays of temper as much as anything else, capitulated out of exhaustion. While a bit-ter Gold told other jurors he felt terrible about ultimately giving in, Brueland [Harold Brueland, another juror who had for a time favored acquittal for McCray] believes it was all part of the process.

"I'd like to tell Ronnie someday that nervous exhaustion is an element built into the court system. They know that," Brueland says of court officials. "They know we're only going to be able to take it for so long. It's just a matter of, you know, who's got the guts to stick with it."

So fixed were the emotions provoked by this case that the idea that there could have been, for even one juror, even a moment's doubt in the state's case, let alone the kind of doubt that could be sustained over ten days, seemed, to many in the city, bewildering, almost unthinkable: the attack on the jogger had by then passed into narrative, and the narrative was about confrontation, about what Governor Cuomo had called "the ultimate shriek of alarm," about what was wrong with the city and about its solution. What was wrong with the city had been identified, and its names were Raymond Santana, Yusef Salaam, Antron McCray, Kharey Wise, Kevin Richardson, and Steve Lopez. "They never could have thought of it as they raged through Central Park, tormenting and ruining people," Bob Herbert wrote in the *News* after the verdicts came in on the first three defendants.

There was no way it could have crossed their vicious minds. Running with the pack, they would have scoffed at the very idea. They would have laughed.

And yet it happened. In the end, Yusef Salaam, Antron McCray and Raymond Santana were nailed by a woman.

Elizabeth Lederer stood in the courtroom and watched Saturday night as the three were hauled off to jail.... At times during the trial, she looked about half the height of the long and lanky Salaam, who sneered at her from the witness stand. Salaam was apparently too dumb to realize that Lederer—this petite, soft-spoken, curly-haired prosecutor—was the jogger's avenger....

You could tell that her thoughts were elsewhere, that she was thinking about the jogger.

You could tell that she was thinking: I did it.

I did it for you.

Do this in remembrance of me: the solution, then, or so such pervasive fantasies suggested, was to partake of the symbolic body and blood of The Jogger, whose idealization was by this point complete, and was rendered, significantly, in details stressing her "difference," or superior class. The Jogger was someone who wore, according to *Newsday*, "a light gold chain around her slender neck" as well as, according to the *News*, a "modest" gold ring and "a thin sheen" of lipstick. The Jogger was someone who would not, according to the *Post*, "even dignify her alleged attackers with a glance." The Jogger was someone who spoke, according to the *News*, in accents "suited to boardrooms," accents that might therefore seem "foreign to many native New Yorkers." In her first appearance on the witness stand she had been subjected, the *Times* noted, "to questions that most people do not have to answer publicly during their lifetimes," principally about her use of a diaphragm on the Sunday preceding the attack, and had answered these questions, according to an editorial in the *News*, with an "indomitable dignity" that had taught the city a lesson "about courage and class."

This emphasis on perceived refinements of character and of manner and of taste tended to distort and to flatten, and ultimately to suggest not the actual victim of an actual crime but a fictional character of a slightly earlier period, the well-brought-up virgin who briefly graces the city with her presence and receives in turn a taste of "real life." The defendants, by contrast, were seen as incapable of appreciating these marginal distinctions, ignorant of both the norms and accoutrements of middle-class life. "Did you have jogging clothes on?" Elizabeth Lederer asked Yusef Salaam, by way of trying to discredit his statement that he had gone into the park that night only to "walk around." Did he have "jogging clothes," did he have "sports equipment," did he have "a bicycle." A pernicious nostalgia had come to permeate the case, a longing for the New York that had seemed for a while to be about "sports equipment," about getting and spending rather than about having and not having: the reason that this victim must not be named was so that she could go unrecognized, it was astonishingly said, by Jerry Nachman, the editor of the *New York Post*, and then by others who seemed to find in this a particular resonance, to Bloomingdale's.

* * *

Some New York stories involving young middle-class white women do not make it to the editorial pages, or even necessarily to the front pages. In April 1990, a young middle-class white woman named Laurie Sue Rosenthal, raised in an Orthodox Jewish household and at age twenty-nine still living with her parents in Jamaica, Queens, happened to die, according to the coroner's report, from the accidental toxicity of Darvocet in combination with alcohol, in an apartment at 36 East 68th Street in Manhattan. The apartment belonged to the man she had been, according to her parents, seeing for about a year, a minor city assistant commissioner named Peter Franconeri. Peter Franconeri, who was at the time in charge of elevator and boiler inspections for the Buildings Department and married to someone else, wrapped Laurie Sue Rosenthal's body in a blanket; placed it, along with her handbag and ID, outside the building with the trash; and went to his office at 60 Hudson Street. At some point an anonymous call was made to 911. Franconeri was identified only after Laurie Sue Rosenthal's parents gave the police his beeper number, which they found in her address book. According to *Newsday*, which covered the story more extensively than the *News*, the *Post*, or the *Times*,

> Initial police reports indicated that there were no visible wounds on Rosenthal's body. But Rosenthal's mother, Ceil, said yesterday that the family was told the autopsy revealed two "unexplained bruises" on her daughter's body.
>
> Larry and Ceil Rosenthal said those findings seemed to support their suspicions that their daughter was upset because they received a call from their daughter at 3 A.M. Thursday "saying that he had beaten her up." The family reported the conversation to police.
>
> "I told her to get into a cab and get home," Larry Rosenthal said yesterday. "The next I heard was two detectives telling me terrible things."
>
> "The ME [medical examiner] said the bruises did not constitute a beating but they were going to examine them further," Ceil Rosenthal said.

"There were some minor bruises," a spokeswoman for the Office of the Chief Medical Examiner told *Newsday* a few days later, but the bruises "did not in any way contribute to her death." This is worth rerunning: A young woman calls her parents at three in the morning, "distraught." She says that she has been beaten up. A few hours later, on East 68th Street between Madison and Park avenues, a few steps from Porthault and Pratesi and Armani and Saint Laurent and the Westbury Hotel, at a time of day in this part of New York 10021 when Jim Buck's dog trainers are assembling their morning packs and Henry Kravis's Bentley is idling outside his Park Avenue apartment and the construction crews are clocking in over near the Frick at the multi-million-dollar houses under reconstruction for Bill Cosby and for the owner of The Limited, this young middle-class white woman's body, showing bruises, gets put out with the trash.

"Everybody got upside down because of who he was," an unidentified police officer later told Jim Dwyer of *Newsday*, referring to the man who put the young woman out with the trash. "If it had happened to anyone else, nothing would have come of it. A summons would have been issued and that would have been the end of it." In fact nothing did come of the death of Laurie Sue Rosenthal, which might have seemed a natural tabloid story but failed, on several levels, to catch the local imagination. For one thing she could not be trimmed into the role of the preferred tabloid victim, who is conventionally presented as fate's random choice (Laurie Sue Rosenthal had, for whatever reason, taken the Darvocet instead of a taxi home, her parents reported treatment for a previous Valium dependency, she could be presumed to have known over the course of a year that Franconeri was married and yet continued to see him); for another, she seemed not to have attended an expensive school or to have been employed in a glamour industry (no Ivy Grad, no Wall Street Exec), which made it hard to cast her as part of "what makes this city so vibrant and so great."

In August 1990, Peter Franconeri pled guilty to a misdemeanor, the unlawful removal of a body, and was sentenced by Criminal Court judge Peter Benitez to seventy-five hours of community service. This was neither surprising nor much of a story (only twenty-three lines even in *Newsday*, on page twenty-nine of the city edition), and the case's lenient resolution was for many people a kind of relief. The district attorney's office had asked for "some incarceration," the amount usually described as a "touch," but no one wanted, it was said, to crucify the guy: Peter Franconeri was somebody who knew a lot of people, understood how to live in the city, who had for example not only the apartment on East 68th Street between Madison and Park but a house in Southampton and who also understood that putting a body outside with the trash was nothing to get upside down about, if it was handled right. Such understandings may in fact have been the city's true "ultimate shriek of alarm," but it was not a shriek the city wanted to recognize.

2

Perhaps the most arresting collateral news to surface, during the first few days after the attack on the Central Park jogger, was that a significant number of New Yorkers apparently believed the city sufficiently well-ordered to incorporate Central Park into their evening fitness schedules. "Prudence" was defined, even after the attack, as "staying south of 90th Street," or having "an awareness that you need to think about planning your routes," or, in the case of one woman interviewed by the *Times*, deciding to quit her daytime job (she was a lawyer) because she was "tired of being stuck out there, running later and later at night." "I don't think there's a runner who couldn't describe the silky, gliding feeling you get running at night," an editor of *Runner's World* told the *Times*. "You see less of what's around you and you become centered on your running."

The notion that Central Park at night might be a good place to "see less of what's around you" was recent. There were two reasons why Frederick Law Olmsted and Calvert Vaux, when they devised their winning entry in the 1858 competition for a Central Park design, decided to sink the transverse roads below grade level. One reason, the most often cited, was aesthetic, a recognition on the part of the designers that the four crossings specified by the terms of the competition, at 65th, 79th, 85th, and 97th streets, would intersect the sweep of the landscape, be "at variance with those agreeable sentiments which we should wish the park to inspire." The other reason, which appears to have been equally compelling, had to do with security. The problem with grade-level crossings, Olmsted and Vaux wrote in their "Greensward" plan, would be this:

> The transverse roads will … have to be kept open, while the park proper will be useless for any good purpose after dusk; for experience has shown that even in London, with its admirable police arrangements, the public cannot be assured safe transit through large open spaces of ground after nightfall.
>
> These public throughfares will then require to be well-lighted at the sides, and, to restrain marauders pursued by the police from escaping into the obscurity of the park, strong fences or walls, six or eight feet high, will be necessary.

The park, in other words, was seen from its conception as intrinsically dangerous after dark, a place of "obscurity," "useless for any good purpose," a refuge only for "marauders." The parks of Europe closed at nightfall, Olmsted noted in his 1882 pamphlet *The Spoils of the Park: With a Few Leaves from the Deep-laden Note-books of "A Wholly Unpractical Man,"* "but one surface road is kept open across Hyde Park, and the superintendent of the Metropolitan Police told me that a man's chances of being garrotted or robbed were, because of the facilities for concealment to be found in the Park, greater in passing at night along this road than anywhere else in London."

In the high pitch of the initial "jogger" coverage, suggesting as it did a city overtaken by animals, this pragmatic approach to urban living gave way to a more ideal construct, one in which New York either had once been or should be "safe," and now, as in Governor Cuomo's "none of us is safe," was not. It was time, accordingly, to "take it back," time to "say no"; time, as David Dinkins would put it during his campaign for the mayoralty in the summer of 1989, to "draw the line." What the line was to be drawn against was "crime," an abstract, a free-floating specter that could be dispelled by certain acts of personal affirmation, by the kind of moral rearmament that later figured in Mayor Dinkins's plan to revitalize the city by initiating weekly "Tuesday Night Out Against Crime" rallies.

By going into the park at night, Tom Wicker wrote in the *Times*, the victim in this case had "affirmed the primacy of freedom over fear." A week after the assault, Susan Chace suggested on the op-ed page of the *Times* that readers walk into

the park at night and join hands. "A woman can't run in the
park at an offbeat time," she wrote. "Accept it, you say. I can't.
It shouldn't be like this in New York City, in 1989, in spring."
Ronnie Eldridge also suggested that readers walk into the park at
night, but to light candles. "Who are we that we allow ourselves
to be chased out of the most magnificent part of our city?" she
asked, and also: "If we give up the park, what are we supposed
to do: fall back to Columbus Avenue and plant grass?" This was
interesting, suggesting as it did that the city's not inconsiderable
problems could be solved by the willingness of its citizens to hold
or draw some line, to "say no"; in other words that a reliance on
certain magical gestures could affect the city's fate.

The insistent sentimentalization of experience, which is to say
the encouragement of such reliance, is not new in New York. A
preference for broad strokes, for the distortion and flattening of
character and the reduction of events to narrative, has been for
well over a hundred years the heart of the way the city presents
itself: Lady Liberty, huddled masses, ticker-tape parades, heroes,
gutters, bright lights, broken hearts, 8 million stories in the naked
city; 8 million stories and all the same story, each devised to
obscure not only the city's actual tensions of race and class but
also, more significantly, the civic and commercial arrangements
that rendered those tensions irreconcilable.

Central Park itself was such a "story," an artificial pastoral in the
nineteenth-century English romantic tradition, conceived, during a decade when the population of Manhattan would increase
by 58 percent, as a civic project that would allow the letting of
contracts and the employment of voters on a scale rarely before undertaken in New York. Ten million cartloads of dirt would
need to be shifted during the twenty years of its construction.
Four to five million trees and shrubs would need to be planted,
half a million cubic yards of topsoil imported, 114 miles of ceramic pipe laid.

Nor need the completion of the park mean the end of the
possibilities: in 1870, once William Marcy Tweed had revised the
city charter and invented his Department of Public Parks, new
roads could be built whenever jobs were needed. Trees could be
dug up, and replanted. Crews could be set loose to prune, to clear,

to hack at will. Frederick Law Olmsted, when he objected, could be overridden, and finally eased out. "A 'delegation' from a great political organization called on me by appointment," Olmsted wrote in *The Spoils of the Park*, recalling the conditions under which he had worked:

> After introductions and handshakings, a circle was formed, and a gentleman stepped before me, and said, "We know how much pressed you must be … but at your convenience our association would like to have you determine what share of your patronage we can expect, and make suitable arrangements for our using it. We will take the liberty to suggest, sir, that there could be no more convenient way than that you should send us our due quota of tickets, if you will please, sir, in this form, *leaving us to fill in the name.*" Here a packet of printed tickets was produced, from which I took one at random. It was a blank appointment and bore the signature of Mr. Tweed.

> As superintendent of the Park, I once received in six days more than seven thousand letters of advice as to appointments, nearly all from men in office…. I have heard a candidate for a magisterial office in the city addressing from my doorsteps a crowd of such advice-bearers, telling them that I was bound to give them employment, and suggesting plainly, that, if I was slow about it, a rope round my neck might serve to lessen my reluctance to take good counsel. I have had a dozen men force their way into my house before I had risen from bed on a Sunday morning, and some break into my drawing room in their eagerness to deliver letters of advice.

Central Park, then, for its underwriters if not for Olmsted, was about contracts and concrete and kickbacks, about pork, but the sentimentalization that worked to obscure the pork, the "story," had to do with certain dramatic contrasts, or extremes, that were believed to characterize life in this as in no other city. These "contrasts," which have since become the very spine of the New York narrative, appeared early on: Philip Hone, the mayor of New York in 1826 and 1827, spoke in 1843 of a city

703

"overwhelmed with population, and where the two extremes of costly luxury in living, expensive establishments and improvident wastes are presented in daily and hourly contrast with squalid mixing and hapless destruction." Given this narrative, Central Park could be and ultimately would be seen the way Olmsted himself saw it, as an essay in democracy, a social experiment meant to socialize a new immigrant population and to ameliorate the perilous separation of rich and poor. It was the duty and the interest of the city's privileged class, Olmsted had suggested some years before he designed Central Park, to "get up parks, gardens, music, dancing schools, reunions which will be so attractive as to force into contact the good and the bad, the gentleman and the rowdy."

The notion that the interests of the "gentleman" and the "rowdy" might be at odds did not intrude: then as now, the preferred narrative worked to veil actual conflict, to cloud the extent to which the condition of being rich was predicated upon the continued neediness of a working class; to confirm the responsible stewardship of "the gentleman" and to forestall the possibility of a self-conscious, or politicized, proletariat. Social and economic phenomena, in this narrative, were personalized. Politics were exclusively electoral. Problems were best addressed by the emergence and election of "leaders," who could in turn inspire the individual citizen to "participate," or "make a difference." "Will you help?" Mayor Dinkins asked New Yorkers, in a September 1990 address from St. Patrick's Cathedral intended as a response to the "New York crime wave" stories then leading the news. "Do you care? Are you ready to become part of the solution?"

"Stay," Governor Cuomo urged the same New Yorkers. "Believe. Participate. Don't give up." Manhattan borough president Ruth Messinger, at the dedication of a school flagpole, mentioned the importance of "getting involved" and "participating," or "pitching in to put the shine back on the Big Apple." In a discussion of the popular "New York" stories written between 1902 and 1910 by William Sidney Porter, or "O. Henry," William R. Taylor of the State University of New York at Stony Brook spoke of the way in which these stories, with their "focus on individuals' plights," their "absence of social or political implications" and "ideological neutrality," provided "a miraculous form of social glue":

These sentimental accounts of relations between classes in the city have a specific historical meaning: empathy without political compassion. They reduce the scale of human suffering to what atomized individuals endure as their plucky, sad lives were recounted week after week for almost a decade ... their sentimental reading of oppression, class differences, human suffering, and affection helped create a new language for interpreting the city's complex society, a language that began to replace the threadbare moralism that New Yorkers inherited from 19th-century readings of the city. This language localized suffering in particular moments and confined it to particular occasions; it smoothed over differences because it could be read almost the same way from either end of the social scale.

Stories in which terrible crimes are inflicted on innocent victims, offering as they do a similarly sentimental reading of class differences and human suffering, a reading that promises both resolution and retribution, have long performed as the city's endorphins, a built-in source of natural morphine working to blur the edges of real and to a great extent insoluble problems. What is singular about New York, and remains virtually incomprehensible to people who live in less rigidly organized parts of the country, is the minimal level of comfort and opportunity its citizens have come to accept. The romantic capitalist pursuit of privacy and security and individual freedom, so taken for granted nationally, plays, locally, not much role. A city where virtually every impulse has been to stifle rather than to encourage normal competition, New York works, when it does work, not on a market economy but on little deals, payoffs, accommodations, *baksheesh*, arrangements that circumvent the direct exchange of goods and services and prevent what would be, in a competitive economy, the normal ascendance of the superior product.

There were in the five boroughs in 1990 only 581 supermarkets (a supermarket, as defined by the trade magazine *Progressive Grocer*, is a market that does an annual volume of $2 million), or, assuming a population of 8 million, one supermarket for every 13,769 citizens. Groceries, costing more than they should because of this absence of competition and also because of the proliferation of payoffs required to ensure this absence of competition (produce, we have come to understand, belongs to the Gambinos, and fish to the Lucheses and the Genoveses, and a piece of the construction of the market to each of the above, but keeping the door open belongs finally to the inspector here, the inspector there), are carried home or delivered, as if in Jakarta, by pushcart.

It has historically taken, in New York as if in Mexico City, ten years to process and specify and bid and contract and construct a new school; twenty or thirty years to build or, in the cases of Bruckner Boulevard and the West Side Highway, to not quite build a highway. A recent public scandal revealed that a batch of city-ordered Pap smears had gone unread for more than a year (in the developed world the Pap smear, a test for cervical cancer, is commonly read within a few days); what did not become a public scandal, what is still accepted as the way things are, is that even Pap smears ordered by Park Avenue gynecologists can go unread for several weeks.

Such resemblances to cities of the third world are in no way casual, or based on the "color" of a polyglot population: these are all cities arranged primarily not to improve the lives of their citizens but to be labor-intensive, to accommodate, ideally at the subsistence level, since it is at the subsistence level that the work force is most apt to be captive and loyalty assured, a third-world population. In some ways New York's very attractiveness, its promises of opportunity and improved wages, its commitments as a city in the developed world, were what seemed destined to render it ultimately unworkable. Where the vitality of such cities in the less developed world had depended on their ability to guarantee low-cost labor and an absence of regulation, New York had historically depended instead on the constant welling up of new businesses, of new employers to replace those phased out, like the New York garment manufacturers who found it cheaper to make their clothes in Hong Kong or Kuala Lumpur or Taipei, by rising local costs.

It had been the old pattern of New York, supported by an expanding national economy, to lose one kind of business and gain another. It was the more recent error of New York to misconstrue this history of turnover as an indestructible resource, there to be taxed at will, there to be regulated whenever a dollar could be seen in doing so, there for the taking. By 1977, New York had lost some 600,000 jobs, most of them in manufacturing and in the kinds of small businesses that could no longer maintain their narrow profit margins inside the city. During the "recovery" years, from 1977 until 1988, most of these jobs were indeed replaced, but in a potentially perilous way: of the 500,000 new jobs created, most were in the area most vulnerable to a downturn, that of financial and business services, and many of the rest in an area not only equally vulnerable to bad times but dispiriting to the city even in good, that of tourist and restaurant services.

The demonstration that many kinds of businesses were finding New York expendable had failed to prompt real efforts to make the city more competitive. Taxes grew still more punitive, regulation more Byzantine. Forty-nine thousand new jobs were created in New York's city agencies between 1983 and 1990, even as the services provided by those agencies were widely perceived to decline. Attempts at "reform" typically tended to create more jobs: in 1988, in response to the length of time it was taking to build or repair a school, a new agency, the School Construction Authority, was formed. A New York City school, it was said, would now take only five years to build. The head of the School Construction Authority was to receive $145,000 a year and each of the three vice presidents $110,000 a year. An executive gym, with Nautilus equipment, was contemplated for the top floor of the agency's new headquarters at the International Design Center in Long Island City. Two years into this reform, the backlog on repairs to existing schools stood at 33,000 outstanding requests. "To relieve the charity of friends of the support of a half-blind and half-witted man by employing him at the public expense as an inspector of cement may not be practical with reference to the permanent firmness of a wall," Olmsted noted after his Central Park experience, "while it is perfectly so with reference to the triumph of sound doctrine at an election."

In fact the highest per capita taxes of any city in the United States (and, as anyone running a small business knows, the widest variety of taxes) provide, in New York, unless the citizen is prepared to cut a side deal here and there, only the continuing multiplication of regulations designed to benefit the contractors and agencies and unions with whom the regulators have cut their own deals. A kitchen appliance accepted throughout the rest of the United States as a basic postwar amenity, the in-sink garbage disposal unit, is for example illegal in New York. Disposals, a city employee advised me, not only encourage rats, and "bacteria," presumably in a way that bags of garbage sitting on the sidewalk do not ("Because it is," I was told when I asked how this could be), but also encourage people "to put their babies down them."

On the one hand this illustrates how a familiar urban principle, that of patronage (the more garbage there is to be collected, the more garbage collectors can be employed), can be reduced, in the bureaucratic wilderness that is any third-world city, to voodoo; on the other it reflects this particular city's underlying criminal ethic, its acceptance of graft and grift as the bedrock of every transaction. "Garbage costs are outrageous," an executive of Supermarkets General, which owns Pathmark, recently told *City Limits* about why the chains preferred to locate in the suburbs. "Every time you need to hire a contractor, it's a problem." The problem, however, is one from which not only the contractor but everyone with whom the contractor does business—a chain of direct or indirect patronage extending deep into the fabric of the city—stands to derive one or another benefit, which was one reason the death of a young middle-class white woman in the East 68th Street apartment of the assistant commissioner in charge of boiler and elevator inspections flickered so feebly on the local attention span.

It was only within the transforming narrative of "contrasts" that both the essential criminality of the city and its related absence of civility could become points of pride, evidence of "energy": if you could make it here you could make it anywhere, hello sucker, get smart. Those who did not get the deal, who bought retail, who did not know what it took to get their electrical work signed off, were dismissed as provincials, bridge-and-tunnels, out-of-towners who did not have what it took not to get taken. "Every tourist's nightmare became a reality for a Maryland couple over the weekend when the husband was beaten and robbed on Fifth Avenue in front of Trump Tower," began a story in the *New York Post* during the summer of 1990. "Where do you think we're from, Iowa?" the prosecutor who took Robert Chambers's statement said on videotape by way of indicating that he doubted Chambers's version of Jennifer Levin's death. "They go after poor people like you from out of town, they prey on the tourists," a clerk explained in the West 46th Street computer store where my husband and I had taken refuge to escape three muggers. My husband said that we lived in New York. "That's why they didn't get you," the clerk said, effortlessly incorporating this change in the data. "That's how you could move fast."

The narrative comforts us, in other words, with the assurance that the world is knowable, even flat, and New York its center, its motor, its dangerous but vital "energy." "Family in Fatal Mugging Loved New York" was the *Times* headline on a story following the September 1990 murder, in the Seventh Avenue IND station, of a twenty-two-year-old tourist from Utah. The young man, his parents, his brother, and his sister-in-law had attended the U.S. Open and were reportedly on their way to dinner at a Moroccan restaurant downtown. "New York, to them, was the greatest place in the world," a family friend from Utah was quoted as having said. Since the narrative requires that the rest of the country provide a dramatic contrast to New York, the family's hometown in Utah was characterized by the *Times* as a place where "life revolves around the orderly rhythms of Brigham Young University" and "there is only about one murder a year." The town was in fact Provo, where Gary Gilmore shot the motel manager, both in life and in *The Executioner's Song.* "She loved New York, she just loved it," a friend of the assaulted jogger told the *Times* after the attack. "I think she liked the fast pace, the competitiveness."

New York, the *Times* concluded, "invigorated" the jogger, "matched her energy level." At a time when the city lay virtually inert, when forty thousand jobs had been wiped out in the financial markets and former traders were selling shirts at Bergdorf Goodman for Men, when the rate of mortgage delinquencies had doubled, when 50 or 60 million square feet of office space remained unrented (60 million square feet of unrented office space is the equivalent of fifteen darkened World Trade Towers) and even prime commercial blocks on Madison Avenue in the Seventies were boarded up, empty; at a time when the money had dropped out of all the markets and the Europeans who had lent the city their élan and their capital during the eighties had moved on, vanished to more cheerful venues, this notion of the city's "energy" was sedative, as was the commandeering of "crime" as the city's central problem.

The extent to which the October 1987 crash of the New York financial markets damaged the illusions of infinite recovery and growth on which the city had operated during the 1980s had been at first hard to apprehend. "Ours is a time of New York ascendant," the New York City Commission on the Year 2000, created during the mayoralty of Edward Koch to reflect the best thinking of the city's various business and institutional establishments, had declared in its 1987 report. "The city's economy is stronger than it has been in decades, and is driven both by its own resilience and by the national economy; New York is more than ever the international capital of finance, and the gateway to the American economy."

And then, its citizens had come gradually to understand, it was not. This perception that something was "wrong" in New York had been insidious, a slow-onset illness at first noticeable only in periods of temporary remission. Losses that might have seemed someone else's problem (or even comeuppance) as the markets were in their initial 1987 free-fall, and that might have seemed more remote still as the markets regained the appearance of strength, had come imperceptibly but inexorably to alter the tone of daily life. By April of 1990, people who lived in and around New York were expressing, in interviews with the *Times*, considerable anguish and fear that they did so: "I feel very resentful that I've lost a lot of flexibility in my life," one said. "I often wonder, 'Am I crazy for coming here?'" "People feel a sense of impending doom about what may happen to them," a clinical psychologist said. People were "frustrated," "feeling absolutely desolate," "trapped," "angry," "terrified," and "on the verge of panic."

It was a panic that seemed in many ways specific to New York, and inexplicable outside it. Even later, when the troubles of New York had become a common theme, Americans from less depressed venues had difficulty comprehending the nature of those troubles, and tended to attribute them, as New Yorkers themselves had come to do, to "crime." "Escape From New York" was the headline on the front page of the *New York Post* on September 10, 1990. "Rampaging Crime Wave Has 59% of Residents Terrified. Most Would Get Out of the City, Says Time/CNN Poll." This poll appeared in the edition of *Time* dated September 17, 1990, which carried the cover legend "The Rotting of the Big Apple." "Reason: a surge of drugs and violent crime that government officials seem utterly unable to combat," the story inside explained. Columnists referred, locally, to "this sewer of a city." The *Times* ran a plaintive piece about the snatch of Elizabeth Rohatyn's Hermès handbag outside Arcadia, a restaurant on East 62nd Street that had for a while seemed the very heart of the New York everyone now missed, the New York where getting and spending could take place without undue reference to having and not having, the duty-free New York; that this had occurred to the wife of Felix Rohatyn, who was widely perceived to have saved the city from its fiscal crisis in the mid-seventies, seemed to many a clarion irony.

This question of crime was tricky. There were in fact eight American cities with higher homicide rates, and twelve with higher overall crime rates. Crime had long been taken for granted in the less affluent parts of the city, and had become in the mid-seventies, as both unemployment and the costs of maintaining property rose and what had once been functioning neighborhoods were abandoned and burned and left to whoever claimed them, endemic. "In some poor neighborhoods, crime became almost a way of life," Jim Sleeper, an editor at *Newsday* and the author of *The Closest of Strangers: Liberalism and the Politics of Race in New York*, noted in his discussion of the social disintegration that occurred during this period:

> ...a subculture of violence with complex bonds of utility and affection within families and the larger, "law-abiding" community. Struggling merchants might "fence" stolen goods, for example, thus providing quick cover and additional incentive for burglaries and robberies; the drug economy became more vigorous, reshaping criminal lifestyles and tormenting the loyalties of families and friends. A walk down even a reasonably busy street in a poor, minority neighborhood at high noon could become an unnerving journey into a landscape eerie and grim.

What seemed markedly different a decade later, what made crime a "story," was that the more privileged, and especially the more privileged white, citizens of New York had begun to feel unnerved at high noon in even their own neighborhoods. Although New York City Police Department statistics suggested that white New Yorkers were not actually in increased mortal danger (the increase in homicides between 1977 and 1989, from 1,557 to 1,903, was entirely among what the NYPD classified as Hispanic, Asian, and black victims; the number of white murder victims had steadily declined, from 361 in 1977 to 227 in 1984 and 190 in 1989), the apprehension of such danger, exacerbated by street snatches and muggings and the quite useful sense that the youth in the hooded sweatshirt with his hands jammed in his pockets might well be a predator, had become general. These more privileged New Yorkers now felt unnerved not only on the street, where the necessity for evasive strategies had become an exhausting constant, but in even the most insulated and protected apartment buildings. As the residents of such buildings, the owners of twelve- and sixteen- and twenty-four-room apartments, watched the potted ficus trees disappear from outside their doors and the graffiti appear on their limestone walls and the smashed safety glass from car windows get swept off their sidewalks, it had become increasingly easy to imagine the outcome of a confrontation between, say, the relief night doorman and six dropouts from Julia Richman High School on East 67th Street.

And yet those New Yorkers who had spoken to the *Times* in April of 1990 about their loss of flexibility, about their panic, their desolation, their anger, and their sense of impending doom, had not been talking about drugs, or crime, or any of the city's more publicized and to some extent inflated ills. These were people who did not for the most part have twelve- and sixteen-room apartments and doormen and the luxury of projected fears. These people were talking instead about an immediate fear, about money, about the vertiginous plunge in the value of their houses and apartments and condominiums, about the possibility or probability of foreclosure and loss; about, implicitly, their fears of being left, like so many they saw every day, below the line, out in the cold, on the street.

This was a climate in which many of the questions that had seized the city's attention in 1987 and 1988, for example that of whether Mortimer Zuckerman should be "allowed" to build two fifty-nine-story office towers on the site of what is now the Coliseum, seemed in retrospect wistful, the baroque concerns of better times. "There's no way anyone would make a sane judgment to go into the ground now," a vice president at Cushman and Wakefield told the *New York Observer* about the delay in the Coliseum project, which had in fact lost its project-ed major tenant, Salomon Brothers, shortly after Black Monday, 1987. "It would be suicide. You're better off sitting in a tub of water and opening your wrists." Such fears were, for a number of reasons, less easy to incorporate into the narrative than the fear of crime.

The imposition of a sentimental, or false, narrative on the disparate and often random experience that constitutes the life of a city or a country means, necessarily, that much of what happens in that city or country will be rendered merely illustrative, a series of set pieces, or performance opportunities. Mayor Dinkins could, in such a symbolic substitute for civic life, "break the boycott" (the Flatbush boycott organized to mobilize resentment of Korean merchants in black neighborhoods) by purchasing a few dollars' worth of pro-duce from a Korean grocer on Church Avenue. Governor Cuomo could "declare war on crime" by calling for five thousand addi-tional police; Mayor Dinkins could "up the ante" by calling for sixty-five hundred. "White slut comes into the park looking for the African man," a black woman could say, her voice loud but still conversational, in the corridor outside the courtroom where, dur-ing the summer of 1990, the first three defendants in the Central Park attack, Antron McCray, Yusef Salaam, and Raymond Santana, were tried on charges of attempted murder, assault, sodomy, and rape. "Boyfriend beats shit out of her, they blame it on our boys," the woman could continue, and then, referring to a young man with whom the victim had at one time split the cost of an apart-ment: "How about the roommate, anybody test his semen? No. He's white. They don't do it to each other."

Glances could then flicker among those reporters and producers and courtroom sketch artists and photographers and cameramen and techs and summer interns who assembled daily at 111 Centre Street. Cellular phones could be picked up, a show of indiffer-ence. Small talk could be exchanged with the marshals, a show of solidarity. The woman could then raise her voice: "White folk, all of them are devils, even those that haven't been born yet, they are *devils*. Little *demons*. I don't understand these devils, I guess they think this is *their court.*"The reporters could gaze beyond her, faces blank, no eye contact, a more correct form of hostility and also more lethal. The woman could hold her ground but avert her eyes, letting her gaze fall on another black, in this instance a black *Daily News* columnist, Bob Herbert. "You," she could say. "You are a *disgrace.* Go ahead. Line up there. Line up with the white folk. Look at them, lining up for their first-class seats while *my* people are downstairs behind *barricades*... kept behind barricades like *cattle*... not even allowed in the room to see their sons lynched... is that an *African* I see in that line? Or is that a *Negro.* Oh, oh, sorry, shush, white folk didn't know, he was *passing*..."

In a city in which grave and disrupting problems had become general—problems of not having, problems of not making it, problems that demonstrably existed, among the mad and the ill and the under-equipped and the overwhelmed, with decreasing reference to color—the case of the Central Park jogger provided more than just a safe, or structured, setting in which various and sometimes only marginally related rages could be vented. "This trial," the *Daily News* announced on its editorial page one morning in July 1990, midway through the trial of the first three defendants, "is about more than the rape and brutalization of a single woman. It is about the rape and the brutalization of a city. The jogger is a symbol of all that's wrong here. And all that's right, because she is nothing less than an inspiration."

The *News* did not define the ways in which "the rape and the brutalization of the city" manifested itself, nor was definition necessary: this was a city in which the threat or the fear of brutalization had become so immediate that citizens were urged to take up their own defense, to form citizen patrols or militia, as in Beirut. This was a city in which between twenty and thirty neighborhoods had already given over their protection, which was to say the right to determine who belonged in the neighborhood and who did not and what should be done about it, to the Guardian Angels. This was a city in which a Brooklyn vigilante group, which called itself Crack Busters and was said to be trying to rid its Bedford-Stuyvesant neighborhood of drugs, would before September was out "settle an argument" by dousing with gasoline and setting on fire an abandoned van and the three homeless citizens inside. This was a city in which the *Times* would soon perceive, in the failing economy, "a bright side for the city at large," the bright side being that while there was believed to have been an increase in the number of middle-income and upper-income families who wanted to leave the city, "the slumping market is keeping many of those families in New York."

In this city rapidly vanishing into the chasm between its actual life and its preferred narratives, what people said when they talked about the case of the Central Park jogger came to seem a kind of poetry, a way of expressing, without directly stating, different but equally volatile and similarly occult visions of the same disaster. One vision, shared by those who had seized upon the attack on the jogger as an exact representation of what was wrong with the city, was of a city systematically ruined, violated, raped by its underclass. The opposing vision, shared by those who had seized upon the arrest of the defendants as an exact representation of their own victimization, was of a city in which the powerless had been systematically ruined, violated, raped by the powerful. For so long as this case held the city's febrile attention, then, it offered a narrative for the city's distress, a frame in which the actual social and economic forces wrenching the city could be personalized and ultimately obscured.

Or rather it offered two narratives, mutually exclusive. Among a number of blacks, particularly those whose experience with or distrust of the criminal justice system was such that they tended to discount the fact that five of the six defendants had to varying degrees admitted taking part in the attack, and to focus instead on the absence of any supporting forensic evidence incontrovertibly linking this victim to these defendants, the case could be read as a confirmation not only of their victimization but of the white conspiracy they saw at the heart of that victimization. For the *Amsterdam News*, which did not veer automatically to the radical analysis (a typical issue in the fall of 1990 lauded the FBI for its minority recruiting and the Harlem National Guard for its high morale and readiness to go to the Gulf), the defendants could in this light be seen as victims of "a political trial," of a "legal lynching," of a case "rigged from the very beginning" by the decision of "the white press" that "whoever was arrested and charged in this case of the attempted murder, rape and sodomy of a well-connected, bright, beautiful, and promising white woman was guilty, pure and simple."

For Alton H. Maddox, Jr., the message to be drawn from the case was that the American criminal justice system, which was under any circumstances "inherently and unabashedly racist," failed "to function equitably at any level when a Black male is accused of raping a white female." For others the message was more general, and worked to reinforce the fragile but functional mythology of a heroic black past, the narrative in which European domination could be explained as a direct and vengeful response to African superiority. "Today the white man is faced head-on with what is happening on the Black Continent, Africa," Malcolm X wrote.

> Look at the artifacts being discovered there, that are proving over and over again, how the black man had great, fine, sensitive civilizations before the white man was out of the caves. Below the Sahara, in the places where most of America's Negroes' foreparents were kidnapped, there is being unearthed some of the finest craftsmanship, sculpture and other objects, that has ever been seen by modern man. Some of these things now are on view in such places as New York City's Museum of Modern Art. Gold work of such fine tolerance and workmanship that it has no rival. Ancient objects produced by black hands ... refined by those black hands with results that no human hand today can equal.
>
> History has been so "whitened" by the white man that even the black professors have known little more than the most ignorant black man about the talents and rich civilizations and cultures of the black man of millenniums ago...

"Our proud African queen," the Reverend Al Sharpton had said of Tawana Brawley's mother, Glenda Brawley: "She stepped out of anonymity, stepped out of obscurity, and walked into history." It was said in the corridors of the courthouse where Yusuf Salaam was tried that he carried himself "like an African king."

"It makes no difference anymore whether the attack on Tawana happened," William Kunstler had told *New York Newsday* when the alleged rape and torture of Tawana Brawley by a varying number of white police officers seemed, as an actual prosecutable crime if not as a window on what people needed to believe, to have dematerialized."If her story was a concoction to prevent her parents from punishing her for staying out all night, that doesn't disguise the fact that a lot of young black women are treated the way she said she was treated."The importance of whether or not the crime had occurred was, in this view, entirely resident in the crime's "description," which was defined by Stanley Diamond in *The Nation* as "a crime that did not occur" but was "described with skill and controlled hysteria by the black actors as the epitome of degradation, a repellent model of what actually happens to too many black women."

A good deal of what got said around the edges of the jogger case, in the corridors and on the call-in shows, seemed to derive exclusively from the suspicions of conspiracy increasingly entrenched among those who believe themselves powerless. A poll conducted in June of 1990 by the *New York Times* and WCBS-TV News determined that 77 percent of blacks polled believed either that it was "true" or "might possibly be true" (as opposed to "almost certainly not true") that the government of the United States "singles out and investigates black elected officials in order to discredit them in a way it doesn't do with white officials." Sixty percent believed that it was true or might possibly be true that the government "deliberately makes sure that drugs are easily available in poor black neighborhoods in order to harm black people."Twenty-nine percent believed that it was true or might possibly be true that "the virus which causes AIDS was deliberately created in a laboratory in order to infect black people." In each case, the alternative response to "true" or "might possibly be true" was "almost certainly not true," which might have seemed in itself to reflect a less than ringing belief in the absence of conspiracy."The conspiracy to destroy Black boys is very complex and interwoven," Jawanza Kunjufu, a Chicago educational consultant, wrote in his *Countering the Conspiracy to Destroy Black Boys*, a 1982 pamphlet that has since been extended to three volumes.

> There are many contributors to the conspiracy, ranging from the very visible who are more obvious, to the less visible and silent partners who are more difficult to recognize.

Those people who adhere to the doctrine of white racism, imperialism, and white male supremacy are easier to recognize. Those people who actively promote drugs and gang violence are active conspirators, and easier to identify. What makes the conspiracy more complex are those people who do not plot together to destroy Black boys, but, through their indifference, perpetuate it. This passive group of conspirators consists of parents, educators, and white liberals who deny being racists, but through their silence allow institutional racism to continue.

For those who proceeded from the conviction that there was under way a conspiracy to destroy blacks, particularly black boys, a belief in the innocence of these defendants, a conviction that even their own statements had been rigged against them or wrenched from them, followed logically. It was in the corridors and on the call-in shows that the conspiracy got sketched in, in a series of fantasy details that conflicted not only with known facts but even with each other. It was said that the prosecution was withholding evidence that the victim had gone to the park to meet a drug dealer. It was said, alternately or concurrently, that the prosecution was withholding evidence that the victim had gone to the park to take part in a satanic ritual. It was said that the forensic photographs showing her battered body were not "real" photographs, that "they," the prosecution, had "brought in some corpse for the pictures." It was said that the young woman who appeared on the witness stand and identified herself as the victim was not the "real" victim, that "they" had in this case brought in an actress.

What was being expressed in each instance was the sense that secrets must be in play, that "they," the people who had power in the courtroom, were in possession of information systematically withheld—since information itself was power—from those who did not have power. On the day the first three defendants were sentenced, C. Vernon Mason, who had formally entered the case in the penalty phase as Antron McCray's attorney, filed a brief that included the bewildering and untrue assertion that the victim's boyfriend, who had not at that time been called to testify, was black. That some whites jumped to engage this assertion on its own terms (the *Daily News* columnist Gail

Collins referred to it as Mason's "slimiest argument of the hour—an announcement that the jogger had a black lover") tended only to reinforce the sense of racial estrangement that was the intended subtext of the assertion, which was without meaning or significance except in that emotional deep where whites are seen as conspiring in secret to sink blacks in misery. "Just answer me, who got addicted?" I recall one black spectator asking another as they left the courtroom. "I'll tell you who got addicted, the inner city got addicted." He had with him a pamphlet that laid out a scenario in which the government had conspired to exterminate blacks by flooding their neighborhoods with drugs, a scenario touching all the familiar points, Laos, Cambodia, the Golden Triangle, the CIA, more secrets, more poetry.

"From the beginning I have insisted that this was not a racial case," Robert Morgenthau, the Manhattan district attorney, said after the verdicts came in on the first jogger trial. He spoke of those who, in his view, wanted "to divide the races and advance their own private agendas," and of how the city was "ill-served" by those who had so "sought to exploit" this case. "We had hoped that the racial tensions surrounding the jogger trial would begin to dissipate soon after the jury arrived at a verdict," a *Post* editorial began a few days later. The editorial spoke of an "ugly claque of 'activists,'" of the "divisive atmosphere" they had created, and of the anticipation with which the city's citizens had waited for "mainstream black leaders" to step forward with praise for the way in which the verdicts had brought New York "back from the brink of criminal chaos":

> Alas, in the jogger case, the wait was in vain. Instead of praise for a verdict which demonstrated that sometimes criminals are caught and punished, New Yorkers heard charlatans like the Rev. Al Sharpton claim the case was fixed. They heard that C. Vernon Mason, one of the engineers of the Tawana Brawley hoax—the attorney who thinks Mayor Dinkins wears "too many yarmulkes"—was planning to appeal the verdicts ...

To those whose preferred view of the city was of an inherently dynamic and productive community ordered by the natural play of its conflicting elements, enriched, as in Mayor Dinkins's "gorgeous mosaic," by its very "contrasts," this case offered a number of useful elements. There was the confirmation of "crime" as the canker corroding the life of the city. There was, in the random and feral evening described by the East Harlem attackers and the clear innocence of and damage done to the Upper East Side and Wall Street victim, an eerily exact and conveniently personalized representation of what the *Daily News* had called "the rape and the brutalization of a city." Among the reporters on this case, whose own narrative conventions involved "hero cops" and "brave prosecutors" going hand to hand against "crime" (the "Secret Agony of Jogger DA," we learned in the *Post* a few days after the verdicts in the first trial, was that "Brave Prosecutor's Marriage Failed as She Put Rapists Away"), there seemed an unflagging enthusiasm for the repetition and reinforcement of these elements, and an equally unflagging resistance, even hostility, to exploring the point of view of the defendants' families and friends and personal or political allies (or, as they were called in news reports, the "supporters") who gathered daily at the other end of the corridor from the courtroom.

This seemed curious. Criminal cases are widely regarded by American reporters as windows on the city or culture in which they take place, opportunities to enter not only households but parts of the culture normally closed, and yet this was a case in which indifference to the world of the defendants extended even to the reporting of names and occupations. Yusuf Salaam's mother, who happened to be young and photogenic and to have European features, was pictured so regularly that she and her son became the instantly recognizable "images" of Jogger One, but even then no one got her name quite right. For a while in the papers she was "Cheroney," or sometimes "Cheronay," McEllhonor, then she became Cheroney McEllhonor Salaam. After she testified, the spelling of her first name was corrected to "Sharonne," although, since the byline on a piece she wrote for the *Amsterdam News* spelled it differently, "Sharrone," this may have been another misunderstanding. Her occupation was frequently given as "designer" (later, after her son's conviction, she went to work as a paralegal for William Kunstler), but no one seemed to take this seriously enough to say what she designed or for whom; not until after she testified, when *Newsday* reported her testimony that on the evening of her son's arrest she had arrived at the precinct house late because she was an instructor at the Parsons School of Design, did the notion of "designer" seem sufficiently concrete to suggest an actual occupation.

The Jogger One defendants were referred to repeatedly in the news columns of the *Post* as "thugs." The defendants and their families were often said by reporters to be "sneering." (The reporters, in turn, were said at the other end of the corridor to be "smirking.") "We don't have nearly so strong a question as to the guilt or innocence of the defendants as we did at Bensonhurst," a *Newsday* reporter covering the first jogger trial said to the *New York Observer*, well before the closing arguments, by way of explaining why *Newsday*'s coverage may have seemed less extensive on this trial than on the Bensonhurst trials. "There is not a big question as to what happened in Central Park that night. Some details are missing, but it's fairly clear who did what to whom."

In fact this came close to the heart of it: that it seemed, on the basis of the videotaped statements, fairly clear who had done what to whom was precisely the case's liberating aspect, the circumstance that enabled many of the city's citizens to say and think what they might otherwise have left unexpressed. Unlike other recent high visibility cases in New York, unlike Bensonhurst and unlike Howard Beach and unlike Bernhard Goetz, here was a case in which the issue not exactly of race but of an increasingly visible underclass could be confronted by the middle class, both white and black, without guilt. Here was a case that gave this middle class a way to transfer and express what had clearly become a growing and previously inadmissible rage with the city's disorder, with the entire range of ills and uneasy guilts that came to mind in a city where entire families slept in the discarded boxes in which new Sub-Zero refrigerators were delivered, at twenty-six hundred per, to more affluent families. Here was also a case, most significantly, in which even that transferred rage could be transferred still further, veiled, personalized: a case in which the city's distress could be seen to derive not precisely from its underclass but instead from certain identifiable individuals who claimed to speak for this underclass, individuals who, in Robert Morgenthau's words, "sought to exploit" this case, to "advance their own private agendas"; individuals who wished even to "divide the races."

If the city's problems could be seen as deliberate disruptions of a naturally cohesive and harmonious community, a community in which, undisrupted, "contrasts" generated a perhaps dangerous but vital "energy," then those problems were tractable, and could be addressed, like "crime," by the call for "better leadership." Considerable comfort could be obtained, given this story line, through the demonization of the Reverend Al Sharpton, whose presence on the edges of certain criminal cases that interested him had a polarizing effect that tended to reinforce the narrative. Jim Sleeper, in *The Closest of Strangers*, described one of the fifteen marches Sharpton led through Bensonhurst after the 1989 killing of an East New York sixteen-year-old, Yusuf Hawkins, who had come into Bensonhurst and been set upon, with baseball bats and ultimately with bullets, by a group of young whites.

An August 27, 1989, *Daily News* photo of the Reverend Al Sharpton and a claque of black teenagers marching in Bensonhurst to protest Hawkins's death shows that they are not really "marching." They are stumbling along, huddled together, heads bowed under the storm of hatred breaking over them, eyes wide, hanging on to one another and to Sharpton, scared out of their wits. They, too, are innocents—or were until that day, which they will always remember. And because Sharpton is with them, his head bowed, his face showing that he knows what they're feeling, he is in the hearts of black people all over New York.

Yet something is wrong with this picture. Sharpton did not invite or coordinate with Bensonhurst community leaders who wanted to join the march. Without the time for organizing which these leaders should have been given in order to rein in the punks who stood waving watermelons; without an effort by black leaders more reputable than Sharpton to recruit whites citywide and swell the march, Sharpton was assured that the punks would carry the day. At several points he even baited them by blowing kisses...

"I knew that Bensonhurst would clarify whether it had been a racial incident or not," Sharpton said by way of explaining, on a recent "Frontline" documentary, his strategy in Bensonhurst. "The fact that I was so controversial to Bensonhurst helped them forget that the cameras were there," he said. "So I decided to help them … I would throw kisses to them, and they would go nuts." *Question*, began a joke told in the aftermath of the first jogger trial. *You're in a room with Hitler, Saddam Hussein, and Al Sharpton. You have only two bullets. Who do you shoot? Answer: Al Sharpton. Twice.*

Sharpton did not exactly fit the roles New York traditionally assigns, for maximum audience comfort, to prominent blacks. He seemed in many ways a phantasm, someone whose instinct for the connections between religion and politics and show business was so innate that he had been all his life the vessel for other people's hopes and fears. He had given his first sermon at age four. He was touring with Mahalia Jackson at eleven. As a teenager, according to Robert D. McFadden, Ralph Blumenthal, M. A. Farber, E. R. Shipp, Charles Strum, and Craig Wolff, the *New York Times* reporters and editors who collaborated on *Outrage: The Story Behind the Tawana Brawley Hoax*, Sharpton was tutored first by Adam Clayton Powell, Jr. ("You got to know when to hit it and you got to know when to quit it and when it's quittin' time, don't push it," Powell told him), then by the Reverend Jesse Jackson ("Once you turn on the gas, you got to cook or burn 'em up," Jackson told him), and eventually, after obtaining a grant from Bayard Rustin and campaigning for Shirley Chisholm, by James Brown. "Once, he trailed Brown down a corridor, through a door, and, to his astonishment, onto a stage flooded with spotlights," the authors of *Outrage* reported. "He immediately went into a wiggle and dance."

It was perhaps this talent for seizing the spotlight and the moment, this fatal bent for the wiggle and the dance, that most clearly disqualified Sharpton from casting as the Good Negro, the credit to the race, the exemplary if often imagined figure whose refined manners and good grammar could be stressed and who could be seen to lay, as Jimmy Walker said of Joe Louis, "a rose on the grave of Abraham Lincoln." It was left, then, to cast Sharpton, and for Sharpton to cast himself, as the Outrageous Nigger, the familiar role—assigned sixty years ago to Father Divine and thirty years later to Adam Clayton Powell—of the essentially manageable fraud whose first concern is his own well-being. It was for example repeatedly mentioned, during the ten days the jury was out on the first jogger trial, that Sharpton had chosen to wait out the verdict not at 111 Centre Street but "in the air-conditioned comfort" of C. Vernon Mason's office, from which he could be summoned by beeper.

Sharpton, it was frequently said by whites and also by some blacks, "represented nobody," was "self-appointed" and "self-promoting." He was an "exploiter" of blacks, someone who "did them more harm than good." It was pointed out that he had been indicted by the state of New York in June of 1989 on charges of grand larceny. (He was ultimately acquitted.) It was pointed out that *New York Newsday*, working on information that appeared to have been supplied by federal law-enforcement agencies, had in January 1988 named him as a federal informant, and that he himself admitted to having let the government tap his phone in a drug-enforcement effort. It was routinely said, most tellingly of all in a narrative based on the magical ability of "leaders" to improve the commonweal, that he was "not the right leader," "not at all the leader the black community needs." His clothes and his demeanor were ridiculed (my husband was asked by *Esquire* to do a piece predicated on interviewing Sharpton while he was having his hair processed), his motives derided, and his tactics, which were those of an extremely sophisticated player who counted being widely despised among his stronger cards, not very well understood.

Whites tended to believe, and to say, that Sharpton was "using" the racial issue—which, in the sense that all political action is based on "using" one issue or another, he clearly was. Whites also tended to see him as destructive and irresponsible, indifferent to the truth or to the sensibilities of whites—which, most notoriously in the nurturing of the Tawana Brawley case, a primal fantasy in which white men were accused of a crime Sharpton may well have known to be a fabrication, he also clearly was. What seemed not at all understood was that for Sharpton, who had no interest in making the problem appear more tractable ("The question is, do you want to 'ease' it or do you want to 'heal' it," he had said when asked if his marches had not worked against "easing tension" in Bensonhurst), the fact that blacks and whites could sometimes be shown to have divergent interests by no means suggested the need for an ameliorative solution.

Such divergent interests were instead a lucky break, a ready-made organizing tool, a dramatic illustration of who had the power and who did not, who was making it and who was falling below the line; a metaphor for the sense of victimization felt not only by blacks but by all those Sharpton called "the left-out opposition." *We got the power*, the chants go on "Sharpton and Fulani in Babylon: Volume I, The Battle of New York City," a tape of the speeches of Sharpton and of Leonora Fulani, a leader of the New Alliance Party. *We are the chosen people. Out of the pain. We that can't even talk together. Have learned to walk together.*

"I'm no longer sure what I thought about Al Sharpton a year or two ago still applies," Jerry Nachman, the editor of the *New York Post*, who had frequently criticized Sharpton, told Howard Kurtz of the *Washington Post* in September of 1990. "I spent a lot of time on the street. There's a lot of anger, a lot of frustration. Rightly or wrongly, he may be articulating a great deal more of what typical attitudes are than some of us thought." Wilbert Tatum, the editor and publisher of the *Amsterdam News*, tried to explain to Kurtz how, in his view, Sharpton had been cast as "a caricature of black leadership":

> He was fat. He wore jogging suits. He wore a medallion and gold chains. And the unforgivable of unforgivables, he had processed hair. The white media, perhaps not consciously, said, "We're going to promote this guy because we can point up the ridiculousness and paucity of black leadership." Al understood precisely what they were doing, precisely. Al is probably the most brilliant tactician this country has ever produced ...

Whites often mentioned, as a clinching argument, that Sharpton paid his demonstrators to appear; the figure usually mentioned was five dollars (by November 1990, when Sharpton was fielding demonstrators to protest the killing of a black woman alleged to have grabbed a police nightstick in the aftermath of a domestic dispute, a police source quoted in the *Post* had jumped the payment to twenty dollars), but the figure floated by a prosecutor on the jogger case was four dollars. This seemed on many levels a misunderstanding, or an estrangement, or as blacks would say a disrespect, too deep to address, but on its simplest level it served to suggest what value was placed by whites on what they thought of as black time.

In the fall of 1990, the fourth and fifth of the six defendants in the Central Park attack, Kevin Richardson and Kharey Wise, went on trial. Since this particular narrative had achieved full resolution, or catharsis, with the conviction of the first three defendants, the city's interest in the case had by then largely waned. Those "charlatans" who had sought to "exploit" the case had been whisked, until they could next prove useful, into the wings. Even the verdicts in this second trial, coinciding as they did with yet another arrest of John ("The Dapper Don") Gotti, a reliable favorite on the New York stage, did not lead the local news. It was in fact the economy itself that had come center stage in the city's new, and yet familiar, narrative work: a work in which the vital yet beleaguered city would or would not weather yet another "crisis" (the answer was a resounding yes); a work, or a dreamwork, that emphasized not only the cyclical nature of such "crises" but the regenerative power of the city's "contrasts." "With its migratory population, its diversity of cultures and institutions, and its vast resources of infrastructure, capital, and intellect, New York has been the quintessential modern city for more than a century, constantly reinventing itself," Michael Stone concluded in his *New York* magazine cover story, "Hard Times." "Though the process may be long and painful, there's no reason to believe it won't happen again."

These were points commonly made in support of a narrative that tended, with its dramatic line of "crisis" and resolution, or recovery, only to further obscure the economic and historical groundwork for the situation in which the city found itself: that long unindictable conspiracy of criminal and semicriminal civic and commercial arrangements, deals, negotiations, gimmes and getmes, graft and grift, pipe, topsoil, concrete, garbage; the conspiracy of those in the know, those with a connection, those with a rabbi at the Department of Sanitation or the Buildings Department or the School Construction Authority or Foley Square, the conspiracy of those who believed everybody got upside down because of who it was, it happened to anybody else, a summons gets issued and that's the end of it. On

November 12, 1990, in its page-one analysis of the city's troubles, the *New York Times* went so far as to locate, in "public spending," not the drain on the city's vitality and resources it had historically been but "an important positive factor":

> Not in decades has so much money gone for public works in the area—airports, highways, bridges, sewers, subways and other projects. Roughly $12 billion will be spent in the metropolitan region in the current fiscal year. Such government outlays are a healthy counterforce to a 43 percent decline since 1987 in the value of new private construction, a decline related to the sharp drop in real estate prices.... While nearly every industry in the private sector has been reducing payrolls since spring, government hiring has risen, maintaining an annual growth rate of 20,000 people since 1987...

That there might well be, in a city in which the proliferation of and increase in taxes were already driving private-sector payrolls out of town, hardly anyone left to tax for such public works and public-sector jobs was a point not too many people wished seriously to address: among the citizens of a New York come to grief on the sentimental stories told in defense of its own lazy criminality, the city's inevitability remained the given, the heart, the first and last word on which all the stories rested. We love New York, the narrative promises, because it matches our energy level.

1990

POLITICAL FICTIONS

*This book is for Robert Silvers. It is also for John Gregory Dunne,
who lived through my discovering what he already knew.*

CONTENTS

A FOREWORD

EARLY IN 1988, Robert Silvers of *The New York Review of Books* asked me if I would do some pieces or a piece about the presidential campaign just then getting underway in New Hampshire. He would arrange credentials. All I had to do was show up, see what there was to see, and write something. I was flattered (a presidential election was a "serious" story, and no one had before solicited my opinions on one), and yet I kept putting off the only essential moment, which was showing up, giving the thing the required focus. In January and February I was selling a house in California, an easy excuse. In March and April I was buying an apartment in New York, another easy excuse. I had packing to do, then unpacking, painting to arrange, many household negotiations and renegotiations. Clippings and books and campaign schedules kept arriving, and I would stack them on shelves unread. I kept getting new deadlines from *The New York Review*, but there remained about domestic politics something resistant, recondite, some occult irreconcilability that kept all news of it just below my attention level. The events of the campaign as reported seemed to have taken place in a language I did not recognize. The stakes of the election as presented seemed not to compute. At the very point when I had in my mind successfully abandoned this project to which I could clearly bring no access, no knowledge, no understanding, I got another, more urgent call from *The New York Review*. The California primary was only days away. The Democratic and Republican national conventions were only weeks away. The office could put me on a campaign charter the next day, Jesse Jackson was flying out of Newark to California, the office could connect me in Los Angeles with the other campaigns. It so happened that my husband was leaving that day to do some research in Ireland. It so happened that our daughter was leaving that day to spend the summer in Guatemala and Nicaragua. There seemed, finally, no real excuse for me not to watch the California primary (and even to vote in it, since

I was still registered in Los Angeles County), and so I went to Newark, and got on the plane. From the notes I typed at three the next morning in a room at the Hyatt Wilshire in Los Angeles, after a rally in South Central and a fundraiser at the Hollywood Palace and a meet-and-greet at the housing project where the candidate was to spend what remained of the night ("Would you call this Watts," the reporters kept saying, and "Who knows about guns? Who makes an AK?"), my introduction to American politics:

> I was told the campaign would be leaving Newark at 11:30 and to be at the Butler Aviation terminal no later than 10:30. Delmarie Cobb was to be the contact. At Butler Aviation the man on the gate knew nothing about the Jackson campaign but agreed to make a phone call, and was told to send me to Hangar 14. Hangar 14, a United hangar, was locked up except for a corrugated fire door open about two feet off the ground. Some men who approached knew nothing about any Jackson plane, they were "just telephone," but they limboed under the fire door and I followed them.

> The empty hangar. I walked around Malcolm Forbes's green 727, "Capitalist Tool," looked around the tarmac, and found no one. Finally a mechanic walked through and told me to try the office upstairs. I did. The metal door to the stairs was locked. I ran after the mechanic. He said he would pick the lock for me, and did. Upstairs, I found someone who told me to go to "Post J."

> At "Post J," an unmarked gate to the tarmac, I found a van open in back and four young men waiting. They said they were Jackson campaign, they were waiting for the Secret Service and then the traveling campaign. I sat down on my bag and asked them to point out Delmarie Cobb when she came. Delmarie, one of them said, was already in California, but he was Delmarie's nephew, Stephen Gaines.

> "Who's she," the Secret Service agents kept saying after they arrived. "She hasn't been cleared by the campaign,

what's she doing here." "All I know is, she's got the right names in Chicago," Stephen Gaines kept saying. In any case the agents were absorbed in sweeping the bags. Finally one said he might as well sweep mine. Once he had done this he seemed confused. It seemed he had no place to put me. I wasn't supposed to be on the tarmac with the swept bags, but I wasn't supposed to be on the plane either. "Look," he said finally. "Just wait on the plane."

I waited, alone on the plane. Periodically an agent appeared and said, "You aren't supposed to be here, see, if there were someplace else to put you we'd put you there." The pilot appeared from the cockpit. "Give me a guesstimate how many people are flying," he said to me. I said I had no idea. "Fifty-five?" the pilot said. I shrugged. "Let's say fifty-five," the pilot said, "and get the fuel guys off the hook." None of this seemed promising.

The piece I finally did on the 1988 campaign, "Insider Baseball," was the first of a number of pieces I eventually did about various aspects of American politics, most of which had to do, I came to realize, with the ways in which the political process did not reflect but increasingly proceeded from a series of fables about American experience. As the pieces began to accumulate, I was asked with somewhat puzzling frequency about my own politics, what they "were," or "where they came from," as if they were eccentric, opaque, somehow unreadable. They are not. They are the logical product of a childhood largely spent among conservative California Republicans (this was before the meaning of "conservative" changed) in a postwar boom economy. The people with whom I grew up were interested in low taxes, a balanced budget, and a limited government. They believed above all that a limited government had no business tinkering with the private or cultural life of its citizens. In 1964, in accord with these interests and beliefs, I voted, ardently, for Barry Goldwater. Had Goldwater remained the same age and continued running, I would have voted for him in every election thereafter. Instead, shocked and to a curious extent personally offended by the enthusiasm with which California Republicans who had jettisoned an authentic conservative (Goldwater) were rushing to embrace Ronald Reagan, I registered as a Democrat, the first member of my family (and perhaps in my generation still the only member) to do so. That this did not involve taking a mark-edly different view on any issue was a novel discovery, and one that led me to view "America's two-party system" with—and this was my real introduction to American politics—a somewhat doubtful eye.

At a point quite soon during the dozen-some years that followed getting on that charter at Newark, it came to my attention that there was to writing about politics a certain Sisyphean aspect. Broad patterns could be defined, specific inconsistencies docu-mented, but no amount of definition or documentation seemed sufficient to stop the stone that was our apprehension of politics from hurtling back downhill. The romance of New Hampshire would again be with us. The crucible event in the candidate's "character" would again be explored. Even that which seemed ineluctably clear would again vanish from collective memory, sink traceless into the stream of collapsing news and comment cycles that had become our national River Lethe. It was clear for example in 1988 that the political process had already become perilously remote from the electorate it was meant to represent. It was also clear in 1988 that the decision of the two major parties to obscure any possible perceived distinction between themselves, and by so doing to narrow the contested ground to a handful of selected "target" voters, had already imposed considerable strain on the basic principle of the democratic exercise, that of assuring the nation's citizens a voice in its affairs. It was also clear in 1988 that the rhetorical manipula-tion of resentment and anger designed to attract these target voters had reduced the nation's political dialogue to a level so dispiritingly low that its highest expression had come to be a pernicious nostalgia. Perhaps most strikingly of all, it was clear in 1988 that those inside the process had congealed into a per-manent political class, the defining characteristic of which was its readiness to abandon those not inside the process. All of this was known. Yet by the time of the November 2000 presidential election and the onset of the thirty-six days that came to be known as "Florida," every aspect of what had been known in

1988 would again need to be rediscovered, the stone pushed up the hill one more time.

Perhaps the most persistent of the fables from which the political process proceeds has to do with the "choice" it affords the nation's citizens, who are seen to remain unappreciative. On the Saturday morning before the November 2000 presidential election, *The Washington Post* ran on its front page a piece by Richard Morin and Claudia Deane headlined "As Turnout Falls, Apathy Emerges As Driving Force." The thrust of this piece, which was based on polls of voter and non-voter attitudes conducted both by the *Post* and by the Joan Shorenstein Center's "Vanishing Voter Project" at Harvard, was reinforced by a takeout about a Missouri citizen named Mike McClusky, a thirty-seven-year-old Army veteran who, despite "the 21-foot flagpole with the Stars and Stripes in the middle of the front yard," had never voted and did not now intend to vote. His wife, Danielle McClusky, did vote, and the *Post* noted the readiness with which she discussed "her take on Social Security, and health care, and health maintenance organizations, and what she heard on Larry King, and what she heard on Chris Matthews, and what George W. Bush would do, and what Al Gore would do." Meanwhile, the *Post* added, making it fairly clear which McClusky merited the approval of its Washington readers, "Mike McClusky pets the dogs and half-listens because he doesn't really have to sift through any of this." Accompanying the main story were graphs, purporting to show why Americans did not vote, and the *Post's* analysis of its own graphs was this: "Apathy is the single biggest reason why an estimated 100 million Americans will not vote on Tuesday."

The graphs themselves, however, told a somewhat more complicated story: only thirty-five percent of nonvoters, or about seventeen percent of all adult Americans, fell into the "apathetic" category, which, according to a director of the Shorenstein study, included those who "have no sense of civic duty," "aren't interested in politics," and "have no commitment in keeping up with public affairs." Another fourteen percent of nonvoters were classified as "disconnected," a group including both those "who can't get to the polls because of advanced age or disability" and those "who recently changed addresses and are not yet registered"—in other words, people functionally unable to vote. The remaining fifty-one percent of these nonvoters, meaning roughly a quarter of all adult Americans, were classified as either "alienated" ("the angry men and women of U.S. politics … so disgusted with politicians and the political process that they've opted out") or "disenchanted" ("these non-voters aren't so much repelled by politics as they are by the way politics is practiced"), in either case pretty much the polar opposite of "apathetic." According to the graphs, more than seventy percent of all nonvoters were in fact registered, a figure that cast some ambiguity on the degree of "apathy" even among the thirty-five percent categorized as "apathetic."

Study of the actual Shorenstein results clouded the *Post*'s "apathy" assessment still further. According to the Shorenstein Center's release dated the same Saturday as the *Post* story, its polling had shown that the attitudes toward politicians and the political process held by those who intended to vote differed— up to an interesting point—only narrowly from the attitudes held by those who did not intend to vote. Eighty-nine percent of nonvoters and seventy-six percent of voters agreed with the statement "most political candidates will say almost anything in order to get themselves elected." Seventy-eight percent of nonvoters and seventy percent of voters agreed with the statement "candidates are more concerned with fighting each other than with solving the nation's problems." Almost seventy percent of nonvoters and voters alike agreed with the state- ment "campaigns seem more like theater or entertainment than something to be taken seriously." The interesting point at which the attitudes of voters and nonvoters did diverge was that revealed by questioning about specific policies. Voters, for example, tended to believe that the federal budget surplus should go to a tax cut. Nonvoters, who on the whole had less education and lower income, more often said that the surplus should be spent on health, welfare, and education. "Nonvoters have different needs," is the way the *Post* summarized this. "But why should politicians listen?"

This notion of voting as a consumer transaction (the voter "pays" with his or her vote to obtain the ear of his or her professional politician, or his or her "leader," or by logical extension his or her "superior") might seem a spiritless social contract, although not— if it actually delivered on the deal—an intrinsically unworkable one. But of course the contract does not deliver: only sentimentally does "the vote" give "the voter" an empathetic listener in the political class, let alone any leverage on the workings of that class. When the chairman of Michael Dukakis's 1988 New York Finance Council stood barefoot on a table at the Atlanta Hyatt during that summer's Democratic convention (see page 761) and said "I've been around this process a while and one thing I've noticed, it's the people who write the checks who get treated as if they have a certain amount of power," she had a clear enough understanding of how the contract worked and did not work. When the only prominent Democrat on the west side of Los Angeles to raise money in 1988 for Jesse Jackson (see page 765) said "When I want something, I'll have a hard time getting people to pick up the phone, I recognize that, I made the choice," he had a clear enough understanding of how the contract worked and did not work.

When the same Democrat, Stanley Sheinbaum, said, in 1992 (see page 828), "I mean it's no longer a thousand dollars. To get into the act now you've got to give a hundred thousand," he had a clear enough understanding of how the contract worked and did not work. When Jerry Brown, who after eight years as governor of California had become the state party chairman who significantly raised the bar for Democratic fundraising in California, said at the 1992 Democratic convention in Madison Square Garden (see page 807) that the time had arrived to listen to "the people who fight our wars but never come to our receptions," he had a clear enough understanding of how the contract worked and did not work. When one of George W. Bush's lawyers told *The Los Angeles Times* in December 2000 that "if you were in this game, you had to be in Florida," he too had a clear enough understanding of how the contract worked and did not work. "Almost every lobbyist, political organizer, consulting group with ties to the Republicans was represented," a Republican official was quoted by Robert B. Reich, writing on the op-ed page of *The New York Times*, as having said to the same point. "If you ever were or wanted to be a Republican, you were down there."

Such clear understandings among the professionals of both major parties notwithstanding, the fact that the 2000 presidential election in Florida could come down to only a handful of votes would still be popularly presented as evidence that "every vote counts," conclusive proof of the absolute power of the American voter. "Whatever else one might conclude about the events of the past two weeks, they have awakened young people to election politics, to the daily news, and to the importance of the vote," a director of the Vanishing Voter project rather mysteriously concluded from data showing that although the attention level of younger respondents rose during the events in Florida, seventy percent of all Americans, young and old, reported themselves to be "discouraged" by those events and fifty percent to believe that the election had been "unfair to voters." Two weeks after the election, according to the Shorenstein Center's comparison of polling conducted just before the election and that conducted in its immediate aftermath, the number of Americans who answered "None" to the question "How much influence do you think people like you have on what the government does?" had increased from one in ten to one in four.

This "civics lesson" aspect of the thirty-six days that followed the election was much stressed, yet what those days actually demonstrated, from the morning on Day One when the candidate whose brother happened to be governor of Florida lined up the critical Tallahassee law firms until the evening on Day Thirty-five when the Supreme Court decided *Bush* v. *Gore* for the same candidate, was the immateriality of the voter against the raw power of being inside the process. "The Republicans didn't have to hire the big firms, or tie them up," a Gore strategist told *The Washington Post* about what happened on the morning of Day One. "Jeb Bush didn't need to send a note for them to know." About what happened on the evening of Day Thirty-five, Cokie Roberts, on *This Week*, made the case of the permanent political class for order, for continuity, for the perpetuation of the contract that delivered only to itself: "I think people do think it's political but they think that's okay. They expect the court to be political and—and they wanted this election to be over." In the absence of actual evidence to back up this arrestingly constructive reading of what "people" expected or wanted, she offered the rationale then common among those inside the process: "At least now, we are beginning to have that post-election coming together. Period."

The events that followed the November 2000 election were widely interpreted by those inside the process as aberrant, a source of outrage or education (the civics-lesson benefit again) but in any case an improbable random sequence thrown up by chance, in no way predictable and therefore dangerous: a "disaster," a "debacle," a disruption that could lead, in the absence of "closure," or of "that post-election coming together" longed for by Mrs. Roberts and by many others, only to "chaos." Yet the events in question were in many ways not only entirely predictable but entirely familiar: the reactive angers that drove this post-election period were not different in kind from the reactive angers that had driven American politics since the 1960s. Now as before, "the rule of law" was repeatedly invoked, although how a matter as demonstrably lawyered up as the Florida recount could be seen to threaten the rule of law was unclear. Now as before, the principal threat to "the rule of law" was construed to be the court system, which Robert H. Bork had described in *Slouching Towards Gomorrah* as the "enforcement arm" of what he called "the 'intellectual' class," the branch of government "responsible in no small measure for the spread of both radical individualism and radical egalitarianism." Now as before, the prevailing tone, on all sides, was self-righteous, victimized, grandiose; a quite florid instance of what Richard Hofstadter had identified in 1965 as the paranoid style in American politics.

This was all familiar, but the events that followed the 2000 presidential election represented something more than another airing of popular resentments to advance one or another element within the political process. The Democrats had lost that election, according to Al From of the Democratic Leadership Council, because their candidate's "populist" message had failed to resonate with the Democratic target voter, who was "affluent, educated, diverse, suburban, 'wired,' and moderate." That the same adjectives described the Republican target voter was, according to Mr. From, the point itself: the "true story" of the 2000 campaign was that the Republican and Democratic parties had at last achieved "parity," which meant that they were now positioned to split the remaining electorate, those "middle- and upper-middle-class Americans" who would be "the dominant voters of the Information Age." In other words we had reached the zero-sum point toward which the process had been moving, the moment in which the determination of the Republican Party to maximize its traditional low-turnout advantage was perfectly matched by the determination of the Democratic Party to shed any association with its traditional low-income base. "Who cares what every adult thinks," as one Republican strategist had presciently said to *The Washington Post* (see page 920) in 1998. "It's totally not germane to this election."

"Florida," in this light, could be seen as a perfectly legible ideogram of the process itself, and of where that process had taken us: the reduction of a national presidential election to a few hundred voters over which both parties could fight for thirty-six days was the logical imaginative representation of a process that had relentlessly worked, to the end of eliminating known risk factors, to restrict the contest to the smallest possible electorate. Fifty-three percent of voters in the 2000 election, Mr. From noted with what seemed genuine enthusiasm, had ("for the first time in our history") incomes above $50,000. Forty-three percent were suburban. Seventy-four percent had some higher education; forty-two percent had actual college degrees. Seventy percent said that they invested in the stock market. That this was not a demographic profile of the country at large, that half the nation's citizens had only a vassal relationship to the government under which they lived, that the democracy we spoke of spreading throughout the world was now in our own country only an ideality, had come to be seen, against the higher priority of keeping the process in the hands of those who already held it, as facts without application.

INSIDER BASEBALL

October 27, 1988

I

IT OCCURRED TO me during the summer of 1988, in California and Atlanta and New Orleans, in the course of watching first the California primary and then the Democratic and Republican national conventions, that it had not been by accident that the people with whom I had preferred to spend time in high school had, on the whole, hung out in gas stations. They had not run for student body office. They had not gone to Yale or Swarthmore or DePauw, nor had they even applied. They had gotten drafted, gone through basic at Fort Ord. They had knocked up girls, and married them, had begun what they called the first night of the rest of their lives with a midnight drive to Carson City and a five-dollar ceremony performed by a justice of the peace still in his pajamas. They got jobs at the places that had laid off their uncles. They paid their bills or did not pay their bills, made down payments on tract houses, led lives on that social and economic edge referred to, in Washington and among those whose preferred locus is Washington, as "out there." They were never destined to be, in other words, communicants in what we have come to call, when we want to indicate the traditional ways in which power is exchanged and the status quo maintained in the United States, "the process."

"The process today gives everyone a chance to participate," Tom Hayden, by way of explaining "the difference" between 1968 and 1988, said to Bryant Gumbel on NBC at 7:50 A.M. on the day after Jesse Jackson spoke at the 1988 Democratic convention in Atlanta. This was, at a convention that had as its controlling principle the notably nonparticipatory goal of "unity," demonstrably not true, but people inside the process, constituting as they do a self-created and self-referring class, a new kind of managerial elite, tend to speak of the world not necessarily as it is but as they want people out there to believe it is. They tend to prefer the theoretical to the observable, and to dismiss that which might be learned empirically as "anecdotal." They tend to speak

743

a language common in Washington but not specifically shared by the rest of us. They talk about "programs," and "policy," and how to "implement" them or it, about "tradeoffs" and constituencies and positioning the candidate and distancing the candidate, about the "story," and how it will "play."

They speak of a candidate's "performance," by which they usually mean his skill at circumventing questions, not as citizens but as professional insiders, attuned to signals pitched beyond the range of normal hearing. "I hear he did all right this afternoon," they were saying to one another in the press section of the Louisiana Superdome in New Orleans on the evening in August 1988 when Dan Quayle was to be nominated for the vice presidency. "I hear he did all right with Brinkley." By the time the balloons fell that night the narrative had changed: "Quayle, zip," the professionals were saying as they brushed the confetti off their laptops. These were people who spoke of the process as an end in itself, connected only nominally, and vestigially, to the electorate and its possible concerns. "She used to be an issues person but now she's involved in the process," a prominent conservative said to me in New Orleans by way of suggesting why an acquaintance who believed Jack Kemp to be "speaking directly to what people out there want" had nonetheless backed George Bush. "Anything that brings the process closer to the people is all to the good," George Bush had declared in his 1987 autobiography, *Looking Forward*, accepting as given this relatively recent notion that the people and the process need not automatically be on convergent tracks.

When we talk about the process, then, we are talking, increasingly, not about "the democratic process," or the general mechanism affording the citizens of a state a voice in its affairs, but the reverse: a mechanism seen as so specialized that access to it is correctly limited to its own professionals, to those who manage policy and those who report on it, to those who run the polls and those who quote them, to those who ask and those who answer the questions on the Sunday shows, to the media consultants, to the columnists, to the issues advisers, to those who give the off-the-record breakfasts and those who attend them; to that handful of insiders who invent, year in and year out, the narrative of public life. "I didn't realize you were a political junkie," Martin Kaplan, the former *Washington Post* reporter and Mondale speechwriter who was married to Susan Estrich, the manager of the Dukakis campaign, said when I mentioned that I planned to write about the campaign; the assumption here, that the narrative should be not just written only by its own specialists but also legible only to its own specialists, is why, finally, an American presidential campaign raises questions that go so vertiginously to the heart of the structure.

2

What strikes one most vividly about such a campaign is precisely its remoteness from the real life of the country. The figures are well known, and suggest a national indifference usually construed, by those inside the process, as ignorance, or "apathy," in any case a defect not in themselves but in the clay they have been given to mold. Only slightly more than half of those eligible to vote in the United States did vote in the 1984 presidential election. An average 18.5 percent of what Nielsen Media Research calls the "television households" in the United States tuned into network coverage of the 1988 Republican convention in New Orleans, meaning that 81.5 percent did not. An average 20.2 percent of those "television households" tuned into network coverage of the 1988 Democratic convention in Atlanta, meaning that 79.8 percent did not. The decision to tune in or out ran along predictable lines: "The demography is good even if the households are low," a programming executive at Bozell, Jacobs, Kenyon & Eckhardt told *The New York Times* in July 1988 about the agency's decision to buy "campaign event" time for Merrill Lynch on both CBS and CNN. "The ratings are about nine percent off 1984," an NBC marketing executive allowed, again to *The New York Times*, "but the upscale target audience is there."

When I read this piece I recalled standing, the day before the 1988 California primary, in a dusty central California schoolyard to which the leading Democratic candidate had come to speak one more time about what kind of president he wanted to be. The crowd was listless, restless. There were gray thunderclouds overhead. A little rain fell. "We welcome you to Silicon Valley," an official had said by way of greeting the candidate, but this was not in fact Silicon Valley: this was San Jose, and a part of San Jose particularly untouched by technological prosperity, a neighborhood in which the lowering of two-toned Impalas remained a central activity. "I want to be a candidate who brings people together," the candidate was saying at the exact moment a man began shouldering his way past me and through a group of women with children in their arms. This was not a solid citizen, not a member of the upscale target audience. This was a man wearing a down vest and a camouflage hat, a man with a definite little glitter in his eyes, a member not of the 18.5 percent and not of the 20.2 percent but of the 81.5 percent, the 79.8. "I've got to see the next president," he muttered repeatedly. "I've got something to tell him."

"... Because that's what this party is all about," the candidate said.

"Where is he?" the man said, confused. "Who is he?"

"Get lost," someone said.

"... Because that's what this country is all about," the candidate said.

Here we had the last true conflict of cultures in America, that between the empirical and the theoretical. On the empirical evidence this country was about two-toned Impalas and people with camouflage hats and a little glitter in their eyes, but this had not been, among people inclined to the theoretical, the preferred assessment. Nor had it even been, despite the fact that we had all stood together on the same dusty asphalt, under the same plane trees, the general assessment: this was how Joe Klein, writing a few weeks later in *New York* magazine, had described those last days before the California primary:

> Breezing across California on his way to the nomination last week, Michael Dukakis crossed a curious American threshold.... The crowds were larger, more excited now; they seemed to be searching for reasons to love him. They cheered eagerly, almost without provocation. People reached out to touch him—not to shake hands, just to touch him....Dukakis seemed to be making an almost subliminal passage in the public mind: he was becoming presidential.

Those June days in 1988 during which Michael Dukakis did or did not cross a curious American threshold had in fact been instructive. The day that ended in the schoolyard in San Jose had at first seemed, given that it was the day before the California primary, underscheduled, pointless, three essentially meaningless events separated by plane flights. At Taft High School in Woodland Hills that morning there had been little girls waving red and gold pom-poms in front of the cameras. "Hold that tiger," the band had played. "Dream … maker," the choir had crooned. "Governor Dukakis … this is … Taft High," the student body president had said. "I understand that this is the first time a presidential candidate has come to Taft High," Governor Dukakis had said. "Is there any doubt … under those circumstances … who you should support?"

"Jackson," a group of Chicano boys on the back sidewalk shouted in unison.

"That's what it's all about," Governor Dukakis had said, and "health care," and "good teachers and good teaching."

This event had been abandoned, and another materialized: a lunchtime "rally" in a downtown San Diego office plaza through which many people were passing on their way to lunch, a borrowed crowd but a less than attentive one. The cameras focused on the balloons. The sound techs picked up "La Bamba." "We're going to take child-support enforcement seriously in this country," Governor Dukakis had said, and "tough drug enforcement here and abroad." "Tough choices," he had said, and "we're going to make teaching a valued profession in this country."

Nothing said in any venue that day had seemed to have much connection with anybody listening ("I want to work with you and with working people all over this country," the candidate had said in the downtown San Diego office plaza, but people who work in offices in downtown San Diego do not think of themselves as "working people"), and late that afternoon, on the bus to the San Jose airport, I had asked a reporter who had traveled through the spring with the various campaigns (among those who moved from plane to plane it was agreed, by June, that the Bush plane had the worst access to the candidate and the best food, that the Dukakis plane had average access and average food, and that the Jackson plane had full access and no time to eat) if the candidate's appearances that day did not seem a little off the point.

"Not really," the reporter said. "He covered three major markets."

Among those who traveled regularly with the campaigns, in other words, it was taken for granted that these "events" they were covering, and on which they were in fact filing, were not merely meaningless but deliberately so: occasions in which film could be shot and no mistakes made ("They hope he won't make any mistakes," the NBC correspondent covering George Bush kept saying the evening of the September 25, 1988, debate at Wake Forest College, and, an hour and a half later, "He didn't make any big mistakes"), events designed only to provide settings for those unpaid television spots which in this case were appearing, even as we spoke, on the local news in California's three major media markets. "On the fishing trip, there was no way for the television crews to get videotapes out," *The Los Angeles Times* noted a few weeks later in a piece about how "poorly designed and executed events" had interfered with coverage of a Bush campaign "environmental" swing through the Pacific Northwest. "At the lumber mill, Bush's advance team arranged camera angles so poorly that in one setup only his legs could get on camera." A Bush adviser had been quoted: "There is no reason for camera angles not being provided for. We're going to sit down and talk about these things at length."

Any traveling campaign, then, was a set, moved at considerable expense from location to location. The employer of each reporter on the Dukakis plane the day before the California primary was billed, for a total flying time of under three hours, $1,129.51; the billing to each reporter who happened, on the morning during the Democratic convention in Atlanta when Michael Dukakis and Lloyd Bentsen met with Jesse Jackson, to ride along on the Dukakis bus from the Hyatt Regency to the World Congress Center, a distance of perhaps ten blocks, was $217.18. There was the hierarchy of the set: there were actors, there were directors, there were script supervisors, there were grips. There was the isolation of the set, and the arrogance, the contempt for outsiders. I recall pink-cheeked young aides on the Dukakis campaign referring to themselves, innocent of irony and so of history, as "the best and the brightest." On the morning after the Wake Forest debate, Michael Oreskes of *The New York Times* gave us this memorable account of Bush aides crossing the Wake Forest campus:

> The Bush campaign measured exactly how long it
> would take its spokesmen to walk briskly from the room in

which they were watching the debate to the center where reporters were filing their articles. The answer was three and a half minutes—too long for Mr. Bush's strategists, Lee Atwater, Robert Teeter, and Mr. Darman. They ran the course instead as young aides cleared students and other onlookers from their path.

There was also the tedium of the set: the time spent waiting for the shots to be set up, the time spent waiting for the bus to join the motorcade, the time spent waiting for telephones on which to file, the time spent waiting for the Secret Service ("the agents," they were called on the traveling campaigns, never the Secret Service, just "the agents," or "this detail," or "this rotation") to sweep the plane. It was a routine that encouraged a certain passivity. There was the plane, or the bus, and one got on it. There was the schedule, and one followed it. There was time to file, or there was not. "We should have had a page-one story," a *Boston Globe* reporter complained to *The Los Angeles Times* after the Bush campaign had failed to provide the advance text of a Seattle "environment" speech scheduled to end only twenty minutes before the departure of the plane for California. "There are times when you sit up and moan, 'Where is Michael Deaver when you need him,'" an ABC producer said to the *Times* on this point.

A final victory, for the staff and the press on a traveling campaign, would mean not a new production but only a new location: the particular setups and shots of the campaign day (the walk on the beach, the meet-and-greet at the housing project) would dissolve imperceptibly, isolation and arrogance and tedium intact, into the South Lawns, the Oval Office signings, the arrivals and departures of the administration day. There would still be the "young aides." There would still be the "onlookers" to be cleared from the path. Another location, another stand-up: "We already shot a tarmac departure," they say on the campaign planes. "This schedule has two Rose Gardens," they say in the White House press room. Ronald Reagan, when asked by David Frost how his life in the Oval Office had differed from his expectation of it, said this: "I was surprised at how familiar the whole routine was—the fact that the night before I would get a schedule telling me what I'm going to do all day the next day and so forth."

3

American reporters "like" covering a presidential campaign (it gets them out on the road, it has balloons, it has music, it is viewed as a big story, one that leads to the respect of one's peers, to the Sunday shows, to lecture fees and often to Washington), which is why there has developed among those who do it so arresting an enthusiasm for overlooking the contradictions inherent in reporting that which occurs only in order to be reported. They are willing, in exchange for "access," to transmit the images their sources wish transmitted. They are even willing, in exchange for certain colorful details around which a "reconstruction" can be built (the "kitchen table" at which the Dukakis campaign was said to have conferred on the night Lloyd Bentsen was added to the 1988 Democratic ticket, the "slips of paper" on which key members of the 1988 Bush campaign, aboard Air Force Two on their way to the Republican convention in New Orleans, were said to have written their choices for vice president), to present these images not as a story the campaign wants told but as fact. This was *Time*, reporting from New Orleans on George Bush's reaction to criticism of Dan Quayle, his chosen running mate:

> Bush never wavered in support of the man he had lifted so high. "How's Danny doing," he asked several times. But the Vice President never felt the compulsion to question Quayle face-to-face. The awkward interrogation was left to Baker. Around noon, Quayle grew restive about answering further questions. "Let's go," he urged, but Baker pressed to know more. By early afternoon, the mood began to brighten in the Bush bunker. There were no new revelations: the media hurricane had for the moment blown over.

"Appeal to the media by exposing the [Bush campaign's] heavy-handed spin-doctoring," William Safire advised the Dukakis campaign. "We hate to be seen being manipulated." This was Sandy Grady, reporting from Atlanta and the Dukakis campaign:

> Ten minutes before he was to face the biggest audience of his life, Michael Dukakis got a hug from his 84-year-old

mother, Euterpe, who chided him, "You'd better be good, Michael." Dukakis grinned and said, "I'll do my best, Ma."

"Periodically," *The New York Times* reported in March 1988, "Martin Plissner, the political editor of CBS News, and Susan Morrison, a television producer and former political aide, organize gatherings of the politically connected at their house in Washington. At such parties, they organize secret ballots asking the assembled experts who will win.... By November 1, 1987, the results of Mr. Dole's organizing efforts were clear in a new Plissner-Morrison poll." The symbiosis here was complete, and the only outsider was the increasingly hypothetical voter, who was seen as responsive not to actual issues but to their adroit presentation: "At the moment the Republican message is simpler and more clear than ours," the Democratic chairman for California, Peter Kelly, said to *The Los Angeles Times* in August 1988, complaining, on the matter of what was called the Pledge of Allegiance issue, not that it was a false issue but that Bush had seized the initiative, or "the symbolism."

"Bush Gaining in Battle of TV Images," *The Washington Post* headlined a front-page story in September 1988, and quoted Jeff Greenfield, the ABC News political reporter: "George Bush is almost always outdoors, coatless, sometimes with his sleeves rolled up, and looks ebullient and Happy Warrior-ish. Mike Dukakis is almost always indoors, with his jacket on, and almost always behind a lectern." According to the same week's issue of *Newsweek*, the Bush campaign, which had the superior gift for getting film shot in "dramatic settings—like Boston Harbor," was winning "the all-important battle of the backdrops." A CBS producer covering the Dukakis campaign was quoted complaining about an occasion when Governor Dukakis, speaking to students on a California beach, had faced the students instead of the camera. "The only reason Dukakis was on the beach was to get his picture taken," the producer had said. "So you might as well see his face." Pictures, *Newsweek* had concluded, "often speak louder than words."

This "battle of the backdrops" story appeared on page 24 of the *Newsweek* dated September 12, 1988. On page 23 of the same issue there appeared, as illustrations for the lead National Affairs story ("Getting Down and Dirty: As the mudslinging campaign moves into full gear, Bush stays on the offensive—and Dukakis

JOAN DIDION

calls back his main street-fighting man"), two half-page color photographs, one of each candidate, which seemed designed to address the very concerns expressed on page 24 and in the *Post*. The photograph of George Bush showed him indoors, behind a lectern, with his jacket on. That of Michael Dukakis showed him outdoors, coatless, sleeves rolled up, looking ebullient, about to throw a baseball on an airport tarmac: something had been learned from Jeff Greenfield, or something had been told to Jeff Greenfield. "We talk to the press, and things take on a life of their own," Mark Siegel, a Democratic political consultant, said to Elizabeth Drew.

About this baseball on the tarmac. On the day that Michael Dukakis appeared at the high school in Woodland Hills and at the office plaza in San Diego and in the schoolyard in San Jose, there was, although it did not appear on the schedule, a fourth event, what was referred to among the television crews as a "tarmac arrival with ball tossing." This event had taken place in late morning, on the tarmac at the San Diego airport, just after the campaign's chartered 737 had rolled to a stop and the candidate had emerged. There had been a moment of hesitation, or decision. Then baseball mitts had been produced, and Jack Weeks, the traveling press secretary, had tossed a ball to the candidate. The candidate had tossed the ball back. The rest of us had stood in the sun and given this our full attention: some forty adults standing on a tarmac watching a diminutive figure in shirtsleeves and a red tie toss a ball, undeflected even by the arrival of an Alaska Airlines 767, to his press secretary.

"Just a regular guy," one of the cameramen had said, his inflection that of the "union official" who confided, in an early Dukakis commercial aimed at blue-collar voters, that he had known "Mike" a long time, and backed him despite his not being "your shot-and-beer kind of guy."

"I'd say he was a regular guy," another cameraman had said. "Definitely."

"I'd sit around with him," the first cameraman said.

Kara Dukakis, one of the candidate's daughters, had at that moment emerged from the 737.

"You'd have a beer with him?"

Jack Weeks had tossed the ball to Kara Dukakis.

"I'd have a beer with him."

Kara Dukakis had tossed the ball to her father. Her father had caught the ball and tossed it back to her.

"OK," one of the cameramen had said. "We got the daughter. Nice. That's enough. Nice."

The CNN producer then on the campaign told me, later in the day, that the first recorded ball tossing on the Dukakis campaign had been outside a bowling alley somewhere in Ohio. CNN had shot it. When the campaign realized that only one camera had it, they restaged it.

"We have a lot of things like the ball tossing," the producer said. "We have the Greek dancing, for example."

I asked if she still bothered to shoot it.

"I get it," she said, "but I don't call in anymore and say, 'Hey, hold it, I've got him dancing.'"

This sounded about right (the candidate might, after all, bean a citizen during the ball tossing, and CNN would need film), and not until I read Joe Klein's version of those days in California did it occur to me that this eerily contrived moment on the tarmac at San Diego could become, at least provisionally, history. "The Duke seemed downright jaunty," Joe Klein reported. "He tossed a baseball with aides. He was flagrantly multilingual. He danced Greek dances...." In the July 25, 1988, issue of *U.S. News & World Report*, Michael Kramer opened his cover story ("Is Dukakis Tough Enough?") with a more developed version of the ball tossing:

> The thermometer read 101 degrees, but the locals guessed 115 on the broiling airport tarmac in Phoenix. After all, it was under a noonday sun in the desert that Michael Dukakis was indulging his truly favorite campaign ritual—a game of catch with his aide Jack Weeks. "These days," he has said, "throwing the ball around when we land somewhere is about the only exercise I get." For 16 minutes, Dukakis shagged flies and threw strikes. Halfway through, he rolled up his sleeves, but he never loosened his tie. Finally, mercifully, it was over and time to pitch the obvious tongue-in-cheek question: "Governor, what does throwing a ball around in this heat say about your men-

tal stability?" Without missing a beat, and without a trace of a smile, Dukakis echoed a sentiment he has articulated repeatedly in recent months: "What it means is that I'm tough."

Nor was this the last word. On July 31, 1988, in *The Washington Post,* David S. Broder, who had also been with the Dukakis campaign in Phoenix, gave us a third, and, by virtue of his seniority in the process, perhaps the official version of the ball tossing:

> Dukakis called out to Jack Weeks, the handsome, curly-haired Welshman who goodnaturedly shepherds us wayward pressmen through the daily vagaries of the campaign schedule. Weeks dutifully produced two gloves and a baseball, and there on the tarmac, with its surface temperature just below the boiling point, the governor loosened up his arm and got the kinks out of his back by tossing a couple hundred 90-foot pegs to Weeks.

What we had in the tarmac arrival with ball tossing, then, was an understanding: a repeated moment witnessed by many people, all of whom believed it to be a setup and yet most of whom believed that only an outsider, only someone too "naive" to know the rules of the game, would so describe it.

4

The narrative is made up of many such understandings, tacit agreements, small and large, to overlook the observable in the interests of obtaining a dramatic story line. It was understood, for example, that the first night of the 1988 Republican convention in New Orleans should be for Ronald Reagan "the last hurrah." "Reagan electrifies GOP" was the headline the next morning on the front page of *New York Newsday;* in fact the Reagan appearance, which was rhetorically pitched not to a live audience but to the more intimate demands of the camera, was, inside the Superdome, barely registered. It was understood, similarly, that Michael Dukakis's acceptance speech on the last night of the 1988 Democratic convention in Atlanta should be the occasion on which his "passion," or "leadership," emerged. "Could the no-nonsense nominee reach within himself to discover the language of leadership?" *Time* had asked. "Could he go beyond the pedestrian promise of 'good jobs at good wages' to give voice to a new Democratic vision?"

The correct answer, since the forward flow of the story here demanded the appearance of a genuine contender (a contender who could be seventeen points "up," so that George Bush could be seventeen points "down," a position from which he could rise to "claim" his own convention), was yes: "The best speech of his life," David S. Broder reported. Sandy Grady found it "superb," evoking "Kennedyesque echoes" and showing "unexpected craft and fire." *Newsweek* had witnessed Michael Dukakis "electrifying the convention with his intensely personal acceptance speech." In fact the convention that evening had been electrified, not by the speech, which was the same series of nonsequential clauses Governor Dukakis had employed during the primary campaign ("My friends … son of immigrants … good jobs at good wages … make teaching a valued and honored profession … it's what the Democratic Party is all about"), but because the floor had been darkened, swept with laser beams, and flooded with "Coming to America," played at concert volume with the bass turned up.

It is understood that this invented narrative will turn on certain familiar elements. There is the continuing story line of the "horse race," the reliable daily drama of one candidate falling behind as another pulls ahead. There is the surprise of the new poll, the glamour of the one-on-one colloquy on the midnight plane, a plot point (the nation sleeps while the candidate and his confidant hammer out its fate) pioneered by Theodore H. White. There is the abiding if unexamined faith in the campaign as personal odyssey, and in the spiritual benefits accruing to those who undertake it. There is, in the presented history of the candidate, the crucible event, the day that "changed the life." Robert Dole's life was understood to have changed when he was injured in Italy in 1945. George Bush's life is understood to have changed when he and his wife decided to "get out and make it on our own" (his words, or those of his speechwriter, Peggy Noonan, from the "lived the dream" acceptance speech at the 1988 convention, suggesting action, shirtsleeves, privilege cast aside) in west Texas. For Bruce Babbitt, "the dam just kind of broke" during a student summer in Bolivia. For Michael Dukakis, the dam was understood to have broken not during his own student summer in South America, in his case Peru, but after his 1978 defeat in Massachusetts: his tragic flaw, we read repeatedly during the 1988 campaign, was neither his evident sulkiness at losing that earlier election nor what many saw later as a rather dissociated self-satisfaction ("We're two people very proud of what we've done," he said on NBC in Atlanta, falling into a favorite speech pattern, "very proud of each other, actually ... and very proud that a couple of guys named Dukakis and Jackson have come this far"), but the more attractive "hubris."

The narrative requires broad strokes. Michael Dukakis was physically small, and had associations with Harvard, which suggested that he could be cast as an "intellectual"; the "immigrant factor," on the other hand, could make him tough (as in "What it means is that I'm tough"), a "street-fighter." "He's cool, shrewd, and still trying to prove he's tough," the July 25, 1988, cover of *U.S. News & World Report* said about Dukakis. "Toughness is what it's all about," one of his advisers was quoted as having said. "People need to feel that a candidate is tough enough to be president. It is the threshold perception." George Bush had presented a more tortured narrative problem. The tellers of the story had not understood, or had not responded to, the essential Bush style, which was complex, ironic, the diffident edge of the Northeastern elite. This was what was at first identified as "the wimp factor," which was replaced not by a more complicated view of the personality but by its reverse: George Bush was by late August of 1988 no longer a "wimp" but someone who had "thrown it over," "struck out" to make his own way: no longer a product of the effete Northeast but someone who had thrived in Texas, and was therefore "tough enough to be president."

That George Bush might have thrived in Texas not in spite of being but precisely because he was a member of the Northeastern elite was a shading that had no part in the narrative: "He was considered back at that time one of the most charismatic people ever elected to public office in the history of Texas," Congressman

Bill Archer of Houston said. "That charisma, people talked about it over and over again." People talked about it, probably, because Andover and Yale and the inheritable tax avoidance they suggested were, during the years George Bush lived in Texas, the exact ideals toward which the Houston and Dallas establishment aspired, but the narrative called for a less ambiguous version: "Lived in a little shotgun house, one room for the three of us," as Bush, or Peggy Noonan, had put it in the celebrated no-subject-pronoun cadences of the "lived the dream" acceptance speech. "Worked in the oil business, started my own…. Moved from the shotgun to a duplex apartment to a house. Lived the dream—high school football on Friday night, Little League, neighborhood barbecue … pushing into unknown territory with kids and a dog and a car…."

All stories, of course, depend for their popular interest upon the invention of personality, or "character," but in the political narrative, designed as it is to maintain the illusion of consensus by obscuring rather than addressing actual issues, this invention served a further purpose. It was by 1988 generally if unspecifically agreed that the United States faced certain social and economic realities that, if not intractable, did not entirely lend themselves to the kinds of policy fixes that people who run for elected office, on whatever ticket, were likely to undertake. We had not yet accommodated the industrialization of parts of the third world. We had not yet adjusted to the economic realignment of a world in which the United States was no longer the principal catalyst for change. "We really are in an age of transition," Brent Scowcroft, Bush's leading foreign policy adviser, told Robert Scheer of *The Los Angeles Times* in the fall of 1988, "from a post-war world where the Soviets were the enemy, where the United States was a superpower and trying to build up both its allies and its former enemies and help the third world transition to independence. That whole world and all of those things are coming to an end or have ended, and we are now entering a new and different world that will be complex and much less unambiguous than the old one."

What continued to dominate the rhetoric of the 1988 campaign, however, was not this awareness of a new and different world but nostalgia for an old one, and coded assurance that any evidence of ambiguity or change, of what George Bush called

757

the "deterioration of values," would be summarily dealt with by increased social control. It was not by accident that the word "enforcement," devoid of any apparent awareness that it had been tried before, played a large role in the language of both the Bush and Dukakis campaigns. Dukakis had promised, by way of achieving his goal of "no safe haven for dope dealers and drug profits anywhere on this earth," to "double the number" of Drug Enforcement Administration agents, not a promising approach. George Bush had repeatedly promised his support for the death penalty, and for both the Pledge of Allegiance and prayer, or "moments of silence," in public schools. "We've got to change this entire culture," he said in the Wake Forest debate; polling indicated that the electorate wanted "change," and this wish for change had been translated, by both campaigns, into the wish for a "change back," a regression to the "gentler America" of which George Bush repeatedly spoke.

To the extent that there was a "difference" between the candidates, the difference lay in just where on the time scale this "gentler America" could be found. The Dukakis campaign was oriented to "programs," and the programs it proposed were similar to those that had worked (the encouragement of private-sector involvement in low-cost housing, say) in the boom years after World War II. The Bush campaign was oriented to "values," and the values to which it referred were those not of a post-war but of a prewar America. In neither case did "ideas" play a part: "This election isn't about ideology, it's about competence," Michael Dukakis had said in Atlanta. "First and foremost, it's a choice between two persons," one of his senior advisers, Thomas Kiley, had told *The Wall Street Journal*. "What it comes down to, after all the shouting and the cheers, is the man at the desk," George Bush had said in New Orleans. In other words, what it "came down to," what it was "about," what was wrong or right with America, was not an historical shift largely unaffected by the actions of individual citizens but "character," and if "character" could be seen to count, then every citizen— since everyone was a judge of character, an expert in the field of personality—could be seen to count. This notion, that the citizen's choice among determinedly centrist candidates makes a "difference," is in fact the narrative's most central element, and its most fictive.

5

The Democratic National Convention of 1968, during which the process was put to a popular vote on the streets of Chicago and after which it was decided that what had occurred could not be allowed to recur, is generally agreed to have prompted the increased emphasis on primaries, and the concomitant increased coverage of those primaries, that led to the end of the national party convention as a more than ceremonial occasion. Early in 1987, as the primary campaigns got underway for the 1988 election, David S. Broder, in *The Washington Post,* offered this compelling analysis of the power these "reforms" in the nominating procedure had vested not in the party leadership, which is where this power of choice ultimately resides, but in "the existing communications system," by which he meant the press, or the medium through which the party leadership sells its choice:

> Once the campaign explodes to 18 states, as it will the day after New Hampshire, when the focus shifts to a super-primary across the nation, the existing communications system simply will not accommodate more than two or three candidates in each party. Neither the television networks, nor the newspapers nor magazines, have the resources of people, space and time to describe and analyze the dynamics of two simultaneous half-national elections among Republicans and Democrats. That task is simply beyond us. Since we cannot reduce the number of states voting on Super Tuesday, we have to reduce the number of candidates treated as serious contenders. These news judgments will be arbitrary—but not subject to appeal. Those who finish first or second in Iowa and New Hampshire will get tickets from the mass media to play in the next big round. Those who don't, won't. A minor exception may be made for the two reverends, Jesse L. Jackson and Marion G. (Pat) Robertson, who have their own church-based communications and support networks and are less dependent on mass-media attention. But no one else.

By the time the existing communications network set itself up in July and August 1988 in Atlanta and New Orleans, the priorities were clear. "NOTICE NOTICE NOTICE," read the typed note given to some print reporters when they picked up their credentials in Atlanta. "Because the Democratic National Convention Committee permitted the electronic media to exceed specifications for their broadcast booths, your assigned seat's sight line to the podium and the convention floor was obliterated." The network's skyboxes, in other words, had been built in front of the sections originally assigned to the periodical press. "This is a place that was chosen to be, for all intents and purposes, a large TV studio, to be able to project our message to the American people and a national audience," Paul Kirk, the chairman of the Democratic National Committee, said by way of explaining why the podium and the skyboxes had so reduced the size of the Omni Coliseum in Atlanta that some thousand delegates and alternates had been, on the evening Jesse Jackson spoke, locked out. Mayor Andrew Young of Atlanta apologized for the lockout, but said that it would be the same on nights to follow: "The one hundred and fifty million people in the country who are going to vote have got to be our major target." Still, convention delegates were seen to have a real role: "The folks in the hall are so important to how it looks," Lane Venardos, senior producer in charge of convention coverage for CBS News, said to *The New York Times* about the Republican convention. The delegates, in other words, were the dress extras who could make the set seem authentic.

During those eight summer evenings in 1988, four in Atlanta and four in New Orleans, when roughly eighty percent of the television sets "out there" were tuned somewhere else, the entire attention of those inside the process was directed toward the invention of this story in which they themselves were the principal players, and for which they themselves were the principal audience. The great arenas in which the conventions were held became self-contained worlds, constantly transmitting their own images back to themselves, connected by skywalks to interchangeable structures composed not of floors but of "levels," mysteriously separated by fountains and glass elevators and escalators that did not quite connect. In the Louisiana Superdome in New Orleans as in the Omni Coliseum in Atlanta, the grids of lights blazed and dimmed hypnotically. Men with rifles patrolled the high catwalks. The nets packed with balloons swung gently overhead, poised for that instant known as "the money shot," the moment, or "window," when everything was working and no network had cut to a commercial. Minicams trawled the floor, fishing in Atlanta for Rob Lowe, in New Orleans for Donald Trump. In the NBC skybox Tom Brokaw floated over the floor, adjusting his tie, putting on his jacket, leaning to speak to John Chancellor. In the CNN skybox Mary Alice Williams sat bathed in white light, the blond madonna of the skyboxes. On the television screens in the press section the images reappeared, but from another angle: Tom Brokaw and Mary Alice Williams again, broadcasting not just above us but also to us, the circle closed.

At the end of prime time, when the skyboxes went dark, the action moved across the skywalks and into the levels, into the lobbies, into one or another Hyatt or Marriott or Hilton or Westin. In the portage from lobby to lobby, level to level, the same people kept materializing, in slightly altered roles. On a level of the Hyatt in Atlanta I saw Ann Lewis in her role as a Jackson adviser. On a level of the Hyatt in New Orleans I saw Ann Lewis in her role as a correspondent for *Ms*. Some pictures were vivid: "I've been around this process a while, and one thing I've noticed, it's the people who write the checks who get treated as if they have a certain amount of power," I recall Nadine Hack, the chairman of New York fundraising for Dukakis, saying in a suite at the Hyatt in Atlanta: here was a willowy woman with long blond hair standing barefoot on a table and explaining to those present how they could buy into the action. "The great thing about those evenings was you could even see Michael Harrington there," I recall Richard Viguerie saying to me at a party in New Orleans: here was the man who managed the action for the American right sounding wishful about evenings he and I had spent together in the early 1960s at the Washington Square apartment of a mutual friend, a woman whose evenings had been at the time a kind of salon for the political edges.

There was in Atlanta in 1988, according to the Democratic National Committee, "twice the media presence" that there had been at the 1984 convention. There were in New Orleans "media work-spaces" assigned not only to 117 newspapers and news services and to the American television and radio industry at full strength but to fifty-two foreign networks. On every corner one turned in the French Quarter someone was doing a standup. There were telephone numbers to be called for quotes: "Republican State and Local Officials," or "Pat Robertson Campaign," or "Richard Wirthlin, Reagan's Pollster." Newspapers came with teams of thirty, forty, fifty. In every lobby there were stacks of fresh newspapers, *The Atlanta Constitution, The New Orleans Times-Picayune, The Washington Post, The Miami Herald, The Los Angeles Times*. In Atlanta these papers were collected in bins and "recycled": made into thirty thousand posters, which were in turn distributed to the press in New Orleans.

This perfect recycling tended to present itself, in the narcosis of the event, as a model for the rest: like American political life itself, and like the printed and transmitted images on which that life depended, this was a world with no half-life. It was understood that what was said here would go on the wire and vanish. Garrison Keillor and his cute kids would vanish. Ann Richards and her peppery ripostes would vanish. Phyllis Schlafly and Olympia Snowe would vanish. All the opinions and all the rumors and all the housemaid Spanish spoken in both Atlanta and New Orleans would vanish, and all that would remain would be the huge arenas themselves, the arenas and the lobbies and the levels and the skywalks to which they connected, the agora, the symbolic marketplace in which the narrative was not only written but immediately, efficiently, entirely, consumed.

6

A certain time lag exists between this world of the arenas and the world as we know it. One evening in New York between the Democratic and Republican conventions I happened to go down to Lafayette Street, to the Public Theater, to look at clips from documentaries on which the English-born filmmaker Richard Leacock had worked during his fifty years in America. We saw folk singers in Virginia in 1941 and oil riggers in Louisiana in 1946 (this was *Louisiana Story,* which Leacock had shot for Robert Flaherty) and tent performers in the Corn Belt in 1954; we saw Eddy Sachs preparing for the Indianapolis 500 in 1960 and Piri Thomas in Spanish Harlem in 1961. We saw parades, we saw baton twirlers. We saw quints in South Dakota in 1963. There on the screen in the Public Theater that night were images and attitudes from an America that had largely vanished, and what was striking was this: these were the very images and attitudes on which "the campaign" was predicated.

That "unknown territory" into which George Bush had pushed "with kids and a dog and a car" had existed in this vanished America, and had long since been subdivided, cut up for those tract houses on which the people who were not part of the process had made down payments. Michael Dukakis's "snowblower," and both the amusing frugality and the admirable husbandry of resources it was meant to suggest, derived from some half-remembered idea of what citizens of this vanished America had found amusing or admirable. "The Pledge" was an issue that referred back to that world. "A drug-free America" had perhaps seemed in that world an achievable ideal. I recall listening in Atlanta to Madeleine Albright, at that time Dukakis's foreign-policy adviser, as she conjured up, in the course of arguing against a "no first use" minority plank in the Democratic platform, a scenario in which "Soviet forces overrun Europe" and the United States has, by promising no first use of nuclear weapons, crippled its ability to act: she was talking about a world that had not turned since 1948. What was at work here seemed on the one hand a grave, although in many ways a comfortable, miscalculation of what people in America might have as their deepest concerns in 1988; it seemed on the other hand just another understanding, another of those agreements to overlook the observable.

It was into this sedative fantasy of a fixable imperial America that Jesse Jackson rode, on a Trailways bus. "You've never heard a sense of panic sweep the party as it has in the past few days," David Garth had told *The New York Times* during those perilous spring weeks in 1988 when there seemed a real possibility that a black candidate with no experience in elected office, a candidate believed to be so profoundly unelectable that he could take the entire Democratic Party down with him, might go to Atlanta with more delegates than any other Democratic candidate. "The party is up against an extraordinary endgame," the pollster Paul Maslin had said. "I don't know where this leaves us," Robert S. Strauss had said. One uncommitted super-delegate, *The New York Times* had reported, "said the Dukakis campaign changed its message since Mr. Dukakis lost the Illinois primary. Mr. Dukakis is no longer the candidate of 'inevitability' but the candidate of order, he said. 'They're not doing the train's leaving the station and you better be on it routine anymore,' this official said. 'They're now saying that the station's about to be blown up by terrorists and we're the only ones who can defuse the bomb.'"

The threat, or the possibility, presented by Jesse Jackson, the "historic" (as people liked to say after it became certain he would not have the numbers) part of his candidacy, derived from something other than the fact that he was black, a circumstance that had before been and could again be compartmentalized, segregated out. For example: "Next week, when we start doing our black media stuff, Jesse Jackson needs to be on the air in the black community on our behalf," Donna Brazile of the Dukakis campaign said to *The New York Times* in September 1988 by way of emphasizing how much the Dukakis campaign "sought to make peace" with Jackson. "Black," in other words, could be useful, and even a moral force, a way for white Americans to attain more perfect attitudes: "How moving it is, and how important, to see a black candidate meet and overcome the racism that lurks in virtually all of us white Americans," Anthony Lewis had noted in a March 1988 column explaining why the notion that Jesse Jackson could win was nonetheless "a romantic delusion" of the kind that had "repeatedly undermined" the Democratic Party. "You look at what Jesse Jackson has done, you have to wonder what a Tom Bradley of Los Angeles could have done, what an Andy Young of Atlanta could have done," I heard someone say on one of the Sunday shows after the Jackson campaign had entered its "historic," or in the candidate's word its "endless," phase.

"Black," by itself and in the right context—the right context being a reasonable constituency composed exclusively of blacks and supportive liberal whites—could be accommodated by the process. Something less traditional was at work in the 1988 Jackson candidacy. I recall having dinner, the weekend before the California primary, at the Pebble Beach house of the chairman of a large American corporation. There were sixteen people at the table, all white, all well off, all well dressed, all well educated, all socially conservative. During the course of the evening it came to my attention that six of the sixteen, or every one of the registered

Democrats present, intended to vote on Tuesday for Jesse Jackson. Their reasons were unspecific, but definite. "I heard him, he didn't sound like a politician," one said. "He's talking about right now," another said. "You get outside the gate here, take a look around, you have to know we've got some problems, and he's talking about them."

What made the 1988 Jackson candidacy a bomb that had to be defused, then, was not that blacks were supporting a black candidate, but that significant numbers of whites were supporting—not only supporting but in many cases overcoming deep emotional and economic conflicts of their own in order to support—a candidate who was attractive to them not because of but in spite of the fact that he was black, a candidate whose most potent attraction was that he "didn't sound like a politician." "Character" seemed not to be, among these voters, the point-of-sale issue the narrative made it out to be: a number of white Jackson supporters to whom I talked would quite serenely describe their candidate as "a con man," or even, in George Bush's phrase, as "a hustler." "And yet…," they would say. What "and yet" turned out to mean, almost without variation, was that they were willing to walk off the edge of the known political map for a candidate who was running against, as he repeatedly said, "politics as usual," against what he called "consensualist centrist politics"; against what had come to be the very premise of the process, the notion that the winning and maintaining of public office warranted the invention of a public narrative based at no point on observable reality.

In other words they were not idealists, these white Jackson voters, but empiricists. By the time Jesse Jackson got to California, where he would eventually win twenty-five percent of the entire white vote and forty-nine percent of the total vote from voters between the demographically key ages of thirty to forty-four, the idealists had rallied behind the sole surviving alternative, who was, accordingly, just then being declared "presidential." In Los Angeles, during May and early June 1988, those Democrats who had not fallen into line behind Michael Dukakis were described as "self-indulgent," or as "immature"; they were even described, in a dispiriting phrase that prefigured the tenor of the campaign to come, as "issues wimps." I recall talking to a rich and politically well-connected Californian who had been, during the primary season there, virtually the only Democrat on the famously liberal west side of Los Angeles who was backing Jackson. He said that he could afford "the luxury of being more interested in issues than in process," but that he would pay for it: "When I want something, I'll have a hard time getting people to pick up the phone. I recognize that. I made the choice."

7

On the June night in 1988 when Michael Dukakis was declared the winner of the California Democratic primary, and the bomb officially defused, there took place in the Crystal Room of the Biltmore Hotel in downtown Los Angeles a "victory party" that was less a celebration than a ratification by the professionals, a ritual convergence of those California Democrats for whom the phones would continue to get picked up. Charles Manatt was there. John Emerson and Charles Palmer were there. John Van de Kamp was there. Leo McCarthy was there. Robert Shrum was there. All the custom-made suits and monogrammed shirts in Los Angeles that night were there, met in the wide corridors of the Biltmore to murmur assurances to one another. The ballroom had been cordoned as if to repel late invaders, roped off in such a way that once the Secret Service, the traveling press, the local press, the visiting national press, the staff, and the candidate himself had assembled, there would be room for only a controllable handful of celebrants, over whom the cameras would dutifully pan.

In fact the actual "celebrants" that evening were not at the Biltmore at all, but a few blocks away at the Los Angeles Hilton, dancing under the mirrored ceiling of the ballroom in which the Jackson campaign had gathered, its energy level in defeat notably higher than that of other campaigns in victory. Jackson parties tended to spill out of ballrooms onto several levels of whatever hotel they were in, and to last until three or four in the morning: anyone who wanted to be at a Jackson party was welcome at a Jackson party, which was unusual among the campaigns, and tended to reinforce the populist spirit that had given this one its extraordinary animation. Of that evening at the Los Angeles Hilton I recall a pretty woman in a gold lamé dress, dancing with a baby in her arms. I recall empty beer bottles, Corona and Budweiser and Excalibur, sitting among the loops of television cable. I recall the candidate, dancing on the stage, and, on this

June evening when the long shot had not come in, this evening when his campaign was effectively over, giving the women in the traveling press the little parody wave they liked to give him, "the press chicks' wave," the stiff-armed palm movement they called "the Nancy Reagan wave"; then taking off his tie and throwing it into the crowd, like a rock star. This was of course a narrative of its own, but a relatively current one, and one that had, because it seemed at some point grounded in the recognizable, a powerful glamour for those estranged from the purposeful nostalgia of the traditional narrative.

In the end the predictable decision was made to go with the process, with predictable, if equivocal, results. On the last afternoon of the 1988 Republican convention in New Orleans I walked from the hotel in the Quarter where I was staying over to Camp Street. I wanted to see 544 Camp, a local point of interest not noted on the points-of-interest maps distributed at the convention but one that figures large in the literature of American conspiracy. "544 Camp Street" was the address stamped on the leaflets Lee Harvey Oswald was distributing around New Orleans between May and September of 1963, the "Fair Play for Cuba Committee" leaflets that, in the years after Lee Harvey Oswald assassinated John Fitzgerald Kennedy, suggested to some that he had been acting for Fidel Castro and suggested to others that he had been set up to appear to have been acting for Fidel Castro. Guy Bannister had his detective agency at 544 Camp. David Ferrie and Jack Martin frequented the coffee shop on the ground floor at 544 Camp. The Cuban Revolutionary Council, the members of which would have made up the provisional government of Cuba had the 1961 invasion of Cuba not ended at the Bay of Pigs, rented an office at 544 Camp. People had taken the American political narrative seriously at 544 Camp. They had argued about it, fallen out over it, hit each other over the head with pistol butts because of it.

In fact I never found 544 Camp, because there was no more such address: the small building had been bought and torn down and replaced by a new federal courthouse. Across the street in Lafayette Square that afternoon there had been a loudspeaker, and a young man on a makeshift platform talking about abortion, and unwanted babies being put down the Disposall and "clogging the main sewer drains of New Orleans," but no one except me had been there to listen. "*Satan, you're the liar,*" the young woman with him on the platform had sung, lip-synching a tape originally made, she told me, by a woman who sang with an Alabama traveling ministry, the Ministry of the Happy Hunters. "*There's one thing you can't deny / You're the father of every lie…*" The young woman had been wearing a black cape, and was made up to portray Satan, or Death, I was unclear which and it had not seemed a distinction worth pursuing.

Still, there were clouds off the Gulf that day and the air was wet and there was about the melancholy of Camp Street a certain sense of abandoned historic moment, heightened, quite soon, by something unusual: the New Orleans police began lining Camp Street, blocking every intersection from Canal Street west. I noticed a man in uniform on a roof. Before long there were Secret Service agents, with wires in their ears. The candidates, it seemed, would be traveling east on Camp Street on their way from the Republican National Committee Finance Committee Gala (Invitation Only) at the Convention Center to the Ohio Caucus Rally (Media Invited) at the Hilton. I stood for a while on Camp Street, on this corner that might be construed as one of those occasional accidental intersections where the remote narrative had collided with the actual life of the country, and waited until the motorcade itself, entirely and perfectly insulated, a mechanism dedicated like the process for which it stood only to the maintenance of itself, had passed, and then I walked to the Superdome. "I hear he did OK with Brinkley," they said that night in the Superdome, and, then, as the confetti fell, "Quayle, zip."

THE WEST WING OF OZ

I

December 22, 1988

IN AUGUST 1986, George Bush, traveling in his role as vice president of the United States and accompanied by his staff, the Secret
Service, the traveling press, and a personal camera crew wearing
baseball caps reading "Shooters, Inc." and working on a $10,000
retainer paid by a Bush PAC called the Fund for America's
Future, spent several days in Israel and Jordan. The schedule in
Israel included, according to reports in *The Los Angeles Times* and
The New York Times, shoots at the Western Wall, at the Holocaust
memorial, at David Ben-Gurion's tomb, and at thirty-two other
locations chosen to produce camera footage illustrating that
George Bush was, as Marlin Fitzwater, at that time the vice-
presidential press secretary, put it, "familiar with the issues." The
Shooters, Inc. crew did not go on to Jordan (there was, an official
explained to *The Los Angeles Times*, "nothing to be gained from
showing him schmoozing with Arabs"), but the Bush advance
team in Amman had nonetheless directed considerable attention
to improving visuals for the traveling press.

Members of the advance team had requested, for example, that
the Jordanian army marching band change its uniforms from white
to red. They had requested that the Jordanians, who did not have
enough equipment to transport Bush's traveling press corps, borrow
the necessary helicopters to do so from the Israeli air force. In an
effort to assure the color of live military action as a backdrop for the
vice president, they had asked the Jordanians to stage maneuvers at
a sensitive location overlooking Israel and the Golan Heights. They
had asked the Jordanians to raise, over the Jordanian base there, the
American flag. They had asked that Bush be photographed studying, through binoculars, "enemy territory," a shot ultimately vetoed
by the State Department, since the "enemy territory" at hand was
Israel. They had also asked, possibly the most arresting detail, that,
at every stop on the itinerary, camels be present.

Some months later I happened to be in Amman, and mentioned reading about this Bush trip to several officials at the

769

American embassy there. They could have, it was agreed, "cordially killed" the reporters in question, particularly Charles P. Wallace from *The Los Angeles Times*, but the reports themselves had been accurate. "You didn't hear this, but they didn't write the half of it," one said.

This is in fact the kind of story we expect to hear about our elected officials. We not only expect them to use other nations as changeable scrims in the theater of domestic politics but encourage them to do so. After the April 1961 failure of the Bay of Pigs, John Kennedy's job approval rating was four points higher than it had been in March. After the 1965 intervention in the Dominican Republic, Lyndon Johnson's job approval rating rose six points. After the 1983 invasion of Grenada, Ronald Reagan's job approval rating rose four points, and what was that winter referred to in Washington as "Lebanon"—the sending of American marines into Beirut, the killing of the 241, and the subsequent pullout—was, in the afterglow of this certified success in the Caribbean, largely forgotten. "Gemayal could fall tonight and it would be a two-day story," I recall David Gergen saying a few months later. In May 1984, Francis X. Clines of *The New York Times* described the view taken by James Baker, who was routinely described during his years in the Reagan White House as a manager of almost supernatural executive ability, the "ultimate pragmatist": "In attempting action in Lebanon, Baker argues, President Reagan avoided another 'impotent' episode, such as the taking of American hostages in Iran, and in withdrawing the Marines, the President avoided another 'Vietnam' ... 'Pulling the Marines out put the lie to the argument that the President's trigger-happy,' he [Baker] said." The "issue," in other words, was one of preserving faith in President Reagan at home, a task that, after the ultimate pragmatist left the White House, fell into the hands of the less adroit.

History is context. At a moment when the nation had seen control of its economy pass to its creditors and when the administration-elect had for political reasons severely limited its ability to regain that control, this extreme reliance on the efficacy of faith over works meant something different from what it might have meant in 1984 or 1980. On the night in New Orleans in August 1988 when George Bush accepted the Republican nomination and spoke of his intention to "speak for freedom, stand for freedom, and be a patient friend to anyone, east or west, who will fight for freedom," the word "patient" was construed by some in the Louisiana Superdome as an abandonment of the Reagan Doctrine, a suggestion that a Bush administration would play a passive rather than an active role in any further dreams of rollback.

This overlooked the real nature of the Reagan Doctrine, the usefulness of which to the Reagan administration had been essentially political. Administrations with little room to maneuver at home have historically looked for sideshows abroad, for the creation of what pollsters call "a dramatic event," an external crisis, preferably one so remote that it remains an abstraction. On the evening of the November 1988 election and on several evenings that followed, I happened to sit at dinner next to men with considerable experience in the financial community. They were agreed that the foreign markets would allow the new Bush administration, which was seen to have limited its options by promising for political reasons not to raise taxes, only a limited time before calling in the markers; they disagreed only as to the length of that time and to the nature of the downturn. One thought perhaps two years, another six months. Some saw a blowout ("blowout" was a word used a good deal), others saw a gradual tightening, a slow transition to that era of limited expectations of which Jerry Brown had spoken when he was governor of California.

These men were, among themselves, uniformly pessimistic. They saw a situation in which the space available for domestic maneuvering had been reduced to zero. In this light it did not seem encouraging that George Bush, on the Thursday before he left for his post-election Florida vacation, found time to meet not with those investors around the world who were that week sending him a message (the dollar was again dropping against the yen, against the mark, and against the pound; the Dow was dropping 78.47 points), not with the Germans, not with the Japanese, not even with anyone from the American financial community, but with representatives of the Afghan resistance. "Once in a while I think about those things, but not much," the president-elect told

771

the CBS News crew which asked him, a few days later in Florida, about the falling market.

2

July 14, 1994

In December 1981 in El Salvador, twenty-one months after the murder of Archbishop Oscar Arnulfo Romero in San Salvador and twelve months after the murder of the four American Maryknoll women outside San Salvador and eleven months after the murder of the head of the Salvadoran land-reform agency and two of his American aides at the Sheraton Hotel in San Salvador, which is to say at a time when the Reagan administration had already demonstrated its ability to tolerate grave insults to its Central American policy, certain events occurred in certain remote villages north of the Torola River in Morazán province. In what has since become the most familiar of those villages, El Mozote, the events in question began late on a Thursday afternoon, December 10, at a time when the village was crowded with refugees from areas believed less safe, and were concluded at dawn on Saturday.

Later that day, in Los Toriles, two kilometers to the southeast, similar events occurred, as similar events had already occurred or would within a few hours occur in Arambala and La Joya and Jocote Amarillo and Cerro Pando and Joateca and La Rancheria. These events were later and variously described to the American writer Mark Danner by the two American embassy officials assigned to investigate them, Todd Greentree and Major John McKay, as "something bad," "something horrible," a case in which "there had probably been a massacre, that they had lined people up and shot them," a case in which "abuses against the civilian population probably took place"; a case that presented as its most urgent imperative the need to craft a report that would "have credibility among people who were far away and whose priorities were—you know, we're talking about people like Tom Enders—whose priorities were definitely not necessarily about getting at exactly what happened."

On December 10, 1992, eleven years to the day after the commencement of what has become known as the Mozote

POLITICAL FICTIONS

massacre (the largest number of those killed on that long
December weekend were killed during the thirty-six hours
spent in El Mozote by members of the Salvadoran army's
Atlacatl Battalion), four American forensic experts submitted
to the United Nations Truth Commission the results of their
analysis of skeletal remains and artifacts recovered by a team
of Argentinian forensic anthropologists originally assembled
to reconstruct evidence of their own country's "dirty war."
Working exclusively with material exhumed from what had
been the sacristy of the Mozote church, the Americans were
able to identify the bones of 143 human beings, 136 of whom
were children and adolescents. Of the remaining seven adults,
six were women, one in the third trimester of pregnancy. The
average age of the children was six.

The report prepared for the United Nations noted that there
may have been a greater number of deaths in the sacristy, which
was one of several sites mentioned by survivors as places where
bodies would be found, since "many young infants may have been
entirely cremated" (much of the village had been burned before
the Atlacatl left El Mozote) and "other children may not have
been counted because of excessive fragmentation of body parts."
Of the ten officers who commanded the units participating in
the Morazán operation, according to the report prepared for the
United Nations, three were by then dead, and four still serving
in the Salvadoran army. None had been officially charged on
any count related to the massacre. A year before, Tutela Legal,
the human rights office of the Archbishopric of San Salvador,
had compiled what may be the final and most comprehensive
list of all those known or believed to have died in El Mozote
and the surrounding villages. The Tutela Legal list numbered
767 men, women, and children, the youngest the two-day-old
grandson of a day laborer named Miguel Marquez (the grandfather was also killed, as were his son, his daughter-in-law, two
of his daughters, and seven of his other grandchildren), the oldest a man named Leoncio Diaz, who was said to be 105 years
old and to have had a 100-year-old companion named Leoncia
Marquez, who was also killed. Of the 767 victims cited on the
Tutela Legal list, 358 were infants and children under the age of
thirteen.

* * *

773

This was of course not a new story, and the fact that it was not a new story seems in many ways what moved Mark Danner to write his dispassionate, meticulously documented, and for these reasons conclusive *The Massacre at El Mozote: A Parable of the Cold War*. The essential facts of the Mozote massacre were published on January 27, 1982, on the front pages of both *The New York Times* and *The Washington Post*, accompanied by photographs taken by Susan Meiselas, who had walked into Morazán from Honduras with Raymond Bonner of the *Times*. Bonner reported seeing the charred skulls and bones of what appeared to him to be several dozen men, women, and children. Allowing that it was "not possible for an observer who was not present at the time of the massacre to determine independently how many people died or who killed them," he reported that the surviving relatives and friends of the victims believed the dead to number 733 and the killing to have been done "by uniformed soldiers" during an Atlacatl sweep of the region.

Alma Guillermoprieto, who was then a stringer for *The Washington Post* and who entered Mozote a few days after Bonner and Meiselas had left, also reported seeing bodies and body parts and quoted the same survivors, as well as the Salvadoran ambassador in Washington, Ernesto Rivas Gallont, who dismissed the reports from Morazán as the "type of story that leads us to believe there is a plan," the plan being either to derail the Salvadoran election scheduled for March 1982 or "to take credit away from the certification President Reagan must make to Congress." This "certification," during 1982 and 1983 a semiannual requirement for continued American aid to El Salvador, involved asserting that its government was "making a concerted and significant effort to comply with internationally recognized human rights" and was "achieving substantial control over all elements of its own armed forces, so as to bring to an end the indiscriminate torture and murder of Salvadoran citizens by those forces."

The Reagan administration made its certification to these points on January 28, 1982, one day after Bonner's and Alma Guillermoprieto's extensive reports from Morazán appeared in the *Times* and the *Post*. Mark Danner's true subject in *The Massacre at El Mozote*, then, was not the massacre itself but the way in which the story of the massacre, which was carried out by troops trained by the U.S. Special Forces and equipped with U.S.-manufactured M-16s and with ammunition manufactured for the U.S. government at Lake City, Missouri, came to be known and discounted in the United States, the way in which the story of El Mozote "was exposed to the light and then allowed to fall back into the dark."

Reports that something bad had happened in Morazán had begun to circulate almost immediately. The Reverend William L. Wipfler at the New York office of the National Council of Churches first heard the story from a contact at Socorro Juridico, which was then the legal aid office at the Archbishopric of San Salvador. Wipfler left a message for Raymond Bonner at the Mexico City bureau of the *Times*, and also sent a cable, dated December 15, 1981, asking Ambassador Deane Hinton in San Salvador for "confirmation or otherwise" of "reliable reports received here [indicating] that between December 10 and 13 a government joint military and security forces operation took place in Morazan Department which resulted in over 900 civilian deaths."

Hinton did not reply until January 8, by which time the guerrillas' Radio Venceremos was back in operation (to at least temporarily knock out the Venceremos transmitter had been one goal, perhaps the single successfully realized goal, of the Atlacatl's Morazán operation) and broadcasting a detailed account of the massacre from a survivor named Rufina Amaya. Rufina Amaya had witnessed the killing of her husband and four of her children, ages nine, five, three, and eight months, but in the confusion and terror of the event had herself been inadvertently overlooked as the soldiers corralled groups of struggling and screaming women, many of them torn from their infants and children, to be killed and then burned. "I do not know what your sources are but the only sources that I have seen alleging something like this are the clandestine Radio Venceremos reports," Hinton's January 8 cable to the National Council of Churches read in part. "Frankly, I do not consider Radio Venceremos to be a reliable source." Since Radio Venceremos did not restore its ability to broadcast until well after the National Council of Churches query was sent, that Hinton would devote ten of this cable's twelve paragraphs to illustrations of Radio Venceremos's unreliability seems in retrospect to suggest a certain crisis of confidence, if not a panic, at the embassy.

In fact, definitely before January 8 and probably closer to mid-December, Todd Greentree, then a junior reporting officer at the embassy in San Salvador and later a desk officer for Nicaragua at the State Department, had relayed to Hinton not only a report from his own sources on the left about a massacre in Morazán but also an offer from the FMLN to guide him there. "I knew the guerrillas would never have masqueraded something like this, would never have fabricated it, if they were offering safe-conduct," Greentree told Danner. "I was convinced that something had gone on, and that it was bad. I mean, it was pretty clear, if they were going to do this, that something must have happened." Hinton's decision was that Greentree could not go in under guerrilla protection. "I should emphasize that I never got the feeling that they just wanted this to go away," Greentree told Danner about the meeting in which this decision was taken. "But there were political and military restraints that we were operating under."

What discussion there may have been of an independent investigation (at least ten of the fifty-five American military advisers Congress then allowed in El Salvador were assigned to the Atlacatl) is unknown, although Danner was told by one of the officers assigned to the Atlacatl that someone from the embassy Milgroup (Military Advisory Group) had called the Atlacatl base at La Libertad a few days after the massacre "and talked to the Special Forces people and told them they wanted Monterrosa [Lieutenant Colonel Domingo Monterrosa Barrios, the Atlacatl commander] to come in—they wanted to talk to him about something that had happened during the operation." Monterrosa had declined to come in, a suggestive illustration of the level of control the United States then had over the military forces it was funding. Whether or not the embassy decision to refuse the FMLN offer to guide Greentree to the site of the massacre was discussed with Washington also remains shrouded in the subjunctive. "However much we might have wanted more information, no one in State was going to make that call," Danner was told by Peter Romero, at the time of Mozote an El Salvador specialist at the State Department.

* * *

Most of the interested players, then, knew about Morazán, in outline if not in detail, well before January 6, when Raymond Bonner and Susan Meiselas, followed a few days later by Alma Guillermoprieto, first walked into El Mozote. Not until January 30, however, three days after the story had appeared on the front pages of the *Times* and the *Post*, did the embassy dispatch Todd Greentree and Major John McKay, who was then in the defense attaché's office at the embassy and was at the time Danner interviewed him a colonel attached to NATO in Brussels, to Morazán. Greentree and McKay did not exactly get to El Mozote, although they did fly over it. Greentree's impression from the air was that "El Mozote had been pretty much destroyed." Once on the ground in Morazán, although not in El Mozote, Greentree and McKay, accompanied by a squad of the Atlacatl, interviewed those residents of the northern villages who had reached the refugee camp outside San Francisco Gotera. Although the Americans later recalled being able to "observe and feel this tremendous fear," they did not elicit eyewitness accounts of a massacre, nor had they expected to.

"You had a bunch of very intimidated, scared people, and now the Army presence further intimidated them," McKay told Danner. "I mean, the Atlacatl had supposedly done something horrible, and now these gringos show up under this pretense of investigating it, but in the presence of these soldiers. It was probably the worst thing you could do. I mean, you didn't have to be a rocket scientist to know what the Army people were there for." Greentree and McKay then set out for El Mozote, and got to within an hour's walk of what had been the village when the Atlacatl soldiers accompanying them stopped, and refused to go further. "In the end, we went up there and we didn't want to find that anything horrible had happened," McKay told Danner. "And the fact that we didn't get to the site turned out to be very detrimental to our reporting—the Salvadorans, you know, were never very good about cleaning up their shell casings." That evening, back at the embassy in San Salvador, Greentree wrote a report, the overriding aim of which appears to have been "credibility," summarizing his and McKay's findings.

Here is the point at which El Mozote entered the thin air of Washington, where the official story was that El Salvador, with the inspiration of the Reagan administration, was at last "turning the corner" toward democracy. "The end of Bob White's tour, and the transition period before Hinton arrived [Robert White had preceded Hinton as ambassador], and the first six months of Hinton's tour—those were the absolute worst days, really out of control," Greentree told Danner by way of explaining why the conviction that what was known or suspected in country would not be "credible" in Washington had by then increased exponentially. "And the fact that Bob White and everybody in the embassy had been so thoroughly traumatized by the murders of the nuns, and the AFL-CIO guys [the two Americans who were killed with the head of the Salvadoran land-reform agency at the Sheraton in San Salvador], and just the general sort of out-of-control way the military was—it meant that everything we reported could be taken as suspect."

The following day, after review and revisions, Greentree's report went to the State Department over Hinton's name. This was the cable containing the careful and soon to be repeated assertions that it was "not possible to prove or disprove excesses of violence against the civilian population of El Mozote by government troops" and that "no evidence could be found to confirm that government forces systematically massacred civilians in the operation zone, nor that the number of civilians killed even remotely approached the number being cited in other reports circulating internationally." The Greentree cable also contained, deep in its text, a curious warning from one of the interviewees, the mayor of Jocoaitique, who according to the cable "intimated that he knew of violent fighting in El Mozote" but was "unwilling to discuss deportment of government troops" and who then made a comment so coded that it could stand as a veiled but exact expression of the embassy position on what did or did not take place in Morazán. What the cable quoted the mayor of Jocoaitique as having said to Todd Greentree and Major McKay was this: "This is something one should talk about in another time, in another country."

That part of the embassy cable did not appear in the statement made two days later to the House Subcommittee on Western Hemisphere Affairs by Assistant Secretary of State for

Inter-American Affairs Thomas O. Enders. (Nor would it appear in the sanitized version of the cable released under the Freedom of Information Act to Raymond Bonner in 1983.) The Enders statement was arresting not only for what it said and did not say but for its tone, which suggested an extreme version of a kind of exaggerated hauteur commonly translated as entitlement in the northeastern United States. "Many of you have read," he said, addressing what he called "special pleading" in the matter of death and disappearance statistics, "about something called the Legal Aid Office of the Archbishopric—Socorro Judico [sic] is its Spanish name; it is often cited in the international media. It strangely lists no victims of guerrilla or terrorist violence. Apparently they do not commit violence."

This was a level of seigneurial dismissal often emulated but never quite mastered by Jeane Kirkpatrick and Elliott Abrams and other regular defenders of administration policy in Central America. "There is another organization, the Central American University, that collects statistics too," Enders continued, referring to UCA, the Jesuit-run José Simeón Cañas University of Central America. "Its bias may be apparent from the fact that it does include a category of persons killed by what I believe Congressman Bonker referred to as paramilitary organizations. And they are called in Spanish *ajusticiados*, referring to persons that have received justice at the hands of their executioners." Only then did Enders turn his attention to what he described as "allegations" of massacres, including Mozote. "We sent two embassy officers down to investigate the reports," Enders said, inadvertently illuminating the particular distance between Washington and Morazán, which in local usage is said to be not "down" but "up" from San Salvador. Enders continued:

> It is clear from the report they gave that there has been a confrontation between the guerrillas occupying Mozote and attacking Government forces last December. There is no evidence to confirm that Government forces systematically massacred civilians in the operations zone, or that the number of civilians remotely approached the 733 or 926 victims cited in the press. I note they asked how many people were in that canton and were told probably not

779

more than 300 in December, and there are many survivors including refugees now.

Enders said this on February 2, 1982. On February 1, Deane Hinton, in response to what he apparently construed as careless use of his reply to the National Council of Churches, had sent a corrective cable to the State Department. This cable read in part:

> I would be grateful if department would use extreme care in describing my views on alleged massacre. Case in point is description in para 3 of *REFTEL* referring to my letter ... as "denying the incident." My letter did not "deny" incident: it reported that at that time I had no confirmation and argued from available evidence from Radio Venceremos and from lack of other reports that I had no reason to believe Venceremos reports. I still don't believe Venceremos version but additional evidence strongly suggests that something happened that should not have happened and that it is quite possible Salvadoran military did commit excesses. Allegations that it was unit from Atlacatl battalion in El Mozote remain to be confirmed or discredited.

Several days later, this Hinton cable notwithstanding, Assistant Secretary of State for Human Rights and Humanitarian Affairs Elliott Abrams echoed Enders in his statement to the Senate Foreign Relations Committee. The Mozote case was, Abrams said, "a very interesting one in a sense." "Interesting" was at the time a word much in use, as were "strange" and "unusual." Enders, for example, had noted that Socorro Juridico "strangely lists no victims of guerrilla and terrorist violence." I recall watching Jeane Kirkpatrick during this period tease an audience to frenzy with little silken whips of innuendo as she described how "*interested*," even "*bemused*," she was by the "*unusual* standards," the "*extraordinarily*, even *uniquely* demanding standards" imposed by the certification requirement. The reason Elliott Abrams found El Mozote "interesting" was this: "... because we found, for example, that the numbers, first of all, were not credible, because as Secretary Enders notes, our information was that there were only three hundred people in the canton." Abrams went on to wonder why a massacre that had occurred in mid-December, if indeed it had occurred at all, had not been "publicized" until late January.

Ten years later, in an interview, Abrams was still asking the same question, to the same innuendo: "If it had really been a massacre and not a firefight, why didn't we hear about it right off from the FMLN? I mean, we didn't start hearing about it until a month later." Abrams, in other words, was still trying to negotiate what had become, with the exhumation of the sacristy, unnegotiable, still trying to return discussion to the familiar question of whether or not a massacre had occurred. Enders, when he talked to Danner, had transcended this now inoperative line of attack, ascending effortlessly to the big-picture argument against the existence of a massacre: "Coming on top of everything else, El Mozote, if true, might have destroyed the entire effort. Who knows? I certainly thought that when I first heard about it." In other words it had been necessary to deny the massacre because had there been a massacre the "effort" would have become, and this was the word Enders used, "unfundable."

The effort did not become unfundable. The effort instead became what was at that time the most expensive effort to support a foreign government threatened by an insurgency since Vietnam. Progressively cruder interpretations of what had been the surgically precise statements made by the embassy came to dominate, during the spring and summer of 1982, discussion of this country's role in Central America. By February 10 of that spring *The Wall Street Journal* was noting editorially that "extremists" in El Salvador had "learned long ago the trick of dressing in military uniforms to confuse their victims." (This appears to have been the source for Ronald Reagan's later assertion that "communist operatives" were dressing in "freedom fighter uniforms" to discredit the Nicaraguan contras.) Shrill excoriations of Raymond Bonner, who necessarily had to be cast as having what George Melloan of *The Wall Street Journal* called "a political orientation," became commonplace.

Bonner was a graduate of Stanford Law School, had been a prosecutor in the San Francisco district attorney's office, and had served as a marine officer in Vietnam. John McKay, the marine major who went up to Morazán with Todd Greentree, had been with Bonner in Vietnam, where McKay lost an eye. "We could not have said, 'My God, there's been a massacre,'" McKay told Danner about the cable the embassy sent to Washington as a report of his and Greentree's trip to Morazán. "But, truth be known, the ambiguity of the cable that went out—in my own conscience I began to question it. And then when I saw the *New York Times* piece, and the picture, that really got me thinking. Bonner and I had gone to Quantico together, went to Vietnam together." In the late summer of 1980, at a time when Bonner had spent time in Bolivia and Guatemala but had made only a few short visits to El Salvador, he had been asked his opinion of U.S. policy in El Salvador. "Ask me about Bolivia, or Guatemala, or any country, I'll probably have an opinion," Bonner recalled having said. "But El Salvador, boy, I just don't know. I guess we're doing the right thing."

Bonner, then, might have seemed an unlikely target for the campaign then being mounted against him in Washington and New York. For those waging this campaign, however, the question of "political orientation" was answered once and for all in August 1982, when the *Times* abruptly withdrew Bonner from Central America. According to A. M. Rosenthal, then the executive editor of the *Times*, Bonner was withdrawn because he "didn't know the techniques of weaving a story together.... I brought him back because it seemed terribly unfair to leave him there without training." Actually Bonner had spent a good part of 1981 on the Metro desk at the *Times*, but Rosenthal suggested that those who believed Bonner to have been withdrawn for reasons other than "training" did so because they resented Rosenthal himself. "I was an agent of change in the *Times*," he said, "and a lot of people didn't like my politics."

This self-referential approach worked to blur the issue. Whatever reason or reasons Rosenthal may have had for withdrawing Bonner, it was the sheer fact of that withdrawal, the fact of that apparent failure to back up a reporter who had put the paper on the line with a story denied by the government, that spoke so eloquently to those who wanted to discredit the reporting on El Mozote. That the *Times* withdrew Bonner was seen, immediately and by larger numbers of people than were actually knowledgeable about El Salvador or administration policy, as "proof" that he had been wrong about El Mozote; as recently as a few years ago it was possible to hear it casually said about Bonner that the *Times* "had to pull him out," that he had "bought into a massacre."

"For more than a year now we've been following the campaign that we victimized former *New York Times* correspondent Raymond Bonner," *The Wall Street Journal* noted editorially in 1993. "The excavation of children's bones in El Mozote is supposed to vindicate Mr. Bonner and discredit what we said.... We did not fire Mr. Bonner in the first place. *The New York Times* did. Or, more precisely, after then Managing Editor A. M. Rosenthal undertook his own reporting visit to El Salvador, it pulled Mr. Bonner off the beat and back to New York, where he left the paper." In defense of its own reasonableness, the *Journal* noted that in its original 1982 attack on Bonner it had "offered not one word of criticism of Alma Guillermoprieto of *The Washington Post.*"

Among the documents reproduced at the end of *The Massacre at El Mozote*, Danner included the full text of both Bonner's and Alma Guillermoprieto's stories. There was no substantive difference between the two in either the reporting or the qualifying of what had been observed, but there were certain marginal distinctions on which critics of Bonner could seize. Guillermoprieto referred to herself as "this correspondent" and said that she had been taken into Morazán by "the Farabundo Martí Liberation Front." Bonner referred to himself as "a visitor who traveled through the area with those who are fighting the junta that now rules El Salvador," i.e., the Farabundo Martí Liberation Front. Guillermoprieto began: "Several hundred civilians, including women and children, were taken from their homes in and around this village and killed by Salvadoran Army troops during a December offensive against leftist guerrillas, according to three survivors who say they witnessed the alleged massacres." She then proceeded to describe the bodies she herself had seen. Bonner began: "From interviews with people who live in this small mountain village and surrounding hamlets, it is clear that a massacre of major proportions occurred here last month." He then proceeded to describe the bodies he himself had seen. Bonner's statement is the less varnished of the two, but to call it different is to resort to a point of journalistic convention so narrowly defined as to be merely legalistic.

There seemed at the time at least two clear reasons that Bonner, not Guillermoprieto, became the target of choice. One reason was that Bonner, unlike Guillermoprieto, continued to report on a daily basis from El Salvador, and so, all through the spring and into the summer of 1982, remained a stubborn mote in Deane Hinton's ability to project the situation as the State Department wanted it projected. "I'm just afraid he's going to get himself killed," I recall an embassy official saying about Bonner during a lunch with Hinton in June of 1982; the tone here was the macho swagger never entirely absent from American embassies on hardship status. "That would be a tragedy." The other clear reason that Bonner was targeted, and Guillermoprieto was not, was this: Benjamin C. Bradlee and *The Washington Post* had backed up their reporter. A. M. Rosenthal and *The New York Times* had not.

The Mozote massacre occurred only six years after most of us watched the helicopters lift off the roof of the Saigon embassy and get pushed off the flight decks of the U.S. fleet into the South China Sea. There were by the time the bodies were exhumed from the sacristy of the Mozote church more than twice as many years between us and Mozote as there were between Mozote and those helicopters. This is not an insignificant time line, and suggests a third reason that Raymond Bonner's report from Morazán elicited an acrimony that Alma Guillermoprieto's did not. Bonner was an American. Alma Guillermoprieto had been born in and was then living in Mexico, a fact that was in some way understood to render her ineligible for casting as a member of what was sometimes called "the adversary culture," the culture that was construed as hostile to the interests of American business and the American government, the culture that had caused the United States to "lose" Vietnam, the culture that was even then drawing parallels between Vietnam and El Salvador.

Certain parallels were inescapable, since El Salvador was seen, by both the American military and the American policy community, as an opportunity to "apply the lesson" of Vietnam.

The counterinsurgency doctrine that rationalized such operations as the 1981 sweep of Morazán was intended as a "revision" of the failed counterinsurgency effort in Vietnam (the "revision" for El Salvador emphasized a need to correct "root causes," or to win popular support by "democratizing" Salvadoran society), yet it had come to sound dispiritingly the same. The word "pacification" was in use, as was the phrase "third force," usually in reference to José Napoleón Duarte. "The only territory you want to hold is the six inches between the ears of the *campesino*," Colonel John C. Waghelstein, who took command of the Milgroup not long after Mozote, said when he spoke at the American Enterprise Institute in 1985 on "LIC [Low-Intensity Conflict] in the Post-Vietnam Period." As late as 1986, in *The Wall Street Journal*, an American military adviser was quoted describing a community event sponsored by a Salvadoran army unit as "winning hearts and minds." The event in question involved clowns, mariachis, and speeches from army officers calling on peasants to reject the guerrillas. "This is low-intensity-conflict doctrine in action," the adviser said.

Again as in Vietnam, the doctrine was met with resistance on the part of those charged with carrying it out. "Attempts to address root causes during [this] period enjoyed less success than did efforts to stabilize the military situation," four American military officers observed in their 1988 *American Military Policy in Small Wars: The Case of El Salvador,* the so-called "colonels' report" prepared for the Institute for Foreign Policy Analysis. "American officers recognized ... [that] the government had to transform itself into an institution perceived as effective, impartial, and committed to bringing about genuine reform. Meaningful implementation of this concept has eluded the Salvadorans and their American advisers." In a 1991 Rand Institute report prepared for the Department of Defense, Benjamin C. Schwarz noted that "the greed and apparent tactical incompetence of Salvadoran officers has so exhausted American experts posted to El Salvador that all the individuals interviewed for this report who have served there in the past two years believe that the Salvadoran military does not wish to win the war because in so doing it would lose the American aid that has enriched it for the past decade."

* * *

In San Salvador as in Saigon, this had long been accepted as one of the many taxing givens that made the posting so difficult to share with those who were planning the effort in Washington. Deane Hinton, who would not talk to Danner, emerges in *The Massacre at El Mozote* as the ultimate example of the career foreign service officer trying to execute an extremely doubtful policy in an even more doubtful situation. In this role as the good soldier of American foreign policy, Hinton left El Salvador in 1983 for Pakistan, a more remote but equally doubtful situation, and then returned to Central America to mop up the debris left by the contra and then the Panama efforts. Alma Guillermoprieto, whose work after El Mozote was especially acute on the immediacy with which Washington dreams became Central and South American responsibilities, noted in *The Heart That Bleeds* that, as late as 1992 in Hinton's Panama embassy, the preferred way to refer to the 1989 invasion was as "*la liberación.*"

"This is a suicide mission," an unidentified embassy official in San Salvador had said when Warren Hoge of *The New York Times* asked, not long after Mozote, if assignment to El Salvador could advance a foreign service career. "Someone's got to be nuts to be here. How many people do you think profited from having worked in Vietnam?" What made the San Salvador embassy a suicide mission was, of course, the certain knowledge that the facts of the situation would be less than welcome at the other end of the cable traffic. "There was no secret about who was doing the killing," Danner was told by Howard Lane, the public affairs officer at the embassy at the time of El Mozote. "I mean, you formed that view within forty-eight hours after arriving in the country, and there was no secret at all about it—except, maybe, in the White House."

What Mark Danner detailed in *The Massacre at El Mozote* was the process by which actual eyewitness accounts (Bonner, Guillermoprieto) and photographs (Meiselas) came to be discounted by large numbers of Americans for no other reason than that the government, presenting no evidence, referred to the accounts (the photographs seemed rather eerily not to exist in anyone's argument) as describing an event that was intrinsically unconfirmable, rendering the accounts by definition untrue. "Accurate information," Thomas Enders said as he began his February 2, 1982, statement on Capitol Hill. "I think we have all found out that is very hard to establish." He continued, first questioning the possibility of ever determining who had been responsible for the deaths—if indeed there had even been "deaths." Then he raised the ultimate question, the coup de grâce question, the question that had to do with the true interests or motives of those who reported such deaths: "The responsibility for the overwhelming number of deaths is never legally determined nor usually accounted for by clear or coherent evidence. Seventy percent of the political murders known to our embassy were committed by unknown assailants. And there is much special pleading going on also in this."

What is especially striking about Enders, as he presents himself in *The Massacre at El Mozote*, is his apparent inability to recognize any contradiction between what he said in 1982 to the House Subcommittee on Western Hemisphere Affairs and what he said a decade later to Danner. At one point Danner asked Enders about a rumor, believed by a number of prominent Salvadorans, that two American advisers had observed the Mozote operation from a base camp below the Torola River. This was the answer Enders gave: "Certainly, one of the issues I remember raising between us and the embassy was: Were there any American advisers on this sortie? The embassy made a great effort to talk to advisers who were with the Atlacatl to try to find out the truth." Any admission of knowledge, Enders conceded, "would have ruined those guys' careers—they would have been cashiered. So no one's going to volunteer, 'Hey, I was up there.'" The effect of such a disclosure on administration efforts to continue funding the war would have been "devastating," Enders said, and then: "American advisers with a unit that committed an atrocity? Can you imagine anything more corrosive of the entire military effort?"

Enders had recognized at the time, then, the existence of a "sortie." He had even recognized the possibility of an "atrocity." (The atrocity if not the sortie was in the subjunctive.) He had raised with the embassy the question of whether there had been "American advisers" present. Yet what Enders had said in 1982

JOAN DIDION

was this:"...frankly, we do not have people who go out with the units as advisers, you know. These are military trainers. They stay behind." The idea that there was a difference between "advisers" and "trainers," another of the many legalistic distinctions at that time employed to rhetorical advantage, seems not to have been consistently held even by Enders.

Danner describes what happened to the story of El Mozote during the days and months after its disclosure as "a parable of the cold war." It was that, and as such a parable Mozote is irresistibly legible, but it was also something else. It was a parable of ideology, and of the apparently inconsolable anger it had become possible to feel toward those who were perceived as not sharing this ideology. "There have also been many fewer allegations of massacres during this reporting period than last," Thomas Enders was able to say in July 1982, when the question of certification once again came before the House Committee on Foreign Affairs. "This may be in part," he said, still the loyalist but still careful—*fewer* allegations, *may* be, *in part*—"because many earlier reports proved to be fabricated or exaggerated." At the same hearing, Nestor Sanchez, then deputy assistant secretary of defense for inter-American affairs, was able to single out "the first quick-reaction battalion trained by U.S. instructors in El Salvador" not only for "its tactical capability in fighting the guerrillas" but also for "its humane treatment of the people."

The "first quick-reaction battalion trained by U.S. instructors in El Salvador" was the Atlacatl. Just six years after Vietnam and in the face of what was beginning to seem a markedly similar American engagement, El Mozote, by which we have come to mean not exactly the massacre itself but the systematic obfuscation and prevarication that followed the disclosure of the massacre, was the first hard evidence that we had emerged a people again so yearning to accept the government version, or again so angry, as to buy into a revision of history in which those Americans who differed—those Americans who for reasons of their "political orientation" would "fabricate" reports of a massacre carried out by a unit noted for its "humane treatment of the people"—were again our true, and only truly sinister, enemy.

3
December 18, 1997

The aides gave us the details, retold now like runes. Promptly at nine o'clock on most mornings of the eight years he spent as president of the United States, Ronald Reagan arrived in the Oval Office to find on his desk his personal schedule, printed on green stationery and embossed in gold with the presidential seal. Between nine and ten he was briefed, first by his chief of staff and the vice president and then by his national security adviser. At ten, in the absence of a pressing conflict, he was scheduled for downtime, an hour in which he answered selected letters from citizens and clipped items that caught his eye in *Human Events* and *National Review*. Other meetings followed, for example with the congressional leadership. "I soon learned that these meetings lasted just one hour, no more, no less," Tony Coelho, at the time majority whip in the House, told us in *Recollections of Reagan: A Portrait of Ronald Reagan*, a 1997 collection of reminiscences edited by Peter Hannaford. "If the agenda—which he had written out on cards—wasn't completed at the end of the hour, he would excuse himself and leave. If it was finished short of an hour, he would fill the rest of the time with jokes (and he tells a good one)." During some meetings, according to his press secretary, Larry Speakes, the president filled the time by reciting Robert Service's "The Cremation of Sam McGee."

When the entry on the schedule was not a meeting but an appearance or a photo opportunity, the president was rehearsed. "You'll go out the door and down the steps," Michael Deaver or someone else would say, we were told by Donald Regan, secretary of the treasury from 1981 until 1985 and White House chief of staff from 1985 until 1987. "The podium is ten steps to the right and the audience will be in a semi-circle with the cameras at the right end of the half-moon; when you finish speaking take two steps back, but don't leave the podium, because they're going to present you with a patchwork quilt." It was Larry Speakes, in his 1988 *Speaking Out: The Reagan Presidency from Inside the White House*, who told us how, at the conclusion of each meeting or appearance, the president would draw on his schedule a vertical line downward and an arrow pointing to the next event. "It gives me a feeling that I am accomplishing something," the president told Speakes. It was Donald Regan, in his 1988 *For the Record: From Wall Street to Washington*, who told us how the schedule reminded the president when it was time to give a birthday present ("a funny hat or a tee shirt bearing a jocular message") to one or another staff member. "These gifts were chosen by others, and sometimes Reagan barely knew the person to whom he was giving them, but his pleasure in these contacts was genuine....On one occasion, when he was somehow given the wrong date for one man's birthday and called to offer congratulations, nobody had the heart to tell him about the mistake."

"I cannot remember a single case in which he changed a time or canceled an appointment or even complained about an item on his schedule," Regan noted, betraying a certain queasy wonder at his initial encounter with this apparently cheerful lack of interest: Regan, still at Treasury, found himself slotted into the schedule, along with James Baker and Michael Deaver, to introduce to the president the novel notion that he and Baker, then chief of staff, switch jobs. "Reagan listened without any sign of surprise," Regan recalled. "He seemed equable, relaxed—almost incurious. This seemed odd under the circumstances." Notwithstanding Regan's efforts to offer the possibility of further deliberation on so serious a move ("'I appreciate that, Don,' the President said with the bright courtesy that is typical of him. 'But I don't see why we shouldn't just go ahead with it'"), the meeting lasted, including an exchange of Christmas-vacation pleasantries, fewer than its allotted thirty minutes. "I did not know what to make of his passivity," Regan wrote. "He seemed to be absorbing a *fait accompli* rather than making a decision. One might have thought that the matter had already been settled by some absent party." On reflection, Regan understood:

> As President, Ronald Reagan acted on the work habits of a lifetime: he regarded his daily schedule as being something like a shooting script in which characters came and went, scenes were rehearsed and acted out, and the plot was advanced one day at a time, and not always in sequence. The Chief of Staff was a sort of producer, making certain that the star had what he needed to do his best; the staff was like the crew, invisible behind the lights, watching the

performance their behind-the-scenes efforts had made possible....Reagan's performance was almost always flawless. If he was scheduled to receive a visitor at ten o'clock, he would finish whatever else he was doing at 9:58, clear off his desk, clear his mind of whatever had gone before, and prepare himself for the next scene.

Dinesh D'Souza, when he arrived at the Reagan White House as a senior domestic policy analyst in 1987, was twenty-six years old, a resident of the United States only since 1978 but already a name within what had come on the right to be called "the movement." He was a native of India who seemed to have arrived in this country with preternatural pitch for the exact charged chords (affirmative action, multiculturalism, gender studies, the academy in general) that drove its politics of resentment, and he played them, first as a founding editor of *The Dartmouth Review*, then as editor of the equally strident Princeton *Prospect*, managing editor of the Heritage Foundation's *Policy Review*, and biographer of the Moral Majority's Jerry Falwell.

The 1980s were years in Washington when careers were made on undergraduate bliss. One of D'Souza's colleagues on *The Dartmouth Review* became a speechwriter for Reagan, another for George Bush. Another, Keeney Jones, the author of the notorious "Dis Sho' Ain't No Jive, Bro," a puerile but predictably inflammatory *Dartmouth Review* parody of black students ("Dese boys be sayin' that we be comin' here to Dartmut an' not takin' the classics. You know, Homa, Shakesphere; but I hea' dey all be co'd in da ground, six feet unda, and whatchu be askin' us to learn from dem?"), became a speechwriter for Secretary of Education William Bennett. Another, Laura Ingraham, who became famous at *The Dartmouth Review* for publishing the secretly taped transcript of a meeting of the Gay Students' Association and to whom D'Souza dedicated *Illiberal Education*, went on to clerk for Clarence Thomas and then to become one of the most visible blonde pundits on MSNBC. "What could be more exciting?" D'Souza, who had been editor of *The Dartmouth Review* at the time "Dis Sho' Ain't No Jive, Bro" was published, later wrote of those years in Washington when to be young and movement was very heaven. "We were a generation of young conservatives who came to Washington in the 1980s inspired by Reagan and the idea of America that he espoused and embodied. The world was changing, and we wanted to be instruments of that change. Reagan was a septuagenarian with a youthful heart. He hired people like me because he wanted fresh faces and new ideas in the White House. Full of vigor and determination, we rallied to his cause."

"He hired people like me" may seem to suggest excessive executive volition on the part of a president who by all accounts expressed no interest in who his secretary of the treasury or chief of staff was to be, but the choice of the active tense is key here. D'Souza's intention in his 1997 *Ronald Reagan: How an Ordinary Man Became an Extraordinary Leader* (which, like his 1991 *Illiberal Education: The Politics of Race and Sex on Campus* and his 1995 *The End of Racism: Principles for a Multiracial Society*, was written within the nurturing framework of the American Enterprise Institute) was to offer what he presented as a "revisionist" view of the Reagan years, a correction of the record for "a new generation of young people" who, because they have had "no alternative source of information," have been unable to detect the "transparent bias" of their teachers and the media.

It was D'Souza's thesis, honed by his useful and apparently inexhaustible ability to present himself as one of a besieged minority, that Reagan had been systematically misread. The misreading only began, in this view, with Reagan's "liberal critics," who were further identified as "the pundits, political scientists, and historians," "the wise men," "the intellectual elite," and "the cognoscenti." The more grave misreading, as D'Souza sees it, came from within Reagan's own party, not only from his more pragmatic aides (the "prags," or "ingrates and apostates," whose remarkably similar descriptions of the detachment at the center of the administration in which they served suggested to D'Souza "an almost defiant disloyalty") but even from his "hard-core" admirers, or "true believers," those movement conservatives who considered Reagan a "malleable figurehead" too often controlled by the pragmatists on his staff. "I was one of those conservatives," D'Souza allowed:

> Even when Reagan proved us wrong and showed how effective a president he was, many of us in his ideological camp nevertheless failed to understand the secret of his

success. We could not fathom how he conceived and realized his grand objectives, effortlessly overcame his powerful adversaries, and won the respect of the American people. Many who worked with him are still bewildered. This study seeks to solve the mystery.

In his casuistical pursuit of the elusive frame in which Reagan can be seen as the "prime mover," the "decisive agent of change," and the "architect of his own success," D'Souza was not actually breaking new ground. Such attempts to "solve the mystery" date back at least to the 1980 transition, during which it became apparent to some that the president-elect, without benefit of constructive interpretation, could appear less than fully engaged. During a transition briefing on secret international agreements and commitments, according to Jimmy Carter, Reagan listened politely but asked no questions and took no notes. Two hours before his 1981 inauguration, according to Michael Deaver, he was still sleeping. Deaver did not actually find this extraordinary, nor would anyone else who had witnessed Reagan's performance as governor of California. "I remember sitting there in the governor's office with him, a couple of days after I had been elected to succeed him," Jerry Brown recalls in *Recollections of Reagan: A Portrait of Ronald Reagan*:

> We didn't have a nuts-and-bolts conversation about the transition that day. I didn't see Ronald Reagan as a nuts-and-bolts kind of guy.... He was definitely performing his ceremonial role as governor, and doing it quite well. I think a great deal of the job is ceremonial. The way I look at it now, most politicians holding office think they are doing things but it's all staffed out.... Most of the day-to-day stuff is very symbolic. That was one of the frustrations I found in being governor. At first, I took literally the nature of the material being presented at meetings, but I soon found that visiting delegations often were satisfied just being in the same room as the governor. There is something illusory about it, like a play. Then again, if that satisfies people, it has some value. Reagan seemed to understand all that.

This was in fact the very understanding that would come to power Reagan's performance as president, and many people knew it, but to have said so at the time would have been out of synch with the somewhat less Zen story line (West Wing lights burn late as dedicated workaholics hit the ground running) preferred in Washington. From the outset, then, the invention of a president who could be seen as active rather than passive, who could be understood to possess mysteriously invisible and therefore miraculously potent leadership skills, became a White House priority. "Reagan's aides have been telling reporters of decisions that the President himself has made, as if they found it necessary to explain that he has made some," Elizabeth Drew reported two months into the administration, when both NBC and *Time* had been enlisted to do "A Day with President Reagan" stories. "A White House aide told me, 'We thought it was important to do those, because of the perception out there that this is a marionette president. It's simply not true.'"

This president who was not a marionette would be shown making decisions, and not only that: the decisions he was shown making (or more often in this instance, where rhetoric was soon understood to be interchangeable with action, the speeches he was shown making) would have demonstrable, preferably Manichean, results. Victory, particularly in the realm of foreign affairs, which offered dramatic "standing tall" roles for the active president to play, would be narrowly defined: the barest suggestion of an election or a reform would serve to signal the enlistment of another fledgling democracy. So defined, all victories could assume equal import: the decision to invade Grenada, D'Souza tells us, reversed the Brezhnev Doctrine. "Reagan had listened intently but said little," D'Souza wrote about the moment of standing tall that preceded the Grenada invasion. "Finally he asked the Joint Chiefs of Staff whether they believed that a military operation was likely to succeed." The Joint Chiefs, according to D'Souza, who credits his account of this meeting to Edwin Meese and Caspar Weinberger, said they believed that the operation, which entailed landing six thousand marines and airborne rangers on an island significantly smaller than Barbados, "could be done."

"Very well," Reagan is said to have said. "In that case, let's go ahead."

The invasion of Grenada is instructive. The operation, which involved one of Reagan's few overt (and his only, on his own terms, "successful") uses of military power, was justified by the administration on the ground that a ten-thousand-foot landing strip was under construction on the island, but secondarily (or primarily, depending on who was talking) because American medical students were "captive" (in fact they could have left on either regularly scheduled or charter flights) at an island medical school. "I don't think it was an invasion," Jeane Kirkpatrick said on *Meet the Press* a few days after the operation. "I think it was a rescue, and I think that we ought to stop calling it an invasion." Norman Podhoretz, on the op-ed page of *The New York Times*, wrote that the invasion, or the rescue, suggested a return to "recovery and health" for "a United States still suffering from the shell-shocked condition that has muddled our minds and paralyzed our national will since Vietnam." D'Souza characterizes it as "Reagan's first opportunity to overthrow a communist regime," an occasion when "Reagan's leadership was exercised in the face of apprehension on the part of his staff and skepticism on the part of the congressional leadership."

Not long after the Grenada invasion, for which the number of medals awarded eventually exceeded the number of actual combatants, the president, in his commander-in-chief role, spoke at a ceremony honoring the nation's Medal of Honor recipients. "Our days of weakness are over," he declared, standing under a huge representation of the medal's pale-blue ribbon and five-pointed star. "Our military forces are back on their feet and standing tall." Grenada, then, virtually as it happened, had materialized into the symbolic centerpiece of the rollback scenario that was the Reagan Doctrine. In the first dozen pages of *Ronald Reagan: How an Ordinary Man Became an Extraordinary Leader*, D'Souza laid out, presumably for that "new generation of young people with no alternative source of information," a kind of Young Adults timeline in which the Reagan administration is seen to begin at modern history's lowest tide ("capitalism and democracy ... on the retreat in much of the world," America itself facing "the greatest economic crisis since the Great Depression") and to conclude at its highest, the triumphal surge of reborn patriotism and purpose that was to raise all boats and end the cold war.

* * *

In this version of what happened between 1980 and 1988, Reagan's role as prime mover is seen to reside, before and after Grenada, less in actual actions than in his speeches, those moments when the president was primed to "go over the heads" of the Congress or the media or whoever was at the moment frustrating the aims of the administration. D'Souza, in *Ronald Reagan: How an Ordinary Man Became an Extraordinary Leader,* devoted four of his 264 pages to a close textual analysis of the 1983 "Evil Empire" speech (further comment appears on four more pages), which was, he assures us, "the single most important speech of the Reagan presidency, a classic illustration of what Vaclev Havel terms 'the power of words to change history.'"

This faith in the laser-like efficacy of Reagan's rhetoric seems undiminished by the fact that it remains largely a priori. "Going after a major policy change, crafting a practical policy initiative, and sticking with it is an accomplishment," Martin Anderson, who was Reagan's chief domestic policy adviser in the early administration, tells us in *Recollections of Reagan.* Yet the accomplishment he cites is the 1983 SDI, or "Star Wars," speech. "Another very important event in 1983 took place two weeks after the SDI speech," he adds, and, again, it develops that he is talking about not an actual "event" but another speech, in this instance the popular "Evil Empire."

William Kristol made recent reference to our need to credit Reagan's "magnificent" 1984 speech at Normandy, as if the speech, which was written by Peggy Noonan, were somehow at one on the "magnificence" scale with the invasion it was delivered to commemorate. ("The State/NSC draft that I'd been given weeks before wanted the president to go off on this little tangent about arms control," Miss Noonan later wrote about her Normandy speech, "and as I read it I thought, in the language of the day, Oh gag me with a spoon, this isn't a speech about arms negotiations, you jackasses, this is a speech about splendor.") As evidence that Reagan had the force of calculation behind his "predictions" and "prophecies," D'Souza offers the "tear down this wall" speech delivered at the Brandenburg Gate in 1987. "Not long after this," he writes, "the wall did come tumbling down, and Reagan's prophecies all came true. The most powerful empire in human history imploded. These were not just results Reagan predicted. He intended the outcome."

The consequences of reinventing Reagan as a leader whose leadership was seen to exist exclusively in his public utterances, the ultimate "charismatic" president, were interestingly studied by the political historian Jeffrey K. Tulis, who, in his 1987 *The Rhetorical Presidency*, outlined in some detail the dilemmas presented by a presidential style that tends to delegitimize both constitutional and bureaucratic authority, to depend for its effect on created crises (to "go over the heads" of the opposition requires the presence of some urgent message to be conveyed), and so to place unusual policy-making power in the hands of speechwriters:

> Many speeches are scheduled long before they are to be delivered. Thus the commitment to speak precedes the knowledge of any issue to speak about, often causing staff to find or create an issue for the speech.... The routinization of crisis, endemic to the rhetorical presidency, is accompanied by attempted repetitions of charisma. In Reagan's case this style was further reinforced by an ideology and a rhetoric opposed to the Washington establishment, to bureaucrats and bureaucracies.... He serves as a better illustration than any other president of the possibility and danger that presidents might come themselves to think in the terms initially designed to persuade those not capable of fully understanding the policy itself. Having reconfigured the political landscape, the rhetorical presidency comes to reconstitute the president's political understanding.

Since D'Souza's account of the Reagan presidency derived from and differed in no substantive factual detail from those of the "ingrates and apostates" who were already on their book tours when that presidency ended, the superimposition of the "leadership" narrative meant grappling with some fairly intractable material already on the record. The peculiarities noticed by others (the president was "detached," or "not entirely informed," or "vague on details," or "passive") would need to be translated into evidence of a grand design. Biographical details would need to be mined for "character" points, often to less than coherent effect. "Here was the son of the town drunk who grew up poor

in the Midwest," D'Souza tells us on page 10. "Without any connections, he made his way to Hollywood and survived its cutthroat culture to become a major star."

This was not literally true: Reagan was never a "major
star," but a reliable studio contract player who hit an era of
diminished demand and was reduced, before finding a role as
a spokesman for General Electric, to introducing a club act,
The Continentals, at the Last Frontier in Las Vegas. "Survived its
cutthroat culture to become a major star," however, fits the point
D'Souza was trying to make on this page, which had to do with
"the personal [and] political mystery" that had enabled Reagan
to change "both his country and the rest of the world." By page
45, where the point to be made had to do with the president's
flexibility and skill at "the art of negotiating and being part of a
team," D'Souza had reworked the bio to yield what he needed:
"Reagan was never a big enough star to permit himself such
consuming narcissism…. When many actors were too fastidious
to be seen on television, regarding it as inferior to film, Reagan
obligingly switched to the new medium, thus guaranteeing
himself more parts."

This constant trimming and tacking leads D'Souza into fairly
choppy water, where logical connections tend to get jettisoned. If
the famous Reagan "gaffes" were calculated, as D'Souza suggests
("When we recall Reagan's gaffes, we see that he sometimes used
them as a kind of code to transmit important political messages
that would be incomprehensible to a hostile media"), then could
the president not be seen as a demagogue, deliberately manipu-
lating the electorate with "facts" (the welfare queens, the student
loans used to buy certificates of deposit, the young man who
went into the grocery store and bought an orange with food
stamps and a bottle of vodka with the change) he knew would
never stand scrutiny? Not at all: the president dealt in "morality
tales," in the "illustration of a broader theme," and "just because
this or that particular detail might be erroneous did not mean
that the moral of the story was invalid." If Reagan failed to
recognize his black secretary of housing and urban development, Samuel Pierce, addressing him as "Mr. Mayor," did that
not suggest a relationship both with his own administration and
with urban America that remained casual at best? No, only an
"oversight": "He was wrong not to recognize Sam Pierce, but

POLITICAL FICTIONS

the reason for his oversight was that he had no interest in the Department of Housing and Urban Development, which he saw as a rat hole of public policy."

If Reagan set out to reduce the size and cost of the government and left it, in 1990 dollars, $1.5 trillion deeper in debt than when he started ("You and I, as individuals, can, by borrowing, live beyond our means, but only for a limited period of time," he had said in his 1981 inaugural address. "Why then should we think that collectively, as a nation, we are not bound by that same limitation?"), could not the president be said to have failed at his own mission? No, because Reagan's unique approach to that mission, which allowed him to cut taxes while increasing domestic entitlements and boosting defense spending to a rough total, for the eight years, of $2 trillion, turned out to have "a silver lining." D'Souza explains: "by a strange turn of fate, the deficit accomplished for Reagan what he was unable to achieve directly: for the first time in this century, Congress began to impose limits on the growth of government." If Reagan lacked, as D'Souza allows, not only "historical learning" and "encyclopedic knowledge" but also "the two characteristics of the liberally educated person: self-consciousness and open-mindedness," did dogmatism not tend to undermine the value of his opinions? Not exactly: Reagan "saw the world through the clear lens of right and wrong," and so possessed a knowledge that "came not from books but from within himself."

The knowledge that "came not from books but from within himself" is where we reenter the real woo-woo of the period, the insistence on the ineffable that began with the perceived need to front the administration with a "leader" and ended by transforming the White House into a kind of cargo cult. "There is no point in pining for 'another Ronald Reagan,'" D'Souza concludes, exactly if unwittingly capturing this aspect of the period. "He isn't returning, and there will never be another quite like him." Since it was the given of the Reagan administration that Reagan was at its helm, and since a good deal of the visible evidence suggested otherwise, the man must be a "mystery," with skills pitched, like a dog whistle, beyond our defective ability to hear them.

JOAN DIDION

D'Souza tells us that Edmund Morris, Reagan's official biographer, in 1990 characterized his subject as the most incomprehensible figure he had ever encountered. He tells us that Lou Cannon, who covered Reagan in Sacramento and in Washington and wrote three books about him, regards Reagan as a puzzle, and is "still trying to understand the man." He tells us that Reagan and Edwin Meese, whose daily lives were inseparable in both Sacramento and Washington, never saw each other socially. Reagan had "countless acquaintances," D'Souza observes, but apparently only one close friend, the actor Robert Taylor. Nancy Reagan spoke regularly to friends on the telephone, but her husband did not: "He would say hello, exchange a few pleasantries, then hand the receiver to her." Frustrated by "the paradoxes of Reagan's personality," D'Souza writes, "some who worked with him for years have given up trying to understand him."

Yet these "paradoxes" existed only within what was essentially a category confusion. Defined as "president," or even as "governor," Reagan did indeed appear to have some flat sides, some missing pieces. Defined as "actor," however, he was from the beginning to the end of his public life entirely consistent, a knowable and in fact quite predictable quantity. D'Souza allows that Reagan's life as an actor was a significant part of his makeup, but sees "actor" as a stepping stone, a role the real Ronald Reagan, or "president," had mastered and shed, although not before absorbing certain lessons that "enabled him to govern more effectively": the importance of appealing to a mass audience, say, or the knowledge that "noble ideals" could be more effectively communicated "if they were not abstract but personalized and visualized." Grappling with the question of how Reagan could be "uniformly fair-minded and pleasant with aides" but "not get close to them personally," D'Souza, laboring from within the definition "president," extracts a "leadership" solution: "He saw them as instruments to achieve his goals."

"People would work for him for a decade, then they would leave, and he would not associate with them—not even a phone call," D'Souza notes, and again draws the "leadership" lesson: "Thus the conventional wisdom must be turned on its head: he wasn't their pawn; they were his." This fails to compute (if they were the pawns and he their leader, would he not instead be inclined to keep them on speed dial, available for further deployment?) and will continue to do so, since the category is wrong: what might be seen as mysterious behavior in one occupation can be standard operating procedure in another, and it is within the unique working rhythms of the entertainment industry that the "mysteries" of the man and the administration evaporate. Reagan could be "uniformly fair-minded and pleasant with aides" without getting close to them personally (or knowing where their offices were or even their names) not because he "saw them as instruments to achieve his goals" but because he saw them as members of the crew ("invisible behind the lights," in Donald Regan's words), as gaffers and best boys and script supervisors and even as day players, actors like himself but not featured performers whose names he need remember.

Similarly, the ability to work with people for a decade and never call them again precisely reflects the intense but temporary camaraderie of the set, the location, where the principals routinely exchange the ritual totems of bonding (unlisted home numbers, cell numbers, car numbers, triple-secret numbers, and hour-by-hour schedules for sojourns in Aspen and Sundance and Martha's Vineyard) in full and mutual confidence that the only calls received after the wrap will be for ADR, or for reshoots. Even that most minor of presidential idiosyncrasies, the absolute adherence to the daily schedule remarked upon by virtually all Reagan's aides, the vertical line drawn through the completed task and the arrow pointing to the next task (D'Souza tells us again about the arrows, as evidence of "the brisk thoroughness with which he discharged his responsibilities"), derives from the habits of the set, where the revised shooting schedule is distributed daily. "SC. 183A—EXT. WASHINGTON STREET—MOTOR-CADE—DAY," such a schedule might read, and, once Scene 183A was completed, a vertical line would be drawn through it on the schedule, with an arrow pointing to "SC. 17—ANDREWS AFB—ESTABLISHING—DAY": not in any sequence the principals need to understand, but the day's next task.

Asked whether he liked being president better than being an actor, Ronald Reagan, according to D'Souza, replied, "Yes, because here I get to write the script too." D'Souza presents this as the president's amusing deprecation of the way in which he

JOAN DIDION

achieved objectives "against the odds," and so it may have been intended, but the deeper peculiarities of Reagan's tenure could even at the time be seen to derive from his tendency to see the presidency as a script waiting to be solved. There is in the development of every motion picture a process known as "licking the script," that period during which the "story" is shaped and altered to fit the idealized character who must be at its center. A president who understands the "character clarity" that results from this process would sense immediately that a scene with, say, Prime Minister Yitzhak Shamir of Israel could be improved by a dramatization of how he, the president, or star, personally experienced the Holocaust.

It would be only logical, then, for Reagan to tell Shamir, as he did in 1983, that during World War II he had filmed Nazi death camps for the Signal Corps (in fact he had spent the entire war in Culver City, making training films at the Hal Roach studio), that he had (presciently) kept one reel in case the Holocaust was ever questioned, and that he had (just recently!) found occasion to convert a doubter by running this reel. A president who understands how a single scene can jump a script would naturally offer reporters in Charlotte, North Carolina, as Lou Cannon tells us that Reagan did during his 1975 primary campaign, this improved version of how segregation ended in the military:

> "When the Japanese dropped the bomb on Pearl Harbor there was a Negro sailor whose total duties involved kitchen-type duties.... He cradled a machine gun in his arms, which is not an easy thing to do, and stood on the end of a pier blazing away at Japanese airplanes that were coming down and strafing him and that [segregation] was all changed." When a reporter pointed out that segregation in the armed services actually had ended when President Truman signed an executive order in 1948 three years after the war, Reagan stood his ground. "I remember the scene," Reagan told me on the campaign plane later. "It was very powerful."

The question most frequently asked in a script meeting is, in one variation or another, always this: *Why do we care, how can we up the stakes, what's going to make America root for this guy?* The "guy," of course, is the main character, the star part, and infinite time and attention is devoted to finding his "hook," the secret to his character that gets hinted at in Act One, revealed at the end of Act Two, and turned in Act Three: "son of the town drunk," say, could even be the secret behind "stood on the burning pier and cradled in his arms the machine gun that would end segregation." Ronald Reagan, we later learned from his personal physician, Brigadier General John Hutton, first grasped the import of the AIDS epidemic in July 1985 (until then he had seemed to construe it as a punishment for bad behavior, and "would say words to the effect: 'Is there a message in this?'"), when he learned from a news report that it had happened to someone America could root for, Rock Hudson.

There is in *Ronald Reagan: How an Ordinary Man Became an Extraordinary Leader* one arresting account, which seems to be based not on D'Souza's access to the famous and less known movers of the period (his two-page list of acknowledgments recalls with considerable poignancy the fervor of the moment, including as it does such evocative names as "Elliott Abrams," "George Gilder," "Josh Gilder," "Michael Ledeen," "Joshua Muravchik," "Grover Norquist," "Robert Reilly," "Joseph Sobran," and "Faith Whittlesey") but on reporting done by Jane Mayer and Doyle McManus for their *Landslide: The Unmaking of the President, 1984–1988.* The place is the White House. The time is October 26, 1983, when the American students "rescued" by the invasion of Grenada were on their way to Charleston Air Force Base in South Carolina. "On the day of their arrival," D'Souza writes, "Oliver North, who had helped plan the Grenada operation, came rushing into the president's office."

> He said that the students had not been briefed on the reasons for the invasion, and no one knew what they would tell the press. "Come with me," Reagan said. He led North into a room with a television monitor. There the two of them watched as the first young man got off the plane, walked over to the runway, dropped to his knees, and kissed the soil of the United States. "You see, Ollie," Reagan said, "you should have more faith in the American people." Reagan knew that with the student's dramatic gesture, the

national debate over the legitimacy of the Grenada invasion was effectively over.

Among the several levels on which this passage invites the
reader to linger (Why would students in need of rescue need
to be briefed on the reasons for the rescue? How exactly would
"more faith in the American people" lead to the expectation that
the first student off the plane would show the cameras what the
administration wanted shown?), the most rewarding has to do
with "Ollie," and his apparently easy access, as early as October
1983, to the president's office. It would, in due time, be repeatedly suggested that Lieutenant Colonel North was a rogue fantast
who had inflated or even invented his proximity to the president.
"He said he sometimes spent time alone with Ronnie in the
Oval Office," Nancy Reagan wrote in *My Turn*, her own essay
into correcting the record. "But that never happened." Larry
Speakes called North's assertion that he had been in the Oval
Office when the medical students arrived home from Grenada
"an outright lie." "We researched the records," he wrote, "and
there was never a time when Ollie was alone with the President
in the Oval Office." Yet D'Souza's vignette casts North, whose
several code names included "Mr. Goode" and "Mr. White," in
what seems to have been his own preferred light: he was on the
scene, he was in the picture, he was able in a moment of threatened crunch to regard the president as his confidant.

By October 1983, the sequence of events that became known
as "Iran-contra," or, as D'Souza calls it, the "historical footnote
that future generations will not even remember," was well
underway, and the White House deep in that perilous territory where certain spectral missions were already coinciding, to
deleterious effect, with the demands of the script. Iran-contra,
D'Souza assures his Young Adult readers, "seems to have been
transacted in the White House without Reagan's knowledge
or approval," but even if we discount the assertions of Reagan's
aides that he was briefed on every detail except possibly (this
point remains unclear) the diversion of funds, and even if we
discount the president's own statement that "it was my idea to
begin with," Iran-contra was not a series of events that professionals of the Washington process would naturally think of
transacting.

It was instead a scenario that suggested the addled inspiration of script meetings, the moment when the elusive line materializes: on the one hand we have the "lion in winter," as D'Souza calls Reagan, the aging freedom fighter (*NB, possible: we learn in Act Two he knows he has something terminal but hasn't told anybody???*) whose life has been dedicated to the eradication of tyranny and who is now, apparently alone (*NB, everyone opposes, scene where even trusted aide backs away*), facing his last and toughest battle with the forces of injustice. The inspiration, of course, the solution to the script, the always startlingly obvious idea that comes only when the table is littered with takeout and the producer is inventing pressing business elsewhere, is this: the lonely lion in winter turns out not to be alone after all, for we also have the young colonel, "Mr. Goode," a born performer, a larger-than-life character, a real character, actually, one who (according to Larry Speakes) "loved to operate big in the Situation Room … standing in the middle of the floor, a phone at each ear, barking cryptic orders to some faraway operative" and who (according to Peggy Noonan) could convincingly deliver such lines as "And don't forget this is in accord conversation Casey-North approximately 1500 this date" or "Don't talk to me about Pastora [the contra leader Eden Pastora, aka 'Comandante Zero'], I'm not speaking to Pastora."

For the "President," a man whose most practiced instincts had trained him to find the strongest possible narrative line in the scenes he was given, to clean out those extraneous elements that undermine character clarity, a man for whom historical truth had all his life run at twenty-four frames a second, Iran-contra would have been irresistible, a go project from concept, a script with two strong characters, the young marine officer with no aim but to serve his president, the aging president with no aim but to free the tyrannized (whether the tyrants were Nicaraguans or Iranians or some other nationality altogether was just a plot point, a detail to work out later), a story about male bonding, a story about a father who found the son he never (in this "cleaned out" draft of the script) had, a buddy movie, and better still than a buddy movie: a mentor buddy movie, with action.

"Reagan didn't violate the public trust in the pursuit of personal power," we are told by D'Souza, who, possibly because he noticed that he had "Ollie" running into the president's office on page 158, seems by page 247 of *Ronald Reagan: How an Ordinary Man Became an Extraordinary Leader* to have somewhat amended his earlier (page 16) assessment of Iran-contra as a series of events "transacted in the White House without Reagan's knowledge or approval." Here, on page 247, we see a change from passive to active voice: "He did it because he empathized with the suffering of the hostages and their families.... He refused to listen to Shultz and Weinberger's prudent recommendations that he avoid the foolish enterprise altogether." D'Souza seems not to entirely appreciate that for this actor, given this script, it would have been precisely the suggestion that he was undertaking a "foolish enterprise" that sealed his determination to go with it. "There are those who say that what we are attempting to do cannot be done," he had said in a hundred variations in as many speeches. This was a president who understood viscerally—as the young colonel also understood—that what makes a successful motion picture is exactly a foolish enterprise, a lonely quest, a lost cause, a fight against the odds: undertaken, against the best advice of those who say it cannot be done, by someone America can root for. *Cut, print.*

September 24, 1992

I

IN THE UNDERSTANDABLY general yearning for "change" in the governing of our country, we might pause to reflect on just what is being changed, and by whom, and for whom. At Madison Square Garden in New York from July 13, 1992, until the balloons fell on the evening of July 16, four days and nights devoted to heralding the perfected "centrism" of the Democratic Party, no hint of what had once been that party's nominal constituency was allowed to penetrate prime time, nor was any suggestion of what had once been that party's tacit role, that of assimilating immigration and franchising the economically disenfranchised, or what used to be called "co-opting" discontent. Jesse Jackson and Jimmy Carter got slotted in during the All-Star Game. Jerry Brown spoke of "the people who fight our wars but never come to our receptions" mainly on C-SPAN.

"This convention looks like our country, not like a country club," Representative Tom Foley declared, and a number of speakers echoed him. Yet the preferred images of the convention were those of a sun-belt country club, for example that of Tipper and Al Gore dancing sedately on the podium. The preferred sound was not "Happy Days Are Here Again" but Fleetwood Mac, Christine McVie's request before the New Hampshire primary that the Clinton campaign stop using her song "Don't Stop" notwithstanding. Those who wanted to dance with the Gores, join the club, made it clear that they were prepared to transcend, as their candidate had often put it, "the brain-dead policies in both parties," most noticeably their own. "Democrat" and "Republican," we heard repeatedly, as if a prayer for electoral rain, were old words, words without meaning, as were the words "liberal" and "conservative." "The choice we offer is not conservative or liberal, in many ways it is not even Republican or Democratic," the candidate told us. "It is different. It is new.... I call it a New Covenant."

What Governor Clinton had been calling "a New Covenant" (for a while he had called it "a Third Way," which had sounded infelicitously Peruvian) was essentially the Democratic Leadership Council's "New Choice," or more recently its "New Social Contract," a series of policy adjustments meant to "reinvent government" (as in *Reinventing Government* by David Osborne, a Clinton adviser) not at all by diminishing but by repackaging its role. There was in the New Covenant or the Third Way or the New Choice or the New Social Contract much that was current in Republican as well as Democratic thinking, but there was also a shell game: part of the "New Covenant," for example, called for the federal government to "cut 100,000 bureaucrats" by attrition, but it was unclear who, if not a new hundred thousand bureaucrats, would administer the new federal programs ($133.7 billion to "Put America to Work," $22.5 billion to "Reward Work and Families," $63.3 billion to encourage "Lifetime Learning") promised in the ticket's *Putting People First: How We Can All Change America*. The "New Covenant" was nonetheless the candidate's "game plan," and it was also, covering another Republican base, his "new choice based on old values."

In certain ways this convention's true keynote address was delivered not by the keynote speakers of record but by the Democratic National Committee's finance chairman, Senator John D. (Jay) Rockefeller IV of West Virginia. Senator Rockefeller, describing himself as "one of those Democrats who doesn't threaten big donors," reported that this was a year in which it was possible to mount "the best financed Democratic presidential campaign ever," one in which the "donor base is bigger than ever," enabling the party to buy "focus groups, polling, research, whatever it takes to get the message out." The message was this: we're tough, kick ass, get a life. "We Democrats have some changing to do," the candidate said, accepting the nomination on behalf of those who "pay the taxes, raise the kids and play by the rules," by which he meant "the forgotten middle class" that had been the target of his campaign since New Hampshire. He had an ultimatum for "the fathers in this country who have chosen to abandon their children by neglecting their child support: take responsibility for your children or we will force you to do so." He had a promise to "end welfare as we know it," to put "100,000 more police on your streets," to set right a situation in which "the prime minister of Japan ... actually said ... he felt sympathy for America."

This world the candidate evoked, one in which the prime minister of Japan conspired with welfare queens and deadbeat dads (referred to in *Putting People First* as "deadbeat parents") to deride those who paid the taxes and raised the kids and played by the rules, began and ended with the woolly resentments of the focus group, and so remained securely distanced from what might be anyone's actual readiness to address actual concerns. The candidate spoke about "taking on the big insurance companies to lower costs and provide health care to all Americans," but *Putting People First* made it clear that this more comprehensive health care was to be paid for not only by decreasing Medicare benefits for those with incomes over $125,000, a proposal with which no one could argue, but also by "cutting medical costs," which, in practice, again means reducing benefits, this time at all income levels. (This is a thorny business. One reason medical costs keep rising is not necessarily because the insured consumer is being "gouged," as *Putting People First* suggests, but precisely because insured consumers now make up certain deficits incurred by the treatment of patients subject to the already restricted payment schedules specified by Medicare and Medicaid.)

The candidate spoke about "less entitlement" and more "empowerment," the preferred word among the Bush administration's own "New Paradigm" theorists for such doubtfully practicable ideas as selling housing projects to their tenants, but it remained unclear just what entitlement this particular candidate could have the political will to cut. The single "entitlement reform" detailed as an actual monetary saving in *Putting People First* was the Medicare cutback for those with incomes over $125,000, and it was hard not to remember that Governor Clinton, just four months before, had saturated Florida retirement condos with the news that Paul Tsongas, who had proposed to limit cost-of-living increases on Social Security benefits to recipients with incomes over $125,000, was against old people.

He spoke about reducing defense spending, but also about maintaining "the world's strongest defense"; the projected figure for "1993 defense cuts (beyond Bush)" offered by *Putting People First*, however, was only two billion dollars, and Governor Clinton, during the press of his losing primary campaign in

Connecticut, had promised to save the Groton-based Seawolf submarine program, one multibillion-dollar defense expenditure marked for a cut by the Bush administration. He spoke about the need to "clean out the bureaucracy," as he had during all his primary campaigns except one, that in New York, where his key union endorsements included the Civil Service Employees Association (some 200,000 members in New York State) and District Council 37 (135,000 members in New York City) of the American Federation of State, County, and Municipal Employees. "There is a real opportunity in the citadel of the failures of the old bureaucratic approaches to talk about new ideas," Will Marshall, the president of the Democratic Leadership Council's Progressive Policy Institute and a Clinton adviser, had acknowledged to Ronald Brownstein of the *Los Angeles Times* on this point. "On the other hand, he's got a lot of support from public employee unions, he's fighting for his life and he needs support wherever he can get it."

These were Democrats, in other words, who accepted the responsibility with which Ron Brown had charged them: to "keep our eye on the prize, so to speak." These were Democrats who congratulated themselves for staying, as they put it, on message. Not much at their convention got left to improvisation. They spoke about "unity." They spoke about a "new generation," about "change," about "putting people first." As evidence of putting people first, they offered "real people" videos, soft-focus videos featuring such actual citizens as "Kyle Harrison," a student at the University of Arkansas in Fayetteville who cooperatively described himself as a member of "the forgotten middle class." Convention delegates were given what a Clinton aide called the "prayerbook," a set of six blue pocket cards covering questions they might be asked, for example about "The Real Bill Clinton." ("His father died before he was born and his mother had to leave home to study nursing.... Bill grew up in a home without indoor plumbing.") The volunteers who worked the DNC's "VVIP" skyboxes at the Garden were equipped with approved conversation, or "Quotable Lines" ("Al Gore complements Bill Clinton, they are a strong team," or "The Republicans have run out of ideas, they're stuck in a rut ... all Americans are losing out"), as well as with answers to more special, more VVIP-oriented questions, as in "Celebrity Talking Points" #3 and #4:

3. "Tipper Gore previously worked on a drive to put warning labels on albums classified violent or obscene. Isn't this a restriction of our 1ˢᵗ Amendment right to freedom of speech?"

First, let's be clear—Al Gore is the Vice-Presidential candidate and this convention will determine the platform for this party and for this campaign. Second, Tipper Gore is entitled to her own opinions as is any other American. She is a good campaigner and will work hard on behalf of the platform of this party and the Clinton-Gore ticket.

4. "Why are some entertainment personalities who normally endorse Democratic candidates sitting this election year out or going to Ross Perot?"

There are many other issues such as Human Rights, the Environment, Women Rights, AIDS and other such important issues which have become a priority for certain individuals. Also, those who have chosen other campaigns must have their reasons and I respect their right to do that.

"When in doubt," skybox volunteers were advised, "the best answer is, 'Thank you, I'll get a staff person to get you the campaign's position on that issue.'" It was frequently said to be the Year of the Woman, and the convention had clearly been shaped to make the ticket attractive to women, but its notion of what might attract women was clumsy, off, devised as it was by men who wanted simultaneously to signal the electorate that they were in firm control of any woman who might have her own agenda. There was the production number from *The Will Rogers Follies* with the poufs on the breasts. There was the transformation of two mature and reportedly capable women, Mrs. Clinton and Mrs. Gore, into double-the-fun blondes who jumped up and down, clapped on cue, and traveled, as Mrs. Reagan had, with a hairdresser on the manifest for comb-outs.

The party did introduce its five women candidates for the Senate (Carol Mosley Braun, Jean Lloyd-Jones, Lynn Yeakel, Barbara Boxer, and Dianne Feinstein) as well as four of its most visible ingenues (Kathleen Brown, Barbara Roberts, Sharon Pratt Kelly, and Pat Schroeder), but had originally hedged the possibility that the presence of too many women might threaten any viewer by ghettoizing them, scheduling them, with Jimmy Carter and Jesse Jackson and the AIDS presentations, on Tuesday night, which on the Monday-through-Thursday convention schedule had traditionally been known as "losers' night." (After some complaints, the Senate candidates, although not the ingenues, got moved to the Monday schedule.) "What used to be losers' night we're making women's night," Ron Brown had said about this to one woman I know, a prominent Democrat in the entertainment industry.

The proceedings ran so relentlessly on schedule that it was sometimes necessary to pad out the pre-primetime events with unmotivated musical interludes, and on one occasion with an actual ten-minute recess. "The people running this convention are just impossible," an aide to Governor Ann Richards of Texas, who as convention chair might in past years have been thought to be one of the people running the convention, said on its second night. "Wouldn't give us a minute of time when the networks were on. Finally she [Governor Richards] said to us, girls, my ego doesn't need this, so don't let yourselves get dragged down." Jodie Evans, who managed Jerry Brown's campaign, was told that to enter his name in nomination would "clutter up the schedule."

Governor Brown, who did not get to be governor of California for eight years by misunderstanding either politics or the meaning of political gestures, remained a flaw in the convention's otherwise seamless projection of its talking points. It was not by accident that he had been the only one of the Democratic primary candidates who, on the evening of the primary campaign's first Washington debate, did not go to dinner at Pamela Harriman's. He maintained so apparently quixotic a guerrilla presence in New York that Maureen Dowd began referring to him in the *Times* as The Penguin. He worked out of the *Rolling*

Stone office. He got messages at Dennis Rivera's Hospital Workers Union Local 1199. He camped one night at a homeless shelter and other nights at my husband's and my apartment. He passed up the balloon drop and the podium handshake to end the convention with his volunteers, finishing the night not at the DNC's four-million-dollar fundraising gala but at Elaine's.

He told Governor Clinton that the ticket would have his "full endorsement" in the unlikely eventuality that the platform was amended to include four provisions: "a $100 ceiling on all political contributions, a ban on political action committees (PACs), universal registration undertaken by government itself (together with same-day registration), and finally election day as a holiday." That these were not provisions the Clinton campaign was prepared to discuss ("I want to work with you on these critical issues throughout my campaign," the response went) freed Brown on what was for him, since he had shaped his campaign as a "fight for the soul of the Democratic Party," a quite sticky and isolating point, that of endorsing a ticket that could be seen as the very model of who his adversary might be in any "fight for the soul of the Democratic Party."

"I'd like to thank someone who's not here tonight," he said on the evening he declined to endorse but nonetheless did opt to clutter up the schedule. "Someone who's missing his first Democratic convention since the Depression. Someone I think of as the greatest Democrat of all. My father, Pat Brown." Referring as it did to a Democratic past, a continuum, a collective memory, this was jarring, off the beat of a party determined to present itself as devoid of all history save that one sunny day in the Rose Garden, preserved on film and repeatedly shown, when President John F. Kennedy shook the hand of the Boy's Nation delegate Bill Clinton, who could be seen on the film elbowing aside less motivated peers to receive the grail: the candidate's first useful photo opportunity.

2

More recent opportunities had given us, early on, the outline of the campaign the Democrats planned to run. There was, first of all, the creation, or re-creation, of Governor Clinton. By all accounts, and particularly by certain contradictory threads within

those accounts, this was a dramatically more interesting character than candidate, a personality so tightly organized around its
own fractures that its most profound mode often appeared to be
self-pity. "I was so young and inexperienced," Governor Clinton
told *The Washington Post* about his 1980 Arkansas defeat, "I didn't
understand how to break through my crisis and turn the situation
around." In his famous and extremely curious letter to the director of the ROTC program at the University of Arkansas, Colonel
Eugene Holmes, who could not reasonably have been thought to
care, he had spoken of his "anguish," of his loss of "self-regard and
self-confidence"; of a period during which, he said, he "hardly
slept for weeks and kept going by eating compulsively and reading until exhaustion set in." He spoke of the continuing inclination of the press to dwell on this and other issues as "the trials
which I endured."

"When people are criticizing me, they get to the old 'Slick
Willie' business," he had explained before the New York primary
to Jonathan Alter and Eleanor Clift of *Newsweek*. "Part of it is
that I'm always smiling and try to make it look easy and all that.
And part of it is the way I was raised. I had such difficulties in my
childhood." Governor Clinton spoke often about these difficulties in his childhood, usually, and rather distressingly, in connection with questions raised about his adulthood. Such questions
had caused him to wonder, he confided to *The Wall Street Journal*,
"whether I'd ever be able to return to fighting for other people
rather than for myself. I had to ask myself: what is it about the
way I communicate or relate? Was it something in my childhood?
I didn't wonder if I was a rotten person. I knew I was involved in
a lifelong effort to be a better person."

He was sometimes demonstrably less than forthcoming
when confronted with contradictions in this lifelong effort. By
mid-May of the 1992 campaign he was still undertaking what
he called an "enormous effort" to reconstruct his draft history,
which had first come into question in Arkansas in October 1978,
but was clear on one point: "Did I violate the laws of my state
or nation? Absolutely not." Still, from the angle of "something
in my childhood," this personal evasiveness could be translated
into evidence of what came to be called his "reaching to please,"
his "need to bring people together": the heroic story required
by the campaign coverage. "I'm always trying to work things out

because that's the role I played for a long time," the candidate told David Maraniss of *The Washington Post* at one point, and, at another: "The personal pain of my childhood and my reluctance to be revealing in that sense may account for some of what may seem misleading."

He frequently referred to "my pain," and also to "my passion," or "my obsession," as in "it would be part of my obsession as president." He spoke of those who remained less than enthusiastic about allowing him to realize his passion or obsession as "folks who don't know me," and of his need to "get the people outside Arkansas to know me like people here do"; most of us do not believe that our best side is hidden. "I can feel other people's pain a lot more than some people can," he told Peter Applebome of *The New York Times*. What might have seemed self-delusion was transformed, in the necessary reinvention of the coverage, into "resilience," the frequently noted ability to "take the hits." "The comeback kid" was said at the convention to be Governor Mario Cuomo's tribute to the candidate, but of course it had initially been the candidate's own tribute, a way of positioning his second-place finish in New Hampshire as a triumph, and there was in Governor Cuomo's echo of it a grudging irony, a New York edge.

What else did we know about this candidate? We knew that he, or his campaign, was adept at what is generally called negative campaigning. There was the knockout punch in Florida, on the eve of Super Tuesday, when Clinton supporters distributed leaflets suggesting that his principal rival there, Senator Tsongas, besides being against old people, was against Israel. (Governor Clinton, who had himself campaigned in Delray Beach wearing a white yarmulke, allowed after the primary that the leaflets had been misleading.) There was, on the weekend before the New York primary, the Clinton radio commercial, run for a few hours before it was pulled off the air, accusing Jerry Brown, the only Clinton challenger then extant, of being against "choice," or the right to abortion. In fact Governor Brown's position on choice in California had been exactly that of Governor Cuomo in New York: each had said that he personally accepted the position of the Catholic Church on abortion but as governor supported both the right to choose and full public funding for abortion. This was a notably less equivocal position than that previously taken by Governor Clinton, who had signed into Arkansas law a measure requiring minors to notify both parents before abortion and had apparently taken no position on the state's 1988 constitutional amendment banning public financing for abortion.

There remained some cloudiness about this amendment. "I opposed the vote of the people to ban public funding on that," Governor Clinton had said, fairly unequivocally, when he was asked about it on WNBC the Sunday before the New York primary. That was April 1992. By July 1992, a letter dated 1986 (the year an earlier version of the Arkansas amendment was proposed) had turned up, and seemed equally unequivocal. This letter, which, according to *The New York Post*, was "made available" to news organizations by "Republican operatives," was from Governor Clinton to Arkansas Right to Life. "I do support the concept of the proposed Arkansas Constitutional Amendment 65 and agree with its stated purpose," the letter read. "I am opposed to abortion and to government funding of abortions. We should not spend state funds on abortions because so many people believe abortion is wrong."

Apparent accidents, and even some apparent mistakes in judgment, had emerged over time as less accidental than strategic. There was Hillary Clinton's "gaffe" in complaining to Gail Sheehy, interviewing her for *Vanity Fair*, that the press was following a "double standard" in dwelling on her husband's alleged friendship with Gennifer Flowers, since Anne Cox Chambers ("sittin' there in her sunroom") had told her about "Bush and his carrying on, all of which is apparently well known in Washington." This was an "embarrassment," a "mistake," and yet the appearance of the *Vanity Fair* piece coincided with Clinton strategists issuing the same preemptive warning to the Bush campaign; with Ron Brown suggesting that if questions about adultery were to persist, he thought similar questions should be put to Bush; and with Democratic consultant Robert Squier suggesting on the NBC *Today* show that Bush be asked what he called "the Jennifer question." Nor was just the single point scored: there was also considerable secondary gain in showing Mrs. Clinton as "feminine," a weaker vessel, gossiping with a friend over tea in the sunroom and then retailing the gossip to a new friend—who, in the "unfeminine" role of reporter, could be seen to have taken unfair advantage of the shared confidence, the wife's moment of indiscretion in her husband's defense. The erring but contrite wife could then be firmly but gently "reprimanded" by the presumptive CINC, her husband ("The main point is, she apologized … she made a mistake and she's acknowledged it"), an improved role for them both.

What else did we know? We knew that this was a candidate who arrived on the national scene with a quite identifiable set of regional mannerisms and attitudes, the residue of a culture that still placed considerable value on playing sports and taking charge and catting around with one kind of woman and idealizing the other kind. It was true that this "southernness" sometimes seemed in Governor Clinton's case less inherited than achieved; it was also true that the achievement seemed to have cost the candidate a certain reliability of pitch. "You're not worth being on the same platform as my wife," which is what he said to Governor Brown when the latter suggested a possible conflict of interest between Mrs. Clinton's law firm and the state of Arkansas, seemed so broad as to raise doubts that he really had the manner down. Yet the rudiments of the style were in place, and they worked to convey the image of a candidate uniquely free of entangling alliances with the exact "special interests" that many voters believed to be receiving undue attention.

Women were one such "special interest." Blacks were another. Appearing to take a firm line on women presented a delicate problem, since the party was increasingly dependent on the support of women who were declaring their intention to vote a single issue, that of choice; the candidate covered this by repeating that he wanted to see abortion made "safe, legal, and rare," an unarguable but safely paternalistic construction. When it came to blacks, the candidate claimed an ambiguous regional expertise. "Where I come from we know about race-baiting," Governor Clinton had said when he announced for the presidency at the Old State House in Little Rock, and in many variations, most of which made reference to "the politics of division," thereafter. "They've used it to divide us for years. I know this tactic well and I'm not going to let them get away with it." This was generally seen, for example in a *New York Newsday* editorial, as the candidate "at his most believable," evidence of his "fidelity to the cause of ending racial divisiveness in America." In *The Washington Post*, Richard Cohen even managed to cite, as "an early indication of why Bill Clinton enjoys such wide support in the black community," the draft letter, in which the twenty-three-year-old Clinton had told Colonel Holmes that his opposition to the Vietnam War had plumbed "a depth of feeling I had preserved solely for racism in America."

Yet there remained an odd undertone in what Governor Clinton actually said on this subject. The "race-baiting" about which he claimed the special southern knowledge, for example, worked more than one way: "race-baiting" was what Governor Clinton accused Senator Tsongas of doing, after Tsongas ran commercials in the South showing film on which Governor Clinton, unaware that a camera was running and enraged by a misunderstanding (he had just been told mistakenly that Jesse Jackson was endorsing Senator Harkin), spoke of Jackson's "backstabbing" and "dirty double-crossing." Similarly, letting "New York be split apart by race" was what Governor Clinton accused Governor Brown of doing, when the Clinton campaign wanted to remind New York primary voters that Brown had named Jesse Jackson as his choice for vice president. There was often this chance, when Governor Clinton spoke about race, to hear what he very clearly said and yet to understand it quite another way. The "them" who would not be allowed to "get away with it," for example, were clearly those who practiced "the politics of division," yet "the politics of division" remained, like "race-baiting," open to conflicting interpretation: it has been within memory the contention of large numbers of white Americans that civil rights legislation itself represented the politics of division.

This has not been a sphere in which very many American politicians have known how to talk straight. Susan Estrich, who managed Michael Dukakis's 1988 campaign, later pointed out to Peter Brown, the chief political writer for Scripps Howard and the author of *Minority Party: Why Democrats Face Defeat in 1992 and Beyond*, that she did not hear voters in the party's 1988 focus groups say they were "against" blacks. What she did hear, she said,

was, "I want to get a decent job, send my kid to a good school."
What was being said, as she saw it, was, "Are you the party that
is going to bend over backwards for blacks when the rest of us
just want to walk straight?" Although the Democratic Party's
1992 candidate told us in Madison Square Garden where he got
what he called "my passionate commitment to bringing people
together without regard to race" (from his grandfather, who ran
a grocery in a black neighborhood and "just made a note of it"
when customers couldn't pay), this was a campaign that took
extraordinary care not to leave the impression that it was bending
over backwards for blacks.

There was the picture, taken the day before the Georgia,
Maryland, and Colorado primaries, showing Governor Clinton
standing with Senator Sam Nunn of Georgia in front of a formation of mostly black prisoners at the Stone Mountain Correctional
Facility, a less than conventional setting in which to make time
for photos on the eve of three contested primaries. Senator Tom
Harkin had promptly blanketed rural South Carolina with some
eighty thousand copies of this Stone Mountain shot (juxtaposed
with one of himself with Jesse Jackson), and its explication had
for a while been a staple of Jerry Brown's stump speech: "Two
white men and forty black prisoners, what's he saying? He's saying, We got 'em under control, folks, don't worry." There was,
when Governor Clinton was campaigning in a white Detroit
suburb before the Michigan primary, his rather unsettling take on
the Bush campaign's 1988 use of Willie Horton: "This guy runs
Willie Horton, scares the living daylights out of people, then cuts
back on aid to local prosecutors, cuts back on aid to local law
enforcement, cuts back Coast Guard, Customs, and Border Patrol
funding to intercept drugs."

There was the apparently unmonitored decision, the day
after the Illinois and Michigan primaries, to play nine holes of
golf, accompanied by at least one television camera crew, at an
unintegrated Little Rock country club, a recreational choice so
outside the range of normal political behavior that it seemed
aberrational, particularly since the issue was not unfamiliar in
Little Rock; a group of twelve Arkansas legislators had a year or
so before boycotted an event at another unintegrated local club,
and both *The Boston Herald* and *The New York Post* had already
run stories about Governor Clinton's honorary memberships in

unintegrated Little Rock clubs. There was the equivocal response to the May 1992 Los Angeles riots (the desirability of "personal responsibility" and "an end to division" remained the unexceptionable but elusive Clinton position on discontent of all kinds), followed six weeks later by the campaign's cleanest surgical strike: the Sister Souljah moment.

Sister Souljah, born Lisa Williamson, was in 1992 a twenty-eight-year-old rap artist, writer, and community activist. She was a graduate of Rutgers. In high school she had won a prize in a constitutional oratory competition sponsored by the American Legion. Not long after the Los Angeles riots, in the course of an interview in *The Washington Post*, she had said this: "I mean, if black people kill black people every day, why not have a week and kill white people? You understand what I'm saying? In other words, white people, this government and that mayor were well aware of the fact that black people were dying every day in Los Angeles under gang violence. So if you're a gang member and you would normally be killing somebody, why not a white person?" What happened next was fortuitous, one of those random opportunities by which campaigns live or die: just a few weeks later, during a meeting of Jesse Jackson's Rainbow Coalition at which Governor Clinton was scheduled to speak, it came to the attention of the Clinton campaign that this same Sister Souljah had spoken the day before. A number of reporters had apparently been told in advance by Clinton aides that Governor Clinton would use his Rainbow Coalition speech to demonstrate his "independence" from Jesse Jackson, and the opportunity to signal white voters by denouncing Sister Souljah's "message of hate" was seamless, a gift from heaven, the most unassailable possible focus for such a signal. That this opportunity had been seized was precisely what constituted, for the campaign and for its observers, the incident's "success," and the candidate's "strength."

The extent to which many prominent Democrats perceived their party as hostage to Jesse Jackson was hard to overestimate. I recall being told by one of the party's 772 "superdelegates," a category devised to move control of the nominating process back from the primary electorate to the party leadership, that Jackson's speech at the 1988 Atlanta convention had been "a disaster" for the party, and had "lost the election for Dukakis." Duane Garrett, a San Francisco attorney and fundraiser, told the Scripps Howard political writer Peter Brown that "the key thing that would have helped Dukakis enormously would have been to go to war with Jesse at the convention. Not to be mean-spirited or petty, but to make it clear that Dukakis was the guy in charge." A good deal of Governor Clinton's 1992 campaign was about creating situations in which he could be seen to do what Dukakis had not done. Eleanor Clift, for example, on one of the Sunday-morning shows, interpreted "You're not worth being on the same platform with my wife" as a success on the not-Dukakis scale. The candidate, she said, had "needed to pass the Dukakis test, needed to show true strong emotion toward his wife." The Sister Souljah moment, in this view, represented a Clinton call for "an end to division" that had at once served to distance him from Jackson and to demonstrate that he was "the guy in charge," capable of dominating, or "standing up to," a kind of black anger that many white voters prefer to see as the basis for this country's racial division.

"It was a brilliant coup," Mary McGrory concluded in *The Washington Post*. "Clinton didn't take on Jackson directly. He didn't pick the fight on a central black concern." That Sister Souljah herself was a straw target was, then, beside the point, and what Clinton actually said at the Rainbow Coalition meeting (he said that Sister Souljah's comments in the *Post* had been "filled with the kind of hatred that you do not honor," that they were an example of "pointing the finger at one another across racial lines," and that "we have an obligation, all of us, to call attention to prejudice wherever we see it") was less important than the coverage of it, and the way in which the candidate capitalized on the coverage: the message had been sent and he reinforced it, just as he had reinforced his willingness to make "tough choices" by allowing the Arkansas execution of Rickey Ray Rector to proceed by lethal injection forty-eight hours before the Super Bowl Sunday on which Governor and Mrs. Clinton would address the Gennifer Flowers question on 60 *Minutes*. The measures Governor Clinton had apparently taken to avoid the draft were adroitly reframed as another "tough choice," a decision to do what he saw as "right" ("I supported the Persian Gulf War because I thought it was right and in our national interest, just as

I opposed the Vietnam War because I thought it was wrong and not in our national interest"); this was his commander-in-chief transformation, a mode in which he was moved to mention, as evidence of his ability to handle crises abroad, the several venues, including Honduras, to which he had deployed the Arkansas National Guard.

"If you want to be president you've got to stand up for what you think is right," Governor Clinton said about his Sister Souljah moment. "They have chosen to react against me, essentially taking the position, I guess, that because I'm white I shouldn't have said it, and I just disagree with that," he told *Larry King Live*. One of his principal advisers, Stuart Eizenstat, a former Carter adviser and then a lobbyist, for example representing the National Association of Manufacturers against a workers' right-to-know law on toxic chemicals, was more forthcoming: "Clinton's strategy is not without risk," he told *The New York Times* about the calculation that reaching out to unhappy white voters should be the campaign's first priority. "But we have no real choice. Our base is too small to win, even in a three-way race, so the old-time religion just won't work any more."

3

This wisdom, that the failure of Democratic candidates in five of the six national elections preceding 1992 derived from an undesirable identification with the party's traditional base, was of course not new. It had its roots during the Vietnam War, with the 1968 and 1972 Nixon victories over the "liberals" Hubert Humphrey and George McGovern; was crystallized by Kevin Phillips's 1970 *The Emerging Republican Majority*; and became a fixed idea among the party's revisionist mainstream after the 1980 and 1984 defections of the so-called Reagan Democrats. These "Reagan Democrats," statistically quite a small group of people, thereafter became the voters to whom all election appeals would be directed, a narrowing of focus with predictable results, not the least significant of which was that presidential elections would come to be conducted almost exclusively in code.

Governor Clinton, for example, did not speak of Reagan Democrats. He spoke instead of being stopped in an airport by a police officer who wanted to tell him that he was "dying to vote

POLITICAL FICTIONS

for a Democrat again." He spoke of "the forgotten middle class," or, in a 1991 speech to the Democratic Leadership Council, of "the very burdened middle class," also known as "the people who used to vote for us." The late Paul Tully, at that time the political director of the Democratic National Committee, described one of those hypothetical "people who used to vote for us" to *The New York Times* as "a suburbanite, in a household with about $35,000 income, younger than forty-five, with a child or two, and in a marriage in which both partners work." James Carville spoke of "a thirty-two-year-old with two kids in day care who works in some suburban office building."

The point on which everyone seemed to agree was that this suburban working parent of two was "middle class," which was, according to Ted Van Dyk, the Democratic strategist who advised Paul Tsongas, the phrase that signaled Reagan Democrats "that it is safe to come home to their party because poor, black, Hispanic, urban, homeless, hungry, and other people and problems out of favor in Middle America will no longer get the favored treatment they got from mushy 1960s and 1970s Democratic liberals." That "middle class" had been drained of any but this encoded meaning was clear when, at a Clinton rally in Atlanta, Governor Zell Miller of Georgia derided Senator Tsongas as "an anti-death-penalty, anti-middle-class politician." Middle class, Governor Clinton told the Rainbow Coalition, by way of answering a direct question, was not "a code word" for racism. In fact this was accurate, since the use of the code was never an appeal exclusively to racism; the appeal was broader, to an entire complex of attitudes held in common by those Americans who sensed themselves isolated and set adrift by the demographic and economic and cultural changes of the last half century. "Middle class," Governor Clinton explained, referred "to values nearly every American holds dear: support for family, reward for work, the willingness to change what isn't working."

This again was accurate, but since the phrase "nearly every American" raised the specter of unspecified other Americans who did not hold these values dear, it appealed to those who would prefer to see the changes of the last half century as reversible error, the detritus of too "liberal" a social policy. "I have spent most of my public life worrying about what it would take to give our children a safe place to live again," Governor Clinton also said, striking the same note of seductive nostalgia. Such reduction of political language to coded messages, to "middle class" and "reward for work," to safe children and Sister Souljah, has much to do with why large numbers of Americans report finding politics deeply silly, yet the necessity for this reduction is now accepted as a given: in his *Minority Party*, Peter Brown quoted suggestions made to Alabama party officials by the Democratic pollster Natalie Davis:

- Instead of talking about Democrats lifting someone out of poverty, describe the party's goal as helping average Americans live the good life.
- Instead of saying Democrats want to eliminate homelessness and educate the underclass, talk about finding a way for young couples to buy their first home and offer financial help to middle-class families to send their kids to college.
- Instead of saying the Democrats want to provide health care for the poor, focus on making sure all working Americans have coverage.

The way of talking here was familiar, that of salesmanship, or packaging. If this seemed a way of talking that the average "young couple" or "middle-class family" or "working American" could instinctively tune out, flick the channel, press the mute button, it was also a way of talking that the Democratic candidate nominated by the 1992 convention instinctively understood: Bill Clinton was the son of a traveling salesman, the stepson of a Buick dealer, he knew in his fingernails how the deal gets closed. "If we lead with class warfare, we lose," he had told Peter Brown after the 1988 campaign. With Governor James Blanchard of Michigan and Senators Nunn of Georgia and Charles Robb of Virginia, he had been a founder in 1985 of the Democratic Leadership Council, which was instrumental in reshaping the "image" of the Democratic Party to attract the money of major lobbyists. The chairman of this repackaged Democratic Party, Ron Brown, was

himself a lobbyist, a partner at one of Washington's most influential law firms, Patton, Boggs, and Blow. Ron Brown was in 1988
lobbying for the Japanese electronics industry, including Hitachi,
Mitsubishi, and Toshiba, but he was on the podium in Madison
Square Garden on the evening when Governor Clinton got the
delegates hissing and booing over how "the prime minister of
Japan actually said he felt sympathy for America"; this was of
course just more code, and accepted as such.

The role played by the Democratic Leadership Council was
central to the eventual narrowing of American politics. It was the
DLC that invented Super Tuesday, the strategy of concentrating
primaries in southern states to "front-load" the process against
visibly liberal candidates. After this backfired in 1988, enabling
Jesse Jackson to gain enough momentum from newly registered
voters on Super Tuesday to go on to Atlanta with a real hand
to play, Jackson opened his remarks at a DLC-sponsored debate
by thanking Senator Robb for Super Tuesday. This had, according to Peter Brown, so amused Governor Clinton, "sitting in the
front row next to Robb," that he nearly fell off his chair, but it
altered the thinking of the new Democratic leadership only to
the extent that Ron Brown took care to deal Jackson out before
play began for 1992.

The wisdom of the DLC analysis, which tacitly called for the
party to jettison those voters who no longer turned out and target those who did, or "hunt where the ducks are," has not been
universally shared. Jesse Jackson had tried to prove it was possible to just register more ducks, and appeared in Madison Square
Garden to endorse the 1992 ticket as that classic tragic figure,
a man who had tried and failed to incorporate his constituency
into the system and who subsequently risked being overtaken
by that constituency. Jerry Brown had tried to prove that what
the political scientist Walter Dean Burnham had called "the
largest political party in America," the party of those who see no
reason to vote, could be given that reason within the Democratic
Party, but had been led by his quite fundamental party allegiance
into a campaign that remained for most Americans inexplicably
internecine and finally recondite, a fight for the "soul" of a party
about which they no longer or had never cared. "The last thing
the Democratic Party has wanted to do is declare that there is a
possibility for class struggle," Burnham noted in a discussion in

New Perspectives Quarterly. "The Republicans, however, are perfectly happy to declare class struggle all the time. They are always waging a one-sided class war against the constituency the Democrats nominally represent. In this sense, the Republicans are the only real political party in the United States. They stand for ideology and interest, not compromise."

4

The 1988 loss of Michael Dukakis was widely seen, both within the Democratic Party and outside it, as another example of the same malaise that had afflicted the party in 1968 and 1972 and in 1980 and 1984. Governor Dukakis, it was said after the fact, was not only "too liberal" but too northeastern, too closely identified with a section of the country that had once been a Democratic stronghold and no longer had the votes to elect a president. (Mario Cuomo, in this view, presented the same problem, one magnified by his very visibility and attractiveness as a candidate.) But in fact Governor Dukakis had not been nominated as a "liberal"; the party had closed ranks around him precisely because he had seemed at the time to offer the possibility of a "centrist" campaign, a campaign "not about ideology but about competence," which was what Governor Dukakis had promised in Atlanta in 1988 and which sounded not unlike what Governor Clinton promised (the choice that was "not conservative or liberal, Democratic or Republican" but "will work") in Madison Square Garden in 1992.

There were in fact a number of such dispiriting similarities between what was said at the Democratic convention in Atlanta in 1988 and what was said at the Democratic convention in New York in 1992. There was the same insistent stress on "unity," on "running on schedule." "This party's trains are running on time," I recall someone saying in Atlanta to dutiful applause. There was the same programmatic emphasis, tricked out in the same sentimental homilies. There were the same successful arguments to keep the platform free of any minority planks that could suggest less than total agreement with the platform, or lack of "unity." There was even the same emphasis on social control, on "enforcement," although nothing said in 1988 went quite so far in this direction, or suggested quite such a worrisome indifference to what such agencies of enforcement have meant in other countries, as the Clinton-Gore proposal to gather up "unemployed veterans and active military personnel" into what they called a "National Police Corps."

"Until now," Mary McGrory wrote in *The Washington Post* on the last day of the 1992 convention, the 1988 Democratic convention in Atlanta had been "considered the best." Clinton, she said, "hopes to top it, and of course, go on to a far different outcome in November." Not long after the 1988 defeat I was told by Stanley Sheinbaum, a major California Democratic fundraiser who had become distressed in the mid-1980s by the direction the party was taking, about having been excluded from a meeting at which leading Democrats had discussed the disaster and what to do next. "Don't ask Sheinbaum, I kept hearing from someone who was there, he'll only want to discuss issues," he said. It seemed that these Democrats had already convinced themselves that they had once again lost on "issues," specifically on what they saw as too close an association with Jesse Jackson, and they wanted now only to discuss mechanics, know-how, money: what Senator Rockefeller would describe, four years later at Madison Square Garden, as "focus groups, polling, research, whatever it takes to get the message out." The problem, as Sheinbaum saw it, was that there was no longer any message to get out:

When you're caught up in this dance of how to run campaigns better, rather than what you can do for that constituency that used to be yours, you're not going to turn anybody on. The whole focus is on big money. The Democrats under Dukakis and this guy Bob Farmer mastered how to get around the campaign finance limitations, both with PACs and soft money. They were magnificent in what they raised and it didn't do them a fucking bit of good. I mean it's no longer a thousand dollars. To get into the act now you've got to give a hundred thousand. So who are the players? The players are the hundred-thousand people. Who are the hundred-thousand people? They're the people who don't go into Harlem, don't go into South Central. They don't even fly MGM [MGM Grand Air,

JOAN DIDION

at the time the transcontinental airline of choice for the
entertainment industry] any more, they have their own
planes. You get this whole DLC crowd, their rationale is
that to talk about the issues will alienate too many people.

What was important, in 1992 as in 1988, was "winning this election," which was why each major DNC fundraiser, or "Managing
Trustee," had been asked to raise for 1992 not $100,000 but
$200,000. What was important, in 1992 as in 1988, was "not sad-
dling the candidate with a position he'll have to defend." What
was important, in 1992 as in 1988, was almost exclusively semantic, a way of presenting the party as free of unprofitable issues for
which it might conceivably need to fight. "I don't only think
George Bush is popular on many of these issues, I think he's
absolutely right," the 1992 Democratic candidate had said in 1991
on one subject that might traditionally have been considered an
issue, the incumbent Republican administration's foreign policy.
By the time the candidate reached Madison Square Garden he
had incorporated into his acceptance speech the very line with
which the incumbent Republican president, in February 1992
at Concord, New Hampshire, had formally opened his campaign for reelection: "If we can change the world we can change
America."

In this determined consensus on all but a few carefully chosen
and often symbolic issues, American elections are necessarily
debated on "character," or "values," a debate deliberately trivialized to obscure the disinclination of either party to mention the
difficulties inherent in trying to resolve even those few problems
that might lend themselves to a programmatic approach. A two-
party system in which both parties are committed to calibrating
the precise level of incremental tinkering required to get elected
is not likely to be a meaningful system, nor is an election likely
to be meaningful when it is specifically crafted as an exercise
in *personalismo*, in "appearing presidential" to that diminishing
percentage of the population that still pays attention. Governor
Clinton, interestingly, began to "appear presidential" on the
very morning he left New Hampshire, despite both his much-
discussed "character problem" and the previous day's vote, which

828

had shown him running eight points behind Senator Tsongas and incapable of raising more than twenty-five percent of the Democratic vote.

He appeared presidential largely because he was sufficiently well financed and sufficiently adroit to exit this disappointing performance via motorcade and private plane, in the authenticating presence of his own press entourage and ten-man Secret Service detail. By the day before the California primary he had begun to assume even the imperial untouchability of the presidency: plunging into a crowd on the UCLA campus, live on C-SPAN, the candidate and his Secret Service cordon became suddenly invisible in the sea of signs and faces. Only voices could be heard: "Bill, Bill, here, Bill," someone had kept saying. "You got a joint? Just one? I promise not to inhale?" And then, the same voice said, apparently to someone in the cordon of aides and agents: "I'm not touching him, hey, I said I'm not touching him, get your fucking hands off me."

Some weeks later, on the hot July morning when he stood outside the governor's mansion in Little Rock to introduce his choice for the vice-presidential nomination, Governor Clinton, in one simple but novel stroke, eliminated what some found the single remaining false note in this performance of presidentiality: he resolved the "character problem" by offering the electorate, as his running mate, an improvement on himself, a putatively more respectable Bill Clinton. In Senator Gore, he could present a version of himself already familiar to large numbers of Americans, a version of himself who had already produced the requisite book on a curve issue (Gore's *Earth in the Balance: Ecology and the Human Spirit*) and need not turn defensive about Arkansas whenever the subject of the environment was raised; a version of himself who, most importantly, had spent fifteen years in Congress free not only of identified character flaws but also of too many positions that might identify him as a Democrat.

Senator Gore, it was generally agreed, grounded the ticket, raised what had been its rather uneasy social comfort level: the Gore family had been with us for two generations now, and did not suggest, as the Clintons sometimes did, the sense of being about to spin free, back to the hollow. (This ungrounded quality reflects the oldest and deepest strain in actual American life, but we do not often see it in our candidates. We saw it in Gary Hart, where it was called "the weird factor," and engendered the distrust that ended his political career.) Senator Gore, moreover, lent Governor Clinton the gravitas of the Senate, and a presumed senatorial depth in foreign policy that the ticket might otherwise have been seen to lack. He supported the Bush administration on the use of force in the Persian Gulf. He had supported nonlethal aid to the Nicaraguan contras. He had supported the Reagan administration on the bombing of Libya. He had supported the Reagan administration on the invasion of Grenada.

Closer to home and to what his party had recently come to view as its terminal incubus, Senator Gore had been seen, during his aborted 1988 campaign for the presidency, as the only Democratic candidate willing to criticize, or "take on," Jesse Jackson. This was a Democratic candidate for vice president who could stand there in the hot midday sun in Little Rock and describe his birthplace— Carthage, Tennessee—as "a place where people know about it when you're born and care about it when you die." He could repeat this at Madison Square Garden, where he could also offer this capsule bio of his father, Senator Albert Gore Sr., who served seven terms in the House and three in the Senate before losing his seat in 1970 after opposing the war in Vietnam (a lesson learned for the son here): "a teacher in a one-room school who worked his way to the United States Senate." As presented by the younger Senator Gore, Carthage had its political coordinates somewhere in Reagan Country, as did the father's one-room school, as for that matter did the entire tableau on the lawn behind the governor's mansion in Little Rock, the candidate and the running mate and the wives and the children with the summer tans and the long straight sun-bleached hair that said *our kind, your kind, good parents, country club, chlorine in the swimming pool.* "This is what America looks like," Governor Clinton said on the eve of the nominating convention when he led the same successful cast off the plane at LaGuardia, "and we're going to give it to you."

5

He said this in a summer during which one American city, Los Angeles, had already burned. He said this in another American city, New York, that had a week before in Washington Heights come close to the flashpoint at which cities burn. This was a year in which 944,000 American citizens and businesses filed for bankruptcy, a figure up twenty-one percent from the year before. This was a year in which 213,000 jobs vanished in the city of New York alone, or 113,000 more than the "100,000 bureaucrats" Governor Clinton proposed to lose by attrition from the federal government. This was a year in which the value of real property had sunk to a point at which Citicorp could agree to sell a vacant forty-four-story office tower at 45th Street and Broadway to Bertelsmann A.G. for $119 million, $134 million less than the $253 million mortgage Citicorp held on the property. Four years before, in the same 1988 interview in *New Perspectives Quarterly*, Walter Dean Burnham had argued that neither of the two existing parties would have sufficient political resources to impose the austerity required to resolve America's financial crisis, the Republicans because their base was narrow to begin with and the Democrats "because a substantial number of people who would be followers of the Democrats if they had credibility, have dropped out of the political system and don't vote":

> It is already clear that when the fiscal crunch gets serious enough, we are going to find ourselves further away from anything that can be called democracy … and the more turned off the public becomes, the more they drop out. There is probably no recourse for this situation. The system is becoming more conspicuously oligarchic all the time. Both the politics of deadlock and, increasingly the bipartisan politics of resolving the fiscal crisis, are accelerating this dynamic.

Half those eligible to vote did not do so in the 1988 presidential election. The percentage of those eligible to vote who actually did vote in the 1992 California primary was forty-four percent. Only twenty-six percent of those registered to vote, or seven percent of the actual voting-age population, voted in the 1992 New York primary. The question of what happens when fifty percent of the electorate (or fifty-six percent, or seventy-four percent, or, in the case of New York, ninety-three percent) believes itself insufficiently connected to either the common weal or the interests of the candidates to render a vote significant could mean, in hard times, something other than it might have meant in good times, and a working instinct for self-preservation might suggest that one's own well-being could well depend on increasing the numbers of those who feel they have a stake in the society.

Yet this was not a year in which the Democratic Party was inclined to address the question of bringing these nonvoting citizens into the process. The party leadership was focused instead on its phantom Reagan Democrats, on what Robert J. Shapiro, a Clinton adviser and vice president of the DLC's Progressive Policy Institute, described to Ronald Brownstein of *The Los Angeles Times* as "an attempt to take the traditional goals of the Democratic Party ... and find means to achieve them that embody the values of the country." The "values of the country," which is to say the values of that fraction of the country that had come to matter, also known as "the swing vote," began to be defined in 1985, when the Michigan House Democratic Caucus commissioned Stanley Greenberg to do what became a seminal study of voters in Macomb County, Michigan. At a motel in Sterling Heights, Michigan, Greenberg assembled a focus group made up of three dozen registered Democrats who had voted for Ronald Reagan. According to Peter Brown,

> The voters were broken into four groups. Each participant was paid $35 for two hours and fed cold cuts. The tone was set when Greenberg read a quote from Robert Kennedy, a man held in reverence by these heavily Roman Catholic voters. The quote was RFK's eloquent call for Americans to honor their special obligation to black citizens whose forefathers had lived through the slave experience and who themselves were the victims of racial discrimination....
> "That's bullshit," shouted one participant.
> "No wonder they killed him," said another.
> "I'm fed up with it," chimed a third....
> The resulting report sent a shudder through state and national Democrats. It was the first of a continuing series of research projects during the latter half of the decade that explained the problem, quite literally, in black and white.

The votes for Reagan among these traditional Democrats, Greenberg reported, stemmed from … a sense that "the Democratic Party no longer responded with genuine feeling to the vulnerabilities and burdens of the average middle-class person. Instead the party and government were preoccupied with the needs of minorities…. They advanced spending programs that offered no appreciable or visible benefit" for middle-class people.

"Traditional" has many meanings here. These were "traditional" Democrats, and yet black voters were those who tended to share what Shapiro had called "the traditional goals of the Democratic Party." A candidate bent on at once luring the former and holding the latter will predictably be less than entirely forthcoming on certain points, which is part of what lent the Clinton "program," as outlined in *Putting People First*, its peculiar evasiveness. In the first place its details were hard to extract, since *Putting People First* was essentially a paste job of speeches and position papers, with only the occasional and odd specific, for example a call to "end taxpayer subsidies for honey producers." Read one way, the program could seem largely based on transferring entitlements from what were called "special interests" to those who "work hard and play by the rules," in other words distributing what wealth there was among the voting percentage of the population. *Putting People First* spoke often and eloquently, and in many variations, of "rewarding work," of "providing tax fairness to working families," of "ending welfare as we know it," of "cracking down on deadbeat parents." Read another way, however, *Putting People First* could be seen to stress benefits to accrue to the formerly needy and about to be "empowered":

> *Empower people* with the education, training, and child care they need for up to two years, so they can break the cycle of dependency; expand programs to help people learn to read, get their high school diplomas or equivalency degrees, and acquire specific job skills; and ensure that their children are cared for while they learn.
>
> After two years, *require those who can work to go to work*, either in the private sector or in community service;

provide placement assistance to help everyone find a job, and give the people who can't find one a dignified and meaningful community service job.

Expand the Earned Income Tax Credit to guarantee a "working wage," so that no American with a family who works full-time is forced to raise children in poverty.

Clues as to how all this might be reconciled seemed absent in the text itself. Much of *Putting People First*, however, appeared to derive from the thinking of the Democratic Leadership Council, particularly as expressed in a document distributed as a "discussion guide" at a May 1992 meeting to which Governor Clinton, the former chairman made candidate, had returned in triumph. The thrust of this document was later refined as the DLC's "New Social Contract," outlined in the July 1992 issue of its bi-monthly publication, *The New Democrat*. It was this "New Social Contract" that provided an instructive subtext for the Clinton program. "Data suggest that the public is ready to shift the moral foundations of entitlements from a one-way street—if you need it, you are entitled to it—to a more balanced social contract," Daniel Yankelovich suggested in *The New Democrat*. "If the society gives you a benefit, you must, if you are able, pay it back in some appropriate form. This means no more 'freebies,' no more ripoffs, and no more unfairness to the middle class."

A few pages earlier, Will Marshall, president of the DLC's Progressive Policy Institute, quoted Yankelovich by way of explaining how to remedy the fact that an "explosion of new rights and entitlements," among which he counted the rights "to remedial and college education, to abortion, to equal pay for women, to child and health care, to free legal counsel, to public facilities for the disabled, and many, many more," had meant "higher taxes to pay for public transfers to 'special interests'": "What the public is saying is that government programs should require some form of reciprocity: people should no longer expect something for nothing."

"Freebies" and "rip-offs" and "something for nothing" are extremely loaded words to use in reference to entitlement programs already weighted, via Social Security and Medicare and tax exemptions for mortgage interest and for contributions to pension funds, to favor the voting class, but they are the words heard in focus groups. Similarly, the "new right" to abortion does not mean "higher taxes to pay for public transfers to 'special interests'"; women who need funded abortions would tend alternately to need funded births and Aid to Families with Dependent Children, clearly the more expensive choice, but the politics are different: abortion remains, among "swing voters," a deeply freighted issue.

The most discussed and ambitious parts of the Clinton program were his proposals to involve the federal government (in ways and at a cost not satisfactorily detailed in *Putting People First*) not only in medical care but in rebuilding infrastructure and retraining and educating the work force. Yet what was said in *The New Democrat* suggested that even these proposals may have been crafted to reflect "what the public is saying." Daniel Yankelovich, describing the results of a focus-group study conducted for the DLC to gauge the mood of the electorate, noted that since "the American people believe activist government is important in solving the great challenges facing our country,"

> they are rejecting calls to eliminate government and leave problems like helping their kids go to college to the whims of the marketplace.... While any proposal to help families send their children to college would appeal both to the growing emphasis on education and to the public's economic worries, national service is especially attractive because it emphasizes the value of reciprocity. [Clinton had proposed national service as a way to pay back universal college loans.] There is a strong belief among the public that "there is no free lunch." In nearly every focus group, people echoed the comments of the man in Detroit who said, "I believe in giving something in return, I don't think anyone should get a free ride."...
>
> Welfare reform proposals that emphasize reciprocal obligation resonate well with the public, because they reinforce core American values....
>
> There is virtual unanimity (76 percent) on the idea that the country's elected leaders are not paying attention to the long-range needs of the country.... They are convinced

that education, training, and the dedication of the work-
force are the keys to economic vitality....

All of this points to a possible solution involving a massive commitment to training, education, and outreach; a
practical and realistic examination of what is meant by
"most-qualified" so that minorities were not disqualified;
and a serious good-faith effort to take black mistrust seriously and work at building a new structure of trust.

This is not an easy or simple strategy to implement. But
it offers a basis for compromise, rather than a sure formula
for confrontation and defeat—moral as well as electoral.

What was striking about this "new social contract," then,
was that its notion of what might resolve our social and economic woes, the "program," had been specifically shaped, like
Governor Clinton's Madison Square Garden speech, to reflect
what was said in focus groups. The "New Social Contract" talked
not about what the Democratic Party should advocate but about
what it "must be seen advocating," not about what might work
but about what might have "resonance," about what "resonates
most clearly with the focus-group participants." The "need for
profound changes in the way progressives view economic policy"
was confirmed, for Will Marshall and presumably for the new
Democratic leadership, not by an economic reality but by an
"evolution in the public's thinking."

The reliance on focus groups is not new, nor is it unique to the
Democratic Party (the Willie Horton issue, most famously, was
born in a 1988 focus group the Bush campaign ran in Paramus,
New Jersey) or even to politics. Motion pictures are tested in
focus groups at every stage of their production, sometimes even
before production, in the "concept" stage. New products have
been for at least the past several decades exhaustively exposed to
focus research. The use of such groups in marketing, however, has
as its general intention the sampling of public opinion at large,
the extrapolation of the opinion of the majority from the opinion of a few. What seemed novel about the use of focus groups
in the 1992 campaign was the increasingly narrow part of the
population to which either party was interested in listening, and

the extent to which this extreme selectivity had transformed the governing of the country, for most of its citizens, into a series of signals meant for someone else. "When people are asked to prioritize U.S. foreign policy," Daniel Yankelovich noted, "they favor furthering our economic interests over support for democracy by a two to one margin."

This was what was meant by the DLC's "revolution in government," the revolution, according to *The New Democrat*, that the Democratic Party must lead if it "expects to win back the confidence of the American people." Out where confidence was harder to come by and the largest political party in America—those who did not vote—got larger as we watched, the questions raised in the focus groups of the two leading minority parties about "freebies" and "rip-offs" and "something for nothing," about Willie Horton and about Sister Souljah, remained less clear. At a time when the country's tolerance of participatory democracy had already shallowed, what remained less clear still, and a good deal more troubling, was what kind of revolution might be made after the focus session in Sterling Heights or Paramus or Costa Mesa when "the American people," which is the preferred way of describing the selected dozens of narrowly targeted registered voters who turn out for the cold cuts and the $35, decide to say something else.

NEWT GINGRICH, SUPERSTAR

August 10, 1995

I

AMONG THE PERSONALITIES and books and events that have "influenced" or "changed" or "left an indelible impression on" the thinking of the Honorable Newton Leroy Gingrich (R-Ga.), the Speaker of the House of Representatives and one of the leading beneficiaries of the nation's cultural and historical amnesia, are, by his own accounts, Abraham Lincoln, Thomas Jefferson, Franklin Roosevelt, Isaac Asimov, Alexis de Tocqueville, Tom Clancy, Allen Drury's *Advise and Consent*, Robert Walpole, William Gladstone, Gordon Wood, Peter Drucker, Arnold Toynbee's *A Study of History*, Napoleon Hill's *Think and Grow Rich*, the "Two Cultures" lectures of C. P. Snow (the lesson here for the Speaker was that "if you're capable of being glib and verbal, the odds are that you have no idea what you're talking about but it sounds good, whereas if you know a great deal of what you're saying the odds are you can't get on a talk show because nobody can understand you"), Adam Smith, *Zen and the Art of Archery*, "the great leader of Coca-Cola for many years, Woodruff," an Omaha entrepreneur named Herman Cain ("who's the head of Godfather Pizza, he's an African-American who was born in Atlanta and his father was Woodruff's chauffeur"), Ray Kroc's *Grinding It Out*, and Johan Huizinga's *The Waning of the Middle Ages*.

There were also: Daryl Conner's *Managing at the Speed of Change*, Sam Walton's *Made in America*, Stephen R. Covey's *The Seven Habits of Highly Effective People*, the 1913 *Girl Scout Handbook*, Alcoholics Anonymous's *One Day At A Time*, Gore Vidal's *Lincoln* ("even though I'm not a great fan of Vidal"), the Sydney Pollack/Robert Redford motion picture *Jeremiah Johnson* ("a great film and a useful introduction to a real authentic American"), commercial overbuilding in the sun belt ("I was first struck by this American passion for avoiding the lessons of history when I watched the Atlanta real-estate boom of the early 1970s"), the science fiction writer Jerry Pournelle, the business consultant W. Edwards Deming ("Quality as Defined by Deming" is Pillar Five of Gingrich's Five Pillars of American Civilization), and, famously, the Tofflers, Alvin and Heidi, "important commentators on the human condition" and "dear friends" as well.

It was these and other influences that gave Mr. Gingrich what Dick Williams, an Atlanta newspaperman and the author of *Newt!*, called "an intellectual base that he has been developing since he was in high school, collecting quotes and ideas on scraps of paper stored in shoeboxes." It was in turn this collection of quotes and ideas on scraps of paper stored in shoeboxes (a classmate estimated that Mr. Gingrich had fifty such boxes, for use "in class and in politics") that led in 1984 to Mr. Gingrich's *Window of Opportunity* (described in its preface by Jerry Pournelle as "a detailed blueprint, a practical program that not only proves that we can all get rich, but shows how"); in 1993 to the televised "Renewing American Civilization" lectures that Mr. Gingrich delivered from Reinhardt College in Waleska, Georgia; and in 1995 to two books, the novel *1945* and the polemic *To Renew America*.

1945 is a fairly primitive example of the kind of speculative fiction known as "alternate history," the premise here being that Hitler "spent several weeks in a coma" after a plane crash on December 6, 1941, and so did not declare war on the United States. Now, in 1945, fully recovered, Hitler is poised to launch Operation Arminius, a manifold effort to seize England (which in 1943 had "agreed to a remarkably lenient armistice" after the collapse of the Churchill government) and cripple the ability of the United States to respond by sinking its fleet and knocking out Oak Ridge, where the development of the atomic bomb is still underway. "Kill every scientist at Oak Ridge and we kill their atomic program," the German officer charged with the facility's infiltration and destruction declares. "That is why the Führer is willing to go to war to stop the Americans before they beat us to this truly ultimate weapon." In *To Renew America*, for which HarperCollins originally offered $4.5 million, Mr. Gingrich recycles familiar themes from both *Window of Opportunity* and the "Renewing American Civilization" lectures as he endeavors to "restore our historic principles," most recently evidenced, as he sees it, in "the certainty and convictions of World War II and the Cold War."

To complain that Mr. Gingrich's thinking is "schematic," as some have, seems not exactly to describe the problem, which is that the "scheme," as revealed in his writing and lectures, remains so largely occult. The videotaped "Renewing American Civilization" lecture in which he discusses "The Historic Lessons of American Civilization" (Pillar One of the Five Pillars of American Civilization) offers, for example, clips from several television movies and documentaries about the Civil War, but not much clue about why the lessons of American civilization might be "historic," and no clue at all why the remaining four Pillars of American Civilization ("Personal Strength," "Entrepreneurial Free Enterprise," "The Spirit of Invention and Discovery," and "Quality as Defined by Deming") might not be more clearly seen as subsections of Pillar One, or lessons of civilization. Similarly, the attempt to track from one to five in Mr. Gingrich's "Five Reasons for Studying American History" ("One: History is a collective memory," "Two: American history is the history of our civilization," "Three: There is an American exceptionalism that can best be understood through history," "Four: History is a resource to be learned from and used," and "Five: There are techniques that can help you learn problem-solving from historic experience") leaves the tracker fretful, uneasy, uncertain just whose synapses are misfiring.

What has lent Mr. Gingrich's written and spoken work (or, as he calls it, his "teaching") the casual semblance of being based on some plain-spoken substance, some rough-hewn horse sense, is that most of what he says reaches us in outline form, with topic points capitalized (the capitalization has been restrained in the more conventionally edited *To Renew America*) and systematically if inappositely numbered. There were "Seven key aspects" and "Nine vision-level principles" of "Personal Strength," Pillar Two of American Civilization. There were "Five core principles" of "Quality as Defined by Deming" (Pillar Five); there were "Three Big Concepts" of "Entrepreneurial Free Enterprise," Pillar Three. There were also, still under Pillar Three, "Five Enemies of Entrepreneurial Free Enterprise" ("Bureaucracy," "Credentialing," "Taxation," "Litigation," and "Regulation"), which might have seemed to replicate one another and would in any case have been pretty much identical to Pillar Four's "Seven welfare state cripplers of progress" had the latter not folded in "Centralization," "Anti-progress Cultural Attitude," and "Ignorance."

In *Window of Opportunity*, Mr. Gingrich advised us that "the great force changing our world is a synergism of essentially six parts," and offered "five simple steps to a bold future." On the health care issue, Mr. Gingrich posited "eight areas of necessary change." On the question of arms control, he saw "seven imperatives that will help the free world survive in the age of nuclear weapons." Down a few paragraphs the seven imperatives gave way to "two initiatives," then to "three broad strategic options for the next generation," and finally, within the scan of the eye, to "six realistic goals which would increase our children's chances of living in a world without nuclear war."

"Outlining" or "listing" remains a favored analytical technique among the management and motivational professionals whose approach Mr. Gingrich has so messianically adopted. (Balancing the budget and "finding a way to truly replace the current welfare state with an opportunity society" could both be done by the year 2002, he advised the Congress on the occasion of his swearing-in as Speaker, "if we apply the principles of Edwards Deming and Peter Drucker.") Yet, on examination, few of his own "areas" and "imperatives" and "initiatives," his "steps" and "options" and "goals," actually advance the discourse. The seventh of the seven steps necessary to solve the drug problem, as outlined in *To Renew America*, calls for the government to "intensify our intelligence efforts against drug lords across the planet and help foreign governments to trap them," in other words exactly what both the Drug Enforcement Administration and the United States Southern Command have been doing for some years now. No piety can long escape inclusion in one or another of Mr. Gingrich's five or four or eleven steps; another of the seven steps necessary to solve the drug problem is the reinvigoration of Mrs. Reagan's "Just Say No" campaign.

The first of the "eight areas of necessary change" in our health care system calls for "focusing on preventive medicine and good health," which meant, in *Window of Opportunity*, offering Medicare recipients $500 for not going to the doctor. *To Renew America* expands this notion to "employee insurance plans" that provide each employee with a $3,000 "Medisave" account to either spend on medical care or receive as a year-end bonus, i.e., a way of phasing out the concept of medical insurance by calling the phase-out "Medisave." Mr. Gingrich cites the "very large savings in medical expenses" achieved through Medisave accounts by the Golden Rule Insurance Company, the executives and employees of which happen to have put their savings to work, during the several years since Mr. Gingrich's ascendance into the national eye, by donating $42,510 to his campaign committee, $117,076 to his GOPAC, an undisclosed amount to the foundation that sponsors his lectures, and $523,775 to the Republican Party. The Golden Rule Insurance Company also sponsors *The Progress Report*, the call-in show Mr. Gingrich co-hosts on National Empowerment Television. "Linking their contributions to performance," Mr. Gingrich told us in *Window of Opportunity*, was "the first step for average Americans in learning to organize and systematize their new relationship with elected politicians."

Those arguments in *To Renew America* not immediately suggestive of ethical conflict tend to speed headlong into another kind of collision. We have, according to Mr. Gingrich, "an absolute obligation to minimize damage to the natural world," a "moral obligation to take care of the ecosystem." Since this collides with his wish to lift the "ridiculous burden" of "environmental regulations hatched in Washington," the fulfillment of our moral obligation to take care of the ecosystem is left to a constituent in Mr. Gingrich's district, Linda Bavaro, who turns two-liter Coca-Cola bottles into T-shirts, which she sells at Disney World. "Linda," Mr. Gingrich notes, "has a good chance of doing well financially by doing good environmentally. That is how a healthy free market in a free country ought to work."

Even Mr. Gingrich's most unexceptionable arguments can take these unpredictable detours. The "Third Wave Information Age" offers "potential for enormous improvement in the lifestyle choices of most Americans," opportunities for "continuous, lifelong learning" that can enable the outplaced or downsized to operate "*outside* corporate structures and hierarchies in the nooks and crannies that the Information Age creates" (so far, so good), but here is the particular cranny of the Information Revolution into which Mr. Gingrich skids:

Say you want to learn batik because a new craft shop has opened at the mall and the owner has told you she will sell some of your work. First, you check in at the "batik station" on the Internet, which gives you a list of recommendations.... You may get a list of recommended video or audio tapes that can be delivered to your door the next day by Federal Express. You may prefer a more personal learning system and seek an apprenticeship with the nearest batik master.... In less than twenty-four hours, you have launched yourself on a new profession.

Similarly, what begins in *To Renew America* as a rational if predictable discussion of "New Frontiers in Science, Space, and the Oceans" takes this sudden turn: "Why not aspire to build a real Jurassic Park? ... Wouldn't that be one of the most spectacular accomplishments of human history? What if we could bring back extinct species?" A few pages further into "New Frontiers in Science, Space, and the Oceans," we are careering into "honeymoons in space" ("Imagine weightlessness and its effects and you will understand some of the attractions"), a notion first floated in *Window of Opportunity*, in that instance as an illustration of how entrepreneurial enterprise could lead to job creation in one's own district: "One reason I am convinced space travel will be a growth industry is because I represent the Atlanta airport, which provides 35,000 aviation-related jobs in the Atlanta area."

The packaging of space honeymoons and recycled two-liter Coca-Cola bottles is the kind of specific that actually engages Mr. Gingrich: absent an idea that can be sold at Disney World, he has tended to lose interest. Asked, during a 1995 appearance at the 92nd Street YMHA in New York, what he would have done early on about Bosnia, he essayed "creating a Balkan-wide development zone." The somewhat anticlimactic ninth of his Nine Principles of Self-Government for an Opportunity Society was this: "Finally, try, try again. Self-government is an arduous, demanding task on which the survival of freedom depends." Many of the proposals in *Window of Opportunity* and *To Renew America* fritter out this way, dwindle into the perfunctory, as if the proposer's attention had already hopped on. Mr. Gingrich, we are told by Dick Williams, manages his day in fifteen-minute increments, a lesson learned from Peter Drucker's *The Effective Executive*. Mr. Gingrich, he himself tells us, believes in dedicating as many as possible of those fifteen-minute increments to reading, particularly to the reading of biography, which is seen to offer direct personal benefit: "I don't care what you want to be. If you want to get rich, read the biographies of people who got rich. If you want to be a famous entertainer, read the biographies of people who got to be famous entertainers."

Reading can provide not only this kind of intravenous inspiration but also "quotes," what *Forbes* used to call "Thoughts on the Business of Life," rhetorical backup to be plucked from the shoebox and deployed, or "used." "I was very struck this morning by something Bill Emerson used," Mr. Gingrich said at his swearing-in as Speaker. "It's a fairly famous quote of Benjamin Franklin." Mr. Gingrich tends to weigh whatever he does on this scale of strategic applicability and immediate usefulness; the fourth and fifth, or clinching, of the "Five Reasons for Studying American History" are "History is a resource to be learned from and used" and "There are techniques that can help you learn problem-solving from historical experience."

A considerable amount of what Mr. Gingrich says has never borne extended study. There was the dispiriting view of the future as a kind of extended Delta hub, where "each news magazine would have a section devoted to the week's news from space," and from which we would "flow out to the Hiltons and Marriotts of the solar system, and mankind will have permanently broken free of the planet." There were the doubtful tales offered in evidence of the point at hand, the "personalization" (a key Gingrich concept) that did not quite add up. Mr. Gingrich learned that America was "in transition from one type of economy and lifestyle to another" from reading Peter Drucker's *The Age of Discontinuity* and John Naisbett's *Megatrends*, but the truth of this came home only when he was "shocked to discover" that he could telephone his oldest daughter on her junior year abroad "by first dialing the 001 code for the international telephone computer, then the code for France, then the area code for the region near Paris, and finally the code for my daughter's telephone."

That this discovery would seem to have taken place in 1982 or 1983 (his oldest daughter was born in 1963) was just one suggestion that this was not a mind that could be productively engaged on its own terms. There was also the casual relationship to accuracy, the spellings and names and ideas seized, in the irresistible momentum of outlining, in mid-flight. In *Window of Opportunity* and in the lectures, Peter Drucker's *The Age of Discontinuity* becomes *The Age of Discontinuities*. Garry Wills's *Inventing America* becomes "Garry Will's *Discovering America*." Gordon Wood becomes Gordon Woods. *To Renew America* shows evidence of professional copy-editing, but it also defines what it calls "situational ethics" and "deconstructionism" as interchangeable terms for "the belief that there are no general rules of behavior." Alexis de Tocqueville is seen as a kind of visiting booster, whose privilege it was to "inform the world that 'Democracy in America' worked." De Tocqueville is also seen, even more peculiarly, as an exemplar of American culture: "From the Jamestown colony and the Pilgrims, through de Tocqueville's *Democracy in America*, up to the Norman Rockwell paintings of the 1940s and 1950s, there was a clear sense of what it meant to be an American."

There was the flirtation with the millennial, the almost astral insistence on the significance of specific but intrinsically meaningless dates and numbers. The "discontinuity" (Peter Drucker again) in American history lasted, according to Mr. Gingrich, from exactly 1965 until exactly 1994: "And what's been happening is that from 1965 to 1994, that America went off on the wrong track. Now that's an important distinction." "A year which ends in three zeroes is a rare thing indeed," he declared in *Window of Opportunity*. "We're starting the 104th Congress," he said at his swearing-in. "I don't know if you've ever thought about the concept: 208 years." This inclination toward the pointlessly specific (we have here a man who once estimated the odds on the survival of his second marriage at "53 to 47") is coupled with a tic to inflate what is actually specific into a general principle, a big concept. The cherry blossoms in Washington, he advised his constituents in 1984, remind us that "there's a rhythm and cycle to life. Winter goes and spring comes." *Forrest Gump* became for Mr. Gingrich "a reaffirmation that the counterculture destroys human beings and basic values." That *Star Wars* made more money than *The Right Stuff* instructs us that "we have allowed bureaucracies to

JOAN DIDION

dominate too many of our scientific adventures." In the absence
of anything specific to either seize or inflate, he tends to spin
perilously out of syntactical orbit:

> I think if you will consider for a moment—and this
> is part of why I wanted to pick up on the concept of
> "virtualness"—if you think about the notion that the
> great challenge of our lifetime is first to imagine a future
> that is worth spending our lives getting to, then because
> of the technologies and the capabilities we have today to
> get it up to sort of a virtual state, whether that's done in
> terms of actual levels of sophistication or whether it's just
> done in your mind, most studies of leadership argue that
> leaders actually are putting out past decisions, that part
> of the reason you get certainty in great leaders is that
> they have already thoroughly envisioned the achievement
> and now it's just a matter of implementation. And so it's
> very different. So in a sense, virtuality at the mental level
> is something I think you'd find in most leadership over
> historical periods.

2

The real substance of Mr. Gingrich's political presence derives
from his skill at massaging exhaustively researched voter preferences and prejudices into matters of lonely principle. The positions
he takes are acutely tuned to the expressed fears and resentments
of a significant number of Americans, yet he stands, in his rhetoric,
alone, opposed by "the system," by "Washington," by "the liberal
elite," by "the East Coast elite" (not by accident does a mention of Harvard in 1945 provoke the antipathy of the sympathetic
president to "East Coast snobbery and intellectual hauteur"), or
simply by an unspecified "they." "I kind of live on the edge,"
Mr. Gingrich told Dick Williams. "I push the system." When, in
a famous GOPAC memo, Mr. Gingrich advised Republican candidates to characterize Democrats with the words "decay," "sick,"
"pathetic," "stagnation," "corrupt," "waste," and "traitors," and
Republicans with the words "share," "change," "truth," "moral,"
"courage," "family," "peace," and "duty," each word had been

tested and oiled in focus groups to function in what the memo called "Language, A Key Mechanism of Control."

The 1994 Contract with America was packaged as, and to a peculiar extent accepted even by its opponents as, a "bold agenda" (opponents said too bold, and were left arguing only to split the difference), a "vision for America's future" (opponents rushed to share the vision, and argued only the means), yet each of its ten items derived from and was later refined in focus groups run by Frank Luntz, who did the 1992 campaign polling first for Pat Buchanan and then for Ross Perot. "The Contract with America was specifically designed to appeal to the swing Perot voter who hates partisan politics," Mr. Gingrich said during his 1995 YMHA appearance. "The ten points basically selected themselves as deeply felt desires of the American people," is his somewhat cryptic version of this process in *To Renew America*. "It can literally be said that the Contract with America grew out of our conversations with the American people and out of our basic conservative values."

The preferences and attitudes discovered through opinion research tend to be, no matter who is paying for the research, fairly consistent. A majority of American voters who end up in political focus groups are displeased with the current welfare system, believe that affirmative action has been carried too far, are opposed to crime and in favor of "opportunity." They say this to researchers working for Republican candidates and they also say it to researchers working for Democratic candidates. Which was why, of course, anyone whose own researcher happened to be having identical conversations with the American people was left, up against the Contract with America, with nowhere to stand. "Now what you've got in this city is a simple principle," Mr. Gingrich told the Republican National Committee in January 1995. "I am a genuine revolutionary; they are the genuine reactionaries. We are going to change their world; they will do anything to stop us. They will use any tool—there is no grotesquerie, no distortion, no dishonesty too great for them to come after us." He described himself to Fred Barnes as "the leading revolutionary in the country. I'm trying to replace the welfare state and the counterculture and the old establishment with a system of opportunity and entrepreneurship and classic American civilization."

* * *

What seems grandiose melts down, on the floor, to business as usual. "Replacing the welfare state" turned out to mean, with the passage in the House of the Personal Responsibility and Senior Citizens Fairness Acts, phasing out a $16 billion welfare program for the poor (Aid to Families with Dependent Children) in order to expand, by lifting the level of its earnings test, what was already a $335 billion welfare program for the middle class, Social Security. The unfairness (Frank Luntz has isolated "fairness" and "unfairness" as hot words) of applying any earnings test at all to Social Security benefits was an issue seized early by Mr. Gingrich, who illustrated or "personalized" it in *Window of Opportunity* with another doubtful tale, this one featuring "Warren," a retiree who "wanted to do something to keep his mind and body busy and to contribute to the community and world he loves" but was forced to give up selling his contribution of choice, which happened to be scrimshaw, when the Social Security Administration threatened to reduce, or in Mr. Gingrich's telling "cut off," his benefits. When Dan Balz and Charles R. Babcock of *The Washington Post* suggested that this preference for what the Speaker calls "65 percent issues" could be construed as pandering to public opinion, Mr. Gingrich corrected them: "Politics," he said, "is about public opinion and gathering public support. It's like saying, isn't it pandering for Wal-Mart to stock everything people want to buy."

3

"I teach a course which is an outline of my thoughts at 51 years of age, based on everything I've experienced, which is, frankly, rather more than most tenured faculty," Mr. Gingrich told *The New York Times* in January 1995. "I'm not credentialed as a bureaucratic academic. I haven't written 22 books that are meaningless." What details we have about the formative experience of the Speaker, who was born Newton Leroy McPherson and took the surname of his mother's second husband, describe a familiar postwar history, one not dissimilar from that of William Jefferson Clinton, who was born William Jefferson Blythe and took the surname of his mother's second husband. Each was the adored first-born son of a mother left largely, in the economic and social dislocations that transformed America during and immediately after World War II, to her own devices. Each was farmed out to relatives while the mother earned a living. Each appears to have reached adolescence firm in the conviction that these would be the make-or-break years, that the point of the exercise was to assert, win over, overcome.

The two relied on different means to this end, but the instinctive technique of each derived from the literature of personal improvement, effective self-presentation, salesmanship, five simple steps. Mr. Clinton, with his considerable personal magnetism, kept extensive lists of people he had met and on whom, when the time arrived, he could call. In the case of Mr. Gingrich, who after his mother remarried was repeatedly uprooted and moved from one army post to another, Kansas to France to Germany to Georgia, such social skills remained undeveloped, forcing him back on his reading, his self-education, his shoeboxes. He recalled being given an article when he was young. "It was about Lincoln's five defeats, I carried it in my wallet for years." At sixteen, en route from Stuttgart to Fort Benning, he concluded "that there was no moral choice except to immerse myself in the process of learning how to lead and how to be effective." His stepfather gave him a set of the *Encyclopedia Americana*, and he read it every night. At Baker High School near Fort Benning he yielded to the southern pressure to play sports, but was sidelined by headaches. His Democratic opponent in 1994 referred to him as a "wuss," and as "the guy who won the science project."

"I think I was very lonely and very driven," Mr. Gingrich told Dick Williams. "If you decide in your freshman year of high school that your job is to spend your lifetime trying to change the future of your people, you're probably fairly weird." The defense he adopted was the persona of "class brain" (his classmates voted him "Most Intellectual"), the one with the pens and slide rule in his shirt pocket, the one who could spark the debating society, tie for highest score in the county on the National Merit Scholarship test, make a strategic detour around his lack of aptitude for high school cool by tutoring the school beauty queen and not-quite-secretly dating the geometry teacher. As a freshman at Emory University he married the geometry teacher and co-founded the Emory Young Republican Club. As a graduate student at Tulane he organized a week-long protest against administration censorship of the college paper, discovered Alvin Toffler, and taught a noncredit class on the Year 2000.

He took for himself, in other words, the ritualized role of breaker of new ground, marcher to a different drummer, which happens to be the cast of mind in which speculative fiction finds its most tenacious hold. *What if* one or another event had not occurred, *what if* one or another historical figure had remained unborn, dropped into a coma, taken another turn: the contemplation of such questions has reliably occupied the different drummers of American secondary education. The impulse is anti-theological, which translates, for these readers, into thrilling iconoclasm. In Isaac Asimov's *Foundation* trilogy, according to Mr. Gingrich, "the Catholic Church's role in maintaining civilized knowledge through the Dark and Middle Ages is played by a secular group of intellectuals called 'The Foundation.'" The tendency is to see history as random but reversible, the sum of its own events and personalities. Isaac Asimov, Mr. Gingrich notes, "did not believe in a mechanistic world. Instead, to Asimov, human beings always hold their fate in their own hands."

It was this high school reading of Isaac Asimov, Mr. Gingrich tells us in *To Renew America*, that first "focused my attention on the fate of civilization. I came to realize that, while most people were immersed in day-to-day activities, daily behavior actually takes place within a much larger context of constantly changing global forces." Mr. Gingrich is frequently and often deprecatingly described as a "futurist," but even as he talks about those "constantly changing global forces," about a transformation "so large and historic that it can be compared with only two other great areas of human history—the Agricultural Revolution and the Industrial Revolution," his view of the future is a view of 1955, factory-loaded with Year 2000 extras. *To Renew America* asks us to "imagine a morning in just a decade or so":

> You wake up to a wall-size, high-definition television showing surf off Maui. (This is my favorite island—you can pick your own scene.) You walk or jog or do Stairmaster while catching up on the morning news and beginning to review your day's schedule. Your home office is filled with

communications devices, so you can ignore rush-hour traffic.... When you are sick, you sit in your diagnostic chair
and communicate with the local health clinic. Sensors take
your blood pressure, analyze a blood sample, or do throat
cultures. The results are quickly relayed to health aides,
who make recommendations and prescribe medicine....
If you need a specialist, a databank at your fingertips gives
you a wide range of choices based on cost, reputation, and
outcome patterns. You can choose knowledgeably which
risk you want to take and what price you want to pay.

The "diagnostic chair," or "personalized health chair," which
could also be programmed to "monitor your diet over time and
change recipes to minimize boredom while achieving the desired
nutritional effect," appeared first in *Window of Opportunity*, which
outlined a future in which we or our descendants would also use
computer technology to correct golf swings, provide tax and IRA
advice, and provide data on "literally thousands of vacation, recreation, and education opportunities," for example the Ocmulgee
Indian Mounds Park in Macon, Georgia, with its "splendid natural walk area, a beautiful collection of ancient Indian ceremonial mounds, and fine museum on the history of the area from
900 A.D. to the present." For any among us whose view of the
future might have been somewhat more forbidding or interesting (no Maui, no Macon, the IRAs all gone bust), Mr. Gingrich
would recommend first the reading of science fiction, since "a
generation that learns its magic from Tom Swift or Jules Verne
has a much more optimistic outlook than one that is constantly
being told that the planet is dying and that everything humanity
is doing is wrong."

If wishes were horses, beggars would ride, as they said in the generation that learned its magic from Tom Swift and Jules Verne. To
know that large numbers of Americans are concerned about getting adequate medical care is one thing; to give them the willies
by talking about their "health chairs" is quite another, suggesting
not the future but the past, the drone of the small-town auto-
didact, the garrulous bore in the courthouse square. There is
about these dismal reductions something disarming and poignant,
a solitary neediness, a dogged determination to shine in public
that leads Mr. Gingrich to reveal to us, again and again, what his

own interests dictate that we should not see. He concludes *To Renew America* with a "personalization" of his concern for voter concerns, an account of how he and his second wife, Marianne, spent the Christmas before he became Speaker in Leetonia, Ohio, "a wonderful small town that is like a scene from a Norman Rockwell *Saturday Evening Post* cover."

For much of this account Mr. Gingrich remains well within the secured territory of H.R. 0003–95 and H.R. 0006–95, the Taking Back Our Streets and American Dream Restoration Acts. He expresses concern for Marianne's eighty-year-old mother, who "worked and saved all her life" but now worries about "the reports that Medicare will go bankrupt by 2002." He worries that his eight-year-old nephew, Sean, "cannot walk around Youngstown the way I once wandered the streets of Harrisburg." He wonders how Marianne's sister and her husband will manage putting their boys, Jon and Mark, through college. Then, midway through this tuned and calculated Christmas reverie, Mr. Gingrich drops, abruptly and inexplicably, through the ice, off message: "At heart," he dismayingly confides, "I am still a happy four-year-old who gets up every morning hoping to find a cookie that friends or relatives may have left for me somewhere." This cookie is worrisome: Was it forgotten? Hidden? Why would they hide it? Where are they? Are they asleep, out, absentee friends, deadbeat relatives? The cookie was the treat and leaving is the trick? What we get from these problematic detours and revelations, from the cookies and the health chairs and the high-resolution views of Maui, from the Ten Steps and the Five Pillars and the thirty gigabytes to an improved golf swing, is a shadow of something unexplained, a scent of failure, which remains one reason why, in a country made even more uncomfortable by losers than Mr. Gingrich claims to be, personal popularity among large numbers of voters may continue to elude him.

POLITICAL PORNOGRAPHY

September 19, 1996

ON THE MORNING of Sunday, June 23, 1996, the day the pre-publication embargo on Bob Woodward's *The Choice* was lifted, *The Washington Post*, the paper for which Mr. Woodward has so famously been, since 1971, first a reporter and then an editor, published on the front page of its "A" section two stories detailing what its editors believed most newsworthy in *The Choice*. In columns one through four, directly under the banner and carrying the legend *The Choice—Inside the Clinton and Dole Campaigns*, there appeared passages from the book itself, edited into a narrative describing the meetings Hillary Clinton had from 1994 to 1996 with Jean Houston, who was characterized in the *Post* as "a believer in spirits, mythic and other connections to history and other worlds" and as "the most dramatic" of Mrs. Clinton's "10 to 11 confidants," a group that included her mother.

This account of Mrs. Clinton's not entirely remarkable and in any case private conversations with Jean Houston appeared under the apparently accurate if unsurprising headline "At a Difficult Time, First Lady Reaches Out, Looks Within," occupied one hundred and fifty-four column inches, was followed by a six-column-inch box explaining the rules under which Mr. Woodward conducted his interviews, and included among similar revelations the news that, according to an unidentified source (Mr. Woodward tells us that some of his interviews were on the record, others "conducted under journalistic ground rules of 'background' or 'deep background,' meaning the information could be used but the sources of the information would not be identified"), Mrs. Clinton had at an unspecified point in 1995 disclosed to Jean Houston ("Dialogue and quotations come from at least one participant, from memos or from contemporaneous notes or diaries of a participant in the discussion") that "she was sure that good habits were the key to survival."

The remaining front-page columns above the fold in that Sunday's *Post* were given over to a news story based on *The Choice*, written by Dan Balz, running seventy-nine column inches and headlined "Dole Seeks 'a 10' Among List of 15: Running Mate Must Not Anger Right, Book Says." Mr. Woodward, according to this story, "quotes Dole as saying he wants a running mate who will be 'a 10' in the eyes of the public, with the candidate telling the head of his search team, Robert F. Ellsworth, 'Don't give me someone who would send up [anger] the conservatives.'" Those *Post* readers sufficiently surprised by this disclosure to continue reading learned that "at the top of the list of 15 names, assembled in the late spring by Ellsworth and Dole's campaign manager, Scott Reed, was Colin L. Powell." When I read this in the *Post* I assumed that I would find some discussion of how or whether the vice-presidential search team had managed to construe their number-one choice of Colin L. Powell as consistent with the mandate "Don't give me someone who would send up the conservatives," but there was no such discussion to be found, neither in the *Post* nor in *The Choice* itself.

Mr. Woodward's aversion to engaging the ramifications of what people say to him has been generally understood as an admirable quality, at best a mandarin modesty, at worst a kind of executive big-picture focus, the entirely justifiable oversight of someone with a more important game to play. Yet what we see in *The Choice* is something more than a matter of an occasional inconsistency left unexplored in the rush of the breaking story, a stray ball or two left unfielded in the heat of the opportunity, as Mr. Woodward describes his role, "to sit with many of the candidates and key players and ask about the questions of the day as the campaign unfolded." What seems most remarkable in this Woodward book is exactly what seemed remarkable in the previous Woodward books, each of which was presented as the insiders' inside story and each of which went on to become a number-one bestseller: these are books in which measurable cerebral activity is virtually absent.

The author himself disclaims "the perspective of history." His preferred approach has been one in which "issues could be examined before the possible outcome or meaning was at all clear or the possible consequences were weighed." The refusal to consider outcome or meaning or consequence has, as a way of writing a book, a certain Zen purity, but tends toward a process in which no research method is so commonplace as to go unexplained ("The record will show how I was able to gain information from records or interviews.... I could then talk with other sources and return to most of them again and again as necessary"), no product of that research so predictable as to go unrecorded. The world rendered is an Erewhon in which not only inductive reasoning but ordinary reliance on context clues appear to have vanished. Any reader who wonders what Vice President Gore thought about Whitewater could turn to page 418 of *The Choice* and find that he believed the matter "small and unfair," but was sometimes concerned that "the Republicans and the scandal machinery in Washington" could keep it front and center. Any reader unwilling to hazard a guess about what Dick Morris's polling data told him about Medicare could turn to page 235 of *The Choice* and find that "voters liked Medicare, trusted it and felt it was the one federal program that worked."

This tabula rasa typing requires rather persistent attention on the part of the reader, since its very presence on the page works to suggest that significant and heretofore unrevealed information must have just been revealed by a reporter who left no stone unturned to obtain it. The weekly lunch shared by President Clinton and Vice President Gore, we learn in *The Choice*, "sometimes did not start until 3 P.M. because of other business." The president, "who had a notorious appetite, tried to eat lighter food." The reader attuned to the conventions of narrative might be led by the presentation of these quotidian details into thinking that a dramatic moment is about to occur, but the crux of the four-page prologue having to do with the weekly lunches turns out to be this: the president, according to Mr. Woodward, "thought a lot of the criticism he received was unfair." The vice president, he reveals, "had some advice. Clinton always had found excess reserve within himself. He would just have to find more, Gore said."

What Mr. Woodward chooses to leave unrecorded, or what he apparently does not think to elicit, is in many ways more instructive than what he commits to paper. "The accounts I have compiled may, at times, be more comprehensive than what a future historian, who has to rely on a single memo, letter, or recollection of what happened, might be able to piece together," he noted in the introduction to *The Agenda*, an account of certain events in the first years of the Clinton administration in which he endeavored, to cryogenic effect, "to give every key participant in these events an opportunity to offer his or her recollections and views." The "future historian" who might be interested in piecing together the details of how the Clinton administration arrived at its program for health care reform, however, will find, despite a promising page of index references, that none of the key participants interviewed for *The Agenda* apparently thought to discuss what might have seemed the central curiosity in that process, which was by what political miscalculation a plan initially meant to remove third-party profit from the health care equation (or to "take on the insurance industry," as *Putting People First*, the manifesto of the 1992 Clinton-Gore campaign, had phrased it) would become one distrusted by large numbers of Americans precisely because it seemed to enlarge and further entrench the role of the insurance industry.

This disinclination of Mr. Woodward's to exert cognitive energy on what he is told reaches critical mass in *The Choice*, where not much said to the author by a candidate or potential candidate appears to have been deemed too insignificant for inclusion, too casual for documentation. ("Most of them permitted me to tape-record the interviews; otherwise I took detailed notes.") President Clinton declined to be interviewed directly for this book, but Senator Dole "was interviewed for more than 12 hours and the typed transcripts run over 200 pages." Accounts of these interviews, typically including date, time, venue, weather, and apparel details (for one Saturday interview in his office the candidate was "dressed casually in a handsome green wool shirt") can be found, according to the index of *The Choice* ("Dole, Robert J. 'Bob,' interviews by author with"), on pages 87–89, 183, 214–215, 338, 345–348, 378, 414, and 423.

Study of these pages suggests the deferential spirit of the enterprise. In the course of the Saturday interview for which Senator Dole selected the "handsome green wool shirt," a ninety-minute session which took place on February 4, 1995, in Dole's office in the Hart Senate Office Building ("My tape recorder sat on the arm of his chair, and his press secretary, Clarkson Hine, took copious notes"), Mr. Woodward asked Dole if he had thought, in

1988, that he was the best candidate. He reports Dole's answer: "Thought I was." This gave Mr. Woodward the opportunity to ask what he had previously (and rather mystifyingly, since little else in *The Choice* tends to this point) defined for the reader as "an important question for my book": "You weren't elected," he reminded Senator Dole, "so you have to come out of that period feeling the system doesn't elect the best?"

Senator Dole, not unexpectedly, answered agreeably: "I think it's true. I think Elizabeth raises that a lot, whether it's president, or Senate or whatever, that a lot of the best—somebody people would describe [as] the best—doesn't make it. That's the way the system works. You also come out of that, even if you lose, if you still have enough confidence in yourself, that you didn't lose because you weren't the best candidate. You lost for other reasons. You can always rationalize these things."

On Saturday, July 1, 1995, again in Dole's Hart office (Senator Dole in "casual khaki pants, a blue dress shirt with cufflinks, and purple Nike tennis shoes"), Mr. Woodward elicited, in the course of a two-and-a-half-hour interview, these reflections from the candidate:

On his schedule: "We're trying to pace ourselves. It's like today I'm not traveling, which is hard to believe. Tomorrow we go to Iowa, get back at 1 A.M. We're off all day Monday. Then we go to New Hampshire."

On his speechwriters: "You can't just read something that somebody's written and say 'Oh, boy, this is dynamite.' You've got to have a feel for it and you've got to think, Jimminy, this might work. And this is the message. And I think we're still testing it, and I think you can't say that if I said this on day one, it's going to be written in stone forever."

On the message, in response to Mr. Woodward's suggestion that "there's something people are waiting for somebody to say that no one has said yet": "Right. I think you're right."

On his strategy: "As long as we're on target, on message, and got money in the bank, and people are signing up, we're mostly doing the right thing. But I also have been around long enough to know that somebody can make a mistake and it'll be all over, too."

On the Senate: "Somebody has to manage it. And it may not be manageable. It isn't, you know, it's a frustrating place sometimes but generally it works out."

"I was not out of questions," Mr. Woodward concludes, "but I too was growing tired, and it seemed time to stand up and thank him."

Mr. Woodward dutifully tries, in the note that prefaces *The Choice*, to provide the "why" paragraph, the "billboard," the sentence or sentences that explain to the reader why the book was written and what it is about. That these are questions with which he experiences considerable discomfort seems clear:

Presidential elections are defining moments that go way beyond legislative programs or the role of the government. They are measuring points for the country that call forth a range of questions which every candidate must try to address. Who are we? What matters? Where are we going? In the private and public actions of the candidates are embedded their best answers. Action is character, I believe, and when all is said and sifted, character is what matters most.

This *quo vadis*, or valedictory, mode is one in which Mr. Woodward, faced with the question of what his books are about, has crashed repeatedly, as if his programming did not extend to this point. The "human story is the core" was his somewhat more perfunctory stab at explaining what he was up to in *The Commanders*. For *Wired*, his 1984 book about the life and death of the comic John Belushi, Mr. Woodward spoke to 217 people on the record and obtained access to "appointment calendars, diaries, telephone records, credit card receipts, medical records, handwritten notes, letters, photographs, newspaper and magazine articles, stacks of accountants' records covering the last several years of Belushi's life, daily movie production reports, contracts, hotel records, travel records, taxi receipts, limousine bills and Belushi's monthly cash disbursement records," only to arrive, not unlike HAL in *2001*, at these questions: "Why? What happened? Who was responsible, if anyone? Could it have been different or better? Those were the questions raised by his family, friends and associates. Could success have been something other than a failure? The questions persist. Nonetheless, his best and most definitive legacy is his work. He made us laugh, and now he can make us think."

In any real sense, these books are "about" nothing but the author's own method, which is not, on the face of it, markedly different from other people's. Mr. Woodward interviews people, he tapes or takes notes ("detailed" notes) on what they say. He takes "great care to compare and verify various sources' accounts of the same events." He obtains documents, he reads them, he files them: for *The Brethren*, the book he wrote with Scott Armstrong about the Supreme Court, the documents filled "eight file drawers." He consults *The Almanac of American Politics* ("the bible, and I relied on it"), he reads what others have written on the subject. "In preparation for my own reporting," he tells us about *The Choice*, "I and my assistant, Karen Alexander, read and often studied hundreds of newspaper and magazine articles."

Should the information he requires necessitate travel, he goes the extra mile: "I traveled from coast to coast many times, visiting everyone possible and everywhere possible," he tells us about the research for *Wired*. Since John Belushi worked in the motion-picture industry and died at the Chateau Marmont in Los Angeles, these coast-to-coast trips might have seemed to represent the minimum in dogged fact-gathering, but never mind: the author had even then, in 1984, transcended method and entered the heady ether of methodology, a discipline in which the reason for writing a book could be the sheer fact of being there. "I would like to know more and *Newsweek* magazine was saying that maybe that is the thing I should look at next," he allowed when a caller on *Larry King Live* asked if he might not want to write about Whitewater. "I don't know. I do not know about Whitewater and what it really means. I am waiting—if I can say this—for the call from somebody on the inside saying 'I want to talk.'"

* * *

Here is where we reach the single unique element in the method, and also the problem. As any prosecutor and surely Mr. Woodward knows, the person on the inside who calls and says "I want to talk" is an informant, or snitch, and is generally looking to bargain a deal, to improve his or her own situation, to place the blame on someone else in return for being allowed to plead down or out certain charges. Because the story told by a criminal or civil informant is understood to be colored by self-interest, the informant knows that his or her testimony will be unrespected, even reviled, subjected to rigorous examination and often rejection. The informant who talks to Mr. Woodward, on the other hand, knows that his or her testimony will be not only respected but burnished into the inside story, which is why so many people on the inside, notably those who consider themselves the professionals or managers of the process—assistant secretaries, deputy advisers, players of the game, aides who intend to survive past the tenure of the patron they are prepared to portray as hapless—do want to talk to him. Many Dole campaign aides did want to talk, for *The Choice*, about the herculean efforts and adroit strategy required to keep the candidate with whom they were saddled even marginally on message, on the program:

> Dole offered a number of additional references to the past, how it had been done before, and Reed [Dole campaign manager Scott Reed] countered with his own ideas about how he would handle similar situations. A sense of diffusion and randomness wouldn't work. Making seat-of-the-pants, airborne decisions was not the way he operated.... Dole needed a coherent and understandable message on which to run, Reed said. Deep down, he added, he knew Dole knew what he wanted to say, but he probably needed some help putting it together and delivering it.... Reed felt he had hit the right weaknesses.

Similarly, many Clinton foreign policy advisers did want to talk, again for *The Choice*, about the equally herculean efforts and strategy required to guide the president, on the question of Bosnia, from one of his "celebrated rages" ("I'm getting creamed!" Clinton, "unleashing his frustration" and "spewing forth profanity," is reported to have said on being told of the fall of Srebrenica) to a more nuanced appreciation of the policy options on which his aides—Deputy National Security Adviser Sandy Berger, say, and National Security Adviser Anthony Lake—had been laboring unappreciated. "Berger reminded him," Woodward tells us, "that Lake was trying to develop an Endgame Strategy." At a meeting a few days later in the Oval Office, when Vice President Gore mentioned a photograph in *The Washington Post* of a refugee from Srebrenica who had hanged herself from a tree, the adroit guidance continued:

> "My 21-year-old daughter asked about that picture," Gore said. "What am I supposed to tell her? Why is this happening and we're not doing anything?"
>
> It was a chilling moment. The vice president was directly confronting and criticizing the president. Gore believed he understood his role. He couldn't push the president too far, but they had built a good relationship and he felt he had to play his card when he felt strongly. He couldn't know precisely what going too far meant unless he occasionally did it.
>
> "My daughter is surprised the world is allowing this to happen," Gore said carefully. "I am too."
>
> Clinton said they were going to do something.

This is a cartoon, but not a cartoon in which anyone who spoke to the author will appear to have taken any but the highest ground. Asked, in the same appearance on *Larry King Live*, why he thought people talked to him, Mr. Woodward responded:

> Only because I get good information and I talk to people at the middle level, lower level, try to talk to the people at the top. They know that I am going to reflect their point of view. One of my earlier books, somebody called me who was in it and said "How am I going to come out?" and I said "Well, essentially, I write self-portraits."... They really are self-portraits, because I go to people and I double-check them but—but who are you? What are you doing? Where do you fit in? What did you say? What did you feel?

Those who talk to Mr. Woodward, in other words, can be confident that he will be civil ("I too was growing tired, and it seemed time to stand up and thank him"), that he will not feel impelled to make connections between what he is told and what is already known, that he will treat even the most patently self-serving account as if untainted by hindsight (that of Richard Darman, say, who in 1992 presented himself to Mr. Woodward, who in turn presented him to America, as the helpless Cassandra of the 1990 Bush budget deal); that he will be, above all, and herein can be found both Mr. Woodward's compass and the means by which he is set adrift, "fair."

I once heard a group of reporters agree that there were at most twenty people who run any story. What they meant by "running the story" was setting the terms, setting the pace, deciding the agenda, determining when and where the story exists, and shaping what the story will be. There were certain people who ran the story in Vietnam, there were certain people in Central America, there were certain people in Washington. An American presidential campaign is a Washington story, which means that the handful of people who run the story in Washington—the people who write the most influential columns, the people who conduct the Sunday shows on which Washington talks to itself—will also run the campaign. Bob Woodward, who is unusual in that he is not a regular participant in the television dialogue and appears in print, outside his books, only infrequently, is one of the people who run the story in Washington.

In this business of running the story, in fact in the business of news itself, certain conventions are seen as beyond debate. "Opinion" will be so labeled, and confined to the op-ed page or the television talk shows. "News analysis" will be so labeled, and will appear in a subordinate position to the "news" story it accompanies. In the rest of the paper as on the evening news, the story will be reported "impartially," the story will be "evenhanded," the story will be "fair." "Fairness" is a quality Mr. Woodward seems particularly to prize ("I learned a long time ago," he told Larry King, "you take your opinions and your attitudes, your predispositions—get them in your back pocket, because they are only going to get in the way of doing your job"), and mentions repeatedly in his thanks to his assistants.

It was "Karen Alexander, a 1993 graduate of Yale University," who "brought unmatched intellect, grace and doggedness and an ingrained sense of fairness" to *The Choice*. On *The Agenda*, it was "David Greenberg, a 1990 graduate of Yale University," who "repeatedly worked to bring greater balance, fairness, and clarity to our reporting and writing." It was "Marc E. Solomon, a 1989 Yale graduate," who "brought a sense of fairness and balance" to *The Commanders*. On *The Veil*, it was "Barbara Feinman, a 1982 graduate of the University of California at Berkeley," whose "friendship and sense of fairness guided the daily enterprise." For *The Brethren*, Mr. Woodward and his coauthor, Scott Armstrong, thank "Al Kamen, a former reporter for the *Rocky Mountain News*," for his "thoroughness, skepticism, and sense of fairness."

The genuflection toward "fairness" is a familiar newsroom piety, in practice the excuse for a good deal of autopilot reporting and lazy thinking but in theory a benign ideal. In Washington, however, a community in which the management of news has become the single overriding preoccupation of the core industry, what "fairness" has often come to mean is a scrupulous passivity, an agreement to cover the story not as it is occurring but as it is presented, which is to say as it is manufactured. Such institutionalized events as a congressional hearing or a presidential trip will be covered with due diligence, but the story will vanish the moment the gavel falls, the hour Air Force One returns to Andrews. "Iran-contra" referred exclusively, for many Washington reporters, to the hearings. The sequence of events that came to be known as "the S&L crisis," which was actually less a "crisis" than the structural malfunction that triggered an uncontrolled meltdown in middle-class confidence, existed as a "story" only on those occasions (hearings, indictments) when it showed promise of rising to its "crisis" slug. Similarly, "Whitewater" (as in "I do not know about Whitewater and what it really means") survived as a story only to the extent that it allowed those who covered it to calibrate the waxing or waning possibility of a "smoking gun," or "evidence."

"If there is evidence it should be pursued," Mr. Woodward told Larry King to this point. "In fairness to the Clintons. And it's—it—you know, we all in the news business, and in politics have to be very sensitive to the unfair smear.... It's not fair and again it goes back to what's the evidence?" Yet the actual interest of Whitewater lies in what has already been documented: it is "about" the S&L crisis, and thereby offers a detailed and specific look at the kinds of political and financial dealing that resulted in the meltdown in middle-class confidence. What Whitewater "really means" or offers, then, is an understanding of that meltdown, which has been reported as if it existed in a vacuum, an inexplicable phenomenon weirdly detached from the periodic growth figures produced in Washington. This could be a valuable story, but it is not one that will be put together by waiting for the call from somebody on the inside saying "I want to talk."

Every reporter, in the development of a story, depends on and coddles, or protects, his or her sources. Only when the protection of the source gets in the way of telling the story does the reporter face a professional, even a moral, choice: he can blow the source and move to another beat or he can roll over, shape the story to continue serving the source. The necessity for making this choice between the source and the story seems not to have come up in the course of writing Mr. Woodward's books, for good reason: since he proceeds from a position in which the very impulse to sort through the evidence and reach a conclusion is seen as suspect, something to be avoided in the higher interest of fairness, he has been able, consistently and conveniently, to define the story as that which the source tells him.

This fidelity to the source, whoever the source might be, leads Mr. Woodward down avenues that might at first seem dead-end. On page 16 of *The Choice* we have President Clinton, presumably on the word of a White House source, "thunderstruck" that Senator Dole, on the morning after Clinton's mother died in early 1994, should have described Whitewater on the network news shows as "unbelievable," "mind-boggling," "big, big news" that "cries out more than ever now for an independent counsel." On page 346 of *The Choice* we have Senator Dole, on December 27, 1995, telling Mr. Woodward "that he had never used Whitewater to attack the president personally," to which Mr. Woodward responds only: "What would be your criteria for picking a vice-president?" On page 423 of *The Choice* we have Mr. Woodward, on April 20,

1996, by which date he had apparently remembered what he said on page 16 that Senator Dole said, although not what he said on page 346 that Senator Dole said, advising Senator Dole that the president had resented his "aggressive call for a Whitewater independent counsel back in early 1994, the day Clinton's mother had died."

Only now do we arrive at what seems to be for Mr. Woodward the point, and it has to do with his own role as honest broker, or conscience to the candidates. He reports that Senator Dole was "troubled" by this disclosure, even "haunted by what he might have done," so much so that he was moved to write Clinton a letter of apology:

> Later that week, Dole was at the White House for an anti-terrorism bill signing ceremony. Clinton took him aside into a corridor so they could speak alone. The president thanked him for the letter. He said he had read it twice. He was touched and appreciated it very much.
>
> "Mothers are important," Dole said.
>
> Emotion rose up in both men. They looked at each other for an instant, then moved back to business. Soon they agreed on a budget for the rest of the year. It was not the comprehensive seven-year deal both had envisioned and worked on for months. But it was a start.

"This human story is the core," as Mr. Woodward said of *The Commanders*. To believe that this moment in the White House corridor occurred is not difficult: we know it occurred, precisely because whether or not it occurred makes no difference, has no significance, appears at first to tell us, like the famous moment described in *Veil*, the exchange between the author and William Casey in Room C6316 at Georgetown Hospital, nothing. "You knew, didn't you," Mr. Woodward thought to ask Casey on that occasion.

> The contra diversion had to be the first question: you knew all along.
>
> His head jerked up hard. He stared, and finally nodded yes.

Why? I asked.
"I believed."
What?
"I believed."
Then he was asleep, and I didn't get to ask another
question.

This account provoked, in the immediate wake of *Veil*'s 1987
publication, considerable talk-show and dinner-table controversy
(was Mr. Woodward actually in the room, did Mr. Casey actually
nod, where were the nurses, what happened to the CIA security detail), including, rather astonishingly, spirited discussion of
whether or not the hospital visit could be "corroborated." In fact
there was so markedly little reason to think the account inauthentic that the very question seemed to obscure, as the account
itself had seemed to obscure, the actual problem with the scene
in Room C6316 at Georgetown Hospital, which had to do with
timing, or with what did Mr. Woodward know and when did he
know it.

The hospital visit took place, according to *Veil*, "several
days" after Mr. Casey's resignation, which occurred on January
29, 1987. This was almost four months after the crash of the
Hasenfus plane in Nicaragua, more than two months after the
Justice Department disclosure that the United States had been
selling arms to Iran in order to divert the profits to the contras,
and a full month after both the House and Senate Permanent
Subcommittees on Intelligence had completed reports on their
investigations into the diversion. The inquiries of the two congressional investigating committees established in the first week
of January 1987, the Senate Select Committee on Secret Military
Assistance to Iran and the Nicaraguan Opposition and the House
Select Committee to Investigate Covert Arms Transactions with
Iran, were already underway. The report of the Tower Commission
would be released in three weeks.

Against this background and this amount of accumulated
information, the question of whether the director of Central
Intelligence "knew" about the diversion was, at the time Mr.
Woodward made his hospital visit and even more conclusively
at the time he committed his account of the visit to paper, no
longer at issue, no longer relevant, no longer a question. The

hospital interview, then, exists on the page only as a prurient distraction from the real questions raised by the diversion, only as a dramatization of the preferred Washington view that Iran-contra reflected not a structural problem but a "human story," a tale of how one man's hubris could have shaken the basically solid foundations of the established order, a disruption of the stable status quo that could be seen to end, satisfyingly, with that man's death.

Washington, as rendered by Mr. Woodward, is by definition basically solid, a diorama of decent intentions in which wise if misunderstood and occasionally misled stewards will reliably prevail. Its military chiefs will be pictured, as Colin Powell was in *The Commanders*, thinking on the eve of battle exclusively of their troops, the "kids," the "teenagers": a human story. The clerks of the Supreme Court will be pictured, as the clerks of the Burger court were in *The Brethren*, offering astute guidance as their justices negotiate the shoals of ideological error: a human story. The more available members of its foreign diplomatic corps will be pictured, as Saudi ambassador Prince Bandar bin Sultan was in *The Commanders* and *Veil*, gaining access to the councils of power not just because they have the oil but because of their "back-slapping irreverence," their "directness," their exemplification of "the new breed of ambassador—activist, charming, profane": yet another human story. Its opposing leaders will be pictured, as President Clinton and Senator Dole are in *The Choice*, finding common ground on the importance of mothers: the ultimate human story.

That this crude personalization works to narrow the focus, to circumscribe the range of possible discussion or speculation, is, for the people who find it useful to talk to Mr. Woodward, its point. What they have in Mr. Woodward is a widely trusted reporter, even an American icon, who can be relied upon to present a Washington in which problematic or questionable matters will be definitively resolved by the discovery, or by the demonstration that there can be no discovery, of "the smoking gun," "the evidence." Should such narrowly defined "evidence" be found, he can then be relied upon to demonstrate, "fairly," that the only fingerprints on the smoking gun are those of the one bad apple in the barrel, the single rogue agent in the tapestry of good intentions.

"I kept coming back to the question of personal responsibility, Casey's responsibility," Mr. Woodward reports having mused (apparently for once prepared, at the moment when he is about to visit a source on his deathbed, to question the veracity of what he has been told) before his last visit to Room C6316 at Georgetown Hospital. "For a moment, I hoped he would take himself off the hook. The only way was an admission of some kind or an apology to his colleagues or an expression of new understanding. Under the last question on 'Key unanswered questions for Casey,' I wrote: 'Do you see now that it was wrong?'" To commit such Rosebud moments to paper is what it means to tell "the human story at the core," and it is also what it means to write political pornography.

CLINTON AGONISTES

September 22, 1998

I

NO ONE WHO ever passed through an American public high school could have watched William Jefferson Clinton running for office in 1992 and failed to recognize the familiar predatory sexuality of the provincial adolescent. The man was, Jesse Jackson said that year to another point, "nothing but an appetite." No one who followed his appearances on *The Road to the White House* on C-SPAN could have missed the reservoir of self-pity, the quickness to blame, the narrowing of the eyes, as in a wildlife documentary, when things did not go his way: a response so reliable that aides on Jerry Brown's 1992 campaign looked for situations in which it could be provoked. The famous tendency of the candidate to take a less than forthcoming approach to embarrassing questions had already been documented and discussed, most exhaustively in the matter of his 1969 draft status, and he remained the front-runner. The persistent but initially unpublished rumors about extramarital rovings had been, once Gennifer Flowers told her story to the *Star*, published and acknowledged, and he remained on his feet. "I have acknowledged wrongdoing," he had told America during his and his wife's rather premonitory 60 *Minutes* appearances on Super Bowl Sunday of that year. "I have acknowledged causing pain in my marriage. I think most Americans who are watching this tonight, they'll know what we're saying, they'll get it, and they'll feel that we have been more than candid. And I think what the press has to decide is, are we going to engage in a game of gotcha?"

Nothing that is now known about the forty-second president of the United States, in other words, was not known before the New Hampshire primary in 1992. The implicit message in his August 1998 testimony to the Office of the Independent Counsel was not different in kind from that made explicit in January 1992:

I think most Americans who are watching this ... they'll know what we're saying, they'll get it, and they'll feel that we have been more than candid. By the time of the 1992 general election, the candidate was before us as he appears today: a more detailed and realized character than that presented in the Office of the Independent Counsel's oddly novelistic *Referral to the United States House of Representatives* but recognizably drawn to similar risk, voraciously needy, deeply fractured, and yet there, a force to contend with, a possessor of whatever manna accrues to those who have fought themselves and survived. The flaws already apparent in 1992 were by no means unreported, but neither, particularly in those parts of the country recently neutralized by their enshrinement as "the heartland," were they seized as occasions for rhetorical outrage. "With 16 million Americans unemployed, 40 million Americans without health care and 3 million Americans homeless, here's what we have to say about presidential aspirant Bill Clinton's alleged previous marital infidelity," the *Peoria Journal-Star* declared on its editorial page at the time of the 60 *Minutes* appearance. "So what? And that's all."

There were those for whom the candidate's clear personal volatility suggested the possibility of a similar evanescence on matters of ideology or policy, but even the coastal opinion leaders seemed willing to grant him a *laissez-passer* on this question of sex: "To what degree, if any, is the private action relevant to the duties of the public office?" *The Los Angeles Times* asked on its editorial page in January 1992. "Shouldn't our right to know about a candidate's sex life be confined ... to offenses such as rape, harassment, or sex discrimination?" *The New York Times* report on the 60 *Minutes* interview, which appeared on page A14 and was headlined "Clinton Defends His Privacy and Says the Press Intruded," was followed the next day by an editorial ("Leers, Smears and Governor Clinton") not only commending the candidate for having drawn a line "between idle curiosity and responsible attention" but noting that "he won't provide details and he need not, unless it develops that his private conduct arguably touches his public performance or fitness for office." The same day, January 28, 1992, A. M. Rosenthal wrote in the *Times* that Governor and Mrs. Clinton had "presented to the American public a gift and a lasting opportunity":

The gift is that they treated us as adults. The opportunity
is for us to act that way.... We can at least treasure the
hope that Americans would be fed up with the slavering
inquisition on politicians' sexual history and say to hell
with that and the torturers. That would be a thank-you
card worthy of the gift from the Clinton couple—the
presumption that Americans have achieved adulthood,
at last.

Few in the mainstream press, in 1992, demanded a demonstration of "contrition" from the candidate. Few, in 1992, demanded
"full remorse," a doubtful concept even in those venues, courtrooms in which criminal trials have reached the penalty phase,
where "remorse" is most routinely invoked. Few, in 1992, spoke
of the United States as so infantilized as to require a president
above the possibility of personal reproach. That so few did this
then, and so many have done this since, has been construed
by some as evidence that the interests and priorities of the
press have changed. In fact the interests and priorities of the
press have remained reliably the same: then as now, the press
could be relied upon to report a rumor or a hint down to
the ground (tree it, bag it, defoliate the forest for it, destroy
the village for it), but only insofar as that rumor or hint gave
promise of advancing the story of the day, the shared narrative,
the broad line of whatever story was at the given moment commanding the full resources of the reporters covering it and the
columnists commenting on it and the on-tap experts analyzing
it on the talk shows. (The 1998 *Yearbook of Experts, Authorities
& Spokespersons* tellingly provides, for producers with underdeveloped Rolodexes of their own, 1,477 telephone numbers to
call for those guests "who will drive the news issues in the next
year.") In *Spin Cycle*, a book in which Howard Kurtz of *The
Washington Post* endeavored to show the skill of the "Clinton
propaganda machine" (similarly described by Joe Klein, despite
what might seem impressive evidence to the contrary, as "the
most sophisticated communications apparatus in the history of
American politics") at setting the agenda for the press, there
appears this apparently ingenuous description of how the press
itself sets its agenda:

A front-page exclusive would ripple through the rest of the press corps, dominate the briefing, and most likely end up on the network news. The newsmagazine reporters were not quite as influential as in years past, but they could still change the dialogue or cement the conventional wisdom with a cover story or a behind-the-scenes report. Two vital groups of reinforcements backed up the White House regulars.... One was the columnists and opinion-mongers—Jonathan Alter at *Newsweek*, Joe Klein at *The New Yorker*, William Safire and Maureen Dowd at *The New York Times*, E. J. Dionne and Richard Cohen at *The Washington Post*—who could quickly change the zeitgeist.... the other was the dogged band of investigative reporters—Jeff Gerth at the *Times*, Bob Woodward at the *Post*, Glenn Simpson at *The Wall Street Journal*, Alan Miller at *The Los Angeles Times*.

Once the "zeitgeist" has been agreed upon by this quite small group of people, any unrelated event, whatever its actual significance, becomes either non-news or, if sufficiently urgent, a news brief. An example of the relegation to non-news would be this: Robert Scheer, in his *Los Angeles Times* review of *Spin Cycle*, noted that its index included eighteen references to Paula Jones and sixteen to John Huang, but none to Saddam Hussein. An example of the relegation to news brief would be this: on August 16, 1998, after hearing flash updates on the Omagh bombing in Northern Ireland ("worst attack in almost thirty years of violence ... latest figures as we have it are 28 people dead ... 220 people injured ... 103 still in hospital") and on the American embassy bombings in East Africa, Wolf Blitzer, on a two-hour *Late Edition with Wolf Blitzer* otherwise exclusively devoted to the "legal ramifications, political considerations, and historic consequences" of Monica Lewinsky, said this: "Catherine Bond, reporting live from Nairobi, thanks for joining us. Turning now to the story that has all of Washington holding its breath..."

In 1992, as in any election year, the story that had all of Washington holding its breath was the campaign, and since the guardians of the zeitgeist, taking their cue from the political professionals, had early on certified Governor Clinton as the most electable of the Democratic candidates, his personal failings could serve only as a step in his quest, a test of his ability to prevail. Before the New Hampshire primary campaign was even underway, Governor Clinton was reported to be the Democratic candidate with "centrist credentials," the Democratic candidate who "offered an assessment of the state of the American economy that borrows as much from Republicans like Jack Kemp as it does from liberals," the Democratic candidate who could go to California and win support from "top Republican fundraisers," the candidate, in short, who "scored well with party officials and strategists." A survey of Democratic National Committee members had shown Clinton in the lead. The late Ronald H. Brown, at the time chairman of the Democratic Party, had been reported, still before a single vote was cast in New Hampshire, to have pressured Mario Cuomo to remove his name from the New York primary ballot, so that a divisive favorite-son candidacy would not impede the chosen front-runner.

By the morning of January 26, 1992, the Sunday of the 60 *Minutes* appearance and shortly after the candidate sealed his centrist credentials by allowing the execution of the brain-damaged Rickey Ray Rector to proceed in Arkansas, William Schneider, in *The Los Angeles Times*, was awarding Governor Clinton the coveted "Big Mo," noting that "the Democratic Party establishment is falling in line behind Clinton." In a party that reserves a significant percentage of its convention votes (eighteen percent in 1996) for "superdelegates," the seven-hundred-some elected and party officials not bound by any popular vote, the message sent by this early understanding among the professionals was clear, as it had been when the professionals settled on Michael Dukakis in 1988: the train was now leaving the station, and, since the campaign, as "story," requires that the chosen candidates be seen as contenders who will go the distance, all inconvenient baggage, including "the character issue," would be left on the platform. What would go on the train was what Joe Klein, echoing the note of romantic credulity in his own 1992 coverage of the candidate Bill Clinton (that was before the zeitgeist moved on), recalled in 1998 in *The New Yorker* as the "precocious fizz" of the War Room, "the all-night-ers... about policy or philosophy," the candidate who "loved to talk about serious things" and "seems to be up on every social program in America."

2

It was January 16, 1998, when Kenneth W. Starr obtained authorization, by means of a court order opaquely titled "*In re* Madison Guaranty Savings & Loan Association," to extend his languishing Whitewater inquiry to the matter of Monica Lewinsky. It was also January 16 when Monica Lewinsky was detained for eleven hours and twenty-five minutes in Room 1016 of the Ritz-Carlton Hotel in Pentagon City, Virginia, where, according to the independent counsel's log of the "meeting," the FBI agent who undertook to read Miss Lewinsky "her rights as found on the form FD-395, Interrogation, Advice of Rights" was, for reasons the log does not explain, "unable to finish reading the FD-395." Miss Lewinsky herself testified:

> Then Jackie Bennett [of the Office of the Independent Counsel] came in and there was a whole bunch of other people and the room was crowded and he was saying to me, you know, you have to make a decision. I had wanted to call my mom, they weren't going to let me call my attorney, so I just—I just wanted to call my mom and they—Then Jackie Bennett said, "You're 24, you're smart, you're old enough, you don't need to call your mommy."

It was January 17 when President Clinton, in the course of giving his deposition in the civil suit brought against him by Paula Corbin Jones, either did or did not spring the perjury trap that Kenneth Starr either had or had not set. By the morning of January 21, when both Susan Schmidt in *The Washington Post* and ABC News correspondent Jackie Judd on *Good Morning America* jumped the stakes by quoting "sources" saying that Monica Lewinsky was on tape with statements that the president and Vernon Jordan had told her to lie, the "character issue" had gone from idle to full throttle, with Sam Donaldson and George Stephanopoulos and Jonathan Alter already on air talking about "impeachment proceedings."

In most discussions of how and why this matter came so incongruously to escalate, the press of course was criticized, and was in turn quick to criticize itself (or, in the phrasing preferred by many, since it suggested that any objection rested on hairsplitting, to "flagellate" itself), citing excessive and in some cases erroneous coverage. Perhaps because not all of the experts, authorities, and spokespersons driving this news had extensive experience with the kind of city-side beat on which it is taken for granted that the D.A.'s office will leak the cases they doubt they can make, selective prosecutorial hints had become embedded in the ongoing story as fact. "Loose attribution of sources abounded," Jules Witcover wrote in the March/April 1998 *Columbia Journalism Review*, although, since he tended to attribute the most egregious examples to "journalistic amateurs" and "journalistic pretenders" (Arianna Huffington and Matt Drudge), he could still express "hope," based on what he discerned two months into the story as "a tapering off of the mad frenzy of the first week or so," that, among "established, proven professional practitioners," any slip had been "a mere lapse of standards in the heat of a fast-breaking, incredibly competitive story of major significance."

For the same *CJR*, the cover line of which was "Where We Went Wrong ... and What We Do Now," a number of other reporters, editors, and news executives were queried, and expressed similar hopes. The possibility of viewer confusion between entertainment and news shows was mentioned. The necessity for more careful differentiation among different kinds of leaks was mentioned. The "new technology" and "hypercompetition" and "the speed of news cycles these days" were mentioned, references to the way in which the Internet and the multiplication of cable channels had collapsed the traditional cyclical presentation of news into a twenty-four-hour stream of provisional raw takes. "We're in a new world in terms of the way information flows to the nation," James O'Shea, deputy managing editor for news of the *Chicago Tribune*, said. (The Lewinsky story had in fact first broken not in the traditional media but on the Internet, in a 1:11 A.M. January 18, 1998, posting on the *Drudge Report*.) "The days when you can decide not to print a story because it's not well enough sourced are long gone. When a story gets into the public realm, as it did with the *Drudge Report*, then you have to characterize it, you have to tell your readers, 'This is out there, you've probably been hearing about it on TV and the Internet. We have been unable to substantiate it independently.' And then give them enough information to judge the validity of it."

That the "story" itself might in this case be anything other than (in Witcover's words) "a fast-breaking, incredibly competitive story of major significance" was questioned by only one panelist, Anthony Lewis of *The New York Times*, who characterized "the obsession of the press with sex and public officials" as "crazy," but allowed that "after Linda Tripp went to the prosecutor, it became hard to say we shouldn't be covering this." The more general attitude seemed to be that there might have been an excess here or an error there, but the story itself was important by defini-tion, significant because it was commanding the full resources of everyone on it—not unlike a campaign, which this story, in that it offered a particularly colorful version of the personalized "horse race" narrative that has become the model for most American political reporting, in fact resembled. "This is a very valid story of a strong-willed prosecutor and a president whose actions have been legitimately questioned," Walter Isaacson of *Time* said. "A case involving sex can be a very legitimate story, but we can't let our journalistic standards lapse simply because the sexual element makes everyone over-excited."

This, then, was a story "involving sex," a story in which there was a "sexual element," but, as we so frequently heard, it was not about sex, just as Whitewater, in the words of one of the several score editorials to this point published over the years by *The Wall Street Journal*, was "not merely about a land deal." What both stories were about, of course (although in the absence of both sex and evidence against the president one of them had proved a harder sell), was which of the contenders, the "strong-willed prosecutor" or his high-placed target, would go the distance, win the race. "The next forty-eight to seventy-two hours are critical," Tim Russert was saying on January 21, 1998, on MSNBC, where the daily recalibration of such sudden-death scenarios would by August raise the cable's Nielsen households from 49,000 a year before to 197,000. "I think his presidency is numbered in days," Sam Donaldson was saying by Sunday of the same week.

"On the high-status but low-interest White House beat, there is no story as exciting as that of the fall of a president," Jacob Weisberg observed in *Slate* in March. The president, everyone by then agreed, was "toast." The president "had to go," or "needed to go." The reasons the president needed to go had seemed, those last days in January and into February, crisp, easy to explain, grounded as they were in the galvanizing felony prospects set adrift without attribution by the Office of the Independent Counsel: obstruction of justice, subornation of perjury. Then, as questions threatened to slow the story (Would it not be unusual to prosecute someone for perjury in a civil suit? Did the chronology present a circumstantial case for, or actually against, obstruction? If someone lied in a deposition about a matter later ruled not essential to and so inadmissible in the case at hand, as Lewinsky had been ruled in *Jones* v. *Clinton*, was it in fact perjury?), the reasons the president "needed to go" became less crisp, more subjective, more a matter of "the mood here in the capital," and so, by definition, less open to argument from those not there in the capital.

This story was definitely moving, as they kept saying on MSNBC. By April 1, 1998, when U.S. District Court Judge Susan Webber Wright rendered the possibility of any felony technically remote by dismissing *Jones* v. *Clinton* altogether, the story had already rolled past its inconvenient legal (or "legalistic," a much-used word by then) limitations: ten weeks after America first heard the name Monica Lewinsky and still in the absence of any allegation bearing on the president's performance of his duties, the reasons the president needed to go were that he had been "weakened," that he would be "unable to function." The president's own former chief of staff, Leon Panetta, had expressed concern about "the slow drip-drip process and the price he's paying in terms of his ability to lead the country." When congressional staff members were asked in late March 1998 where they believed the situation was leading, twenty-one percent of Democratic staff members (forty-three percent of Republican) had foreseen, in the absence of resignation, impeachment proceedings.

The story was positioned, in short, for the satisfying long haul. By August 17, 1998, when the president confirmed the essential fact in the testimony Monica Lewinsky had given the grand jury eleven days before, virtually every "news analyst" on the eastern seaboard was on air (we saw the interiors of many attractive summer houses) talking about "the president's credibility," about "can he lead" or "still govern in any reasonably effective manner," questions most cogently raised that week by Garry Wills in *Time* and, to a different point, by Thomas L. Friedman in *The New York Times*. Proceeding from a belief both in President Clinton's underlying honor and in the redemptive power, if he was to be faced by crippling harassment, of the "principled resignation," Wills had tried to locate the homiletic possibilities in the dilemma, the opportunities for spiritual growth that could accrue to the country and to the president through resignation. The divergence between this argument and that made by Friedman was instructive. Friedman had seemed to be offering "can he lead" mainly as a strategy, an argument with which the professionals of the political process, who were increasingly bewildered by the public's apparent disinclination to join the rush to judgment by then general in the columns and talk shows, might most adroitly reeducate that "substantial majority" who "still feel that Mr. Clinton should remain in office."

In other words we had arrived at a dispiriting and familiar point, and would be fated to remain there even as telephone logs and Epass Access Control Reports and pages of grand-jury testimony floated down around us: "the disconnect," as it was now called, between what the professionals—those who held public office, those who worked for them, and those who wrote about them—believed to be self-evident and what a majority of Americans believed to be self-evident. John Kennedy and Warren Harding had both conducted affairs in the Oval Office (more recently known as "the workplace," or "under the same roof where his daughter lay sleeping"), and these affairs were by no means the largest part of what Americans thought about either of them. "If you step back a bit, it still doesn't look like a constitutional crisis," former federal prosecutor E. Lawrence Barcella told *The Los Angeles Times* to this point. "This is still a case about whether the President had sex with someone half his age. The American people have understood—certainly better than politicians, lawyers, and the press—that if this is ultimately about sex, it's really no one else's business. There are acceptable lies and unacceptable lies, and lying about someone's sex life is one of those tolerated lies."

Ten days after the president's August 17 admission to the nation, or ten days into the endless tape loop explicating the inadequacies of that admission, Mr. Clinton's own polls, according to *The Washington Post*, showed pretty much what everyone else's polls showed and would continue to show, notwithstanding the release first of Kenneth Starr's "narrative" and "grounds for impeachment" and then of Mr. Clinton's videotaped testimony and 3,183 pages of "supporting documents": that a majority of the public had believed all along that the president had some kind of involvement with Monica Lewinsky ("Cheat once, cheat twice, there's probably a whole line of them," a thirty-four-year-old woman told Democratic pollster Peter Hart in a focus session attended by *The Los Angeles Times*), continued to see it as a private rather than a political matter, believed Kenneth Starr to be the kind of sanctimonious hall monitor with sex on the brain they had avoided in their formative years (as in the jump-rope rhyme *Rooty-toot-toot! Rooty-toot-toot! / There go the boys from the Institute! / They don't smoke and they don't chew / And they don't go with the girls who do*), and, even as they acknowledged the gravity of lying under oath, did not wish to see the president removed from office.

The charge that he tried to conceal a personally embarrassing but not illegal liaison had not, it seemed, impressed most Americans as serious. Whether or not he had ever asked Vernon Jordan to call Ron Perelman and whether Vernon Jordan had in fact done so before or after the subpoena was issued to Monica Lewinsky had not, it seemed, much mattered to these citizens. Outside the capital, there had seemed to be a general recognition that the entire "crisis," although mildly entertaining, represented politics as usual, particularly since it had evolved from a case, the 1994 *Jones* v. *Clinton*, that would probably never have been brought and certainly never been funded had Mr. Clinton not been elected president. For Thomas L. Friedman, then, the way around this was to produce more desirable polling results by refocusing the question, steering the issue safely past the shoals of "should he be president," which was the essence of what the research was asking. "What might influence the public most,"

Friedman wrote, "is the question of 'can' Mr. Clinton still govern in any reasonably effective manner."

Since taking this argument to its logical conclusion raised, for a public demonstrably impatient with what it had come to see as a self-interested political class, certain other questions (If the president couldn't govern, who wouldn't let him? Was it likely that they would have let a lame duck govern anyway? What in fact was "governing," and did we want it?), most professionals fell back to a less vulnerable version of what the story was: a story so simple, so sentimental, as to brook no argument, no talking back from "the American people," who were increasingly seen as recalcitrant children, fecklessly resistant to responsible guidance. The story, William J. Bennett told us on *Meet the Press*, was about the "moral and intellectual disarmament" that befalls a nation when its president is not "being a decent example" and "teaching the kids the difference between right and wrong." The story, Cokie Roberts told us in the *New York Daily News*, was about reinforcing the lesson "that people who act immorally and lie get punished." The story, William Kristol told us on *This Week*, was about the president's "defiance," his "contempt," his "refusal to acknowledge some standards of public morality."

Certain pieties were repeated to the point where they could be referred to in shorthand. Although most Americans had an instinctive sense that Monica Lewinsky could well have been, as the *Referral* would later reveal her to have been, a less than entirely passive participant in whatever happened, we heard about the situational inviolability of interns (interns were "given into our care," interns were "lent to us by their parents") until Cokie Roberts's censorious cry to an insufficiently outraged congresswoman ("But with an *intern*?") could stand alone, a verdict that required no judge or jury. We heard repeatedly about "our children," or "our kids," who were, as presented, avid consumers of the *Nightly News* in whose presence sex had never before been mentioned and discussions of the presidency were routine. "I'd like to be able to tell my children, 'You should tell the truth,'" Stuart Taylor of the *National Journal* told us on *Meet the Press*. "I'd like to be able to tell them, 'You should respect the president.' And I'd like to be able to tell them both things at the same time." Jonathan Alter, in *Newsweek*, spoke of the president as someone "who has made it virtually impossible to talk to your kids about the American presidency or let them watch the news."

"I approach this as a mother," Cokie Roberts said on *This Week*. "We have a right to say to this president, 'What you have done is an example to our children that's a disgrace,'" William J. Bennett said on *Meet the Press*. The apparent inability of the public to grasp this *Kinder-Kirche* point (perhaps because not all Americans could afford the luxury of idealizing their own children) had itself become an occasion for outrage and scorn: the public was too "complacent," or too "prosperous," or too "fixed on the Dow Jones." The public in fact became the unindicted co-conspirator: "This ought to be something that outrages us, makes us ashamed of him," Mona Charen complained on *Late Edition with Wolf Blitzer*. "This casts shame on the entire country because he behaved that way and all of the nation seems to be complicit now because they aren't rising up in righteous indignation."

This was the impasse (or, as it turned out, the box canyon) that led many into a scenario destined to prove wishful at best: "The American people," we heard repeatedly, would cast off their complicity when they were actually forced by the report of the independent counsel to turn their attention from the Dow and face what Thomas L. Friedman, in the *Times*, called "the sordid details that will come out from Ken Starr's investigation." "People are not as sophisticated as this appears to be," William Kristol had said hopefully the day before the president's televised address. "We all know, inside the Beltway, what's in that report," Republican strategist Mary Matalin said. "And I don't think ... the country needs to hear any more about tissue, dresses, cigars, ties, anything else." George Will, on *This Week*, assured his co-panelists that support for the president would evaporate in the face of the *Referral*. "Because Ken Starr must—the president has forced his hand—must detail graphically the sexual activity that demonstrates his perjury. Once that report is written and published, Congress will be dragged along in the wake of the public.... Once the dress comes in, and some of the details come in from the Ken Starr report, people—there's going to be a critical mass, the yuck factor—where people say, 'I don't want him in my living room any more.'"

The person most people seemed not to want in their living rooms any more was "Ken" (as he was now called by those with an interest in protecting his story), but this itself was construed as evidence of satanic spin on the part of the White House. "The president's men," William J. Bennett cautioned in *The Death of Outrage: Bill Clinton and the Assault on American Ideals*, "…attempt relentlessly to portray their opposition as bigoted and intolerant fanatics who have no respect for privacy." He continued:

> At the same time they offer a temptation to their supporters: the temptation to see themselves as realists, worldly-wise, sophisticated: in a word, European. This temptation should be resisted by the rest of us. In America, morality is central to our politics and attitudes in a way that is not the case in Europe, and precisely this moral streak is what is best about us…. Europeans may have something to teach us about, say, wine or haute couture. But on the matter of morality in politics, America has much to teach Europe.

American innocence itself, then, was now seen to hang on the revealed word of the *Referral*. The report, Fox News promised, would detail "activities that most Americans would describe as unusual." These details, *Newsweek* promised, would make Americans "want to throw up." "Specifics about a half-dozen sex acts," *Newsday* promised, had been provided "during an unusual two-hour session August 26 in which Lewinsky gave sworn testimony in Starr's downtown office, not before the grand jury."

This is arresting, and not to be brushed over. On August 6, Monica Lewinsky had told the grand jury that sexual acts had occurred. On August 17, the president had tacitly confirmed this in both his testimony to the grand jury and his televised address to the nation. Given this sequence, the "unusual two-hour session August 26" might have seemed, to some, unnecessary, even excessive, not least because of the way in which, despite the full knowledge of the prosecutors that the details elicited in this session would be disseminated to the world in two weeks under the *Referral* headings "November 15 Sexual Encounter," "November 17 Sexual Encounter," "December 31 Sexual Encounter," "January 7 Sexual Encounter," "January 21 Sexual Encounter," "February 4 Sexual Encounter and Subsequent Phone Calls," "March 31

Sexual Encounter," "Easter Telephone Conversations and Sexual Encounter," "February 28 Sexual Encounter," and "March 29 Sexual Encounter," certain peculiar and warped proprieties had been so pruriently observed. "In deference to Lewinsky and the explicit nature of her testimony," *Newsday* reported, "all the prosecutors, defense lawyers and stenographers in the room during the session were women."

Since the "explicit nature of the testimony," the "unusual activity," the "throw-up details" everyone seemed to know about (presumably because they had been leaked by the Office of the Independent Counsel) turned out to involve masturbation, it was hard not to wonder if those in the know might not be experiencing some sort of rhetorical autointoxication, a kind of rapture of the feed. The average age of first sexual intercourse in this country has been for some years sixteen, and is younger in many venues. Since the average age of first marriage in this country is twenty-five for women and twenty-seven for men, sexual activity outside marriage occurs among Americans for an average of nine to eleven years. Six out of ten marriages in this country are likely to end in divorce, a significant percentage of those who divorce doing so after engaging in extramarital sexual activity. As of the date of the 1990 census, there were in this country 4.1 million households headed by unmarried couples. More than thirty-five percent of these households included children. Seventh-graders in some schools in this country were as early as the late 1970s reading the Boston Women's Health Book Collective's *Our Bodies, Ourselves*, which explained the role of masturbation in sexuality and the use of foreign objects in masturbation. The notion that Americans apparently willing to overlook a dalliance in the Oval Office would go pale at its rather commonplace details seemed puzzling in the extreme, as did the professed inability to understand why these Americans might favor the person who had engaged in a common sexual act over the person who had elicited the details of that act as evidence for a public stoning.

But of course these members of what Howard Fineman recently defined on MSNBC as "the national political class," the people "who read the *Hotline* or watch cable television political shows such as this one," were not talking about Americans at large. They did not know Americans at large. They occasionally heard from one, in a focus group or during the Q&A after a lecture date, but their attention, since it was focused on the political process, which had come to represent the concerns not of the country at large but of the organized pressure groups that increasingly controlled it, remained remote. When Howard Fineman, during the same MSNBC appearance, spoke of "the full-scale panic" that he detected "both here in Washington and out around the country," he was referring to calls he had made to "a lot of Democratic consultants, pollsters, media people and so forth," as well as to candidates: "For example one in Wisconsin, a woman running for the Democratic seat up there, she said she's beginning to get calls and questions from average folks wanting to know what her view of Bill Clinton is."

"Average folks," however, do not call their elected representatives, nor do they attend the events where the funds get raised and the questions asked. The citizens who do are the citizens with access, the citizens with an investment, the citizens who have a special interest. When Representative Tom Coburn (R-Okla.) reported to *The Washington Post* that during three days in September 1998 he received five hundred phone calls and 850 e-mails on the question of impeachment, he would appear to have been reporting, for the most part, less on "average folks" than on constituents who already knew, or had been provided, his telephone number or e-mail address; reporting, in other words, on an organized blitz campaign. When Gary Bauer of the Family Research Council seized the moment by test-running a drive for the presidency with a series of Iowa television spots demanding Mr. Clinton's resignation, he would appear to have been interested less in reaching out to "average folks" than in galvanizing certain caucus voters, the very caucus voters who might be expected to have already called or e-mailed Washington on the question of impeachment.

When these people on the political talk shows spoke about the inability of Americans to stomach "the details," then, they were speaking, in code, about a certain kind of American, a minority of the population but the minority to whom recent campaigns have been increasingly pitched. They were talking politics. They were talking about the "values" voter, the "pro-family" voter, and so complete by now was their isolation from the country in which they lived that they seemed willing to reserve its franchise for, in other words give it over to, that key core vote.

3

The cost of producing a television show on which Wolf Blitzer or John Gibson referees an argument between an unpaid "former federal prosecutor" and an unpaid "legal scholar" is significantly lower than that of producing conventional programming. This is, as they say, the "end of the day," or the bottom-line fact. The explosion of "news comment" programming occasioned by this fact requires, if viewers are to be kept from tuning out, nonstop breaking stories on which the stakes can be raised hourly. The Gulf War made CNN, but it was the trial of O. J. Simpson that taught the entire broadcast industry how to perfect the pushing of the stakes. The crisis that led to the Clinton impeachment began as and remained a situation in which a handful of people, each of whom believed that he or she had something to gain (a book contract, a scoop, a sinecure as a network "analyst," contested ground in the culture wars, or, in the case of Starr, the justification of his failure to get either of the Clintons on Whitewater), managed to harness this phenomenon and ride it. This was not an unpredictable occurrence, nor was it unpredictable that the rather impoverished but generally unremarkable transgressions in question would come in this instance to be inflated by the rhetoric of moral rearmament.

"You cannot defile the temple of justice," Kenneth Starr told reporters during his many front-lawn and driveway appearances. "There's no room for white lies. There's no room for shading. There's only room for truth.... Our job is to determine whether crimes were committed." This was the authentic if lonely voice of the last American wilderness, the voice of the son of a Texas preacher in a fundamentalist denomination (the Churches of Christ) so focused on the punitive that it forbade even the use of instrumental music in church. This was the voice of a man who himself knew a good deal about risk-taking, an Ahab who had been mortified by his great Whitewater whale and so in his pursuit of what Melville called "the highest truth" would submit to the House, despite repeated warnings from his own supporters (most visibly on the editorial page of *The Wall Street Journal*) not to do so, a report in which his attempt to take down the government was based in its entirety on ten occasions of backseat intimacy as detailed by an eager but unstable participant who appeared to have memorialized the events on her hard drive.

This was a curious document. It was reported by *The New York Times*, on the day after its initial and partial release, to have been written in part by Stephen Bates, identified as a "part-time employee of the independent counsel's office and the part-time literary editor of *The Wilson Quarterly*," an apparent polymath who after his 1987 graduation from Harvard Law School "wrote for publications as diverse as *The Nation*, *The Weekly Standard*, *Playboy*, and *The New Republic*." According to the *Times*, Mr. Bates and Mr. Starr had together written a proposal for a book about a high school student in Omaha barred by her school from forming a Bible study group. The proposed book, which did not find a publisher, was to be titled *Bridget's Story*. This is interesting, since the "narrative" section of the *Referral*, including as it does a wealth of nonrelevant or "story" details (for example the threatening letter from Miss Lewinsky to the president which the president said he had not read, although "Ms. Lewinsky suspected that he had actually read the whole thing"), seems very much framed as "Monica's Story." We repeatedly share her "feelings," just as we might have shared Bridget's: "I left that day sort of emotionally stunned," Miss Lewinsky is said to have testified at one point, for "I just knew he was in love with me."

Consider this. The day in question, July 4, 1997, was six weeks after the most recent of the president's attempts to break off their relationship. The previous day, after weeks of barraging members of the White House staff with messages and calls detailing her frustration at being unable to reach the president, her conviction that he owed her a job, and her dramatically good intentions ("I know that in your eyes I am just a hindrance—a woman who doesn't have a certain someone's best interests at heart, but please trust me when I say I do"), Miss Lewinsky had dispatched a letter that "obliquely," as the narrative has it, "threatened to disclose their relationship." On this day, July 4, the president has at last agreed to see her. He accuses her of threatening him. She accuses him of failing to secure for her an appropriate job, which in fact she would define in a later communiqué as including "anything at *George* magazine." "The most important things to me," she would then specify, "are that I am engaged and interested in my work, I am *not* someone's administrative/executive assistant, and my salary can provide me a comfortable living in NY."

At this point she cried. He "praised her intellect and beauty," according to the narrative. He said, according to Miss Lewinsky, "he wished he had more time for me." She left the Oval Office, "emotionally stunned," convinced "he was in love with me." The "narrative," in other words, offers what is known among students of fiction as an unreliable first-person narrator, a classic literary device whereby the reader is made to realize that the situation, and indeed the narrator, are other than what the narrator says they are. It cannot have been the intention of the authors to present their witness as the victimizer and the president her hapless victim, and yet there it was, for all the world to read. That the authors of the *Referral* should have fallen into this basic craft error suggests the extent to which, by the time the *Referral* was submitted, the righteous voice of the grand inquisitor had isolated itself from the more wary voices of his cannier allies.

That the voice of the inquisitor was not one to which large numbers of Americans would respond had always been, for these allies, beside the point: what it offered, and what less authentic voices obligingly amplified, was a platform for the reintroduction of fundamentalism, or "values issues," into the general discourse. "Most politicians miss the heart and soul of this concern," Ralph Reed wrote in 1996, having previously defined "the culture, the family, a loss of values, a decline in civility, and the destruction of our children" as the chief concerns of the Christian Coalition, which in 1996 claimed to have between a quarter and a third of its membership among registered Democrats. Despite two decades during which the promotion of the "values" agenda had been the common cause of both the "religious" (or Christian) and the neoconservative right, too many politicians, Reed believed, still "debate issues like accountants." John Podhoretz, calling on Republicans in 1996 to resist the efforts of Robert Dole and Newt Gingrich to "de-ideologize" the Republican Party, had echoed, somewhat less forthrightly, Reed's complaint about the stress on economic issues. "They do not answer questions about the spiritual health of the nation," he wrote. "They do not address the ominous sense we all have that Americans are, with every intake of breath, unconsciously inhaling a philosophy that stresses individual pleasure over individual responsibility; that our capacity to be our best selves is weakening."

That "all" of us did not actually share this "ominous sense" was, again, beside the point, since neither Reed nor Podhoretz was talking about all of us. Less than fifty percent of the voting-age population in this country actually voted (for anyone) for president in 1996. The figures in the previous five presidential-year elections ranged from fifty to fifty-five percent. Only between thirty-three and thirty-eight percent voted in any mid-term election since 1974. The figures for those who vote in primary elections, where the terms on which the campaign will be waged are determined, drop even further, in some cases into the single digits. Ralph Reed and John Podhoretz had been talking in 1996, as William Kristol and Mary Matalin would be talking in 1998, about that small group of citizens for whom "the spiritual health of the nation" would serve as the stalking horse for a variety of "social," or control-and-respect, issues. They were talking, in other words, about that narrow subsection of the electorate known in American politics as most-likely-to-vote.

What the Christian Coalition and *The Weekly Standard* were asking the Republican Party and (by logical extension) its opponents to do in 1996 was to further narrow most-likely-to-vote, by removing from debate those issues that concerned the country at large. This might have seemed, at the time, a ticket only to marginalization. It might have seemed, as recently as 1996, a rather vain hope that the nation's opinion leaders would soon reach general agreement that the rearming of the citizenry's moral life required that three centuries of legal precedent and even constitutional protections be overridden in the higher interest of demonstrating the presence of moral error, or "determining whether a crime has been committed," as Kenneth Starr put it in the brief he submitted to the Supreme Court in the matter of whether Vincent Foster's lawyer could be compelled to turn over notes on conversations he had with Foster before his death. Yet by August 1998, here were two of those opinion leaders, George Will and Cokie Roberts, stiffening the spines of those members of Congress who might be tempted to share the inclination of their constituents to distinguish between mortal and venial sins:

> G.W.: Cokie, the metastasizing corruption spread by this man [the president] is apparent now. And the corruption of the very idea of what it means to be a representative. We hear people in Congress saying, "Our job is solely to read the public opinion polls and conform thereto." Well, if so, that's not intellectually complicated, it's not morally demanding. But it makes a farce of being a ...
>
> C.R.: No, at that point, we should just go for direct democracy.
>
> G.W.: Exactly. Get them out of here and let's plug computers in....
>
> C.R.: ... I must say I think that letting the [impeachment] process work makes a lot of sense because it brings—then people can lead public opinion rather than just follow it through the process.
>
> G.W.: What a concept.
>
> C.R.: But we will see.

To talk about the failure of Congress to sufficiently isolate itself from the opinion of the electorate as a "corruption of the very idea of what it means to be a representative" is to talk (another kind of "end of the day," or bottom-line fact) about disenfranchising America. "The public was fine, the elites were not," an unnamed White House adviser had told *The Washington Post* about the difference of opinion, on the matter of the president's "apology" or "nonapology," between the political professionals and what had until recently been deferred to, if only pro forma, as the electorate. "You've got to let the elites win one."

No one should have doubted that the elites would in fact win this one, since, even before the somewhat dampening polling on the Starr report and on the president's videotaped testimony, the enterprise had achieved the perfect circularity toward which it had long been tending. "I want to find out who else in the political class thinks the way Mr. Clinton does about what is acceptable behavior," George Will had said in August, explaining why he favored impeachment proceedings over a resignation. "Let's smoke them out." That a majority of Americans seemed capable of separating Mr. Clinton's behavior in this matter from his performance as president had become, by that point, irrelevant, as had the ultimate outcome of the congressional deliberation. What was going to happen had already happened: since future elections could now be focused on the entirely spurious issue of correct sexual, or "moral," behavior, those elections would be increasingly decided by that committed and well-organized minority brought most reliably to the polls by "pro-family," or "values," issues. The fact that an election between two candidates arguing which has the more correct "values" left most voters with no reason to come to the polls had even come to be spoken about, by less wary professionals, as the beauty part, the bonus that would render the process finally and perpetually impenetrable. "Who cares what every adult thinks?" a Republican strategist asked *The Washington Post* to this point in early September 1998. "It's totally not germane to this election."

VICHY WASHINGTON

June 24, 1999

I

ON AN EVENING late in April 1999, some 350 survivors of what they saw as a fight for the soul of the republic gathered at the Mayflower Hotel in Washington to honor Representative Henry J. Hyde and the twelve House managers who, under his leadership, had carried the charges of impeachment to the floor of the Senate. C-SPAN caught the distinctive, familial fervor of the event, which was organized to benefit the Independent Women's Forum, an organization funded in part by Richard Mellon Scaife and the "women's group" in the name of which Kenneth Starr volunteered in 1994 to file an amicus curiae brief arguing that *Jones* v. *Clinton* should go forward. Live from the Mayflower, there on-screen were the familiar faces from the year-long entertainment that had preceded the impeachment, working the room amid the sedate din and the tinkling of glasses. There were the pretty women in country-club dinner dresses, laughing appreciatively at the bons mots of their table partners. There was the black-tie quartet, harmonizing on "Vive la, vive la, vive l'amour" and "Goodbye My Coney Island Baby" as Henry Hyde doggedly continued to spoon up his dessert, chocolate meeting mouth with metronomic regularity, his perseverance undeflected even by Bob Barr, leaning in to make a point.

The word "courage" was repeatedly invoked. Midge Decter, a director of the Independent Women's Forum, praised Henry Hyde's "manliness," and the way in which watching "him and his merry hand" on television during the impeachment trial had caused her to recall "whole chunks" of Rudyard Kipling's "If." Robert L. Bartley, the editor of *The Wall Street Journal*, had found similar inspiration in the way in which the managers had "exposed truths to the American people, and they did this in the face of all the polls and focus groups, and they were obviously doing an unpopular thing, and I think that is why they deserve our greatest credit." The words of Henry V before the Battle of Agincourt were recalled by Michael Novak, as they had been by Henry Hyde in his closing statement during the Senate impeachment trial, but for this occasion adapted to "our Prince Hal, our own King Henry": "He that outlives this day, and comes safe home, will stand at tiptoe when this day is named…. Then shall our names, familiar in his mouth as household words, Henry the King, Rogan and Hutchinson, Canady, Cannon, McCollum, Lindsey Graham, Gekas, Chabot, Bryant, Buyer, Barr, and Sensenbrenner."

This evening could have seemed, for those who still misunderstood the Reagan mandate to have been based on what are now called "social" issues, the last redoubt. Familiar themes were sounded, favorite notes struck. Even the most glancing reference to the depredations of "the Sixties" ("…according to Sean Wilentz, a scholar who exemplifies all the intellectual virtues and glories of the Sixties…") proved a reliable crowd-pleaser. In deference to the man who had not only sponsored the Hyde Amendment (banning Medicaid payments for abortions) but who had a year before testified as a character witness for a defendant accused of illegally blockading abortion clinics ("He's a hero to me," Hyde had said. "He has the guts I wish more of us had"), the "unborn" were characterized as "the stranger, the other, the unwanted, the inconvenient."

Mentions of "Maxine Waters" were cues for derision. "Barney Frank" was a laugh line that required no explication. The loneliness of the shared position was assumed, and proudly stressed. Yet the mood of the evening was less elegiac than triumphal, less rueful than rededicated, as if there in a ballroom at the Mayflower was the means by which the American political dialogue could be finally reconfigured: on the sacrificial altar of the failed impeachment, in the memory of the martyred managers, the message of moral rearmament that has driven the conservative movement to what had seemed no avail might at last have met its moment. "As we were coming in," William J. Bennett told the guests that night, "I said to my friend Dan Oliver, I said 'Good group.' Dan said, 'Good group? This is it, pal. This is the army. This is all of it.'"

The notion that a failed attempt to impeach the president might nonetheless have accomplished exactly what it was meant to accomplish, that the desired phoenix might even then be rising from the ashes of acquittal, might have seemed to many, in the immediate wake of the November 1998 elections, when the disinclination

of the American people to see the president impeached translated into the loss of five Republican congressional seats, wishful.
"It's pretty clear that impeachment dropped off the public's radar
screen," Henry Hyde said to a *Los Angeles Times* reporter as he
realized on election night that he was losing not only his anticipated mandate but five of his votes. The next morning, in the
O'Hare Hilton, he told three aides that his Judiciary Committee
inquiry, which party leaders had inexplicably construed as so in
tune with public sentiment as to promise a gain of twenty seats,
would have to be telescoped, and impeachment delivered out of
the House while his lame ducks could still vote.

Over the next several weeks, as they contemplated the unexpected hit they had taken by feeding the greed of their conservative base for impeachment, Republicans would float many fanciful
scenarios by which the party could be extricated from its own
device. Senator Arlen Specter of Pennsylvania argued on the op-
ed page of *The New York Times* for "abandoning impeachment," in
effect handing off this suddenly sticky wicket to the courts, where,
since not many lawyers saw a makeable case for perjury, it could
conveniently dematerialize. Robert Dole laid out a plan based on
the distinctly improbable agreement of the president in his own
censure. Even Henry Hyde saw a way for the president to save the
day, by resigning: "I think he could be really heroic if he did that.
He would be the savior of his party.... It would be a way of going
out with honor." By mid-December 1998, former Senator Alan K.
Simpson was expressing what had become by default the last-ditch
position of most Republicans, which was that any hemorrhaging
they were suffering outside their conservative base could be contained before 2000 by the putative inability of these less ideological
voters to remember that long. "The attention span of Americans,"
Simpson said, "is 'which movie is coming out next month?' and
whether the quarterly report on their stock will change."

This casual contempt for the electorate at large was by then sufficiently general to pass largely unremarked upon. A good deal
of what seemed at the time opaque in the firestorm that consumed the attention of the United States from January 1998 until
the spring of 1999 has since been illuminated, but what remains
novel, and unexplained, was the increasingly histrionic insistence

of the political establishment that it stood apart from, and indeed above, the country that had until recently been considered its validation. Under the lights at CNN and MSNBC and the Sunday shows, it became routine to declare oneself remote from "them," or "out there." The rhetorical expression of outrage, or "speaking out," became in itself a moral position, even when the reasons for having spoken out could not be recalled. "...Whether or not it happens," Robert H. Bork said to *The Washington Post* in December 1998 about impeachment, which he favored, "I will still think I was right.... I just spoke out. I think on a television show, maybe Larry King. I wish I could recall what I was concerned with, but I can't at the moment."

The electorate, as anyone who had turned on a television set since the spring of 1998 had heard repeatedly, was "complicit" in the "corruption" of the president, or of the administration, or of the country itself, which was therefore in need of the "purging" to be effected, as in myth, by the removal of the most visible figure on the landscape. "It would be an enormous emetic—culturally, politically, morally—for us to have an impeachment," the Reverend John Neuhaus, editor of the conservative monthly *First Things*, told Michael Powell of *The Washington Post*. "It would purge us." The reason the public was "complicit," and the country in need of "purging," was that the public was "materialistic," interested only in "the Dow," or, later, "their pension funds." The reason the public was "materialistic" was that the public had, well, no morals. "My wife likes to say they must be polling people coming out of Hooters on Saturday night," Senator Robert C. Smith of New Hampshire said at the time he was announcing his bid for the presidency. "I will not defend the public," William J. Bennett told *The New York Times* in February 1999, after Paul M. Weyrich had written to supporters of his Free Congress Foundation that since the nation was in the grip of an "alien ideology" they should abandon the idea that a moral majority existed and take steps to "quarantine" their families. "Absolutely not. If people want to pander to the public and say they're right they can. But they're not right on this one."

"What's popular isn't always what's right," Representative J. C. Watts of Oklahoma said, arguing in the House for impeachment. "Polls would have rejected the Ten Commandments. Polls would have embraced slavery and ridiculed women's rights."

On the weekend in January 1999 when the "favorable" rating of the Republican Party dropped to thirty-six percent, the lowest point since Watergate, Senator Phil Gramm said on *Meet the Press* that the people of Texas "didn't elect me to read those polls." Not even when the bumper stickers of the John Birch Society were common road sightings had we been so insistently reminded that this was not a democracy but a republic, or a "representative form of government." For the more inductive strategists in the movement, the next logical step was obvious: since a republic depended by definition on an electorate, and since the electorate at hand had proved itself "complicit," the republic itself could be increasingly viewed as doubtful, open for rethinking. "The Clinton affair and its aftermath will, I think, turn out to be a defining moment that exposed the rot in the institutions of American republican government," Charles Murray wrote in *The Weekly Standard* in February 1999. "Whether the response will be to shore up the structure or abandon it remains an open question."

2

On the morning of February 11, 1994, Michael Isikoff, at that time a reporter for *The Washington Post* and later the author of *Uncovering Clinton: A Reporter's Story*, received, from the conservative strategist Craig Shirley, a heads-up on what would be said that afternoon at the Conservative Political Action Conference at the Hotel Omni Shoreham, where a woman brought to Washington by Cliff Jackson, the Hot Springs lawyer who orchestrated Troopergate, was scheduled to give a press conference. Isikoff went over to the Shoreham, witnessed what would turn out to be the debut performance of Paula Jones, and the next morning conducted a three-hour interview with her, in a suite at the Shoreham where she was flanked by her husband and her then lawyer, Danny Traylor. Isikoff asked Paula Jones about her eighteen-month-old son, Madison, and told her about his own baby daughter. He asked her whether her parents had been Democrats or Republicans, a point about which she was uncertain. "I guess any man probably would be more [interested in politics] than a woman," she said. "That's just not my interest in life." Isikoff tells us that he questioned Traylor and Jackson independently about their initial involvement, and reports that the answers they gave "point toward an innocent explanation." If Isikoff did indeed choose to ask Paula Jones herself why, given her lack of interest in politics, her lawyer had hooked her up with Cliff Jackson and Craig Shirley and the Conservative Political Action Conference, he chose not to record her answer, although he renders certain details from that initial interview with some avidity:

> *Paula Jones:* "He had boxer shorts and everything and he exposed hisself [sic] with an erection ... holding it ... fiddling it or whatever. And he asked me to—I don't know his exact word—give him a blow job or—I know you gotta know his exact words."
>
> *Isikoff:* "Exact words."
>
> *Paula Jones:* "He asked me to do something. I know that. I'll tell you, I was so shocked. I think he wanted me to kiss it.... And he was saying it in a very disgusting way, just a horny-ass way ..."
>
> *Isikoff:* "What do you mean in a very disgusting way?"
>
> *Paula Jones:* "Disgusting way, he just, it was *please, I want it so bad*—just that type of way, like he was wanting it bad, you know."

Over the next several years, first on the Paula Jones story for the *Post* and then on the Paula Jones and the Kathleen Willey and the Monica Lewinsky stories for *Newsweek*, Isikoff would encounter a number of such choices, moments in which a less single-minded reporter might well have let attention stray to the distinctly peculiar way the story was unfolding itself, the way in which corroborating witnesses and incriminating interviews would magically materialize, but Isikoff kept his eye on the ball, his story, which was, exactly, "uncovering" Clinton. There was for example the moment when Joe Cammarata, one of the lawyers chosen by those working behind the scenes on the Jones case to replace Danny Traylor, had accommodated Isikoff's need to find "evidence that Clinton did this to other women" by recalling a "mysterious phone call" he had received from a woman who would not give her name but said that "a similar thing" had happened to her when she was working in the White

House. "This was weird, I thought," Isikoff recalls. "The caller had imparted a hell of a lot of detail. Cammarata, for his part, was more than happy to let me figure it out. If I could track this woman down, he reasoned, I'd probably pass it along to him. Then he could subpoena her. As he saw it, I would save him some legwork."

Examine this. Isikoff thought the call was "weird," but any suspicions this aroused seem not to have suggested to him that the Jones defense team, or someone working through the Jones defense team, might be planting a story. As might have been predicted, this tip led Isikoff to Kathleen Willey, at which point we enter another reportorial twilight zone. "A journalistic dance between aggressive reporter and reluctant source began," Isikoff writes, "a dance that was to continue for months." In the average reporting experience, reluctant sources hang up, or say no comment, then screen their calls, leave town. This "reluctant source," however, having extracted the promise that Isikoff would not publish her story "until she gave the green light," allowed herself to be interviewed for more than two hours, telling her story "in gripping and microscopic detail."

Asked by the "aggressive reporter" if anyone could corroborate her story, another point at which, if she did not want the story out, she could have recouped her losses by saying no, Kathleen Willey obligingly named two women. One of the women she named was Julie Hiatt Steele, to whom, on the spot, she placed a call, arranging a meeting later that day between Steele and Isikoff. The second woman was Linda Tripp, then at the Pentagon. Dutifully, a relentless op on the case, Isikoff followed up his conveniently arranged meeting with Julie Hiatt Steele by tagging along with a *Newsweek* reporter who had access to the Pentagon. There, in a cubicle in the basement, Isikoff confronted Linda Tripp, who, within minutes, although "alarmed" by his visit, delivered the story's next reveal: "'There's something here, but the story's not what you think it is,' she said cryptically. 'You're barking up the wrong tree.'"

Note "cryptically." That was in March 1997. By April, Linda Tripp had delivered considerably more ("twenty-three-year-old former White House intern," got her job through "a wealthy campaign contributor," a "big insurance executive," "thrown out of the White House," "had gotten her a job at another federal agency," "hideaway off the Oval Office," "oral sex"), and had even let Isikoff listen in on a phone call from the former intern, "an excited and somewhat whiny young woman complaining about another woman named 'Marsha.'" Marsha, Linda Tripp explained, was Marsha Scott, the president's personnel aide. Marsha was supposed to have brought the young woman back to the White House after the 1996 election. Marsha had not. Marsha was giving the young woman the runaround.

No matter how many clues the remarkably patient Tripp provided, the story remained, Isikoff tells us, presenting himself as an impartial fact-gatherer to whom speculative connections were anathema, in the cryptic range. "I'm a reporter, not a voyeur," he tells us, appropriating the high-road benefit, and, also, "Tripp wouldn't give me the ex-intern's name or the agency she worked for." And there was something else: "Tripp was certain the relationship was entirely consensual.... That, it seemed to me, placed it outside the scope of the Paula Jones lawsuit—my main justification for proceeding down this path."

But wait, he surely said to himself at this point, or perhaps not. You got to Tripp via Willey. You got to Willey via the Jones defense team. Who gains here? Who wants what out? Why? Four months later, Isikoff was still refusing to acknowledge the possibility of connections. In August 1997, in a CNBC green room, he happened to be discussing legal strategy on the Jones case with Ann Coulter, one of the "movement," or conservative, lawyers who had become a fixture on the news-comment shows. According to Isikoff, he remarked to Coulter that she seemed to have inside knowledge of *Jones* v. *Clinton*, and she laughed. "Oh, yes," he reports her responding. "There are lots of us busy elves working away in Santa's workshop." "Busy elves?" Isikoff recalls having thought, and then: "I remembered something about George Conway in New York. Now Coulter. Who else? And what were they doing?"

Some might have seen this as a line of inquiry worth pursuing, but Isikoff, after a call to Conway's office at Wachtell, Lipton, Rosen & Katz in New York ("Conway and Coulter were fast friends" who "bonded over their common disdain for Clinton, and they loved nothing more than to gossip into the night about the latest developments in the Jones lawsuit"), seems to have satisfied himself that Conway and the other ardently conservative lawyers with whom Conway was in touch might be useful sources, but not themselves the story. Not until October 1997, when Linda Tripp summoned him to a meeting with Lucianne Goldberg and provided him with a beer, a bowl of pistachio nuts, and the name Monica Lewinsky, did his reporter's instincts briefly revive: "I stopped eating the nuts and started taking notes." There were, Linda Tripp said, tapes, and she was prepared to play them, but Isikoff, who "had been invited to appear on a CNBC talk show, *Hardball*," and so was "a bit pressed for time," refused, famously, to listen:

> It's an interesting journalistic issue. My hesitation was instinctive—but rooted in principles I had drummed into me when I first started as a young reporter at the *Post*. We don't tape without permission, the late Howard Simons, then the paper's managing editor, had decreed.... We reporters shouldn't deceive our sources, any more than we should deceive the public. Or so Simons—a wise and revered editor—had taught me.
>
> Of course, I wasn't being asked by Tripp to tape anybody secretly. But the distinction was a bit fuzzy. Tripp's taping of Lewinsky was ongoing. If I started to listen in on her conversations as she was taping them—as opposed to when she was finished—then I inevitably would have become part of the process.... And I was in a bit of a hurry to make it to *Hardball*.

"What do you do when you find yourself sucked into the story?" Isikoff asks rhetorically toward the end of *Uncovering Clinton*, the part in which he says mea culpa but not quite. "What happens when you become beholden to sources with an agenda? There are no easy answers here." Much that he learned later, he tells us, "cast a somewhat different light" on events. He was, for example, "chagrined to discover" that Linda Tripp and Lucianne Goldberg "had been talking about a book deal from the start." But what could there have been, in that, to "discover"? If Isikoff was, as he presents himself here, "an aggressive reporter" still unaware that there was more in this than met the eye, would not "a book deal" have been his first assumption? During his first meetings with Tripp, Isikoff had read part of her proposal for a book to be called *The President's Women.* He knew Lucianne Goldberg to be a literary agent. The idea of a book was nonetheless, Isikoff tells us, "well off my radar screen; indeed, it seemed a bit counterintuitive. Why were they wasting their time sharing information with me, if that was their purpose?"

If Isikoff asked himself this question, he seems to have adroitly avoided the answer, which might have led him to another aspect of the story that he was managing to keep well off his radar screen. What there was to "discover," of course, he already knew: by the time Linda Tripp and Lucianne Goldberg gave him Monica Lewinsky's name, any idea of "a book deal" would have been, as Lucianne Goldberg noted in her review of *Uncovering Clinton* in *Slate,* "a moot point that I can safely say faded to the vanishing point." The reason the point was moot was that, even by Isikoff's own account, Lucianne Goldberg was by then operating less as a lone agent than as a kind of useful front, a cutout for those unable to reveal themselves as running the same move: a cutout for Linda Tripp, a cutout for the ardent young movement lawyers (the "busy elves" Ann Coulter had mentioned) who made up the shadow legal team for *Jones* v. *Clinton*, and a cutout ultimately for the Office of the Independent Counsel.

"I had relied on the elves for information at critical junctures," Isikoff tells us on page 357 of *Uncovering Clinton*, still in his modified mea culpa mode, "even while they concealed from me their role in bringing the Lewinsky allegations to the Jones lawyers and later to Ken Starr." Among the "elves," whose contributions to *Jones* v. *Clinton* included writing briefs and arranging a moot court at which the nominal Jones lawyers were prepped for their argument before the Supreme Court by Robert H. Bork, the most frequently named were Jerome M. Marcus, an associate at Berger & Montague in Philadelphia, George T. Conway III at Wachtell Lipton in New York, and Richard W. Porter, a Chicago partner, as Kenneth Starr was a Washington partner, at Kirkland & Ellis. Jerome Marcus and Richard Porter had been classmates at the University of Chicago, as had Paul Rosenzweig, who was approached to work on *Jones* v. *Clinton* in 1994, decided against it, and in 1997 joined the Office of the Independent Counsel.

Review Isikoff's admission of imperfect prescience, the reporter's dilemma for which there were "no easy answers." The elves, he told us on page 357, had "concealed" from him their role in bringing the Lewinsky allegations to the Jones lawyers and later to Ken Starr. Go back to page 182 of *Uncovering Clinton*, the CNBC green room: when Ann Coulter said to Isikoff that there were "lots of us busy elves working away in Santa's workshop," was this not said to have been a response to his remark that she seemed to have "inside knowledge" of *Jones* v. *Clinton*? Or go back to page 135, where Isikoff gives a quite detailed account of what Linda Tripp told him during their early meetings, when she was not yet telling him the name of the intern. Linda Tripp told him, he reports, that "she herself had been asked by her White House-provided lawyer not to volunteer information about a memo she had seen about the White House travel office that implicated First Lady Hillary Rodham Clinton." Travel office? Travelgate? White House-provided lawyer? Did this not suggest a prior relationship with the Office of the Independent Counsel?

Given the players and the relationships already in place, would it not have been, as Isikoff said about the red herring that was the book deal, "counterintuitive" not to suspect that a certain amount of information was passing between the Jones team and the Office of the Independent Counsel and Linda Tripp? Did he not suspect it? If he suspected it, why did he not pursue it? Could it have been because he already knew it? This is an area that *Uncovering Clinton* was cannily designed, by virtue of the way its author chose to present himself, to leave safely uncharted. "As a reporter," the author tells us, "I don't think ideologically." And then, about his primary sources, Linda Tripp and Lucianne Goldberg: "I could not have cared less about their motives or their ultimate goal. My interest in them was quite simple and fairly well focused: Was the stuff they were telling me true? Could it be corroborated? Would it make a story for *Newsweek*?"

3

When Paula Jones was brought to the 1994 Conservative Political Action Conference to air her charge against the president, Ralph

Reed, under whose leadership the Christian Coalition had grown from fewer than five thousand members to a potent political force and whose presence might have lent the fateful press conference at the Shoreham a degree of legitimacy, was asked to participate. For what he seems to have seen as pragmatic reasons, he declined. As he explained in his 1996 *Active Faith: How Christians Are Changing the Soul of American Politics*, Reed considered it a mistake for conservatives to build their case against Clinton around Paula Jones: "When one of the nation's leading evangelical preachers suggests that the President may be a murderer, when a pro-life leader says that to vote for Clinton is to sin against God, and when conservative talk-show hosts lampoon the sexual behavior of the leader of the free world, the manner of their speech reflects poorly on the gospel and on our faith."

This was at a time when Jerry Falwell, on his *Old Time Gospel Hour*, was marketing *The Clinton Chronicles*, a forty-dollar video asserting that Clinton had ordered the murders of Arkansas opponents and governed the state "hooked on cocaine." A second video, *Circle of Power*, was suggesting that "countless people" who "had some connection to Bill Clinton" had "mysteriously died," and that "this is going on today." Even well in from the ideological frontiers of telemarketing, "impeachment" was already the word of the hour: a contributor to *The Weekly Standard*, Gary Schmitt, was calling for Clinton's impeachment on the grounds that the president had told Jim Lehrer during a PBS interview that he believed Kenneth Starr's Whitewater investigation to be a partisan effort and so would not rule out the possibility of presidential pardons for those convicted in connection with that investigation. Reed, in his 1996 book, recalled attending a conservative dinner where the speaker had called for Clinton's impeachment and imprisonment on the grounds that he was "the most criminal president in our history."

Reed saw the feeding of this particular fire as a strategy only for self-immolation. "Like an army that overwhelms its enemies but leaves the land uninhabitable, some religious conservatives have come dangerously close to defining themselves in purely anti-Clinton terms," he wrote. "Those who are identified as followers of Christ should temper their disagreements with Clinton with civility and the grace of God, avoiding the temptation to personalize issues or demonize their opponents. This is critical to remember if our movement is to avoid the fate of its predecessors." Some of the harshest attacks on Clinton, Reed noted, had their origins in the "Christian nation" or "Reconstructionist" movement, the more unyielding proponents of which advocated "legislating the ancient Jewish law laid out in the Old Testament: stoning adulterers, executing homosexuals, even mandating dietary laws":

> There are historical precedents for Reconstructionist ideas stretching back to the millenialistic strains of Puritan thinking, American Revolutionary ideology, and even the anti-slavery movement. But those currents did not reflect the mainstream of Christian thinking then, and they certainly do not today. Reconstructionism is an authoritarian ideology that threatens the most basic civil liberties of a free and democratic society. If the pro-family movement hopes to realize its goals of relimiting government and reinstilling traditional values in our culture and in public policy, it must unequivocally dissociate itself from Reconstructionism and other efforts to use the government to impose biblical law through direct political action. It must firmly and openly exclude the triumphalist and authoritarian elements....

That the fire had already jumped this break should have been, in retrospect, clear, since, even then, the word "authoritarian" no longer carried the exact freight it carried for Reed. The problem with rock music, Robert H. Bork told us in his 1996 *Slouching Towards Gomorrah*, was that it had encouraged the "subversion of authority," which in turn was the problem with the "baby boomers," who were already, principally because Clinton could be shoehorned into their number, a target of choice for the derision and excoriation engaged in even by many who were themselves members of the same generation. As this view took hold, the word "authority" was frequently preceded, as in William J. Bennett's *The Death of Outrage*, by the word "moral," "moral authority" being the manna allegedly possessed by all American presidents before William Clinton. Clinton, according to David S. Broder and Richard Morin of *The Washington Post*, confronted "his fellow citizens with choices between deeply held moral standards and an abhorrence of judging others' behavior, a conflict the baby boomers have stirred all their adult lives."

These "boomers," who had "no respect for authority," or who "flouted established moral standards," made increasingly frequent appearances. "The battle to dethrone Bill Clinton takes its place in the ongoing Boomer War, a three-decade struggle to define our culture and control our history and symbols," Michael Powell wrote in *The Washington Post*, citing Robert Bork, who had suggested in defense of Kenneth Starr that his was a useful effort to "kill off the lax moral spirit of the Sixties." The pollster Daniel Yankelovich, whose 1981 *New Rules* and later opinion surveys for the Democratic Leadership Council inspired the 1992 Clinton-Gore campaign's *Putting People First*, was quoted by Broder and Morin as having said that "we are beginning to measure a shift back toward absolute as opposed to relative values." The "shift back" was to a period before the mid-sixties, which had been marked, according to Yankelovich, by a "radical extension of individualism."

Reenter Robert Bork, who in *Slouching Towards Gomorrah* identified "radical individualism," or "the drastic reduction of limits to personal gratification," as one of the two "defining characteristics of modern liberalism" (the other being "radical egalitarianism") and, as such, a root cause of "Western decline." That Bork has tended to support his arguments with something other than a full deck of facts (as evidence of "Western decline," he asked us in 1996 to consider "the latest homicide figures for New York City, Los Angeles, or the District of Columbia," as well as "the rising rate of illegitimate births," both of which were dropping steadily during the 1990s) has never deflected his enthusiasm for taking positions, since facts seemed to exist for him in the same mutable state positions did, unfixed weapons to be deployed as needed in that day's sortie against the "leftist dream world."

Bork is worth some study, since it is to him that we owe the most forthright statements of what might be required to effect "a moral and spiritual regeneration," the necessity for which has since entered the talk-show and op-ed ether. Such a regeneration could be produced, Bork speculated in *Slouching Towards Gomorrah*, by one of four events: "a religious revival; the revival of public discourse about morality; a cataclysmic war; or a deep economic depression." As for the first of these options, Bork saw possibilities in "the rise of an energetic, optimistic, and politically sophisticated religious conservatism," but not in the "mainline churches," which no longer posited "a demanding God ... who dictates how one should live and puts a great many bodily and psychological pleasures off limits." "The carrot alone has never been a wholly adequate incentive to desired behavior," Bork wrote. "It is not helpful that the ideas of salvation and damnation, of sin and virtue, which once played major roles in Christian belief, are now almost never heard of in the mainline churches."

It is of course not true that ideas of salvation and damnation or sin and virtue are "now almost never heard of in the mainline churches." Anyone who repeats the responses in the Episcopal litany asks for deliverance "from all evil and wickedness, from sin, from the crafts and assaults of the devil, from thy wrath and from everlasting damnation," and the Catholic baptismal sponsor swears in the name of the child to "reject Satan, father of sin and prince of darkness." Nor is it true, as Bork also wrote, that "the intellectual classes" view religion as "primitive superstition," or believe either that "science has left atheism as the only respectable intellectual stance" or that the question of faith was definitely answered by "Freud, Marx, and Darwin." These "atheists" and "mainline churches" that had abandoned sin and virtue had nonetheless become fixed stations in the conservative canon, recognizable cues, along with "Freud, Marx, and Darwin" and "the ACLU" and all the other calculated outrages; what John J. DiIulio Jr. described in *The Weekly Standard* as "the radical-feminist faithful, the non-judgmental clergy, the Hollywood crowd, and the abortion-on-demand minions."

The literal "truth" or "untruth" of what Bork wrote or said was, then, beside the point, since this was metaphor, and was so understood within the movement: polemic, political litany, a rhetorical incitement to the legislation of "desired behavior," which was to say the scourging of "immoral" behavior. That Bork himself understood this seems clear enough, since he seems to believe that Thomas Jefferson had some kind of similar intention—*this will raise the rabble*—when he wrote the Declaration of Independence. "It was indeed stirring rhetoric," Bork allows,

entirely appropriate for the purpose of rallying the col-
onists and justifying their rebellion to the world. But some
caution is in order. The ringing phrases are hardly useful,
indeed may be pernicious, if taken, as they commonly are,
as a guide to action, governmental or private. Then the
words press inevitably towards extremes of liberty and the
pursuit of happiness that court personal license and social
disorder.

The extent to which "personal license" might be sought out for
punishment was suggested by Bork in his earlier *The Tempting of
America: The Political Seduction of the Law*: "Moral outrage is a sufficient ground for prohibitory legislation," he wrote. "Knowledge
that an activity is taking place is a harm to those who find it
profoundly immoral."

4

"The Republican right wing in this country doesn't like it when
we say coup d'etat, so I'll make it easier for them," Representative
Jose E. Serrano (D-N.Y.) said on the floor of the House the day
the impeachment vote was taken. "*Golpe de estado*. That's Spanish
for overthrowing a government." The word "coup," which had
begun to surface in the dialogue as the more ambiguous aspects
of the Starr investigation became known, had predictably provoked impassioned objections, some of them reasoned (impeachment was a legitimate constitutional process, a conviction by the
Senate on the impeachment charges brought by the House would
result in the removal of the president but not of the political
party holding the presidency) and others less reasoned (Hillary
Rodham Clinton had said that there was a "vast right-wing conspiracy" to get her husband, ergo, there was not, or, alternately, it
was not "vast," or it was not a "conspiracy"); and yet there were,
in the sequence of events that culminated in impeachment, certain factors that seemed distinctly exotic to the politics of the
United States.

There was, first of all, the sense of a "movement," an unchar-
tered sodality that was dedicated to the "remoralization" (William
Kristol's word) of the nation and that, for a variety of reasons (judicial activism, feminism, "nonjudgmentalism," what Bork called

POLITICAL FICTIONS

"the pernicious effects of our passion for equality"), believed
itself inadequately represented in the nation's conventional electoral process. There was the reliance, as in the more authoritarian
Latin American structures, on *orejas*, "ears," tale-tellers like Linda
Tripp, citizens encouraged, whether directly or through the rhetoric of the movement, to obtain evidence against those perceived
as enemies of the movement. There was the aid from the private
sector, the dependence on such rich sympathizers as Richard
Mellon Scaife and John Whitehead and the Chicago investment
banker Peter W. Smith. There was the way in which it was seen
as possible that the electoral process could be bypassed, that the
desired change in the government could be effected by a handful
of unseen individuals, like George Conway and Jerome Marcus
and Richard Porter, working in concert.

There was the shared conviction of urgency, of mission, of an
end so crucial to the fate of the republic as to sweep away possible reservations about means. If the Office of the Independent
Counsel was violating Justice Department prosecutorial guidelines by prosecuting its case in the press, this had been justified,
Kenneth Starr told Steven Brill, because it was "a situation where
what we are doing is countering misinformation that is being
spread about our investigation in order to discredit our office and
our dedicated career prosecutors." If the treatment of Monica
Lewinsky had seemed to some to violate her legal rights, this
too had been justified by the imperative of the "prosecution," the
"investigation." "When you're asked to cooperate in an investigation of this kind it's going to be hellish no matter how nice you
are to her," Michael Emmick of the Office of the Independent
Counsel told members of the American Bar Association in
February 1999. "That's one of the ugly truths about law enforcement. It's very ugly at times. We tried to make it as undifficult as
we could." Since the moral necessity and therefore the absolute
priority of the "investigation" were assumed, any assertion of the
right of the accused to defend himself could be construed only as
prima facie evidence of guilt, which is what people meant when
they condemned the president's defense as "legalistic."

In fact we had seen this willingness to sacrifice means to ends
before, in the late 1980s, when it had seemed equally exotic.
"Sometimes you have to go above the written law," Fawn Hall
had testified on behalf of Lieutenant Colonel Oliver North,

expressing a view shared, in that instance, by most conservatives. Representative Henry J. Hyde, for example, had argued that Fawn Hall was echoing Thomas Jefferson, who had written in an 1810 letter to John Colvin that to insist on "a strict observance of the written law" over "the laws of necessity, of self-preservation, of saving our country when in danger" would be "absurdly sacrificing the end to the means." "All of us," Hyde wrote in the "Supplemental Views" he attached to the 1987 *Report of the Congressional Committees Investigating the Iran-Contra Affair*, "at some time confront conflicts between rights and duties, between choices that are evil and less evil, and one hardly exhausts moral imagination by labeling every untruth and deception an outrage." Hyde continued:

> We have had a disconcerting and distasteful whiff of moralism and institutional self-righteousness in these hearings.... It has seemed to me that the Congress is usually more eager to assert authority than to accept responsibility, more ready to criticize than to constructively propose, more comfortable in the public relations limelight than in the murkier greyness of the real world, where choices must often be made, not between relative goods, but between bad and worse....

The "less evil" choice at hand, of course, had been the covert support of the Nicaraguan contras, or "freedom fighters," who were for the conservative movement in the 1980s what the shifting cast of starring (Paula Jones, Monica Lewinsky) and day players (the Arkansas state troopers, Kathleen Willey, Dolly Kyle Browning, Juanita Broaddrick) who "proved" the moral perfidy of William Jefferson Clinton would become in the 1990s: flags around which the troops could be mobilized and an entire complex of "movement values" attached. For these symbolic purposes, the contras had proved the less fragile standard, since their support involved issues that could be sufficiently inflated to launch the entire matter into the ozone of "national security." Unlike "covert support for the freedom fighters," "Monica Lewinsky" remained resistant to inflation: no matter how many mentions of "perjury" and "rule of law" and "constitutional obligation" got pumped into the noise, the possibility of dallying and lying about it continued to be understood by, and regarded as irrelevant to the survival of the nation by, a majority of the nation's citizens.

This presented a problem. On a broad range of loosely cultural issues (the balanced budget, welfare reform, the death penalty), the positions shared by the president and the citizens in question could by no alchemy be presented as the products of "left-liberal ideology," which had been firmly established in the litany of the movement as the root cause of the nation's moral crisis. "For the model of cultural collapse to work," Andrew Sullivan observed in October 1998 in an analysis of the conservative dilemma in *The New York Times Magazine*, "Clinton must represent its nadir." It was the solution to this problem, the naming of the citizens themselves as co-conspirators in the nation's moral degradation, that remains the most strikingly exotic aspect of the events that came to dominate the late 1990s. "No analysis can absolve the people themselves of responsibility for the quandary we appear to be in," Don Eberly, director of the Civil Society Project in Harrisburg, Pennsylvania, told David S. Broder and Richard Morin of *The Washington Post*. "Non-judgmentalism, the trump card of moral debate, seems to have gained strength among the people, especially in the sexual realm, and this clearly does not bode well for America."

The citizens, it seemed, were running behind the zeitgeist, incapable of understanding momentous events. "The objection that the American people are opposed to impeachment ignores culture lags of historical frequency, including general opposition to the liberation of the slaves," William F. Buckley Jr. told *The New York Times*. The citizens were incapable of understanding momentous events because they had succumbed to the lures of hedonism, materialism, false modernity, "radical individualism" itself. "A certain portion of the American public is cowed by popular culture," Craig Shirley, the conservative strategist who gave Michael Isikoff the heads-up on the unveiling of Paula Jones at the 1994 Conservative Political Action Conference, told the *Times*. "They do not want to be thought of as not being modern or sophisticated." "Given their obstinate lack of interest in the subject, asking a group of average Americans about politics is like asking a group of stevedores to solve a problem in astrophysics," a senior editor of *The Weekly Standard*, Andrew Ferguson, had written in 1996. "Before long they're explaining, not merely that the moon is made of cheese, but what kind of cheese it is, and whether it is properly aged, and how it would taste on a Triscuit."

Within the movement, then, this censorious approach to the electorate was not entirely recent. What was recent was the extent to which the movement crusade to save America from its citizens would come to be acquiesced in by, which is to say aided and abetted by, that small but highly visible group of people who, day by day and through administration after administration, relay Washington to the world, tell its story, agree among themselves upon and then disseminate its narrative. They report the stories. They write the op-ed pieces. They appear on the talk shows. They consult, they advise, they swap jobs, they travel with unmarked passports between the public and the private, the West Wing and the green room. They make up the nation's permanent professional political class, and they are for the most part people who would say of themselves, as Michael Isikoff said of himself, that they "don't think ideologically."

And yet this was an instance in which the narrative they agreed upon, that the president's behavior had degraded and crippled the presidency and the government and the nation itself, worked at every point to obscure, in some cases by omission and in other cases through dismissal as "White House spin," what we now know to have been going on. It would have been possible to read the reports from Washington in four or five daily newspapers and still not know, until it was detailed by Renata Adler in *The Los Angeles Times Book Review* on March 14, 1999, that by the time Linda Tripp surfaced on the national screen as Monica Lewinsky's confidante she had already testified in four previous Office of the Independent Counsel investigations: Filegate, Travelgate, the Vincent Foster suicide, and Whitewater.

In the face of even this single piece of information, a good many of the attitudes struck during the past year might have seemed, if not deliberate obfuscation, at best perplexing digressions. "I couldn't buy the party line that this was more about Clinton's accusers than his own actions," George Stephanopoulous told us in his own mea culpa but not quite, *All Too Human*. On the first Sunday in February 1999, when it seemed clear that there were not enough votes for conviction in the Senate, Cokie Roberts was still on air calling for a censure vote, "a Democratic vote saying what he did was wrong." Otherwise, she said, "the way it will be written for history is that this was a partisan witch hunt, that it was an illegitimate process," and "the spinners could certainly win if you do it that way."

These people lived in a small world. Consider again the sentence that appears on page 357 of *Uncovering Clinton*, particularly its second clause: "*I had relied on the elves for information at critical junctures—even while they concealed from me their role in bringing the Lewinsky allegations to the Jones lawyers and later to Ken Starr.*" What we now know occurred was, in other words, a covert effort to advance a particular agenda by bringing down a president. We know that this covert effort culminated in the kind of sting operation that reliably creates a crime where a crime may or may not have otherwise existed. We knew all along that the "independence" of the independent prosecutor could have been, or should have been, open to some question, since, before his appointment as independent prosecutor, Kenneth Starr had consulted with the Jones legal team on the projected amicus curiae brief to be filed on behalf of the Independent Women's Forum arguing that *Jones* v. *Clinton* should go forward. This had been reported, but was allowed to pass unremarked upon in what passed for the dialogue on the case. The Jones lawyer with whom Starr consulted, Isikoff tells us, was Gil Davis, whose billing records showed that the conversations with Starr covered four and a half hours, for which Davis billed Paula Jones $775.

The clues were always there, as they had been for Isikoff. There was always in the tale of the foolish intern and her disloyal friend a synchronicity that did not quite convince. There was from the outset the occasional odd reference in a news story, the name here or there that did not quite belong in the story, the chronology that did not quite tally, the curiously inexorable escalation of *Jones* v. *Clinton*. At least some of this, in other words, would appear to have been knowable, but it remained unacknowledged in the narrative that was the official story. "What drives Ken Starr onward?" Michael Winerip asked in *The New York Times Magazine* in September 1998. "Who is this minister's son in such relentless pursuit that he forced the president to admit his sins on national television?"

Everyone has a theory on Starr. After the Lewinsky affair broke, Hillary Clinton called Starr "a politically motivated prosecutor who is allied with the right-wing opponents of my husband." Harold Ickes, the former Clinton aide, says he sees Starr as a dangerous moralist who views the Clintons "like Sodom and Gomorrah and is hell-bent on running them out of Washington."

Even Starr's best friends don't know what to make of it all. They were caught off guard when he took the independent counsel's job in 1994 and are not sure why he wanted it. "I have no idea," says Theodore Olson, a prominent Washington lawyer. "He never asked me. I was shocked when I heard the news."

"*I was shocked when I heard the news.*" This was the same small world. Theodore Olson, whose wife, Barbara Olson, was a member of the National Advisory Board of the Independent Women's Forum, the group for which Kenneth Starr was to have written the amicus curiae brief urging that *Jones* v. *Clinton* go forward, was a Washington partner of the Los Angeles-based Gibson, Dunn & Crutcher. Gibson, Dunn had also been the firm of William French Smith, attorney general during the Reagan administration. Kenneth Starr had been William French Smith's chief of staff at the Justice Department, and it was William French Smith who in 1983 arranged Starr's appointment to the U.S. Circuit Court of Appeals for the District of Columbia, where he served with, and often voted with, Robert H. Bork. Olson was one of the lawyers, along with Robert Bork, enlisted by George Conway to prepare the Jones lawyers for the Supreme Court arguments that led to the Court's 9–0 decision denying a sitting president immunity from civil suits. The preparation took place at the Army-Navy Club in Washington. At a point after Christmas 1997, concerned about the ideological reliability of Linda Tripp's lawyer and under pressure to find a replacement before the cards started falling into place, Jerome Marcus and Richard Porter approached Theodore Olson about taking on Tripp's legal representation. Olson could not.

Ann Coulter, via George Conway, then suggested James Moody, who could, and did. James Moody was a Washington lawyer and a member, along with George Conway and Robert H. Bork and Kenneth Starr and Theodore and Barbara Olson, of the Federalist Society, an organization of conservative legal scholars and students that became influential during the Reagan administration and had been the recipient, according to *The Washington Post*, of at least $1.5 million from Richard Mellon Scaife's foundations and trusts. Moody was also an admirer of the Grateful Dead, and, with Ann Coulter, had flown to San Francisco for the memorial concert that followed the 1995 death of Jerry Garcia. James Moody and Ann Coulter called themselves, according to Isikoff, "the only two right-wing Deadheads in Washington."

"Even Starr's best friends don't know what to make of it all." Nor did we, since this was the tone in which the nation's permanent professional political class had chosen to tell us the story. To suggest that the investigation might be politically motivated, we were told repeatedly, was to misrepresent "Ken" Starr, whose own tendency to encourage this reading was understood in Washington as a badge of scholarly innocence, a "clumsiness," at worst an "amateurishness" (that was the editorial page of *The Washington Post*), the endearing "tin ear," not important. "What's important," the *Post* declared in a February 1999 editorial calling for a bipartisan censure, "is to have a clear record and a clear statement of the standard of conduct—the expectations—that this president has violated by the lying to escape being held to account that is a hallmark of his career." In the absence of censure, the *Post* warned: "The president and his people will end up portraying this sorry episode as mostly a partisan proceeding, an effort by his enemies to win through entrapment and impeachment what they could not at the polls. Mr. Clinton will be the victim in this telling, not a president who dishonored the office but one who was caught up in a politics of personal destruction."

This merits study. The word "partisan," as in "partisan proceeding," suggests, in the United States, a traditional process, "taking sides," "knows how to count," Democrats, Republicans, the ballot box. The word "partisan," then, worked to contain the suggestion that anything outside that tradition was at work here.

Both the "president who dishonored the office" and the "one who was caught up in a politics of personal destruction" further trivialized what had taken place, reducing it to the "personal," to a parable about the "character" of either the president or his attackers. By reducing the matter to the personal as by labeling it "partisan" or "bipartisan," it was possible to divest what had taken place of its potentially disruptive gravity, possible to avoid all consideration of whether or not a move on the presidency had been covertly run, of whether or not the intent of such a move had been to legitimize a minority ideological agenda, and of whether or not—most disruptive of all—such a move was ongoing.

On November 2, 1998, the day before the midterm elections, *The Washington Post* published a much-discussed piece by Sally Quinn, a *Post* writer and the wife of former *Post* executive editor Benjamin Bradlee. Whether or not this piece should have been published became a matter of momentary controversy within the Washington establishment, precisely because it reported so accurately the collegial, even collaborative approach the establishment was taking toward the matter at hand, the unwillingness to consider the ramifications of the refusal to conjugate the verb *to conspire*, the way in which an institutional forgetfulness was serving to preserve the sanctity of the Washington status quo. "Privately," Quinn wrote, "many in Establishment Washington would like to see Bill Clinton resign and spare the country, the presidency, and the city any more humiliation."

In 1972, when word reached the *Post* that there had been a break-in at the Watergate office of the Democratic National Committee, those assigned to work the story were Metro reporters, Bob Woodward and Carl Bernstein. Woodward, Benjamin Bradlee wrote in his autobiography, *A Good Life*, was then "one of the new kids on the staff," and Bernstein "the Peck's Bad Boy of the Metro staff." Woodward and Bernstein, in other words, were at that time Washington outsiders, and it was to their status as Washington outsiders that their ability to get "the real story" was commonly attributed. Those to whom Quinn spoke, on the other hand, seemed to believe that it was their own status as Washington insiders that gave them unique knowledge of the "real story" behind the drive for impeachment, which came down to what they saw as the president's betrayal, by his failure to tell the truth, of the community and the country.

Those to whom Quinn spoke also seemed to believe that, despite their best efforts to disseminate it, this unique knowledge remained unshared by and unappreciated by the rest of the country. "Clinton's behavior is unacceptable," the pollster Geoff Garin told her. "If they did this at the local Elks Club hall in some other community it would be a big cause for concern." "He came in here and he trashed the place, and it's not his place," David Broder of the *Post* said. "It's a canard to say this is a private matter," the *Wall Street Journal* columnist Albert R. Hunt said. "It's had a profound effect on governance." "There's no way any president going through this process can be able to focus, whether on Kosovo or the economic crisis," the NBC correspondent Andrea Mitchell said. "It's just a tragedy for everyone."

But not necessarily for everyone in Washington. The president would soon be, as David Broder would write in the *Post*, "disgraced and enfeebled." The time would soon come for the president, as Broder would also write, to "step aside for the man he clearly believes is well qualified to be his successor, Vice-President Gore." Since the matter had been so firmly established as "personal," there would be no need to pursue the possibility that the "process," or the "tragedy," or the "profound effect on governance," had been initiated by someone other than the president. In fact such a possibility need not even enter the picture, for this was a view from inside Washington, where those who did not "think ideologically" appreciated the drift, the climate, the wheeling of the ideological seasons, and also their access to whoever turns the wheel. As Quinn explained, "Starr is a Washington insider too."

GOD'S COUNTRY

October 5, 2000

I

THE WORDS "compassionate conservatism" sound like and have often been dismissed as political rhetoric, a construction without intrinsic meaning, George W. Bush's adroit way of pitching the center, allowing middle-class voters to feel good about themselves while voting their interests. Former governor Lamar Alexander of Tennessee called them "weasel words." Joe Andrews, the national chairman of the Democratic National Committee, called them "a contrived copout." "You can't have these massive tax cuts and at the same time ... be a compassionate conservative," Senator Paul Wellstone of Minnesota told *The New York Times*. To the extent that the words were construed to mean anything at all, then, they were misunderstood to suggest a warmer, more generous, more ameliorative kind of conservative. "I'm a conservative, and proud of it, but I'm a compassionate conservative," Senator Orrin Hatch told Judith Miller of *The New York Times* in March 1981. "I'm not some kind of ultra-right-wing maniac." Former governor Pete Wilson of California offered a still more centrist reading: compassionate conservatism, he was quoted as saying by *The Washington Post*, is "old-fashioned budget-balancing with spending for preventive health measures and protection of the environment, and a strong pro-choice position on abortion."

This suggests a pragmatic but still traditional economic conservatism into which many Americans could comfortably buy. Yet the phrase "compassionate conservatism" describes a specific and deeply radical experiment in social rearrangement, the aim of which was defined by Governor Bush, in his acceptance speech at the Republican convention in Philadelphia, with sufficient vagueness to signal the troops without alerting the less committed: what he meant by compassionate conservatism, he said, was "to put conservative values and conservative ideas into the thick of the fight for justice and opportunity." Marvin Olasky, the journalism professor at the University of Texas who became a Bush adviser in 1993 and is the author of the seminal work on the subject, *The Tragedy of American Compassion* (this was the 1992 book that Newt Gingrich received as a Christmas present from William J. Bennett in 1994 and promptly recommended to all Republican members of Congress), and of the more recent *Compassionate Conservatism*, has been more forthright. "Compassionate conservatism is neither an easy slogan nor one immune from vehement attack," he advises readers on page 1 of *Compassionate Conservatism*:

> It is a full-fledged program with a carefully considered philosophy. It will face in the twenty-first century not easy acceptance but dug-in opposition. It will have to cross a river of suspicion concerning the role of religion in American society. It will have to get past numerous ideological machine-gun nests. Only political courage will enable compassionate conservatism to carry the day and transform America.

The source of this "river of suspicion" and these "ideological machine-gun nests" becomes clear on reading the text, which is largely devoted to detailing a 1999 road trip during which Olasky, who before "God found me and changed me when I was twenty-six," had wrestled first with atheism ("I was bar mitzvahed at thirteen and an atheist by fourteen") and then with the Communist Party U.S.A. ("What if Lenin is wrong? What if there is a God?"), introduced his fourteen-year-old son, Daniel, to anti-poverty programs in Texas, the Midwest, and the Northeast. The drift soon emerges. "God's in charge," a couple who run a community center in South Dallas tell Olasky and Daniel. "I had to learn that God's in charge," they are told by a former user of heroin and cocaine who now runs the day-to-day operation of a recovery center in Minneapolis. A teacher at an evangelical summer school in Dallas explains how "curriculum is cleverly tied" to a pending mountain field trip, for example by assigning "Bible passages concerning mountains, eagles, and hawks."

Outside Houston, they visit "Youth-Reach Houston" and its founder, "Curt Williams, forty, who wears his long black hair pulled back in a pony tail" and who in 1984 "followed a pretty girl into a church and found welcome there.... Having hit bottom, he went to church and felt spiritually compelled to throw away his drugs and pornography." In Indianapolis, they meet with Mayor Stephen Goldsmith, chief domestic policy adviser to the Bush campaign and a civic leader who had studied "the negatives (high taxes, red tape, bad schools) that drive middle-class people away from the city" and found the answer in "using his bully pulpit to promote Catholic schools," since, as he tells Olasky and Daniel, "only hardened skeptics have trouble accepting that widespread belief in a Supreme Being improves the strength and health of our communities."

Again and again, Olasky and Daniel learn of successful recoveries effected in one or another "have-not" program, which is to say a program prevented from receiving the funding it deserves for the sole reason, Olasky suggests, that it is "faith-based." Again and again, they hear the same language ("hitting bottom," "putting God in charge," "changing one life at a time"), which is, not coincidentally, that of the faith-based twelve-step movement, from which a good deal of the "new thinking" on welfare derives. (Alcoholics Anonymous, according to James Q. Wilson, is "the single most important organized example of personal transformation we have.") Visiting a faith-based prison program outside Houston, they meet Donnie Gilmore, who was "pushing thirty with a resume of breaking into houses and stealing cars" when "his four-year-old daughter asked him about Jesus, and he realized he had never opened a Bible."

Gilmore then joined the "InnerChange" program ("Texas Governor George W. Bush gave the program a try, and state officials kept the American Civil Liberties Union at bay…") developed by Prison Fellowship Ministries, which is the organization founded by Charles ("Chuck") Colson after his release from the Maxwell Federal Prison Camp in Alabama and in which "the keys to success" are "God's grace and man's mentoring." "I have a couple of editions of the Bible with me," Colson reportedly said on the day he left for Maxwell to serve seven months of a one-to-three-year sentence for obstruction of justice in the prosecution of Daniel Ellsberg. "That's all."

"Repeatedly," Olasky notes with approval, "Daniel and I had found that the impetus for a compassionate conservative program came out of a Bible study or some other church or synagogue function." Both father and son are made "uneasy" by more secular programs, for example KIPP (Knowledge Is Power Program) Academy, a charter school in Houston, where, despite the fact that it seemed "excellent," its public nature meant that "students miss out on that added dimension," i.e., prayer and Bible study. Similarly, in Minneapolis, they visit a Goodwill program that seemed to be successfully introducing women to the basic workplace manners (be on time, answer the phone politely) needed to make the transition from welfare to work. "All of this was impressive," Olasky allows, and yet, "as Daniel noted in comparing this helpful program to the faith-based equivalents we were seeing elsewhere, 'The absence of interest in God is glaring.'"

This use of "faith-based" is artful, and worth study. Goodwill was founded by a Methodist minister and run during its early years out of the Morgan Memorial Chapel in Boston, which would seem to qualify it as based in faith, although not, in the sense that Olasky apparently construes the phrase, as "faith-based." "Faith-based," then, is, as Olasky uses it, a phrase with a special meaning, a code phrase, employed to suggest that certain worthy organizations have been prevented from receiving government funding solely by virtue of their religious affiliation. This is misleading, since "religiously affiliated" organizations (for example Catholic Charities) can and do receive such funding. The organizations that have not are those deemed "pervasively sectarian," a judgment based on the extent to which they proselytize, or make religious worship or instruction a condition of receiving aid. This, the Supreme Court has to date maintained, would violate the establishment clause of the First Amendment, the original intent of which Olasky believes to have been warped. "Daniel and I spent some time talking about what happened 210 years ago," he wrote. "There's nothing about 'separation of church and state.' That was Thomas Jefferson's personal expression in a letter written over a decade after the amendment was adopted.... The founding fathers would be aghast at court rulings that make our part of the world safe for moral anarchy."

Olasky is insistent that the faith propagated by these "faith-based" organizations need by no means be exclusively Christian, and here we enter another area of artful presentation. "My tendency is to be inclusive," he told *The Los Angeles Times*. "That can include Wiccans and Scientologists. If people are going to get mad at me, then so be it." The goal of compassionate conservatism, he has written repeatedly, is "faith-based diversity," a system in which the government would offer those in need of aid a choice of programs: "Protestant, Catholic, Jewish, Islamic, Buddhist, atheist." Perhaps because the theological imperative to convert nonbelievers runs with considerably more force among evangelical Christians than among Buddhists or atheists, most of the programs described in *Compassionate Conservatism* are nonetheless Christian, and, to one degree or another, evangelical. "All organizations, religious or atheistic, [had] the opportunity to propose values-based pre-release programs," Olasky notes by way of explaining how Texas state officials "kept the American Civil Liberties Union at bay" on behalf of Prison Fellowship, "but only Prison Fellowship went all the way."

In Philadelphia, Olasky and Daniel visit Deliverance Evangelistic, where John J. DiIulio Jr. "took his first steps toward faith in Christ" and where the pastor speaks of how "the ACLU is using and abusing" the First Amendment. They also visit the Bethel Community Bible Church, where they meet a paraplegic weight lifter who "sold drugs and saw no meaning to life until God grabbed him twelve years ago." Now he runs the Bethel weight room, which is "used by forty men each week, with no payment or conditions for use except one: the men need to attend church, Bible study, or church counseling at least once per week." Some of the programs Olasky describes refuse to compromise their evangelical mission by accepting government funding ("the reason we're here is that kids need to come to Christ"); others take the money, and devise ways of nominally separating it from the teaching mission.

Olasky and Daniel for example visit "the praying tailback," Herb Lusk, "the first National Football League player to use the end zone as the pulpit by crouching prayerfully following a touchdown." As pastor of the Greater Exodus Baptist Church in Philadelphia, Lusk does accept government funding for the church's welfare-to-work program, but works around it: "No, we don't talk about Christ during the training, but we promote our offer of a free lunch for participants, with Bible teaching during it." "Evangelism is central to everything we do," Olasky is told by a Dallas woman, Kathy Dudley, who left her suburban home for the inner city, where she defines her mission as "discipleship." "Early in the 1990s," Olasky reports, "one official offered her a $170,000 grant, but she asked, 'If I take this money and hire a housing director, I will hire a Christian and expect a certain standard of behavior. If the director has sex outside of marriage, I will fire him immediately. Do you have a problem with this?' Yes, the official told her. She spurned the grant."

2

In addition to teaching at Austin, Marvin Olasky has written a number of books, none of which tapped into the national moment with the exact force that *The Tragedy of American Compassion* did but the range of which suggests the dexterity with which the excitable mind can divine the sermon in every stone. There was *Prodigal Press: The Anti-Christian Bias of the American News Media.* There was *Telling the Truth: How to Revitalize Christian Journalism.* There was *Corporate Public Relations: A New Historical Perspective*, drawn from five years Olasky spent writing speeches in the public affairs office at DuPont, an experience that led him to the Manichean conclusion that corporations were engaged in a liberal conspiracy to eliminate competition by supporting government regulation. "I wanted to work at DuPont because I was on the side of free enterprise," he told Michael King of *The Texas Observer*. "But I found out ... you were largely lobbying government officials and others so that when they do the next set of regs—say environmental regs—that they write the regs in such a way that benefits you and hurts your smaller competitor."

There was *Fighting for Liberty and Virtue: Political and Cultural Wars in Eighteenth-Century America.* There was *The American Leadership Tradition: Moral Vision from Washington to Clinton*, which locates the "moral vision" of American presidents in their "religious beliefs and sexual morality" and offers a foreword by former Nixon aide Charles Colson, he of the career-making seven months at Maxwell, who speaks of "dedicated Olaskyites" and suggests that "a generation or two hence, historians will look back at this era and put Marvin Olasky among the pantheon of seminal thinkers who have changed the way people and societies think."

From Austin, communicating largely by e-mail, Olasky also manages to both edit and write a column for every issue of a weekly magazine, *World*, which is published out of Asheville, North Carolina, and has as its national editor Bob Jones IV, the great-grandson of the founder and son of the current president of Bob Jones University. The "mission statement" of *World*, until it was edited into a slightly more elliptical version in February 1999, read this way:

> To help Christians apply the Bible to their understanding of and response to everyday current events. To achieve this by reporting the news on a weekly basis in an interesting, accurate, and arresting fashion. To accompany reporting with practical commentary on current events and issues from a perspective committed to the final authority of the Bible as the inerrant written Word of God. To assist in developing a Christian understanding of the world, rather than accepting existing secular ideologies.

Ninety-five percent of *World*'s 103,000 subscribers, according to its own 1999 survey, identify themselves as Caucasian. Ninety-eight percent attend church "usually every week." Twenty-two percent are Baptist, seventeen percent are Presbyterian or Reformed, twelve percent members of the Presbyterian Church in America (a fundamentalist breakaway from the mainline Presbyterian Church U.S.A. and the denomination to which Olasky himself belongs), and eleven percent pentecostal or charismatic. Forty-five percent of those with children "homeschool," or teach at least one child at home. Asked to rate twenty-six individuals and movements named by *World*, these readers think most highly of James Dobson (who as head of Focus on the Family threatened to leave the Republican Party if Bush chose a pro-choice running mate), of "crisis pregnancy centers," and of Charles Colson. They think least highly of President William Clinton, of the National Organization for Women, and of "the religious left."

Since *World* largely reflects or encourages these predispositions, its coverage tends to the predictable. "*Homosexuals take the offensive*," a 1999 cover line read. Onward *World* went, marching as to war through 1999 and into 2000: "*A teenage martyr: The funeral of Cassie Bernall." "Battling the cultural menace." "Abortion Speech Police." "An inside look at the scary summer gathering of a fading feminist organization,"* i.e., the National Organization for Women. *"Armey: End Christian bashing." "Texas students fight for pre-game prayers." "Darwinists circle wagons against science teacher."* Some stories are, for the general reader, more arresting, involving as they do people or issues or points of view somewhat outside the general discourse. This is a community of readers to whom a call to counter a "gay activist campaign" against "Dr. Laura" Schlessinger, the Orthodox Jewish talk-show host who referred to homosexuality as a "biological error," can serve as a summons to the barricades, in this case the main gate of Paramount Pictures. This is a community to which a "Pandora's box of controversies" can be opened by the question of whether Christians should continue to buy CDs featuring divorced Christian singers, or "fallen stars." "How credible can evangelicals be in condemning such sins as homosexuality and extramarital sex," *World* asked, "when many seem so tolerant of the sin of divorce?"

Olasky himself is divorced from his first wife. "I've been married since 1976, and in the early 1970s had a brief marriage followed by divorce," is the way he put it in a letter to *The New York Times Magazine* objecting to a piece that suggested he had "hidden his divorce from the press." He met his second wife, Susan, at the University of Michigan, where she was an undergraduate and he a graduate student in the throes of abandoning communism. "When I met him, he was definitely an anti-Communist, but I wouldn't say he was a Christian, at that point," Susan Olasky later told *The Texas Observer.* She said that Whittaker Chambers's *Witness,* which Olasky had recommended that she read, "described where he was then." After their arrival in Austin, Susan Olasky founded the Austin Crisis Pregnancy Center, the purpose for which Olasky believes "God brought about" the move. Charles Colson is also divorced from his first wife, which would not be worth mentioning had he not in summer 2000 called upon Charles Stanley, a fellow Christian broadcaster whose wife had recently divorced him, to resign as pastor of the thirteen-thousand-member First Baptist Church of Atlanta. "Given the already high divorce rate among Baptists," Colson declared (the highest 1998 divorce rates in the United States, according to the U.S. Census Bureau, were, outside Nevada, in the heavily Baptist states of Tennessee, Arkansas, Alabama, and Oklahoma), "the last thing we need to do is to give one of our own leaders a pass, no matter how much we may respect him." What Charles Stanley needed, Colson said, was "a time for personal repentance and healing."

Olasky, having had this time, now seems sufficiently cleansed of the sin of which too many evangelicals are tolerant to write frequently and enthusiastically about marriage, both his own and in general, as well as about the correct relative roles of men and women. "God does not forbid women to be leaders in society, generally speaking," he explained in a 1998 issue of the evangelical *Journal for Biblical Manhood and Womanhood*, "but when that occurs it's usually because of the abdication of men.... There's a certain shame attached. Why don't you have a man who's able to step forward?" An entire May 2000 issue of *World* was devoted to marriage and the family, with special emphasis on what remains a lively issue among evangelicals, this "headship and submission" question, which has to do with whether the language in Ephesians 5:22 and 5:23 commanding wives to "be subject" to their husbands "for the husband is the head of the wife as Christ is the head of the church" should be understood strictly or placed in the context of other biblical teachings. In the course of arguing for the latter position and against the extremity of the first ("The Bible advocates neither feminism nor sexual segregation"), Olasky inadvertently opened a window on a view of women not far from that of the Taliban:

> The Bible clearly shows the error both of feminists who claim no differences between men and women, and of sexual segregationists who argue that women are to be concerned "only" with marriage and motherhood.... Men go wrong, biblically, by either abdicating or waxing arrogant, either by running from God-given functions or refusing to hear what women have to say. In 1 Samuel 25, Abigail knows that her husband, Nabal, is a fool; when she acts to save her whole household, David tells her, "May you be blessed for your good judgment." I know that my wife often has better judgment than I, and that if I am not to be Nabal Olasky I should listen. And so should we all. Today,

some Christian men believe women should be co-leaders in everything. That leaves many men feeling emasculated and many women wishing that guys would step up and make a decision, already. Other Christian men go to the opposite extreme and assert that married women should not even be studying the Bible by themselves or in groups with other women; they should be taught only by their husbands.

3

The intention that led Olasky to write *The Tragedy of American Compassion* ("I hoped to see welfare transformed, as much as possible, from government monopoly to faith-based diversity") might have well been dismissed as the evangelical impulse of someone operating at a considerable remove from the centrist American political tradition. Yet the book had a certain think-tank imprimatur that caused it to begin percolating through neoconservative circles. *The Tragedy of American Compassion* had been largely written during a year, 1990, that Olasky spent in Washington as a fellow at the Heritage Foundation. The book's central notions bore a reassuring resemblance to arguments already so much a part of the discourse that they had two years before inspired Peggy Noonan to incorporate the "thousand points of light" into the acceptance speech delivered by Governor Bush's father at the 1988 Republican convention. Alfred Regnery, who ultimately published the book, appeared in the acknowledgments, as did Patricia Bozell. Charles Murray, who was at the time writing *The Bell Curve* with Richard J. Herrnstein as a fellow at the American Enterprise Institute, wrote the preface.

The Tragedy of American Compassion was published in 1992, a year when certain key rhetorical assumptions, those having to do with the "moral depredations" of the 1960s and the "moral squalor" of American life since, were already in place. Robert H. Bork, having been sanctified as one of the two living martyrs of the judicial confirmation process, was already handing down the dicta that would shape his 1996 *Slouching Towards Gomorrah: Modern Liberalism and American Decline*. William J. Bennett was about to publish his first book of moral teachings, *The Book of Virtues*, with *The Moral Compass* and *The Death of Outrage* still in the pipeline. This was a febrile moment, and the characteristically schematic ideas that emerged from it often seemed specifically crafted to support the mood of moral rearmament that was coming to dominate the dialogue. In January 1995, on C-SPAN, Marvin Olasky gave Brian Lamb an instructive precis of the process by which this moment had come to pass: "John Fund of *The Wall Street Journal* read it [*The Tragedy of American Compassion*] and wrote about it and liked it and talked about it with others. Bill Bennett read it and was talking about it. Some other people were, and then it got to the Speaker and he got excited about it and has been talking about it."

"Our models are Alexis de Tocqueville and Marvin Olasky," Newt Gingrich had just told the nation in his first 1995 address as Speaker of the House, apparently having already incorporated into his program the Christmas present William J. Bennett had given him a few weeks before. The "most important book on welfare and social policy in a decade," Bennett himself said about Olasky's book. Three years after the largely unnoticed initial publication of *The Tragedy of American Compassion*, then, its reductive and rather spookily utilitarian thesis, that the government should fund the faithful because faith "works," had become the idea whose time had come, the ultimate weapon in the "values" wars, a super stealth missile with first-strike capability, precisely aimed to simultaneously get welfare out of the system and get religion into it.

By his own account, Olasky wrote the book after comparing the evangelism of nineteenth-century philanthropy to secular welfare efforts, which he believed to be rendered useless by their lack of emphasis on personal responsibility. This belief was confirmed, he wrote, by taking "a first-hand look at contemporary compassion toward the poor" during two days he spent disguised as a beggar in order to visit Washington soup kitchens: "I put on three used T-shirts and two dirty sweaters, equipped myself with a stocking cap and a plastic bag, removed my wedding ring, got lots of dirt on my hands, and walked with the slow shuffle that characterizes the forty-year-old white homeless male of the streets." During his two days (no nights) as a street person, he was offered, he reported (and here we reach the germ of the experiment), "lots of food, lots of pills of various kinds, and lots of offers of clothing and shelter," but never a Bible.

* * *

There could never have been much doubt that the parable of the white homeless male in search of a Bible would resonate with George W. Bush. This was a man who not only grew up in Texas and did business in Texas but managed a Texas sports franchise, pretty much rendering him a market-maker in the secular God business. This was a man who, in the course of a primary-season debate, would famously name Jesus Christ as the "political philosopher" he most admires. This was a man who, when the Texas economy went belly-up in the mid-1980s, joined a group of Midland businessmen who met once a week under the guidance of a national group called Community Bible Study, the class format of which includes the twelve-step technique of personal testimony, in this case "seeing the truths of the Bible lived out in the lives of leaders and class members." The participants in Bush's class were "baby boomers, men with young families," a former member told Hanna Rosin of *The Washington Post*. "And we suddenly found ourselves in free fall. So we began to search for an explanation. Maybe we had been too involved with money. Maybe we needed to look inwardly and find new meaning in life."

It was 1993 when Marvin Olasky was first called to meet with Bush, who was at the time shopping for issues with which to defeat the incumbent governor of Texas, Ann Richards. Olasky and Bush, along with Bush adviser Karl Rove, talked for an hour, during which, according to Olasky, Bush "asked questions that went to the heart of issues involving children born out of wedlock and men slowly dying from drug abuse on the streets." Bush did not have occasion to call again on Olasky until 1995, when, as governor, he saw the political potential in taking up the side of a Christian drug program called Teen Challenge, which state regulators had tried to shut down because it refused to comply with certain state regulations, including one that required drug counselors to be trained in conventional anti-addiction techniques. (Conventional anti-addiction techniques in this country are largely based on the twelve-step regime, which carefully refers to an unspecified "Higher Power," or "God as we understand Him." The anti-addiction technique of choice at Teen Challenge was, in the words of its executive director, "Jesus Christ.") Over his next few years as governor, Bush not only made Texas the first state to sanction the redirection of state funds into faith-based programs but virtually dismantled state regulation of such programs, accruing, in the course of this pioneering endeavor, considerable political capital from the religious right. "An opportunity arose for a far-sighted governor to take the lead" is how Olasky describes this. "George W. Bush was a natural, both because of his father's earlier interest in the 'thousand points of light' and his own personal, faith-based change in 1986 from heavy drinking at times to abstinence from alcohol."

Olasky was never a full-time Bush adviser, yet his involvement would seem to have been something more than "maybe they met once or twice," the version preferred by those Bush aides made nervous by the enthusiasm with which Olasky airs his less marketable positions, on the role of women, say, or on the necessity of conversion. T. Christian Miller of *The New York Times*, reporting in July 2000 on the campaign's "pattern of distancing Bush from the controversies that have dogged Olasky," quoted a Bush spokesman saying that the two had met only twice, once in 1996 and once in 1999, although the 1993 and 1995 meetings have been extensively documented. "Marvin is an evangelical Christian, and Bush is an evangelical Christian," John J. DiIulio Jr., a Bush adviser, told David Grann by way of suggesting the philosophical distance. "But Bush does not believe that every faith-based program is about religious conversion."

Olasky does believe this, and, on the basis of what Governor Bush himself has said, it would be hard to argue that Bush did not at some level, however unexamined, agree. "When asked why some faith-based groups succeed where secular organizations fail," Olasky wrote of Bush, "he praised programs that help to 'change the person's heart.'" "A person with a changed heart," Olasky quotes Bush as having told him, "is less likely to be addicted to drugs and alcohol.... I've had some personal experience with this. As has been reported, I quit drinking. The main reason I quit was because I accepted Jesus Christ into my life in 1986." To accept Jesus Christ as personal savior is pretty much the heart and soul of evangelical conversion (or of being "born again," which both Governor Bush and Vice President Gore claim to be), and incurs the obligation, for evangelical Christians who want to be saved, of converting others, which is to say, in Bush's words, changing the person's heart. The evangelical obligation to convert, the biblical basis for which is Matthew 28:19 ("Go therefore and make disciples of all nations, baptizing them in the name of the Father and of the Son and of the Holy Spirit"), rests on the belief that Bush notoriously expressed to a reporter for the *Austin American-Statesman* in 1993, that those who do not believe in Christ will go to hell. "Bush was giving the orthodox biblical answer," Marvin Olasky later explained to *Salon* on this point. "On the face of it, you have to believe in Christ to go to heaven; Jews don't believe in Christ; therefore, Jews don't go to heaven. So of course there was an uproar."

Olasky was made the head of Bush's policy subcommittee on religion in February 1999, after the two met for a four-hour session during which they and Bush aides hammered out policy with John J. DiIulio Jr., James Q. Wilson, and Robert L. Woodson Sr., the founder of the National Center for Neighborhood Enterprise and one of the people Olasky cites as a formative influence. In an October 1999 *World* column urging conservative Christians not to abandon the political process, Olasky himself described his role as "trying to walk the above talk by giving informal advice to one of the contenders for the G.O.P. nomination," a circumstance that had led him, he explained, to recuse himself from editing *World*'s campaign coverage. By the end of March 2000, however, in the wake of a small media storm over a column he had written for the *Austin American-Statesman* accusing three political commentators who happened to be Jews (David Brooks, William Kristol, and Frank Rich) of favoring John McCain because he lacked Bush's "Christian albatross" and so afforded them "a post-Clinton glow without pushing them to confront their own lives," Olasky downgraded his involvement to "my very minor Bush advising role last year" and declared that, since this involvement was no longer an issue and since Christian conservatives would "clearly favor the Bush position," he was now free to comment on the campaign.

However casually or occasionally delivered, Olasky's message demonstrably locked into certain of the candidate's established preferences, notably those for spinning off the government to the private sector and for taking a firm line with its less productive citizens. "Marvin offers not just a blueprint for government,"

Bush declared in the foreword he provided for *Compassionate Conservatism*, "but also an inspiring picture of the great resources of decency, caring, and commitment to one another that Americans share." Just how closely Olasky's "blueprint for government" would be followed was made clear on July 22, 1999, when Bush delivered, in Indianapolis, the speech that Olasky describes as the culmination of a process that began with the four-hour February meeting. "First, the ivy cabinet of policy conceptualizers came up with ideas and proposals," he wrote. "Second, Bush's kitchen cabinet of Austin advisers reviewed the proposals and tried to meld them. Third, Governor Bush decided which ones to run with and which to table."

"In every instance where my administration sees a responsibility to help people," Bush promised that day in Indianapolis, "we will look first to faith-based organizations, charities, and community groups that have shown their ability to save and change lives.... We will change the laws and regulations that hamper the cooperation of government and private institutions." The stories told that day as illustration of this "ability to save and change lives" now seem familiar, not only because they were so often repeated during the campaign but because they are identical in tone and venue to those told by Marvin Olasky. Bush for example cited the case in Texas of "a young man named James Peterson, who'd embezzled his way into a prison term" and who, as the time approached for his parole hearing, joined InnerChange, the faith-based program through which Olasky and Daniel met the similarly converted "Donnie Gilmore." Offered parole, "James" turned it down, electing to stay in prison "to finish the InnerChange course," a version of whatever happened that Bush seemed both to believe and to construe as a happy ending. "As James put it, 'There is nothing I want more than to be back in the outside world with my daughter Lucy, [but] I realized that this was an opportunity to become a living [witness] for my brothers [in prison] and to the world. I want to stay in prison to complete the transformation [God] has begun in me.'"

Among those present that day in Indianapolis were political reporters from America's three major newspapers, Adam Clymer for *The New York Times*, Terry M. Neal for *The Washington Post*, and Ronald Brownstein from *The Los Angeles Times*. "First major policy speech," their stories would read the next morning. "Most elaborate definition to date of his 'compassionate conservatism' credo." They would have heard the candidate say that federal money should be "devolved," not just to states but to "charities and neighborhood healers." They would have heard the candidate promise that his administration would expand the "role and reach" of such organizations "without changing them or corrupting them": a significant victory for Olasky, since the phrase would open the door to what he calls "theological conservatives," i.e., those whose aim is conversion. They would have heard the candidate, by way of forestalling any possible concern that an "unchanged" (or "uncorrupted") "neighborhood healer" might render "faith" the ultimate means test, offer the by now familiar but empirically ambiguous utilitarian argument. "It works," the candidate had said, and then: "Sometimes our greatest hope is not found in reform. It is found in redemption." That a mainstream American political candidate should make these remarkable statements might have seemed worth reporting, but did not: talk of "redemption" as a political platform had by July 1999 become sufficiently commonplace that neither the word "redemption" nor the words "without changing them or corrupting them" appeared the next day in any of the three major papers.

4

> *Jeff Flock, CNN Correspondent:* Well, Kyra, we've got our ear to the ground here in Wisconsin, this is Port Washington, north of Milwaukee, as you point out. We are inside the Allen-Edmonds shoe manufacturing plant ... trying to get a sense [from] undecided voters if they made up their mind based on what they saw yesterday.... First of all is ... the COO of Allen-Edmonds, I have got to ask you, you're on the fence. Have you made up your mind as a result of what you saw last night?

> *Unidentified Male:* Well, I'm still undecided ...

> *Flock:* Now you tend to the Republican and vote Republican, but at this point, you are still undecided. Al Gore could get your vote.

Unidentified Male: Possibly, yes…. Certainly I'm going to listen to the next two debates, and I think not only are the issues important, but also the sincerity of the candidates…. Just a whole lot of honesty needs to be brought back into the candidacy.

— CNN *Early Edition,* OCTOBER 4, 2000

This question of the "undecided," or "swing," voter, about whom we have heard so much in recent elections, is interesting. "Scientific" political forecasting, that done not by professional pollsters but by a handful of political scientists around the country, for some months prior to the November 2000 election showed Vice President Gore the probable winner. In May 2000, when Robert G. Kaiser of *The Washington Post* reported on this academic forecasting, the only disagreement among the political scientists to whom he spoke had to do with the point spread by which Gore would win. Thomas M. Holbrook of the University of Wisconsin at Milwaukee gave Gore 59.6 percent, Christopher Wlezien of the University of Houston 56.1 percent, Alan I. Abramowitz of Emory University 53 or 54 percent, and Michael Lewis-Beck of the University of Iowa 56.2 percent. By the end of August 2000, when seven of these academic forecasters (including Robert S. Erickson of Columbia University, James E. Campbell of the University of Buffalo, and Helmut Norpoth of the State University of New York at Stony Brook) presented their forecasts at the annual meeting of the American Political Science Association in Washington, six of the seven had somewhat narrowed but not significantly changed the Gore lead, their August forecasts ranging from a 52.3 to a 55.4 Gore victory. The seventh, Holbrook, citing the record number of Americans who reported themselves satisfied with their personal financial situation, had slightly increased the Gore lead, to 60.3 percent.

This kind of forecasting, which was based on analyzing mathematical models of the thirteen presidential elections since 1948 and of the state of the economy (both actual and perceived) during each of these elections, had in the past proved remarkably accurate. Wlezien's early forecasts were accurate within six-tenths of one percent in 1988 and one-tenth of one percent in 1996. Lewis-Beck's early call on the 1996 election (in collaboration with Charles Tien of Hunter College) was, according to *The Washington Post*, not only closer to the ultimate result than polls conducted immediately before the election (Lewis-Beck and Tien gave Clinton 54.8 percent, the eventual recorded result was 54.7) but also closer, by almost three percentage points, than exit polls conducted while the election was actually in progress. "The outcome of a presidential election can be accurately predicted based on factors that are known well before the official campaign gets underway," Abramowitz told the *Post*. "Despite the time, effort and money devoted to campaigning, there is very little that the candidates can do during September and October to alter the eventual outcome of a presidential election."

Political reporters and operatives are nonetheless dismissive of this academic forecasting, since the models on which it is based, focusing as they do on economic indicators, relentlessly exclude the questions of personality or "positioning" that are seen as key to the "undecided" vote and so dominate discussion of presidential elections. The models largely discount the number of "undecided" answers that are elicited by polling, since, as James E. Campbell noted in *Before the Vote: Forecasting American National Elections*, "the 'socially desirable' answer … may be a late decision, both out of a sense of open-mindedness and because one may appear more deliberative in obtaining all possible information about the candidate before deciding how to vote." "Character," on which many polls seem to turn, plays no role in these projections. "Values," although much discussed in focus groups, go unmentioned.

Adam Clymer, covering the Washington meeting of the American Political Science Association for *The New York Times*, characterized the forecasters as "seven visitors [i.e., not Washington insiders] seeking to impose a precision and predictability on political life that even those working in its midst [i.e., the insiders the "visitors" will never be] cannot discern." At a time when conventional polling showed Bush running ahead of Gore by double digits, the Bush pollster Fred Steeper told *The Washington Post* that the academic models would necessarily prove wrong, since none factored in the opinion of voters on the question to which the professionals were at that time giving full focus, that of the country's presumed "decline in moral values."

* * *

Steeper said this in May 2000. The kind of polling or focus research that elicits opinions about "moral values" (where the "socially desirable" answer is even more clear than in preference polls) would have been, in May, not much more effective at projecting a November outcome than asking a ouija board. Until the final weeks of a presidential campaign, conventional opinion research has been notoriously unreliable. In May 1988, a not atypical *New York Times*/CBS News poll showed Dukakis leading Vice President Bush by ten points. In June 1992, the Field Institute showed Perot and by then President Bush dividing the bulk of the electoral vote, with Clinton "getting so few that he is currently not a factor." To the professionals of the political process, this indicates not an ambiguity in the research but an exciting volatility, the "horse race" construct, in which the election is seen to turn on the skill or lack of skill with which the candidates and their handlers "send signals," or deploy counters derived from the research.

Governor George W. Bush's acceptance speech at the 2000 Republican convention in Philadelphia was a string of such notational counters, each on the face of it deeply meaningless ("When I act, you will know my reasons.... When I speak, you will know my heart") but among which could be embedded such signals as "valuing the life of the unborn," or "We must renew our *values* to restore our *country*." Bush, it was immediately agreed, had sent the right signals, had at once positioned himself to seem, as they were saying on NBC while the confetti was still falling, "a very simple guy—loves his ranch, loves his family" and "also presidential." This instant positive judgment was entirely predictable, a phenomenon that occurs on the last night of every convention, but it was nonetheless seen, by those who made it and by those whose business it was to calibrate it, to significantly change the dynamic of the election. "My view of this process has totally changed," Robert Teeter, the longtime Republican pollster, told *The Washington Post* after the similarly predictable instant positive judgment on the naming of Richard Cheney (Cheney, it was said on CNN, was "one of the governing class") as Governor Bush's running mate. "You used to look for twenty-eight electoral votes or some demographic bloc. Now, the crucial question is how the press and public react in the first forty-eight hours."

That the press and the public might ultimately react in sharply divergent ways seemed not to enter Teeter's analysis, yet we had just lived through a period, that of the events leading up to and following impeachment, during which no political commentator in America failed to express bafflement at the mystery of what was called "the disconnect," which is to say the divergence between what the press thought and what the public thought about President Clinton. "It is impossible to overstate the extent to which the political community felt betrayed by the president and convinced that he would be forced from office," Thomas E. Mann of the Brookings Institution wrote in *Newsday* immediately after the November 1998 congressional elections, the occasion on which the prevailing view of the political community got put to a vote and lost. Mann continued:

> The public, on the other hand, while morally offended by the president's misbehavior and skeptical of the content of his character, has been steadfast in its belief that Clinton's personal failings did not compromise his ability to function successfully as chief executive. Each new public revelation of titillating details served mainly to reinforce their view that the effort to force the president from office was both unwise and, at least in part, politically motivated. This gap between Washington and public opinion had to close before the president's future could be resolved. Now that the election returns are in, we know how that gap will close. The message from the election is crystal-clear: The Washington community will have to accommodate itself to the views of the country.

In April 1999, two months after the Senate tried and acquitted President Clinton on the articles of impeachment brought by the House and three months before Governor George W. Bush would launch his redemption platform in Indianapolis, I happened to hear several prominent Democratic and Republican pollsters and strategists agree that the 2000 election would necessarily turn, in the absence of hard times, on "values." That these specialists in opinion research were hearing a certain number of Americans express concern about their own future and about the future of America seemed clear. What seemed less clear was the source of this concern, or what inchoate insecurity or nostalgia is actually being voiced when respondents address such questions as whether they fear that "this society will become too accepting of behaviors that are bad for people," say, or believe that "a president should set a moral tone for the country."

On the latter point, a 1998 poll conducted by *The Washington Post* in conjunction with Harvard University and the Kaiser Foundation found that fifty percent of those queried did believe the president should set a moral tone and forty-eight percent did not, a statistically insignificant difference but one cited in a later *Post* story bearing the headline "Polls Suggest Public Seeks Moral Leadership in Wake of White House Scandal." When Americans told researchers that they worried about the future of their family or the country, say, or that they did not believe their fellow citizens to be "as honest or moral as they used to be," what they were actually expressing, according to the *Post*, was their "yearning for a moral compass and virtuous leadership," a notion that tallied with what the nation's opinion leaders had been wishing they yearned for all year. Almost a year before the New Hampshire primary, then, the shape the campaign would take had already been settled upon, and it was not a shape that would require the Washington community to accommodate itself to the views of the country: what was concerning Americans, it had been decided, was the shame they had to date failed to recognize.

5

More than two-thirds of Americans polled by *The Los Angeles Times* in February 1999, immediately after President Clinton was tried and acquitted by the Senate, said that his misconduct had not caused them to lose respect for the office of the presidency. Sixty-eight percent said that they did not want the issue raised in the 2000 presidential campaign. More than three in five said that Republicans pursued impeachment "primarily because they wanted to hurt President Clinton politically." Only one-third, or a number approximately the size of the Republican base, said that Republicans were motivated by concern about the effect of "Clinton's actions on the legal and moral fabric of the country."

The notional conviction that most Americans felt "revulsion" toward the Clinton administration, and the collateral conviction that this was damaging the Gore candidacy, nonetheless remained general, and, as became clear with the addition of Senator Joseph I. Lieberman to the Democratic ticket, would come to warp Gore's own conduct of his campaign. "The fundamentals are in Gore's favor," the political analyst Allan J. Lichtman acknowledged to *The New York Times* in September 2000. "Peace, prosperity, tranquility at home and a united incumbent party. Why has the race even been close? The Clinton scandals." A Republican pollster, Ed Goeas, suggested that Gore was suffering "the after-effect of impeachment. Voters didn't want Republicans to impeach Clinton because they thought it would rock the boat. Now that that is no longer an issue, they are indulging in a second emotion—they didn't want Clinton impeached, but they think what he did was wrong."

The choice of Senator Lieberman was widely construed as Gore's way of transcending this presumed public sentiment, of "sending a message" to the electorate. The actual message that got sent, however, was not to the electorate but to its political class—to that narrow group of those who wrote and spoke and remained fixed in the belief that "the Clinton scandals" constituted a weight that must be shed. Senator Lieberman, who had previously come to the nation's attention as the hedge player who had briefly seized center stage by managing both to denounce the president for "disgraceful" and "immoral" behavior and to vote against his conviction (similarly, he had in 1991 both voiced support for and voted against the confirmation of Clarence Thomas), was not, except to the press, an immediately engaging personality. There were, in those first wobbly steps as a vice-presidential candidate, the frequent references to "private moments of prayer" and to the "miracle" of his nomination. There were the insistent reminders of his own filial devotion, as displayed to the nation during his "only in America moment" at the Democratic convention: "Mom, thank you, I love you, and you and I know how proud Pop would be tonight. Yes we do love you, Mom." There was the unsettling way in which he seemed to patronize his running mate, as if insensitive to the possibility that his unsolicited testimonials to Gore's character ("This is a man of courage! He showed it by picking me to be with him!") could suggest that it would otherwise be seen as doubtful.

His speech patterns, grounded as they were in the burden he bore for the rest of us and the personal rewards he had received from God for bearing it, tended to self-congratulation. In his *In Praise of Public Life*, a modest work in which he peculiarly defends his career as a professional politician, he noted that he must "endure the disdain" of those who distrust politicians, that he risks being "sullied by the fight for election," that winning the fight means only stepping "into yet another arena that has turned uglier than before." After his 1988 election to the Senate, he girded himself for the arena that had turned uglier than before by making "private visits to three religious leaders who meant a lot to me, to ask them for their prayers as I began this new chapter of my life." The religious leaders on whom he chose to call, already exhibiting his preference for hedge betting, were the Catholic archbishop of Hartford, an evangelical Protestant minister in Milford, and the Lubavitch rabbi Menachem Schneerson in Brooklyn.

There was, the reader of *In Praise of Public Life* learns, "no single reason" for the failure after sixteen years of his first marriage, and yet he does give reasons, each of which redounds to his credit. The president may have committed "disgraceful" and "immoral" acts, but Senator Lieberman had not, and the suggestion on a call-in radio show that he might have so upset his ex-wife that she had immediately called the show to say that "she knew I had never committed adultery." There had been instead "the fact that I had become much more religiously observant than I was when we met and married." There had been "the demands my political career put on our private life. That is surely one of the great costs and risks of public life."

There were, in the aftermath of Gore's decision to name Lieberman, many dispiriting reiterations of the benefit that would accrue. "Integrity on the Ticket" was the headline on the *Washington Post*'s lead editorial on the morning after the announcement. "A Gore-Lieberman ticket is not going to be associated with bad behavior," Al From of the Democratic Leadership Council told *The New York Times*, which obtained a similar encomium (to the "credibility" that "Mr. Lieberman brings to everything he touches") from the Reverend Jerry

Falwell. Senator Lieberman, it was repeatedly said, gave the ticket "moral authority," the most frequently cited source for which was his having "fearlessly spoken out" or "fearlessly acted on his beliefs" to denounce both Clinton and popular culture. Hollywood, he had asserted, "doesn't understand piety." Although Hollywood, like Clinton at the time of his impeachment, might be considered something less than a moving target, there had been a further "fearless" aspect to Lieberman's crusade: just as he had teamed with Lynne Cheney to denounce "political correctness" (another fairly lethargic target), he had teamed with William J. Bennett to decry "the rising tide of sex and violence in our popular culture." This showed, it was said, Lieberman's "independence," his ability to "follow his conscience," which as presented came to seem a kind of golden retriever bounding ever to the right, determined to outrun his master and his ninety-five percent A.D.A. rating. "On issues that cut very close to the bone," Bennett explained to E. J. Dionne Jr., "he's there."

The rather histrionic humility with which Senator Lieberman accepted this nonpartisan admiration served only to further encourage those who wrote and spoke and offered opinions. "In the choice of a single man," Richard Cohen wrote on the *Washington Post*'s op-ed page, "...Gore shows he is comfortable with a running mate who was uncomfortable with Clinton's behavior." David Broder mentioned "the moral character he adds.... Lieberman embodies and defines the standards by which politicians should be judged." George Will spoke of the "unfeigned revulsion" with which Lieberman had denounced Clinton, and of the way in which that unfeigned revulsion could address "the national longing" to be rid of this president. To the same point, the editorial page of *The New York Times* saw the choice of Lieberman as "a signal that this ticket was moving beyond Mr. Clinton's behavioral—as opposed to his policy—legacy. Mr. Lieberman's authority in this regard derives from his moral bearing, embodied in his criticism of Mr. Clinton's conduct two years ago." Nor was this enthusiasm confined to the editorial and op-ed pages: on page 1 of a single issue, the *Times*, in its own reportorial voice, certified Mr. Lieberman's "moral rectitude," his "seriousness of purpose," his "integrity." He was "untainted." He was "regarded as one of the most upstanding public officials in the nation." He was a "moral compass in the wastelands of politics."

That the ticket would otherwise woefully lack this moral compass, and unless shriven by Senator Lieberman would reap the whirlwind of the assumed national yearning to punish Clinton, was accepted as given, since, for those who wrote and spoke and offered opinions, the furies and yearnings of the nation were necessarily indivisible from the furies and yearnings of its political class. The possibility that the yearnings of the nation might instead be expressed by the occasional actual citizen who managed to penetrate the cloud cover of the coverage seemed not to occur. On the morning of September 4, 2000, in a news-analysis piece headline "Still Riding Wave, a Confident Gore Heads to Florida for Fall Push," Katharine G. Seelye of the *Times*, flying safely within the cloud cover, reminded readers of what was according to the story line the campaign's "central concern": that "while voters appreciate the good times, there is lingering resentment toward Mr. Clinton over his personal behavior, creating a complex web of emotions that still seems to ensnare Mr. Gore." This story appeared on page A14. Also on page A14, the same morning, in a report on a Gore-Lieberman event at a construction site in downtown Philadelphia, Richard Perez-Pena of the *Times* quoted a twenty-one-year-old electrician whom he had interviewed on the site. "Clinton did a real good job with the economy, and Gore was his V.P.," this actual citizen was reported to have said, "so he's the next best thing to Clinton if we can't have Clinton."

6

Well, there's nothing wrong with candidates indicating what their faith [or] belief is. It's something else when they begin to put it into the public arena in terms of politics. And then what it starts becoming, as we've heard, Governor Bush this week talked about America being God's country. God created it.... Vice-Presidential candidate Cheney talked about [how] tolerance in this country should be the way Jesus Christ taught it. Now, that sounds like preaching from a pulpit. What's starting to happen is campaigning and candidates are beginning to outdo each other as [to] how godly they are and how much God has a part in their life.... All of a sudden, this new emphasis on faith and religion in—in—in a campaign that should deal with issues may move us off that experience of two hundred years.

—ABRAHAM H. FOXMAN, ON *This Week,*
SUNDAY, SEPTEMBER 3, 2000

Bill Clinton lowballed it to the White House with his yeomen telling themselves that "It's the economy, stupid," but the winning party has generally been the one that could claim the high moral ground. That's why Joe Lieberman's talk of God, which helps voters forget Bill Clinton's ungodly activity, has been so fruitful for Al Gore.

—MARVIN OLASKY, IN *World,* SEPTEMBER 23, 2000

This was an election in which there were running for president and vice president on the Democratic ticket two professional politicians, one of whom was born to the game and the other of whom said that he was inspired to play it by the "figures of respect" already on the field, beginning with "the succession of dignified, personable mayors who ran Stamford." There was running for president on the Republican ticket someone whose most successful previous venture was based on his questionable readiness to accept, in the first year of his own father's presidency, a sweetheart ten percent "general partner interest" (aka "promote fee") in the 1989 purchase of the Texas Rangers by a consortium of investors, an $86 million deal in which the candidate's personal investment was only $606,000. There was running for vice president on the Republican ticket someone who had parlayed his Gulf War credits in the Middle East into a $45.5 million stake in Halliburton, and who thought the thing to say when asked why he did not vote in the 2000 presidential primary in Texas (or for that matter in fourteen of the sixteen elections held while he was a resident of Dallas County) was that he had been focused on "global concerns," just as he had been focused on "other priorities" during the Vietnam years he spent failing to get a doctorate at the University of Wisconsin instead of getting drafted.

The grounds on which any one of the four could be construed as a candidate for the "high moral ground" remain obscure, yet their respective claims to this phantom venue, with Governor Bush and Senator Lieberman on point but Vice President Gore and Mr. Cheney not far behind, had come to dominate the campaign. Each had testified to the centrality of "faith" in his life and in that of the nation. Each had declared his intention to install "faith-based organizations" (by this point so obligatory a part of policy discussions that they were referred to by acronym, "FBOs") in the front lines of what had previously been the nation's social support system. "The Constitution guarantees freedom *of* religion, not freedom *from* religion," one or another of them could rather too frequently be heard saying, appropriating as new a line already familiar during the 1950s debate over adding the clause "under God" to the Pledge of Allegiance. ("It's not constitutional, so don't say it," I recall my grandfather instructing me to that point.) "I believe that faith in itself is sometimes essential to spark a personal transformation," Vice President Gore was already saying in May 1999 in Atlanta. By August 2000, Senator Lieberman was saying in Detroit that America was "moving to a new spiritual awakening," requiring only that we its people "reaffirm our faith and renew the dedication of our nation and ourselves to God and God's purpose."

There is a level at which many Americans simply discount what is said during a political campaign, dismiss it as loose talk. When Senator Lieberman tells us "never to indulge the supposition that morality can be maintained without religion," or when Governor Bush says "our nation is chosen by God," or when Vice President Gore talks about What Would Jesus Do or Mr. Cheney appears on a platform in Kansas City with a succession of athletes attesting to the personal role played in their lives by Jesus Christ and the Gospels, what gets said is often understood as no more than a tactical signal, a "message" sent to a certain constituency, a single fleeting moment in a moving campaign; a marker in a game with no causal connection to policy or legislation as it will actually evolve. Evangelical Christians, a spokesman for the National Association of Evangelicals told *The New York Times* in a discussion of Senator Lieberman's religiosity, "are very happy with everything the senator's been saying." They may well have been, and were meant to be, yet the senator had supported neither of two causes, authorization of student-led prayer or the mandatory posting of the Ten Commandments, recently of urgent interest to the evangelical community. Nor, despite what he has called in reference to abortion his "growing personal anxiety that something very wrong is happening in our country," had his votes on abortion legislation, a crucial evangelical concern, been other than generally pro-choice.

The expressed "personal anxiety that something very wrong is happening in our country," then, was exclusively rhetorical, or loose talk. As such, it could be set aside, understood as a nod to those "pro-family" or "values" voters who, although a minority, have been increasingly encouraged, by the way in which both parties have deliberately narrowed campaign dialogue to issues that concern those voters, to decide our elections. There is considerable evidence that this narrowing, which tends to alienate younger voters, has already had a deleterious effect on the electoral process. In the 1996 presidential election, the president of the ACLU Foundation of Southern California pointed out in *The Los Angeles Times*, the number of voters aged eighteen to twenty-one dropped from thirty-eight to thirty-one percent and the number of those aged twenty-one to twenty-four dropped from forty-five to thirty-three percent. In the 1998 congressional elections, the turnout in these age groups was less than seventeen percent, roughly half that of older voters. The competitive pieties of the 2000 campaign are not calibrated to reverse this estrangement of the young: in *What's God Got to Do with the American Experiment?*, a collection of studies and essays compiled under the auspices of the Brookings Institution, Richard N. Ostling noted that members of the generation now approaching voting age, to a greater extent than members of any previous generation, are "thoroughly detached from traditional Christian concepts ... do not believe Jesus is the unique savior of mankind, do not read the Bible as God's word, and do not accept the idea of moral absolutes."

The September Sunday morning on which Abraham H. Foxman suggested to Cokie Roberts and the Reverend Pat Robertson that an excessive campaign emphasis on faith could "move us off that experience of two hundred years" ("So there's a tiny, tiny minority who consider themselves atheist," Pat Robertson said, "and you can't surrender the deeply held religious beliefs

of the entire majority to please some tiny minority") followed
several days of op-ed and talk-show debate prompted by the letter, making the same point, that Mr. Foxman had sent to Senator
Lieberman after the latter's "new spiritual awakening" event in
Detroit. In the course of this debate, the appropriate role of religion in American life had been discussed at some length. It had
been widely agreed that the establishment clause of the First
Amendment had been, to the extent that it had ensured the dis-
establishment of the Anglican or Episcopal Church, a good idea.
It had also been widely agreed that the aim of the Founders had
been not "atheism" (the straw man from the Scopes trial curiously back among us) but "diversity of faith." There had been
areas of disagreement, hotly argued but narrow. Some held that
one's faith was best practiced in private, others that faith practiced in private was no faith at all; a difference, as differences
go, not entirely unlike the 1844 Philadelphia riot in which six
people were killed over the issue of which version of the Ten
Commandments should be posted in public schools.

Yet virtually all of the many positions and postures taken in
this debate rested on a single and largely unchallenged assumption, that religion, whether public or private, was at the heart
of the American experience, and that the "experience of two
hundred years" to which Mr. Foxman referred had been in fact
a record of serial awakenings, the eventual rightful end of which,
once the obstructive element increasingly referred to as "the
ACLU" had been shown the light, would be what both presidential candidates were now calling the "personal transformation"
of the nation's citizens. "I need my civil liberties friends to tell
me again the mortal danger of prayer—of religion generally—in
public places," William Raspberry wrote in The Washington Post.
"I keep forgetting it." "Separation between church and state never
meant that religion had no place in American life," E. J. Dionne Jr.
wrote in the Post. "Remember, this is a nation that still stamps 'In
God We Trust' on its currency." The fact that the words "In God
We Trust" were added to American currency during the same
recent period and for the same political reason that the words
"under God" were added to the Pledge of Allegiance, home-
front ammunition in the Eisenhower administration's cold war
arsenal, had vanished (like the fact that the number of Americans
who belonged to churches during the American Revolution

constituted only seventeen percent of the population) from the collective memory stream. "I confess," Dionne also wrote, "I love what Joe Lieberman is doing to our national debate about religion and public life":

> Lieberman is not the first politician to say how important faith is to our democracy. President Dwight Eisenhower offered the nation this notable sentiment: "Our government makes no sense unless it is founded on a deeply felt religious belief—and I don't care what it is." Today's discussion about religion and politics is much more serious than it was in the "I don't care what it is" past memorialized by Eisenhower. That's what makes so many people uncomfortable.

This was a meaningful shift in the national political dialogue. Politics, it had been until recently understood, is push and pull, give and take, the art of the possible, an essentially pragmatic process by which the differing needs and rights of the nation's citizens get balanced and to some degree met. The insertion into this process of a claim to faith, or to "the high moral ground," it also had been until recently understood, is perilous, permissible if at all only at moments of such urgent gravity as to warrant its inherent danger, which is that the needs and rights of some citizens might be overridden to accommodate the needs and rights of those holding the high ground. This was not such a moment in American life. The nation was not at war. A majority of its citizens seemed to understand that the demonstration of "full remorse" recently demanded of its president would prove less personally meaningful to their families than the skill or lack of skill with which he guided them through the rapids of the global economy.

The possible "legacy" of that president was popularly discussed in negative terms, as the redeeming grail he had hoped for and lost, but on any reasonable scale his legacy was already sizable: the country he would hand over to either Governor Bush or Vice President Gore was one in which median household income had reached an all-time high, the unemployment rate was at its lowest point in three decades, the rate of violent crime was down, and the digital national-debt clock in Manhattan was running, until its creator allowed that the device had outlived its effectiveness and stopped it, backward. It had been Clinton's "legacy," in short, to create the very conditions that had early on led the academic forecasters to call a presidential victory by the incumbent party the most probable outcome of the November 2000 election.

Yet so thin was the air on the high moral ground that none of this was seen as relevant, not even by the candidate who might have seemed poised to benefit from it. What had been for the past several decades the origin myth of the neoconservative right had become, in part because it so uniquely filled the need of the political class to explain its own estrangement from the electorate, the official story, shared by all participants in the process: America, in this apocalyptic telling, had been from its inception until the 1960s a deeply religious nation. During the 1960s, through the efforts of what Robert H. Bork called "the 'intellectual' class and that class's enforcement arm, the judiciary, headed by the Supreme Court of the United States," the nation and its citizens had been inexplicably and destructively "secularized," and were accordingly in need of "transformation," of "moral and intellectual rearmament," of "renewed respect for moral authority." In a country already so increasingly steeped in evangelical teaching that a significant number of its citizens had come to believe that "God created man pretty much in his present form at one time within the last ten thousand years" (forty-seven percent of Americans surveyed by Gallup in 1991 said they believed in such a fell swoop, or "recent special creation"), those who wrote and spoke were arguing about how the nation's political system could best revive those religious values allegedly destroyed (in an interestingly similar fell swoop) during the 1960s.

The delusionary notion that such a revival was now in progress, and would soon prove the correctness of the political class on the Clinton issue, is what lent the 2000 campaign its peculiar, and for the Democratic candidate its dangerous, distance from the electorate. President Clinton may have "escaped conviction," Marvin Olasky wrote in the preface to the most recent edition of *The American Leadership Tradition*, but was nonetheless "convicted in the court of public opinion." The electorate, he wrote, would no longer accept "an anything-goes moral vision." Accordingly, the 2000 election was one in which "the populace seemed to want the next president to be someone who would not disgrace the Oval Office, and that desire gave hope to those who want to revive a tradition of moral leadership."

The logic here, and it was the same logic that surfaced in response to the Lieberman nomination, was that of the origin myth, in which "the populace," once warned, could yet cast out its wicked allegiance to its disgraced leader and be saved before the final Rapture. This fable had been adjusted and trimmed with each retelling, yet one element, the disgraced leader, remained fixed, the rock on which the Bush campaign might have foundered early had the Gore campaign itself, in search of the chimerical "undecided" voter, not rushed to enter the fable's fatal eddy. The distinct possibility that an entire generation of younger voters might see no point in choosing between two candidates retelling the same remote story could benefit only one campaign, the Republican, and the failure of the Democratic campaign to recognize this could yet neutralize the advantage of the legacy it has worked so assiduously to disavow.

WHERE I WAS FROM

*This book is for my brother James Jerrett Didion, and for our mother
and father, Eduene Jerrett Didion and Frank Reese Didion, with love*

Part I

I

MY GREAT-GREAT-great-great-great-grandmother Elizabeth Scott was born in 1766, grew up on the Virginia and Carolina frontiers, at age sixteen married an eighteen-year-old veteran of the Revolution and the Cherokee expeditions named Benjamin Hardin IV, moved with him into Tennessee and Kentucky and died on still another frontier, the Oil Trough Bottom on the south bank of the White River in what is now Arkansas but was then Missouri Territory. Elizabeth Scott Hardin was remembered to have hidden in a cave with her children (there were said to have been eleven, only eight of which got recorded) during Indian fighting, and to have been so strong a swimmer that she could ford a river in flood with an infant in her arms. Either in her defense or for reasons of his own, her husband was said to have killed, not counting English soldiers or Cherokees, ten men. This may be true or it may be, in a local oral tradition inclined to stories that turn on decisive gestures, embroidery. I have it on the word of a cousin who researched the matter that the husband, our great-great-great-great-great-grandfather, "appears in the standard printed histories of Arkansas as 'Old Colonel Ben Hardin, the hero of so many Indian wars.'" Elizabeth Scott Hardin had bright blue eyes and sick headaches. The White River on which she lived was the same White River on which, a century and a half later, James McDougal would locate his failed Whitewater development. This is a country at some level not as big as we like to say it is.

I know nothing else about Elizabeth Scott Hardin, but I have her recipe for corn bread, and also for India relish: her granddaughter brought these recipes west in 1846, traveling with the Donner-Reed party as far as the Humboldt Sink before cutting north for Oregon, where her husband, the Reverend Josephus Adamson Cornwall, was determined to be the first Cumberland Presbyterian circuit rider in what was then called Oregon country. Because that granddaughter, Nancy Hardin Cornwall, was my great-great-great-grandmother, I have, besides her recipes, a piece of appliqué she made on the crossing. This appliqué, green and red calico on a muslin field, hangs now in my dining room in New York and hung before that in the living room of a house I had on the Pacific Ocean.

I also have a photograph of the stone marker placed on the site of the cabin in which Nancy Hardin Cornwall and her family spent the winter of 1846–47, still short of their destination in the Willamette Valley but unable to get their wagons through a steep defile on the Umpqua River without abandoning Josephus Cornwall's books. (This option seems to have presented itself only to his daughters.) "Dedicated to the memory of Rev. J. A. Cornwall and family," the engraving on the marker reads. "They built the first immigrant cabin in Douglas County near this site, hence the name Cabin Creek. The family wintered here in 1846–1847, were saved from extreme want by Israel Stoley, a nephew who was a good hunter. The Indians were friendly. The Cornwalls traveled part way westward with the ill-fated Donner Party."

My mother was sent the photograph of this marker by her mother's cousin Oliver Huston, a family historian so ardent that as recently as 1957 he was alerting descendants to "an occasion which no heir should miss," the presentation to the Pacific University Museum of, among other artifacts, "the old potato masher which the Cornwall family brought across the plains in 1846." Oliver Huston's letter continued: "By this procedure, such items can then be seen by all Geiger and Cornwall heirs at any time in the future by simply visiting the Museum." I have not myself found occasion to visit the potato masher, but I do have a typescript of certain memories, elicited from one of Nancy Hardin Cornwall's twelve children, Narcissa, of those months on what would later be called Cabin Creek:

> We were about ten miles from the Umpqua River and the Indians living there would come and spend the greater part of the day. There was one who spoke English, and he told Mother the Rogue River Indians were coming to kill us. Mother told them if they troubled us, in the spring the Bostons (the Indian name for the white people) would come out and kill them all off. Whether this had any effect

or not I don't know, but anyway they did not kill us. But we
always thought they would come one day for that purpose.
One day Father was busy reading and did not notice the
house was filling with strange Indians until Mother spoke
about it.... As soon as Father noticed them he got up and
got his pistols and asked the Indians to go out and see him
shoot. They followed him out, but kept at a distance. The
pistols were a great curiosity to them. I doubt if they had
ever seen any before. As soon as they were all out of the
cabin Mother barred the door and would not let them in
any more. Father entertained them outside until evening,
when they got on their ponies and rode away. They never
returned to trouble us any more.

In another room of this house I had on the Pacific Ocean
there hung a quilt from another crossing, a quilt made by my
great-great-grandmother Elizabeth Anthony Reese on a wagon
journey during which she buried one child, gave birth to another,
twice contracted mountain fever, and took turns driving a yoke
of oxen, a span of mules, and twenty-two head of loose stock. In
this quilt of Elizabeth Reese's were more stitches than I had ever
seen in a quilt, a blinding and pointless compaction of stitches,
and it occurred to me as I hung it that she must have finished it
one day in the middle of the crossing, somewhere in the wilderness of her own grief and illness, and just kept on stitching. From
her daughter's account:

Tom was sick with fever the first day of the crossing, no
chance for a doctor. He was only sick a day or two when
he died. He had to be buried right away, as the train of
wagons was going right on. He was two years old, and we
were glad to get a trunk to bury him in. A friend gave a
trunk. My aunt, the following year, when her baby died,
carried it for a long time in her arms without letting anyone know for fear they would bury the baby before coming
to a station.

These women in my family would seem to have been pragmatic and in their deepest instincts clinically radical, given to
breaking clean with everyone and everything they knew. They

could shoot and they could handle stock and when their children outgrew their shoes they could learn from the Indians how to make moccasins. "An old lady in our wagon train taught my sister to make blood pudding," Narcissa Cornwall recalled. "After killing a deer or steer you cut its throat and catch the blood. You add suet to this and a little salt, and meal or flour if you have it, and bake it. If you haven't anything else to eat, it's pretty good." They tended to accommodate any means in pursuit of an uncertain end. They tended to avoid dwelling on just what that end might imply. When they could not think what else to do they moved another thousand miles, set out another garden: beans and squash and sweet peas from seeds carried from the last place. The past could be jettisoned, children buried and parents left behind, but seeds got carried. They were women, these women in my family, without much time for second thoughts, without much inclination toward equivocation, and later, when there was time or inclination, there developed a tendency, which I came to see as endemic, toward slight and major derangements, apparently eccentric pronouncements, opaque bewilderment and moves to places not quite on the schedule.

> Mother viewed character as being the mainspring of life, and, therefore, as regulating our lives here and indicating our destiny in the life to come. She had fixed and settled principles, aims and motives in life. Her general health was excellent and in middle life she appeared almost incapable of fatigue. Winter and summer, at all seasons and every day, except Sunday, her life was one ceaseless round of activity. The care of her family, to provide for hired help, to entertain visitors, and to entertain preachers and others during meetings which were frequent.

That was the view of Nancy Hardin Cornwall taken by her son Joseph, who was thirteen years old during the crossing. Nancy Hardin Cornwall's daughter Laura, two years old during the crossing, took a not dissimilar view: "Being a Daughter of the American Revolution, she was naturally a brave woman, never seeming afraid of Indians or shrinking from hardships."

A photograph:

A woman standing on a rock in the Sierra Nevada in perhaps 1905.

Actually it is not just a rock but a granite promontory: an igneous outcropping. I use words like "igneous" and "outcropping" because my grandfather, one of whose mining camps can be seen in the background of this photograph, taught me to use them. He also taught me to distinguish gold-bearing ores from the glittering but worthless serpentine I preferred as a child, an education to no point, since by that time gold was no more worth mining than serpentine and the distinction academic, or possibly wishful.

The photograph. The promontory. The camp in the background.

And the woman: Edna Magee Jerrett. She is Nancy Hardin Cornwall's great-granddaughter, she will in time be my grandmother. She is Black Irish, English, Welsh, possibly (this is uncertain) a fraction Jewish through her grandfather William Geiger, who liked to claim as an ancestor a German rabbi but was himself a Presbyterian missionary in the Sandwich Islands and along the Pacific coast; possibly (this is still more uncertain) a lesser fraction Indian, from some frontier somewhere, or maybe, because her skin darkens in the sun as she was told not to let it, she just likes to say that. She grew up in a house on the Oregon coast filled with the educational curiosities of the place and period: strings of shells and seeds from Tahiti, carved emu eggs, Satsuma vases, spears from the South Pacific, an alabaster miniature of the Taj Mahal and the baskets her mother was given by the local Indians. She is quite beautiful. She is also quite indulged, clearly given, although she knows enough about mountains to shake out her boots for snakes every morning, to more amenities than could have been offered in this mining camp in the Sierra Nevada at the time in question. In this photograph she is wearing, for example, a long suede skirt and jacket made for her by the most expensive tailor in San Francisco. "You couldn't pay for her *hats*," her father, a ship's captain, had told her suitors by way of discouragement, and perhaps they had all been discouraged but my grandfather, an innocent from the Georgetown Divide who read books.

It was an extravagance of spirit that would persist through her life. Herself a child, she knew what children wanted. When I was six and had the mumps she brought me, as solace, not a coloring book, not ice cream, not bubble bath, but an ounce of expensive perfume, Elizabeth Arden "On Dit," in a crystal bottle sealed with gold thread. When I was eleven and declined to go any longer to church she gave me, as inducement, not the fear of God but a hat, not any hat, not a child's well-mannered cloche or beret, but a *hat*, gossamer Italian straw and French silk cornflowers and a heavy satin label that read "Lilly Dache." She made champagne punch for the grandchildren left to sit with her on New Year's Eve. During World War II she volunteered to help salvage the Central Valley tomato crop by working the line at the Del Monte cannery in Sacramento, took one look at the moving conveyer belt, got one of those sick headaches her great-grandmother brought west with the seeds, and spent that first and only day on the line with tears running down her face. As atonement, she spent the rest of the war knitting socks for the Red Cross to send to the front. The yarn she bought to knit these socks was cashmere, in regulation colors. She had vicuña coats, hand-milled soap, and not much money. A child could make her cry, and I am ashamed to say that I sometimes did.

She was bewildered by many of the events in her adult life. One of her seafaring brothers became unstable when his ship hit a mine crossing the Atlantic; the son of another committed suicide. She witnessed the abrupt slide into madness of her only sister. Raised to believe that her life would be, as her great-grandmother's was said to have been, one ceaseless round of fixed and settled principles, aims, motives, and activity, she could sometimes think of nothing to do but walk downtown, check out the Bon Marché for clothes she could not afford, buy a cracked crab for dinner and take a taxi home. She died when I was twenty-three and I have of hers a petit-point evening bag, two watercolors she painted as a young girl in an Episcopal convent school (the watermelon still life, the mission she had never seen at San Juan Capistrano), twelve butter knives she had made at Shreve's in San Francisco, and fifty shares of Transamerica stock. I was instructed by her will to sell the stock for something I wanted and could not afford. "What will she have to look forward to," my mother scolded my grandmother on the occasions of the ounce of "On Dit," the Lilly Dache hat, the black scarf embroidered with jet to assuage the pain of dancing school. In the generational theater my mother, despite what I came to recognize as a recklessness quite outside my grandmother's range, had been assigned the role described in the stage directions as sensible. "She'll find something," my grandmother always said, a reassuring conclusion if not one entirely supported by her own experience.

Another photograph, another grandmother: Ethel Reese Didion, who I never knew. She caught fever during the waning days of the 1918 influenza epidemic and died, leaving a husband and two small boys, one of them my father, on the morning of the false armistice. Many times my father told me that she died thinking the war was over. He told me this each time as if it were a matter of considerable importance, and perhaps it was, since on reflection that is all he ever told me about what she thought on any subject. My great-aunt Nell, her younger sister, would say only that my grandmother had been "nervous," and "different." Different from what, I used to ask. Aunt Nell would light another cigarette, consign it immediately to a heavy quartz ashtray, and slide her big rings up and down her thin fingers. Ethel was nervous, she would finally repeat. You could never tease Ethel. Ethel was, well, different.

In this photograph, taken in about 1904, Ethel is at a Grange picnic in Florin, at that time a farm settlement south of Sacramento. She has not yet married the man, my grandfather, whose startling taciturnity would remain so inexplicable to her family, the man to whom I sometimes referred as "Grandfather Didion" but never addressed directly, from the time I was a small child until the day he died in 1953, by any form more familiar than "Mr. Didion." She is still Ethel Reese in this picture and she is wearing a white shirtwaist and a straw hat. Her brothers and cousins, ranchers' sons with a bent for good times and a gift for losing things without rancor, laugh at something outside the camera's range. Aunt Nell, the smallest, darts among their legs. My grandmother smiles tentatively. Her eyes are shut against the sun, or against the camera. I was said to have her eyes, "Reese eyes," eyes that reddened and watered at the first premonition of sun or primroses or raised voices, and I was also said to have some of her "difference," her way of being less than easy at that moment when the dancing starts, but there would be no way of knowing any of that from this picture of Ethel Reese at the Florin Grange picnic in about 1904. This is the memory of her aunt, Catherine Reese, a child during the Reese family's 1852 crossing, of the last stage and aftermath of the journey during which her mother made the quilt with the blinding compaction of stitches:

> Came by Carson City climbing mountains all the time, to Lake Tahoe and on down. Lived in the mountains as Father was sick with chills and fever. Had to give up our stock driver and Mother looked after the stock. Found two or three families of old country folk and lived with them until we got located in a sheep herder's house and lived the winter with him until Father got a house built on the hill ranch near Florin, $2 an acre government land. Father paid cash for 360 acres as he had sold the team and had some money. Went to raising grain and stock, had twelve cows and made and sold butter and eggs and chickens, once in a while a calf. Drove to Sacramento once a week to sell the stuff. Father and Dave did the churning, Mother and I did the milking. I walked six miles to school, to where the graveyard is now on Stockton Boulevard.

That first Reese ranch in Florin, enlarged after a few years from 360 to 640 acres, was into my adult life still owned by my family, or, more precisely, by a corporation called the Elizabeth Reese Estate Company, the shareholders in which were all members of my family. Occasionally, late at night, my father and brother and I would talk about buying out the interests of our cousins in what we still called "the hill ranch" (there was no actual "hill," but there was on the original acreage a rise of perhaps a foot), a move that would have pleased them, since most of them wanted to sell it. I was never able to ascertain whether my father's interest in holding this particular ranch was in any way sentimental; he spoke of it only as a cold property in the short term but a potentially hot one in the long. My mother had no interest in keeping the hill ranch, or in fact any California land: California, she said, was now too regulated, too taxed, too expensive. She spoke enthusiastically, on the other hand, about moving to the Australian outback.

"Eduene," my father would say, a remonstration.

"I would," she would insist, reckless.

"Just leave California? Give it all up?"

"In a *minute*," she would say, the pure strain talking, Elizabeth Scott's great-great-great-great-granddaughter. "Just *forget* it."

2

"ONE HUNDRED YEARS ago, our great-great-grandparents were pushing America's frontier westward, to California." So began the speech I wrote to deliver at my eighth-grade graduation from the Arden School, outside Sacramento. The subject was "Our California Heritage." Developing a theme encouraged by my mother and grandfather, I continued, made rather more confident than I should have been by the fact that I was wearing a new dress, pale green organdy, and my mother's crystal necklace:

> They who came to California were not the self-satisfied, happy and content people, but the adventurous, the restless, and the daring. They were different even from those who settled in other western states. They didn't come west for homes and security, but for adventure and money. They pushed in over the mountains and founded the biggest cities in the west. Up in the Mother Lode they mined gold by day and danced by night. San Francisco's population multiplied almost twenty times, until 1906, when it burned to the ground, and was built up again nearly as quickly as it had burned. We had an irrigation problem, so we built the greatest dams the world has known. Now both desert and valley are producing food in enormous quantities. California has accomplished much in the past years. It would be easy for us to sit back and enjoy the results of the past. But we can't do this. We can't stop and become satisfied and content. We must live up to our heritage, go on to better and greater things for California.

That was June 1948.
The pale green of the organdy dress was a color that existed in the local landscape only for the few spring days when the rice first showed.

The crystal necklace was considered by my mother an effective way to counter the Valley heat.

Such was the blinkering effect of the local dreamtime that it would be some years before I recognized that certain aspects of "Our California Heritage" did not add up, starting with but by no means limited to the fact that I had delivered it to an audience of children and parents who had for the most part arrived in California during the 1930s, refugees from the Dust Bowl. It was after this realization that I began trying to find the "point" of California, to locate some message in its history. I picked up a book of revisionist studies on the subject, but abandoned it on discovering that I was myself quoted, twice. You will have perhaps realized by now (a good deal earlier than I myself realized) that this book represents an exploration into my own confusions about the place and the way in which I grew up, confusions as much about America as about California, misapprehensions and misunderstandings so much a part of who I became that I can still to this day confront them only obliquely.

A GOOD DEAL about California does not, on its own preferred terms, add up. The Sacramento River, the main source of surface water in a state where distrust of centralized governmental authority has historically passed for an ethic, has its headwaters in the far northern ranges of Siskiyou County. It picks up the waters of the McCloud and the Pit Rivers above Redding, of the Feather and the Yuba and the Bear below Knight's Landing, of the American at Sacramento, of the San Joaquin below Steamboat Slough; and empties through San Francisco Bay into the Pacific, draining the deep snowpacks of the southern Cascades and the northern Sierra Nevada. "The river here is about 400 yards wide," one of my great-great-grandfathers, William Kilgore, whose daughter Myra married into the Reese family, wrote in the journal of his arrival in Sacramento in August of 1850. "The tide raises the water about 2 ft. and steamboats and vessels are here daily. From this place to San Francisco is about 150 miles by water. All of this distance the river has low banks and is subject to inundation for several miles back." That the land to which he intended eventually to bring his wife and two children was "subject to inundation for several miles back" seems not to have presented itself as an argument against immediate settlement. "This is one of the trying mornings for me, as I now have to leave my family, or back out," he had written in his journal four months before. "Suffice it to say, we started." Yet this river that had been from the beginning his destination was one regularly and predictably given, during all but the driest of those years before its flow was controlled or rearranged, to turning its valley into a shallow freshwater sea a hundred miles long and as wide as the distance between the coast ranges and the foothills of the Sierra Nevada: a pattern of flooding, the Army Corps of Engineers declared in 1927, more intense and intractable than that on any other American river system including the Mississippi.

This annual reappearance of a marsh that did not drain to the sea until late spring or summer was referred to locally not as flooding but as "the high water," a seasonal fact of life, no more than an inconvenient but minor cost of the rich bottom land it created, and houses were routinely built with raised floors to accommodate it. Many Sacramento houses during my childhood had on their walls one or another lithograph showing the familiar downtown grid with streets of water, through which citizens could be seen going about their business by raft or rowboat. Some of these lithographs pictured the high water of 1850, after which a three-foot earthen levee between the river and the settlement was built. Others showed the high water of 1852, during which that first levee was washed out. Still others showed the high water of 1853 or 1860 or 1861 or 1862, nothing much changing except the increasing number of structures visible on the grid. "If you will take, on a map of California, Stockton, Sacramento, and San Francisco as guiding points, you will see that a large part of the land lying between these cities is marked 'swamp and overflowed,'" Charles Nordhoff, the grandfather of the co-author of *Mutiny on the Bounty*, wrote in his 1874 *Northern California, Oregon and the Sandwich Islands*:

Until within five or six years these lands attracted but little attention. It was known that they were extremely fertile, but it was thought that the cost and uncertainty of reclaiming them were too great to warrant the enterprise. Of late, however, they have been rapidly bought up by capitalists, and their sagacity has been justified by the results on those tracts which have been reclaimed. These Tule lands ... are simply deposits of muck, a mixture of the wash or sediment brought down by the Sacramento and San Joaquin rivers with the decayed vegetable matter resulting from an immense growth of various grasses, and of the reed called the "tule," which often grows ten feet high in a season, and decays every year.... The swamp and overflowed lands were given by Congress to the State, and the State has, in its turn, virtually given them to private persons. It has sold them for one dollar per acre, of which twenty percent was paid down, or twenty cents per acre; and this money, less some small charges for recording the transfer and for inspecting the reclamation, is returned by the State to the purchaser if he, within three years after the purchase, reclaims his land. That is to say, the State gives away the land on condition that it shall be reclaimed and brought into cultivation.

The creation of the entirely artificial environment that is now the Sacramento Valley was not achieved at one stroke, nor is it complete to this day. Bulletins on when and where the rivers would crest, on the conditions of levees and the addresses of evacuation centers, remained into my adult life the spring commonplaces of Sacramento life, as did rumors that one or another levee had been (or was being, or would be) covertly dynamited by one or another agency looking to save one or another downstream community. During years when repeated storms rolling in from the Pacific coincide with an early melting of the Sierra snowpack, levees still break, sections of interstate highways get destabilized by the rising water table, and the big dams go to crisis mode, trying to save themselves by releasing water as they get it, unchecked, no control, the runoff from the pack running free to the sea.

Reclamation of the tule lands has been a war, for those waging it, in which no armament could be too costly, no strategy too quixotic. By 1979, when the State of California published William L. Kahrl's *The California Water Atlas*, there were 980 miles of levee, 438 miles of canal. There were fifty miles of collecting canals and seepage ditches. There were three drainage pumping plants, five low-water check dams, thirty-one bridges, ninety-one gauging stations, and eight automatic shortwave water-stage transmitters. There were seven weirs opening onto seven bypasses covering 101,000 acres. There were not only the big headwater dams, Shasta on the Sacramento and Folsom on the American and Oroville on the Feather, but all their predecessors and collateral dams, their afterbays and forebays and diversions: Thermalito and Lake Almanor and Frenchman Lake and Little Grass Valley on the Feather, New Bullard's Bar and Englebright and Jackson Meadows and Lake Spaulding on the Yuba, Camp Far West and Rollins and Lower Bear on the Bear, Nimbus and Slab Creek and L. L. Anderson on the American, Box Canyon and Keswick on the Sacramento. The cost of controlling or rearranging the Sacramento, which is to say the "reclamation" of the Sacramento Valley, was largely borne, like the cost of controlling or rearranging many other inconvenient features of California life, by the federal government.

This extreme reliance of California on federal money, so seemingly at odds with the emphasis on unfettered individualism that constitutes the local core belief, was a pattern set early on, and derived in part from the very individualism it would seem to belie. ("They didn't come west for homes and security, but for adventure and money," as "Our California Heritage" put it.) Charles Nordhoff complained of California in 1874 that "a speculative spirit invades even the farm-house," too often tempting its citizens "to go from one avocation to another, to do many things superficially, and to look for sudden fortunes by the chances of a shrewd venture, rather than be content to live by patient and continued labor." There had been from the beginning virtually no notion of "pushing America's frontier westward," my eighth-grade conception of it notwithstanding: the American traders and trappers who began settling in California as early as 1826 were leaving their own country for a remote Mexican province, Alta California. Many became naturalized Mexican citizens. Many married into Mexican and Spanish families. A fair number received grants of land from the Mexican authorities. As late as 1846, American emigrants were starting west with the idea of reaching territory at least provisionally Mexican, only to find on their arrival that the Bear Flag Revolt and the Mexican War had placed Alta California under American military authority. There it would remain—along with the other American spoil of that conquest, the territory that eventually became Nevada and Utah and New Mexico and Arizona and part of Colorado—until California was admitted to the union as a state in 1850.

Predicated as it was on this general notion of cutting loose and striking it rich, the California settlement had tended to attract drifters of loosely entrepreneurial inclination, the hunter-gatherers of the frontier rather than its cultivators, and to reward most fully those who perceived most quickly that the richest claim of all lay not in the minefields but in Washington. It was a quartet of Sacramento shopkeepers, Charles Crocker and Leland Stanford and Collis P. Huntington and Mark Hopkins, who built the railroad that linked California with the world markets and opened the state to extensive settlement, but it was the citizens of the rest of the country who paid for it, through a federal cash subsidy (sixteen thousand dollars a mile in the valley and forty-eight thousand dollars a mile in the "mountains," which were contractually defined as beginning six miles east of Sacramento) plus a federal land grant, ten or twenty checkerboarded square-mile sections, for each mile of track laid.

Nor did the role of the government stop with the construction of the railroad: the citizens of the rest of the country would also, in time, subsidize the crops the railroad carried, make possible the irrigation of millions of acres of essentially arid land, underwrite the rhythms of planting and not planting, and create, finally, a vast agricultural mechanism in a kind of market vacuum, quite remote from the normal necessity for measuring supply against demand and cost against return. As recently as 1993, eighty-two thousand acres in California were still planted in alfalfa, a low-value crop requiring more water than was then used in the households of all thirty million Californians. Almost a million and a half acres were planted in cotton, the state's second largest consumer of water, a crop subsidized directly by the federal government. Four hundred thousand acres were planted in rice, the cultivation of which involves submerging the fields under six inches of water from mid-April until the August harvest, months during which, in California, no rain falls. The 1.6 million acre feet of water this required (an acre foot is roughly 326,000 gallons) was made available, even in drought years, for what amounted to a nominal subsidized price by the California State Water Project and the Central Valley Project, an agency of the federal government, which, through the commodity-support program of the Department of Agriculture, also subsidized the crop itself. Ninety percent of this California rice was glutinous medium-grain Japonica, a type not popular in the United States but favored in both Japan and Korea, each of which banned the import of California rice. These are the kinds of contradictions on which Californians have tended to founder when they try to think about the place they come from.

4

JOSIAH ROYCE, WHO was from 1885 until his death in 1916 a central figure in what later became known as the "golden period" of the Harvard philosophy department, was born in Grass Valley, not far from Sacramento, grew up there and in San Francisco, and in some sense spent the rest of his life trying to make coherent the discontinuities implicit in this inheritance. "My native town was a mining town in the Sierra Nevada—a place five or six years older than myself," he said at a dinner given in his honor at the Walton Hotel in Philadelphia in 1915.

> My earliest recollections include a very frequent wonder as to what my elders meant when they said that this was a new community. I frequently looked at the vestiges left by the former diggings of miners, saw that many pine logs were rotten, and that a miner's grave was to be found in a lonely place not far from my own house. Plainly men had lived and died thereabouts. I dimly reflected that this sort of life had apparently been going on ever since men dwelt thereabouts. The logs and the grave looked old. The sunsets were beautiful. The wide prospects when one looked across the Sacramento Valley were impressive, and had long interested the people of whose love for my country I heard so much. What was there then in this place that ought to be called new, or for that matter crude? I wondered, and gradually came to feel that part of my life's business was to find out what all this wonder meant.

Here we come close to a peculiar California confusion: what Royce had actually made it his "life's business" to do, his work, did not resolve "what all this wonder meant." Instead, Royce invented an idealized California, an ethical system in which "loyalty" was the basic virtue, the moral law essential to the creation of "community," which was in turn man's only salvation and by extension the redeeming essence of the California settlement. Yet the California community most deeply recalled by the author of this system was what he acknowledged to have been "a community of irresponsible strangers" (or, in another reference, "a blind and stupid and homeless generation of selfish wanderers"), a community not of the "loyal" but of "men who have left homes and families, who have fled from before the word of the Lord, and have sought safety from their old vexatious duties in a golden paradise."

Such calls to dwell upon the place and its meaning (and, if the meaning proved intractable, to reinvent the place) had been general in California since the first American settlement, the very remoteness of which was sufficiently extreme to raise questions about why one was there, why one had come there, what the voyage would ultimately mean. The overland crossing itself had an aspect of quest: "One was going on a pilgrimage whose every suggestion was of the familiar sacred stories," Royce wrote. "One sought a romantic and far-off golden land of promise, and one was in the wilderness of this world, often guided only by signs from heaven…. The clear blue was almost perpetually overhead; the pure mountain winds were about one; and again, even in the hot and parched deserts, a mysterious power provided the few precious springs and streams of water."

Each arriving traveler had been, by definition, reborn in the wilderness, a new creature in no way the same as the man or woman or even child who had left Independence or St. Joseph however many months before: the very decision to set forth on the journey had been a kind of death, involving the total abandonment of all previous life, mothers and fathers and brothers and sisters who would never again be seen, all sentiment banished, the most elementary comforts necessarily relinquished. "I had for months anticipated this hour, yet, not till it came, did I realize the blank dreariness of seeing night come on without house or home to shelter us and our baby-girl," Josiah Royce's mother, Sarah, wrote of the day in 1849 on which she set off for Sacramento with her husband and first child.

The blank dreariness, Sarah Royce wrote.

Without house or home, Sarah Royce wrote.

Suffice it to say, we started, my great-great-grandfather William Kilgore wrote.

This moment of leaving, the death that must precede the rebirth, is a fixed element of the crossing story. Such stories are artlessly told. There survives in their repetition a problematic elision or inflation, a narrative flaw, a problem with point of view: the actual observer, or camera eye, is often hard to locate. This was Josephus Adamson Cornwall's goodbye to his mother, as related by a son who seems to have heard the story from his mother, Nancy Hardin Cornwall, she of the fixed and settled principles, aims, and motives in life, who had not herself been present: "Just ready to go, he entered his mother's parlor. She went out with him to his horse to say the last words and to see him depart. She told him that she would never again see him in this world, gave him her blessing, and commended him to God. He then mounted his horse and rode away, while she followed him with a last look, until he vanished from sight."

Who witnessed this moment of departure? Was the camera on Josephus Cornwall's mother, following her son with the last look? Or on the son himself, glancing back as he vanishes from sight? The gravity of the decisive break demands narrative. Conflicting details must be resolved, reworked into a plausible whole. Aging memories will be recorded as gospel. Children recount as the given of their personal and cultural history what neither they nor even their parents could possibly have known, for example the "providential interposition" that was said to have saved Josephus Cornwall's life when he was an infant in Georgia: "It was a peculiarity of that section of the state that mad dogs were very common. One day when his parents were busy he was left in the house alone in his cradle. A mad dog entered the room, walked around it and went away, but never molested him." What witness saw the mad dog enter the room? Did the witness take action, or merely observe and report, trusting the "providential interposition" to save the baby?

Yet it was through generations of just such apparently omniscient narrators that the crossing stories became elevated to a kind of single master odyssey, its stations of veneration fixed. There were the Platte, the Sandy, the Big and Little Sandys. There was the Green River. Fort Hall. Independence Rock. The Sweetwater. There were the Humboldt, the Humboldt Sink, the Hastings cut-off. The names were so deeply embedded in the stories I heard as a child that when I happened at age twenty to see the Green River, through the windows of a train crossing Wyoming, I was astonished by this apparent evidence that it actually existed, a fact on the ground, there to be seen—entirely unearned—by anyone passing by. Just as there were stations of veneration, so there were objects of veneration, relics of those who had made the redeeming journey. "The old potato masher which the Cornwall family brought across the plains in 1846" was not the only family totem given by my grandmother's cousins to the Pacific University Museum in 1957. "After consulting with certain of the heirs," Oliver Huston wrote, the cousins had also determined "that it will be advisable to turn over to the Museum at that time the small desk sent Grandfather in 1840 by William Johnson from Hawaii, and also certain mementoes of Grandmother Geiger," specifically "the blouse which formed part of her wedding costume" and "the old shawl or shoulder wrap she wore in her later years." So Saxon Brown, the heroine of Jack London's curious "California" novel *The Valley of the Moon*, could hold in her hands her mother's red satin corset ("the pioneer finery of a frontier woman who had crossed the plains") and see pass before her, "from East to West, across a continent, the great hegira of the land-hungry Anglo-Saxon. It was part and fiber of her. She had been nursed on its traditions and its facts from the lips of those who had taken part."

As repeated, this was an odyssey the most important aspect of which was that it offered moral or spiritual "tests," or challenges, with fatal consequences for failure. Josiah Royce's parents, traveling with only their two-year-old daughter, three other emigrants, and a manuscript list of landmarks that stopped at the Humboldt Sink, found themselves lost on the Carson desert, "confused, almost stupefied," "dazed," "half-senseless," suffering for a period "the same fatal horror of desolation and death that had assailed the Donner Party in the Truckee pass." Children who died of cholera got buried on the trail. Women who believed they could keep some token of their mother's house (the rosewood chest, the flat silver) learned to jettison memory and keep moving. Sentiment, like grief and dissent, cost time. A hesitation, a moment spent looking back, and the grail was forfeited. Independence Rock, west of Fort Laramie on the Sweetwater

River, was so named because the traveler who had not reached that point by the Fourth of July, Independence Day, would not reach the Sierra Nevada before snow closed the passes.

The diaries of emigrants refer to the Sierra Nevada as "the most dreaded moment," "the Great Bugaboo," the source of "sleepless nights," "disturbed dreams." *Without house or home*: Sarah Royce and her husband and child abandoned their wagon and made it through the Sierra, with the help of a United States Army relief party, only ten days before the passes closed. Even while the passes remained open, there would be snow. There would be the repeated need to ford and again ford the Truckee or the Carson. There would be the repeated need to unload and reload the wagons. There would be recent graves, wrecked wagons, and, at Donner Lake, after the winter of 1846–47, human as well as animal bones, and the trees notched to show the depth of the fatal winter's snowpack. This is the entry in William Kilgore's diary for August 1, 1852:

> Ice and frost this morning. Four miles to Red Lake. This is ... the head of Salmon Trout, or Carson River. It is a small lake and is within one mi. of the summit of the Sierra Nevada. From this lake to the summit the ascent is very great, some places being almost perpendicular.... Four mi. from the summit we cross a small creek, a tributary of the Sacramento.... At this creek we stop to noon. Here we help inter a young man who died last night of bilious fever. He was from Michigan. His name was Joseph Ricker. His parents reside in the state of Maine. Here we ascend another ridge of this mt. It is higher than the one we have just passed, being 9,339 ft. above the sea. From the foot to the summit it is five miles, and in ascending and descending we travel over four miles of snow, and it from two to 20 ft. deep.... 21 miles today.

To read these crossing accounts and diaries is to be struck by the regularity with which a certain apprehension of darkness enters the quest, a shadow of moral ambiguity that becomes steadily more pervasive until that moment when the traveler realizes that the worst of the Sierra is behind him. "The Summit is crossed!" one such diary reads. "We are in California! Far away in the haze the dim outlines of the Sacramento Valley are discernible! We are on the down grade now and our famished animals may pull us through. We are in the midst of huge pines, so large as to challenge belief. Hutton is dead. Others are worse. I am better." By this point, in every such journey, there would have been the accidents, the broken bones, the infected and even the amputated hands and feet. There would have been the fevers. Sarah Royce remembered staying awake all night after a man in her party died of cholera, and hearing the wind whip his winding sheet like "some vindictive creature struggling restlessly in bonds." There would have been the hurried burials, in graves often unmarked and sometimes deliberately obliterated. "Before leaving the Humboldt River there was one death, Miss Mary Campbell," Nancy Hardin Cornwall's son Joseph recalled. "She was buried right in our road and the whole train of wagons was driven over her grave to conceal it from the Indians. Miss Campbell died of mountain fever, and Mother by waiting on her caught the fever and for a long time she lingered, apparently between life and death, but at last recovered. Miss Campbell was an orphan, her mother having died at Green River."

There would have been, darkest of all, the betrayals, the suggestions that the crossing might not after all be a noble odyssey, might instead be a mean scrambling for survival, a blind flight on the part of Josiah Royce's "blind and stupid and homeless generation of selfish wanderers." Not all emigrants, to take just one example, cared for all orphans. It was on the Little Sandy that an emigrant named Bernard J. Reid, who had put down two hundred dollars to secure a place on an 1849 crossing, saw first "an emigrant wagon apparently abandoned by its owners" and then "a rude head-board indicating a new grave," which turned out to be that of the Reverend Robert Gilmore and his wife Mary, who had died the same day of cholera. This account comes to us from Reid's diary, which was found by his family in the 1950s, entrusted to Mary McDougall Gordon for editing, and published in 1983 by the Stanford University Press as *Overland to California with the Pioneer Line*. On turning from the grave to the apparently abandoned wagon, Reid tells us, he was "surprised to see a neatly dressed girl of about 17, sitting on the wagon tongue, her feet resting on the grass, and her eyes apparently directed at vacancy."

She seemed like one dazed or in a dream and did not seem to notice me till I spoke to her. I then learned from her in reply to my questions that she was Miss Gilmore, whose parents had died two days before; that her brother, younger than herself, was sick in the wagon, probably with cholera; that their oxen were lost or stolen by the Indians; and that the train they had been traveling with, after waiting for three days on account of the sickness and death of her parents, had gone on that morning, fearful, if they delayed longer, of being caught by winter in the Sierra Nevada mountains…. The people of her train had told her that probably her oxen would yet be found, or at any rate some other train coming along with oxen to spare would take her and her brother and their wagon along.

"Who could tell the deep sense of bereavement, distress and desolation that weighed on that poor girl's heart, there in the wilderness with no telling what fate was in store for her and her sick brother?" Reid asks his readers and surely also himself. Such memories might have seemed difficult to reconcile with the conviction that one had successfully met the tests or challenges required to enter the new life. The redemptive power of the crossing was, nonetheless, the fixed idea of the California settlement, and one that raised a further question: for what exactly, and at what cost, had one been redeemed? When you jettison others so as not to be "caught by winter in the Sierra Nevada mountains," do you deserve not to be caught? When you survive at the cost of Miss Gilmore and her brother, do you survive at all?

5

I WAS BORN in Sacramento, and lived in California most of my life. I learned to swim in the Sacramento and the American, before the dams. I learned to drive on the levees up and down-river from Sacramento. Yet California has remained in some way impenetrable to me, a wearying enigma, as it has to many of us who are from there. We worry it, correct and revise it, try and fail to define our relationship to it and its relationship to the rest of the country. We make declamatory breaks with it, as Josiah Royce did when he left Berkeley for Harvard. "There is no philosophy in California—from Siskiyou to Ft. Yuma, and from the Golden Gate to the summit of the Sierras," he had written to William James, who eventually responded to this *cri de coeur* with the offer from Harvard. We make equally declamatory returns, as Frank Norris did, determined before his thirtieth birthday "to do some great work with the West and California as a background, and which will be at the same time thoroughly American." The intention, Norris wrote to William Dean Howells, who had reviewed *McTeague* favorably, was "to write three novels around the one subject of *Wheat*. First, a story of California (the producer), second, a story of Chicago (the distributor), third, a story of Europe (the consumer) and in each to keep the idea of this huge Niagara of wheat rolling from West to East. I think a big Epic trilogy could be made out of such a subject, that at the same time would be modern and thoroughly American. The idea is so big that it frightens me at times but I have about made up my mind to have a try at it."

Frank Norris's experience with his subject appears to have been exclusively literary. He was raised in Chicago and then San Francisco, where he met the young woman he would eventually marry at a debutante dance. He spent a year in Paris, studying art and writing a medieval romance, *Yvernelle, A Tale of Feudal*

France, which his mother arranged to have published. He spent four years at Berkeley without taking the courses necessary for a degree, then a year as a non-degree student at Harvard. He covered the prelude to the Boer War for *Collier's* and *The San Francisco Chronicle,* the Santiago campaign in Cuba for *McClure's.* At the time he was seized by the trilogy-of-wheat notion, he was living in New York, at 61 Washington Square South.

The Octopus, published in 1901 and based on what was at the time quite recent history in the San Joaquin Valley, was, in the best sense, worked up: through well-situated friends, Ernest Peixotto and his wife (the Peixottos were a prominent San Francisco Jewish family, and Ernest Peixotto's older sister Jessica, an economist, was one of the first women on the faculty of the University of California), Norris managed an introduction to a couple who ran five thousand acres of wheat in San Benito County, and arranged to spend the summer of 1899 on their ranch near Hollister. San Benito County presented a gentler, more coastal landscape than the San Joaquin, which was where Norris intended to set his novel ("San Juan de Guadalajara," the mission in *The Octopus,* was a borrow from Mission San Juan Bautista near Hollister, there being no missions in the San Joaquin), but it was nonetheless a setting in which an attentive reporter could absorb the mechanics of a big wheat operation.

The Octopus opens on a day in "the last half of September, the very end of the dry season," a day when "all Tulare County, all the vast reaches of the San Joaquin Valley—in fact all South Central California, was bone dry, parched, and baked and crisped after four months of cloudless weather, when the day seemed always at noon, and the sun blazed white hot over the valley from the Coast Range in the west to the foothills of the Sierras in the east." The stuff of the novel, the incidents on which the narrative turns, came directly from actual events in what was then Tulare County. In 1893 in Tulare County there had been the killing by a sheriff's posse of John Sontag, an embittered Southern Pacific brakeman who had spent the previous three years dynamiting track and robbing trains, killing and wounding several lawmen. In *The Octopus* Sontag would become "Dyke," who commandeers an engineer to escape his pursuers, foils their attempt to derail him by reversing the engine, abandons it, and is taken by the posse.

Thirteen years before, in 1880, there had been, at a place then called Mussel Slough but after the incident renamed "Lucerne," the shootout between federal marshals acting for the Southern Pacific, which had become through its federal land grants the largest landowner in California, and a group of local ranchers who were growing wheat on land leased from the railroad. The ranchers, under the rather willful misapprehension that their lease agreements gave them the right to buy the land at $2.50 an acre (the agreements were vaguely worded, but quite clearly stated that the land would be made available "at various figures from $2.50 upward per acre," "upward" being the word the ranchers preferred to miss), refused to pay the price, $17 to $40 an acre, ultimately set on the land. The railroad obtained eviction orders, the ranchers resisted, and both the ranchers and the federal marshals sent to evict them began firing. Six ranchers ultimately died in this confrontation, which not only provided the climactic incident for *The Octopus*—the showdown between eleven ranchers and the U.S. marshals sent in to enforce eviction orders—but also influenced the final scenes in Josiah Royce's only work of fiction, *The Feud of Oakfield Creek: A Novel of California Life*, based on the Sacramento squatters' riots of 1850.

For the San Francisco threads in his narrative, Norris drew on even more recent events: in 1899, there had been the celebrated publication in *The San Francisco Examiner* of Edwin Markham's "The Man with the Hoe," a rhetorical poem that decried the exploitation of labor. An epic poem in the style of "The Man with the Hoe" appears in *The Octopus* as "The Toilers," the newspaper poem that makes an instant celebrity of its author, Presley, the irresolute graduate of "an Eastern college" who is the novel's protagonist. The publication of "The Toilers" enables Presley to dine at the table of "the Railroad King" (Blue Point oysters, *purée à la Derby*, ortolan patties, *grenadins* of bass and stuffed salmon, Londonderry pheasants, *escalopes* of duck, *rissolettes à la pompadour*, asparagus rushed to the kitchen of the Railroad King by special train within hours of its cutting), even as, outside in the fog, the dispossessed widow of one of the evicted and killed San Joaquin wheat growers is literally starving to death, falling into her terminal coma on a vacant lot at the top of the Clay Street hill, her small daughter at her side, her older daughter already descended into prostitution.

Presley knows nothing of the fate of the widow, but had by fortuitous narrative design run into the older daughter, her degradation apparent, that very afternoon, rendering this dinner an occasion for him of considerable clarity. He sits at the opulent table of the Railroad King as the Château Latour is poured and imagines the clink of the glasses "drowned in the explosion of revolvers" in the San Joaquin Valley. He sees, for an instant, "that splendid house sacked to its foundations, the tables overturned, the pictures torn, the hangings blazing, and Liberty, the red-handed Man in the Street, grimed with powder smoke, foul with the gutter, rush yelling, torch in hand, through every door." The intercutting from the dinner table inside to the dying widow and child outside is insistently allegorical, operatic, outsized, as is the subsequent death of the railroad's agent in the hold of a cargo ship taking on wheat destined for Asia, consigned there by the blind force of the market even as widows and orphans starve for want of a heel of bread on the streets of San Francisco:

> Deafened with the roar of the grain, blinded and made dumb with its chaff, he threw himself forward with clutching fingers, rolling upon his back, and lay there, moving feebly, the head rolling from side to side. The Wheat, leaping continuously from the chute, poured around him. It filled the pockets of the coat, it crept up the sleeves and trouser legs, it covered the great, protuberant stomach, it ran at last in rivulets into the distended, gasping mouth. It covered the face.
>
> Upon the surface of the Wheat, under the chute, nothing moved but the Wheat itself. There was no sign of life. Then, for an instant, the surface stirred. A hand, fat, with short fingers and swollen veins, reached up, clutching, then fell limp and prone. In another instant it was covered.

The Octopus has been, from the outset, a troubling work, in part because its apparent relentlessness could be so readily dismissed. As recently as 1991, in a discussion of the railroad's role in the development of California, the quarterly publication of the California Historical Society was trying to separate the significance of that role from Norris's "shrill, anti-corporate rhetoric," his "superficial and distorted tale," and pointing out that the cartoon image of the Southern Pacific as an octopus, with portraits of Leland Stanford and Charles Crocker for its eyes, long predated Norris's use of it. There would seem on the face of it to be nothing subtle in *The Octopus*: the novel is barely under way when Presley catches sight of a train, and immediately translates it into:

> the galloping monster, the terror of steel and steam, with its single eye, cyclopean, red, shooting from horizon to horizon … the symbol of a vast power, huge, terrible, flinging the echo of its thunder over all the reaches of the valley, leaving blood and destruction in its path; the leviathan, with tentacles of steel clutching into the soil, the soulless Force, the iron-hearted Power, the monster, the Colossus, the Octopus.

Yet *The Octopus* remains perhaps the most complex statement to date of the California condition, and a deeply ambiguous work. Nothing about the novel, on examination, is quite what it seems. Edwin Markham's "The Man with the Hoe" may have galvanized sentiment against the exploitation of labor, but it was said by its author to have been inspired, curiously, in one of the many apparent connections in California life that serve only as baffles to further inquiry, by study of a Millet painting owned by Charles Crocker, one of the Central and Southern Pacific's "Big Four," in other words a Railroad King. Frank Norris may have considered the Southern Pacific "the soulless Force, the iron-hearted Power, the monster, the Colossus, the Octopus," but two years before he conceived the novel he was an editor of, and writing regularly for, *The Wave*, a San Francisco weekly financed by the Southern Pacific to promote Charles Crocker's new Del Monte Hotel in Monterey. *The Octopus* is not, as it might logically seem to be, a story of an agrarian society overtaken by the brute momentum of industrialization: the octopus, if there is one, turns out to be neither the railroad nor corporate ownership but indifferent nature, which is characterized, to somewhat unsettling effect, in much the same language as the railroad was earlier: "a gigantic engine, a vast cyclopean power, huge, terrible, a leviathan with a heart of steel, knowing no compunction, no forgiveness, no tolerance;

crushing out the human atom standing in its way, with nirvanic calm, the agony of destruction sending never a jar...."

There are, as drawn by Norris, serious ambiguities about even the climactic shootout, not the least of which are that the ranchers had never owned the land in dispute, had chosen to misread the lease agreements on the gamble that other growers would band together in such force as to render the papers useless ("Oh, rot!" one of them cries when warned to take a closer look at the leases. "Of course the railroad will sell at two-fifty. We've got the contracts"), and had taken up raising wheat on railroad land in the first place only because the railroad was there to transport the wheat. These wheat ranchers in *The Octopus* are in no sense simple farmers. They are farmers with tickers in their offices, connecting the San Joaquin by wire with San Francisco and Chicago and New York and finally with Liverpool, at that time the nerve center of the wheat market. "Fluctuations in the price of the world's crop during and after the harvest," Norris wrote, "thrilled straight to the office of Los Muertos, to that of the Quien Sabe, to Osterman's, and to Broderson's [the ranches in the novel]. During a flurry in the Chicago wheat pits in the August of that year, which had affected even the San Francisco market, Harran and Magnus had sat up nearly half of one night watching the strip of white tape jerking unsteadily from the reel."

Nor are Magnus Derrick and his son Harran and Osterman and Broderson and Annixter even "farmers" at all, in the conventional sense of the word: they had come to the San Joaquin as an entrepreneurial move, after other ventures (in mining, in politics, in whatever had presented itself) had failed or gone dry, and after, most significantly and most ambiguously, the railroad had opened the San Joaquin to profitable cultivation by offering, for the first time, a way to move its crops to market. The proprietor of Los Muertos, Magnus Derrick, the nearest the novel gets to a tragic hero, is nonetheless characterized by Norris as a high-stakes gambler, a miner at heart, come to the San Joaquin in search of the quick killing that had eluded him in the Comstock Lode:

> It was the true California spirit that found expression through him, the spirit of the West, unwilling to occupy itself with details, refusing to wait, to be patient, to achieve by legitimate plodding; the miner's instinct of wealth

acquired in a single night prevailed, in spite of all. It was in this frame of mind that Magnus and the multitude of other ranchers of whom he was a type, farmed their ranches. They had no love for their land. They were not attached to the soil. They worked their ranches as a quarter of a century before they had worked their mines…. To get all there was out of the land, to squeeze it dry, to exhaust it, seemed their policy. When, at last, the land worn out, would refuse to yield, they would invest their money in something else; by then, they would all have made fortunes. They did not care.

Norris's San Joaquin wheat growers, then, were of a type common enough in California: the speculators noted by Charles Nordhoff in 1874, entrepreneurs in search of the shrewd venture, men who might themselves have been running the railroad had they seen the opportunity, held the right cards, been quicker players. Confronted with the demands of the railroad (which was pressing not only to evict the ranchers but to raise freight rates) and its bought members of the Railroad Commission, the first response of the ranchers in *The Octopus* is to buy a commissioner of their own. Even in this venture not quick enough players, they buy the wrong man: Magnus Derrick's politically ambitious older son, who sells out to the railroad. That the only actual conflict in *The Octopus* turns out to be between successful and failed members of the same entrepreneurial class (members in some cases of the same families) creates a deep and troubled confusion in the novel, a dissonance its author grasped but failed to resolve. This dissonance, which had to do with the slippage between the way Californians perceived themselves and the way they were, between what they believed to be their unlimited possibilities and the limitations implicit in their own character and history, might have been Norris's great subject, but he died, at thirty-two, of peritonitis, before he could work it through. The confusions here have not been mine alone.

In the 1860s … William Henry Brewer [the chief assistant to Josiah Dwight Whitney in his 1860–64 geological survey of California] … described the southwestern San Joaquin Valley as a "plain of absolute desolation." At the turn-of-the-century, the crusading novelist Frank Norris pictured the valley as "bone dry, parched, and baked and crisped" where the "day seemed always at noon." But, a century after Brewer's report, and less than half a century after Norris's observations, it became clear that by just adding water, this vale of sterility would bloom as the nation's garden.

Just by adding water. The above appears on the United States Bureau of Reclamation's web site, on the page prepared by the Bureau's History Program to deal with the Central Valley Project's San Luis Unit, West San Joaquin Division. *We had an irrigation problem, so we built the greatest dams the world has known*, was my equally can-do approach to the subject in "Our California Heritage." This, according to the same Bureau of Reclamation web page, is what it takes to "just add water" to the San Joaquin:

Melting snow and runoff high in the mountains of Northern California are the first steps of a trek through the heart of the state. Once in the Sacramento–San Joaquin River Delta, water is released from storage and lifted 197 feet by the Tracy Pumping Plant. The flow is then conveyed about 70 miles south to the O'Neill Forebay via the California Aqueduct (a State Water Project, or SWP, feature) and the Federal Delta-Mendota Canal. Delta-Mendota carries water southeasterly from the Tracy Pumping Plant, eventually arriving at the O'Neill Pumping-Generating Plant. Running parallel to the Delta-Mendota Canal, the Edmund G. Brown California Aqueduct travels directly into the O'Neill Forebay. The O'Neill Dam, Pumping-Generating Plant and Forebay are all a half mile from the San Luis Dam and Reservoir. Units of the William R. Gianelli Pumping-Generating Plant (formerly known as the San Luis Pumping-Generating Plant) raises water from O'Neill Forebay into San Luis Reservoir. Releases from San Luis Reservoir are directed into the 101.3-mile-long San Luis Canal. Seventeen miles south of San Luis Reservoir, the Dos Amigos Pumping Station lifts the water again, so the flow can continue another 85 miles across central California. Journey's end for the San Luis Canal is the Federal terminus at Kettleman City. At Kettleman City, the SWP's California Aqueduct carries on to service farms, recreational users and municipalities as far south as Los Angeles. When drought strikes California, and Delta flows cannot supply State and Federal water projects, water is released back into the O'Neill Forebay, coursing southward through the California Aqueduct. During irrigation season, water is released from the reservoir back through the pump-generator units of Gianelli to the O'Neill Forebay, generating electric power. Protecting the canal from streams crossing its path are the Los Banos and Little Panoche Detention Dams and Reservoirs. Other Unit features include the San Luis Drain, Pleasant Valley Pumping Plant, and the Coalinga Canal. The operation of the San Luis Unit is a fairly simple procedure for those brief periods when man and nature are in harmony, but both seldom have been in synchronization.

Just by adding water.
This vale of sterility would bloom as the nation's garden.
A fairly simple procedure for those brief periods when man and nature are in harmony.

The San Luis Dam, at the time it was completed in 1968, cost three billion dollars. What this taxpayer-financed investment meant to the San Joaquin's Westlands Water District was that several hundred growers, most of them corporate, would have the assurance of water, ditches, big automated Rain Birds moving all day with the sun. These growers would also have the assurance of "irrigation subsidies," which by 1987, according to Gerald Haslam's *The Great Central Valley*, amounted to twenty-seven million dollars, eleven million of which went to the Southern Pacific Land Company. "You can't buck the railroad" was a common phrase in my childhood, but I never ventured into its local application.

HOLLISTER, THE SAN Benito County town near which Frank Norris spent the summer of 1899 researching *The Octopus*, was named for, and built on land at that time only recently owned by, an emigrant from Ohio named William Welles Hollister. In 1852, William Welles Hollister had driven some three hundred head of cattle from Ohio to California, sold them, and returned home. In 1853, he again made the crossing, this time driving not cattle but sheep, five thousand head. This time he stayed, and over the next twenty years he and two partners, Albert and Thomas Dibblee, accumulated some two hundred thousand acres of ranch land ranging from Monterey and San Benito Counties south to Santa Barbara. William Welles Hollister was the sole owner of thirty-nine thousand acres in Santa Barbara County alone, the several ranches collectively referred to as "the Hollister ranch," which at the time of its sale in the late 1960s incorporated the twenty miles of coastline running south from Point Conception and constituted one of the last intact coastal properties of its size between the Oregon and Mexican borders.

Such extensive holdings, typically acquired on very little equity, were not, at the time of their acquisition, entirely unusual, nor did William Welles Hollister and the Dibblee brothers even count among the largest private owners. In 1882, Richard O'Neill and James Flood together bought more than two hundred thousand acres straddling the line between Orange and San Diego Counties, a holding undivided until 1940, when the Flood heirs took the San Diego acreage and the O'Neill heirs took the Orange. Further north in Orange County, the heirs of James Irvine held the ninety-three thousand acres he had acquired in the 1870s by combining acreage originally granted to the Sepulveda and Yorba families, a property that stretched from the mountains to the sea and covered one-fifth of the county. By the time James Ben Ali Haggin and Lloyd Tevis consolidated their properties in 1890 as the Kern County Land Company, they had acquired, throughout the Southwest, almost a million and a half acres, roughly a third of them in the San Joaquin Valley. Henry Miller, another big holder, who once said that he could drive his cattle from Oregon to the Mexican border and sleep them every night on his own land, had arrived in San Francisco in 1850 with six dollars in his pocket and gone to work as a butcher. Within twenty years, he and his partner, Charles Lux, also a butcher in San Francisco, had gained control of ten to twelve million acres in California, a million and a half owned outright and grazing rights on the rest, vast tracts largely acquired through imaginative interpretation of the small print in federal legislation.

Miller, for example, made deals with cash-hungry veterans, buying up, at a discount, the land options to which they were entitled as a service benefit. He also made deft use of the federal Reclamation Act of 1850, which had granted California's "swamp and overflowed" land to the state, which in turn sold it (the "virtual gift" noted by Charles Nordhoff in 1874) for $1.15 to $1.25 an acre, an amount returned to any buyer who could demonstrate use of the land. Henry Miller was instrumental in getting large parts of California classified as swamp, in one favored telling by hooking up a team of horses to tow a rowboat over the land in question. Nor, at the time, was this even an obscure angle: *Power and Land in California*, the 1971 report prepared by the Ralph Nader Task Force and later published as *Politics of Land*, noted that two of the state surveyors responsible for classifying land as "swamp and over-flowed" each left office with three hundred thousand acres.

Such landowners tended to have not much interest in presenting themselves as the proprietors of farms or estates on the eastern, which was to say the English, model. William Henry Brewer, when he came out from Pennsylvania in 1860 to assist Josiah Dwight Whitney in the first geological survey of California, complained that the owner of eighty thousand acres between Gaviota Pass and San Luis Obispo lived "about half as well as a man would at home who owned a hundred-acre farm paid for." Almost a century later, Carey McWilliams, in *California: The Great Exception*, remarked on the almost total absence of conventional "rural" life in California, which would have been, were it a country, the world's seventh-largest agricultural producer: "The large shipper-growers 'farm by phone' from headquarters in San Francisco or Los Angeles. Many of them travel, nowadays, exclusively by plane in visiting their various 'operations.' … Their relationship to the land is as casual as that of the migratory workers they employ." To live as farmers would have been, for the acquisitors of these operations, a bewilderingly alien concept, since their holdings were about something else altogether: they were temporary chips in the greater game of capital formation.

This is well known, yet remains an elusive point for many Californians, particularly those with a psychic investment in one or another heightened version of the founding period. The heroine of Jack London's *The Valley of the Moon*, Saxon Brown, when hard times and union troubles come to Oakland, finds herself "dreaming of the arcadian days of her people, when they had not lived in cities nor been vexed with labor unions and employers' associations. She would remember the old people's tales of self-sufficingness, when they shot or raised their own meat, grew their own vegetables, were their own blacksmiths and carpenters, made their own shoes—yes, and spun the cloth of the clothes they wore…. A farmer's life must be fine, she thought. Why was it that people had to live in cities? Why had times changed?" In fact almost no one in California speaks of "farmers," in the sense the word is used in the rest of the country, and yet this persistent suggestion of constructive husbandry continues to cloud the retrospect. What amounted to the subsidized monopolization of California tends to be reinvented either as "settlement" (the settlers came, the desert bloomed) or, even more ideally, as a kind of foresighted commitment on the part of the acquisitors, a dedication to living at one with both the elemental wilderness and an improved patrician past.

"We had all shared in the glamour of immense, privately owned land," one of William Welles Hollister's seven grandchildren, Jane Hollister Wheelwright, wrote in *The Ranch Papers: A California Memoir*, the book she published in 1988, some twenty years after the sale of the Hollister ranch. "We lived in a fantastic but real world of our own discovery: square miles of impassable terrain, wild cattle threatening on the trail, single coyotes caterwauling like a pack, pumas screaming, storms felling giant oaks, washouts that marooned us for days, wildfires that lasted weeks and scorched whole mountain ranges." Her father, she tells us, "rarely wore his *chapaderos*," and did not use his silver-inlaid saddle, "but our Mexican ranch hands knew him for what he was. They called him '*El Patrón*.'" In 1961, after the death of the father, the daughter returns alone to the ranch, the point at which there appears in her memoir the first shadow on the glamour: "No one was there to meet me—not even the ranch hands," she writes. "I had none of the honor and recognition given automatically to *El Patrón*. The ranch seemed deserted. I was being deliberately avoided. Wandering aimlessly, I found myself walking into the canyon that stretched in back of the old family home.... The disappointment at seeing no one quickly faded. At least the land was there to greet me."

Jane Hollister Wheelwright's sense of her entitlement seems, in *The Ranch Papers*, more layered than that of many inheritors, more complicated, even tortured. The Hollisters, she concludes, "had been given a chance to live a part of history, to experience an era virtually extinct elsewhere in California." She remains reluctant to confront the contradictions in that history. Her idea of what the land meant remains heightened, and in the familiar way. She mentions in passing that the ranch supported "a large herd of white-faced Hereford cattle," but offers no sense of a working cattle operation. She sees her father as "one of the last of the gentlemen cattlemen of the era of large family ranches in California." She tells us that she and her twin brother "had grown up in a trance, like sleepwalkers, muffled by the land's huge embrace," and accompanies a photograph of herself at twenty with an apparently meaningful quotation from Aldo Leopold's *A Sand County Almanac*: "There are two kinds of people: those who can live without wild things and those who cannot."

Yet she seems to have quite deliberately chosen, at age twenty-four, to live without wild things: she married a psychiatrist, Joseph Wheelwright, was herself analyzed by Carl Jung, became a lay analyst, gave birth to a daughter in China and a son in London, and returned to California with her husband to found, in 1943 in San Francisco, the world's first Jungian training center. The description she gives of her 1961 return to the ranch is suggestive. All such returns, she tells us, involved a learned process of "reaching into the mood of the place," of shedding "city demands." She had come to understand the necessity of cultivating "calming" through "the monotony of walking," of encouraging the accelerated onset of what others might call by other names but she called "the big letdown": "Our coast requires a descent always. For those new to the place the letdown is more often experienced as an unpleasant locked-in feeling, an immobilizing depression."

What we seem to have here, then, is a story of an acquisitive grandfather, a father who retreated into the huge holding that allowed him to play *El Patrón* (even the daughter who reveres him mentions, in the guise of a virtue, "his power of passivity"), and a daughter, Jane Hollister, who ran guiltily for daylight. It was nonetheless Jane Hollister Wheelwright, not her brothers or cousins, who inherited from the father in 1961 the power to vote more than half the shares in the ranches. "My father must have known that I was as stubborn as he and would try to tackle the problems; and as the only woman I would be outside male competition," she wrote in *The Ranch Papers*. "But the outrage it caused only compounded the existing situation, and so the struggle began amongst the seven of us." That the nature of this struggle is not described in *The Ranch Papers* is a telling lacuna. It would appear to have focused, since the need to sell was a given, on the terms of the sale: to whom, for how much, in return for what contingent agreements. One senses that the daughter may have favored, probably more than her brothers and cousins did, the ultimate buyer: a Los Angeles developer, described in *The Ranch Papers*, again ideally, as "an enterprising but environment-minded Los Angeles man," whose plan was to rezone the property into hundred-acre parcels and present the whole as an exclusive planned retreat.

In California as elsewhere, a buyer with a plan for this kind of low-density development signifies something quite specific: this is a buyer who means to pay less for the land than one with a plan for more intensive development. During the same years when the Hollisters were falling out over this issue, James Irvine's great-granddaughter, Joan Irvine Smith, someone else who had "shared in the glamour of immensely, privately owned land," was fighting the same kind of family fight, but from a different angle: it was Joan Irvine who successfully insisted, against the opposition of some in her own family, that the eighty-eight thousand acres that remained of the Irvine ranch in Orange County be intensively developed. Whether Jane Hollister's decision to divide her grandfather's ranch into hundred-acre parcels was in the end more intrinsically tuned to the spirit of the place than Joan Irvine's quite different decision remains an unresolved question. I recall in the early seventies seeing advertising for what came to be called "Hollister Ranch," emphasizing how very few select achievers could hope to live there. As it happens my father had been at Berkeley with one of the Hollisters, someone of an age to have been one of Jane Hollister's brothers or cousins; I do not remember his name and my father is dead. I remember this at all only because, every time we drove south and again at the time the ranch was sold, my father mentioned that the effort to keep their holding intact had left the Hollisters unable to afford, in the early 1930s, during the Depression, to let one of their children finish Berkeley. This was offered as a lesson, I am unsure to what point.

The lesson Jane Hollister Wheelwright took from the sale of her family's ranch, proceeding as she did from within what amounts to a fable of confusion, concerned what she called the "debatable" questions: "whether land can belong to anyone, or whether one belongs to the land." She concluded, unsurprisingly, that land belonged to no one. Yet it did: at the time the Hollister ranch was sold, in the late 1960s, according to a Ralph Nader Study Group report on land use in California, roughly two and a half million acres of California still belonged to the Southern Pacific. Almost half a million acres belonged to the Shasta Forest Company. A third of a million acres belonged to Tenneco, another third of a million each to the Tejon Ranch Company, Standard Oil, and Boise Cascade. Two hundred seventy-eight thousand acres belonged to Georgia Pacific. Two hundred and fifty thousand belonged to Pacific Gas & Electric. Two hundred thousand belonged to Occidental Petroleum, 192,000 to Sunkist, 171,062 to Pacific Lumber, 155,000 to Fibreboard Incorporated, and 152,000 to the Newhall Land and Farming Company. Another 1,350,045 acres belonged to, among them, American Forest Products, Times Mirror, the Penn Central, Hammond Lumber, Kaiser Industries, the Masonite Corporation, J. G. Boswell, International Paper, Diamond International Corporation, Vail, Miller & Lux, and the Irvine Ranch Company. Some of these were California companies; some were not. All played a role in determining

989

which of California's possibilities would be realized and which limited. Most were diversified, no more interested in what grew or grazed on their land than Jane Hollister had been, to another point, in what grew or grazed on hers, but quicker players, all of them, than the Hollisters had proved to be.

Jane Hollister's mother, Lottie Steffens Hollister, was the sister of Lincoln Steffens, who wrote *The Shame of the Cities* and later said of the Soviet Union that he had seen the future and it worked. Lincoln Steffens was Jane Hollister's "Uncle Steffie," and she his "Lady Jane." The Steffens children had grown up in a house in Sacramento a few blocks from the house in which, in 1908, my father was born. The Steffens house later became the Governor's Mansion, in which both Jerry Brown and his sister Kathleen lived during the years their father, Edmund G. ("Pat") Brown, was the thirty-second governor of California. Jerry Brown was himself the thirty-fourth governor of California. Kathleen Brown, in 1994, tried and failed to become the thirty-seventh. I went to Berkeley with their sister Barbara. There are many connections in California life, and yet, like Charles Crocker's Millet as the source for Edwin Markham's "The Man with the Hoe," not much connects: my mother's father, who lived in Sacramento but grew up on the Georgetown Divide in El Dorado County, remained convinced to his death that Edwin Markham, who had been superintendent of schools in El Dorado County from 1882 until 1886, did not himself write "The Man with the Hoe," but was given the poem by, in my grandfather's words, "an emigrant wayfarer from whom Markham purchased it for a small amount of money, and thereby helped the traveler along his way." My grandfather seemed to have in his memory bank a fairly complete dossier on Edwin Markham (the names of his three wives, the dates of his and their arrivals in California, even the houses in which they had lived), and could be quite insistent about what he believed to be the true provenance of "The Man with the Hoe," but his attitude toward the alleged appropriation was sufficiently opaque to encourage me, as a child, to ask my mother if my grandfather had in fact been the emigrant wayfarer. "He wasn't an emigrant," my mother said, settling at least that question.

* * *

Jane Hollister Wheelwright, who was herself born in Sacramento, saw as a kind of death the intrusion onto the Hollister ranch of two Chevron pipelines ("I can only believe that their appearance on the ranch means just one thing: another expression of man's historical arrogance and hatred of nature") but, still operating within the fable of an ideal personal past, was untroubled, even comforted, by the presence of the Southern Pacific, which her grandfather had actively supported and to which he had given a sixty-foot right-of-way along the coast. On her farewell rides through the ranch she observed the daily appearance of *The Daylight*, the Southern Pacific's principal passenger train to Los Angeles, and noted that it "seemed to belong there, and did not jar the feeling of the coast in the slightest. The noises it made recalled my childhood when we had no other way of telling time, and the sound of a whistle in the distance meant we were hopelessly late for lunch."

The eighth governor of California, Leland Stanford, was at the time of his election the president of the Central Pacific and later the president of the Southern Pacific. Hiram Johnson, the twenty-third governor of California, was elected as a reform candidate pledged to break the power of the Southern Pacific. Hiram Johnson's father, Grove Johnson, had fled upstate New York under indictment for forgery in 1863, settled in Sacramento, become clerk of the county Swamp Land Board, been implicated in two vote-rigging scandals, and been elected, in 1877, to the California State Assembly. "The interests of the railroad and Sacramento are identical, and should always remain so," the elder Johnson declared during this campaign. "They should labor together like man and wife, only to be divorced by death."

When Hiram Johnson went to Berkeley in 1884 he lived in the Chi Phi house, as did, forty-five years later, my father and my uncle and the Hollister who had to drop out of school. When I went to Berkeley some years later I lived, as did Barbara Brown, at the Tri Delt house. Her father, not yet governor of California but its attorney general, spoke at our annual father-daughter dinners. When my brother went to Berkeley five years after I did he lived at the Phi Gamma Delta, or Fiji, house, as had, sixty-some years before, Frank Norris, who remained famous in the house for having initiated its annual celebratory "Pig Dinner." This was a California, into the nineteen-fifties, so hermetic, so isolated by geography and by history and also by inclination, that when I first read *The Octopus*, at age twelve or thirteen, in Sacramento, I did not construe it to have a personal relevance, since the events described took place not in the Sacramento Valley but somewhere else, the San Joaquin.

Not much about California, on its own preferred terms, has encouraged its children to see themselves as connected to one another. The separation, of north from south—and even more acutely of west from east, of the urban coast from the agricultural valleys and of both the coast and the valleys from the mountain and desert regions to their east—was profound, fueled by the rancor of water wars and by less tangible but even more rancorous differences in attitude and culture. My mother made the trip from Sacramento to Los Angeles in 1932, to see the Olympics, and did not find reason to make it again for thirty years. In the north we had San Francisco, with its Beaux Arts buildings and eucalyptus, its yearnings backward and westward, its resolutely anecdotal "color"; a place as remote and mannered as the melancholy colonial capitals of Latin America, and as isolated. When I was at Berkeley and had gone home to Sacramento for a weekend I would sometimes take the Southern Pacific's transcontinental *City of San Francisco* back down, not the most convenient train (for one thing it was always late) but one that suggested, carrying as it did the glamour of having come across the mountains from the rest of America, that our isolation might not be an indefinite sentence.

I see now that the life I was raised to admire was entirely the product of this isolation, infinitely romantic, but in a kind of vacuum, its only antecedent aesthetic, and the aesthetic only the determined "Bohemianism" of nineteenth-century San Francisco. The clothes chosen for me as a child had a strong element of the Pre-Raphaelite, muted greens and ivories, dusty rose, what seems in retrospect an eccentric amount of black. I still have the black mantilla I was given to wear over my shoulders when I started to go to dances, not the kind of handkerchief triangle Catholic woman used to keep in their pockets and glove compartments but several yards of heavy black lace. It had been my great-grandmother's, I have no idea why, since this particular

992

great-grandmother was from Oregon, with no reason to have bought into a romance-of-the-ranchos scenario. We lived in dark houses and favored, a preference so definite that it passed as a test of character, copper and brass that had darkened and greened. We also let our silver darken, which was said to "bring out the pattern." To this day I am put off by highly polished silver: it looks "new." This predilection for the "old" extended into all areas of domestic life: dried flowers were seen to have a more subtle charm than fresh, prints should be faded, rugs worn, wallpaper streaked by the sun. Our highest moment in this area was the acquisition, in 1951, of a house in Sacramento in which the curtains on the stairs had not been changed since 1907. These curtains, which were of unlined (and faded, naturally) gold silk organza, hung almost two stories, billowed iridescent with every breath of air, and, if touched, crumbled.

Stressing as it did an extreme if ungrounded individualism, this was not an ambiance that tended toward a view of life as defined or limited or controlled, or even in any way affected, by the social and economic structures of the larger world. To be a Californian was to see oneself, if one believed the lessons the place seemed most immediately to offer, as affected only by "nature," which in turn was seen to exist simultaneously as a source of inspiration or renewal ("Born again!" John Muir noted in the journal of his first trip into Yosemite) and as the ultimate brute reckoning, the force that by guaranteeing destruction gave the place its perilous beauty. Much of the California landscape has tended to present itself as metaphor, even as litany: the redwoods (*for a thousand years in thy sight are but as yesterday*), the Mojave (*in the midst of life we are in death*), the coast at Big Sur, Mono Lake, the great vistas of the Sierra, especially those of the Yosemite Valley, which, Kevin Starr has pointed out, "offered Californians an objective correlative for their ideal sense of themselves: a people animated by heroic imperatives." Thomas Starr King saw Yosemite in 1860 and went back to the First Unitarian Church of San Francisco determined to inspire "Yosemites in the soul." Albert Bierstadt saw Yosemite in 1863 and came back to do the grandiose landscapes that made him for a dozen years the most popularly acclaimed painter in America. "Some of Mr. Bierstadt's mountains swim in a lustrous, pearly mist," Mark Twain observed with some acerbity, "which is so enchantingly beautiful that I am sorry the Creator hadn't made it instead of him, so that it would always remain there."

Lessons could be found even in less obviously histrionic features: climbing Mt. Tamalpais in Marin County at sunrise was seen, in my grandmother's generation, as a convenient transformative experience, as was any contemplation of the opening to the Pacific that John C. Frémont, when he mapped the area in 1846, had named "Chrysopylae," or Golden Gate, "on the same principle that the harbor of Byzantium (Constantinople afterwards) was called Chrysoceras (golden horn)." Josiah Royce, in his 1879 essay "Meditation Before the Gate," reflected on the view of the Gate from Berkeley and pledged himself to pursue his philosophical inquiries "independently, because I am a Californian, as little bound to follow mere tradition as I am liable to find an audience by preaching in this wilderness; reverently, because I am thinking and writing face to face with a mighty and lovely Nature, by the side of whose greatness I am but as a worm."

This is interesting, a quite naked expression of what has been the California conundrum. Scaled against Yosemite, or against the view through the Gate of the Pacific trembling on its tectonic plates, the slightest shift of which could and with some regularity did destroy the works of man in a millisecond, all human beings were of course but as worms, their "heroic imperatives" finally futile, their philosophical inquiries vain. The population of California has increased in my lifetime from six million to close to thirty-five million people, yet the three phrases that come first to mind when I try to define California to myself refer exclusively to its topography, a landscape quite empty of people. The first of these phrases comes from the language of broadcast weather reports, the second from John Muir. The third, and most persistent, comes from Robinson Jeffers. *Point Conception to the Mexican border. The Range of Light. Beautiful country burn again, / Point Pinos down to the Sur Rivers.*

This is the point in the California experience when discussion stops, and many voices fade. Broadcast weather reports could be seen as nominally neutral on the question of whether human beings have any rightful place in California, but John Muir and Robinson Jeffers could not. Muir traded the Calvinism of his Scottish childhood for an equally Calvinist wilderness, a landscape in which he could tolerate only Indians, because Indians "walk softly and hurt the landscape hardly more than the birds and squirrels, and their brush and bark huts last hardly longer than those of woodrats, while their more enduring monuments, excepting those wrought on the forests by the fires they made to improve their hunting grounds, vanish in a few centuries." Jeffers tolerated no one at all, taking this aversion to the point at which he came to favor war, which alone, as he saw it, could return the world to its "emptiness," to "the bone, the colorless white bone, the excellence." "Be in nothing so moderate as in love of man," he advised his twin sons, and referred to mankind as a "botched experiment that has run wild and ought to be stopped." He was accused of "proto-fascism." He called himself an "Inhumanist." (As in, from a posting on the Jeffers Studies web site, "I'm interested in the relationship between Inhumanism and Deep Ecology and would welcome any thoughts or comments.") He seemed to many an easy target: his poetry could be pretentious, his postures ugly. Read in situ, however, Jeffers makes fatally seductive sense: *Burn as before with bitter wonders, land and ocean and the Carmel water.* And: *When the cities lie at the monster's feet there are left the mountains.*

I am thinking and writing face to face with a mighty and lovely Nature, Josiah Royce wrote, *by the side of whose greatness I am but as a worm.* Royce in fact seems to have maintained an exhausting but finally vain alert against the undertow of this localized nihilism. His 1886 *California: A Study of American Character* bore on its title page these peculiar but premonitory lines, spoken by Mephistopheles in the Prologue to *Faust*: *On suns and worlds I can shed little light / I see but humans, and their piteous plight.* At sixty, in despair at the prospect of World War One and a few months short of what would be a fatal stroke, he encountered in Harvard Yard one of his students, Horace Kallen, who, according to Robert V. Hine's *Josiah Royce: From Grass Valley to Harvard*, reported of Royce that "When I greeted him, his round blue eyes looked staring, and without recognition. And then he said in a voice somehow thinner ... 'You are on the side of humanity, aren't you?'" A few months before, describing himself as "socially ineffective as regards genuine 'team play,' ignorant of politics, an ineffective member of committees, and a poor helper of concrete social enterprises," as well as "a good deal of a non-conformist, and disposed to a certain rebellion," Royce had acknowledged that the idea of community to which he had devoted his career remained in some way alien to him: "When I review this whole process, I strongly feel that my deepest motives and problems have centered about the Idea of the Community, although this idea has only come gradually to my clear consciousness. This is what I was intensely feeling, in the days when my sisters and I looked across the Sacramento Valley, and wondered about the great world beyond our mountains.... So much of the spirit that opposes the community I have and have always had in me, simply, deeply, elementally."

So much of the spirit that opposes the community: of course he had it in him, considering what he was: "*...because I am a Californian,*" he himself had written, "*as little bound to follow mere tradition....*" In 1970 I spent a month in the South, in Louisiana and Alabama and Mississippi, under the misapprehension that an understanding of the differences between the West and the South, which had given California a good deal of its original settlement, would improve my understanding of California. Royce had fretted over the same question: "Very early ... this relatively peaceful mingling of Americans from North and South had already deeply affected the tone of California life," he noted in *California: A Study of American Character*. "The type of the Northern man who has assumed Southern fashions, and not always the best Southern fashions at that, has often been observed in California life.... He often followed the Southerner, and was frequently, in time, partly assimilated by the Southern civilization." One difference between the West and the South, I came to realize in 1970, was this: in the South they remained convinced that they had bloodied their land with history. In California we did not believe that history could bloody the land, or even touch it.

THOMAS KINKADE WAS born in the late 1950s and raised in Placerville, El Dorado County, where his mother supported him and his siblings by working as a notary public, piecework, five dollars a document. The father had left. The family lived much of the time in a trailer. By the early 1990s "Thomas Kinkade" was a phenomenon, a brand on his own, a merchandiser who could touch a snow globe or a stoneware mug or a night-light or a La-Z-Boy chair with the magic of his name and turn it to money, a painter so successful that by the end of the decade there would be throughout the United States 248 Thomas Kinkade "signature galleries," seventy-eight of them in California alone, most of those in malls or tourist areas, four for example in Monterey and another four in Carmel, two exits down Highway 1. Since very few of Thomas Kinkade's original oil paintings were by that time available, and since those that were had risen in price from about $15,000 in the early 1990s to more than $300,000 by 1997, the pictures sold in these 248 "signature galleries" were canvas-backed reproductions, which themselves sold for $900 to $15,000 and were produced by the 450 employees who labored in the hundred-thousand-square-foot Morgan Hill headquarters of Media Arts Group Incorporated ("MDA" on the New York Stock Exchange), the business of which was Thomas Kinkade.

The passion with which buyers approached these Kinkade images was hard to define. The manager of one California gallery that handled them told me that it was not unusual to sell six or seven at a clip, to buyers who already owned ten or twenty, and that the buyers with whom he dealt brought to the viewing of the images "a sizeable emotional weight." A Kinkade painting was typically rendered in slightly surreal pastels. It typically featured a cottage or a house of such insistent coziness as to seem actually sinister, suggestive of a trap designed to attract Hansel and Gretel. Every window was lit, to lurid effect, as if the interior of the structure might be on fire. The cottages had thatched roofs, and resembled gingerbread houses. The houses were Victorian, and resembled idealized bed-and-breakfasts, at least two of which in Placerville, the Chichester-McKee House and the Combellack-Blair House, claimed to have been the models for Kinkade "Christmas" paintings. "There's a lot of beauty here that I present in a way that's whimsical and charming," Kinkade allowed to the Placerville *Mountain Democrat*. He branded himself the "Painter of Light," and the postcards Media Arts provided to his galleries each for a while bore this legend: "Thomas Kinkade is recognized as the foremost living painter of light. His masterful use of soft edges and luminous colors give his highly detailed oil paintings a glow all their own. This extraordinary 'Kinkade Glow' has created an overwhelming demand for Thomas Kinkade paintings and lithographs worldwide."

This "Kinkade Glow" could be seen as derived in spirit from the "lustrous, pearly mist" that Mark Twain had derided in the Bierstadt paintings, and, the level of execution to one side, there are certain unsettling similarities between the two painters. "After completing my recent plein air study of Yosemite Valley, the mountains' majesty refused to leave me," Kinkade wrote in June 2000 on his web site. "When my family wandered through the national park visitor center, I discovered a key to my fantasy—a recreation of a Miwok Indian Village. When I returned to my studio, I began work on *The Mountains Declare His Glory*, a poetic expression of what I felt at that transforming moment of inspiration. As a final touch, I even added a Miwok Indian Camp along the river as an affirmation that man has his place, even in a setting touched by God's glory."

Affirming that man has his place in the Sierra Nevada by reproducing the Yosemite National Park Visitor Center's recreation of a Miwok Indian Village is identifiable as a doubtful enterprise on many levels (not the least of which being that the Yosemite Miwok were forcibly run onto a reservation near Fresno during the Gold Rush, and allowed to return to Yosemite only in 1855), but is Thomas Kinkade's Sierra in fact any more sentimentalized than that of Albert Bierstadt? Were not the divinely illuminated passes of Bierstadt's Sierra meant to confirm the successful completion of our manifest destiny? Was it by chance that Collis P. Huntington commissioned Bierstadt to undertake a painting celebrating the domination of Donner Pass by the Central Pacific

Railroad? Was not Bierstadt's triumphalist *Donner Lake from the Summit* a willful revision to this point of the locale that most clearly embodied the moral ambiguity of the California settlement? This was the lesson drawn from the pass in question by one of the surviving children of the Donner Party, Virginia Reed, who wrote to her cousin: "Oh, Mary, I have not wrote you half of the trouble we've had, but I have wrote you enough to let you know what trouble is. But thank God, we are the only family that did not eat human flesh. We have left everything, but I don't care for that. We have got through with our lives. Don't let this letter dishearten anybody. Remember, never take no cutoffs and hurry along as fast as you can."

Remember, never take no cutoffs and hurry along as fast as you can.

Did the preferred version of our history reflect the artless horror and constricted moral horizon of Virginia Reed's first-hand account?

Or had it come more closely to resemble the inspirational improvement that was Bierstadt's *Donner Lake from the Summit*?

The confusions embedded in the crossing story can be seen in unintended relief in Jack London's *The Valley of the Moon*, the 1913 novel that has at its center the young woman Saxon Brown. At the time we meet Saxon she is orphaned, boarding with her hard-pressed socialist brother and his bad-tempered wife, and spending six hard days a week as a piecework ironer in an Oakland laundry. On their Saturday night off, Saxon and a friend from the laundry splurge on tickets to a Bricklayers' picnic, where Saxon meets a similarly orphaned teamster, Billy Roberts, to whom she confides that she was named for "the first English, and you know the Americans came from the English. We're Saxons, you an' me, an' Mary, an' Bert, and all the Americans that are real Americans, you know, and not Dagoes and Japs and such." If this seems a thin reed on which to hang one's identity, it would not have seemed so to London, who, Kevin Starr noted in *Americans and the California Dream*, once protested an arrest for vagrancy by arguing to the court "that no old American whose ancestors had fought in the American Revolution should be treated this way." The moment in which the judge nonetheless sentenced him to thirty days is described by Starr as "one of the most traumatic" in London's life.

Assured by Billy Roberts that he too is a "real" American, that his mother's family "crossed to Maine hundreds of years ago," Saxon asks where his father was from. This extraordinary exchange ensues:

"Don't know." Billy shrugged his shoulders. "He didn't know himself. Nobody ever knew, though he was American, all right, all right."

"His name's regular old American," Saxon suggested. "There's a big English general right now whose name is Roberts. I've read it in the papers."

"But Roberts wasn't my father's name. He never knew what his name was. Roberts was the name of a gold-miner who adopted him. You see, it was this way. When they was Indian-fightin' up there with the Modoc Indians, a lot of miners an' settlers took a hand. Roberts was captain of one outfit, and once, after a fight, they took a lot of prisoners—squaws, an' kids an' babies. An' one of the kids was my father. They figured he was about five years old. He didn't know nothin' but Indian."

Saxon clapped her hands, and her eyes sparkled: "He'd been captured on an Indian raid!"

"That's the way they figured it," Billy nodded. "They recollected a wagon-train of Oregon settlers that'd been killed by the Modocs four years before. Roberts adopted him, and that's why I don't know his real name. But you can bank on it, he crossed the plains just the same."

"So did my father," Saxon said proudly.

"An' my mother, too," Billy added, pride touching his own voice. "Anyway, she came pretty close to crossin' the plains, because she was born in a wagon on the River Platte on the way out."

"My mother, too," said Saxon. "She was eight years old, an' she walked most of the way after the oxen began to give out."

Billy thrust out his hand.

"Put her there, kid," he said. "We're just like old friends, what with the same kind of folks behind us."

With shining eyes, Saxon extended her hand to his, and gravely they shook.

"Isn't it wonderful?" she murmured. "We're both old American stock."

To assume that London was employing irony here, that his intention was to underline the distance between Saxon and Billy's actual situation and their illusions of superior lineage, would be to misread *The Valley of the Moon*. "Times have changed," Saxon complains to Billy. "We crossed the plains and opened up this country, and now we're losing even the chance to work for a living in it." This strikes a chord in Billy, which resonates again when the two happen into a prosperous Portuguese settlement: "It looks like the free-born American ain't got no room left in his own land," Billy says to Saxon. A further thought from Billy: "It was our folks who made this country. Fought for it, opened it up, did everything—"

This truculence on the question of immigration was by no means an unfamiliar note in California, which by the time London wrote already had a tenacious history of vigilance committees and exclusionary legislation. "The fearful blindness of the early behavior of the Americans in California towards foreigners is something almost unintelligible," Josiah Royce wrote in 1886 of the violence and lynchings to which "foreigners"—mainly Sonorans but also Chinese and native Digger Indians—had been subjected in the gold fields. Sixty-some years after Royce, Carey McWilliams, in *California: The Great Exception*, characterized the pervasive local hostility toward Asians as "a social and psychic necessity of the situation," the "negative device" by which a state made up of newly arrived strangers had been able to achieve the illusion of a cohesive community joined against the menace of the foreign-born.

Such hostility was by no means unknown in more settled parts of the country, but rarely was it so intricately codified by law. The Foreign Miners' License Tax of 1850 had exacted a monthly fee of any non-citizen who wanted to work a claim. In 1854, an existing law prohibiting Negroes and Indians from testifying in court had been extended to also prohibit testimony by Chinese. The state legislature had barred "Mongolians, Indians, and Negroes" from public schools in 1860; had barred Chinese from employment in corporations or on public works projects in 1879; and had amended an existing miscegenation law to include Chinese in 1906. The state Alien Land Acts of 1913 and 1920 would for more than thirty years effectively prohibit land ownership in California to both Asians and their American-born children.

It was in this spirit that the two "real" Americans, Saxon and Billy, set out in search of government land, the 160 free acres which were, as they saw it, their due. This conviction of entitlement was another familiar California note, and a particularly complicated one, since the idea of depending on the government of course ran counter to the preferred self-image of most Californians. Yet such dependence was, even then, almost total. It had been, as we have seen, federal money, spent on behalf of a broad spectrum of business interests, that built the railroad and opened the state to the rest of the world. It had been and would be, as we have seen, federal money, again spent on behalf of a large spectrum of business interests, that created what was no longer locally even called agribusiness, just "ag." The rationalization that resolves this contradiction is, in *The Valley of the Moon*, fairly primitive: the government owes Saxon and Billy free land, Billy reasons, "for what our fathers an' mothers done. I tell you, Saxon, when a woman walks across the plains like your mother done, an' a man an' wife gets massacred by the Indians like my grandfather an' mother done, the government does owe them something."

The land on which Saxon and Billy finally settle is the actual Valley of the Moon, in Sonoma County, and their discovery of it prefigures many of the doubtful sentiments that would later surface in the paintings of Thomas Kinkade. They arrive in the valley just as "sunset fires, refracted from the cloud-driftage of the autumn sky" turn the landscape "crimson." They see a stream, "singing" to them. They see "fairy circles" of redwoods. They see, at a distance, a man and a woman, "side by side, the delicate hand of the woman curled in the hand of the man, which looked as if made to confer benedictions." This magical bonding continues, again as if touched by the Kinkade Glow:

> Perhaps the picture made by Saxon and Billy was equally arresting and beautiful, as they drove down through the golden end of day. The two couples had eyes only for each

other. The little woman beamed joyously. The man's face glowed into the benediction that had trembled there. To Saxon, like the field up the mountain, like the mountain itself, it seemed that she had always known this adorable pair. She knew that she loved them.

Only later does Saxon discover what the reader (by this point almost four hundred pages into *The Valley of the Moon*) may well have suspected early on: "this adorable pair" are in fact "old stock that had crossed the Plains," keepers perhaps of their own iconic potato masher, in any event kindred souls who "knew all about the fight at Little Meadow, and the tale of the massacre of the emigrant train of which Billy's father had been the sole survivor." Their rightful place in the California fable validated, Saxon and Billy settle in, determined to redeem the birthright of the "old stock" through the practice of scientific agronomy, which London himself imagined that he and his second wife, the woman he called his "Mate-Woman," Charmian Kittredge, were perfecting on their own Sonoma ranch. London's letters from this period speak of "making the dead soil live again," of leaving the land "better for my having been," of unremitting industry, transcendent husbandry. "No picayune methods for me," he wrote. "When I go in silence, I want to know that I left behind me a plot of land which, after the pitiful failures of others, I have made productive…. Can't you see? Oh, try to see!—In the solution of great economic problems of the present age, I see a return to the soil."

This was another confusion. His crops failed. His Wolf House, built to last a thousand years, burned to the ground before he and the Mate-Woman (or, as he alternately called Charmian, the Wolf-Mate) could move in. His health was gone. He battled depression. He battled alcoholism. At one point in 1913, the year Wolf House was completed and burned, he had only three dollars and forty-six cents left in the bank. In the end only the Mate-Woman kept the faith: "I am crazy for everyone to know about Jack's big experiment up here," Charmian Kittredge London wrote to a friend, Tom Wilkinson, on December 15, 1916. "So few persons think of it at all in connection with him—they slobber about his this and his that and his the other, and say nothing about his tremendous experiment—practical experiment—up here on Sonoma Mountain." Just three weeks before this letter was written, Jack London had died, at forty, of uremic poisoning and one final, fatal, dose of the morphine prescribed to calm his renal colic. In the last novel he was to write, *The Little Lady of the Big House*, he had allowed his protagonist and author-surrogate to ask these questions, a flash of the endemic empty in a work that is otherwise a fantasy of worldly and social success: "Why? What for? What's it worth? What's it all about?"

8

THE BOHEMIAN CLUB of San Francisco was founded, in 1872, by members of the city's working press, who saw it both as a declaration of unconventional or "artistic" interests and as a place to get a beer and a sandwich after the bulldog closed. Frank Norris was a member, as was Henry George, who had not yet published *Progress and Poverty*. There were poets: Joaquin Miller, George Sterling. There were writers: Samuel Clemens, Bret Harte, Ambrose Bierce, Jack London, who only a few months before his death managed to spend a week at Bohemian Grove, the club's encampment in the redwoods north of San Francisco. John Muir belonged to the Bohemian Club, and so did Joseph LeConte. For a few years the members appear to have remained resolute in their determination not to admit the merely rich (they had refused membership to William C. Ralston, the president of the Bank of California), but their over-ambitious spending, both on the club in town and on its periodic encampments, quite soon overwhelmed this intention. According to a memoir of the period written by Edward Bosqui, San Francisco's most prominent publisher during the late nineteenth century and a charter member of the Bohemian Club, it was at this point decided to "invite an element to join the club which the majority of the members held in contempt, namely men who had money as well as brains, but who were not, strictly speaking, Bohemians."

By 1927, a year after George Sterling committed suicide during a club dinner for H. L. Mencken by going upstairs to bed and swallowing cyanide (he had been depressed, he had been drinking, Frank Norris's brother had replaced him as toastmaster for the Mencken dinner), the Bohemian Club was banning from its annual art exhibit any entry deemed by the club "in radical and unreasonable departure from laws of art." By 1974, when G. William Domhoff, then a professor of sociology at the University of California at Santa Cruz, wrote *The Bohemian Grove and Other Retreats: A Study in Ruling-Class Cohesiveness*, one in

JOAN DIDION

five resident members and one in three nonresident members of the Bohemian Club was listed in *Standard & Poor's Register of Corporations, Executives, and Directors*. Among those attending the summer encampment at Bohemian Grove in 1970, the year for which Domhoff obtained a list, "at least one officer or director from forty of the fifty largest industrial corporations in America was present.... Similarly, we found that officers and directors from twenty of the top twenty-five commercial banks (including all of the fifteen largest) were on our lists. Men from twelve of the first twenty-five life-insurance companies were in attendance (eight of these twelve were from the top ten)."

The summer encampment, then, had evolved into a special kind of enchanted circle, one in which these captains of American finance and industry could entertain, in what was to most of them an attractively remote setting, the temporary management of that political structure on which their own fortunes ultimately depended. When Dwight Eisenhower visited the Grove in 1950, eleven years before he made public his concern about the military-industrial complex, he traveled on a special train arranged by the president of the Santa Fe Railroad. Domhoff noted that both Henry Kissinger and Melvin Laird, then secretary of defense, were present at the 1970 encampment, as were David M. Kennedy, then secretary of the treasury, and Admiral Thomas H. Moorer, chairman of the Joint Chiefs of Staff. John Erlichman, as the guest of Leonard Firestone, represented the White House. Walter J. Hickel, at the time secretary of the interior, was the guest of Fred L. Hartley, the president of Union Oil.

The rituals of the summer encampment were fixed. There were, every day at twelve-thirty, "Lakeside Talks," informal speeches and briefings, off the record. Kissinger, Laird, and William P. Rogers, then secretary of state, gave Lakeside Talks in 1970; Colin Powell and the chairman of Dow Chemical were scheduled for 1999. Local color was measured: the fight songs sung remained those of the traditional California schools, Berkeley (or, in this venue, "Cal") and Stanford, yet it was a rule of the Bohemian Club that no Californian, unless he was a member, could be asked as a guest during the two-week midsummer encampment. (As opposed to the May "Spring Jinks" weekend, to which California non-members could be invited.) The list for the 1985 encampment, the most recent complete roster I have seen, shows the members and their "camps," the hundred-some self-selected groupings situated back through the hills and canyons and off the road to the Russian River. Each camp has a name. for example Stowaway, or Pink Onion, or Silverado Squatters, or Lost Angels.

For the 1985 encampment, Caspar Weinberger was due at Isle of Aves, James Baker III at Woof. "George H. W. Bush" appeared on the list for Hillbillies (his son, George W. Bush, seems not to have been present in 1985, but he was on the list, along with his father and Newt Gingrich, for 1999), as did, among others, Frank Borman, William F. Buckley, Jr., and his son Christopher, Walter Cronkite, A. W. Clausen of the Bank of America and the World Bank, and Frank A. Sprole of Bristol-Myers. George Shultz was on the list for Mandalay, along with William French Smith, Thomas Watson, Jr., Nicholas Brady, Leonard K. Firestone, Peter Flanigan, Gerald Ford, Najeeb Halaby, Philip M. Hawley, J. K. Horton, Edgar F. Kaiser, Jr., Henry Kissinger, John McCone, and two of the Bechtels. This virtual personification of Eisenhower's military-industrial complex notwithstanding, the Spirit of Bohemia, or California, could still be seen, in the traditional tableaux performed at every Grove encampment, to triumph over Mammon, God of Gold, and all his gnomes and promises and bags of treasure:

> SPIRIT: *Nay, Mammon. For one thing it cannot buy*.
> MAMMON: *What cannot it buy?*
> SPIRIT: *A happy heart!*

The transformation of the Bohemian Club from a lively if frivolous gathering of local free spirits to a nexus of the nation's corporate and political interests in many ways mirrored a larger transformation, that of California itself from what it had been, or from what its citizens preferred to believe that it had been, to what it is now, an entirely dependent colony of the invisible empire in which those corporate and political interests are joined. In 1868, four years before he helped to found the Bohemian Club, Henry George, twenty-nine years old and previously unpublished, wrote a piece in the *Overland Monthly* in which he tried to locate "the peculiar charm of California, which all who have lived here long enough feel." He concluded that California's charm resided in the character of its people: "…there has been a feeling of personal independence and equality, a general hopefulness and self-reliance, and a certain large-heartedness and open-handedness which were born of the comparative evenness with which property was distributed, the high standard of wages and of comfort, and the latent feeling of everyone that he might 'make a strike.'" This piece, "What the Railroad Will Bring Us," was intended, of course, as an antidote to the enthusiasm then general about the windfall to be realized by giving the state to the Southern Pacific:

> Let us see clearly whither we are tending. Increase in population and in wealth past a certain point means simply an approximation to the condition of older countries—the eastern states and Europe…. The truth is, that the completion of the railroad and the consequent great increase of business and population, will not be a benefit to all of us, but only to a portion…. This crowding of people into immense cities, this aggregation of wealth into large lumps, this marshalling of men into big gangs under the control of the great "captains of industry," does not tend to foster personal independence—the basis of all virtues—nor will it tend to preserve the characteristics which particularly have made Californians proud of their state.

Henry George asked what the railroad would bring, but not too many other people did. Many people would later ask whether it had served the common weal to transform the Sacramento and San Joaquin Valleys from a seasonal shallow sea to a protected hothouse requiring the annual application on each square mile of 3.87 tons of chemical pesticides, but not too many people asked this before the dams; those who did ask, for whatever reason, were categorized as "environmentalists," a word loosely used in this part of California to describe any perceived threat to the life of absolute personal freedom its citizens believe they lead. "California likes to be fooled," Cedarquist, the owner in *The Octopus* of a failed San Francisco ironworks, advises Presley when they happen to meet at (where else?) the Bohemian Club. "Do you suppose Shelgrim [the Collis P. Huntington figure] could convert the whole San Joaquin Valley into his back yard otherwise?"

"What the Railroad Will Bring Us" remained, into my generation at least, routine assigned reading for California children, one more piece of evidence that assigned reading makes nothing happen. I used to think that Henry George had overstated the role of the railroad, and in one sense he had: the railroad, of course, was merely the last stage of a process already underway, one that had its basis in the character of the settlement, in the very quality recommended by "What the Railroad Will Bring Us" as "a general hopefulness and self-reliance," or "a feeling of personal independence or equality," or "the latent feeling of everyone that he might 'make a strike.'" This process, one of trading the state to outside owners in exchange for their (it now seems) entirely temporary agreement to enrich us, in other words the pauperization of California, had in fact begun at the time Americans first entered the state, took what they could, and, abetted by the native weakness for boosterism, set about selling the rest.

Josiah Royce understood this negative side of the California character, but persisted in what was for him the essential conviction that the California community was so positive a force as to correct its own character. He allowed that "a general sense of social irresponsibility is, even today, the average Californian's easiest failing." Still, he seemed temperamentally unable to consider an "average Californian" who would not, in the end, see that his own best interests lay in cooperation, in the amelioration of differences, in a certain willingness to forgo the immediate windfall for the larger or even his own long-term good. This was the same "average Californian" who, by the year Royce wrote, 1886, had already sold half the state to the Southern Pacific and was in the process of mortgaging the rest to the federal government. For most of the next hundred years, kept aloft first by oil and then by World War Two and finally by the Cold War and the largesse of the owners and managers who would arrive in Gulfstreams for the annual encampment at Bohemian Grove, that average Californian had seen his "easiest failing" yield only blue skies.

Part II

IN THE MAY 1935 issue of the *American Mercury*, William Faulkner published one of the few pieces of fiction he set in California, a short story he called "Golden Land." "Golden Land" deals with a day in the life of Ira Ewing, Jr., age forty-eight, a man for whom "twenty-five years of industry and desire, of shrewdness and luck and even fortitude," seem recently to have come to ashes. At fourteen, Ira Ewing had fled Nebraska on a westbound freight. By the time he was thirty, he had married the daughter of a Los Angeles carpenter, fathered a son and a daughter, and secured a foothold in the real estate business. By the time we meet him, eighteen years later, he is in a position to spend fifty thousand dollars a year, a sizable amount in 1935. He has been able to bring his widowed mother from Nebraska and install her in a house in Glendale. He has been able to provide for his children "luxuries and advantages which his own father not only could not have conceived in fact but would have condemned completely in theory."

Yet nothing is working out. Ira's daughter, Samantha, who wants to be in show business and has taken the name "April Lalear," is testifying in a lurid trial reported on page one ("April Lalear Bares Orgy Secrets") of the newspapers placed on the reading table next to Ira's bed. Ira, less bewildered than weary, tries not to look at the accompanying photographs of Samantha, the "hard, blonde, and inscrutable" daughter who "alternately stared back or flaunted long pale shins." Nor is Samantha the exclusive source of the leaden emptiness Ira now feels instead of hunger: there is also his son, Voyd, who continues to live at home but has not spoken unprompted to his father in two years, not since the morning when Voyd, drunk, was delivered home to his father wearing, "in place of underclothes, a woman's brassiere and step-ins."

Since Ira prides himself on being someone who will entertain no suggestion that his life is not the success that his business achievement would seem to him to promise, he discourages discussion of his domestic trials, and has tried to keep the newspapers featuring April Lalear and the orgy secrets away from his mother. Via the gardener, however, Ira's mother has learned about her granddaughter's testimony, and she is reminded of the warning she once gave her son, after she had seen Samantha and Voyd stealing cash from their mother's purse: "You make money too easy," she had told Ira. "This whole country is too easy for us Ewings. It may be all right for them that have been born here for generations, I don't know about that. But not for us."

"But these children were born here," Ira had said.

"Just one generation," his mother had said. "The generation before that they were born in a sod-roofed dugout on the Nebraska wheat frontier. And the one before that in a log house in Missouri. And the one before that in a Kentucky blockhouse with Indians around it. This world has never been easy for Ewings. Maybe the Lord never intended it to be."

"But it is from now on," the son had insisted. "For you and me too. But mostly for them."

"Golden Land" does not entirely hold up, nor, I would guess, will it ever be counted among the best Faulkner stories. Yet it retains, for certain Californians, a nagging resonance, and opens the familiar troubling questions. I grew up in a California family that derived, from the single circumstance of having been what Ira Ewing's mother called "born here for generations," considerable pride, much of it, it seemed to me later, strikingly unearned. "The trouble with these new people," I recall hearing again and again as a child in Sacramento, "is they think it's supposed to be easy." The phrase "these new people" generally signified people who had moved to California after World War Two, but was tacitly extended back to include the migration from the Dust Bowl during the 1930s, and often further. New people, we were given to understand, remained ignorant of our special history, insensible to the hardships endured to make it, blind not only to the dangers the place still presented but to the shared responsibilities its continued habitation demanded.

If my grandfather spotted a rattlesnake while driving, he would stop his car and go into the brush after it. To do less, he advised me more than once, was to endanger whoever later entered the brush, and so violate what he called "the code of the West." New people, I was told, did not understand their responsibility to kill rattlesnakes. Nor did new people understand that the water that came from the tap in, say, San Francisco, was there only because part of Yosemite had been flooded to put it there. New people did not understand the necessary dynamic of the fires, the seven-year cycles of flood and drought, the physical reality of the place. "Why didn't they go back to Truckee?" a young mining engineer from back East asked when my grandfather pointed out the site of the Donner Party's last encampment. I recall hearing this story repeatedly. I also recall the same grandfather, my mother's father, whose family had migrated from the hardscrabble Adirondack frontier in the eighteenth century to the hardscrabble Sierra Nevada foothills in the nineteenth, working himself up into writing an impassioned letter-to-the-editor over a fifth-grade textbook in which one of the illustrations summed up California history as a sunny progression from Spanish Señorita to Gold Miner to Golden Gate Bridge. What the illustration seemed to my grandfather to suggest was that those responsible for the text-book believed the settlement of California to have been "easy," history rewritten, as he saw it, for the new people. There were definite ambiguities in this: Ira Ewing and his children were, of course, new people, but so, less than a century before, had my grandfather's family been. New people could be seen, by people like my grandfather, as indifferent to everything that had made California work, but the ambiguity was this: new people were also who were making California rich.

Californians whose family ties to the state predate World War Two have an equivocal and often uneasy relationship to the post-war expansion. Joan Irvine Smith, whose family's eighty-eight-thousand-acre ranch in Orange County was developed during the 1960s, later created, on the twelfth floor of the McDonnell Douglas Building in Irvine, a city that did not exist before the Irvines developed their ranch, the Irvine Museum, dedicated to the California impressionist or plein air paintings she had begun collecting in 1991. "There is more nostalgia for me in these paint-ings than in actually going out to look at what used to be the ranch now that it has been developed, because I'm looking at what I looked at as a child," she told *Art in California* about this collection. Her attraction to the genre had begun, she said, when she was a child and would meet her stepfather for lunch at the

California Club, where the few public rooms in which women were at that time allowed were decorated with California landscapes lent by the members. "I can look at those paintings and see what the ranch was as I remember it when I was a little girl."

The California Club, which is on Flower Street in downtown Los Angeles, was then and is still the heart of Southern California's old-line business establishment, the Los Angeles version of the Bohemian and Pacific Union Clubs in San Francisco. On any given day since World War Two, virtually everyone lunching at the California Club, most particularly not excluding Joan Irvine, has had a direct or indirect investment in the development of California, which is to say in the obliteration of the undeveloped California on display at the Irvine Museum. In the seventy-four paintings chosen for inclusion in *Selections from the Irvine Museum*, the catalogue published by the museum to accompany a 1992 traveling exhibition, there are hills and desert and mesas and arroyos. There are mountains, coastline, big sky. There are stands of eucalyptus, sycamore, oak, cottonwood. There are washes of California poppies. As for fauna, there are, in the seventy-four paintings, three sulphur-crested cockatoos, one white peacock, two horses, and nine people, four of whom are dwarfed by the landscape and two of whom are indistinct Indians paddling a canoe.

Some of this is romantic (the indistinct Indians), some washed with a slightly falsified golden light, in the tradition that runs from Bierstadt's "lustrous, pearly mist" to the "Kinkade Glow." Most of these paintings, however, reflect the way the place actually looks, or looked, not only to Joan Irvine but also to me and to anyone else who knew it as recently as 1960. It is this close representation of a familiar yet vanished landscape that gives the Irvine collection its curious effect, that of a short-term memory misfire: these paintings hang in a city, Irvine (population more than one hundred and fifty thousand, with a University of California campus enrolling some nineteen thousand students), that was forty years ago a mirror image of the paintings themselves, bean fields and grazing, the heart but by no means all of the cattle and sheep operation amassed by the great-grandfather of the founder of the Irvine Museum.

The disposition of such a holding can be, for its inheritors, a fraught enterprise. "On the afternoon of his funeral we gathered to honor this man who had held such a legacy intact for the main part of his ninety-one years," Jane Hollister Wheelwright wrote in *The Ranch Papers* about the aftermath of her father's death and the prospect of being forced to sell the Hollister ranch. "All of us were deeply affected. Some were stunned by the prospect of loss; others gloated, contemplating cash and escape. We were bitterly divided, but none could deny the power of that land. The special, spiritually meaningful (and often destructive) impact of the ranch was obvious. I proved it by my behavior, as did the others."

That was 1961. Joan Irvine Smith had replaced her mother on the board of the Irvine Company four years before, in 1957, the year she was twenty-four. She had seen, a good deal more clearly and realistically than Jane Hollister Wheelwright would see four years later, the solution she wanted for her family's ranch, and she had seen the rest of the Irvine board as part of the problem: by making small deals, selling off bits of the whole, the board was nibbling away at the family's principal asset, the size of its holding. It was she who pressed the architect William Pereira to present a master plan. It was she who saw the potential return in giving the land for a University of California campus. It was she, most importantly, who insisted on maintaining an interest in the ranch's development. And, in the end, which meant after years of internecine battles and a series of litigations extending to 1991, it was she who more or less prevailed. In 1960, before the Irvine ranch was developed, there were 719,500 people in all of Orange County. In 2000 there were close to 3 million, most of whom would not have been there had two families, the Irvines in the central part of the county and the inheritors of Richard O'Neill's Rancho Santa Margarita and Mission Viejo acreage in the southern, not developed their ranches.

This has not been a case in which the rising tide floated all boats. Not all of Orange County's new residents came to realize what would have seemed the middle-class promise of its growth. Not all of those residents even had somewhere to live: some settled into the run-down motels built in the mid-1950s, at the time Disneyland opened, and were referred to locally, because they had nowhere else to live and could not afford the deposits required for apartment rental, as "motel people." In his 1986 *The New California: Facing the 21st Century*, the political columnist Dan Walters quoted *The Orange County Register* on motel people:

"Mostly Anglo, they're the county's newest migrant workers: instead of picking grapes, they inspect semiconductors." This kind of week-by-week or even day-by-day living arrangement has taken hold in other parts of the country, but remains particularly entrenched in Southern California, where apartment rents rose to meet the increased demand from people priced out of a housing market in which even the least promising bungalow can sell for several hundred thousand dollars. By the year 2000, according to *The Los Angeles Times*, some hundred Orange County motels were inhabited almost exclusively by the working poor, people who made, say, $280 a week sanding airplane parts, or $7 an hour at Disney's "California Adventure" park. "A land celebrating the richness and diversity of California, its natural resources, and pioneering spirit of its people," the web site for "California Adventure" read. "I can look at these paintings and look back," Joan Irvine Smith told *Art in California* about the collection she bought with the proceeds of looking exclusively, and to a famous degree, forward. "I can see California as it was and as we will never see it again." Hers is an extreme example of the conundrum that to one degree or another confronts any Californian who profited from the boom years: if we could still see California as it was, how many of us could now afford to see it?

What is the railroad to do for us?—this railroad that we
have looked for, hoped for, prayed for so long?

—Henry George,
"What the Railroad Will Bring Us"

LAKEWOOD, CALIFORNIA, THE Los Angeles County community
where in early 1993 an amorphous high school clique iden-
tifying itself as the Spur Posse achieved a short-lived national
notoriety, lies between the Long Beach and San Gabriel
Freeways, east of the San Diego, part of that vast grid familiar
to the casual visitor mainly from the air, Southern California's
industrial underbelly, the thousand square miles of aerospace
and oil that powered the place's apparently endless expansion. Like much of the southern end of this grid, Lakewood
was until after World War Two agricultural, several thousand
acres of beans and sugar beets just inland from the Signal Hill
oil field and across the road from the plant behind the Long
Beach airport that the federal government completed in 1941
for Donald Douglas.

This Douglas plant, with the outsized American flag whipping
in the wind and the huge forward-slanted letters *MCDONNELL
DOUGLAS* wrapped around the building and the MD-11s
parked like cars off Lakewood Boulevard, was at the time I first
visited Lakewood in 1993 the single most noticeable feature
on the local horizon, but for a while, not long after World War
Two, there had been another: a hundred-foot pylon, its rotating
beacon visible for several miles, erected to advertise the opening, in April 1950, of what was meant to be the world's biggest
subdivision, a tract larger in conception than the original Long
Island Levittown, 17,500 houses waiting to be built on the 3,400
dead-level acres that three California developers, Mark Taper and

Ben Weingart and Louis Boyar, had purchased for $8.8 million from the Montana Land Company.

Lakewood, the sign read at the point on Lakewood Boulevard where Bellflower would become Lakewood, *Tomorrow's City Today*. What was offered for sale in Tomorrow's City, as in most subdivisions of the postwar period, was a raw lot and the promise of a house. Each of the 17,500 houses was to be 950 to 1,100 square feet on a fifty-by-hundred-foot lot. Each was to be a one-story stucco (seven floor plans, twenty-one different exteriors, no identical models to be built next to or facing each other) painted in one of thirty-nine color schemes. Each was to have oak floors, a glass-enclosed shower, a stainless-steel double sink, a garbage disposal unit, and either two or three bedrooms. Each was to sell for between eight and ten thousand dollars. *Low FHA, Vets No Down*. There were to be thirty-seven playgrounds, twenty schools. There were to be seventeen churches. There were to be 133 miles of street, paved with an inch and a half of No. 2 macadam on an aggregate base.

There was to be, and this was key not only to the project but to the nature of the community which eventually evolved, a regional shopping center, "Lakewood Center," which in turn was conceived as America's largest retail complex: 256 acres, parking for ten thousand cars, anchored by a May Company. "Lou Boyar pointed out that they would build a shopping center and around that a city, that he would make a city for us and millions for himself," John Todd, a resident of Lakewood since its beginning and later its city attorney, wrote of the planning stage. "Everything about this entire project was perfect," Mark Taper said in 1969, when he sat down with city officials to work up a local history. "Things happened that may never happen again."

What he meant, of course, was the perfect synergy of time and place, the seamless confluence of World War Two and the Korean War and the G.I. Bill and the defense contracts that began to flood Southern California as the Cold War set in. Here on this raw acreage on the flood plain between the Los Angeles and San Gabriel Rivers was where two powerfully conceived national interests, that of keeping the economic engine running and that of creating an enlarged middle or consumer class, could be seen to converge.

The scene beneath the hundred-foot pylon during that spring of 1950 was Cimarron: thirty thousand people showed up for the first day of selling. Twenty thousand showed up on weekends throughout the spring. Near the sales office was a nursery where children could be left while parents toured the seven completed and furnished model houses. Thirty-six salesmen worked day and evening shifts, showing potential buyers how their G.I. benefits, no down payment, and thirty years of monthly payments ranging from $43 to $54 could elevate them to ownership of a piece of the future. Deals were closed on 611 houses the first week. One week saw construction started on 567. A new foundation was excavated every fifteen minutes. Cement trucks were lined up for a mile, waiting to move down the new blocks pouring foundations. Shingles were fed to roofers by conveyer belt. And, at the very point when sales had begun to slow, as Taper recalled at the 1969 meeting with city officials, "the Korean War was like a new stimulation."

"There was this new city growing—growing like leaves," one of the original residents, who with her husband had opened a delicatessen in Lakewood Center, said when she was interviewed for an oral history project undertaken by the city and Lakewood High School. "So we decided this is where we should start.... There were young people, young children, schools, a young government that was just starting out. We felt all the big stores were coming in. May Company and all the other places started opening. So we rented one of the stores and we were in business." These World War Two and Korean War veterans and their wives who started out in Lakewood were, typically, about thirty years old. They were, typically, not from California but from the Midwest and the border South. They were, typically, blue-collar and lower-level white collar. They had 1.7 children, they had steady jobs. Their experience tended to reinforce the conviction that social and economic mobility worked exclusively upward.

Donald J. Waldie, while he was working as the City of Lakewood's public information officer, wrote an extraordinary book, *Holy Land: A Suburban Memoir*, published in 1996, a series of interconnected essays about someone who, like their author, lived in Lakewood and worked at City Hall. "Naively, you could say that Lakewood was the American dream made affordable for a generation of industrial workers who in the preceding generation could never aspire to that kind of ownership," he said one morning when we were talking about the way the place was developed. "They were fairly but not entirely homogenous in their ethnic background. They were oriented to aerospace. They worked for Hughes, they worked for Douglas, they worked at the naval station and shipyard in Long Beach. They worked, in other words, at all the places that exemplified the bright future that California was supposed to be."

Donald Waldie grew up in Lakewood, and, after Cal State Long Beach and graduate work at the University of California at Irvine, had chosen to come back, as had a striking number of people who lived there. In a county increasingly populated by low-income Mexican and Central American and Asian immigrants and pressed by the continuing needs of its low-income blacks, almost sixty thousand of Lakewood's seventy-some thousand citizens were still, in the spring of 1993, white. More than half had been born in California, and most of the rest in the Midwest and the South. The largest number of those employed worked, just as their fathers and grandfathers had, for Douglas or Hughes or Rockwell or the Long Beach naval station and shipyard or for the many subcontractors and vendors that did business with Douglas and Hughes and Rockwell and the Long Beach naval station and shipyard.

People who lived in Lakewood did not necessarily think of themselves as living in Los Angeles, and could often list the occasions on which they had visited there, to see the Dodgers play, say, or to show a relative from out of state the Music Center. Their apprehension of urban woes remained remote: the number of homeless people in Lakewood either in shelters or "visible on street," according to the 1990 Census, was zero. When residents of Lakewood spoke about the rioting that had begun in Los Angeles after the 1992 Rodney King verdicts, they were talking about events that seemed to them, despite the significant incidence of arson and looting in such neighboring communities as Long Beach and Compton, to have occurred somewhere else. "We're far away from that element," one woman to whom I spoke said when the subject of the riots came up. "If you've driven around …"

"Little suburbia," a neighbor said.

"America U.S.A., right here."

The neighbor's husband worked at a nearby Rockwell plant, not the Rockwell plant in Lakewood. The Rockwell plant in Lakewood had closed in 1992, a thousand jobs gone. The scheduled closing of the Long Beach naval station would mean almost nine thousand jobs gone. The Federal Base Closure and Realignment Commission had granted a provisional stay to the Long Beach naval shipyard, which adjoined the naval station and employed another four thousand people, but its prospects for survival remained dim. One thing that was not remote in Lakewood in 1993, one thing so close that not many people even wanted to talk about it, was the apprehension that what had already happened to the Rockwell plant and would happen to the Long Beach naval station and shipyard could also happen to the Douglas plant. I recall talking one day to Carl Cohn, then superintendent of the Long Beach Unified School District, which included Lakewood. "There's a tremendous fear that at some point this operation might go away entirely," he said. "I mean that's kind of one of the whispered things around town. Nobody wants it out there."

Douglas had already, in 1993, moved part of its MD-80 production to Salt Lake City. Douglas had already moved part of what remained of its C-17 production to St. Louis. Douglas had already moved the T-45 to St. Louis. In a 1992 study called *Impact of Defense Cuts on California*, the California Commission on State Finance had estimated nineteen thousand layoffs still to come from Hughes and McDonnell Douglas, but by 1992 there had already been, in Southern California, some twenty-one thousand McDonnell Douglas layoffs. According to a June 1993 report on aerospace unemployment prepared by researchers at the UCLA School of Architecture and Urban Planning, half the California aerospace workers laid off in 1989 were, two years later, either still unemployed or no longer living in California. Most of those who did find jobs had ended up in lower-income service jobs; only seventeen percent had gone back to work in the aerospace industry at figures approaching their original salaries. Of those laid off in 1991 and 1992, only sixteen percent, a year later, had found jobs of any kind.

It was the Douglas plant on the Lakewood city line, the one with the flag whipping in the wind and the logo wrapped around the building, that had by 1993 taken the hit for almost eighteen thousand of McDonnell Douglas's twenty-one thousand layoffs. "I've got two kids, a first and a third grader," Carl Cohn told me. "When you take your kid to a birthday party and your wife starts talking about so-and-so's father just being laid off—there are all kinds of implications, including what's going to be spent on a kid's birthday party. These concrete things really come home to you. And you realize, yeah, this bad economic situation is very real." The message on the marquee at Rochelle's Restaurant and Motel and Convention Center, between Douglas and the Long Beach airport, still read "Welcome Douglas Happy Hour 4–7," but the place was nailed shut, a door banging in the wind. "We've developed good citizens," Mark Taper said about Lakewood in 1969. "Enthusiastic owners of property. Owners of a piece of their country—a stake in the land." This was a sturdy but finally unsupportable ambition, sustained for forty years by good times and the good will of the federal government.

When people in Lakewood spoke about what they called "Spur," or "the situation at the high school," some meant the series of allegations that had led to the March 1993 arrests— with requests that charges be brought on ten counts of rape by intimidation, four counts of unlawful sexual intercourse, one count of forcible rape, one count of oral copulation, and one count of lewd conduct with a minor under the age of fourteen— of nine current or former Lakewood High School students who either happened to be or were believed to be members of an informal fraternity known locally as the Spur Posse. Others meant not the allegations, which they saw as either outright inventions or representations of events open to interpretation (the phrase "consensual sex" got heavy usage), but rather the national attention that followed those allegations, the invasion of Lakewood by what its residents called "you people," or "you folks," or "the media," and the appearance, on *Jenny Jones* and *Jane Whitney* and *Maury Povich* and *Nightline* and *Montel Williams* and *Dateline* and *Donahue* and *The Home Show*, of two hostile and briefly empowered arrangements of hormones, otherwise known as "the boys" and "the girls."

For a moment that spring they had seemed to be on view everywhere, those blank-faced Lakewood girls, those feral Lakewood boys. There were the dead eyes, the thick necks, the jaws that closed only to chew gum. There was the refusal or inability to process the simplest statement without rephrasing it. There was the fuzzy relationship to language, the tendency to seize on a drifting fragment of something once heard and repeat it, not quite get it right, worry it like a bone. The news that some schools distributed condoms had been seized in mid-drift, for example, and pressed into service as an extenuating circumstance, the fact that Lakewood High School had never distributed condoms notwithstanding. "The schools, they're handing out condoms and stuff like that, and like, if they're handing out condoms, why don't they tell us you can be arrested for it?" one Spur asked Gary Collins and Sarah Purcell on *The Home Show*. "They pass out condoms, teach sex education and pregnancy this, pregnancy that, but they don't teach us any rules," another told Jane Gross of *The New York Times*. "Schools hand out condoms, teach safe sex," the mother of a Spur complained on *The Home Show*. "It's the society, they have these clinics, they have abortions, they don't have to tell their parents, the schools give out condoms, jeez, what does that tell you?" the father of one Lakewood boy, a sixteen-year-old who had just admitted to a juvenile-court petition charging him with lewd conduct with a ten-year-old girl, asked a television interviewer. "I think people are blowing this thing way out of proportion," David Ferrell of *The Los Angeles Times* was told by one Spur. "It's all been blown out of proportion as far as I'm concerned," he was told by another. "Of course there were several other sex scandals at the time, so this perfectly normal story got blown out of proportion," I was told by a Spur parent. "People, you know, kind of blow it all out of proportion," a Spur advised viewers of *Jane Whitney*. "They blow it out of proportion a lot," another said on the same show. A Spur girlfriend, "Jodi," called in to offer her opinion: "I think it's been blown way out of proportion, like way out of proportion."

Each of these speakers seemed to be referring to a cultural misery apprehended only recently, and then dimly. Those who mentioned "blowing it out of proportion" were complaining specifically about "the media," and its "power," but more generally about a sense of being besieged, set upon, at the mercy of forces beyond local control. "The whole society has changed," one Spur parent told me. "Morals have changed. Girls have changed. It used to be, girls would be more or less the ones in control. Girls would hold out, girls would want to be married at eighteen or nineteen and they'd keep their sights on having a home and love and a family." What seemed most perplexing to these Lakewood residents was that the disruption was occurring in what they uniformly referred to as "a middle-class community like this one," or sometimes "an upper-middle-class community like this one." "We're an upper-middle-class community," I was told one morning outside the Los Padrinos Juvenile Court in Downey, where a group of Lakewood women were protesting the decision of the Los Angeles County district attorney's office not to bring most of the so-called "sex charges" requested by the sheriff's department. "*It Wasn't The Bloods, Crips, Longos, It Was The Spurs,*" the hand-lettered signs read that morning, "the Longos" being a Long Beach gang. "*What If One of the Victims Had Been Your Granddaughter, Huh, Mr. District Attorney?*" "It's a very hush-hush community," another protester said. "Very low profile, they don't want to make waves, don't want to step on anybody's toes." The following is an extract from the first page of Donald J. Waldie's *Holy Land: A Suburban Memoir*:

> He knew his suburb's first 17,500 houses had been built in less than three years. He knew what this must have cost, but he did not care.
>
> The houses still worked.
>
> He thought of them as middle class even though 1,100-square-foot tract houses on streets meeting at right angles are not middle class at all.
>
> Middle-class houses are the homes of people who would not live here.

This is in fact the tacit dissonance at the center of every moment in Lakewood, which is why the average day there raises, for the visitor, so many and such vertiginous questions:

What does it cost to create and maintain an artificial ownership class?

Who pays?

Who benefits?

What happens when that class stops being useful?

What does it mean to drop back below the line?

What does it cost to hang on above it, how do you behave, what do you say, what are the pitons you drive into the granite?

One of the ugliest and most revelatory of the many ugly and revelatory moments that characterized the 1993 television appearances of Lakewood's Spur Posse members occurred on *Jane Whitney*, when a nineteen-year-old Lakewood High School graduate named Chris Albert ("Boasts He Has 44 'Points' For Having Sex With Girls") turned mean with a member of the audience, a young black woman who had tried to suggest that the Spurs on view were not exhibiting what she considered native intelligence.

"I don't get—I don't understand what she's saying," Chris Albert had at first said, letting his jaw go slack as these boys tended to do when confronted with an unwelcome, or in fact any, idea.

Another Spur had interpreted: "We're dumb. She's saying we're dumb."

"What education does she have?" Chris Albert had then demanded, and crouched forward toward the young woman, as if trying to shake himself alert. "Where do you work at? McDonald's? Burger King?" A third Spur had tried to interrupt, but Chris Albert, once roused, could not be deflected. "Five twenty-five?" he said. "Five fifty?" And then, there it was, the piton, driven in this case not into granite but into shale, already disintegrating: "*I go to college.*" Two years later Chris Albert would be dead, shot in the chest and killed during a Fourth of July celebration on the Pacific Coast Highway in Huntington Beach.

3

LAKEWOOD EXISTS BECAUSE at a given time in a different economy it had seemed an efficient idea to provide population density for the mall and a labor pool for the Douglas plant. There are a lot of towns like Lakewood in California. They were California's mill towns, breeder towns for the boom. When times were good and there was money to spread around, these were the towns that proved Marx wrong, that managed to increase the proletariat and simultaneously, by calling it middle class, to co-opt it. Such towns were organized around the sedative idealization of team sports, which were believed to develop "good citizens," and therefore tended to the idealization of adolescent males. During the good years, the years for which places like Lakewood or Canoga Park or El Segundo or Pico Rivera existed, the preferred resident was in fact an adolescent or post-adolescent male, ideally one already married and mortgaged, in harness to the plant, a good worker, a steady consumer, a team player, someone who played ball, a good citizen.

When towns like these came on hard times, it was the same adolescent males, only recently the community's most valued asset, who were most visibly left with nowhere to go. Among the Spur Posse members who appeared on the talk shows that spring, a striking number had been out of high school a year, or even two years, but did not seem actively engaged in a next step. "It was some of the older kids who were so obnoxious, so arrogant," one Spur father, Donald Belman, told me. "They're the ones who were setting up talk-show appearances just for the money. I had to kick them out of my house, they were answering my phone, monitoring my mail. They were just in it for the money, quick cash." Jane Gross of *The New York Times* asked one of these postgraduate Spurs what he had been doing since high school. "Partying," he said. "Playing ball."

Good citizens were encouraged, when partying failed, when playing ball failed, when they finally noticed that the jobs had gone to Salt Lake or St. Louis, to see their problem as one caused by "the media," or by "condoms in the schools," or by less-good citizens, or non-citizens. "Orange County is using illegal aliens now as a smokescreen, as a scapegoat, because that's the way we get the white lower-income people to jump on board and say the immigrants are the problem," the wife of an aerospace engineer in Costa Mesa told Robert Scheer of *The Los Angeles Times*. "But we had our class differences before the immigrants. One of our sons was on the football team in the high school in Costa Mesa about twelve years ago. They had a great team and they were beating the pants off one of the schools in Newport Beach and the Newport stands started to cheer. '*Hey, hey, that's OK, you're gonna work for us one day.*' "

This is what it costs to create and maintain an artificial ownership class.

This is what happens when that class stops being useful.

Most adults to whom I spoke in Lakewood during that spring of 1993 shared a sense that something in town had gone wrong. Many connected this apprehension to the Spur Posse, or at least to certain Spur Posse members who had emerged, even before the arrests and for a variety of reasons, as the community's most visible males. Almost everyone agreed that this was a town in which what had been considered the definition of good parenting, the encouragement of assertive behavior among male children, had for some reason gotten badly out of hand. The point on which many people disagreed was whether sex was at the center of this problem, and some of these people felt troubled and misrepresented by the fact that public discussion of the situation in Lakewood had tended to focus exclusively on what they called "the sex charges," or "the sexual charges." "People have to understand," I was told by one plaintive mother. "This isn't about the sexual charges." Some believed the charges intrinsically unprovable. Others seemed simply to regard sex among teenagers as a combat zone with its own rules, a contained conflict from which they were prepared, as the district attorney was, to look away. Many seemed unaware of the extent to which questions of gender had come to occupy the nation's official attention, and so had failed to appreciate the ease with which the events in Lakewood could feed seamlessly into a discussion already in progress, offer a fresh context in which to recap Tailhook, Packwood, Anita Hill.

What happened that spring had begun, most people agreed, at least a year before, maybe more. Much of what got talked about had seemed, at first, suggestive mainly of underemployed teenagers playing at acting street. There had been threats, bully tactics, the systematic harassment of girls or younger children who made complaints or "stood up to" or in any way resisted the whim of a certain group of boys. Young children in Lakewood had come to know among themselves who to avoid in those thirty-seven playgrounds, what cars to watch for on those 133 miles of No. 2 macadam. "I'm talking about throughout the community," I was told by Karin Polacheck, who represented Lakewood on the board of education for the Long Beach Unified School District. "At the baseball fields, at the parks, at the markets, on the corners of schoolgrounds. They were organized enough that young children would say, 'Watch out for that car when it comes around,' 'Watch out for those boys.' I've heard stories of walking up and stealing base-ball bats and telling kids, 'If you tell anyone I'll beat your head in.' I'm talking about young children, nine, ten years old. It's a small community. Younger kids knew that these older kids were out there."

"You're dead," the older boys would reportedly say, or "You're gonna get fucked up." "You're gonna get it." "You're gonna die." "I don't like who she's hanging with, why don't we just kill her now." There was a particular form of street terror mentioned by many people: invasive vehicular maneuvers construed by the targets as attempts to "run people down." "There were skid marks outside my house," one mother told me. "They were trying to scare my daughter. Her life was hell. She had chili-cheese nachos thrown at her at school." "They just like to intimidate people," I was repeatedly told. "They stare back at you. They don't go to school, they ditch. They ditch and then they beg the teacher to pass them, because they have to have a C average to play on the teams." "They came to our house in a truck to do something to my sister," one young woman told me. "She can't go anywhere. Can't even go to Taco Bell any more. Can't go to Jack-in-the-Box. They'll jump you. They followed me home not long ago, I just headed for the sheriff's office."

There had also been more substantive incidents, occurrences that could not be written off to schoolyard exaggeration or adolescent oversensitivity. There had been assaults in local parks, bicycles stolen and sold. There had been burglaries, credit cards and jewelry missing from the bedroom drawers of houses where local girls had been babysitting. There had even been, beginning in the summer of 1992, felony arrests: Donald Belman's son Dana, who was generally said to have "founded" the Spur Posse, was arrested on suspicion of stealing a certain number of guns from the bedroom of a house where he was said to have attended a party. Not long before that, in Las Vegas, Dana Belman and another Spur, Christopher Russo, had been detained for possession of stolen credit cards. Just before Christmas 1992, Dana Belman and Christopher Russo were detained yet again, and arrested for alleged check forgery.

There were odd quirks here, details not entirely consistent with the community's preferred view of itself. There were the high school trips to Vegas and to Laughlin, which is a Nevada casino town on the Colorado River below Las Vegas. There was the question of the certain number of guns Dana Belman was suspected of having stolen from the bedroom of the house where he was said to have attended the party: the number of guns mentioned was nineteen. Still, these details seemed to go unremarked upon, and the events unconnected. People who had been targeted by the older boys believed themselves, they said later, "all alone in this." They believed that each occasion of harassment was discrete, unique. They did not yet see a pattern in the various incidents and felonies. They had not yet made certain inductive leaps. That was before the pipe bomb.

The pipe bomb exploded on the front porch of a house not far from Lakewood High School between three and three-thirty on the morning of February 12, 1993. It destroyed one porch support. It tore holes in the stucco. It threw shrapnel into parked cars. One woman remembered that her husband was working the night shift at Rockwell and she had been sleeping light as usual when the explosion woke her. The next morning she asked a neighbor if she had heard the noise. "And she said, 'You're not going to believe it when I tell you what that was.' And she explained to me that a pipe bomb had blown up on someone's front porch. And that it had been a gang retaliatory thing. 'Gang thing?' I said. 'What are you *talking* about, a gang thing?' And she said, 'Well, you know, Spur Posse.' And I said, 'Spur Posse, what *is* Spur Posse?'"

This was the point at which the principal of Lakewood High School and the local sheriff's office, which had been trying to get a handle on the rash of felonies around town, decided to ask certain parents to attend a special meeting at the high school. Letters were sent to twenty-five families, each of which was believed to have at least one Spur Posse son. Only some fifteen people showed up at the March 2 meeting. Sheriff's deputies from both the local station and the arson-explosives detail spoke. The cause for concern, as the deputies then saw it, was that the trouble, whatever it was, seemed to be escalating: first the felonies, then a couple of car cherry bombs without much damage, now this eight-inch pipe bomb, which appeared to have been directed at one or more Spur Posse members and had been, according to a member of the arson-explosives detail, "intended to kill." It was during this meeting that someone, it was hard to sort out who, said the word "rape." Most people to whom I talked at first said that the issue had been raised by one of the parents, but those who said this had not actually been present at the meeting. Asking about this after the fact tended to be construed as potentially hostile, because the Los Angeles attorney Gloria Allred, a specialist in high-profile gender cases, had by then appeared on the scene, giving press conferences, doing talk shows, talking about possible civil litigation on behalf of the six girls who had become her clients, and generally making people in Lakewood a little sensitive about who knew what and when they had known it and what they had done about what they knew.

What happened next was also unclear. Lakewood High School students recalled investigators from the sheriff's Whittier-based sex-abuse unit coming to the school, calling people in, questioning anyone who had even been seen talking to boys who were said to be Spurs. "I think they came up with a lot of wannabe boys," one mother told me. "Boys who wanted to belong to something that had notoriety to it." The presence of the investigators at the school might well have suggested that arrests could be pending, but school authorities said that they knew nothing until the morning of March 18, when sheriff's deputies appeared in the principal's office and said that they were going into class-rooms to take boys out in custody. "There was never any allegation that any of these incidents took place on school ground or at school events or going to and from school," Carl Cohn said on the morning we talked in his Long Beach Unified School District office. He had not been present the morning the boys were taken from their classrooms in cutoffs and handcuffs, but the television vans had been, as had *The Los Angeles Times* and *The Long Beach Press-Telegram*. "Arresting the youngsters at school might have been convenient, but it very much contributed to what is now this media circus," he said. "The sheriff's department had a press briefing. Downtown. Los Angeles. Where they notified the media that they were going in. All you have to do is mention that the perpetrators are students at a particular school and everybody gets on the freeway."

The boys arrested were detained for four nights. All but one sixteen-year-old, who was charged with lewd conduct against a ten-year-old girl, were released without charges. When those still enrolled at Lakewood High went back to school, they were greeted with cheers by some students. "Of *course* they were treated as heroes, they'd been wrongly accused," I was told by Donald Belman, whose youngest son, Kristopher, was one of those arrested and released. "These girls pre-planned these things. They wanted to be looked on favorably, they wanted to be part of the clique. They wanted to be, hopefully, the girlfriends of these studs on campus." The Belman family celebrated Kristopher's release by going out for hamburgers at McDonald's, which was, Donald Belman told *The Los Angeles Times*, "the American way."

Some weeks later the district attorney's office released a statement which read in part: "After completing an extensive investigation and analysis of the evidence, our conclusion is that there is no credible evidence of forcible rape involving any of these boys.... Although there is evidence of unlawful sexual intercourse, it is the policy of this office not to file criminal charges where there is consensual sex among teenagers.... The arrogance and contempt for young women which have been displayed, while appalling, cannot form the basis for criminal charges." "The district attorney on this did her homework," Donald Belman told me. "She questioned all these kids, she found out these girls weren't the victims they were made out to be. One of these girls had tattoos for chrissake." "If it's true about the ten-year-old, I feel bad for her and her family," one Spur told David Ferrell of *The Los Angeles Times*. "My regards go out to the family." As far as Lakewood High was concerned, it was time to begin, its principal said, "the healing process."

Donald and Dottie Belman, at the time they became the most public of the Spur Posse parents, had lived for twenty-two of their twenty-five years of marriage in a beige stucco house on Greentop Street in Lakewood. Donald Belman, who worked as a salesman for an aerospace vendor, selling to the large machine shops and to prime contractors like Douglas, had graduated in 1963 from Lakewood High School, spent four years in the Marine Corps, and come home to start a life with Dottie, herself a 1967 Lakewood High graduate. "I held out for that white dress," Dottie Belman told Janet Wiscombe of *The Long Beach Press-Telegram*. "The word 'sex' was never spoken in my home. People in movies went into the bedroom and closed the door and came out with a smile on their face. Now people are having brutal sex on TV. They aren't making love. There is nothing romantic about it."

This was a family that had been, by its own and other accounts, intensively focused on its three sons, Billy, then twenty-three, Dana, twenty, and Kristopher, eighteen, all of whom, at that time, still lived at home. "I'd hate to have my kids away from me for two or three days in Chicago or New York," Donald Belman told me by way of explaining why he had given his imprimatur to the appearance of his two younger sons on *The Home Show*, which was shot in Los Angeles, but not initially on *Jenny Jones*, which was shot in Chicago. "All these talk shows start calling, I said, 'Don't do it. They're just going to lie about you, they're going to set you up.' The more the boys said no, the more the shows enticed them. *The Home Show* was where I relented. They were offering a thousand dollars and a limo and it was in L.A. *Jenny Jones* offered I think fifteen hundred, but they'd have to fly."

During the years before this kind of guidance was needed, Donald Belman was always available to coach the boys' teams. There had been Park League, there had been Little League. There had been Pony League, Colt League, Pop Warner. Dottie Belman had regularly served as Team Mother, and remembered literally running from her job as a hairdresser so that she could have dinner on the table every afternoon at five-fifteen. "They would make a home run or a touchdown and I held my head high," she told the *Press-Telegram*. "We were reliving our past. We'd walk into Little League and we were hot stuff. I'd go to Von's and people would come up to me and say, 'Your kids are great.' I was so proud. Now I go to Von's at five a.m. in disguise. I've been Mother of the Year. I've sacrificed everything for my kids. Now I feel like I have to defend my honor."

The youngest Belman, Kristopher, who graduated from Lakewood High in June 1993, had been one of the boys arrested and released without charges that March. "I was crazy that weekend," his father told me. "My boy's in jail, Kris, he's never been in any trouble whatsoever, he's an average student, a star athlete. He doesn't even have to be in school, he has enough credits to graduate, you don't have to stay in school after you're eighteen. But he's there. Just to be with his friends." Around the time of graduation, Kristopher was arraigned on a charge of "forcible lewd conduct" based on an alleged 1989 incident involving a girl who was then thirteen; this charge was later dropped and Kristopher Belman agreed to do one hundred hours of community service. The oldest Belman son, Billy, according to his father, was working and going to school. The middle son, Dana, had graduated from Lakewood High in 1991 and had been named, as his father and virtually everyone else who mentioned him pointed out, "Performer of the Year 1991," for wrestling, in the Lakewood Youth Sports Hall of Fame. The Lakewood Youth Sports Hall of Fame is not at the high school, not at City Hall, but in a McDonald's, at the corner of Woodruff and Del Amo. "They're all standouts athletically," Donald Belman told me. "My psychology and philosophy is this: I'm a standup guy, I love my sons, I'm proud of their accomplishments." Dana, his father said, was at that time "looking for work," a quest complicated by the thirteen felony, burglary and forgery charges on which he was then awaiting trial.

Dottie Belman, who had cancer surgery in April 1993, had filed for divorce in 1992 but for a year continued to live with her husband and sons on Greentop Street. "If Dottie wants to start a new life, I'm not going to hold her back," Donald Belman told the *Press-Telegram*. "I'm a solid guy. Just a solid citizen. I see no reason for any thought that our family isn't just all-American, basic and down-to-earth." Dottie Belman, when she spoke to the *Press-Telegram*, had been more reflective. "The wrecking ball shot right through the mantel and the house has crumbled," she said. "Dana said the other day, 'I want to be in the ninth grade again, and I want to do everything differently. I had it all. I was Mr. Lakewood. I was a star. I was popular. As soon as I graduated, I lost the recognition. I want to go back to the wonderful days. Now it's one disaster after another.' "

"You saw the papers," Ira Ewing says in "Golden Land" to the woman, a divorcée with a fourteen-year-old child of her own, who has become his sole consolation. "I can't understand it! After all the advantages that ... after all I tried to do for them—"

The woman tries to calm him, offers him lunch.

"No. I don't want any lunch.—After all I have tried to give—"

Which was another way of saying: "The wrecking ball shot right through the mantel and the house has crumbled." It was 1996 when Dana Belman, convicted on three counts of burglary in the first degree, began serving a ten-year sentence at the California Men's Colony in San Luis Obispo. It was 1999 when he was discharged from prison, and a year later when he was released from parole.

4

ONCE WHEN I was twelve or thirteen and had checked the Lynds'
Middletown and *Middletown in Transition* out of the Sacramento
library, I asked my mother to what "class" we belonged.

"It's not a word we use," she said. "It's not the way we think."

On one level I believed this to be a willful misreading of
what even a twelve-year-old could see to be the situation and
on another level I understood it to be true: it was not the way
we thought in California. We believed in fresh starts. We believed
in good luck. We believed in the miner who scratched together
one last stake and struck the Comstock Lode. We believed in the
wildcatter who leased arid land at two and a half cents an acre
and brought in Kettleman Hills, fourteen million barrels of crude
in its first three years. We believed in all the ways that apparently played-out possibilities could while we slept turn green and
golden. *Keep California Green and Golden*, was the state's Smokey
the Bear fire motto around the time I was reading the Lynds.
Put out your campfire, kill the rattlesnake and watch the money
flow in.

And it did.

Even if it was somebody else's money.

The extent to which the postwar boom years confirmed this
warp in the California imagination, and in the expectations of
its citizens, would be hard to overestimate. Good times today and
better times tomorrow were supposed to come with the territory,
roll in with the regularity of the breakers on what was once the
coast of the Irvine ranch and became Newport Beach, Balboa,
Lido Isle. Good times were the core conviction of the place, and
it was their only gradually apparent absence, in the early 1990s,
that began to unsettle California in ways that no one exactly
wanted to plumb. The recognition that the trend was no longer
reliably up came late and hard to California. The 1987 market

crash was widely if not consciously seen by its citizens as just one more of the problems that plagued the America they had left behind, evidence of a tiresome eastern negativity that would not travel. Even when the defense plants started closing down off the San Diego Freeway and the for-lease signs started going up in Orange County, very few people wanted to see a connection with the way life was going to be lived in the California that was not immediately identifiable as "aircraft."

This was in fact a state in which virtually every county was to one degree or another dependent on defense contracts, from the billions upon billions of federal dollars that flowed into Los Angeles County to the five-digit contracts in counties like Plumas and Tehama and Tuolomne, yet the sheer geographical isolation of different parts of the state tended to obscure the elementary fact of its interrelatedness. Even within Los Angeles County, there had seemed no meaningful understanding that if General Motors shut down its assembly plant in Van Nuys, say, as it did in fact do in 1992, twenty-six hundred jobs lost, the bell would eventually toll in Bel Air, where the people lived who held the paper on the people who held the mortgages in Van Nuys. I recall asking a real estate broker on the west side of Los Angeles, in June 1988, what effect a defense cutback would have on the residential real estate boom then in progress. She said that such a cutback would have no effect on the west side of Los Angeles, because people who worked for Hughes and Douglas did not live in Pacific Palisades or Santa Monica or Malibu or Beverly Hills or Bel Air or Brentwood or Holmby Hills. "They live in Torrance maybe, or Canoga Park or somewhere."

Torrance is off the San Diego Freeway, west of Lakewood and south of El Segundo and Hawthorne and Lawndale and Gardena. Canoga Park is in the San Fernando Valley. People who worked for Hughes did in 1988 live in Torrance and Canoga Park. Five years later, after passage by the Arizona state legislature of a piece of tax-incentive legislation known locally as "the Hughes bill," Hughes was moving a good part of its El Segundo and Canoga Park operations to Tucson, and a well-known residential real estate broker on the west side of Los Angeles was advising clients that the market in Beverly Hills was down 47.5 percent. I remember being told, by virtually everyone to whom I spoke in Los Angeles during the few months that followed the 1992 riot, how much the riot had "changed" the city. Most of those who said this had lived in Los Angeles, as I had, during the 1965 Watts riot, but 1992, they assured me, had been "different," 1992 had "changed everything." The words they used seemed overfreighted, ominous in an unspecific way, words like "sad" and "bad." Since these were largely not people who had needed a riot to tell them that a volatile difference of circumstance and understanding existed between the city's haves and its have-nots, what they said puzzled me, and I pressed for a closer description of how Los Angeles had changed. After the riot, I was told, it was impossible to sell a house in Los Angeles. The notion it might have been impossible to sell a house in Los Angeles that year for a simpler reason, the reason being that the money had gone away, was still in 1992 so against the grain of the place as to be largely rejected.

The sad, bad times had actually begun, most people later allowed, in 1989, when virtually every defense contractor in Southern California began laying off. TRW had already dropped a thousand jobs. Rockwell had dropped five thousand as its B-1 program ended. Northrop dropped three thousand. Hughes dropped six thousand. Lockheed's union membership had declined, between 1981 and 1989, from fifteen thousand to seven thousand. McDonnell Douglas asked five thousand managers to resign, then to compete against one another for 2,900 jobs. Yet there was still, in McDonnell Douglas towns like Long Beach and Lakewood, space to maneuver, space for a little reflexive optimism and maybe even a trip to Vegas or Laughlin, since the parent corporation's Douglas Aircraft Company, the entity responsible for commercial as opposed to defense aircraft, was hiring for what was then its new MD-11 line. "Douglas is going great guns right now because of the commercial sector," I had been told in 1989 by David Hensley, who then headed the UCLA Business Forecasting Project. "Airline traffic escalated tremendously after deregulation. They're all beefing up their fleets, buying planes, which means Boeing up in Washington and Douglas here. That's a buffer against the downturn in defense spending."

These early defense layoffs were described at the time as "correctives" to the buildup of the Reagan years. Later they became "reorganizations" or "consolidations," words that still suggested the normal trimming and tacking of individual companies; the acknowledgment that the entire aerospace industry might be in trouble did not enter the language until a few years later, when "the restructuring" became preferred usage. The language used, like the geography, had worked to encyst the problem in certain communities, enabling Los Angeles at large to see the layoffs as abstractions, the predictable if difficult detritus of geopolitical change, in no way logically connected to whether the mini-mall at the corner made it or went under. It had been August 1990 before anybody much noticed that the commercial and residential real estate markets had dried up in Los Angeles. It had been October 1990 before a *Los Angeles Times* business report tentatively suggested that a local slowdown "appears to have begun."

Before 1991 ended, California had lost sixty thousand aerospace jobs. Many of these jobs had moved to southern and southwestern states offering lower salary scales, fewer regulations, and state and local governments, as in Arizona, not averse to granting tax incentives. Rockwell was entertaining bids on its El Segundo plant. Lockheed had decided to move production on its Advanced Tactical Fighter from Burbank to Marietta, Georgia. By 1992, more than seven hundred manufacturing plants had relocated or chosen to expand outside California, taking with them 107,000 jobs. Dun & Bradstreet reported 9,985 California business failures during the first six months of 1992. Analysts spoke approvingly of the transition from large companies to small businesses. *The Los Angeles Daily News* noted the "trend toward a new, more independent work force that will become less reliant on the company to provide for them and more inclined toward entrepreneurship," in other words, no benefits and no fixed salary, a recipe for motel people. Early in 1991, the Arco oil refinery in Carson, near where the Harbor and San Diego Freeways intersect, had placed advertisements in *The Los Angeles Times* and *The Orange County Register* for twenty-eight jobs paying $11.42 to $17.45 an hour. By the end of a week some fourteen thousand applicants had appeared in person at the refinery, and an unspecified number more had mailed in resumes. "I couldn't get in the front gate," an Arco spokesman told the *Times*. "Security people were directing traffic. It was quite a sight to see."

According to the Commission on State Finance in Sacramento, which monitors federal spending and its impact on the state, some 800,000 jobs were lost in California between 1988 and 1993. More than half the jobs lost were in Los Angeles County. The commission's May 1993 report estimated the further loss, between 1993 and 1997, of another 90,000 aerospace jobs, as well as 35,000 civilian jobs at bases scheduled for closure, but warned that "the potential loss could be greater if the defense industry continues to consolidate operations outside California." The Bank of America estimated six to eight hundred thousand jobs lost between 1990 and 1993, but made an even more bleak projection: four to five hundred thousand more jobs lost, in the state's "downsizing industries," between 1993 and 1995. This was what people in Los Angeles were talking about when they talked about the 1992 riot.

5

PEOPLE WHO WORKED on the line in the big California aerospace plants had constituted, in the good years, a kind of family. Many of them were second generation, and would mention the father who worked on the Snark missile, the brother who was foreman of a fabricating shop in Pico Rivera, the uncle who used to get what seemed like half the A-4 line out to watch Little League. These people might move among the half dozen or so major suppliers, but almost never outside them. The conventions of the marketplace remained alien to them. They worked to military specifications, or "milspec," a system that, *The Washington Post* noted, provided fifteen pages of specs for the making of chocolate cookies. They took considerable pride in working in an industry where decisions were not made in what Kent Kresa, then chairman of Northrop, dismissed as "a green eyeshade way." They believed their companies to be consecrated to what they construed as the national interest, and to deserve, in turn, the nation's unconditional support. They believed in McDonnell Douglas. They believed in Rockwell, Hughes, Northrop, Lockheed, General Dynamics, TRW, Litton Industries. They believed in the impossibility of adapting even the most elementary market principles to the manufacturing of aircraft. They believed the very notion of "fixed price," which was the shorthand contractors used to indicate that the government was threatening not to pay for cost overruns, to be antithetical to innovation, anathema to a process that was by its own definition undefined and uncertain.

Since this was an industry in which machine parts were drilled to within two-thousandths or even one-thousandth of an inch, tolerances that did not immediately lend themselves to automation, the people who worked in these plants had never, as they put it, gone robotic. They were the last of the medieval hand workers, and the spaces in which they worked, the huge structures with the immaculate white floors and the big rigs and the overhead cameras and the project banners and the flags of the foreign buyers, became the cathedrals of the Cold War, occasionally visited by but never entirely legible to the uninitiated. "Assembly lines are like living things," I was once told by the manager of assembly operations on the F/A-18 line at Northrop in El Segundo. "A line will gain momentum and build toward a delivery. I can touch it, I can feel it. Here on the line we're a little more blunt and to the point, because this is where the rubber meets the road. If we're going to ship an airplane every two days, we need people to respond to this." *Navy Pilots Are Depending On You*, a banner read in the high shadowy reaches above the F/A-18 line. *Build It As If You Were Going to Fly It*, another read. A toolbox carried this message: *With God & Guts & Guns Our Freedom Was Won!*

This was a world bounded by a diminishing set of coordinates. There were from the beginning a finite number of employers who needed what these people knew how to deliver, and what these people knew how to deliver was only one kind of product. "Our industry's record at defense conversion is unblemished by success," Norman Augustine, then the chairman and CEO of Martin Marietta, told *The Washington Post* in 1993. "Why is it rocket scientists can't sell toothpaste? Because we don't know the market, or how to research, or how to market the product. Other than that, we're in good shape."

Increasingly, the prime aerospace contractors had come to define themselves as "integrators," meaning that a larger and larger proportion of what they delivered, in some cases as much as seventy-five percent, had been supplied by subcontractors. The prime contractors were of course competitive with one another, but there was also an interdependence, a recognition that they had, vis-à-vis their shared principal customer, the federal government, a mutual interest. In this spirit, two or three competing contractors would typically "team" a project, submitting a joint bid, supporting one another during the lobbying phase, and finally dividing the spoils of production.

McDonnell Douglas had been the prime contractor on the F/A-18, an attack aircraft used by both the Navy and the Marine Corps and sold by the Air Force to such foreign users as the Republic of Korea, Malaysia, Australia, Canada, Spain, and Kuwait. McDonnell Douglas, however, teamed the F/A-18 with Northrop, which would every week send, from its El Segundo plant, two partial airplanes, called "shipsets," to the McDonnell Douglas facility in St. Louis. Each Northrop shipset for the F/A-18 included the fuselage and two tails, "stuffed," which is what aircraft people say to indicate that a piece of an airplane comes complete with its working components. McDonnell Douglas would then assemble the shipsets with the wings and other components, and roll the finished F/A-18s off its own line. Northrop and McDonnell Douglas again teamed on a prototype for the YF-23 Advanced Tactical Fighter, but lost the contract to Lockheed, which had teamed its own ATF prototype with Boeing and General Dynamics. Boeing, in turn, teamed its commercial 747 with Northrop, which supplied several 747 shipsets a month, each consisting of the center fuselage and associated sub-assemblies, or stuffing. General Dynamics had the prime contract with the Navy for the A-12 attack jet, but had teamed it with McDonnell Douglas.

The perfect circularity of the enterprise, one in which politicians controlled the letting of government contracts to companies which in turn utilized the contracts to employ potential voters, did not encourage natural selection. When any single element changed in this hermetic and interrelated world, for example a shift in the political climate enabling even one member of Congress to sense a gain in questioning the cost of even one DOD project, the interrelatedness tended to work against adaptation. One tree falls and the food chain fails: on the day in 1991 when Richard B. Cheney, then secretary of defense, finally canceled the Navy's contract with General Dynamics for the A-12, thousands of McDonnell Douglas jobs got wiped out in St. Louis, where McDonnell Douglas had been teaming the A-12 with General Dynamics.

To protect its headquarters plant in St. Louis, McDonnell Douglas moved some of the production on its own C-17 program from Long Beach to St. Louis. To protect the program itself, the company opened a C-17 plant in Macon, Georgia, what was called in the industry a "double-hitter," situated as it was in both the home state of Senator Sam Nunn, chairman of the Senate Armed Services Committee, and the home district of Rep. J. Roy Rowland, a member of the House Veterans' Affairs Committee. "It was smart business to put a plant in Macon," a former McDonnell Douglas executive told Ralph Vartabedian of *The Los*

Angeles Times. "There wouldn't be a C-17 without Nunn's support. There is nothing illegal or immoral about wanting to keep your program funded."

The C-17 was a cargo plane with a capacity for landing, as its supporters frequently mentioned, "on short runways like in Bosnia." It entered development in the mid-1980s. By the time the first plane was delivered in 1993 the number of planes on order from the Air Force had dropped from 210 to 120 and the projected cost of each had risen from $150 million to $380 million. The C-17, even more than most programs, had been plagued by cost overruns and technical problems. There were flaws in the landing gear, a problem with the flaps, trouble meeting range and payload specifications. One test aircraft leaked fuel. Another emerged from a ground strength-certification test with broken wings. Once off the ground, the plane showed a distressing readiness to pitch up its nose and go into a stall.

On June 14, 1993, the day the Air Force accepted delivery of its first C-17 Globemaster III, the plane was more than a year behind schedule, already $1.4 billion over budget, and not yet within sight of a final design determination. Considerable show attended this delivery. Many points were made. The ceremony took place at Charleston Air Force Base in South Carolina, the home state of Senator Strom Thurmond, then the ranking minority member of the Senate Armed Services Committee, as well as of Representatives Floyd Spence, John M. Spratt, Jr., and Arthur Ravenal, Jr., all members of the House Armed Services Committee. Some thirty-five hundred officials turned out. The actual aircraft, which was being delivered with 125 "waivers and deviations" from contract specifications and had been flown east with a load of ballast positioned to keep the nose from pitching up, was piloted on its delivery leg by General Merrill McPeak, the Air Force chief of staff. "We had it loaded with Army equipment … a couple of Humvees, twenty or thirty soldiers painted up for battle," General McPeak reported a few days later at a Pentagon briefing. "And I would just say that it's a fine airplane, wonderful capability when we get it fielded, it will make a big difference to us in terms of the global mobility requirement we have, and so I just think, you know, it's a home run."

At the time General McPeak pronounced the plane a home run, 8,700 of the remaining employees at McDonnell Douglas's

Long Beach plant were working on the C-17. What those 8,700 employees would be doing the month or the year after that remained, at that time, an open question, since even as the Air Force was demonstrating support of its own program, discussions had begun about how best to dispose of it. There were a number of options under consideration. One was to transfer program management from McDonnell Douglas to Boeing. Another was to further reduce the number of C-17s on order from 120 to as few as 25. The last-ditch option, the A-12 solution, was to just pull the plug. The Long Beach plant was the plant on the Lakewood city line, the plant with the American flag whipping in the wind and the forward-slanted logo and the boarded-up motel with the marquee that still read "Welcome Douglas Happy Hour 4–7." This was what people in Lakewood were talking about when they talked about the Spur Posse.

6

OF THE EIGHTY-NINE members of the Lakewood High School Class of 1989 who had responded, a year after graduation, to a school district questionnaire asking what they were doing, seventy-one said that they were attending college full or part time. Forty-two of those were enrolled at Long Beach Community College. Five were at community colleges in the neighboring communities of Cerritos and Cypress. Twelve were at various nearby California State University campuses: Fullerton, Long Beach, San Diego, Pomona. Two had been admitted to the University of California system, one to Irvine and one to Santa Barbara. One was at U.S.C. Nine were at unspecified other campuses. During the 1990–91 school year, 234 Lakewood High students were enrolled in the district's magnet program in aerospace technology, which channeled into Long Beach Community College and McDonnell Douglas. Lakewood High's SAT scores for that year averaged 362 verbal and 440 math, a total of ninety-five points below the state average.

This was not a community that pushed its children hard, or launched them into the far world. Males were encouraged to continue, after graduation and indeed into adulthood, playing ball (many kinds of ball, all kinds of ball) in the parks and on the schoolgrounds where they had grown up. Females were encouraged to participate in specific sports of their own, as well as to support the team activities of the ball players. Virtually everyone to whom I spoke in the spring of 1993 mentioned the city's superior sports program. "It's been a very clean community," I was told by John Todd, who had been instrumental in the city's 1954 incorporation and had served as city attorney ever since. "The people that made it up were sound American citizens. We were oriented to our schools and churches and other local activities. We have a tremendous park and recreation program here in Lakewood. And it tended to keep people here." Another longtime resident, whose oldest son worked for McDonnell

Douglas and whose other grown children were all in school nearby, echoed this: "It's just a mass recreation program to keep them all busy."

People in Lakewood often mentioned to me how much there was going on in the area. There were the batting cages. There was bowling. There were many movies around. There was, nearby in Downey, the campaign to preserve the nation's last operating original McDonald's, a relic of 1953 at the corner of Lakewood Boulevard and Florence Avenue. "If they're going to tear this down, they might as well tell Clinton please take your business to Taco Bell," one observer told the *Press-Telegram*. And there was, always, the mall, Lakewood Center, the actual and figurative center of town. During the days I spent in Lakewood I had occasion to visit the mall now and then, and each time I found it moderately busy, the fact that its sales figures had decreased every quarter since 1990 notwithstanding. There was a reflecting pool, a carousel, a Burger King, a McDonald's, if not an original McDonald's. There was a booth offering free information on prescriptions. There was another displaying photographs of houses for sale. I said to a woman leafing through the listings that I had not before seen houses for sale in a mall. "H.U.D. and V.A. repos," she said.

One day at the mall I walked over to the freestanding Bullock's, which, because it was about to close its doors for good, was in the process of selling everything in the store at thirty-five percent off the ticket price. There were women systematically defoliating the racks in the men's swear department, women dropping discards and hangers in tangles on the floor, women apparently undiscouraged by the scrawled sign warning that register lines were "currently in excess of 3+ hours long," women who had already staked out positions for the wait, women curled with their children on the floor, women who had bulwarked their positions with forts of quilts, comforters, bedspreads, mattress pads, Cuisinarts, coffee makers, sandwich grills, Juice Tigers, and Heart Wafflers. These were the women and the daughters and granddaughters of the women who had seen the hundred-foot pylon in 1950 and decided that this was the place to start. The clerks and security personnel monitoring the register lines were men. These were the men and the sons and grandsons of the men who used to get what seemed like half the A-4 line out to watch Little League.

"WE WANT GREAT cities, large factories, and mines worked cheaply, in this California of ours!" That was Henry George, in "What the Railroad Will Bring Us," rhetorically setting forth what was in 1868 popular local sentiment. Then he proceeded to count the cost:

> Would we esteem ourselves gainers if New York, ruled and robbed by thieves, loafers and brothel-keepers; nursing a race of savages fiercer and meaner than any who ever shrieked a war-whoop on the plains; could be set down on our bay tomorrow? Would we be gainers, if the cotton-mills of Massachusetts, with their thousands of little children who, official papers tell us, are being literally worked to death, could be transported to the banks of the American; or the file and pin factories of England, where young girls are treated worse than even slaves on southern plantations, be reared as if by magic at Antioch? Or if among our mountains we could by wishing have the miners, men, women and children, who work the iron and coal mines of Belgium and France, where the condition of production is that the laborer shall have meat but once a week—would we wish them here?

> Can we have one thing without the other?

In those towns off the San Diego Freeway that had seemed when times were good to answer Henry George's question in the affirmative, 1993 was a sullen spring. In April, about the time the Lakewood Center Bullock's was selling the last of its Heart Wafflers, the ten-year-old girl who said that she had been assaulted by a Spur Posse member gave her first press conference, in Gloria Allred's office. Her mother had been seen, on *Donahue*, *The Home Show*, and *20/20*, but the child, by that time eleven, had not. "I have been upset because I wanted to be on TV," she said at her press conference. "To show how I feel. I wanted to say it for myself." Also in April, Spur Posse members approached various talent agencies, trying to sell their story for a TV movie. An I.C.M. agent asked these Spurs if they were not concerned about how they might be presented. Their concern, they told him, was how much money they would make. I.C.M. declined to represent the Spurs, as did, it was later reported, C.A.A., United Talent Agency, and William Morris.

It was April, too, at the Douglas plant on the Lakewood city line, when Teamsters Local 692 went on strike, over the issue of whether or not Douglas could contract out work previously done by union members. "They can't do that to people after twenty-seven years," the wife of one driver, for whom the new contract would mean a cut from $80,000 to $35,000 a year, told the *Press-Telegram*. "It's just not right." It was in April, again, that Finnair disclosed discussions about a switch from its mostly Douglas fleet to buying Boeing. It was in May that Continental, just out of bankruptcy reorganization, ordered ninety-two new planes, with options for ninety-eight more, all from Boeing.

In a town where it was possible to hear, unprompted, a spirited defense of the DC-10 ("Very quiet plane," John Todd told me, "nice flying plane, compared to those Boeings and those other airplanes it makes about half as much noise"), the involvement with Douglas went deeper than mere economic dependence. People in Lakewood had defined their lives as Douglas. I had lunch one day with a 1966 graduate of Lakewood High who had later spent time in the Peace Corps. It seemed that somewhere in the heart of Africa, he had hopped a ride on a DC-3. The DC-3 had a plate indicating that it had come off the Long Beach line, and he had thought, There it is, I've come as far as I can go and it's still Douglas. "It's a town on the plantation model," he said to me at lunch. "Douglas being the big house."

"They're history," an aircraft industry executive said that spring to *The Washington Post*. "I see a company going out of business, barring some miracle," Don E. Newquist, chairman of the International Trade Commission, said at a hearing on commercial aerospace competitiveness. Each was talking about Douglas, and by extension about the plant on the Lakewood city line, the plant with the flag and the forward-slanted logo and the

MD-11s parked like cars and the motel with the marquee that still read "Welcome Douglas Happy Hour 4–7." "It's like a lifetime thing," one Lakewood High graduate said on *Jane Whitney*, trying to explain the Spur Posse and what held its members together. "We're all going to be friends for life, you know."

It was 1997 when Douglas was finally melted into Boeing, and the forward-slanted letters reading *MCDONNELL DOUGLAS* vanished from what was now the Boeing plant on the Lakewood city line.

It was 1999 when Boeing shut down Douglas's MD-90 program.

It was 2000 when Boeing shut down Douglas's MD-80 program, 2001 when Boeing shut down Douglas's MD-11 program.

It was 2000 when Boeing began talking about its plan to convert two hundred and thirty acres of what had been the Douglas plant into non-aircraft use, in fact a business park, "PacifiCenter," with its own condominium housing and the dream of attracting, with what inducements became increasingly unclear as the economy waned, such firms as Intel and Sun Microsystems.

It was 2002 when Boeing obtained an order from the Pentagon for sixty additional C-17s, another temporary stay of execution for what had been the Douglas program, which had been scheduled for closure in 2004. "It's a great day," the manager on the program told employees on the day he announced the order. "This is going to keep you employed through 2008, so rest tonight and start on sixty more tomorrow."

It was also 2002 when the first stage of a multi-billion-dollar public works project called the "Alameda Corridor" was completed, a $2.4 billion twenty-mile express railway meant to speed freight containers from the ports of Long Beach and Los Angeles to inland distribution points. This "Alameda Corridor" had been for some years a kind of model civic endeavor, one of those political mechanisms designed to reward old friends and make new ones. During the period when the Alameda Corridor was still only an idea, but an idea moving inexorably toward a start date, its supporters frequently framed it as the way to bring a "new economy" to the twenty-six "Gateway Cities" involved, all of which had been dependent on aerospace and one of which was

Lakewood. This "new economy" was to be built on "international trade," an entirely theoretical replacement for the gold-standard money tree, the federal government, that had created these communities. Many seminars on "global logistics" were held. Many warehouses were built. The first stage of the Alameda Corridor was near completion before people started wondering what exactly these warehouses were to bring them; started wondering, for example, whether eight-dollars-an-hour forklift operators, hired in the interests of a "flexible" work force only on those days when the warehouse was receiving or dispatching freight, could ever become the "good citizens" of whom Mark Taper had spoken in 1969, the "enthusiastic owners of property," the "owners of a piece of their country—a stake in the land." *California likes to be fooled*, as Cedarquist, the owner in *The Octopus* of the failed San Francisco iron works, told Presley at the Bohemian Club.

In 1970 I was working for *Life*, and went up to eastern Oregon to do a piece on the government's storage of VX and GB nerve gas on twenty thousand acres near Hermiston, a farm town in Umatilla County, population then 5,300. It seemed that many citizens wanted the nerve gas, or, in the preferred term, "the defense material," the storage of which provided 717 civilian jobs and brought money into town. It seemed that other citizens, some of whom lived not in Hermiston but across the mountains in Portland and Salem, making them members of what was referred to in Hermiston as "the academic community and Other Mothers for Peace or whatever," saw the presence in Oregon of VX and GB as a hazard. The story was routine enough, and I had pretty much wrapped it up (seen the mayor, seen the city manager, seen the anti-gas district attorney in Pendleton, seen the colonel in charge of the depot and seen the rabbits they left in the bunkers to test for leaks) before I realized that the situation had for me an actual resonance: since well before Elizabeth Scott was born, members of my family had been moving through places in the same spirit of careless self-interest and optimism that now seemed to be powering this argument in Hermiston. Such was the power of the story on which I had grown up that this thought came to me as a kind of revelation: the settlement of the west, however inevitable, had not uniformly tended to the greater good, nor had it on every level benefited even those who reaped its most obvious rewards.

One afternoon in September of 2002 I drove the length of the Alameda Corridor, north from the port through what had been the industrial heart of Southern California: Carson, Compton, Watts. Lynwood, South Gate. Huntington Park. Vernon. It was a few weeks before that fall's dockworkers' strike shut down Pacific trade, and I saw that afternoon no trains, no containers, only this new rail line meant to carry the freight and these new warehouses meant to house the freight, many of them bearing for-lease signs. On the first hill north of Signal Hill there was what appeared to be a new subdivision, with a sign, "Vista Industria." Past the sign that read Vista Industria there were only more warehouses, miles of warehouses, miles of empty intersections, one Gateway City after another, each indistinguishable from the last. Only when the Arco Towers began emerging from the distant haze over downtown Los Angeles did I notice a sign on a warehouse that seemed to suggest actual current usage. *165,000 Square Feet of T-Shirt Madness*, this sign read.

Save the Aero—See "Tadpole." This was the sign on the Aero Theatre on Montana Avenue in Santa Monica in September of 2002. The Aero Theatre was built in 1939 by Donald Douglas, as recreation for his workers when Douglas Aircraft was Santa Monica's biggest employer. During the ten years when I was living not far from the Aero, 1978 to 1988, I never saw anyone actually enter or leave the theatre. Douglas built Santa Monica and then left it, and the streets running south of what had been the first Douglas plant were now lined with body shops, minimarts, Pentecostal churches and walk-in dentists. Still, Santa Monica had its ocean, its beaches, its climate, its sun and its fog and its climbing roses. The Gateway Cities will have only their warehouses.

Part III

"WHAT HAD IT all been about: all the manqué promises, the failures of love and faith and honor; Martha buried out there by the levee in a $250 dress from Magnin's with river silt in the seams; Sarah in Bryn Mawr, Pennsylvania; her father, who had not much cared, the easy loser (*He never could have been*, her mother had said and still loved him); her mother sitting alone this afternoon in the big house upriver writing out invitations for the Admission Day Fiesta and watching *Dick Clark's American Bandstand* because the Dodgers were rained out; Everett down there on the dock with his father's .38. She, her mother, Everett, Martha, the whole family gallery: they carried the same blood, come down through twelve generations of circuit riders, county sheriffs, Indian fighters, country lawyers, Bible readers, one obscure United States senator from a frontier state a long time ago; two hundred years of clearings in Virginia and Kentucky and Tennessee and then the break, the void into which they gave their rosewood chests, their silver brushes; the cutting clean which was to have redeemed them all. They had been a particular kind of people, their particular virtues called up by a particular situation, their particular flaws waiting there through all those years, unperceived, unsuspected, glimpsed only cloudily by one or two in each generation, by a wife whose bewildered eyes wanted to look not upon Eldorado but upon her mother's dogwood, by a blue-eyed boy who was at sixteen the best shot in the county and who when there was nothing left to shoot rode out one day and shot his brother, an accident. It had been above all a history of accidents: of moving on and of accidents. What is it you want, she had asked Everett tonight. It was a question she might have asked them all."

That passage is from the last few pages of a novel, *Run River*, published in 1963. The author of the novel was me. The protagonist, the "she" of the passage, is Lily McClellan, born Lily Knight, the wife of a hop grower on the Sacramento River. As the novel opens, Lily's husband, Everett McClellan, has just shot and killed the man with whom both Lily and his sister Martha have had affairs. This story, the "plot" of the novel, was imagined, but the impulse that initially led me to imagine this story and not another was real: I was a year or two out of Berkeley, working for *Vogue* in New York, and experiencing a yearning for California so raw that night after night, on copy paper filched from my office and the Olivetti Lettera 22 I had bought in high school with the money I made stringing for *The Sacramento Union* ("Big mistake buying Italian," my father had advised, "as you'll discover the first time you need a part replaced"), I sat on one of my apartment's two chairs and set the Olivetti on the other and wrote myself a California river.

The "stuff" of the novel, then, was the landscape and weather of the Sacramento Valley, the way the rivers crested and the way the tule fogs obscured the levees and the way the fallen camellias turned the sidewalks brown and slick during the Christmas rains. The stuff, too, was in the way those rains and those rivers had figured in the stories I had been told my entire life, stories predicated on the childhood memories of relatives (Kilgores and Reeses, Jerretts and Farnsworths, Magees and Cornwalls) who were by then long dead themselves, fragments of local oral history preserved by daughters and granddaughters on legal pads and the backs of envelopes:

> That winter was a very wet winter, raining night and day for weeks. It was always called the winter of the Flood as the levee broke on the east side of Sacramento and the city was a lake of water, boats running up and down the streets and small houses floating around like dry goods boxes. This was in 1861 and 1862.

> During the flood it was impossible to get any provisions out of Sacramento, only by boat, so three of our neighbors who were out of tobacco, Wm. Scholefield, Myron Smith and a man by the name of Sidell, built a boat out of

rough boards and launched it in the creek on Scholefield's place and went to Sacramento by water, two rowing and one bailing the water out. They made the round trip and brought home their tobacco and some provisions.

The downpour continued and the river swelled until the banks overflowed. The families were soon engulfed by the water. They gathered as much of their belongings as were salvageable and moved by rowboat to a two-story house on the Grape Vine Ranch, about one-half mile away.

The importance of recording these memories was unquestioned: the flood and the levees and the two-story house on the Grape Vine Ranch had become, like the potato masher that crossed the plains, like the books that did not get jettisoned on the Umpqua River, evidence of family endurance, proof of our worth, indistinguishable from the crossing story itself.

During this time Elizabeth became critically ill. It was typhoid. Allen and one of the Kilgore cousins rowed through the storm to Sacramento for necessary supplies. The current of the rampant river flood raged about them and it took two days and nights to reach the settlement city. The morning following Allen's return, Elizabeth died. Allen built a coffin for Elizabeth and the women dressed her in a garment of coarse white cotton. The coffin was rowed to hilly ground where there were already other graves. The ground was so full of water that the grave was like a well. Here Elizabeth was buried as there was no other place available.

"Two hundred years of clearings in Virginia and Kentucky and Tennessee and then the break, the void into which they gave their rosewood chests, their silver brushes, the cutting clean which was to have redeemed them all." This was the crossing story as origin myth, the official history as I had learned it. Although certain other lines in that passage from *Run River* suggest that I was beginning to entertain some doubt ("what had it all been about," "a history of accidents: of moving on and of accidents"), the passage now raises questions that did not at the time occur to me. From what exactly was "the break" or "the void" or "the cutting clean" to have redeemed them? From their Scotch-Irish genes? From the idealization that had alchemized the luckless of Wales and Scotland and Ireland into classless western yeomen? From the confusions that led both Jack London and *The Valley of the Moon*'s Saxon Brown to claim the special rights they believed due them as "old American stock"? Or were they to have been redeemed from the break itself, the "cutting clean," "the void"? And the related question: for *what* were they to have been redeemed? To make of their lives, as Nancy Hardin Cornwall was said to have made of hers, "one ceaseless round of activity"? To "live up to our heritage," as I put it in my eighth-grade graduation speech, and "go on to better and greater things for California"? What exactly was our heritage? *Remember,* as Virginia Reed wrote to her cousin, *never take no cutoffs and hurry along as fast as you can.*

Much in *Run River*, as I believed when I was writing it and as I read it now, some four decades later, has to do with the ways California was or is "changing," the detailing of which permeates the novel with a tenacious (and, as I see it now, pernicious) mood of nostalgia. The current action (much of the novel is past action) takes place in August 1959. Everett McClellan's sister Martha has been dead more than ten years, drowned when she took a boat onto the river in flood stage. On the March morning after Martha's death, as Everett and the ranch foreman dig the grave by the levee in which they will bury her, Lily concentrates on the river, on where and when the levee will go, on the "file of information, gathered and classified every year there was high water.... At what point had they opened the Colusa Weir. How many gates were open at the Sacramento Weir. When would the Bypass reach capacity. What was the flood stage at Wilkins Slough. At Rough and Ready Bend. Fremont Weir. Rio Vista."

As presented, Martha McClellan's burial on the ranch, with the river still rising and talk confined to speculation about whether the Army Engineers will dynamite an upstream levee, would seem to represent an idea of traditional, or "old," California. We are told that Martha herself, as a child, invented a game called "Donner

Party," in which she herself starred as Tamsen Donner, and hung on the walls of her room "neither Degas ballet dancers nor scenes from *Alice in Wonderland* but a framed deed signed by John Sutter in 1847, a matted list of the provisions carried on an obscure crossing in 1852, a detailed relief map of the Humboldt Sink, and a large lithograph of Donner Pass on which Martha had printed, in two neat columns, the names of the casualties and survivors of the Donner-Reed crossing." To a similar point, Martha is buried in the sea chest in which her mother, long dead, had kept her linens, along with "ends of lace, a box of jet beading from a dress, and the ivory fan carried by Martha's great-great-grandmother Currier at Governor Leland Stanford's Inaugural Ball in 1862." To lay in the grave, Everett has torn down "whole branches" of camellias, which are presented in the novel as having, since they were planted locally in memory of the pioneers, a totemic significance. If the grave washes out, which it surely will if the river continues rising, Martha (and the totemic camellias) will be "free again in the water," at one with the river, a prospect that seems to deter, as "true" Californians, neither her brother nor her sister-in-law.

The year Martha dies is 1949. By 1959, as presented in *Run River*, this "true" California has been largely obliterated. The pear orchards on which Lily herself grew up are being relentlessly uprooted: her mother is selling off the acreage for development as fast as the bank will allow her to subordinate it. The ranches immediately upriver and downriver from the McClellan ranch are already subdivisions, Rancho Del Rio No. 1 and Rancho Del Rio No. 3. This is unsettling to Everett but not so to his and Lily's son, Knight. "They're just biding their time," Knight says. "Waiting it out for Rancho Del Rio No. 2." Knight is about to go east to college, to Princeton, a "new" kind of choice (the "traditional" choice would have been Berkeley or Stanford) and so, again, unsettling. Knight is full of himself, and lectures his mother, who has asked him, since he is driving to Berkeley, to pick up some new paperback books on Telegraph Avenue. From Knight's point of view:

> She did not seem to realize that there were now paperback bookstores in Sacramento. She and his father would never seem to get it through their heads that things were

changing in Sacramento, that Aerojet General and Douglas Aircraft and even the State College were bringing in a whole new class of people, people who had lived back East, people who read things. She and his father were going to be pretty surprised if and when they ever woke up to the fact that nobody in Sacramento any more had even heard of the McClellans. Or the Knights. Not that he thought they ever would wake up. They'd just go right along dedicating their grubby goddamn camellia trees in Capitol Park to the memory of their grubby goddamn pioneers.

There are other signs of change, which, in the construct of the novel, is understood to mean decline. There is Everett's older sister, Sarah, who lives outside Philadelphia, another "new" kind of choice, with her third husband: again, a new kind of choice. Sarah has stopped by the ranch on her way to Maui (still another new choice, since the traditional Hawaiian destination would be Honolulu, on the *Lurline*), apologized to her husband for the Valley heat ("true" children of the Valley are made uneasy by summer temperatures that do not reach three digits), and made it clear to Everett that she tolerates his wish to keep as ranches rather than subdivide their joint inheritance, seven thousand acres on the Sacramento and Cosumnes Rivers, only as a provisional indulgence. "Surely we've had offers," Sarah suggests to Everett. Everett allows that interest has been expressed in the ranch on the Cosumnes. "I don't *care* so much about the Cosumnes," Sarah says. "The Cosumnes at least brings in a little cash."

There is also the man Everett will eventually shoot, Ryder Channing. Ryder Channing is the only character in the novel not "from" California, in other words one of the "new people." He first meets Martha in 1944, when he is stationed at Mather Field in Sacramento, and his appearances on the ranch to see her, which continue, inexplicably to Everett, after the war has ended and this person not from California should have gone home to wherever he came from, are presented as troubling elements. He has no intention of leaving, he tells Everett, because California is where the future is being made:

Starting now. Channing had the hunch they were in on the ground floor of the biggest boom this country had ever seen. Talk about your gold rush. And he wasn't the only one who believed in Northern California. Just one example, the Keller Brothers believed in Northern California to the tune of five million berries.

"The Keller Brothers," Everett said. "I don't believe I know them."

The Keller Brothers, Channing explained patiently, were developers. Los Angeles developers who believed in Northern California, in the Valley specifically, to the tune of five million smackeroos. Which they were putting into the Natomas District.

"I never heard of any Kellers in the Natomas," Everett said.

With what appeared to be infinite restraint, Channing inspected and crumpled three empty cigarette packages before answering. "They aren't in the Natomas right now. They want to develop the Natomas."

"Who's putting up the money? How can they raise five million dollars on land they haven't got?"

"Those sweethearts could raise five million dollars with a plot plan on the back of a goddamn napkin. Anyway," Channing added, apparently abandoning his effort to justify the Kellers' ways to Everett, "that's just one example. The point is we're sitting right here on the ground floor with the button pushed go."

Ryder, who because he has no California heritage is incapable of betraying it, not only sees the future but seizes it: he abandons Martha in 1948 to marry the daughter of a recently rich developer. ("Construction money, Everett believed. Wartime. It was all mixed up in his mind with Henry Kaiser.") Martha, about whom there have been previous suggestions of histrionic instability (at parties the year she was sixteen "it had been impossible not to notice her, as it might have been impossible not to notice someone running a high fever, or wearing a cellophane dress"), spends the winter between Ryder's marriage and her own death trying in vain to embrace this New California from which Ryder had come and to which she has now lost him: "She went everywhere, met everyone. She met builders, promoters, people looking for factory sites and talking about a deep-water channel and lobbying for federal dams; people neither Everett nor Lily would have known existed had she not told them. She went to large parties at new country clubs, went to small parties at new apartment houses, and went, almost every afternoon, to inspect subdivisions opened by one or another of the boys she knew who were going into the real estate business."

This is a not inaccurate characterization of the way Sacramento, or for that matter California itself, felt to a child growing up during the postwar boom years, the late 1940s and early 1950s; sometimes, say when I hear about what the Alameda Corridor will bring us, I still catch the echo of those years. It was true that it was suddenly possible, as if overnight, to buy paperback books at Levinson's bookstore downtown. It was true that it was suddenly possible, as if overnight, to see foreign movies—*Open City*, *The Bicycle Thief*, a lachrymose Swedish young-love picture called *One Summer of Happiness*—at the Guild Theater in Oak Park, although the only member of my family to regularly see them was a half-deaf great-aunt for whom subtitles offered the novel possibility of actually following the action onscreen. It was true that the habits and customs of "old Sacramento" (the school-vacation jobs on the ranches and at the canneries, the swimming in the rivers and wading in the ditches, the dutiful study of the agricultural exhibits at the California State Fair) were giving way to a more urban, or suburban, life, in which children swam in clear water in backyard pools lined with gunite and bought Italian typewriters and ate pears bought in supermarkets rather than dropped off in lugs by the relatives who grew them.

All this was true, and yet there was in *Run River* something that was not true, a warp, a persistent suggestion that these changes brought about by World War Two had in some way been resisted by "true" Californians. Had not any such resistance been confined to the retrospect? Were not "changes" and "boom years" what the California experience had been about since the first American settlement? Were we not still willing to traffic our own history to get what the railroad could bring us?

Take for example this business of laying the iconic camellias in Martha's grave: in point of fact the whole notion of planting camellias for the pioneers—there was in the park across from the state capitol building in Sacramento a "Camellia Grove" set aside for this purpose—had originated with my father's stepmother,

Genevieve Didion, who was for many years the president of the Sacramento City Board of Education and was said by the rest of the family, not entirely approvingly, to be "political." All association of camellias with pioneers, in other words, derived from the same spirit of civic boosterism that would later turn Front Street, along the river, into the entirely ersatz "redevelopment" known as "Old Sacramento," twenty-eight riverfront acres of shops selling trinkets and souvenirs and popcorn. "The pioneers," in other words, had become a promotional tool, Sacramento's own unique selling proposition, a way of attracting tourists, conventions, a new kind of cash that did not depend on crops: one more version of the weakness for the speculative venture that Charles Nordhoff had noted in 1874.

"The pool kills me," Everett McClellan's sister Sarah says, in *Run River*, when she visits the ranch on which he and Lily live. "It looks like Pickfair."

The year Sarah says this is 1959. Although swimming pools were fairly general throughout California by 1959, this pool on the ranch represents, as presented, Everett's first concession to the postwar mood, and so cues the reader to yet another sign of decline. This did not exactly reflect any attitude toward pools with which I was familiar.

In 1948, when my mother and father and brother and I were living on some acreage outside Sacramento on which my father had built a house until the time seemed right to subdivide the property, my brother and I wanted a pool. We could have a pool, my father said, but only if we ourselves dug it. Every morning all that hot summer my brother, Jim, who was eight, took a shovel out to the middle of the field in front of the house and chipped in vain at the hardpan that underlay the inch or two of topsoil.

Five years older than Jim, doubtful that either he or I could dig a twenty-by-forty-foot hole eight feet deep, equally doubtful that our father—were such a hole to miraculously materialize—had any intention of following through (as I saw it, he might string a hose out there and turn on the tap, but no gunite, no filter, no tile coping), I declined to dig. Instead I spent the summer reading the plays of Eugene O'Neill and dreamed of escaping to Bennington, where I would prepare myself for a New York

life in the theater by sitting in a tree in a leotard and listening to Francis Fergusson explain the difference between drama
and melodrama. This was the year, 1948, when, already plotting
my departure, I delivered the eighth-grade graduation speech on
"Our California Heritage." This was also the year, 1948, when
the Sacramento City Parks Department awarded, as prizes in its
annual Easter egg hunt, what *The Sacramento Bee* described as
"live bunnies named after pioneers," a teaching tool, it occurs
to me now, that had "Genevieve Didion" written all over it. Ten
years later I did have a New York life, although not in the theater,
and I was writing the novel that would put such a protective distance between me and the place I came from.

THIS QUESTION OF "changes," involving as it does some reflexive suggestion of a birthright squandered, a paradise lost, is a
vexed issue. I was many times told as a child that the grass in the
Sacramento Valley had at the time the American settlers arrived
in the 1840s grown so high that it could be tied over a saddle,
the point being that it did no more. California, in this telling, had
even then been "spoiled." The logical extension of this thought,
that we were the people who had spoiled it, remained unexplored.
Nor would it be explored in *Run River*, the inchoate intent of
which was to return me to a California I wished had been there
to keep me. "*Everything changes, everything changed*," one passage,
obviously acutely felt at the time I wrote it, begins. "*Summer evenings driving downriver to auctions, past the green hops in leaf, blackbirds
flying up from the brush in the dry twilight air, red Christmas-tree balls
glittering in the firelight, a rush of autumn Sundays, all gone, when you
drove through the rain to visit the great-aunts.*" The "change," the "all
gone" part, is seen in *Run River* to have come only with the postwar boom years, the prosperous years when California "as it was"
got bulldozed out of existence either for better (as Ben Weingart
and Louis Boyar and Mark Taper saw it when they conceived
Lakewood) or (as I then wished to see it) for worse.

Californians of more programmatic mind for many years
presented these postwar changes as positive, the very genius of
the place: it was conventional to mention the freeway system,
the aerospace industry, the University of California Master Plan,
Silicon Valley, the massive rearrangement of the water that got
funded when Pat Brown was governor, the entire famous package, the celebrated promise that California was committed to creating and educating an apparently infinitely expandable middle
class. The more recent programmatic attitude was to construe
the same changes as negative, false promises: the freeways had
encouraged sprawl, the aerospace industry had gone away, the
University of California had lost faculty and classrooms to budget

cuts, Silicon Valley had put housing beyond the means of non-tech California, and most of the state was still short water.

In a book of readings for students in freshman composition classes at California colleges, the editors and contributors speak of "the threats to the California dream," of the need to keep "the California dream in sight," of "the fashionable new mythology emerging nationwide in which California is being recast as a nightmare rather than a dream," and of which O. J. Simpson—O. J. Simpson as "the self-invented celebrity who climbed from poverty to the summit of fame and fortune" or O. J. Simpson in the white Bronco—"better reflects the truth about the California dream." In either case, genius of the place or its dystopian blight, the postwar changes that transformed California were understood to have been brought about by what was popularly seen as an unprecedented influx of population, what Pat Brown, in a 1962 issue of *Look*, called "the greatest mass migration in the history of the world" and George B. Leonard, in the same issue of *Look*, called "the migrating millions who vote with their wheels for California." During World War Two and the immediate postwar years, 1940 to 1950, the population of California did in fact increase 53 percent. During the next ten years, 1950 to 1960, the population of California did in fact increase 49 percent.

Yet such growth was in no way unprecedented. Nor, in a state that had seen its population increase in the first ten years of statehood by 245 percent, was it even remarkable. The decade between 1860 and 1870 brought a population increase to California of 47 percent, the decade that followed an increase of 54 percent. The years between 1900 and 1910 brought another 60 percent. Those were the years during which Faulkner's Ira Ewing, in "Golden Land," would have fled Nebraska on the night train to end up twenty-five years later sleepless in Beverly Hills. The years between 1910 and 1920 brought 44 percent. Those were the years when it came to the attention of Saxon Brown and Billy Roberts in *The Valley of the Moon* that "it looks like the free-born American ain't got no room left in his own land"—two babes convinced that they had been deprived of their Eden by industrialization, by immigration, by whatever it was that they could not name. The ten years that followed, between 1920 and 1930, when only shallowly settled arrivals were to find themselves further marginalized by the onset of the Depression, brought 66 percent. There had been, then, from the beginning, these obliterating increases, rates of growth that systematically erased freshly laid traces of custom and community, and it was from such erasures that many California confusions would derive.

There used to be on the main street through Gilroy, a farm town in Santa Clara County that billed itself as "The Garlic Capital of the World," a two- or three-story hotel, the Milias, where the dining room off the lobby had a black-and-white tiled floor and fans and potted palm trees and, in the opinion of my father, short ribs so succulent that they were worth a stop on any drive between Sacramento and the Monterey Peninsula. I remember sitting with him in the comparative cool of the Milias dining room (any claim of "cool" was at that time comparative, air conditioning not yet having taken widespread hold in Santa Clara County), eating short ribs and the cherries from his old-fashioned bourbon cocktail, the singular musky smell of garlic being grown and picked and processed permeating even the heavy linen napkins.

I am unsure at what point the Milias Hotel vanished (probably about the time Santa Clara County started being called Silicon Valley), but it did, and the "farm town" vanished too, Gilroy having reinvented itself as a sprawl of commuter subdivisions for San Jose and the tech industry. In the summer of 2001, a local resident named Michael Bonfante opened a ninety-million-dollar theme park in Gilroy, "Bonfante Gardens," the attractions of which were designed to suggest the agricultural: stage shows with singing tomatoes, rides offering the possibility of being spun in a giant garlic bulb or swung from a thirty-nine-foot-high mushroom. The intention behind Bonfante Gardens, according to its creator, was "to show how the county was in the 1950s and 1960s." The owner of a neighboring property was interviewed by *The New York Times* on the subject of Bonfante Gardens. "If it gets to be Disneyland, I am going to hate it," she said. "Right now it is pretty and beautiful. But who knows? Someone who has been here as long as I have has mixed feelings."

This interviewee, according to the *Times*, had been a resident of Gilroy, in other words "been here," for fifteen years. If fifteen years seems somewhat short of the long-time settlement suggested by "someone who has been here as long as I have," consider this: when my brother and I applied to change the zoning from agricultural to residential on a ranch we owned east of Sacramento, one of the most active opponents to the change, a man who spoke passionately to the folly of so altering the nature of the area, had moved to California only six months before, which suggested that he was living on a street that existed only because somebody else had developed a ranch. Discussion of how California has "changed," then, tends locally to define the more ideal California as that which existed at whatever past point the speaker first saw it: Gilroy as it was in the 1960s and Gilroy as it was fifteen years ago and Gilroy as it was when my father and I ate short ribs at the Milias Hotel are three pictures with virtually no overlap, a hologram that dematerializes as I drive through it.

Victor Davis Hanson is a professor of classics on the Fresno campus of California State University, a contributor of occasional opinion pieces to *The New York Times* and *The Wall Street Journal*, and the author of a number of books, including *The Land Was Everything: Letters from an American Farmer*, an impassioned polemic modeled on and informed by J. Hector St. John de Crèvecoeur's 1782 *Letters from an American Farmer*. Hanson has in fact for most of his life thought of himself as a farmer, either active or failed (he rejects the word "grower," more common in California, as "a term of self-approbation, used by those in California who often do not themselves grow anything"), with his brother and cousins a cultivator of grapevines and fruit trees on the same San Joaquin Valley land, fewer than two hundred acres, that their great-great-grandfather homesteaded in the 1870s. He sees himself as heir to the freeholding yeomen farmers who, in Crèvecoeur's and his own view, "created the American republican spirit." He tells us that his children are the sixth consecutive generation to live in the same house. The single photograph I have seen of him shows a man in his forties, wearing khakis and a T-shirt, his features and general stance so characteristic of the Central Valley (a good deal of sun exposure goes into this look, and a certain wary defiance) that the photograph could seem indistinguishable from snapshots of my father and cousins.

There is much in *The Land Was Everything* that catches exactly this Valley note. There is the smell of insecticides, fungicides, the toxic mists that constitute the smell of the place. ("What they're trying to do is generate a new fear of the word 'carcinogen,'" the corporate counsel for the J. G. Boswell Company, which operates fifty thousand acres in the Tulare Basin, famously said in response to certain restrictions placed during the mid-1980s on the use of toxic chemicals. "Chemicals are absolutely necessary for everyday life.") There is the sense of walking the ditches in an orchard, losing oneself among the propped limbs of the overburdened fruit trees. There is the visceral pleasure of cold Sierra water as it comes from the flume. There is the monosyllabic speech pattern, the directness to the point of rudeness, the abrupt way of launching and ending telephone calls with no niceties, no identification, no salutation, no goodbye, just a hangup. I never once heard my father's father, the grandfather who remained "Mr. Didion" to me, identify himself on the telephone. My mother frequently hung up without saying goodbye, sometimes in midsentence. "I do not think I shall leave the San Joaquin Valley of California," Hanson writes. "Courage, a friend tells me, requires me to grow up and leave, to get a better job elsewhere; cowardice, he says, is to stay put, possumlike, as the world goes on by. But at least my credentials as a San Joaquin Valley loyalist are unimpeachable, and thus my lament over its destruction is genuine."

Hanson lives on the family farm, but no longer actually farms it. "When we all went to the universities, when we abandoned what made us good and embraced what made us comfortable and secure, we lost something essential, knew we lost it and yet chose to lose," he writes. "Material bounty and freedom are so much stronger incentives than sacrifice and character." What was lost by the "we" of this passage, and in Hanson's view by America itself, was the pure hardship of the agrarian life, the yeoman ideal that constituted the country's "last link with the founding fathers of our political and spiritual past," its last line of defense against "market capitalism and entitlement democracy, the final stage of Western culture that is beyond good and evil."

This gets tricky. Notice the way in which the author implicitly frames his indictment of himself and his family for turning away from the pure agrarian life as an indictment of the rest of us, for failing to support that life. Notice, too, that the "destruction" of the San Joaquin Valley, as he sees it, began at the point when the small family farms on the east side of the Valley (the arid west side of the Valley, the part described by William Henry Brewer in the 1860s as a "plain of absolute desolation," belonged to the corporate growers) began giving way first to industrial parks and subdivisions and then to strip malls and meth labs. "Its Golden Age was therefore brief, no more than the beautiful century between 1870 and 1970, when gravity-fed irrigation in hand-dug ditches from the Sierra first turned a weed-infested desert into an oasis of small tree and vine farms and their quiet satellite communities."

This "Golden Age," in other words, began with the arrival of Hanson's own family, and ended with his own adolescence. "Times have changed," as the similarly focused Saxon Brown complained to Billy Roberts in *The Valley of the Moon*. "They've changed even since I was a little girl." There is a further possible mirage here: the San Joaquin Valley's "beautiful century" could have seemed, to those who were actually living it, perhaps not entirely golden: "Here, in this corner of a great nation, here, on the edge of the continent, here, in this valley of the West, far from the great centers, isolated, remote, lost, the great iron hand crushes life from us, crushes liberty and the pursuit of happiness from us.... Tell them, five years from now, the story of the fight between the League of the San Joaquin and the railroad and it will not be believed." That was Frank Norris, writing in *The Octopus*, on the slaughter that took place in 1880 at Mussel Slough, now Lucerne, now and then just fifteen miles from Selma, the site of the farmhouse in which six generations of Victor Davis Hanson's family have lived.

"There in my own small town," Hanson tells us in *The Land Was Everything*, "we have torn up vineyards and now have planted the following crops: Wal-Mart, Burger King, Food-4-Less, Baskin-Robbins, Cinema 6, Denny's, Wendy's, Payless, Andersen's Pea Soup, the Holiday Inn, McDonald's, Carl's Jr., Taco Bell, four gas stations, three shopping centers, two videotape stores, and a car wash." In line with the thrust of his argument, Hanson offers this list as evidence of "change," specifically of the moral or spiritual impoverishment to which he believes the loss of the yeoman ethic in the San Joaquin Valley has led. Some readers—those, say, who remain unconvinced that there was ever a yeoman ethic in the San Joaquin Valley to lose—might take from the list evidence of a less elusive impoverishment: the enterprises named are in the main national chains, or franchises, not the kinds of entrepreneurial activity calculated to return either money or opportunity to the community.

According to a study conducted by the Public Policy Institute of California, the poverty rate in the San Joaquin Valley in the year 2000 was in fact twenty-two percent of the population, the highest in the state, which in turn had an overall poverty rate, when adjusted for cost of living, exceeded in the United States only by that of the District of Columbia. This overall California poverty rate began exceeding that of the rest of the nation only in the late 1980s, but being poor in the Central Valley was not a new condition. In 1980, of the ten American metropolitan areas most reliant on public assistance, six were in the Sacramento and San Joaquin Valleys, running south from Redding and Yuba City–Marysville and Stockton straight down through Modesto and Fresno and Visalia. Many assumed California's rising poverty rate to be a function of immigration, and to some degree, in the short term, it was: the foreign-born, particularly those from Southeast Asia and Hispanic America, who did have the highest rate of poverty in the state.

In the Central Valley, however, immigration did not tell the whole story. In 1998, Tulare County began paying its welfare clients the cost of relocating in other states, providing an average of $2,300 a client to rent a U-Haul van and buy gas and stay in motels en route and pay first-and-last-month rent on a place to live once they get there. This policy, which also includes e-mailing job applications and mining the Internet for apartment rentals, has since been adopted by four other San Joaquin counties, Kings, Madera, Fresno, and Kern. In June 2001 and June 2002, reporters from first *The New York Times* and then *The Washington Post* interviewed samplings of these relocated clients. There were David Langley and his wife and child, who moved from Visalia to Colorado, as did Jackie and Michael Foster, "with their year-old red-haired son." There was Lorrie Gedert, who moved with her two daughters from Ivanhoe, about ten miles outside Visalia, to Little Rock. There were Gloria and Nathan Dickerson, who moved with their two children, Emily and Drake, from Visalia to Ocala, Florida. There were Richard and Zena White, who moved from Fresno to Slidell, Louisiana, where, according to the *Post*, both are now working full-time, "Zena as an assistant manager at a Chevron gas station and Richard as a shift manager at McDonald's." What first strikes the reader of these reports is that the names of the former Californians interviewed do not uniformly suggest recent immigration from Southeast Asia or Hispanic America. What next strikes the reader is that even such marginal jobs as assistant manager at the Chevron station and shift manager at the McDonald's appear to have been unobtainable in the San Joaquin Valley, here where the vineyards got torn up so the Wal-Marts and the Burger Kings and the Taco Bells could grow, here, as Frank Norris saw it in 1901, *in this corner of a great nation, here, on the edge of the continent, here, in this valley of the West, far from the great centers, isolated, remote, lost.*

3

FOR MOST OF my life California felt rich to me: that was the point of it, that was the promise, the reward for having left the past on the Sweetwater, the very texture of the place. This was by no means to say that I believed all or even most Californians to be rich, only to suggest that the fact of having no money seemed to me to lack, in California, the immutable gravity that characterized the condition elsewhere. It was not designed to be a life sentence. You were meant, if you were a Californian, to know how to lash together a corral with bark, you were meant to know how to tent a raft and live on the river, you were meant to show spirit, kill the rattlesnake, keep moving. There were in California a lot of "dead brokes," Henry George had pointed out in 1868, in a passage from "What the Railroad Will Bring Us" that got read to me (rather selectively, in retrospect) by my grandfather, "but there never was a better country to be 'broken' in, and where almost every man, even the most successful, had been in the same position, it did not involve the humiliation and loss of hope which attaches to utter poverty in older and more settled communities."

That I should have continued, deep into adult life, to think of California as I was told as a child that it had been in 1868 suggests a confusion of some magnitude, but there it was. *It's not a word we use*, my mother had said about class. *It's not the way we think.* Only in the 1980s did certain facts—two of them, not unrelated—manage to penetrate what was clearly a fairly tenacious wish not to examine whatever it was I needed to believe. The first fact, which entered my attention as an almost personal affront, was that California no longer felt rich enough to adequately fund its education system. The second, or corollary, fact was that there seemed to be many towns in California—including towns I knew, towns I thought of as my own interior landscape, towns I had thought I understood, towns in the Sacramento and San Joaquin Valleys—so impoverished in spirit as well as in fact that the only way their citizens could think to reverse their fortunes was by getting themselves a state prison. Since the building and staffing of new prisons were major reasons why California no longer felt rich enough to adequately fund its education system, this second fact initially presented itself as an even deeper affront than the first, evidence that a "new" California had finally and fatally sold out the old.

Then I remembered, then I realized.

We were seeing nothing "new" here.

We were seeing one more version of making our deal with the Southern Pacific.

We were seeing one more version of making our bed with the federal government.

We were seeing one more enthusiastic fall into a familiar California error, that of selling the future of the place we lived to the highest bidder, which was in this instance the California Correctional Peace Officers Association.

The California Correctional Peace Officers Association is the prison guards' union, a 29,000-member force that has maintained for some years now the most effective lobbying operation in Sacramento. In the 1998 election cycle, for example, the union funneled over two million dollars to Grey Davis's gubernatorial campaign and another three million dollars to various other candidates and propositions. "All I've ever asked is that we get to play in the ballpark with all the big guys and gals out there," Don Novey told *The Los Angeles Times* in 2000. Don Novey is the former guard at Folsom State Prison who became in 1980 the president of the California Correctional Peace Officers Association. "They call us the 800-pound gorilla. But we're just taking care of our own like everybody else." Don Novey refers to those who consider the need for new prisons an arguable proposition as "the other element." He gave $75,000 to the opponent of a state senator who had once spoken against a prison bond issue. "If Don Novey ran the contractors' union," a Republican strategist told the *Times*, "there'd be a bridge over every puddle in the state." The prison guards were in California the political muscle behind the victims' rights movement. The prison guards were in California the political muscle behind the 1994 "three strikes" legislation and initiative, the act that mandated a sentence of twenty-five years to life for any third felony conviction, even for crimes as minor as growing a marijuana plant on a window-sill or shoplifting a bottle of Ripple. The prison guards were the political muscle that had by the year 2000 made the California corrections system, with thirty-three penitentiaries and 162,000 inmates, the largest in the western hemisphere.

Incarceration was not always a growth industry in California. In 1852 there was only San Quentin, by 1880 there was also Folsom. During the 104 years that followed, a century during which the population of California increased from 865,000 to 25,795,000 people, the state found need for only ten additional facilities, most of them low or medium security. It was only in 1984, four years after Don Novey took over the union, that the new max and supermax prisons began rolling online, Solano in 1984, "New Folsom" (a quarter mile removed from "Old Folsom") in 1986, Avenal and Ione and Stockton and San Diego in 1987, Corcoran and Blythe in 1988, Pelican Bay in 1989, Chowchilla in 1990, Wasco in 1991, Calipatria in 1992, Lancaster and Imperial and Centinela and Delano in 1993, Coalinga and a second prison at Blythe in 1994, second prisons at both Susanville and Chowchilla in 1995, Soledad in 1996, a second prison at Corcoran in 1997.

Delano, the town in the San Joaquin between Tulare and Bakersfield that became synonymous outside California with Cesar Chavez's farmworkers' union, still yearns for its own second prison, "New Delano," to be built just across the road from what is already called "Old Delano," the ten-year-old North Kern State Prison. Mendota, west of Fresno and south of Chowchilla, still waits for what was to have been its privately built and operated prison, on which construction was begun and then postponed by the Nashville-based Corrections Corporation of America, which had hit a snag trying to contract with the state for prisoners to fill the $100 million maximum-security prison it had already built in the Mojave desert. "They can build whatever prisons they want," Don Novey had said to this point. "But the hell if they're going to run them."

That these prisons should remain the objects of abject civic desire is curious, since they have not actually enriched the towns that got them. A new prison creates jobs, but few of those jobs go to local hires. The Department of Corrections allows that it imports half the "corrections workers" in any new prison, but "tries" to hire the rest from the community. Opponents to "New Delano" point out that only seven to nine percent of the jobs at these new prisons have typically been local hires, and that the local hires get the low-paid service jobs. Of the 1,600 projected jobs at "New Delano," only 72 would be local hires. There are, moreover, costs, both economic and social: when the families of inmates move into a prison town, they not only strain the limited resources of local schools and social service agencies but bring emotionally stressed children into the community and school system. "The students are all very high risk," a school official in Lassen County, where Susanville is located, told *The Los Angeles Times*. "They come from single-parent homes. They're latchkey kids, often on AFDC. It's very obvious they're from a whole different area. It creates societal conflicts. The child does not fit in."

It was 1993 when the California Department of Corrections activated its first "death fence," at Calipatria. It was 1994 when the second "death fence" was activated, at Lancaster, carrying a charge of 650 milliamperes, almost ten times the voltage required to cause instant death. "What the fence does is take out the human-error part," the warden at Lancaster was quoted as having said, explaining that the million-dollar fences would save money in the long run because armed officers could be removed from prison gun towers. "The fence never goes to sleep. It doesn't go to the bathroom. It doesn't do any of those things. It's always working." It was also 1994 when standardized testing of reading skills among California fourth-graders placed them last in the nation, below Mississippi, tied only with Louisiana. It was 1995 when, for the first time, California spent more on its prisons than on its two university systems, the ten campuses of the University of California and the twenty-four campuses of California State University.

Through most of my life I would have interpreted the growth of the prison system and the diminution of the commitment to public education as evidence of how California had "changed." Only recently did I come to see them as the opposite, evidence of how California had "not changed," and to understand "change" itself as one of the culture's most enduring misunderstandings about itself.

4

"THE AMERICAN COMMUNITY in early California fairly represented, as we shall see, the average national culture and character. But no other part of our land was ever so rapidly peopled as was California in the first golden days. Nowhere else were we Americans more affected than here, in our lives and conduct, by the feeling that we stood in the position of conquerors in a new land. Nowhere else, again, were we ever before so long forced by circumstance to live at the mercy of a very wayward chance, and to give to even our most legitimate business a dangerously speculative character. Nowhere else were we driven so hastily to improvise a government for a large body of strangers; and nowhere else did fortune so nearly deprive us for a little time of our natural devotion to the duties of citizenship. We Americans therefore showed, in early California, new failings and new strength. We exhibited a novel degree of carelessness and overhastiness, an extravagant trust in luck, a previously unknown blindness to our social duties, and an indifference to the rights of foreigners, whereof we cannot be proud. But we also showed our best national traits—traits that went far to atone for our faults. As a body, our pioneer community in California was persistently cheerful, energetic, courageous, and teachable. In a few years it had repented of its graver faults, it had endured with charming good humor their severest penalties, and it was ready to begin with fresh devotion the work whose true importance it had now at length learned—the work of building a well-organized, permanent, and progressive State on the Pacific Coast. In this work it has been engaged ever since."

—Josiah Royce,
California: A Study of American Character, 1886

Just east of Sacramento, off Kilgore Road in what is now Rancho Cordova, a town with a population of almost fifty thousand that exists only because Aerojet General began manufacturing rockets there after World War Two, there is a three-acre family graveyard, the Matthew Kilgore Cemetery, its gates long gone, its two-hundred-some graves overgrown and many of its stone markers, a few of which are dated as recently as the 1970s, overturned. Two of my great-great-great-grandparents, Matthew Kilgore and his wife Massa McGuire Kilgore, were buried there, Massa Kilgore in 1876, Matthew Kilgore in 1882. When I was in high school and college and later I would sometimes drive out there, park the car and sit on the fender and read, but after the day I noticed, as I was turning off the ignition, a rattlesnake slide from a broken stone into the dry grass, I never again got out of the car.

In the 1980s, when the condition of the Kilgore Cemetery had become a matter of local concern (vandals had dug up a body and stolen its head), the president of the Rancho Cordova Chamber of Commerce appealed to "Cordovans" (residents of Rancho Cordova, in other words "new people") to join a volunteer effort to clean up the beer bottles and debris left by trespassers. "There are a lot of residents who would like to see this historic site preserved as it deserves to be," he was quoted as having said in the newspaper story my mother clipped and sent to me in Los Angeles.

I asked, when my mother and I next spoke, if the family—the seventy-some of my father's cousins who annually attended the Kilgore Family Reunion in McKinley Park in East Sacramento, say—was joining the effort to clean up the Kilgore Cemetery.

The family, my mother said, did not own the Kilgore Cemetery.

It occurred to me that neither did the president of the Rancho Cordova Chamber of Commerce own the Kilgore Cemetery, but I opted to go in a different direction. I asked how exactly it had come to pass that the family did not own the Kilgore Cemetery.

"I presume somebody sold it," my mother said.

I thought about this.

I also thought about having seen the rattlesnake slide from the broken stone into the grass.

I had seen the rattlesnake but I had failed to get out of the car and kill it, thereby violating, in full awareness that I was so doing, what my grandfather had told me was "the code of the West."

If "not killing the rattlesnake" violated "the code of the West," how about "selling the cemetery"? Would that qualify? Not surprisingly, the Kilgore Cemetery makes an appearance of a kind in *Run River*. Lily's father, Walter Knight, after he misses a curve on the river road and drowns trapped in his car, is buried in what is described as a small family cemetery where the last previous burial had taken place in 1892. The burial is described from Lily's point of view: "There was a certain comfort in the unkempt graveyard. Dried grass obscured the markers, and the wings had been broken years before from the stone angels guarding the rusted wire gate; there was about the place none of the respect for death implicit in a well-tended plot."

Could this have been what I thought letting the Kilgore Cemetery go to ruin demonstrated? Some admirable wagons-west refusal to grant death its dominion? The idealization of the small family cemetery in *Run River* continues: "Once, a long time before, Walter Knight had brought Lily to see this graveyard. He had made her trace out with her finger the letters on the stones, the names and their dates, until she found the small, rough stone which marked the oldest grave." This "oldest grave" was that of a child not yet two, the first family member to die in California. "I think nobody owns land until their dead are in it," Walter Knight had said to Lily on this occasion. "Sometimes I think this whole valley belongs to me," Lily had said, and her father had responded sharply: "It does, you hear me? We made it."

Had I known when I was writing *Run River* that the Kilgore Cemetery had been or would be sold, was this the rationalization I would have worked out? Our dead were in it, so we owned it? Our deal, so we could sell it? Or would I have somehow managed to incorporate "selling the cemetery" into my bill of particulars against the "new people," against the "changes"? At what point exactly might I have asked: was it new people who sold the cemetery? Was it new people who ploughed under and grazed out the grass that could be tied over the saddle? How would Josiah Royce have construed "selling the cemetery"? "Novel degree of carelessness"? "Previously unknown blindness to social duties"? Or "building a well-organized, permanent, and progressive State on the Pacific Coast"? Or was that the same thing?

From the 1870s to the 1920s, according to Richard W. Fox's 1978 study *So Far Disordered in Mind: Insanity in California 1870–1930*, California had a higher rate of commitment for insanity than any other state in the nation, a disproportion most reasonably explained, Fox suggests, "by the zeal with which California state officials sought to locate, detain, and treat not only those considered 'mentally ill,' but also a wide variety of other deviants— including, as state hospital physicians put it, 'imbeciles, dotards, idiots, drunkards, simpletons, fools,' and 'the aged, the vagabond, the helpless.'" Not only did California have this notably higher rate of commitment but the institutions to which it committed its citizens differed fundamentally from those in the East, where the idea of how to deal with insanity had been from the beginning medicalized, based on regimes—however more honored in the breach—of treatment and therapy. The idea of how to deal with insanity in California began and ended with detention.

So broad were the standards for committal, and so general was the inclination to let the state take care of what might in another culture have been construed as a family burden, that even many of the doctors who ran the system were uneasy. As early as 1862, according to *So Far Disordered in Mind*, the resident physician at the Stockton State Asylum for the Insane complained of receiving patients "who, if affected in their minds at all, it is the weakness of old age, or intemperance, or perhaps most commonly both together." In 1870, the federal census classified one in every 489 Californians as insane. By 1880, the rate had risen to one in 345. After 1903, when the rate had reached one in 260 and the asylums had passed capacity, the notion of sterilizing inmates gained currency, the idea being that a certain number could then be released without danger of reproducing. Sterilization, or "asexualization," of inmates, which was legalized in some other states as early as 1907, was made legal in California in 1909. By 1917, the right of the state to sterilize had been extended twice, first to cases in which the patient did not agree to the procedure, then to cases in which the patient had not even been necessarily diagnosed with a hereditary or incurable disorder, but only with "perversion or marked departures from normal mentality." By the end of 1920, of the 3,233 sterilizations for insanity or feeblemindedness performed to that date throughout the United States, 2,558, or seventy-nine percent, had taken place in California.

What was arresting in this pattern of commitment was the extent to which it diverged from the California sense of itself as loose, less socially rigid than the rest of the country, more adaptable, more tolerant of difference. When Fox analyzed the San Francisco commitment records for the years 1906 to 1929, he found that the majority of those hospitalized, fifty-nine percent, had been committed not because they were violent, not because they presented a threat to others or to themselves, but simply because they had been reported, sometimes by a police officer but often by a neighbor or relative, to exhibit "odd or peculiar behavior." In 1914, for example, San Francisco medical examiners granted the wish of a woman to commit her thirty-seven-year-old unmarried sister, on the grounds that the sister, despite her "quiet and friendly" appearance during detention, had begun "to act silly, lost interest in all things which interest women, could no longer crochet correctly as formerly, takes no interest in anything at present." In 1915, a forty-year-old clerk was committed because "for three weeks he has been annoying the City Registrar, calling every day and insisting that he is a Deputy." In 1922, a twenty-three-year-old divorcée was committed after a neighbor reported that she was "lazy, slovenly, careless of personal appearance, stays away from home for days, neglecting self and consorting with men." The same year, a forty-eight-year-old pianist was committed on the grounds that "she has been irresponsible for years; has been a source of great annoyance to many institutions such as Y.W.C.A. Association, churches, etc."

The apparently pressing need to commit so many and in many cases such marginally troubled Californians to indefinite custodial detention seems not at the time to have struck their fellow citizens as an excessive lust for social control. Nor did these fellow citizens appear to see their readiness to slough off bothersome relatives and neighbors as a possible defect in their own socialization. Madness, it became convenient to believe quite early on, came with the territory, on the order of earthquakes. The first State Lunatic Asylum in California, that at Stockton, was established in 1853 specifically to treat those believed to have been driven mad

JOAN DIDION

by the goldfields. According to an 1873 State Board of Health report, this endemic madness had to do with "the speculative and gambling spirit" of the California settlement. It had to do with "heterogeneous elements," it had to do with "change of climate, habits, and modes of life," it had to do with being "isolated, without sympathy, and deprived of all home influences." California itself, then, according to its own Board of Health, was "well-calculated to break some link in reason's chain, and throw into confusion even the best balanced properties of mind."

I have on my desk a copy of the 1895 *California Blue Book, or State Roster*, family detritus, salvaged from a Good Will box during a move of my mother's. I assumed at the time I retrieved it that the roster had been my grandfather's but I see now that the bookplate reads "Property of Chas. F. Johnson, Bakersfield, Calif., No. 230," in other words the detritus of someone else's family. The book is illustrated with etchings and photographs, a startling number of which feature what were in 1895 the state's five asylums for the insane, huge Victorian structures that appear to have risen from the deserts and fields of California's rural counties in a solitude more punitive than therapeutic. Among the illustrations are the facts, in neat columns: there were at the Napa State Asylum for the Insane thirty-five "Attendants," each of whom received an annual salary of $540. All were identified by name. There were, listed under the "Attendants" and also identified by name, sixty "Assistant Attendants," thirteen of whom received $480 a year and the rest $420. There were on the staff at the State Insane Asylum at Agnews, in Santa Clara County, more "Cooks" and "Assistant Cooks" and "Bakers" and "Assistant Bakers" than there appear to have been doctors (the only doctors listed are the "Medical Director," at $3,500, and two "Assistant Physicians," at $2,500 and $2,100 respectively), but the staff roster also includes—a note that chills by the dolorous entertainments it suggests—one "Musician, and Assistant Attendant," budgeted at $60 a year more than the other, presumably unmusical, Assistant Attendants.

These places survived through my childhood and adolescence into my adult life, sources of a fear more potent even than that of drowning in the rivers (drowning meant you had misread the river, drowning made sense, drowning you could negotiate), the fear of being sent away—no, worse—"put away." There

1084

was near Sacramento an asylum where I was periodically taken with my Girl Scout troop to exhibit for the inmates our determined cheerfulness while singing rounds, nine-year-olds with merit badges on our sleeves pressed into service as Musicians and Assistant Attendants. *White coral bells upon a slender stalk*, we sang in the sunroom, trying not to make eye contact, *lilies of the valley line your garden walk*. I could not have known at nine that my grandmother's sister, who arrived lost in melancholia to live with us after her husband died, would herself die in the asylum at Napa, but the possibility that such a fate could strike at random was the air we breathed.

Oh don't you wish that you could hear them ring, we sang, one by one faltering, only the strongest or most oblivious among us able to keep the round going in the presence of the put away, the now intractably lost, the abandoned, *that will happen only when the angels sing*. If it was going to be us or them, which of us in that sunroom would not have regressed in Royce's view to that "novel degree of carelessness," that "previously unknown blindness to social duties"? Which of us in that sunroom could not have abandoned the orphaned Miss Gilmore and her brother on the Little Sandy? Which of us in that sunroom did not at some level share in the shameful but entrenched conviction that to be weak or bothersome was to warrant abandonment? Which of us in that sunroom would not see the rattlesnake and fail to kill it? Which of us in that sunroom would not sell the cemetery? Were not such abandonments the very heart and soul of the crossing story? Jettison weight? Keep moving? Bury the dead in the trail and run the wagons over it? Never dwell on what got left behind, never look back at all? *Remember,* Virginia Reed had warned attentive California children, we who had been trained since virtual infancy in the horrors she had survived, *never take no cutoffs and hurry along as fast as you can*. Once on a drive to Lake Tahoe I found myself impelled to instruct my brother's small children in the dread lesson of the Donner Party, just in case he had thought to spare them. "Don't worry about it," another attentive California child, Patricia Hearst, recalled having told herself during the time she was locked in a closet by her kidnappers. "Don't examine your feelings. Never examine your feelings—they're no help at all."

Part IV

TO ME AS a child, the State was the world as I knew it, and I pictured other States and countries as pretty much "like this." I never felt the warm, colorful force of the beauty of California until I had gone away and come back over my father's route: dull plains; hot, dry desert; the night of icy mountains; the dawning foothills breaking into the full day of sunshine in the valley; and last, the sunset through the Golden Gate. And I came to it by railroad, comfortably, swiftly. My father, who plodded and fought or worried the whole long hard way at oxen pace, always paused when he recalled how they turned over the summit and waded down, joyously, into the amazing golden sea of sunshine— he would pause, see it again as he saw it then, and say, "I saw that this was the place to live."

—Lincoln Steffens,
The Autobiography of Lincoln Steffens

My mother died on May 15, 2001, in Monterey, two weeks short of her ninety-first birthday. The preceding afternoon I had talked to her on the telephone from New York and she had hung up midsentence, a way of saying goodbye so characteristic of her— especially by way of allowing her callers to economize on what she still called "long distance"—that it did not occur to me until morning, when my brother called, that in this one last instance she had been just too frail to keep the connection.

Maybe not just too frail.

Maybe too aware of what could be the import of this particular goodbye.

Flying to Monterey I had a sharp apprehension of the many times before when I had, like Lincoln Steffens, "come back," flown west, followed the sun, each time experiencing a lightening of spirit as the land below opened up, the checkerboards of the midwestern plains giving way to the vast empty reach between the Rockies and the Sierra Nevada; then *home, there, where I was from, me,* California. It would be a while before I realized that "me" is what we think when our parents die, even at my age, *who will look out for me now, who will remember me as I was, who will know what happens to me now, where will I be from.*

In the aftermath of my mother's death I found myself thinking a good deal about the confusions and contradictions in California life, many of which she had herself embodied. She despised, for example, the federal government and its "giveaways," but saw no contradiction between this view and her reliance on my father's military reserve status to make free use of Air Force doctors and pharmacies, or to shop at the commissaries and exchanges of whatever military installation she happened to be near. She thought of the true California spirit as one of unfettered indi-vidualism, but carried the idea of individual rights to dizzying and often punitive lengths. She definitely aimed for an appearance of being "stern," a word she seemed to think synonymous with what was not then called "parenting." As a child herself in the upper Sacramento Valley she had watched men hung in front of the courthouse. When John Kennedy was assassinated she insisted that Lee Harvey Oswald had "every right" to assassinate him, that Jack Ruby in turn had "every right" to kill Lee Harvey Oswald, and that any breakdown of natural order in the event had been on the part of the Dallas police, who had failed to exercise their own right, which was "to shoot Ruby on the spot." When I introduced her to my future husband, she advised him immediately that he would find her political beliefs so far to the right that he would think her "the original little old lady in tennis shoes." At Christmas that year he gave her the entire John Birch library, dozens of call-to-action pamphlets, boxed. She was delighted, amused, displaying the pamphlets to everyone who came by the house that season, but to the best of my knowledge she never opened one.

She was passionately opinionated on a number of points that reflected, on examination, no belief she actually held. She thought of herself as an Episcopalian, as her mother had been. She was married at Trinity Episcopal Pro-Cathedral in Sacramento. She had me christened there. She buried her mother there. My brother and I had her own funeral service at Saint John's Episcopal Chapel in Monterey, a church she had actually attended only two or three times but favored as an idea not only because it was a "California" church (it was built in the 1880s by Charles Crocker and C. P. Huntington on the grounds of the Southern Pacific's Del Monte Hotel) but also because the litany used was that from the 1928, as opposed to the revised, *Book of Common Prayer.* Yet she had herself at age twelve refused outright to be confirmed an Episcopalian: she had gone through the instruction and been presented to the bishop, but, when asked for the usual rote affirmation of a fairly key doctrinal point, had declared resoundingly, as if it were a debate, that she found herself "incapable of believing" that Christ was the son of God. By the time of my own confirmation, she had further hardened this position. "The only church I could possibly go to would be Unitarian," she announced when my grandmother asked why she never went to church with us.

"Eduene," my grandmother said, a soft keening. "How can you say that."

"I *have* to say it, if I want to be honest," my mother said, the voice of sweet reason. "Since I don't believe that Christ is the son of God."

My grandmother brightened, seeing space for resolution. "Then it's fine," she said. "Because nobody has to believe all *that.*"

Only in recent years did I come to realize that many of these dramatically pronounced opinions of my mother's were defensive, her own version of her great-grandmother's "fixed and settled principles, aims and motives in life," a barricade against some deep apprehension of meaninglessness. There had been glimpses of this apprehension all along, overlooked by me, my own barricade. She did not see a point in making beds, for example, since "they just get slept in again." Nor did she see a point in dusting, since dust just returned. "What difference does it make," she would often say, by way of ending a discussion of whether an acquaintance should leave her husband, say, or whether a cousin should drop out of school and become a manicurist. "What difference does it make," five words that had come to chill me at the bone, was what she said when I pressed her on the point about selling the cemetery. On the Good Friday after her own mother died she happened to be driving across the country with a friend from Sacramento. At the place where they stopped for dinner there had been no fish on the menu, only meat. "I took one bite and I thought of Mother and I wanted to throw up," my mother said when she arrived at my apartment in New York a few days later. Her mother, she said, would never eat meat on Good Friday. Her mother did not like to cook fish, but she would get a crab and crack it. I was about to suggest that cracked Dungeness crab was hard to come by on the average midwestern road trip, but before I could speak I noticed that she was crying. "What difference does it make," she said finally.

I had seen my mother cry only once before. The first time had been during World War Two, on a downtown street in some town where my father was stationed, Tacoma or Durham or Colorado Springs. My brother and I had been left in the car while our mother went into the military housing office that dealt with dependents. The office was crowded, women and children leaning against the plate glass windows and spilling outside. When our mother came back out onto the sidewalk she was crying: it seemed to be the end of some rope, one day too many on which there would be no place for us to stay.

The blank dreariness, Sarah Royce wrote.

Without house or home.

When she got into the car her eyes were dry and her expression was determinedly cheerful. "It's an adventure," she said. "It's wartime, it's history, you children will be thankful you got to see all this." In one of those towns we finally got a room in a hotel, with a shared bathtub, into which she poured a bottle of pine disinfectant every day before bathing us. In Durham we had one room, with kitchen privileges, in the house of a fundamentalist preacher and his family who sat on the porch after dinner and ate peach ice cream, each from his or her own quart carton. The preacher's daughter had a full set of *Gone With the Wind* paper dolls, off limits to me. It was in Durham where the neighborhood children crawled beneath the back stoop and ate the dirt, scooping it up with a cut raw potato and licking it off, craving some element their diet lacked.

Pica.

I knew the word even then, because my mother told me. "Poor children do it," she said, with the same determinedly cheerful expression. "In the South. You never would have learned that in Sacramento."

It was in Durham where my mother noticed my brother reaching for something through the bars of his playpen and froze, unable to move, because what he was reaching for was a copperhead. The copperhead moved on, possibly another instance of the "providential interposition" that had spared my mother's great-great-grandfather from the mad dog in Georgia. Something occurs to me as I write this: my mother did not kill the copperhead.

Only once, in Colorado Springs, did we actually end up living in a house of our own—not much of a house, a four-room stucco bungalow, rented furnished, but a house. I had skipped part of first grade because we were moving around and I had skipped second grade because we were moving around but in Colorado Springs we had a house, in Colorado Springs I could go to school. I did. They were already doing multiplication and I had skipped learning how to subtract. Out at the base where my father was stationed pilots kept spiraling down through the high thin Colorado air. The way you knew was that you heard the crash wagons. A classmate told me that her mother did not allow her to play with military trash. My grandmother came by train to visit, bringing as usual material solace, thick blue towels and Helena Rubinstein soap in the shape of apple blossoms. I have snapshots of the two of us in front of the Broadmoor Hotel, my grandmother in a John Fredericks hat, me in a Brownie uniform. "You are just out of luck to be home because it's so nice and warm here," I wrote to her when she was gone. The letter, which I found with my mother's snapshots of the period, is decorated with gold and silver stars and cutout Christmas trees, suggesting that I had been trying hard for the upbeat. "But Mommy heard a girl say on the base that 'Remember last New Year's? It was eighteen below, and we had just this kind of weather.' We have a blue spruce Christmas tree. Jimmy and me are going to a party the 23rd at the base. They have a new name for the base. It's Peterson field."

I remember that my mother made me give the apple-blossom soap to the wife of a departing colonel, a goodbye present. I remember that she encouraged me to build many of those corrals that Californians were meant to know how to build, branches lashed together with their own stripped bark, ready for any loose livestock that might come our way, one of many frontier survival techniques I have never had actual occasion to use. I remember that once when we were snowbound she taught me how to accept and decline formal invitations, a survival technique from a different daydream: *Miss Joan Didion accepts with pleasure the kind invitation of, Miss Joan Didion regrets that she is unable to accept the kind invitation of.* Another time when we were snowbound she gave me several old copies of *Vogue*, and pointed out in one of them an announcement of the competition *Vogue* then had for college seniors, the Prix de Paris, first prize a job in *Vogue*'s Paris or New York office.

You could win that, she said. When the time comes. You could win that and live in Paris. Or New York. Wherever you wanted. But *definitely* you could win it.

A dozen-plus years later, my senior year at Berkeley, I did win it, and drove to Sacramento with the telegram from *Vogue* in my bag. I had found the yellow envelope with the glassine window slipped under my apartment door when I got back from a class that afternoon. *We are delighted to inform you*, the little strips of yellow tape read. *Miss Jessica Daves, Editor-in-Chief, Vogue.* When I showed the telegram to my mother I reminded her that it had been her idea in the first place.

"Really?" she said, doubtful.

This calls for a drink, my father said, his solution, as hanging up was my mother's solution, to any moment when emotion seemed likely to surface.

Colorado Springs, I said, prompting her. When we were snowbound.

"Imagine your remembering," she said.

I see now that World War Two was our own Big Sandy, Little Sandy, Humboldt Sink.

Imagine your remembering.

Something else I remembered: I remembered her telling me that when the war was over we would *all* go to live in Paris. *Toute la famille.* Paris had not yet been liberated but she already had a plan: my father was to reinvent himself as an architect, study architecture at

the Sorbonne on the G.I. Bill. To this end she tried to teach me the
French she had learned at Lowell High School in San Francisco.

Pourquoi did we never go to live in Paris?

Je ne sais pas.

A few years after the war ended, when we were again living
in Sacramento, I asked this question. My mother said that we had
never gone to live in Paris because my father felt an obligation to
his family to remain in Sacramento. I recall wondering how much
of the plan she had actually discussed with him, since I had never
been able to quite bring the picture of my father dropping everything and starting over in Paris into clear focus. The problem in
the picture was not that he was risk-averse. Risk was in fact our
bread and butter, risk was what put the lamb chops on the table.
He had supported my mother and me during the Depression by
playing poker with older and more settled acquaintances at the
Sutter Club, a men's club in Sacramento to which he did not
belong. Right now, after the war, he was supporting my mother
and brother and me by buying houses and pieces of property
with no money to speak of, then leveraging them, and buying
some more. His idea of a relaxing way to make a payment was to
drive to Nevada and shoot craps all night.

No.

"Risk" he definitely would have gone for.

The problem in the picture was "Paris."

One of the few perfectly clear points in his belief system (there
was much that remained opaque) was the conviction that France,
where he had never been, was a worthless country peopled
exclusively by the devious, the corrupt, the frivolous, and the collaborating. The name "Didion," he insisted, was not French but
German, the name of an ancestor who, although German, "happened to live in Alsace after the French took it over." The first
time I went to Paris I sent him a page from a telephone book on
which many apparently French Parisians named "Didion" were
listed, but he never mentioned it.

One element in my mother's version of the chimerical Paris
adventure did hold up: it was true that my father felt an obligation to his family to remain in Sacramento. The reason he felt
this obligation had been distilled, within the family and over
the years, into a plausible sequence of events, a story so reasonable that it seemed unconvincing, a kind of cartoon. Here was

the story: when his mother was dying of influenza in 1918 she had told him to take care of his younger brother, and when his brother lost an eye in a fireworks accident my father thought he had failed. In fact whatever unfulfilled and unfulfillable obligation he felt was less identifiable than that. There was about him a sadness so pervasive that it colored even those many moments when he seemed to be having a good time. He had many friends. He played golf, he played tennis, he played poker, he seemed to enjoy parties. Yet he could be in the middle of a party at our own house, sitting at the piano—playing "Darktown Strutter's Ball," say, or "Alexander's Ragtime Band," a bourbon highball always within reach—and the tension he transmitted would seem so great that I would have to leave, run to my room and close the door.

It was during my first year at Berkeley when the physical manifestations of this tension became sufficiently troubling that he was referred to Letterman Hospital, at the Presidio in San Francisco, to undergo a series of tests. I am unsure how long he spent at Letterman, but it was a period covering some weeks or months. My mother would drive down from Sacramento on the weekends, either Saturday or Sunday, and pick me up at the Tri Delt house in Berkeley. We would cross the Bay Bridge and go out to the Presidio and pick up my father for lunch. I remember that all he would eat that year were oysters, raw. I remember that after the oysters we would spend the rest of the afternoon driving—not back into the city, because he did not like San Francisco, but through Golden Gate Park, down the beach, over into Marin County, anywhere he was likely to see a pickup baseball game he could stop and watch. I remember that at the end of the afternoon he would instruct my mother to drop him not at the Presidio but at the southwesternmost end of Golden Gate Park, so that he could walk back to the hospital along the beach. Sometimes during the week he would walk across the Golden Gate Bridge, visit a cousin at his Sausalito office, and walk back. Once I walked across the bridge with him. I remember that it swayed. In his letters to my mother he dismissed the Letterman psychiatrists as "the mind guys," or sometimes "the mind-over-matter guys," but a year or so before he died, in his eighties, he told me that there had been "this woman doctor" at Letterman who had been "actually very helpful" to him. "We talked about my mother," he said. It was several years after he died before I was able to fully articulate what could not have escaped either my or my mother's fixedly narrowed attention on those week-end afternoons in 1953: those were bad walks for someone under observation for depression.

It occurs to me how brave he must have been, to make those walks and come back.

It also occurs to me how brave my mother must have been, to drive back alone to Sacramento while he made those walks.

My father died in December of 1992. A few months later, in March, I happened to drive my mother from Monterey to Berkeley, where we were to spend a few nights at the Claremont Hotel and I was to speak at a University of California Charter Day ceremony.

"Are we on the right road," my mother had asked again and again as we drove up 101.

I had repeatedly assured her that we were, at last pointing out an overhead sign: *101 North.*

"Then where did it all go," she had asked.

She meant where did Gilroy go, where was the Milias Hotel, where could my father eat short ribs now. She meant where did San Juan Bautista go, why was it no longer so sweetly remote as it had been on the day of my wedding there in 1964. She meant where had San Benito and Santa Clara Counties gone as she remembered them, the coastal hills north of Salinas, the cattle grazing, the familiar open vista that had been relentlessly replaced (during the year, two years, three, the blink of the eye during which she had been caring for my father) by mile after mile of pastel subdivisions and labyrinthine exits and entrances to free-ways that had not previously existed.

For some miles she was silent.

California had become, she said then, "all San Jose."

In the bar at the Claremont that evening someone was playing, as if to reinforce what had become a certain time-travel aspect in our excursion, "Only Make Believe," and "Where or When."

The smile you are smiling you were smiling then—
But I can't remember where or when—

I had last been in the bar at the Claremont in 1955, with the son of a rancher from Mendocino County. I recall that I had my roommate's driver's license and a crème de menthe frappé. Thirty-eight years later, from the platform at the Charter Day ceremony, I glanced at the row where my mother was seated and found her chair empty. When I located her outside she told me that it had been essential to leave. She said that "something terrible" had happened during the academic procession, something that had made her fear that she would "cry in front of everybody." It seemed that she had seen a banner reading "Class of 1931," and had realized that the handful of men straggling along behind it (if there were any women she did not mention them) were having trouble walking.

The Class of 1931 had been my father's class at Berkeley. "They were all old men," my mother said about those few of his former classmates who had made the procession. "They were just like your father." *Frank Reese "Jim" Didion*, the memorial note for my father had read in the alumni magazine. *December 19, in Carmel. A native of Sacramento, where he was active as a real estate investor, he majored in business at Cal and was a member of Chi Phi. He is survived by his wife, Eduene, two children, Joan Didion Dunne '56 and James '62, and four grandchildren, including Steven '88 and Lori '93.* There was no believable comfort I could offer my mother: she was right. They were all old men and it was all San Jose. Child of the crossing story that I was, I left my mother with Lori '93 and took the United redeye from San Francisco to Kennedy, the last plane to land before a storm CNN was calling "The Nor'easter of the Century" closed every airport and highway north of Atlanta. I remembered this abandonment the day she died.

2

I ALSO REMEMBERED this one.

Sacramento, July or August, 1971 or 1972.

I had brought Quintana—my daughter, then five or six—to spend a few days with my mother and father. Because it would be 105 at two and 110 before the sun went down, my mother and I decided to take Quintana out to lunch, somewhere with air conditioning.

My father did not believe in air conditioning.

My father in fact believed that Sacramento summers had been too cold since the dams.

We would go downtown, my mother said. We would have lunch in the Redevelopment. Old Sacramento. You haven't even *seen* Old Sacramento, she said.

I asked if she had seen Old Sacramento.

Not exactly, she said. But she definitely wanted to. We would see it together, it would be an adventure.

Quintana was wearing a pinafore, pale green, Liberty lawn.

My mother gave her a big straw hat to wear against the sun.

We drove downtown, we parked, we started walking on what had been Front Street, its view of the Tower Bridge pretty much constituting the "adventure" part.

The sidewalks in the Redevelopment were wooden, to give the effect of 1850.

Quintana was walking ahead of us.

The lawn pinafore, the big hat, the wooden sidewalk, the shimmer of the heat.

My father's great-grandfather had owned a saloon on Front Street.

I was about to explain this to Quintana—the saloon, the wooden sidewalk, the generations of cousins who had walked just as she was walking down just this street on days just this hot—when I stopped. Quintana was adopted. Any ghosts on this wooden sidewalk were not in fact Quintana's responsibility.

This wooden sidewalk did not in fact represent anywhere Quintana was from. Quintana's only attachments on this wooden sidewalk were right now, here, me and my mother.

In fact I had no more attachment to this wooden sidewalk than Quintana did: it was no more than a theme, a decorative effect.

It was only Quintana who was real.

Later it seemed to me that this had been the moment when all of it—the crossing, the redemption, the abandoned rosewood chests, the lost flatware, the rivers I had written to replace the rivers I had left, the twelve generations of circuit riders and county sheriffs and Indian fighters and country lawyers and Bible readers, the two hundred years of clearings in Virginia and Kentucky and Tennessee and then the break, the dream of America, the entire enchantment under which I had lived my life—began to seem remote.

ON THE AFTERNOON after our mother's funeral my brother and I divided what few pieces of furniture she still had among her grandchildren, my brother's three children and Quintana. There was not much left; during the previous few years she had been systematically giving away what she had, giving back Christmas presents, jettisoning belongings. I do not remember what Quintana's cousins Kelley and Steven and Lori took. I do remember what Quintana took, because I have seen the pieces since in her apartment in New York. There was an oval Victorian table with a marble top that had come to my mother from some part of the family, I no longer remember which. There was a carved teak chest that had been in my mother and father's bedroom when I was a child. There was a small piecrust table that had been my grandmother's. There was, from among my mother's clothes, an Italian angora cape that she had been wearing ever since my father gave it to her, one Christmas in the late 1940s.

Actually I took the angora cape.

I remembered her wearing it the spring before, at the wedding in Pebble Beach, of my brother's youngest child. I remembered her wearing it in 1964 at my own wedding, wrapping herself in it for the drive from San Juan Bautista to the reception in Pebble Beach.

A representative from Allied came.

The pieces got tagged for shipment.

I put what I did not want to be thrown away—letters, photographs, clippings, folders and envelopes I could not that day summon up the time or the heart to open—in a large box.

Some weeks later the box arrived at my apartment in New York, where it sat in the dining room for perhaps a month, unopened. Finally I opened it. There were pictures of me on the beach at Carmel in 1936, pictures of me and my brother on the beach at Stinson Beach in 1946, pictures of me and my brother and my rabbit in the snow in Colorado Springs. There were pictures of great-aunts and cousins and great-great-grandparents who could be identified only because our mother, on the evening before she died, had thought to tell the names to my brother, who wrote them on the backing of the frames. There were pictures of my mother as a two-year-old visiting her grandmother in Oregon in 1912, there were pictures of my mother at a Peterson Field barbecue in 1943, a young woman in her early thirties wearing flowers in her hair as she makes hamburgers. There was an unframed watercolor of my grandmother's. There were letters my grandmother's brother Jim, like her father a merchant sea captain, had sent her in 1918 from England, where his ship, the S.S. *Armenia*, was in drydock at Southampton after having been torpedoed. There were letters my father had written to his own father in 1928, from a summer job on a construction crew outside Crescent City—my father asking, in letter after letter, if his father could please put in a word for him with an acquaintance who did the hiring for the State Fair jobs, a plea I happen to know was in vain.

I know this because I once wanted my father to make the same call for me.

My mother had told me to forget asking him, because *he's just like his own father, everybody in Sacramento picks up the phone to get their children jobs at the Fair but your father and his father never will, they won't ask for favors.*

There were also letters from me, letters I had written my mother from Berkeley, from the time I went down for summer school in 1952, making up credits between high school and college, until the time I graduated in 1956. These letters were in many ways unsettling, even dispiriting, in that I both recognized myself and did not. *Have never been so depressed as when I got back here Sunday night*, one of the first letters reads, from the summer of 1952. *I keep thinking about Sacramento and what people are doing. I got a letter from Nancy—she misses Sacramento too. They saw "The King and I," "Where's Charley," "Guys and Dolls," and "Pal Joey." A woman committed suicide by jumping out a window across from the Waldorf while they were there. Nancy said it was terrible, they had to clean up the street with fire hoses.*

Nancy was my best friend from Sacramento, traveling with her parents (this is only a guess, but an informed one, since another letter to my mother that summer mentions having "heard from Nancy who is at the Greenbrier and so bored") before beginning Stanford.

Nancy and I had known each other since we were five, when we had been in the same ballet class at Miss Marion Hall's dancing school in Sacramento.

In fact there was also, in the box that came from my mother's house, a program for a recital of that very ballet class: *Joan Didion and Nancy Kennedy*, the program read. *"Les Petites."* There were also in the box many photographs of Nancy and me: modeling children's clothes in a charity fashion show, wearing matching corsages around our wrists at a high-school dance, standing on the lawn outside Nancy's house on the day of her wedding, Nancy in bouffant white, the bridesmaids in pale green organza, all of us smiling.

The last time I saw Nancy was at the Outrigger Canoe Club in Honolulu, during the Christmas season of the Iran hostage crisis. She was at the next table, having dinner with her husband and children. They were laughing and arguing and interrupting just as she and her brothers and her mother and father had laughed and argued and interrupted in the late 1940s and early 1950s, when I would have dinner at their house two or three times a week.

We kissed, we had a drink together, we promised to keep in touch.

A few months later Nancy was dead, of cancer, at Lenox Hill Hospital in New York.

I sent the recital program to Nancy's brother, to send on to her daughter.

I had my grandmother's watercolor framed and sent it to the next oldest of her three granddaughters, my cousin Brenda, in Sacramento.

I closed the box and put it in a closet.

There is no real way to deal with everything we lose.

When my father died I kept moving. When my mother died I could not. The last time I saw her was eight weeks before she died. She had been in the hospital, my brother and I had gotten her home, we had arranged for oxygen and shifts of nurses, we had filled the prescriptions for morphine and Ativan. On the morning Quintana and I were to leave for New York, my mother insisted that we bring her a painted metal box that sat on a small table in her bedroom, a box in which she kept papers she thought might have importance, for example a copy of the deed to a gold mine in El Dorado County that she and her sister had inherited from their father and no longer owned. My brother said that she did not need the box, that he had already extracted any still operable papers and put them in safekeeping. She was insistent. She wanted the metal box. Quintana brought the box and set it on the bed. From it my mother took two pieces of silver flatware, a small ladle and a small serving spoon, each wrapped in smoothed scraps of used tissue paper. She gave the serving spoon to Quintana and the ladle to me. I protested: she had already given me all her silver, I had ladles, she had given me ladles. "Not this one," she said. She pointed out the curve of the handle. It seemed that she had what she called "a special feeling" for the way the handle curved on this particular ladle. It seemed that she found this ladle so satisfying to touch that she had set it aside, kept it. I said that since it gave her pleasure she should continue to keep it. "*Take* it," she said, her voice urgent. "I don't want it lost." I was still pretending that she would get through the Sierra before the snows fell. She was not.

NOTES TO *MIAMI*

These notes are meant only as a guide, and reflect only the smallest part of those published sources on which I have drawn and to whose authors I owe thanks. Aside from published sources, I would like particularly to thank, among the many people who were helpful to me in Miami and in Washington, the editors and staff of the Miami Herald, *especially Madeleine Blais and John Katzenbach; Frank Calzón at the Cuban American National Foundation; Ernesto Betancourt at Radio Martí; Carlos Luis at the Museo Cubano de Arte y Cultura in Miami; Ricardo Pau-Llosa at Miami-Dade Community College in Miami; and Mr. and Mrs. George Stevens, Jr., in Washington. I would like also to thank, in New York, Robert Silvers, Michael Korda, Lois Wallace, Sophie Sorkin, and especially Rebecca Stowe, whose tireless willingness to research even the smallest point has made any error in this book entirely my own.*

CHAPTER 1, PAGES 415 TO 421

I am indebted for much of the historical detail in this chapter to Hugh Thomas, *Cuba* (London: Eyre & Spottiswoode, 1971). The photograph of the Prío family leaving Havana appeared in *Cuba*, and before that in *Life*, March 24, 1952.

"They say that I was a terrible president …": *A Thousand Days* by Arthur M. Schlesinger, Jr. (Boston: Houghton Mifflin, 1965), p. 216.

An account of the attempt to land a third force in Camagüey Province appears in *The Winds of December* by John Dorschner and Roberto Fabricio (New York: Coward, McCann & Geoghegan, 1980). Dorschner and Fabricio also provide a detailed account of Fulgencio Batista's departure from Havana on January 1, 1959.

The Kennedy campaign statement mentioned on page 420 is discussed by Schlesinger in *A Thousand Days*, p. 72.

The Nicaraguan Refugee Fund dinner at which Ronald Reagan spoke was covered by both the *Miami Herald* and *The New York Times* on April 16, 1985.

The *Miami Herald* report mentioning "guerrilla discounts" was by Juan Tamayo and appeared July 21, 1985, under the headline, "Cuban exiles said to ship guns to rebels."

The pamphlet giving tips for maintaining a secure profile was reported by Brian Duffy in the *Miami Herald*, June 5, 1985, under the headline, "Smuggling guide-book offers 'how to' hints."

"Well-heeled investors returning north" appeared in the *Herald* on June 16, 1985. "Costly condos threatened with massive fore-closures" appeared August 2, 1985, and "Foreclosures soaring in S. Florida" on March 28, 1986. "Arena financing plan relies on hotel guests" appeared June 7, 1985, and "S. Florida hotel rooms get emptier" on October 19, 1985. The real-estate analyst quoted on page 428 was Mike Cannon, president of Appraisal and Real Estate Economics Associates, Inc., quoted by Dory Owens in "Wirth betting that office glut will end," *Miami Herald*, July 17, 1985.

Reports on Theodore Gould and Miami Center appeared in the *Miami Herald* on August 9 and October 11, 1985.

Reports by Brian Duffy and Nancy Ancrum on the cache of hand grenades and the pawnbroker appeared in the *Miami Herald* on October 25 and November 2, 1985. Debbie Sontag's report ("Former guard accidentally kills self in Beach supermarket lot") on the shooting in the Miami Beach parking lot appeared October 9, 1985. The arrest of Jose "Coca Cola" Yero was reported by Jeff Leen in the October 22, 1985, *Herald*. Charisse L. Grant's report on the young woman who was car-bombed in South Palm Beach ("Bomb victim feared for her life, cops say") appeared June 28, 1986.

Black tensions in Miami have been extensively covered since 1980 not only in the *Herald* but in *The New York Times* and the *Los Angeles Times*. For background see *The Miami Riot of 1980* by Bruce Porter and Marvin Dunn (Lexington, Mass.: D. C. Heath and Company–Lexington Books, 1984); "Overwhelmed

NOTES

in Miami" by John Katzenbach in *Police Magazine*, September 1980; "Under Siege in an Urban Ghetto" by Bruce Porter and Marvin Dunn in *Police Magazine*, July 1981; and "Open Wounds" by Madeleine Blais in the *Miami Herald*'s Sunday magazine, *Tropic*, May 12, 1985.

The quote from the president of the Orange Bowl committee appeared in "CRB 'slaps' OB for party at restrictive club," by Marc Fisher, *Miami Herald*, March 21, 1985. Membership policies at South Florida private clubs were covered in Marc Fisher's three-part report on private clubs, appearing in the *Herald* on April 7, 8, and 9, 1985. The Surf Club party on page 439 was mentioned in "Miami's Elite Holds Fast to Tradition," April 4, 1985, part of a *Herald* series on "Society in South Florida."

For background on Mariel, see *The Cuban-American Experience: Culture, Images and Perspectives* by Thomas D. Boswell and James R. Curtis (Totowa, N.J.: Rowman & Allanheld, 1984); *Cuban Americans: Masters of Survival* by José Llanes (Cambridge, Mass.: Abt Books, 1982); and "The Cubans: A People Divided" and "The Cubans: A People Changed," two *Miami Herald* Special Reports published as supplements to the editions of December 11 and 18, 1983. This chapter also draws on a 1985 study by Helga Silva called "Children of Mariel: From Shock to Integration," provided to me by the Cuban American National Foundation in Washington, D.C.

CHAPTER 5, PAGES 442 TO 450

"The Most Influential People in Dade's History" and "The Most Important Events in Dade's History" appeared in the *Miami Herald*, February 3, 1986. The population statistics on page 443 are those given for 1986 by the Miami Chamber of Commerce.

The *Herald* reports on "Cuban Miami: A Guide for Non-Cubans" appeared each Friday from October 10 to November 21, 1986. The *Herald* piece in which Luis Botifoll was quoted was by Guillermo Martinez and appeared in *Tropic* on January 16, 1983. The *Herald* food section mentioned was that for March 20, 1986. A note on the Miami Springs Holiday Inn and its 26 Julio bar special appeared in Fred Tasker's *Herald* column on July 26, 1985.

The address quoted by Vice President George Bush was delivered in Miami on May 20, 1986.

The column by George Will ("The First Contras") appeared in *Newsweek*, March 31, 1986. George Gilder's piece ("Making It") appeared in the Winter 1985 issue of *The Wilson Quarterly*. The "samba" report on the Calle Ocho Festival appeared in the *Herald*, March 10, 1986.

CHAPTER 6, PAGES 451 TO 453

The lines quoted are from p. 34 of the transcript for a January 19, 1984, meeting of the Miami City Commission, and the speaker was Maurice Ferre, then mayor of Miami.

Robert Melby was quoted in the *Miami Herald*, March 21, 1985, in a report ("English proponent renews drive") by Andres Viglucci. The reference to Xavier Suarez's "flawless English" appeared in the *Los Angeles Times*, November 13, 1985, in a story ("Attorney Suarez Elected Mayor in Miami") credited to Times Wire Services. The *Herald* political editor quoted was Tom Fiedler, and the quoted lines appeared in his column ("On the fringes of politics"), October 6, 1985. The quoted note about Raul Masvidal's unlisted telephone number appeared in Fred Tasker's *Herald* column on September 23, 1985. The closing of Gator Kicks Longneck Saloon (which was, incidentally, the bar for whose advertising Donna Rice was photographed, before she met Gary Hart, with the Confederate flag) was covered in the *Herald* ("Colorful country roadhouse closes" by Ivonne Rovira Kelly), February 8, 1986. The quoted column by Charles Whited appeared February 9, 1986.

CHAPTER 7, PAGES 454 TO 462

Jim Hampton's column ("Voters' kiss of death? Kiss off!") appeared in the *Herald* November 17, 1985. The quotes from Andres Nazario Sargen and from police spokesmen on page 456 appeared in the *Herald*, March 21, 1986, in "Opposing rallies OKd at same site" by Andres Viglucci. The headlines and photograph mentioned on page 456 appeared March 23, 1986. Other sources on the Torch of Friendship demonstrations included "Suarez clarifies his stand on 'free speech'" by Justin Gillis, *Miami Herald*, April 5, 1986; the letters columns of the *Herald* for March 27 and 28, 1986 (a letter from Mayor Suarez appeared March 27);

Charles Whited's *Herald* column ("Impeding right to free speech is undemocratic") for March 25, 1986; and Carl Hiaasen's *Herald* column ("Goons who hit man at rally aren't patriots") for March 26, 1986.

The José Martí letter quoted on page 458 was to Manuel Mercado and appears in volume I of *Obras Completas*. The translation here is Hugh Thomas's.

The mayoralty candidate with the plan to confine minors to their houses was Evelio Estrella, and his statement appeared in the *Miami News* (in the "Miami Mayoral Forum" series) on October 10, 1985. General Benítez's statement appeared in the same series October 8, 1985.

"Resort sells sun, fun—in Cuba" by Alfonso Chardy appeared in the *Herald*, April 17, 1985. "Free markets allow Havana to spiff up," also by Alfonso Chardy (whose ethnic background remained a source of some speculation in the Cuban community), appeared March 25, 1985.

The José Martí lines on page 461 are from volume III of *Obras Completas*, and also appear on p. 109 of *José Martí: Thoughts / Pensamientos* (New York: Eliseo Torres & Sons-Las Américas Publishing Co., 1980 and 1985), by Carlos Ripoll, whose translation this is.

For the Kennedy and Reagan quotes see notes on chapter 1.

CHAPTER 8, PAGES 465 TO 475

Allen Dulles is quoted by Schlesinger in *A Thousand Days*, p. 242; John F. Kennedy on p. 257.

The poll mentioned on p. 465 appeared in *Tropic, Miami Herald*, January 16, 1983. The existence of The Non-Group was first reported by Celia W. Dugger in "The 38 who secretly guide Dade," *Miami Herald*, September 1, 1985.

The Theodore C. Sorensen quotes on pages 467 and 469 appear in his *Kennedy* (New York: Harper & Row, 1965), p. 722.

For background on JM/WAVE, see William R. Amlong, "How the CIA operated in Dade," *Miami Herald*, March 9, 1975; Taylor Branch and George Crile III, "The Kennedy Vendetta," *Harper's*, August 1975; *Portrait of a Cold Warrior* by Joseph Burkholder Smith (New York: G. P. Putnam's Sons, 1976); and *Investigation of the Assassination of President John F. Kennedy: Hearings before the Select*

Committee on Assassinations of the U.S. House of Representatives, 95th Congress (Washington, D.C.: U.S. Government Printing Office, 1979), particularly volume X. CIA activities out of Miami during this period are also discussed in *The Investigation of the Assassination of President John F. Kennedy: Performance of the Intelligence Agencies*, which is book V of the *Final Report of the Select Committee to Study Governmental Operations with respect to Intelligence Activities, U.S. Senate, 94th Congress* (Washington, D.C.: U.S. Government Printing Office, 1976).

The December 1962 appearance of President and Mrs. Kennedy at the Orange Bowl is discussed by Sorensen in *Kennedy*, p. 308, and by Schlesinger in both *A Thousand Days*, p. 839, and *Robert Kennedy and His Times* (New York: Ballantine Books, 1979), p. 579. "But had CIA been up to its old tricks?" appears in *Robert Kennedy and His Times*, p. 586.

The financing of Southern Air Transport was reported by William R. Amlong in "CIA sold airline cheap," *Miami Herald*, March 10, 1975, and also by Martin Merzer in "Airline does job—quietly," *Miami Herald*, December 10, 1986.

The Schlesinger quotes on page 471 are from *Robert Kennedy and His Times*, p. 588. The Church committee testimony quoted on page 471 was given on May 16, 1976, and quoted on p. 11 of book V, *The Investigation of the Assassination of President John F. Kennedy: Performance of the Intelligence Agencies*.

There is a section on JURE, and on "autonomous operations," beginning on p. 77 of volume X of the 1979 *Investigation of the Assassination of President John F. Kennedy: Hearings before the Select Committee on Assassinations of the U.S. House of Representatives*. There is an account of the June 1963 Special Group meeting authorizing CIA supervision of exile actions within Cuba in the Church committee's 1975 *Interim Report: Alleged Assassination Plots Involving Foreign Leaders*.

The CIA internal report quoted appears on p. 126 of volume IV of the 1979 *Investigation of the Assassination of President John F. Kennedy: Hearings before the Select Committee on Assassinations of the U.S. House of Representatives*.

The Schlesinger quote on page 473 appears on p. 586 of *Robert Kennedy and His Times*. The Kennedy quote appears on p. 14 of volume X of the 1979 *Investigation of the Assassination of President John F. Kennedy: Hearings before the Select Committee on Assassinations of the U.S. House of Representatives.* James Angleton was quoted by Dick Russell, after a series of interviews which took place at the Army-Navy Club in Washington, in "Little Havana's Reign of Terror," *New Times*, October 29, 1976.

The footnote from *Robert Kennedy and His Times* appears on p. 513. The testimony before the Church committee mentioned on page 97 was given May 6, 1976, and quoted on p. 14, book V, *Final Report of the U.S. Senate Select Committee to Study Governmental Operations with respect to Intelligence Activities.*

The Kennedy quote on p. 474 appears in *A Thousand Days*, p. 839. The Sorensen quote appears in *Kennedy*, p. 722. The Schlesinger quote appears in *Robert Kennedy and His Times*, p. 579.

CHAPTER 9, PAGES 476 TO 482

A report on the arrest of Eduardo Arocena ("Arocena 'Armory' Uncovered" by Jim McGee) appeared in the *Miami Herald*, July 24, 1983, and the quotes from Miriam Arocena, from the head of the 2506, from Andres Nazario Sargen, and from Tomas Garcia Fuste, the news director of WQBA, appeared in this piece. For Xavier Suarez and the Arocena defense fund, see Helga Silva and Guy Gugliotta, "'La Causa' binds exile community," *Miami Herald* Special Report, December 11, 1983. Omega 7 itself has been covered since the late 1970s in both the *Herald* and *The New York Times*, which published a particularly complete report ("'Highest Priority' Given by U.S. to Capture of Anti-Castro Group" by Robin Herman) on March 3, 1980.

For background on Max Lesnik, see Hugh Thomas, *Cuba*; John Dorschner and Roberto Fabricio, *The Winds of December*; and Helga Silva, "Those called 'soft' are often shunned," *Miami Herald* Special Report, December 11, 1983.

The incident with Luciano Nieves in the Versailles is mentioned by José Llanes in *Cuban Americans: Masters of Survival*, p. 127. According to the *Miami Herald* ("Killer asks for clemency," November 26, 1986), an exile named Valentin Hernandez was in 1978 convicted of the killing of Luciano Nieves and sentenced to twenty-five years without possibility of parole. Eight years later, when he petitioned the court for an early release, six thousand letters were received in support of his request, along with petitions describing him as "a political prisoner guilty of fighting against the oppression of communism."

CHAPTER 10, PAGES 483 TO 487

The *diálogo*, and Orlando Padron and the cigar, are discussed by Barry Bearak, "Anti-Fidel Fervor Still Burns in Little Havana," *Los Angeles Times*, November 30, 1982. Also see David Vidal, "In Union City, the Memories of the Bay of Pigs Don't Die," *The New York Times*, December 21, 1979, and Jorge Fierro, "For the *Comunidad*, the Visit Is a Sad Show," *The New York Times*, January 20, 1980. Also: Max Azicri, "Un análisis pragmático del diálogo entre la Cuba del interior y la del exterior," *Areíto* IX, no. 36 (1984).

The quote from Fidel Castro appears on p. 67, *Diary of the Cuban Revolution* by Carlos Franqui (New York: The Viking Press, 1980).

For background on Carlos Muñiz Varela, see Luis Angel Torres, "Semblanza de Carlos Muñiz," *Areíto* IX, no. 36 (1984). The murder of Eulalio José Negrin was reported in *The New York Times*, November 26, 1979, "Cuban Refugee Leader Slain in Union City." The *El Diario-La Prensa* bombing was discussed by Robin Herman in the March 3, 1980, *New York Times* piece cited in the notes for Chapter 9. For the TWA bombing, see Robert D. McFadden, "Kennedy Bomb Hurts Four Workers in Baggage Area," *The New York Times*, March 26, 1979.

CHAPTER 11, PAGES 488 TO 494

The translations of *Areíto*'s 1974 and 1984 statements of purpose are those provided by *Areíto*. The piece referring to exile Miami as "the deformed foetus ..." appears in *Areíto* IX, no. 36 (1984) ("El Miami cubano" by Lourdes Argüelles and Gary MacEoin), and the translation is mine.

"Introduction to the Sandinista Documentary Cinema" (p. 489) appeared in *Areíto* X, no. 37 (1984). Marifeli Pérez-Stable was quoted by Helga Silva in "Those called soft ...," *Miami Herald* Special Report, December 11, 1983. For background on Lourdes Casal see *Areíto* IX, no. 36 (1984). Dolores Prida and the controversy over *Coser y Cantar* were extensively covered in the *Miami Herald* during the first two weeks of May 1986.

The issue of *Areíto* referred to on page 491 is volume IX, no. 36, and the pieces referred to are "El Instituto de Estudios Cubanos o los estrechos límites del pluralismo" (Consejo de Dirección de Areíto) and "Sobre las relaciones entre el Instituto de Estudios Cubanos y Areíto: convergencias y divergencias" (María Cristina Herrera/Consejo de Dirección de Areíto).

For the Unaccompanied Children's Program, see Michael J. McNally's *Catholicism in South Florida: 1868–1968* (Gainesville: University of Florida Press, 1982). The extracts from *Contra Viento y Marea* were reprinted in *Areíto* (vol. IX, no. 36), and the translation is mine.

CHAPTER 12, PAGES 495 TO 504

For "the *P.M.* affair," see *Area Handbook for Cuba*, Foreign Area Studies of The American University (Washington, D.C.: U.S. Government Printing Office, 1976), p. 330; *Family Portrait with Fidel* by Carlos Franqui (New York: Vintage Books, 1985), pp. 131–33; and *A Man with a Camera* by Nestor Almendros (New York: Farrar, Straus & Giroux, 1984), p. 139. For *Bohemia*, see Franqui, *Family Portrait*, and also Hugh Thomas, *Cuba*, p. 1292.

About the Jorge Valls controversy: see Liz Balmaseda and Jay Ducassi, "Hero in jail, freed poet provokes exile ire," *Miami Herald*, September 2, 1984. About Armando Valladares: Carl Gershman, president of the National Endowment for Democracy, stated to the Senate Foreign Relations Committee on March 29, 1985, that Endowment efforts "in the fields of education, culture and communications" included "assistance to a program organized by the distinguished Cuban writer and former political prisoner Armando Valladares to inform European public opinion about the human rights situation in Cuba."

For background on Dr. Orlando Bosch, see pp. 89–93, volume X of the 1979 *Investigation of the Assassination of President John F. Kennedy: Hearings before the Select Committee* ..., cited in the notes for Chapter 8. For background on Luis Posada Carriles, see Tim Golden, "Sandinistas say escapee ran supplies," *Miami Herald*, October 16, 1986; Sam Dillon, "Fugitive may be contra supplier," *Miami Herald*, October 21, 1986; Sam Dillon and Guy Gugliotta, "How jail escapee joined rebels' supply network," *Miami Herald*, November 2, 1986 (the spokesman for George Bush mentioned on page 501 is quoted in this report); and p. 44, volume X of the 1979 *Investigation of the Assassination of President John F. Kennedy* ..., also cited for Chapter 8.

The president of the Committee to Free Orlando Bosch was quoted by Sandra Dibble, "Bosch's friends turn out to view exhibit of his artworks," *Miami Herald*, December 13, 1986. The letter in defense of Dr. Bosch appeared in *El Herald*, November 20, 1985; translation mine. Cosme Barros and Norma Garcia were quoted by Reinaldo Ramos, "To Miami Cubans, Bosch is folk hero," *Miami Herald*, July 27, 1986. The 1977 CIA document mentioned is discussed by Sam Dillon and Guy Gugliotta, "How jail escapee ...," cited above.

Orlando Bosch's CIA experience is discussed on p. 90, volume X of the 1979 *Investigation of the Assassination of President John F. Kennedy* ..., cited above. The Richard Helms quote appears on p. 159 of volume IV, the same House Select Committee hearings.

CHAPTER 13, PAGES 505 TO 512

Robert C. McFarlane was quoted by Joanne Omang in one of the first pieces to name Lieutenant Colonel Oliver North, "The White House's Nicaragua Middleman: A Marine Officer Implements Policy," *Washington Post National Weekly Edition*, August 26, 1985.

CHAPTER 14, PAGES 513 TO 520

For Guillermo Novo and the Letelier case, see Taylor Branch and Eugene M. Propper, former assistant U.S. attorney for the District of Columbia, *Labyrinth* (New York: The Viking Press, 1982).

For Felipe Rivero and Cuban radio in Miami, see Fabiola Santiago, "When stations talk, listeners act" and "Some voices of Miami's Spanish-language radio," *Miami Herald*, June 22, 1986.

The Reagan radio talks about the death of Orlando Letelier are reprinted on pp. 521–23 of *On Reagan: The Man and His Presidency* by Ronnie Dugger (New York: McGraw-Hill, 1983). Jesse Helms was quoted by Taylor Branch and Eugene M. Propper in *Labyrinth*. Ronald Reagan on the blacklist was quoted by Robert Scheer on p. 259 of his *With Enough Shovels: Reagan, Bush & Nuclear War* (New York: Random House, 1982).

For Ronald Reagan on the Salvadoran death squads, see George Skelton, "Reagan Suspects Rebels of Death Squad Killings," *Los Angeles Times*, December 3, 1983. For Ronald Reagan on Sandinistas dressing up in freedom fighter uniforms, see "Nicaraguan killers really Sandinista agents," *Miami Herald*, March 16, 1986, and Rudy Abramson, "Sandinistas Kill in Contra Guise, Reagan Charges," *Los Angeles Times*, March 16, 1986.

Ronnie Dugger quotes David Gergen on pp. 463–64, *On Reagan*. For Ronald Reagan on "Medical science doctors confirm ...," see Francis X. Clines, "Reagan Tells Broadcasters Aborted Fetuses Suffer Pain," *The New York Times*, January 31, 1984. Hannah Arendt's discussion of propaganda appears on pp. 341–64 of *The Origins of Totalitarianism* (New York: Harcourt Brace, the 1966 edition).

For Ronald Reagan's 1983 visit to Miami see George Skelton, "Reagan Vows to Defend Latin American Liberty," *Los Angeles Times*, May 21, 1983; Reginald Stuart, "Cubans in Miami Await Reagan's Visit Eagerly," *The New York Times*, May 20, 1983, and Helga Silva and Liz Balmaseda, "Superstar Wows Little Havana," *Miami Herald*, May 21, 1983.

CHAPTER 15, PAGES 523 TO 531

"A couple of hours into our meeting ...": see José Llanes, *Cuban Americans: Masters of Survival*, cited in the notes for Chapter 4, p. 74. "Our hearts sank ..." and "I had never seen ...," see Schlesinger, *A Thousand Days*, pp. 283–84. For "rekindled doubts in Congress ...," see Philip Taubman, "Latin Debate Refocused," *New York Times*, April 9, 1984.

The Associated Press story quoting Larry Speakes and Michael Deaver (mentioned on page 527) was by Michael Putzel, and was on the wire April 12, 1984, for release April 15. David Gergen was quoted in *The New York Times* by Steven R. Weisman and Francis X. Clines in "Q. & A.: David R. Gergen— Key Presidential Buffer Looks Back," January 10, 1984. The quote from Morton Kondracke comes from his review of Robert Dallek's *Ronald Reagan: The Politics of Symbolism*, in *The New York Times Book Review*, March 4, 1984. The 1984 American Enterprise Institute discussion mentioned took place at the Mayflower Hotel in Washington on March 1, 1984, and was editors of each: *Esquire, The Saturday Evening Post, Life* (more specifically, the "old" *Saturday Evening Post* and the "old" *Life*), *Travel & Leisure, The Los Angeles Times Book Review, The New York Times Book Review, New West,* and *The New York Review of Books*.

J.D.

Thanks are due the following publishers for permission to include excerpts from:

"Caracas I" from *Notebook* by Robert Lowell. Copyright © 1967, 1968, 1969, 1970 by Robert Lowell. Reprinted with the permission of Farrar, Straus & Giroux, Inc.

From Here to Eternity by James Jones. Copyright © 1951 by James Jones. Reprinted with the permission of Charles Scribner's Sons.

"California Winter" from *Collected Poems 1940–1978* by Karl Shapiro. Copyright © 1957 by Karl Shapiro. Reprinted with the permission of Wieser & Wieser, Inc., 118 East 25th St., New York, N.Y. 10010.

Lyric from "Moonlight Drive" by The Doors. Copyright © 1967 by Doors Music Company. Reprinted by permission.

SALVADOR

I am indebted for general background particularly to Thomas P. Anderson's *Matanza: El Salvador's Communist Revolt of 1932* (University of Nebraska Press: Lincoln, 1971) and *The War of the Dispossessed: Honduras and El Salvador, 1969* (University of Nebraska Press: Lincoln, 1981); to David Browning's *El Salvador: Landscape and Society* (Clarendon Press: Oxford, 1971); and to the officers and staff of the United States embassy in San Salvador. I am indebted most of all to my husband, John Gregory Dunne, who was with me in El Salvador and whose notes on, memories about, and interpretations of events there enlarged and informed my own perception of the place.

Portions of this book were published in *The New York Review of Books* in 1982.

called "The Reagan Administration and the Press: What's the Problem?"

CHAPTER 16, PAGES 532 TO 550

A New Inter-American Policy for the Eighties can be obtained in some libraries (Library of Congress Catalog Card No. 81–68443) or from the Council for Inter-American Security, 729 Eighth St., S.E., Washington, D.C. 20003. The Edward Cody piece mentioning the Santa Fe document is "Disappointment in Havana: No Thaw in U.S. Relations," *Washington Post National Weekly Edition*, June 17, 1985.

For the National Security Planning Group document mentioned on page 536, Project Truth, and the establishment of the Office of Public Diplomacy, see Alfonso Chardy, "Secrets leaked to harm Nicaragua, sources say," *Miami Herald*, October 13, 1986. Faith Ryan Whittlesey and Otto Juan Reich are quoted by Tim Golden, "Reagan Countering Critics of Policies in Central America," *Los Angeles Times*, December 21, 1983.

For background on Jack Wheeler, see Paul Dean, "Adventurer Devotes Energy to Anti-Communist Causes," *Los Angeles Times*, August 1, 1985. The *Washington Post* story mentioned on page 541 is Joanne Omang's "The White House's Nicaragua Middleman ...," cited in the notes for Chapter 13.

For background on Steven Carr and Jesus Garcia, see Juan Tamayo, "Cuban exiles said to ship guns to rebels," *Miami Herald*, July 21, 1985; Lori Rozsa, "Contra mercenary wants new life," *Miami Herald*, August 10, 1986; Steven J. Hedges, "Witness claimed U.S. aided escape," *Miami Herald*, January 6, 1987; Alfonso Chardy, "Contra weapons probe may bring first prosecution," *Miami Herald*, July 13, 1986; Lynn O'Shaughnessy and Mark Henry, "Witness in Nicaragua Arms Trafficking Dies," *Los Angeles Times*, December 15, 1986; Sandra Dibble, "Contra supporter lands in jail," *Miami Herald*, August 4, 1986; Stephen J. Hedges, "Independent counsel may end Miami probe," *Miami Herald*, December 30, 1986; Alfonso Chardy, "Rebel guns may spur U.S. probe," *Miami Herald*, July 12, 1986; "Inquiry Reported into Contra Arms," *The New York Times*, April 11, 1986; Caitlin Randall, "5 await trial in 'sensitive' Costa Rican case," *Miami Herald*, April 23, 1986; and, on Robert Owen: Alfonso Chardy,

"Idealism drew him into contra struggle," *Miami Herald*, June 8, 1986, and Tim Golden, "State Department adviser tied to misuse of rebel aid," *Miami Herald*, February 16, 1987.

The column by Anthony Lewis mentioned on page 546, "What Not to Do," appeared in *The New York Times* September 25, 1975. The memorandum prepared by W. David Slawson and William Coleman is quoted at length on p. 5, volume X, of the 1979 *Investigation of the Assassination of President John F. Kennedy...*, cited in the notes for Chapter 8. The Schlesinger line quoted appears in *A Thousand Days*, p. 207.

ACKNOWLEDGMENTS

SLOUCHING TOWARDS BETHLEHEM

"Where the Kissing Never Stops" appeared first in *The New York Times Magazine* under the title "Just Folks at a School for Non-Violence." "On Keeping a Notebook" and "Notes from a Native Daughter" appeared first in *Holiday*. "I Can't Get That Monster out of My Mind" and "On Morality" first appeared in *The American Scholar*, the latter under the title "The Insidious Ethic of Conscience." "On Self-Respect" and "Guaymas, Sonora" appeared first in *Vogue*. "Los Angeles Notebook" includes a section which was published as "The Santa Ana" in *The Saturday Evening Post*. All the other essays appeared originally in *The Saturday Evening Post*, several under different titles: "Some Dreamers of the Golden Dream" was published as "How Can I Tell Them There's Nothing Left"; "7000 Romaine, Los Angeles 38," was published as "The Howard Hughes Underground"; "Letter from Paradise, 21° 19′ N., 157° 52′ W." was called "Hawaii: Taps Over Pearl Harbor"; "Goodbye to All That" was called "Farewell to the Enchanted City."

The author is grateful to all these publications for permission to reprint the various essays.

"The Second Coming" is reprinted with permission of Mr. M. B. Yeats and Macmillan & Co. Ltd. and The Macmillan Company (New York) from *Collected Poems* by William Butler Yeats. Copyright 1924 by The Macmillan Company, renewed 1952 by Bertha Georgie Yeats.

THE WHITE ALBUM

Most of these pieces appeared, in various forms and at various times, in the following magazines, and I would like to thank the called "The Reagan Administration and the Press: What's the Problem?"

CHAPTER 16, PAGES 532 TO 550

A New Inter-American Policy for the Eighties can be obtained in some libraries (Library of Congress Catalog Card No. 81–68443) or from the Council for Inter-American Security, 729 Eighth St., S.E., Washington, D.C. 20003. The Edward Cody piece mentioning the Santa Fe document is "Disappointment in Havana: No Thaw in U.S. Relations," *Washington Post National Weekly Edition*, June 17, 1985.

For the National Security Planning Group document mentioned on page 536, Project Truth, and the establishment of the Office of Public Diplomacy, see Alfonso Chardy, "Secrets leaked to harm Nicaragua, sources say," *Miami Herald*, October 13, 1986. Faith Ryan Whittlesey and Otto Juan Reich are quoted by Tim Golden, "Reagan Countering Critics of Policies in Central America," *Los Angeles Times*, December 21, 1983.

For background on Jack Wheeler, see Paul Dean, "Adventurer Devotes Energy to Anti-Communist Causes," *Los Angeles Times*, August 1, 1985. The *Washington Post* story mentioned on page 541 is Joanne Omang's "The White House's Nicaragua Middleman …," cited in the notes for Chapter 13.

For background on Steven Carr and Jesus Garcia, see Juan Tamayo, "Cuban exiles said to ship guns to rebels," *Miami Herald*, July 21, 1985; Lori Rozsa, "Contra mercenary wants new life," *Miami Herald*, August 10, 1986; Steven J. Hedges, "Witness claimed U.S. aided escape," *Miami Herald*, January 6, 1987; Alfonso Chardy, "Contra weapons probe may bring first prosecution," *Miami Herald*, July 13, 1986; Lynn O'Shaughnessy and Mark Henry, "Witness in Nicaragua Arms Trafficking Dies," *Los Angeles Times*, December 15, 1986; Sandra Dibble, "Contra supporter lands in jail," *Miami Herald*, August 4, 1986; Stephen J. Hedges, "Independent counsel may end Miami probe," *Miami Herald*, December 30, 1986; Alfonso Chardy, "Rebel guns may spur U.S. probe," *Miami Herald*, July 12, 1986; "Inquiry Reported into Contra Arms," *The New York Times*, April 11, 1986; Caitlin Randall, "5 await trial in 'sensitive' Costa Rican case," *Miami Herald*, April 23, 1986; and, on Robert Owen: Alfonso Chardy,

"Idealism drew him into contra struggle," *Miami Herald*, June 8, 1986, and Tim Golden, "State Department adviser tied to misuse of rebel aid," *Miami Herald*, February 16, 1987.

The column by Anthony Lewis mentioned on page 546, "What Not to Do," appeared in *The New York Times* September 25, 1975. The memorandum prepared by W. David Slawson and William Coleman is quoted at length on p. 5, volume X, of the 1979 *Investigation of the Assassination of President John F. Kennedy...*, cited in the notes for Chapter 8. The Schlesinger line quoted appears in *A Thousand Days*, p. 207.

ACKNOWLEDGMENTS

SLOUCHING TOWARDS BETHLEHEM

"Where the Kissing Never Stops" appeared first in *The New York Times Magazine* under the title "Just Folks at a School for Non-Violence." "On Keeping a Notebook" and "Notes from a Native Daughter" appeared first in *Holiday*. "I Can't Get That Monster out of My Mind" and "On Morality" first appeared in *The American Scholar*, the latter under the title "The Insidious Ethic of Conscience." "On Self-Respect" and "Guaymas, Sonora" appeared first in *Vogue*. "Los Angeles Notebook" includes a section which was published as "The Santa Ana" in *The Saturday Evening Post*. All the other essays appeared originally in *The Saturday Evening Post*, several under different titles: "Some Dreamers of the Golden Dream" was published as "How Can I Tell Them There's Nothing Left"; "7000 Romaine, Los Angeles 38," was published as "The Howard Hughes Underground"; "Letter from Paradise, 21° 19′ N., 157° 52′ W." was called "Hawaii: Taps Over Pearl Harbor"; "Goodbye to All That" was called "Farewell to the Enchanted City."

The author is grateful to all these publications for permission to reprint the various essays.

"The Second Coming" is reprinted with permission of Mr. M. B. Yeats and Macmillan & Co. Ltd. and The Macmillan Company (New York) from *Collected Poems* by William Butler Yeats. Copyright 1924 by The Macmillan Company, renewed 1952 by Bertha Georgie Yeats.

THE WHITE ALBUM

Most of these pieces appeared, in various forms and at various times, in the following magazines, and I would like to thank the editors of each: *Esquire, The Saturday Evening Post, Life* (more specifically, the "old" *Saturday Evening Post* and the "old" *Life*), *Travel & Leisure, The Los Angeles Times Book Review, The New York Times Book Review, New West,* and *The New York Review of Books.*

J.D.

Thanks are due the following publishers for permission to include excerpts from:

"Caracas I" from *Notebook* by Robert Lowell. Copyright © 1967, 1968, 1969, 1970 by Robert Lowell. Reprinted with the permission of Farrar, Straus & Giroux, Inc.

From Here to Eternity by James Jones. Copyright © 1951 by James Jones. Reprinted with the permission of Charles Scribner's Sons.

"California Winter" from *Collected Poems 1940–1978* by Karl Shapiro. Copyright © 1957 by Karl Shapiro. Reprinted with the permission of Wieser & Wieser, Inc., 118 East 25th St., New York, N.Y. 10010.

Lyric from "Moonlight Drive" by The Doors. Copyright © 1967 by Doors Music Company. Reprinted by permission.

SALVADOR

I am indebted for general background particularly to Thomas P. Anderson's *Matanza: El Salvador's Communist Revolt of 1932* (University of Nebraska Press: Lincoln, 1971) and *The War of the Dispossessed: Honduras and El Salvador, 1969* (University of Nebraska Press: Lincoln, 1981); to David Browning's *El Salvador: Landscape and Society* (Clarendon Press: Oxford, 1971); and to the officers and staff of the United States embassy in San Salvador. I am indebted most of all to my husband, John Gregory Dunne, who was with me in El Salvador and whose notes on, memories about, and interpretations of events there enlarged and informed my own perception of the place.

Portions of this book were published in *The New York Review of Books* in 1982.

The author wishes to thank the following for their permission
to reprint lines from:

The song "American Pie," written by Don McLean, published
by Mayday Music and Benny Bird Company, © 1971. Used by
permission. All rights reserved.

The specified abridged excerpt from pp. 63–64 in *The Autumn
of the Patriarch* by Gabriel García Márquez. Translated from the
Spanish by Gregory Rabassa. Copyright © 1975 by Gabriel García
Márquez. English translation copyright © 1976 by Harper & Row,
Publishers, Inc. Reprinted by permission of the publisher.

The excerpt from "Heart of Darkness" from *Youth* by Joseph
Conrad. Reprinted by permission of Doubleday & Company,
Inc.

The lines from the poem by Roque Dalton García from the
book *El Salvador: The Face of the Revolution* by Robert Armstrong
and Janet Shenk. Copyright © 1982, South End Press. Reprinted
by permission of the publisher.

MIAMI

Excerpts from this book have appeared in *The New York Review of
Books* in slightly different form.

AFTER HENRY

"In the Realm of the Fisher King," "Girl of the Golden West,"
and "Sentimental Journeys" appeared originally in *The New
York Review of Books*. "Los Angeles Days," "Down at City
Hall," "L.A. *Noir*," "Fire Season," "Times Mirror Square," and
part of "Pacific Distances" appeared originally as "Letters from
Los Angeles" in *The New Yorker*. Most of "Pacific Distances"
and the introductory piece, "After Henry," appeared originally in *New West*, which later became *California* and eventually
folded. I would like to thank my editors at all three magazines,
Jon Carroll at *New West*, Robert Gottlieb at *The New Yorker*,
and most especially, since he has put up with me over nineteen

years and through many long and eccentric projects, Robert Silvers at *The New York Review*.

POLITICAL FICTIONS

WHERE I WAS FROM